Argentina

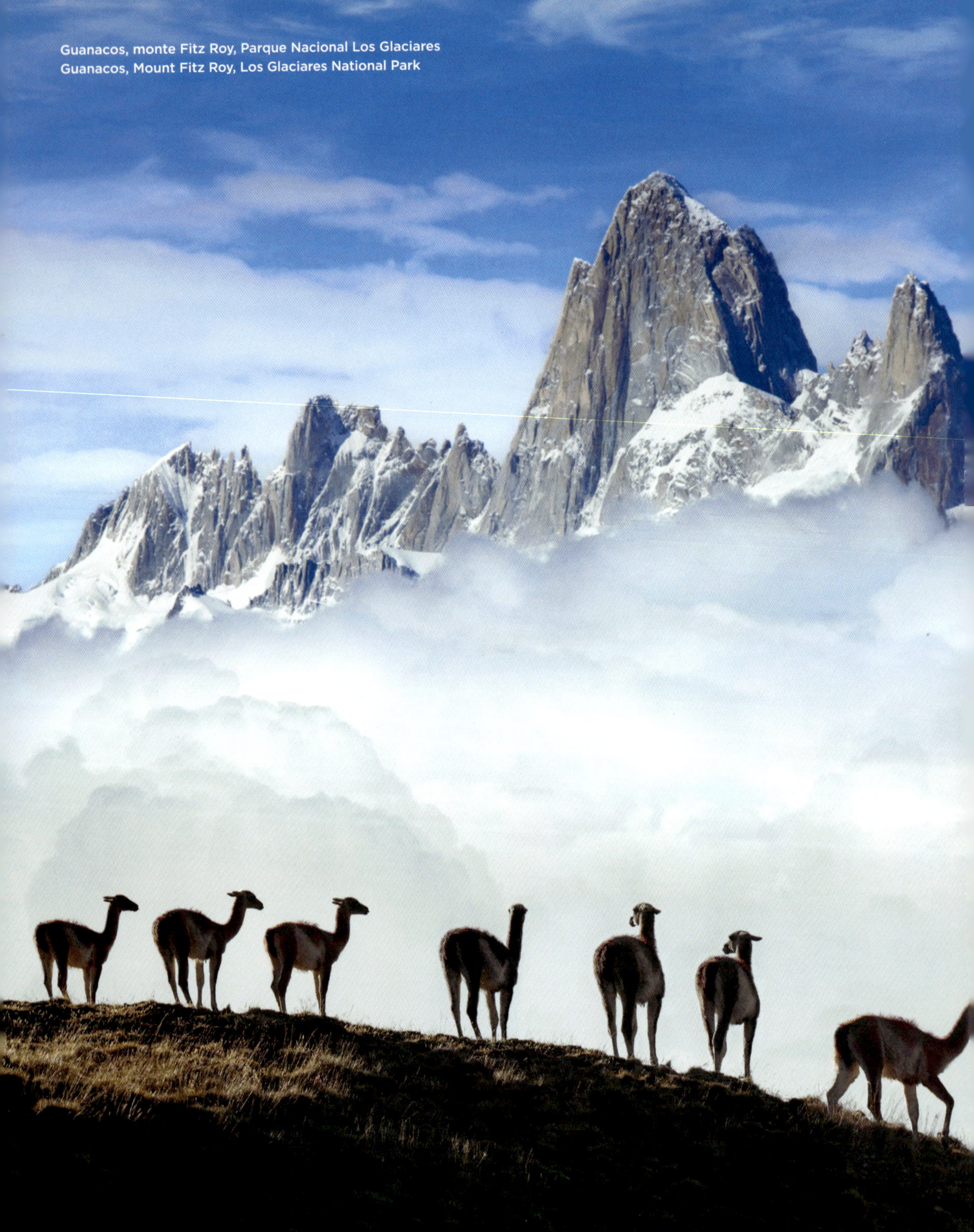

Guanacos, monte Fitz Roy, Parque Nacional Los Glaciares
Guanacos, Mount Fitz Roy, Los Glaciares National Park

Argentina

Argentine

Argentinien

Argentinië

Katja Sassmannshausen
Ellen Spielmann

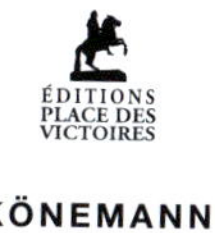

ÉDITIONS
PLACE DES
VICTOIRES

KÖNEMANN

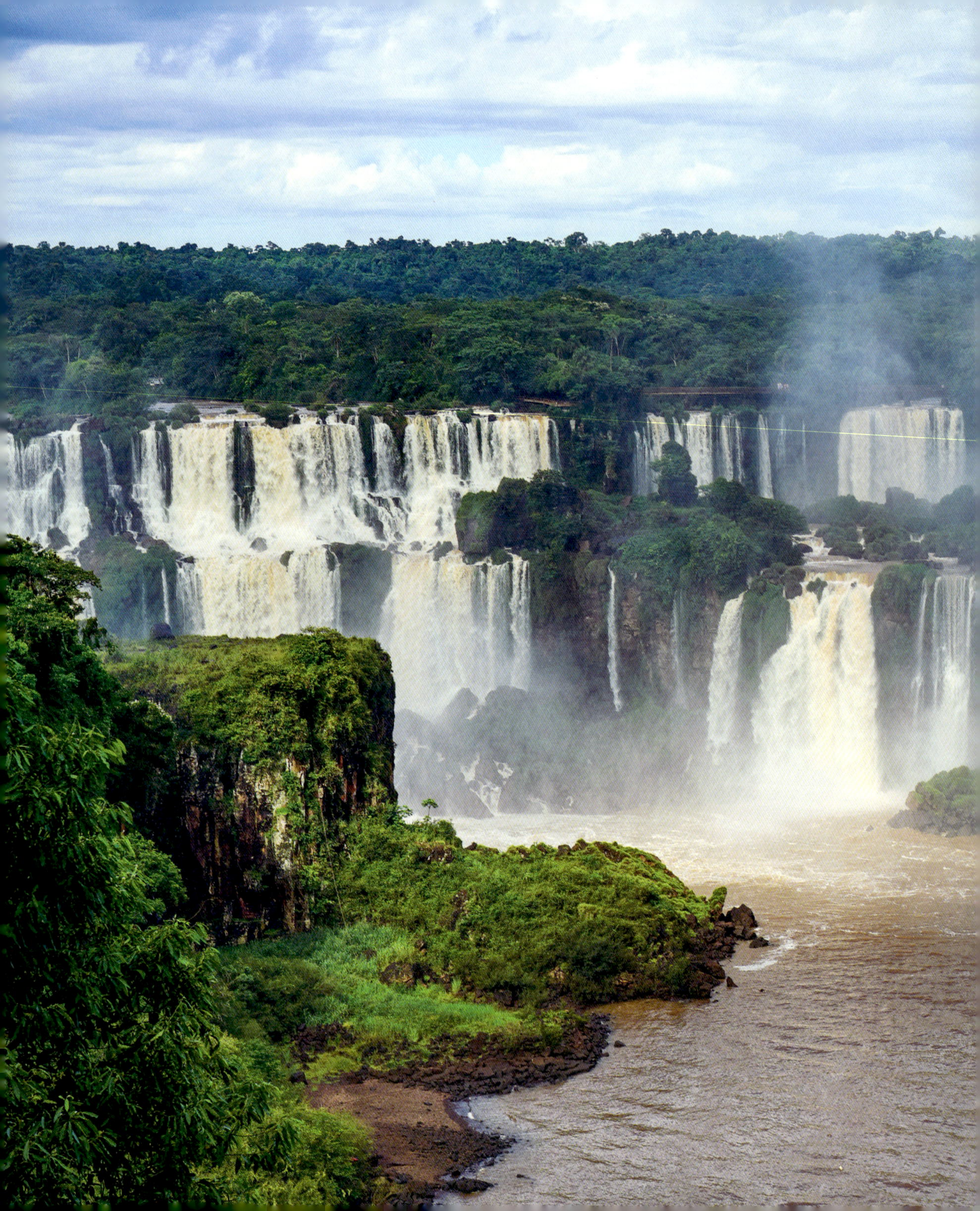

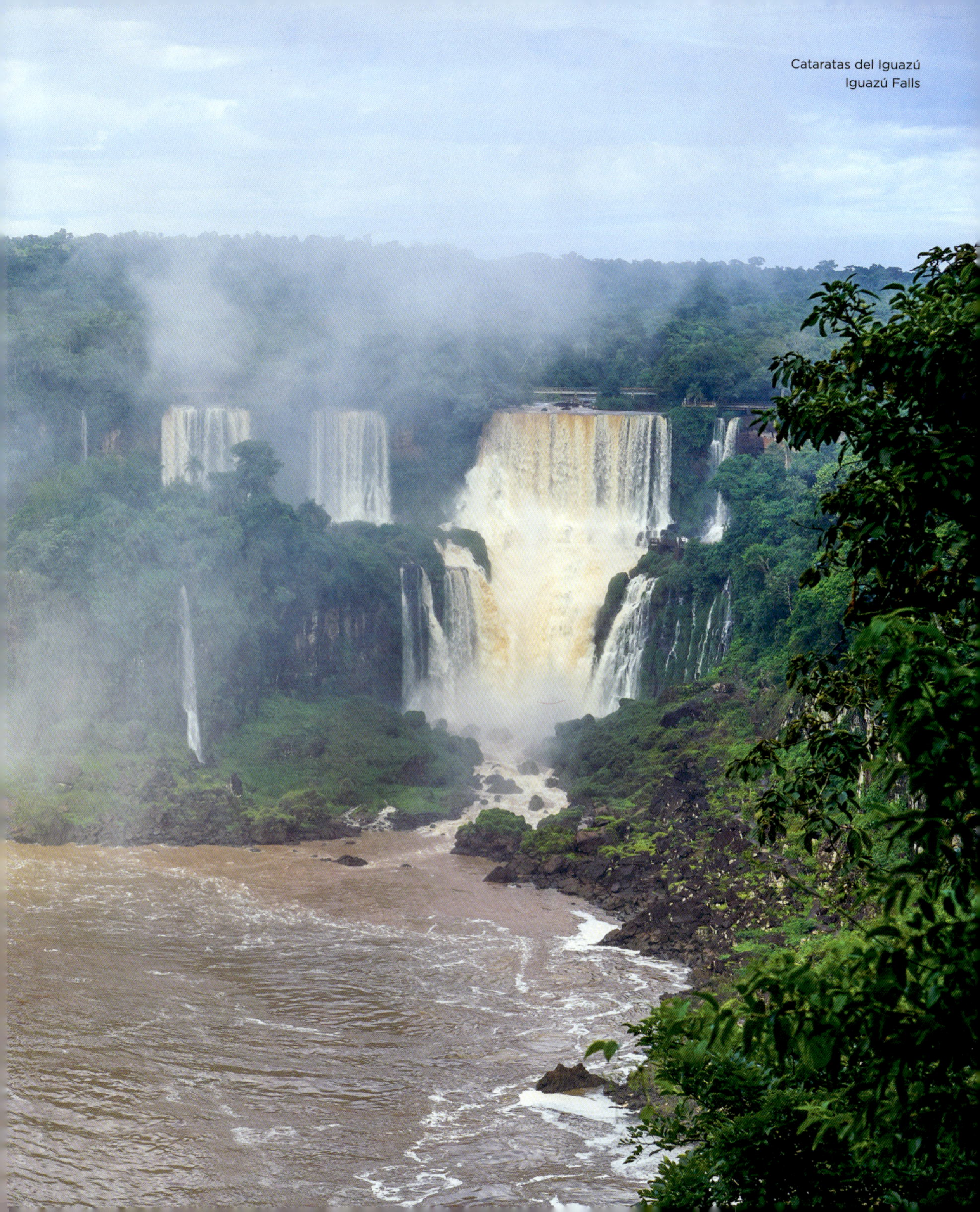

Cataratas del Iguazú
Iguazú Falls

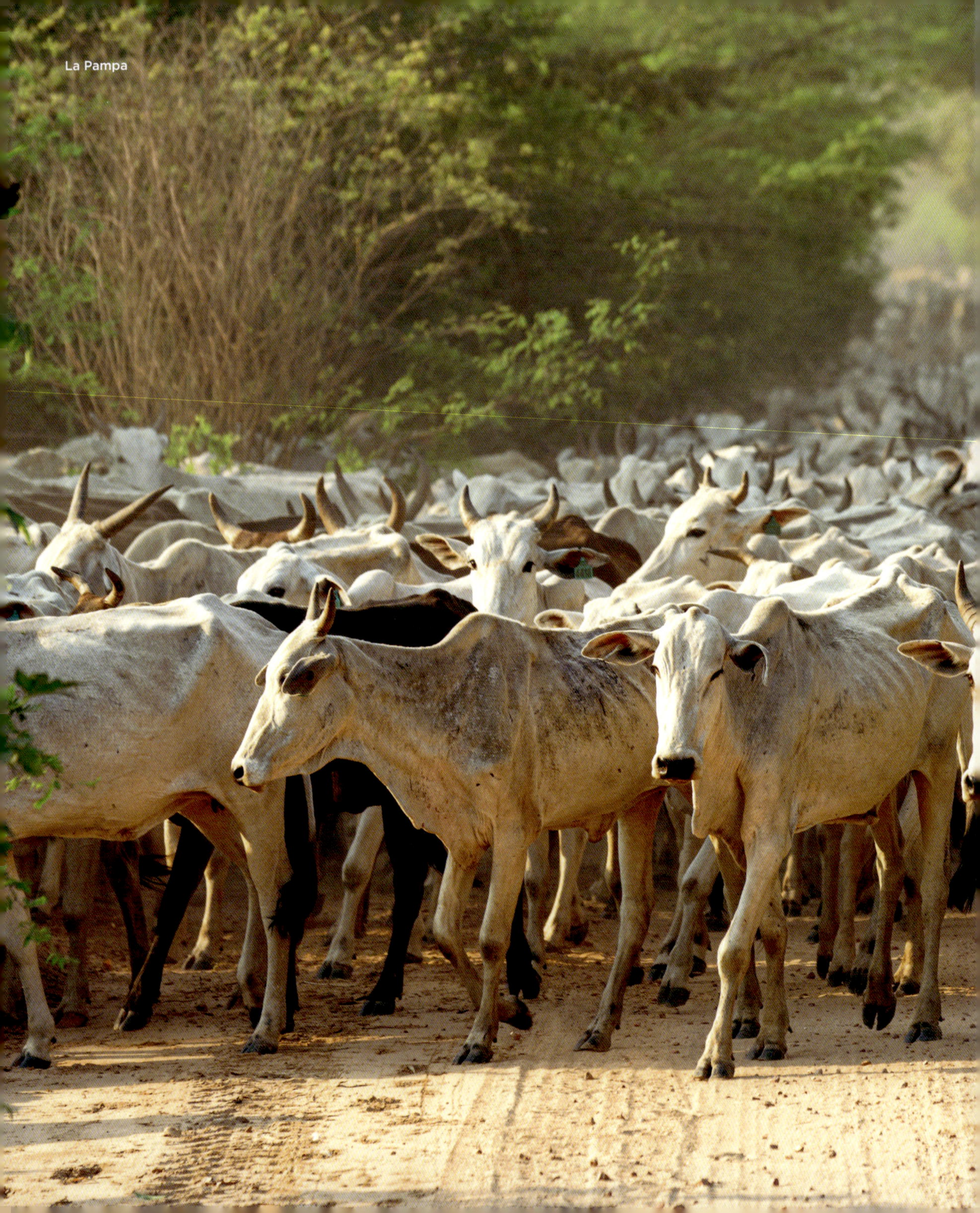
La Pampa

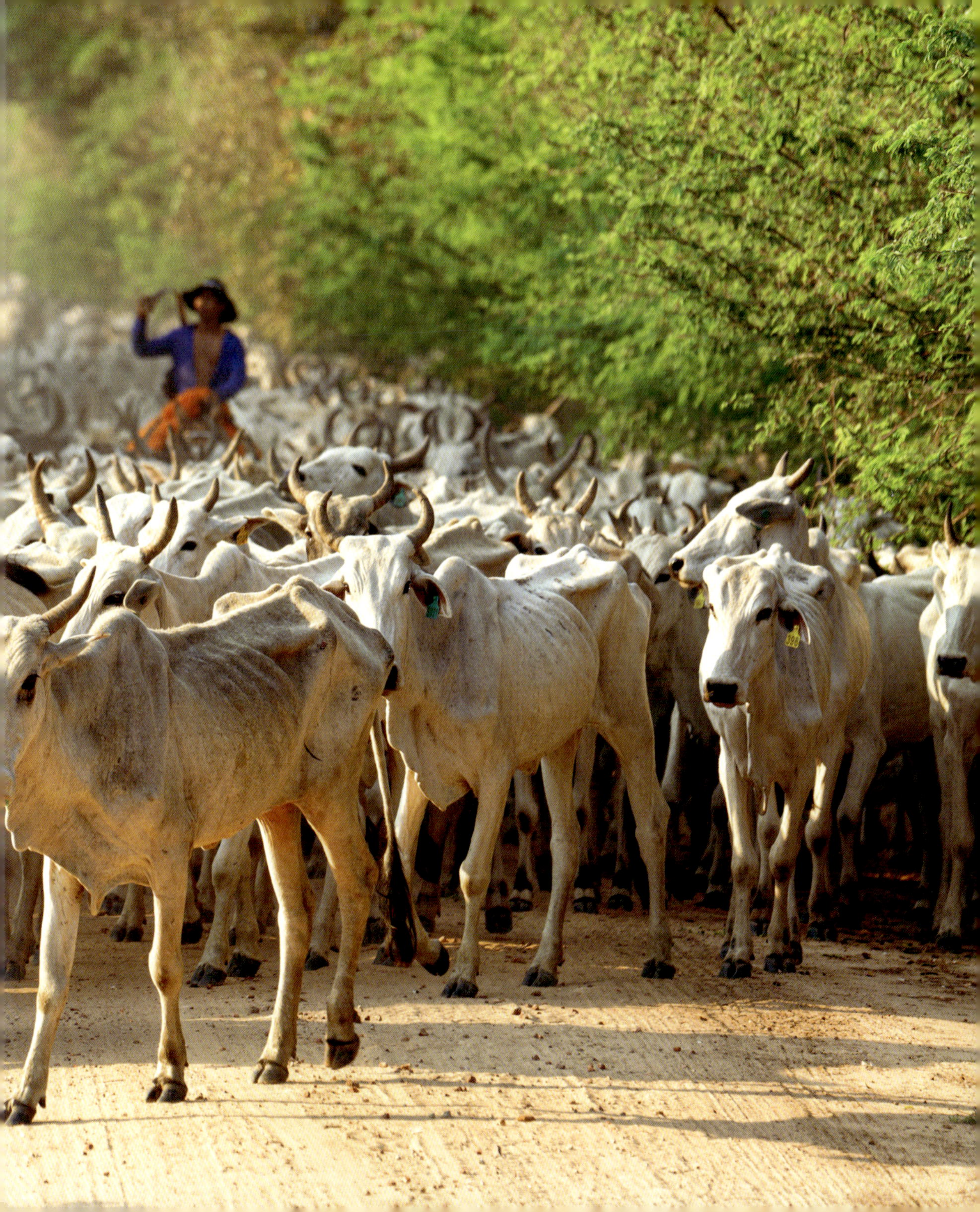

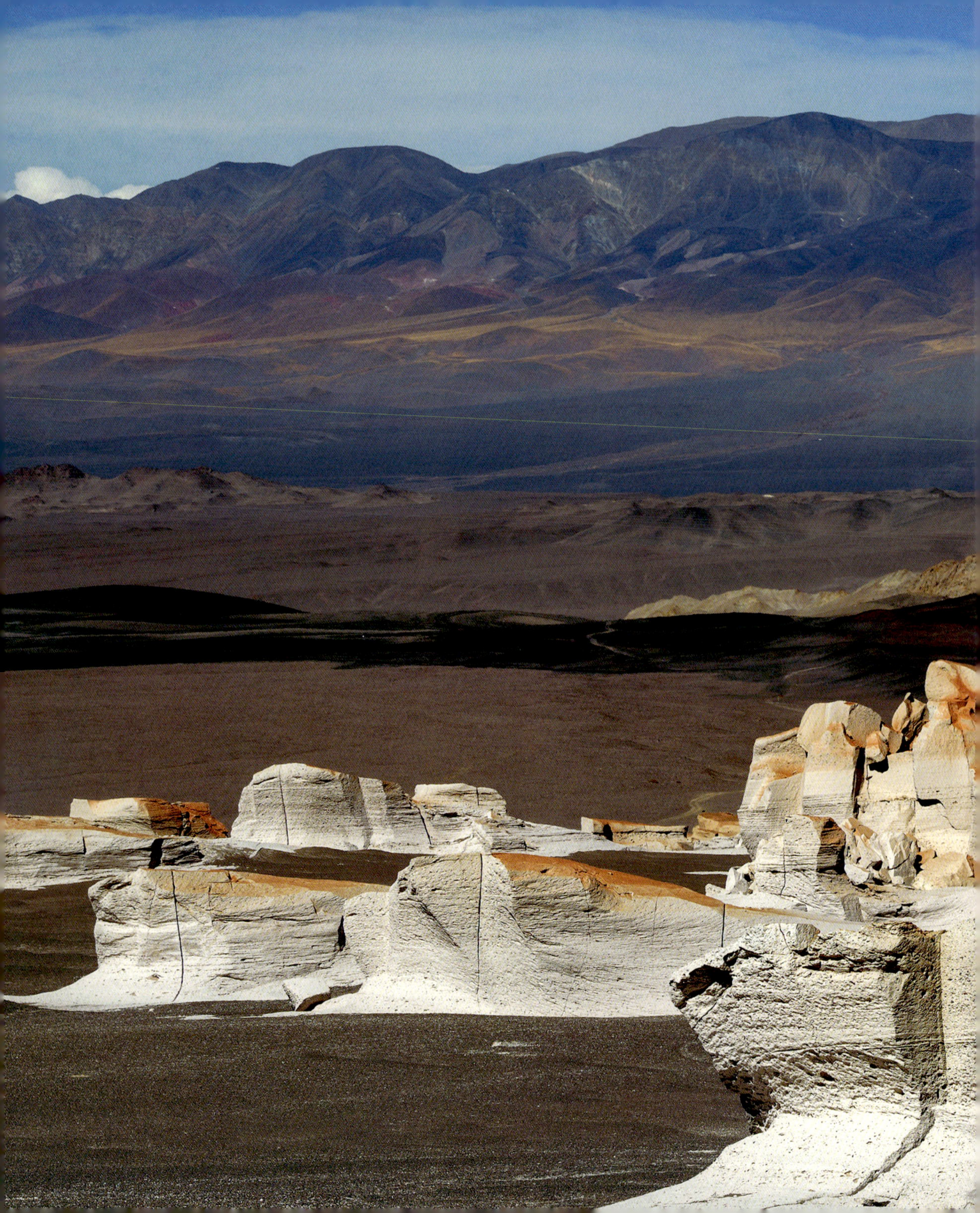

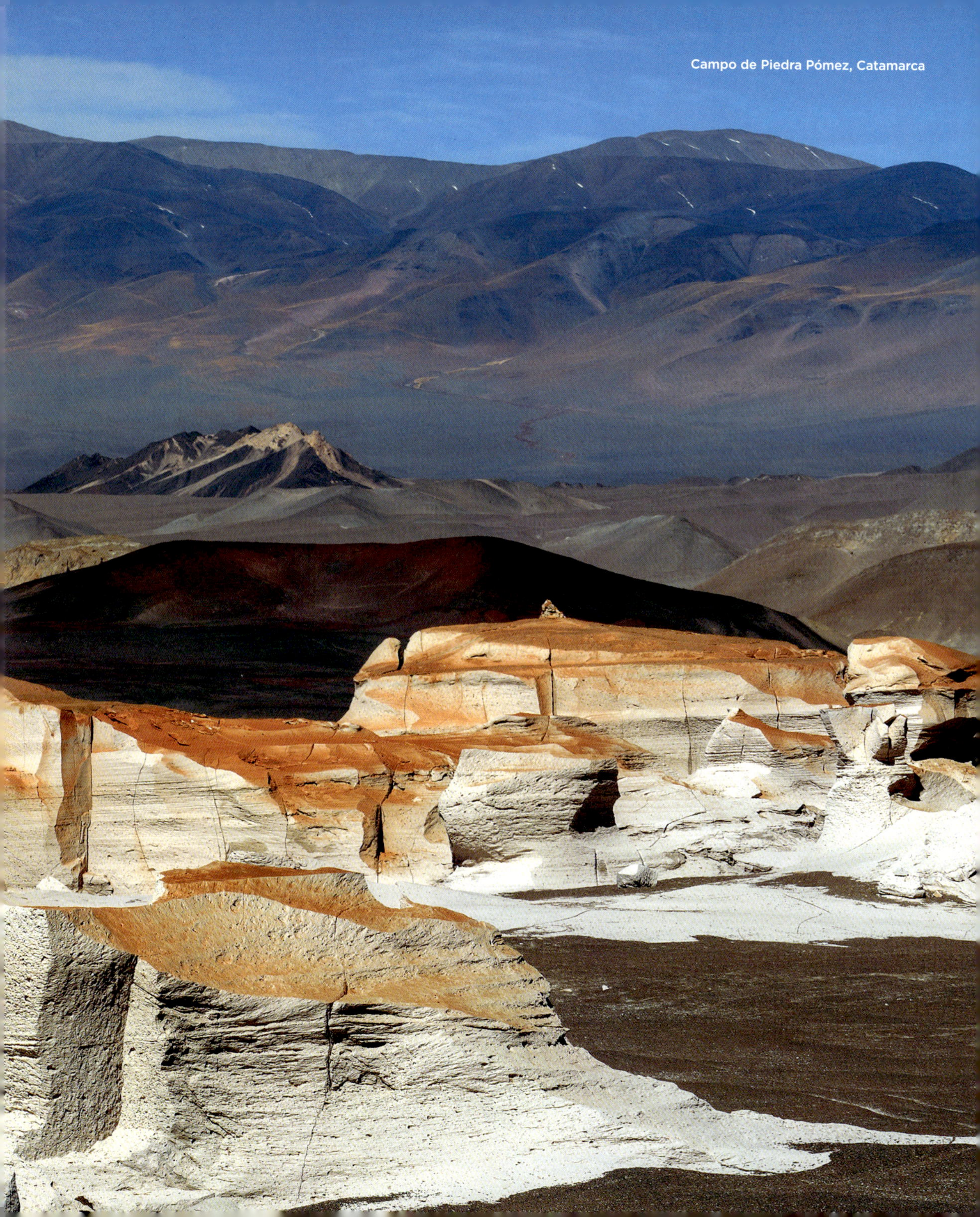
Campo de Piedra Pómez, Catamarca

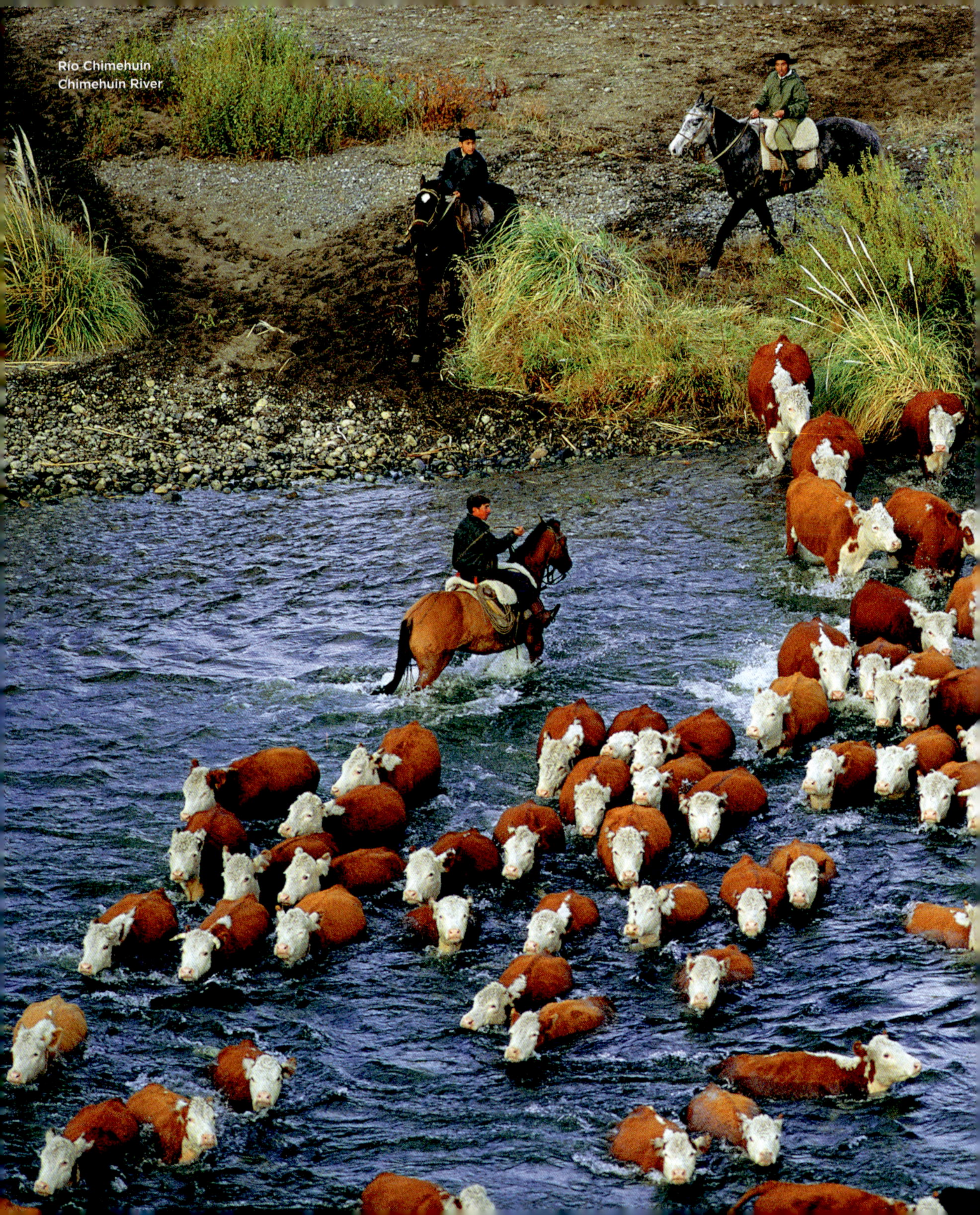

Río Chimehuin
Chimehuin River

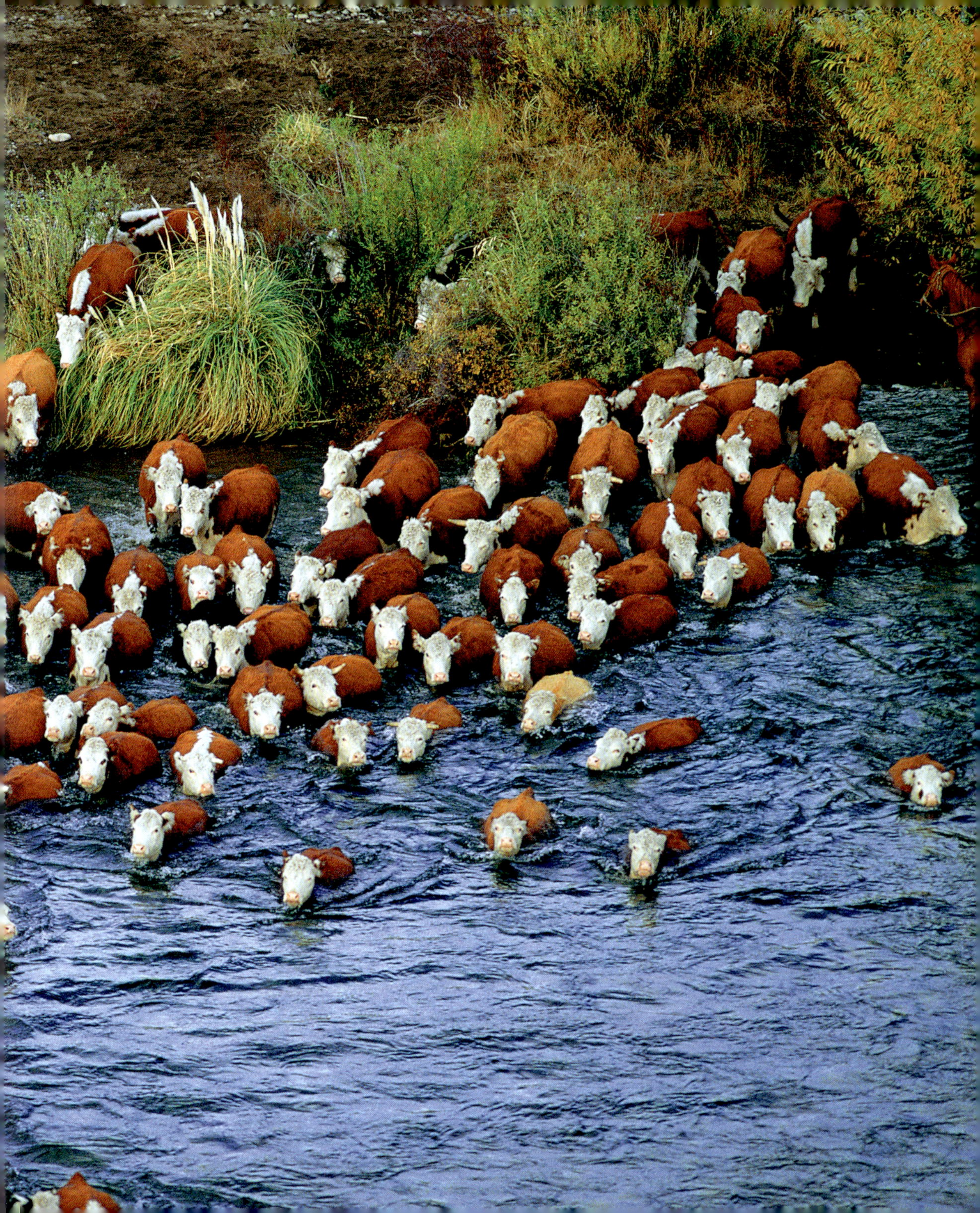

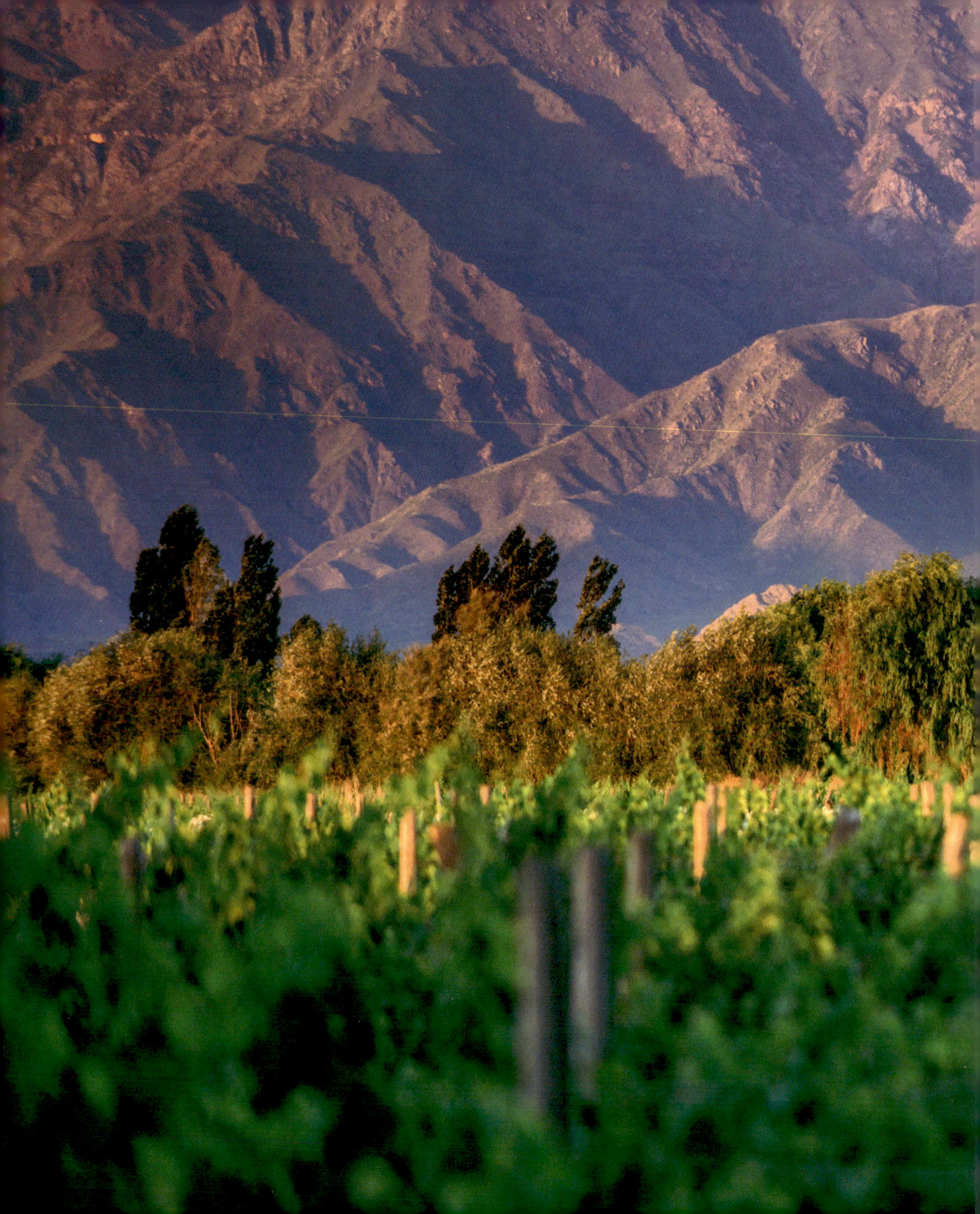

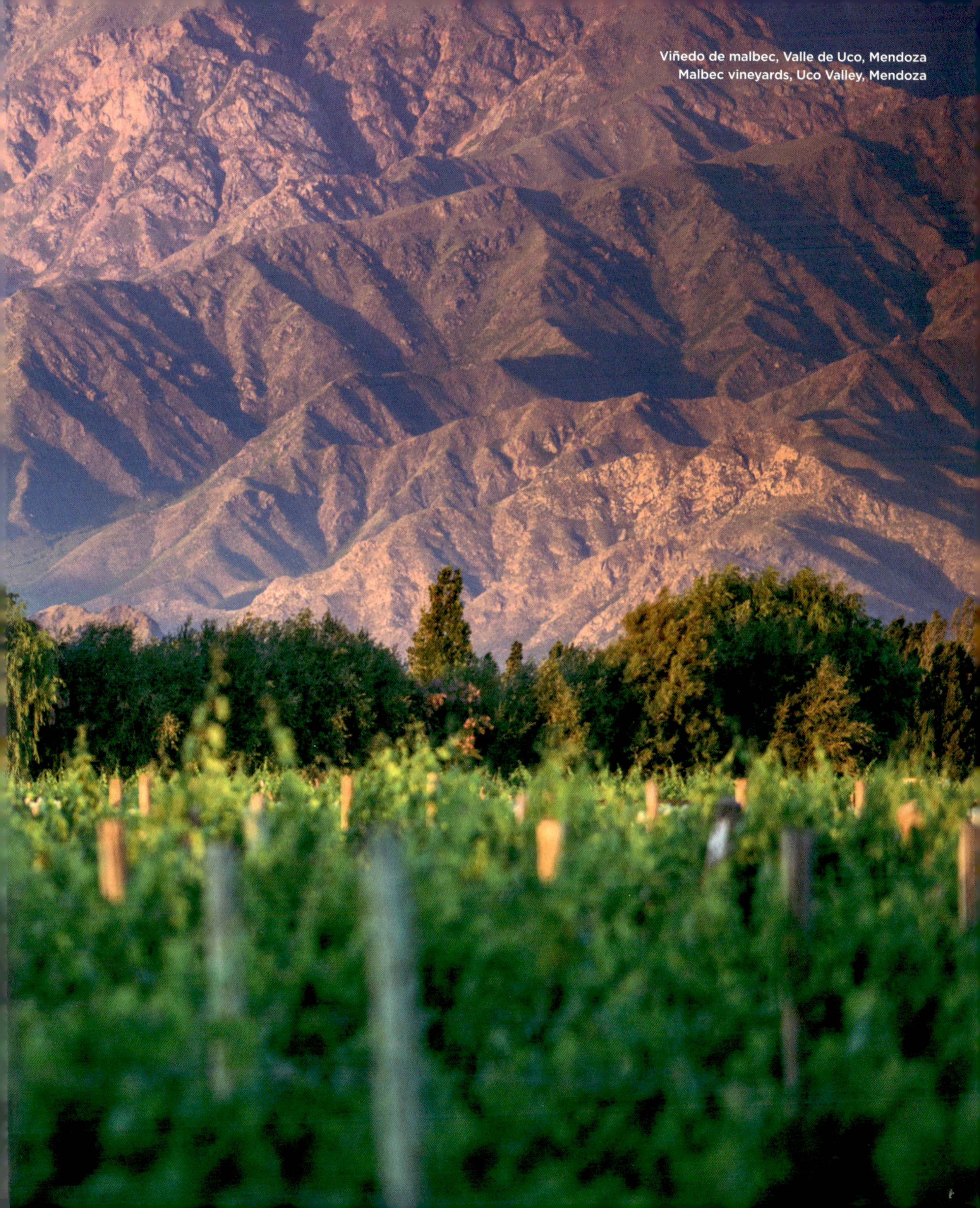

Viñedo de malbec, Valle de Uco, Mendoza
Malbec vineyards, Uco Valley, Mendoza

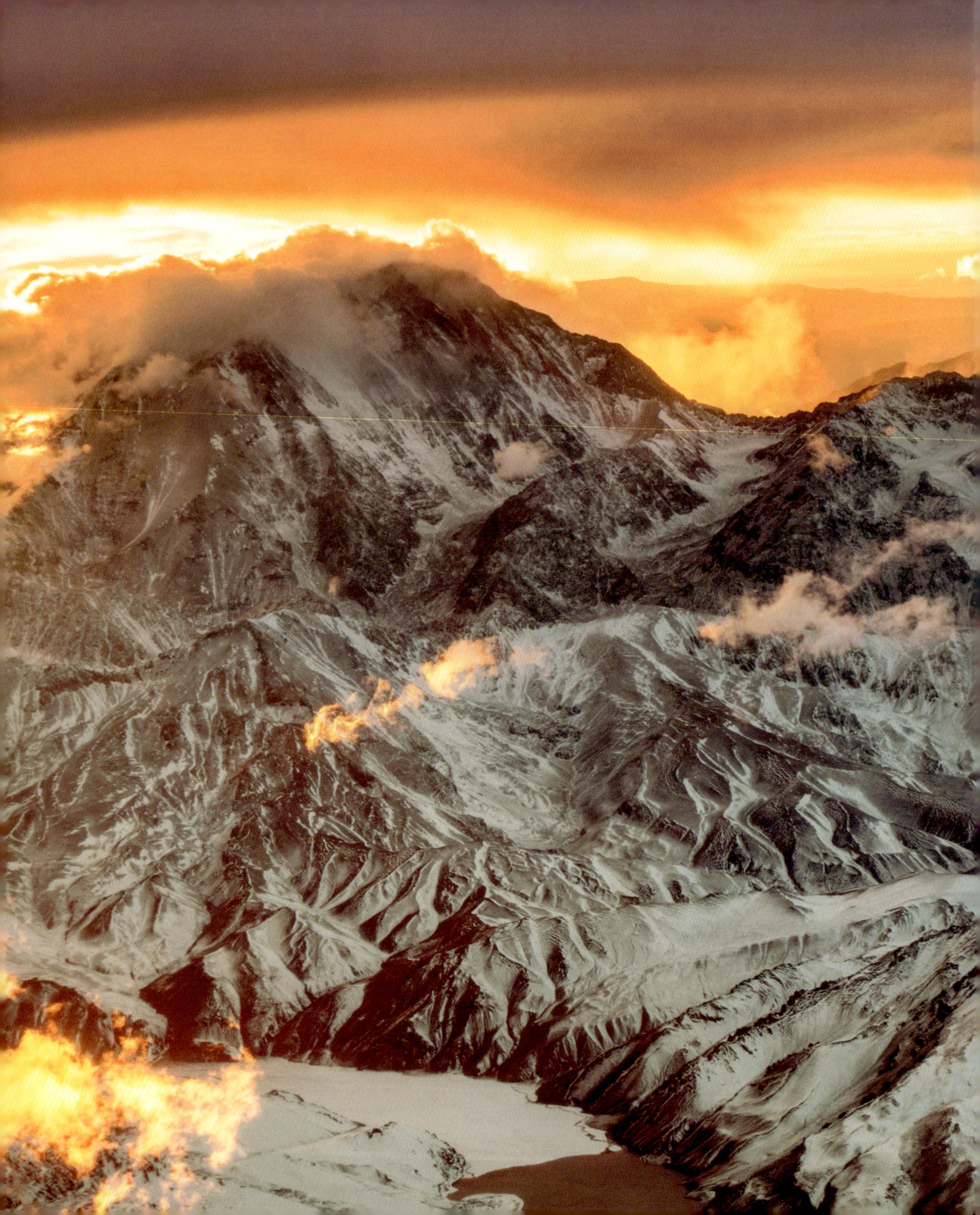

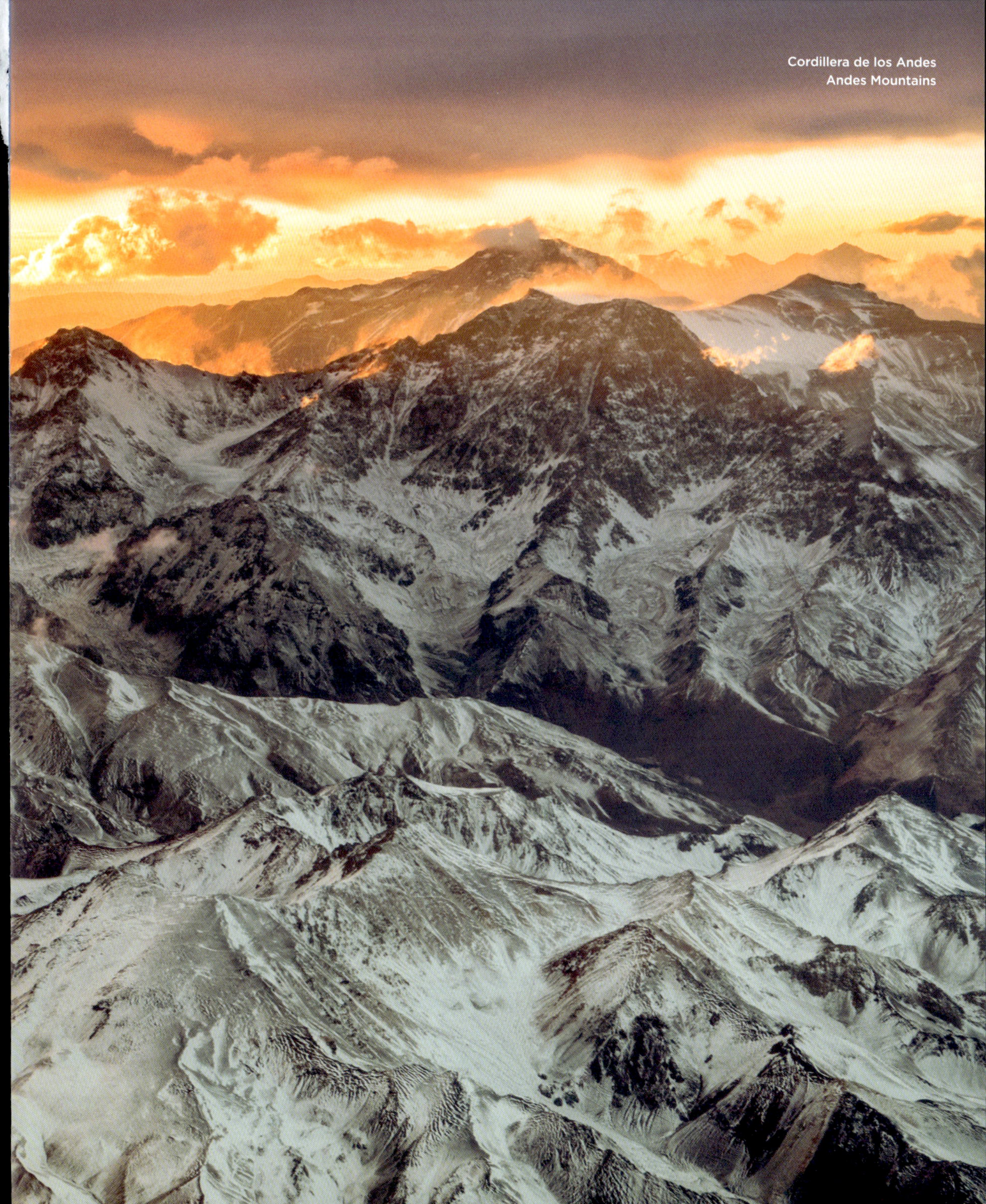

Cordillera de los Andes
Andes Mountains

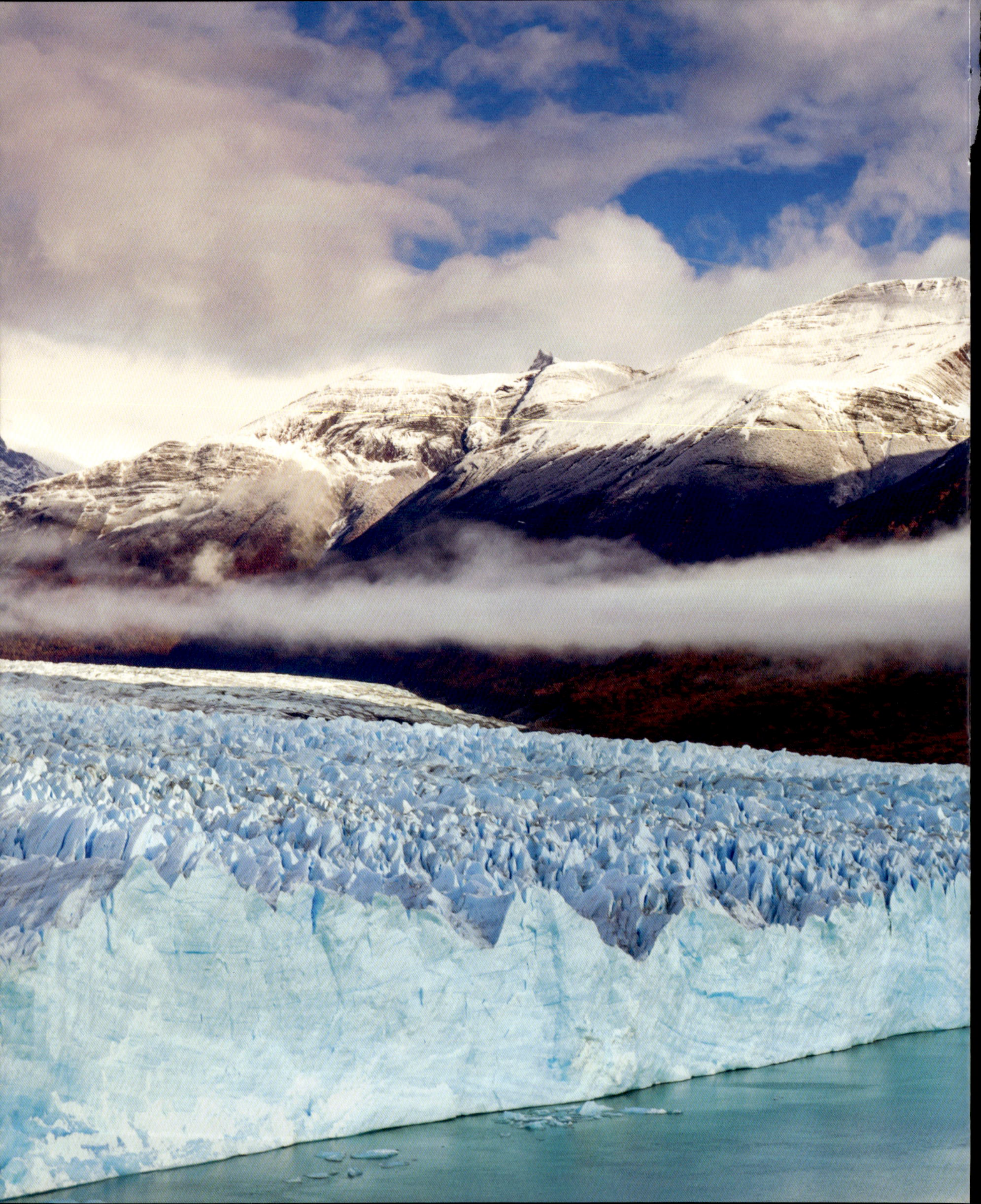

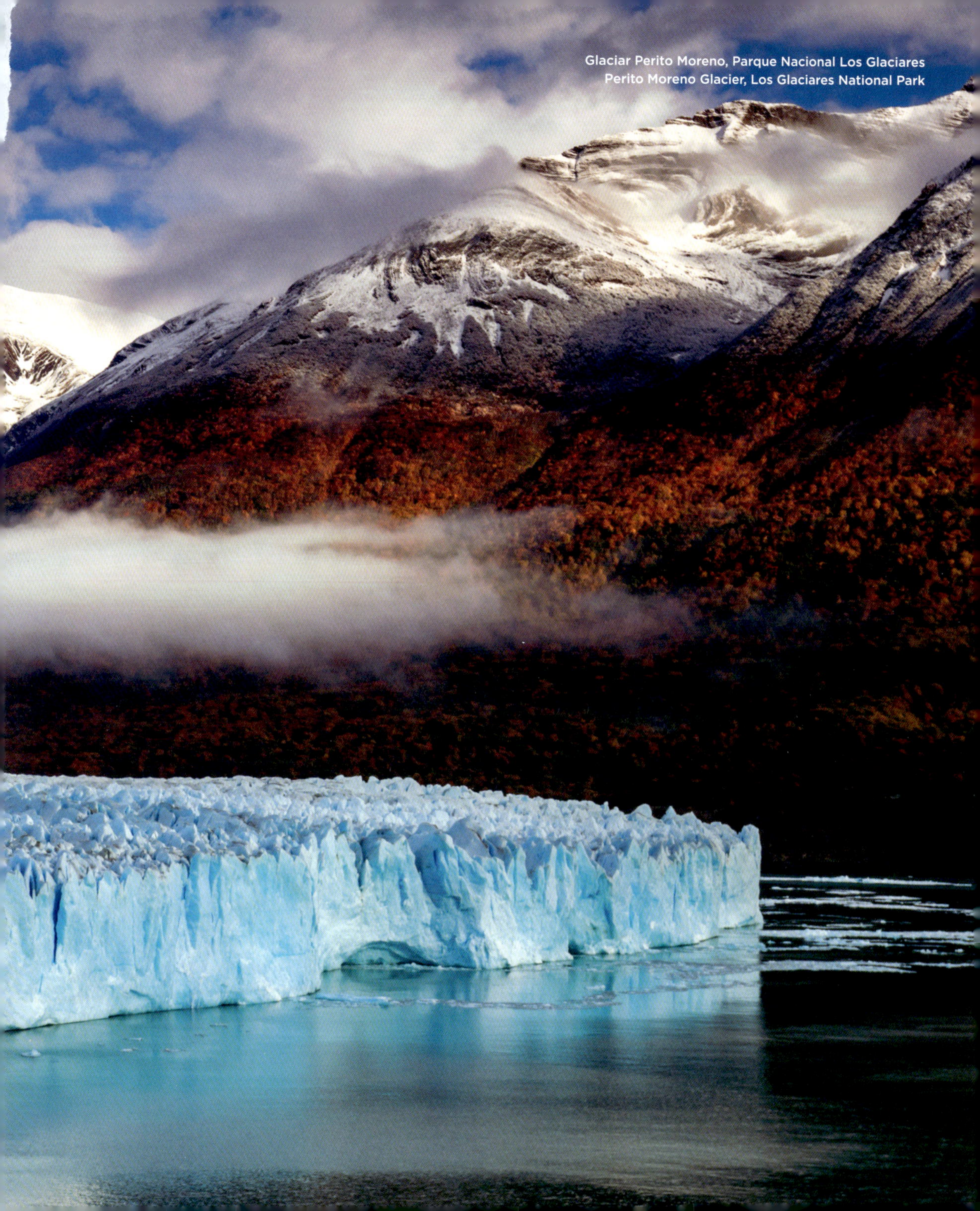
Glaciar Perito Moreno, Parque Nacional Los Glaciares
Perito Moreno Glacier, Los Glaciares National Park

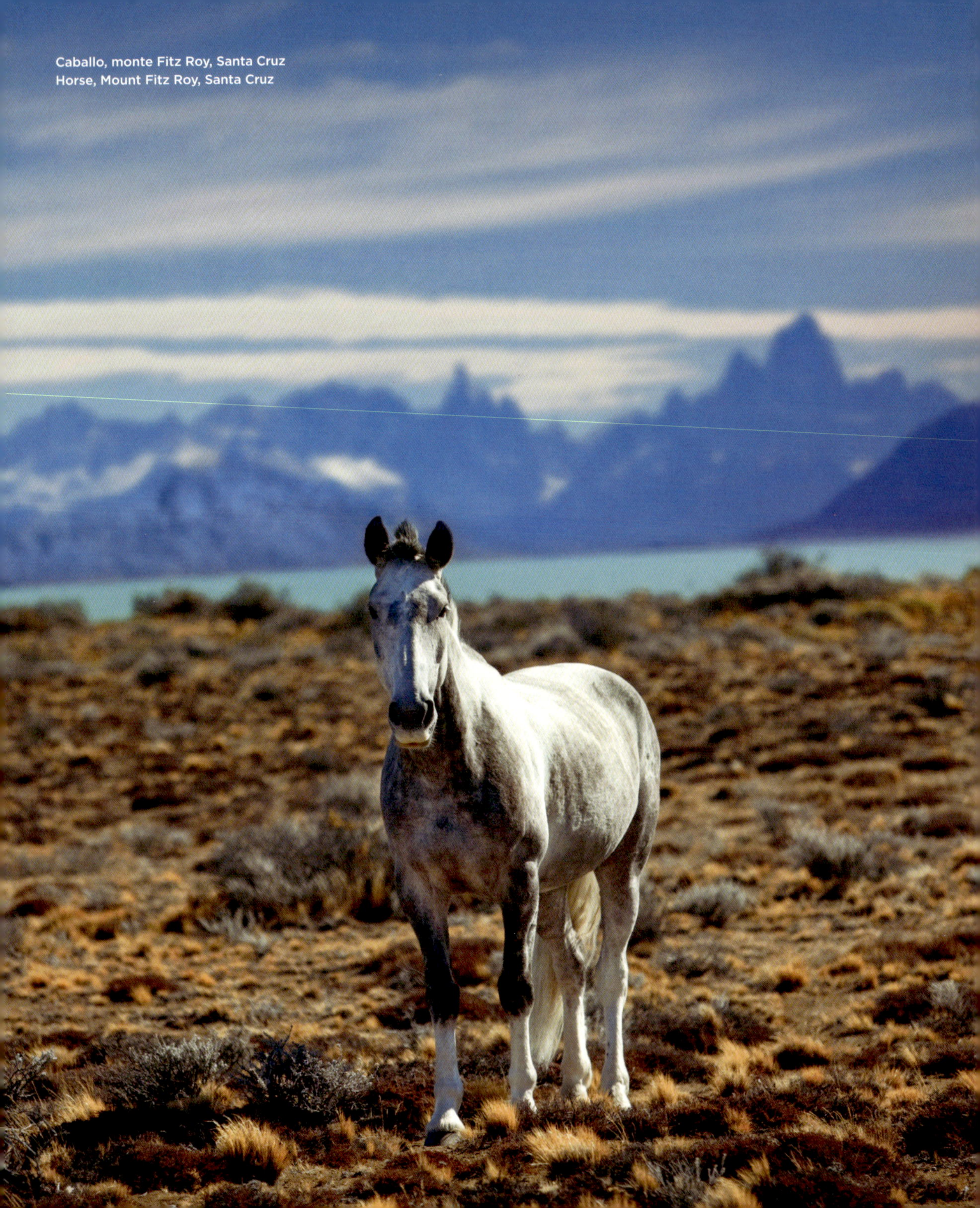

Caballo, monte Fitz Roy, Santa Cruz
Horse, Mount Fitz Roy, Santa Cruz

Contents · Sommaire · Inhalt · Índice · Inhoud

20 Introduction
Introducción
Einleitung
Introduçao
Inleiding

24 Jujuy

46 Salta & Catamarca

80 Argentinian cuisine
La cuisine argentine
Argentinische Küche
Cocina argentina
Cozinha argentina
Argentijnse keuken

90 Región del Litoral

120 Buenos Aires

134 Churrasco

158 Tango origins
Tango : le succès
Ursprünge des Tango
Orígenes del tango
Origens do Tango
Tango oorsprong

162 Tango

202 Polo
Pólo

212 La Rioja

226 Córdoba

240 San Luis

250 Mendoza

268 La Pampa

332 Neuquén

354 Río Negro

372 Chubut

388 Santa Cruz

448 Tierra del Fuego
Terre de Feu
Feuerland
Terra do Fogo
Vuurland

474 Malvinas
Les îles Malouines
Malwinen
Islas Malvinas

502 Argentine Antarctica
L'Antarctique argentine
Argentinische Antarktis
Antártida Argentina
Argentijns Antarctica

512 Index

514 Photo credits

Argentina

The name Argentina already sounds auspicious, being derived from the Latin argentum, or silver. Spanish colonizers vainly hoped to find precious metals when they arrived at the Rio de la Plata (Silver River). However, the country became very rich in the middle of the 19th century through the meat and wool industries, located in the heartlands of the Pampas and Patagonia. Europeans were hired to work seasonally on the *estancias.* The port city of Buenos Aires rose like a phoenix from the ashes, and The 'City of the Tango' soon soared to become the richest and most modern metropolis in Latin America. With an area of 2 791 910 km² (1,077,962 sq mi), Argentina is the second largest country on the subcontinent after Brazil. Its absolute peculiarity lies in its north-south extension of 3700 km (2,300 mi), which brings with it the extreme climatic contrasts of the tropics in the north and arctic ice in the south. Between the 5100 km (3170 mi) long Atlantic coast in the east and the Andes in the west, hosting the highest peak of the Americas, stretches the vast grassland of the Pampas and Patagonia. Here you can still experience the wild romanticism of the gaucho culture. In the northwest, on the border with Bolivia and Chile, there are traces of pre-historic and pre-Columbian civilization, and a richly diverse fauna. The natural wonders of the impressive Iguazú waterfalls in the border region to Brazil, the whales and elephant seals near the Valdés peninsula, all offer unique worlds of experience, as do the spectacular glacier landscapes of Patagonia and Tierra del Fuego's 'lighthouse at the end of the world'.

Argentine

L'Argentine porte un nom prometteur, hérité du latin *argentum* (argent). À leur arrivée aux abords du río de la Plata («fleuve de l'argent»), les colons espagnols espéraient en effet y trouver le précieux métal. En vain. Le pays connut toutefois la prospérité au milieu du xixᵉ siècle, grâce aux industries de la viande et de la laine installées dans les régions centrales des pampas et de la Patagonie. Dans les estancias, les Européens travaillaient comme saisonniers. Buenos Aires, ville portuaire, a réussi, tel le phénix, à renaître de ses cendres. La ville du tango est rapidement devenue la plus riche et la plus moderne métropole d'Amérique latine. Avec une superficie de 2 791 910 km², l'Argentine est, après le Brésil, le deuxième plus grand pays du sous-continent. Sa principale particularité tient à son étendue nord-sud de 3 700 km et aux contrastes climatiques extrêmes qui en découlent. Le nord du pays vit sous les tropiques, alors que le sud est couvert de glace antarctique. Entre la côte atlantique – longue de 5 100 km – à l'est et les Andes à l'ouest, qui comptent le plus haut sommet d'Amérique, s'étendent les vastes prairies et steppes des pampas et de la Patagonie. Aujourd'hui encore, on y goûte le romantisme sauvage de la culture *gaucho.* Le Nord-Ouest, frontalier de la Bolivie et du Chili, recèle les vestiges des peuples préhistoriques et précolombiens, ainsi qu'une faune très riche. De nombreuses merveilles de la nature, dont les imposantes chutes d'Iguazú à la frontière brésilienne, ou la presqu'île de Valdès, séjour des baleines et des éléphants de mer, offrent des terres d'aventure uniques, tout comme le spectaculaire paysage des glaciers de la Patagonie et du phare de la Terre de Feu, au bout du monde.

Argentinien

Verheißungsvoll klingt schon der Name Argentinien, er leitet sich vom lateinischen *argentum* (Silber) ab. Spanische Kolonisatoren hofften bei ihrer Ankunft am Rio de la Plata (Silberfluss) Edelmetalle zu finden. Vergebens. Doch zu großem Reichtum kam das Land Mitte des 19. Jahrhunderts durch Fleischwirtschaft und Wolle im Kernland der Pampa und in Patagonien. Europäer wurden angeheuert, um saisonal auf den Estanzias zu arbeiten. Buenos Aires, die Hafenstadt, erhob sich wie Phönix aus der Asche. Die Stadt des Tangos stieg bald zur reichsten und modernsten Metropole Lateinamerikas auf. Mit einer Fläche von 2 791 910 km² ist Argentinien nach Brasilien das zweitgrößte Land des Subkontinents. Seine absolute Besonderheit liegt in der Nord-Südausdehnung von 3700 km, die extreme klimatische Gegensätze mit sich bringt: Tropen im Norden und arktisches Eis im Süden. Zwischen der 5100 km langen Atlantikküste im Osten und den Anden im Westen mit dem höchsten Gipfel Amerikas erstreckt sich das weite Grasland der Pampa und Patagoniens. Hier ist auch heute die wilde Romantik der Gaucho-Kultur zu erleben. Im Nordwesten an der Grenze zu Bolivien und Chile finden sich prä-historische und prä-kolumbische Spuren und eine reiche Tierwelt. Das Naturwunder der imposanten Iguazú-Wasserfälle im Grenzgebiet zu Brasilien, die Wale und Seeelefanten bei der Halbinsel Valdés bieten einzigartige Erlebniswelten ebenso wie die spektakuläre Gletscherlandschaft Patagoniens und Feuerlands Leuchtturm am Ende der Welt.

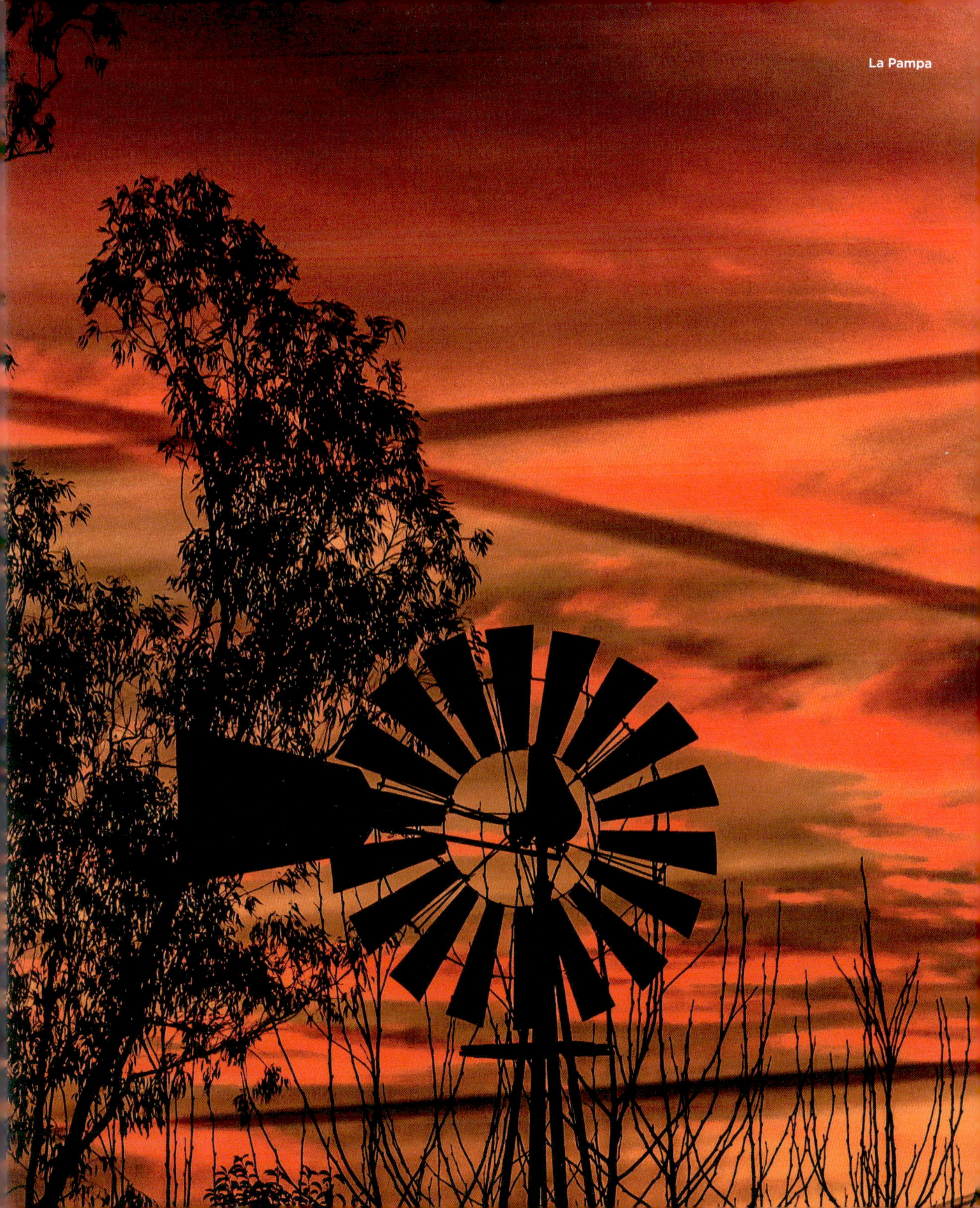
La Pampa

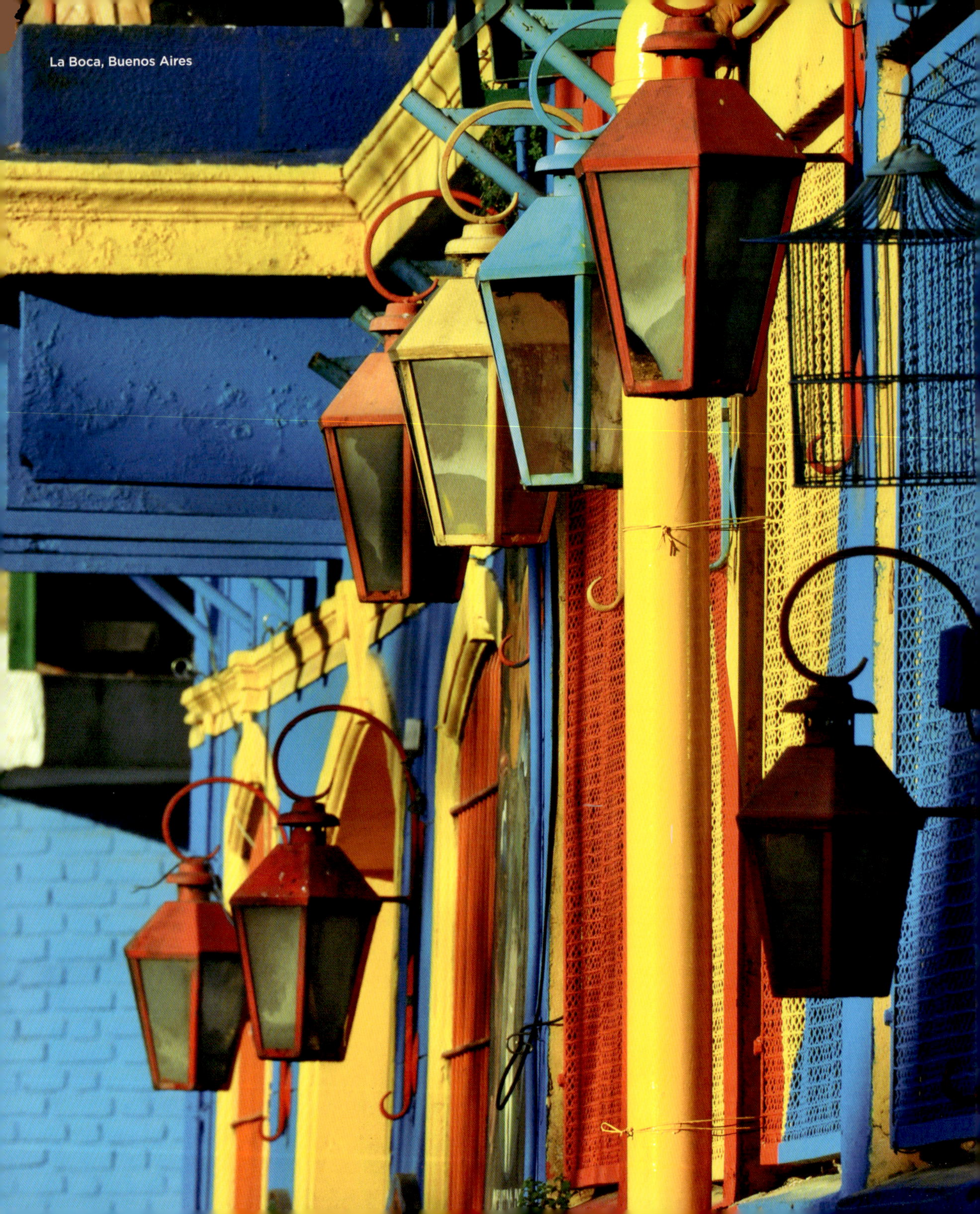
La Boca, Buenos Aires

Argentina

El nombre Argentina, que proviene de la palabra latina *argentum* (plata), ya suena prometedor. Los colonizadores españoles esperaban encontrar metales preciosos cuando llegaron al Río de la Plata. Fue en vano; pero el país se hizo muy rico a mediados del siglo XIX, gracias a la industria de la carne y la lana en el corazón de la Pampa y la Patagonia. Los europeos fueron contratados para trabajar por temporadas en las estancias. La ciudad portuaria de Buenos Aires se levantó de sus cenizas como un fénix. La ciudad del tango pronto se elevó para convertirse en la metrópoli más rica y moderna de América Latina. Con una superficie de 2 791 910 km², Argentina es el segundo país más grande del subcontinente después de Brasil. Su absoluta peculiaridad radica en su extensión de norte a sur de 3700 km, lo que trae consigo contrastes climáticos extremos: trópicos en el norte y hielo ártico en el sur. Entre los 5100 km de la costa atlántica en el este y los Andes en el oeste con el pico más alto de América, se extiende la vasta pradera de las Pampas y la Patagonia. Aquí todavía se puede vivir el salvaje romanticismo de la cultura gaucha. En el noroeste, en la frontera con Bolivia y Chile, hay huellas prehistóricas y precolombinas, y una rica fauna. Las maravillas naturales de las impresionantes cataratas de Iguazú en la región fronteriza con Brasil, las ballenas y los elefantes marinos cerca de la península Valdés ofrecen mundos de experiencia únicos, así como el espectacular paisaje de los glaciares de la Patagonia y el faro de Tierra del Fuego en el fin del mundo.

Argentina

O nome Argentina já soa promissor, é derivado do latim *argentum* (prata). Os colonizadores espanhóis esperavam encontrar metais preciosos quando chegassem ao Rio da Prata. Em vão. Mas o país tornou-se muito rico em meados do século XIX, através da indústria da carne e da lã no coração dos Pampas e da Patagônia. Os europeus foram contratados para trabalhar sazonalmente nas fazendas. Buenos Aires, a cidade portuária, levantou-se como uma fênix das cinzas. A cidade do tango logo se tornou a metrópole mais rica e moderna da América Latina. Com uma área de 2 791 910 km², a Argentina é o segundo maior país do subcontinente, depois do Brasil. Sua peculiaridade absoluta está em sua extensão norte-sul de 3700 km, o que traz consigo contrastes climáticos extremos: trópicos no norte e gelo ártico no sul. Entre os 5100 km de costa atlântica no leste e os Andes no oeste, com o pico mais alto da América, estendem-se vastas pastagens dos Pampas e da Patagônia. Aqui você ainda pode experimentar o romantismo selvagem da cultura gaúcha. No noroeste, na fronteira com a Bolívia e o Chile, existem vestígios pré-históricos e pré-colombianos e uma fauna rica. As maravilhas naturais das impressionantes cachoeiras do Iguaçu na região fronteiriça com o Brasil, as baleias e elefantes-marinhos perto da península de Valdés oferecem mundos de experiência únicos, assim como a espetacular paisagem glacial da Patagônia e o farol da Terra do Fogo no fim do mundo.

Argentinië

De naam Argentinië klinkt al veelbelovend. Hij is afgeleid van het Latijnse *argentum* (zilver). De Spaanse kolonisten hoopten edelmetalen te vinden toen ze bij de Rio de la Plata (Zilverrivier) aankwamen. Tevergeefs. In het midden van de 19e eeuw kwam het land echter tot grote rijkdom door de vlees- en wolindustrie in het hart van de pampa en Patagonië. Europeanen werden ingehuurd om seizoensgebonden op de zgn. estancias te werken. Buenos Aires, de havenstad, steeg als een feniks op uit de as. De stad van de tango groeide al snel tot de rijkste en modernste metropool van Latijns-Amerika. Met een oppervlakte van 2 791 910 km² is Argentinië na Brazilië het grootste land van het subcontinent. Zijn absolute bijzonderheid ligt in de uitgestrektheid van noord tot zuid van 3700 km, die extreme klimatologische contrasten met zich meebrengt: de tropen in het noorden en het arctische ijs in het zuiden. Het uitgebreide grasland van de pampa en Patagonië strekt zich uit tussen de 5100 km lange Atlantische kust in het oosten en de Andes met de hoogste top van Amerika in het westen. Hier valt ook vandaag de dag nog de wilde romantiek van de gaucho-cultuur te beleven. In het noordwesten, aan de grens met Bolivia en Chili, bevinden zich prehistorische en pre-Columbiaanse sporen en een rijke fauna. De natuurwonderen van de indrukwekkende Watervallen van de Iguaçu in het grensgebied met Brazilië en de walvissen en zeeolifanten bij het schiereiland Valdés bieden unieke belevingswerelden, net als het spectaculaire gletsjerlandschap van Patagonië en de vuurtoren van Vuurland aan het "einde van de wereld".

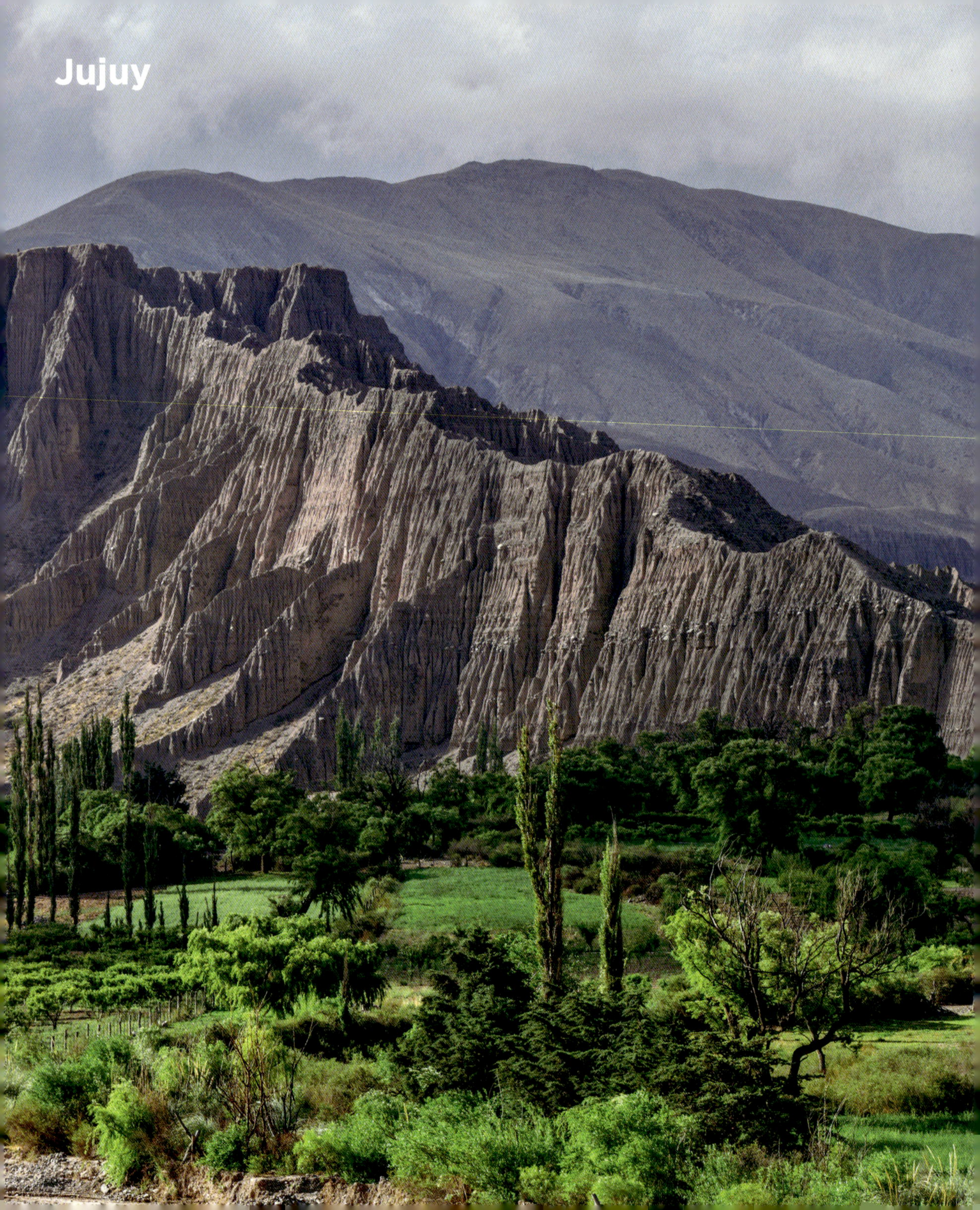
Jujuy

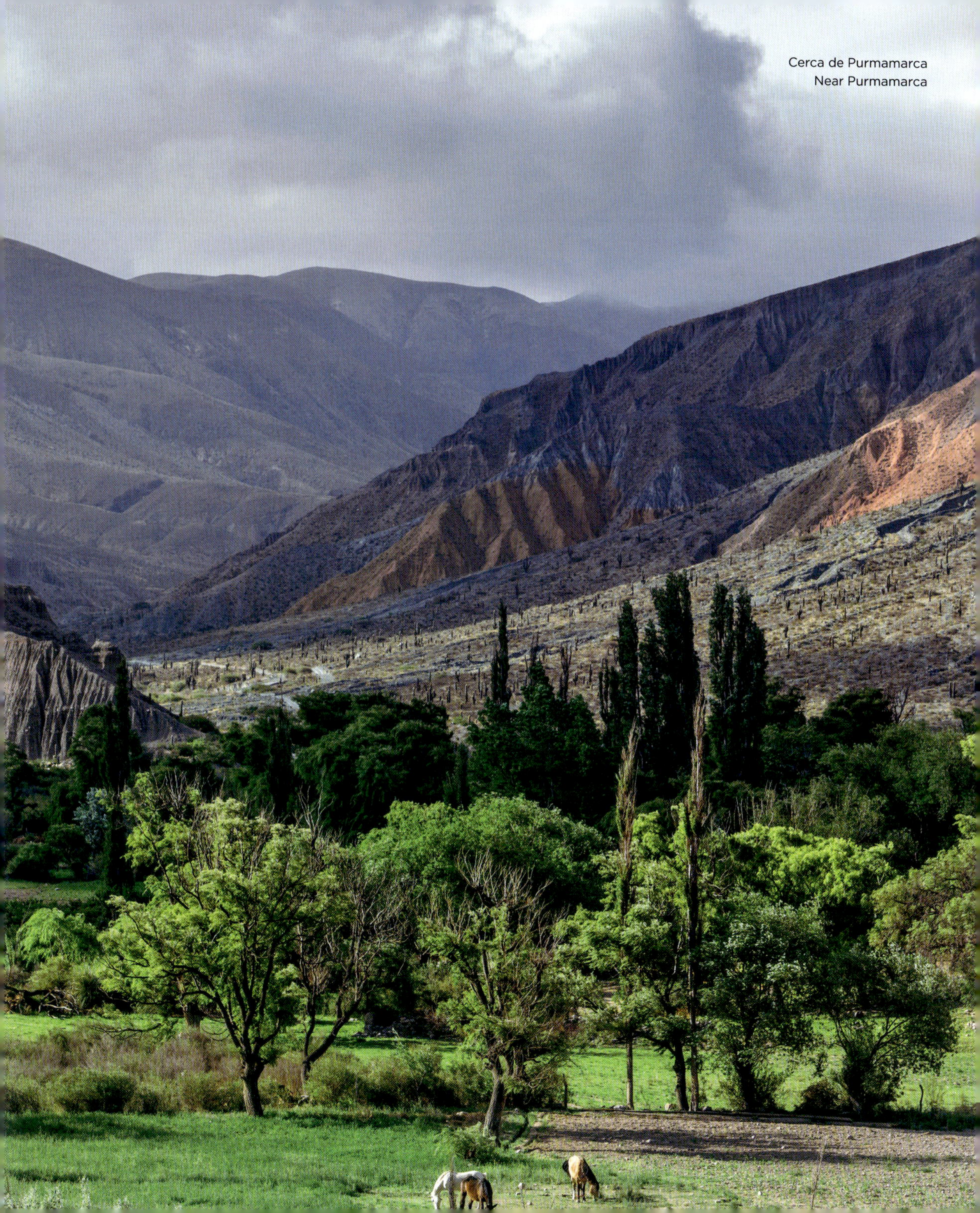

Cerca de Purmamarca
Near Purmamarca

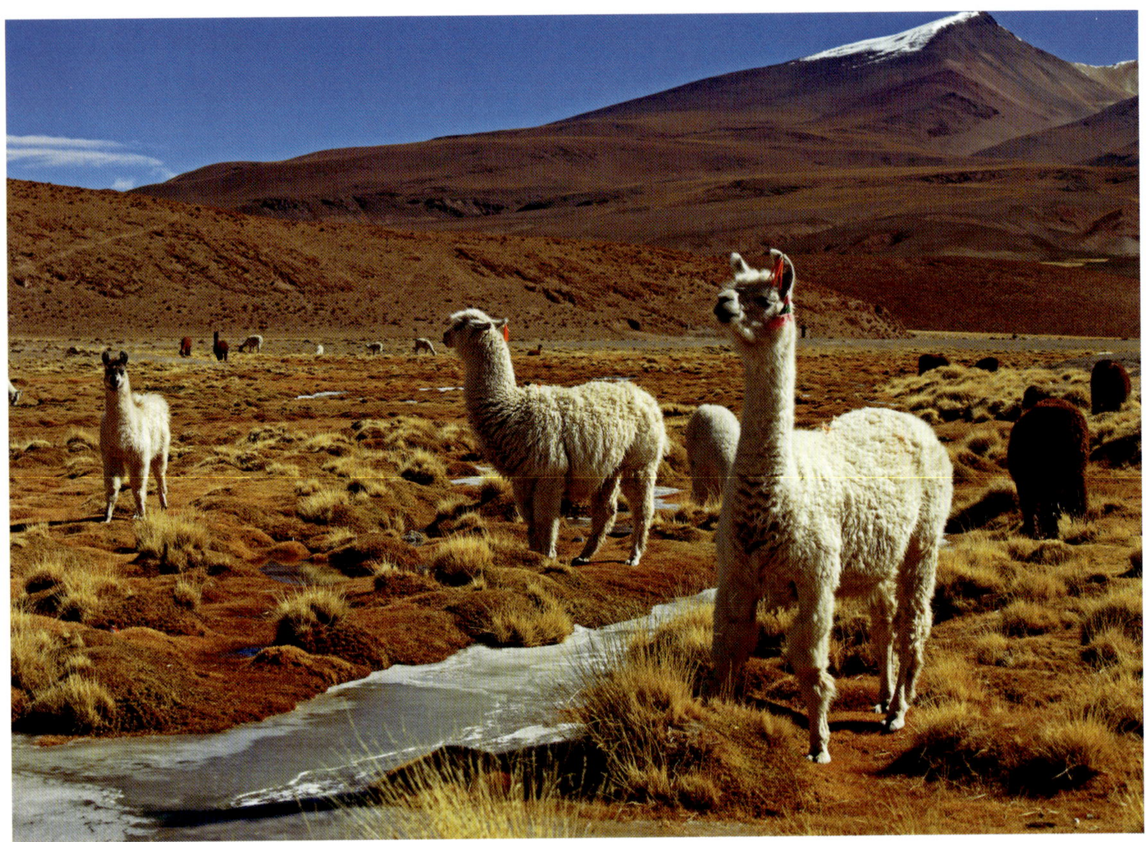

Llamas, puna de Atacama
Llamas, Atacama Plateau

Jujuy

The small, remote province borders Bolivia to the north and Chile to the west. The spectacular topography of the Andes chain, plateaus and river valleys determine the landscape and way of life. Jujuy is derived from the Quechua word "Xuxuyoc", which denoted the regional Inca ruler. Indigenous life is still present today, with 40,000 of these people living in the province. Its capital, San Salvador de Jujuy, is located at the confluence of the rivers Xibi Xibi and Rio Grande. Via the Andes pass of Paso de Jama, one arrives at the desert-like plateau of Puna de Atacama, which lies 4000 m (13,000 ft) above sea level, in the shadow of the Andes Cordillera. Here, the days are hot and the nights cold.

Jujuy

La petite province isolée est bordée au nord par la Bolivie et à l'ouest par le Chili. Une nature spectaculaire, la cordillère des Andes, les hauts plateaux et les vallées fluviales définissent paysage et mode de vie. « Jujuy » provient du mot quechua *xuxuyoc,* qui évoquait les souverains incas. La culture indienne est aujourd'hui encore bien vivante, puisque 40 000 Indiens habitent la province. Sa capitale, San Salvador de Jujuy, a été bâtie au confluent des fleuves río Xibi Xibi et río Grande. Au-delà du col andin Jama s'étend le haut plateau désertique de Puna de Atacama. Il s'élève à 4 000 m au-dessus du niveau de la mer, dans l'ombre de la cordillère des Andes. Les jours y sont brûlants et les nuits froides.

Jujuy

Die abgeschiedene, kleine Provinz grenzt im Norden an Bolivien und im Westen an Chile. Spektakuläre Natur, die Andenkette, Hochebenen und Flusstäler bestimmen Landschaft und Lebensweise. Jujuy leitet sich von dem Quechua-Wort „Xuxuyoc" ab. Es bezeichnete den regionalen Inka-Herrscher. Indianisches Leben ist auch heute gegenwärtig, denn 40 000 Indios bewohnen die Provinz. Ihre Hauptstadt, San Salvador de Jujuy, liegt an der Mündung der Flüsse Xibi Xibi und Rio Grande. Über den Anden-Pass Jama gelangt man in die wüstenartige Hochebene Puna de Atacama. Sie liegt 4000 m über dem Meeresspiegel im Schatten der Andenkordillere. Hier sind die Tage heiß und die Nächte kalt.

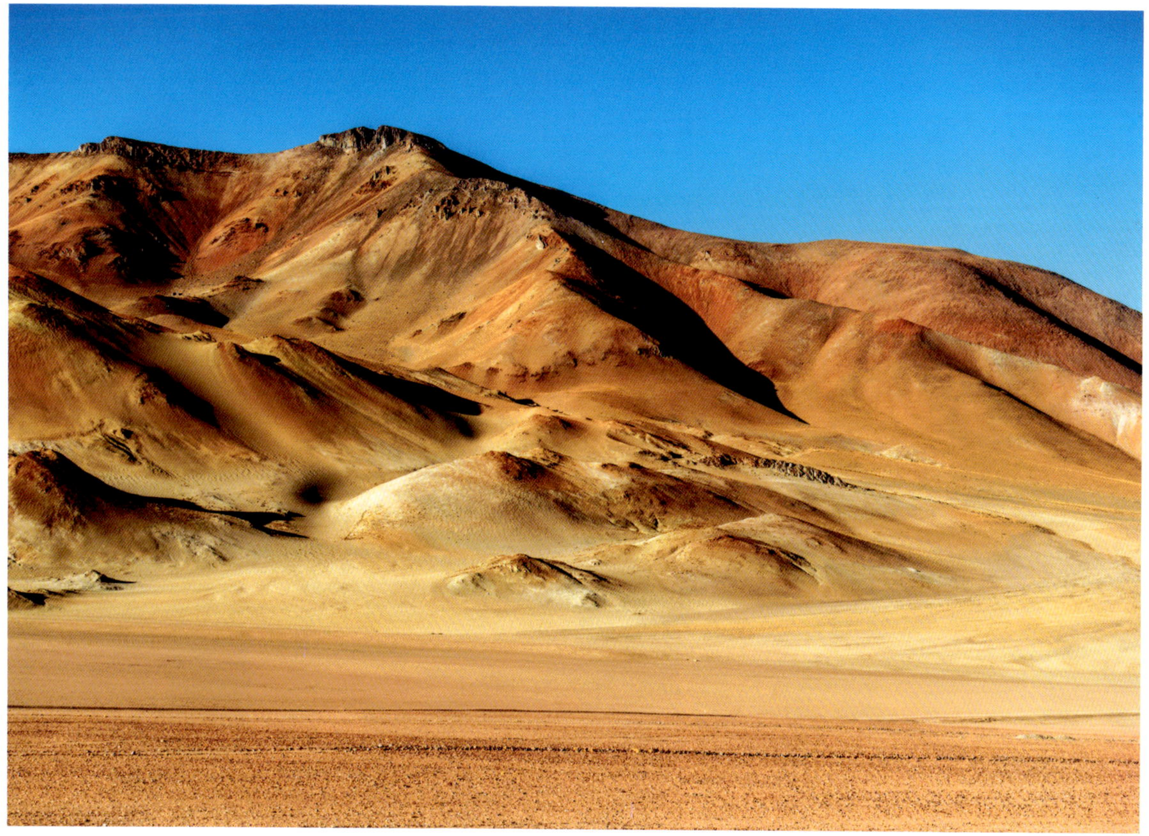

Paso de Jama

Jujuy

La remota y pequeña provincia limita con Bolivia al norte y con Chile al oeste. La espectacularidad de la naturaleza, la cadena de los Andes, las mesetas y los valles de los ríos determinan el paisaje y la forma de vida. Jujuy proviene de la palabra quechua "Xuxuyoc", que denotaba al gobernante inca regional. La vida indígena sigue presente hoy en día, ya que en la provincia viven 40 000 aborígenes. Su capital, San Salvador de Jujuy, se encuentra en la desembocadura de los ríos Xibi Xibi y Río Grande. A través del Paso de Jama de los Andes se llega a la desértica Puna de Atacama. Se encuentra a 4000 m sobre el nivel del mar, a la sombra de la cordillera de los Andes. Aquí los días son calurosos y las noches frías.

Jujuy

A remota e pequena província faz fronteira com a Bolívia no norte e com o Chile no oeste. A natureza espetacular, a cadeia andina, os planaltos e os vales dos rios determinam a paisagem e o modo de vida. Jujuy é derivado da palavra quechua "Xuxuyoc". Referia-se ao governante inca regional. A vida indígena ainda hoje está presente, com 40 000 índios vivendo na província. Sua capital, San Salvador de Jujuy, está localizada na foz dos rios Xibi Xibi e Rio Grande. Atravessando o Paso de Jama na Cordilheira dos Andes, chega-se ao planalto desértico de Puna de Atacama. Encontra-se a 4000 m acima do nível do mar, à sombra da Cordilheira dos Andes. Aqui os dias são quentes e as noites frias.

Jujuy

De kleine, afgelegen provincie grenst in het noorden aan Bolivia en in het westen aan Chili. Spectaculaire natuur, de Andesketen, hoogvlakte en rivierdalen bepalen het landschap en de levenswijze. Jujuy is afgeleid van het Quechua woord "Xuxuyoc". Het beschreef de regionale Inca heerser. Het indianenleven is vandaag de dag nog alom vertegenwoordigd, want in de provincie wonen 40 000 indianen. Hun hoofdstad, San Salvador de Jujuy, ligt aan de monding van de rivieren Xibi Xibi en Rio Grande. Via de Andes-pas Jama komt men in het woestijnachtige hooggebergte van Puna de Atacama. Dit ligt 4000 m boven de zeespiegel in de schaduw van het Andesgebergte. Hier zijn de dagen warm en de nachten koud.

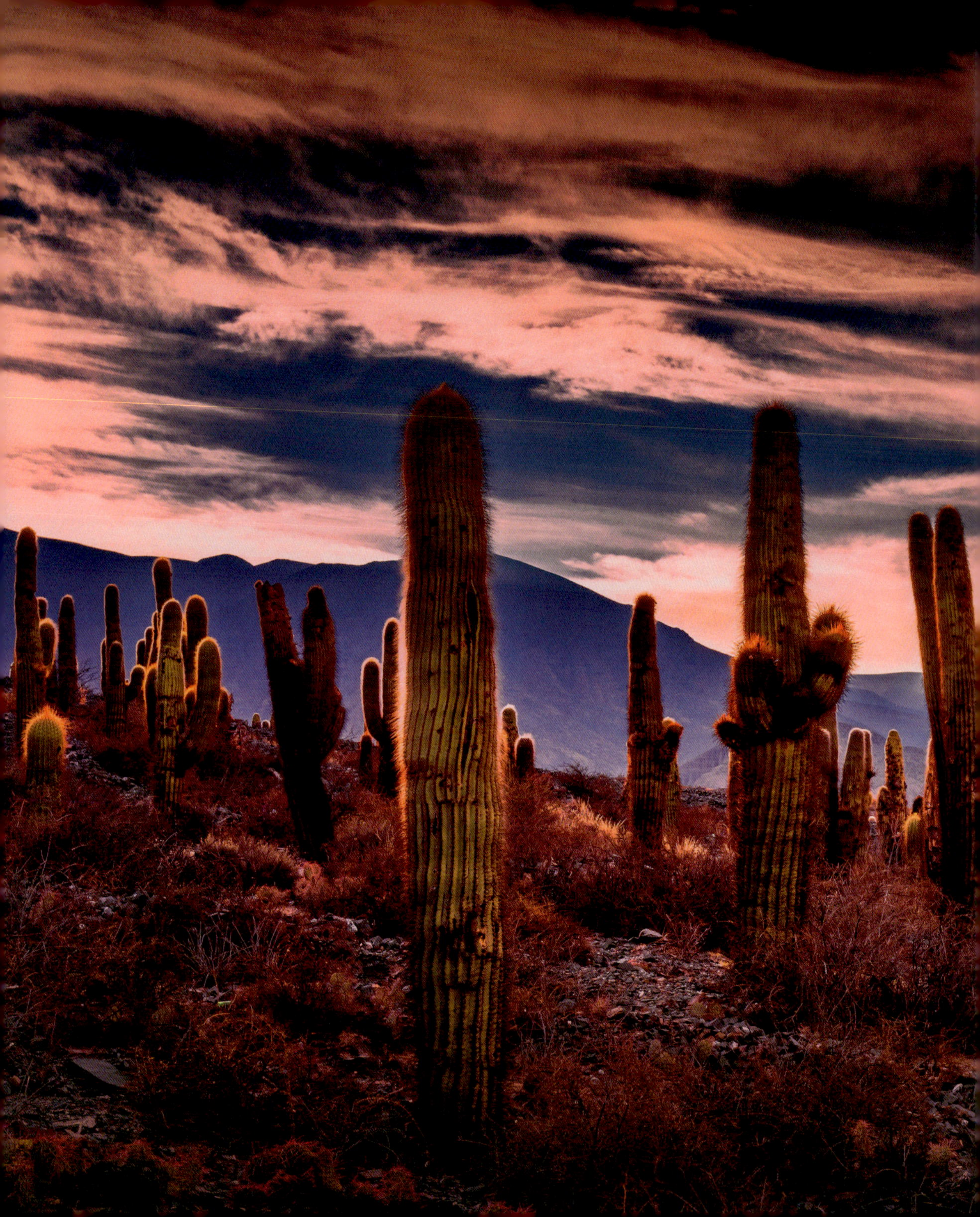

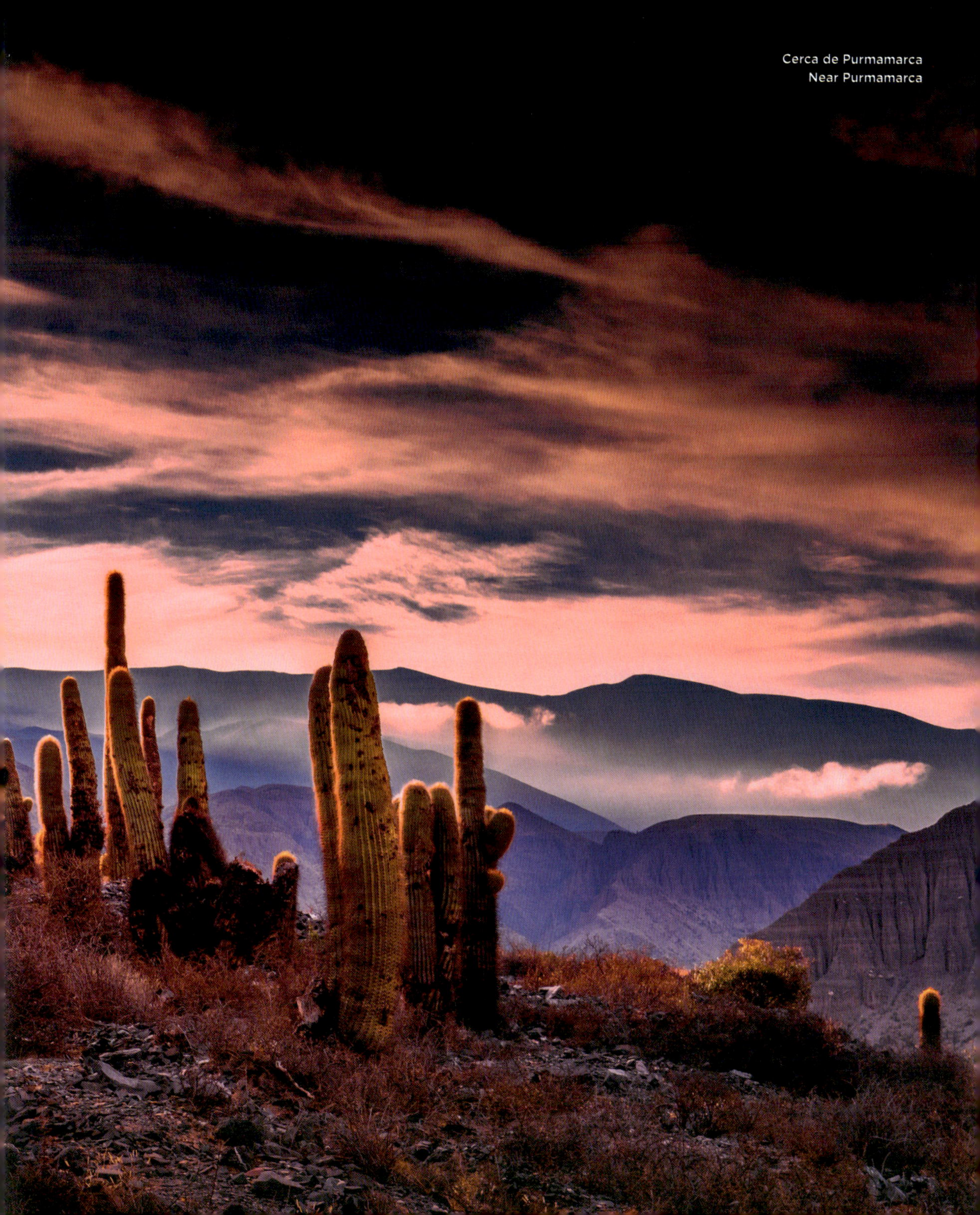

Cerca de Purmamarca
Near Purmamarca

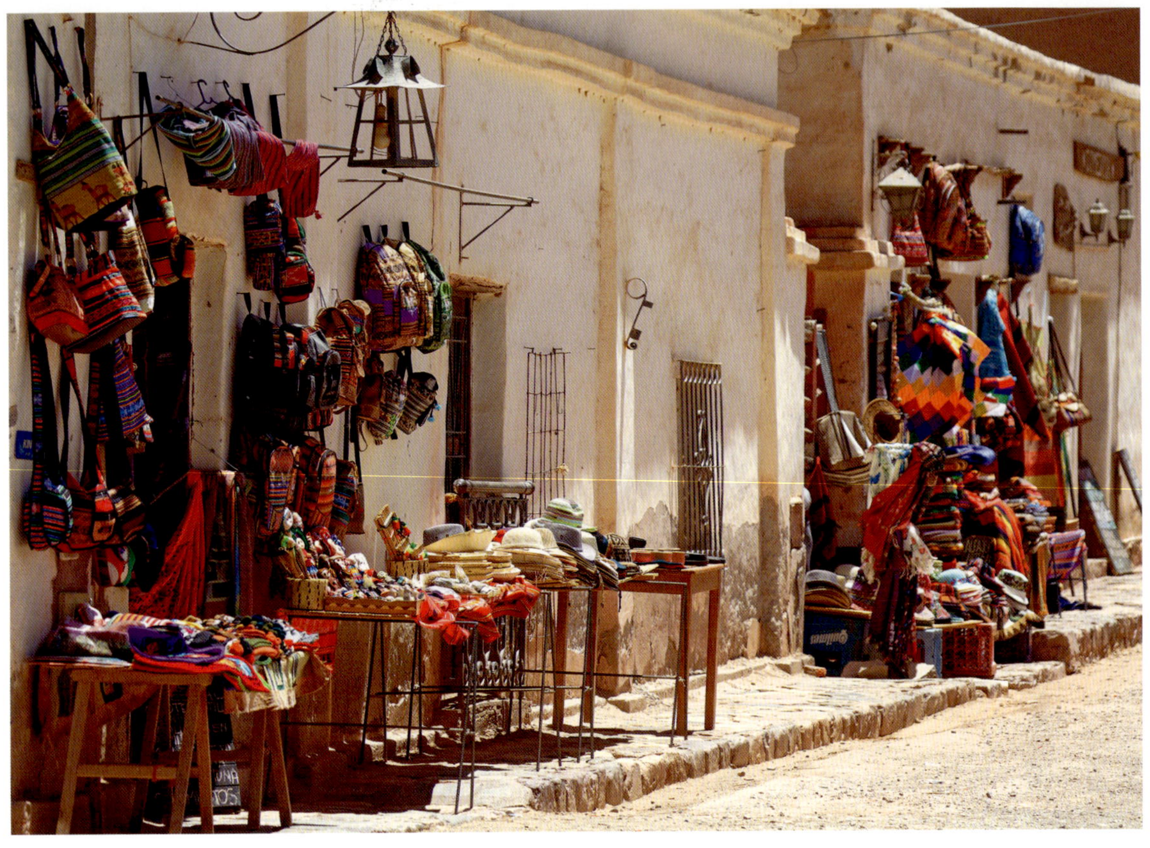

Purmamarca

Ancient Inca settlement

The name of the old Inca settlement
Purmamarca means desert region. It lies in
the mountain gorge of the same name at
2190 m (7185 ft) altitude. Fabulous cactus
landscapes can be admired here. In the
small mountain village, colorful Indian
weaving mills and handicrafts are offered
for sale, which the inhabitants of the region
produce traditionally. Purmamarca is part
of the gorge of Humahuaca, which was
used as a road during the Inca period and
afterwards by colonizers and missionaries.
Numerous village churches from the 17th
and 18th century, with paintings of the
famous Peruvian school of Cuzco can be
found in the area.

Ancien village inca

Le nom de l'ancien village inca
Purmamarca signifie «lieu de la terre
vierge». Situé dans le canyon homonyme,
à 2190 m d'altitude, il offre un paysage
exceptionnel, caractérisé par une flore
de cactées. La petite localité vend des
créations artisanales et des tissages
indiens colorés, fabriqués par les
habitants de la région selon des pratiques
traditionnelles. Purmamarca est proche du
canyon Humahuaca, utilisé comme voie de
circulation à l'époque préhispanique, puis
par les conquistadors et les missionnaires.
La région compte plusieurs églises des XVIIe
et XVIIIe siècles ornées de peintures de la
célèbre école de Cuzco péruvienne.

Alte Inka-Siedlung

Der Name der alten Inka-Siedlung
Purmamarca bedeutet Wüstengegend.
Sie liegt in der gleichnamigen
Bergschlucht auf 2190 m Höhe. Sagenhafte
Kakteenlandschaften sind hier zu
bewundern. In dem kleinen Bergdorf
werden farbenfrohe indianische Webereien
und Kunsthandwerk feilgeboten, die die
Bewohner der Region traditionsbewusst
anfertigen. Purmamarca ist Teil der
Schlucht von Humahuaca, die während
der Inka-Zeit und anschließend von
Kolonisatoren und Missionaren als Weg
genutzt wurde. Zahlreiche Dorfkirchen aus
dem 17. und 18. Jahrhundert mit Malereien
der berühmten peruanischen Schule von
Cuzco finden sich in der Gegend.

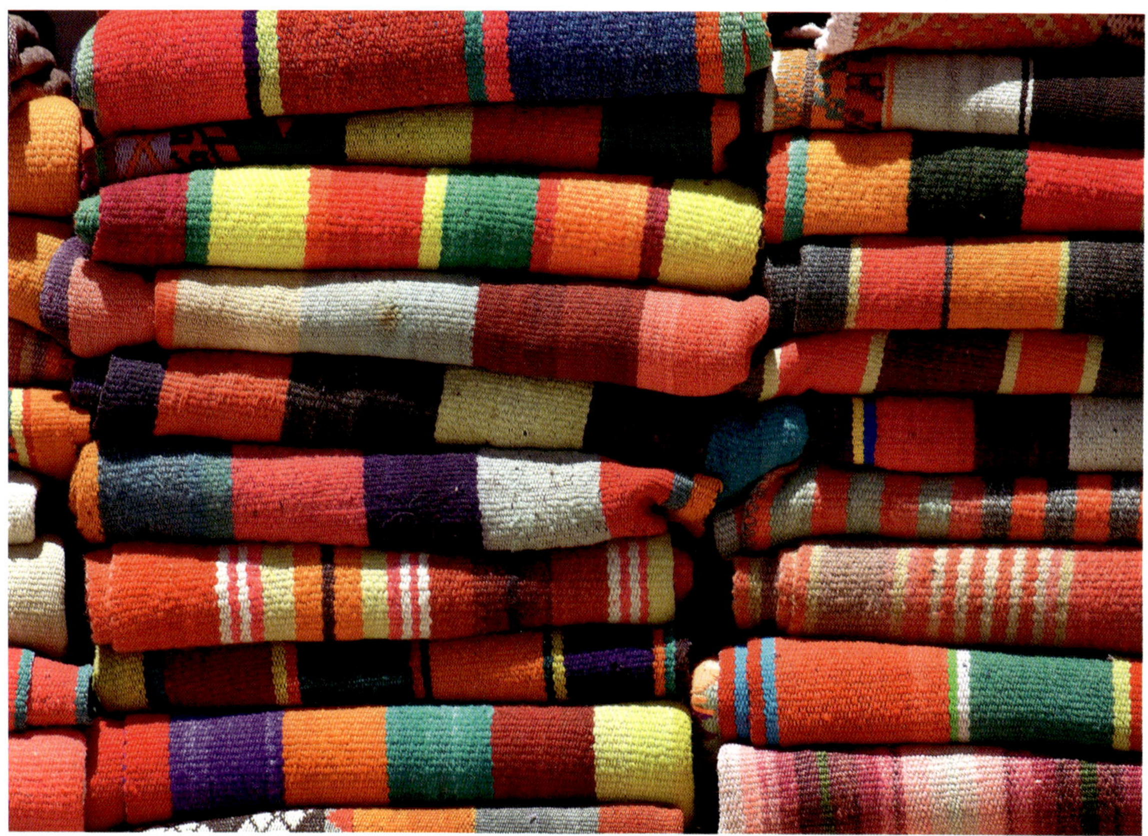

Tejidos, Purmamarca
Textiles, Purmamarca

Antiguo asentamiento inca

El nombre del antiguo asentamiento inca
Purmamarca significa "región desértica".
Se encuentra en el desfiladero que lleva el
mismo nombre, a 2190 m de altitud. Aquí
se pueden admirar fabulosos paisajes de
cactus. En el pequeño pueblo de montaña
se venden coloridos tejidos y artesanías de
los pueblos orignarios, que los habitantes
de la región producen tradicionalmente.
Purmamarca es parte de la quebrada
de Humahuaca, que fue utilizada como
camino durante el período incaico y luego
por los colonizadores y misioneros. En
la zona se pueden encontrar numerosas
iglesias de los pueblos de los siglos XVII
y XVIII con pinturas de la famosa escuela
peruana de Cuzco.

Antiga povoação inca

O nome do antigo assentamento inca
Purmamarca significa região desértica.
Encontra-se no desfiladeiro da montanha
com o mesmo nome, a 2190 m de altitude.
As fabulosas paisagens de cactos podem
ser admiradas aqui. Na pequena aldeia
de montanha, estão à venda tecelagens
e artesanatos indianos coloridos, que
os habitantes da região fabricam de
maneira tradicional. Purmamarca faz
parte da Quebrada de Humahuaca, que
foi usada como rota durante o período
inca e depois pelos colonizadores e
missionários. Numerosas igrejas de aldeia
dos séculos XVII e XVIII com pinturas da
famosa escola peruana de Cuzco podem
ser encontradas na área.

Oude Inca nederzetting

De naam van de oude Inca-nederzetting
Purmamarca betekent woestijngebied.
Deze ligt in de gelijknamige bergkloof
op 2190 m hoogte. Hier zijn fantastische
cactuslandschappen te bewonderen.
In het kleine bergdorpje worden
kleurrijke Indiase weverijproducten
en handnijverheidsproducten te koop
aangeboden, die de inwoners uit de
regio op traditionele wijze produceren.
Purmamarca behoort tot de kloof van
Humahuaca die tijdens de Inca-periode en
daarna door kolonisten en missionarissen
als weg werd gebruikt. In de omgeving zijn
talrijke dorpskerken uit de 17e en 18e eeuw
met schilderijen van de beroemde
Peruaanse school van Cuzco te vinden.

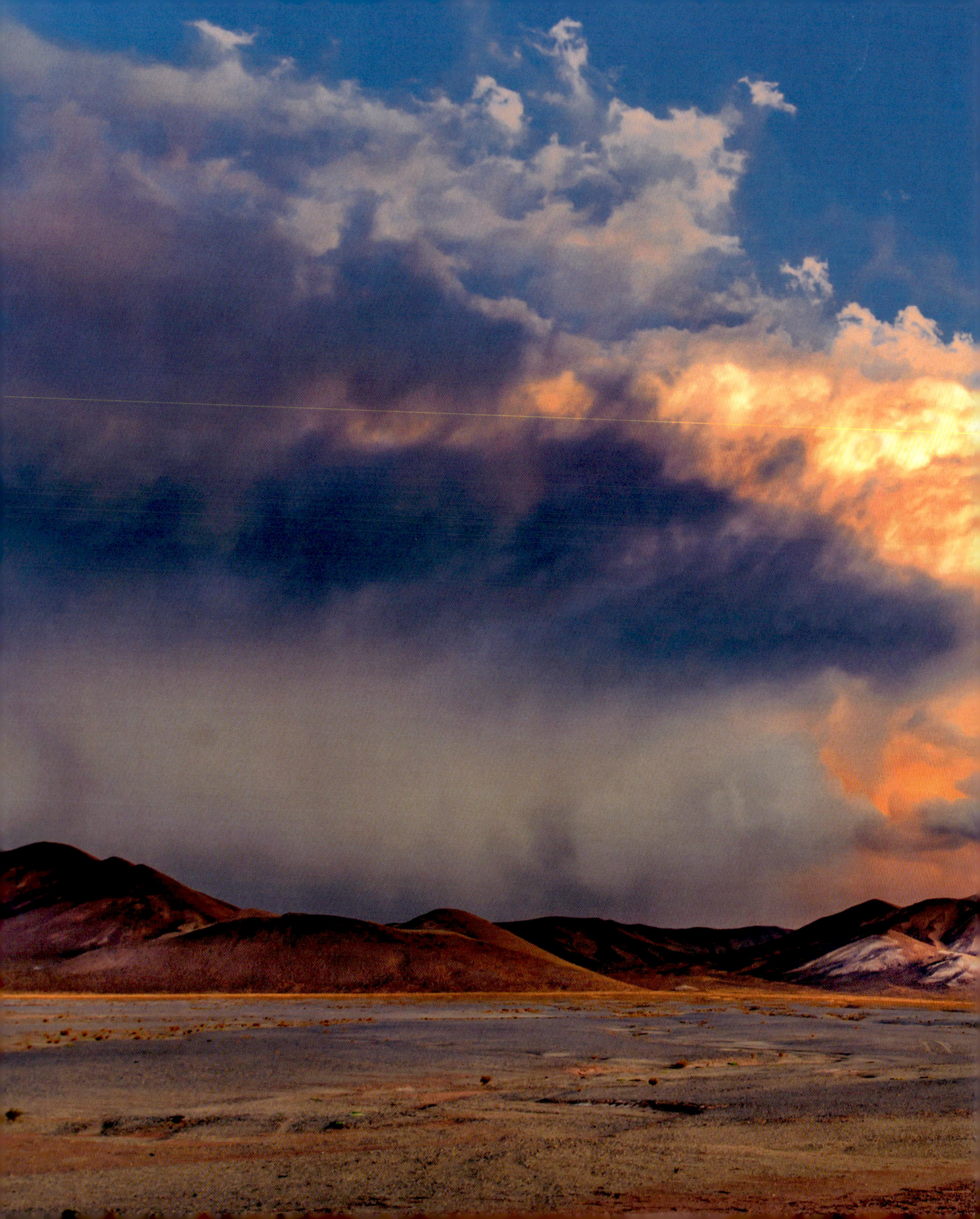

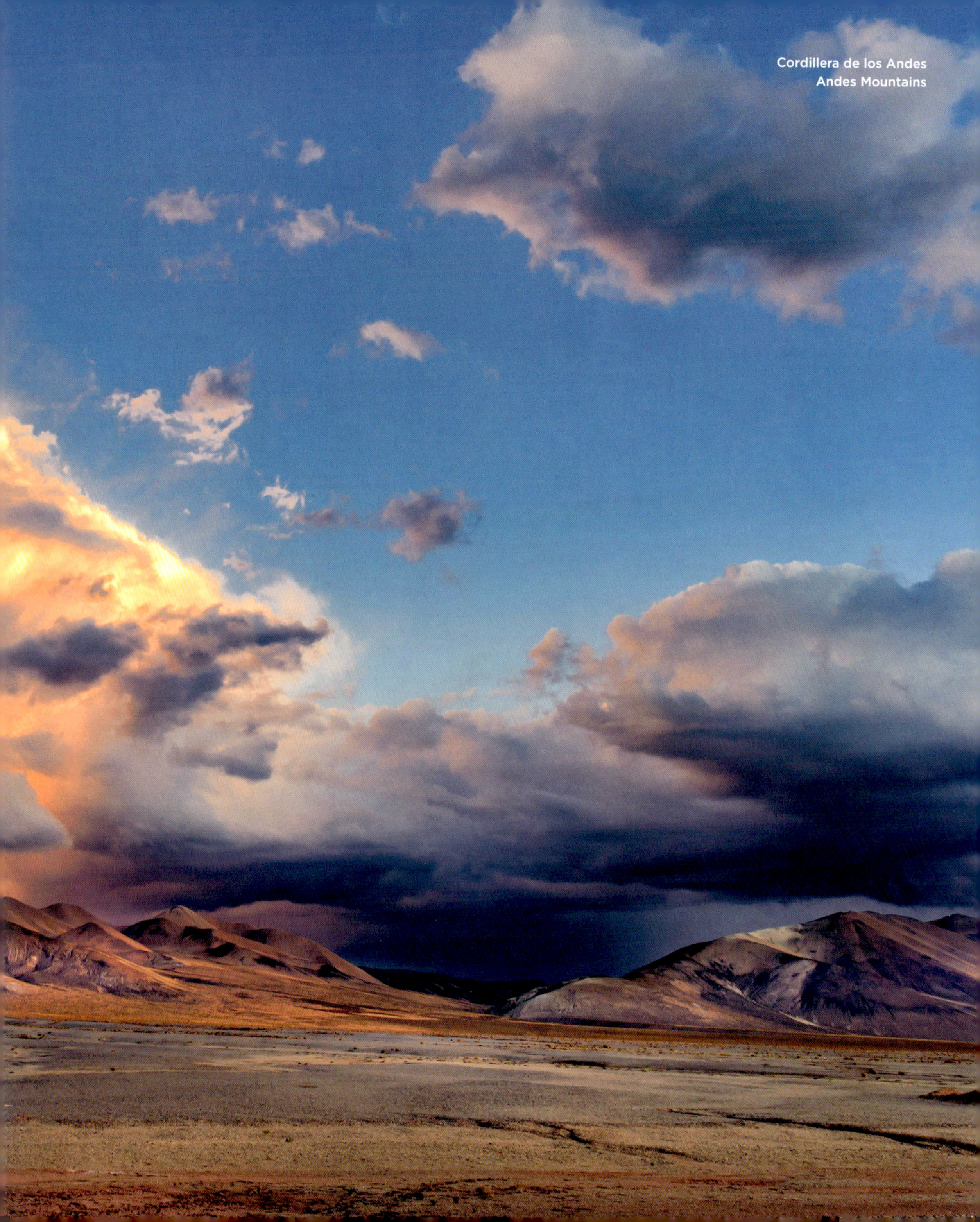
Cordillera de los Andes
Andes Mountains

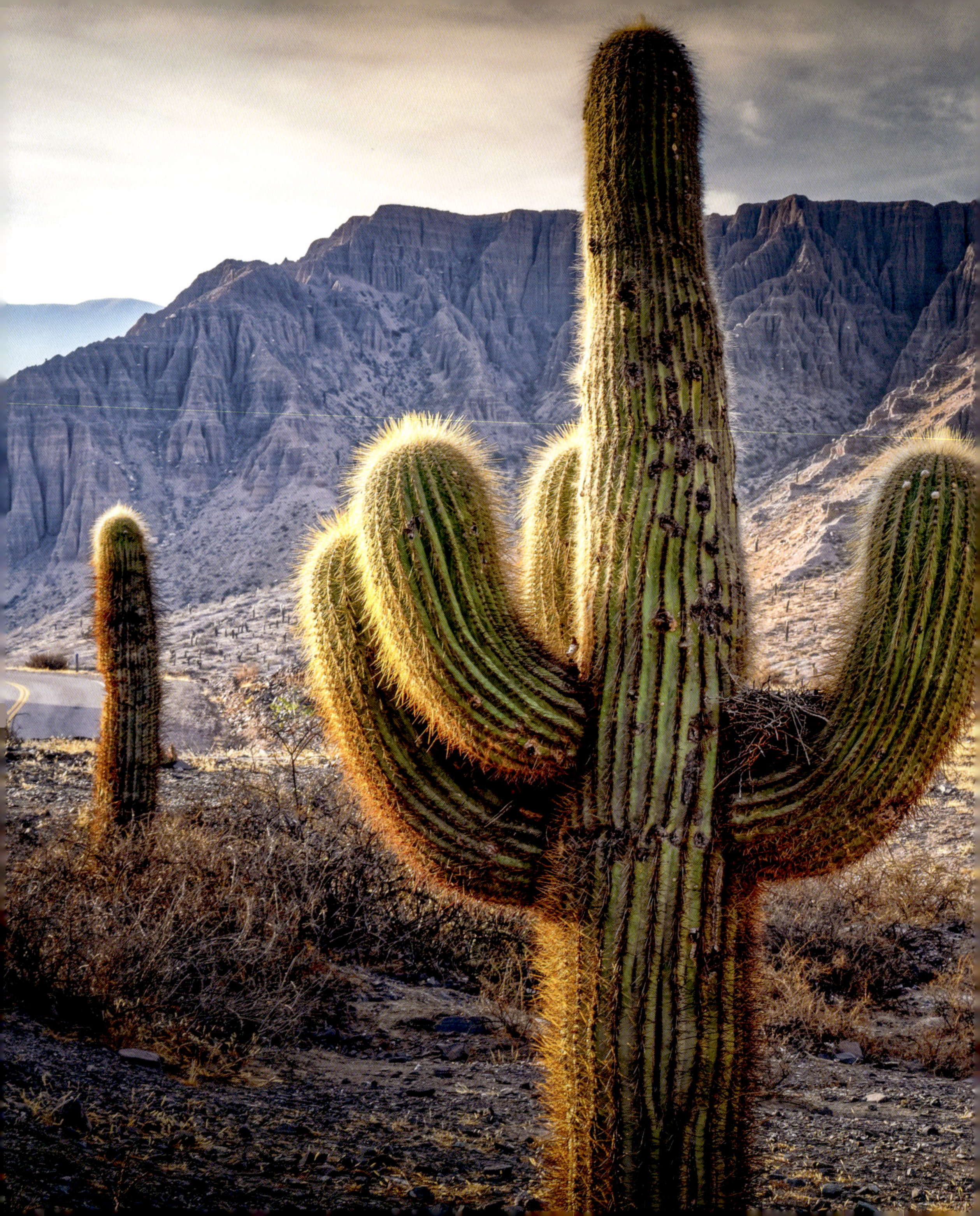

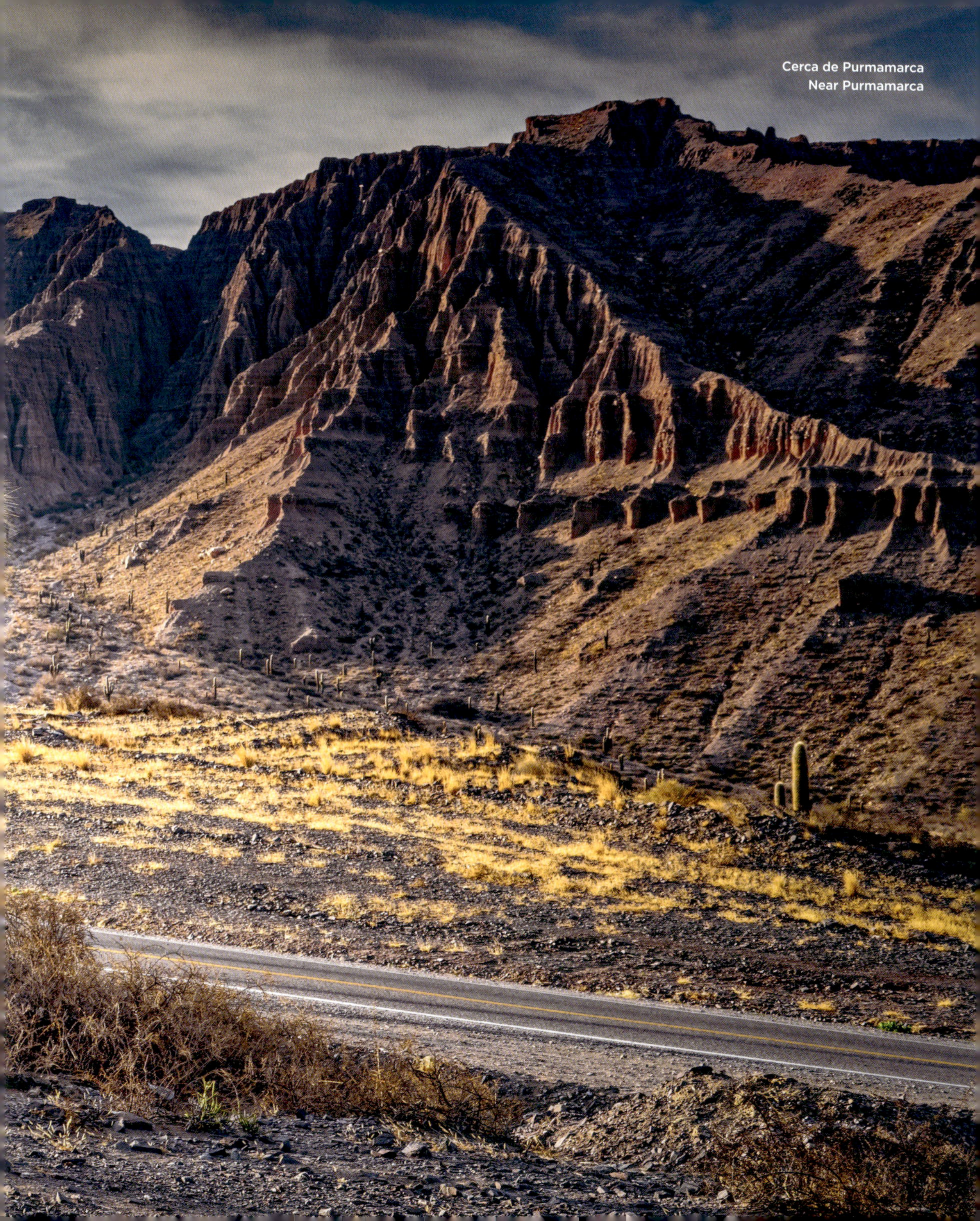

Cerca de Purmamarca
Near Purmamarca

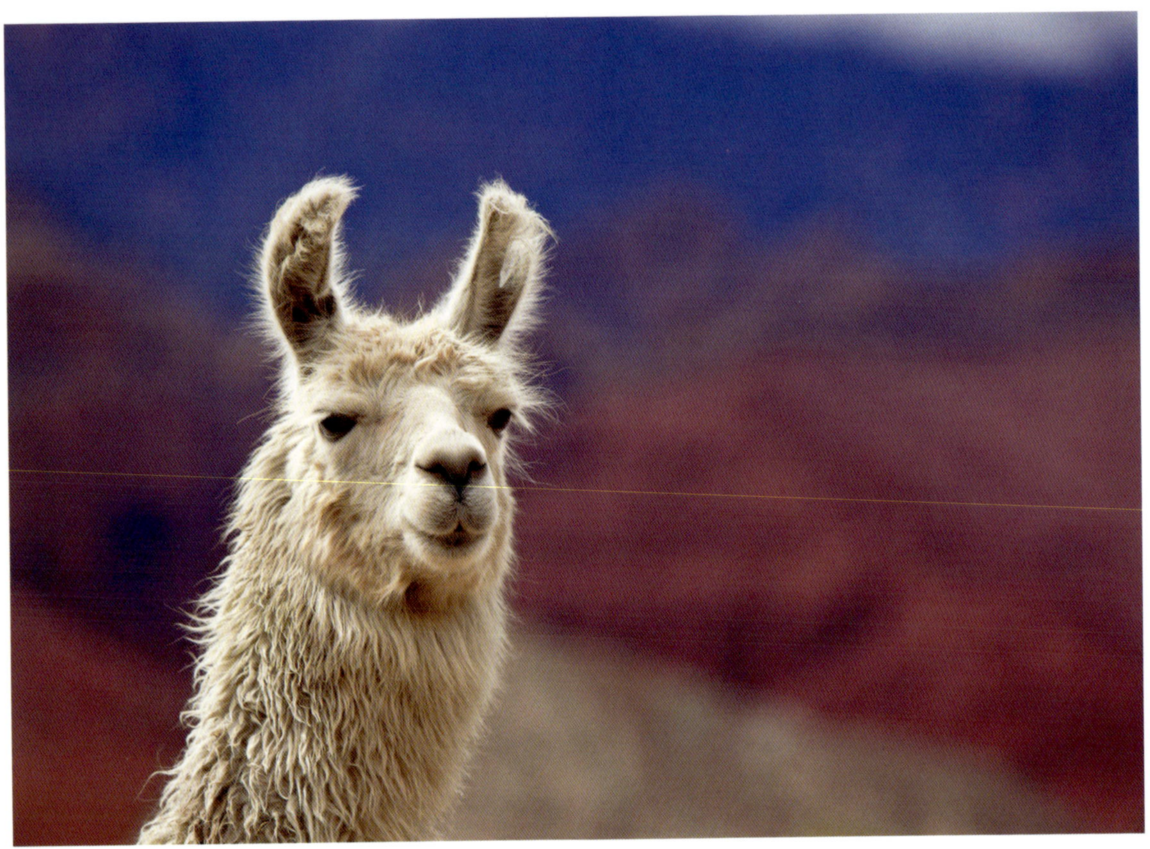

Llama

Life in the mountains

Jujuy lives mainly from mining, but there is modest agriculture in the high valleys and the plateau. Llamas are used as pack animals in the steep, often impassable terrain and are descended from the wild guanacos. Llamas reach a shoulder height of 140 cm (55 in) and weigh 150 kg (330 lb). Before the arrival of the Spaniards, llamas were of great importance: even in the High Andes, up to 5000 m (16,400 ft), they transported an average of 50 kg (110 lb) of luggage over distances of 30 km (19 mi) per day. Their meat was eaten, the skin was made into leather, candles were made from the fat and the dung was used for heating and cooking.

Vivre dans les montagnes

Le Jujuy vit essentiellement de l'exploitation minière mais, en altitude, la population exerce une modeste activité agricole. Les lamas, descendants des guanacos sauvages, sont des animaux domestiques peu exigeants, utilisés comme bêtes de somme dans les régions escarpées et souvent non aménagées. Ils mesurent environ 140 cm au garrot et pèsent 150 kg. Avant l'arrivée des Espagnols, les lamas jouaient un rôle primordial pour la population, qui les utilisait pour le transport : ils pouvaient porter quotidiennement des charges moyennes de 50 kg, sur 30 km et jusqu'à 5 000 m d'altitude. Leur chair était consommée, leur peau transformée en cuir, leur graisse en bougies, et leurs déjections étaient brûlées pour cuisiner et se chauffer.

Leben in der Bergwelt

Jujuy lebt hauptsächlich vom Bergbau, doch in den Hochtälern und der Hochebene gibt es bescheidene Landwirtschaft. Lamas, die genügsamen Haustiere, werden in dem steilen, oft unwegsamen Gelände als Lastentiere eingesetzt. Sie stammen von den wilden Guanakos ab. Lamas erreichen eine Schulterhöhe von 140 cm und bringen 150 kg auf die Waage. Vor der Ankunft der Spanier waren Lamas von großer Wichtigkeit: Sie transportierten selbst in den Hochanden bis auf 5000 m im Schnitt 50 kg Gepäck über Entfernungen von 30 km am Tag. Ihr Fleisch wurde gegessen, die Haut zu Leder verarbeitet, aus dem Fett wurden Kerzen hergestellt und der Dung zum Heizen und Kochen verwendet.

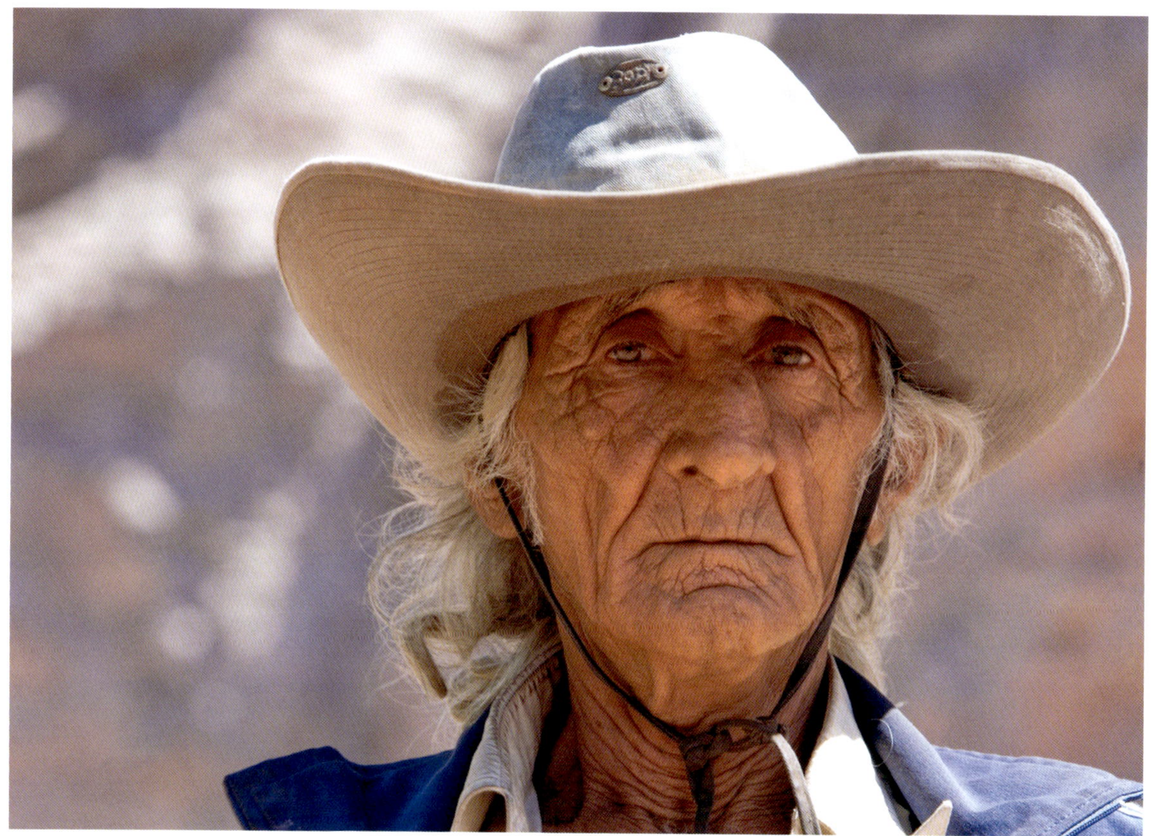

Hombre jujeño
Jujuy man

La vida en las montañas

Jujuy vive principalmente de la minería, pero hay una modesta agricultura en los valles altos y la meseta. Las llamas domesticadas se utilizan como animales de carga en los terrenos escarpados y a menudo intransitables. Son descendientes de los guanacos salvajes. Las llamas alcanzan una altura de hombro de 140 cm y pesan 150 kg. Antes de la llegada de los españoles, las llamas eran de gran importancia: incluso en los altos Andes, hasta los 5000 m, transportaban un promedio de 50 kg de equipaje en distancias de 30 km por día. Se comía su carne, la piel se convertía en cuero, se hacían velas con la grasa y el estiércol se utilizaba para calentar y cocinar.

A vida nas montanhas

Jujuy vive principalmente da mineração, mas há uma agricultura modesta nos vales altos e no planalto. As lhamas, os animais de estimação frugais, são utilizados como animais de carga em terrenos íngremes e muitas vezes intransitáveis. Elas são descendentes dos guanacos selvagens. As lhamas atingem uma altura de ombro de 140 cm e chegam a pesar até 150 kg. Antes da chegada dos espanhóis, as lhamas eram de grande importância: transportavam em média 50 kg de bagagem em distâncias de 30 km por dia, mesmo no alto da Cordilheira dos Andes até 5000 m. A sua carne era comida, a pele transformada em couro, da gordura eram feitas velas e o esterco era usado para aquecimento e cozedura.

Leven in de bergen

Jujuy leeft voornamelijk van de mijnbouw, maar in de hooggelegen dalen en het hooggebergte is bescheiden sprake van landbouw. Lama's, de sober levende huisdieren, worden op het steile, vaak onbegaanbare terrein als lastdier ingezet. Ze stammen af van de wilde guanaco's. Lama's bereiken een schouderhoogte van 140 cm en wegen 150 kg. Vóór de komst van de Spanjaarden waren lama's van groot belang: ze transporteerden zelfs in het hoge Andesgebergte tot 5000 meter gemiddeld 50 kg bagage over afstanden van 30 km per dag. Hun vlees werd gegeten, de huid tot leer verwerkt, van het vet werden kaarsen gemaakt en de mest werd gebruikt voor het verwarmen en koken.

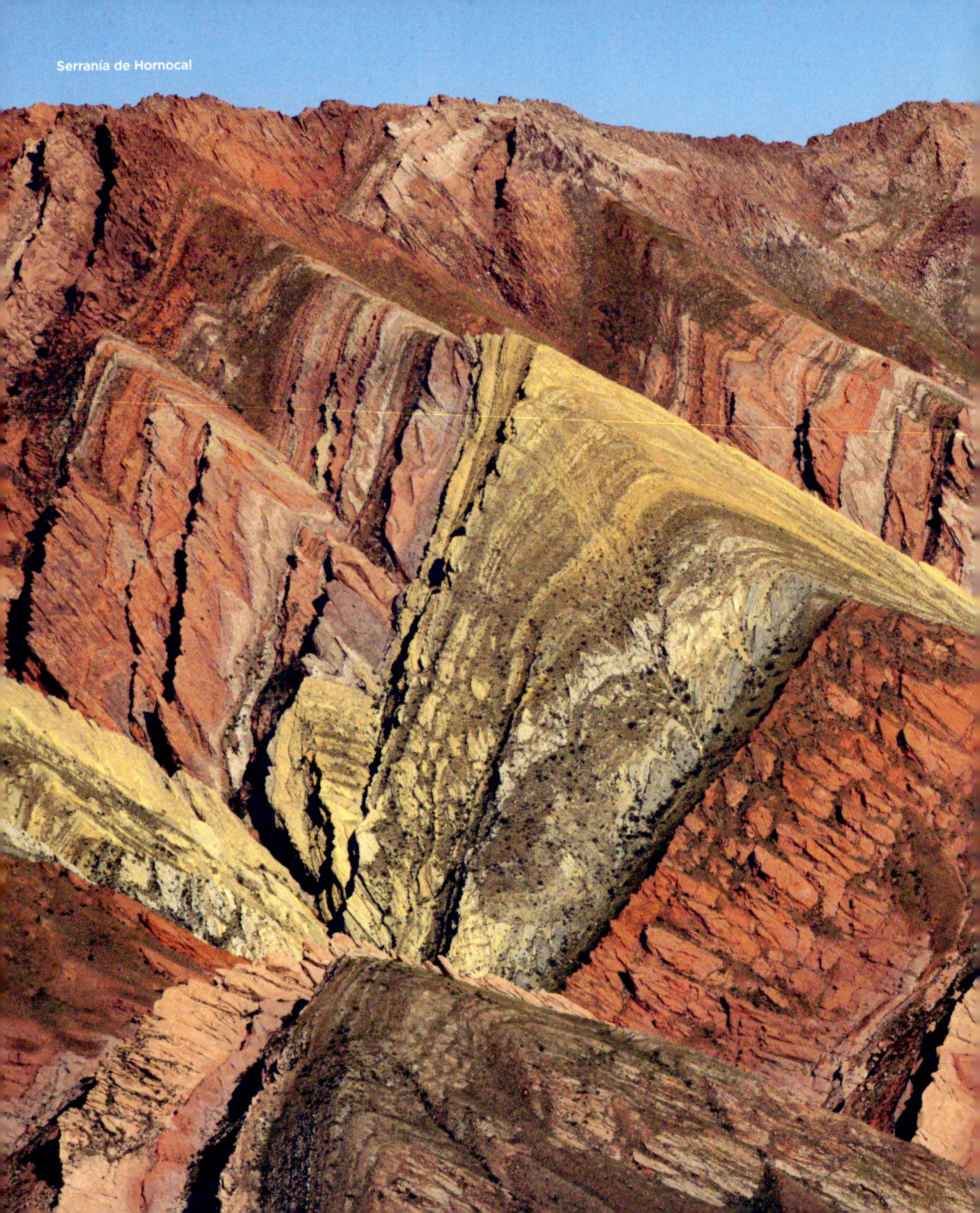

Serranía de Hornocal

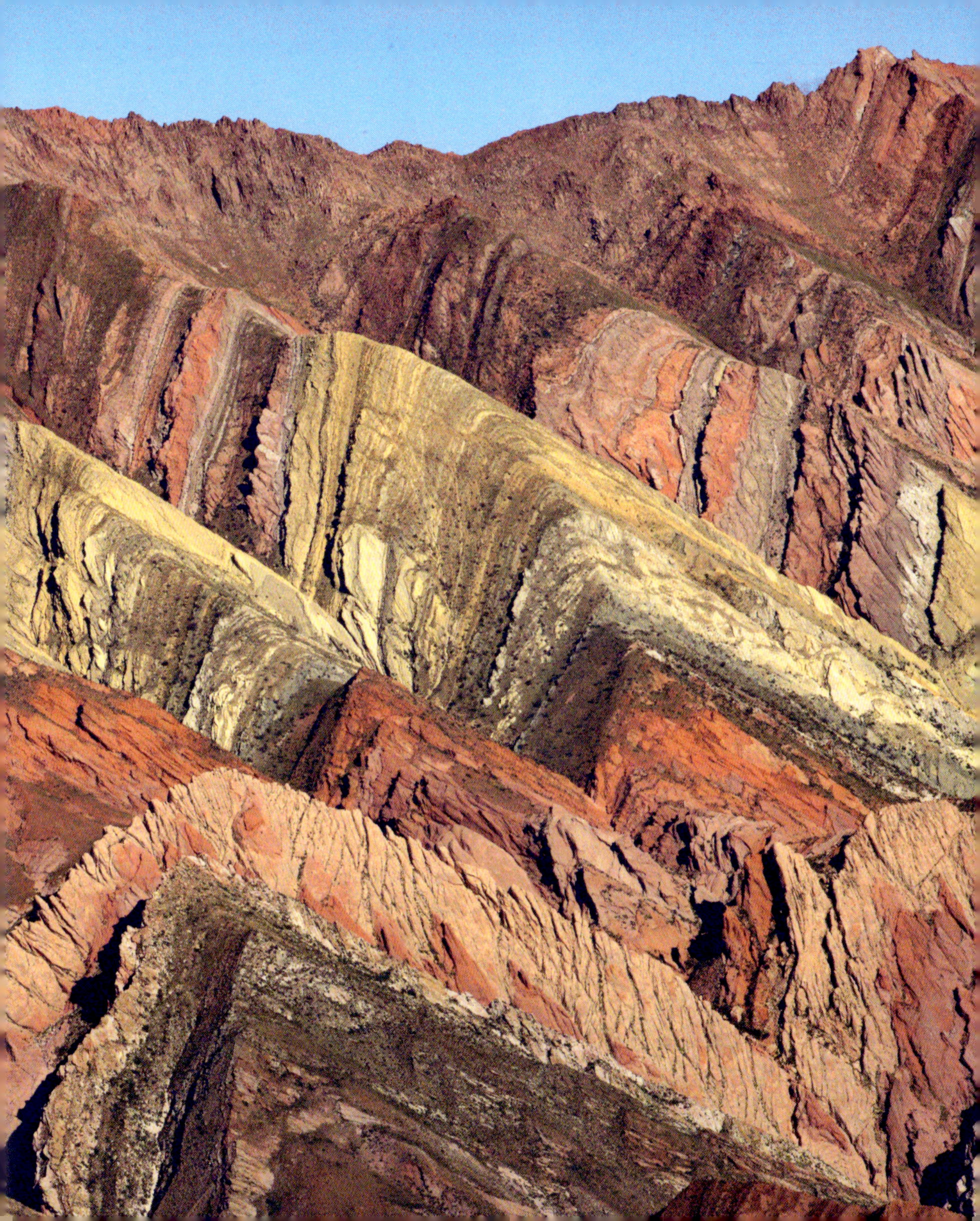

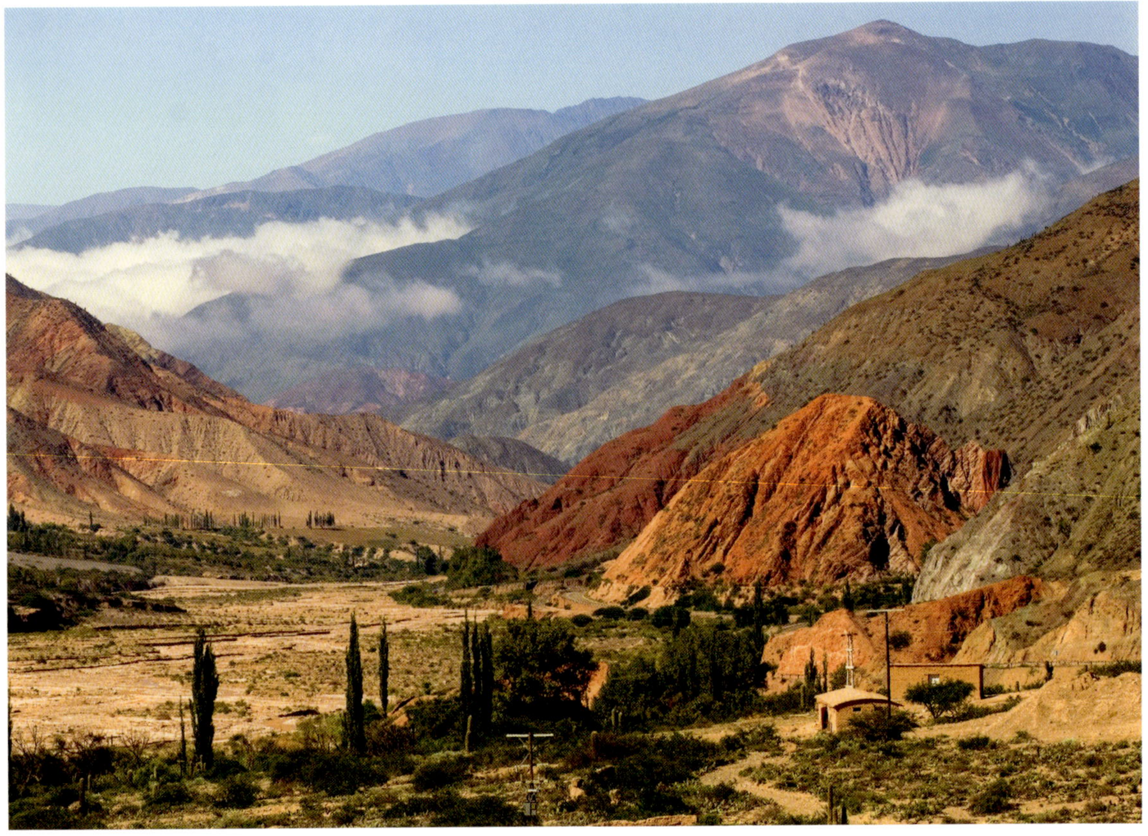

Quebrada de Humahuaca, cerca de Maimará
Quebrada de Humahuaca near Maimará

The Humahuaca Gorge

The Quebrada de Humahuaca is the real highlight of the province. In 2003, the bizarre, steep valley, which digs into the plateau of the northwest, was declared a UNESCO World Heritage Site. This is because the 130 km (81 mi) long corridor between the Andean highlands and the lower river valley has been a place of exchange and trade for the Andean populations for centuries. From the green valley at 1552 m (5092 ft) altitude, the Quebrada de Humahuaca rises steadily to 2939 m (9642 ft). The description "painter's color palette" applies to the colorful shimmering hills near the city of Maimará. The highlight of the gorge is the Cerro de los Siete Colores, or "mountain of seven colors" (2460 m/8071 ft).

Le canyon de Humahuaca

La Quebrada de Humahuaca est le joyau de la province. Depuis 2003, l'étrange canyon abrupt, creusé dans les hauts plateaux du Nord-Ouest, est inscrit au patrimoine de l'Unesco. Ce corridor, circulant sur 130 km entre les hauts plateaux andins et la vallée fluviale en contrebas, est en outre exceptionnel parce qu'il servit de lieu d'échange et de commerce aux populations locales pendant des siècles. Depuis la vallée verte située à 1552 m d'altitude, la Quebrada de Humahuaca s'élève régulièrement jusqu'à 2939 m. Le paysage de collines polychromes et chatoyantes de la ville de Maimará porte le nom évocateur de « palette du peintre », et le Cerro de los Siete Colores (« colline des sept couleurs »), à 2460 m, constitue le point d'orgue de la région.

Die Humahuaca-Schlucht

Die Quebrada de Humahuaca ist das eigentliche Highlight der Provinz. 2003 wurde das bizarre, steile Tal, das sich in die Hochebene des Nordwestens eingräbt, zum UNESCO-Weltkulturerbe erklärt. Auch weil in dem 130 km langen Korridor zwischen Anden-Hochebene und tiefer gelegenem Flusstal über Jahrhunderte Austausch und Handel der andinen Bevölkerung stattfand. Vom grünen Tal auf 1552 m Höhe steigt die Quebrada de Humahuaca stetig an und erreicht 2939 m. Die Beschreibung „Farbpalette des Malers" trifft zu auf die farbig schimmernden Hügel nahe der Stadt Maimará. Den Höhepunkt der Bergschlucht bildet der Cerro de los Siete Colores, „Berg der sieben Farben" (2460 m).

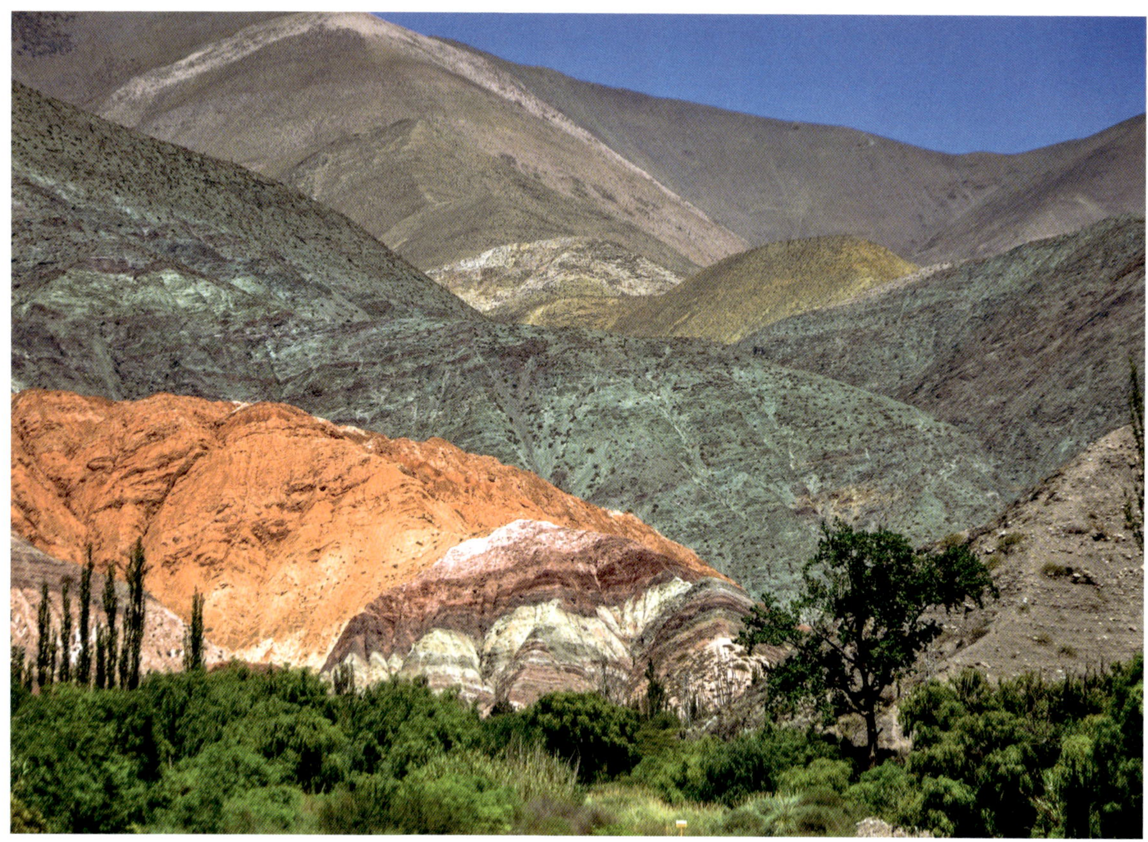

Cerro de los Siete Colores, Purmamarca

La Quebrada de Humahuaca

La Quebrada de Humahuaca es el verdadero punto culminante de la provincia. En 2003, el extraño y escarpado valle, que se adentra en la meseta del noroeste, fue declarado Patrimonio de la Humanidad por la UNESCO. Esto también se debe a que el paso de 130 km de largo entre el altiplano andino y el valle del río inferior ha sido un lugar de intercambio y comercio para la población andina durante siglos. La Quebrada de Humahuaca se eleva constantemente desde el verde valle (a 1552 m de altura) hasta los 2939 m. La descripción "paleta de colores del pintor" se aplica a las coloridas y brillantes colinas cerca de la ciudad de Maimará. El punto culminante del desfiladero es el Cerro de los Siete Colores, "montaña de siete colores" (2460 m).

A Quebrada de Humahuaca

A Quebrada de Humahuaca é o verdadeiro destaque da província. Em 2003, o bizarro e íngreme vale, que se escava no planalto do noroeste, foi declarado Património Mundial da UNESCO. Isto também porque o longo corredor de 130 km de comprimento entre o platô andino e o vale do baixo rio tem sido um lugar de trocas e comércio para a população andina durante séculos. Do vale verdejante a 1552 m de altitude, a Quebrada de Humahuaca sobe constantemente até 2939 m. A descrição "paleta de cores do pintor" aplica-se às colinas coloridas e cintilantes perto da cidade de Maimará. O ponto alto do desfiladeiro é o Cerro de los Siete Colores, "montanha de sete cores" (2460 m).

Het Humahuaca ravijn

De Quebrada de Humahuaca is het eigenlijke hoogtepunt van de provincie. In 2003 werd het bizarre, steile dal, dat zich in de hoogvlakte van het noordwesten heeft genesteld, uitgeroepen tot UNESCO-werelderfgoed. Dit komt ook, omdat in de 130 km lange gang tussen het Hoogland van de Andes en het lager gelegen rivierdal al eeuwenlang ruil en handel van de bevolking uit de Andes plaatsvond. Vanuit het groene dal op 1552 m hoogte stijgt de Quebrada de Humahuaca gestaag naar 2939 m. De beschrijving "kleurenpalet van de schilder" past bij de kleurrijke glinsterende heuvels in de buurt van de stad Maimará. Het hoogtepunt van het ravijn is de Cerro de los Siete Colores, "berg van zeven kleuren" (2460 m).

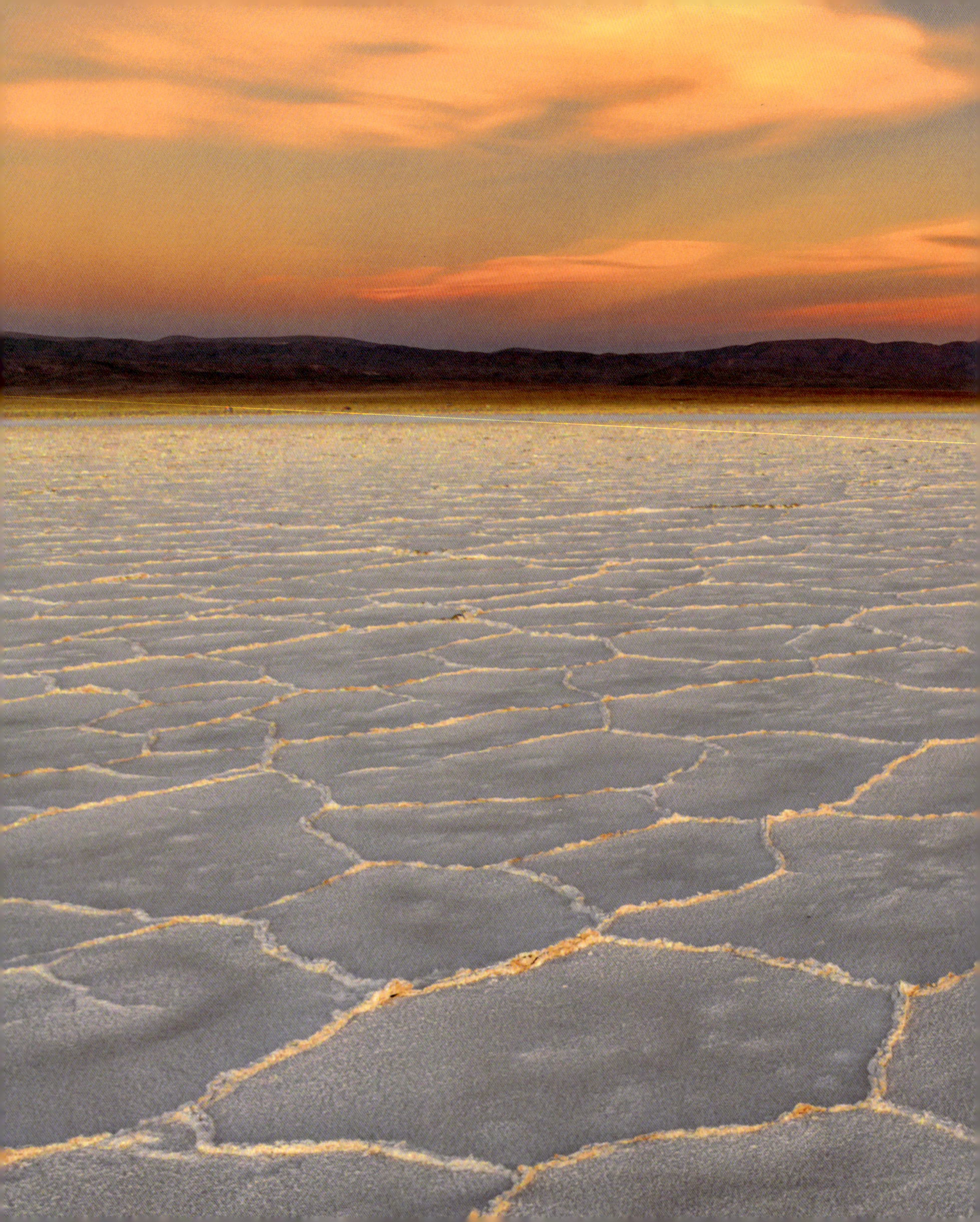

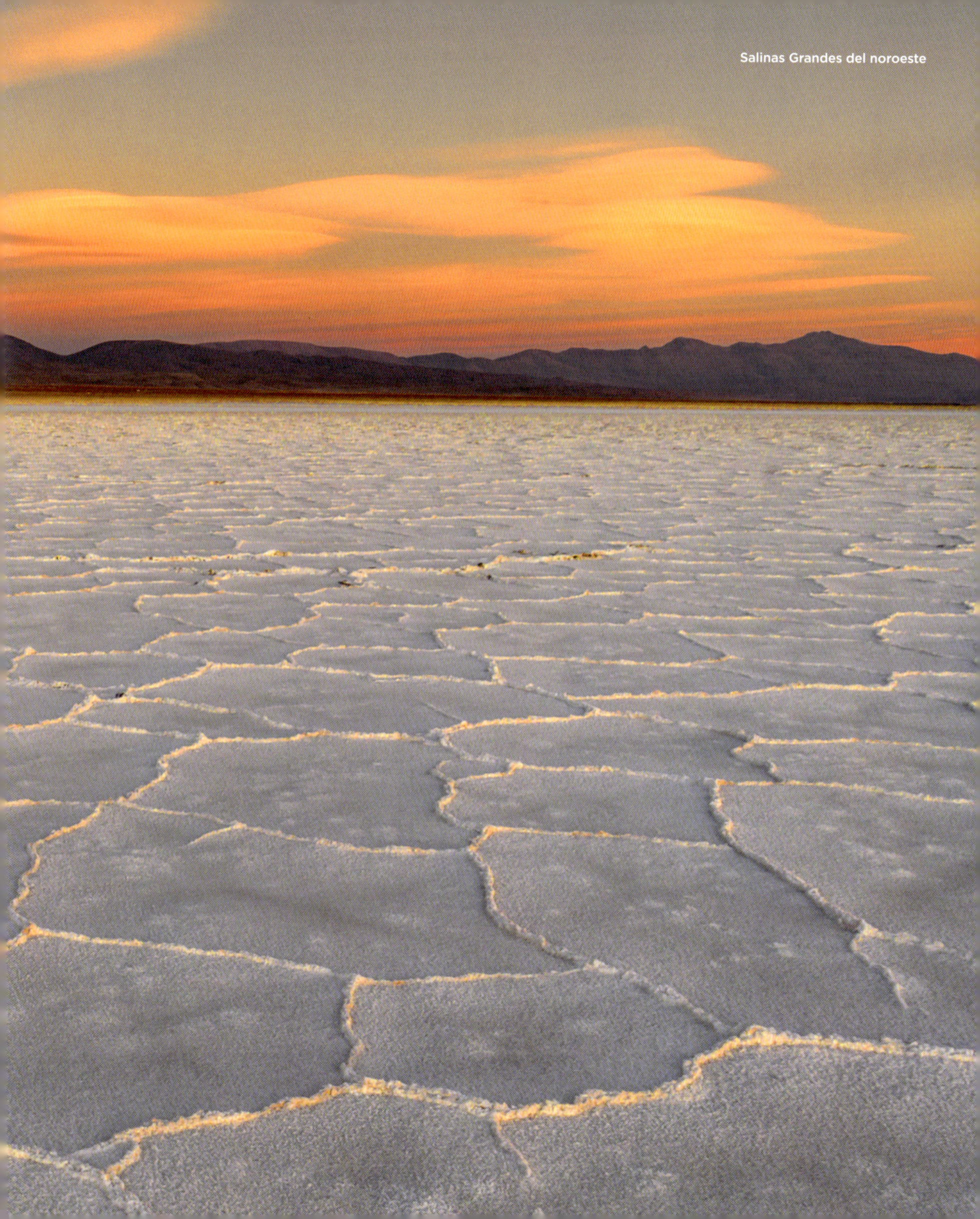
Salinas Grandes del noroeste

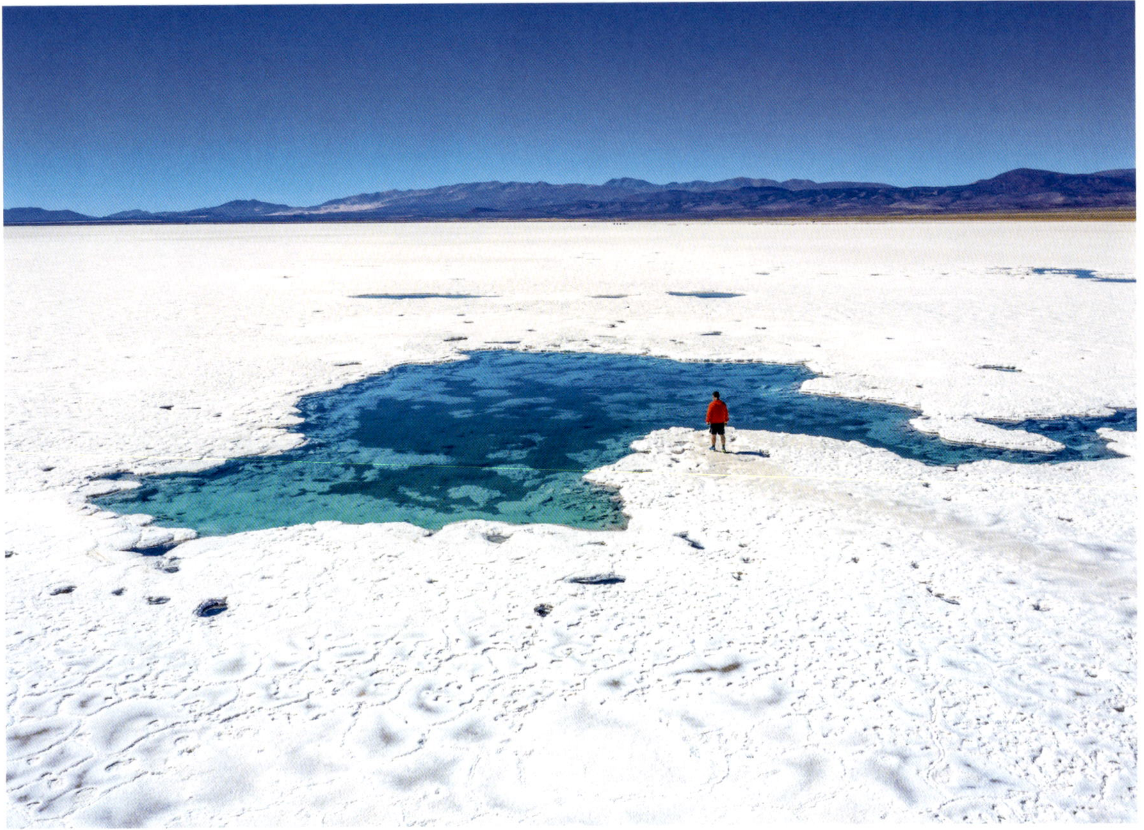

Salinas Grandes del noroeste

Salt Lake Desert

At an altitude of 3450 m (11,319 ft), 190 km (118 mi) northwest of the provincial capital, lie the Salinas Grandes, the great salt lakes. Their salty water is of volcanic origin. Due to tectonic shifting of the Andes, the outflow of three rivers was blocked, thus forming the salt lake. Over an area of 212 km² (82 sq mi), a shining white salt desert extends, which becomes a lake when it rains. After only a few days of sunshine the water evaporates completely, so that a 30 cm (1 ft) thick salt crust is formed on the surface, consisting of sodium chloride. Salt is mined in many small, but also a few larger industrially operated salt works. It is cut off in blocks and dried.

Déserts de sel

Les Salinas Grandes, ou grands lacs salés, se déploient à 3 450 m d'altitude, à 190 km au nord-ouest de la capitale de la province. Leur eau salée est d'origine volcanique. Les mouvements tectoniques dans les Andes ont bloqué le cours de trois fleuves, provoquant la formation de lacs salés. Sur une superficie de 212 km² s'étend aujourd'hui un désert de sel blanc éblouissant que la pluie transforme en lac. Après quelques jours de soleil, l'eau s'évapore totalement et la surface présente une croûte de sel de 30 cm, constituée de chlorure de sodium. Le sel est récolté dans de nombreuses petites exploitations salines et quelques grandes entreprises industrielles. Il est extrait sous forme de pains puis séché.

Salzseewüste

Auf 3450 m Höhe, 190 km nordwestlich der Provinzhauptstadt, liegen die Salinas Grandes, die großen Salzseen. Ihr salziges Wasser ist vulkanischen Ursprungs. Durch tektonische Verschiebung der Anden war der Abfluss von drei Flüssen blockiert, so bildete sich der Salzsee. Auf einer Fläche von 212 km² erstreckt sich eine strahlend weiße Salzwüste, die sich bei Regen in einen See verwandelt. Schon nach wenigen Tagen Sonne verdunstet das Wasser vollständig, so dass auf der Oberfläche eine 30 cm dicke Salzkruste entsteht. Sie besteht aus Natriumchlorid. In vielen kleinen und auch wenigen größeren industriell betriebenen Salinen wird Salz abgebaut. Es wird blockweise abgestochen und getrocknet.

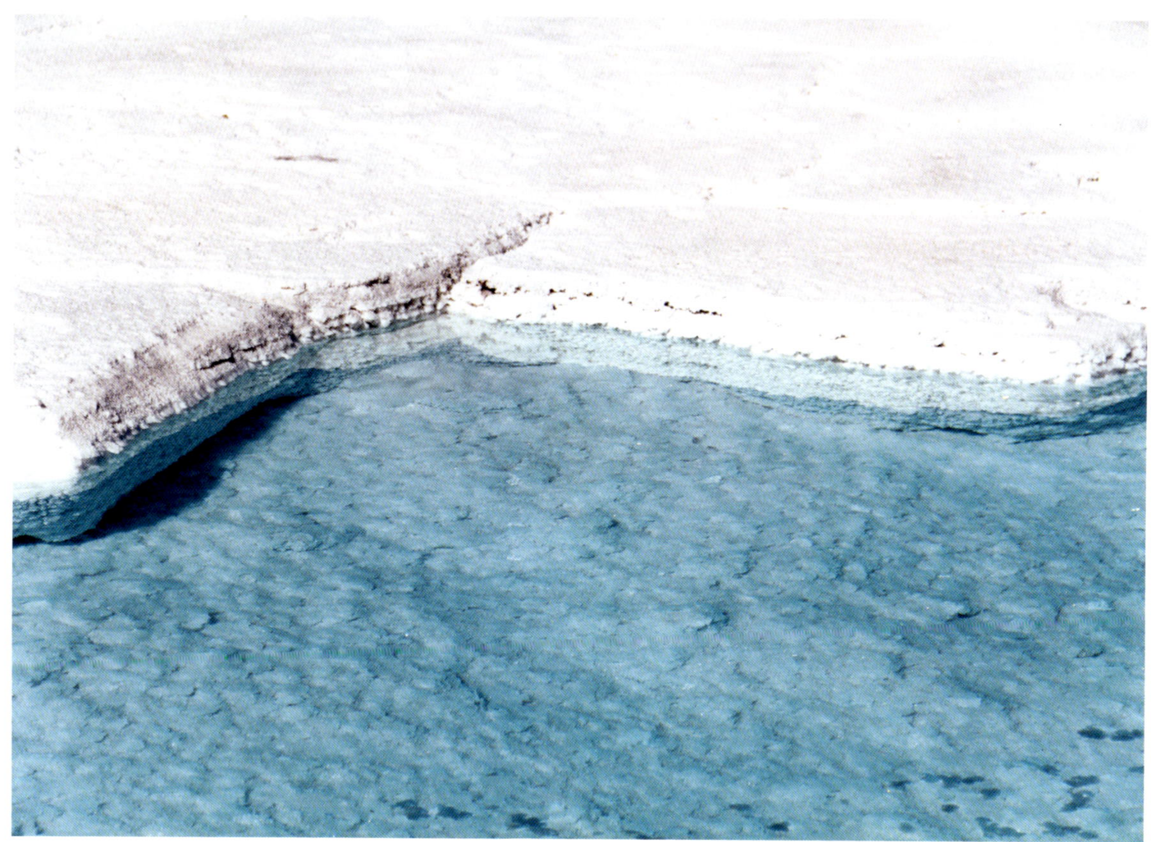

Salinas Grandes del noroeste

Desierto de sal

A una altura de 3450 m, 190 km al noroeste de la capital de la provincia, se encuentran las Salinas Grandes, los grandes salares. Su agua salada es de origen volcánico. Debido al desplazamiento tectónico de los Andes, se bloqueó la salida de tres ríos, formando así el lago salado. En una superficie de 212 km² se extiende un brillante y blanco desierto de sal, que se transforma en un lago cuando llueve. Después de unos pocos días de sol, el agua se evapora completamente, de modo que se forma una costra de sal de 30 cm de espesor en la superficie. Consiste en cloruro de sodio. La sal se extrae en muchas salinas industriales pequeñas y también en algunas grandes. Se corta en bloques y seseca.

Deserto do Lago Salgado

A uma altitude de 3450 m, 190 km a noroeste da capital provincial, encontram-se as Salinas Grandes, os grandes lagos salgados. A sua água salgada é de origem vulcânica. Devido ao deslocamento tectônico dos Andes, a vazão de três rios foi bloqueada, formando assim o lago salgado. Em uma área de 212 km² estende-se um deserto de sal branco brilhante, que se transforma em um lago quando chove. Após apenas alguns dias de sol a água evapora completamente, de modo que se forma uma crosta salina de 30 cm de espessura na superfície. É constituído por cloreto de sódio. O sal é extraído em muitas salinas pequenas e também em algumas salinas grandes operadas industrialmente. É cortado e seco em blocos.

Zoutmeer woestijn

Op 3450 m hoogte, 190 km ten noordwesten van de provinciehoofdstad, liggen de Salinas Grandes, de grote zoutmeren. Hun zoute water is van vulkanische oorsprong. Door de tektonische verschuiving van de Andes werd de uitstroom van drie rivieren geblokkeerd en zo ontstond het zoutmeer. Op een oppervlakte van 212 km² strekt zich een glimmende, witte zoutwoestijn uit, die bij regen verandert in een meer. Al na enkele dagen zon verdampt het water volledig, zodat op het oppervlak een 30 cm dikke zoutkorst ontstaat. Deze bestaat uit natriumchloride. In veel kleine en ook enkele grotere industrieel geëxploiteerde zoutmeren wordt zout gewonnen. Het wordt in blokken afgesneden en gedroogd.

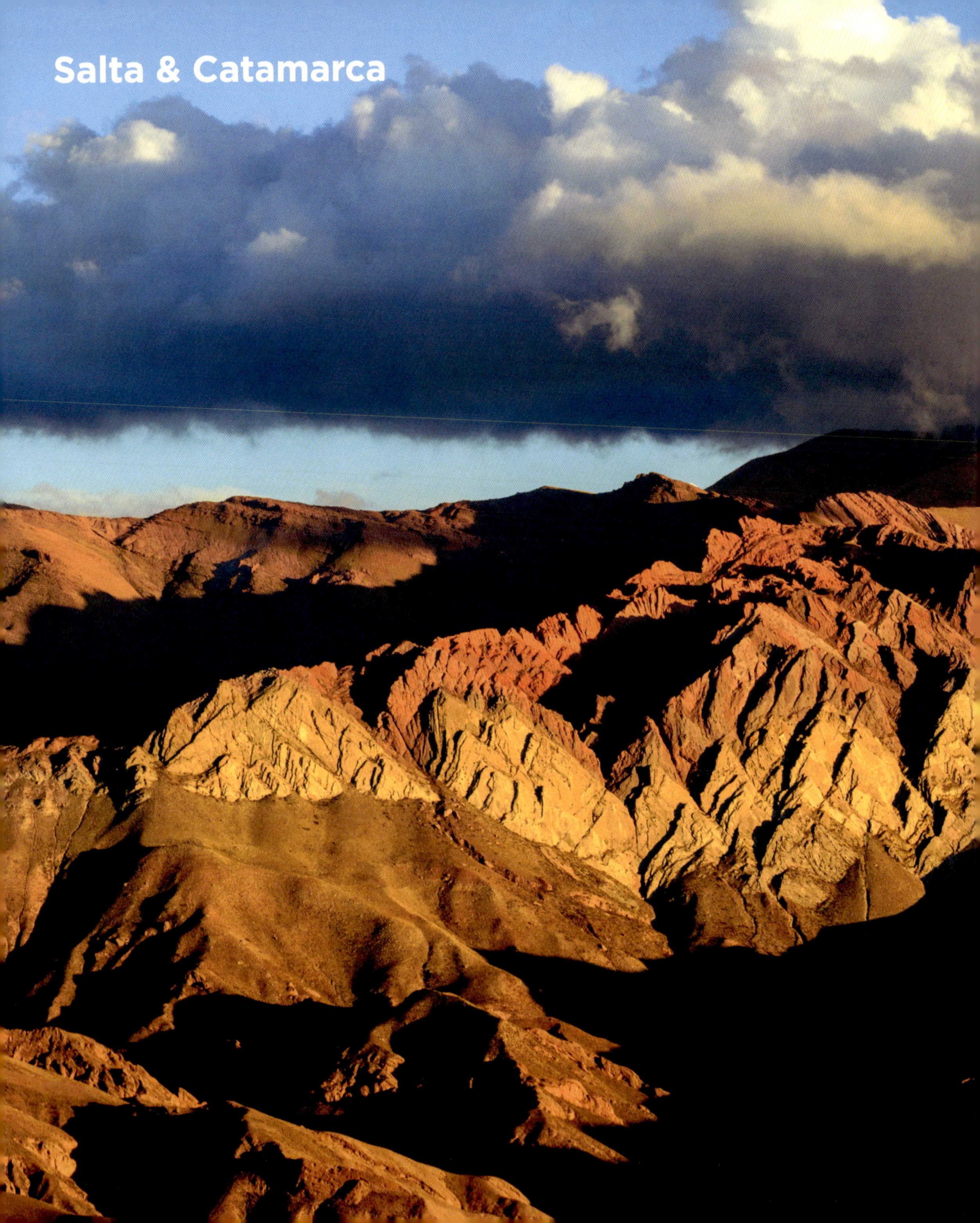
Salta & Catamarca

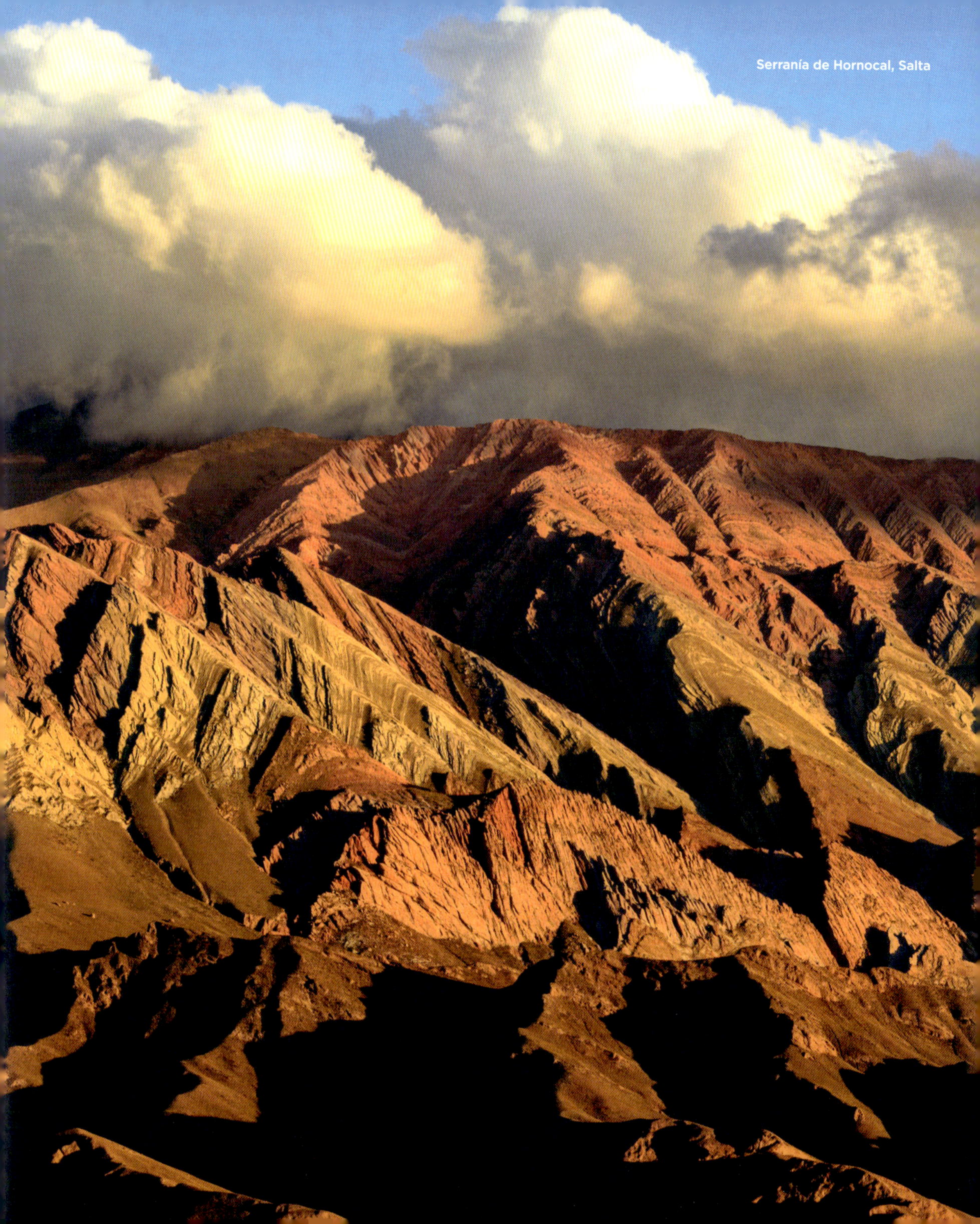
Serranía de Hornocal, Salta

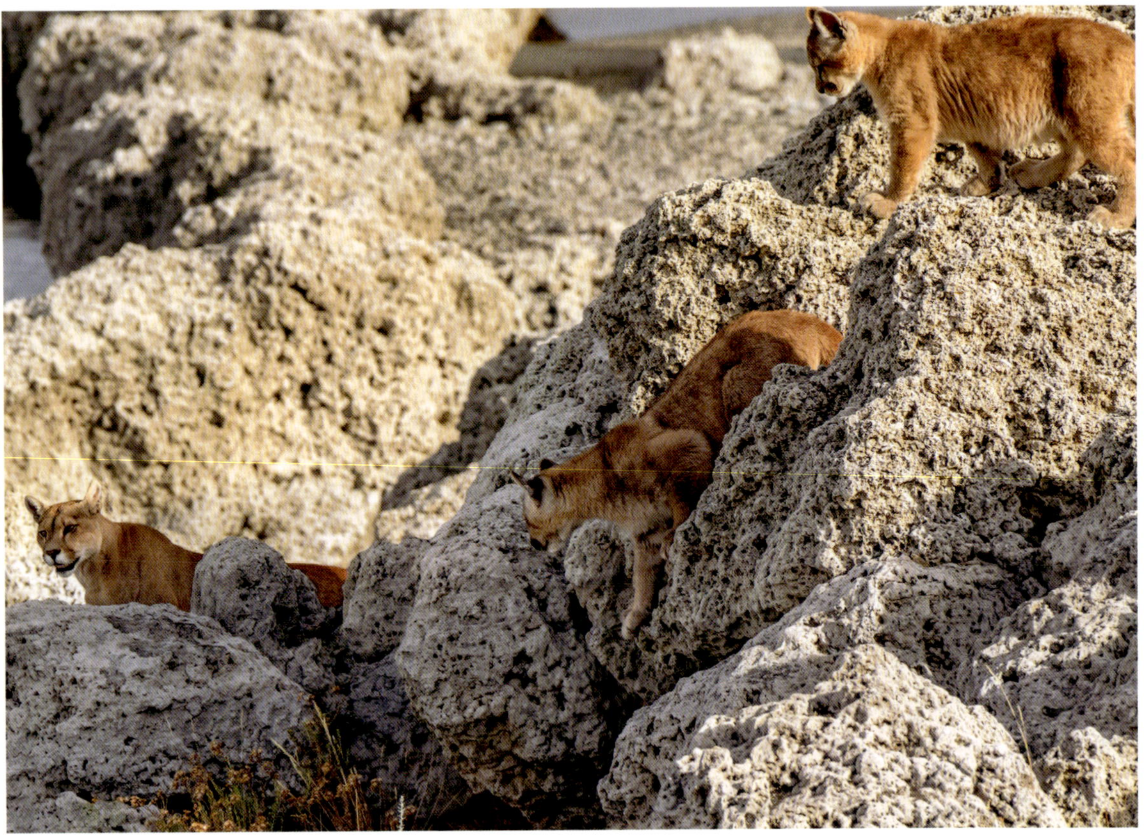

Pumas

Salta and Catamarca

These belong to the northwestern provinces. Salta borders Chile in the west and Bolivia and Paraguay in the north. With an area of 155 488 km² (60,034 sq mi) it is one of the larger provinces. Catamarca translates to "rock fortress" and it is located south of Salta, covering 102 600 km² (39,614 sq mi). Both provinces are historically strongly influenced by Indian cultures. Spanish settlements and trade brought early wealth in the colonial period, which ebbed away with the foundation of the viceroyalty of Río de la Plata. The chain of the Andes and the plateaus, sparse population, nature parks and the possibility to observe rare animals such as pumas make both provinces very popular with travelers.

Salta et Catamarca

Ces deux provinces font partie du Nord-Ouest argentin. Salta est frontalière à l'ouest du Chili et au nord de la Bolivie et du Paraguay. Avec une superficie de 155 488 km², elle compte parmi les plus grandes provinces du pays. Catamarca (forteresse de pierre) se situe au sud de Salta et occupe 102 600 km². Historiquement, les deux provinces sont fortement imprégnées des cultures indiennes. À l'époque coloniale, les cités et le commerce espagnols y apportèrent une prospérité qui décrut à la fondation de la vice-royauté de Río de la Plata. Salta et Catamarca attirent de nombreux voyageurs venant admirer la cordillère des Andes et les hauts plateaux, les petits villages et les parcs naturels, ainsi qu'une faune rare, dont des pumas.

Salta und Catamarca

Sie gehören zu den nordwestlichen Provinzen. Salta grenzt im Westen an Chile, im Norden an Bolivien und Paraguay. Mit 155 488 km² Fläche gehört sie zu den großen Provinzen. Catamarca bedeutet übersetzt „Felsenfestung", sie liegt südlich Saltas und ist 102 600 km² groß. Beide Provinzen sind historisch stark von indianischen Kulturen geprägt. Spanische Siedlungen und Handel brachten in der Kolonialzeit frühen Reichtum. Er verebbte mit der Gründung des Vizekönigreichs Río de la Plata. Die Kette der Anden und Hochebenen, dünne Besiedlung, Naturparks und die Möglichkeit, seltene Tiere wie Pumas zu beobachten, machen beide Provinzen bei Reisenden sehr beliebt.

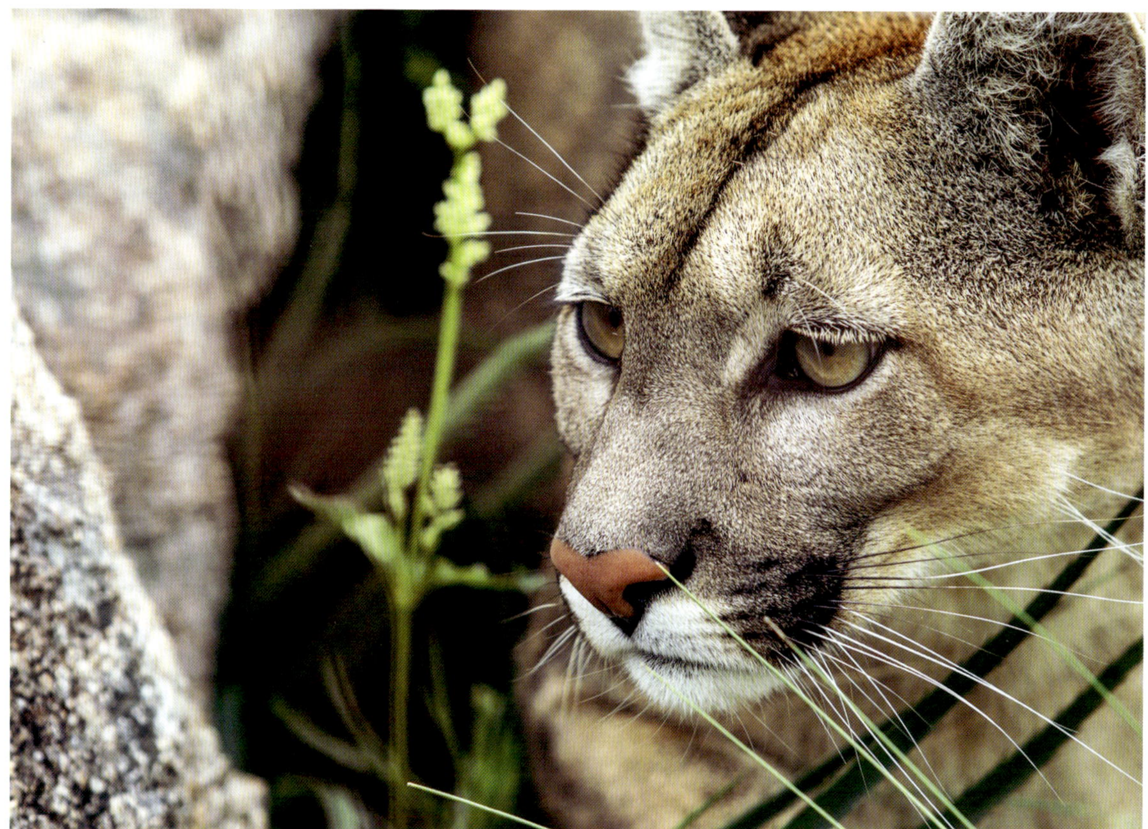

Puma

Salta y Catamarca

Pertenecen a las provincias del noroeste.
Salta limita con Chile al oeste y con Bolivia
y Paraguay al norte. Con una superficie
de 155 488 km² es una de las grandes
provincias. Catamarca significa "fortaleza
de roca", está situada al sur de Salta
y tiene una superficie de 102 600 km².
Ambas provincias están históricamente
muy influenciadas por las culturas
indígenas. Los asentamientos y el comercio
españoles trajeron la riqueza temprana en
el período colonial, pero esta se atenuó
con la fundación del Virreinato del Río
de la Plata. La cadena de los Andes y las
mesetas, la escasa población, los parques
naturales y la posibilidad de observar
animales raros, como pumas, hacen que
ambas provincias sean muy populares
entre los viajeros.

Salta e Catamarca

Elas pertencem às províncias do noroeste.
Salta faz fronteira com o Chile no oeste
e com a Bolívia e o Paraguai no norte.
Com uma área de 155 488 km², é uma
das maiores províncias. Catamarca
significa traduzida "fortaleza de pedra",
está localizada ao sul de Salta e tem
102 600 km² de extensão. Ambas as
províncias são historicamente fortemente
influenciadas pelas culturas indianas. Os
assentamentos e o comércio espanhóis
trouxeram riqueza precoce no período
colonial. Com a fundação do vice-reinado
de Río de la Plata ela chegou ao fim. A
cadeia dos Andes e planaltos, a escassa
população, os parques naturais e a
possibilidade de observar animais raros
como as suçuaranas ou pumas, tornam
ambas as províncias muito populares entre
os viajantes.

Salta en Catamarca

Ze behoren tot de noordwestelijke
provincies. Salta grenst in het westen
aan Chili en in het noorden aan Bolivia
en Paraguay. Met een oppervlakte van
155 488 km² is het één van de grote
provincies. Catamarca betekent vertaald
"fort op de helling", het ligt ten zuiden
van Salta en is 102 600 km² groot. Beide
provincies zijn historisch gezien sterk
beïnvloed door de Indiaanse culturen.
De Spaanse nederzettingen en handel
brachten in de koloniale tijd vroege
rijkdom. Dat ebde weg met de komst van
het onderkoninkrijk van Río de la Plata.
De keten van de Andes en hoogvlaktes,
de schaarse bevolking, de natuurparken
en de mogelijkheid om zeldzame dieren
zoals poema's te observeren, maken beide
provincies zeer populair bij reizigers.

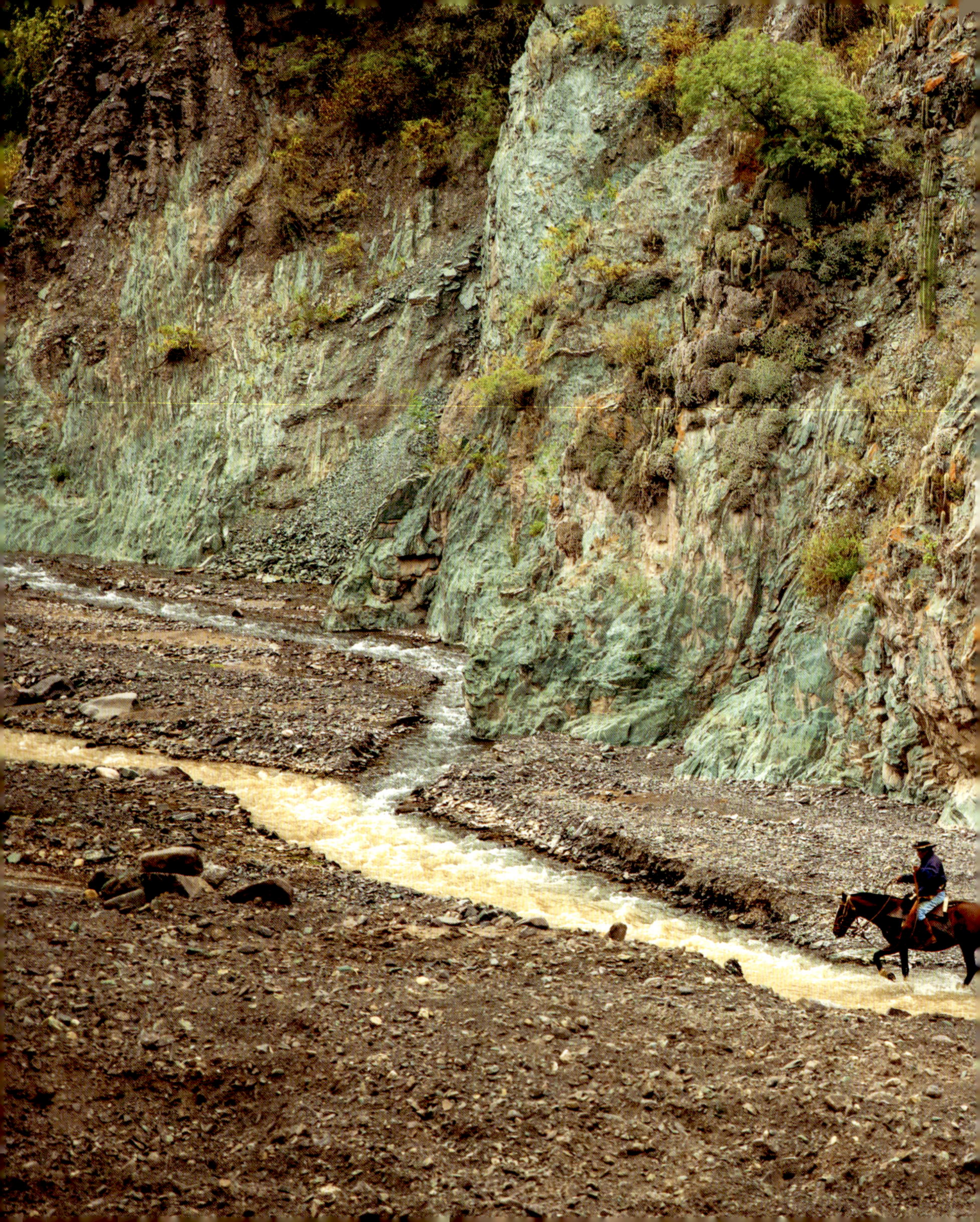

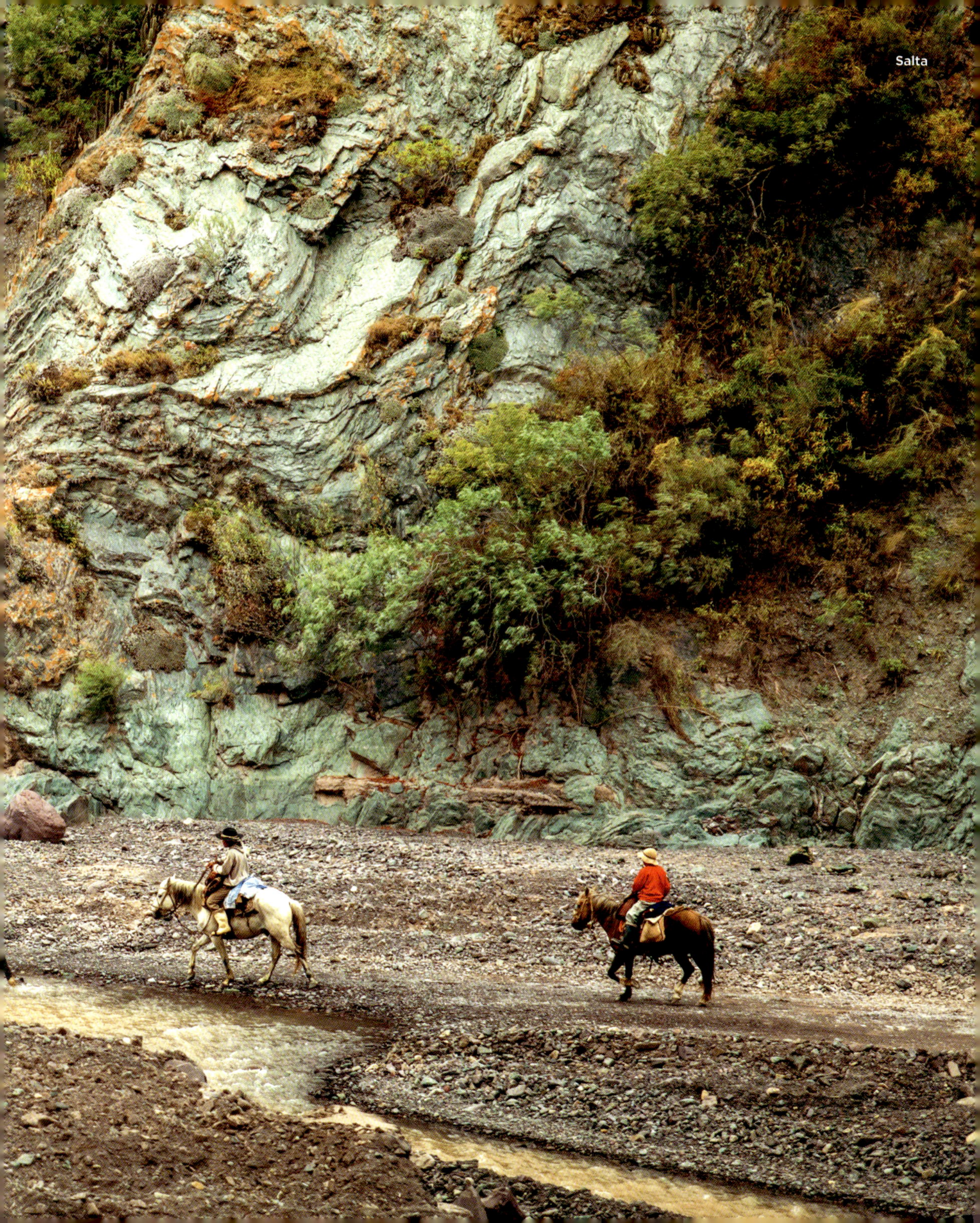
Salta

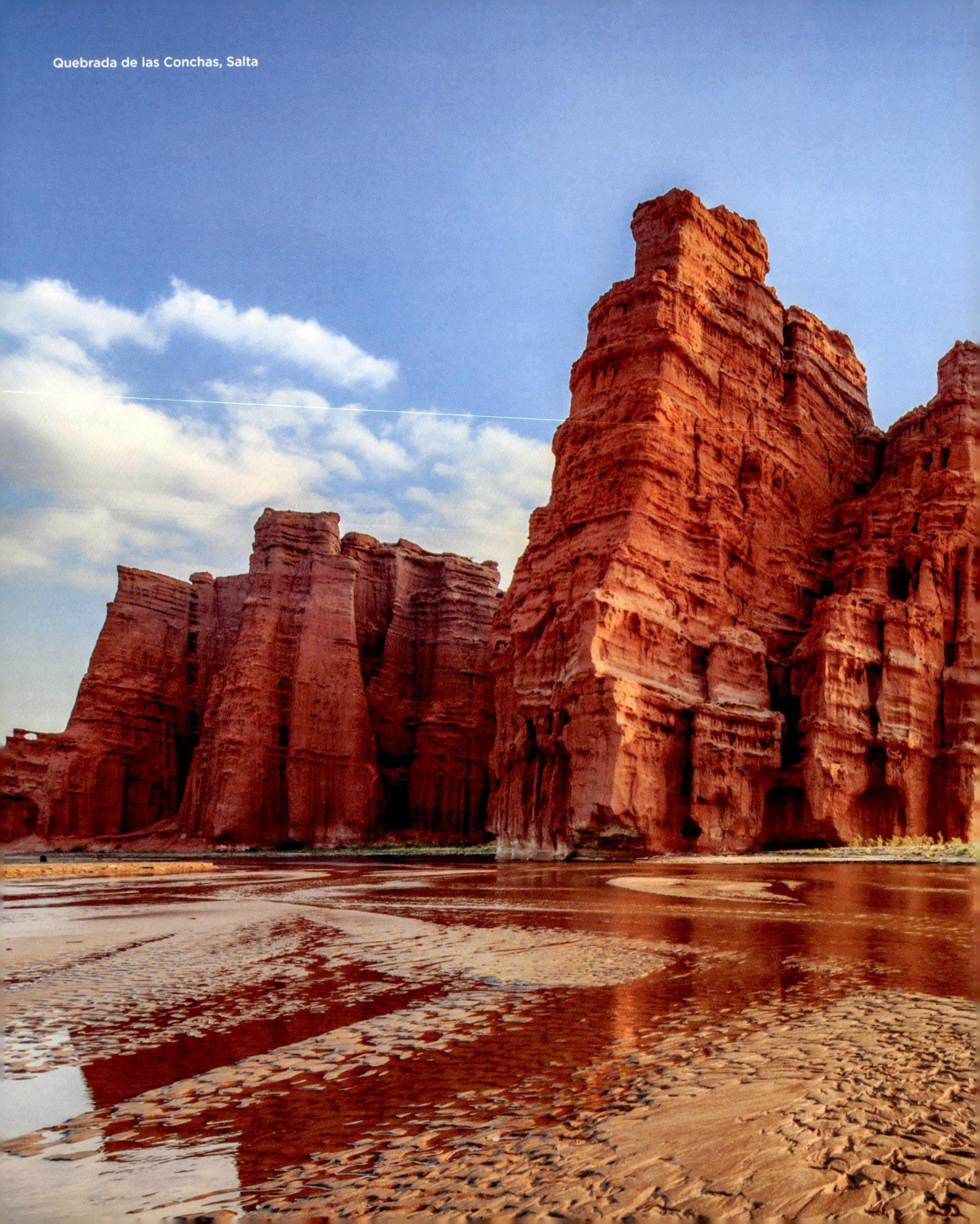
Quebrada de las Conchas, Salta

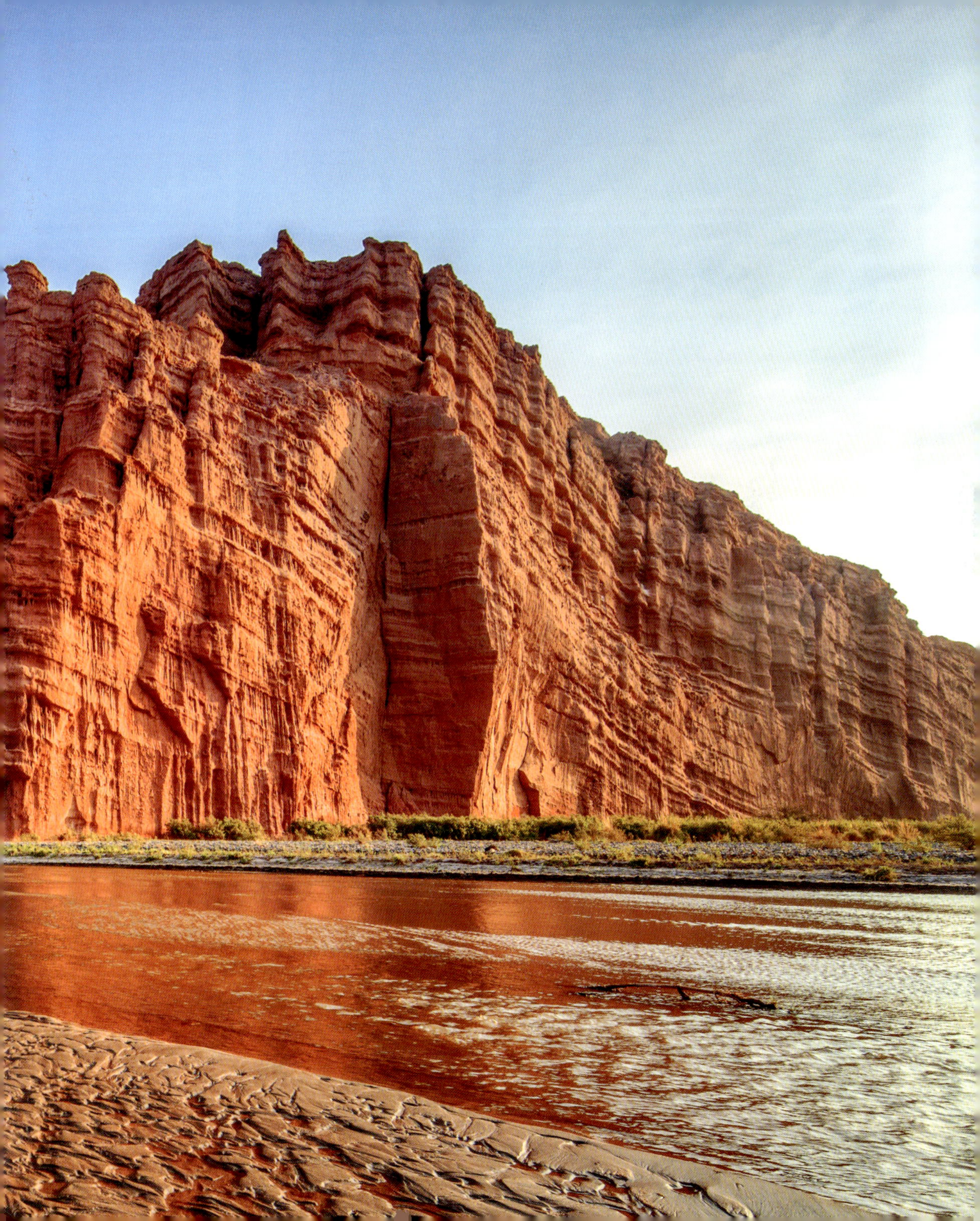

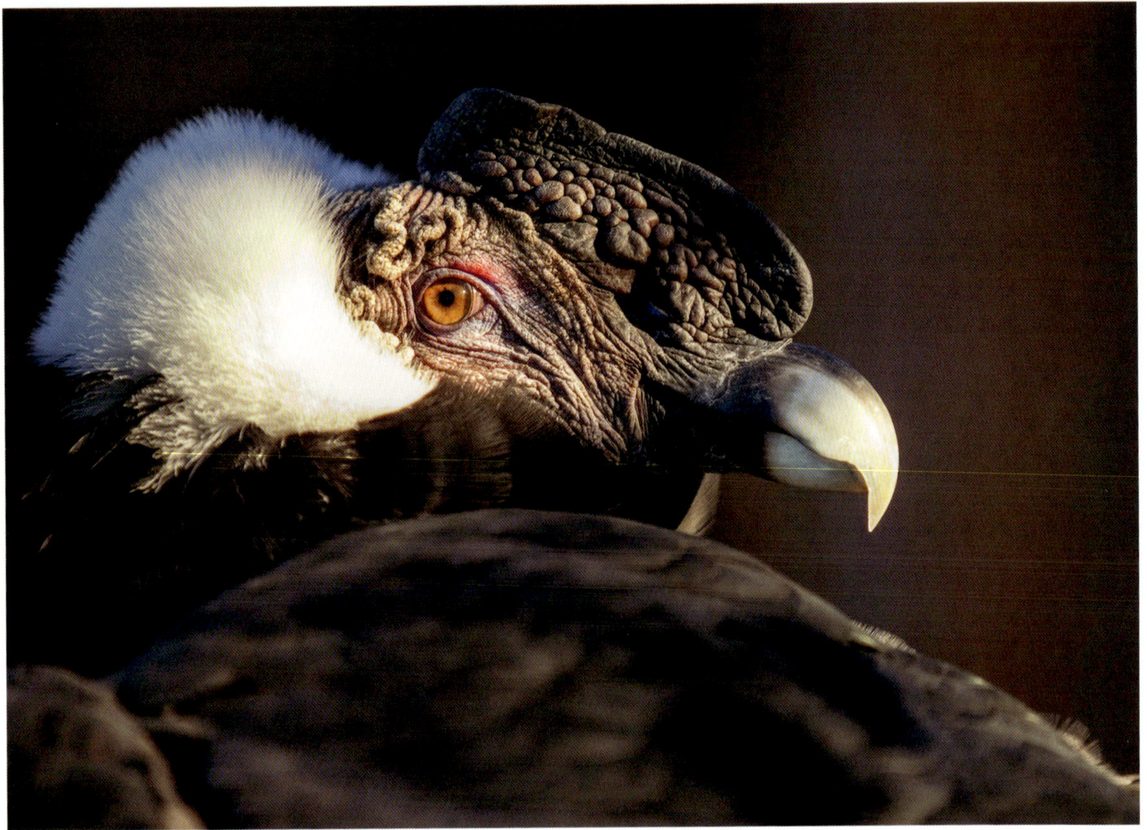

Cóndor andino
Andean condor

Andean Condor

The condor is said to be the king of the Andes and the Incas believed it was immortal. The black majestic bird of prey, with the characteristic white ruffled neck, belongs to the family of New World Vultures, which are scavengers. Circling over the canyons of the Andes, this aerial artist seeks out dead guanacos, or other animals, with its sharp eyes. It weighs around 15 kg (33 lb), with the span of its wings reaching 3 m (10 ft). Nesting places are rock ledges or platforms. Every two years condors raise a chick, which is looked after by the parents for two years. The condor, the national symbol of Argentina, is threatened with extinction.

Le condor des Andes

Le condor des Andes est surnommé « roi des Andes ». Les Incas le pensaient immortel. Ce rapace noir et majestueux, reconnaissable à sa collerette blanche, fait partie de la famille des Cathartidés. Les condors sont des charognards. En planant en cercle au-dessus des ravins de la cordillère des Andes, ils repèrent les cadavres des guanacos ou autres animaux grâce à leur regard extrêmement perçant. Ils pèsent environ 15 kg et leur envergure atteint 3 m. Ils nichent sur les corniches ou les plateformes rocheuses. La femelle met au monde un oisillon tous les deux ans, qui est nourri par ses deux parents pendant deux ans. Le condor, symbole national de l'Argentine, est menacé d'extinction.

Andenkondor

Er gilt als der König der Anden. Die Inkas glaubten, er sei unsterblich: der Andenkondor. Der schwarze majestätische Greifvogel mit der charakteristischen weißen Halskrause gehört zur Familie der Neuweltgeier. Kondore sind Aasfresser. Über den Felsschluchten der Andenkette kreisend entdeckt der Flugkünstler mit scharfem Blick verendete Guanakos oder andere Tiere. Sein Gewicht liegt bei 15 kg, die Spannweite seiner Flügel erreicht 3 m. Nistplätze sind Felssimse oder Plattformen. Alle zwei Jahre ziehen Kondore ein Junges groß. Es wird von den Eltern zwei Jahre lang versorgt. Der Kondor, das Nationalsymbol Argentiniens, ist vom Aussterben bedroht.

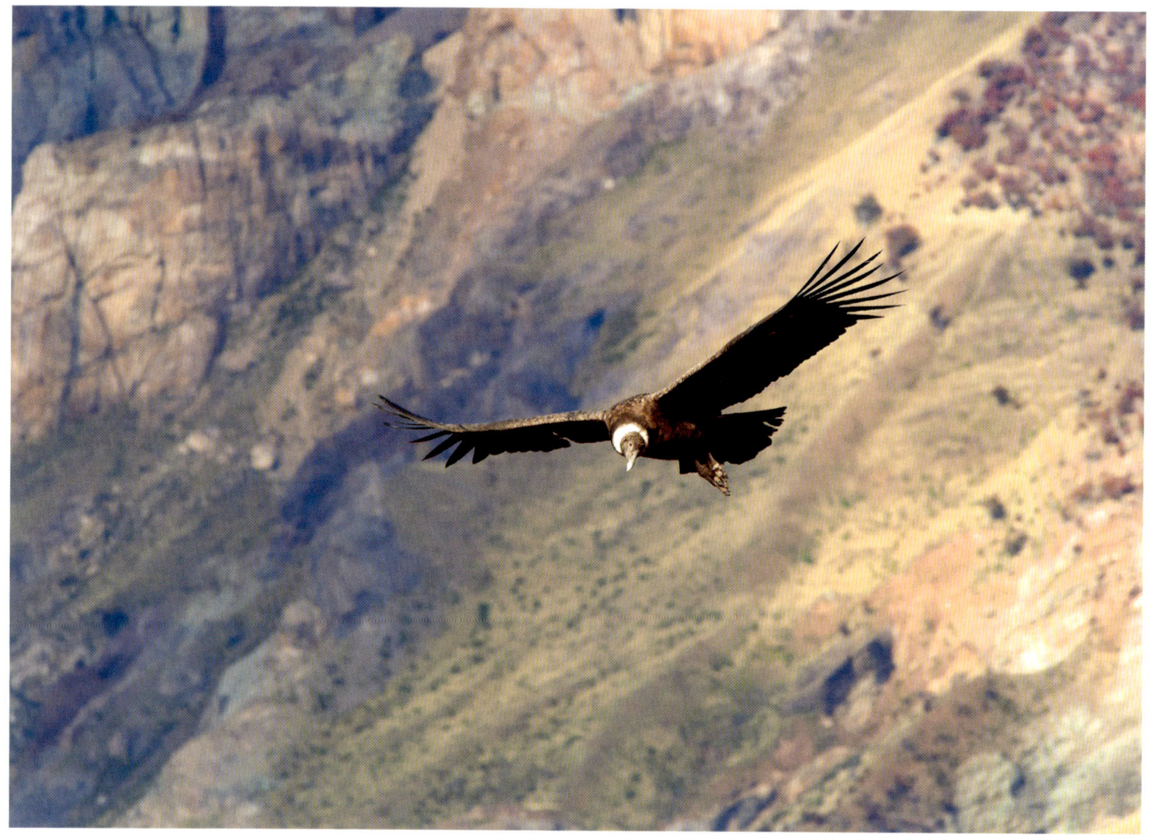

Cóndor andino
Andean condor

Cóndor Andino

Se dice que es el rey de los Andes y
los incas creían que era inmortal. La
majestuosa ave de rapiña negra con
el característico cuello blanco erizado
pertenece a la familia de los buitres del
Nuevo Mundo. El cóndor es carroñero y, al
circular sobre los cañones de los Andes,
este artista aéreo descubre guanacos
muertos u otros animales con su gran
agudeza visual. Su peso es de 15 kg y la
envergadura de sus alas alcanza los 3 m.
Los lugares de anidación son salientes
de roca o plataformas. Cada dos años
los cóndores crían un polluelo al que
los padres cuidan durante dos años. El
cóndor, símbolo nacional de Argentina,
se encuentra actualmente en peligro
de extinción.

Condor Andino

Ele é considerado o rei dos Andes. Os
incas acreditavam que ele era imortal:
o condor-dos-andes. A majestosa ave de
rapina negra, com o característico pescoço
branco desbotado pertence à família
Cathartidae. Os condores são necrófagos.
Circulando pelos desfiladeiros dos Andes,
o artista aéreo descobre guanacos mortos
ou outros animais com um olho afiado. O
seu peso é de 15 kg, o vão das suas asas
atinge os 3 m. Os locais de nidificação são
saliências ou plataformas de rocha. A cada
dois anos os condores criam um filhote.
É cuidado pelos pais durante dois anos.
O condor, o símbolo nacional da Argentina,
está ameaçado de extinção.

Andescondor

Hij geldt als de koning van de Andes.
De Inca's geloofden dat hij onsterfelijk
was: de andescondor. De zwarte,
majestueuze roofvogel met de
karakteristieke witte, gerimpelde nek
behoort tot de familie van de Gieren
van de Nieuwe Wereld. Condors zijn
aaseters. Cirkelend boven de rotsachtige
ravijnen van het Andesgebergte ontdekt
de vluchtkunstenaar met scherpe blik
omgekomen guanaco's of andere dieren.
Zijn gewicht ligt bij 15 kg, de spanwijdte
van de vleugels reikt tot 3 m. Nestplaatsen
zijn hooggelegen kliffen of platforms. Elke
twee jaar brengen condors een kleintje
groot. Deze wordt twee jaar lang door de
ouders verzorgd. De condor, het nationale
symbool van Argentinië, wordt met
uitsterven bedreigd.

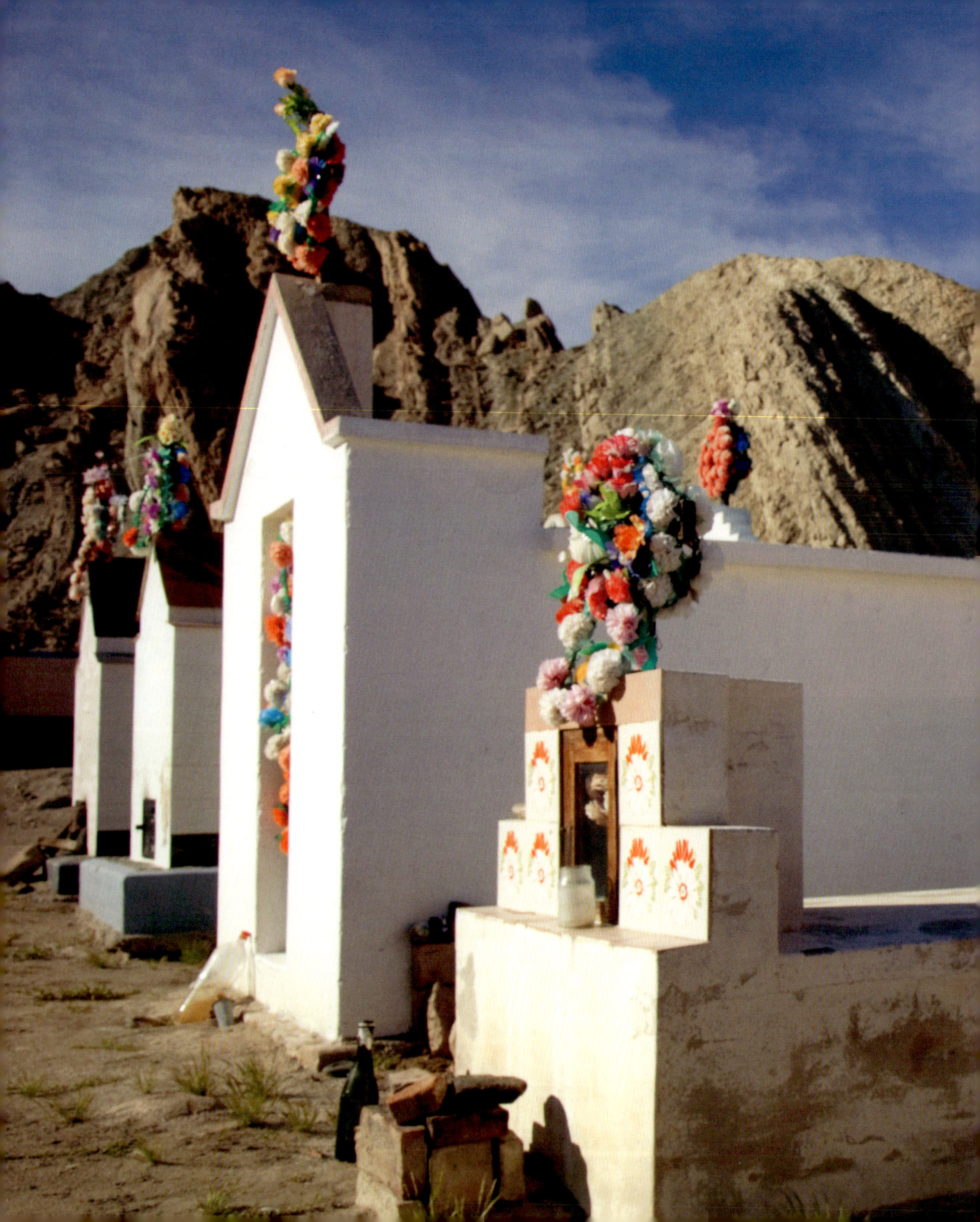

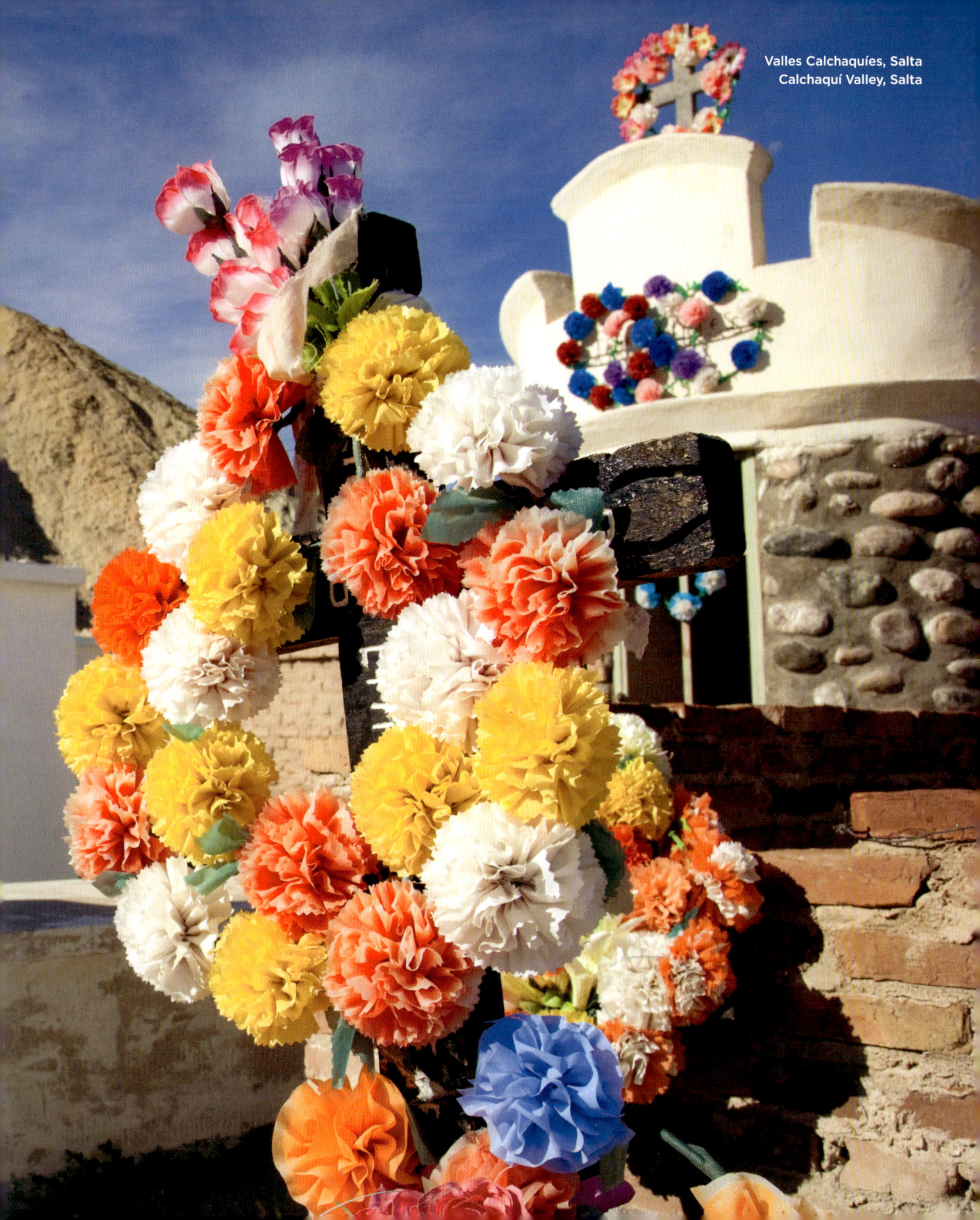

Valles Calchaquíes, Salta
Calchaquí Valley, Salta

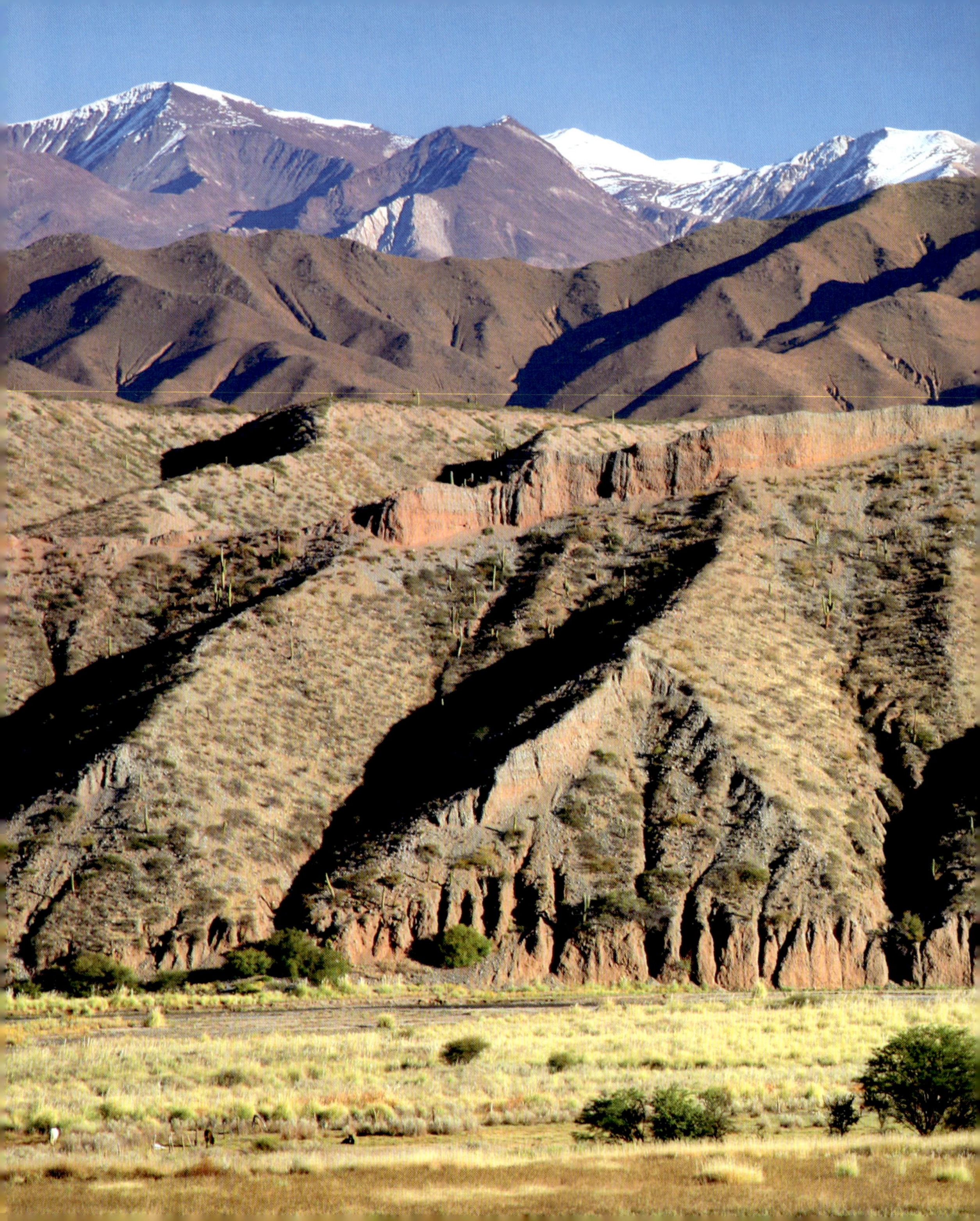

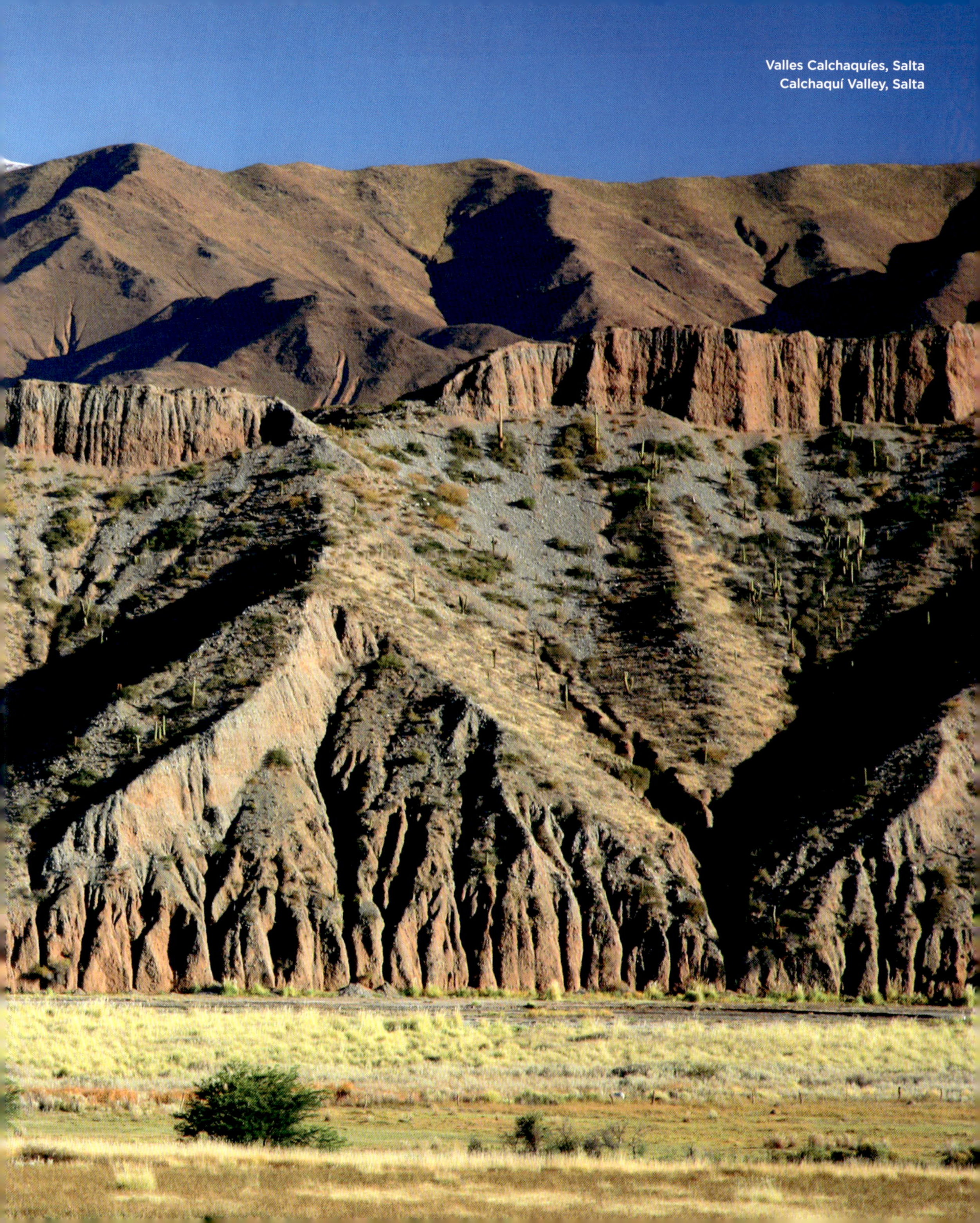

Valles Calchaquíes, Salta
Calchaquí Valley, Salta

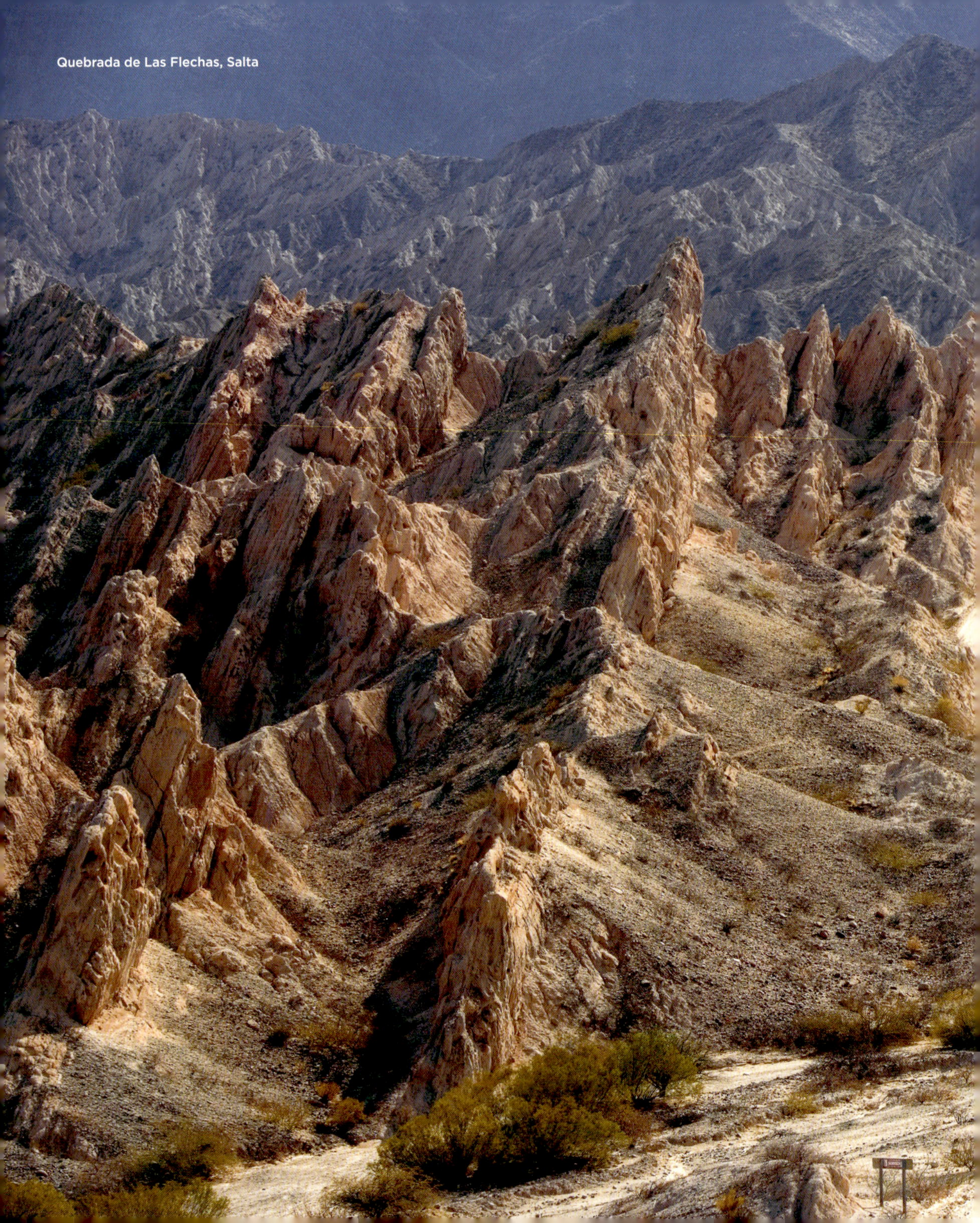
Quebrada de Las Flechas, Salta

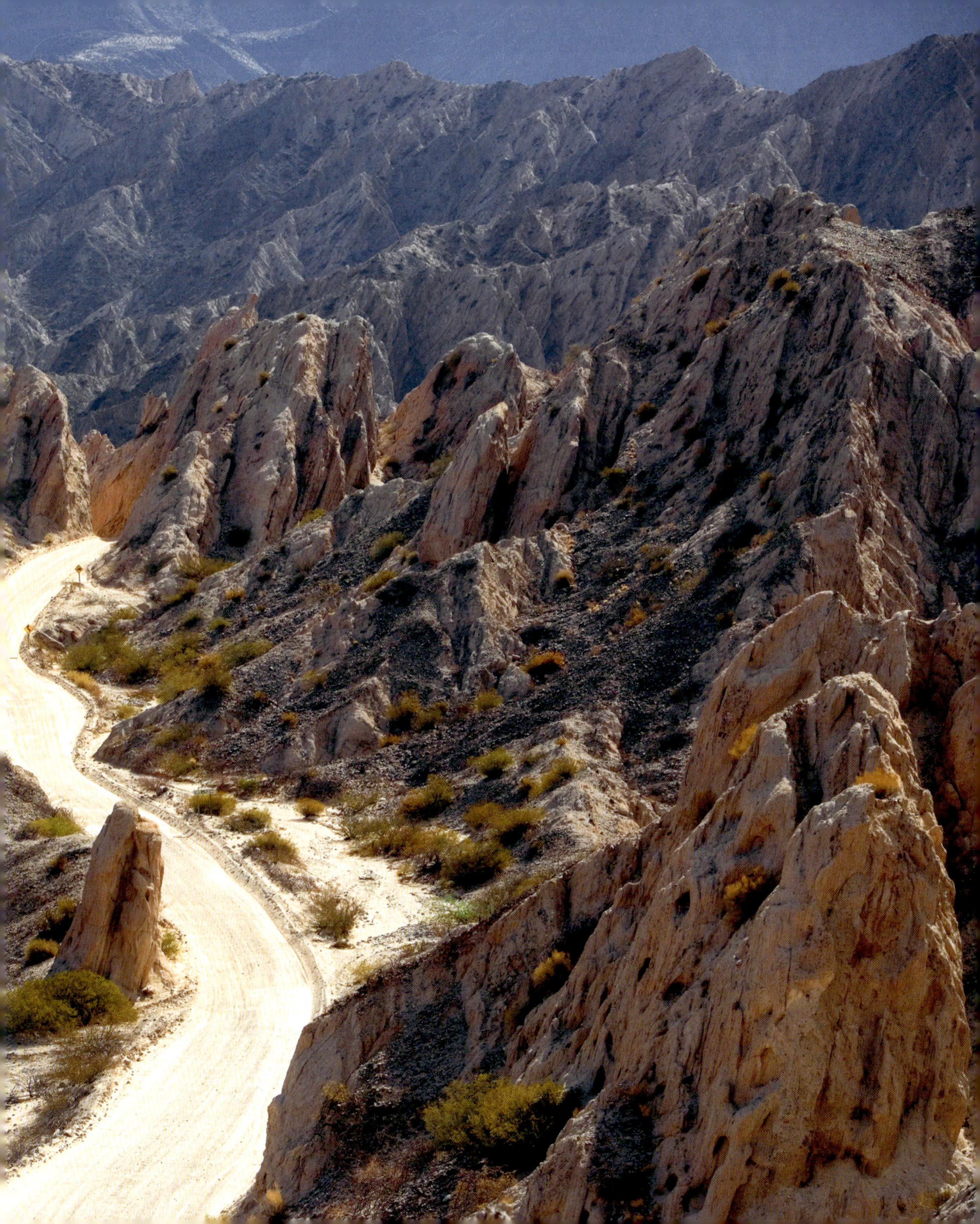

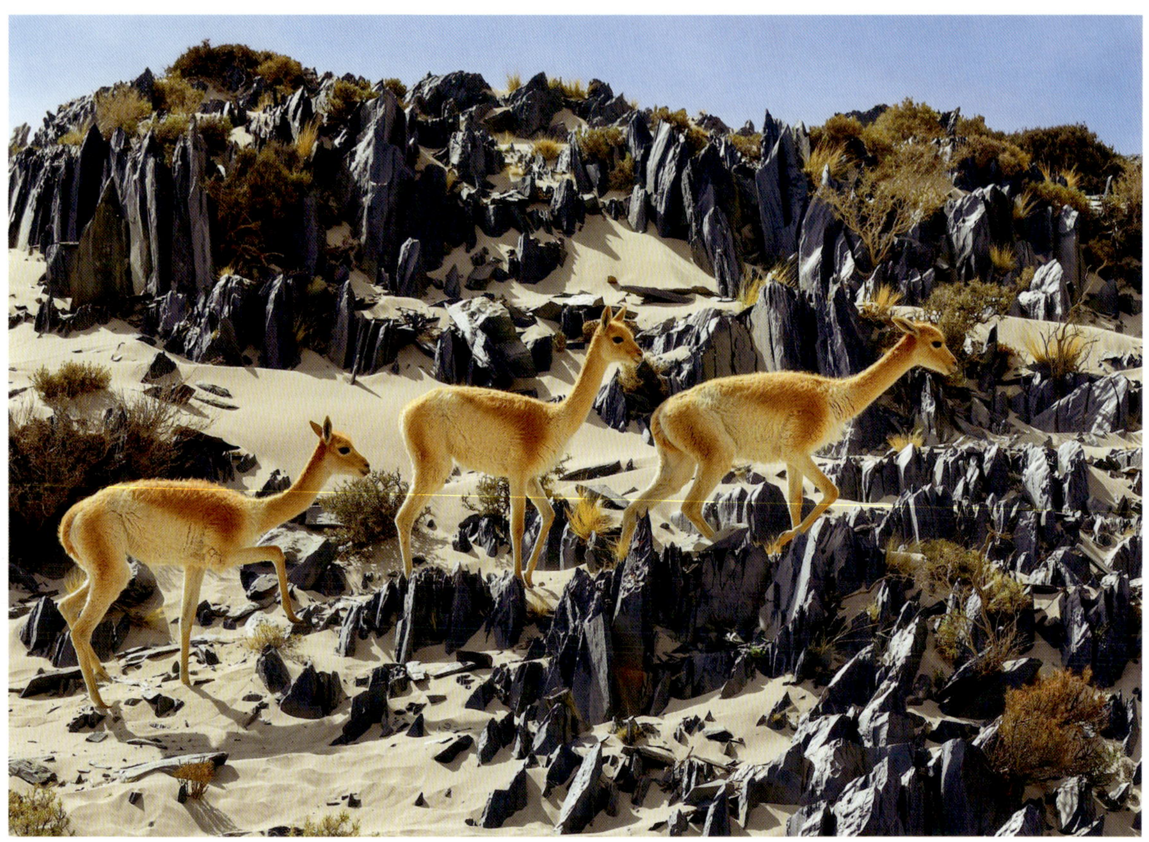

Vicuñas

Vicuñas

In the extensive Calchaquí valleys on the
eastern slopes of the Andes, the Calchaquí
Indians had their hunting grounds. Here
you can find traces of pre-Columbian
cultures and an environment which offers
the ideal habitat for vicuñas. This is what
the Quechua-speaking Indians called
the animals, which like alpacas belong
to the camel family. The vicuña is similar
to the guanaco, but more delicate. The
Incas herded large numbers together
to shear them, after which the animals
were released again. Their fine wool was
reserved for nobles. With the arrival of
the Spaniards, the animal population was
decimated, as the vicuñas were hunted and
killed for shearing.

Vicuñas

Les vastes vallées Calchaquíes, sur le
versant est des Andes, constituaient le
terrain de chasse des Indiens calchaquís.
On y retrouve des vestiges de ces cultures
préhispaniques, et la nature y compose
un habitat parfait pour les *vicuñas*. C'est
ainsi que les peuples parlant le quechua
dénomment les vigognes qui, à l'instar
des alpagas, font partie de la famille des
chameaux. La vigogne, comme le guanaco,
est cependant bien plus gracieuse. Les
Incas les réunissaient en grand nombre
pour les tondre, puis les relâchaient.
La laine fine faisait ensuite l'objet d'un
traitement délicat. Avec l'arrivée des
Espagnols, la population animale a été
décimée, car les vigognes étaient chassées,
tondues, puis tuées.

Vicuñas

In den weitläufigen Calchaquíe-Tälern
am Ostabhang der Anden hatten die
Calchaqui-Indianer ihre Jagdgründe.
Hier finden sich Spuren prähispanischer
Kulturen und die Natur bietet das ideale
Habitat für Vicuñas. So nannten die
Quechua-sprachigen Indios die Tiere,
die wie die Alpakas zur Familie der
Kamele zählen. Das Vicuña gleicht dem
Guanako, ist aber zierlicher. Die Inka
trieben große Herden zusammen, um
sie zu scheren. Danach wurden die Tiere
wieder freigelassen. Die feine Wolle war
Adligen vorbehalten. Mit der Ankunft der
Spanier dezimierte sich der Tierbestand,
denn Vicuñas wurden zum Scheren gejagt
und getötet.

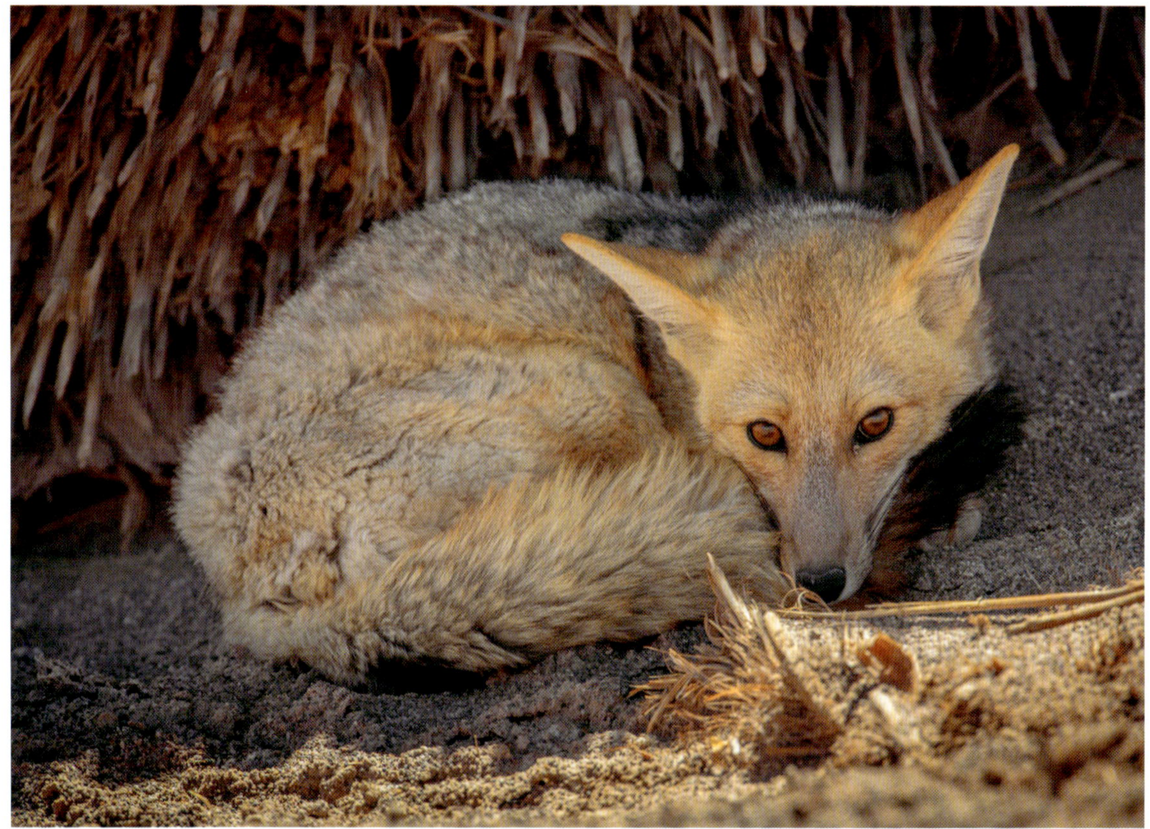

Zorro culpeo

Vicuñas

En los extensos valles Calchaquíes de las laderas orientales de los Andes, los calchaquíes tenían sus cotos de caza. Aquí se pueden encontrar vestigios de las culturas prehispánicas y la naturaleza ofrece el hábitat ideal para las vicuñas. Así es como los quechuas llamaban a estos animales que, como las alpacas, pertenecen a la familia de los camellos. La vicuña es similar al guanaco, pero más delicada. Los incas reunían grandes rebaños para esquilarlos y después los animales se liberaban de nuevo. La fina lana estaba reservada para los nobles. Con la llegada de los españoles, la población animal se diezmó, porque las vicuñas se cazaban y mataban para la esquila.

Vicuñas

Nos extensos Vales Calchaquíes das encostas orientais dos Andes, os índios Calchaquíes tinham suas áreas de caça. Aqui você pode encontrar vestígios de culturas pré-hispânicas e a natureza oferece o habitat ideal para as Vicuñas. Foi assim que os índios de língua quechua chamavam estes animais, que como as alpacas pertencem à família dos camelos. A vicunha é semelhante ao guanaco, mas mais delicada. Os incas juntavam grandes rebanhos para os tosquiar. Depois, os animais eram soltos novamente. A lã fina era reservada para os nobres. Com a chegada dos espanhóis, a população animal foi dizimada, porque as vicunhas, para serem tosquiar, foram caçadas e mortas.

Vicuñas

In de uitgestrekte Calchaquíe-valleien op de oostelijke hellingen van de Andes hadden de Calchaqui-indianen hun jachtgebied. Hier bevinden zich sporen van pre-Hispaanse culturen en biedt de natuur de ideale leefomgeving voor vincuñas. Zo noemden de Quechua sprekende Indianen de dieren die net als alpaca's tot de kameelfamilie behoren. De vicuña is vergelijkbaar met de guanaco, maar dan eleganter. De Inca's dreven grote kuddes bij elkaar om ze te scheren. Daarna werden de dieren weer vrijgelaten. De fijne wol was aan de adelijken voorbehouden. Met de komst van de Spanjaarden nam de dierenpopulatie af, want om ze te scheren werd op de vicuña's gejaagd en vervolgens werden ze gedood.

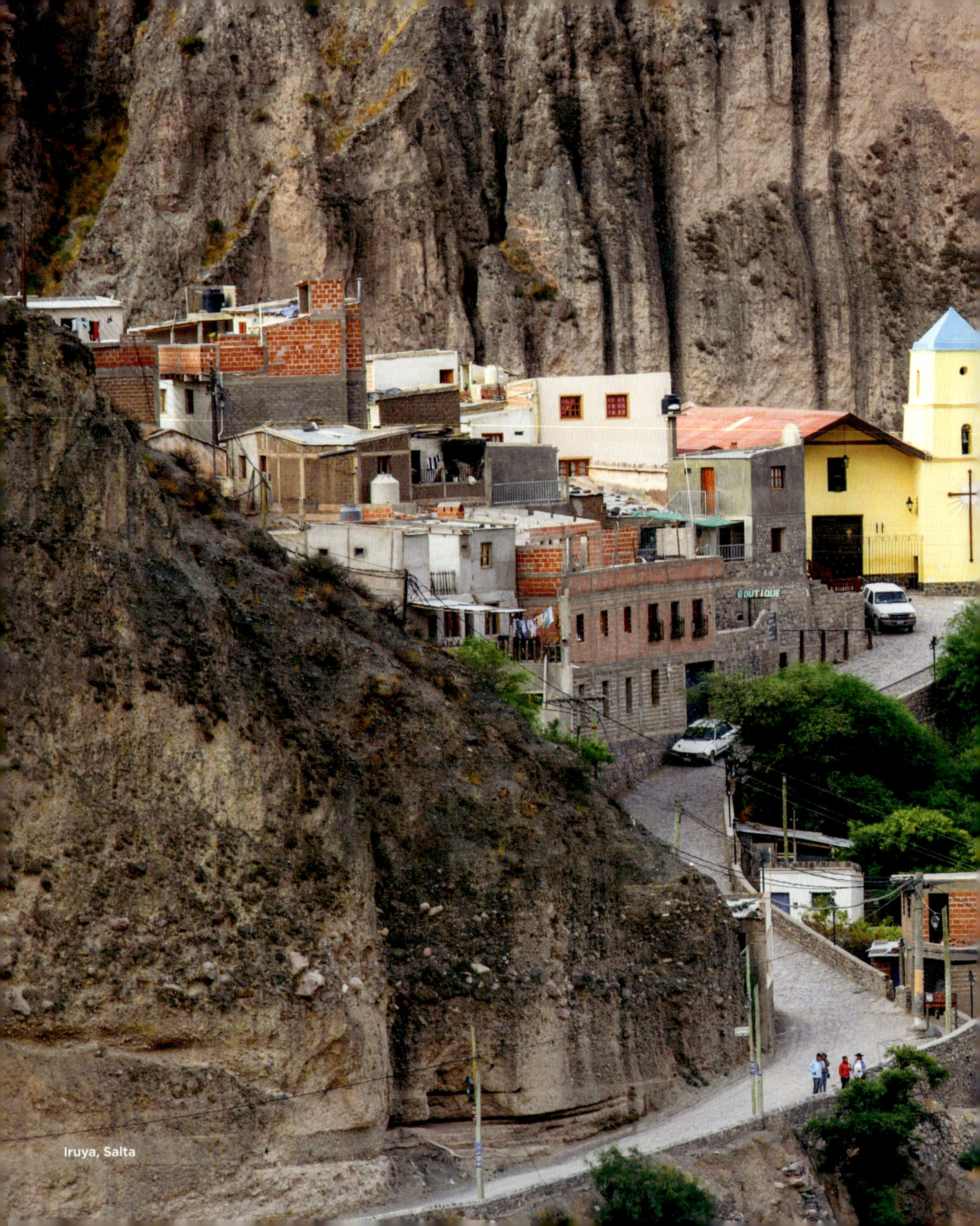

Iruya, Salta

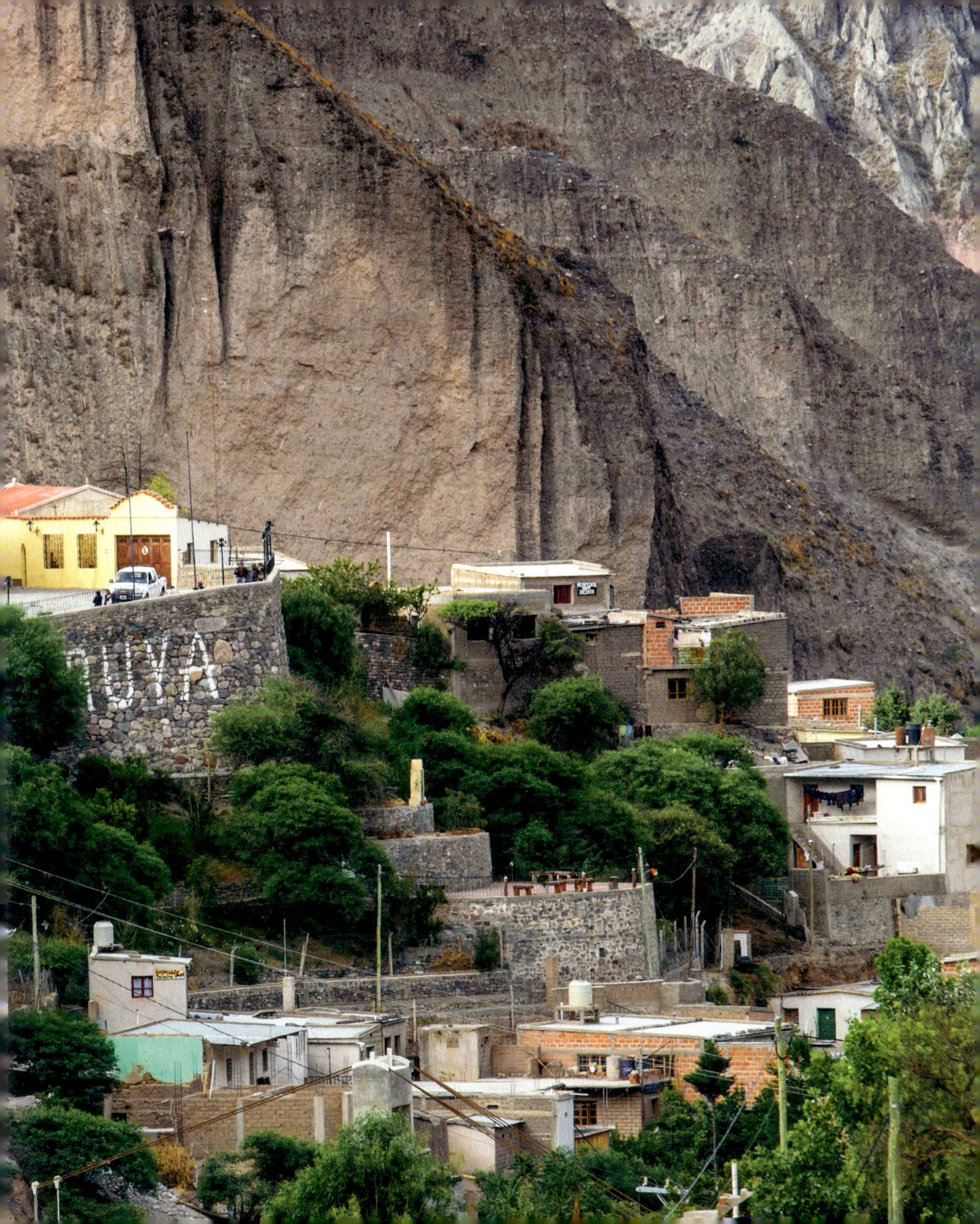
IRUYA

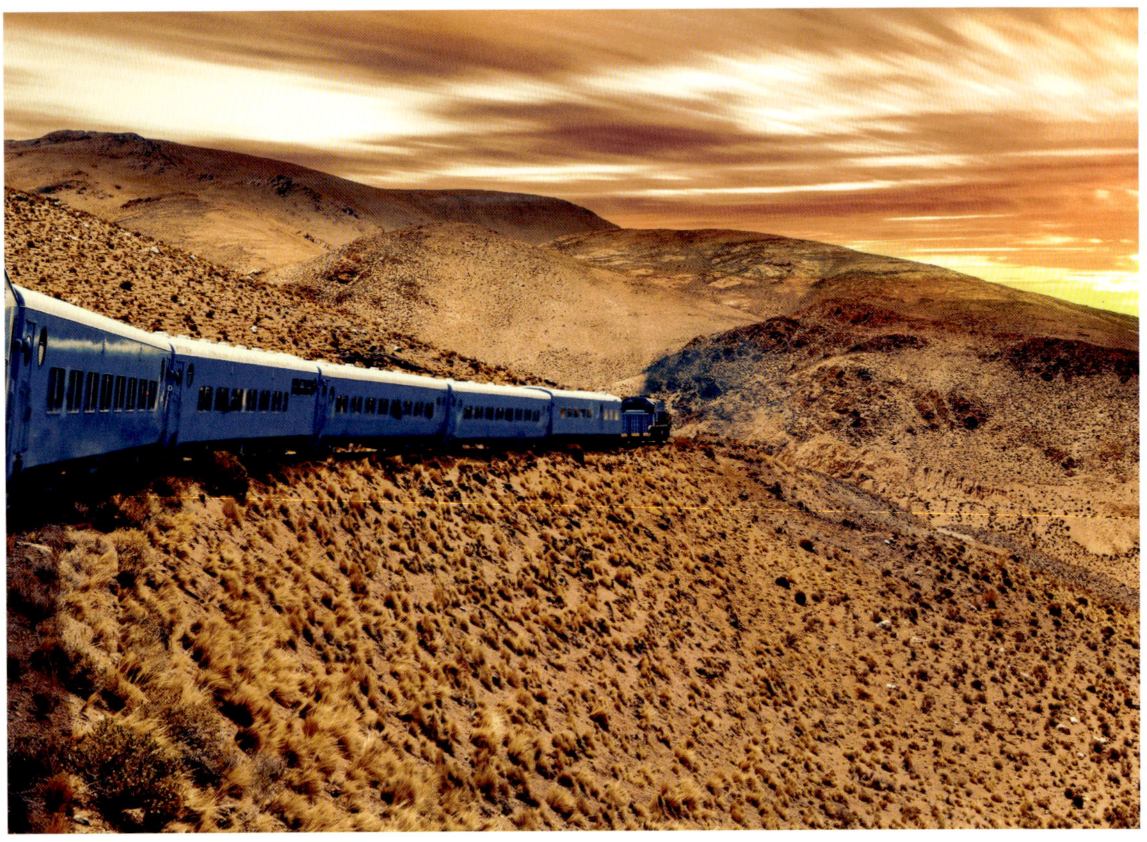

Tren a las Nubes, Salta

Train ride into the cloud

For all fans of rail travel, the "train ride
into the cloud" is an absolute hit. The
tourist train "Tren a las Nubes" covers
217 km (135 mi), taking in 44 bridges and
21 tunnels. With a speed of 35 km (22 mi)
per hour it travels from Salta, via San
Antonio de los Cobres, to the Polvorilla
viaduct at 4200 m (13,779 ft) above sea
level. This steel construction bridges a
224 m (735 ft) long valley at an altitude of
63 m (207 ft). The viaduct was completed
in 1932, as part of the railway line that
was to connect Salta, via the Andes,
with the Chilean port of Antofagasta.
Started in 1921, the plan was to create a
transport link to carry the products of the
mining industry.

Le train des nuages

Pour les amateurs de trains, le train
des nuages (Tren a las Nubes) est un
incontournable. Cette boucle touristique
de 217 km traverse 44 ponts et 21 tunnels.
Avec une vitesse de 35 km/h, le train
circule entre Salta et San Antonio de los
Cobres, en passant notamment par le
viaduc de la Polvorilla, à 4200 m d'altitude.
Cette construction en acier franchit à
63 m de haut une vallée large de 224 m.
Elle fut érigée en 1932 au moment de la
construction de la ligne de chemin de fer
destinée à relier Salta à la ville portuaire
chilienne d'Antofagasta par les Andes. Le
plan de création d'une voie de circulation
pour le transport des produits de l'industrie
minière avait débuté en 1921.

Zugfahrt in die Wolke

Für alle Fans des Eisenbahnfahrens ist
die „Zugfahrt in die Wolke" ein absoluter
Hit. Der Touristenzug „Tren a las Nubes"
legt 217 km zurück, passiert 44 Brücken
und 21 Tunnel. Mit einer Geschwindigkeit
von 35 km pro Stunde führt er von Salta
über San Antonio de los Cobres zum
Viadukt Polvorilla auf 4200 m Höhe.
Diese Stahlkonstruktion überbrückt auf
63 Höhenmetern ein 224 m langes Tal.
Das Viadukt wurde 1932 im Zuge der
Eisenbahnstrecke gebaut, die Salta über
die Anden hinweg mit der chilenischen
Hafenstadt Antofagasta verbinden
sollte. Seit 1921 bestand der Plan, eine
Verkehrsverbindung herzustellen, um
die Produkte der Bergbauindustrie
zu transportieren.

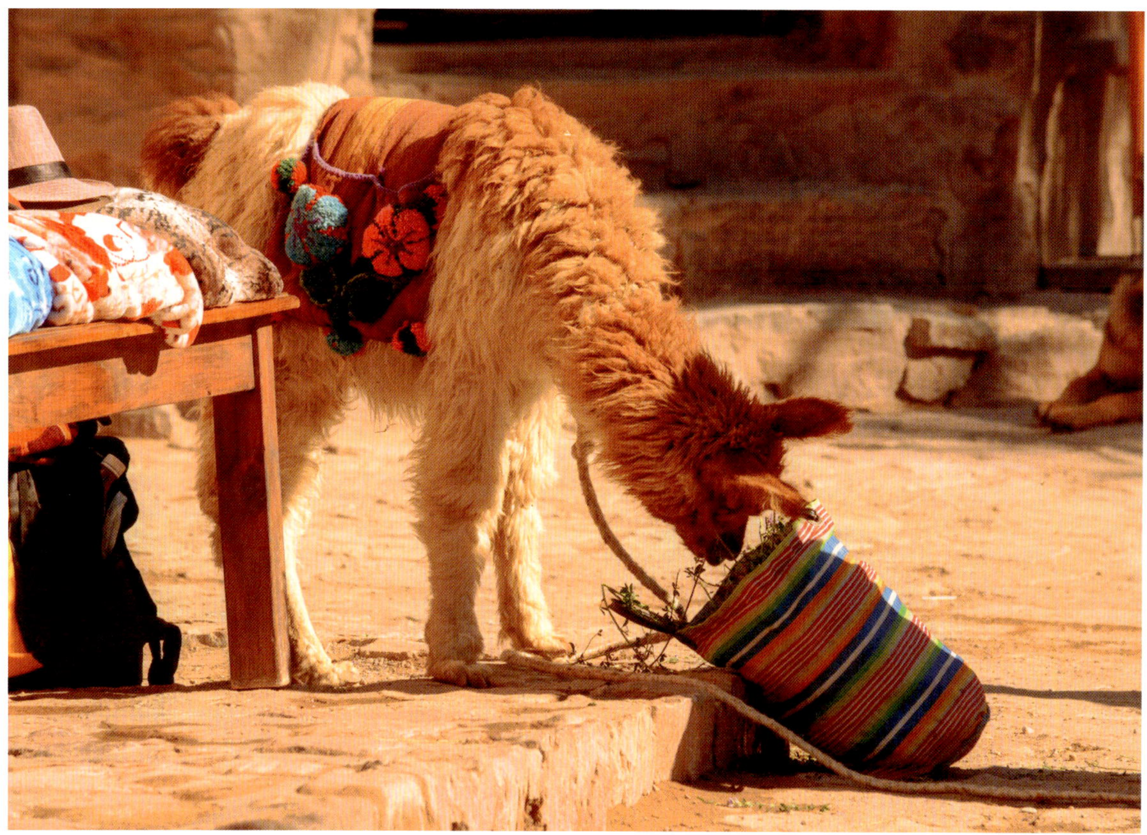

Llama

Viaje en tren a las nubes

Para todos los aficionados a los viajes en tren, el "Viaje en tren a las nubes" es un éxito absoluto. El tren turístico "Tren a las Nubes" recorre 217 km, pasa por 44 puentes y 21 túneles. Con una velocidad de 35 km por hora, conduce desde Salta, a través de San Antonio de los Cobres, hasta el viaducto de la Polvorilla, a 4200 m sobre el nivel del mar. Esta construcción de acero atraviesa un valle de 224 m de largo a una altitud de 63 metros. El viaducto fue construido en 1932 como parte de la línea ferroviaria que iba a conectar Salta a través de los Andes con el puerto chileno de Antofagasta. Desde 1921, el plan era crear una conexión de transporte para llevar los productos de la industria minera.

Viagem de comboio para a nuvem

Para todos os fãs de viagens de trem, a "Viagem de trem para a nuvem" é um sucesso absoluto. O comboio turístico "Tren a las Nubes" cobre 217 km, passa por 44 pontes e 21 túneis. Com uma velocidade de 35 km por hora vai de Salta via San Antonio de los Cobres até ao viaduto de Polvorilla a 4200 m acima do nível do mar. Esta estrutura de aço faz a ponte entre um vale de 224 m de comprimento a uma altitude de 63 metros. O viaduto foi construído em 1932 como parte da linha ferroviária que ligaria Salta através dos Andes com a cidade portuária de Antofagasta. Desde 1921, o plano era estabelecer uma ligação de transporte para transportar os produtos da indústria de mineração.

Treinreis naar de wolken

Voor alle liefhebbers van treinreizen is de "Treinreis naar de wolken" een absolute must. De toeristische trein "Tren a las Nubes" legt 217 km af en komt langs 44 bruggen en 21 tunnels. Met een snelheid van 35 km per uur gaat het van Salta via San Antonio de los Cobres naar het Polvorilla-viaduct op 4200 m boven de zeespiegel. Deze staalconstructie overbrugt op 63 meter hoogte een 224 meter lange vallei. Het viaduct werd in 1932 gebouwd als onderdeel van de spoorlijn die Salta over de Andes zou verbinden met de Chileense haven Antofagasta. Sinds 1921 bestond het plan om een verkeersverbinding aan te leggen om de producten van de mijnbouwindustrie te transporteren.

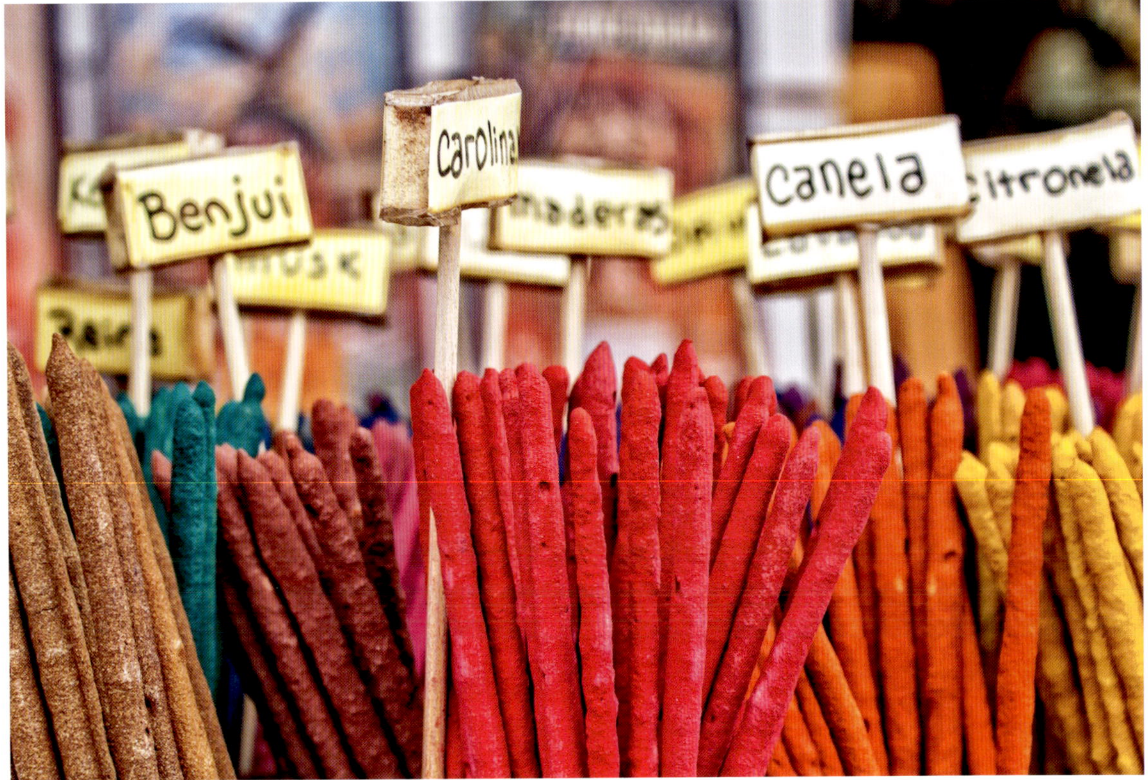

Incienso
Incense

Medicinal herbs

Everything that is good for body and soul can be bought at an indigenous market: handmade incense sticks with the scent of cinnamon or lemon, medicinal plants and herbs. The medicinal herb mixtures go back to ancient traditions. There are recipes against inflammations of all kinds and others that strengthen the heart and circulation.

Hierbas medicinales

Todo lo que es bueno para el cuerpo y el alma se puede comprar en el mercado aborigen: palitos de incienso hechos a mano con aroma de canela o limón, plantas medicinales y hierbas. Las mezclas de hierbas medicinales se remontan a las tradiciones de los pueblos originarios. Hay recetas para inflamaciones de todo tipo y otras que son buenas para el corazón y la circulación.

Herbes médicinales

Sur le marché indien, on trouve tout ce qui est bon pour le corps et pour l'âme: bâtons d'encens fabriqués à la main aux parfums de cannelle ou de citron, plantes médicinales et herbes aromatiques. Les mélanges d'herbes médicinales puisent leurs recettes dans les traditions indiennes. Certains luttent contre les inflammations de toutes sortes et d'autres renforcent le cœur et la circulation sanguine.

Ervas medicinais

Tudo o que é bom para o corpo e a alma pode ser encontrado no mercado indiano: incensos feitos à mão com cheiro de canela ou limão, plantas medicinais e ervas aromáticas. As misturas de ervas medicinais remontam às tradições indianas. Existem receitas para todos os tipos de inflamações e outras que fortalecem o coração e a circulação.

Heilkräuter

Alles, was Körper und Seele guttut, bekommt man auf dem Indio-Markt: handgefertigte Räucherstäbchen mit Zimt- oder Zitronenduft, medizinische Pflanzen und Kräuter. Die Heilkrautmischungen gehen auf indianische Traditionen zurück. Es gibt Rezepturen gegen Entzündungen aller Art und andere, die Herz und Kreislauf stärken.

Geneeskrachtige kruiden

Op de Indiase markt is van alles te koop wat goed is voor lichaam en ziel is: handgemaakte wierookstokjes met de geur van kaneel of citroen, geneeskrachtige planten en kruiden. De medicinale kruidenmengsels gaan terug naar de Indiase tradities. Er zijn recepten tegen allerlei soorten ontstekingen en andere die het hart en de bloedsomloop versterken.

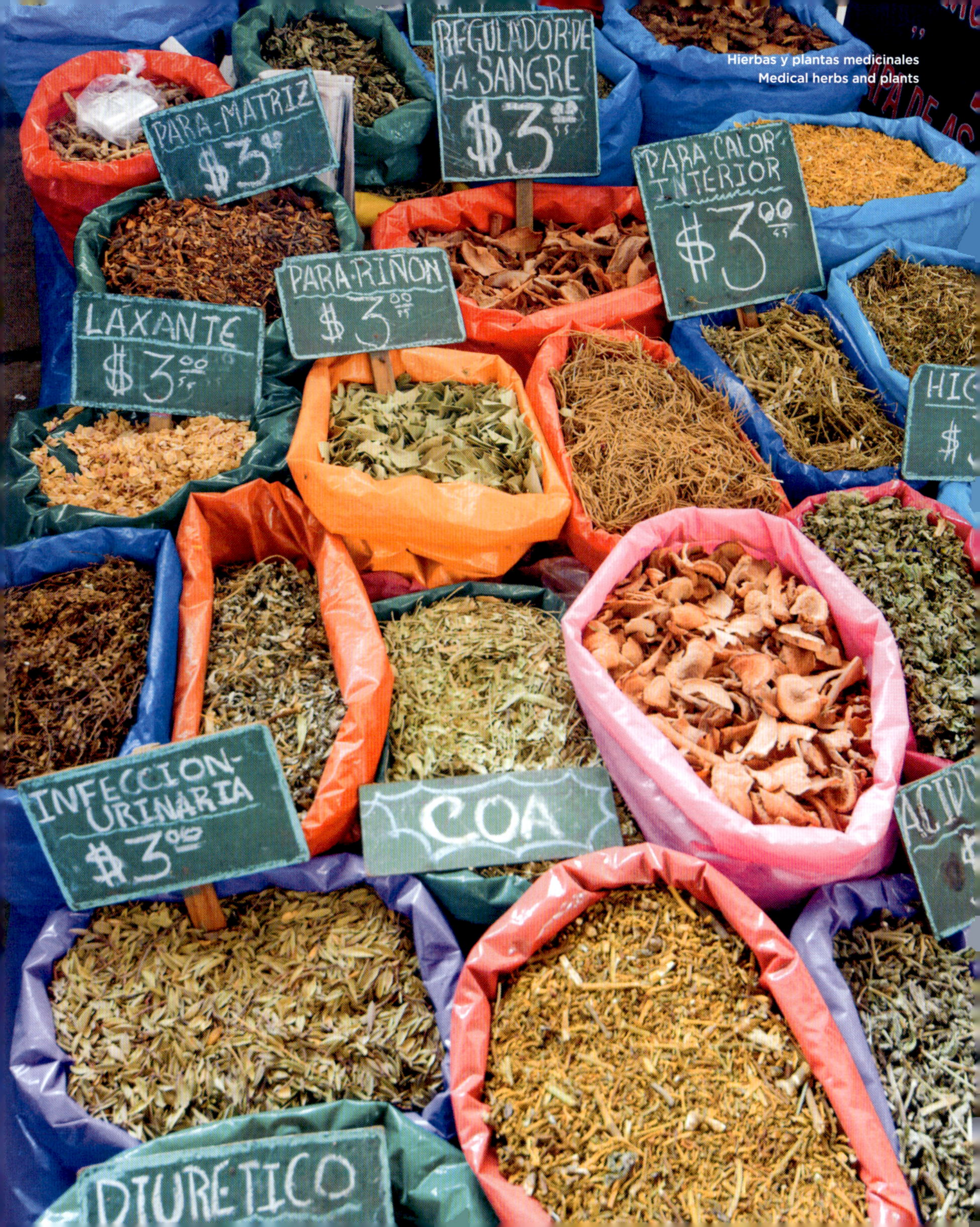

Hierbas y plantas medicinales
Medical herbs and plants
REGULADOR·DE LA SANGRE $3°°
PARA·MATRIZ $3°°
PARA·CALOR INTERIOR $3°°
PARA·RIÑON $3°°
LAXANTE $3°°
HIG
INFECCION· URINARIA $3°°
COA
DIURETICO

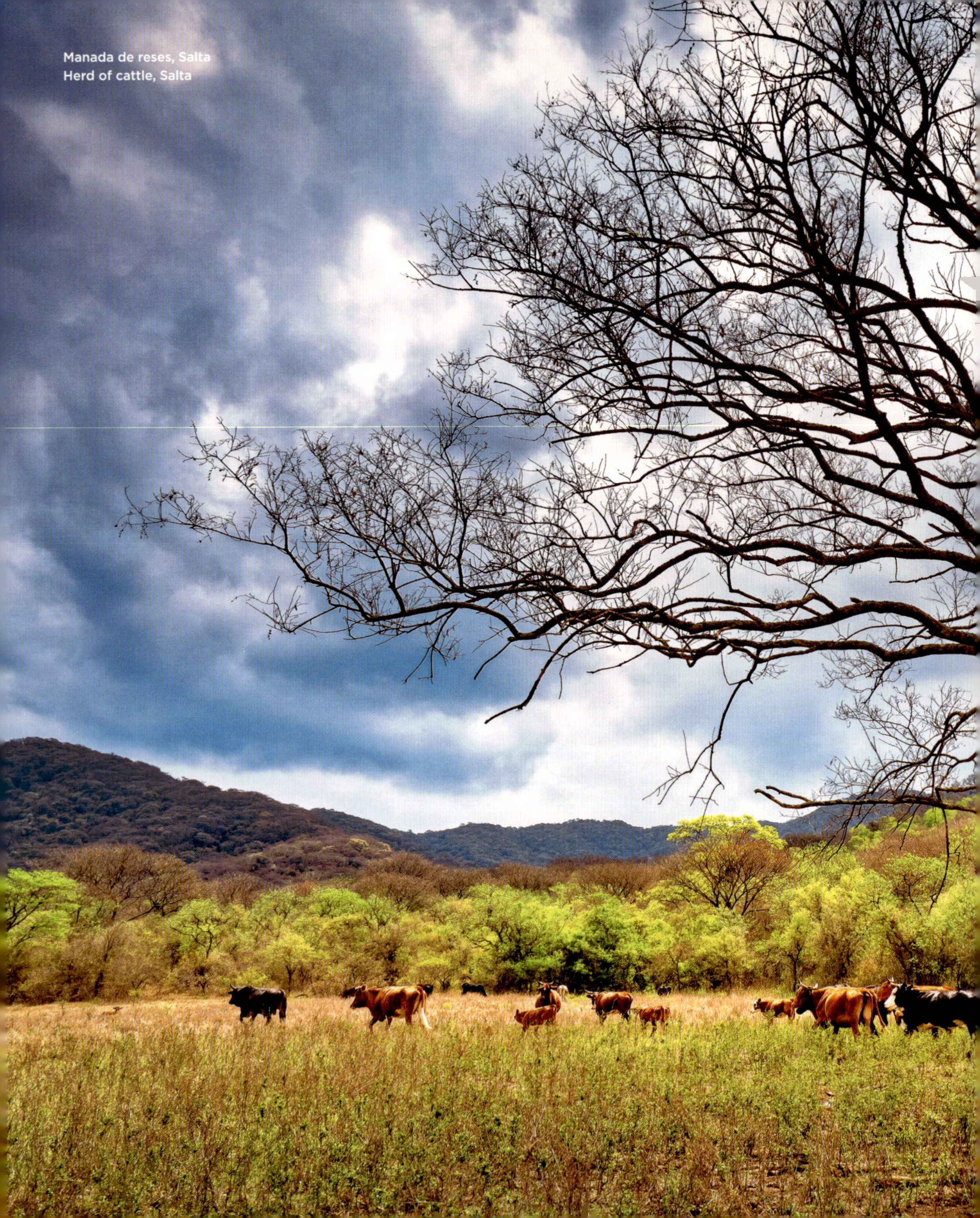

Manada de reses, Salta
Herd of cattle, Salta

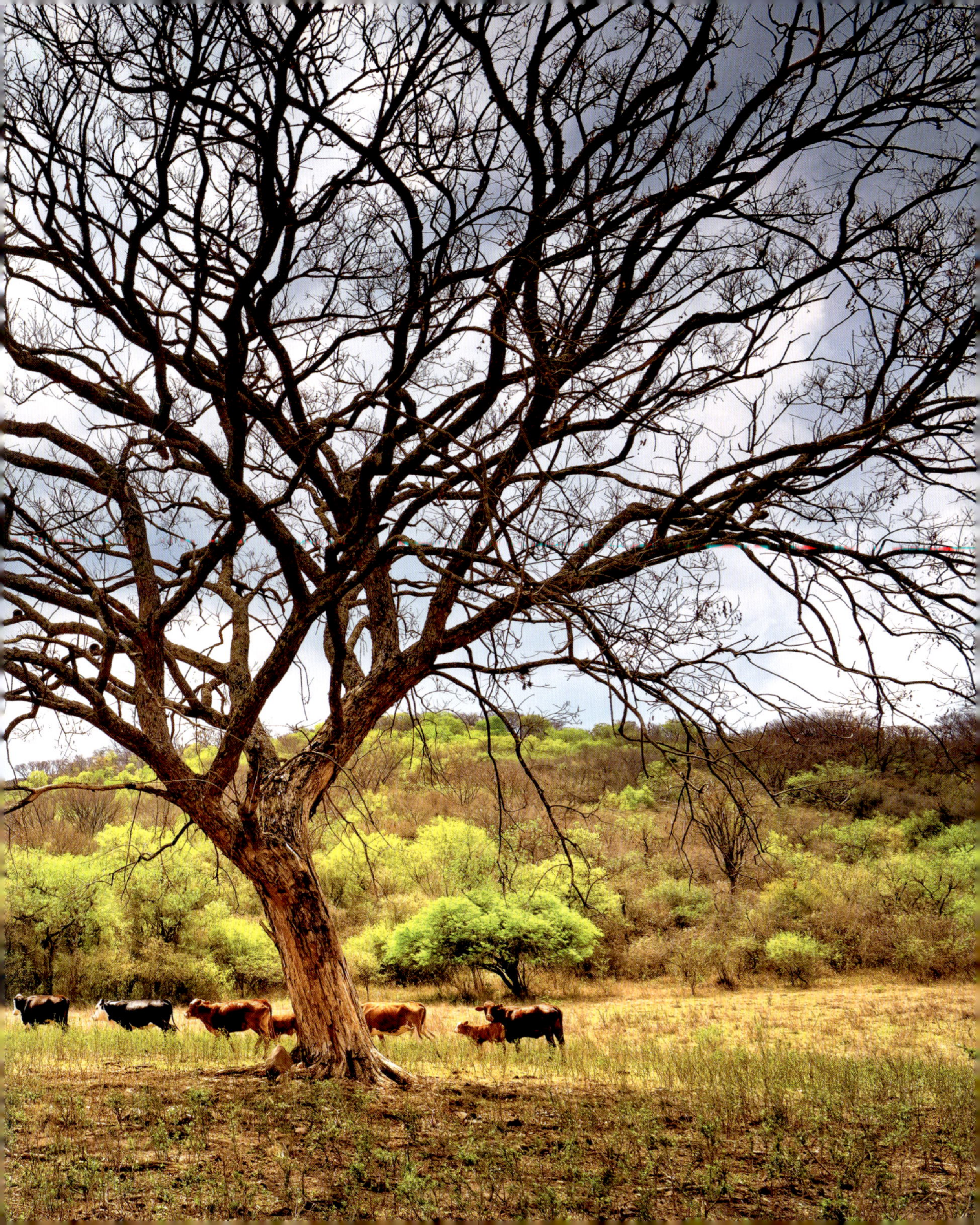

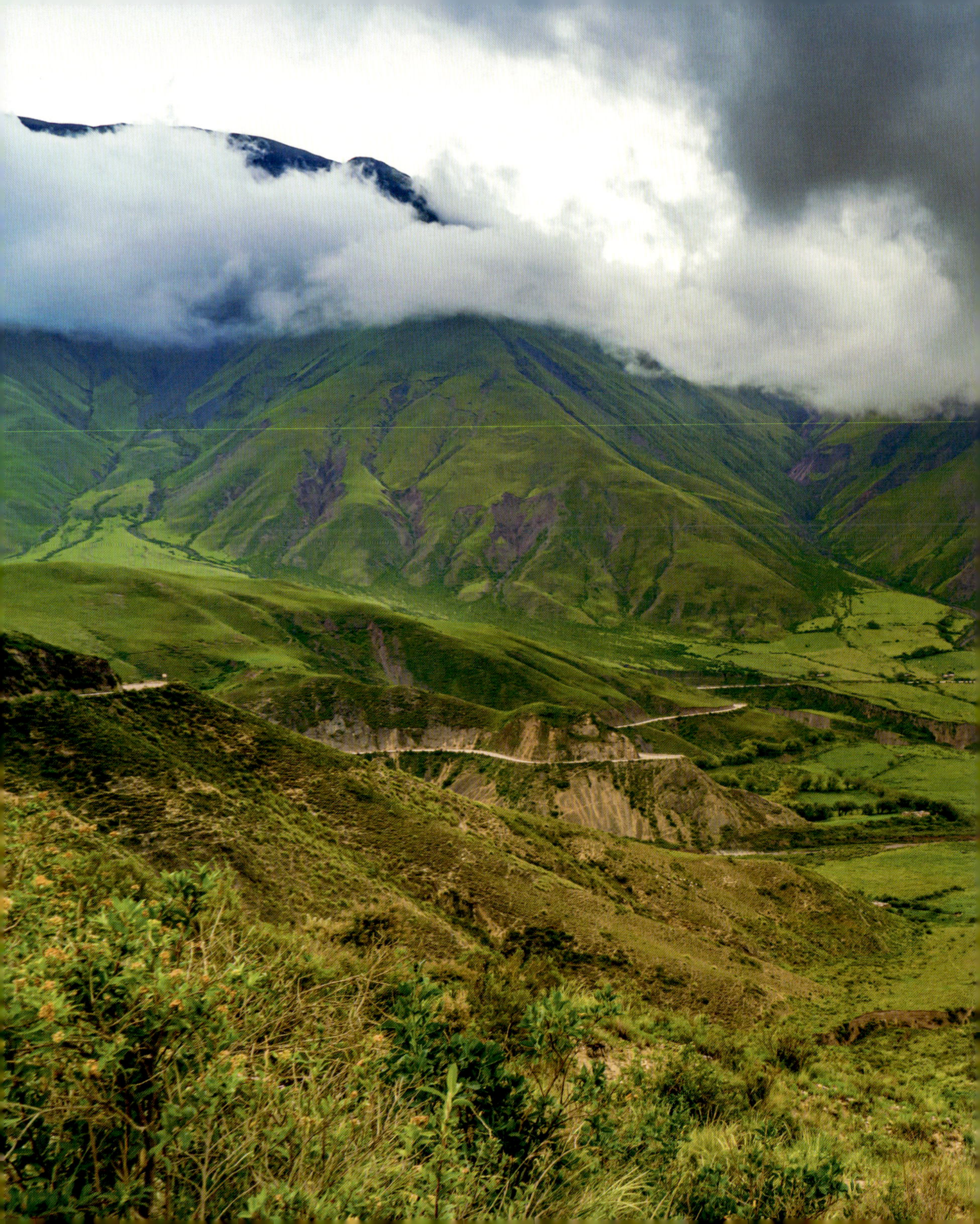

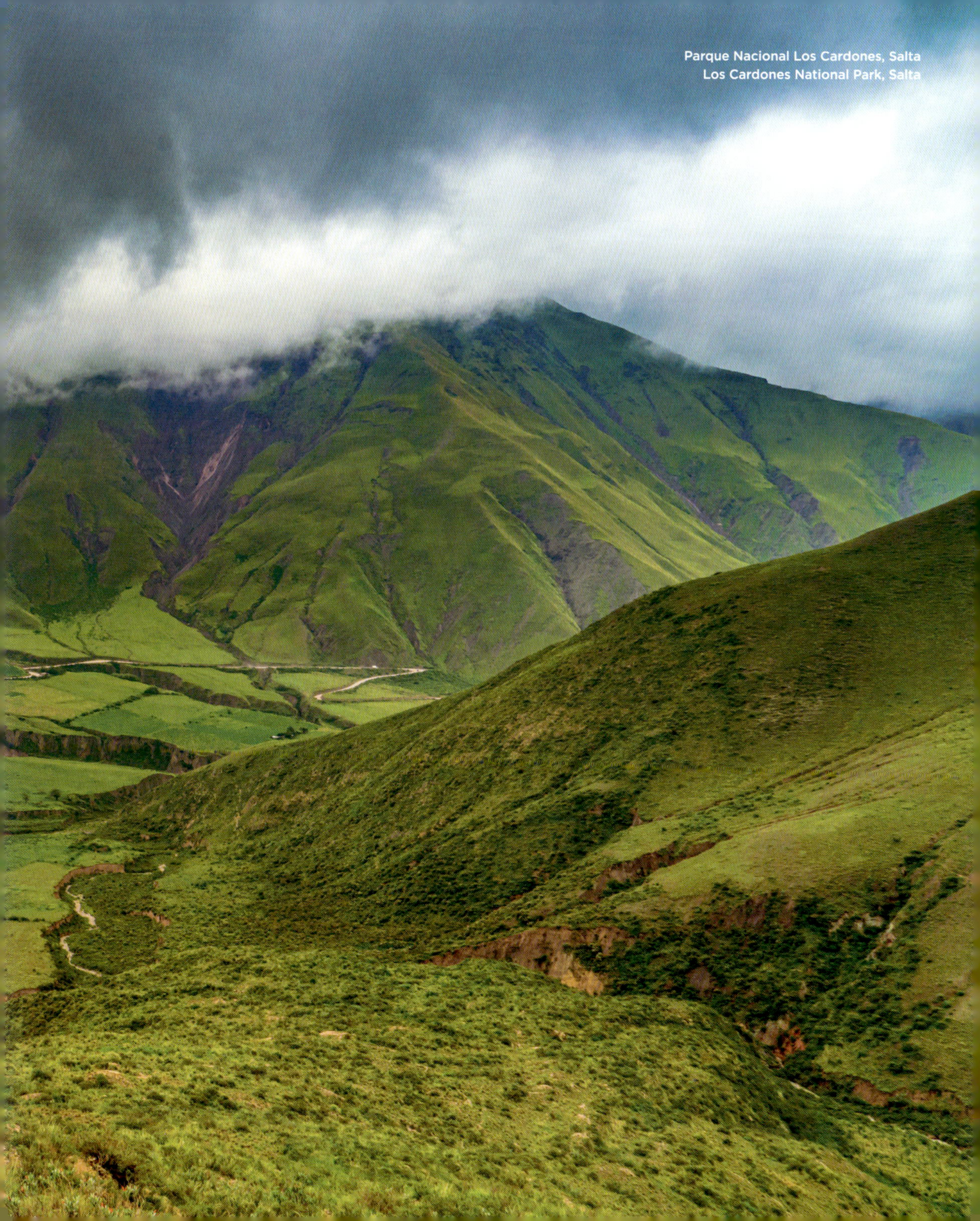

Parque Nacional Los Cardones, Salta
Los Cardones National Park, Salta

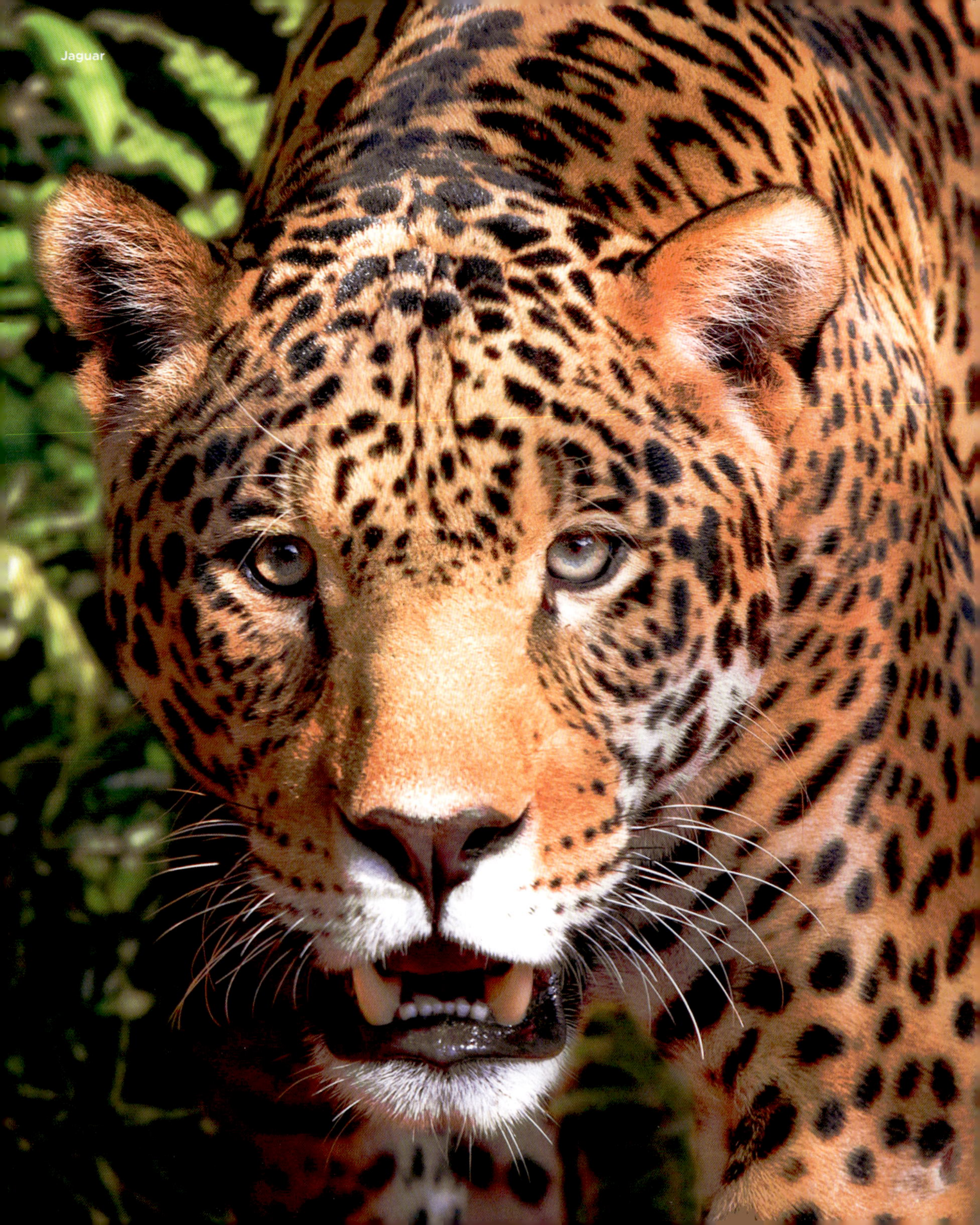
Jaguar

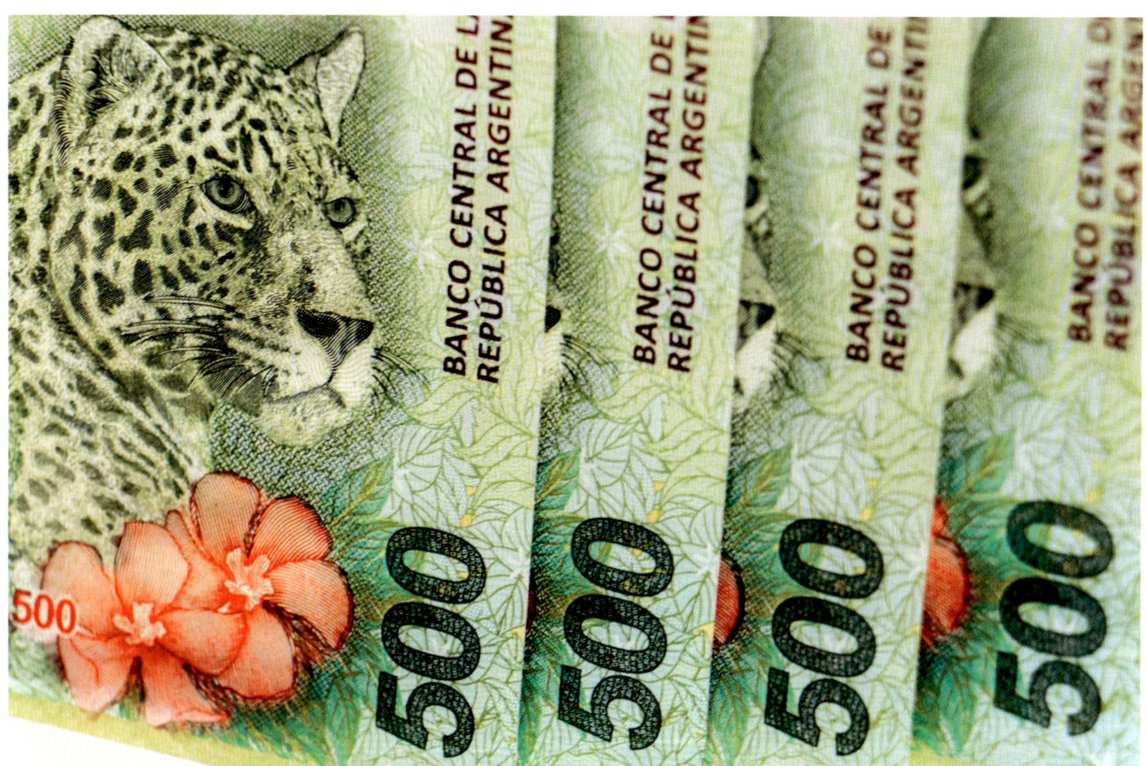

Billete de 500 pesos
500 peso bill

Jaguars

In the biosphere reserve of the Yungas, which lies in the north of Salta on the Bolivian border, there are still 120–150 jaguars surviving. At the beginning of the 19th century, 2000 Jaguar skins were shipped from the port of Buenos Aires alone. Even today, the endangered big cat is still hunted, but with monitoring programs wildlife conservationists are trying to save the jaguar.

Jaguares

En la Reserva de la Biosfera de las Yungas todavía viven entre 120 y 150 jaguares. Se encuentra al norte de Salta, en la frontera con Bolivia. A principios del siglo XIX, solo desde el puerto de Buenos Aires se enviaron 2000 pieles de jaguar. Incluso hoy en día se sigue cazando este gran felino en peligro de extinción. Los conservacionistas de vida silvestre tratan de salvar al jaguar a través de programas de control.

Jaguar

Dans la réserve de biosphère des Yungas vivent encore 120 à 150 jaguars. La réserve est située au nord de la province de Salta, à la frontière bolivienne. Au début du xixe siècle, le port de Buenos Aires expédiait à lui seul 2 000 peaux de jaguars. Le félin est encore aujourd'hui menacé d'extinction. Les défenseurs de la faune sauvage s'efforcent de sauver l'espèce à l'aide de programmes de surveillance.

Jaguares

Na Reserva da Biosfera de las Yungas ainda vivem 120–150 jaguares. Fica no norte de Salta, na fronteira boliviana. No início do século XIX, 2000 peles de onça-pintada foram embarcadas somente do porto de Buenos Aires. Ainda hoje o grande gato, que se encontra em perigo de extinção, é caçado. Com programas de monitoramento, os defensores da vida selvagem tentam salvar a onça-pintada.

Jaguare

Im Biosphärenreservat der Yungas leben noch 120–150 Jaguare. Es liegt im Norden Saltas an der bolivianischen Grenze. Anfang des 19. Jahrhunderts wurden allein vom Hafen in Buenos Aires 2000 Jaguar-Felle verschifft. Auch heute wird die vom Aussterben bedrohte Großkatze gejagt. Mit Monitoring-Programmen versuchen Wildtierschützer den Jaguar zu retten.

Jaguars

In het biosfeerreservaat van de Yungas leven nog 120–150 jaguars. Het ligt in het noorden van Salta aan de Boliviaanse grens. In het begin van de 19e eeuw werden alleen al vanuit de haven van Buenos Aires 2000 jaguarhuiden verscheept. Ook vandaag de dag wordt er op de bedreigde, grote kat gejaagd. Met monitoringsprogramma's proberen beschermers van wild gedierte de jaguar te redden.

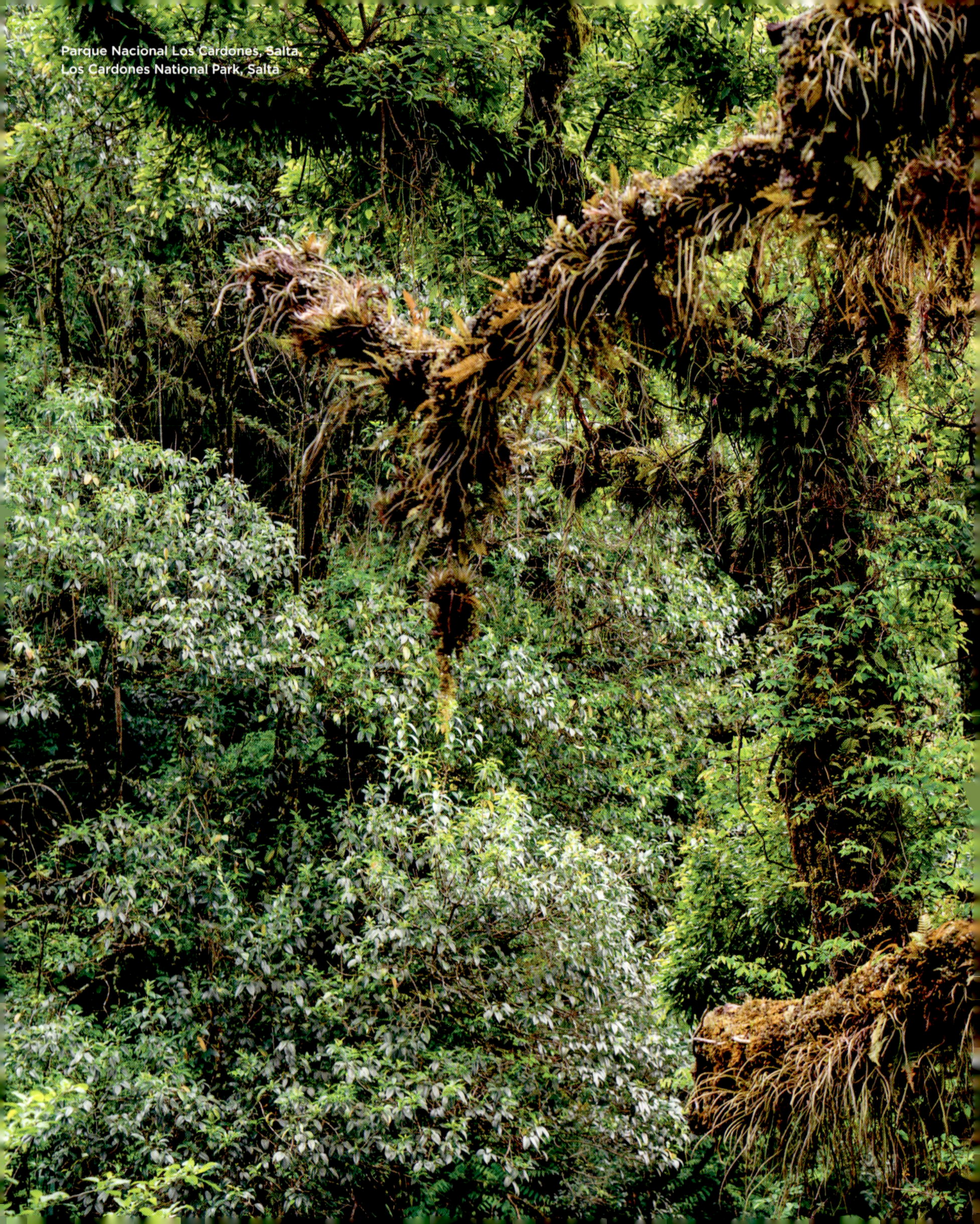
Parque Nacional Los Cardones, Salta
Los Cardones National Park, Salta

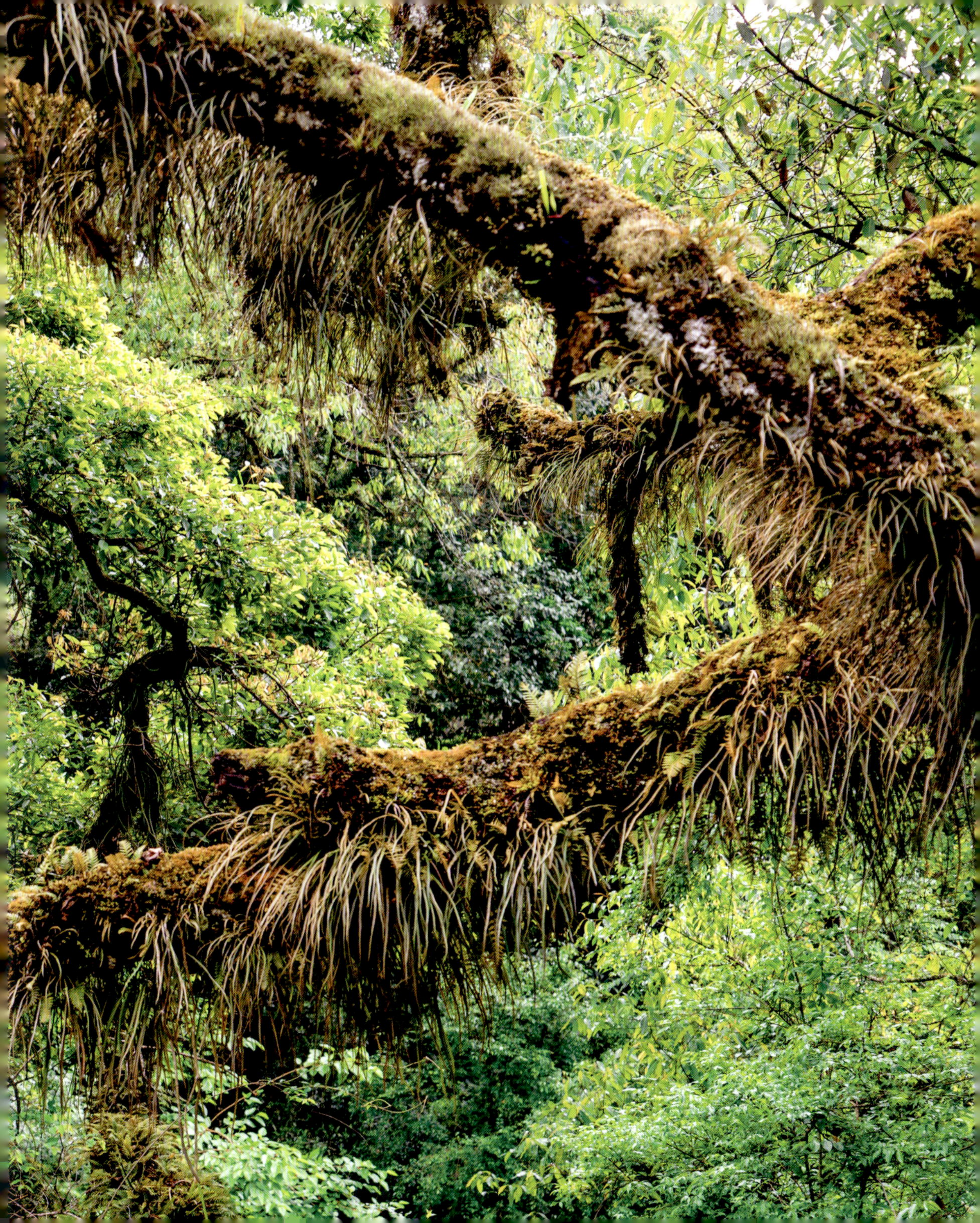

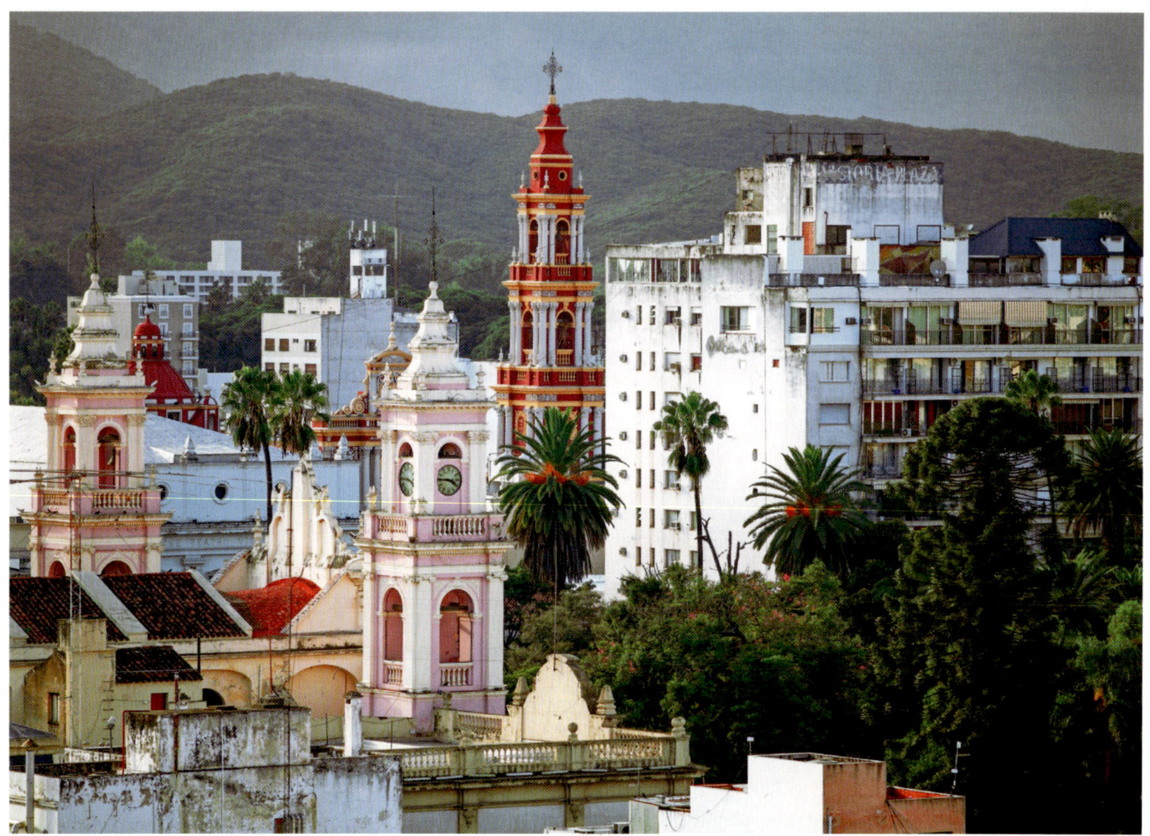

Salta

Salta

The provincial capital is also Known as "La Linda", the beautiful. It lies in a valley at 1200 m (3937 ft) altitude, surrounded by picturesque mountain peaks. Salta was founded by the Spanish in 1582 and played a key role in the war of independence. Historic buildings dominate the cityscape, including the imposing three-aisled cathedral with its large dome and the Cabildo, with its courtyards, which today houses a museum tracing the history of the city and the province. However, the most beautiful colonial building is the red and gold painted San Francisco Church, with its 57 m (187 ft) high freestanding bell tower. Salta is famous for its "empanada salteñas", small pastries, which are typically filled with spicy meat.

Salta

La capitale de la province est surnommée *La Linda* (La Belle). Elle est située au cœur d'une vallée à 1200 m d'altitude et cernée de sommets pittoresques. Salta fut fondée en 1582 par les Espagnols et joua un rôle prépondérant dans la guerre d'indépendance. Elle compte de nombreux bâtiments historiques, dont une imposante cathédrale, dotée de trois nefs et d'une coupole, et le Cabildo avec ses cours intérieures, qui abrite aujourd'hui le musée de l'histoire de la ville et de la province. Toutefois, le plus bel édifice colonial reste l'Iglesia San Francisco, aux façades peintes en rouge et or et flanquée d'un clocher indépendant de 57 m de haut. Salta est célèbre pour ses *salteñas,* petits *empanadas* traditionnellement fourrés de viande fortement épicée.

Salta

Die Provinzhauptstadt wird auch „La Linda", die Schöne genannt. Sie liegt in einem Tal auf 1200 m Höhe, umgeben von malerischen Berggipfeln. Salta wurde 1582 von den Spaniern gegründet und spielte im Unabhängigkeitskrieg eine Schlüsselrolle. Historische Bauten bestimmen das Stadtbild: die imposante dreischiffige Kathedrale mit der großen Kuppel, der Cabildo mit den Innenhöfen. Er beherbergt heute ein Museum zur Stadt- und Provinzgeschichte. Doch das schönste koloniale Bauwerk ist die rot-golden bemalte San Francisco Kirche mit dem 57 m hohen, freistehenden Glockenturm. Berühmt ist Salta für seine „Salteñas", kleine Empanadas, die typischerweise mit scharf gewürztem Fleisch gefüllt sind.

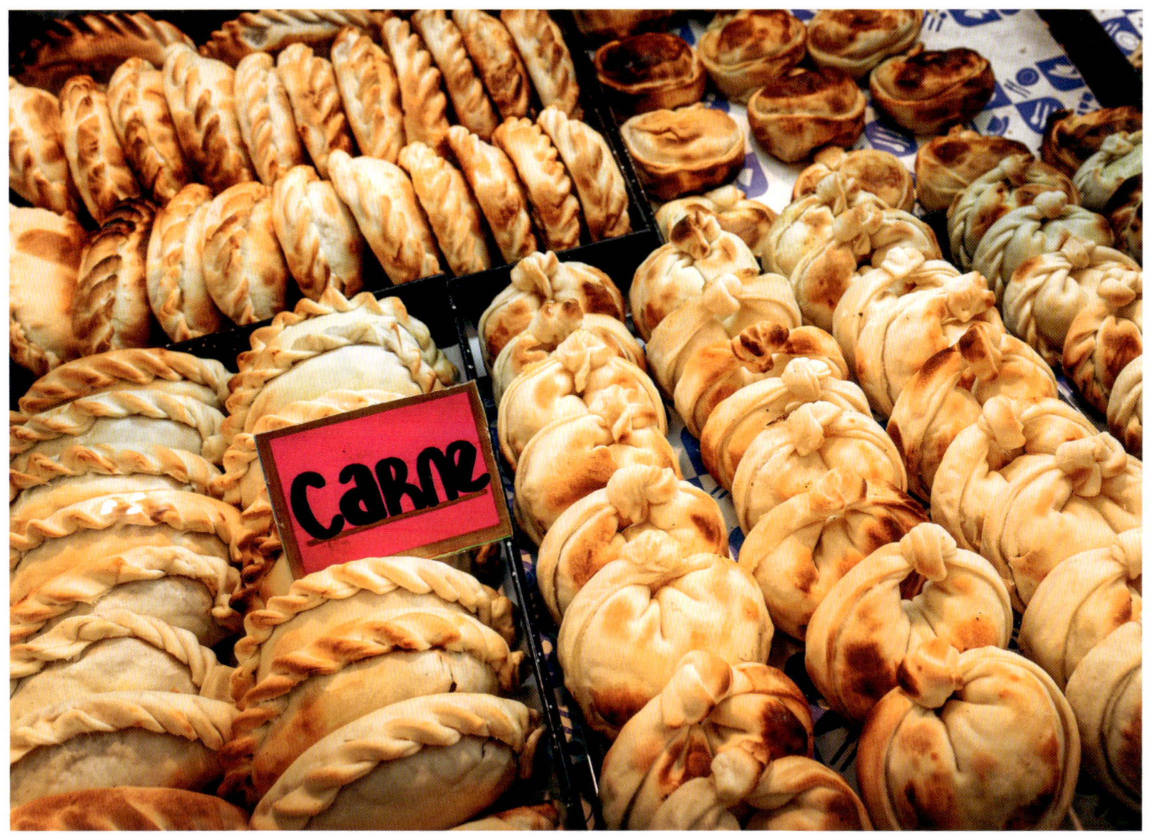

Empanadas

Salta

La capital de la provincia, a la que también se le llama "La Linda", se encuentra en un valle a 1200 m de altitud, y está rodeada de pintorescos picos de montaña. Salta fue fundada por los españoles en 1582 y desempeñó un papel clave en la Guerra de la Independencia. Los edificios históricos dominan el paisaje de la ciudad: la imponente catedral de tres pisos con su gran cúpula, el cabildo con sus patios. Hoy en día alberga un museo sobre la historia de la ciudad y de la provincia. Pero el edificio colonial más bello es la iglesia de San Francisco, pintada de rojo y dorado, con su campanario independiente de 57 m de altura. Salta es famosa por sus "salteñas", pequeñas empanadas, que son típicamente rellenas de carne picante.

Salta

A capital da província também é chamada "La Linda", a bela. Encontra-se num vale a 1200 m de altitude, rodeado de pitorescos picos de montanha. Salta foi fundada pelos espanhóis em 1582 e desempenhou um papel fundamental na Guerra da Independência. Edifícios históricos dominam a paisagem da cidade: a imponente catedral de três naves com sua grande cúpula, o Cabildo com seus pátios. Hoje abriga um museu sobre a história da cidade e da província. Mas o edifício colonial mais bonito é a Igreja de São Francisco pintada de vermelho dourado com a sua torre sineira de 57 m de altura. Salta é famosa por suas "Salteñas", pequenas empanadas, que normalmente são recheadas com carne picante.

Salta

De provinciehoofdstad wordt ook wel "La Linda", de mooie, genoemd. De stad ligt in een dal op 1200 m hoogte, omgeven door pittoreske bergtoppen. Salta werd in 1582 door de Spanjaarden gesticht en speelde een sleutelrol in de onafhankelijkheidsoorlog. Historische gebouwen domineren het stadsbeeld: de imposante kathedraal met drie schepen en grote koepel, de Cabildo met zijn binnenplaatsen. Vandaag de dag herbergt hij een museum over de stads- en provinciegeschiedenis. Maar het mooiste koloniale gebouw is de rood-gouden geschilderde San Francisco kerk met de 57 m hoge, vrijstaande klokkentoren. Salta is beroemd om zijn "Salteñas", kleine empanadas die typisch genoeg gevuld zijn met scherp gekruid vlees.

Argentinian cuisine

Even today, Argentinean cuisine cannot do without meat. *Locro,* a spicy stew of corn, beef, potatoes, pumpkin and sweet potatoes, originates from the north. Empanadas filled with meat, corn or chicken are popular all over the country, but the crowning glory is *dulce de leche,* which is the sweet cream made from boiled milk, sugar and vanilla beans and is not only a dessert but also a spread.

La cuisine argentine

Aujourd'hui encore, la cuisine argentine n'est rien sans viande. Le *locro,* ragoût épicé comprenant maïs, porc, pommes de terre, courges et patates douces, est originaire du Nord. Les *empanadas,* farcis de viande de bœuf, de maïs ou de poulet, sont appréciés dans tout le pays. Mais rien ne saurait égaler la *dulce de leche ;* cette crème à base de lait concentré, de sucre et de gousses de vanille se déguste en dessert ou comme pâte à tartiner.

Argentinische Küche

Ohne Fleisch kommt die argentinische Küche auch heute nicht aus. Locro, ein scharfer Eintopf aus Mais, Rindfleisch, Kartoffeln, Kürbis und Süßkartoffeln, stammt aus dem Norden. Empanadas, mit Fleisch, Mais oder Huhn gefüllt, sind landesweit beliebt. Doch die Krönung bildet Dulce de leche: die süße Creme aus eingekochter Milch, Zucker und Vanilleschoten ist nicht nur Dessert, sondern auch Brotaufstrich.

Cocina argentina

Aún hoy en día, la cocina argentina no puede prescindir de la carne. El locro, un guiso picante de maíz, carne, patatas, calabaza y batatas, es originario del norte. Las empanadas rellenas de carne, maíz o pollo son populares en todo el país. Pero la reina es el dulce de leche: la dulce crema hecha de leche hervida, azúcar y vainas de vainilla no es solo un postre, sino también una crema para untar.

Cozinha argentina

Ainda hoje, a cozinha argentina não pode passar sem carne. Locro, um guisado picante de milho, carne de vaca, batata, abóbora e batata doce, é originário do norte. Empanadas, recheadas com carne, milho ou frango, são populares em todo o país. Mas o ponto culminante é o "Dulce de leche": o creme doce feito com leite cozido, açúcar e baunilha não é apenas uma sobremesa, mas também uma pasta para barrar.

Argentijnse keuken

Ook vandaag de dag kan de Argentijnse keuken niet zonder vlees. Locro, een kruidige stoofpot van maïs, rundvlees, aardappelen, pompoen en zoete aardappelen, stamt uit het noorden. Empanadas, gevuld met vlees, maïs of kip, zijn in het hele land populair. Maar de bekroning vormt dulce de leche: de zoete crème op basis van gekookte melk, suiker en vanillestokjes is niet alleen een dessert, maar ook broodbeleg.

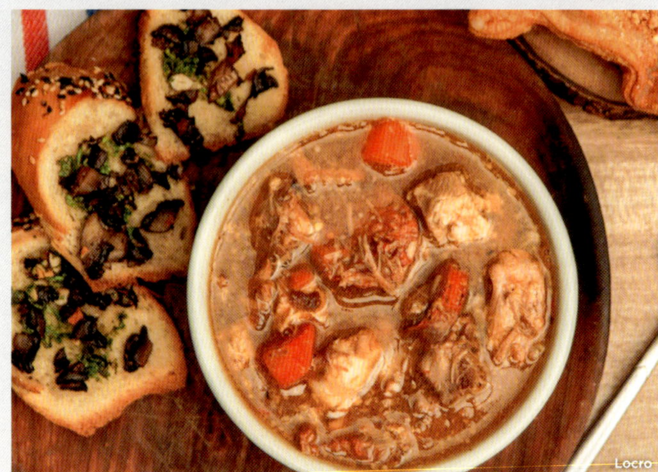
Locro

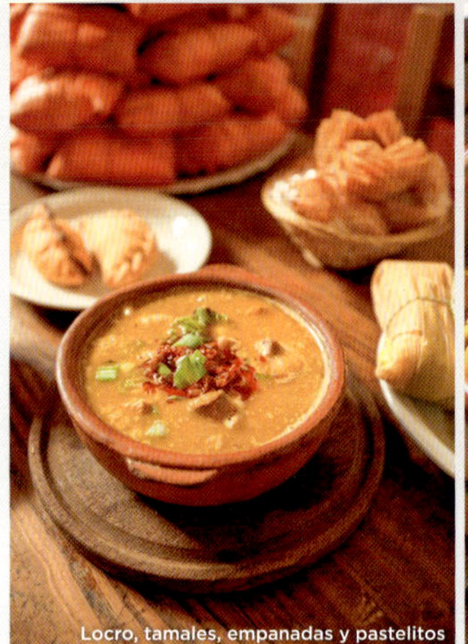
Locro, tamales, empanadas y pastelitos

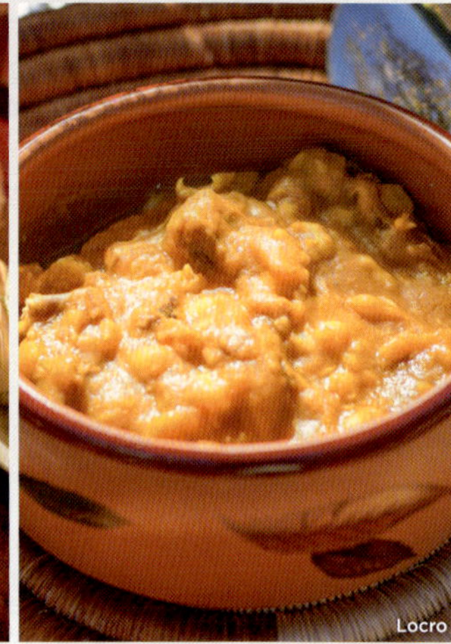
Locro

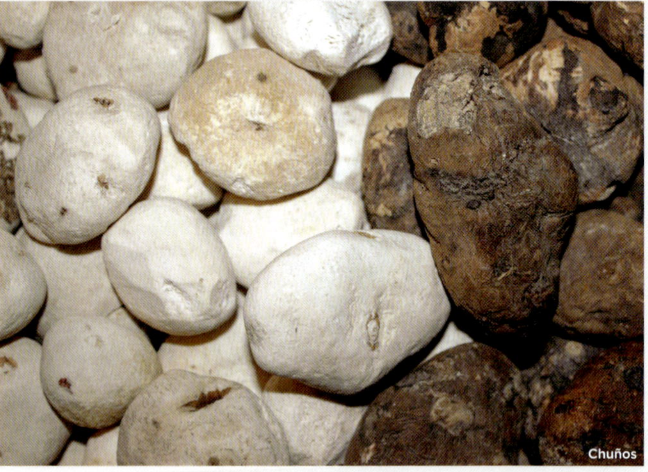
Chuños

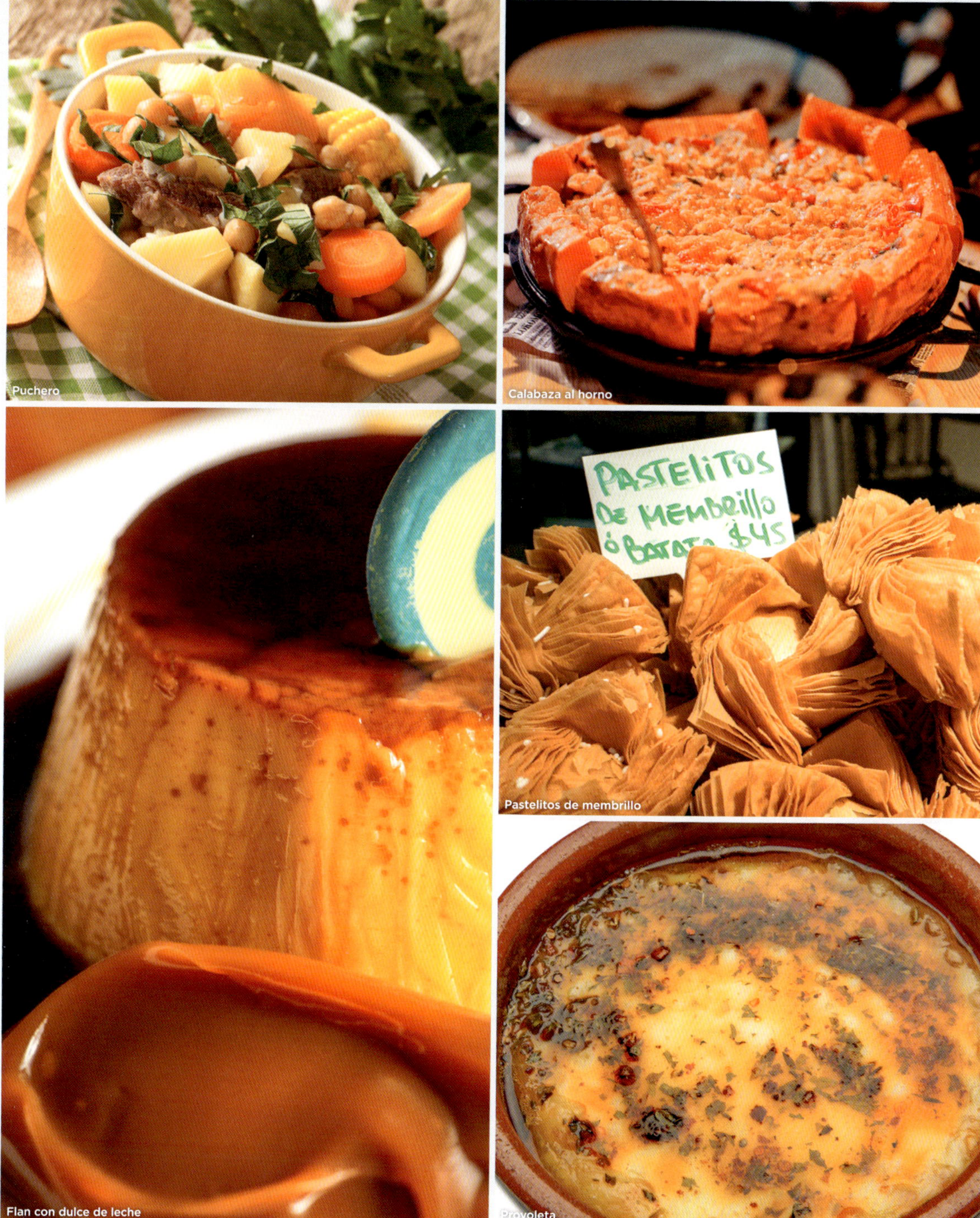

Puchero

Calabaza al horno

Pastelitos de membrillo

Flan con dulce de leche

Provoleta

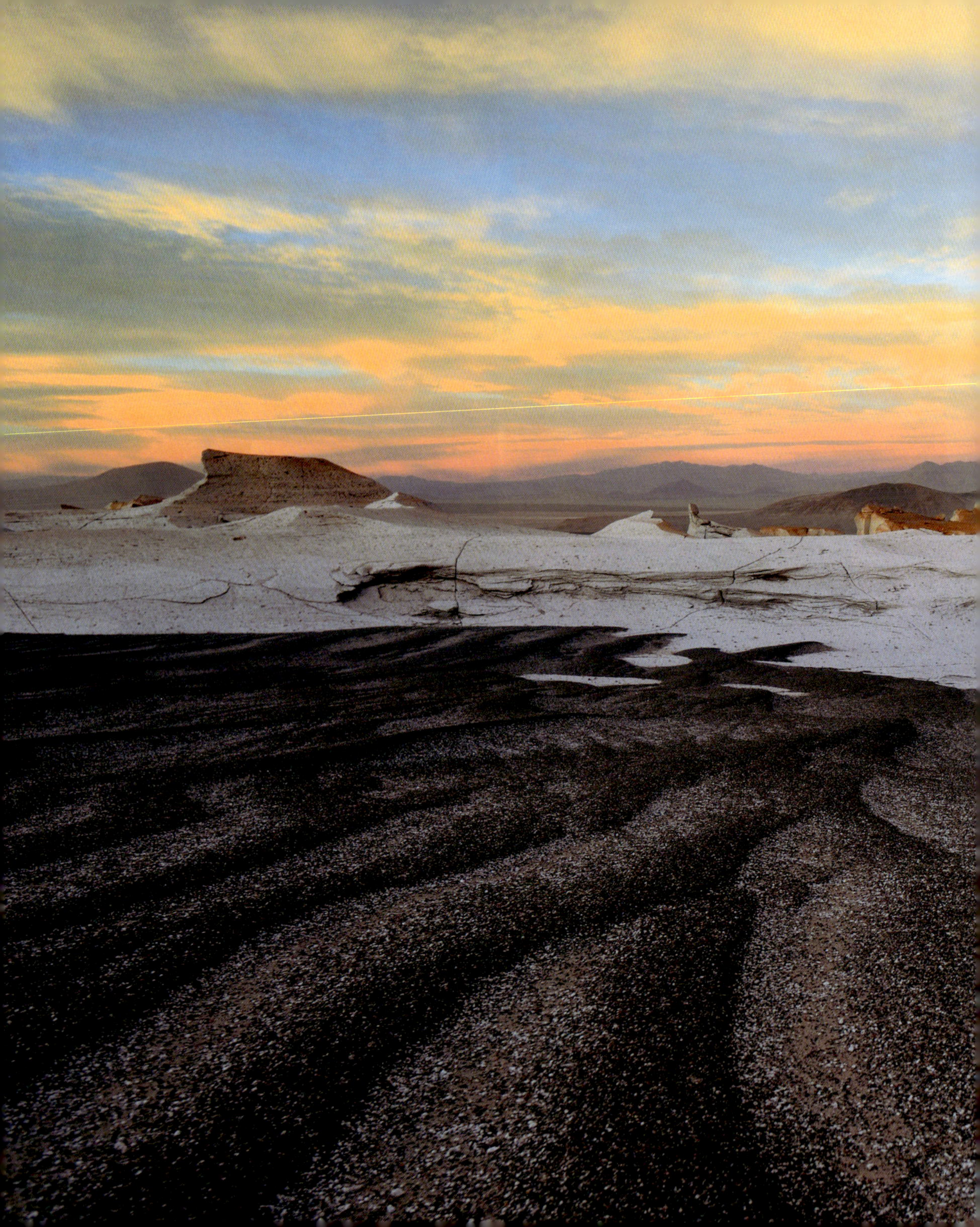

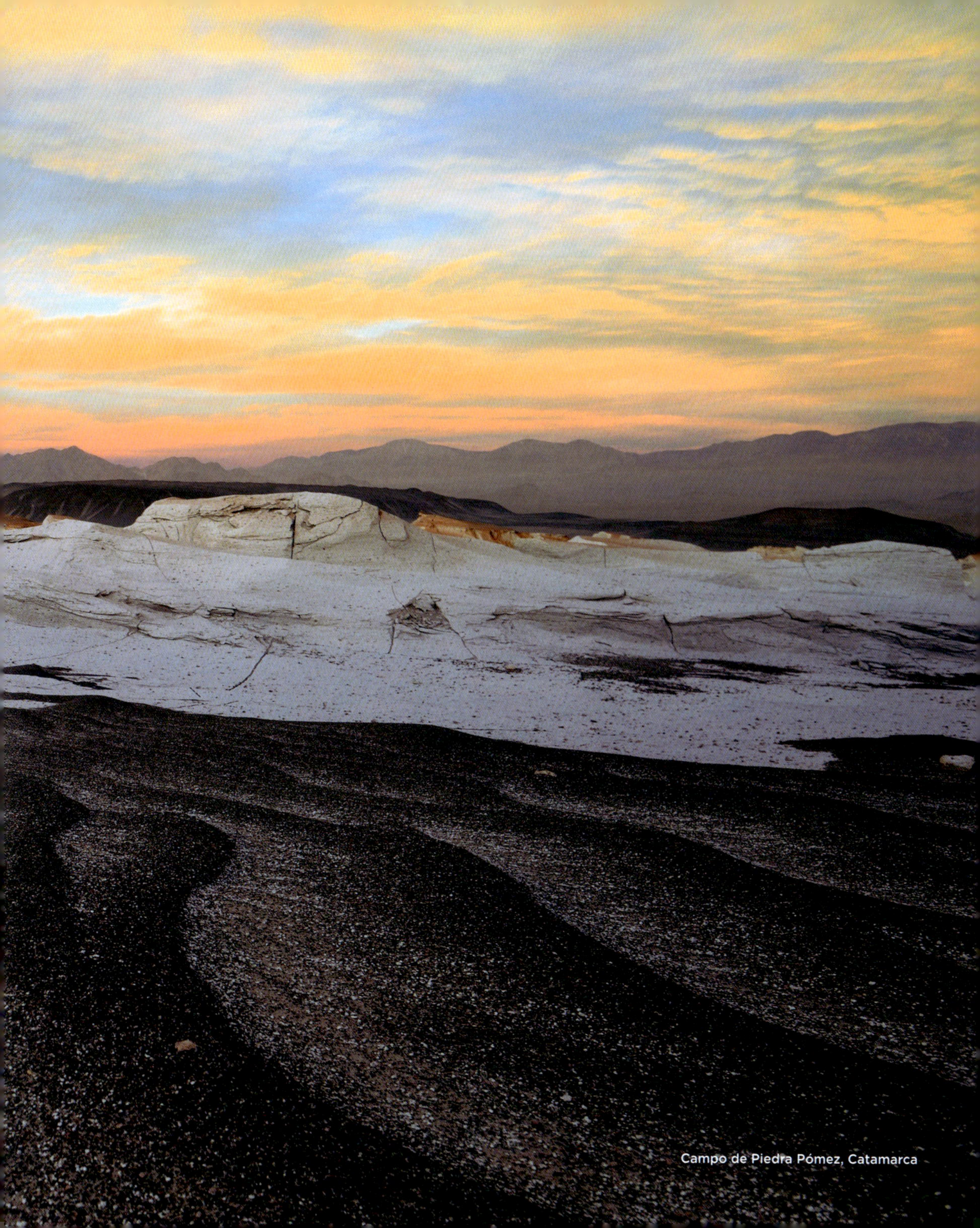

Campo de Piedra Pómez, Catamarca

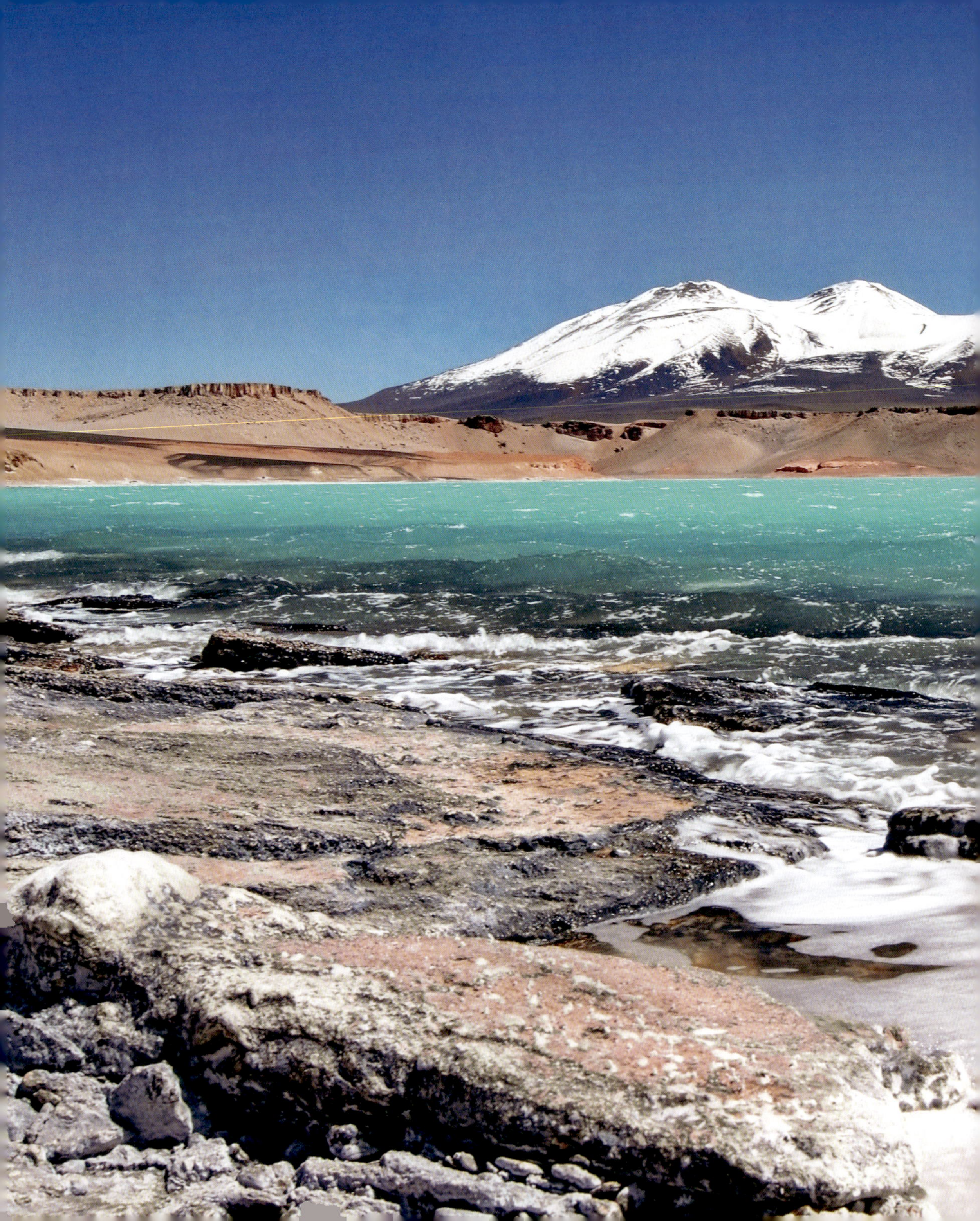

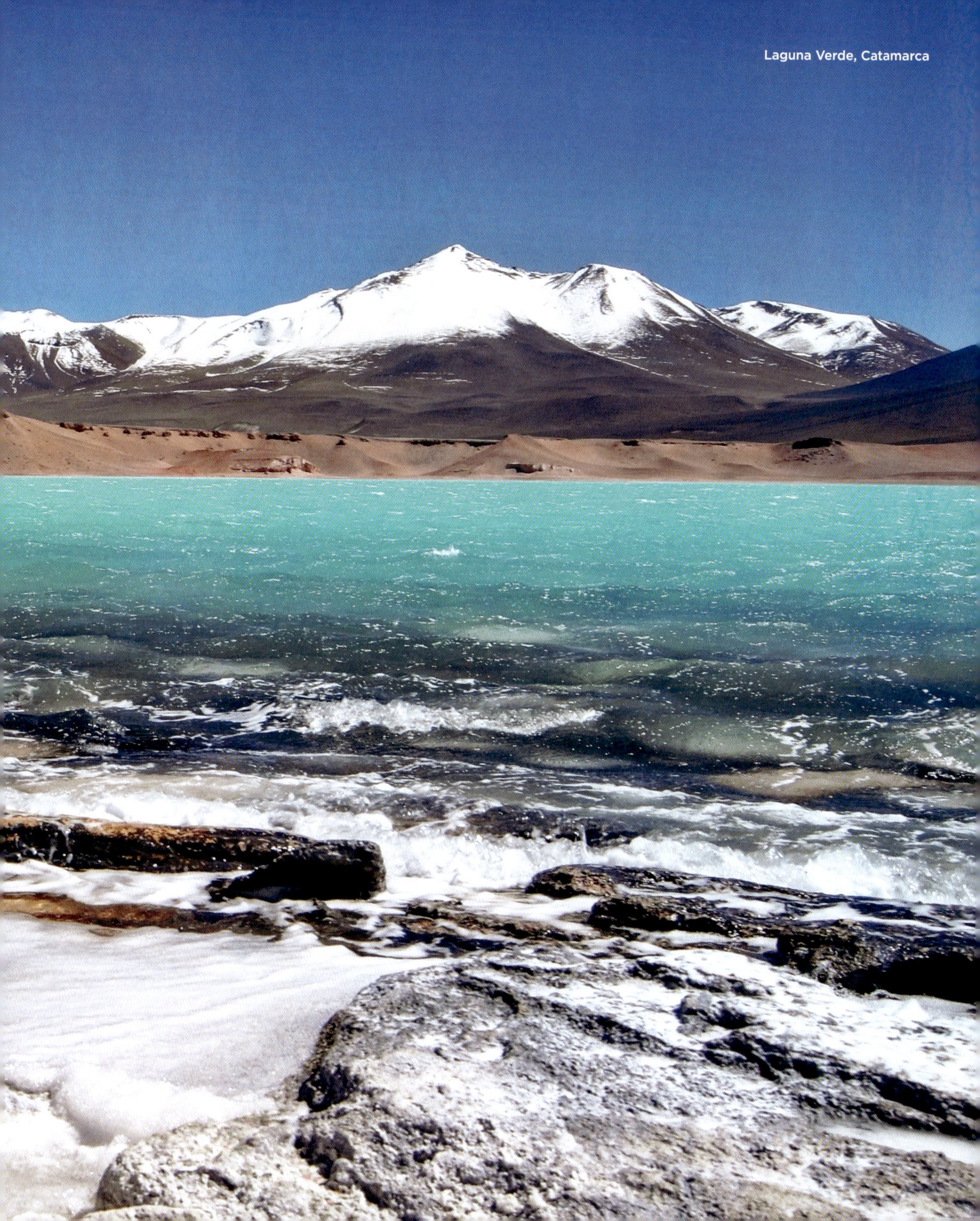

Laguna Verde, Catamarca

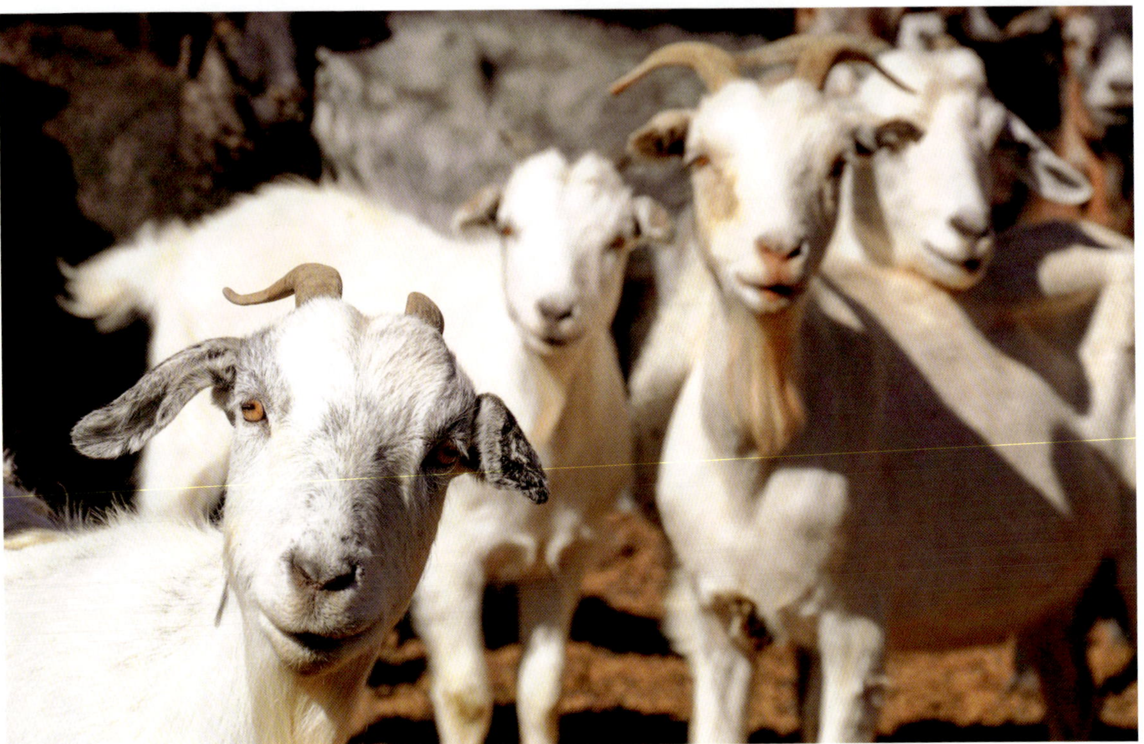

Cabras
Goats

Goat breeding

The natives named the dry region on
the eastern slope of the Andes after the
Cachi mountains, where they irrigated
the agricultural terraces with the water of
the Cachi River, and the Spanish followed
their example. Through the *encomienda*
system of the Spanish colonial rulers and
its distribution of land ownership, the area
and its haciendas and fincas remained
rural. Today the district of Cachi lives from
goat breeding.

Cría de cabras

Los nativos nombraron la región seca en
la vertiente oriental de los Andes en honor
a la montaña de Cachi. Regaron el cultivo
en terrazas con el agua del río Cachi.
Los españoles siguieron su ejemplo. A
través del sistema de encomienda de los
colonizadores españoles y la distribución
de la propiedad de la tierra, el área con sus
haciendas y fincas se mantuvo rural. Hoy
en día, el distrito de Cachi vive de la cría
de cabras.

L'élevage de chèvres

Les populations autochtones appelaient la
région sèche sur le versant est des Andes
« la montagne de Cachi ». Ils irriguaient
leurs cultures en terrasses avec l'eau du
fleuve Cachi. Les Espagnols suivirent leur
exemple. La région est restée agricole avec
une organisation des terres en *haziendas* et
fincas, héritée du système de l'*encomienda*
appliqué par les maîtres coloniaux
espagnols. Le département de Cachi vit de
l'élevage de chèvres.

Criação de caprinos

Os nativos batizaram a região seca na
encosta leste dos Andes com o nome da
montanha Cachi. Eles irrigaram a cultura
em terraços com a água do rio Cachi. Os
espanhóis seguiram o seu exemplo. Através
do sistema de encomenda dos mestres
coloniais espanhóis e a distribuição da
propriedade da terra, a área com suas
fazendas e fincas permaneceu rural.
Hoje, o distrito de Cachi vive da criação
de caprinos.

Ziegenzucht

Die Ureinwohner bezeichneten die
trockene Region am Ostabhang der Anden
nach dem Cachi-Berg. Sie bewässerten
die Terrassenkultur mit dem Wasser
des Cachi-Flusses. Die Spanier folgten
ihrem Beispiel. Durch das Encomienda-
System der spanischen Kolonialherren
und die Landbesitzverteilung blieb das
Gebiet mit seinen Haziendas und Fincas
ländlich. Heute lebt der Bezirk Cachi
von Ziegenzucht.

Geitenfokkerij

De oerinwoners noemden de droge regio
op de oostelijke helling van de Andes
naar de Cachi-berg. Ze besproeiden
de terrascultuur met het water van de
Cachi rivier. De Spanjaarden volgden het
voorbeeld. Door het encomienda systeem
van de Spaanse koloniale meesters en
de verdeling van het grondbezit, bleef
het gebied met zijn haciënda's en finca's
landelijk. Vandaag de dag leeft het district
Cachi van de geitenfokkerij.

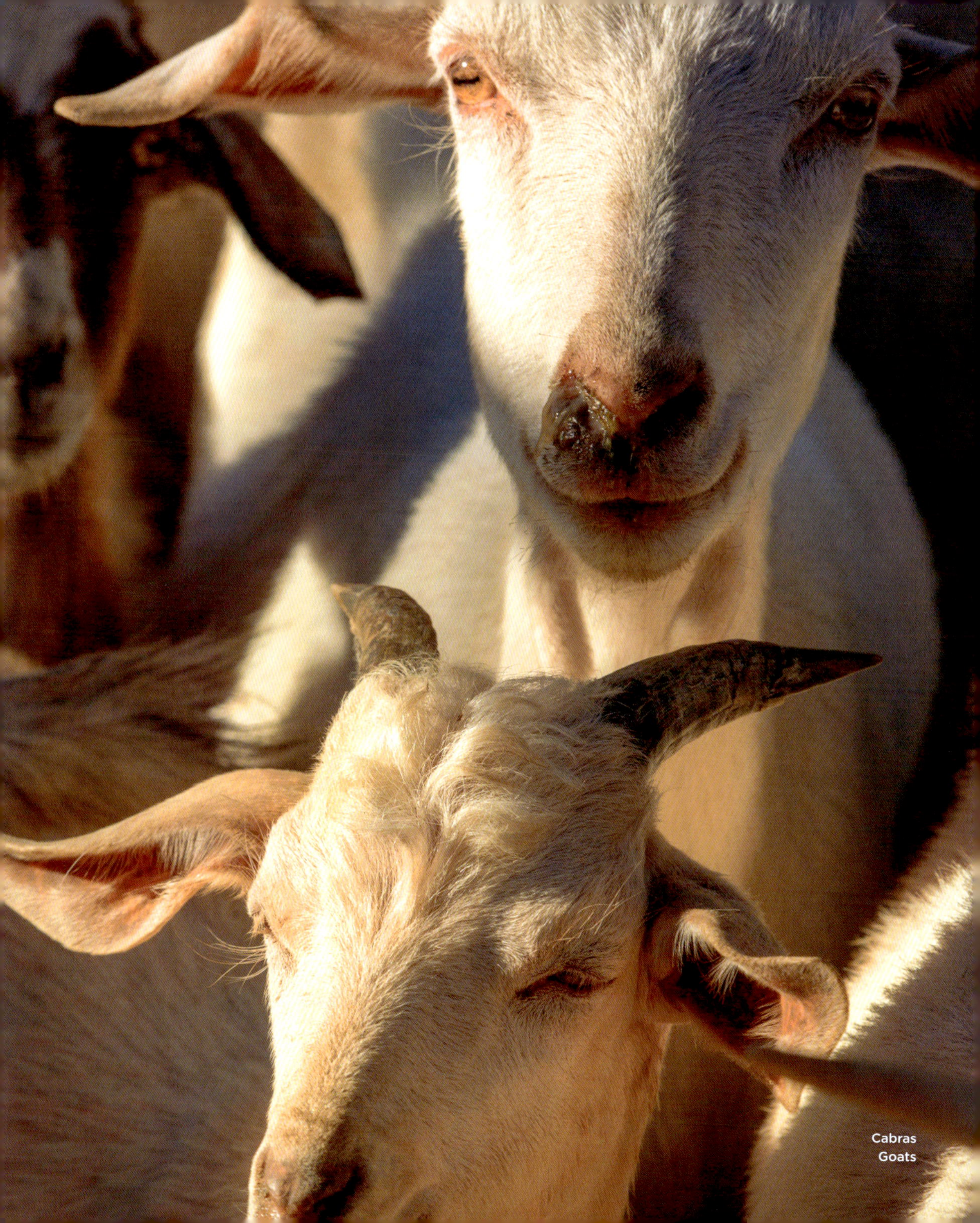

Cabras
Goats

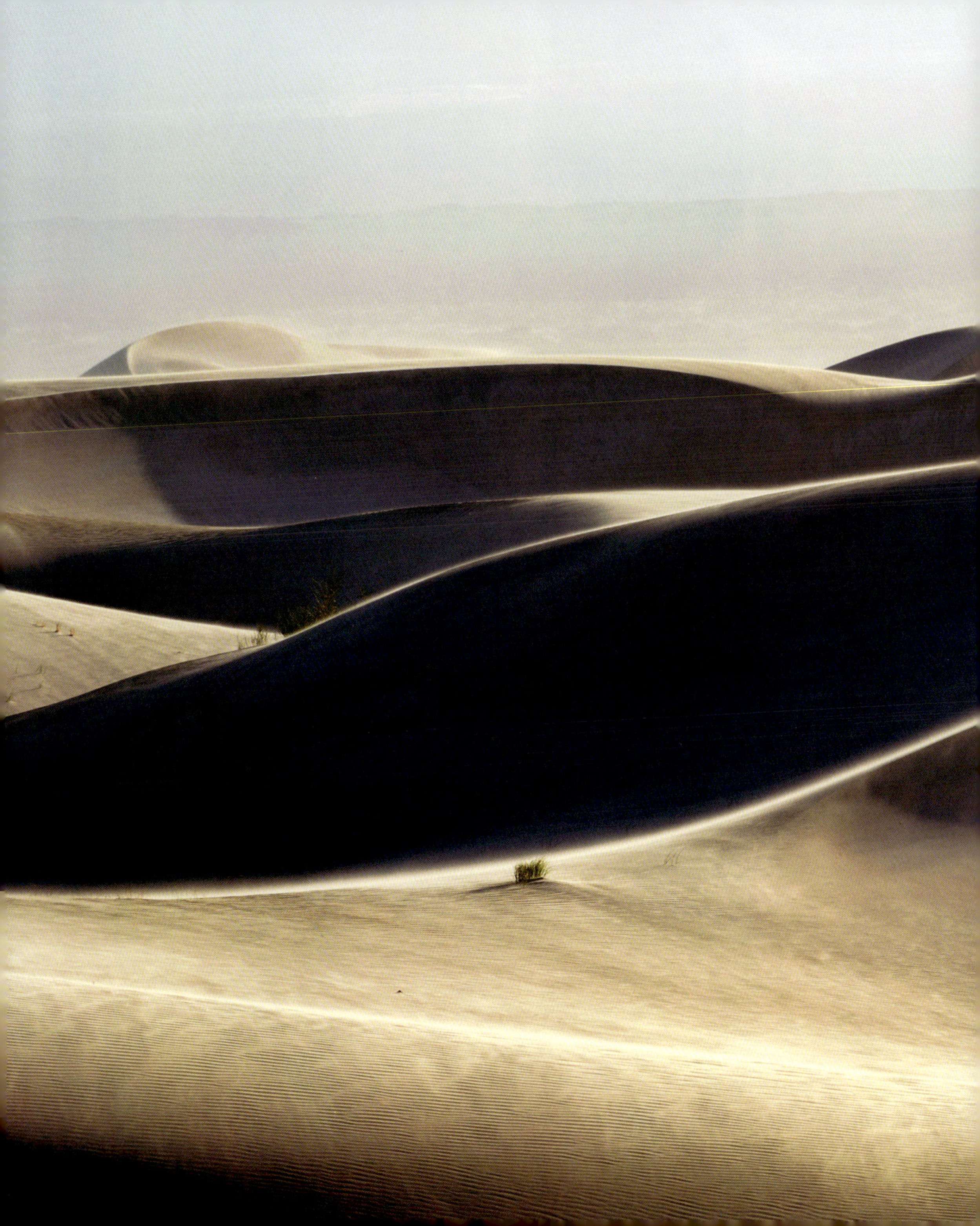

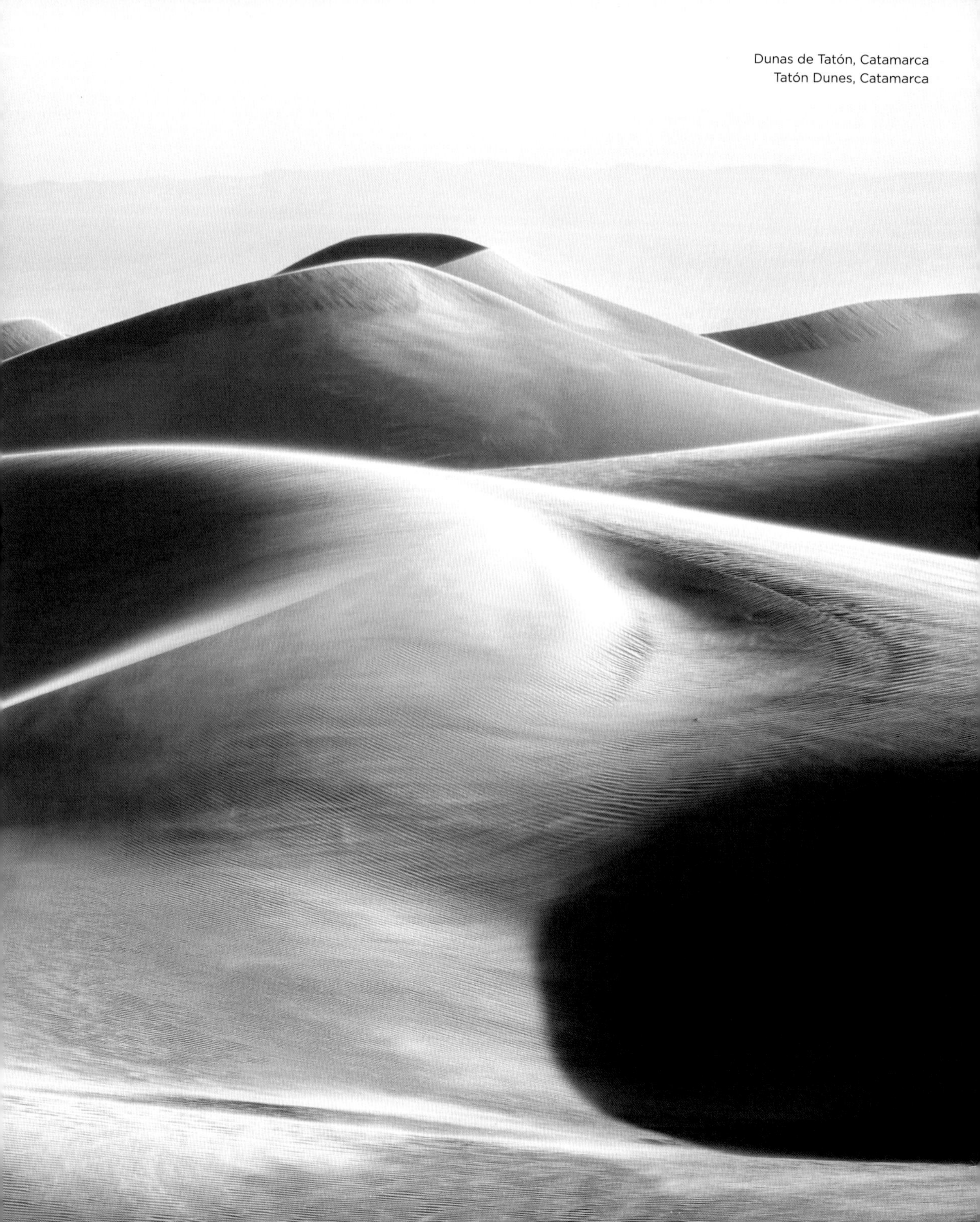

Dunas de Tatón, Catamarca
Tatón Dunes, Catamarca

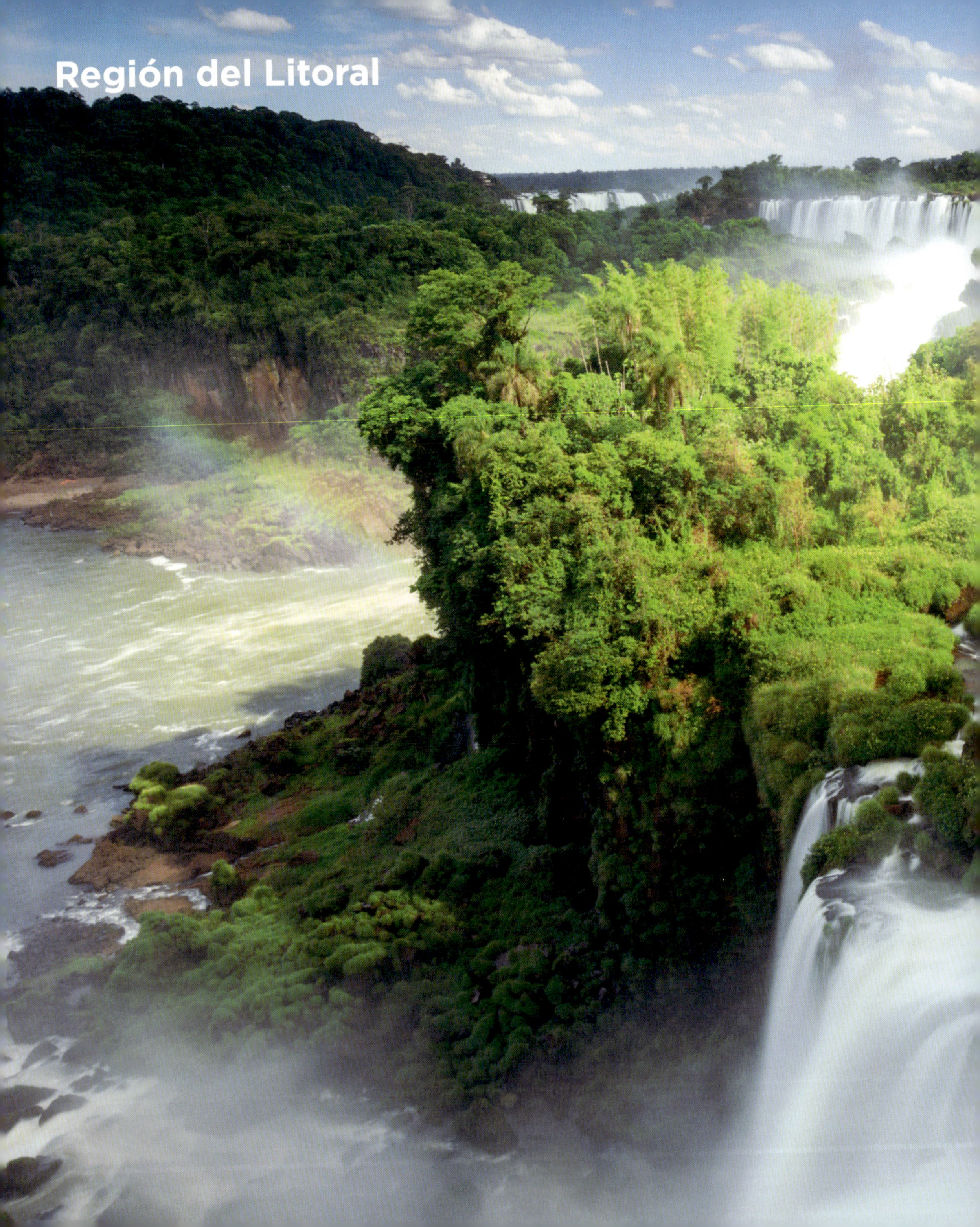

Región del Litoral

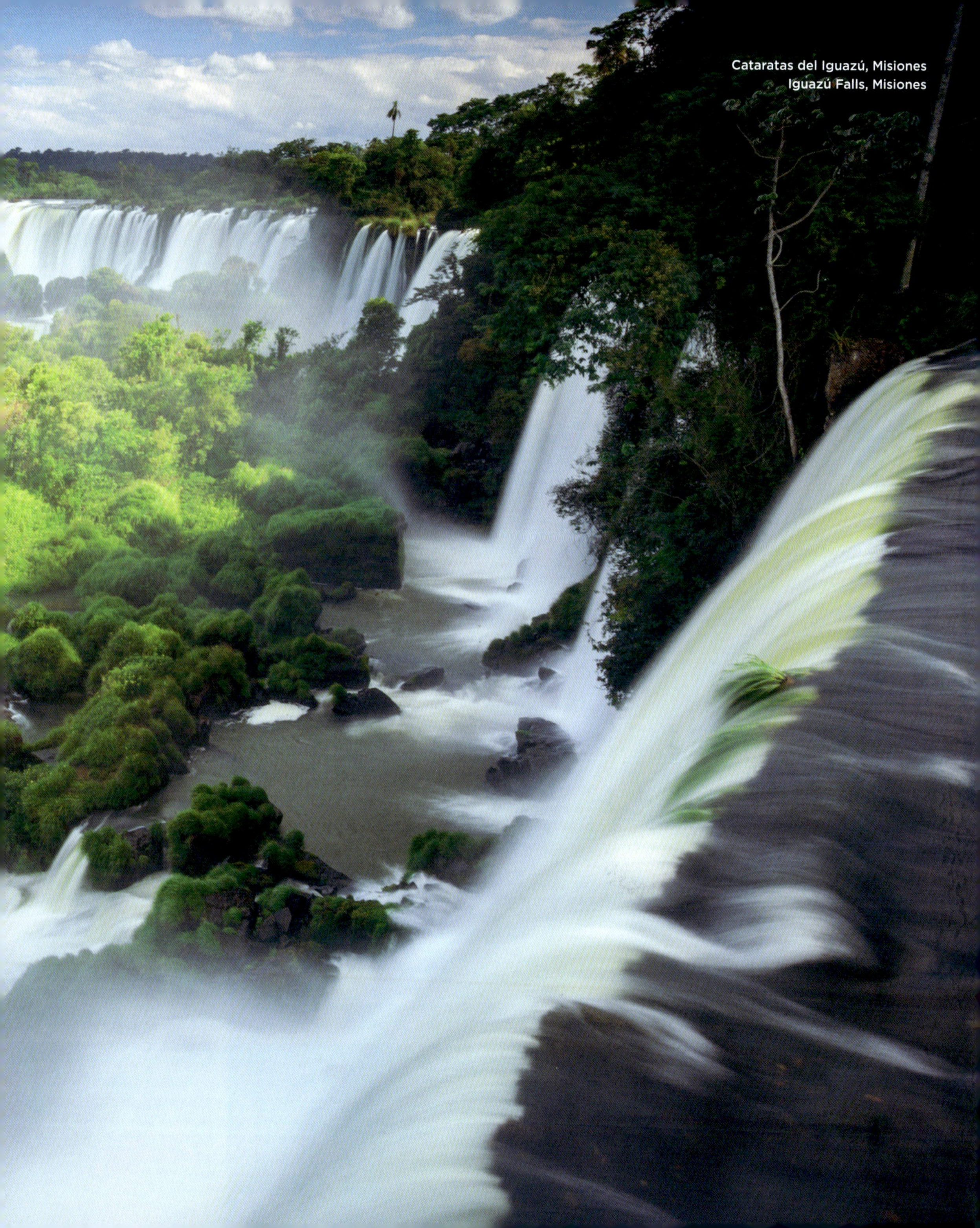

Cataratas del Iguazú, Misiones
Iguazú Falls, Misiones

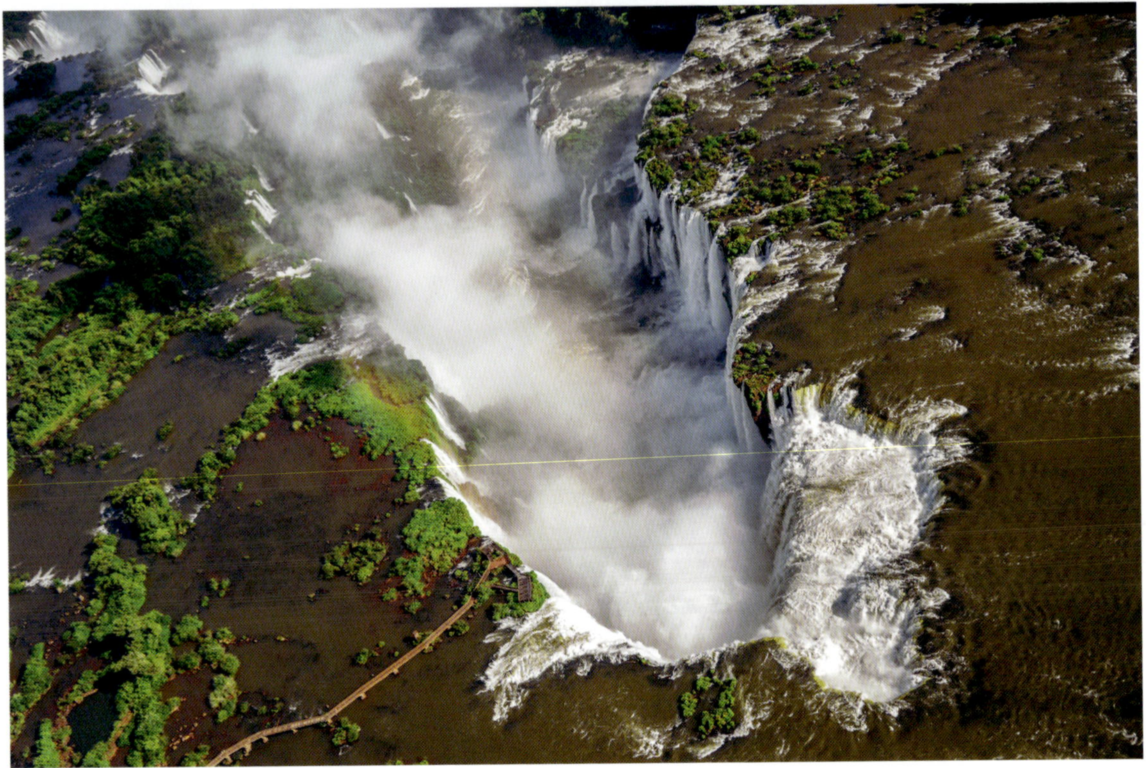

Cataratas del Iguazú, Misiones
Iguazú Falls, Misiones

Región del Litoral
The provinces of Misiones, Corrientes and Entre Ríos form 'La Mesopotamia', or the land between two rivers. The Argentine Mesopotamia stretches between the Rio Uruguay and the Rio Paraná. The provinces of Formosa, Chaco and Santa Fé are close to the rivers Paraná and to Paraguay. The Iguazú Waterfalls in the border triangle of Argentina, Brazil and Paraguay are particularly attractive.

Región del Litoral
Les provinces de Misiones, Corrientes et Entre Ríos constituent le «pays entre les fleuves», la Mésopotamie argentine. La région est délimitée par les fleuves Uruguay et Paraná. Les provinces de Formosa, Chaco et Santa Fe sont situées entre les rivières Paraná et Paraguay. Les chutes d'Iguazú confèrent un pouvoir d'attraction exceptionnel à une région transfrontalière partagée entre l'Argentine, le Brésil et le Paraguay.

Región del Litoral
Misiones, Corrientes und Entre Ríos bilden das Zweistromland. Das argentinische Mesopotamia erstreckt sich zwischen dem Rio Uruguay und dem Rio Paraná. Die Provinzen Formosa, Chaco und Santa Fé liegen nah an den Flüssen Paraná und Paraguay. Besondere Anziehungskraft geht von den Iguazú-Wasserfällen im Dreiländereck Argentinien, Brasilien, Paraguay aus.

Región del Litoral
Misiones, Corrientes y Entre Ríos forman la Mesopotamia. La Mesopotamia argentina se extiende entre el río Uruguay y el río Paraná. Las provincias de Formosa, Chaco y Santa Fe están cerca de los ríos Paraná y Paraguay. Las cataratas del Iguazú, en el triángulo fronterizo de Argentina, Brasil y Paraguay, son particularmente atractivas.

Región del Litoral
Misiones, Corrientes e Entre Ríos formam a Mesopotâmia. A Mesopotâmia Argentina se estende entre o Rio Uruguai e o Rio Paraná. As províncias de Formosa, Chaco e Santa Fé estão próximas aos rios Paraná e Paraguai. As Cataratas do Iguaçu, no triângulo fronteiriço da Argentina, Brasil e Paraguai, são particularmente atraentes.

Región del Litoral
De provincies Misiones, Corrientes en Entre Ríos vormen het Tweestromenland. Het Argentijnse Mesopotamië strekt zich uit tussen de Rio Uruguay en de Rio Paraná. De provincies Formosa, Chaco en Santa Fé liggen in de buurt van de rivieren Paraná en Paraguay. De Iguazú watervallen in het grensgebied van Argentinië, Brazilië en Paraguay hebben een bijzondere aantrekkingskracht.

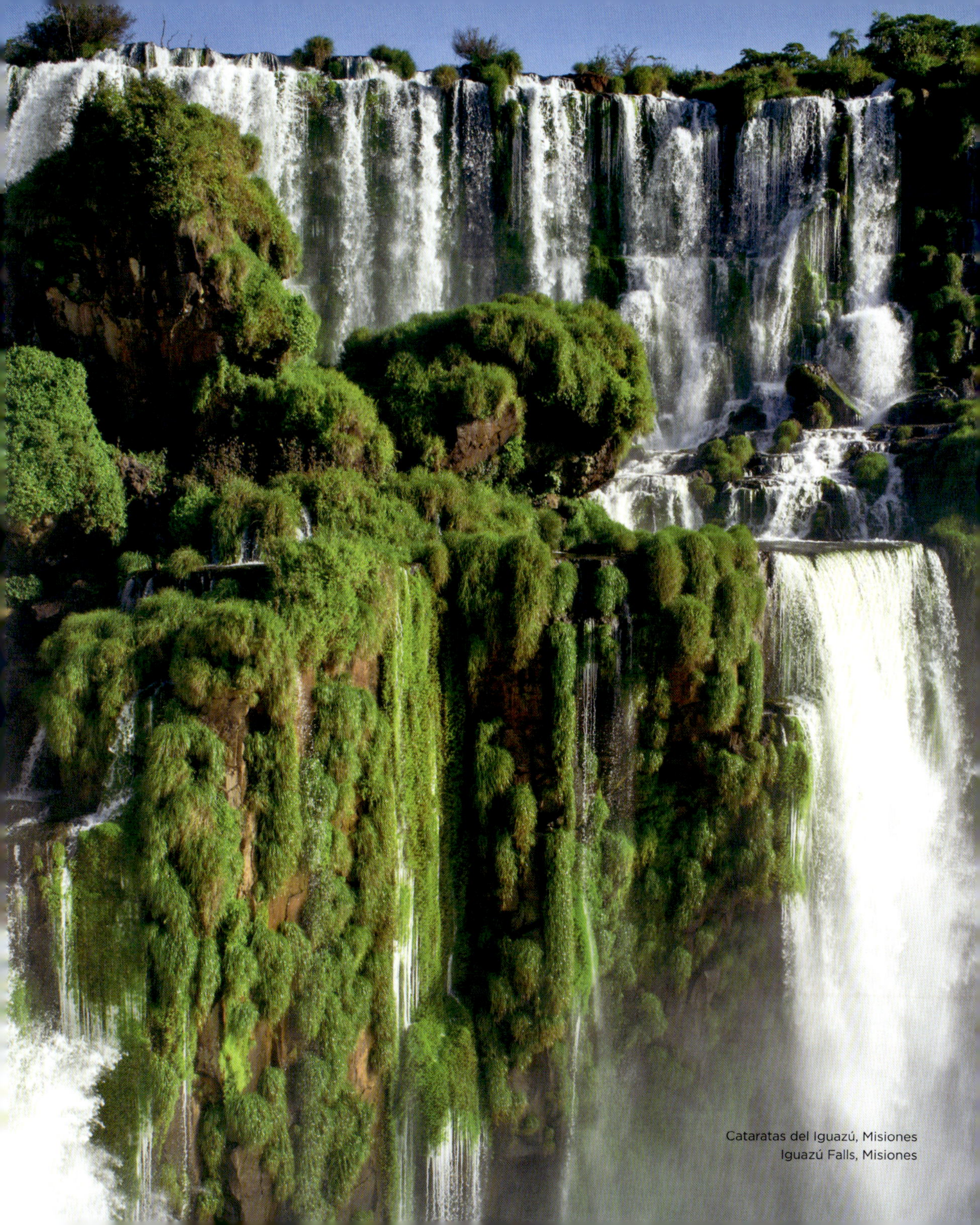

Cataratas del Iguazú, Misiones
Iguazú Falls, Misiones

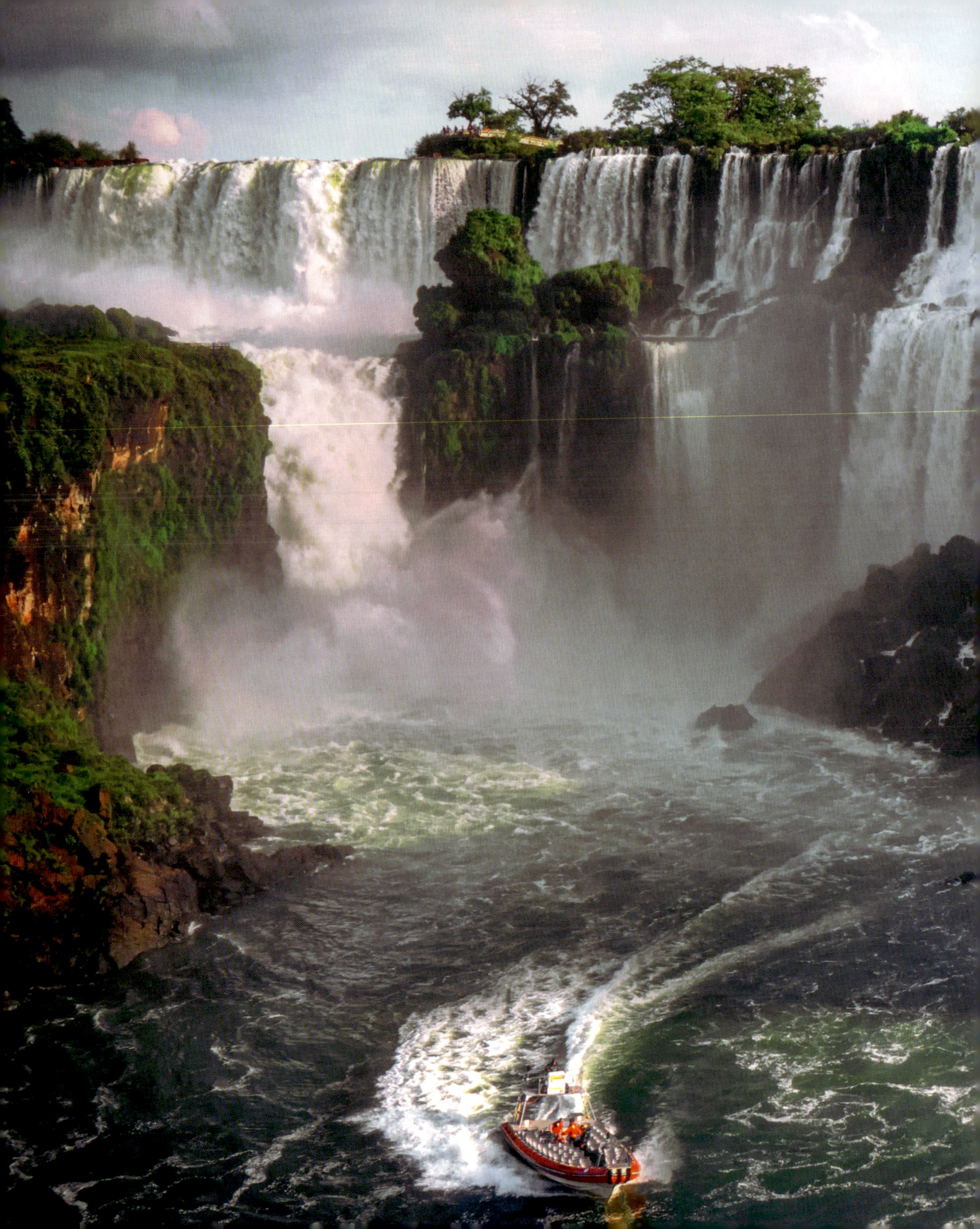

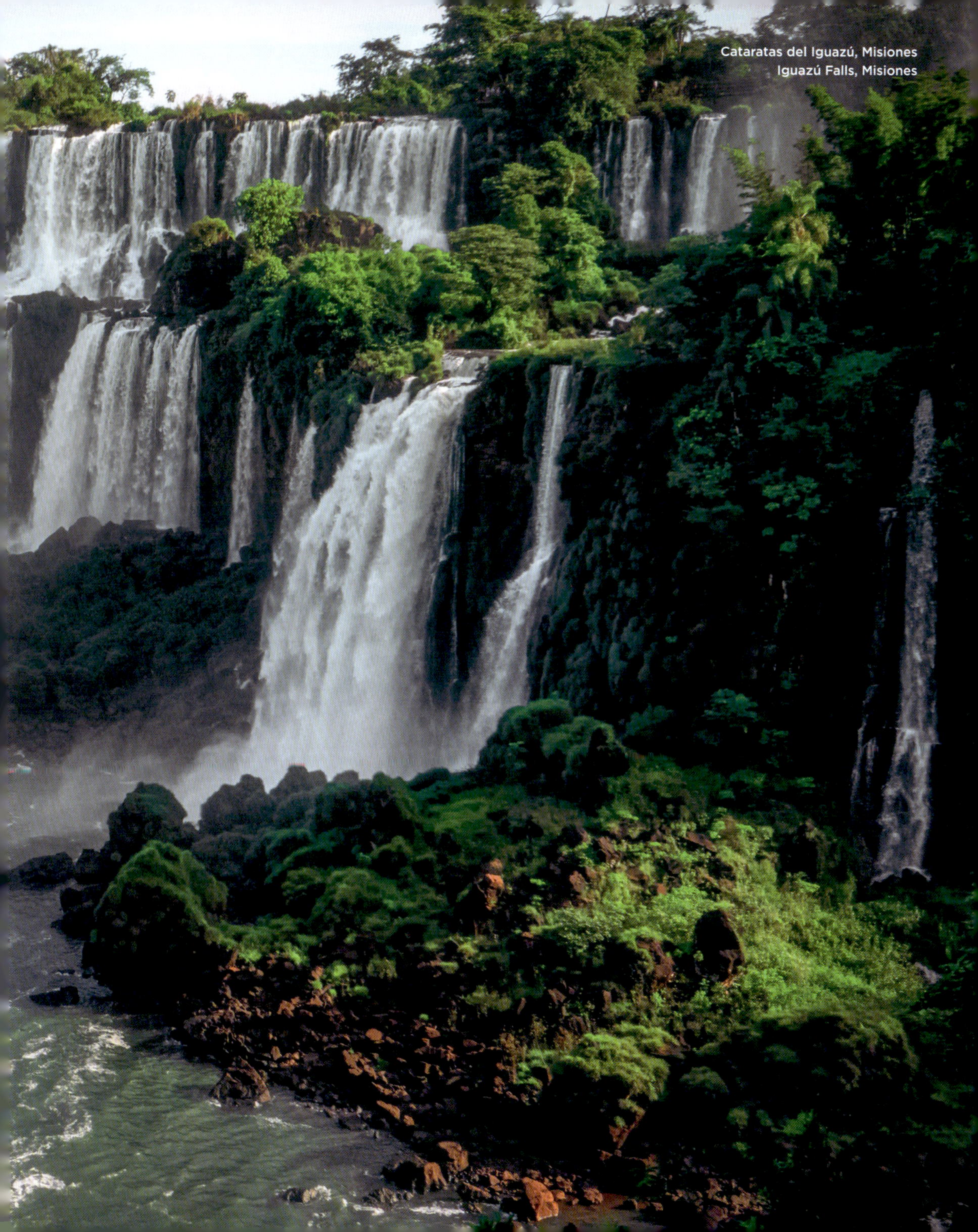

Cataratas del Iguazú, Misiones
Iguazú Falls, Misiones

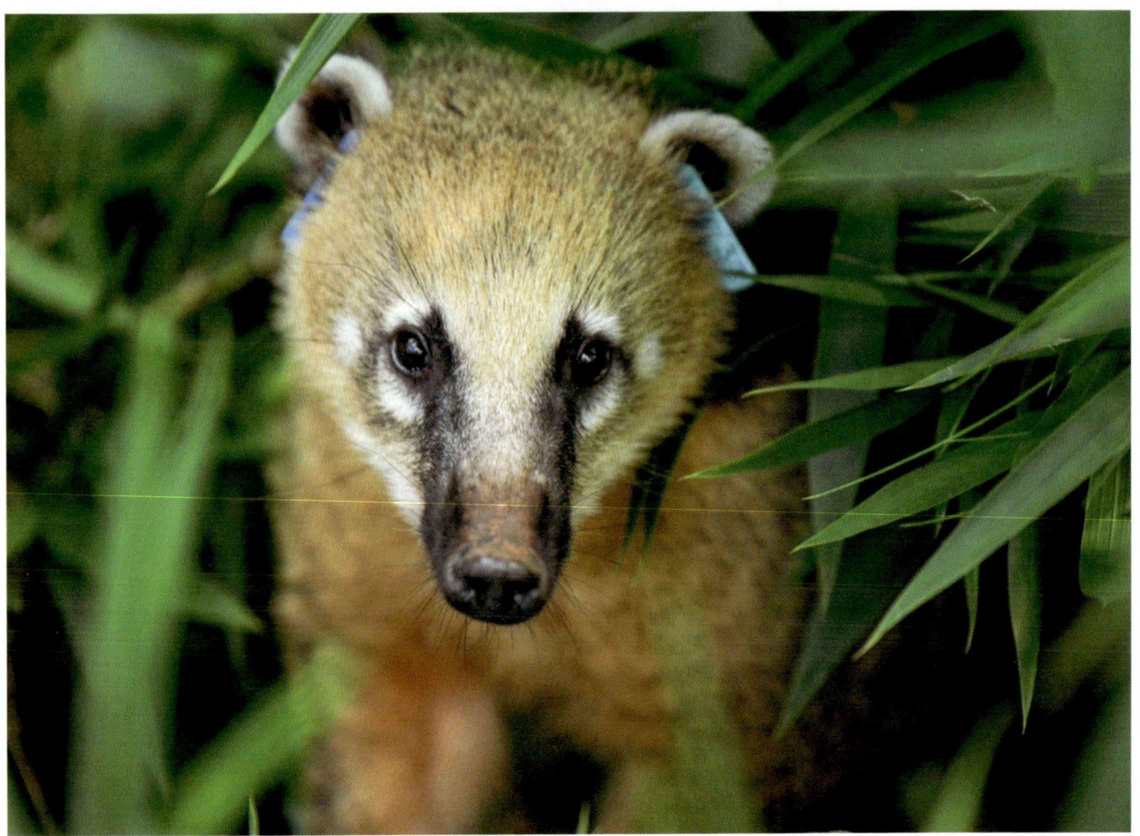

Coatí
Coati

Iguazú National Park

The Iguazú Falls in the province of Misiones are a real natural wonder. After 1300 km (808 mi) of river course, with many tributaries, the Iguazú River plunges 82 m (269 ft) in 275 waterfalls over a width of 2.7 km (1.68 mi). In 1934, the Argentinean national park was founded here, which today covers 677 km² (261 sq mi). A large part of the waterfalls is on the Brazilian side. Since 1984, the Argentine-Brazilian Iguazú National Park has been a UNESCO World Natural Heritage Site and is a subtropical rainforest that provides space for large mammals. Coatis and sloths may be seen here. The herbivores find sufficient food here in the jungle.

Parc national de l'Iguazú

Les chutes d'Iguazú, dans la province de Misiones, sont une véritable merveille de la nature. Après un trajet de 1300 km comprenant de nombreux confluents, la rivière Iguazú chute de 82 m, en 275 cataractes réparties sur une grande courbe de 2,7 km. En 1934, un parc national argentin y fut fondé ; il compte aujourd'hui 677 km². Une grande partie des chutes d'eau est située sur le territoire du Brésil. Depuis 1984, le parc national argentino-brésilien d'Iguazú, est inscrit au patrimoine mondial de l'Unesco. La forêt pluvieuse subtropicale abrite de grands mammifères. On y rencontre également les coatis et les paresseux. La forêt vierge regorge de nourriture pour ces arboricoles.

Iguazú-Nationalpark

Die Iguazú-Wasserfälle in der Provinz Misiones sind ein echtes Naturwunder. Nach 1300 km Flusslauf mit vielen Zuflüssen stürzt der Iguazú-Fluss auf einer Breite von 2,7 km in 275 Wasserfällen 82 m in die Tiefe. 1934 wurde hier der argentinische Nationalpark gegründet, der heute 677 km² groß ist. Ein großer Teil der Wasserfälle liegt auf brasilianischer Seite. Seit 1984 gehört der argentinisch-brasilianische Iguazú Nationalpark zum UNESCO-Weltnaturerbe. Es ist ein subtropischer Regenwald, der großen Säugetieren Raum bietet. Nasenbären und Faultiere sind hier zu sehen. Die Pflanzenfresser finden im Urwald ausreichend Kost.

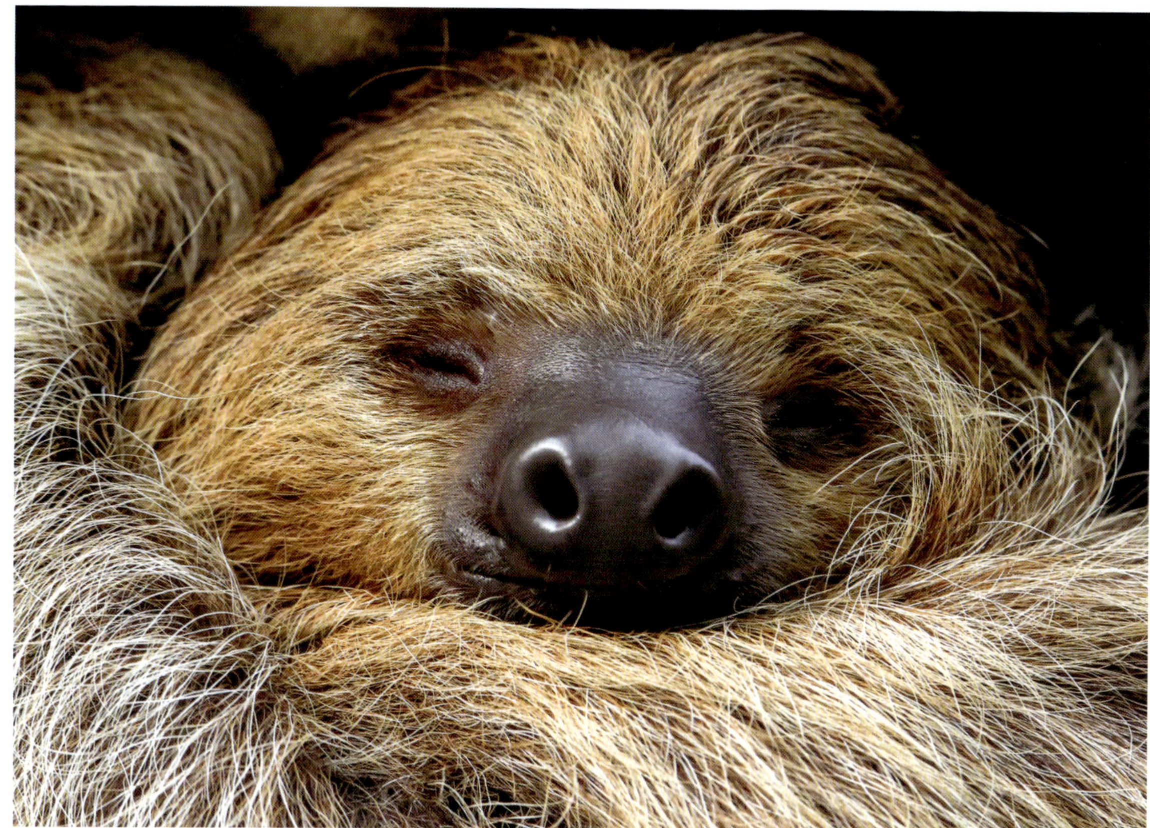

Perezoso de dos dedos de Linnaeus
Linnaeus's two-toed sloth

Parque Nacional Iguazú

Las Cataratas del Iguazú en la provincia de Misiones son una verdadera maravilla natural. Después de 1300 km de curso fluvial con muchos afluentes, el río Iguazú se sumerge 82 m en 275 cascadas, en un ancho de 2,7 km. En 1934, se fundó aquí el Parque Nacional argentino, que hoy en día cubre 677 km². Una gran parte de las cascadas se encuentra en el lado brasileño. Desde 1984, el Parque Nacional Iguazú Argentino-Brasileño es Patrimonio Natural de la Humanidad de la UNESCO. Es una selva subtropical que proporciona espacio para grandes mamíferos. Aquí se pueden ver coatíes y folívoros. También hay perezosos. Los herbívoros encuentran suficiente comida en la selva.

Parque Nacional do Iguaçu

As Cataratas do Iguaçu, na província de Misiones, são uma verdadeira maravilha natural. Após 1300 km de curso de rio com muitos afluentes, o rio Iguaçu mergulha 82 m em 275 cachoeiras, numa largura de 2,7 km. Em 1934, foi fundado aqui o Parque Nacional Argentino, que hoje abrange 677 km². Uma grande parte das cachoeiras fica no lado brasileiro. Desde 1984, o Parque Nacional Argentino-Brasileiro do Iguaçu é Patrimônio Natural Mundial da UNESCO. É uma floresta tropical subtropical que fornece espaço para grandes mamíferos. Coatis e preguiças podem ser vistos aqui. As preguiças também vivem aqui. Os herbívoros encontram comida suficiente na selva.

Nationaal park Iguazú

De Watervallen van de Iguaçu in de provincie Misiones zijn een echt natuurwonder. Na 1300 km rivierstroming met veel zijrivieren stort de Iguazú-rivier zich over een breedte van 2,7 km in 275 watervallen in de 82 m diepte. In 1934 werd hier het Argentijnse Nationaal park opgericht dat vandaag de dag 677 km² beslaat. Een groot deel van de watervallen ligt aan de Braziliaanse kant. Sinds 1984 staat het Argentijns-Braziliaans Nationaal park Iguazú op de UNESCO Werelderfgoedlijst. Het is een subtropisch regenwoud dat ruimte biedt aan grote zoogdieren. Hier zijn neusberen en luiaards te zien. De herbivoren vinden voldoende voedsel in het oerwoud.

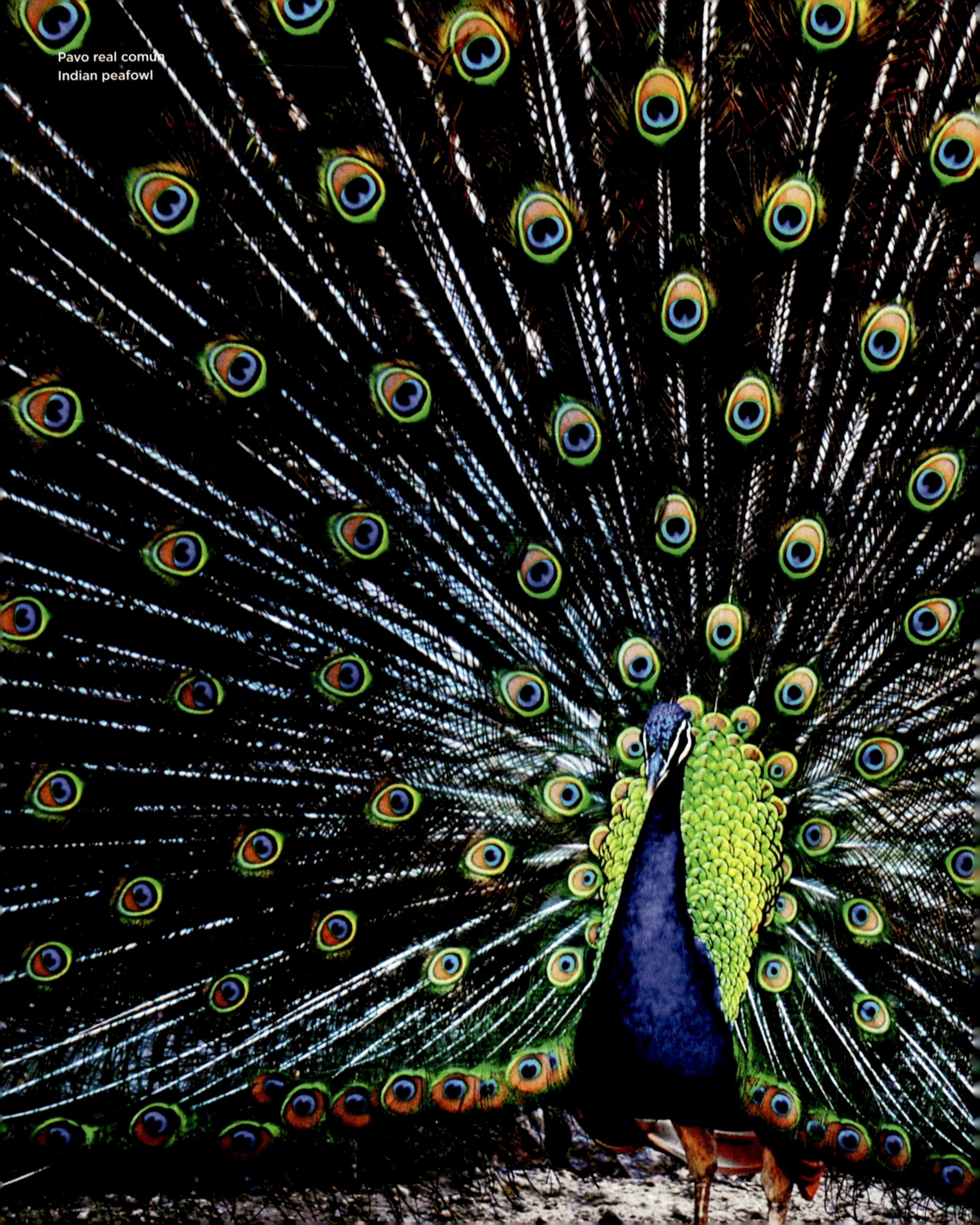
Pavo real común
Indian peafowl

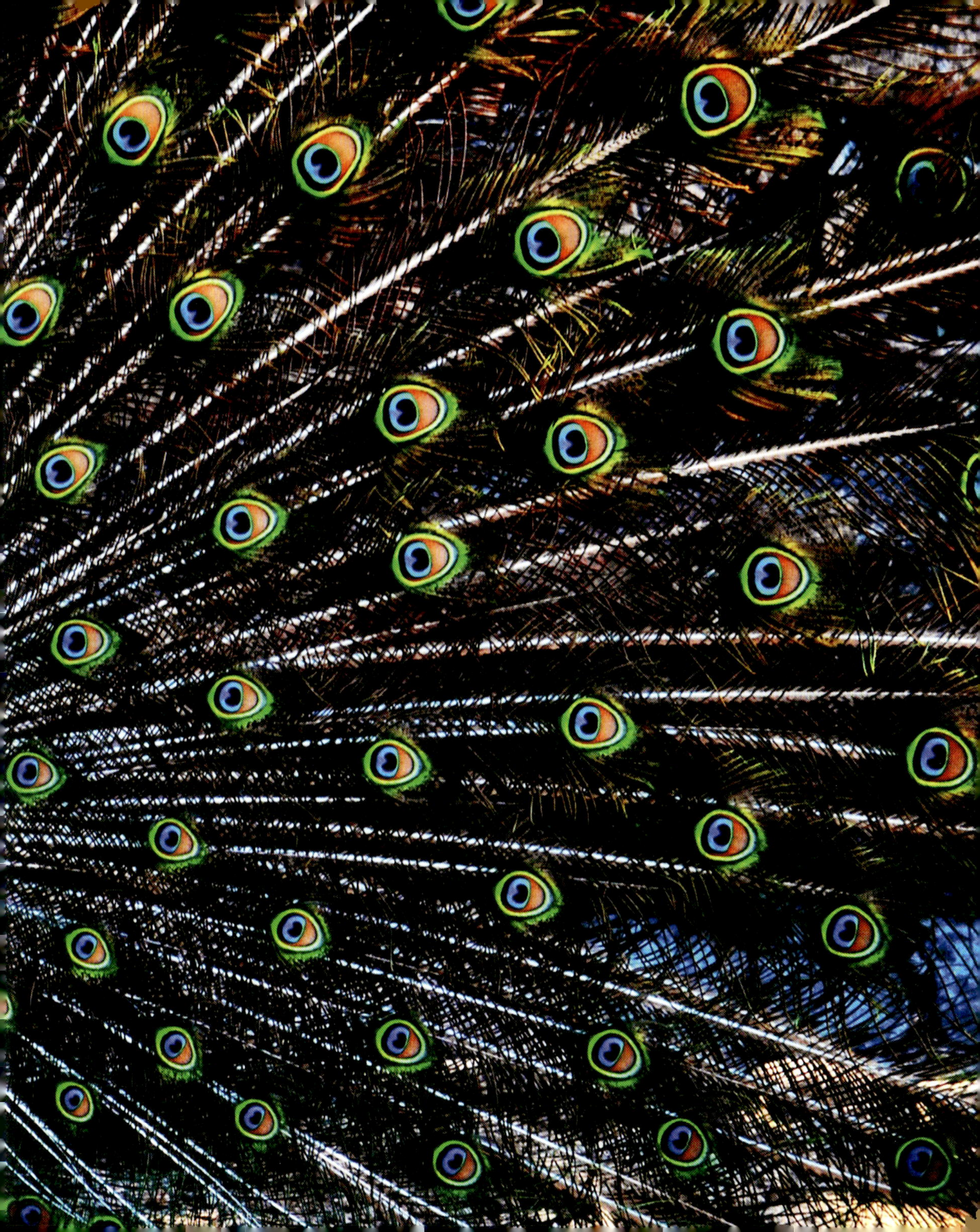

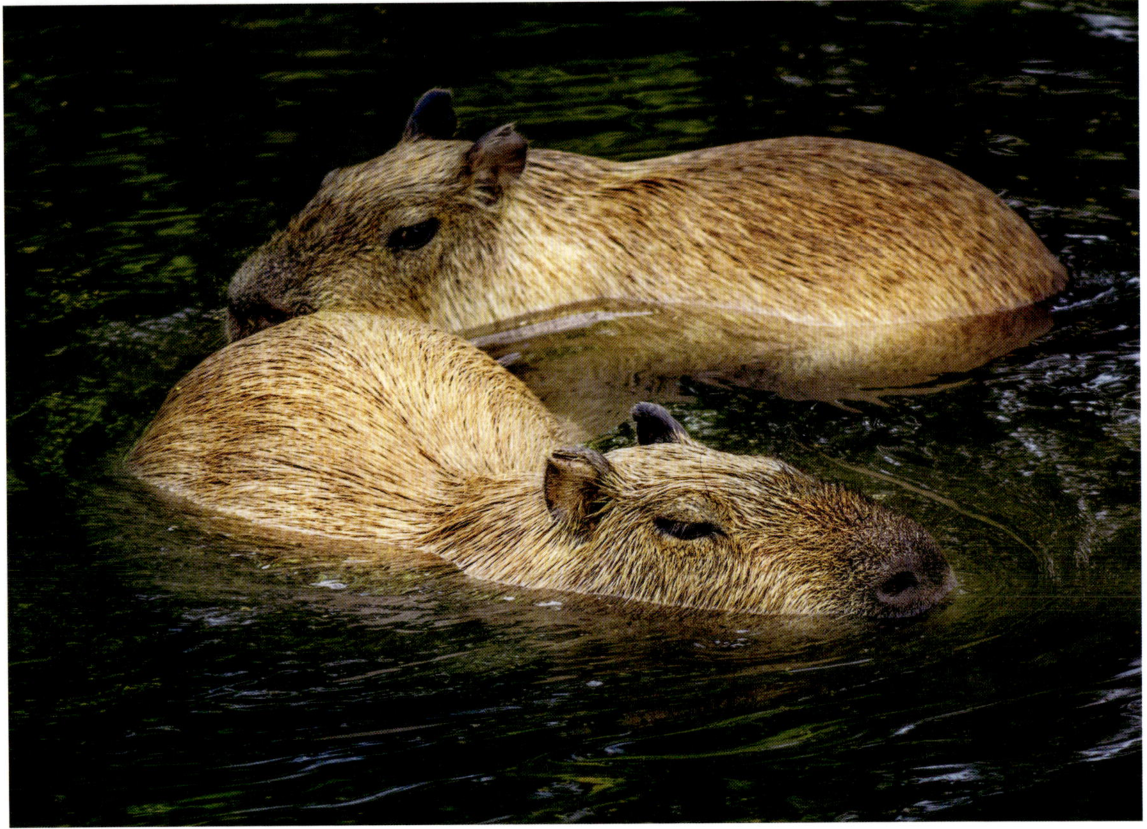

Carpincho
Capybara

Capybaras

Around 63 km² (24 sq mi) of the Iguazú
National Park are National Reserve. The
subtropical vegetation differs in respect
of the tree-type distribution depending
upon their proximity to the waterfalls.
There are 422 bird species. Two thirds of
all species existing in Argentina occur only
here. Among the 68 mammal species are
large mammals such as the tapir and also
the capybara, which may grow to 1.25 m
(4 ft) long and is the largest living rodent.
Capybaras maintain a semi-aquatic lifestyle
and have webbed feet between their
toes. They live in herds of 6 to 20 animals,
feeding on grasses and water plants.

Capybaras

Les 63 km² du parc national d'Iguazú
sont une réserve nationale. La végétation
subtropicale varie en fonction des
essences d'arbres et de la proximité des
chutes d'eau. Le parc compte 422 espèces
d'oiseaux. Deux tiers de toutes les espèces
vivant en Argentine sont endémiques. Les
68 espèces de mammifères incluent de
grands animaux, dont le tapir et le cabiai
(ou capybara), plus grand rongeur au
monde, pouvant mesurer jusqu'à 1,25 m.
Doté de pattes palmées, le capybara
possède un mode de vie semi-aquatique.
Il vit en troupeau de 6 à 20 individus et se
nourrit d'herbes et de plantes aquatiques.

Capybaras

63 km² des Iguazú Nationalparks sind
Nationalreservat. Die subtropische
Vegetation unterscheidet sich durch
den Baumbestand und die Nähe bzw.
Ferne zu den Wasserfällen. Es gibt 422
Vogelarten. Zwei Drittel aller in Argentinien
existierenden Arten kommen nur hier
vor. Unter den 68 Säugetierarten sind
große Säugetiere wie der Tapir und das
Wasserschwein. Das auch Capybara
genannte Tier wird 1,25 m lang, es ist das
größte lebende Nagetier. Wasserschweine
pflegen eine semiaquatische Lebensweise,
sie haben Schwimmhäute zwischen den
Zehen. Capybaras leben in Herden von
6 bis 20 Tieren. Ihre Nahrung sind Gräser
und Wasserpflanzen.

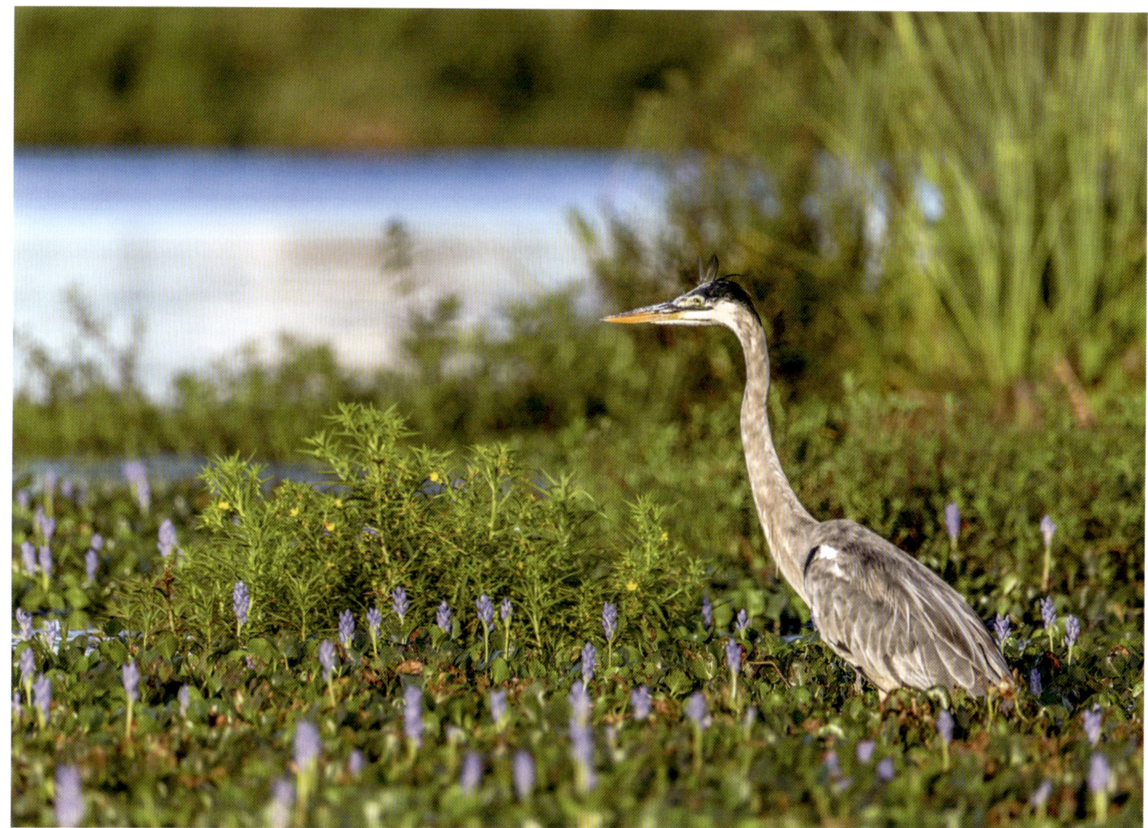

Ardeida, Esteros del Iberá, Corrientes
Heron, Iberá Wetlands, Corrientes

Carpinchos

63 km² del Parque Nacional Iguazú son
reserva nacional. La vegetación subtropical
difiere en la población de árboles y en la
proximidad o distancia a las cascadas. Hay
422 especies de aves. Dos tercios de todas
las especies que existen en Argentina
se encuentran solamente aquí. Entre las
68 especies de mamíferos se encuentran
grandes mamíferos como el tapir y el
carpincho. El animal, también llamado
carpincho, crece hasta 1,25 m de largo y es
el roedor vivo más grande. Los carpinchos
mantienen un estilo de vida semiacuático,
tienen membranas interdigitales entre los
dedos de los pies. Los carpinchos viven
en grupos de entre 6 y 20 integrantes. Su
alimento es el pasto y las plantas del agua.

Capivaras

63 km² do Parque Nacional do Iguaçu
são Reservas Nacionais. A vegetação
subtropical difere na população arbórea
e na proximidade ou distância das
cachoeiras. Existem 422 espécies de aves.
Dois terços de todas as espécies existentes
na Argentina são encontradas somente
aqui. Entre as 68 espécies de mamíferos
estão os grandes mamíferos, como a anta
e a capivara. A capivara, também chamada
de carpincho ou porco-capivara, chega a
ter até 1,25 m de comprimento e é o maior
roedor vivo. As capivaras mantêm um
estilo de vida semi-aquático, elas possuem
pele como membranas entre os dedos
dos pés. As capivaras vivem em rebanhos
de 6 a 20 animais. Os seus alimentos são
gramíneas e plantas aquáticas.

Capibara's

63 km² van het Nationaal park Iguazú
bestaat uit Nationaal natuurreservaat.
De subtropische vegetatie onderscheidt
zich door de bomenpopulatie en de
nabijheid resp. afstand tot de watervallen.
Er zijn 422 vogelsoorten. Twee derde
van alle in Argentinië voorkomende
soorten komen alleen hier voor. Onder
de 68 zoogdiersoorten bevinden zich
grote zoogdieren zoals de tapir en
het waterzwijn. Het ook wel capibara
genoemde dier wordt 1,25 m lang en is het
grootste levende knaagdier. Waterzwijnen
hebben een semi-aquatische levensstijl
en hebben deels zwemvliezen tussen hun
tenen. Capibara's leven in kuddes van 6
tot 20 dieren. Hun voedsel bestaat uit gras
en waterplanten.

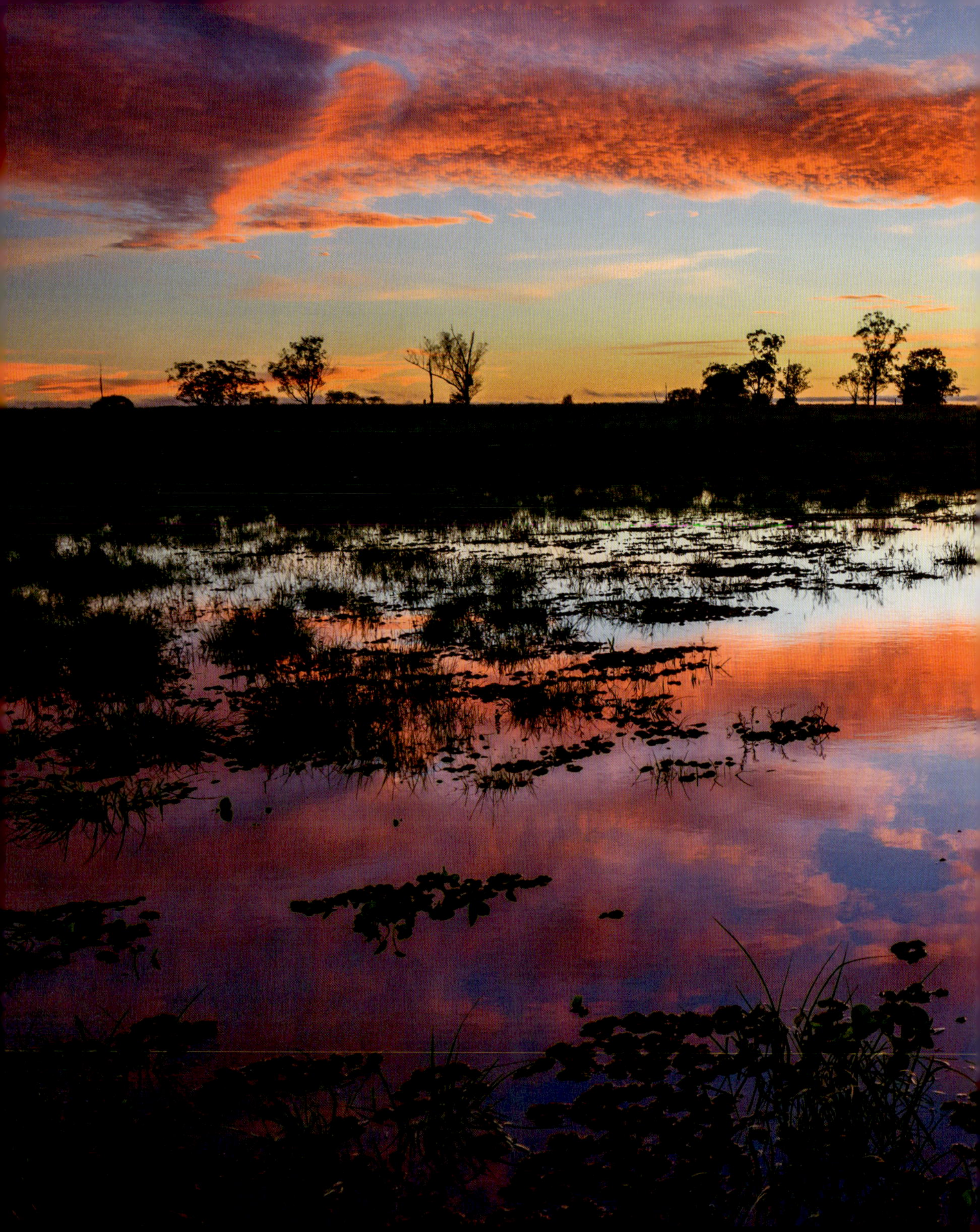

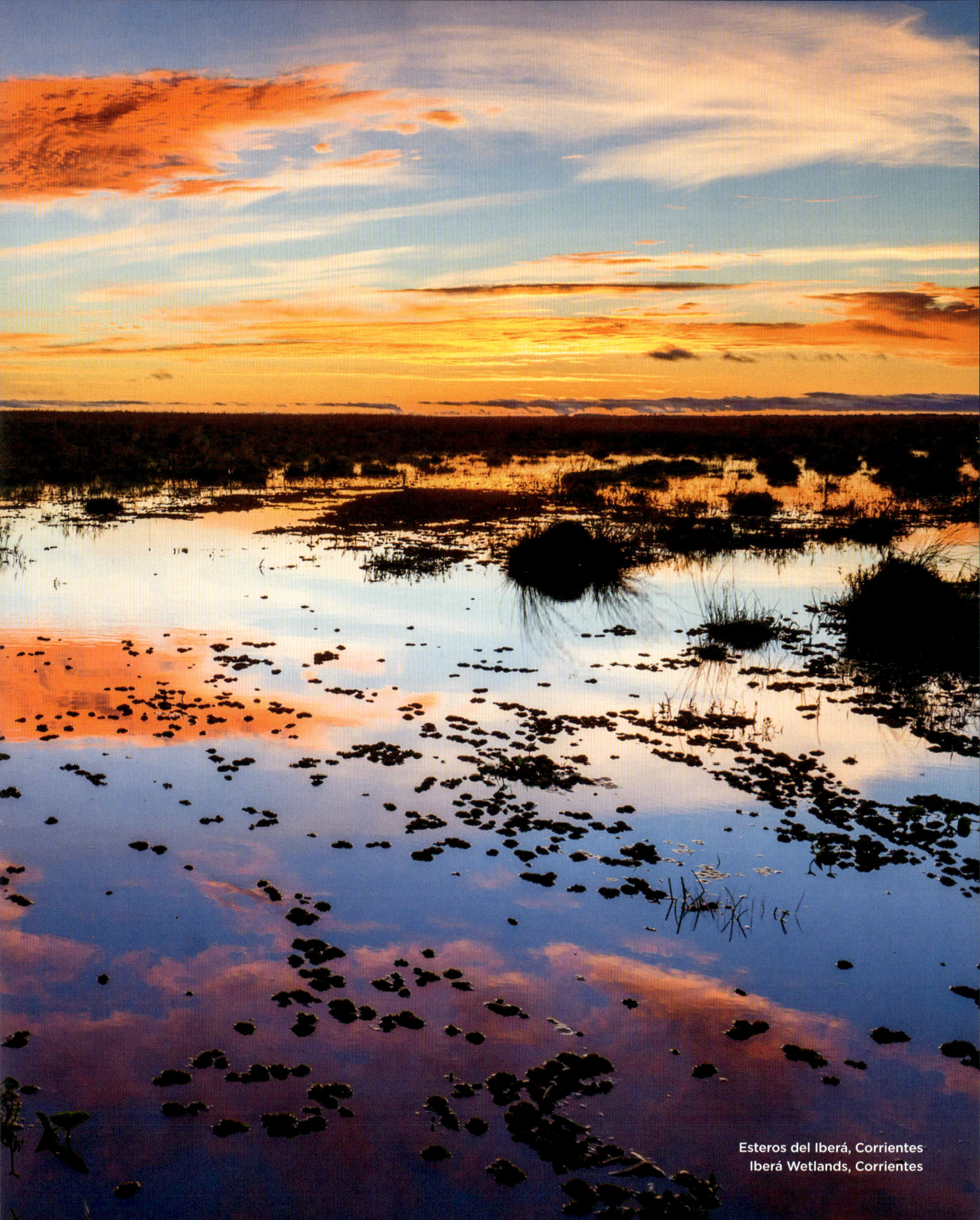

Esteros del Iberá, Corrientes
Iberá Wetlands, Corrientes

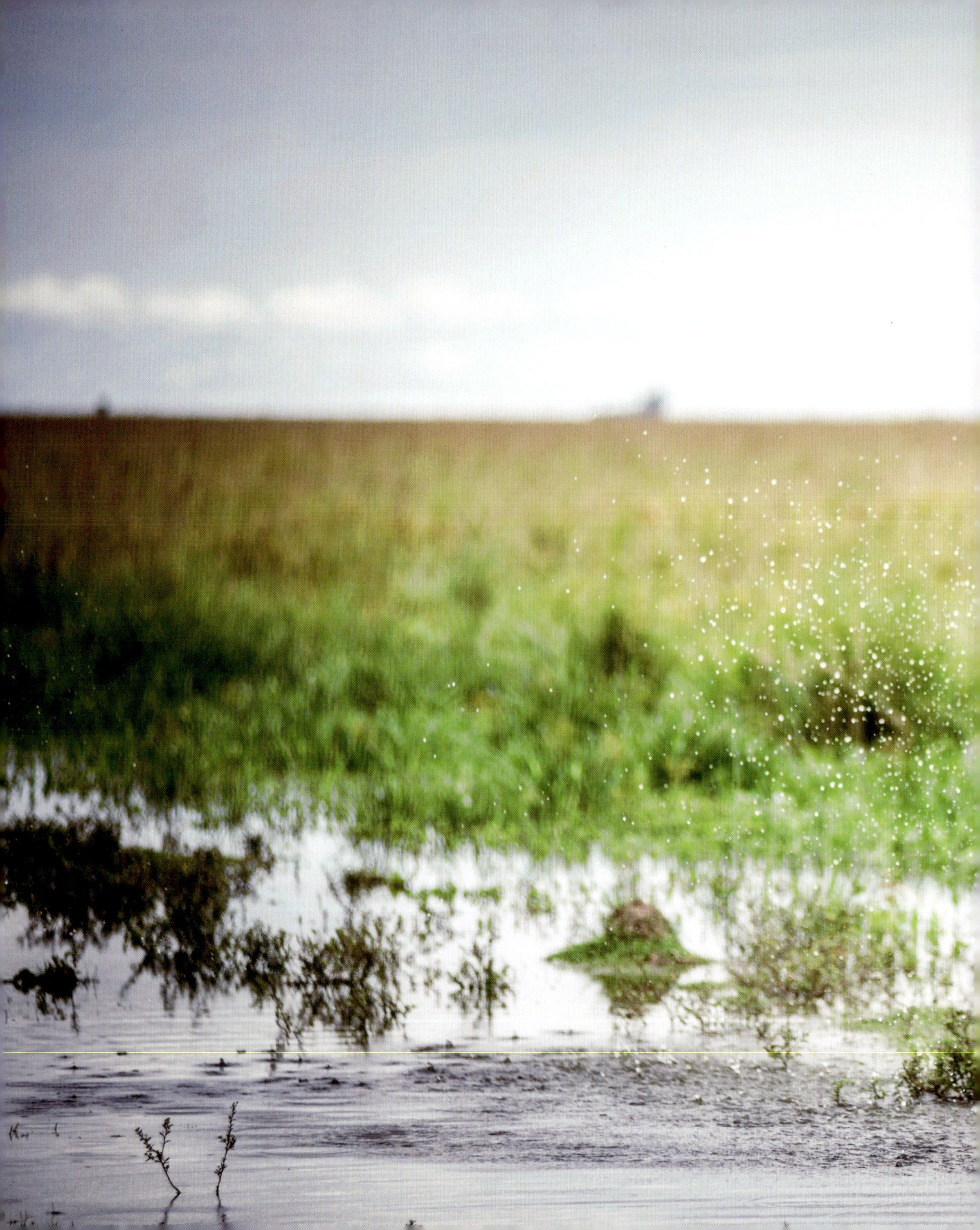

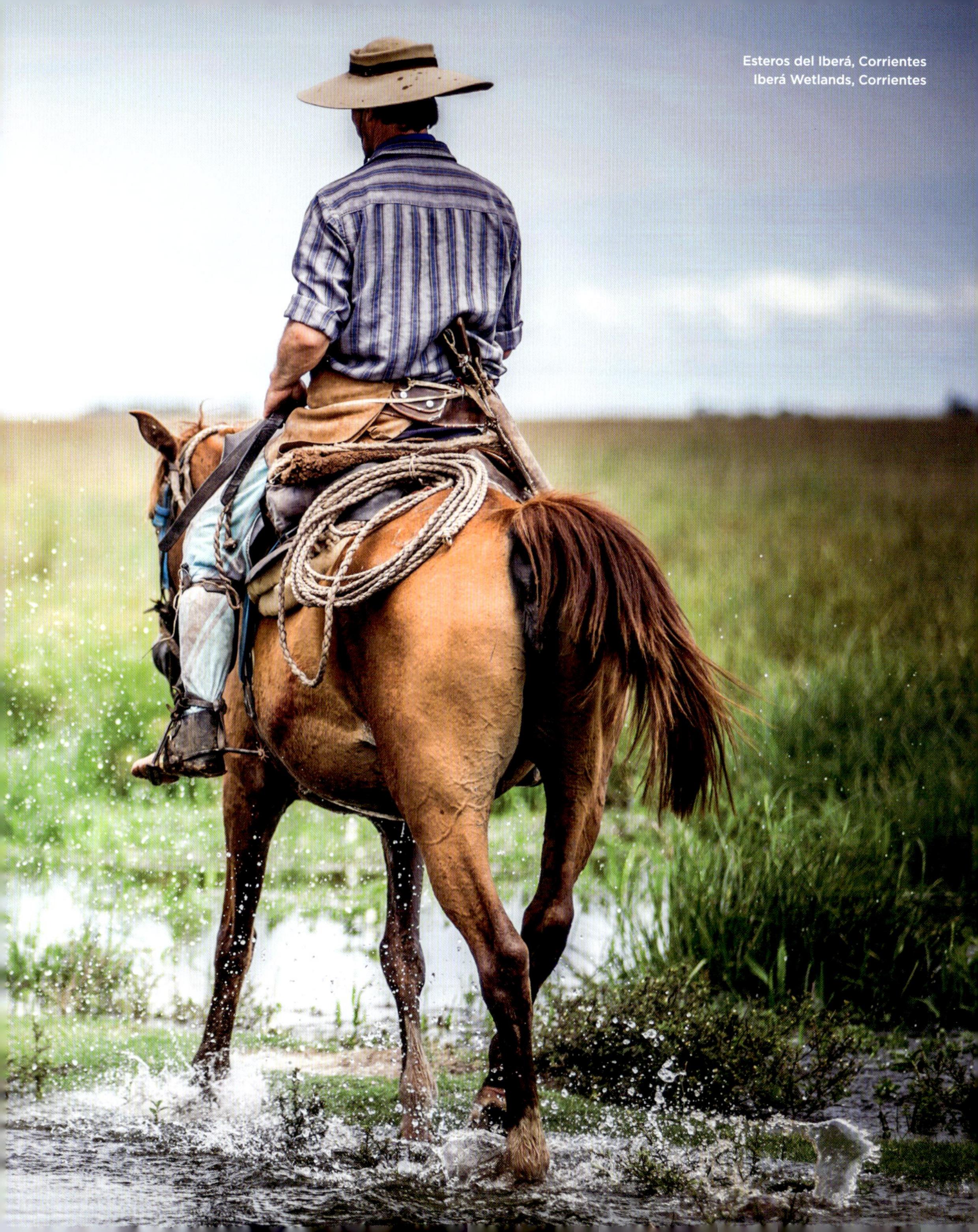

Esteros del Iberá, Corrientes
Iberá Wetlands, Corrientes

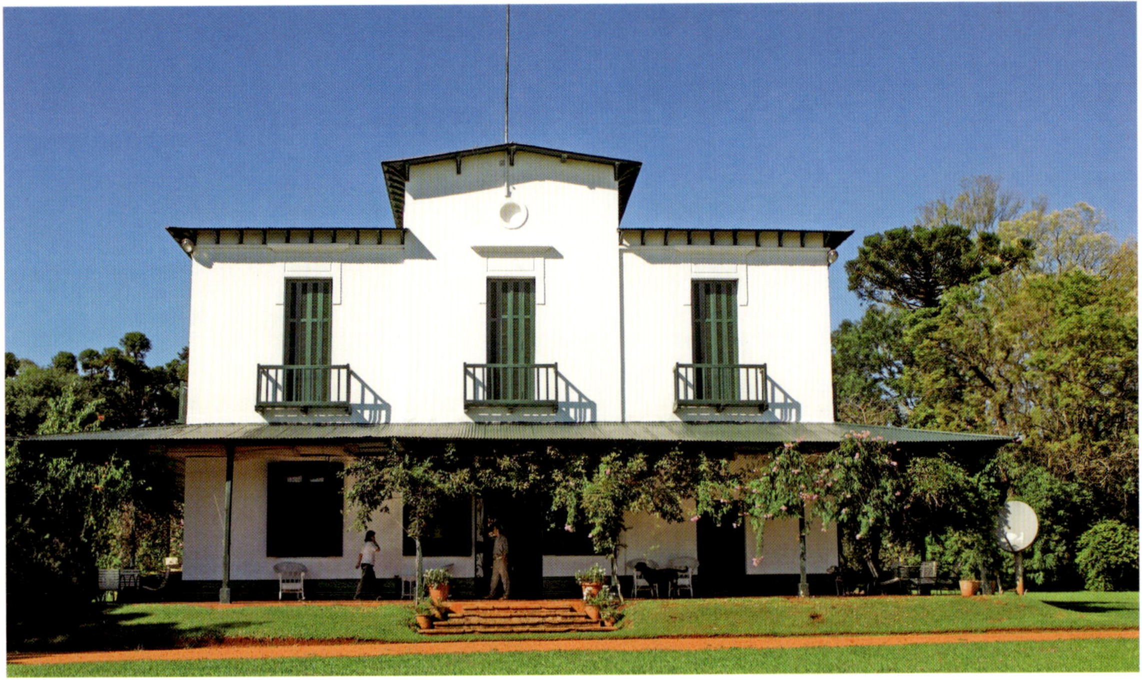

Estancia Santa Cecilia, Misiones

Iberá Swamps

The province of Corrientes, situated in the Mesopotamia, has a mainly agricultural economy. Estancias grow rice, cotton, sweet potatoes and mate. The region is one of the most water-rich in the country. The largest swamp area, covering around 5000 km² (1930 sq mi), is the Iberá Wetlands, which is fed from the Miriñay River. The word Iberá comes from the Guaraní language and means "sparkling water". This beautiful landscape may be explored on horseback.

Esteros del Iberá

La provincia de Corrientes, situada en la Mesopotamia, vive económicamente sobre todo de la agricultura. Las estancias cultivan arroz, algodón, batatas y mate. La región es una de las más ricas en agua del país. La mayor área de pantanos con una superficie de 5000 km² son los Esteros del Iberá. Se alimentan del río Miriñay. La palabra Iberá proviene del guaraní y significa "aguas brillantes". El hermoso paisaje se puede explorar a caballo.

Marais de l'Iberá

La province de Corrientes, située dans la région Mésopotamie, tire l'essentiel de ses revenus de l'agriculture. Les *estancias* cultivent riz, coton, patates douces et maté. La région est l'une des plus humides du pays. Les plus vastes marais, les Esteros del Iberá, s'étendent sur 5000 km² et sont alimentés par la rivière Miriñay. Le mot *iberá* provient de la langue guarani et signifie « eaux scintillantes ». La randonnée équestre est l'un des meilleurs moyens de découvrir cette magnifique région agricole.

Esteros del Iberá

A província de Corrientes, situada na Mesopotâmia Argentina, vive economicamente principalmente da agricultura. As fazendas cultivam arroz, algodão, batata doce e mate. A região é uma das mais ricas em água do país. A maior área de pântano com uma área de 5000 km² são os Esteros del Iberá. Eles alimentam-se do rio Miriñay. A palavra Iberá vem do guarani e significa "água brilhante". A bela paisagem pode ser explorada da melhor maneira a cavalo.

Iberá-Sümpfe

Die im Zweistromland gelegene Provinz Corrientes lebt wirtschaftlich hauptsächlich von der Landwirtschaft. Estanzias bauen Reis, Baumwolle, Süßkartoffeln und Mate an. Die Region gehört zu den wasserreichsten des Landes. Das größte Sumpfgebiet mit einer Fläche von 5000 km² sind die Esteros del Iberá. Sie speisen sich aus dem Miriñay-Fluss. Das Wort Iberá kommt aus dem Guaraní und bedeutet „glitzerndes Wasser". Auf dem Pferderücken lässt sich die landschaftlich schöne Gegend bestens erkunden.

Iberá moerassen

De in het Tweestromenland gelegen provincie Corrientes is economisch vooral afhankelijk van de landbouw. Estancias verbouwen rijst, katoen, zoete aardappelen en mate. De regio behoort tot de waterrijkste van het land. Het grootste moerasgebied met een oppervlakte van 5000 km² is de Esteros del Iberá. Dat wordt gevoed door de Miriñay-rivier. Het woord Iberá stamt uit het Guaraní en betekent "schitterend water". Het prachtige landschap kan uitstekend te paard worden verkend.

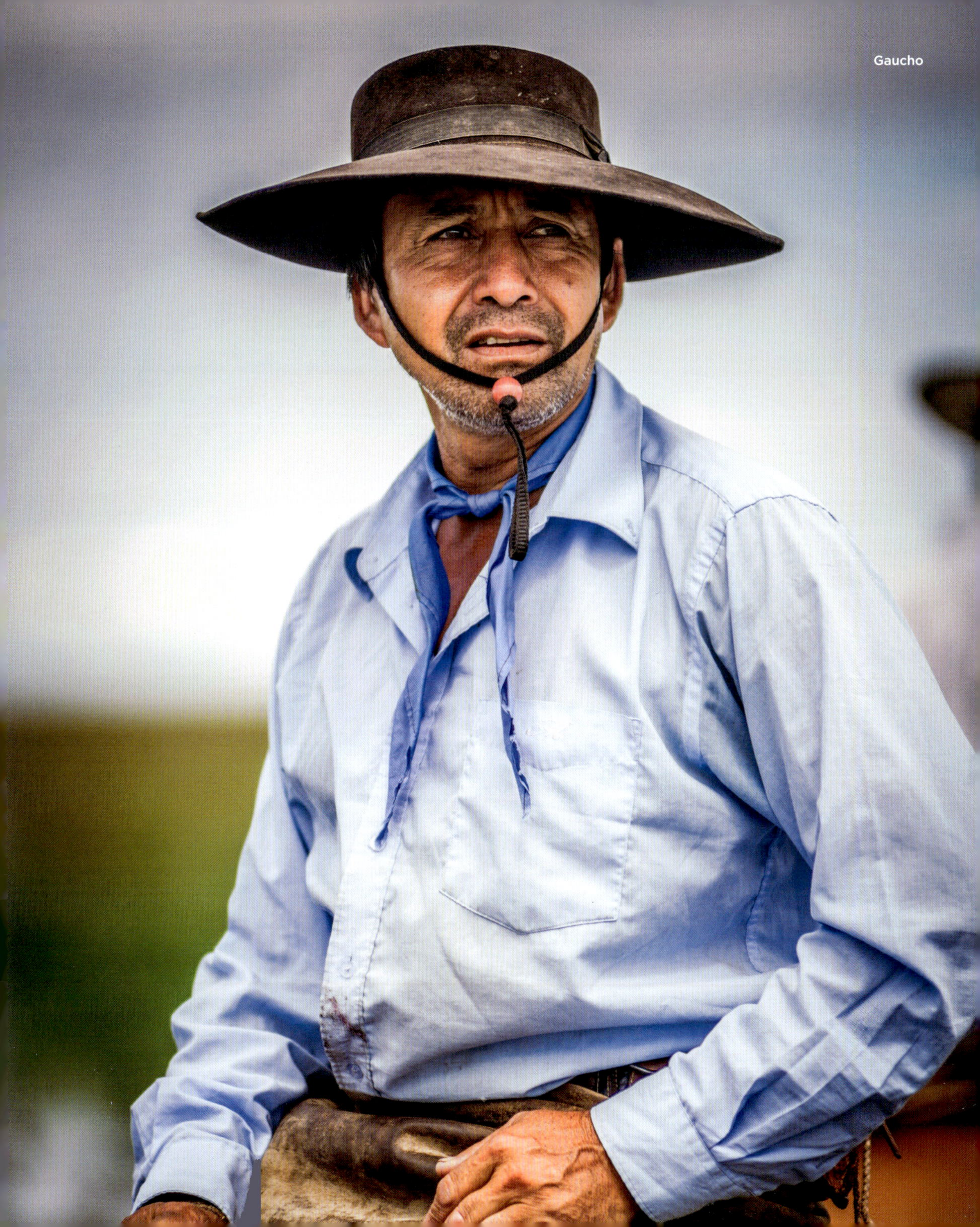

Gaucho

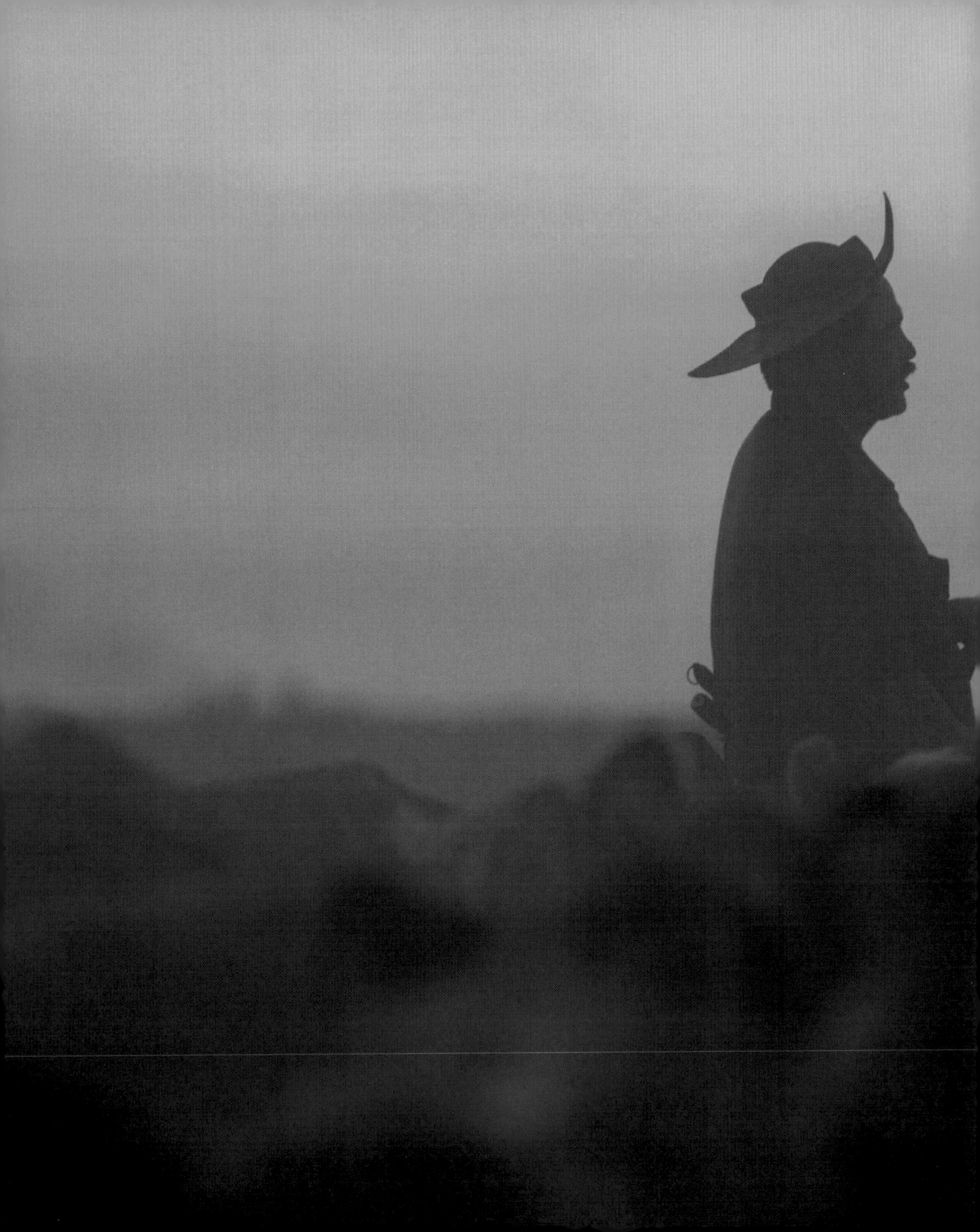

Gaucho

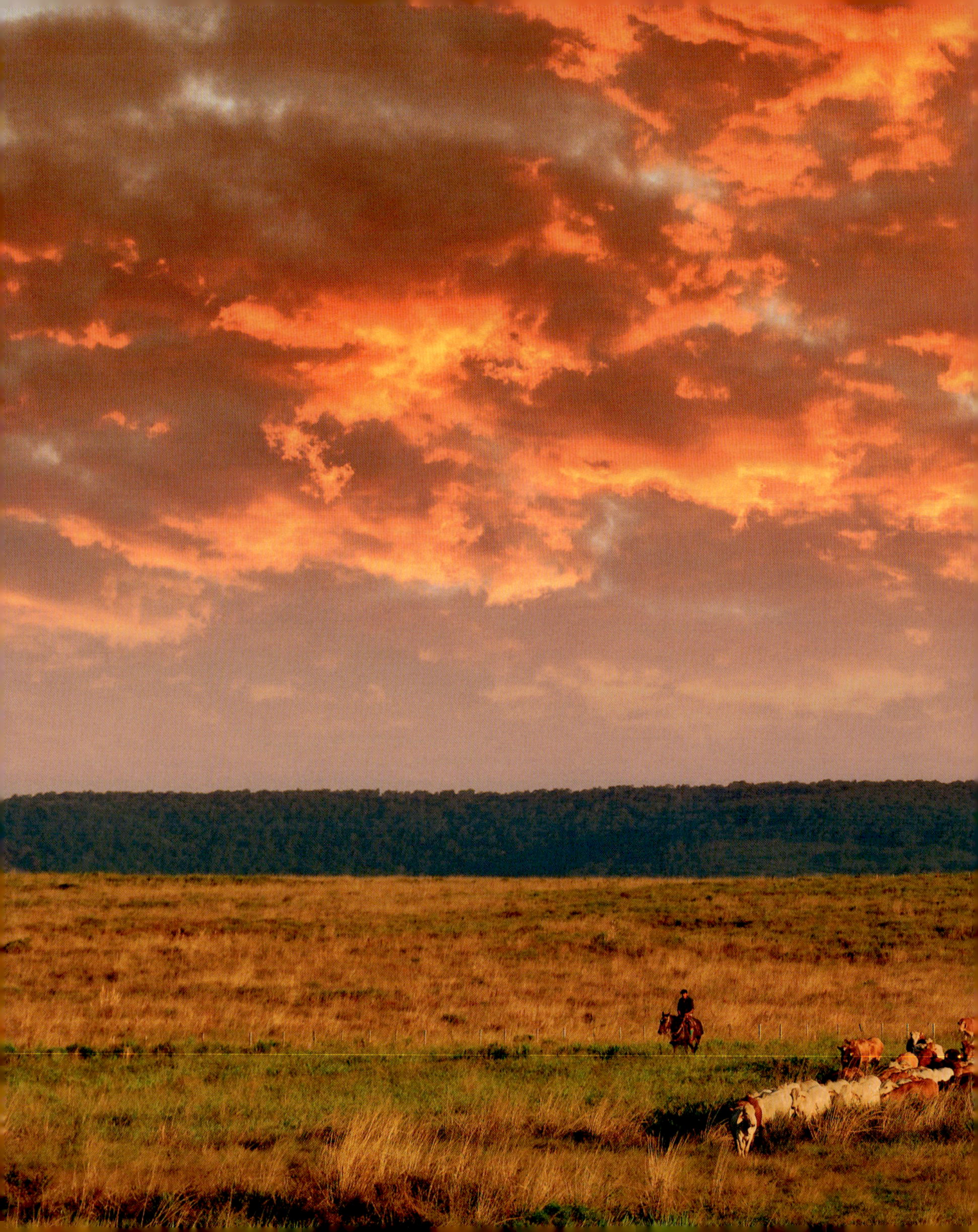

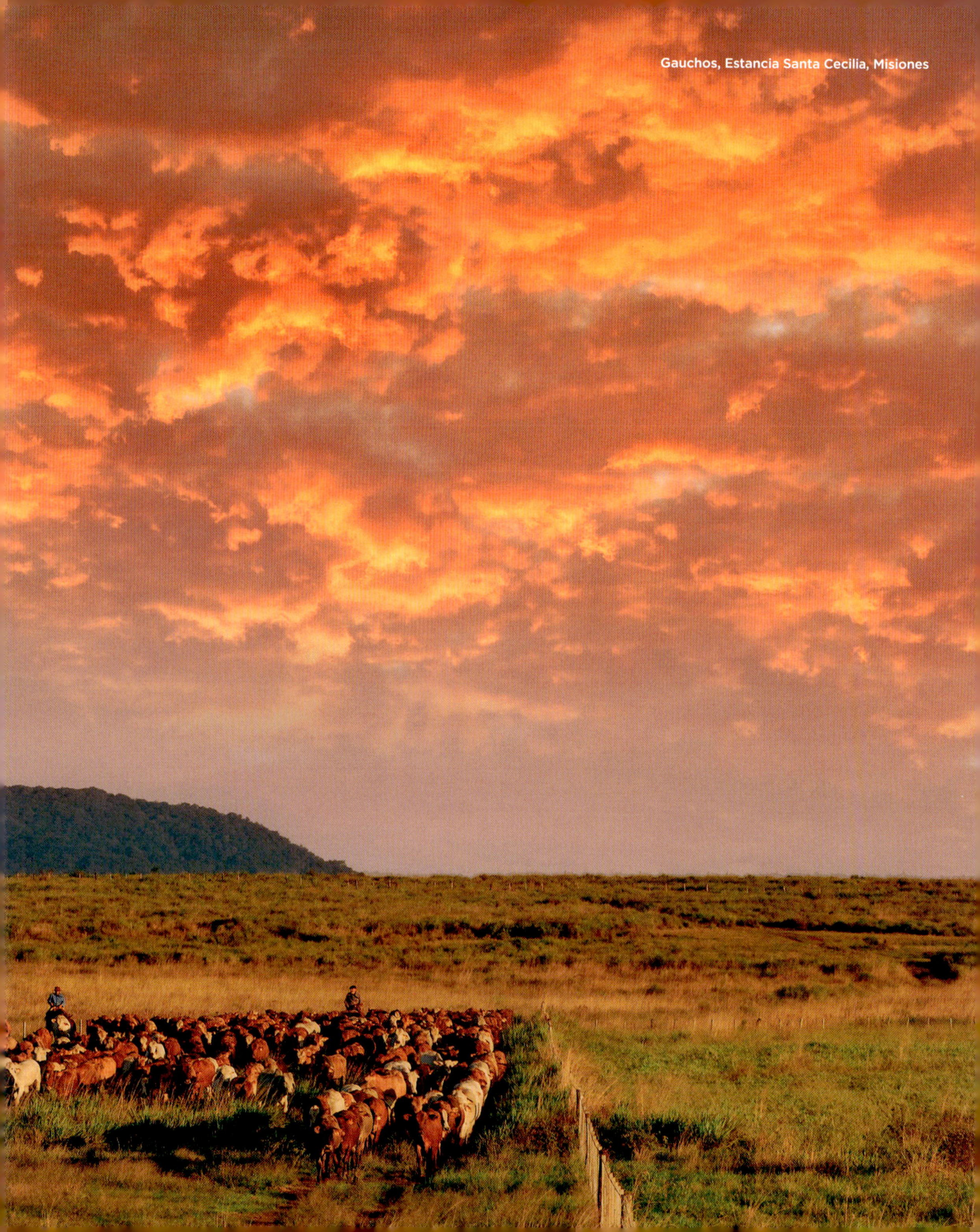
Gauchos, Estancia Santa Cecilia, Misiones

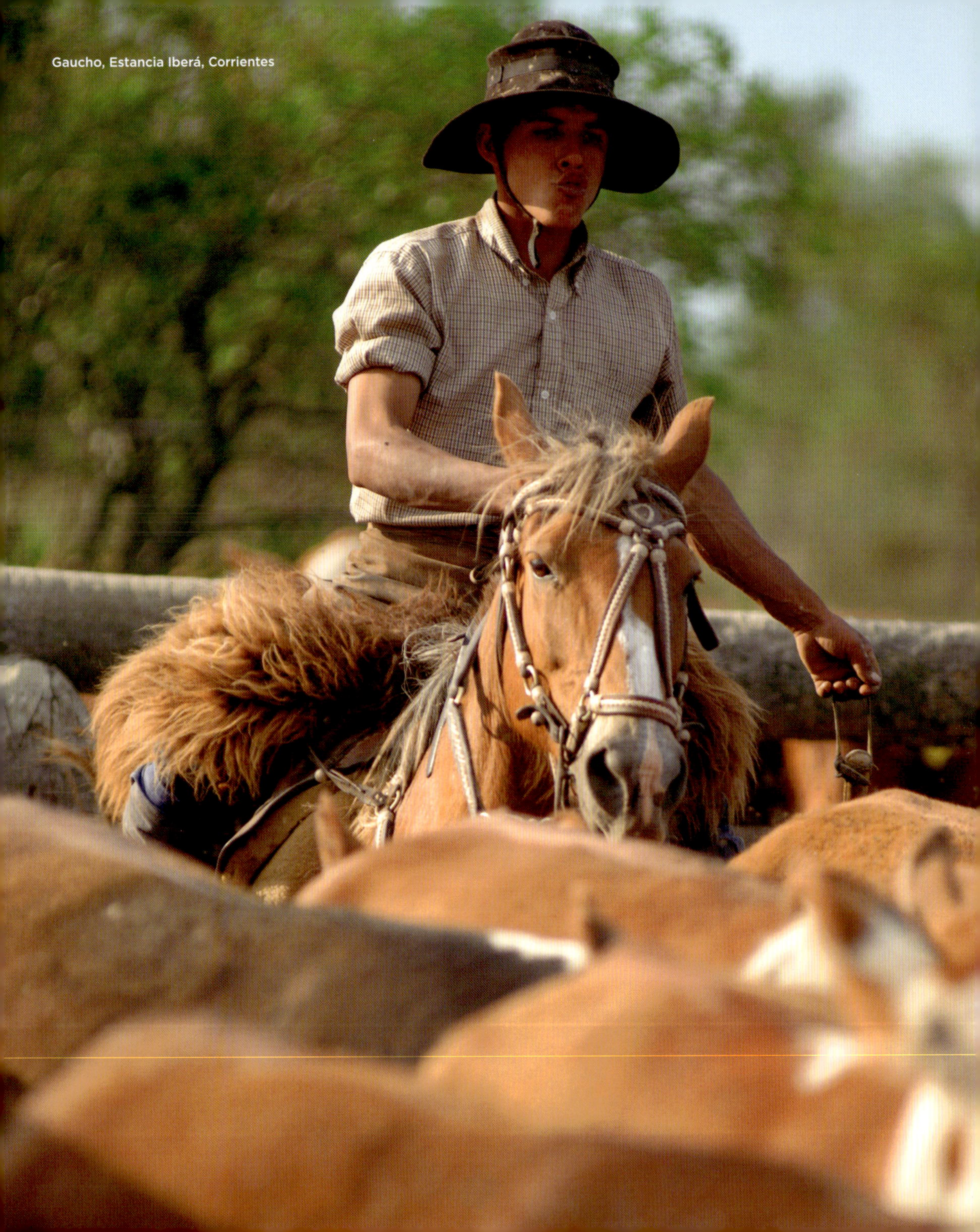

Gaucho, Estancia Iberá, Corrientes

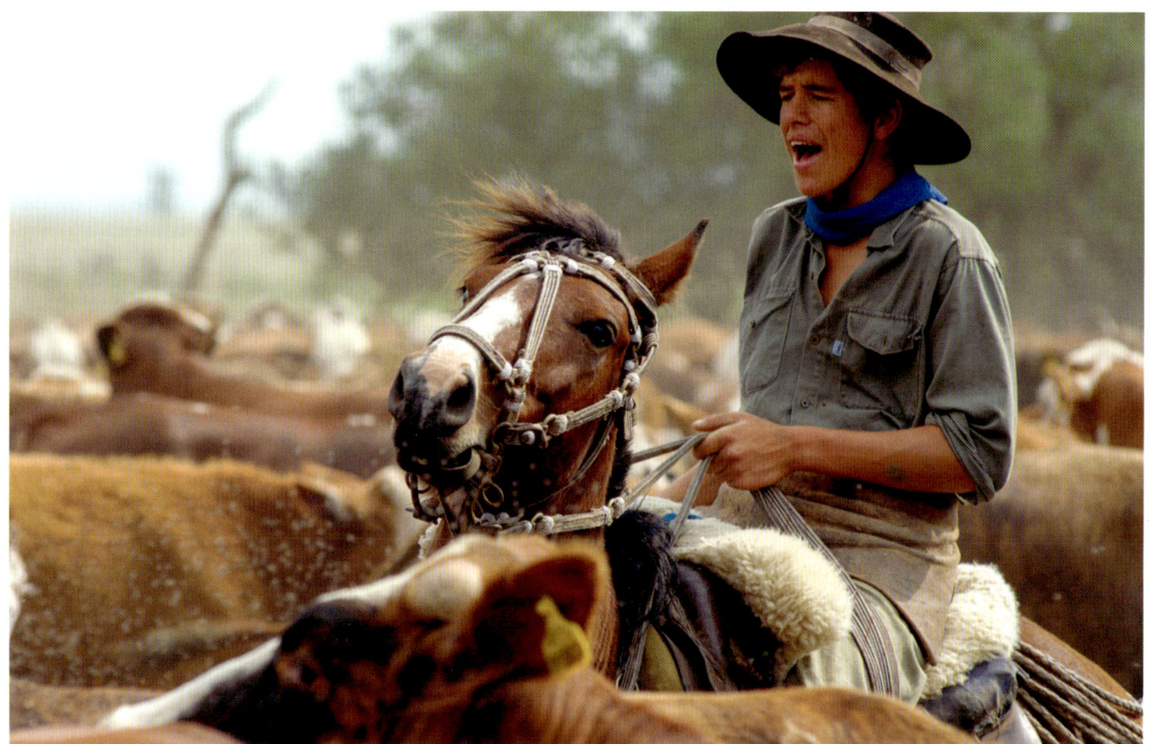

Gaucho, Estancia Iberá, Corrientes

Animal husbandry

In the municipality of San Martín - named after the famous general of the independence struggle - there are large areas of pastureland and considerable livestock farming, in addition to marshes. The region used to be almost cut off from the outside world. It was not until 1927 that settlements such as the Colonia Carlos Peligrini on Lake Iberá were founded, which today comprises a 550,000 ha (2124 sq mi) nature reserve.

Ganadería

En el municipio de San Martín (nombrado así por el famoso general de la lucha por la independencia) hay grandes zonas de pastos y una considerable actividad ganadera, además de pantanos. La región solía estar casi aislada del mundo exterior. Recién en 1927 se fundaron asentamientos, como la Colonia Carlos Peligrini en el lago Iberá, que hoy constituye una reserva natural de 550 000 ha.

Élevage

Le département de San Martín, baptisé en l'honneur du célèbre général qui mena la lutte pour l'indépendance argentine, compte, outre des marécages, de vastes pâturages où s'exerce une activité d'élevage dynamique. La région fut longtemps coupée du reste du monde. Ce n'est qu'en 1927 que les premières colonies s'y installèrent, dont Colonia Carlos Pellegrini, bâtie sur les rives du lac Iberá. Elle comprend aujourd'hui un parc naturel de 550 000 ha.

Criação de gado

No município de San Martín - que recebeu o nome em homenagem ao famoso general das lutas pela independência – existem grandes áreas de pastagem e uma considerável pecuária, além de áreas de pântanos. A região já estava quase isolada do mundo exterior. Só em 1927 foram fundados assentamentos como o Colonia Carlos Pelligrini no lago Iberá, que hoje compreende uma reserva natural de 550 000 ha.

Viehwirtschaft

In der Gemeinde San Martín – benannt nach dem berühmten General der Unabhängigkeitskämpfe – gibt es neben Sumpfgebieten große Weideflächen und eine beachtliche Viehwirtschaft. Die Region war früher von der Außenwelt nahezu abgeschnitten. Erst 1927 wurden Siedlungen wie die Colonia Carlos Peligrini am Iberá-See gegründet, die heute ein 550 000 ha großes Naturschutzgebiet umfasst.

Veehouderij

In de gemeente San Martín - vernoemd naar de beroemde generaal van de onafhankelijkheidsstrijd - zijn er naast moerassen ook grote weilanden en een aanzienlijke veehouderij. Vroeger was de regio bijna afgesneden van de buitenwereld. Pas in 1927 werden aan het Iberá meer nederzettingen zoals Colonia Carlos Peligrini gesticht, dat vandaag de dag een natuurreservaat van 550 000 ha omvat.

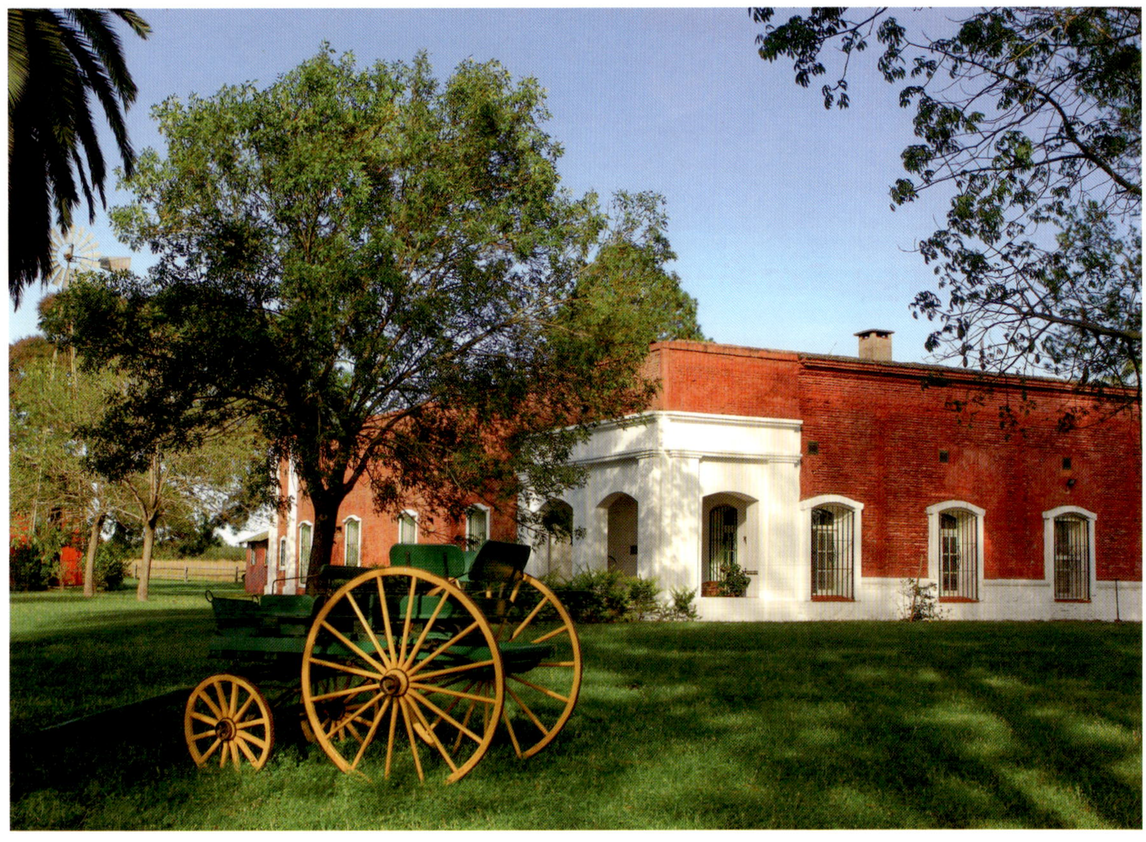

Estancia Yapeyú, Corrientes

Estanzias

In the course of the development of the hinterland, spacious mansions with huge estates were built in the 19th century. Lucrative businesses centered on beef and wool production brought the owners fabulous wealth. An average estancia has 60,000 sheep, 40,000 cattle and 10,000 horses. A 'short ride' from the main house can easily last over 5 hours.

Estancias

Au xixᵉ siècle, la mise en exploitation de l'arrière-pays s'est organisée autour d'immenses demeures à la tête de vastes surfaces agricoles. Le commerce lucratif de la viande de bœuf et de la laine de mouton apporta aux propriétaires une fabuleuse richesse. Une *estancia* moyenne gère 60 000 moutons, 40 000 bovins et 10 000 chevaux. Un petit tour de la propriété à cheval peut facilement nécessiter cinq heures.

Estanzias

Im Zuge der Erschließung des Hinterlands entstanden im 19. Jahrhundert großzügige Herrenhäuser mit riesigen Ländereien. Lukrative Geschäfte mit Rindfleisch und Schafwolle bescherten den Besitzern sagenhaften Reichtum. Eine durchschnittliche Estanzia hat 60 000 Schafe, 40 000 Rinder und 10 000 Pferden. Ein kleiner Ausritt vom Herrenhaus kann sich leicht über 5 Stunden erstrecken.

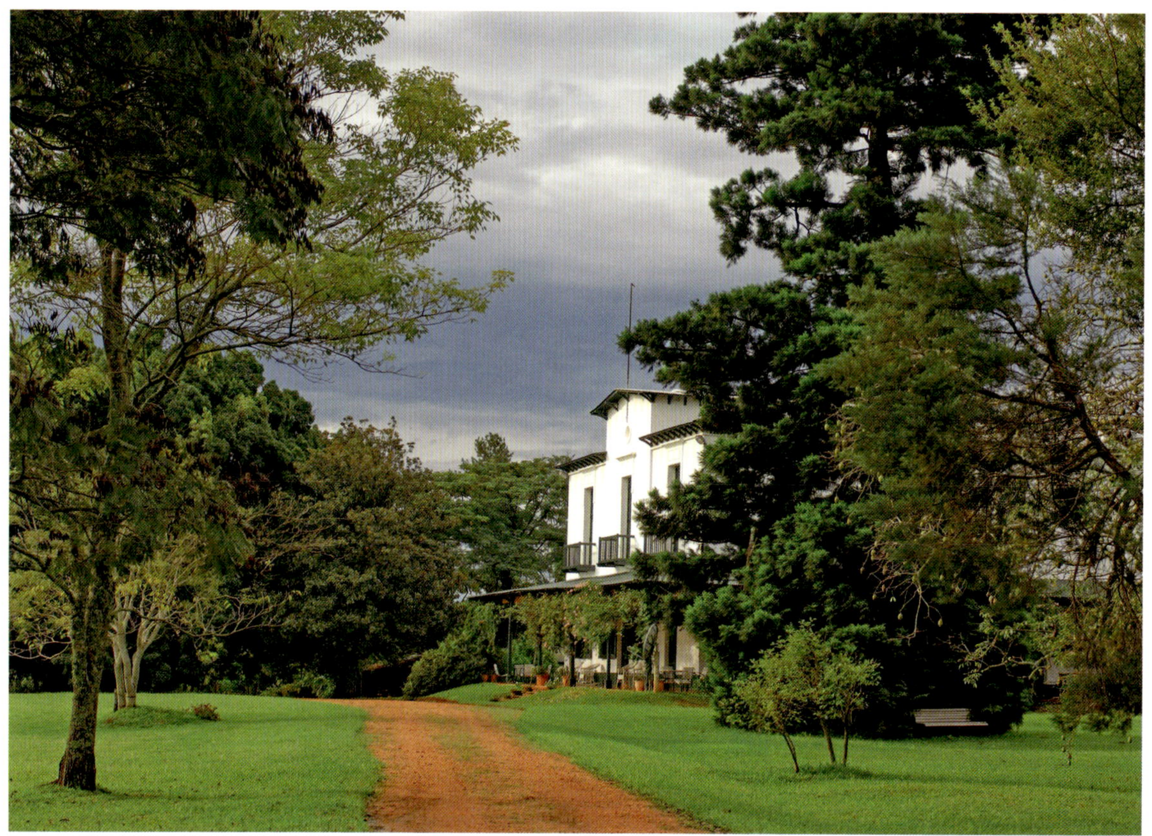

Estancia Santa Cecilia, Misiones

Estancias

Durante el desarrollo del interior, en el siglo XIX se construyeron amplias mansiones con grandes propiedades. Los lucrativos negocios con carne de vacuno y lana de oveja trajeron a los propietarios una fabulosa riqueza. Una estancia media tiene 60 000 ovejas, 40 000 vacas y 10 000 caballos. Un corto viaje desde la casa solariega puede durar 5 horas fácilmente.

Estâncias

No decorrer do desenvolvimento do interior, no século XIX, foram construídas mansões espaçosas com grandes propriedades. Negócios lucrativos com carne de vaca e lã de ovelha trouxeram aos proprietários uma riqueza fabulosa. Uma estância tem em média 60 000 ovelhas, 40 000 bovinos e 10 000 cavalos. Um pequeno passeio desde a casa senhorial pode facilmente durar mais de 5 horas.

Estancias

Naarmate het achterland zich ontwikkelde, ontstonden in de 19e eeuw ruime herenhuizen met enorme landerijen. Lucratieve bedrijven met rundvlees en schapenwol leverden de eigenaren ongelooflijk veel rijkdom op. Een gemiddelde estancia heeft 60 000 schapen, 40 000 runderen en 10 000 paarden. Een korte rit vanaf het landhuis kan gemakkelijk 5 uur duren.

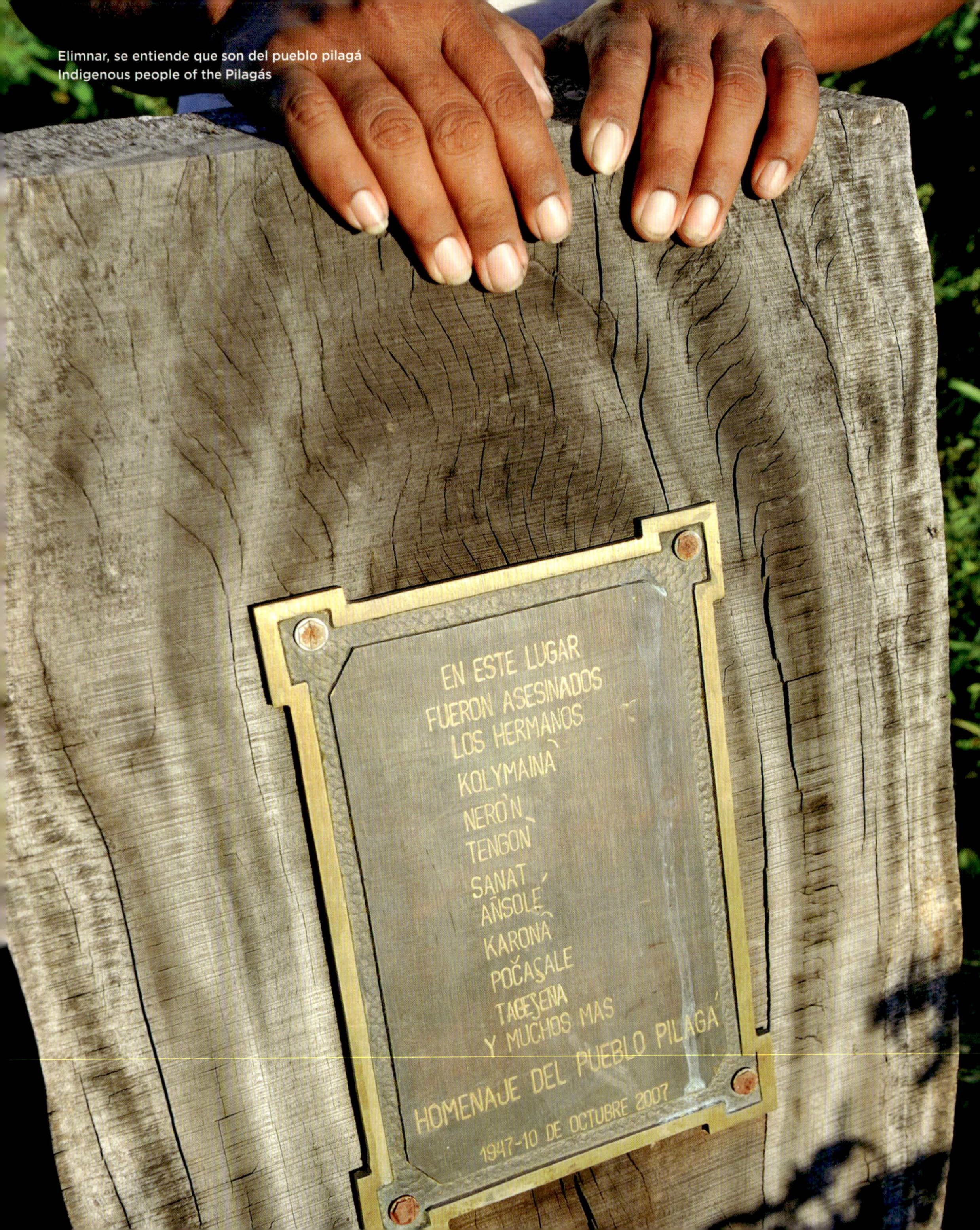

Elimnar, se entiende que son del pueblo pilagá
Indigenous people of the Pilagás
EN ESTE LUGAR
FUERON ASESINADOS
LOS HERMANOS
KOLYMAINA
NERON
TENGON
SANAT
AÑSOLE
KARONA
POCASALE
TAGESENA
Y MUCHOS MAS
HOMENAJE DEL PUEBLO PILAGA
1947-10 DE OCTUBRE 2007

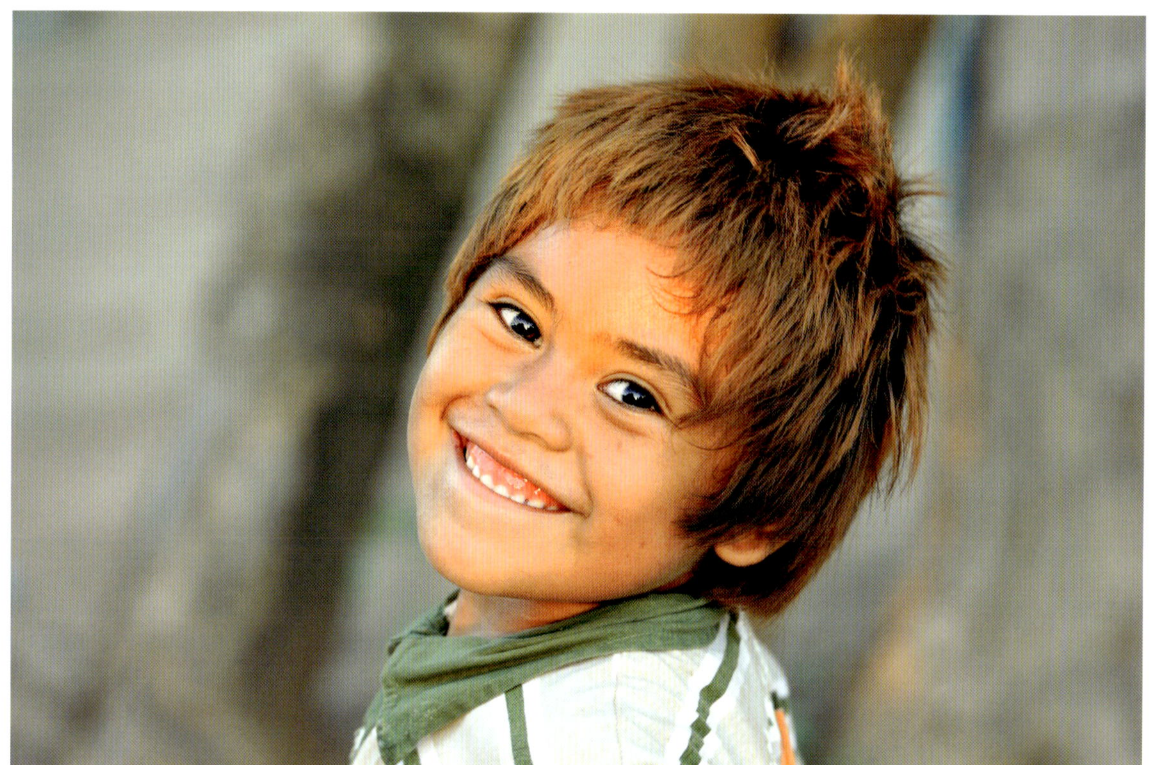

Niño pilagá
Indigenous people of the Pilagás

Pilagás Indians

The indigenous group Pilagás lives in small communities along the Paraguay River. In the 17th century this ethnic group of hunter-gatherers numbered 30,000 people. Their extermination took place during the course of European conquest and Christian conversion, during the 19th and 20th centuries. A monument to the Pilagás in Formosa commemorates the last great massacre in 1947.

Los Pilagás

El pueblo originario pilagá vive en pequeñas comunidades a lo largo del río Paraguay. En el siglo XVII, el grupo étnico contaba con 30 000 personas. Eran cazadores-recolectores. Su exterminio tuvo lugar en el curso de la conquista y la cristianización en los siglos XIX y XX. Un monumento a los Pilagás en Formosa conmemora la última gran masacre de 1947.

Les Indiens pilagás

Les Pilagás vivent dans de petites communautés sur les rives de la rivière Paraguay. Au xviiᵉ siècle, la population comptait 30 000 individus. Ils étaient chasseurs-cueilleurs mais furent décimés au cours des épisodes d'appropriation des terres et de christianisation aux xixᵉ et xxᵉ siècles. Un monument à Formosa rappelle le dernier grand massacre perpétré contre les Pilagás en 1947.

Índios Pilagás

O grupo indígena Pilagás vive em pequenas comunidades ao longo do rio Paraguai. No século XVII, o grupo étnico contava com 30 000 pessoas. Eles eram caçadores-colectores. O seu extermínio ocorreu no decurso da conquista e da cristianização nos séculos XIX e XX. Um monumento aos Pilagás em Formosa recorda o último grande massacre de 1947.

Pilagás-Indianer

Die indigene Gruppe Pilagás lebt in kleinen Gemeinden am Paraguay-Fluss. Im 17. Jahrhundert zählte die Volksgruppe 30 000 Menschen. Sie waren Jäger und Sammler. Ihre Ausrottung fand im Zuge der Eroberung und Christianisierung im 19. und 20. Jahrhundert statt. Ein Denkmal für die Pilagás in Formosa erinnert an das letzte große Massaker von 1947.

Pilagás indianen

De inheemse groep Pilagás leeft in kleine gemeenschappen langs de Paraguay rivier. In de 17e eeuw telde de nationale minderheid 30 000 mensen. Het waren jagers en verzamelaars. Hun uitroeiing vond plaats in de loop van de verovering en de kerstening in de 19e en 20e eeuw. Een monument voor de Pilagás in Formosa herdenkt het laatste grote bloedbad van 1947.

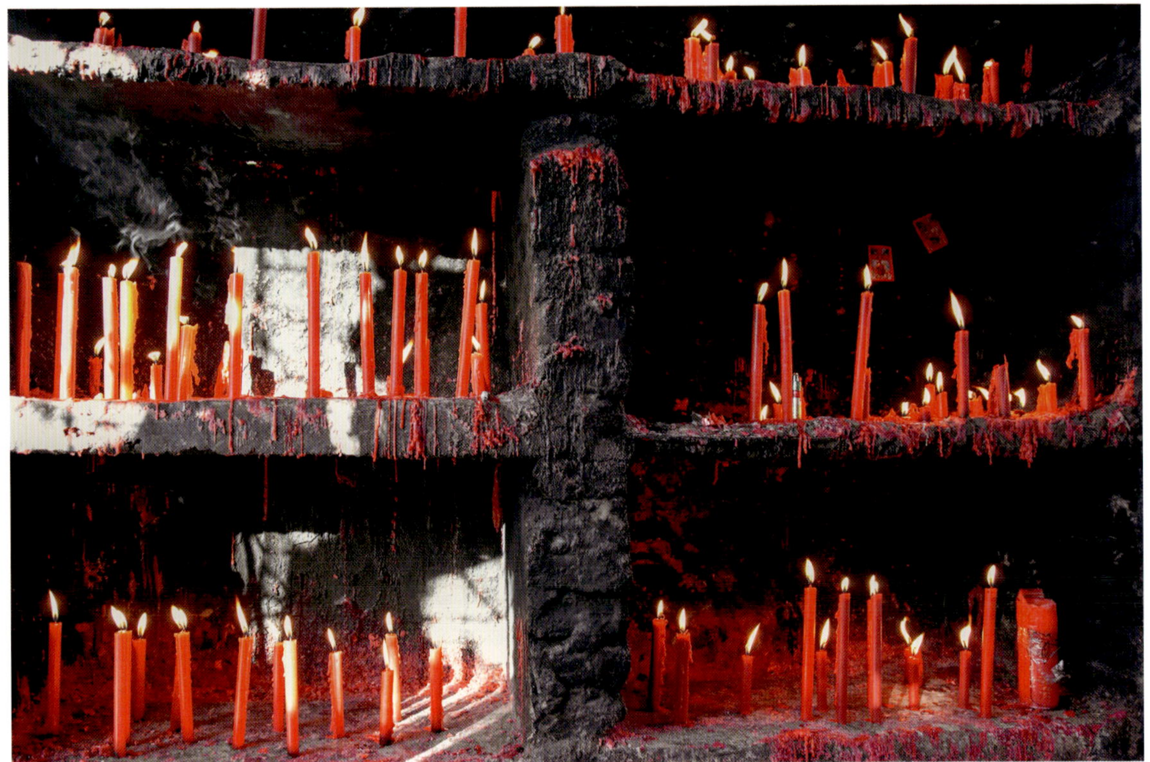

Altar para el Gauchito Gil
Altar for Gauchito Gil

The Legend of the Little Gaucho Gil

A legend circulates about the adventures of the Gauchito Gil. It centers upon the historical figure of Gaucho Antonio Plutarco Cruz Mamerto Gil Núñez, who was born in the 1840s in Mercedes and was executed there in 1878. With a group of like-minded people he traveled the land, robbing the rich and giving presents to the poor. Gauchito Gil is revered like a saint.

La leyenda del Gaucho Gil

Una leyenda circula sobre las aventuras del Gauchito Gil. Se entrelaza en torno a la figura histórica del Gaucho Antonio Plutarco Cruz Mamerto Gil Núñez, que nació en Mercedes en la década de 1840 y fue ejecutado allí en 1878. Con un grupo de personas de ideas afines fue por tierra, robó a los ricos y dio regalos a los pobres. El Gauchito Gil es venerado como un santo.

La légende du Gauchito Gil

Une légende raconte les aventures du Gauchito Gil. Elle s'est développée autour de la figure historique du *gaucho* Antonio Plutarco Cruz Mamerto Gil Núñez, qui est né à Mercedes dans les années 1840 et y a été exécuté en 1878. Accompagné d'un groupe d'hommes animés des mêmes valeurs, il parcourait le pays et volait les riches pour donner aux pauvres. Gauchito Gil est honoré comme un saint.

A Lenda do Pequeno Gaucho Gil

Uma lenda que circula sobre as aventuras do Gaucho Gil. Ela conta sobre a figura histórica do gaúcho Antonio Plutarco Cruz Mamerto Gil Núñez, que nasceu na Mercedes na década de 1840 e lá foi executado em 1878. Com um grupo de pessoas com os mesmos interesses, ele foi por terra, roubando os ricos e dando presentes aos pobres. Gaucho Gil é venerado como um santo.

Die Legende des Kleinen Gaucho Gil

Über die Abenteuer des Gauchito Gil kursiert eine Legende. Sie rankt um die historische Figur des Gaucho Antonio Plutarco Cruz Mamerto Gil Núñez, der in den 1840er Jahren in Mercedes geboren und dort 1878 hingerichtet wurde. Mit einer Gruppe Gleichgesinnter zog er über Land, raubte die Reichen aus und beschenkte die Armen. Gauchito Gil wird wie ein Heiliger verehrt.

De legende van de kleine Gaucho Gil

Er doet een legende de ronde over de avonturen van Gauchito Gil. Het gaat om de historische figuur Gaucho Antonio Plutarco Cruz Mamerto Gil Núñez, die in de jaren 1840 in Mercedes werd geboren en daar in 1878 werd geëxecuteerd. Met een groep gelijkgestemden trok hij door het land, beroofde de rijken en gaf cadeautjes aan de armen. Gauchito Gil wordt vereerd als een heilige.

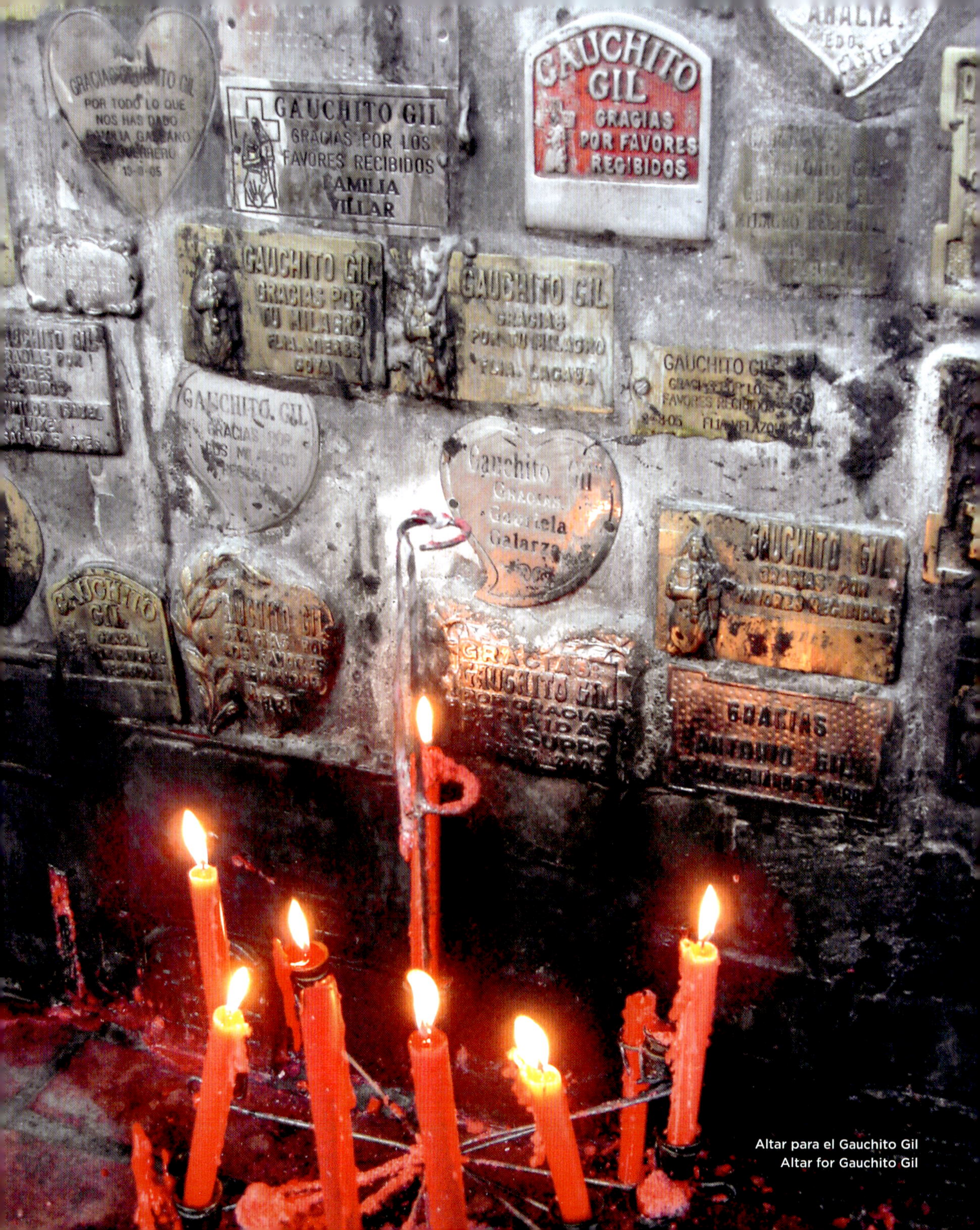

Altar para el Gauchito Gil
Altar for Gauchito Gil

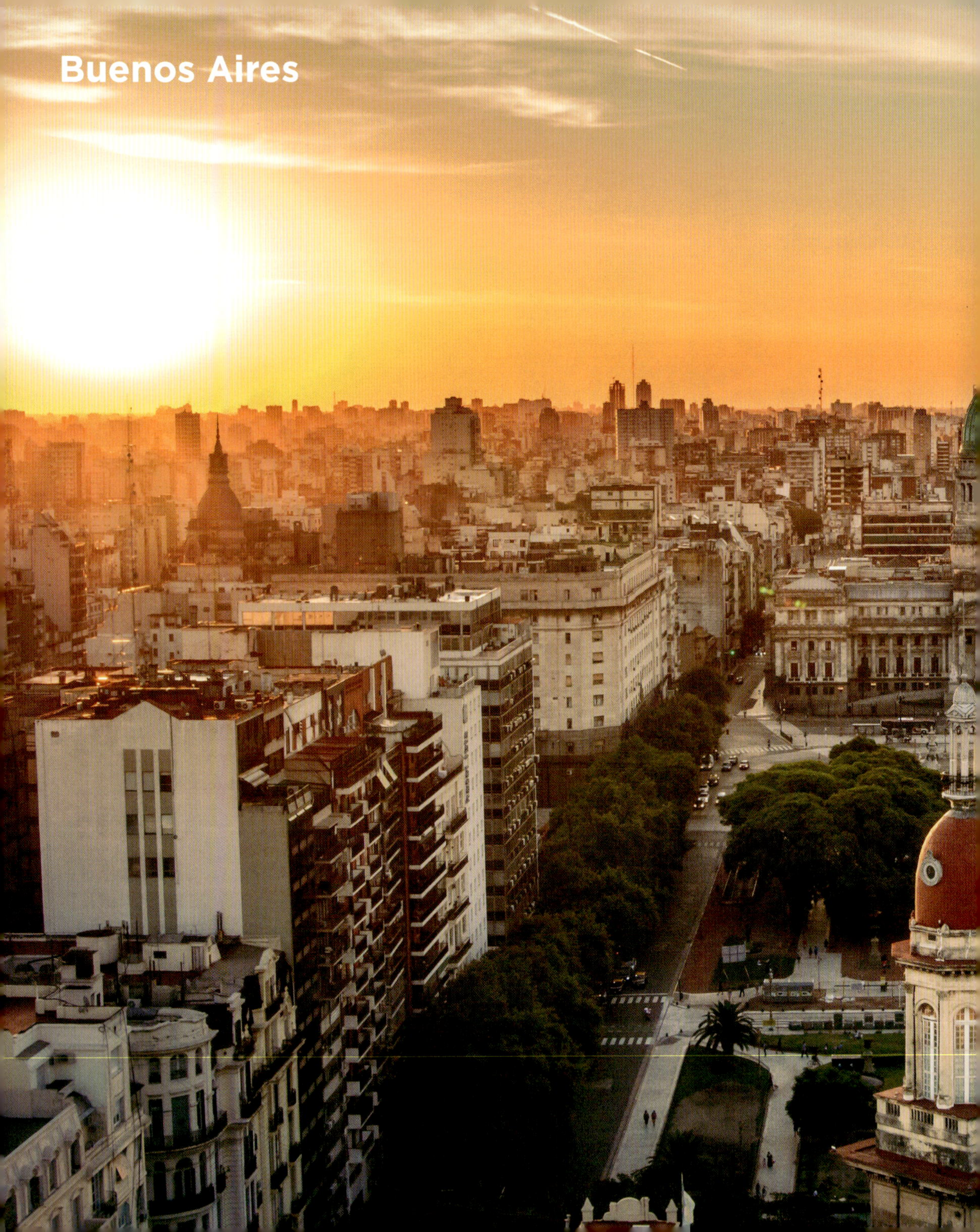
Buenos Aires

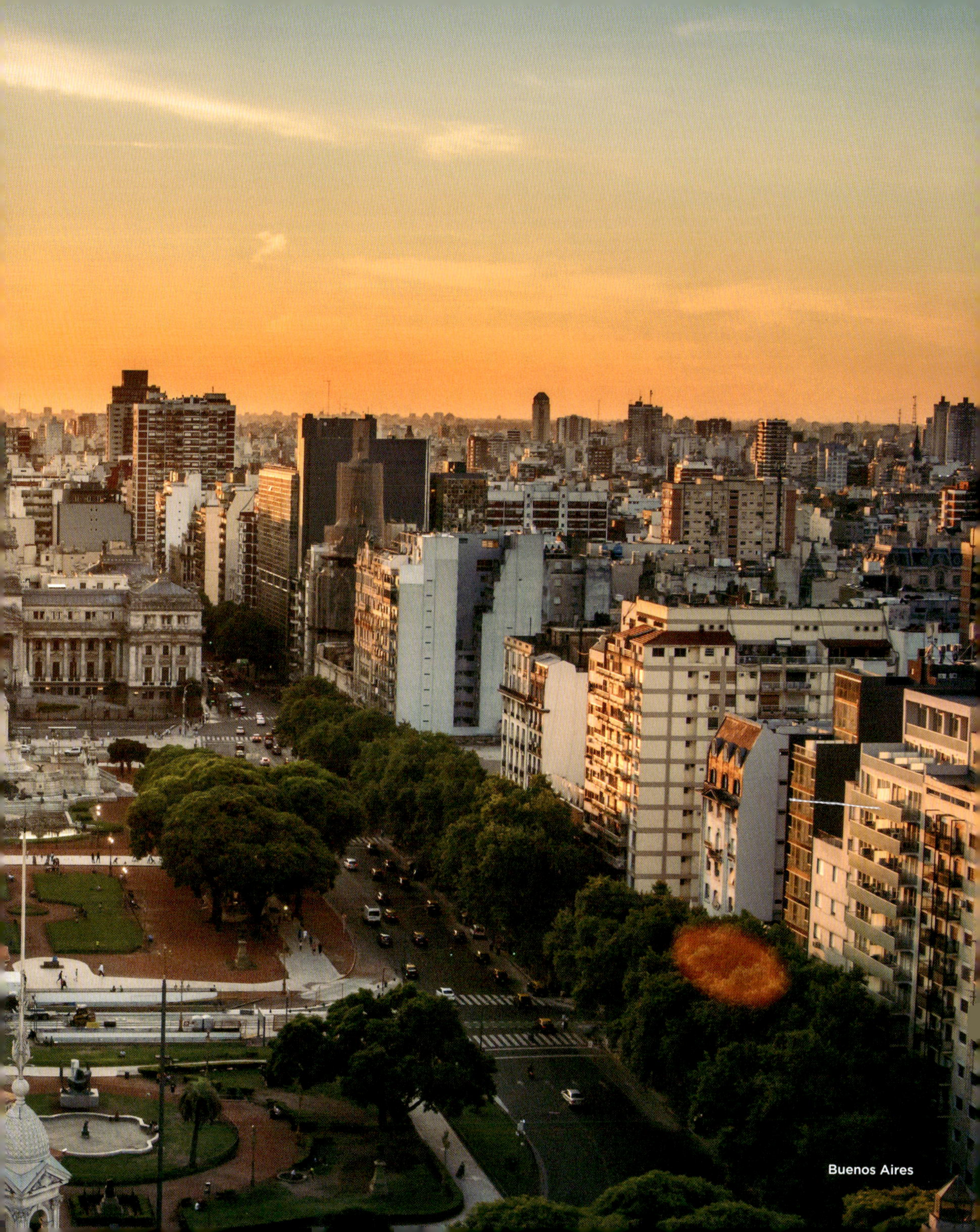
Buenos Aires

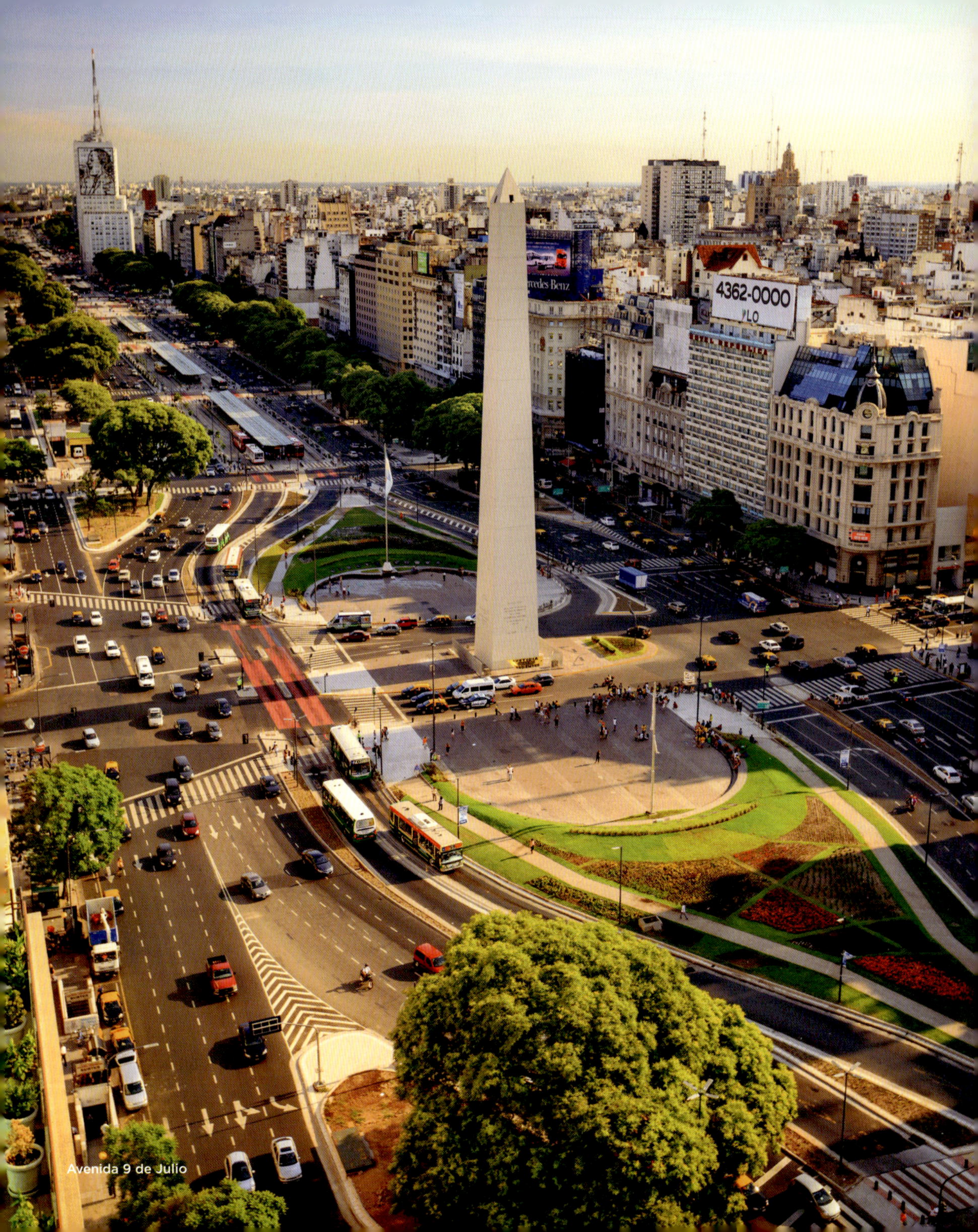

Avenida 9 de Julio

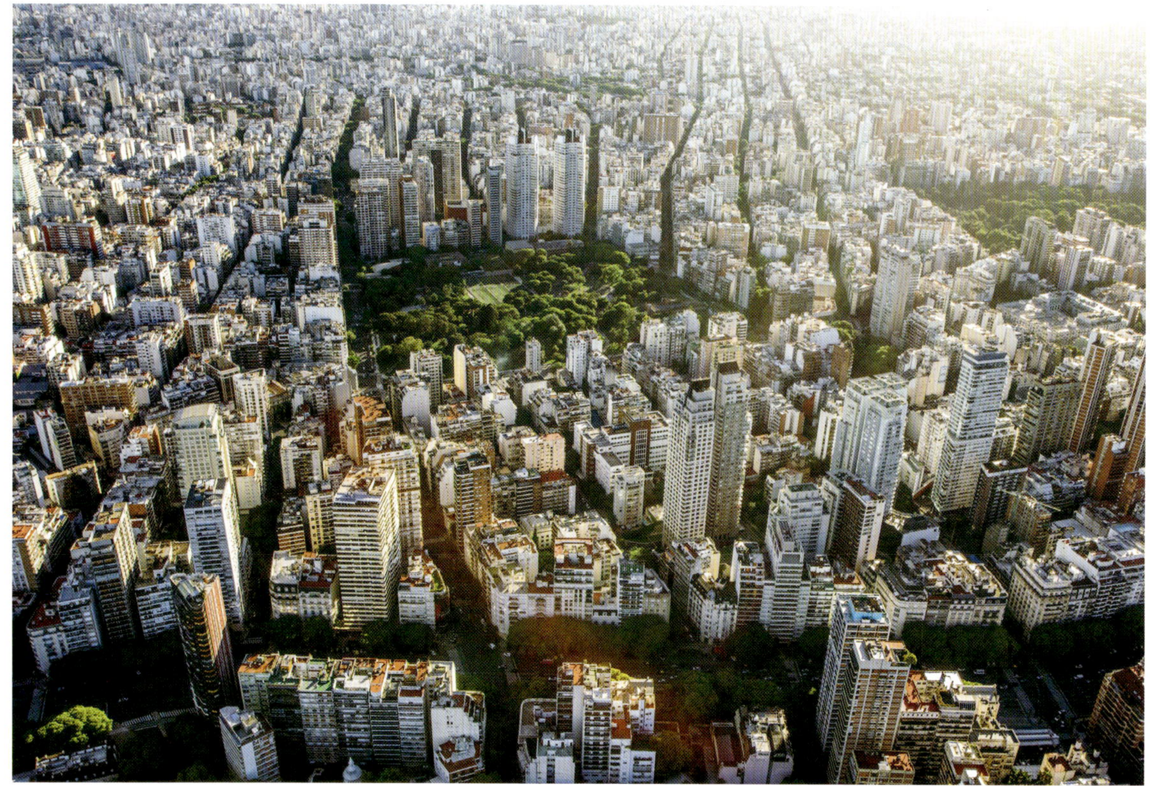

Palermo, Buenos Aires

Buenos Aires

Buenos Aires was not chosen as the capital until 1861, after the first settlements on the coastal strip of the Rio de la Plata had all failed. The port city achieved a great boom thanks to the meat industry and its railway connections to the pampas. In the early 20th century, Buenos Aires was considered the largest, richest and most modern city in Latin America.

Buenos Aires

Buenos Aires no fue elegida capital hasta 1861, ya que los primeros asentamientos en la franja costera del Río de la Plata habían fracasado. La ciudad portuaria alcanzó un gran auge gracias a la industria cárnica y a la conexión ferroviaria con La Pampa. En el siglo XX, Buenos Aires fue considerada la ciudad más grande, rica y moderna de América Latina.

Buenos Aires

Buenos Aires a été désignée capitale nationale en 1861, après l'échec des premières colonies installées sur les rives du río de la Plata. La ville portuaire a connu un formidable essor grâce à l'industrie de la viande et à la liaison ferroviaire traversant la pampa. Au xxᵉ siècle, Buenos Aires était considérée comme la ville la plus grande, la plus riche et la plus moderne d'Amérique latine.

Buenos Aires

Buenos Aires só foi escolhida como capital em 1861, pois os primeiros assentamentos na faixa costeira do Rio de la Plata haviam fracassado. A cidade portuária alcançou um grande boom graças à indústria de carne e à conexão ferroviária com os pampas. No século XX, Buenos Aires foi considerada a maior, mais rica e mais moderna cidade da América Latina.

Buenos Aires

Zur Hauptstadt wurde Buenos Aires erst 1861 gekürt, denn die ersten Siedlungen am Küstenstreifen des Rio de la Plata waren allesamt gescheitert. Der Hafenstadt gelang der große Aufschwung dank der Fleischindustrie und der Eisenbahnverbindung in die Pampa. Im 20. Jahrhundert galt Buenos Aires als die größte, reichste und modernste Stadt Lateinamerikas.

Buenos Aires

Buenos Aires werd pas in 1861 als hoofdstad gekozen, omdat de eerste nederzettingen op de kuststrook van de Rio de la Plata allemaal waren mislukt. Dankzij de vleesindustrie en de spoorverbinding naar de pampa kende de havenstad een grote bloei. In de 20e eeuw gold Buenos Aires als de grootste, rijkste en modernste stad van Latijns-Amerika.

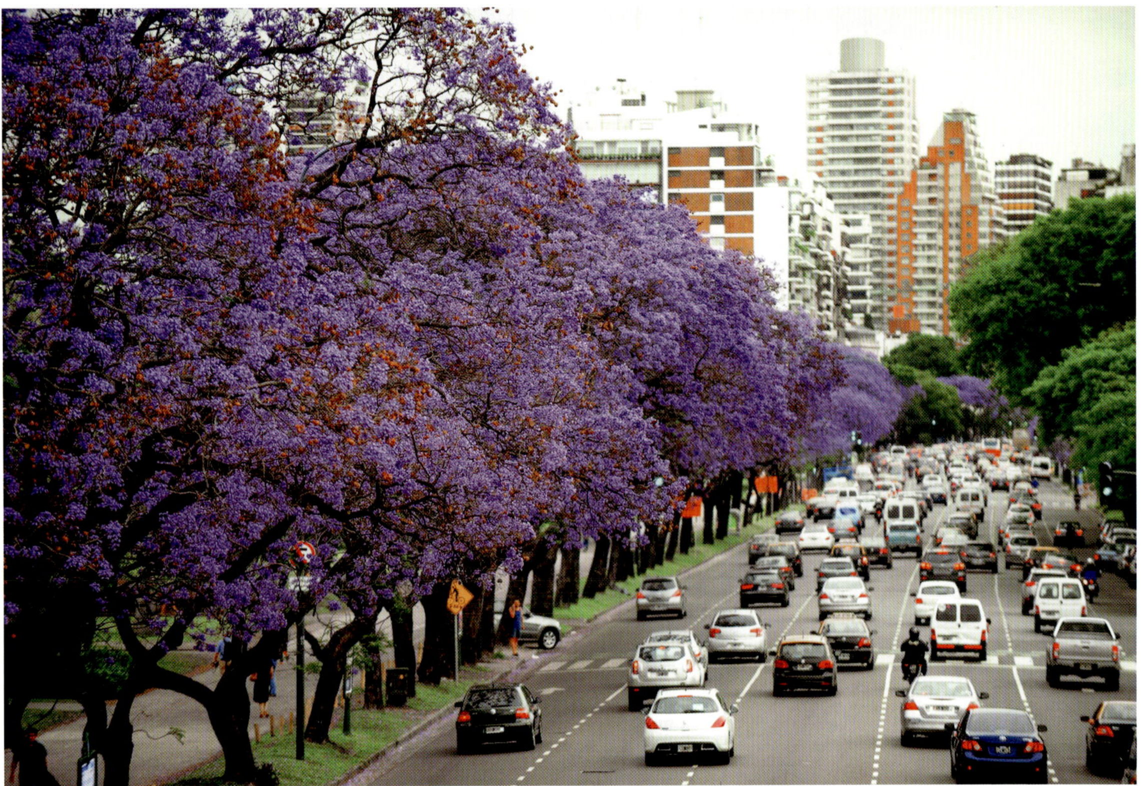

Buenos Aires

Symbols of the city

Characteristic for the capital are wide avenues with shady, flowering trees. At the Plaza de Mayo there is the Casa Rosada, the presidential palace. Its pink color symbolizes the unity of Argentina. From the balcony of the palace, the country's presidents traditionally address the people with grand gestures and speeches.

Símbolos de la ciudad

La capital se caracteriza por sus amplias avenidas con árboles sombreados y florecientes. En la Plaza de Mayo se encuentra la Casa Rosada, el palacio presidencial. Su color rosado simboliza la unidad de Argentina. Desde el balcón del palacio, los presidentes del país tradicionalmente se dirigen al pueblo con grandes gestos y discursos.

Les symboles de la ville

La capitale est traversée par de larges avenues caractéristiques, bordées d'arbres qui y projettent leur ombre et se couvrent de fleurs au printemps. Sur la Plaza de Mayo trône la Casa Rosada, le palais présidentiel. Sa couleur rose symbolise l'unité de l'Argentine. Depuis son balcon, les présidents s'adressent traditionnellement à la population avec force gestes et discours.

Símbolos da cidade

As características da capital são avenidas largas com árvores sombreadas e floridas. Na Plaza de Mayo fica a Casa Rosada, o palácio presidencial. A sua cor rosa simboliza a unidade da Argentina. Da varanda do palácio, os presidentes do país dirigem-se tradicionalmente ao povo com grandes gestos e discursos.

Symbole der Stadt

Charakteristisch für die Hauptstadt sind breite Alleen mit schattenspendenden, blühenden Bäumen. An der Plaza de Mayo steht die Casa rosada, der Präsidentenpalast. Seine rosa Farbe symbolisiert die Einheit Argentiniens. Vom Balkon des Palasts wenden sich traditionell die Präsidenten des Landes mit großen Gesten und Reden an das Volk.

Symbolen van de stad

Karakteristiek voor de hoofdstad zijn de brede alleeën met schaduwrijke, bloeiende bomen. Op de Plaza de Mayo staat het Casa rosada, het presidentiële paleis. Zijn roze kleur symboliseert de eenheid van Argentinië. Vanaf het balkon van het paleis richten de presidenten van het land zich traditioneel met grote gebaren en toespraken tot het volk.

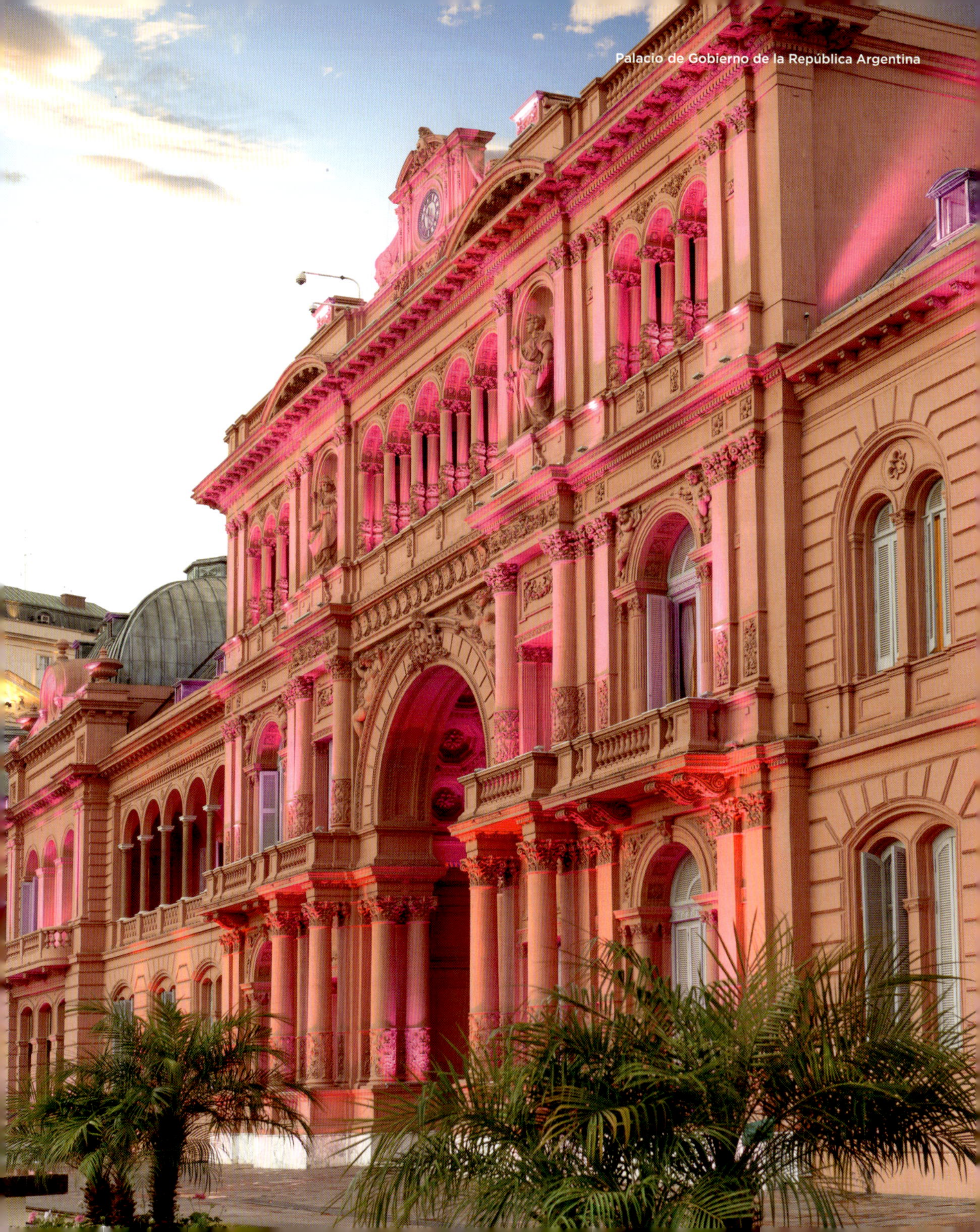
Palacio de Gobierno de la República Argentina

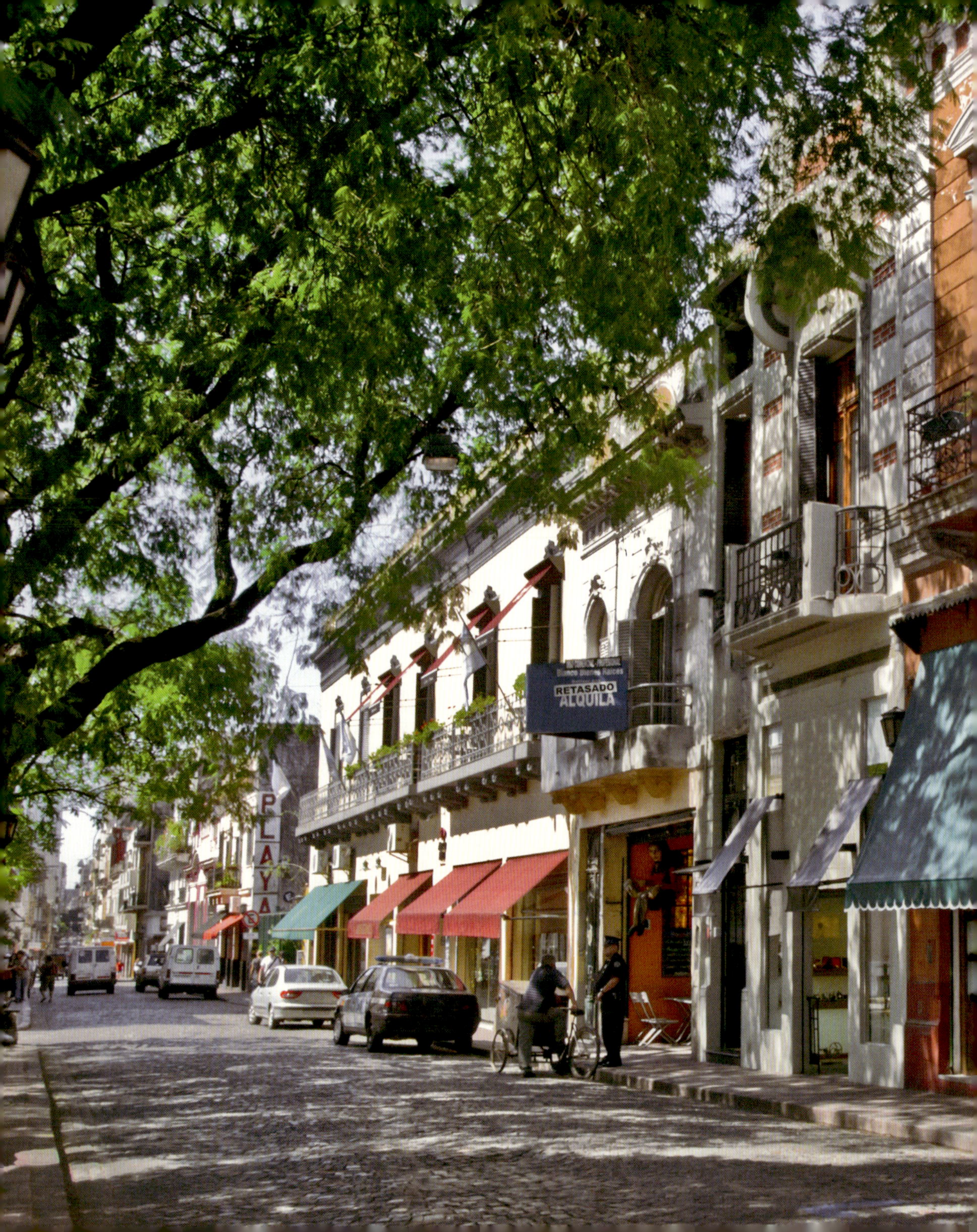

RETASADO
ALQUILA
PLAYA

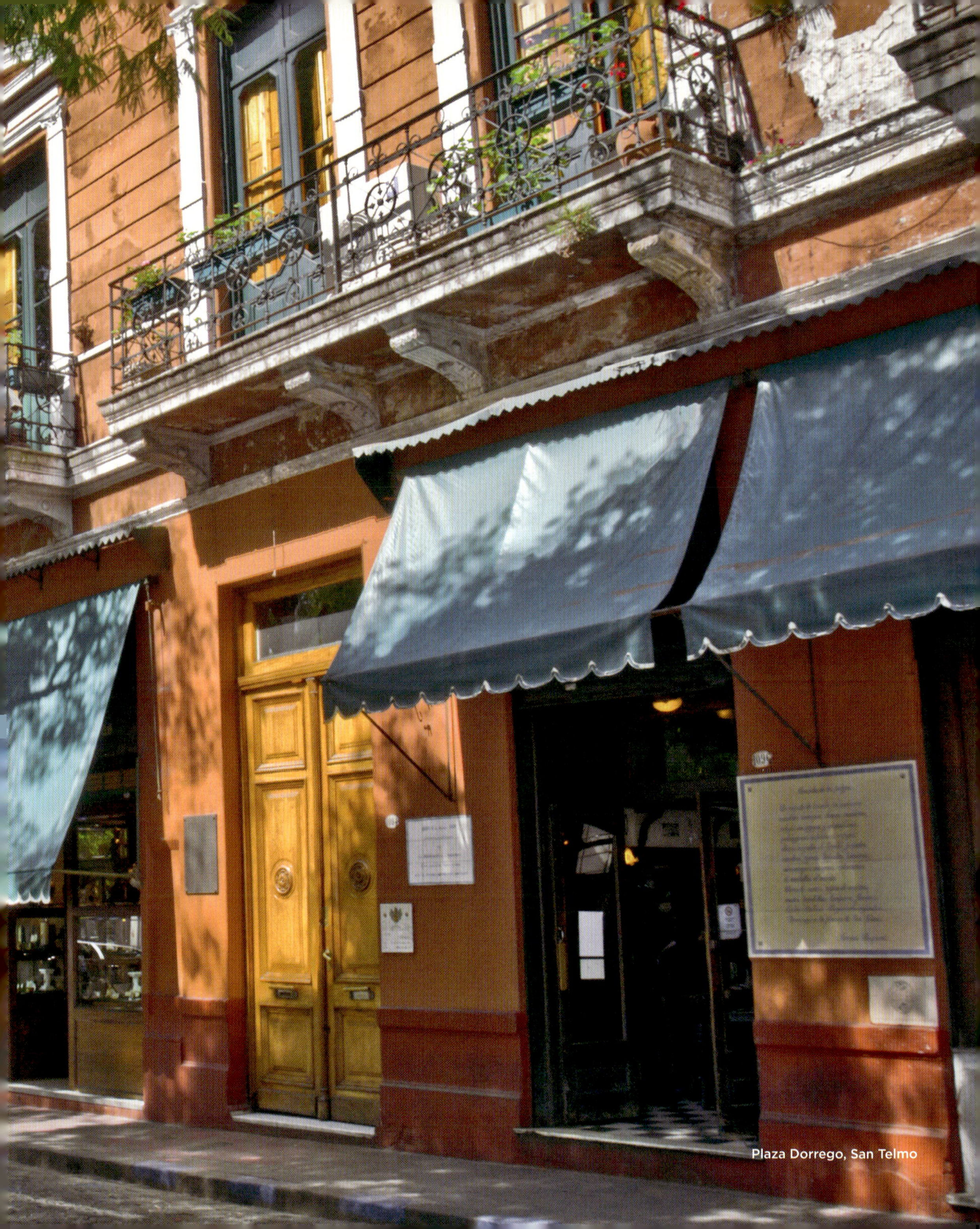

Plaza Dorrego, San Telmo

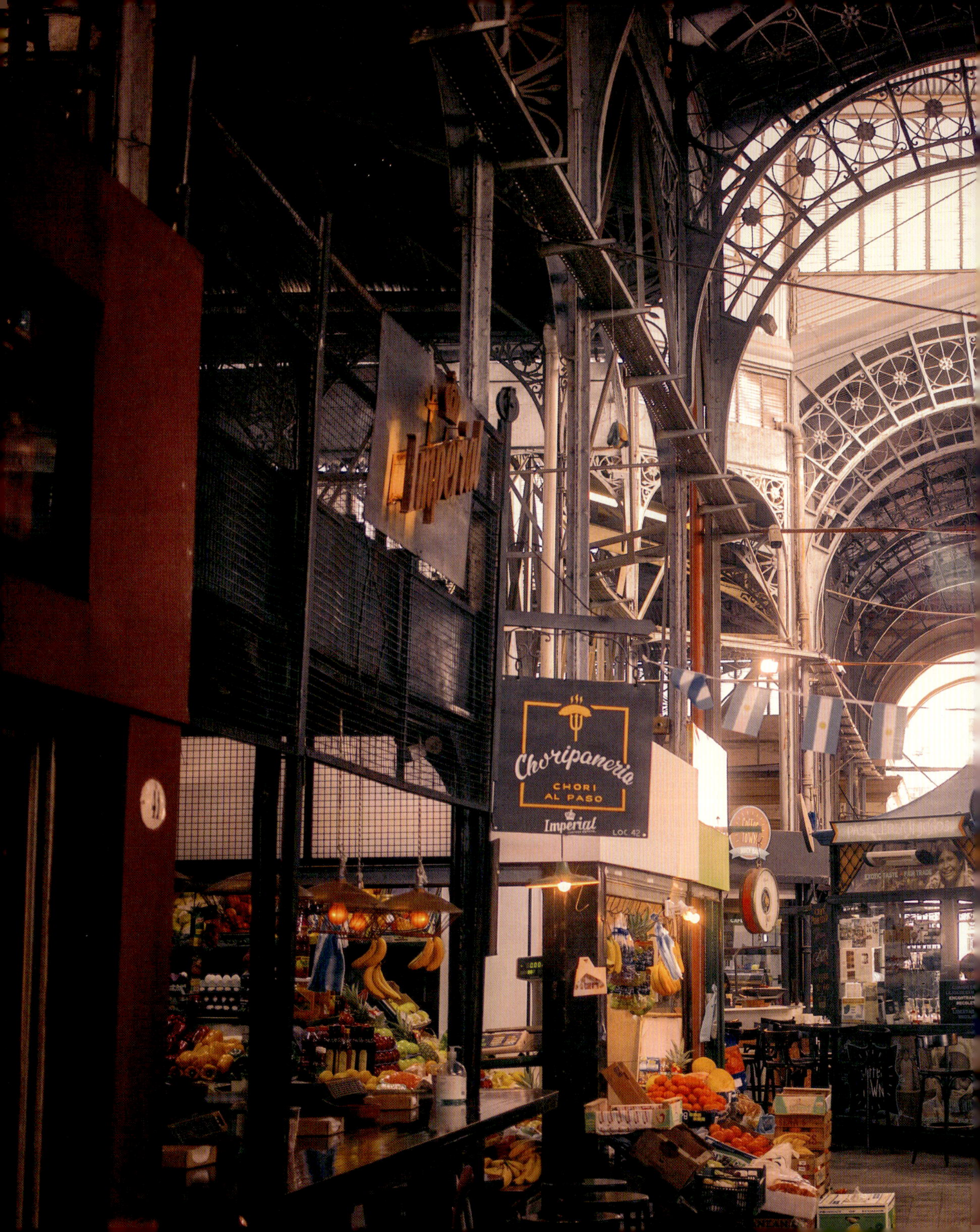
Imperial
Choripanería
CHORI
AL PASO
Imperial
LOC. 42

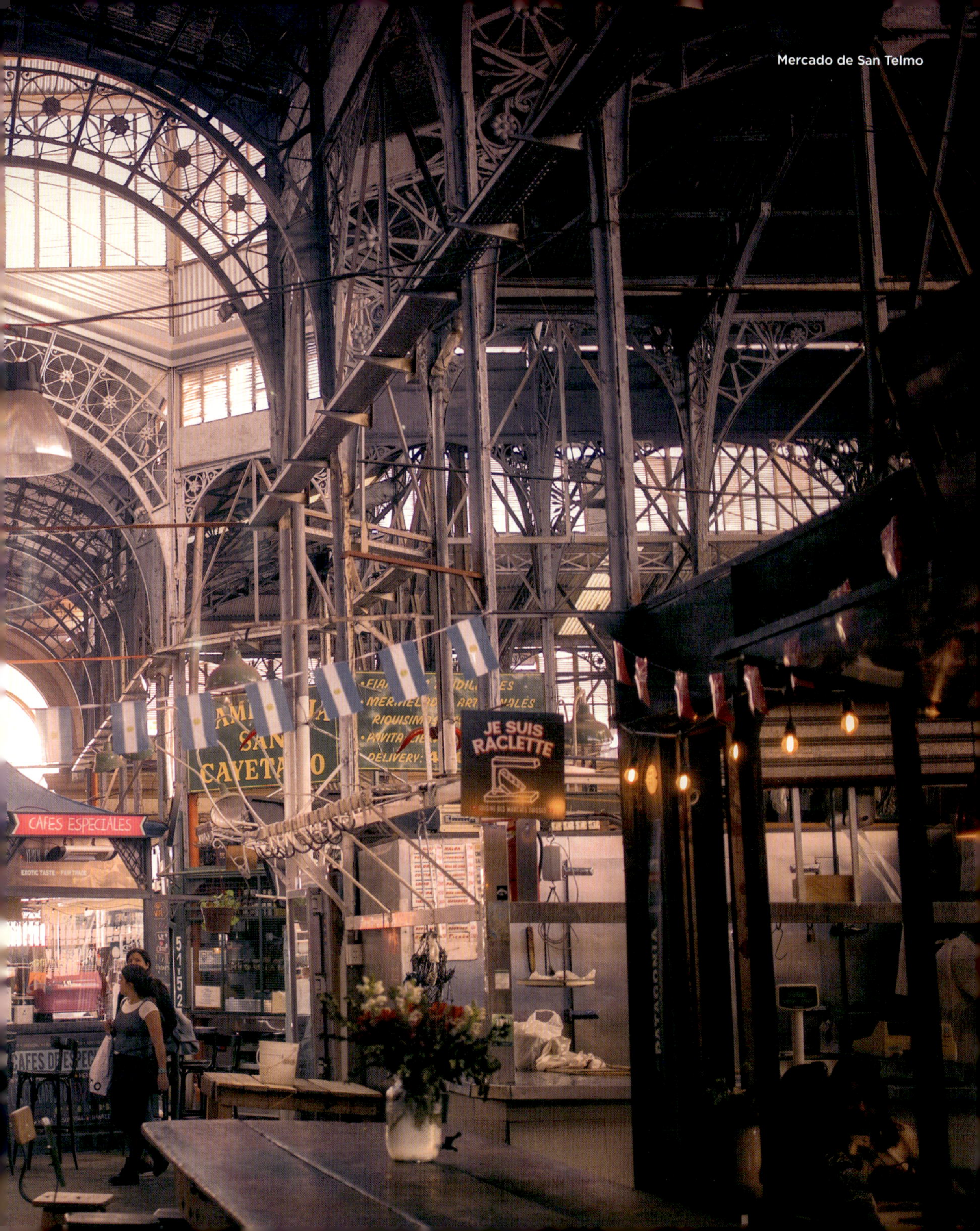
Mercado de San Telmo
CAFES ESPECIALES
EXOTIC TASTE · FAIR TRADE
SAN CAYETANO
MERMELADAS ARTESANALES
RIQUISIMOS
DELIVERY:
JE SUIS RACLETTE
5152

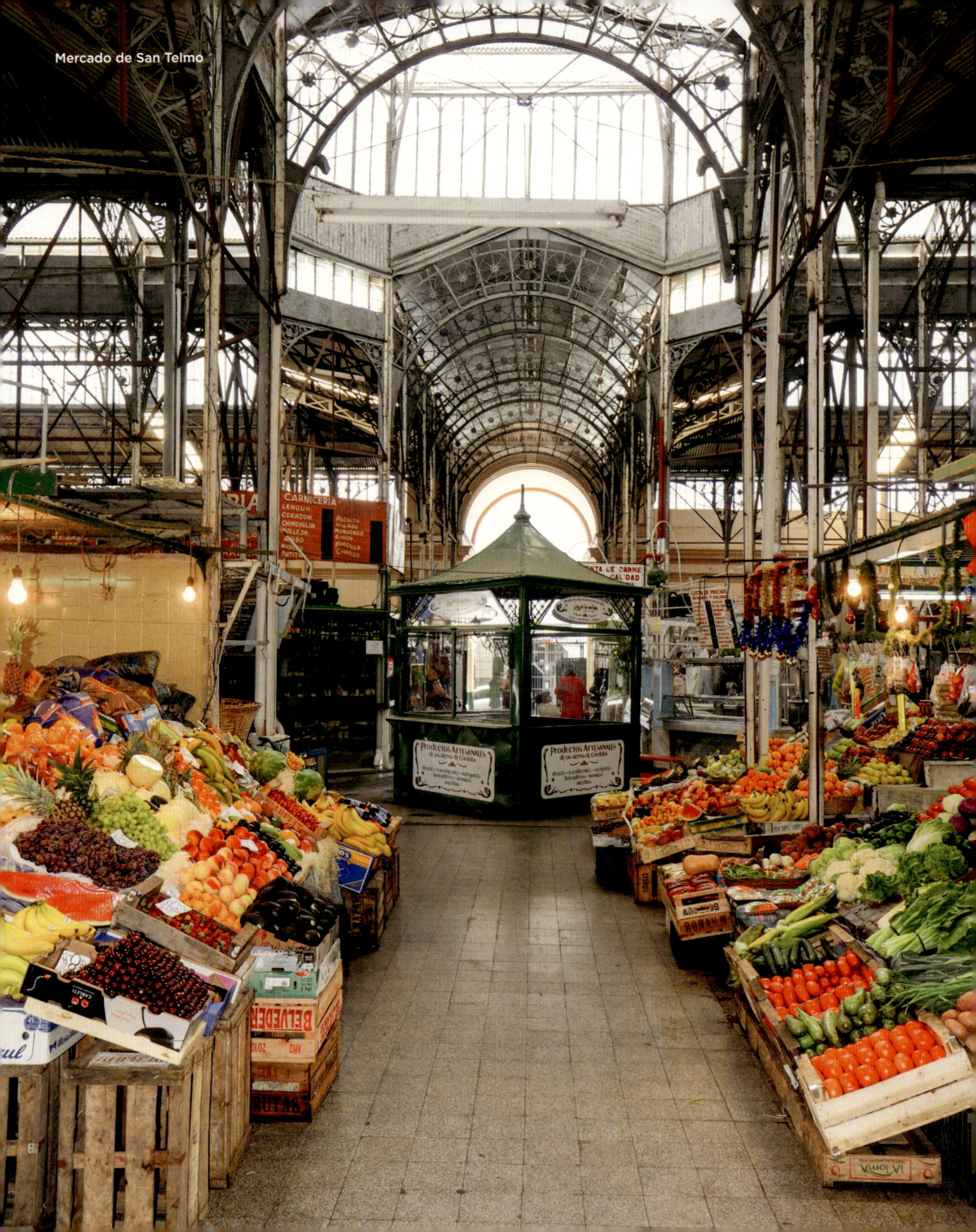

Mercado de San Telmo

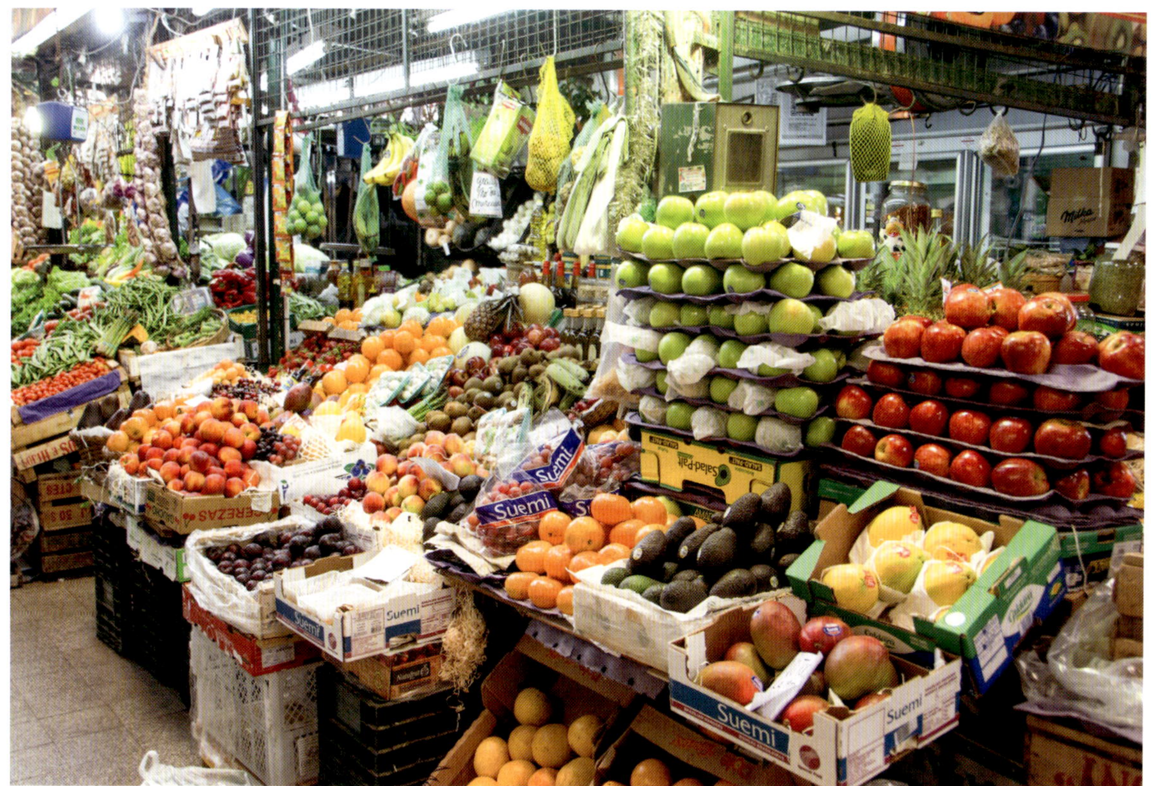

Mercado de San Telmo

San Telmo

The Plaza Dorrego is historically the centre of this quarter. Once the square was a traffic junction. In 1897 the Italian architect Juan Antonio Buschiazzo built the wonderful market hall, which is made of iron, with glass structures inside. Today, traders in the historic halls offer fruit and vegetables as well as antiques and souvenirs.

San Telmo

La Plaza Dorrego es históricamente el centro del barrio. En su día, la plaza fue un cruce de tráfico. En 1897 el arquitecto italiano Juan A. Buschiazzo construyó el maravilloso mercado cubierto, que está hecho de estructuras de hierro y vidrio en su interior. Hoy en día, los comerciantes de las salas históricas ofrecen tanto frutas y verduras como antigüedades y recuerdos.

San Telmo

La Plaza Dorrego constitue historiquement le cœur du quartier. Elle était autrefois un important lieu de convergence des voies de circulation. En 1897, l'architecte italien Juan A. Buschiazzo y bâtit une magnifique halle de marché, arborant une structure interne d'acier et de verre. Aujourd'hui, les marchands installés dans la halle historique proposent, outre des fruits et des légumes, des antiquités et des souvenirs.

San Telmo

A Plaza Dorrego é, historicamente, o centro do bairro. A praça já foi um cruzamento de tráfego. Em 1897, o arquiteto italiano Juan A. Buschiazzo construiu o maravilhoso mercado, que é feito de estruturas de ferro e vidro no seu interior. Hoje, os comerciantes nos pavilhões históricos são somente frutas e legumes, mas também antiguidades e lembranças.

San Telmo

Die Plaza Dorrego bildet historisch den Mittelpunkt des Viertels. Einst war der Platz Verkehrsknotenpunkt. 1897 baute der italienische Architekt Juan A. Buschiazzo die wunderbare Markthalle, die innen aus Eisen- und Glaskonstruktionen besteht. Heute bieten Händler in den historischen Hallen neben Obst- und Gemüses auch Antiquitäten und Souvenirs an.

San Telmo

De Plaza Dorrego is historisch gezien het centrum van de wijk. Ooit was het plein een verkeersknooppunt. In 1897 bouwde de Italiaanse architect Juan A. Buschiazzo de prachtige markthal, die binnenin uit ijzeren en glazen constructies bestaat. Vandaag de dag bieden de handelaren in de historische hallen naast groente en fruit ook antiquiteiten en souvenirs aan.

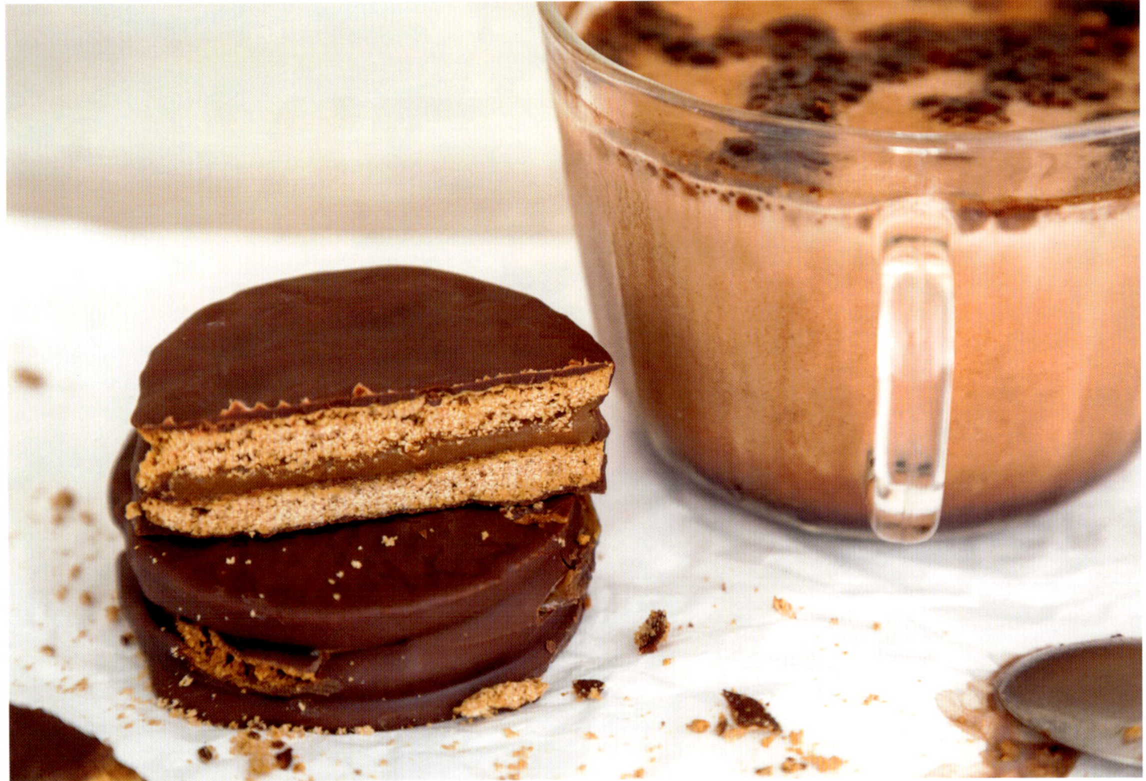

Alfajores

Sweets with coffee

Alfajores are classic cookies filled with caramel and usually decorated with chocolate icing. Next to mate, coffee is the everyday drink which is consumed between meals, as in Italy or Spain. This habit was introduced by the many Italian and Spanish immigrants who came to the country in the 19th century.

Dulces con café

Un clásico de la repostería son los alfajores, galletas rellenas de dulce, que normalmente van decoradas con glaseado de chocolate. Junto al mate, el café es la bebida cotidiana que se consume entre comidas, como en Italia o España. Este hábito fue introducido por los numerosos inmigrantes italianos y españoles que llegaron al país en el siglo XIX.

Sucreries pour le café

Les *alfajores* sont des pâtisseries traditionnelles. Ce sont des biscuits fourrés de caramel et souvent recouverts d'un glaçage au chocolat. Le café, tout comme le maté, est une boisson courante que l'on consomme à tout moment, comme en Italie ou en Espagne. L'habitude fut en effet importée par les émigrés italiens et espagnols qui s'installèrent dans le pays au xixe siècle.

Especiarias para café

Uma massa clássica são alfajores, bolachas recheadas com caramelo e normalmente decoradas com cobertura de chocolate. Ao lado do mate, o café é a bebida diária que se consome entre as refeições, como na Itália ou na Espanha. O hábito foi introduzido pelos muitos imigrantes italianos e espanhóis que vieram para o país no século XIX.

Süßes zum Kaffee

Ein klassisches Gebäck sind Alfajores, mit Karamell gefüllte und meist mit Schokoguss verzierte Kekse. Kaffee ist neben Mate das Alltagsgetränk, das wie in Italien oder Spanien zwischendurch konsumiert wird. Der Habitus wurde von den vielen italienischen und spanischen Einwanderern eingeführt, die im 19. Jahrhundert ins Land kamen.

Iets zoetigs bij de koffie

Een klassiek koekjes zijn de alfajores, gevuld met karamel en meestal versierd met een laagje chocolade. Koffie is naar mate de alledaagse drank die net als in Italië of Spanje tussendoor wordt geconsumeerd. Deze gewoonte werd door de vele Italiaanse en Spaanse immigranten geïntroduceerd, die in de 19e eeuw naar het land kwamen.

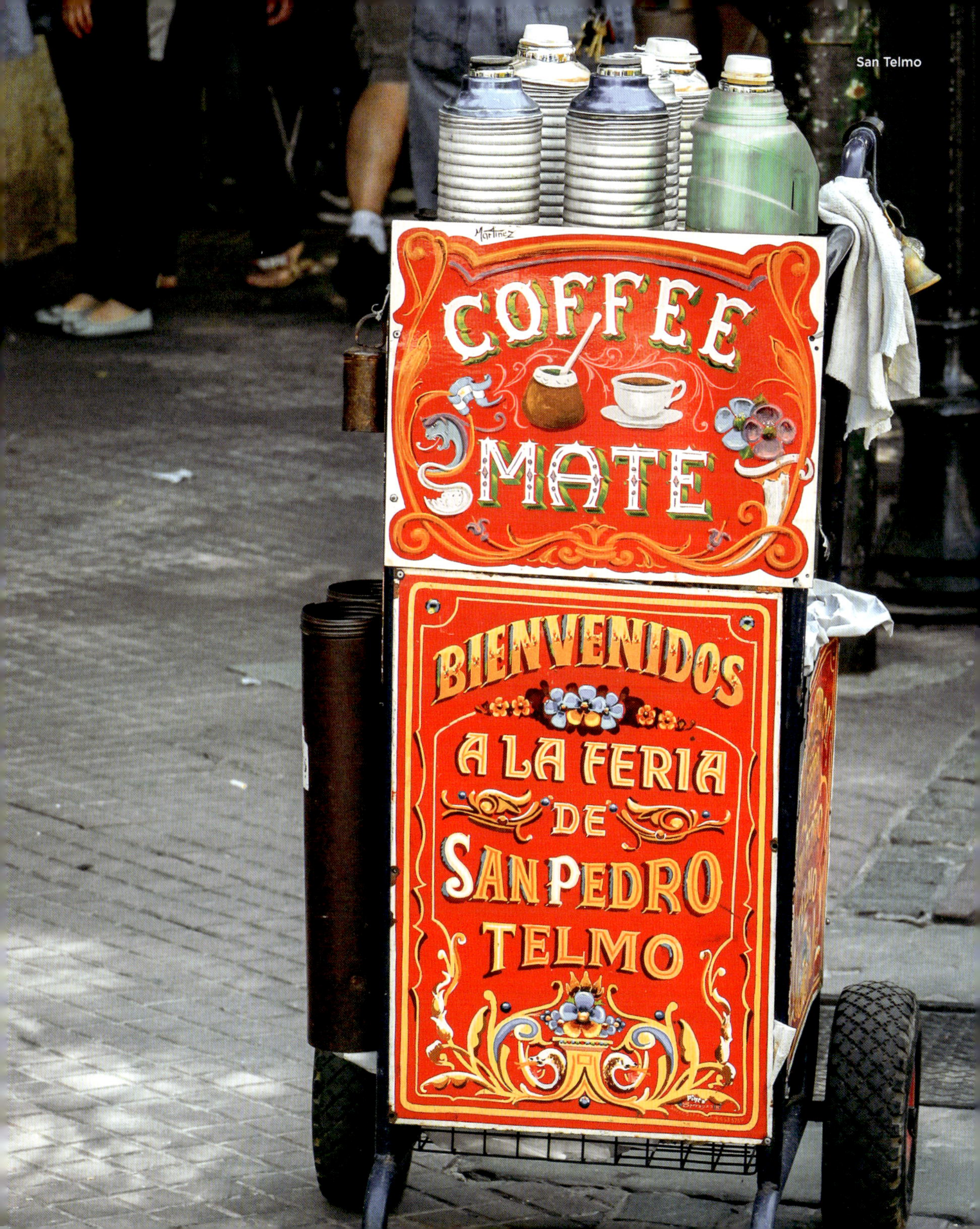

Martinez
COFFEE
MATE
BIENVENIDOS
A LA FERIA
DE
SAN PEDRO
TELMO

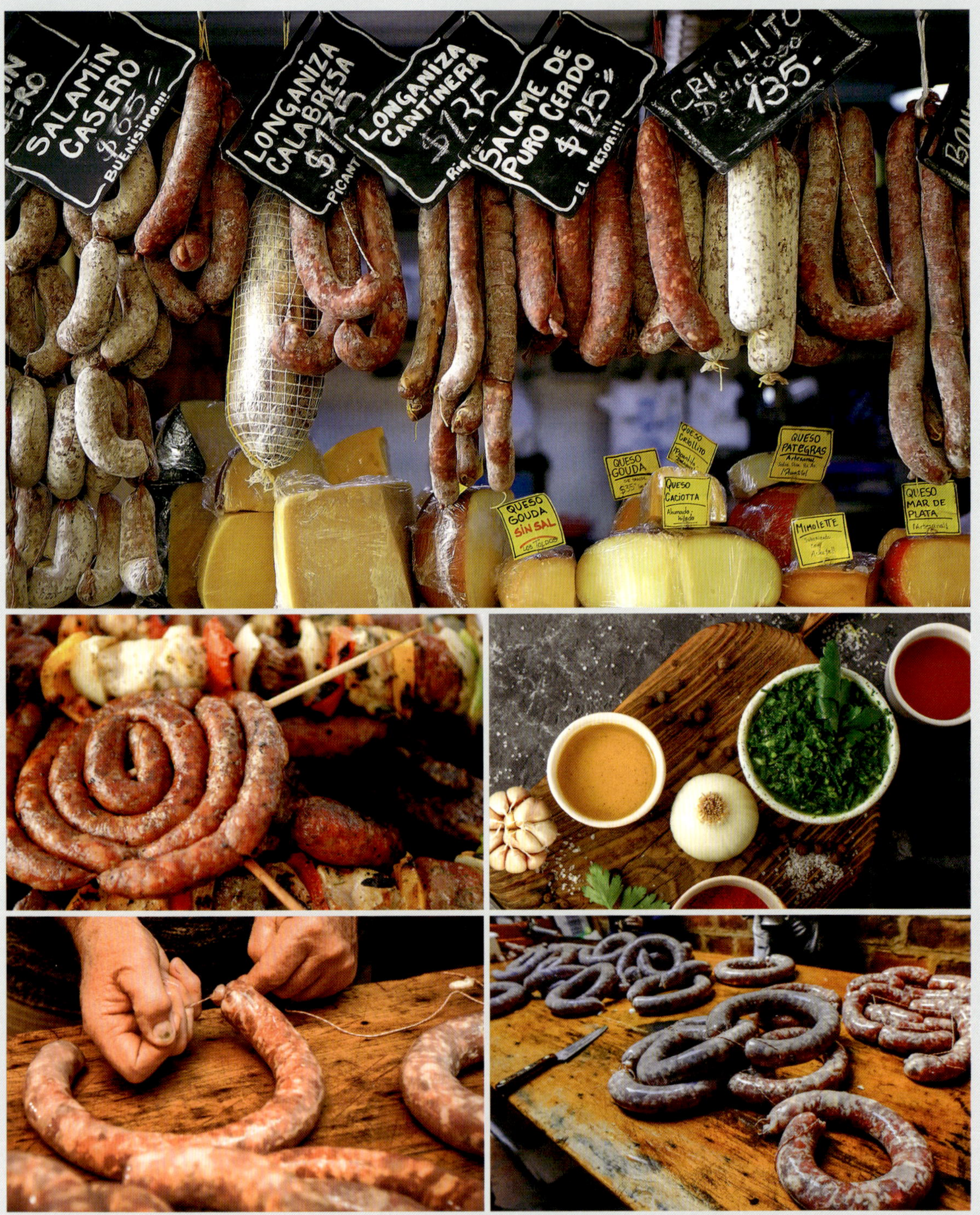
SALAMÍN CASERO
$65
BUENÍSIMO!!!
LONGANIZA CALABRESA
LONGANIZA CANTINERA
$135
SALAME DE PURO CERDO
$125
EL MEJOR!!!
CRIOLLITO
135.
QUESO GOUDA
SIN SAL
QUESO GOUDA
QUESO CRIOLLITO
QUESO CACIOTTA
QUESO PATEGRAS
MIMOLETTE
QUESO MAR DE PLATA

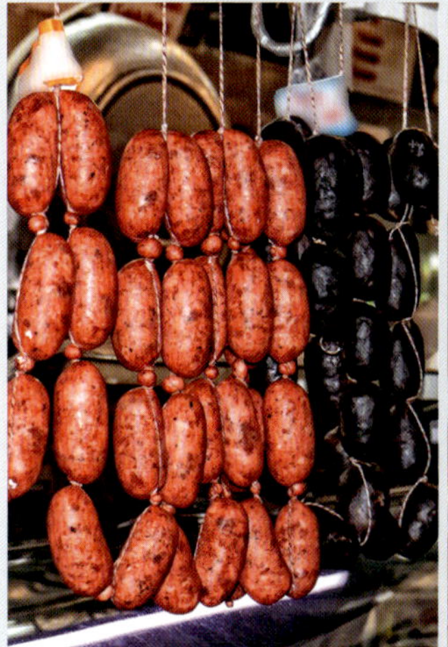
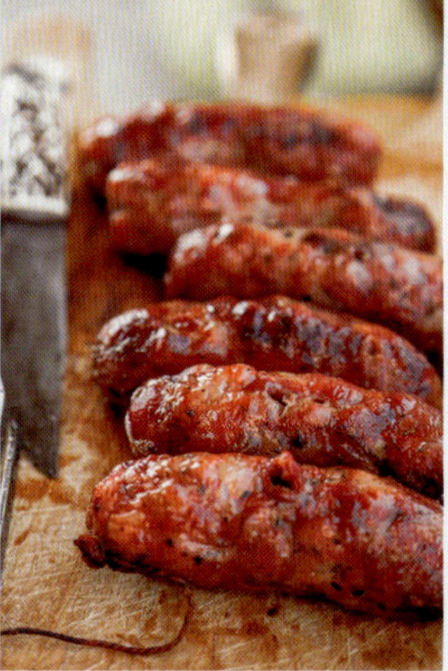
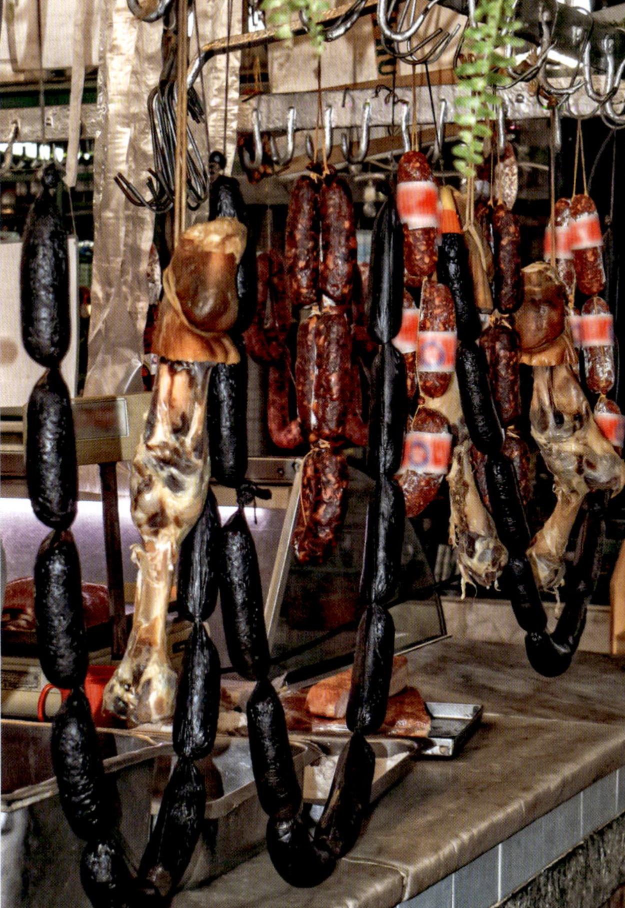

Churrasco

Classically, it is a piece of beef cooked on a skewer over open embers. The first gauchos, who roamed the pampas herding cattle, prepared their meal in this way. Salt is the only spice used for the spit-roasts on the grill today, which may also be made of chicken. Mashed potatoes and pumpkin are the usual side dishes, along with rice, chips and salad.

Churrasco

Il s'agit historiquement d'un morceau de viande de bœuf, grillé en brochette directement sur la braise. Les premiers *gauchos,* qui parcouraient la pampa en traquant les animaux pour leur peau, se préparaient ainsi leur repas. Le sel est l'unique épice de ces grillades aujourd'hui cuites sur un gril et parfois déclinées avec du poulet. Pommes de terre et courges écrasées sont des accompagnements courants, tout comme le riz, les frites et la salade.

Churrasco

Klassisch ist es ein Stück Rindfleisch, das am Spieß über der offenen Glut gegart wird. Die ersten Gauchos, die auf der Jagd nach Fellen die Pampa durchstreiften, bereiteten sich auf diese Weise ihr Mahl zu. Salz ist das einzige Gewürz für den Spießbraten, der heute auf den Grill kommt und auch mal aus Huhn sein darf. Kartoffel- und Kürbisstampf sind neben Reis, Pommes frites und Salat die üblichen Beilagen.

Churrasco

Clásicamente, es un trozo de carne de res cocinado en un pincho sobre brasas abiertas. Los primeros gauchos, que deambulaban por La Pampa en busca de pieles, preparaban su comida de esta manera. La sal es la única especia para el churrasco, que actualmente se pone en la parrilla y también puede ser de pollo. El puré de patatas y la calabaza son los acompañamientos habituales junto con el arroz, las patatas fritas y la ensalada.

Churrasco

O churrasco clássico é um pedaço de carne de vaca cozida num espeto sobre brasas. Os primeiros gaúchos, que passavam pelos pampas em busca de peles, preparavam a sua refeição desta forma. O sal é o único tempero para o assado, que é colocado hoje em dia na grelha e também pode ser feito de frango. O puré de batata e abóbora são os acompanhamentos usuais, juntamente com arroz, batatas fritas e salada.

Churrasco

Klassiek gezien is het een stuk rundvlees dat op een spies boven de open vuurgloed wordt gegaard. De eerste gaucho's, die op jacht naar huiden door de pampa's zwierven, bereidden hun maaltijd op deze manier. Zout is de enige specerij die voor het gebraad aan het spit, dat vandaag de dag op de grill komt, en soms ook uit kip bestaat. Aardappel- en pompoenpuree zijn naast rijst, friet en salade de gebruikelijke bijgerechten.

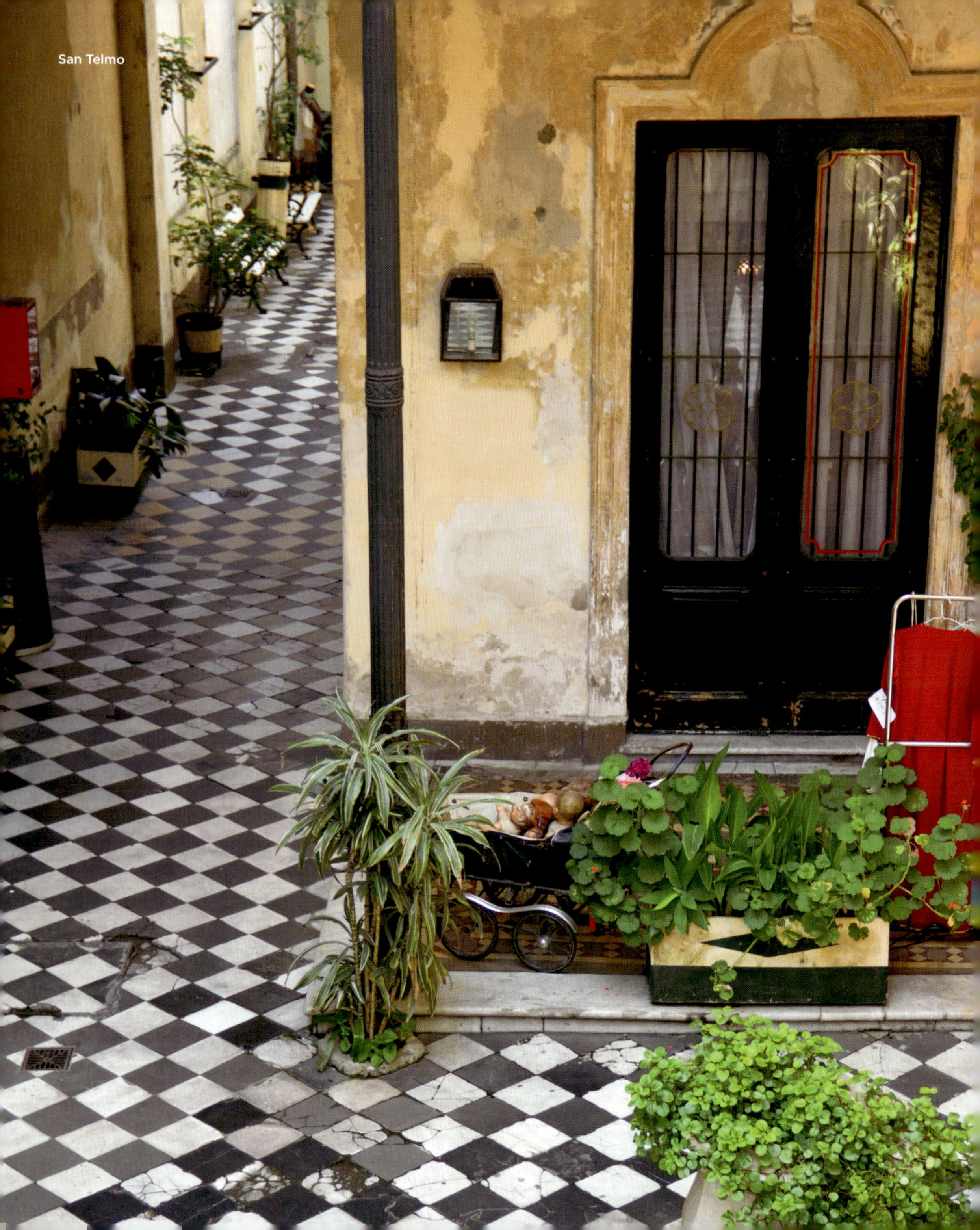
San Telmo

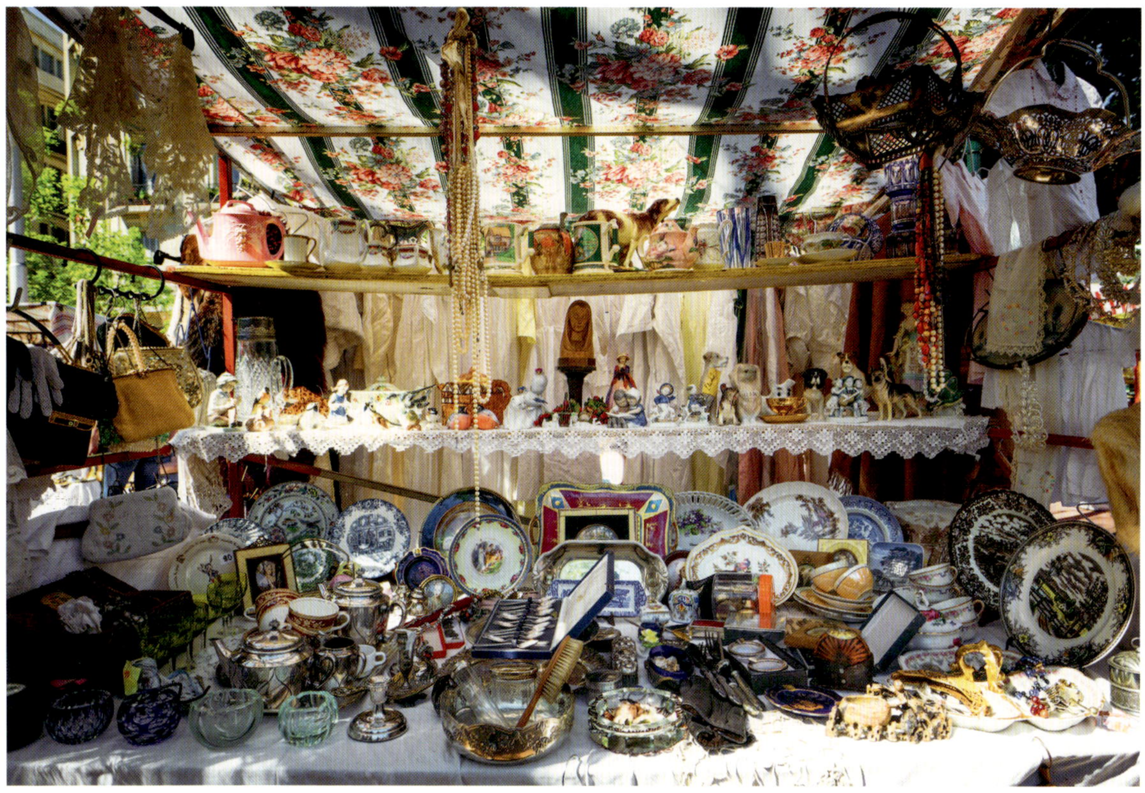

Mercado de San Telmo

Flair San Telmos

In this former harbor area fishermen
and slaves lived alongside merchants
and landowners, until 1871 when yellow
fever broke out and the rich moved away.
Houses, alleys and tiled courtyards still
bear witness to the good old days. The
antiques market invites one to stroll around
on Sundays. With a little luck you can find
wonderful vintage objects here.

Ambiente de San Telmo

En la antigua zona portuaria vivían
pescadores y esclavos, así como
comerciantes y terratenientes hasta 1871,
cuando estalló la fiebre amarilla y los ricos
se marcharon. Aún hay casas, callejones
y patios embaldosados que son testigos
de los buenos tiempos. El mercado de
antigüedades invita a pasear el domingo.
Con un poco de suerte pueden encontrarse
aquí maravillosos objetos de época.

L'ambiance de San Telmo

L'ancien quartier portuaire était autrefois
habité par les pêcheurs et les esclaves,
mais également par les marchands et les
propriétaires, jusqu'à ce que la ruée vers
l'or ne le vide des plus fortunés en 1871.
Les maisons, ruelles et cours intérieures
carrelées témoignent encore de cette
époque faste. Un marché d'antiquités y
offre le dimanche l'occasion d'une balade.
Avec un peu de chance, on peut y déceler
de magnifiques objets du passé.

Flair de San Telmo

Na antiga área portuária, pescadores,
escravos, mas também comerciantes e
proprietários de terras, viveram até 1871,
quando a febre amarela surgiu e os ricos
se mudaram. Casas, becos e pátios de
azulejos ainda testemunham os bons
velhos tempos. O mercado de antiguidades
convida-o a passear no domingo. Com
um pouco de sorte, você pode encontrar
maravilhosos objetos vintage aqui.

Flair San Telmos

Im ehemaligen Hafenviertel wohnten
Fischer, Sklaven, aber auch Kaufleute und
Grundbesitzer bis 1871 das Gelbfieber
ausbrach und die Reichen wegzogen.
Häuser, Gassen und gekachelte Innenhöfe
zeugen bis heute von der guten alten Zeit.
Der Antiquitätenmarkt lädt am Sonntag
zum Bummeln ein. Mit etwas Glück findet
man hier wunderbare Vintage-Objekte.

Flair San Telmos

In de voormalige havenwijk woonden
vissers, slaven maar ook kooplieden en
landeigenaren, totdat in 1871 de goldrush
uitbrak en de rijken wegtrokken. Huizen,
steegjes en betegelde binnenplaatsen
getuigen nog tot vandaag aan de goede
oude tijd. De antiekmarkt nodigt uit
tot een wandeling op zondag. Met een
beetje geluk vindt men hier prachtige
vintage objecten.

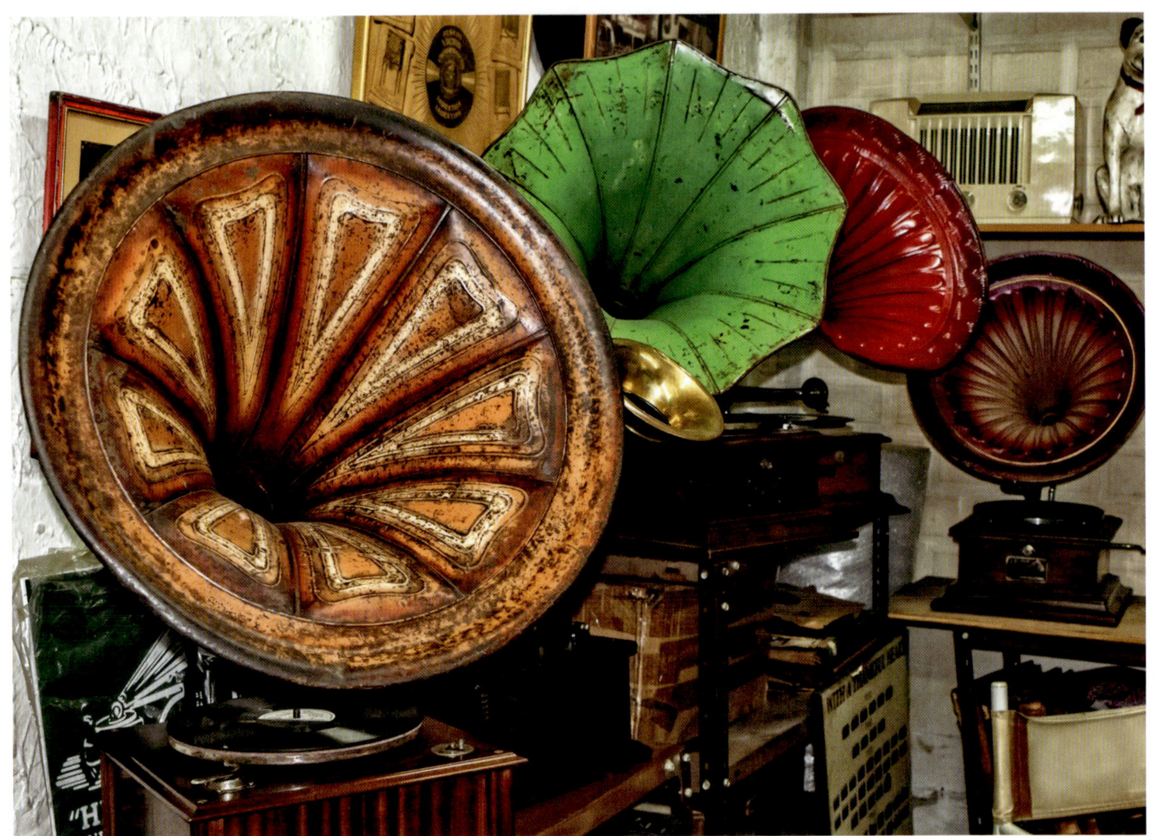

Mercado de San Telmo

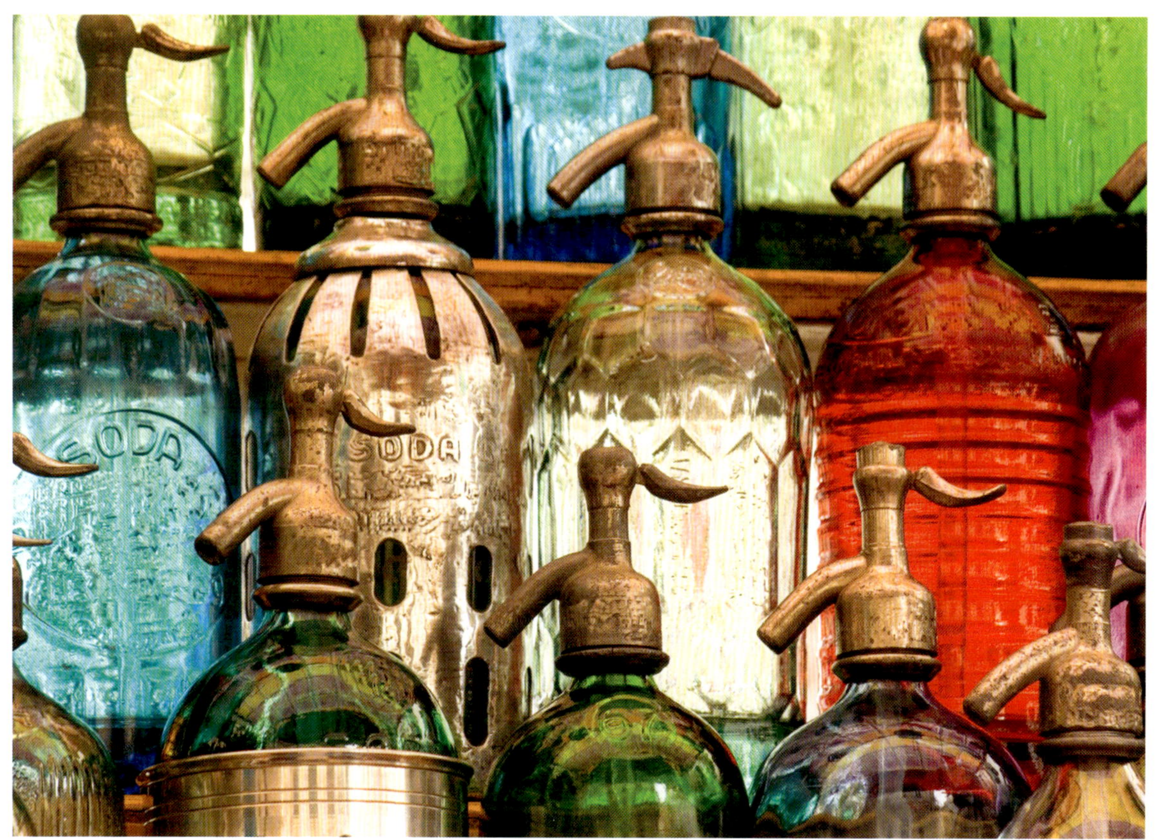

Mercado de San Telmo

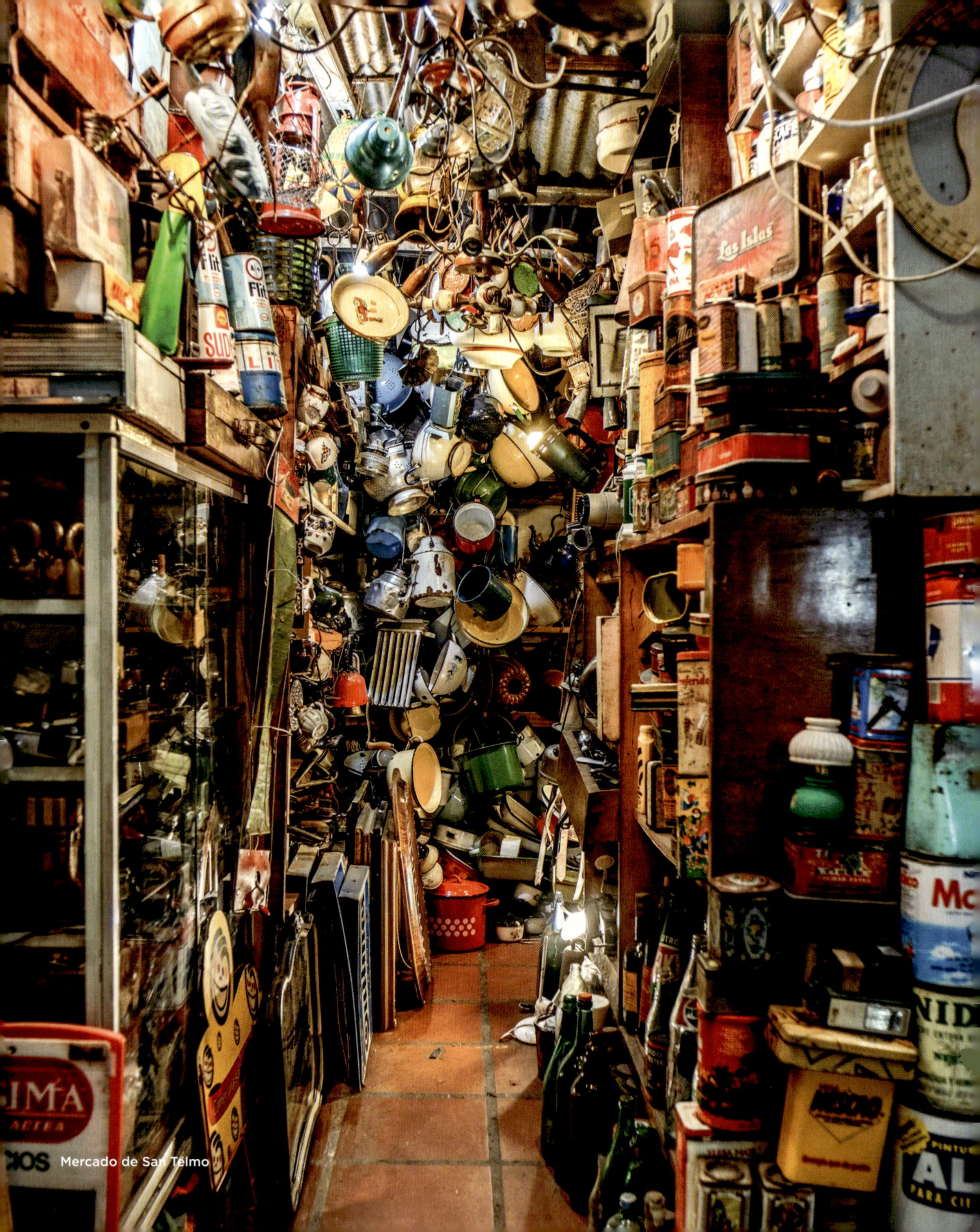

Mercado de San Telmo

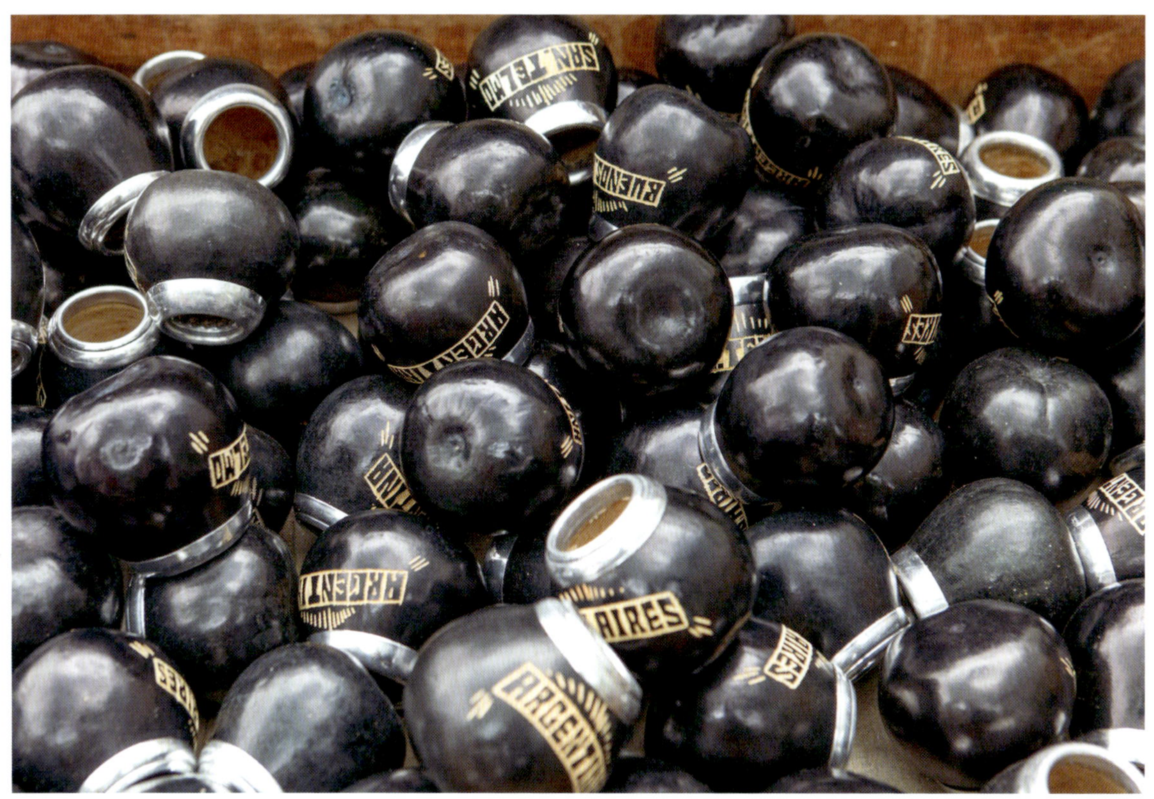

Mates
Mate bowls

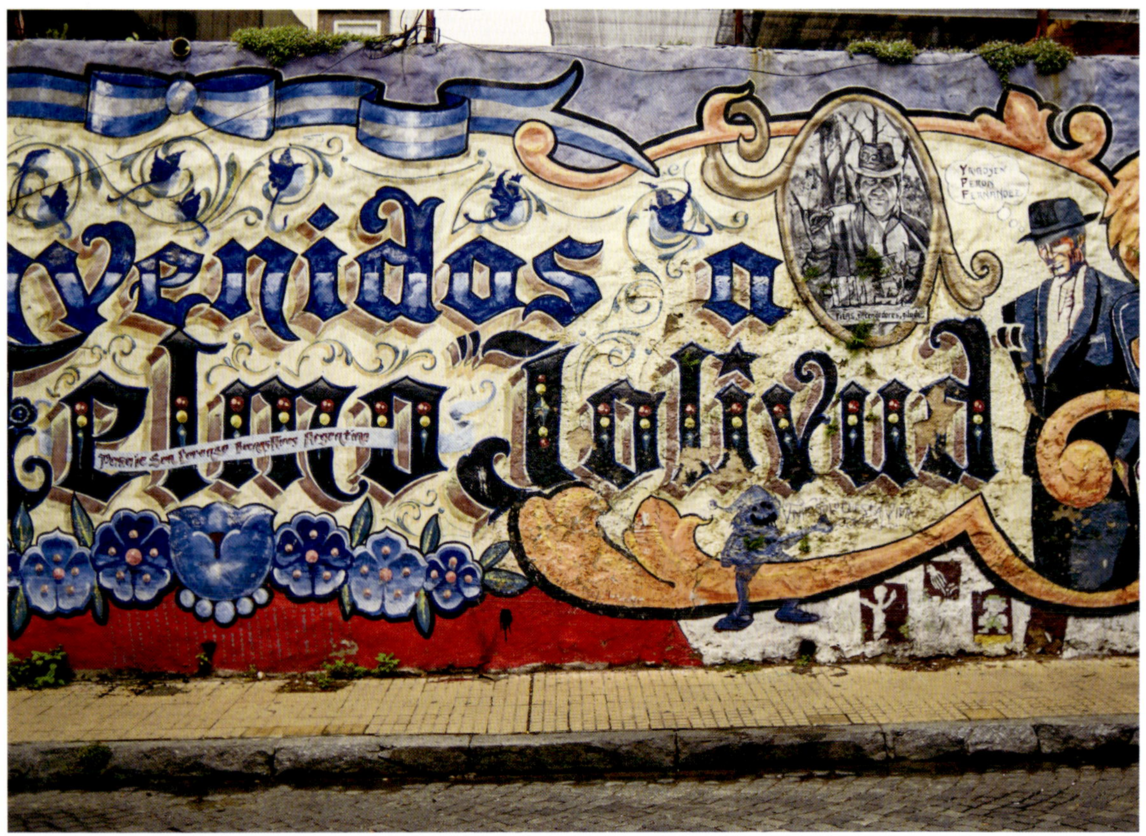

Grafiti, San Telmo
Graffiti, San Telmo

Graffiti

"Welcome to San Telmo", reads an already historic mural painting in this artistic quarter, greeting its visitors. Graffiti artists and fans are attracted by the lively residential area. Not only large-scale murals with icons of the revolution, but also small-format graffiti art can be found. Regularly street art festivals take place here, which generate great enthusiasm in the international graffiti scene. New faces from the globally networked community appear in San Telmo and leave their artistic messages, reviving and renewing the already positive image of the quarter.

Graffiti

« Bienvenue à San Telmo ». Une fresque murale déjà ancienne accueille les visiteurs dans le quartier des spectacles et des artistes. Graffeurs et amateurs se sentent particulièrement bien au cœur de ces rues résidentielles. Les murs y sont ornés de vastes fresques représentant les icônes révolutionnaires, mais arborent également des graffitis de petit format. Le quartier accueille régulièrement des festivals de *street art* qui font l'admiration de la scène internationale. Certains nouveaux visages de la communauté mondiale connectée s'aventurent à San Telmo et y laissent leur message artistique, avivant et renouvelant l'image déjà positive du lieu.

Graffiti

„Willkommen in San Telmo" begrüßt eine heute schon historische Wandmalerei im Künstler- und Szeneviertel seine Besucher. Graffiti-Künstler und Fans fühlen sich von dem lebendigen Wohnviertel angezogen. Nicht nur großflächige Wandbilder mit Ikonen der Revolution, sondern auch kleinformatige Graffiti-Kunst ist zu finden. Regelmäßig finden hier Street-Art-Festivals statt, die in der internationalen Szene für Begeisterung sorgen. Neue Gesichter aus der global vernetzten Community tauchen in San Telmo auf und hinterlassen ihre künstlerischen Botschaften. Sie beleben und erneuern das ohnehin positive Image des Viertels.

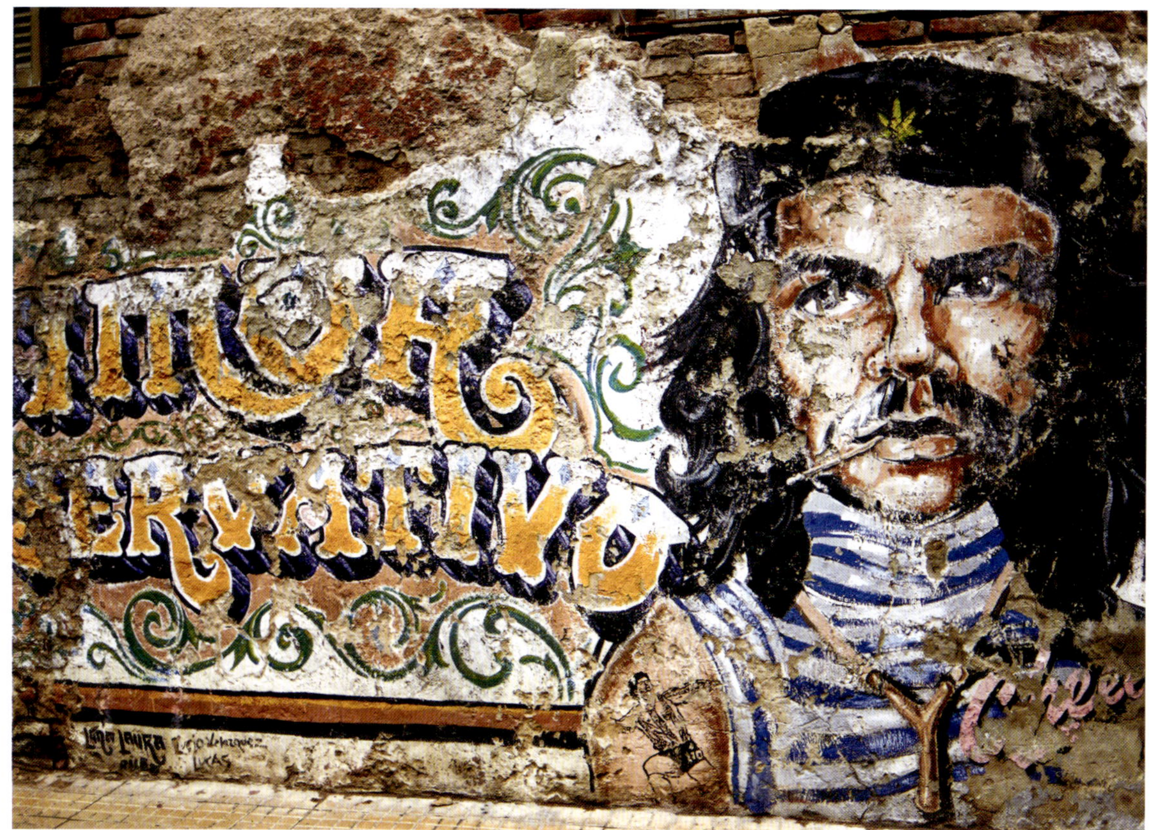

Grafiti, San Telmo
Graffiti, San Telmo

Grafitis

"Bienvenidos a San Telmo", un mural ya histórico en el barrio de los artistas y de la escena da la bienvenida a sus visitantes. Los grafiteros y los aficionados se sienten atraídos por la animada zona residencial. No solo se pueden encontrar murales a gran escala con iconos de la revolución, sino también grafitis en pequeño formato. Aquí se celebran regularmente festivales de arte callejero, que causan entusiasmo en la escena internacional. Nuevos rostros de la comunidad globalmente conectada aparecen en San Telmo y dejan sus mensajes artísticos. Reactivan y renuevan la imagen ya positiva del barrio.

Graffiti

"Bienvenido San Telmo", uma pintura mural já histórica no bairro dos artistas e da cena acolhe os seus visitantes. Os artistas e fãs de graffiti são atraídos pela animada área residencial. Não apenas murais de grande escala com ícones da revolução, mas também grafites de pequeno formato podem ser encontrados. Aqui acontecem regularmente festivais de arte de rua, que causam entusiasmo na cena internacional. Novos rostos da comunidade mundialmente ligada aparecem em San Telmo e deixam suas mensagens artísticas. Eles reanimam e renovam a imagem já positiva do bairro.

Graffiti

"Welkom in San Telmo", groet een vandaag al historische muurschildering in de kunstenaars- en scènewijk zijn bezoekers. Graffitikunstenaars en fans worden door de levendige woonwijk aangetrokken. Hier zijn niet alleen grootschalige muurschilderingen met iconen van de revolutie te vinden, maar er is ook ruimte voor kleinschalige graffitikunst. Regelmatig vinden hier straatkunstfestivals plaats die in de internationale scene enthousiasme opwekken. Nieuwe gezichten uit de globaal gekoppelde community duiken in San Telmo op en laten hun artistieke boodschappen achter. Ze laten het toch al positieve imago van de wijk herleven en vernieuwen.

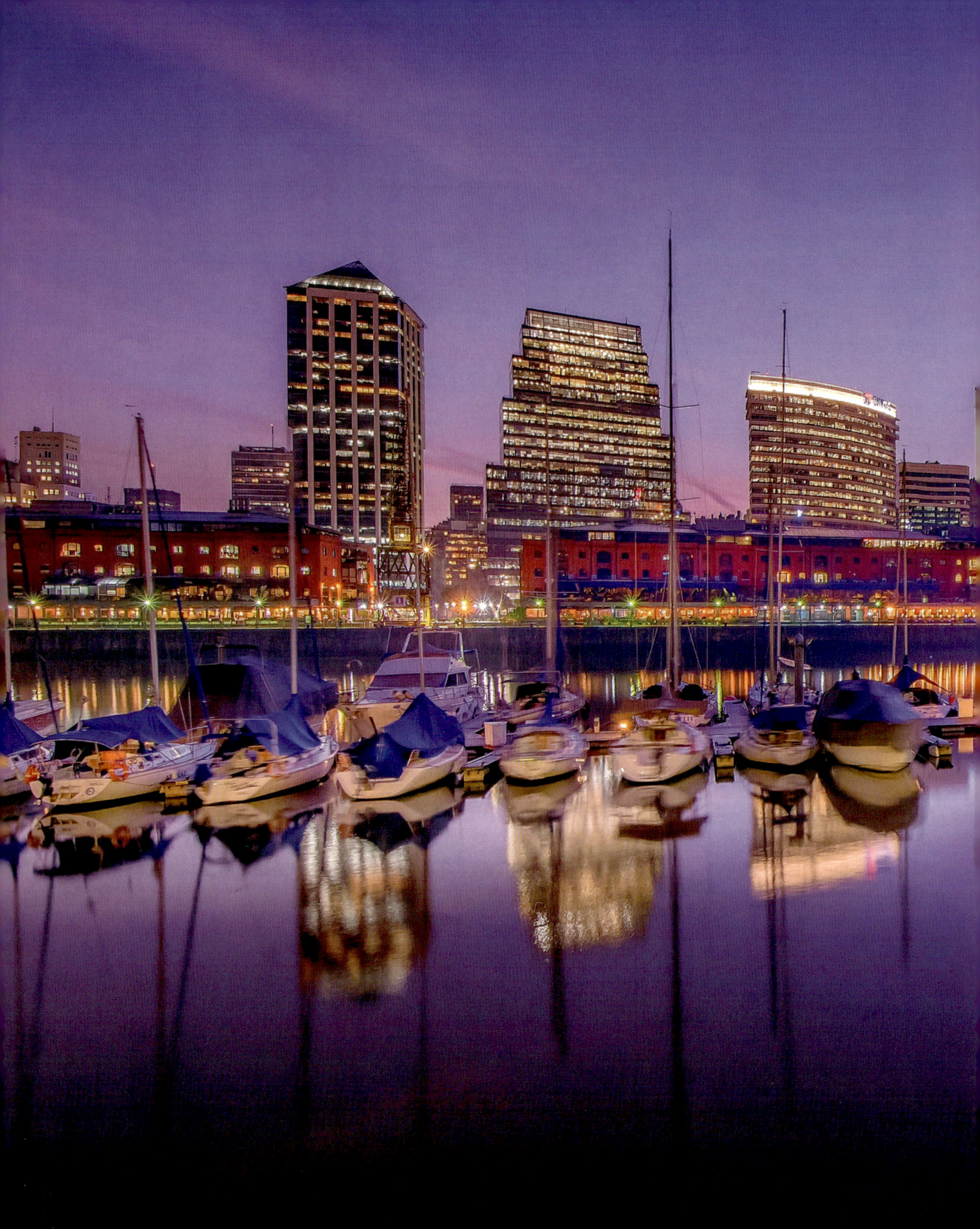

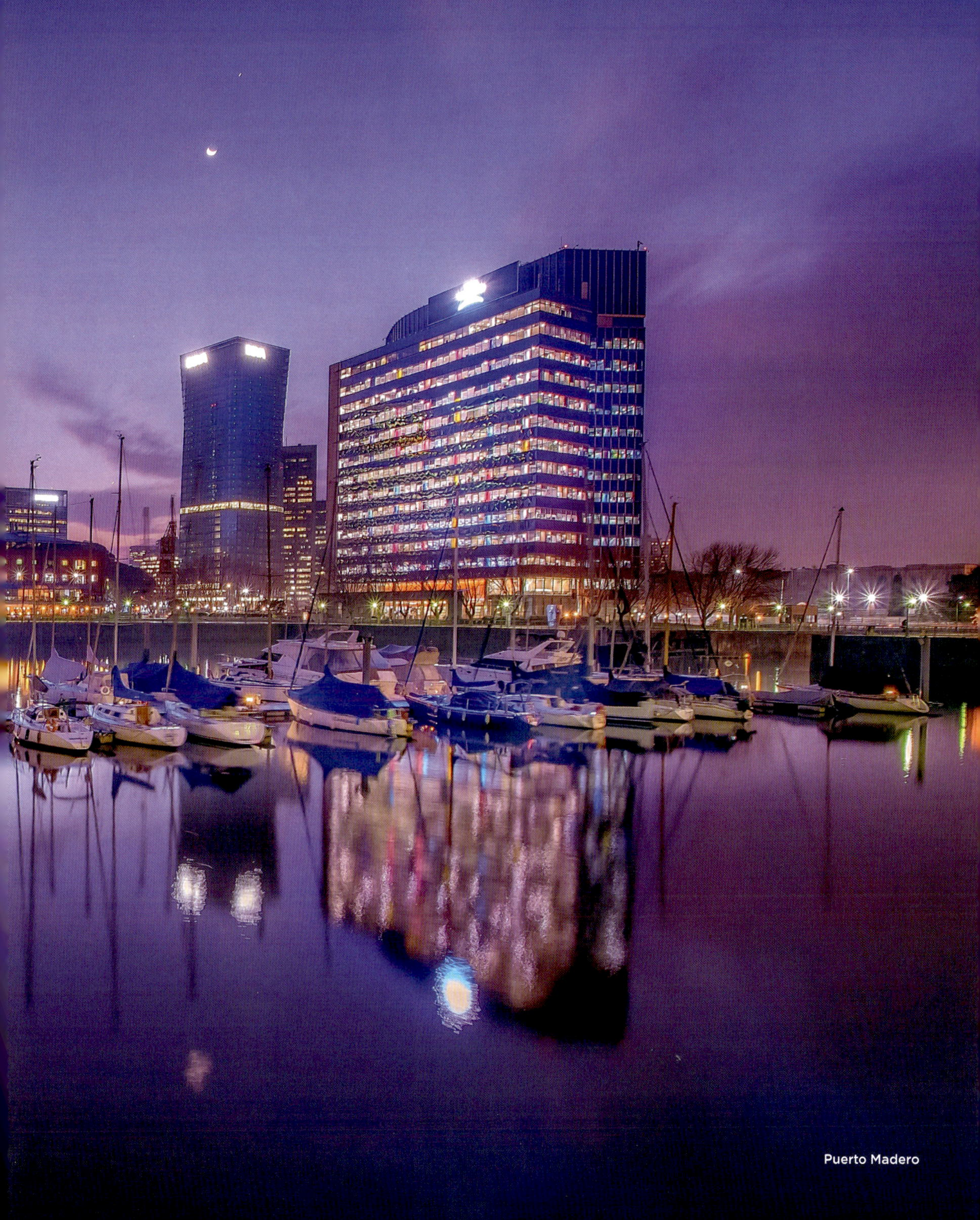

Puerto Madero

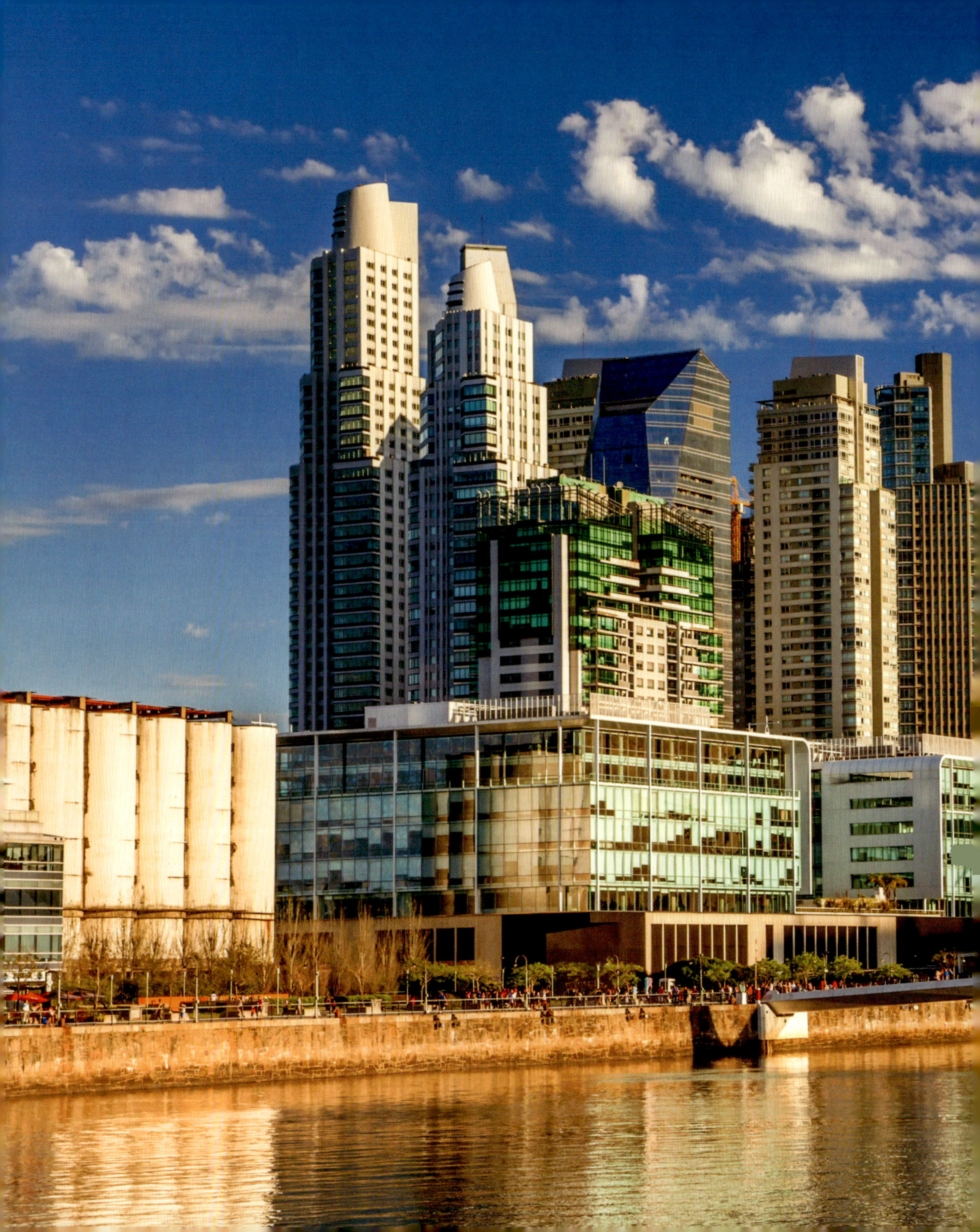

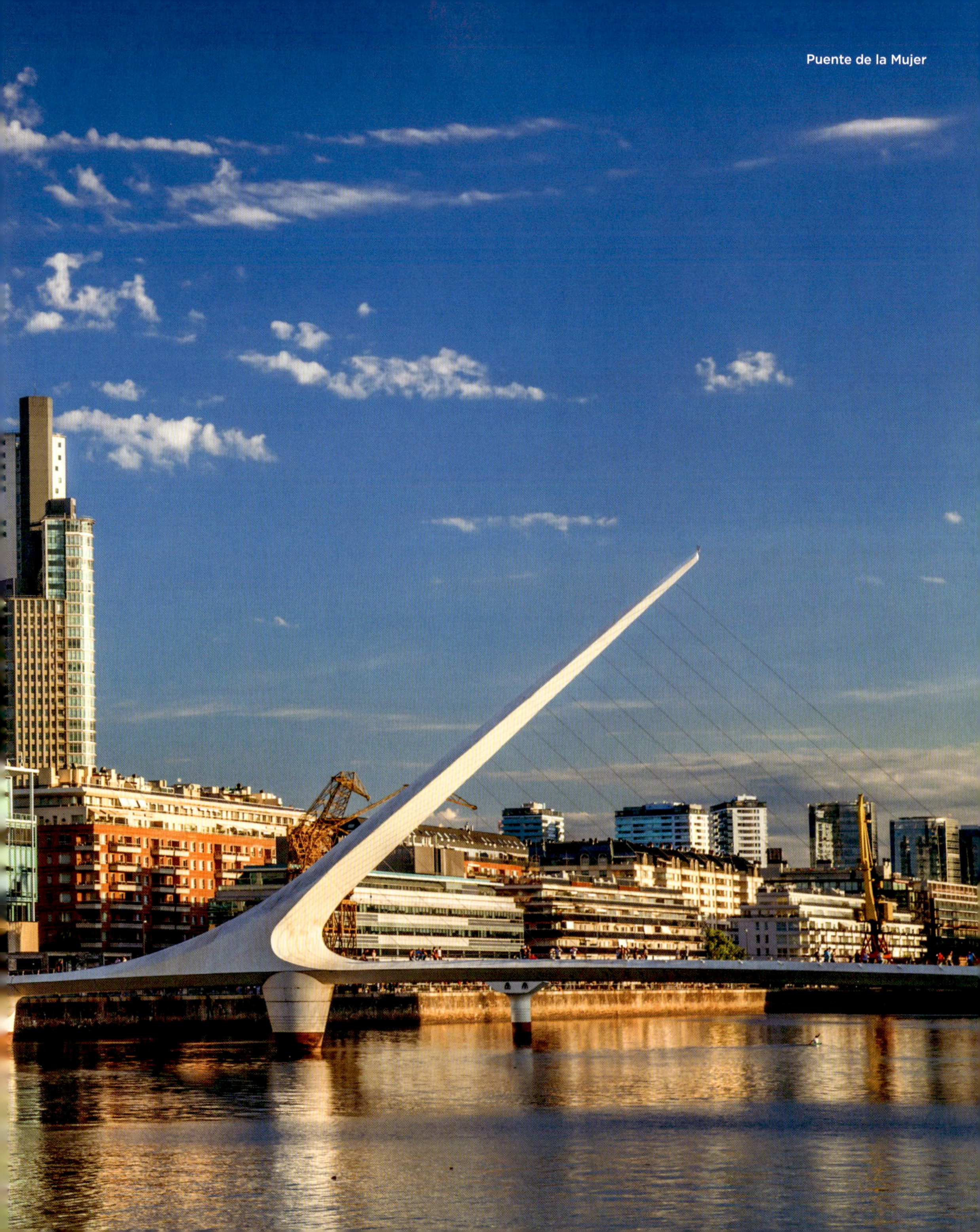
Puente de la Mujer

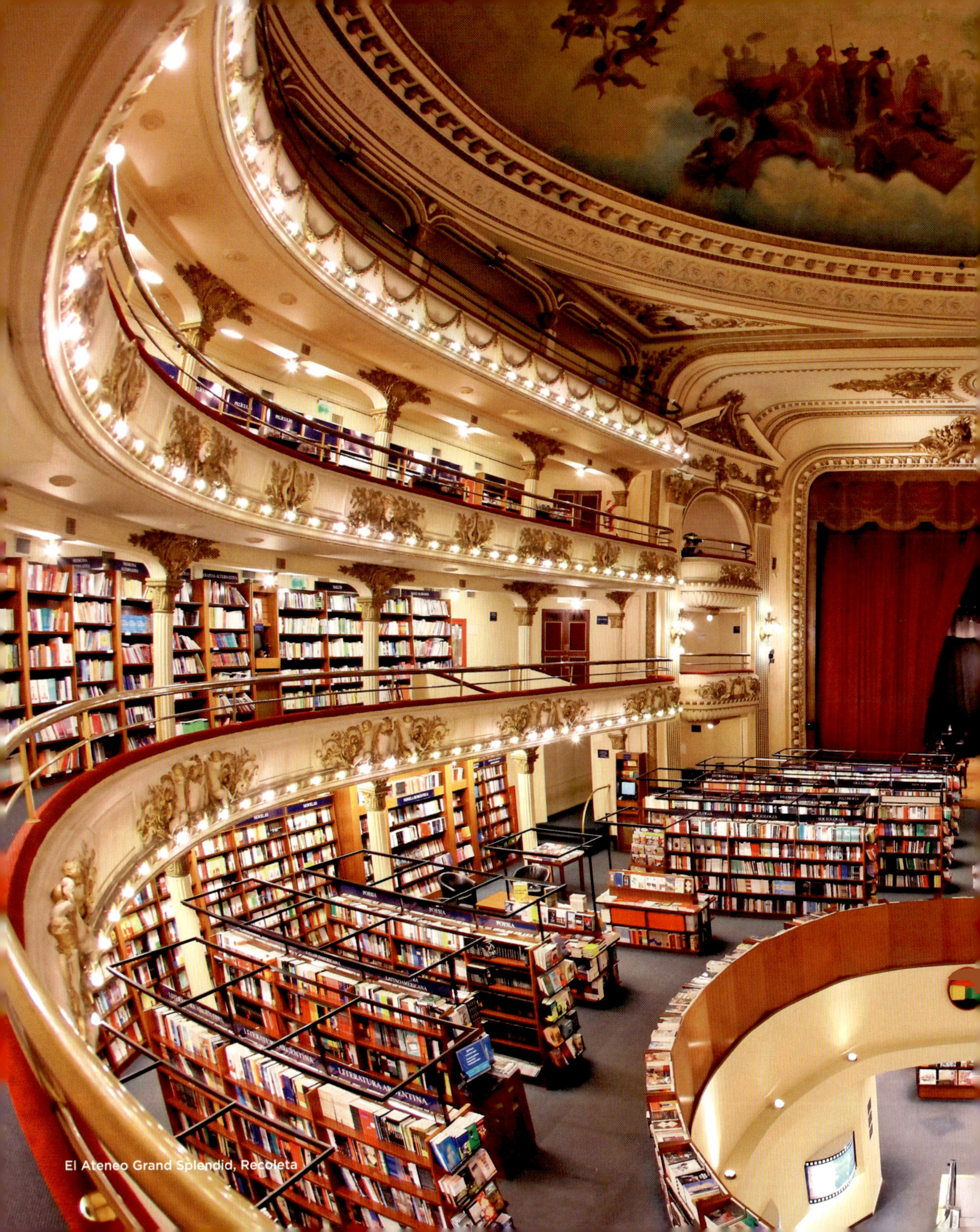

El Ateneo Grand Splendid, Recoleta

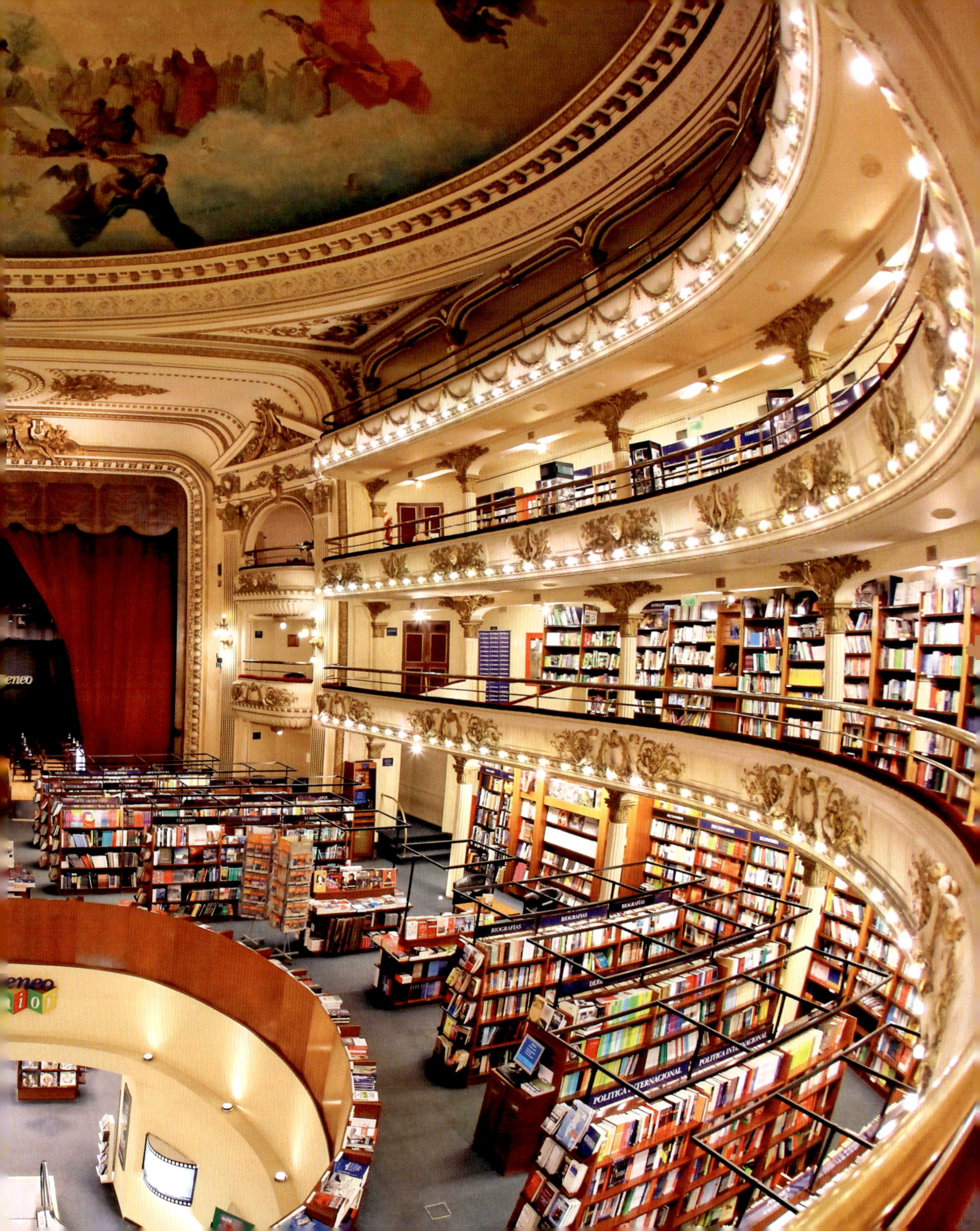

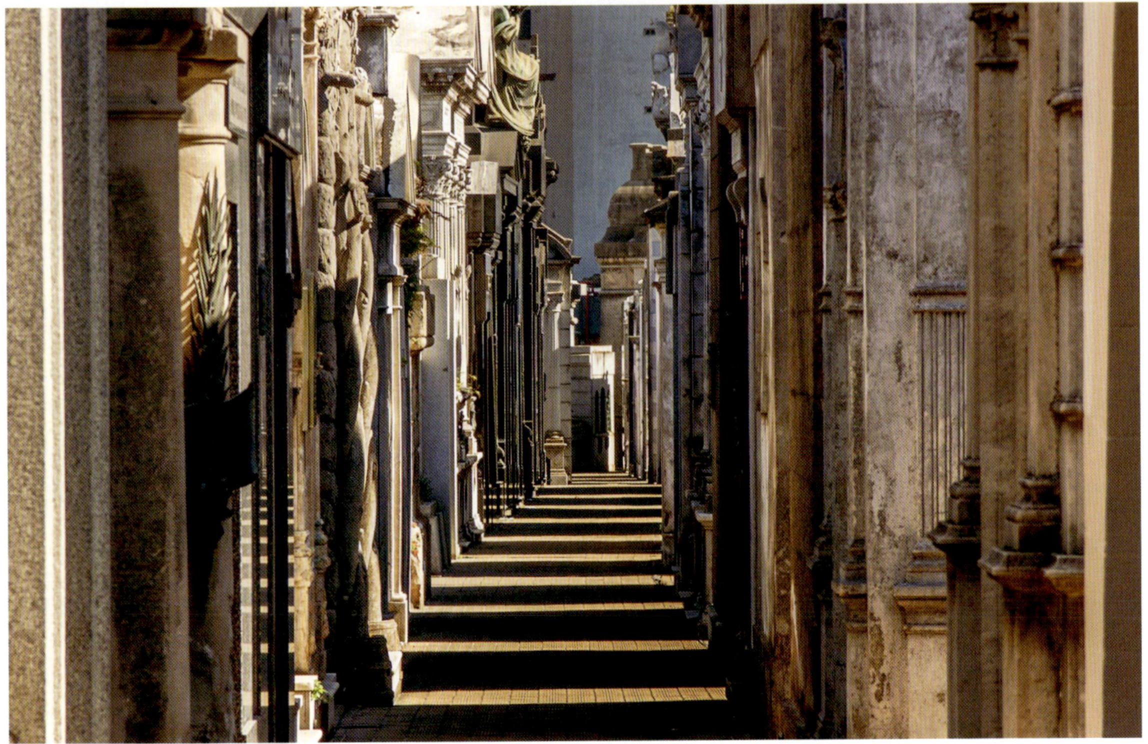

Cementerio de la Recoleta
La Recoleta Cemetery

Recoleta

The cemetery of the same name is located in the rich residential area of the northern zone. This is where Argentina's wealthy families bury their loved ones. Politicians, high-ranking military officers, bankers, industrialists and football stars find their last resting place in monumental mausoleums. The magnificent tombs of marble, featuring angels and elaborately designed crosses attract many visitors.

Recoleta

El cementerio del mismo nombre está situado en la rica zona residencial de la zona norte. Aquí es donde las grandes familias argentinas entierran a sus seres queridos. Políticos, altos oficiales militares, banqueros, industriales y estrellas de fútbol encuentran su último lugar de descanso en los gigantescos mausoleos. Las magníficas tumbas de mármol, los ángeles y las cruces de elaborado diseño atraen a muchos visitantes.

Recoleta

Le cimetière Recoleta est installé dans le quartier homonyme aisé de la zone nord de la ville. C'est là que les grandes familles d'Argentine enterrent leurs défunts. Politiques, gradés militaires, banquiers, industriels et stars du football trouvent ici leur dernier repos à l'abri de mausolées monumentaux. Les tombeaux en marbre somptueux, les anges et les croix richement décorées attirent de nombreux visiteurs.

Recoleta

O cemitério do mesmo nome está localizado na rica área residencial da zona norte. É aqui que as grandes famílias argentinas enterram os seus entes queridos. Políticos, altos oficiais militares, banqueiros, industriais e estrelas do futebol encontram seu último lugar de descanso em mausoléus monumentais. As magníficas tumbas de mármore, anjos e cruzes elaboradamente desenhadas atraem muitos visitantes.

Recoleta

Im reichen Wohnviertel der Nordzone liegt der gleichnamige Friedhof. Hier begraben die großen Familien Argentiniens ihre Angehörigen. Politiker, hohe Militärs, Bankiers, Industrielle und Fußballstars finden in monumentalen Mausoleen die letzte Ruhe. Die prachtvollen Gruften aus Marmor, Engel und aufwendig gestaltete Kreuze ziehen viele Besucher an.

Recoleta

In de rijke woonwijk in de noordelijke zone ligt de gelijknamige begraafplaats. Hier begraven de grote families uit Argentinië hun naaste verwanten. Politici, hoge militairen, bankiers, industriëlen en voetbalsterren vinden hun laatste rustplaats in monumentale mausolea. De prachtige graftombes van marmer, engelen en uitvoerig vormgegeven kruizen trekken veel bezoekers.

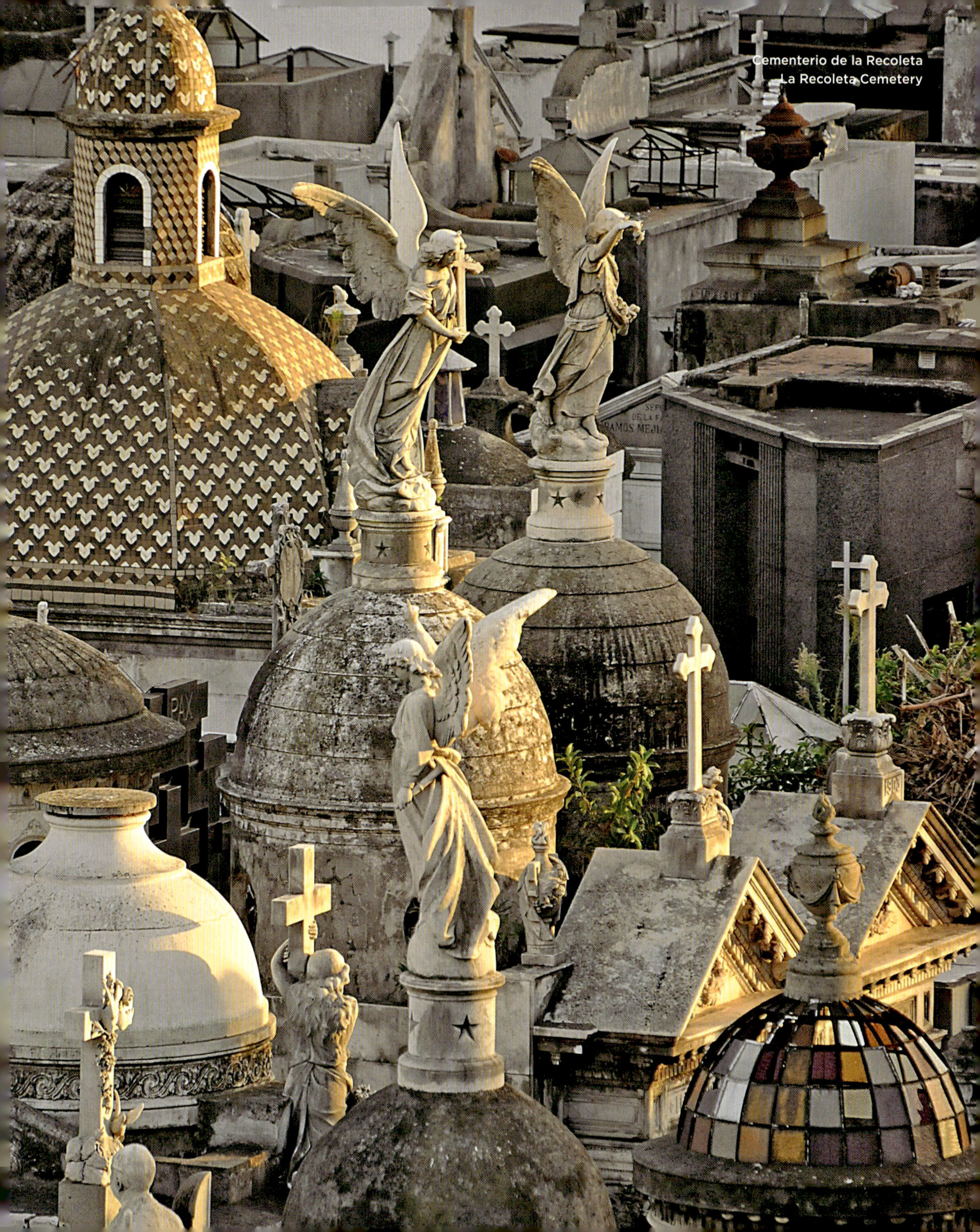

Cementerio de la Recoleta
La Recoleta Cemetery

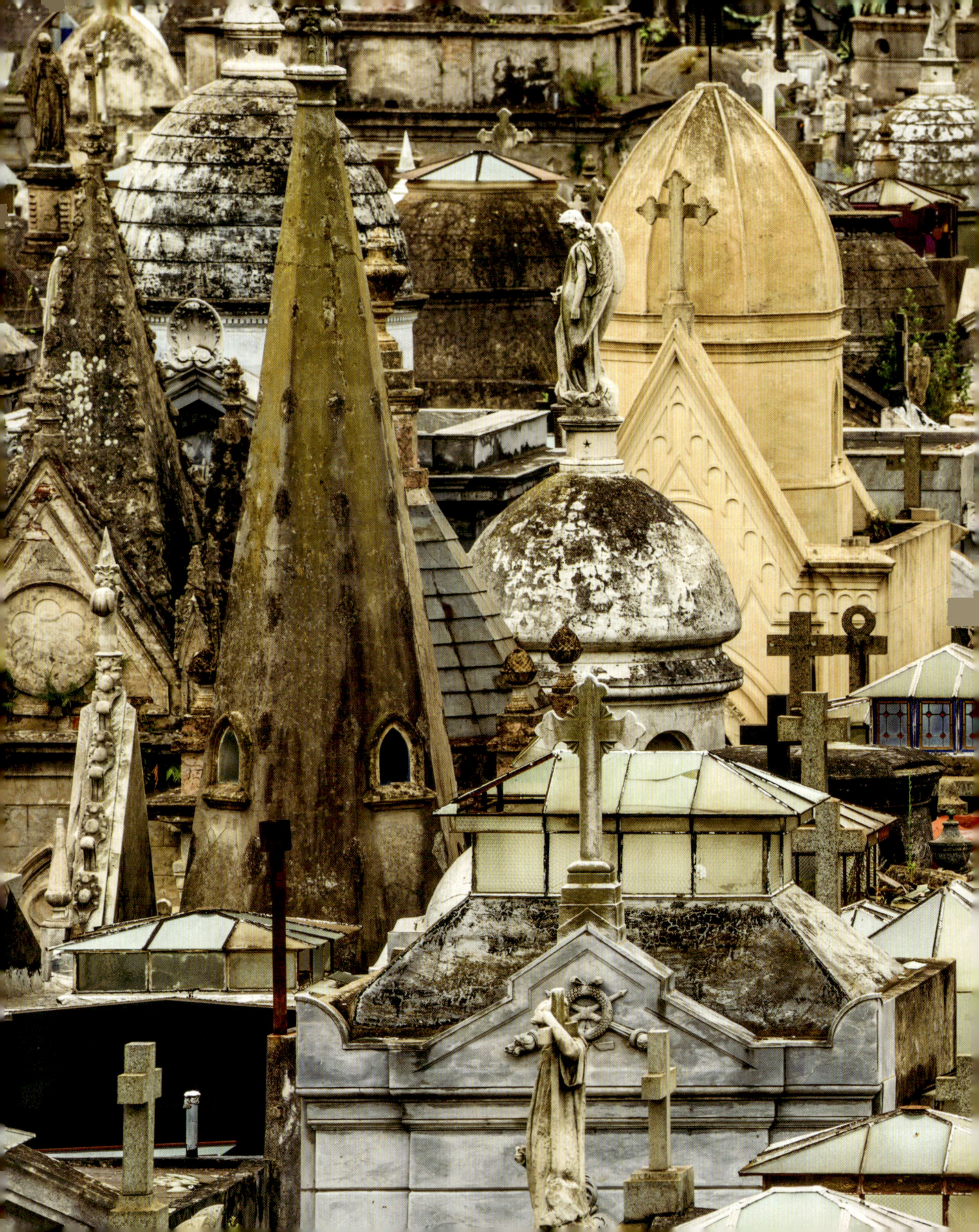

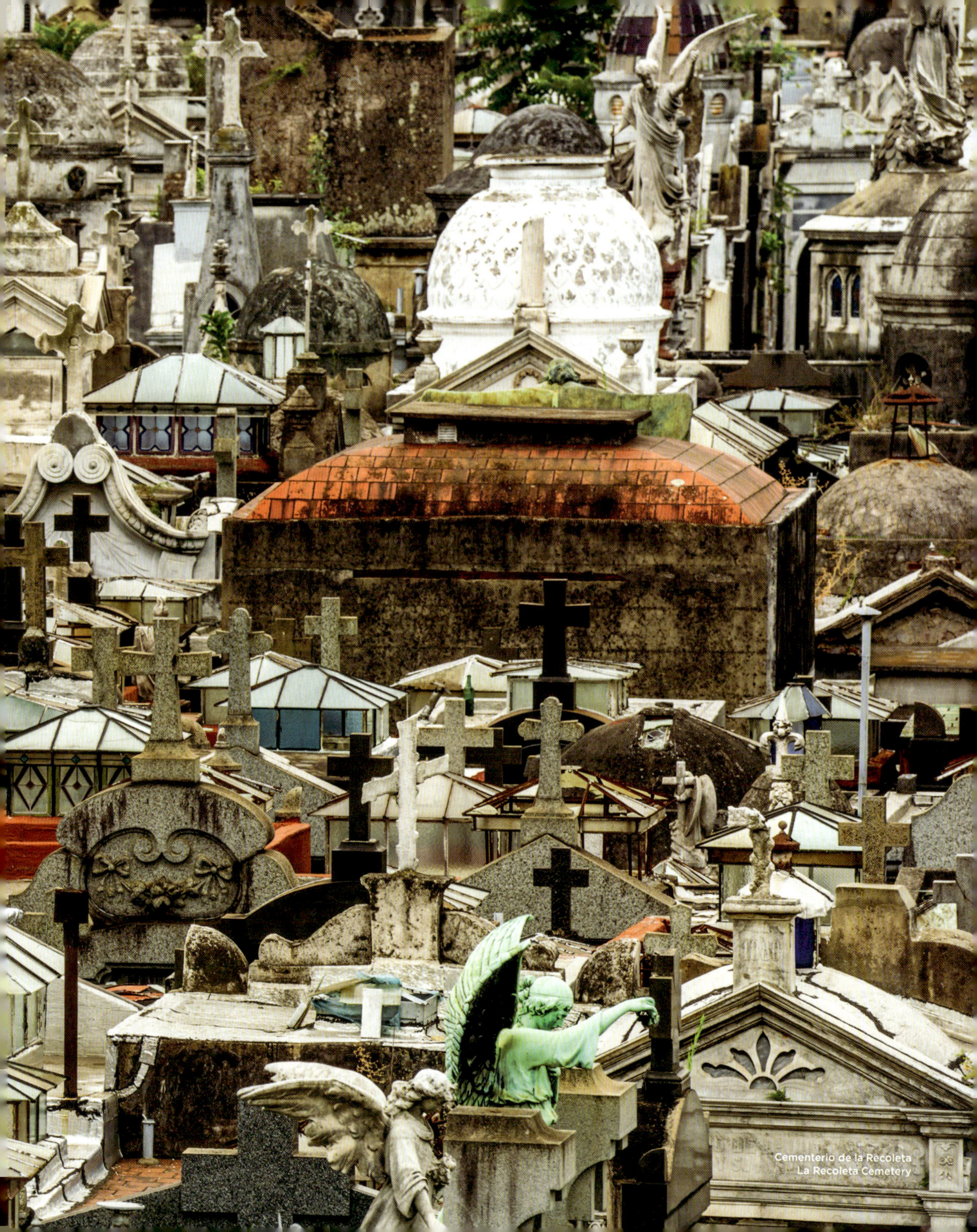

Cementerio de la Recoleta
La Recoleta Cemetery

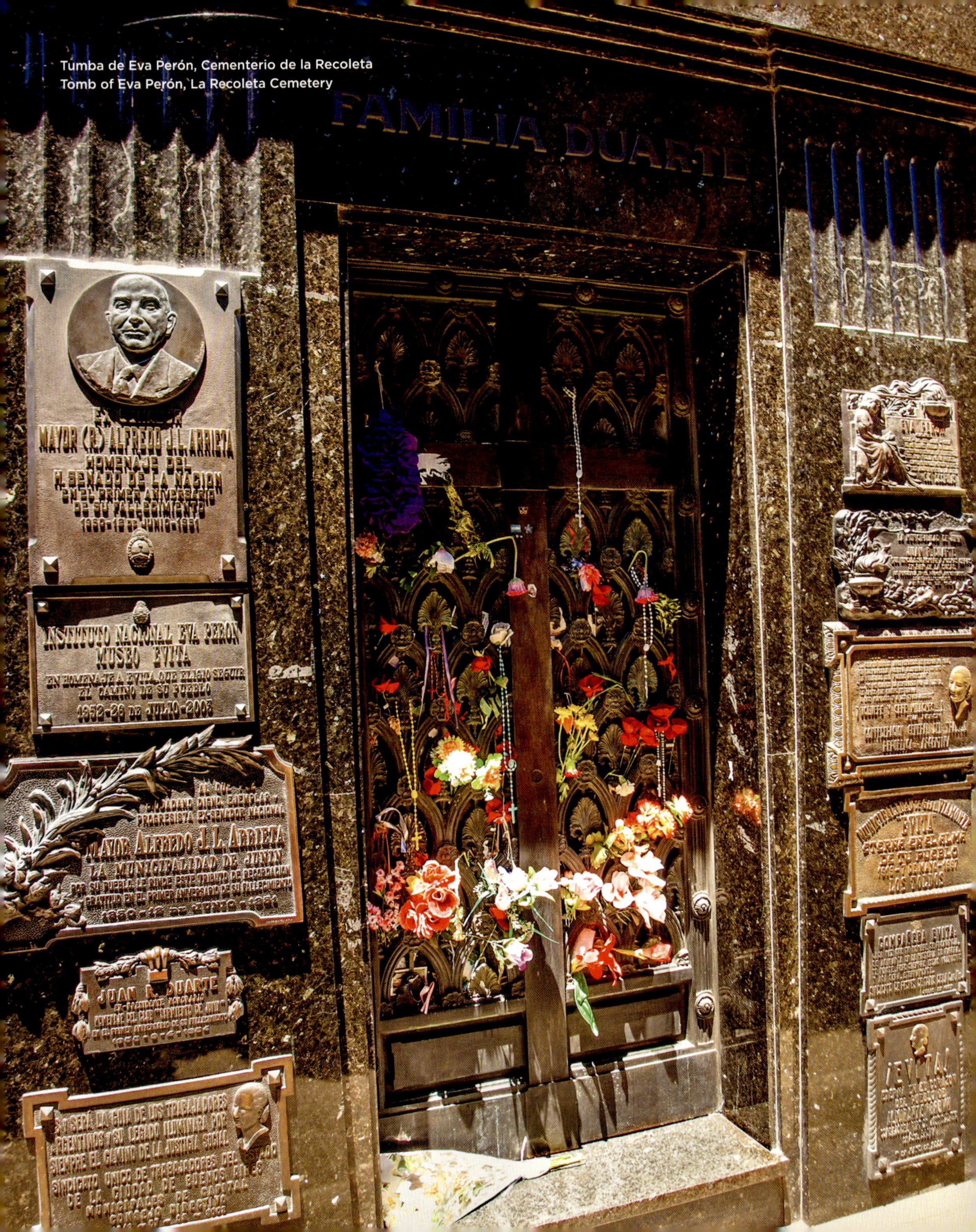

Tumba de Eva Perón, Cementerio de la Recoleta
Tomb of Eva Perón, La Recoleta Cemetery

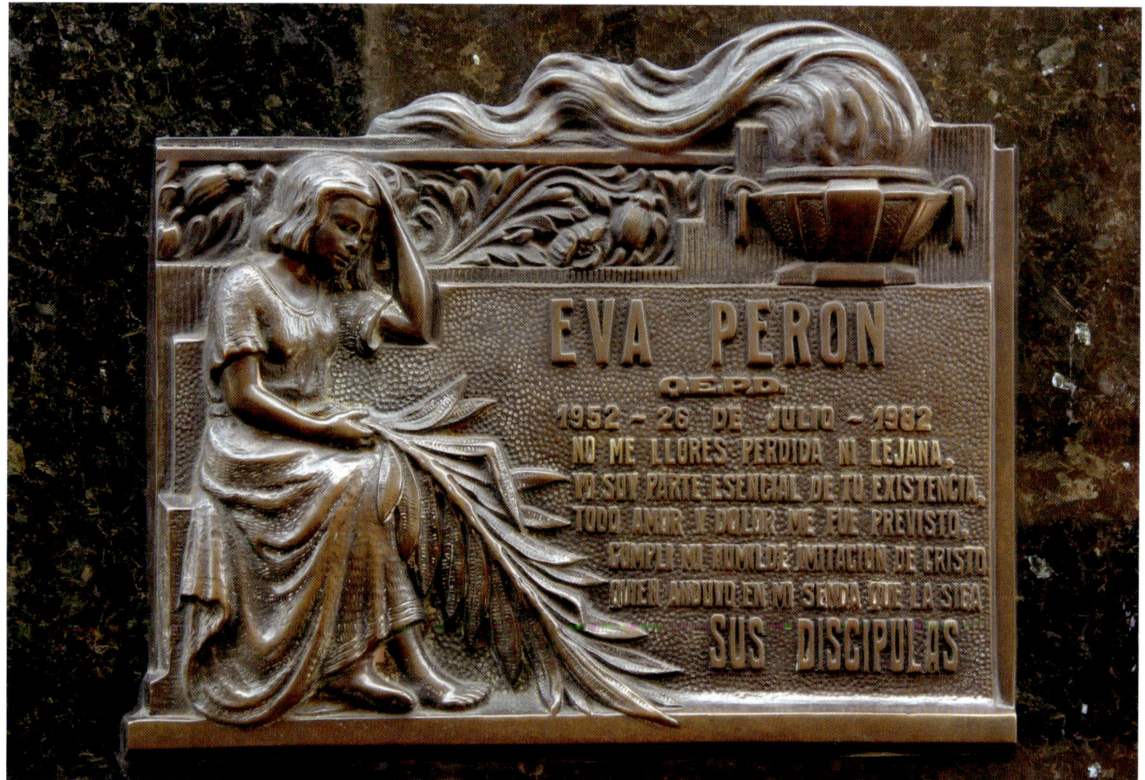

Tumba de Eva Perón, Cementerio de la Recoleta
Tomb of Eva Perón, La Recoleta Cemetery

Eva Perón

To this day she is still considered the "angel of the poor", because Eva Duarte de Perón, as the wife of the president, launched welfare programs and introduced the right to vote for women. In 1944 she married Juan Domingo Perón and celebrated great political successes at his side. Since 1976 she has lain in La Recoleta Cemetery.

Eva Perón

Hasta el día de hoy, se le sigue considerando un "ángel de los pobres", porque Eva Duarte de Perón, como esposa del presidente, introdujo programas de asistencia social y el derecho al voto para las mujeres. En 1944 se casó con Juan Domingo Perón y celebró grandes éxitos políticos a su lado. Desde 1976 se encuentra en la Recoleta.

Eva Perón

Aujourd'hui encore, on la surnomme « l'ange des démunis ». Eva Duarte de Perón, dite Evita, dirigea, en tant qu'épouse du président, des programmes d'assistance sociale et mena le combat en faveur du droit de vote des femmes. En 1944, elle avait épousé Juan Domingo Perón et vécut à ses côtés d'immenses succès politiques. Depuis 1976, elle repose à Recoleta.

Eva Perón

Até hoje ela ainda é considerada o "anjo dos pobres", porque Eva Duarte de Perón, como esposa do presidente, lançou programas de assistência social e introduziu o direito de voto para as mulheres. Em 1944 ela se casou com Juan Domingo Perón e celebrou grandes sucessos políticos ao seu lado. Desde 1976 está no cemitério Recoleta.

Eva Perón

Bis heute gilt sie als „Engel der Armen", denn Eva Duarte de Perón legte als Präsidentengattin Wohlfahrtsprogramme auf und führte das Frauenwahlrecht ein. 1944 heiratete sie Juan Domingo Perón und feierte an seiner Seite große politische Erfolge. Seit 1976 liegt sie in Recoleta.

Eva Perón

Tot op de dag van vandaag geldt zij als "engel van de armen", want Eva Duarte de Perón schreef als presidentsvrouw welzijnsprogramma's en voerde het vrouwenstemrecht in. In 1944 trouwde ze met Juan Domingo Perón en vierde aan zijn zijde grote politieke successen. Sinds 1976 ligt zij in Recoleta.

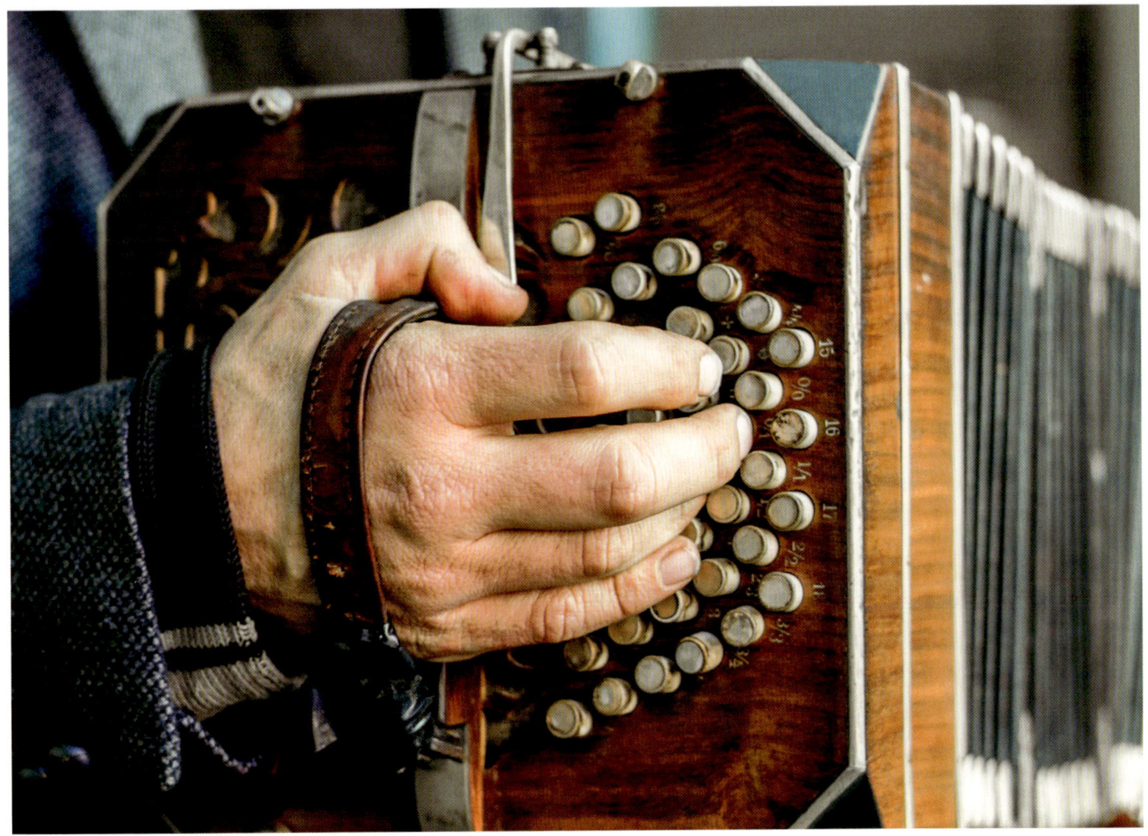

Bandoneón

Tango instrument

The bandoneon is the key instrument of the tango. The instrument gives the tango music its unmistakable sound. Initially, tango was played with guitar, violin, flute and piano. Only afterwards was the bandoneon, or button accordion, added, which had been invented by the German, Hans Band, in Krefeld in 1845. Buenos Aires offers a number of tango clubs of different types, including the traditional schools of Carlos Gardel or Tita Merello, along with modern, jazz, rock or electro forms. The bars open their doors for tango lessons as well as for dancing. Famous tango greats can sometimes be experienced there quite unexpectedly.

Tango : la musique

Le bandonéon est l'instrument roi du tango. C'est de sa voix que cette musique tire sa sonorité unique. À l'origine, le tango était joué par un orchestre réunissant guitare, violon, flûte et piano. Puis le bandonéon est arrivé, « harmonica à boutons » inventé par l'Allemand Hans Band en 1845, à Krefeld. Buenos Aires est riche de plusieurs styles de tango, pratiqués dans différentes salles : outre l'école traditionnelle, portée par Carlos Gardel et Tita Merello, le tango se décline en une version plus moderne et diverses interprétations teintées de jazz, rock ou électro. Les salles de tango organisent cours et bals. Il est encore possible d'y croiser, à l'improviste, de grands maîtres de la discipline.

Tango instrumental

Das Bandoneon ist das Schlüsselinstrument des Tangos. Durch das Instrument gewinnt die Tangomusik ihren unverwechselbaren Klang. Zunächst spielte man Tango mit Gitarre, Geige, Flöte und Klavier. Dann erst kam das Bandoneon, die Knopfharmonika, hinzu, die der Deutsche Hans Band 1845 in Krefeld erfand. Buenos Aires wartet mit etlichen Tangolokalen verschiedenster couleur auf: ob traditionelle Schule à la Carlos Gardel oder Tita Merello, moderne, Jazz-, Rock-, Elektroklänge. Die Lokale öffnen ihre Pforten sowohl zum Tangounterricht als auch zum Tanz. Berühmte Tangogrößen lassen sich dort manchmal auch ganz unverhofft erleben.

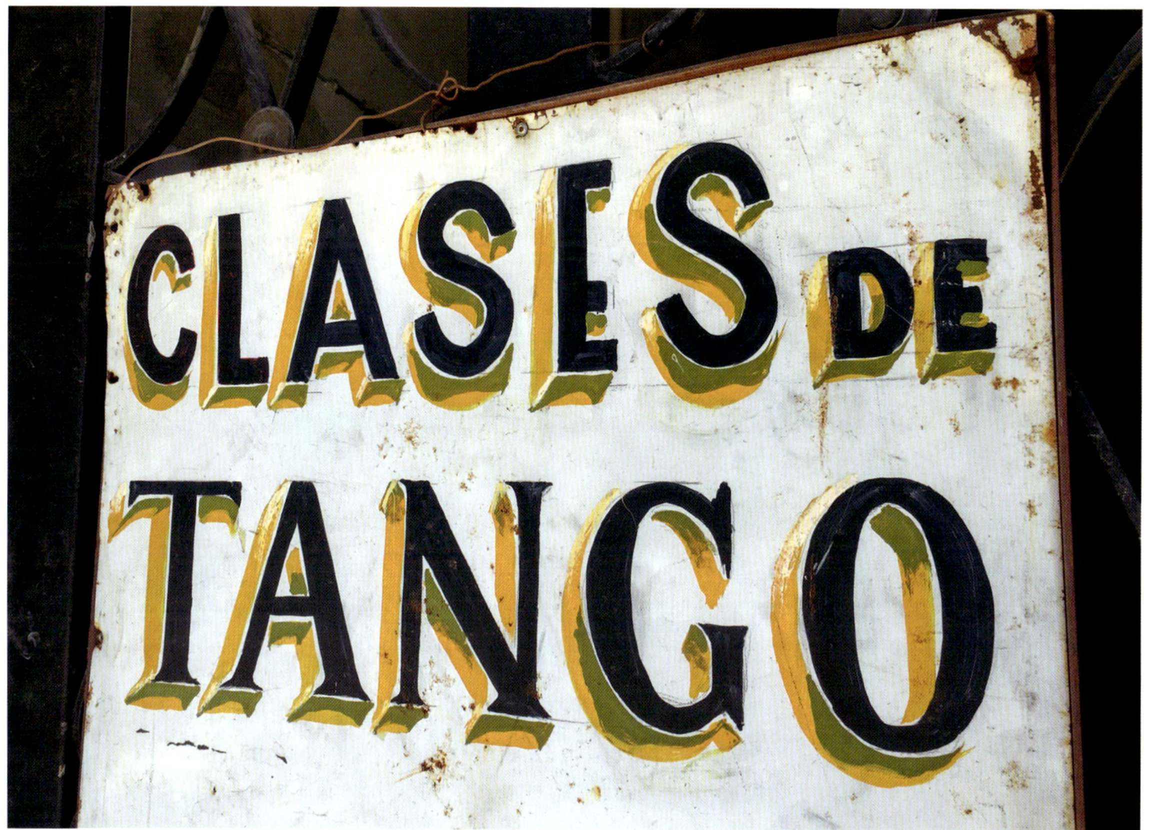

Cartel en el que se ofrecen clases de tango
Sign offering tango lessons

Tango instrumental

El bandoneón es el instrumento clave del tango. Este instrumento da a la música de tango su sonido inconfundible. Al principio el tango se tocaba con guitarra, violín, flauta y piano, pero entonces se añadió el bandoneón (una armónica con botones), que la banda alemana Hans Band inventó en Krefeld en 1845. Buenos Aires ofrece un gran número de clubes de tango de diferentes estilos: ya sea la escuela tradicional de Carlos Gardel o Tita Merello, sonidos modernos, jazz, rock o electro. Los restaurantes abren sus puertas tanto para las clases de tango como para el baile. Los grandes éxitos del tango también se pueden disfrutar en estos lugares de manera inesperada.

Tango instrumental

O bandoneón é o principal instrumento do tango. O instrumento dá à música do tango o seu som inconfundível. No início eles tocavam tango com violão, violino, flauta e piano. Só então foi acrescentado o bandoneón, o acordeão de botões, que a banda alemã Hans Band inventou em Krefeld em 1845. Buenos Aires oferece uma série de clubes de tango de diferentes cores: seja a escola tradicional Carlos Gardel ou Tita Merello, moderna, jazz, rock ou sons eletrônicos. Os restaurantes abrem suas portas para aulas de tango, bem como para dançar. Grandes nomes do tango podem às vezes ser vivenciados lá de forma bastante inesperada.

Tango instrumentaal

De bandoneon is het belangrijkste instrument van de tango. Het instrument geeft de tangomuziek zijn onmiskenbare klank. In het begin speelde men tango met gitaar, viool, fluit en piano. Pas toen werd de bandoneon, de knopharmonica die de Duitse Hans Band in 1845 in Krefeld uitvond, toegevoegd. Buenos Aires beschikt over een diverse tangoclubs: of het nu gaat om een traditionele school à la Carlos Gardel of Tita Merello, moderne, jazz-, rock- of electro-klanken. De zalen openen hun deuren voor zowel tangolessen als voor dansen. Soms kun je daar heel onverwacht beroemde tangogrootheden beleven.

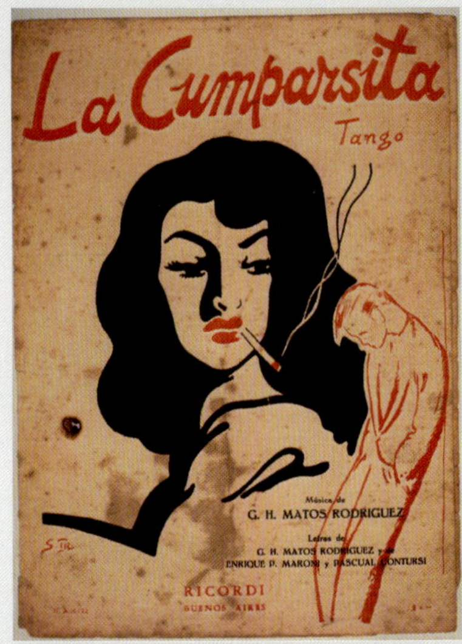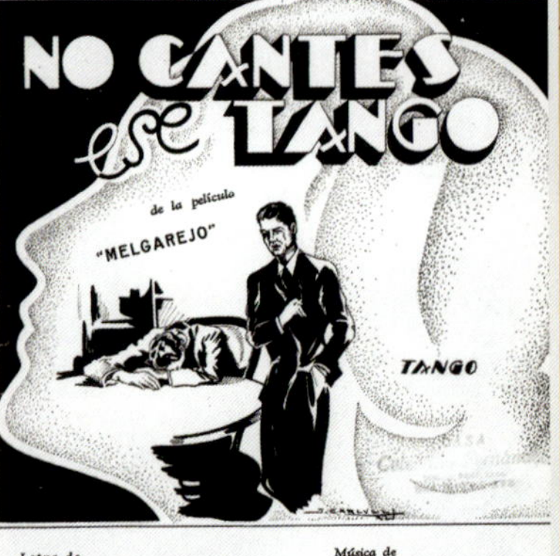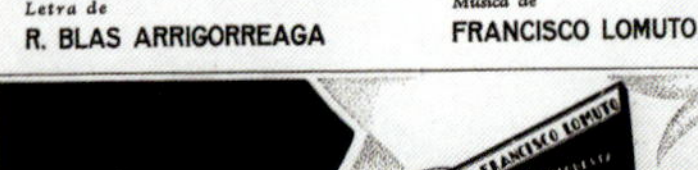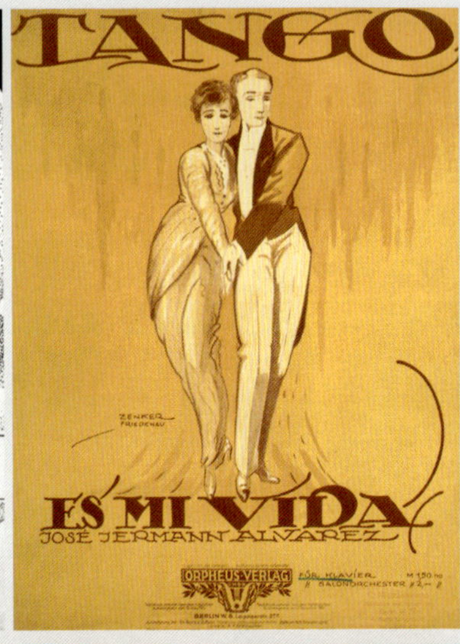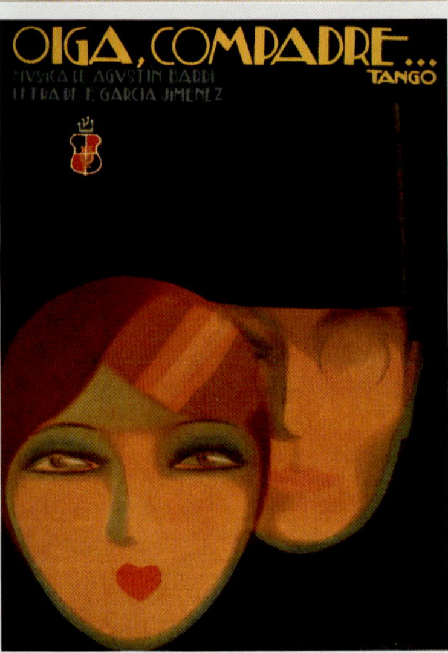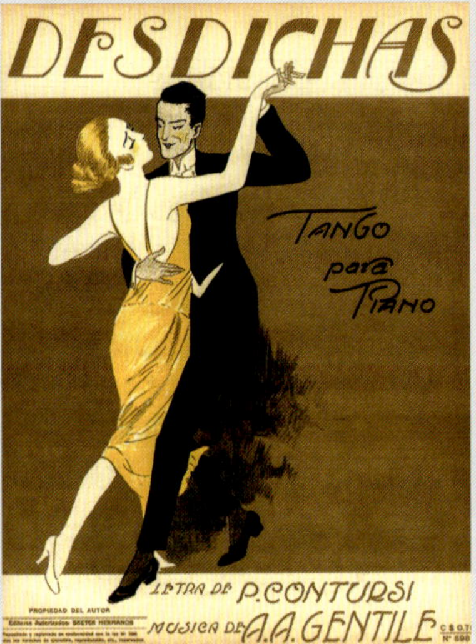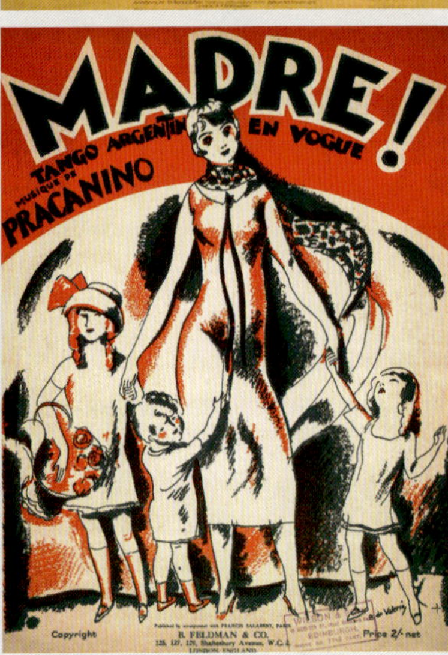

Tango origins

The tango developed during the time when Argentina became one of the richest countries in the world, at the end of the 19th century, which brought Italian, Spanish and French immigrants to the pampas for work. They brought the tango back to Europe, where its success story began. In 1905-06 the first tango orchestra was founded in Paris. After the great successes in Europe, the tango swung back to Argentina, where it experienced several high points until the 1950s.

Tango : le succès

Le tango s'est développé alors que l'Argentine devenait, au XIXᵉ siècle, l'un des pays les plus riches du monde et où Italiens, Espagnols et Français venaient travailler pendant la saison des récoltes dans les exploitations des pampas. Ils ramenèrent le tango en Europe, où il eut beaucoup de succès. Le premier orchestre de tango fut créé à Paris vers 1905. Après son immense triomphe en Europe, le tango revint en Argentine où il connut plusieurs temps forts jusque dans les années 1950.

Ursprünge des Tango

Der Tango entwickelte sich, als Argentinien Ende des 19. Jahrhunderts zu einem der reichsten Länder der Welt wurde und italienische, spanische und französische Gastarbeiter zur Ernte in die Pampa holte. Sie brachten den Tango zurück nach Europa, wo seine Erfolgsgeschichte begann. 1905–06 gab es in Paris das erste Tangoorchester. Nach den großen Erfolgen in Europa schwappte der Tango zurück nach Argentinien, dort erlebte er bis in die 1950er Jahre mehrere Höhepunkte.

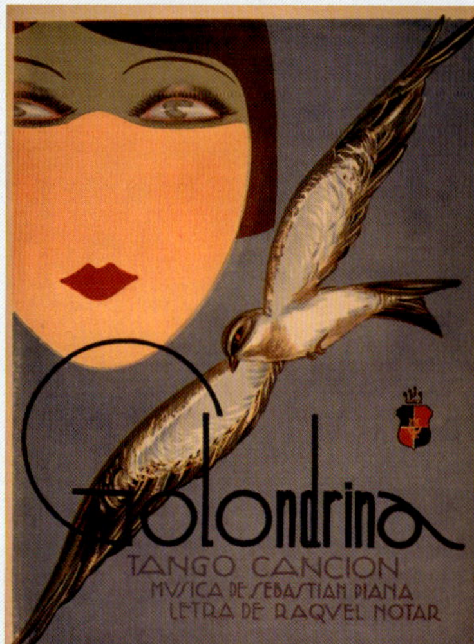

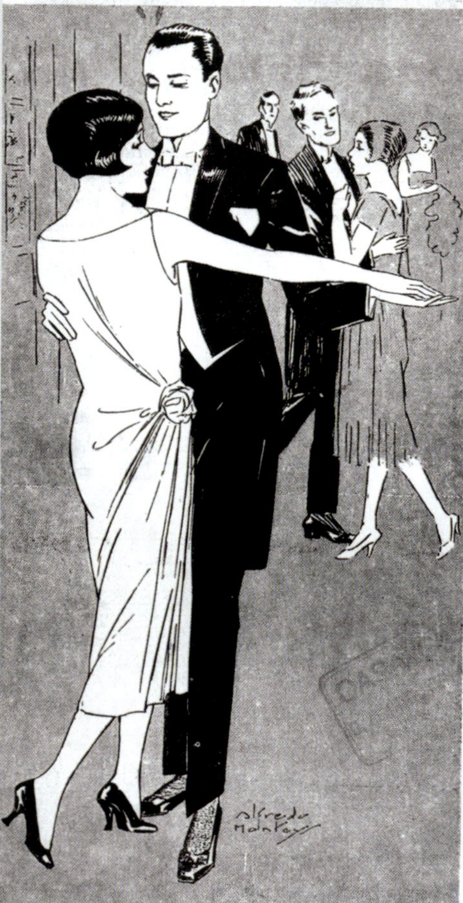

Orígenes del tango

El tango se desarrolló cuando Argentina se convirtió en uno de los países más ricos del mundo a finales del siglo XIX y atrajo a La Pampa a trabajadores italianos, españoles y franceses para la cosecha. Llevaron el tango de vuelta a Europa, donde comenzó su historia de éxito. En 1905-1906 se fundó la primera orquesta de tango en París. Después de los grandes éxitos en Europa, el tango regresó a Argentina, donde experimentó varios éxitos hasta la década de 1950.

Origens do Tango

O tango se desenvolveu quando a Argentina se tornou um dos países mais ricos do mundo no final do século XIX, trazendo trabalhadores italianos, espanhóis e franceses convidados para os pampas para a colheita. Eles trouxeram o tango de volta para a Europa, onde sua história de sucesso começou. Em 1905-06 foi fundada a primeira orquestra de tango em Paris. Depois dos grandes sucessos na Europa, o tango voltou à Argentina, onde experimentou vários destaques até a década de 1950.

Tango oorsprong

De tango ontwikkelde zich toen Argentinië aan het eind van de 19e eeuw één van de rijkste landen ter wereld werd en Italiaanse, Spaanse en Franse gastarbeiders naar de pampa haalde voor de oogst. Ze brachten de tango terug naar Europa, waar het succesverhaal begon. In 1905-06 werd in Parijs het eerste tango-orkest opgericht. Na de grote successen in Europa keerde de tango terug naar Argentinië waar hij tot in de jaren vijftig van de vorige eeuw meerdere hoogtepunten beleefde.

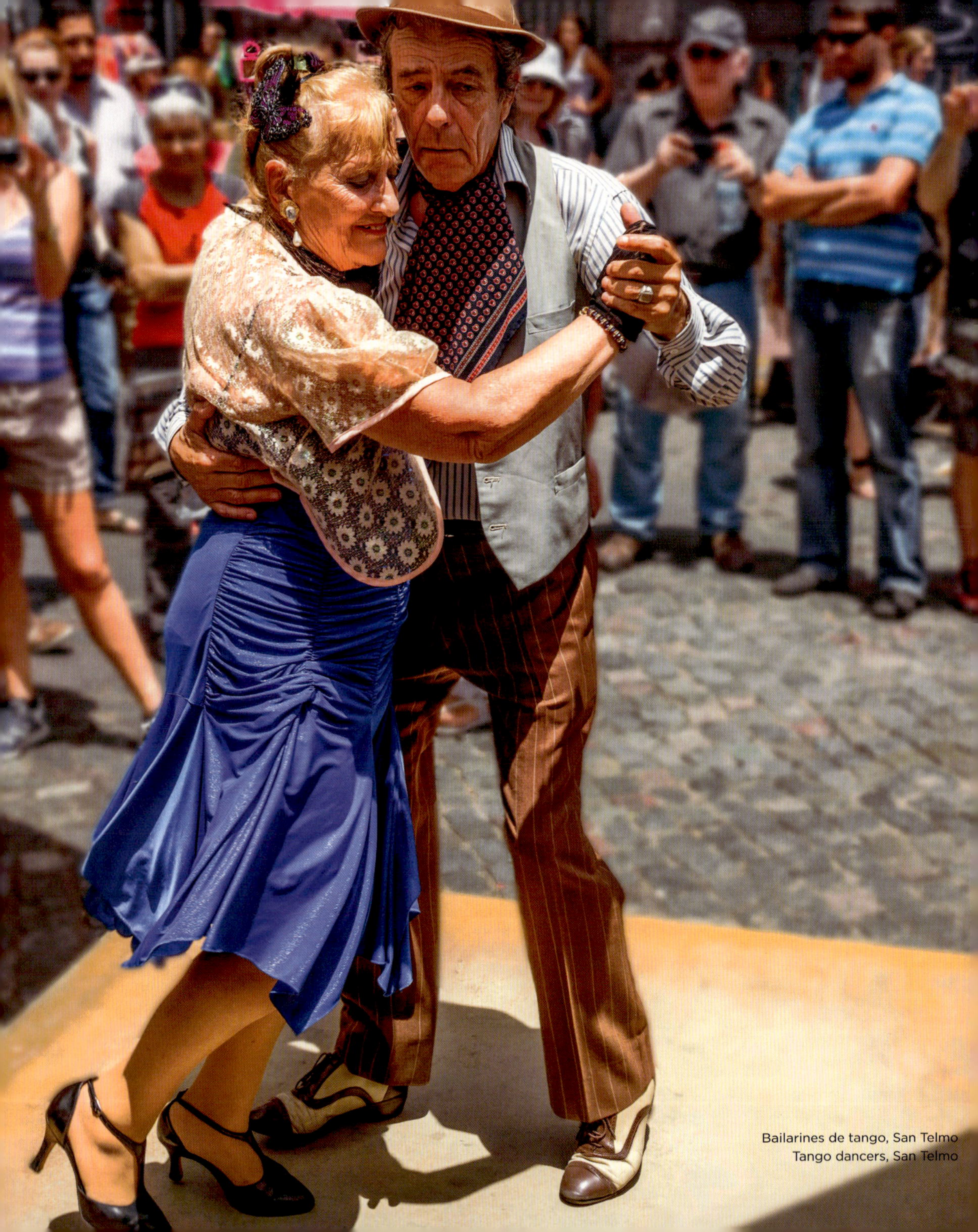

Bailarines de tango, San Telmo
Tango dancers, San Telmo

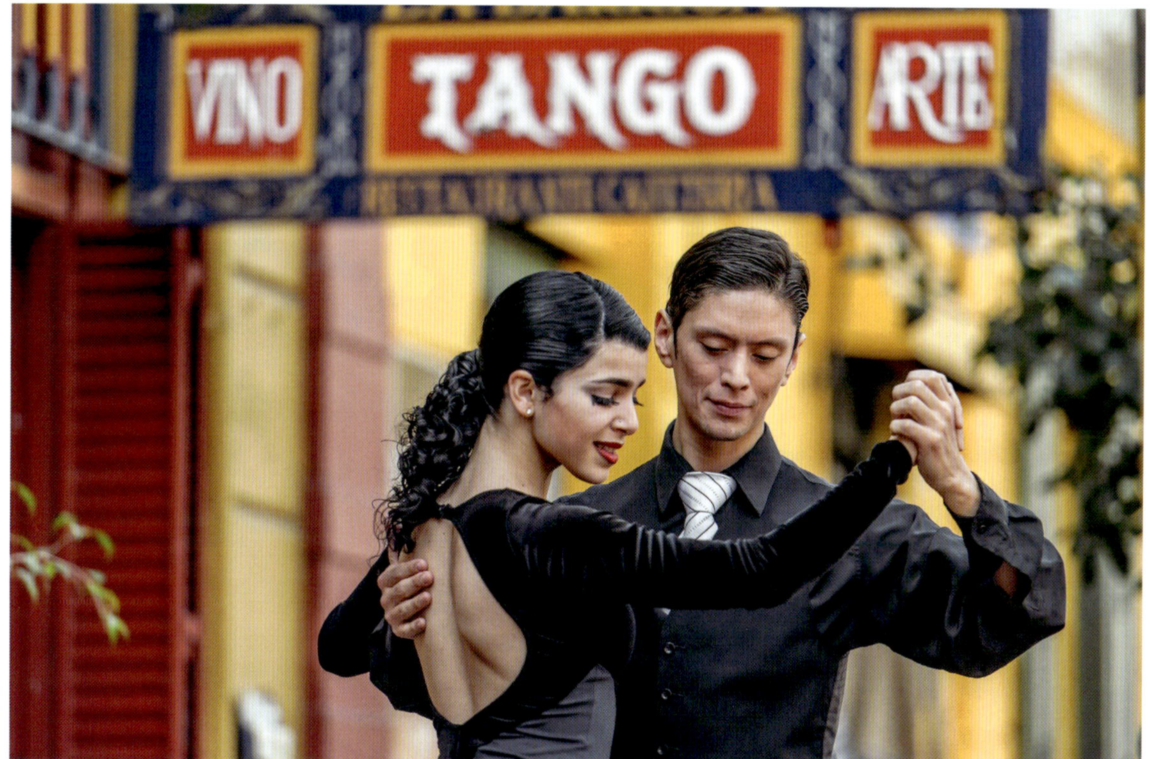

Bailarines de tango, San Telmo
Tango dancers, San Telmo

Tango Dance

Whether in the San Telmo or La Boca neighborhood, dancing is found not only in tango bars, but also on Sundays in the streets and squares. Young and old dancing couples, often also professionals, perform their art clad in outfits of the 1930s, 40s or 50s. The climax is the supposedly erotic pose of the "gancho", or hook, which is the swinging of the woman's lower leg around the man.

El baile del tango

Ya sea en el barrio de San Telmo o en el de La Boca, no solo se baila en los bares de tango, sino también los domingos en las calles y plazas. Parejas de baile jóvenes y mayores, a menudo también profesionales, muestran su arte en trajes de los años 30, 40 o 50. El clímax es la supuesta postura erótica del "gancho": el balanceo de la parte inferior de la pierna de la mujer alrededor del hombre.

Tango : la danse

À San Telmo, ou dans le quartier de la Boca, on ne danse pas le tango uniquement en salle, mais également, le dimanche, dans les rues et sur les places. Les couples plus ou moins jeunes, dont souvent des professionnels, présentent leur art dans des tenues des années 1930 à 1950. Le *gancho*, pose supposée érotique, marque l'apogée de la danse, lorsque la danseuse enveloppe une jambe autour de celle de son cavalier.

Dança do Tango

Seja no bairro de San Telmo ou La Boca, dançar não é só em bares de tango, mas também aos domingos, nas ruas e praças. Casais de dançarinos jovens e velhos, muitas vezes também profissionais, mostram sua arte em trajes dos anos 30, 40 ou 50. O destaque é a pose supostamente erótica do "gancho" – o movimento da perna da mulher em torno do homem.

Tangotanz

Ob im San Telmo- oder La Boca-Viertel, getanzt wird nicht nur in Tangolokalen, sondern auch sonntags auf der Straße und auf Plätzen. Junge und alte Tanzpaare, oft auch Profis, zeigen in Outfits der 1930er, 40er oder 50er Jahre ihre Kunst. Höhepunkt ist die vermeintlich erotische Pose des „gancho" – das Hochschlagen des Frauenunterschenkels um den Mann.

Tangodans

Of in de wijk San Telmo of La Boca; gedanst wordt niet alleen in tangozalen, maar ook zondags op straat en op pleinen. Jonge en oude dansparen, vaak ook professionals, tonen in outfits uit de jaren dertig, veertig of vijftig hun kunsten. Het hoogtepunt is de zogenaamde erotische houding van de "gancho" – het omhoogslaan van het onderbeen van de vrouw om de man heen.

Tango

Tango is considered the first 'scandal' dance.
To be good tango, a beautiful voice with an
excellent performance of the singers, dancers and
musicians, who like actors transfer great emotions
to the audience, is indispensable. Constant
renewals of the genre ensure that Buenos
Aires remains the place of pilgrimage for the
international tango scene.

Tango

Le tango fut la première danse « scandaleuse ». Un
bon tango exige une belle voix et une excelente
performance des chanteurs, danseurs et musiciens
qui s'appliquent, à la manière de comédiens,
à exprimer au public de puissants sentiments.
Le genre connaît en permanence de nouvelles
variations. Grâce à cette vitalité, Buenos Aires a su
rester un haut lieu de pèlerinage pour les amateurs
de tango du monde entier.

Tango

Tango gilt als der erste Skandaltanz. Zu einem
guten Tango sind eine schöne Stimme und eine
exzellente Performance der Sänger, Tänzer und
Musiker, die wie Schauspieler große Gefühle aufs
Publikum übertragen, unabdingbar. Ständige
Erneuerungen des Genres sorgen dafür, dass
Buenos Aires weiter die Pilgerstätte für die
internationale Tangoszene bleibt.

Tango

El tango es considerado el primer baile
escandaloso. Para un buen tango son
indispensables una hermosa voz y una excelente
actuación de los cantantes, bailarines y músicos,
que como actores transmiten grandes emociones
al público. Las constantes renovaciones del género
hacen que Buenos Aires siga siendo el lugar de
peregrinación de la escena internacional del tango.

Tango

Para um bom tango, uma bela voz e uma excelente
performance dos cantores, dançarinos e músicos,
que como atores transferem grandes emoções
para o público, são indispensáveis. As constantes
renovações do gênero garantem que Buenos Aires
continue sendo o lugar de peregrinação para o
cenário do tango internacional.

Tango

De tango wordt beschouwd als de eerste
schandaaldans. Voor een goede tango is een
mooie stem en een uitstekend optreden van de
zangers, dansers en muzikanten, die als acteurs
grote emoties op het publiek overbrengen,
noodzakelijk. Steeds nieuwe veranderingen van
het genre zorgen ervoor dat Buenos Aires het
bedevaartsoord voor de internationale tango-
scène blijft.

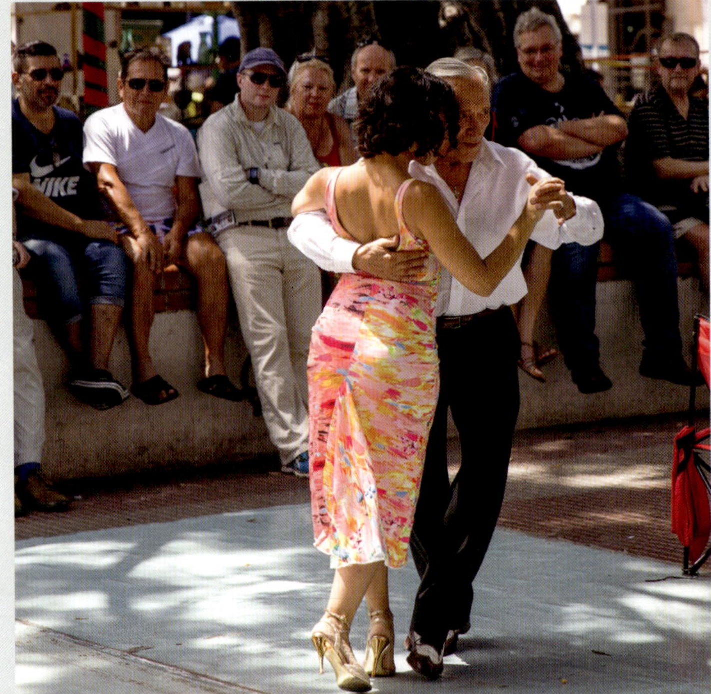

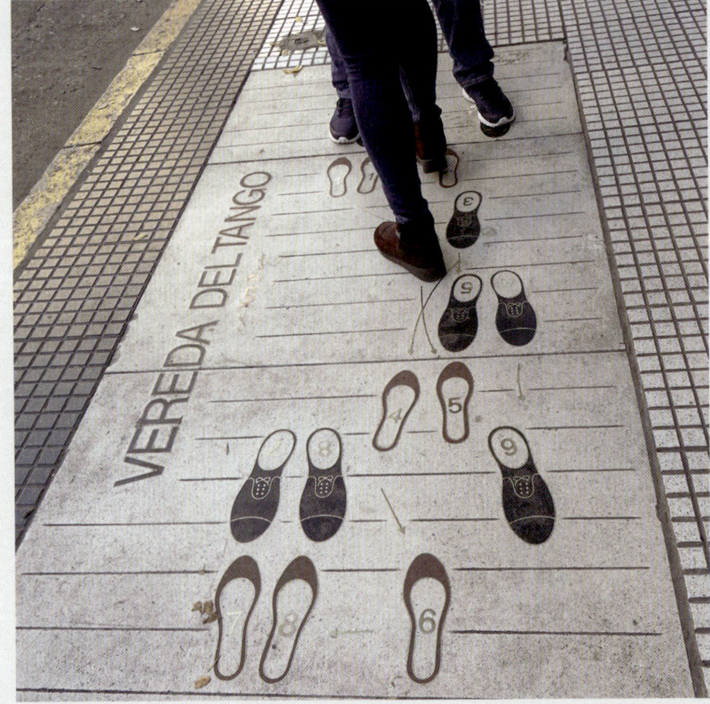

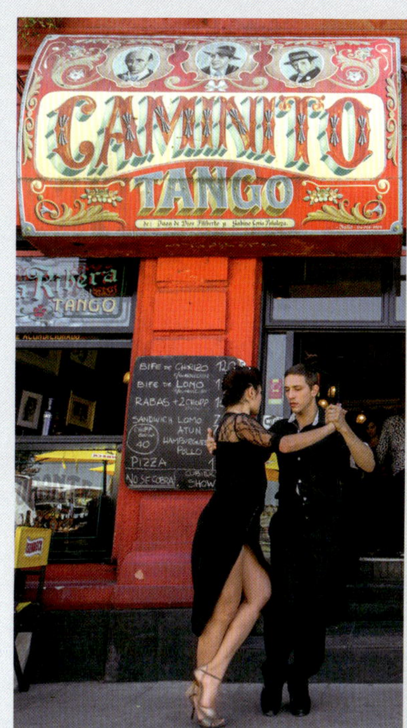
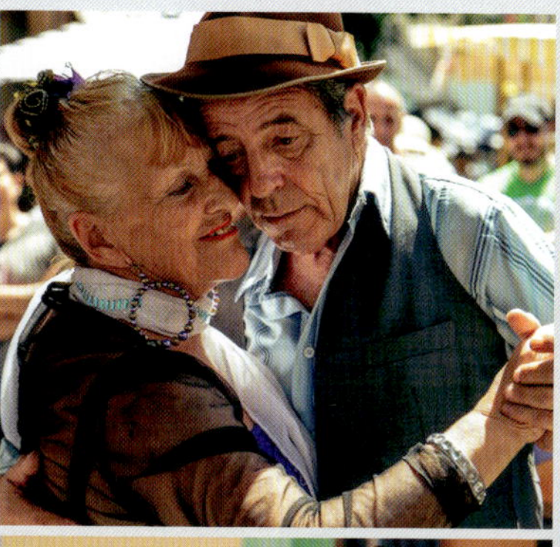
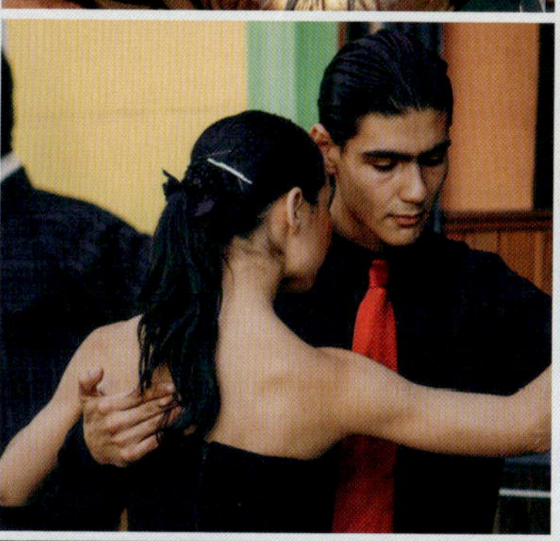
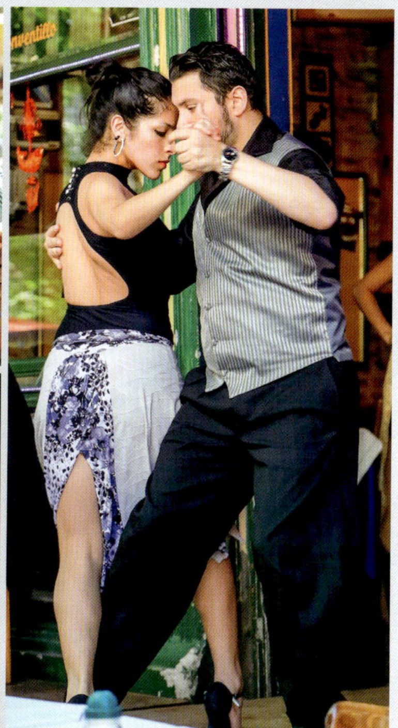
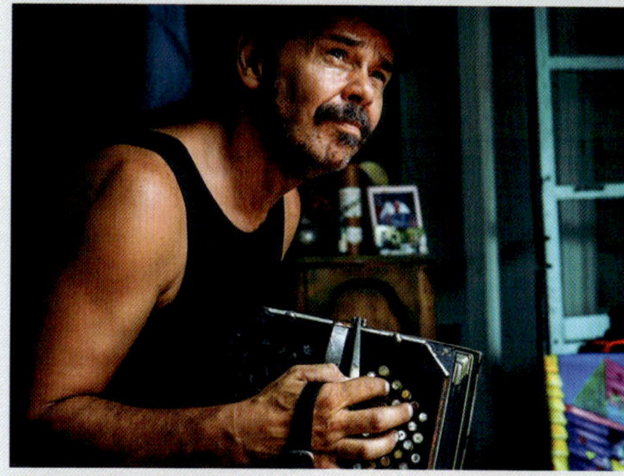
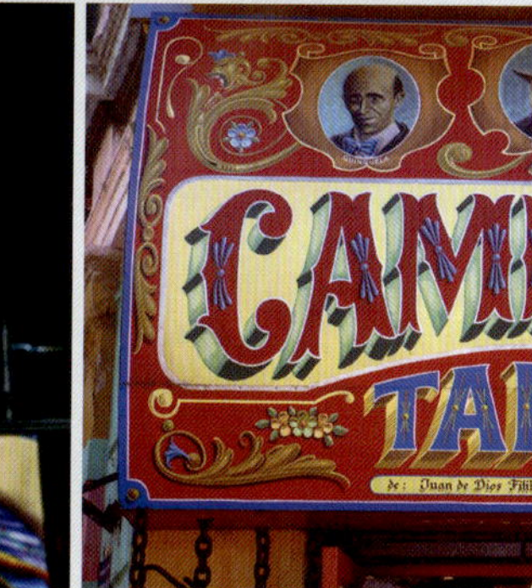
CAMINITO
TANGO
de : Juan de Dios Filiberto y Gabino Coria Peñaloza.
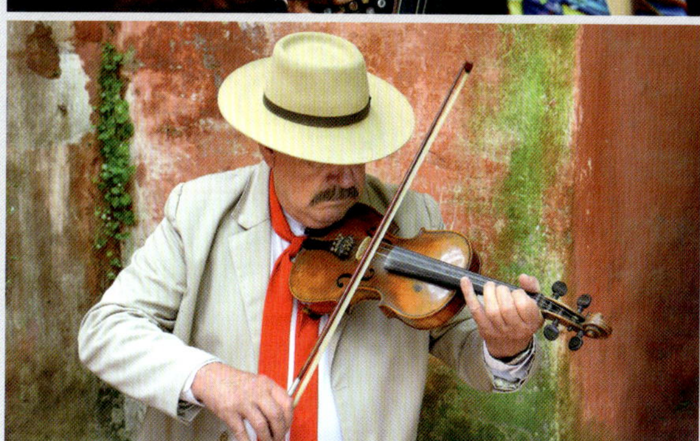
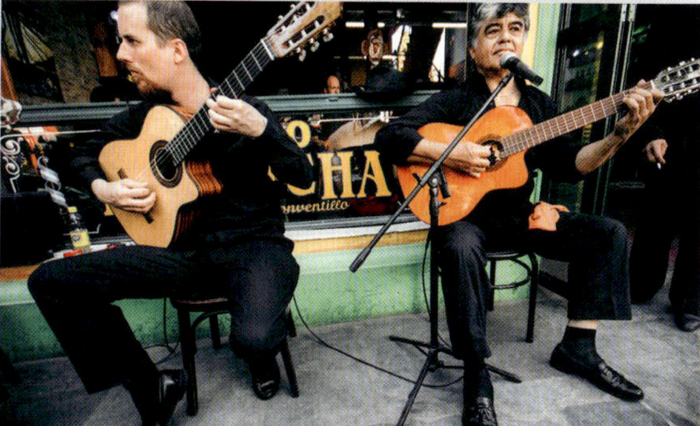

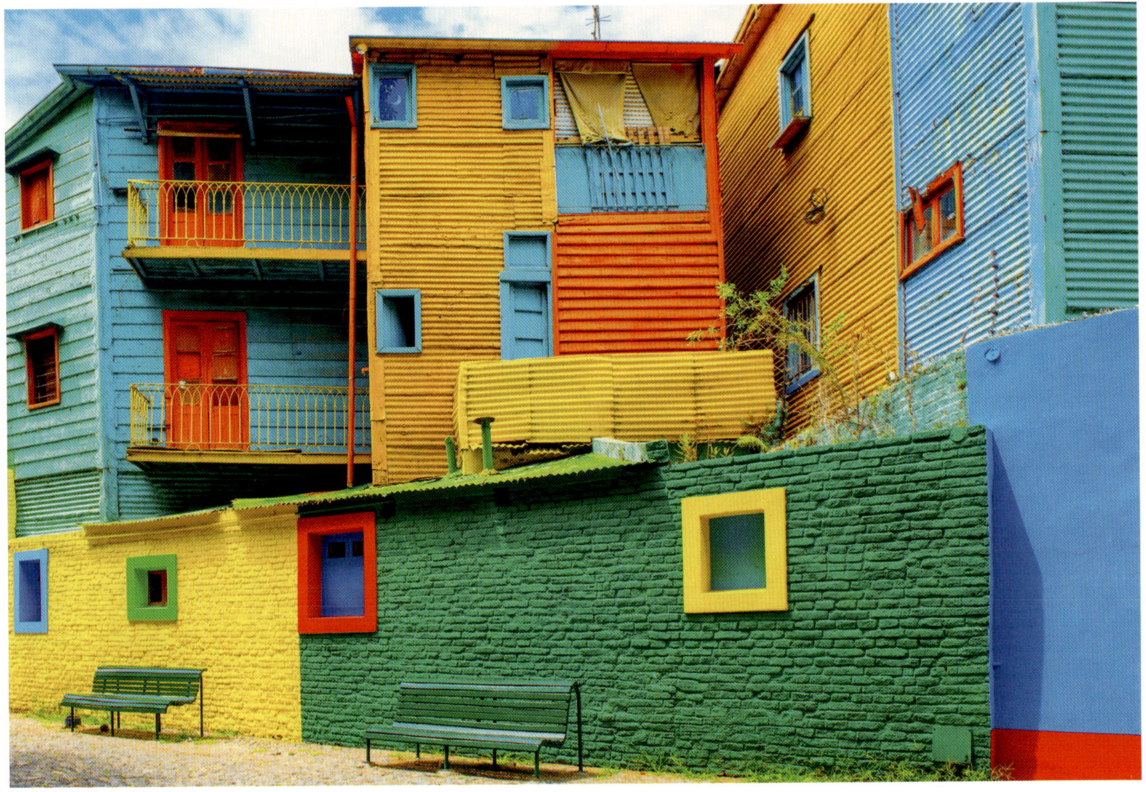

La Boca

La Boca

In the old harbor district, where the mouth *(boca)* of the river Riachuelo feeds into the Rio de la Plata, mainly poor Italian immigrants lived in the 19th century. Unusual houses were built here using the building material of sheet metal taken from shipwrecks, which was then painted with ship's paint in bright colors. La Boca is also famous for its numerous harbor pubs and the tango.

La Boca

En el antiguo barrio portuario, en la desembocadura (boca) del Río de la Plata, vivían principalmente inmigrantes italianos pobres en el siglo XIX. Aquí se construyeron casas especiales: el material de construcción era la chapa de los naufragios, que se pintaba con barniz para barcos en colores vivos. La Boca también es famosa por sus numerosos pubs del puerto y por el tango.

La Boca

L'ancien quartier portuaire, à l'embouchure *(boca)* du fleuve Riachuelo dans l'estuaire Río de la Plata, était, au XIXᵉ siècle, essentiellement habité par des immigrés italiens démunis. Ils y aménagèrent des maisons d'un type particulier, construites avec des tôles de vieux navires peintes à la laque marine en couleurs vives. La Boca est également célèbre pour les nombreux bistrots de son port et pour le tango.

La Boca

No século XIX principalmente imigrantes italianos pobres viviam no antigo bairro portuário, na foz *(boca)* do rio Riachuelo até o Rio da Prata. Aqui foram construídas casas especiais: o material de construção era chapa de metal de navios naufragados, que foi pintada com verniz de navio em cores vivas. La Boca também é famosa por seus numerosos pubs portuários e pelo tango.

La Boca

Im alten Hafenviertel, an der Mündung *(boca)* des Flusses Riachuelo in den Rio de la Plata lebten im 19. Jahrhundert vor allem arme italienische Einwanderer. Hier entstanden besondere Häuser: Baumaterial war Blech von Schiffswracks, das mit Schiffslack in knallbunten Farben bemalt wurde. Berühmt ist La Boca auch für seine zahlreichen Hafenkneipen und den Tango.

La Boca

In de oude havenwijk aan de monding *(boca)* van de rivier Riachuelo in de Rio de la Plata woonden in de 19e eeuw voornamelijk arme, Italiaanse immigranten. Hier ontstonden speciale huizen: bouwmateriaal was blik uit scheepswrakken dat met scheepslak in felle kleuren werd geschilderd. La Boca is ook beroemd om talrijke havencafés en de tango.

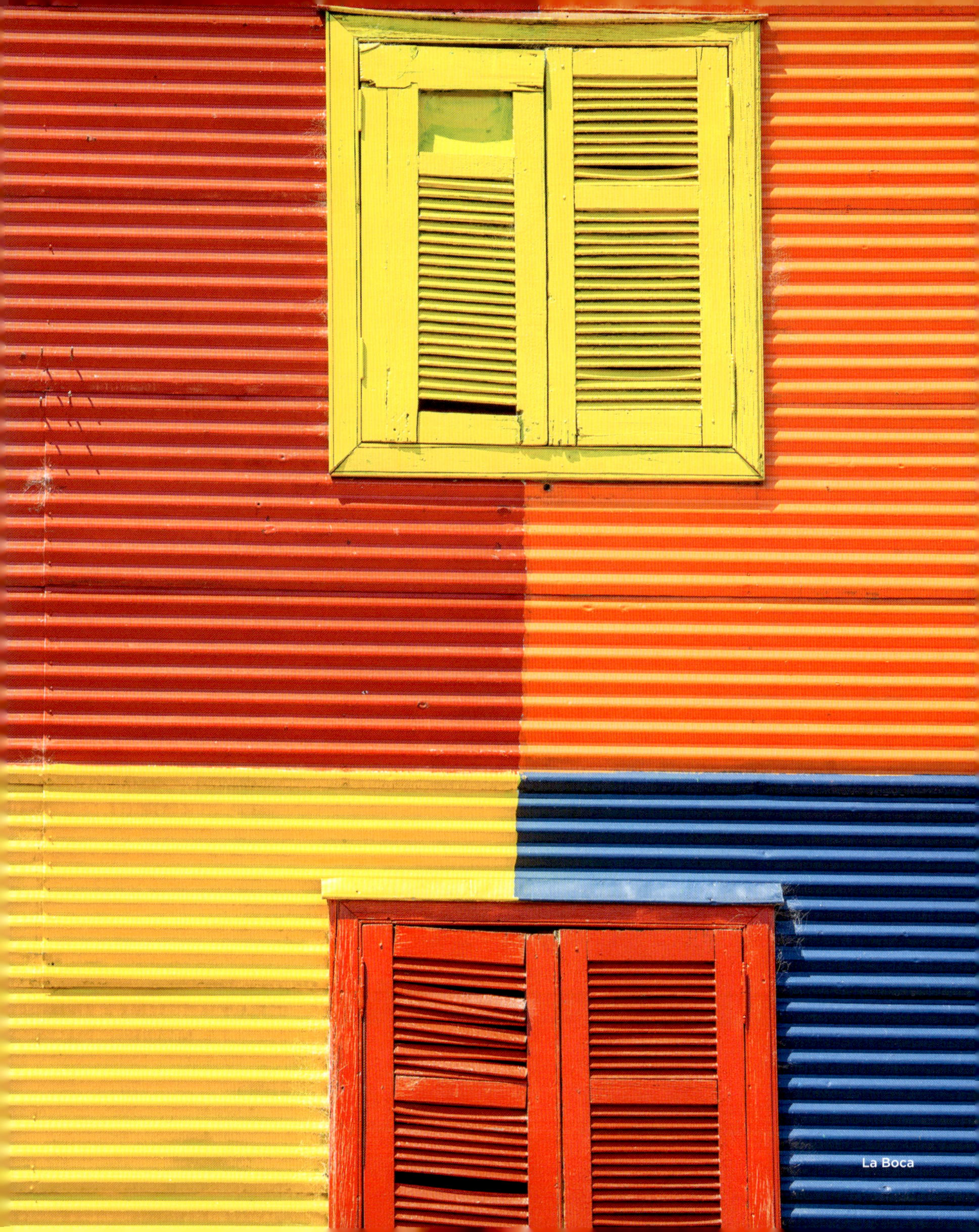
La Boca

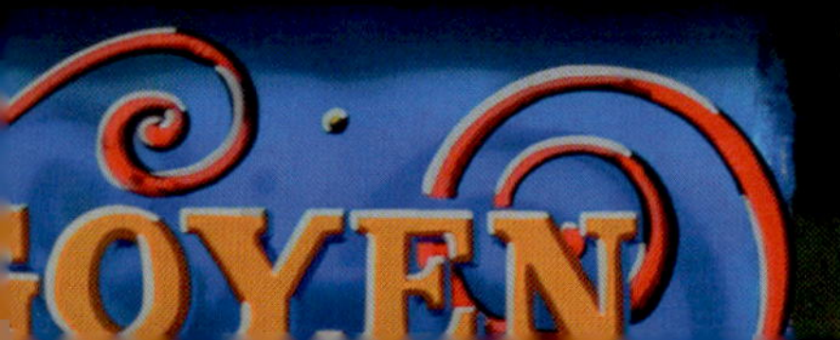
PARK
AL CA
FE
16!
OYEN

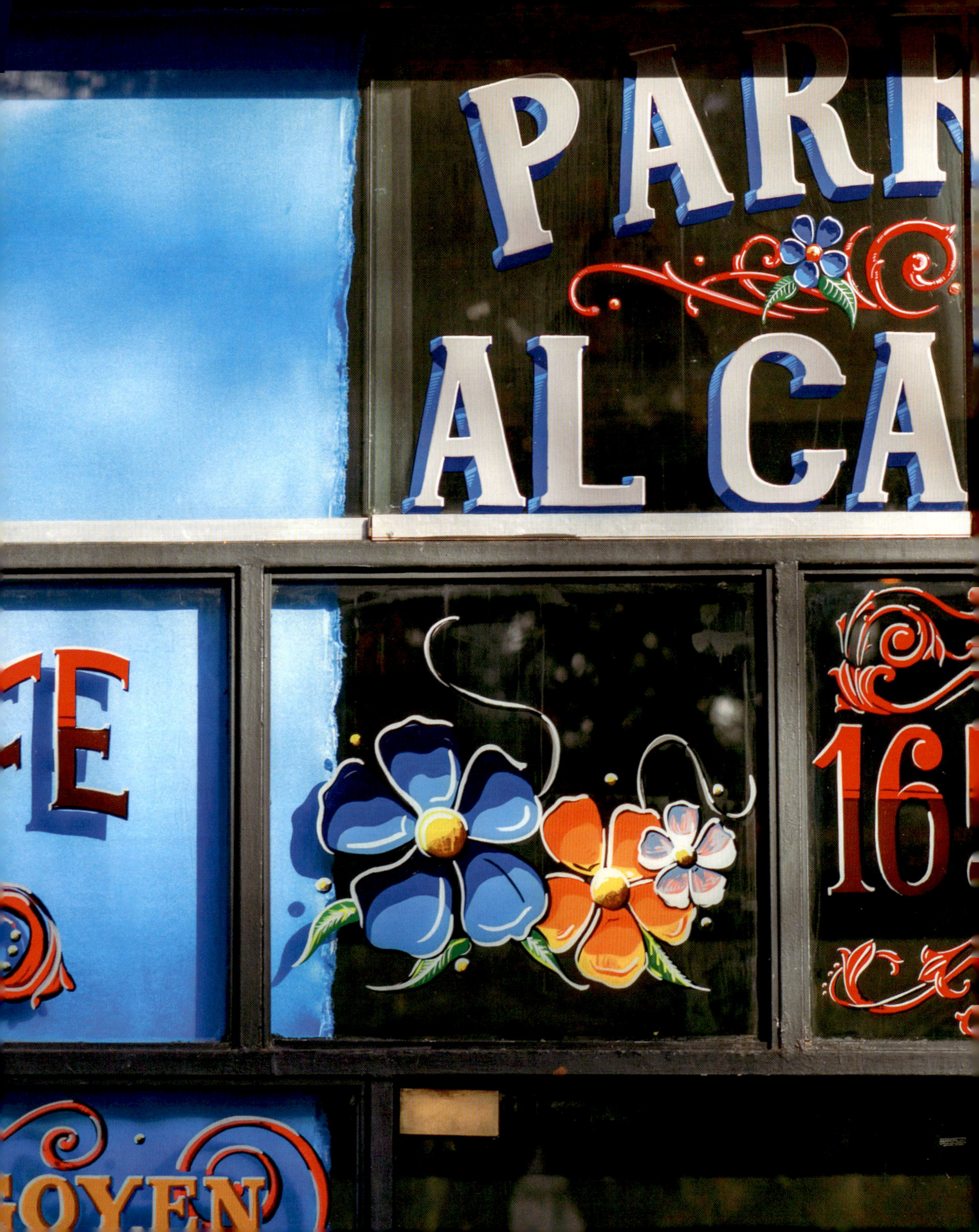

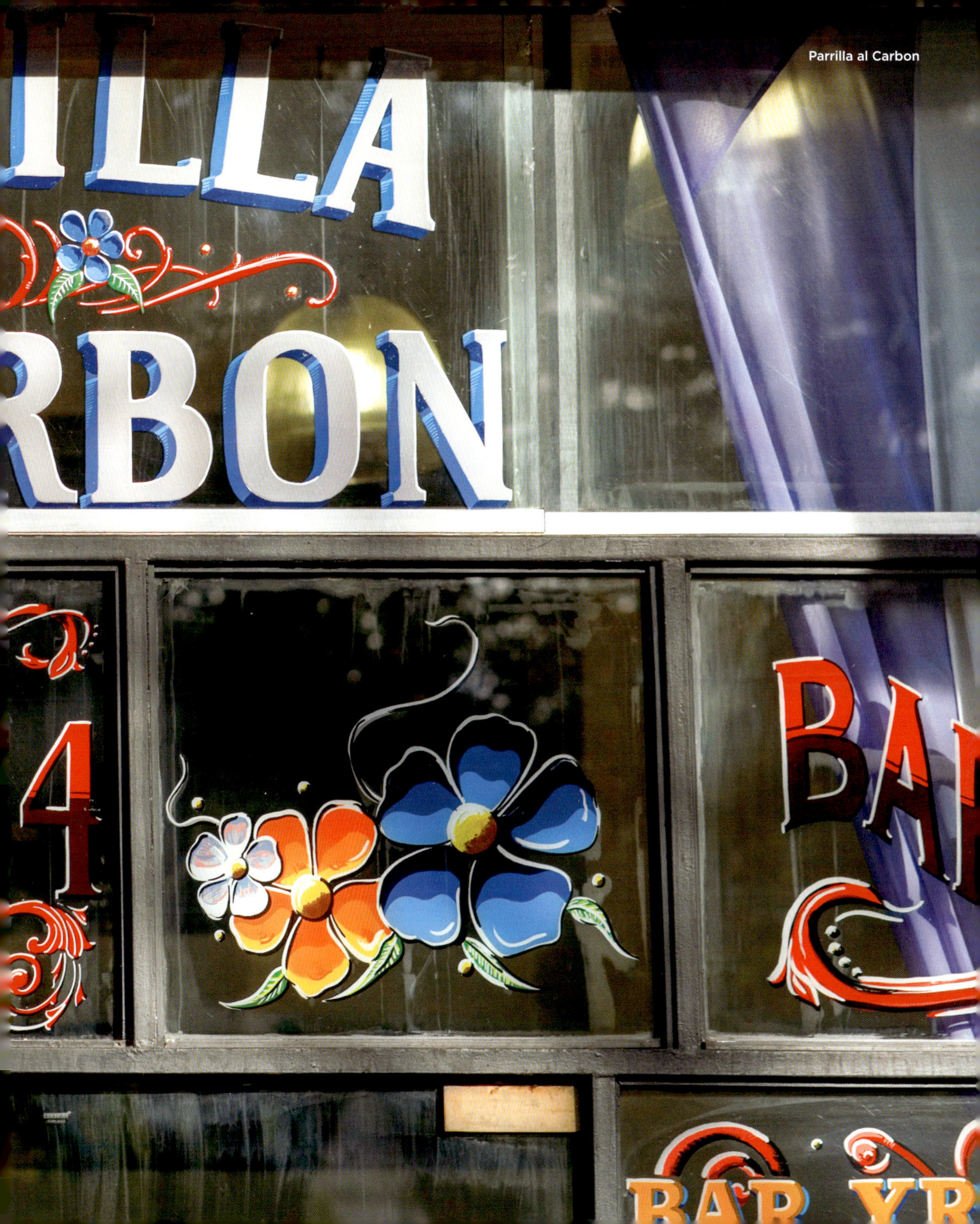

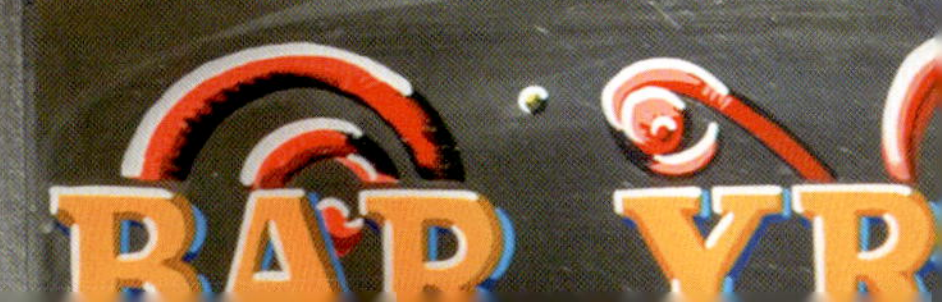

Parrilla al Carbon

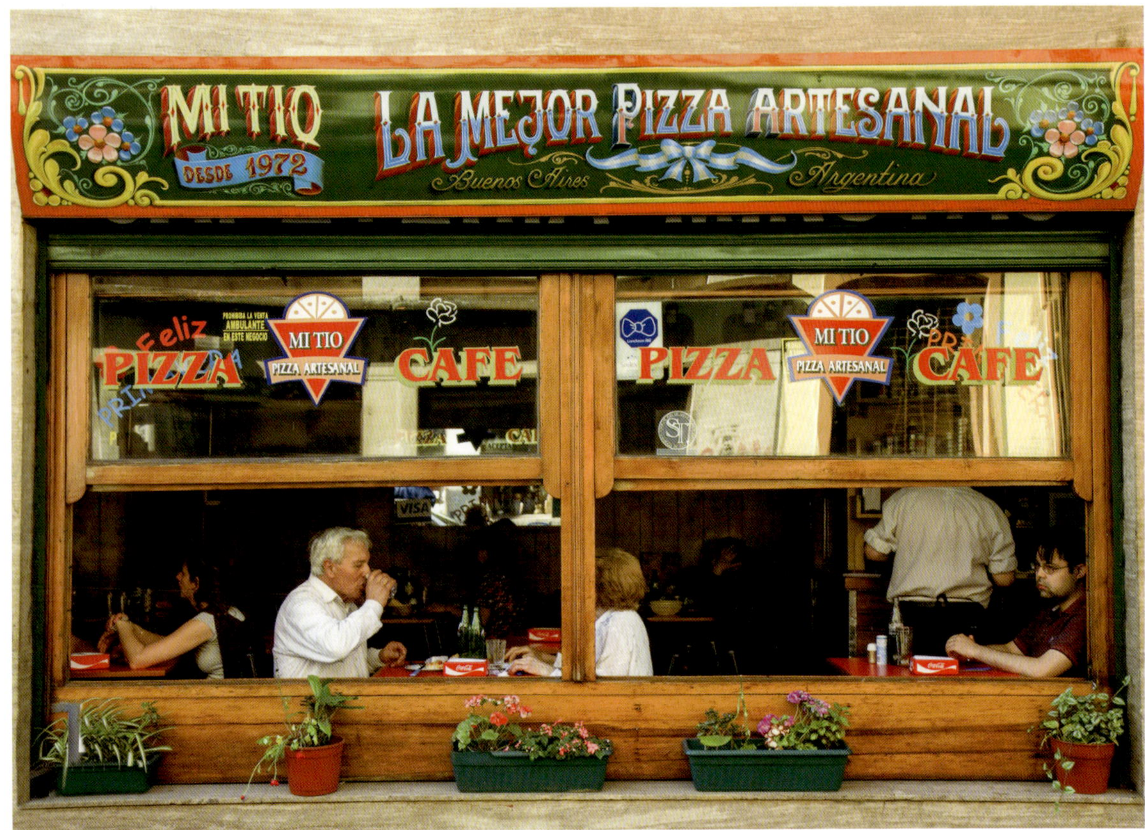

Restaurante, San Telmo
Restaurant, San Telmo

Parrilla

The highlight in this declared country of meat is a visit to a grill restaurant, or parrilla, which offers plate-sized pieces of beef of the best quality, with steaks that weigh easily 400 g (14 oz). Parrilla is the name for the external stone barbecue, around which the family gathers to eat and drink together on holidays and celebrations. In the city centre and in the northern zone of the city there are specialized parrillas, which cater for this family ritual with the highest quality meat and hospitable atmosphere. Traditional restaurants of the Italian communities in San Telmo or Palermo also offer classic Italian cuisine.

Parrilla

La visite d'un restaurant de grillades, ou *parrilla,* reste un temps fort au pays proclamé de la viande. On y sert des pièces de bœuf de qualité aussi larges qu'une assiette et des steaks généreux de 400 g. La *parrilla* se caractérise par son gril de plein air en pierres maçonnées, autour duquel s'attablent les familles les jours fériés ou à l'occasion de diverses célébrations. Au centre et au nord de la ville, des *parrillas* spécialisées rendent hommage au rituel familial avec une atmosphère hospitalière et un niveau de qualité exceptionnel. Les restaurants traditionnels des quartiers italiens de San Telmo ou Palermo servent également de la cuisine italienne.

Parrilla

Das Highlight im deklarierten Fleischland ist der Besuch im Grillrestaurant, Parrilla. Angeboten werden tellergroße Stücke Rindfleisch bester Qualität, Steaks, die locker 400 g auf die Waage bringen. Parrilla bezeichnet den aus Stein gemauerten Grill im Freien, um den sich die Familie an Feiertagen und zu Festen versammelt, gemeinsam isst und trinkt. Im Zentrum und in der Nordzone der Stadt gibt es spezialisierte Parrillas, die mit höchster Qualität und gastlicher Atmosphäre dem Familienritual gerecht werden. Traditionelle Restaurants der italienischen Gemeinde in San Telmo oder Palermo bieten aber auch klassische italienische Küche.

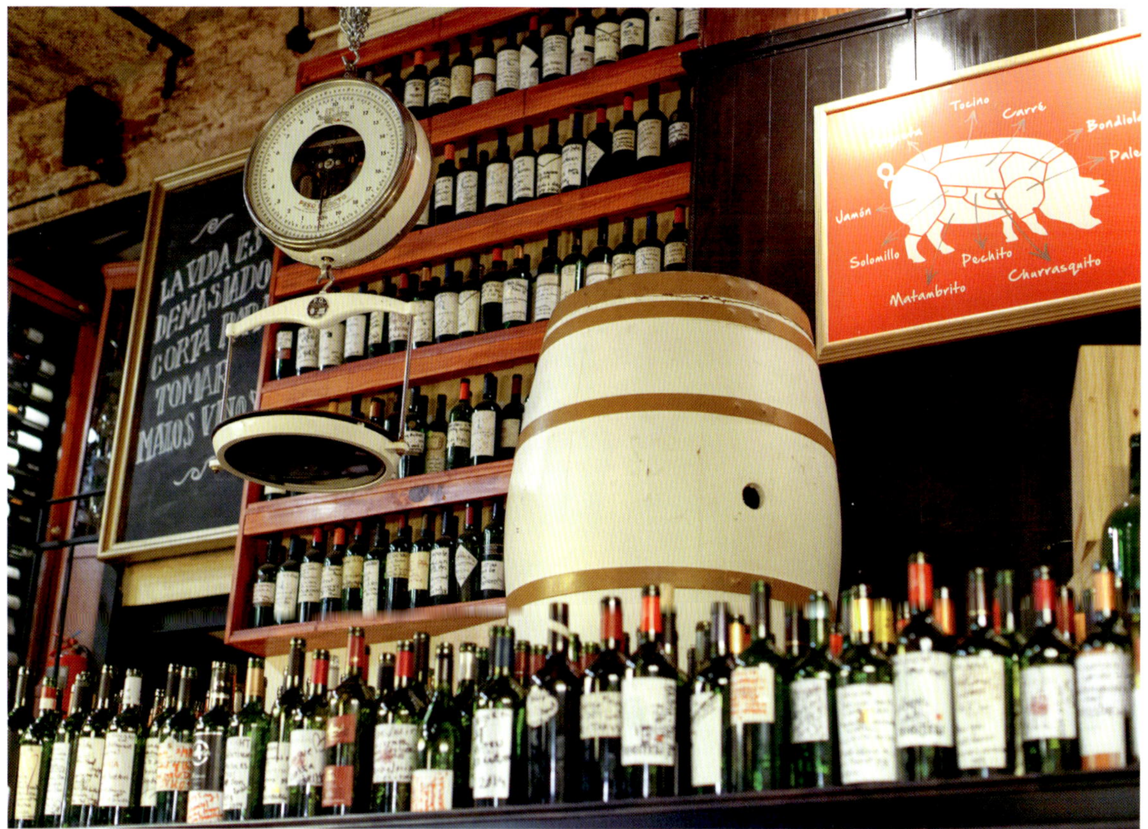

Parrilla Don Julio, Palermo

Parrilla

El punto culminante en el declarado país
de la carne es una visita a una parrilla.
Se ofrecen piezas de carne de vacuno de
la mejor calidad del tamaño de un plato,
filetes que pueden pesar fácilmente 400 g.
La parrilla es la barbacoa de piedra que se
encuentra en el exterior, alrededor de la
cual la familia se reúne, come y bebe junta
en los días festivos y celebraciones. En el
centro y en la zona norte de la ciudad hay
parrillas especializadas, que cumplen con
el ritual familiar con la más alta calidad y
ambiente hospitalario. Los restaurantes
tradicionales de la comunidad italiana en
San Telmo o Palermo también ofrecen
comida italiana clásica.

Parrilla

O destaque no declarado "país da carne"
é uma visita ao restaurante de grelhados,
Parrilla. São oferecidos pedaços de
carne de vaca da melhor qualidade do
tamanho de um prato, bifes que pesam
facilmente 400 g. Parrilla quer dizer uma
churrasqueira construída em pedra, que é
usada ao ar livre, ao redor do qual a família
se reúne, todos comem e bebem juntos
nos feriados e festas. No centro da cidade
e na zona norte da cidade, existem parrillas
especializadas, que atende os requisitos
do ritual familiar com a mais alta qualidade
e atmosfera hospitaleira. Os restaurantes
tradicionais da comunidade italiana em
San Telmo ou Palermo também oferecem a
clássica cozinha italiana.

Parrilla

Het hoogtepunt in het uitgesproken
vleesland is een bezoek aan het
grillrestaurant, parrilla. Hier worden
stukken rundvlees van de beste kwaliteit en
zo groot als het bord aangeboden, steaks
die gemakkelijk 400 gram wegen. Parrilla
verwijst naar de stenen barbecue buiten,
waar de familie zich op feestdagen en bij
feesten omheen schaart en samen eet en
drinkt. In het centrum en de noordelijke
zone van de stad zijn gespecialiseerde
parrilla's die met de hoogste kwaliteit
en gastvrije sfeer aan het familieritueel
voldoen. De traditionele restaurants van
de Italiaanse gemeenschap in San Telmo
of Palermo bieden echter ook de klassieke
Italiaanse keuken aan.

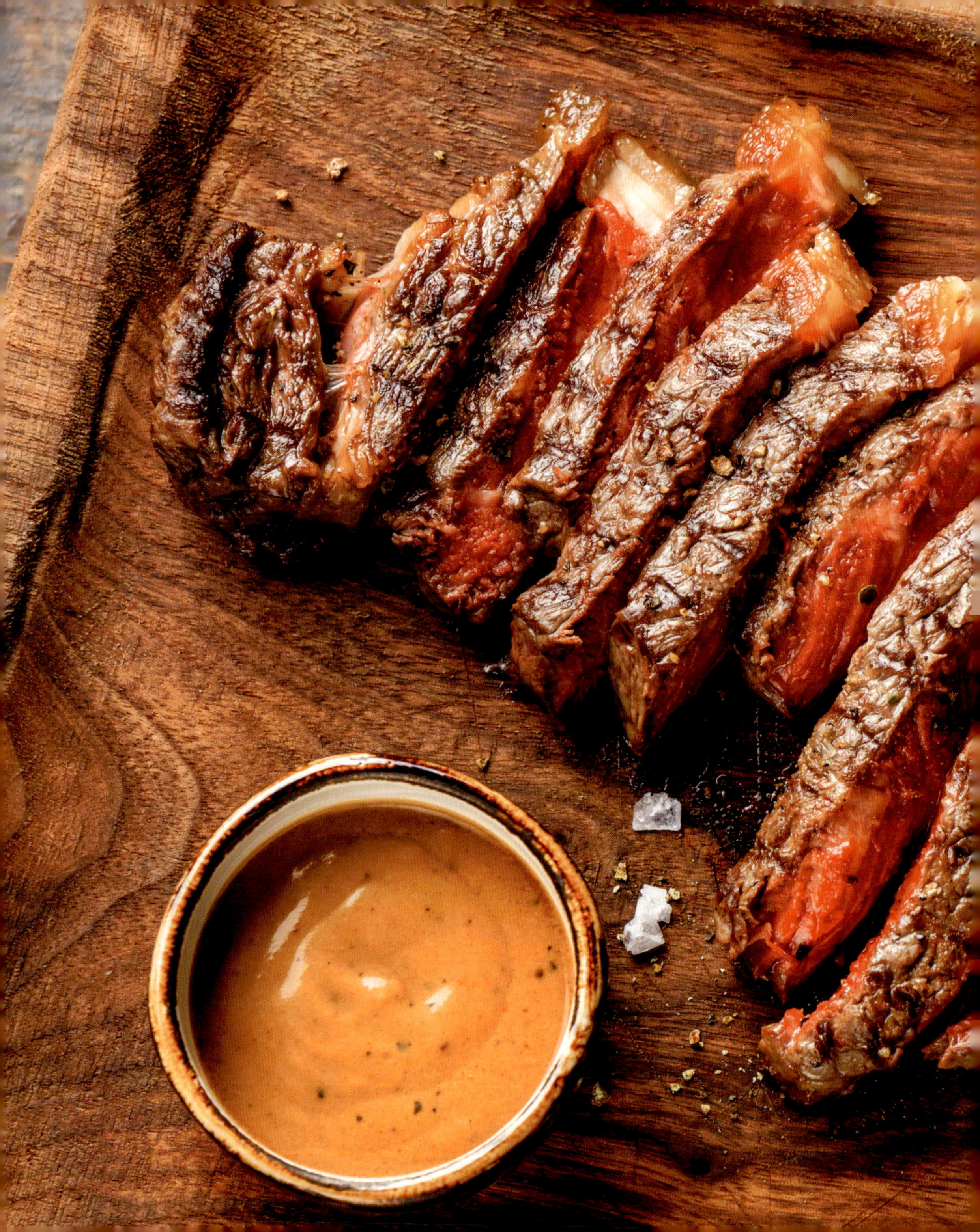

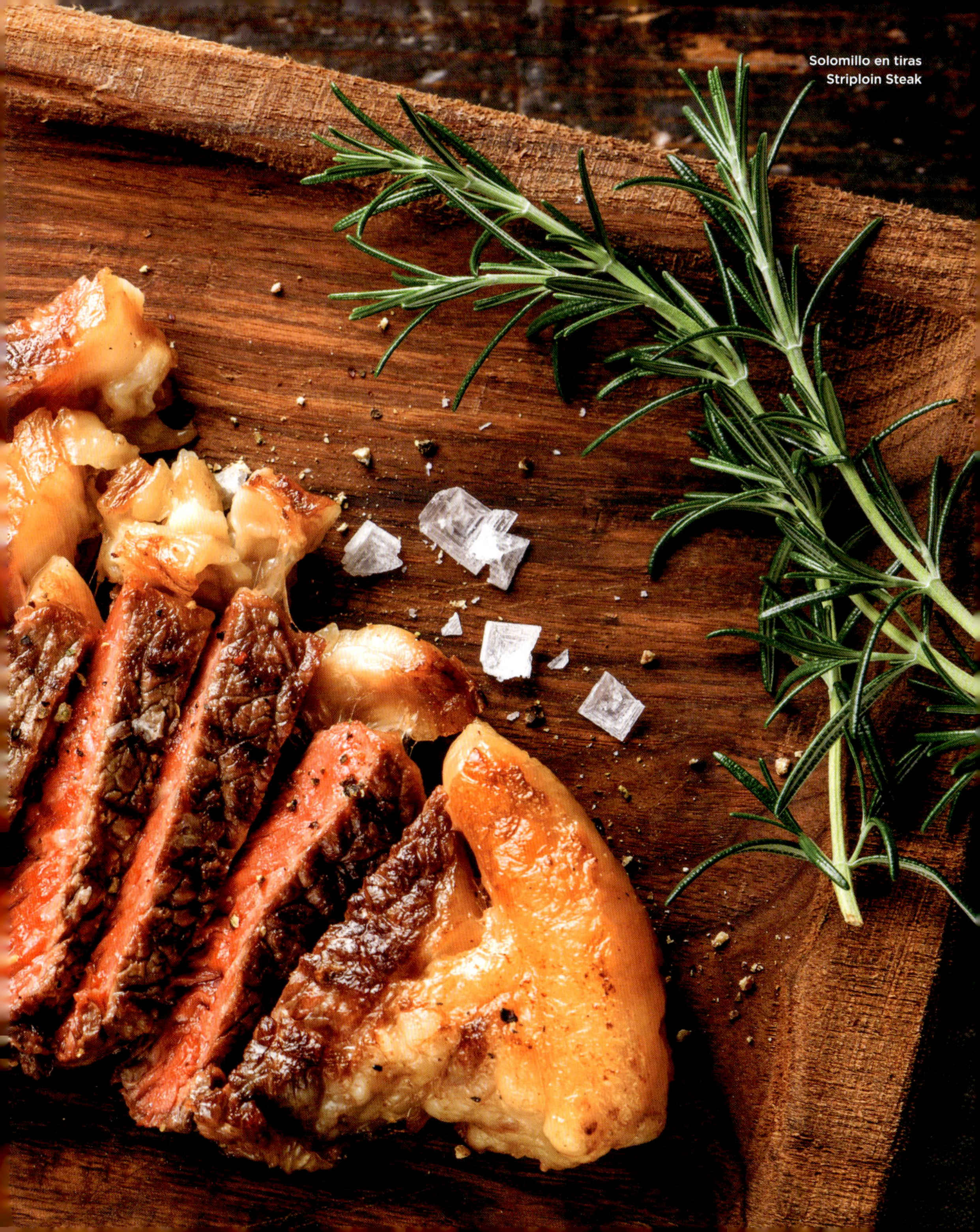

Solomillo en tiras
Striploin Steak

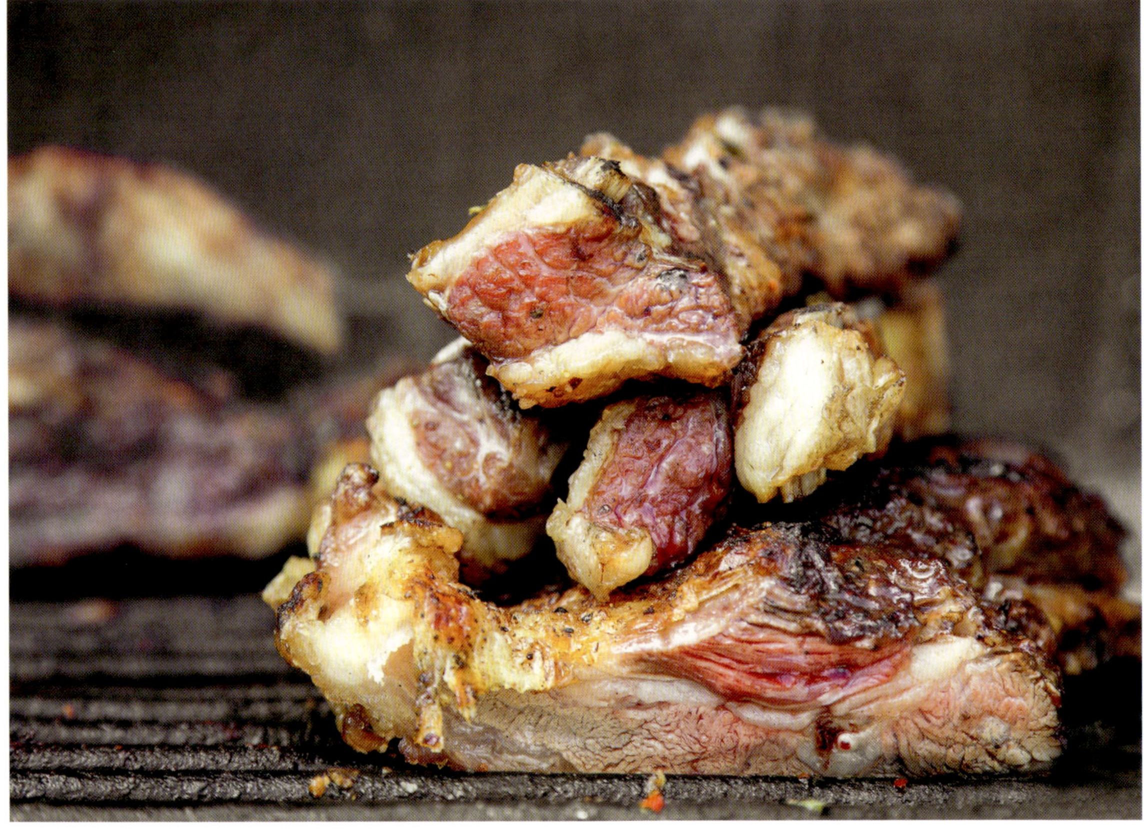

Asado argentino

Argentine asado

The typical grilled meat platter is rich in variations. Everything from the animal is used, as not everyone can afford expensive fillet pieces. What is decisive is the optimal cut, about which there are many differing opinions, along with the method of preparation. The meat, cooked over charcoal, should be juicy and aromatic. Classics are the grilled steaks of Black Angus beef with pepper sauce. *Bife de chorizo,* the sirloin, is the tastiest. *Bife de costilla,* also called *chuleta,* the T-bone steak and *tira de asado,* shortribs, as well as *vacío,* flank steak, are popular, as are also marinated pork ribs, blood sausage and offal in a wheat flour coat. Kidneys, sweetbreads and marrow bones are also grilled.

Asado argentin

Cette assiette de grillades typique contient des morceaux variés. Tout ce qui vient de l'animal est utilisé, car tout le monde ne peut pas s'offrir les morceaux coûteux. La technique de découpe, sur laquelle les avis divergent, et la préparation sont décisives. La viande cuite sur charbon de bois doit être juteuse et parfumée. Le steak grillé de bœuf Angus noir, avec sa sauce au poivre, est un autre grand classique. Le *bife de chorizo,* morceau d'aloyau, est particulièrement savoureux. Le *bife de costilla,* ou *chuleta* (steak T-Bone), la *tira de asado* (plat de côte) ainsi que le *vacío* (steak dans le flanc) sont tout aussi appréciés. Côtes de porc marinées, boudin, abats enveloppés de farine, rognons, ris de veau et os à moelle sont également cuisinés sur le gril.

Asado Argentino

Die typische Grillfleischplatte ist variantenreich. Alles vom Tier wird verwertet, denn nicht jeder kann teure Filetstücke kaufen. Entscheidend sind der optimale Schnitt, über den es verschiedenste Meinungen gibt, und die Zubereitungsart. Das auf Holzkohle gegarte Fleisch soll saftig und aromatisch sein. Klassiker sind gegrillte Steaks vom schwarzen Angus-Rind mit Pfeffersauce. *Bife de chorizo,* das Lendenstück, ist am schmackhaftesten. *Bife de costilla,* auch *chuleta* genannt, das T-Bone Steak und *tira de asado,* Shortribs, sowie *vacío,* Flankensteak, sind beliebt. Aber auch marinierte Schweinerippchen, Blutwurst, Innereien im Weizenmehlmantel, Nieren, Kalbsbries und Markknochen kommen auf den Grill.

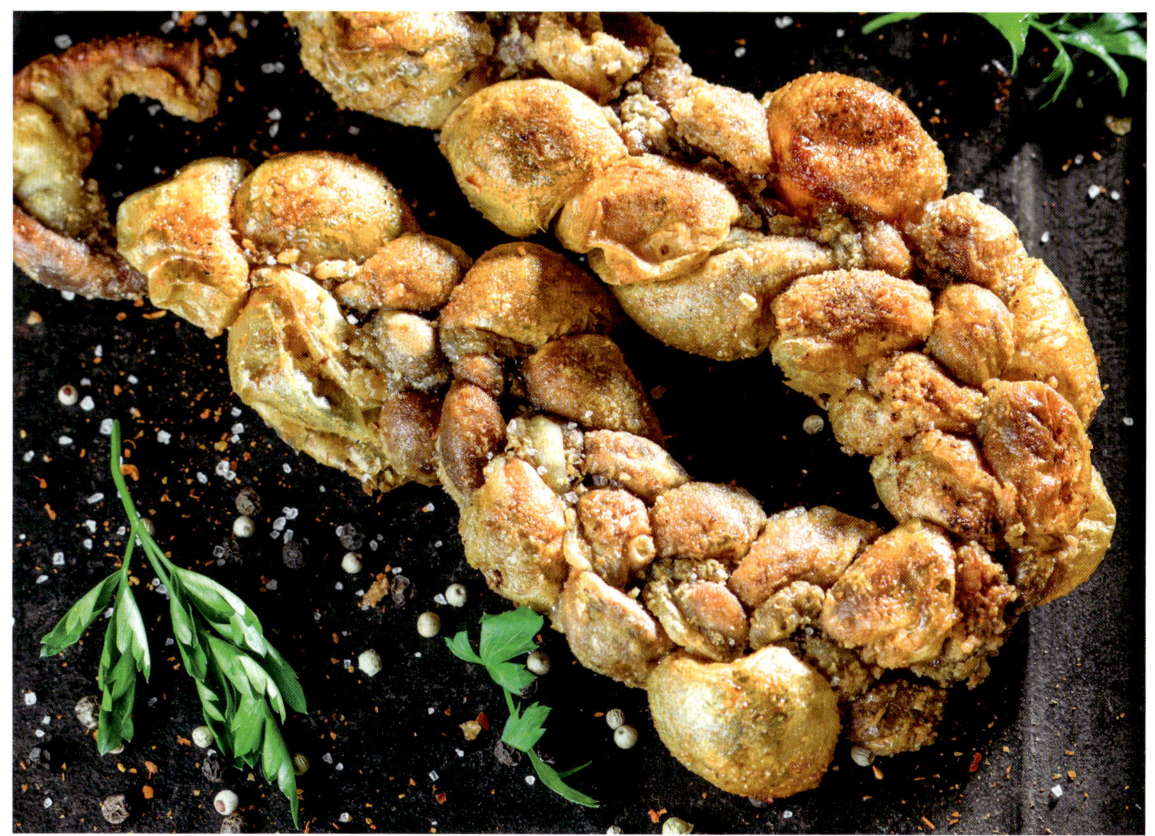

Chinchulines rellenos

Asado argentino

El típico plato de carne a la parrilla tiene muchas variaciones. Se aprovechan todas las partes del animal, porque no todos pueden comprar piezas de filete costosas. Lo que es decisivo es el corte óptimo (sobre el que existen numerosas opiniones diferentes) y el método de preparación. La carne, cocida al carbón, debe ser jugosa y aromática. Los clásicos son los filetes de carne de vacuno angus a la parrilla con salsa de pimienta. El bife de chorizo es el más sabroso, pero también son populares el bife de costilla o chuleta y la tira de asado, así como el vacío (el bistec de falda). También se asan costillas de cerdo marinadas, morcilla, riñones, mollejas y hueso de osobuco.

Asado argentino

A típica travessa de carne grelhada é rica em variações. Tudo do animal é aproveitado, porque nem todos podem comprar peças de filete caras. O que é decisivo é o corte ideal, sobre o qual existem várias opiniões diferentes, e o método de preparação. Diz-se que carne cozida em carvão vegetal é suculenta e aromática. Os clássicos são bifes grelhados da carne Angus preta com molho de pimenta. *Bife de chorizo*, o lombo de vaca, é o mais saboroso. *Bife de costilla*, também chamado *chuleta*, o T-bone steak e *tira de asado,* shortribs, assim como *vacío,* bife de flanco, são populares. Costelas de porco marinadas, morcela, miudezas numa camada de farinha de trigo, rins, molejas e ossos de medula também são servidos na grelha.

Argentijnse asado

De typische schotel gegrilld vlees is rijk aan variaties. Alles van het dier wordt gebruikt, want niet iedereen kan dure filetstukken kopen. Doorslaggevend is de optimale insnijding waarover veel verschillende meningen bestaan én de bereidingswijze. Het op houtskool gegaarde vlees moet sappig en aromatisch zijn. Klassiekers zijn gegrilde steaks van het zwarte Angus-rund met pepersaus. *Bife de chorizo,* het lendenstuk, is het smaakvolste. *Bife de costilla,* ook *chuleta* genoemd, de T-bone steak en *tira de asado,* shortribs, evenals *vacío* en flank steak, zijn populair. Maar ook gemarineerde varkensribben, bloedworst, inwendige organen en ingewanden in een mantel van tarwemeel, nieren, zwezerik en mergbeenderen komen op de grill.

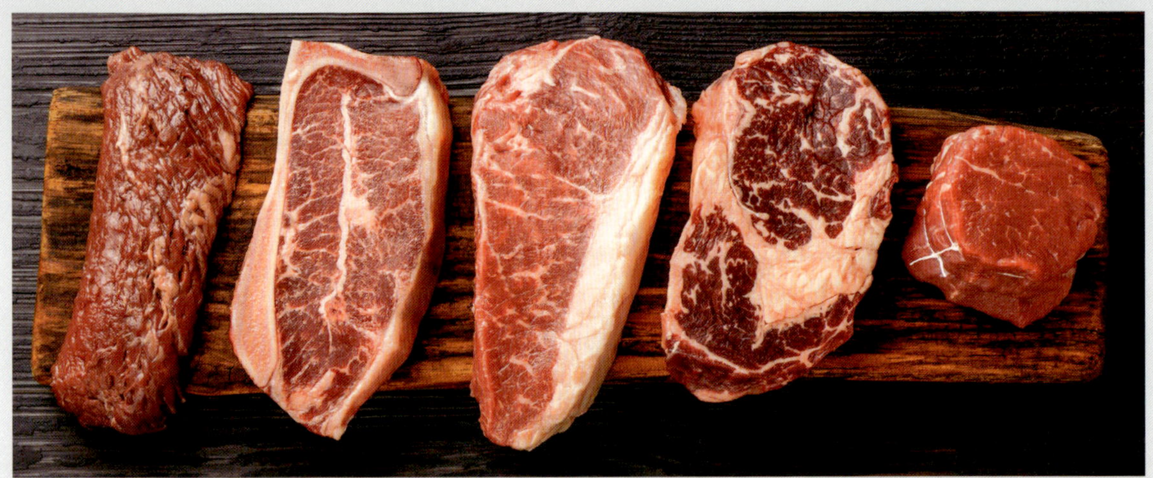

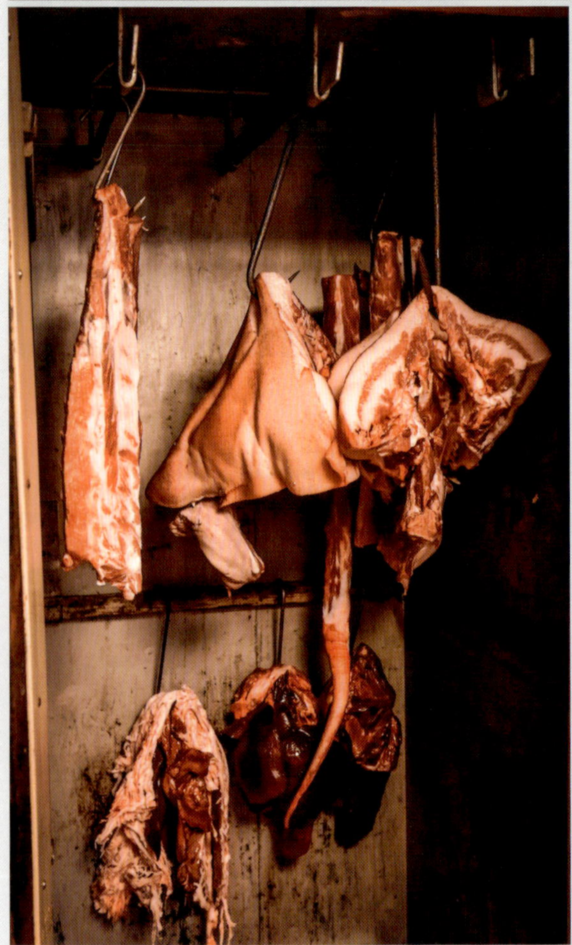

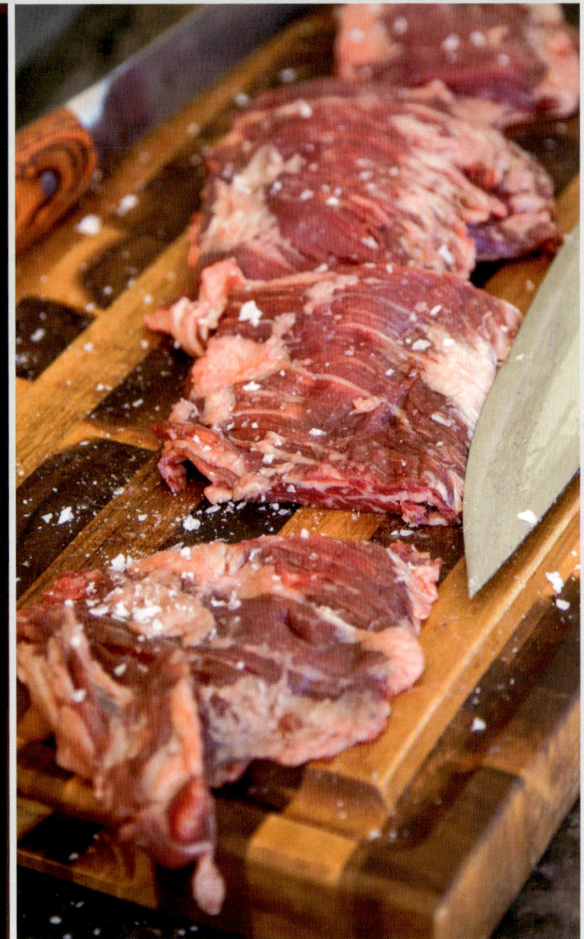

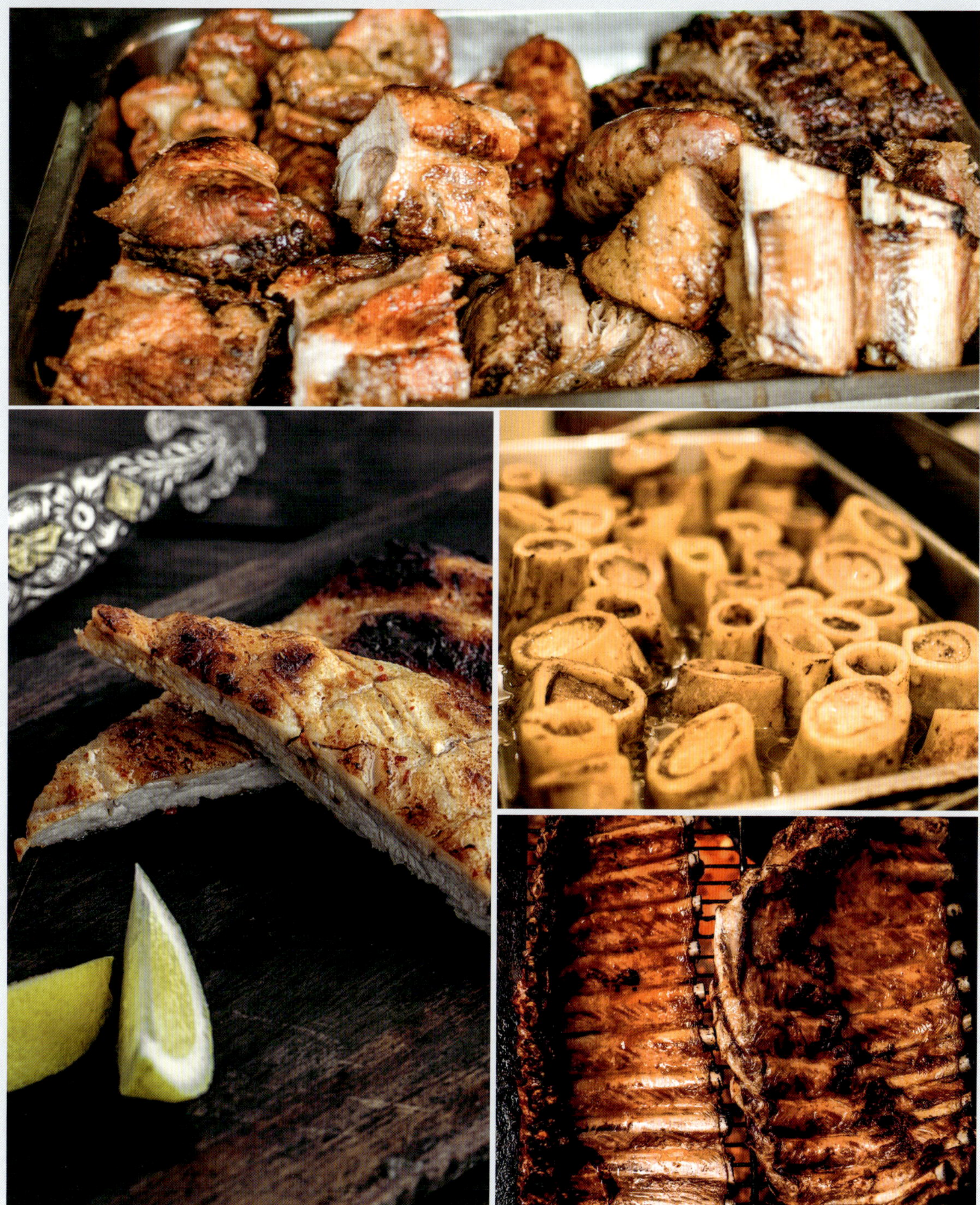

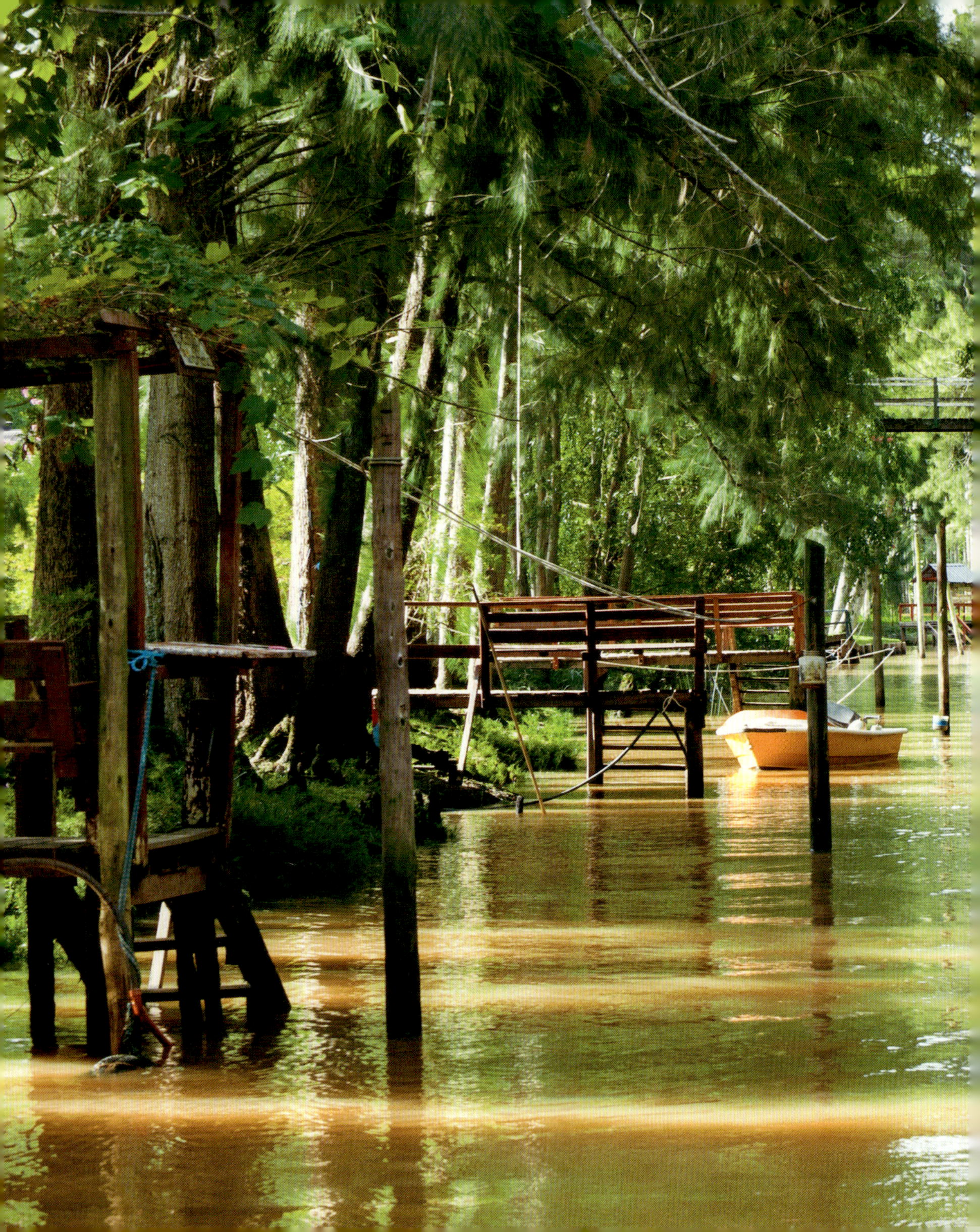

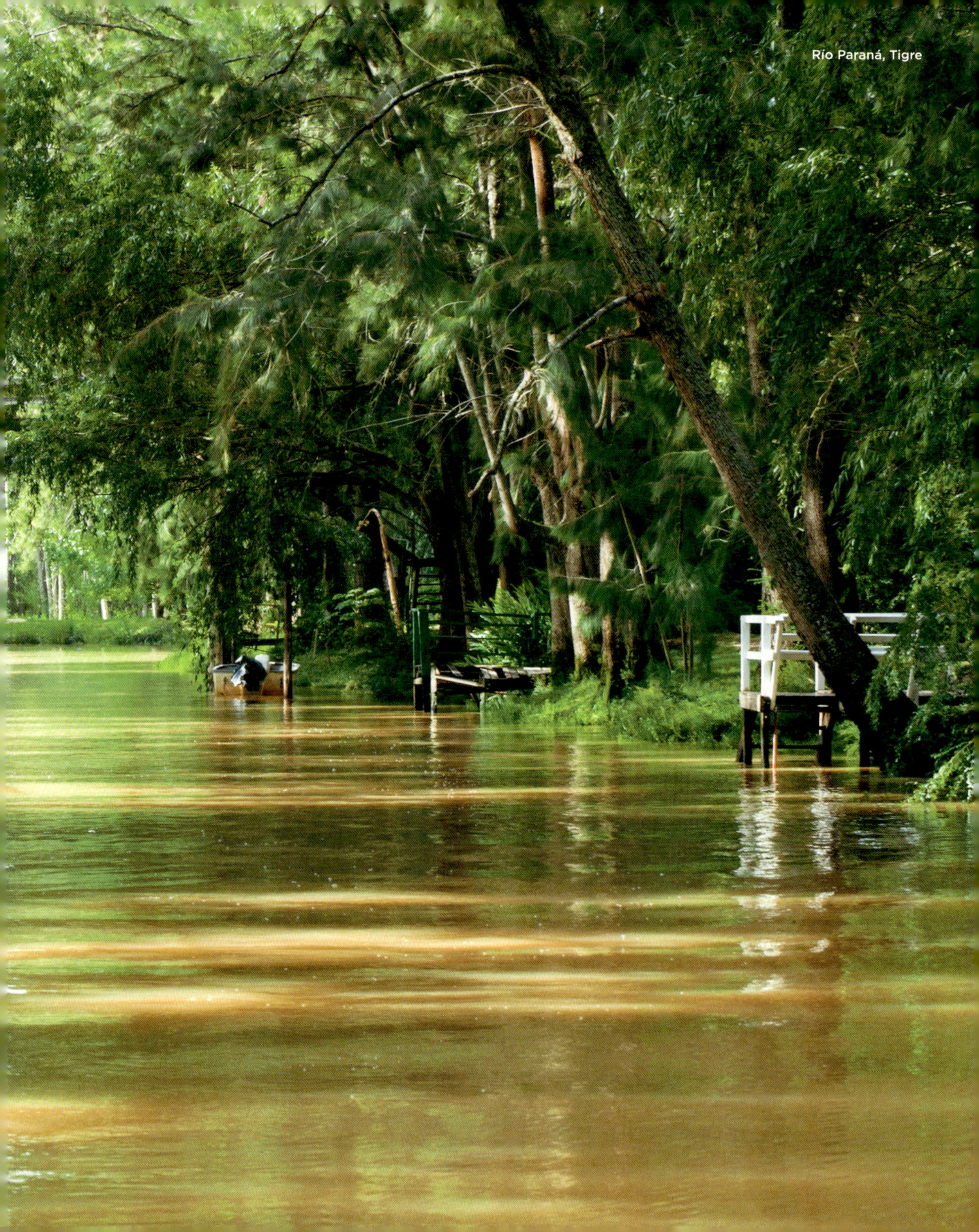

Río Paraná, Tigre

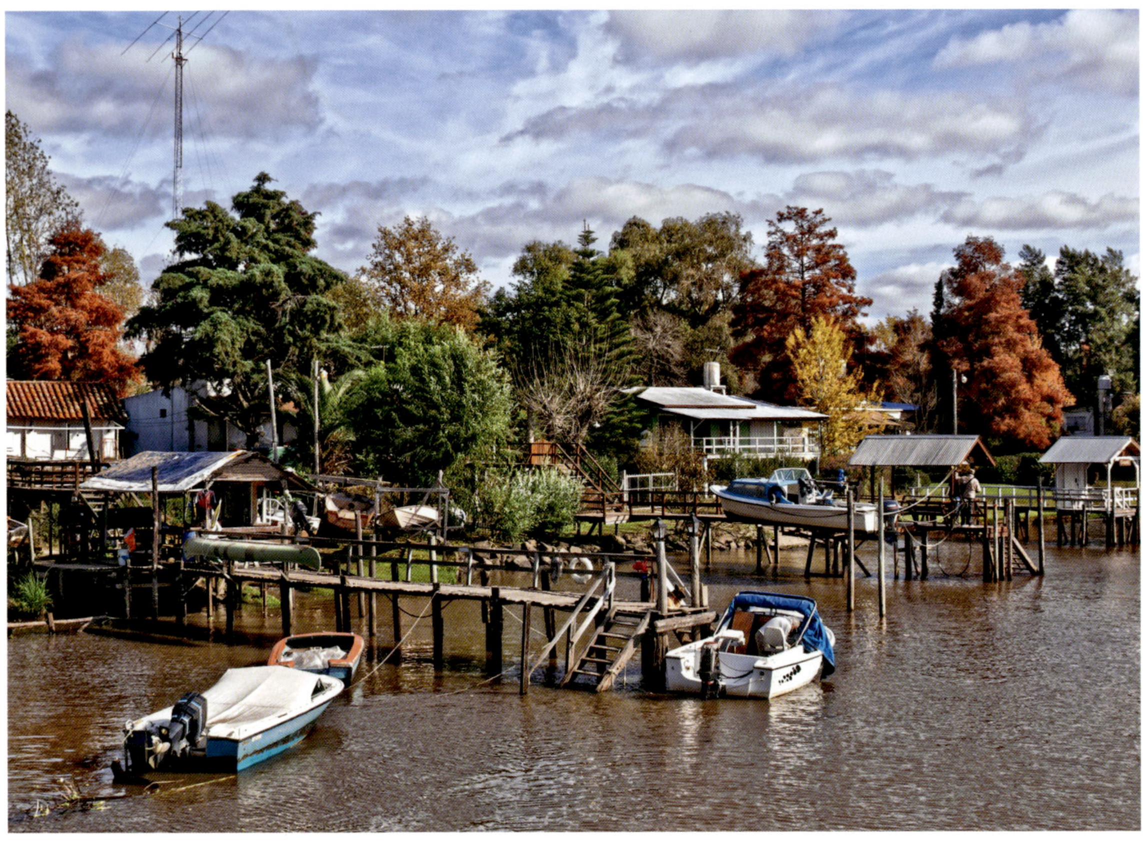

Río Sarmiento, Tigre

Paraná Delta

At the mouth of the Paraná River, 30 km (19 mi) north of Buenos Aires, lies the small town of Tigre. In the more than 10,000 km² (3860 sq mi) delta, crossed by rivers and canals, there are countless verdant islands. Here, wealthy capital city dwellers have their summer homes. One can navigate the various waterways, shady canals or wide arms of the shallow and slow flowing Paraná River by speedboat, steamer, sailboat or canoe. Numerous landing stages invite one to linger. The subtropical vegetation creates an almost paradisiacal atmosphere.

Tigre et le delta du Río Paraná

La petite ville de Tigre a été bâtie à l'embouchure du río Paraná, à 30 km au nord de Buenos Aires. Le delta, d'une superficie de 10 000 km², sillonné de rivières et de canaux, compte d'innombrables îles verdoyantes. Les citadins fortunés y font construire leur résidence secondaire. Les différentes voies d'eau, canaux ombragés ou larges bras du Paraná, calme et lent, se parcourent en vedette, bateau à vapeur, voilier ou canot. De nombreux embarcadères invitent à s'attarder. La végétation subtropicale compose un décor absolument paradisiaque.

Delta del Paraná

An der Mündung des Paraná-Flusses 30 km nördlich von Buenos Aires liegt das Städtchen Tigre. Im 10 000 km großen, von Flüssen und Kanälen durchzogenen Delta gibt es unzählig viele grüne Inseln. Hier haben wohlhabende Hauptstädter ihre Sommerhäuser. Per Schnellboot, Dampfer, Segelboot oder Kanu lassen sich die verschiedenen Wasserwege, schattige Kanäle oder breite Flussarme, des flachen und langsam fließenden Paraná befahren. Zahlreiche Anlegestellen laden zum Verweilen ein. Die subtropische Vegetation erschafft ein geradezu paradiesisches Ambiente.

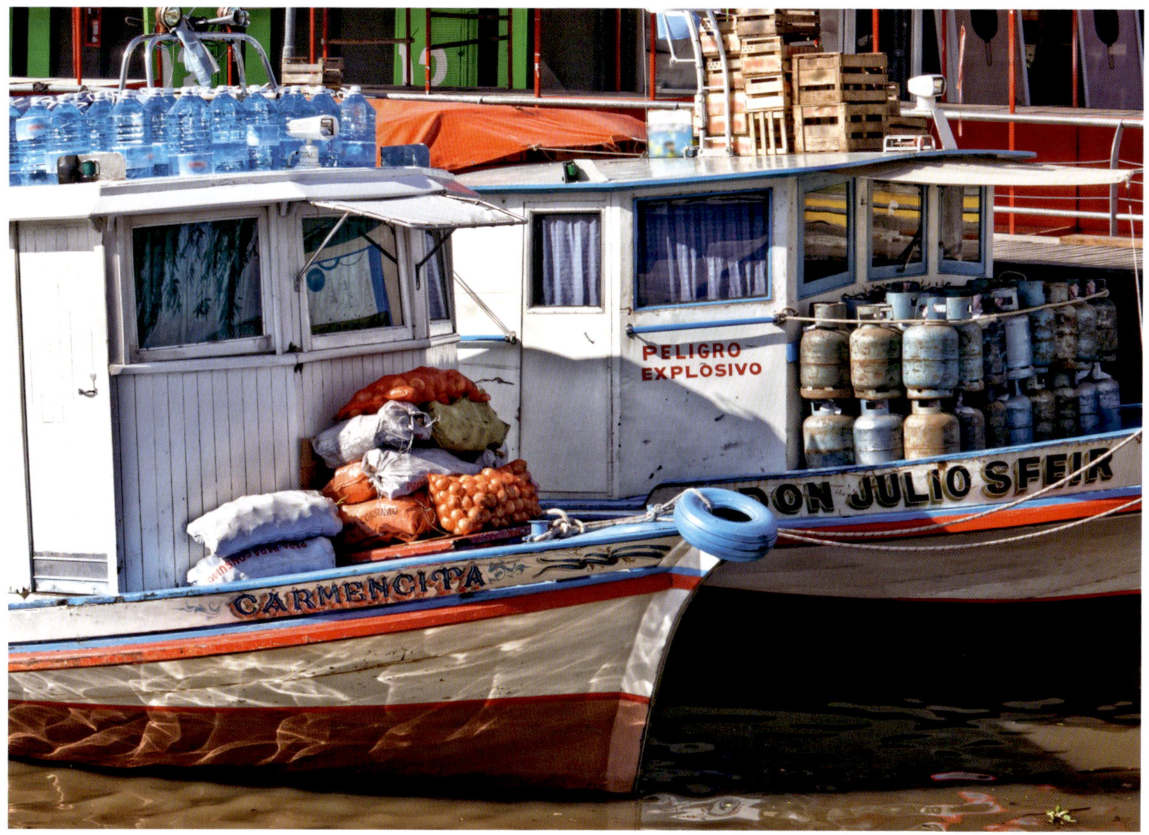

Puerto de Frutos, Tigre

Delta del Tigre

En la desembocadura del río Paraná,
a 30 km al norte de Buenos Aires, se
encuentra la pequeña ciudad de Tigre. En
los 10 000 km del gran delta atravesado
por ríos y canales hay innumerables islas
verdes. Aquí tienen sus casas de verano
los habitantes ricos de la capital. En
lancha rápida, barco de vapor, velero o
canoa se puede navegar por las diferentes
vías fluviales, canales sombreados o
brazos anchos del poco profundo y
lento río Paraná. Numerosos escenarios
de aterrizaje invitan a quedarse. La
vegetación subtropical crea una atmósfera
casi paradisíaca.

Delta do Tigre

Na foz do Rio Paraná, 30 km ao norte
de Buenos Aires, encontra-se a pequena
cidade de Tigre. Nos 10 000 km do grande
delta que são atravessados por rios e
canais, existem inúmeras ilhas verdes.
Aqui os ricos habitantes da capital têm
as suas casas de verão. Por lancha, vapor,
veleiro ou canoa você pode navegar
pelos diferentes cursos d'água, canais
sombreados ou braços largos do rio
Paraná, de fluxo raso e lento. Numerosas
cais convidam-no a permanecer. A
vegetação subtropical cria um ambiente
quase paradisíaco.

Tigre delta

Aan de monding van de Paraná rivier,
30 km ten noorden van Buenos Aires, ligt
het stadje Tigre. In de 10 000 km grote
door rivieren en kanalen doorkruiste delta
liggen ongelooflijk veel groene eilanden.
Hier hebben welgestelde stadsbewoners
hun zomerhuis. Met een speedboot,
stoomboot, zeilboot of kano zijn de
verschillende waterwegen, schaduwrijke
kanalen of brede rivierarmen van de
ondiepe en langzaam stromende Paraná-
rivier te bevaren. Talrijke steigers nodigen
uit om zich ergens op te houden. De
subtropische vegetatie zorgt voor een
bijna paradijselijke sfeer.

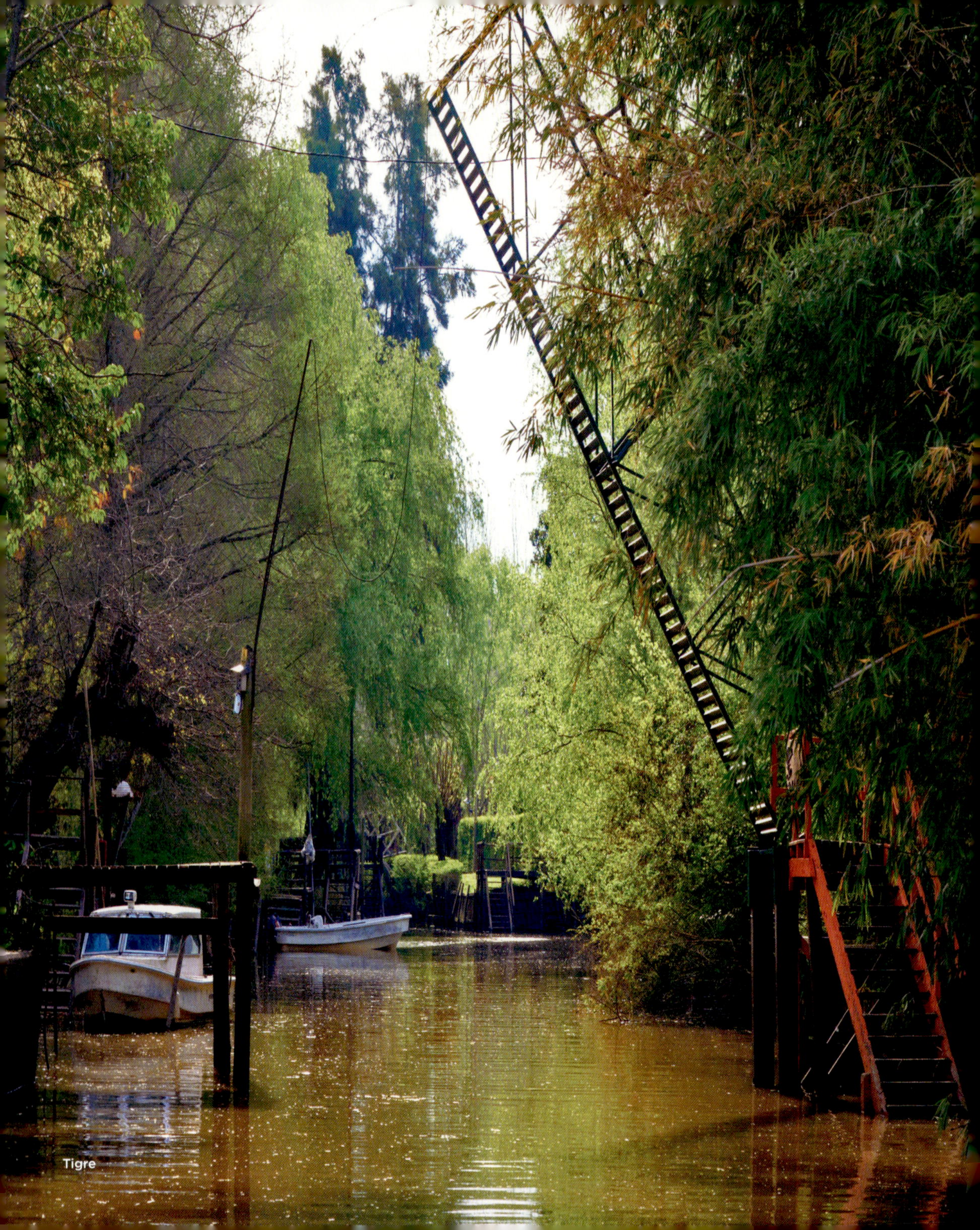
Tigre

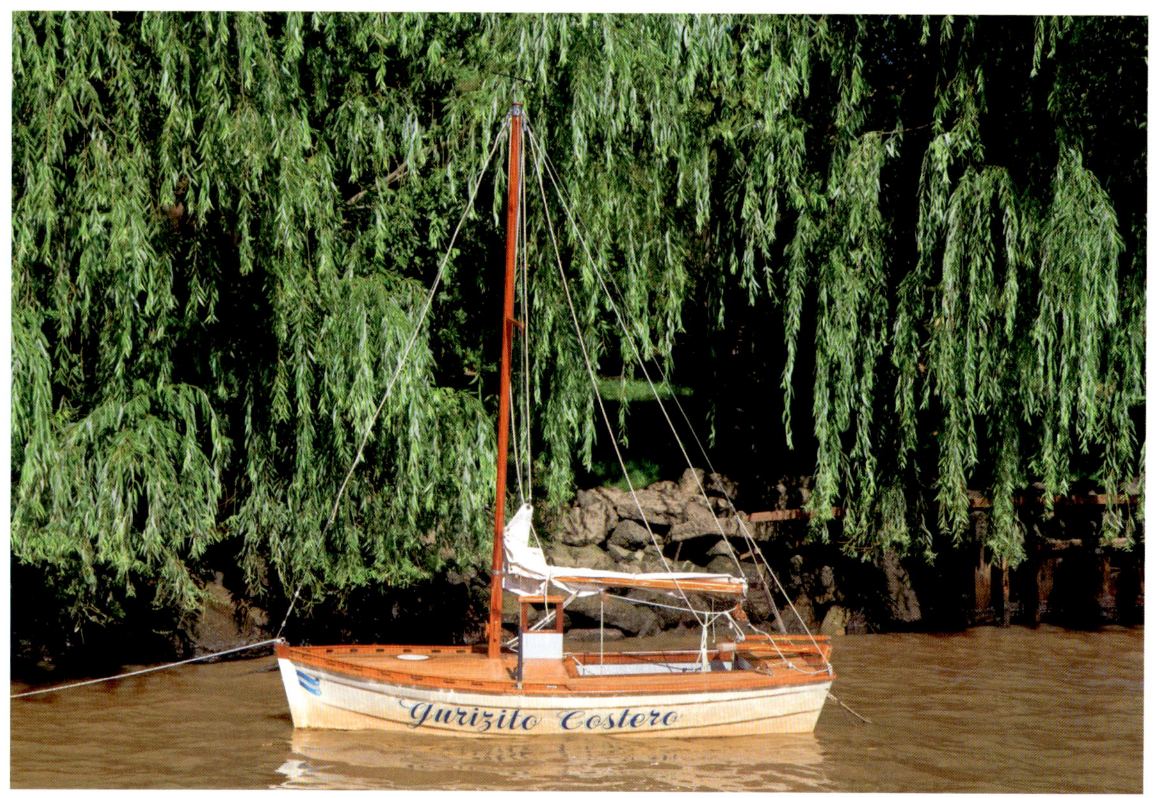

Río Paraná, Tigre

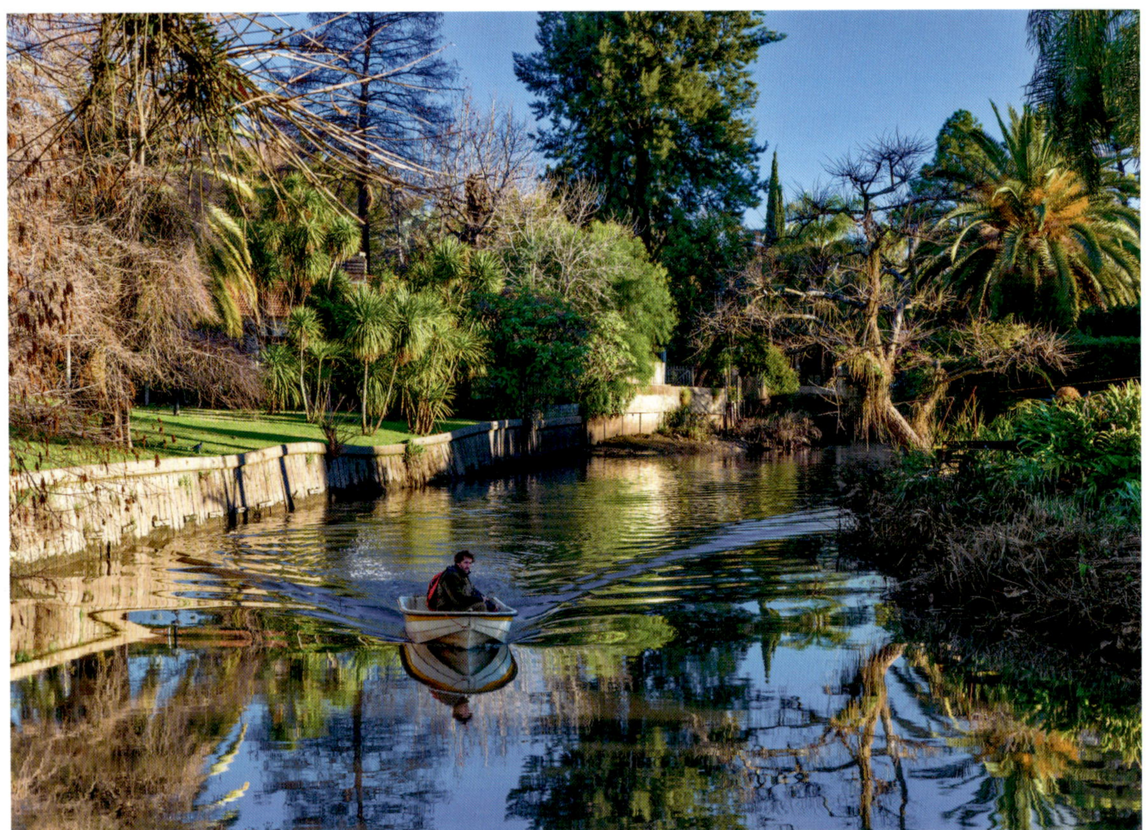

Tigre

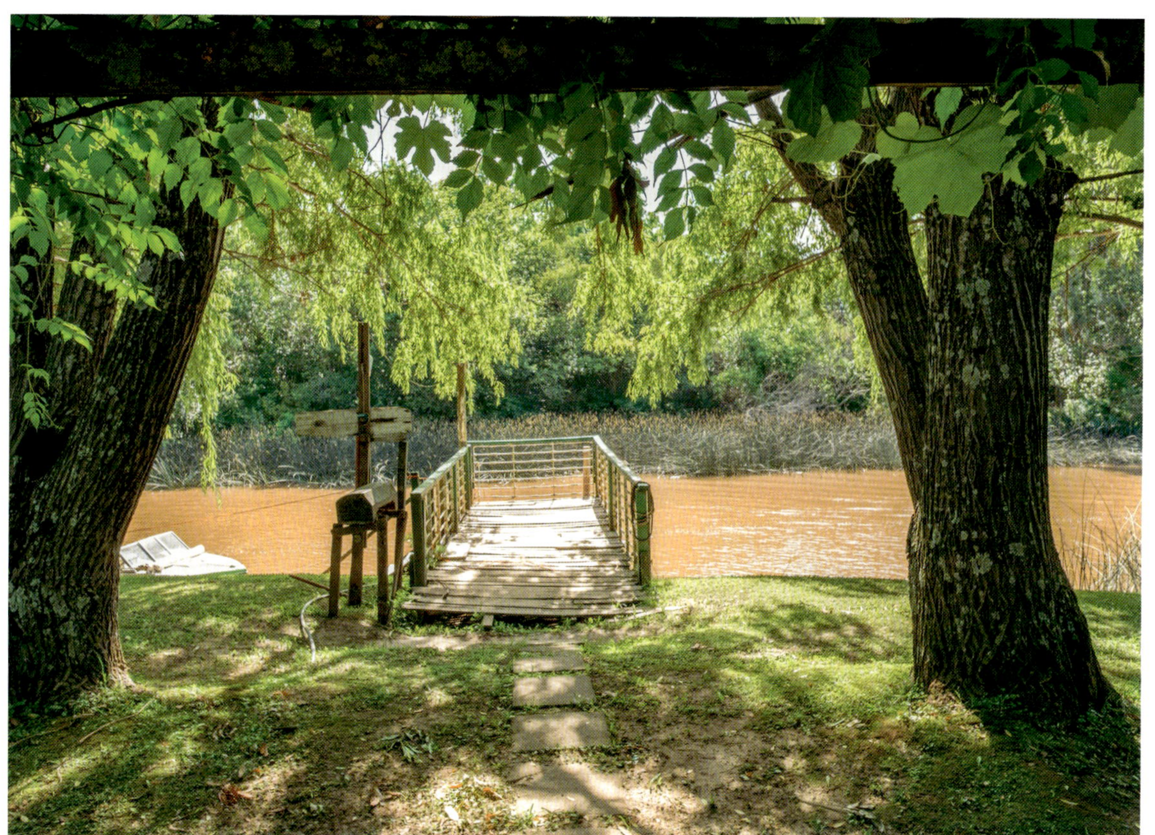

Tigre

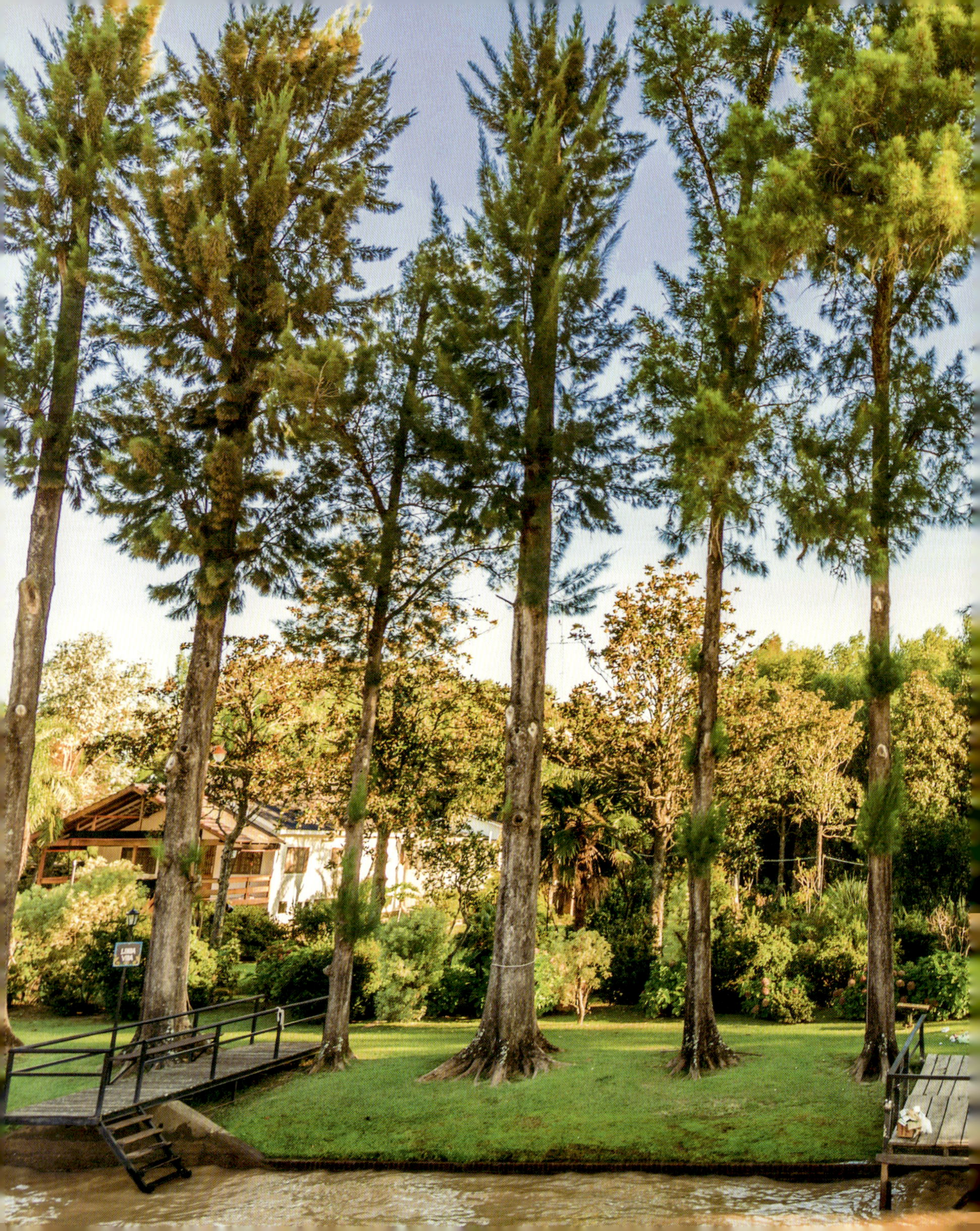

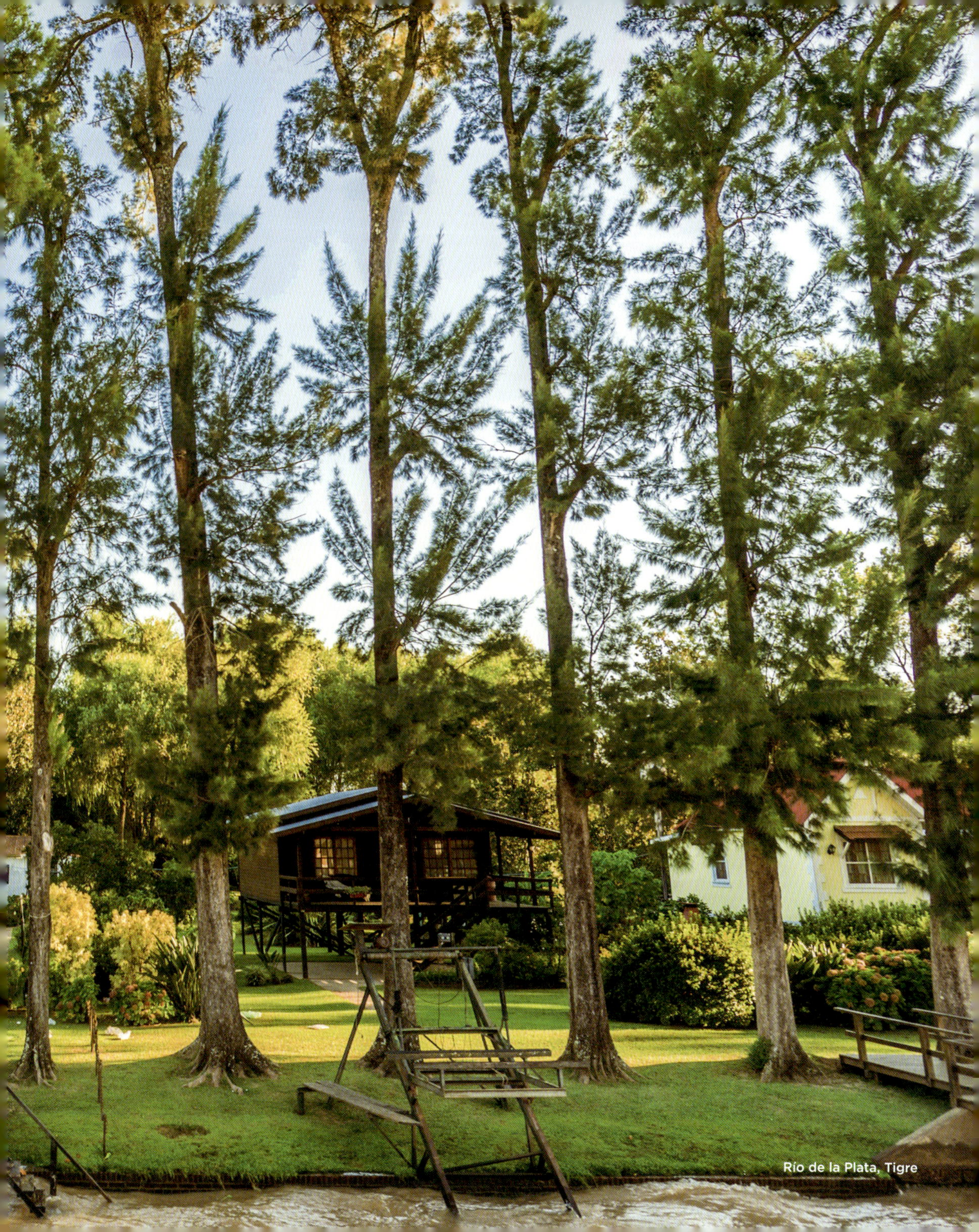
Río de la Plata, Tigre

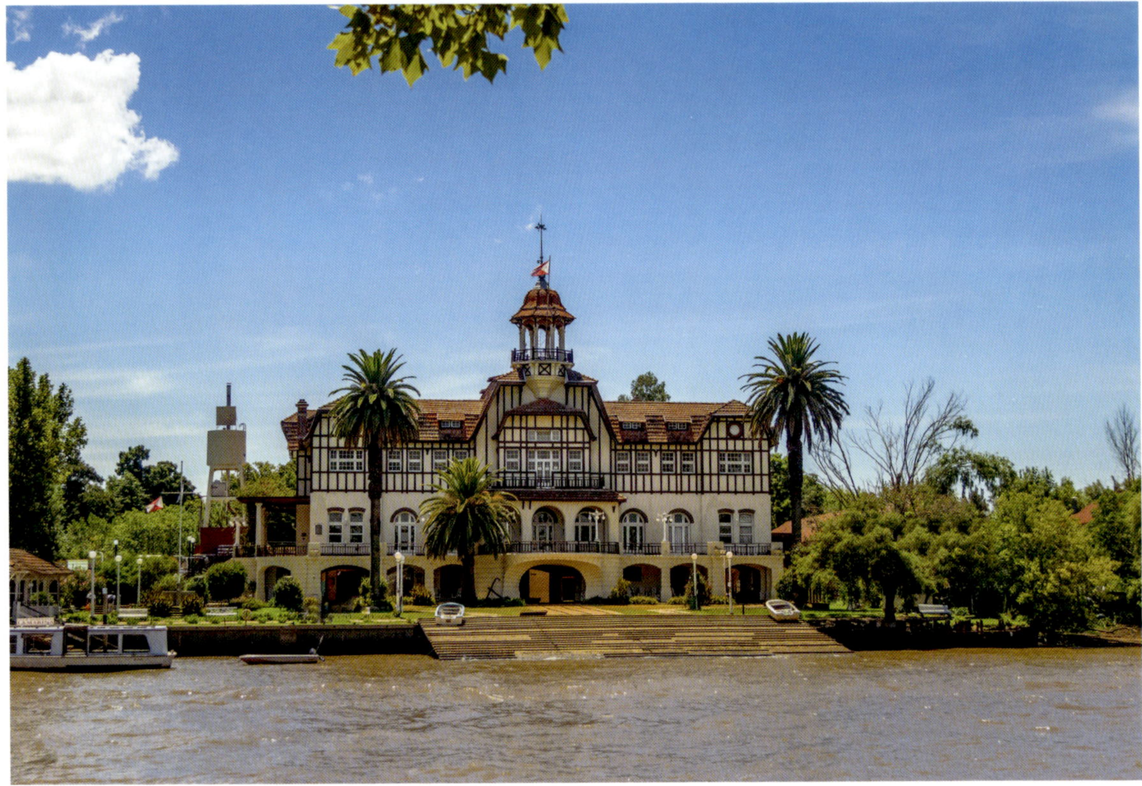

Club de Regatas La Marina, Tigre

Sport and art

On the left bank of the Luján River in Tigre, the legendary Yacht Club with its castle-like architecture awaits. This achieved fame through its rowing regattas, which were introduced by English immigrants. Tigre also has a remarkable art museum, housed in the casino built in 1927.

El deporte y el arte

En el margen izquierdo del río Luján, en Tigre, le espera el legendario Yacht Club con su arquitectura tipo castillo. Alcanzó la fama a través de sus regatas de remo, que fueron introducidas por los inmigrantes ingleses. Tigre también tiene un importante museo de arte, alojado en el casino construido en 1927.

Sports et arts

Sur la rive gauche du fleuve Luján, à Tigre, est installé un légendaire yacht-club à l'architecture monumentale. Il a bâti sa gloire autour des régates d'aviron qu'organisaient les riches immigrés anglais. Tigre s'est également dotée d'un musée d'art remarquable, aménagé en 1927 dans un ancien casino.

Esporte e arte

Na margem esquerda do rio Luján em Tigre, o lendário clube de iates com sua arquitetura de castelo espera por você. Ele alcançou fama através das suas regatas de remo, que foram introduzidas por imigrantes ingleses. A cidade de Tigre tem também um notável museu de arte, localizado no casino construído em 1927.

Sport und Kunst

Am linken Ufer des Luján-Flusses in Tigre wartet der legendäre Yacht-Club mit seiner schlossähnlichen Architektur auf. Berühmtheit erlangte er durch seine Ruderregatten, die englische Einwanderer einführten. Tigre hat auch ein bemerkenswertes Kunstmuseum, das im 1927 erbauten Casino untergebracht ist.

Sport en kunst

Op de linkeroever van de Luján rivier in Tigre wacht de legendarische Yacht Club met zijn kasteelachtige architectuur. Hij werd beroemd door zijn roeiregatta's die door de Engelse immigranten werden geïntroduceerd. Tigre heeft ook een opmerkelijk kunstmuseum waarin het in 1927 gebouwde casino is ondergebracht.

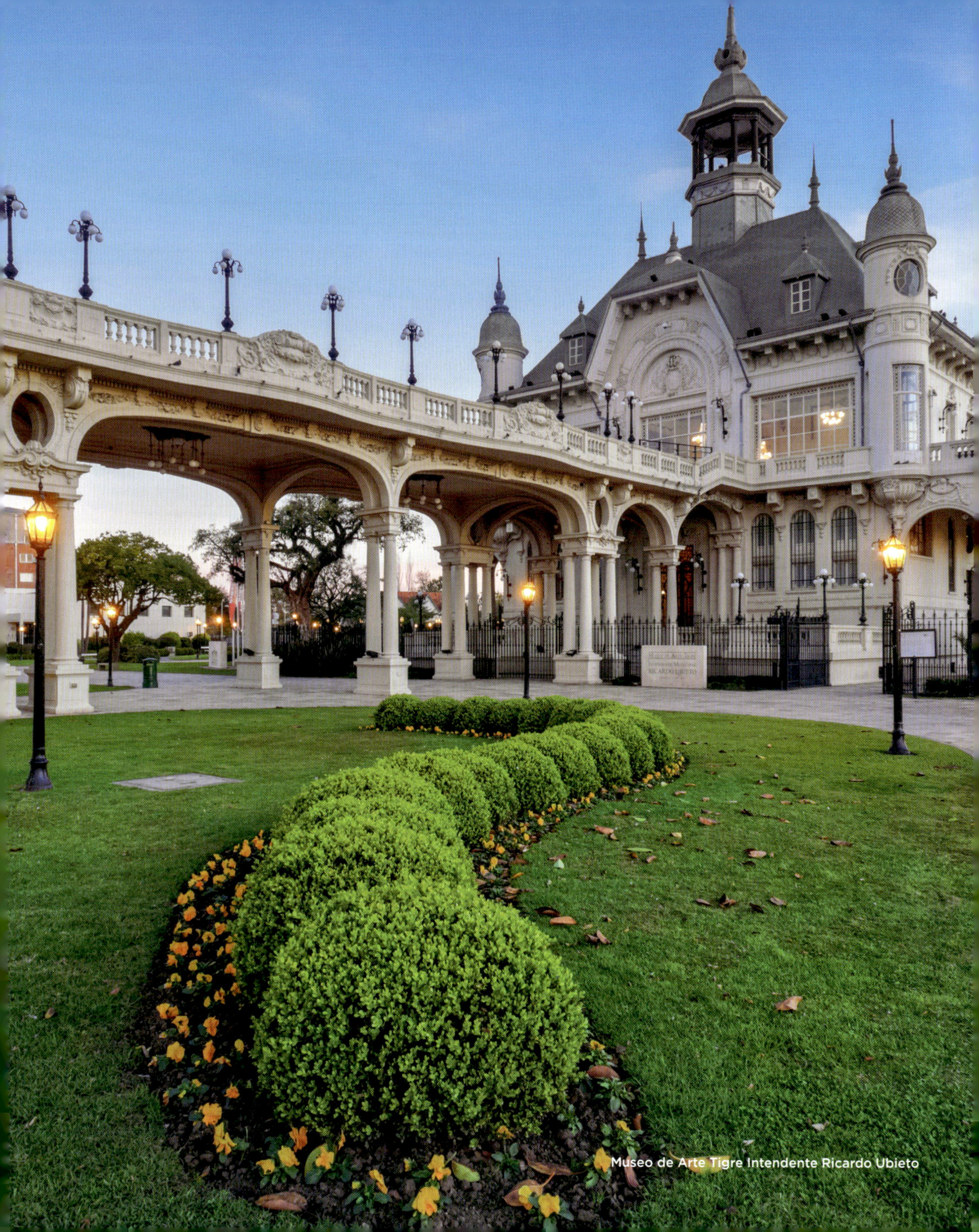

Museo de Arte Tigre Intendente Ricardo Ubieto

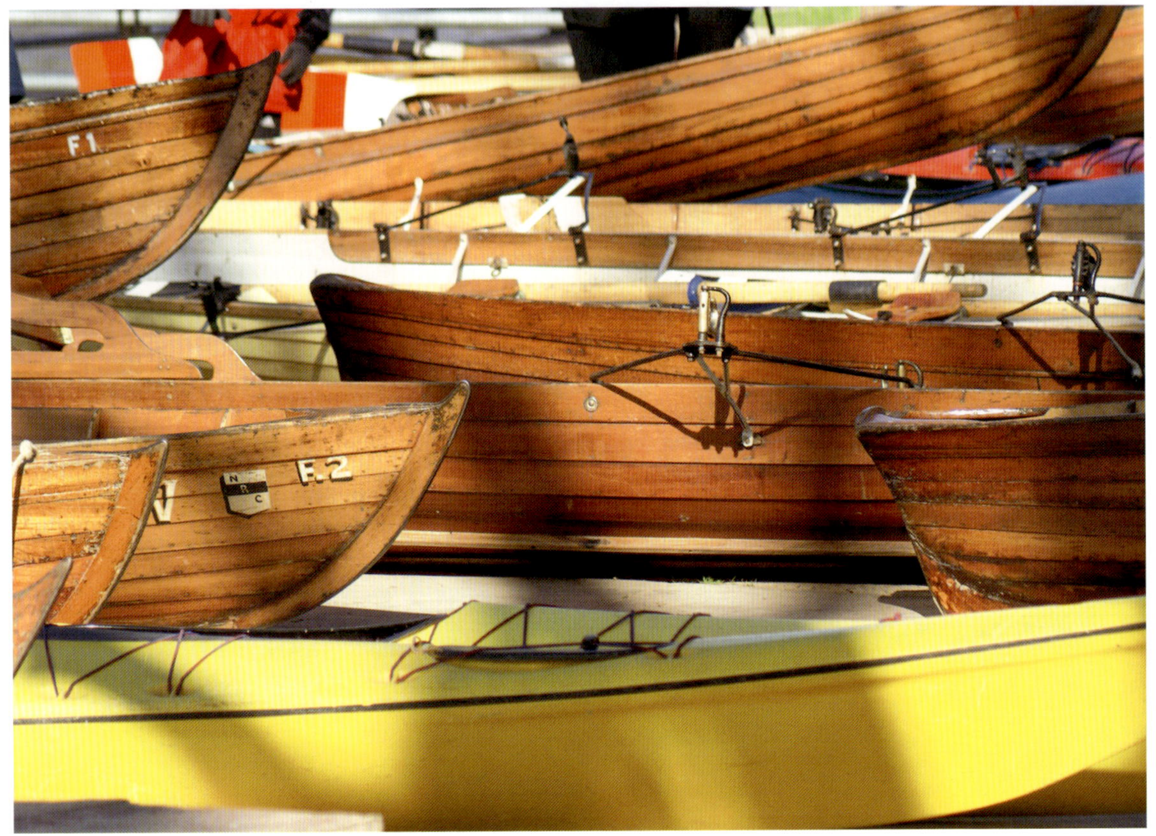

Tigre

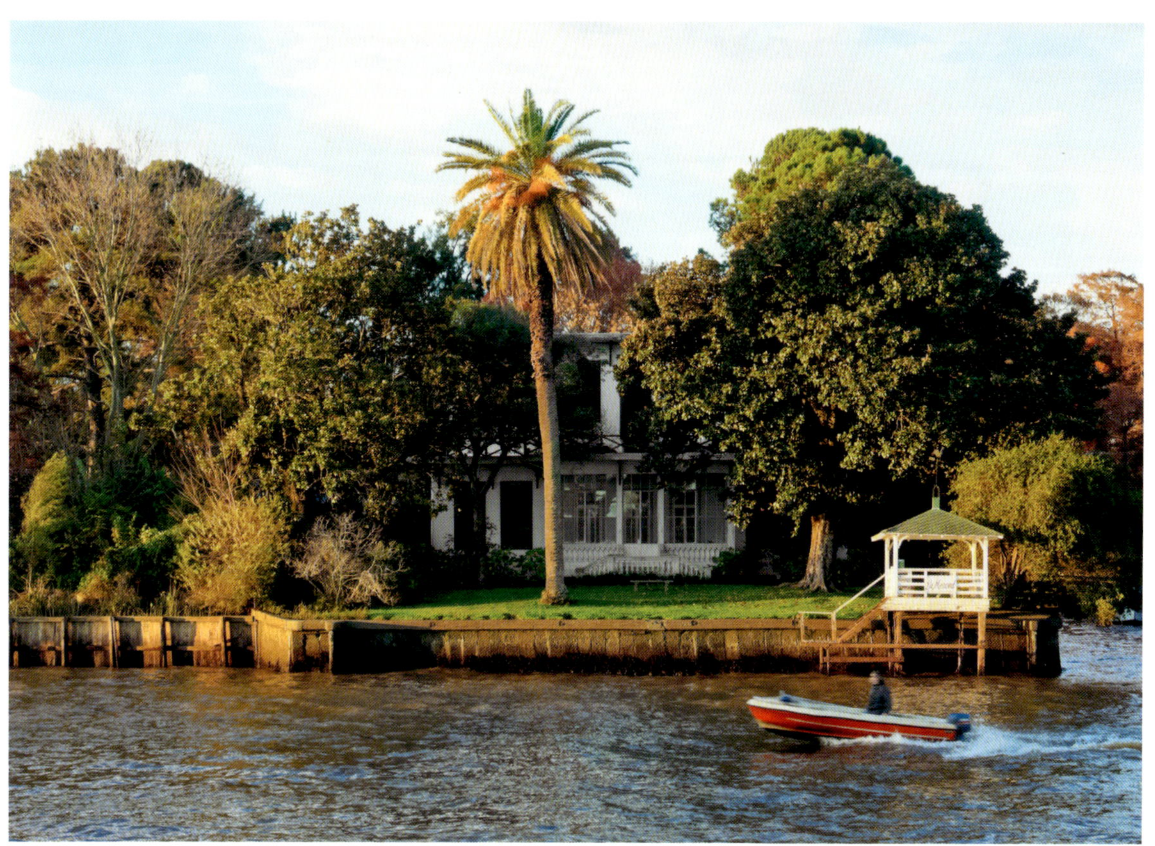

Río Luján, Tigre

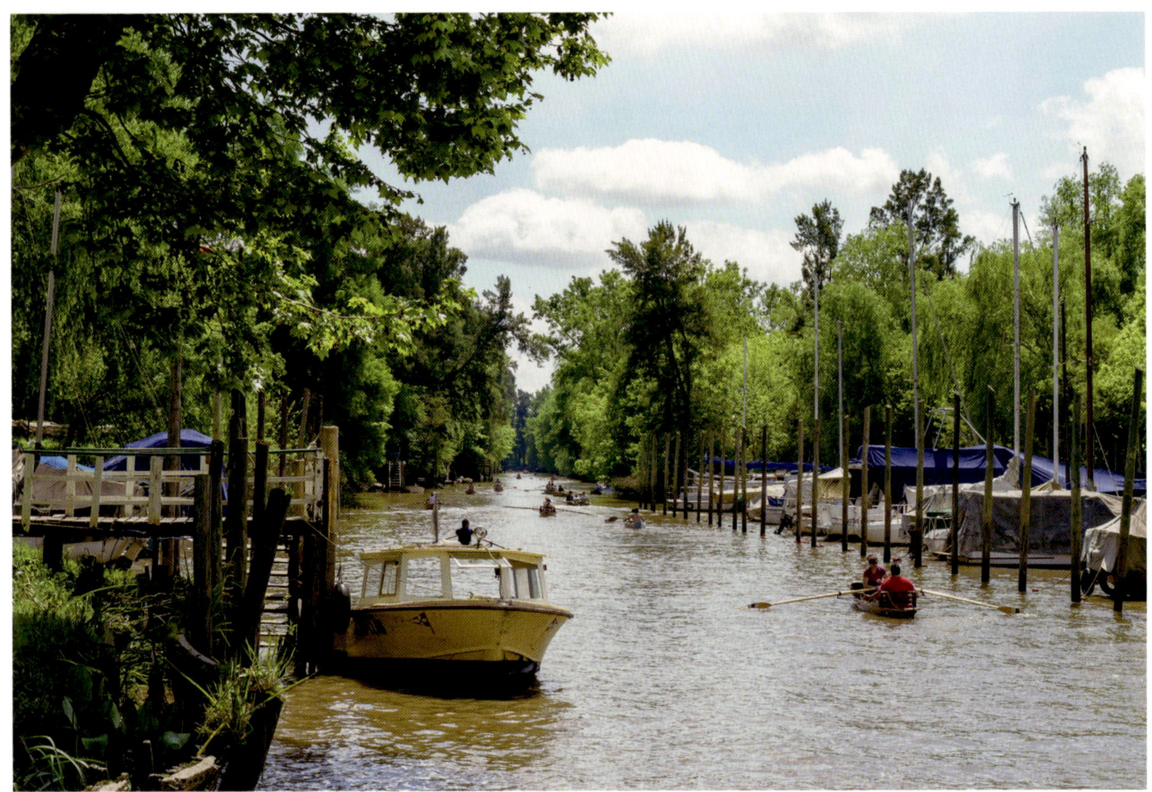

Tigre

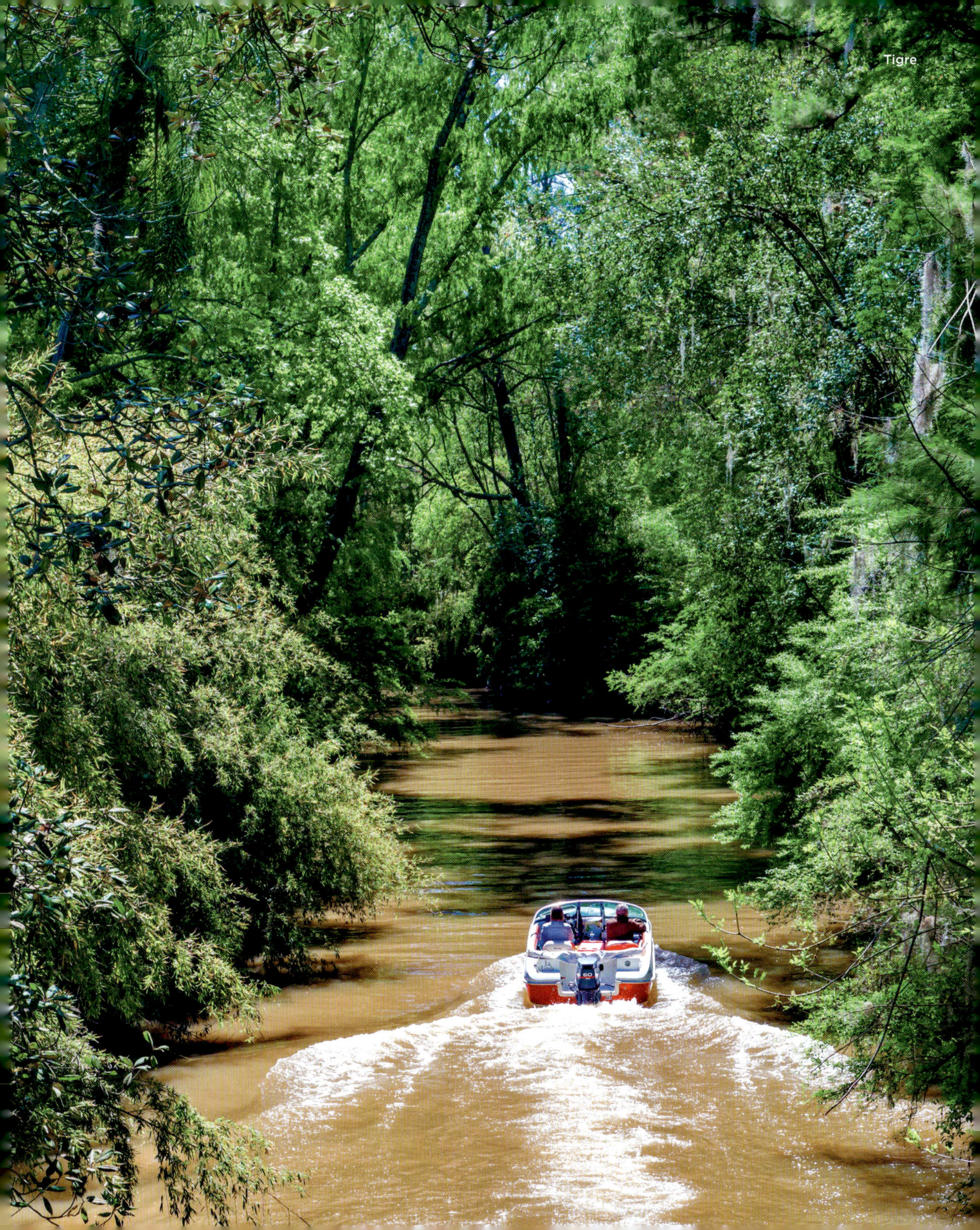
Tigre

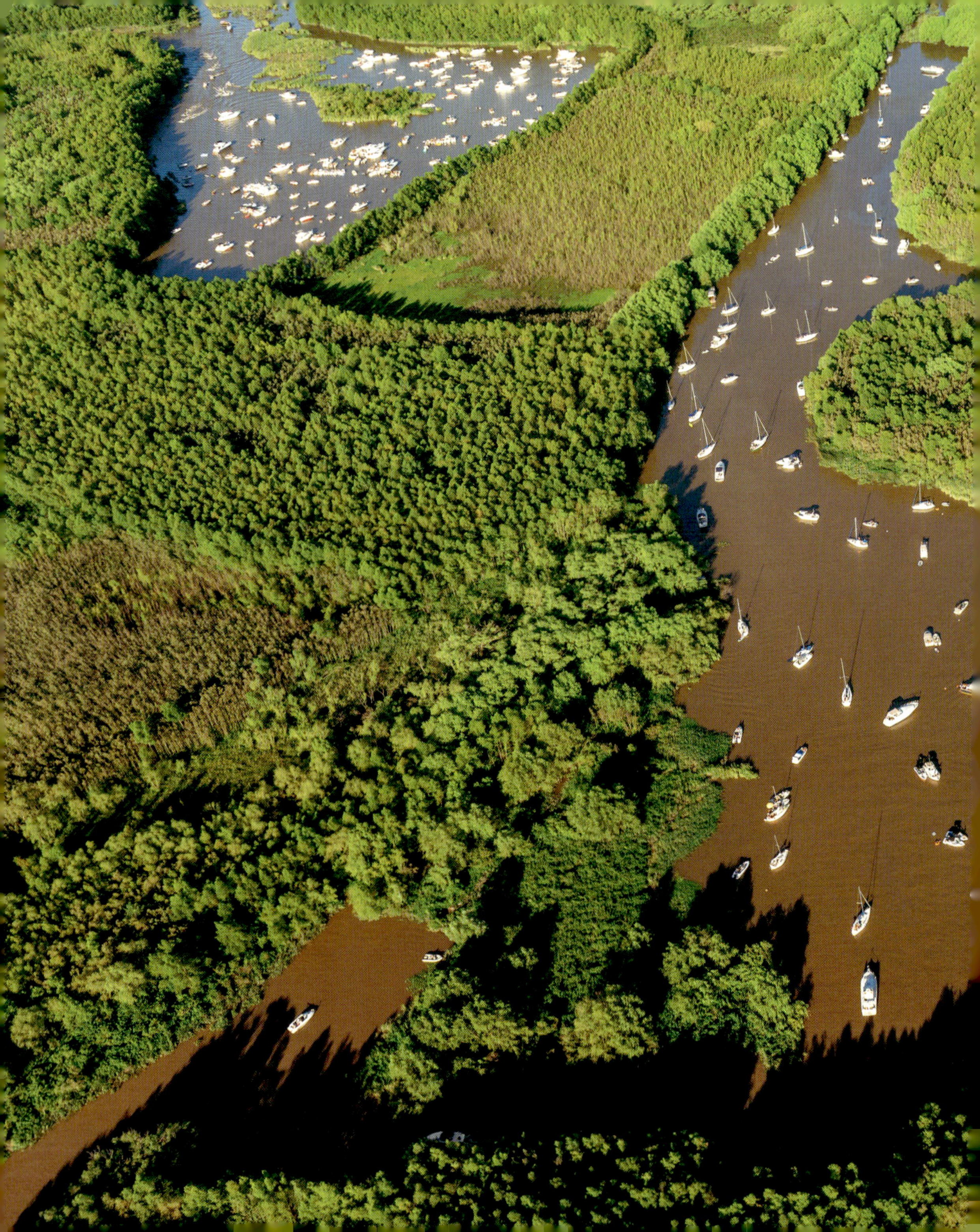

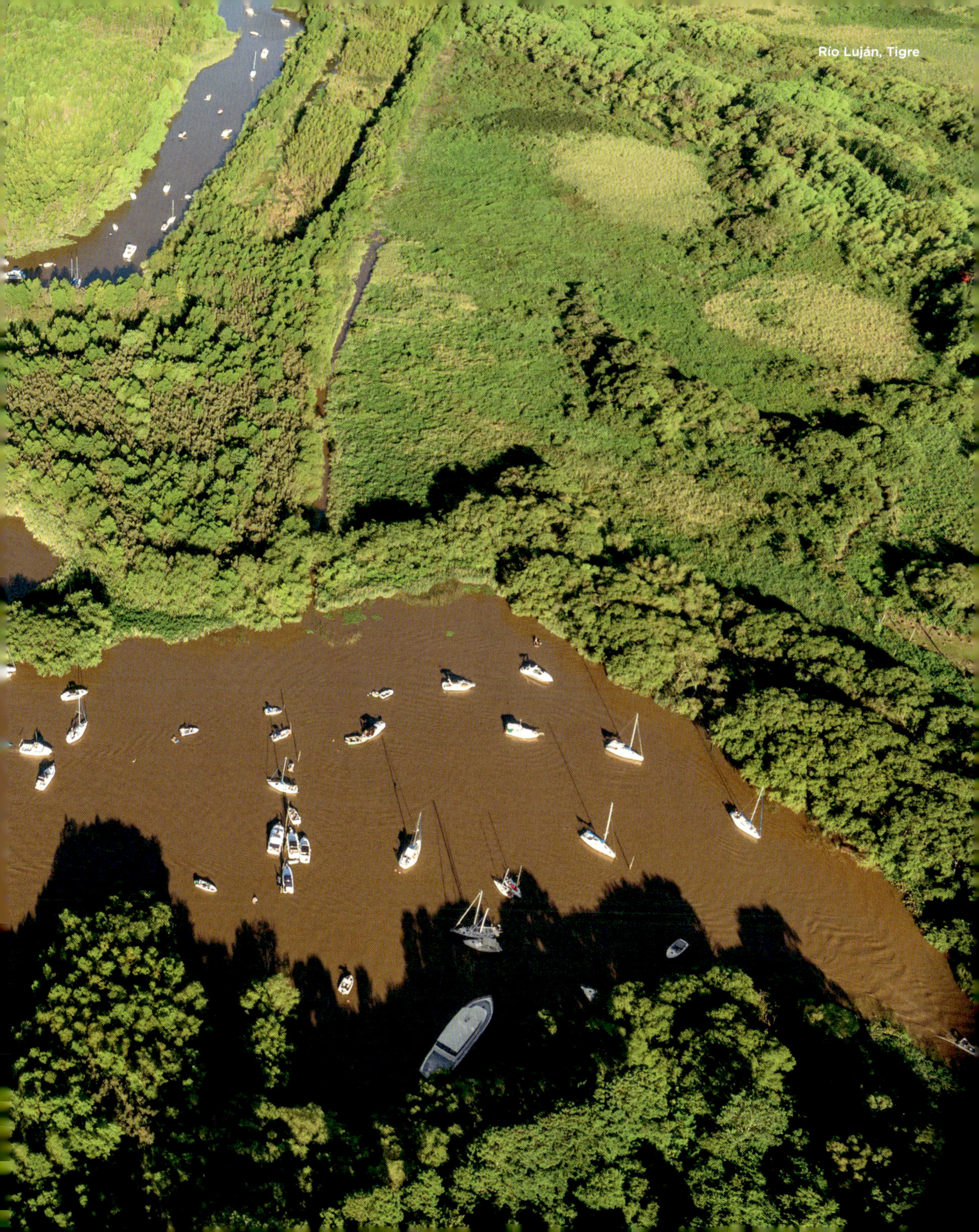
Río Luján, Tigre

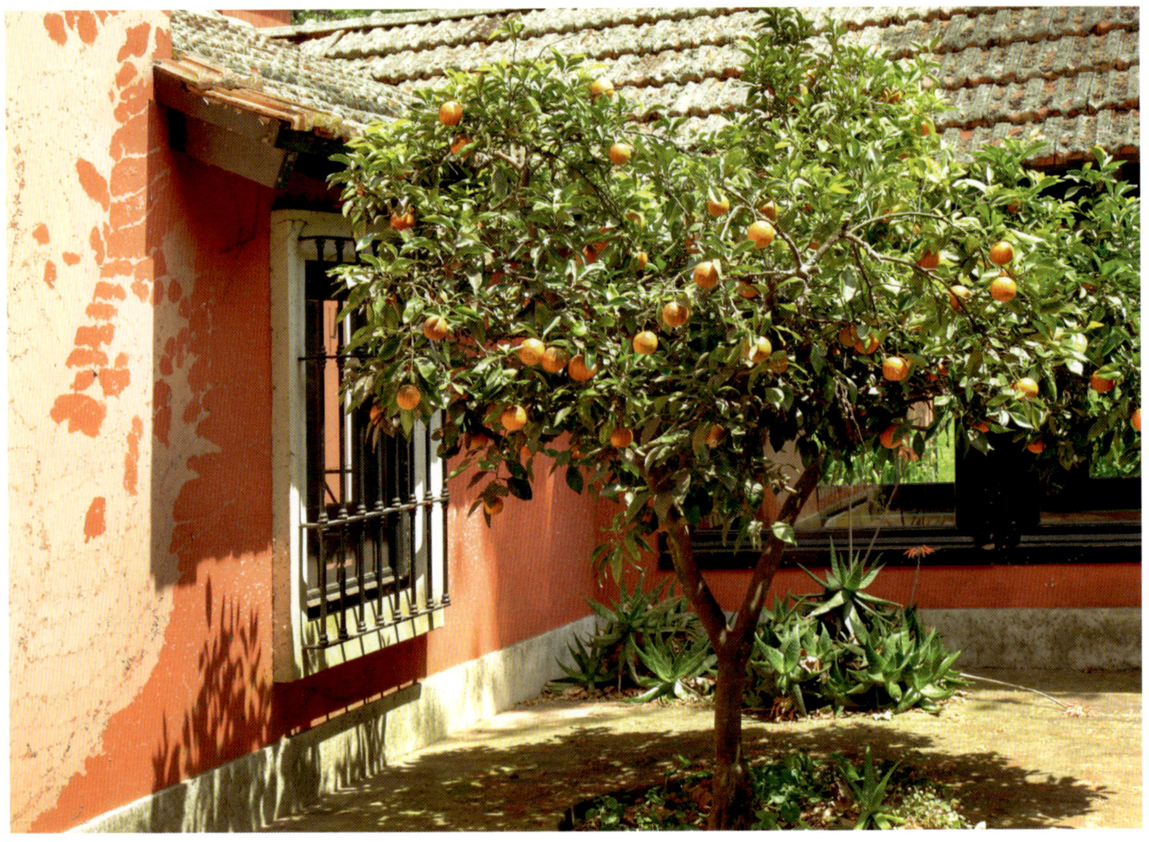

Estancia La Candelaria del Monte

Country life in the pampas

In the province of Buenos Aires, within a radius of 100–200 km (62–125 mi) of the capital Buenos Aires, there are wonderful estancias, or country estates in the middle of the pampas. La Bamba de Areco was in colonial times a horse-changing station and sentry post on the "royal road" that connected Buenos Aires with the north. This luxurious country estate, with large stables and a 200-year-old park, is located near the city of San Antonio de Areco. In this town of cattle breeders, founded in 1730, the "Festival of the Gaucho Tradition" takes place every year in November, when the gauchos, the cattle drivers of the pampas, present their rodeo arts in traditional dress.

Mode de vie rural dans la pampa

Dans la province de Buenos Aires, dans un rayon de 100 à 200 km au nord ou au sud de la capitale, de magnifiques *estancias,* propriétés foncières, prospèrent au cœur de la pampa. La Bamba de Areco était à l'époque coloniale un relais pour cavaliers et un poste de garde sur la « route royale » reliant Buenos Aires au nord du pays. La luxueuse propriété, dotée de grandes écuries et d'un parc vieux de 200 ans, est située près de la localité San Antonio de Areco. Cette ville d'éleveurs, fondée dans les années 1730, accueille chaque année en novembre la fête de la tradition *gaucho,* au cours de laquelle les *gauchos,* gardiens de bétail de la pampa, présentent leur art du rodéo en tenue traditionnelle.

Landleben in der Pampa

In der Provinz Buenos Aires liegen im Umkreis von 100–200 km nördlich oder südlich der Hauptstadt Buenos Aires wunderbare Estanzias, Landgüter mitten in der Pampa. La Bamba de Areco war in der Kolonialzeit Pferdewechselstelle und Wachposten auf dem „Königsweg", der Buenos Aires mit dem Norden verband. Der luxuriöse Landsitz mit großen Stallungen und einem 200 Jahre alten Park liegt nahe der Ortschaft San Antônio de Areco. In der 1730 gegründeten Stadt der Viehzüchter findet jährlich im November das „Fest der Gaucho-Tradition" statt, bei dem Gauchos, Viehtreiber der Pampa, in traditioneller Kleidung ihre Rodeo-Künste vorstellen.

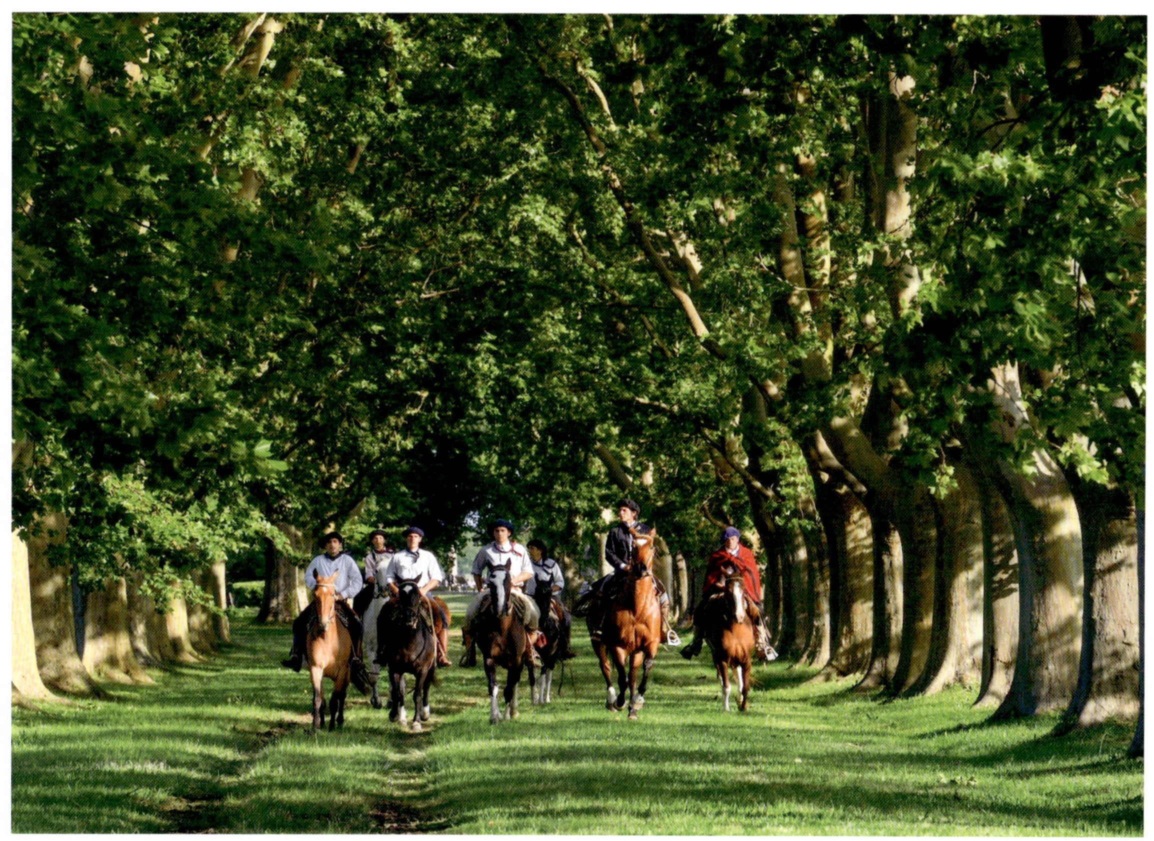

Estancia La Bamba de Areco

La vida en el campo en La Pampa

En la provincia de Buenos Aires, en un radio de 100–200 km al norte o al sur de la capital, hay maravillosas estancias, fincas en medio de La Pampa. La Bamba de Areco fue en la época colonial una estación de cambio de caballos y centinela del "camino real", que conectaba Buenos Aires con el norte. Esta lujosa finca, con grandes establos y un parque de 200 años de antigüedad, se encuentra cerca del pueblo de San Antonio de Areco. En la ciudad de los ganaderos, fundada en 1730, se realiza todos los años en el mes de noviembre la "Fiesta de la tradición gaucha", donde los gauchos, ganaderos de la pampa, presentan sus artes de rodeo en traje tradicional.

A vida no campo nos pampas

Na província de Buenos Aires, num raio de 100–200 km ao norte ou sul da capital Buenos Aires, há maravilhosas fazendas, propriedades rurais no meio dos pampas. La Bamba de Areco era no período colonial uma estação de troca e sentinela de cavalos na "estrada real", que ligava Buenos Aires com o norte. Esta luxuosa propriedade rural com grandes estábulos e um parque com 200 anos está localizada perto do vilarejo de San Antônio de Areco. O "Festival da Tradição Gaúcha" acontece todos os anos em novembro na cidade dos criadores de gado, fundada em 1730, onde os gaúchos, condutores de gado dos pampas, apresentam as suas artes de rodeio com trajes tradicionais.

Het landleven in de pampa

In de provincie Buenos Aires liggen binnen een straal van 100-200 km ten noorden of ten zuiden van de hoofdstad Buenos Aires prachtige estancias, landgoederen midden in de pampa. La Bamba de Areco was in de koloniale tijd een paardenwisselstation en wachtpost op de "koninklijke weg" die Buenos Aires met het noorden verbond. Dit luxe landgoed met grote stallen en een 200 jaar oud park ligt dicht bij het dorp San Antônio de Areco. In de in 1730 gestichte stad van de veefokkers vindt in november jaarlijks het "Feest van de Gaucho-traditie" plaats, waarbij gaucho's, veedrijvers van de pampa, in traditionele kledij hun rodeokunsten laten zien.

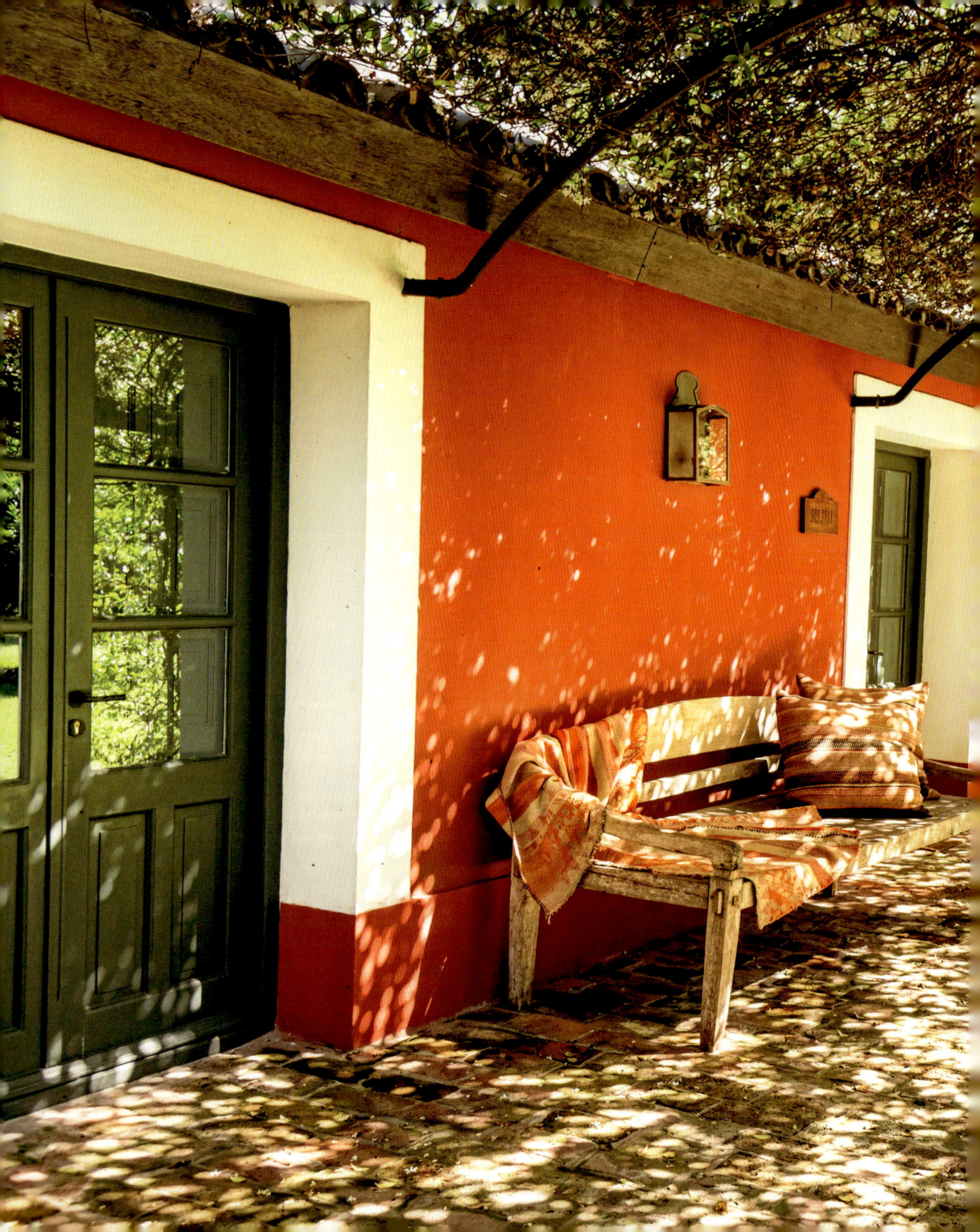

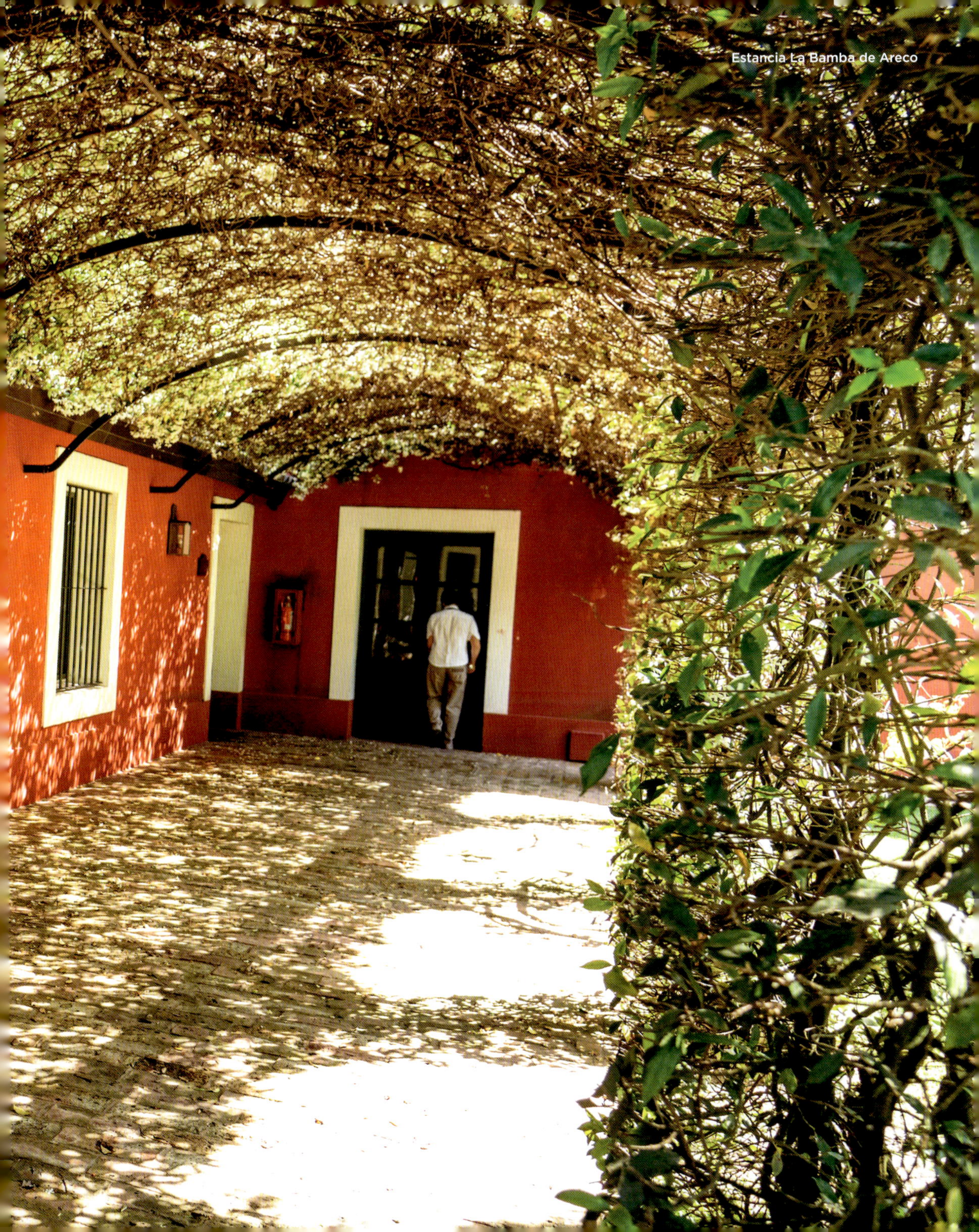

Estancia La Bamba de Areco

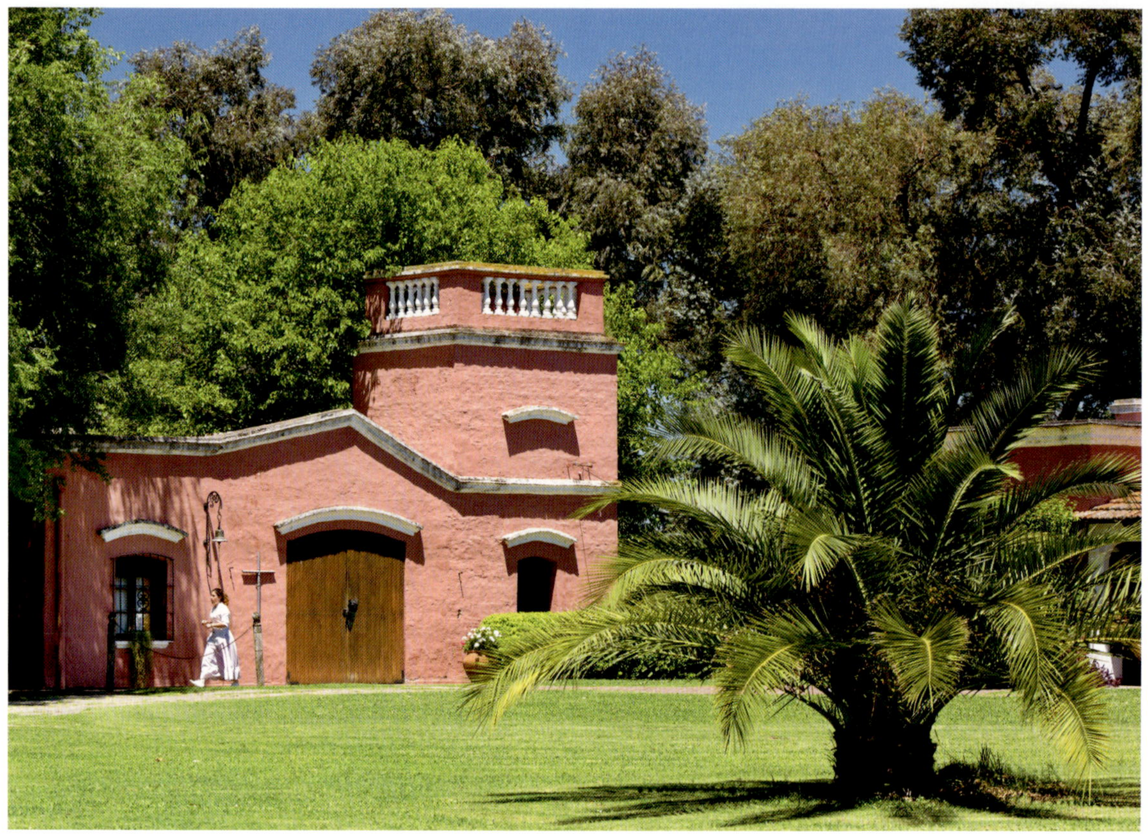

Estancia Santa Susana

Little Paradises

The plains of the pampas are occasionally interrupted by trees, the presence of which indicates an estancia. The planting of trees was done to protect against wind and to provide shade during the hot summer. The Estancia Santa Susana near Campana, 80 km (50 mi) northwest of Buenos Aires, covers 1200 ha (2965 ac). It was founded in the 19th century by an Irish cattle breeder and is open to visitors today. In the manor house there is a museum, with antique furniture, that tells about country life. The history of the Estancia La Porteña near San Antonio de Areco is closely linked to the famous novelist and poet Ricardo Güiraldes, whose book 'Don Segundo Sombra' was inspired by the gaucho Segundo Ramirez, who lived and worked on the estancia.

Petits paradis

Les plaines pampéennes sont parsemées de petites forêts, qui indiquent la présence d'une *estancia*. Les arbres ont été plantés pour protéger les résidents du vent et leur apporter de l'ombre pendant les étés brûlants. L'*estancia* Santa Susana, près de Campana, à 80 km au nord-ouest de Buenos Aires, regroupe 1200 ha. Elle fut fondée au XIXe siècle par un éleveur bovin irlandais et est aujourd'hui ouverte aux visiteurs. La demeure est devenue un musée meublé d'antiquités, consacré à la vie rurale de l'époque. L'histoire de l'*estancia* La Porteña, près de San Antonio de Areco, est étroitement liée au célèbre poète Ricardo Güiraldes. Celui-ci honora dans son œuvre le *gaucho* Ramirez, qui vivait et travaillait dans la propriété.

Kleine Paradiese

Die Ebene der Pampa wird ab und zu durch Wälder unterbrochen. Sie weisen auf eine Estanzia hin. Zum Schutz vor Wind und als Schattenspender im heißen Sommer wird aufgeforstet. Die Estanzia Santa Susana bei Campana, 80 km nordwestlich von Buenos Aires umfasst 1200 ha. Sie wurde im 19. Jahrhundert von einem irischen Rinderzüchter gegründet und steht heute Besuchern offen. Im Herrenhaus ist ein Museum mit antiken Möbeln eingerichtet, das vom Landleben erzählt. Die Geschichte der Estancia La Porteña bei San Antônio de Areco verknüpft sich aufs engste mit dem berühmten Dichter Ricardo Güiraldes. Er setzte dem Gaucho Ramirez, der auf der Estanzia lebte und arbeitete, in seinem Werk ein Denkmal.

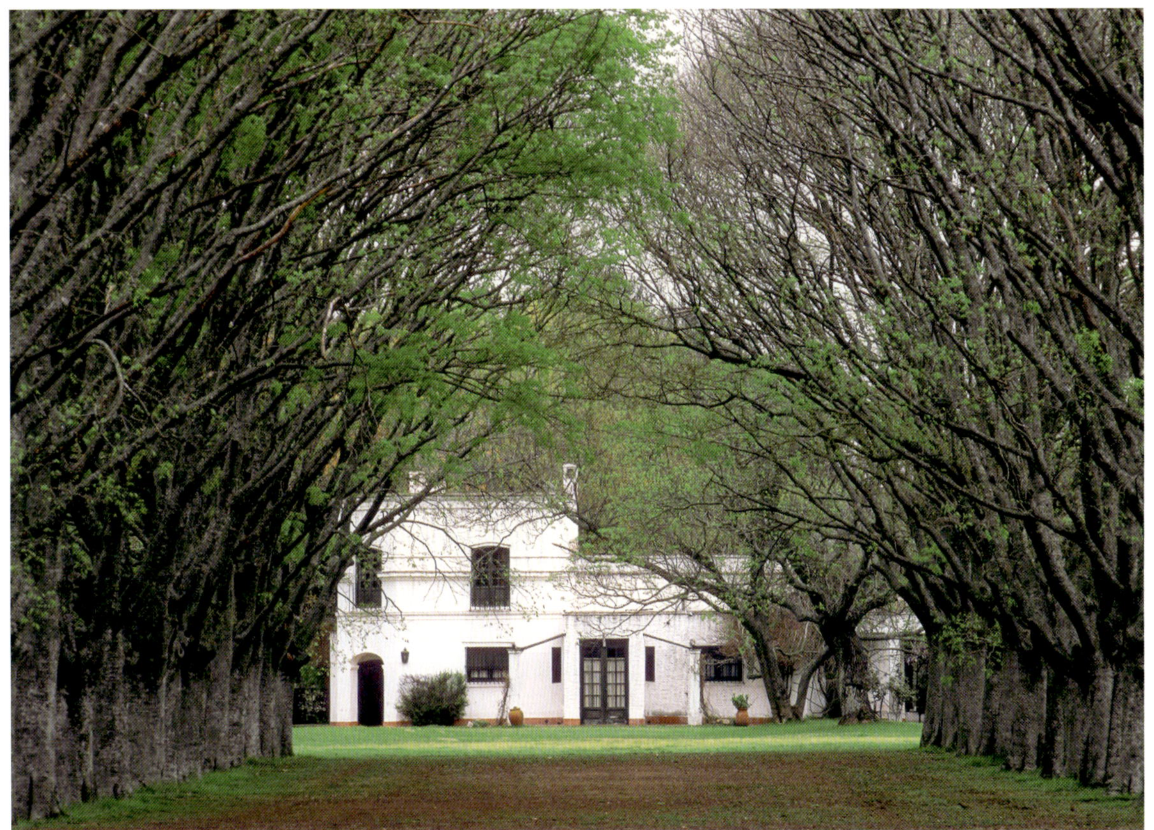

Estancia La Porteña

Pequeños paraísos

La llanura pampeana es interrumpida ocasionalmente por bosques. Señalan una estancia. La reforestación se lleva a cabo para protegerse del viento y proporcionar sombra en el caluroso verano. La Estancia Santa Susana, cerca de Campana, a 80 km al noroeste de Buenos Aires, cubre 1200 ha. Fue fundada en el siglo XIX por un ganadero irlandés y hoy en día está abierta a los visitantes. En la casa solariega hay un museo con muebles antiguos que cuenta la vida en el campo. La historia de la Estancia La Porteña, cerca de San Antonio de Areco, está estrechamente ligada al famoso poeta Ricardo Güiraldes. En su obra erigió un monumento al Gaucho Ramírez, que vivió y trabajó en la estancia.

Pequenos Paraísos

A planície dos pampas é às vezes interrompida por florestas. Elas indicam que há uma estância por perto. O plantio de árvores é realizado para proteger as estâncias contra o vento e para proporcionar sombra no verão quente. A Estância Santa Susana, perto de Campana, 80 km a noroeste de Buenos Aires, abrange 1200 ha. Foi fundada no século XIX por um criador de gado irlandês e agora está aberta aos visitantes. Na casa senhorial há um museu com móveis antigos que conta sobre a vida no campo. A história da Estância La Porteña perto de San Antônio de Areco está intimamente ligada ao famoso poeta Ricardo Güiraldes. Em sua obra ele criou um monumento ao Gaúcho Ramirez, que viveu e trabalhou na estância.

Kleine paradijzen

De vlakte van de pampa wordt af en toe onderbroken door bossen. Ze duiden op een estancia. Ter bescherming tegen wind en als schaduwbrenger wordt in de hete zomer herbebost. De Estancia Santa Susana bij Campana, 80 km ten noordwesten van Buenos Aires, beslaat 1200 ha. Het werd in de 19e eeuw gesticht door een Ierse veefokker en staat vandaag de dag open voor bezoekers. In het landhuis is een museum met antieke meubels ingericht en vertelt over het plattelandsleven. De geschiedenis van de Estancia La Porteña bij San Antônio de Areco is nauw verbonden met de beroemde dichter Ricardo Güiraldes. In zijn werk richtte hij voor de gaucho Ramirez, die op de estancia leefde en werkte, een gedenkteken op.

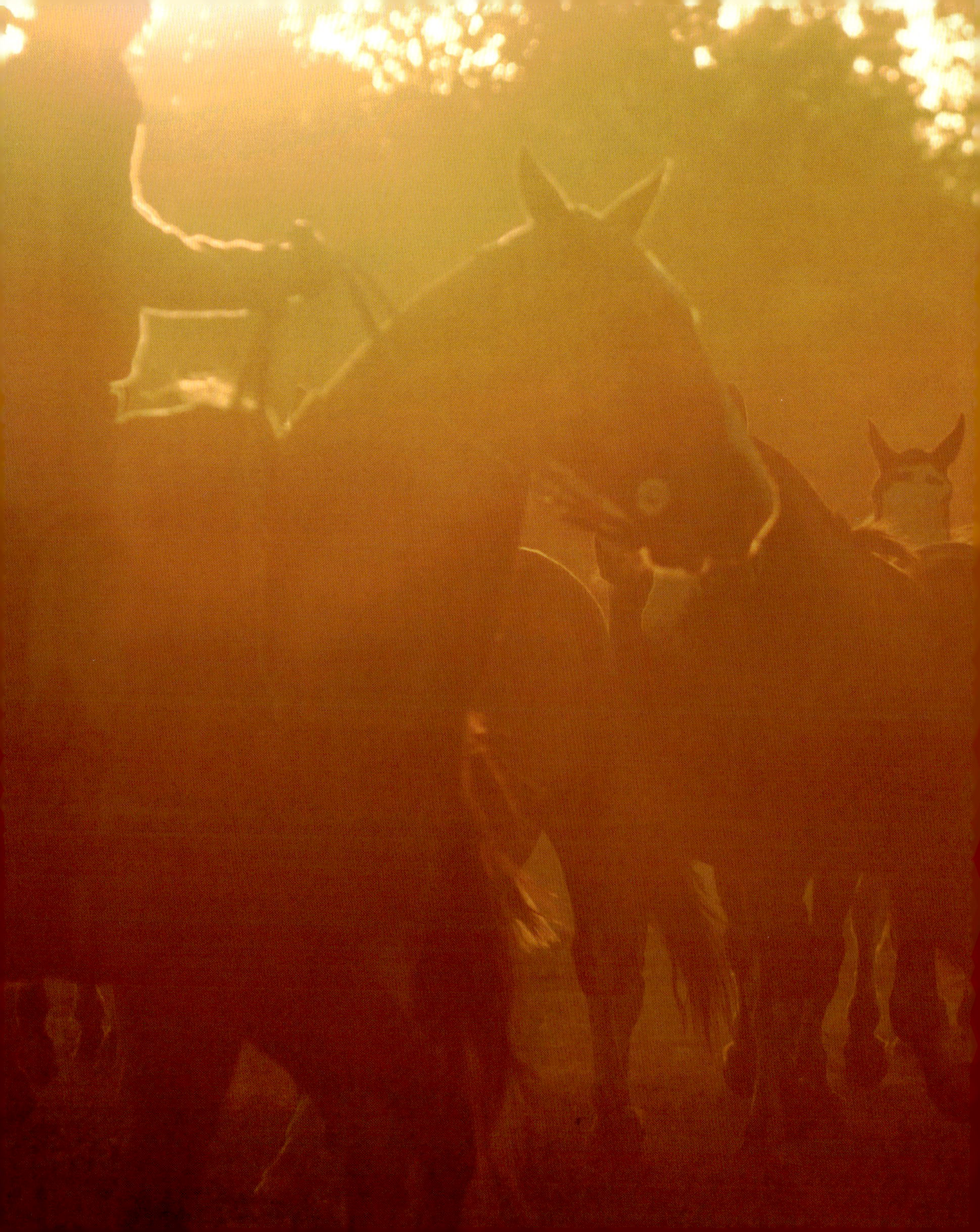

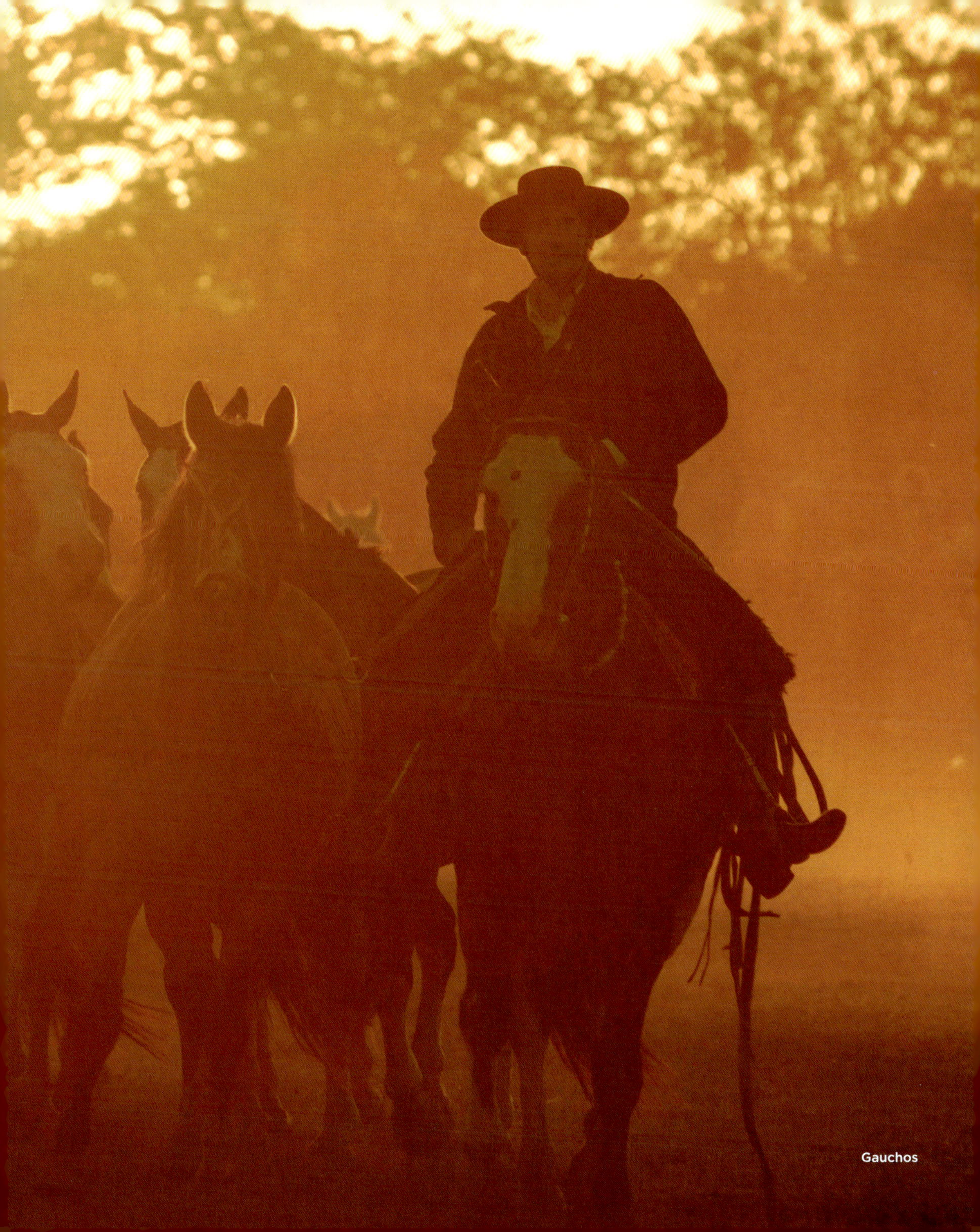
Gauchos

Polo

The English popularized this sport in Argentina, which is particularly popular in upper-class circles. From the horse, the polo player seeks to hit the ball into the opponent's goal. League matches between the famous clubs are big social events and are celebrated pompously in the clubhouses. Similarly to football, well-known names from the Argentinean Champions League are in great demand as professional players abroad.

Polo

Ce sport, essentiellement prisé dans les hautes sphères de la société, fut importé par les Anglais en Argentine. Il s'agit pour le cavalier d'envoyer la balle dans le but de l'adversaire. Les derby entre les meilleurs clubs sont de grands événements sociaux, pompeusement fêtés par les *club-houses.* Tout comme en football, les célèbres joueurs de la Ligue des champions argentine sont souvent recrutés à l'étranger par des équipes professionnelles.

Polo

Die vor allem in oberen Kreisen beliebte Sportart haben die Engländer in Argentinien bekannt gemacht. Vom Pferd aus schlägt der Polospieler den Ball auf das gegnerische Tor. Derbyligaspiele zwischen den berühmten Clubs sind große gesellschaftliche Ereignisse und werden in den Clubhäusern pompös gefeiert. Ähnlich wie im Fußball sind bekannte Namen der argentinischen Champions-League als Profispieler im Ausland äußerst gefragt.

Polo

Los ingleses han hecho famoso en Argentina este deporte, que es particularmente popular en los círculos altos de la sociedad. Desde el caballo, el jugador de polo golpea la pelota hacia la portería del oponente. Los partidos de la Derby League entre los clubes famosos son grandes eventos sociales y se celebran con pomposidad en las casas club. Al igual que el fútbol, los nombres conocidos de la Liga de Campeones argentina son muy solicitados como jugadores profesionales en el extranjero.

Pólo

Os ingleses tornaram este esporte famoso na Argentina, que é particularmente popular nos círculos superiores. Do cavalo, o jogador de pólo acerta a bola na baliza do adversário. Os jogos da liga Derby entre os clubes famosos são grandes eventos sociais e são comemorados pomposamente nos clubes. Semelhante ao futebol, nomes conhecidos da Liga dos Campeões da Argentina estão em grande demanda como jogadores profissionais no exterior.

Polo

De vooral in hogere kringen geliefde sport hebben de Engelsen in Argentinië bekendgemaakt. Vanaf het paard slaat de polospeler de bal op het doel van de tegenstander. Derby's tussen de beroemde clubs zijn grote sociale evenementen en worden in de clubhuizen pompeus gevierd. Net als bij voetbal zijn bekende namen uit de Argentijnse Champions League veelgevraagde profs in het buitenland.

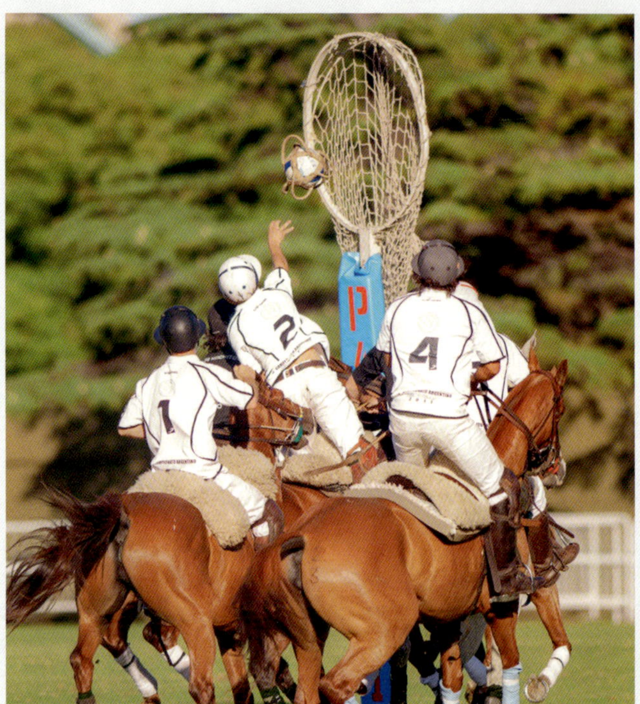

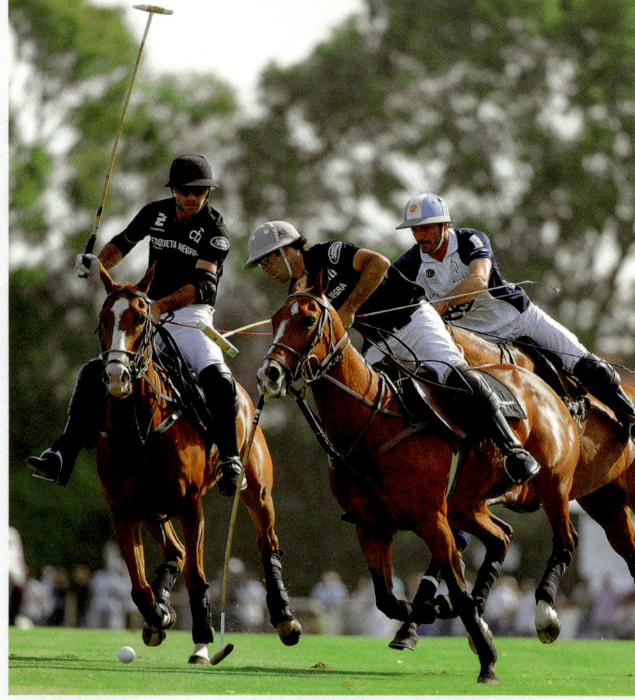

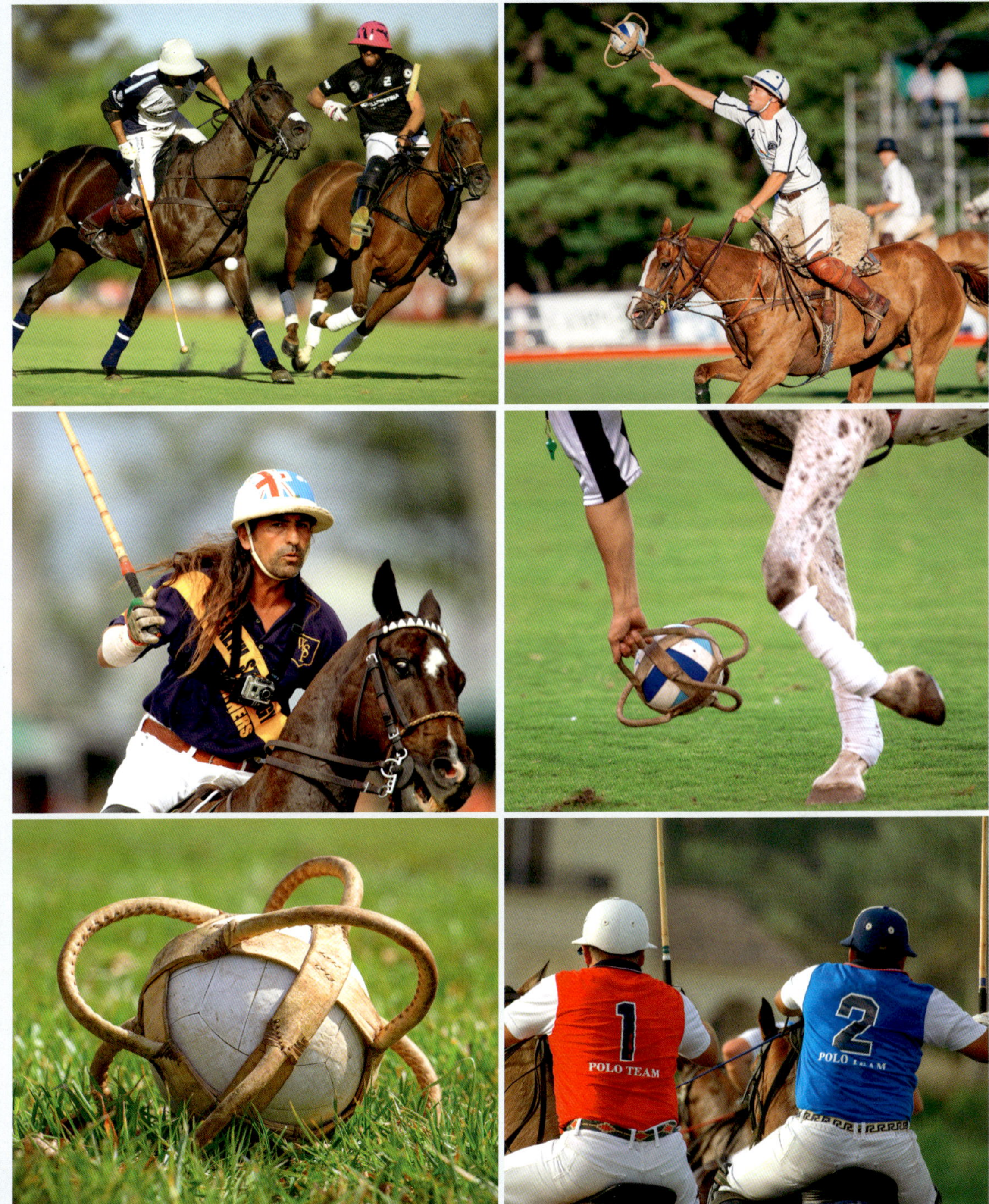

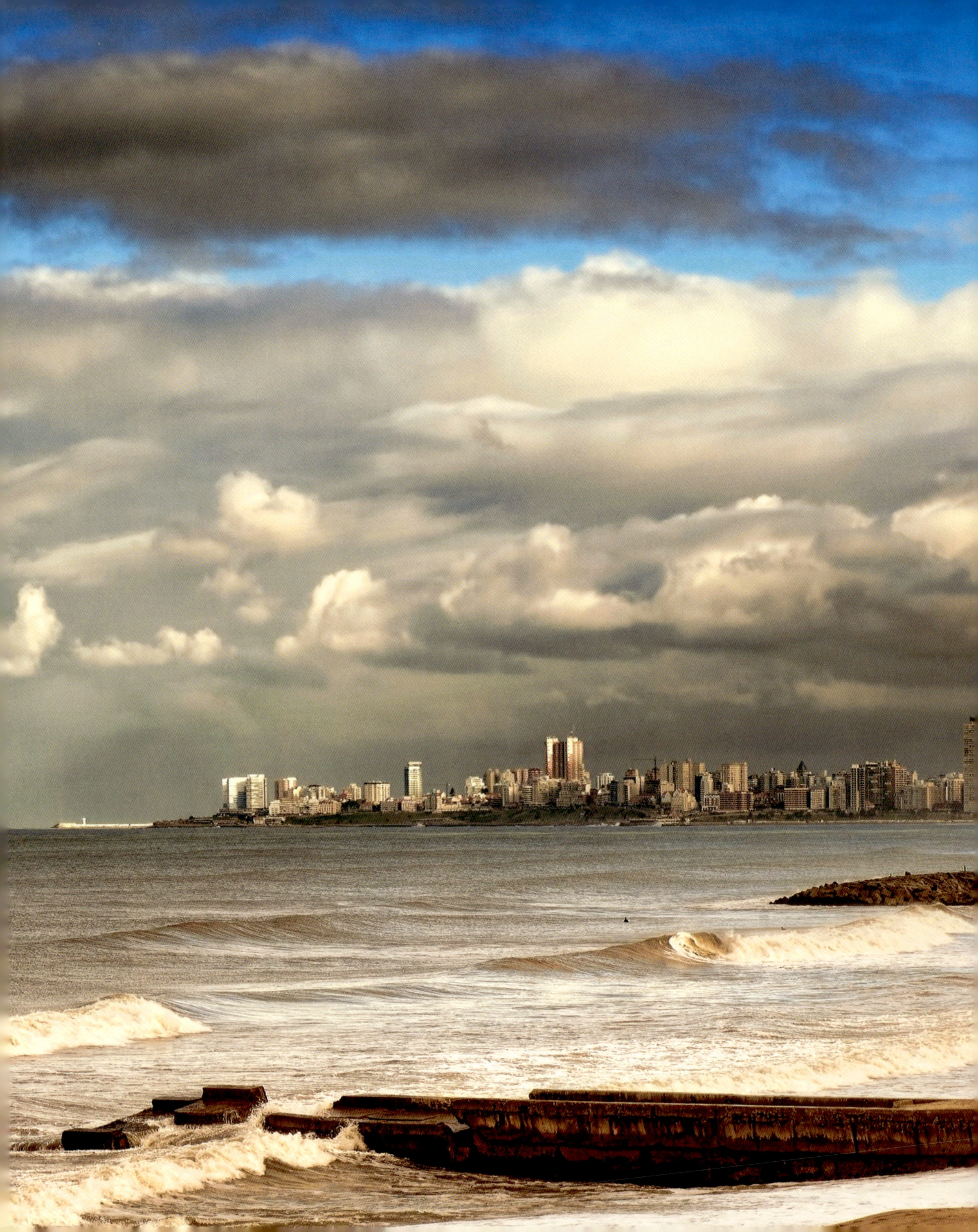

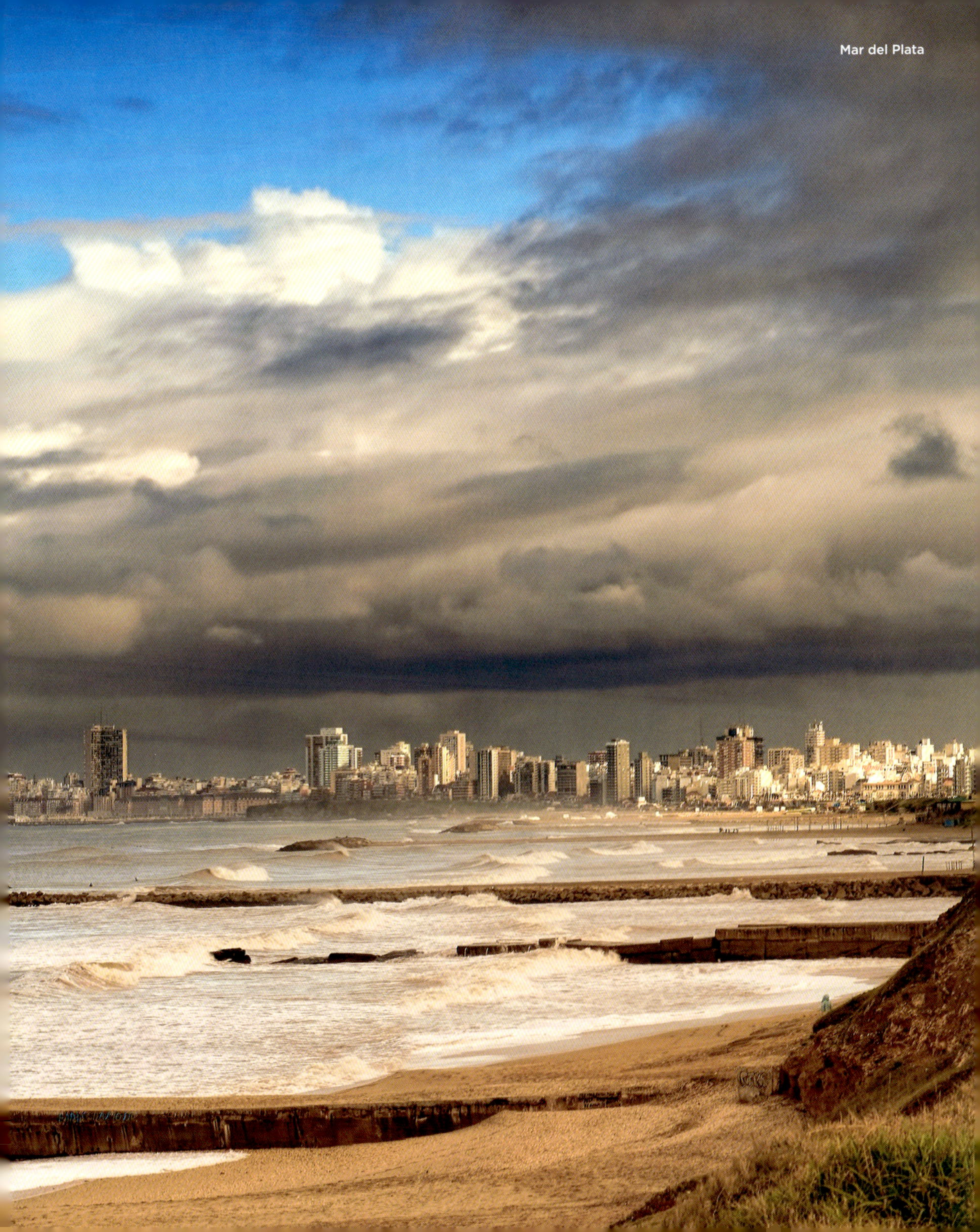
Mar del Plata

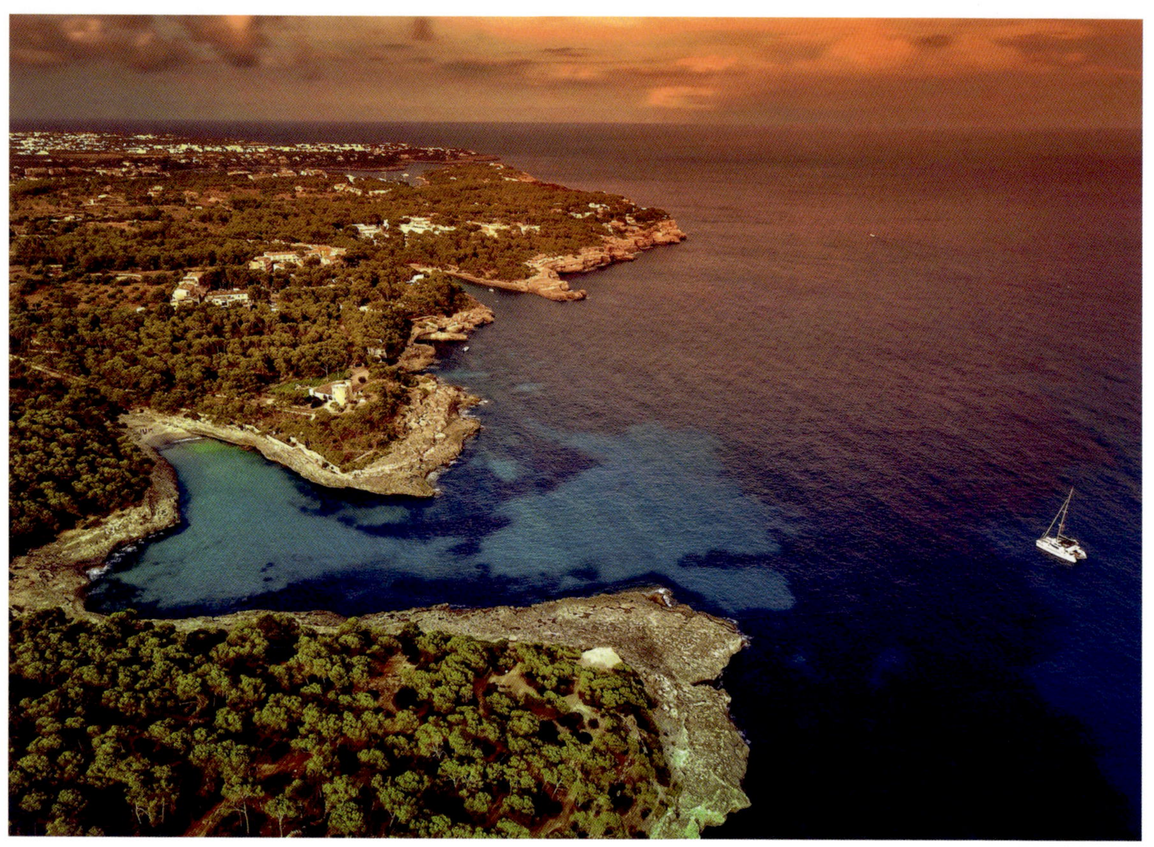

Buenos Aires

Mar del Plata

During the hot summer months, the *porteños,* or citizens of Buenos Aries, are drawn to the Atlantic coast south of the capital. The most famous destination is the big seaside resort Mar del Plata, which is 410 km (255 mi) away. At the beginning of the 20th century, prominent families from Buenos Aires spent the summer months here. Thanks to the railway connection, the journey was possible without great effort. The seaside resort, with its attractive rocky outcrop, saw Biarritz as its model. After the Second World War, the idyllic little Mar del Plata became the most popular and largest seaside resort in Argentina. This earlier romantic flair may still be felt at the harbor, where traditional fishing boats, equipped to spend 100 hours at sea, lie at anchor.

Mar del Plata

Au cœur des mois d'été brûlants, les Porteños se retrouvent sur la côte atlantique au sud de Buenos Aires. La grande cité balnéaire Mar del Plata, à 410 km de la capitale, est la plus connue. Au début du XXᵉ siècle, la bonne société de Buenos Aires y passait la saison. Le chemin de fer permettait de parcourir facilement la distance. La station balnéaire, jouissant de belles vagues, se voyait comme le Biarritz argentin. Après la Seconde Guerre mondiale, l'idyllique petite ville est devenue la plus grande et la plus populaire cité balnéaire d'Argentine. Toutefois, le port a su garder son atmosphère romantique d'autrefois et abrite des bateaux de pêcheurs traditionnels, aménagés pour pouvoir passer des centaines d'heures en mer.

Mar del Plata

In den heißen Sommermonaten zieht es die *porteños* an die Atlantikküste südlich von Buenos Aires. Am berühmtesten ist das große Seebad Mar del Plata, das 410 km entfernt liegt. Zu Beginn des 20. Jahrhunderts verbrachten Familien aus Buenos Aires, die Rang und Namen hatten, hier die Sommermonate. Dank der Eisenbahnverbindung war die Reise ohne großen Aufwand möglich. Das Seebad mit der attraktiven Felsbrandung sah in Biarritz sein Vorbild. Aus dem idyllischen kleinen Mar del Plata wurde nach dem Zweiten Weltkrieg der populärste und größte Badeort Argentiniens. Am Hafen ist der einstige romantische Flair noch spürbar: Traditionelle Fischerboote, ausgestattet um 100 Stunden auf See zu verbringen, liegen vor Anker.

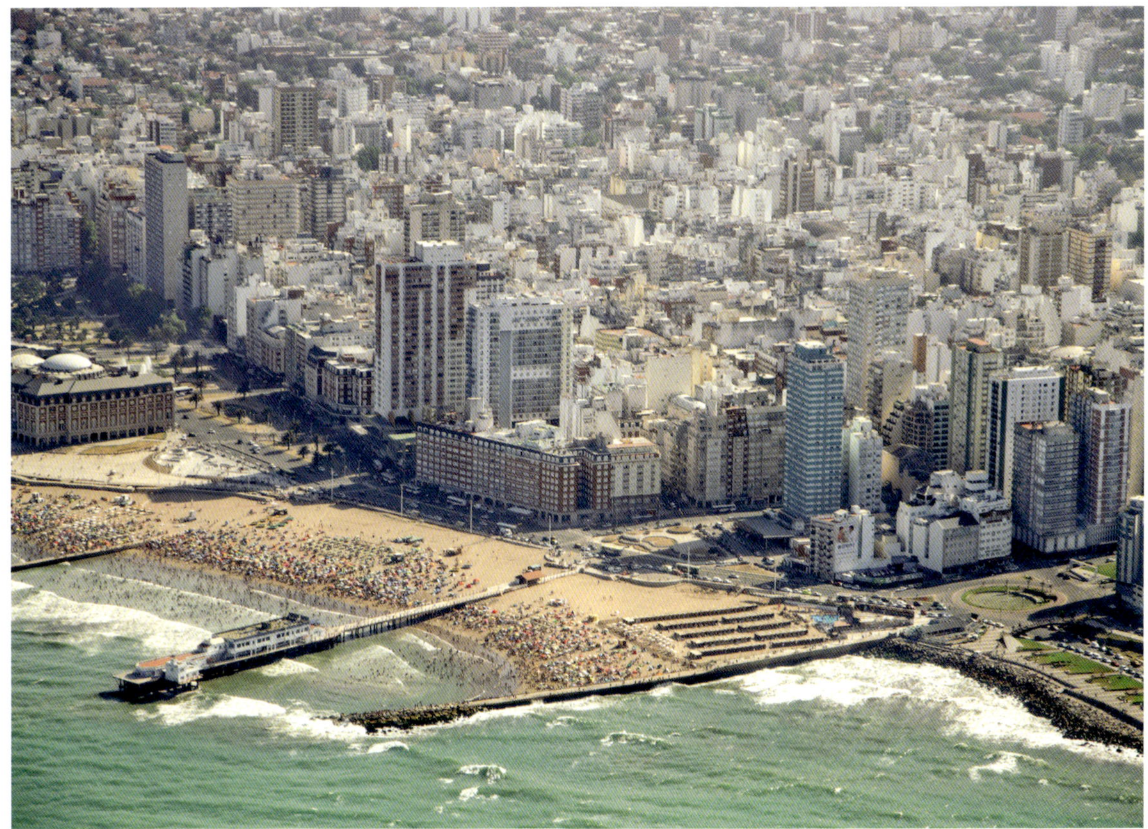

Mar del Plata

Mar del Plata

Durante los calurosos meses de verano, los porteños son atraídos por la costa atlántica al sur de Buenos Aires. El más famoso es el gran balneario de Mar del Plata, que se encuentra a 410 km. A principios del siglo XX, las familias prominentes de Buenos Aires pasaban los meses de verano aquí. Gracias a la conexión ferroviaria, el viaje era posible sin grandes esfuerzos. La estación balnearia, con su atractivo afloramiento rocoso, tuvo como modelo a Biarritz. Después de la Segunda Guerra Mundial, el idílico Mar del Plata se convirtió en el balneario más popular y más grande de Argentina. El antiguo ambiente romántico todavía se puede sentir en el puerto: los tradicionales barcos de pesca, equipados para pasar 100 horas en el mar, están anclados.

Mar del Plata

Durante os meses quentes de verão, os "porteños" são atraídos para a costa atlântica ao sul de Buenos Aires. O mais famoso é o grande balneário Mar del Plata, que fica a 410 km de distância. No início do século XX, famílias com boa reputação de Buenos Aires, passavam os meses de verão aqui. Graças à ligação ferroviária, a viagem era possível sem grandes esforços. O balneário com o seu atraente afloramento rochoso tomou Biarritz como seu modelo. Após a Segunda Guerra Mundial, o pequeno e idílico Mar del Plata tornou-se o mais popular e maior balneário da Argentina. O antigo toque romântico ainda pode ser sentido no porto: onde barcos de pesca tradicionais, equipados para passar 100 horas no mar, estão ancorados.

Mar del Plata

Tijdens de hete zomermaanden lokt voor de porteños de Atlantische kust ten zuiden van Buenos Aires. Het beroemdst is de grote badplaats Mar del Plata op 410 km afstand. Aan het begin van de 20e eeuw brachten vooraanstaande families uit Buenos Aires hier de zomermaanden door. Dankzij de treinverbinding was de reis zonder veel moeite mogelijk. De badplaats met zijn aantrekkelijke rotspartij zag Biarritz als voorbeeld. Na de Tweede Wereldoorlog ontstond uit het idyllische, kleine Mar del Plata de populairste en grootste badplaats van Argentinië. In de haven is de vroegere romantische flair nog steeds voelbaar: traditionele vissersboten, uitgerust om 100 uur op zee door te brengen, liggen voor anker.

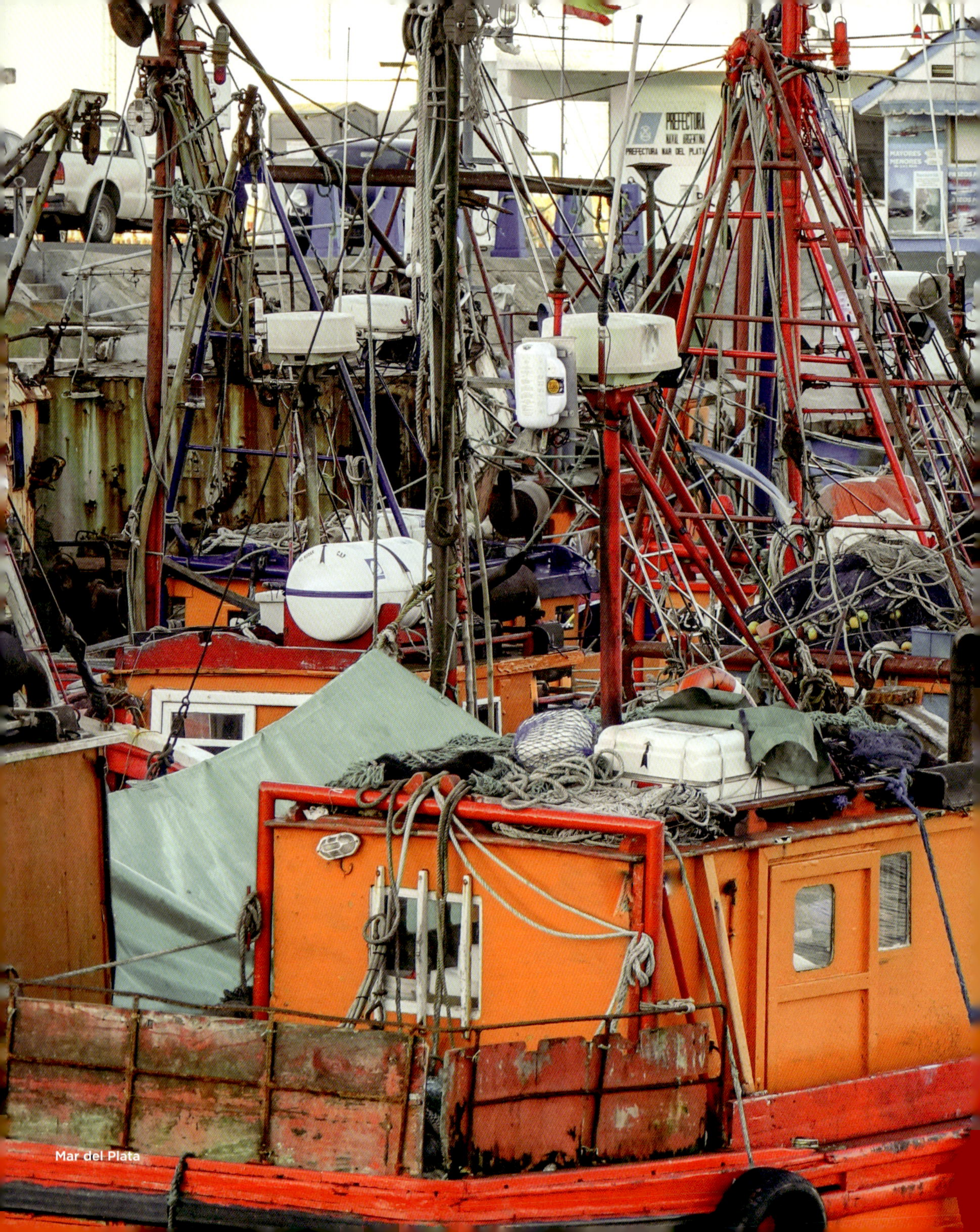

Mar del Plata

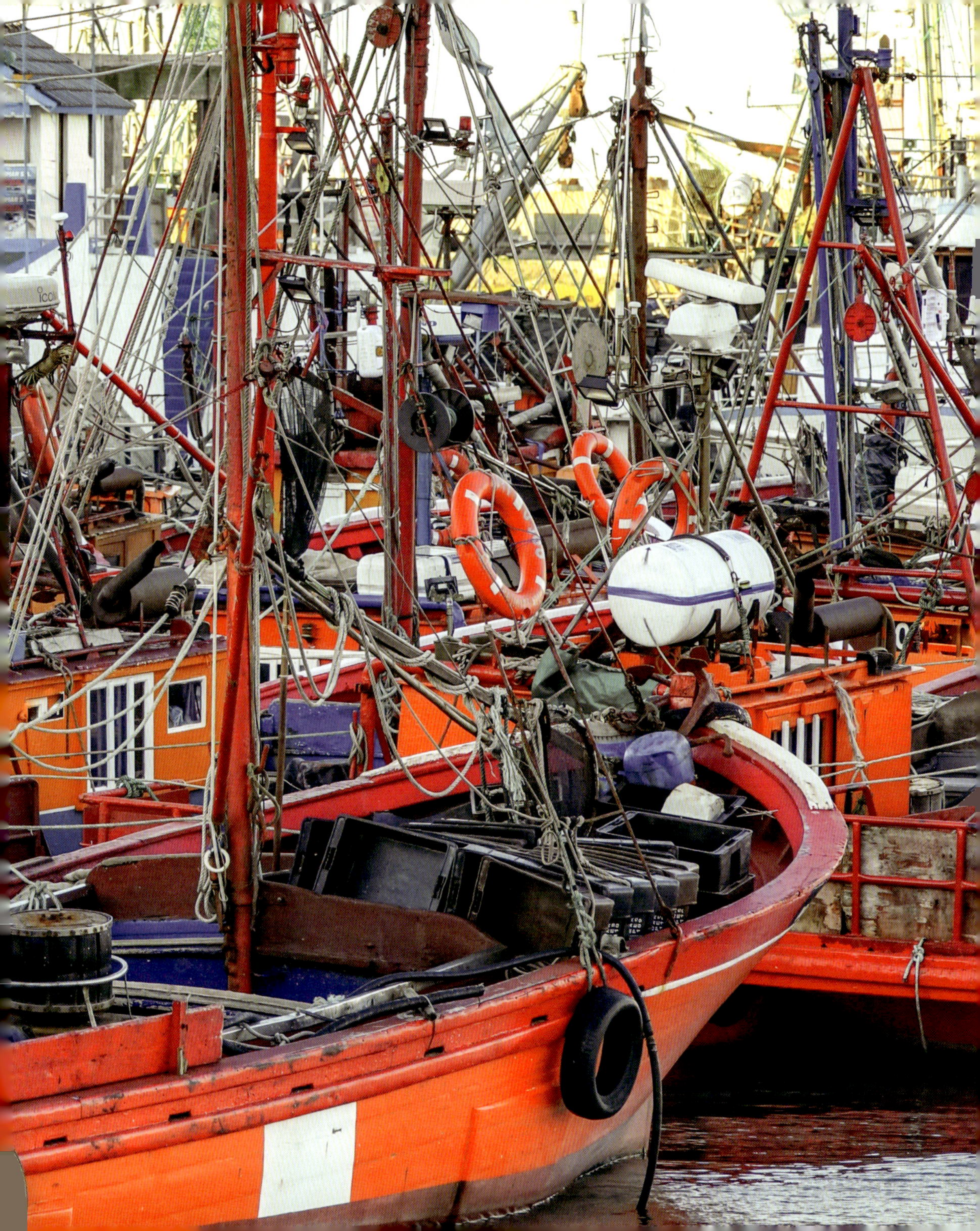

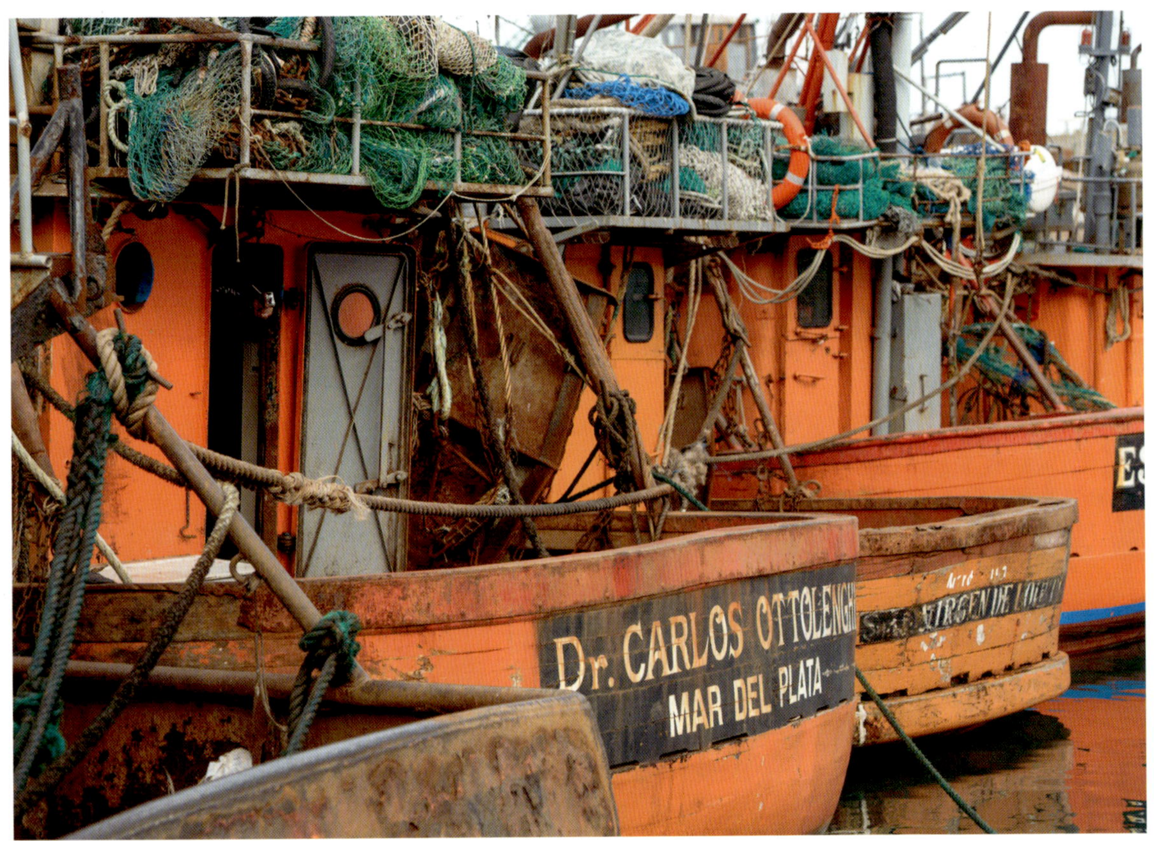
Mar del Plata

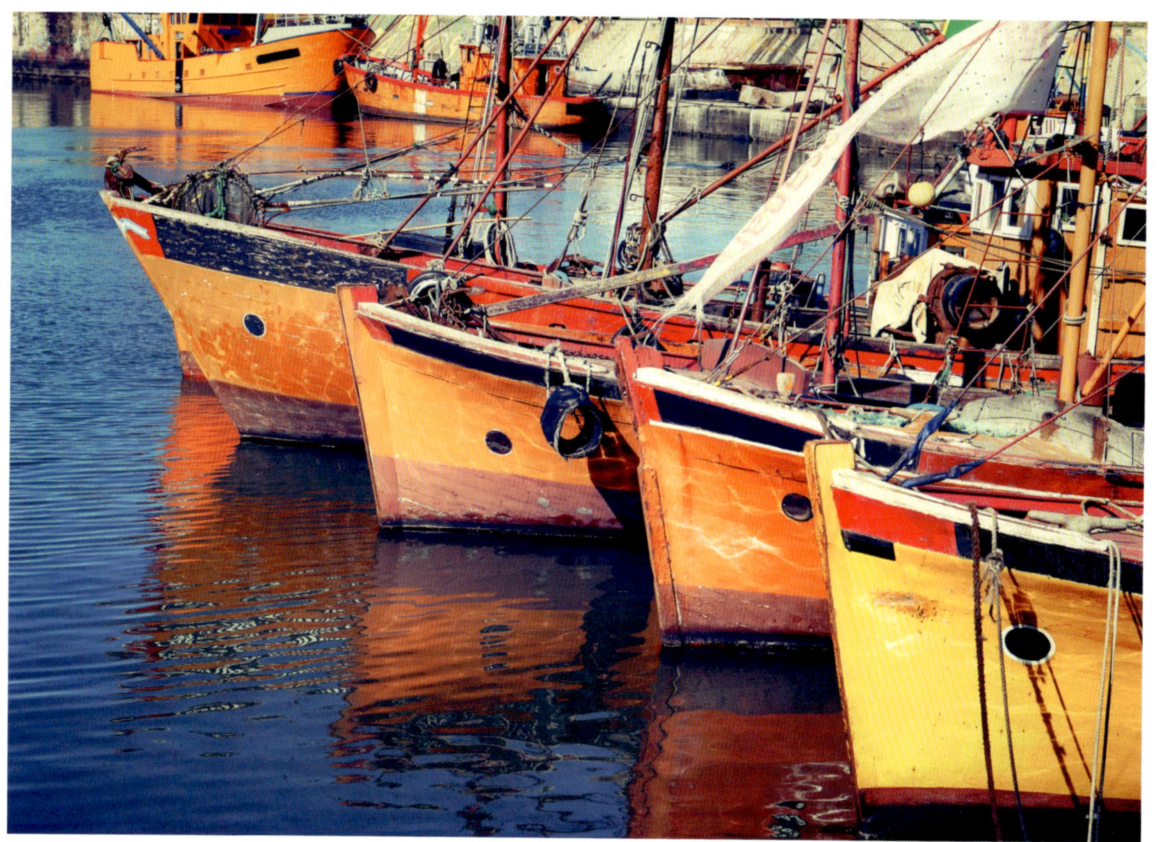

Mar del Plata

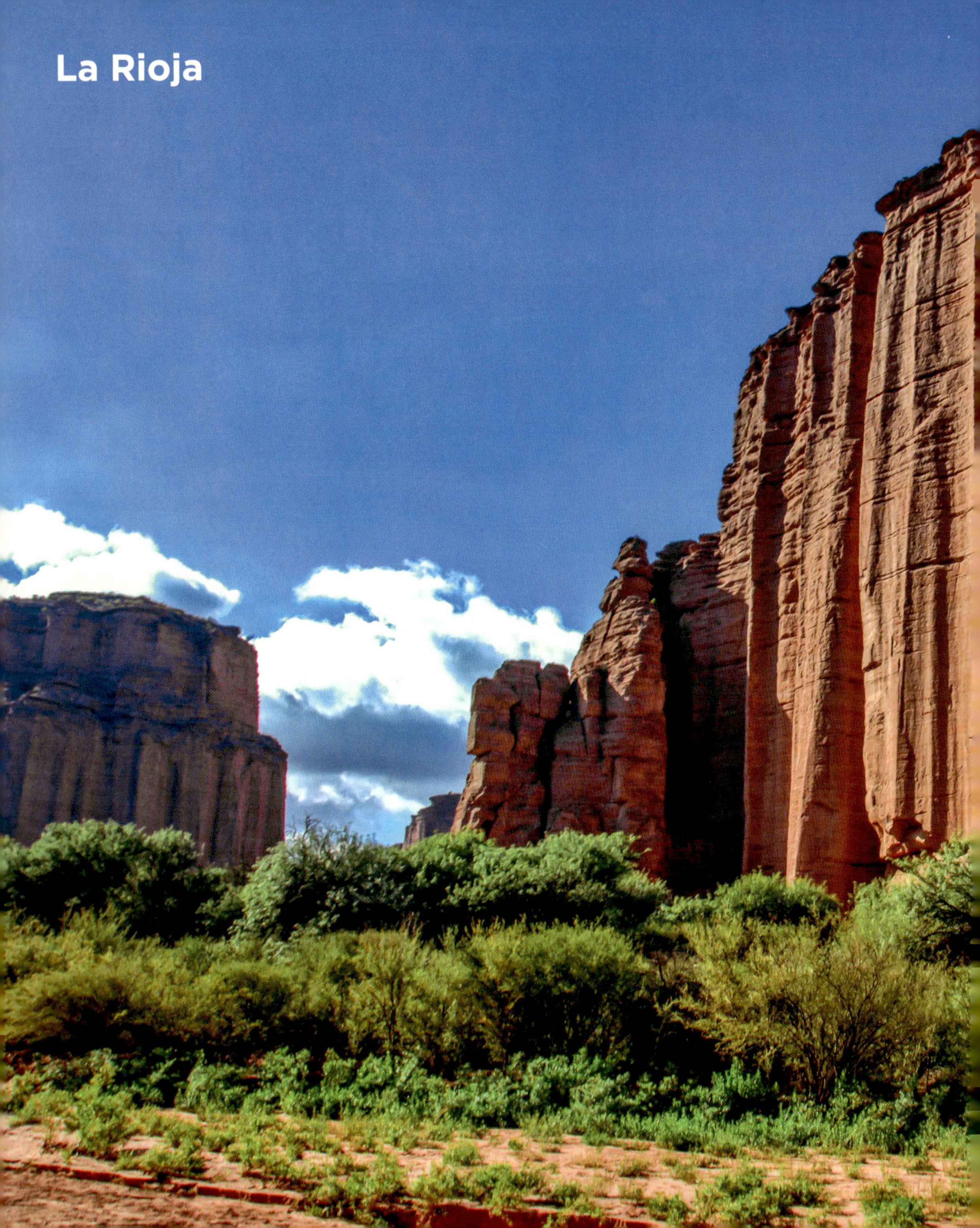
La Rioja

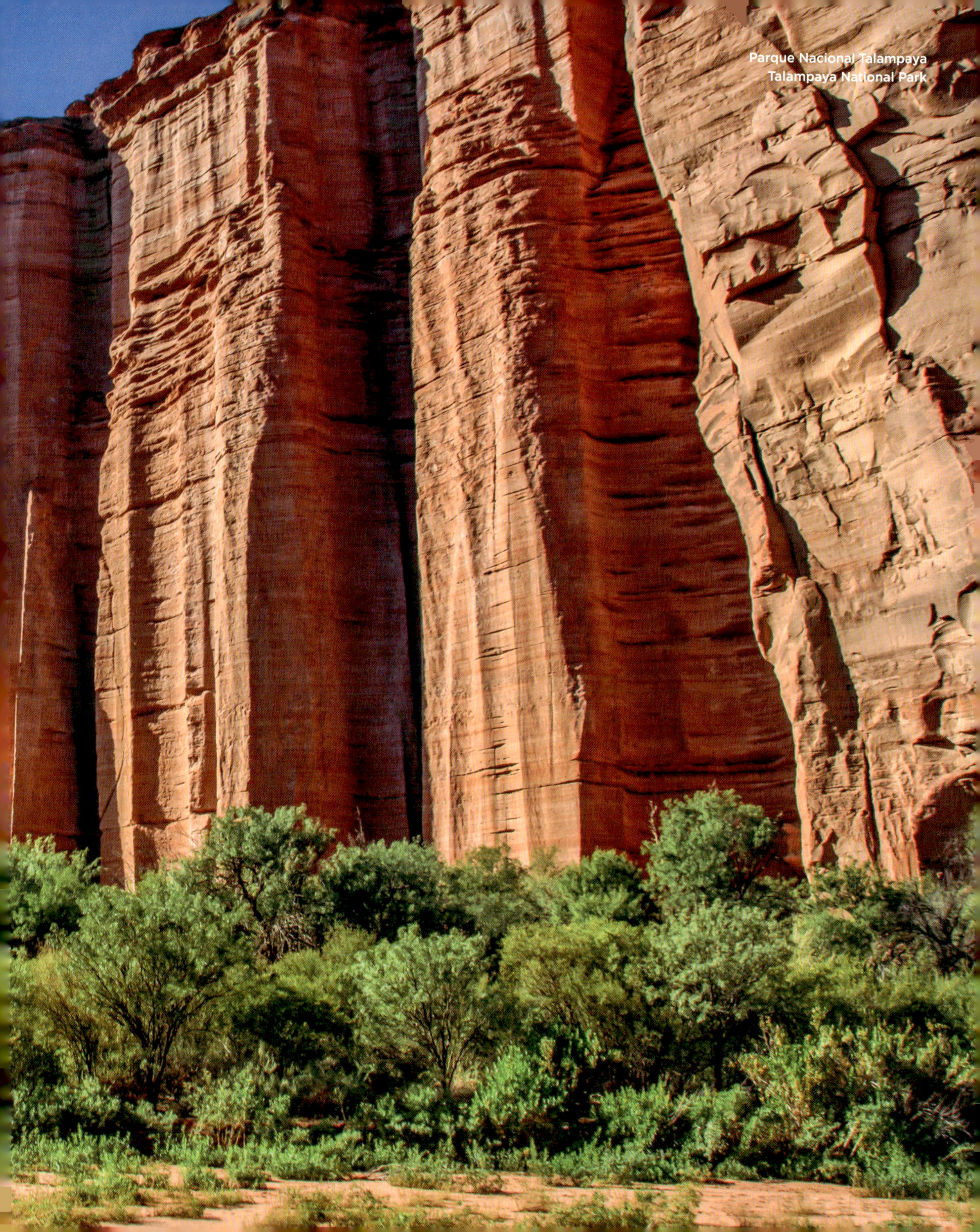
Parque Nacional Talampaya
Talampaya National Park

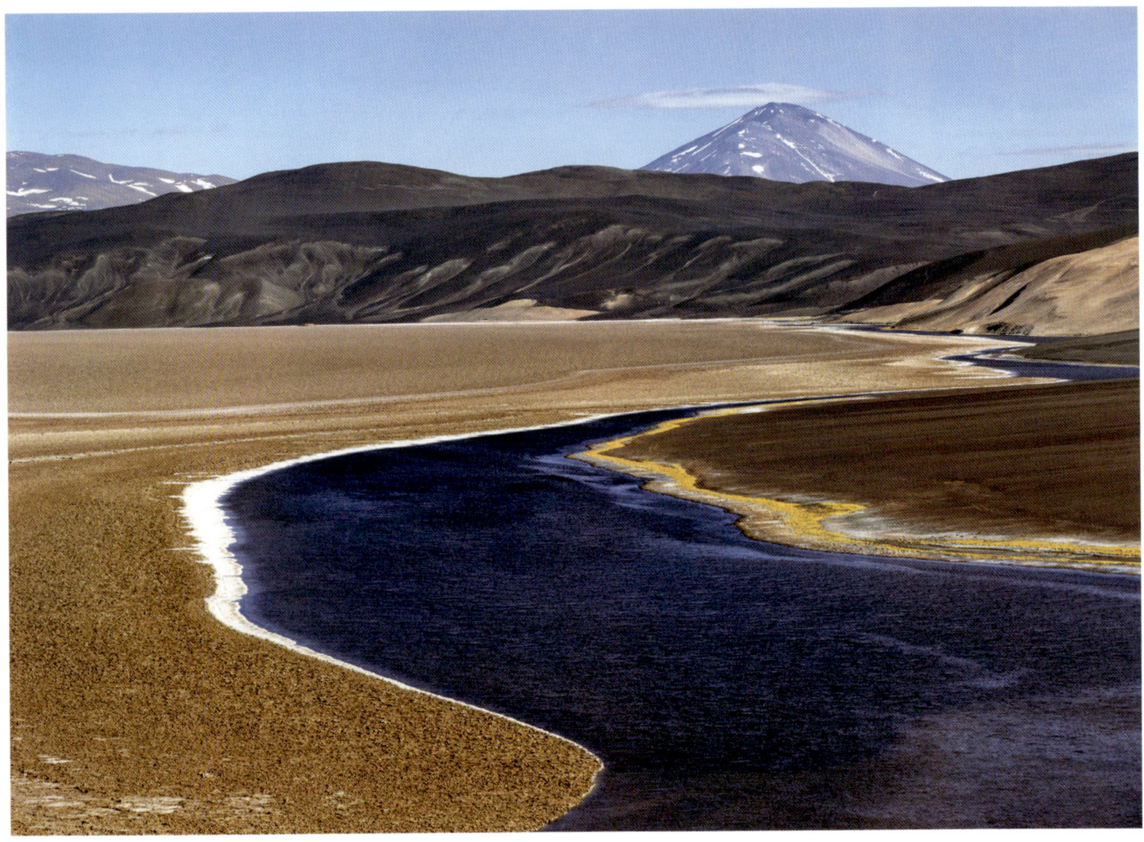

Laguna Brava, monte Pissis

La Rioja

The northwestern province, with the
its capital bearing the same name, was
named by its Spanish conqueror, Juan
Ramírez de Velazco. Agriculture, with the
cultivation of wine, olives and nuts, is their
main source of income, whilst spectacular
canyons, mountain formations, desert
landscapes and lagoons attract visitors.
The Laguna Brava, a huge lake with salt
deposits, shows traces of the Inca culture,
according to archaeological research.
Red earth and red rocks characterize the
mountain slopes of the Cuesta de Miranda.
From here there is a view of the Sierra de
Famatina mountain range, near the village
of Famatina, 320 km (200 mi) north of the
provincial capital.

La Rioja

La province, située au nord-ouest du pays
et dotée d'une capitale homonyme, doit
son nom à ses conquérants espagnols.
L'agriculture – et en particulier les vignes,
les olives et les noix – constitue sa
principale source de revenus, alors que
ses canyons spectaculaires, ses formations
montagneuses, ses paysages désertiques
et ses lagons attirent les visiteurs. La
Laguna Brava, immense lac renfermant
des gisements de sel, recèle, selon des
recherches archéologiques, des vestiges
de la culture inca. Terre et rochers rouges
caractérisent les versants de la Cuesta de
Miranda. Depuis son sommet, on aperçoit
la montagne Famatina, proche de la
localité homonyme située à 320 km au
nord de la capitale provinciale.

La Rioja

Die nordwestliche Provinz mit der
gleichnamigen Hauptstadt ist nach
ihrem spanischen Eroberer Juan Ramírez
de Velazco benannt. Landwirtschaft,
Anbau von Wein, Oliven und Nüssen,
bilden ihre Haupteinnahmequelle.
Spektakuläre Canyons, Bergformationen,
Wüstenlandschaft und Lagunen locken
Besucher an. Die Laguna brava, ein
riesiger See mit Salzvorkommen, birgt
laut archäologischer Untersuchungen
Spuren der Inka-Kultur. Rote Erde, roter
Fels bestimmt die Berghänge der Cuesta
de Miranda. Von hier blickt man auf das
Famatina Gebirge nahe der Ortschaft
Famatina, die 320 km nördlich der
Provinzhauptstadt liegt.

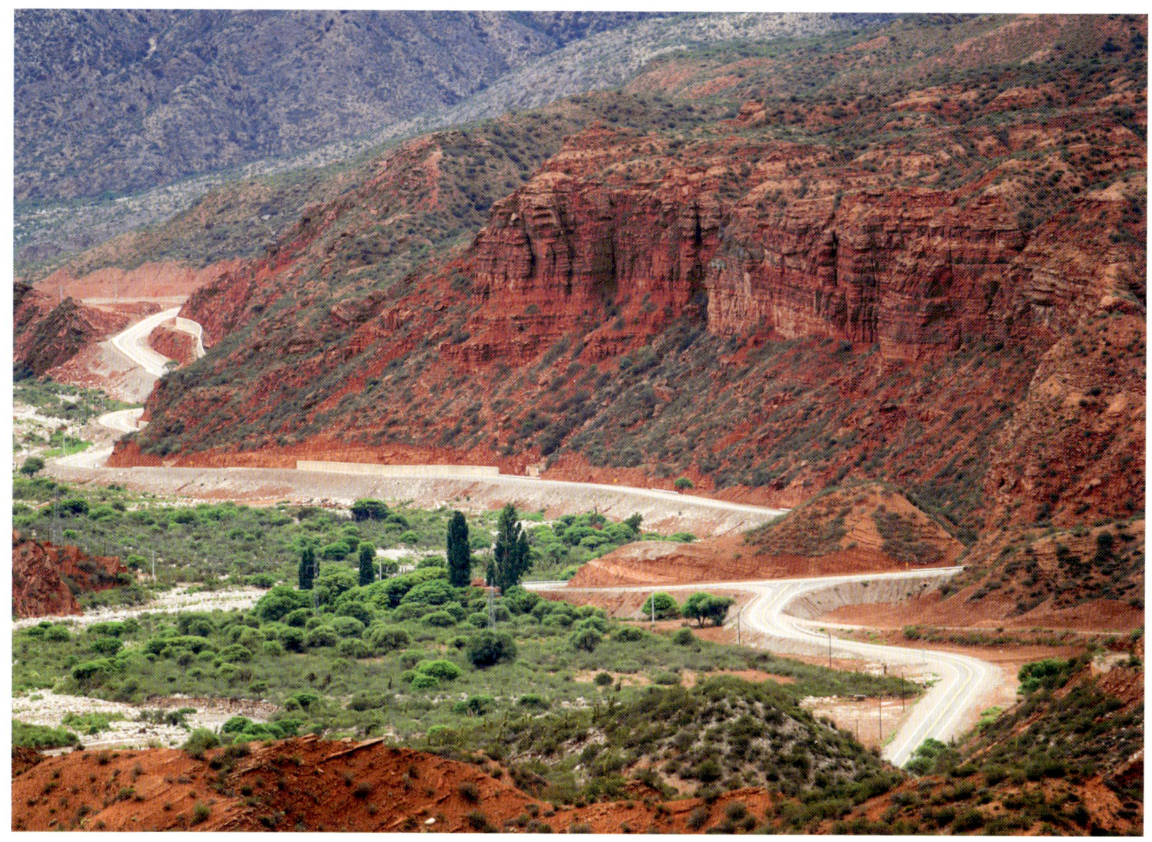

Cuesta de Miranda

La Rioja

La provincia situada al noroeste fue nombrada por su conquistador español, Juan Ramírez de Velasco. La agricultura, el cultivo del vino, las aceitunas y los frutos secos son sus principales fuentes de ingresos. Espectaculares cañones, formaciones montañosas, paisajes desérticos y lagunas atraen a los visitantes. La Laguna Brava, un enorme lago con depósitos de sal, contiene rastros de la cultura inca según las investigaciones arqueológicas. Tanto la tierra como la roca roja caracterizan las laderas de las montañas de la Cuesta de Miranda. Desde aquí hay una vista de las montañas de Famatina cerca del pueblo de Famatina, a 320 km al norte de la capital de la provincia.

La Rioja

A província do noroeste com a capital, com o mesmo nome; tem o nome do seu conquistador espanhol. A agricultura, o cultivo de vinho, azeitonas e frutos secos, são a sua principal fonte de rendimento. Cânions espetaculares, formações montanhosas, paisagens desérticas e lagoas atraem visitantes. Segundo pesquisas arqueológicas, o Laguna brava, um enorme lago com depósitos de sal, contém vestígios da cultura inca. Terra e rocha vermelhas caracterizam as encostas das montanhas da Cuesta de Miranda. Daqui tem-se uma vista da Serra de Famatina perto da aldeia de Famatina, 320 km ao norte da capital provincial.

La Rioja

De noordwestelijke provincie met de gelijknamige hoofdstad is genoemd naar de Spaanse veroveraar. De landbouw, de teelt van wijn, olijven en noten vormen de belangrijkste bron van inkomsten. Spectaculaire ravijnen, bergformaties, woestijnlandschappen en lagunes trekken bezoekers aan. De Laguna brava, een groot meer met zoutlaag, bevat volgens archeologisch onderzoek sporen van de Inca-cultuur. Rode aarde en rood gesteente bepalen de berghellingen van de Cuesta de Miranda. Vanaf hier kijkt men op het Famatina gebergte nabij het dorp Famatina, dat 320 km ten noorden van de provinciehoofdstad ligt.

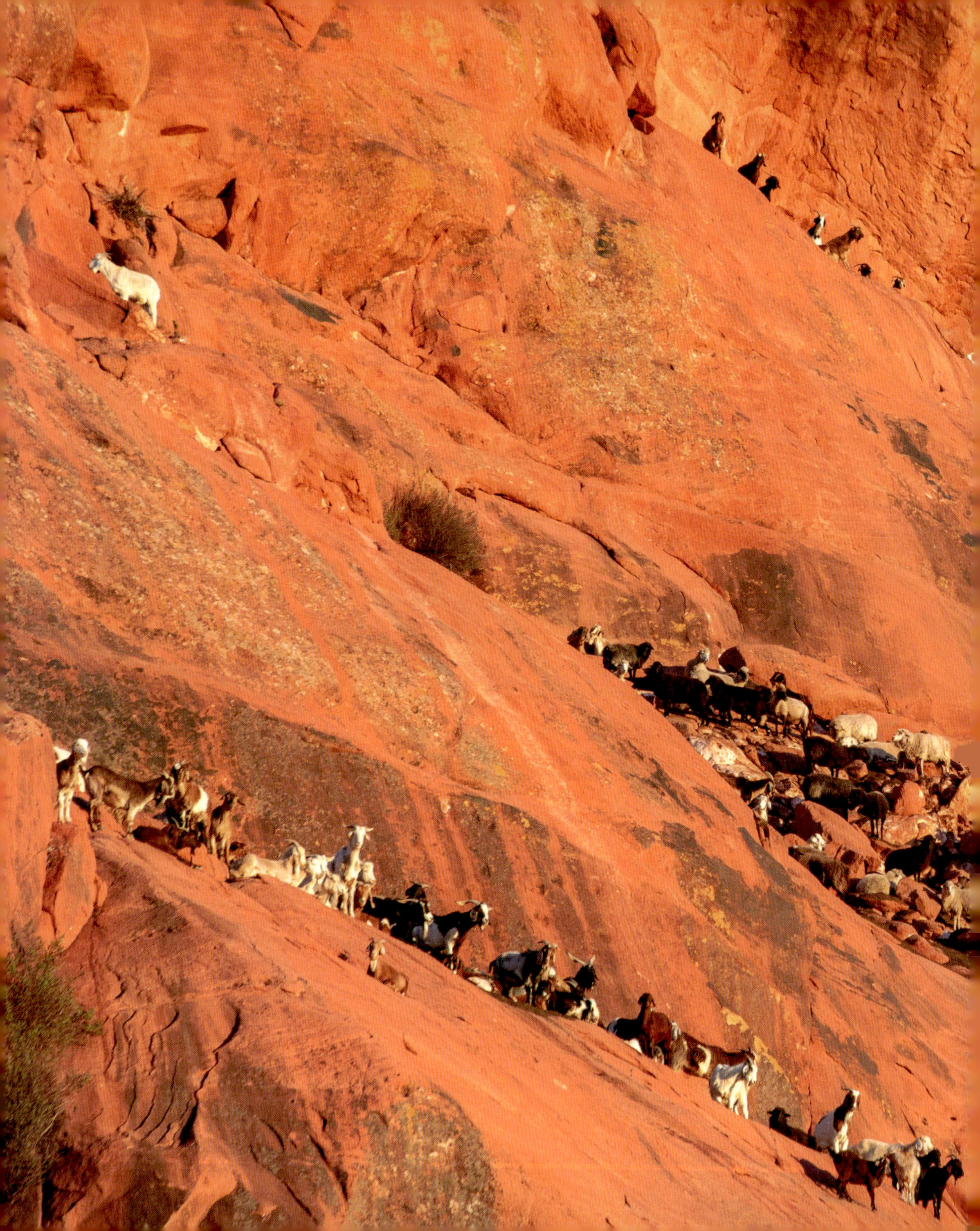

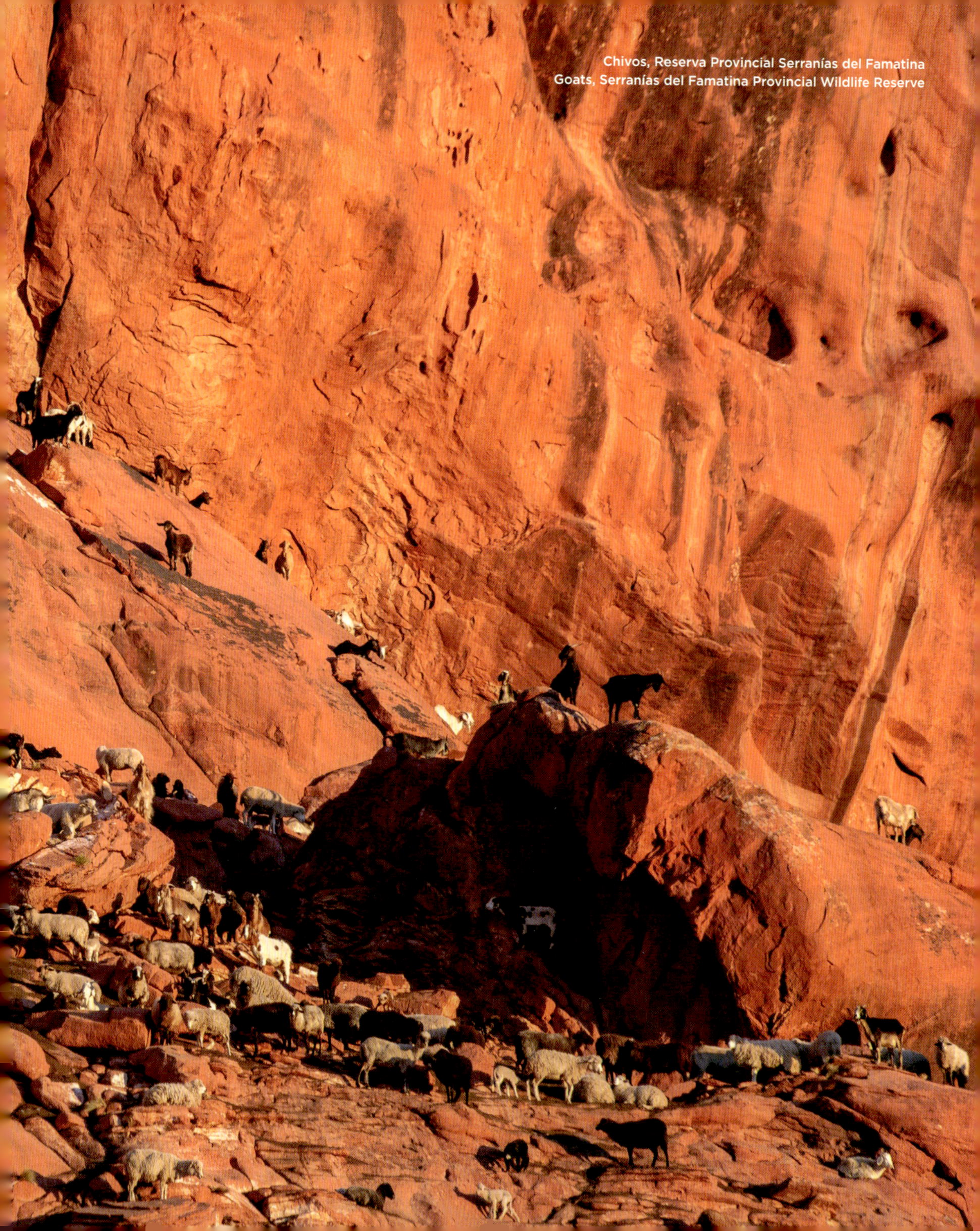

Chivos, Reserva Provincial Serranías del Famatina
Goats, Serranías del Famatina Provincial Wildlife Reserve

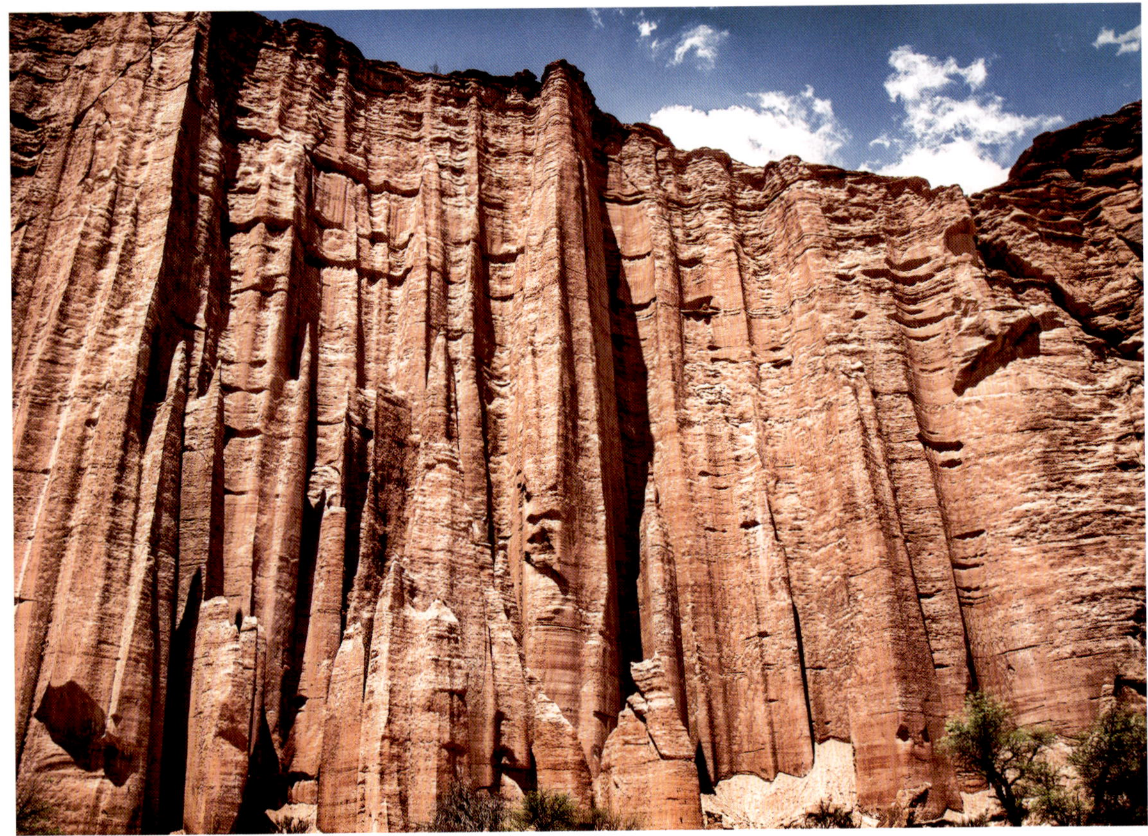

Parque Nacional Talampaya
Talampaya National Park

Talampaya Canyon

The Talampaya Canyon is 12 km (7.5 mi)
long and 160 m (525 ft) high and contains
fossils and traces of prehistoric and
pre-hispanic cultures. The people of La
Aguada, descendants of the Ciénaga
people
(100–500 AD), settled here around 600–
900 AD, leaving behind fascinating rock
paintings. Named after the canyon, the
215,000 ha (830 sq mi) national park was
established in 1975. Since 2000 it has been
a UNESCO World Heritage Site. Its bizarre
rock formations bear majestic names such
as "Gateway to the Cayon", "Wise Man"
or "Cathedral". Thanks to archaeological
studies it is known that the region was not
always as dry as it is today.

Canyon de Talampaya

Long de 12 km et profond de 160 m,
le canyon de Talampaya renferme des
fossiles et des vestiges des cultures
préhistoriques et préhispaniques. Le
peuple aguada, descendant des Ciénaga
(100–500 ap. J.-C.), s'y était installé entre
600 et 900. Il y a laissé d'intéressantes
fresques rupestres. Le parc national
Talampaya fut fondé en 1975 sur une
superficie de 215 000 ha. Depuis 2000, il
est inscrit au patrimoine de l'Unesco. Ses
formations rocheuses étranges portent
des noms majestueux : « Porte du canyon »,
« Homme sage » ou « Cathédrale ». Les
études archéologiques ont montré que
la région n'a pas toujours vécu sous son
climat sec actuel.

Talampaya Canyon

12 km lang und 160 m hoch ist der
Talampaya Canyon. Er birgt Fossilien und
Spuren prähistorischer und prähispanischer
Kulturen. Das Volk La Aguada, Nachfahren
der Ciénaga (100–500), siedelte hier um
600–900. Sie hinterließen interessante
Felszeichnungen. Der nach dem Canyon
benannte, 215 000 ha große Nationalpark
wurde 1975 gegründet. Seit 2000
zählt er zum UNESCO-Weltkulturerbe.
Seine bizarren Felsformationen tragen
majestätische Namen wie „Tor zum
Canyon", „Weiser Mann" oder „Kathedrale".
Dank archäologischer Studien weiß man,
dass in der Region nicht immer die heutige
Trockenheit herrschte.

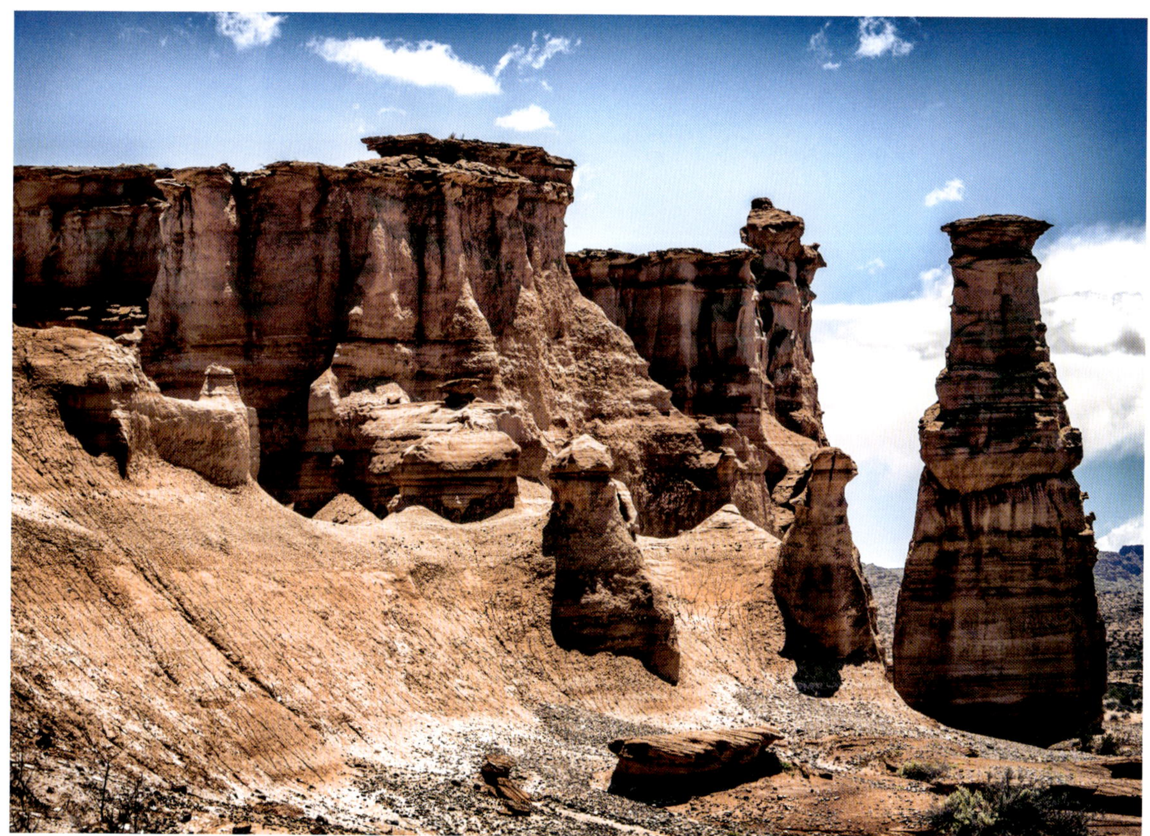

Parque Nacional Talampaya
Talampaya National Park

Cañón de Talampaya

El Cañón de Talampaya tiene 12 km de largo y 160 m de altura. Contiene fósiles y rastros de culturas prehistóricas y prehispánicas. Los habitantes de La Aguada, descendientes de la Ciénaga (100–500), se asentaron aquí alrededor de 600–900 y dejaron interesantes pinturas rupestres. Llamado así por el cañón, el parque nacional de 215 000 ha se creó en 1975, y desde el año 2000 es Patrimonio de la Humanidad de la UNESCO. Sus extrañas formaciones rocosas llevan nombres majestuosos como Puerta del Cañón, Hombre Sabio o Catedral. Gracias a los estudios arqueológicos se sabe que la región no siempre fue tan seca como lo es hoy en día.

Talampaya Canyon

O Cânion de Talampaya tem 12 km de comprimento e 160 m de altura. Ele contém fósseis e vestígios de culturas pré-históricas e pré-hispânicas. O povo de La Aguada, descendentes de Ciénaga (100–500), se estabeleceram aqui por volta de 600–900, deixando para trás interessantes pinturas rupestres. Em homenagem ao cânion, o parque nacional de 215 000 ha foi criado em 1975 com o seu mesmo nome. Desde 2000 é um Património Mundial da UNESCO. Suas bizarras formações rochosas ostentam nomes majestosos como “Portal para o Cânion”, “Homem Sábio” ou “Catedral”. Graças aos estudos arqueológicos, sabe-se que a região nem sempre foi tão seca como é hoje.

Talampaya Canyon

Talampaya Canyon is 12 km lang en 160 m hoog. Het bevat fossielen en sporen van prehistorische en pre-Hispaanse culturen. Het La Aguada volk, afstammelingen van Ciénaga (100–500), vestigde zich hier rond 600–900 en lieten interessante rotsschilderingen achter. Het 215 000 ha naar de Canyon genoemde natuurpark werd in 1975 opgericht. Sinds 2000 is het UNESCO-Werelderfgoed. Zijn bizarre rotsformaties dragen majestueuze namen zoals “Poort tot de Canyon”, “Wijze man” of Kathedraal”. Dankzij archeologische studies is bekend dat de regio niet altijd zo droog was als nu.

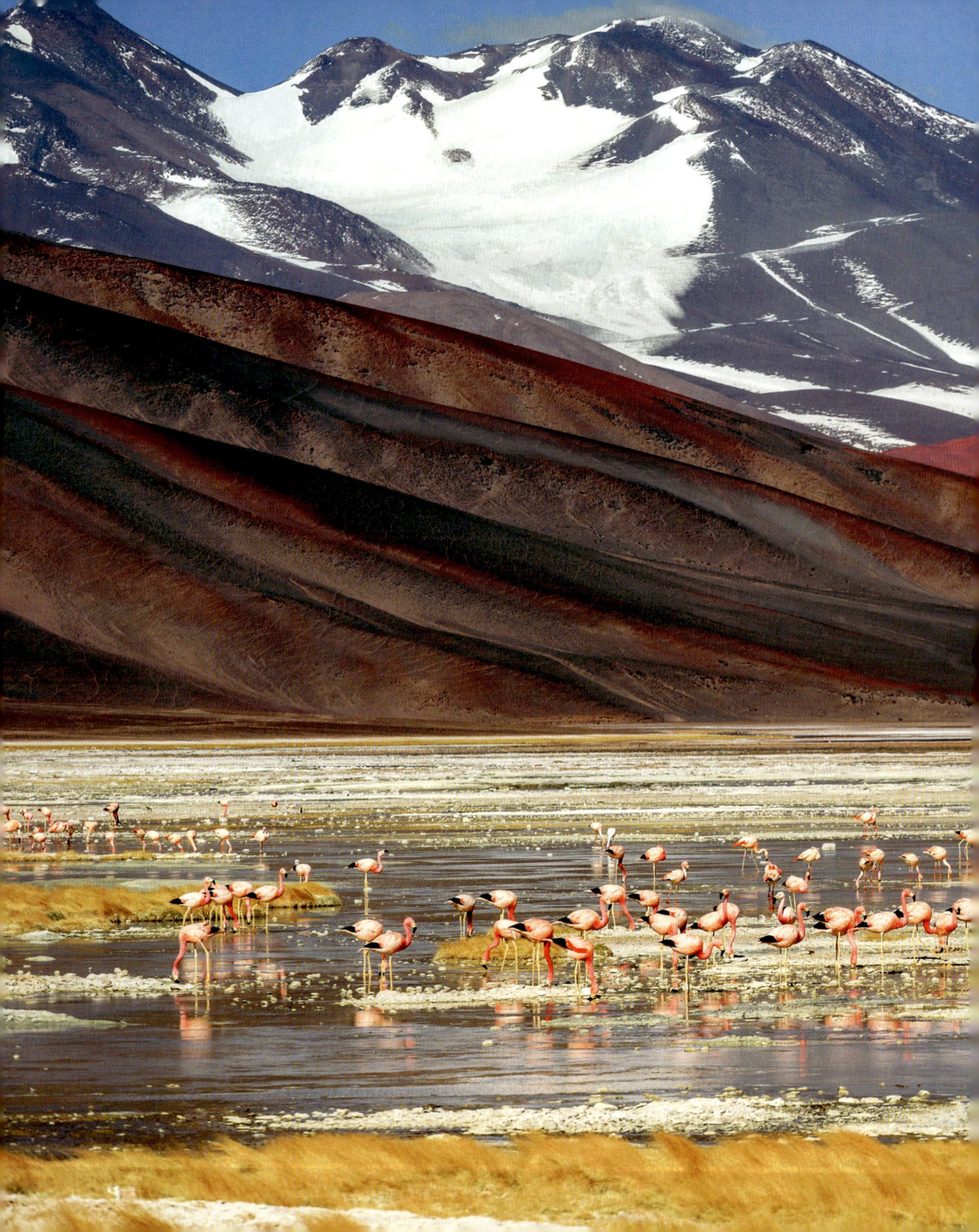

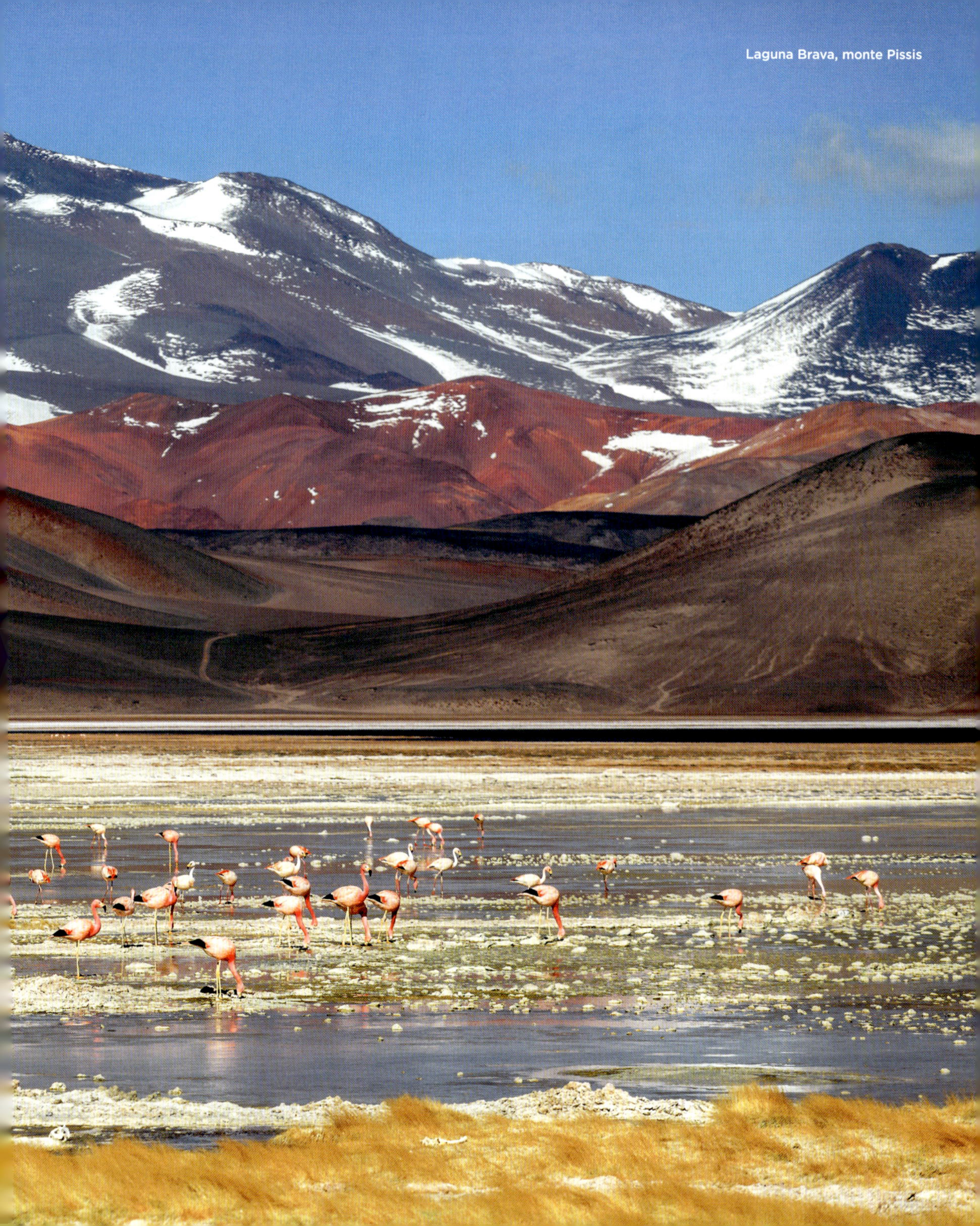
Laguna Brava, monte Pissis

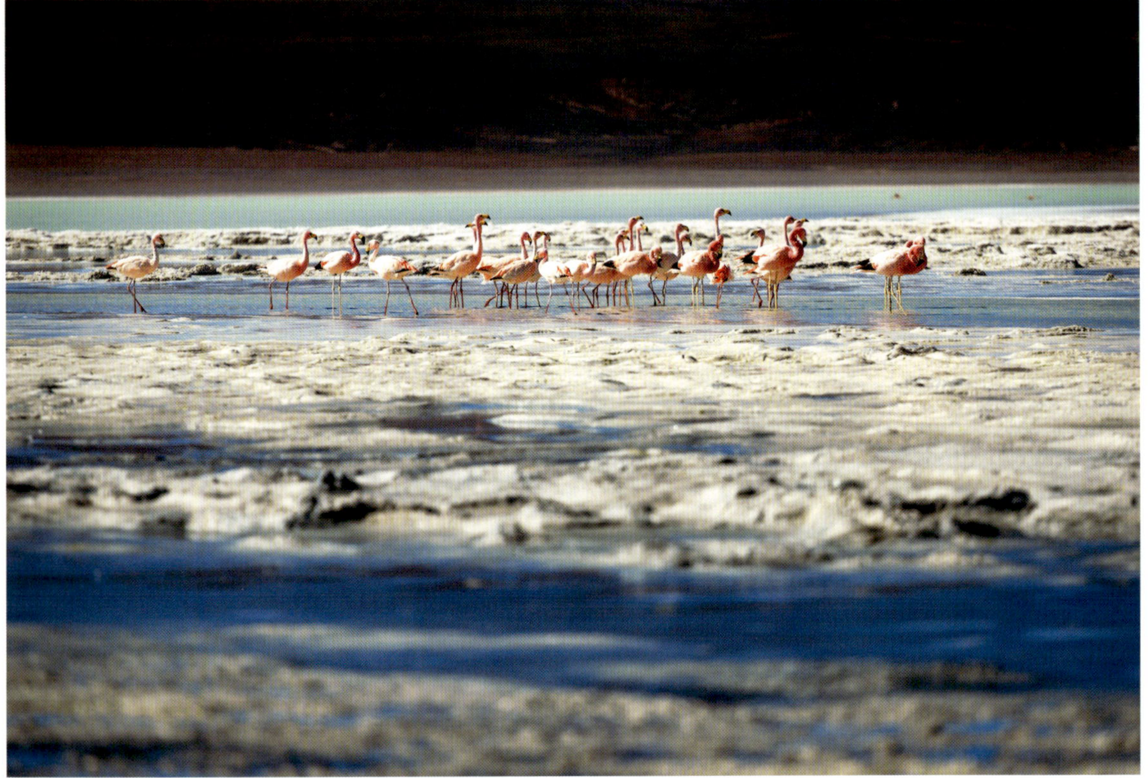

Laguna Brava

Lagoon of Wrath

In the middle of the stormy Andes region, at 3000 m (9840 ft) altitude, hides the Laguna Brava. The lake is, at 60 km² (23 sq mi), the largest in the region. The name *brava* means angry and refers to the frequent storms which rage over it. Legend has it that the angry spirit of the lake wants to keep its visitors away, but the white and pink flamingos still come in flocks.

Laguna de la Ira

En medio de la tormentosa región de los Andes, a 3000 m de altitud, se esconde la Laguna Brava. Con sus 60 km², la laguna es la más grande de la región. Su nombre brava hace referencia a las frecuentes tormentas que se desatan sobre ella. Cuenta la leyenda que el espíritu enojado del lago quiere mantener a sus visitantes alejados. Sin embargo, los flamencos blancos y rosas vienen en grandes cantidades.

Le lac de la colère

Au cœur de cette région andine accidentée se cache, à 3000 m d'altitude, la Laguna Brava. Avec une superficie de 60 km², ce lac est le plus vaste de la région. Son nom, *brava* (en colère), fait référence aux orages qui s'abattent régulièrement sur ses eaux. Selon la légende, l'esprit agressif du lac souhaiterait ainsi tenir à distance les visiteurs. Pourtant, flamants roses et blancs y prospèrent en nuées.

Lagoa da Ira

No meio da região tempestuosa dos Andes a 3000 m de altitude, esconde-se o "Laguna Brava". O lago é com 60 km² o maior da região. Seu nome "brava" significa raiva, referindo-se às frequentes tempestades que o assolam. A lenda diz que o espírito irado do lago quer manter os seus visitantes afastados. Mas os flamingos brancos e cor-de-rosa vêm em massa.

Lagune des Zorns

Inmitten der stürmischen Anden-Region auf 3000 m Höhe versteckt sich die Laguna brava. Der See ist mit 60 km² der größte in der Region. Sein Name *brava* bedeutet zornig, er nimmt Bezug auf die häufigen Stürme, die über ihm wüten. Die Legende sagt, der zornige Geist des Sees wolle seine Besucher fernhalten. Doch weiße und rosa Flamingos kommen in Scharen.

Lagune van de woede

In het midden van de stormachtige Andes regio verstopt zich op 3000 m hoogte de Laguna Brava. Het meer is met 60 km² het grootste in de regio. Zijn naam *brava* betekent woedend, het verwijst naar de veelvuldige stormen die over hem woeden. Volgens de legende wil de boze geest van het meer zijn bezoekers op afstand houden. Maar witte en roze flamingo's komen hier in groten getale.

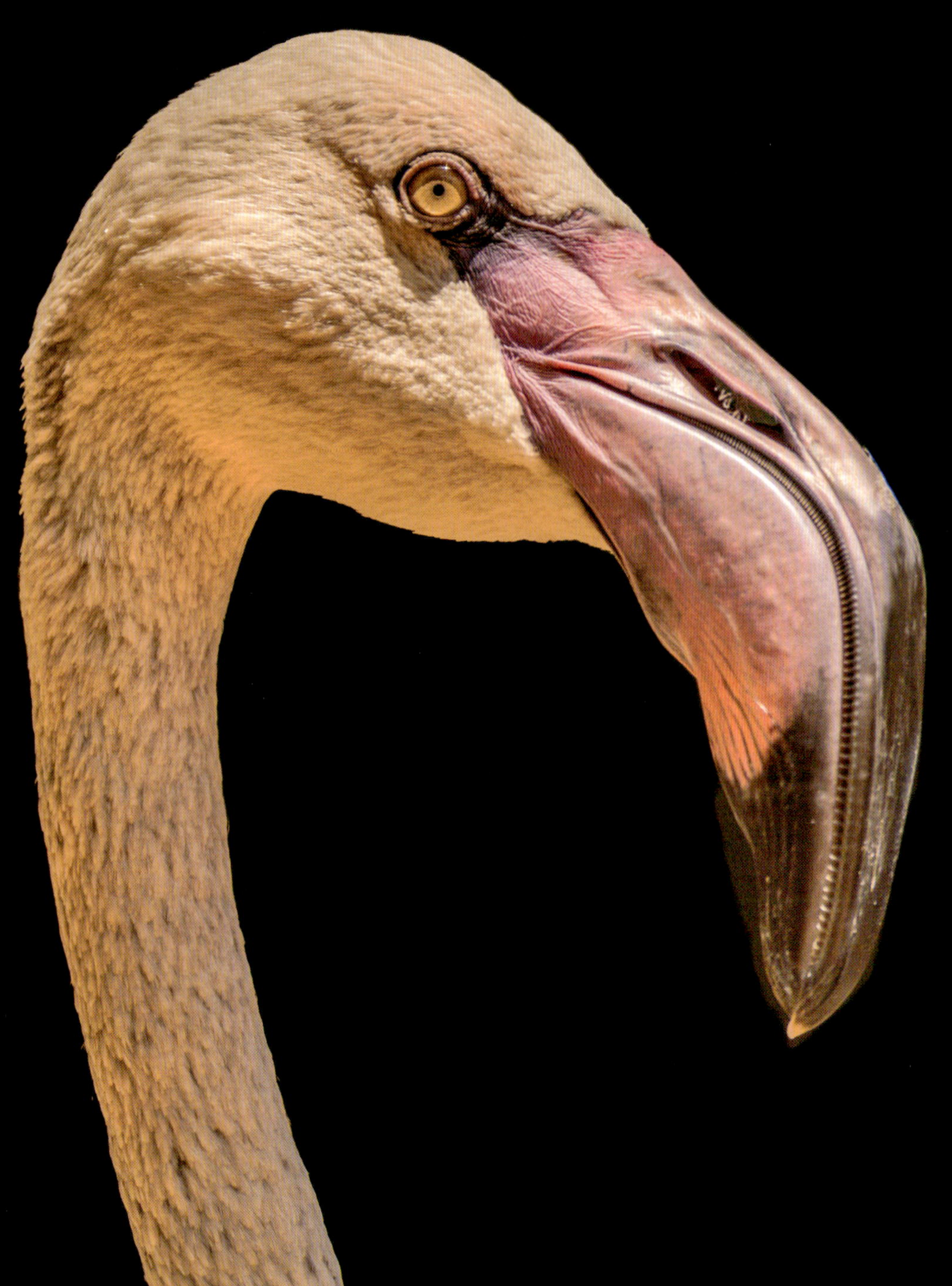
Flamenco
Flamingo

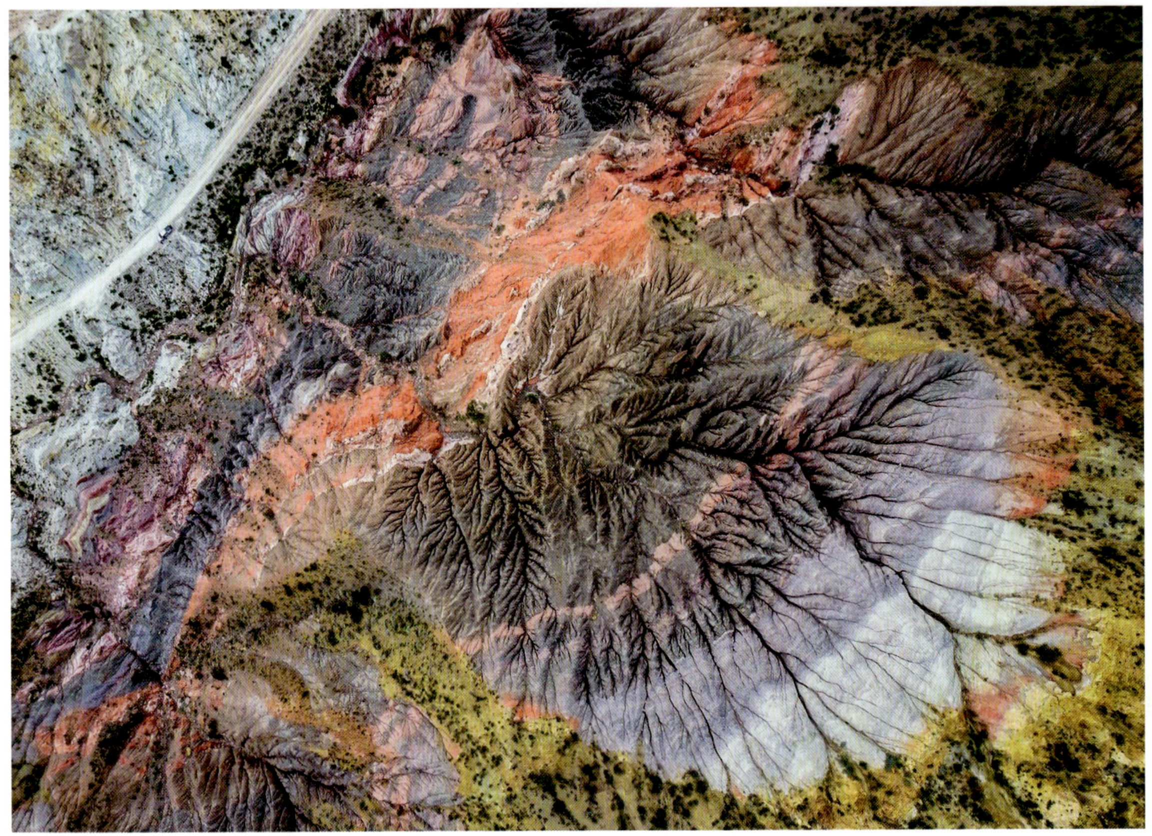

Cerca de Chilecito
Near Chilecito

Little Chile

In the mining region, 196 km (122 mi) northwest of the capital La Rioja, many Chileans settled in the 18th century, hence the name Chilecito, or "Little Chile". In 1717, the Spanish conqueror Domingo Castro y Bazán had claimed the area for himself, during his search for gold. In the 19th century, the place was considered the 'gold city' of Argentina. Chilecito lies at 1074 m (3520 ft), surrounded by the 6300 m (20,670 ft) high peaks of the Famatina massif. The former wealth and faith of the miners led to the construction of many chapels in the area, which may be visited on the 'church-route'.

Le petit Chili

Le nom « Chilecito » (le petit Chili) provient de l'importante communauté de Chiliens qui s'installa au xviiie siècle dans cette région minière, située à 196 km au nord-ouest de la capitale, La Rioja. En 1717, le conquistador espagnol Domingo de Castro y Bazán réclama cette terre pour y chercher de l'or. Au xixe siècle, la ville était surnommée « la ville de l'or argentin ». Chilecito, située à 1074 m d'altitude, est cernée par les sommets du massif Famatina, culminant à 6 300 m. La richesse et la ferveur religieuse des mineurs de l'époque les ont incités à bâtir de nombreuses chapelles dans la région. Une route de col, surnommée « route des chapelles », permet de les admirer.

Kleines Chile

In der Bergbauregion 196 km nordwestlich der Hauptstadt La Rioja siedelten im 18. Jahrhundert viele Chilenen, daher stammt der Name Chilecito, „Kleines Chile". 1717 hatte der spanische Eroberer Domingo Castro y Bazán auf der Suche nach Gold das Gebiet für sich reklamiert. Im 19. Jahrhundert galt der Ort als Goldstadt Argentiniens. Chilecito liegt auf 1074 m, es ist von 6300 m hohen Bergspitzen des Famatina Massivs umgeben. Ehemaliger Reichtum und Gläubigkeit der Minenarbeiter führten dazu, dass in der Gegend viele Kapellen errichtet wurden. Sie lassen sich auf der Kappelen-Route, einer Passstrasse, besichtigen.

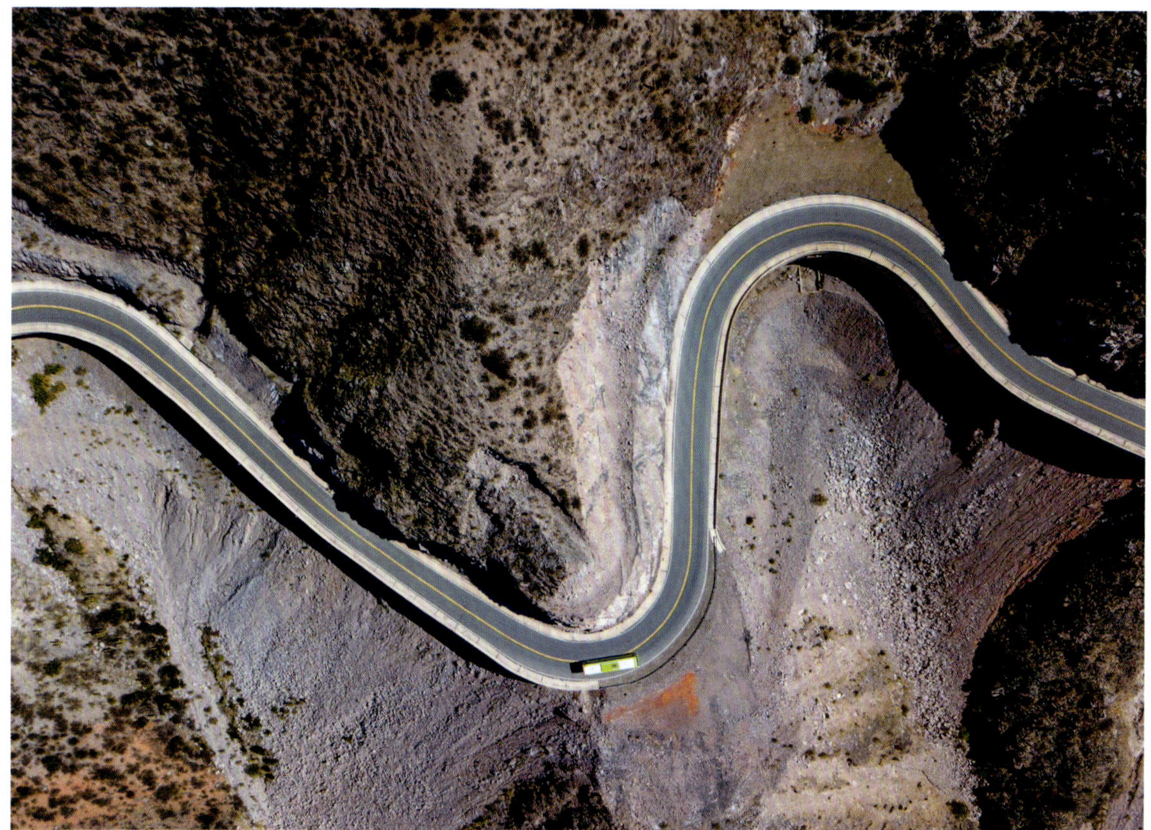

Cerca de Chilecito
Near Chilecito

Chilecito

En la región minera, a 196 km al noroeste
de la capital La Rioja, se asentaron muchos
chilenos en el siglo XVIII; de ahí el nombre
de Chilecito. En 1717, el conquistador
español Domingo Castro y Bazán, en
busca de oro, había reclamado la zona.
En el siglo XIX, el lugar era considerado la
ciudad de oro de Argentina. Chilecito se
encuentra a 1074 m y está rodeado por las
cumbres de 6300 m de altura del macizo
del Famatina. La antigua riqueza y la fe
de los mineros llevaron a la construcción
de muchas capillas en la zona. Se pueden
visitar en la ruta de Kappelen, una
carretera de paso.

Pequeno Chile

Muitos chilenos se estabeleceram no
século XVIII na região de mineração a
196 km a noroeste da capital La Rioja, daí o
nome Chilecito, "Pequeno Chile". Em 1717, o
conquistador espanhol Domingo Castro y
Bazán, em busca de ouro, havia reclamado
a área para si mesmo. No século XIX, o
lugar foi considerado a cidade de ouro
da Argentina. Chilecito situa-se a 1074 m,
rodeado por picos de 6300 m de altura
do maciço de Famatina. A antiga riqueza
e a fé dos mineiros levou à construção de
muitas capelas na área. Elas podem ser
visitadas na rota das capelas, uma estrada
de passagem.

Klein Chili

In de mijnstreek 196 km ten noordwesten
van de hoofdstad La Rioja vestigden zich
in de 18e eeuw veel Chilenen, vandaar de
naam Chilicito, "Klein Chili". Op zoek naar
goud had de Spaanse veroveraar Domingo
Castro y Bazán in 1717 het gebied voor
zichzelf opgeëist. In de 19e eeuw werd
de plaats beschouwd als de goudstad
van Argentinië. Chilicito ligt op 1074 m
en is omgeven door 6300 m hoge
bergtoppen van het Famatina gebergte.
Vroegere rijkdom en de gelovigheid van
de mijnwerkers leidden ertoe dat in de
omgeving veel kapellen werden gebouwd.
Via de kappelen-route, een weg over een
bergpas, zijn ze te bewonderen.

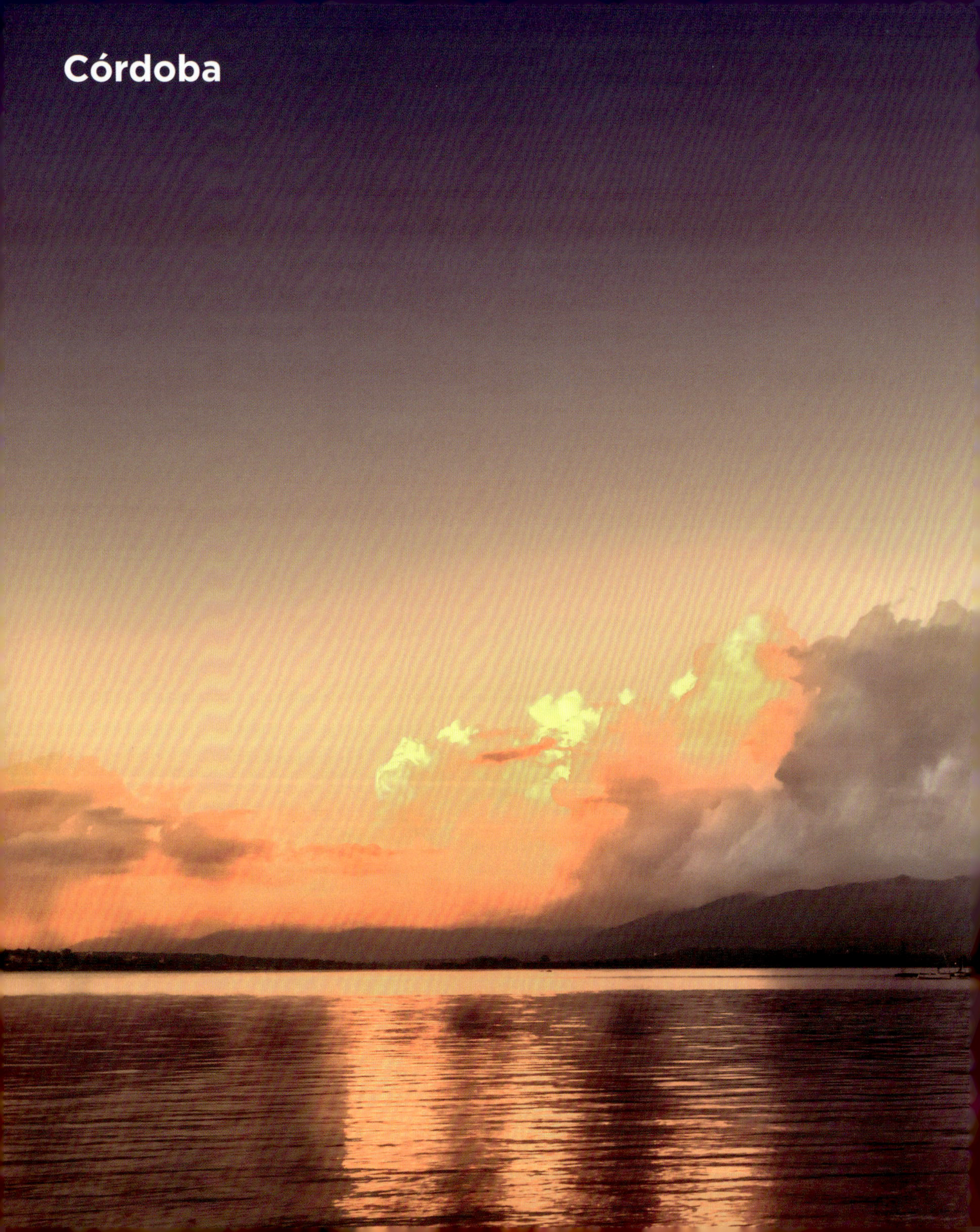

Córdoba

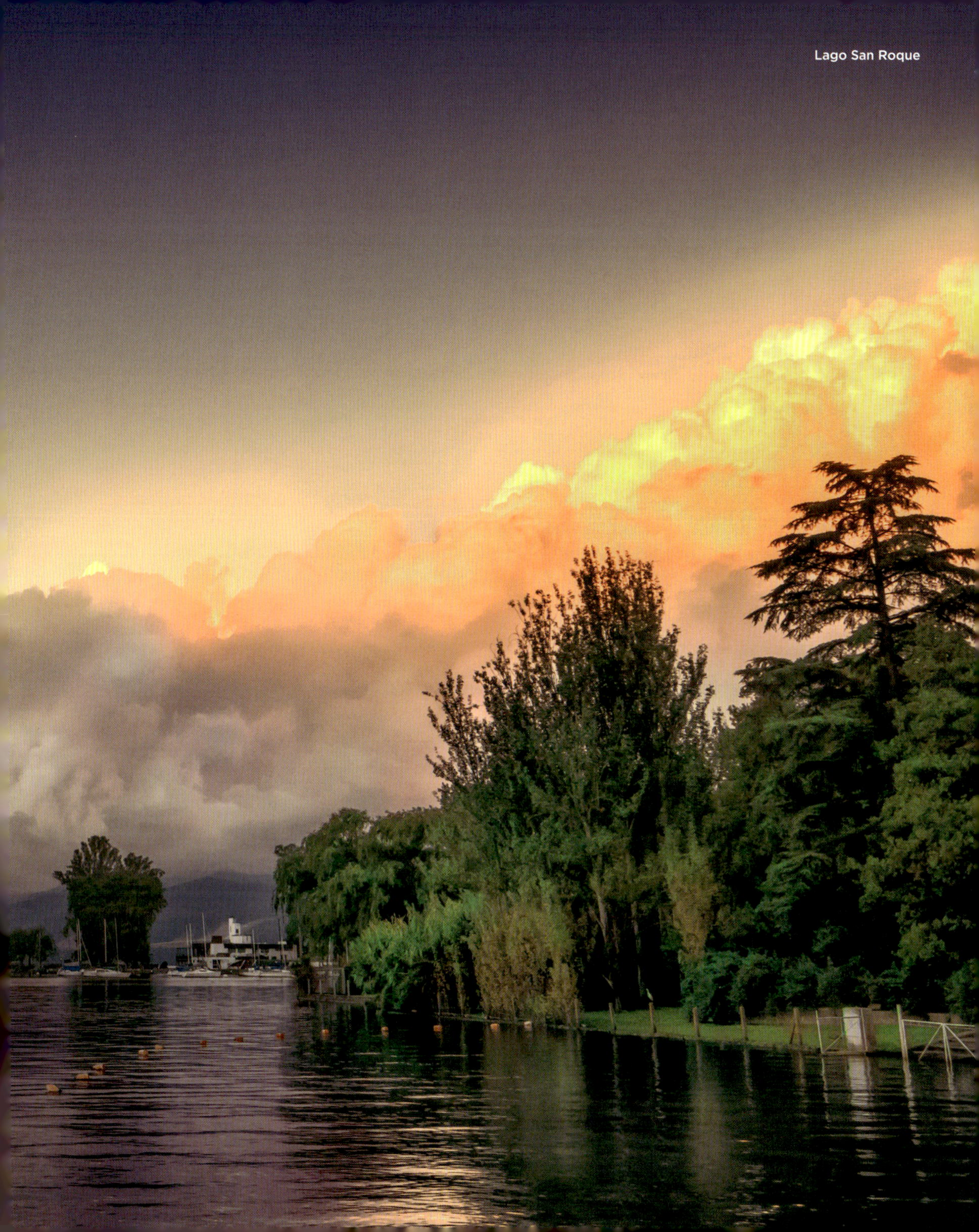
Lago San Roque

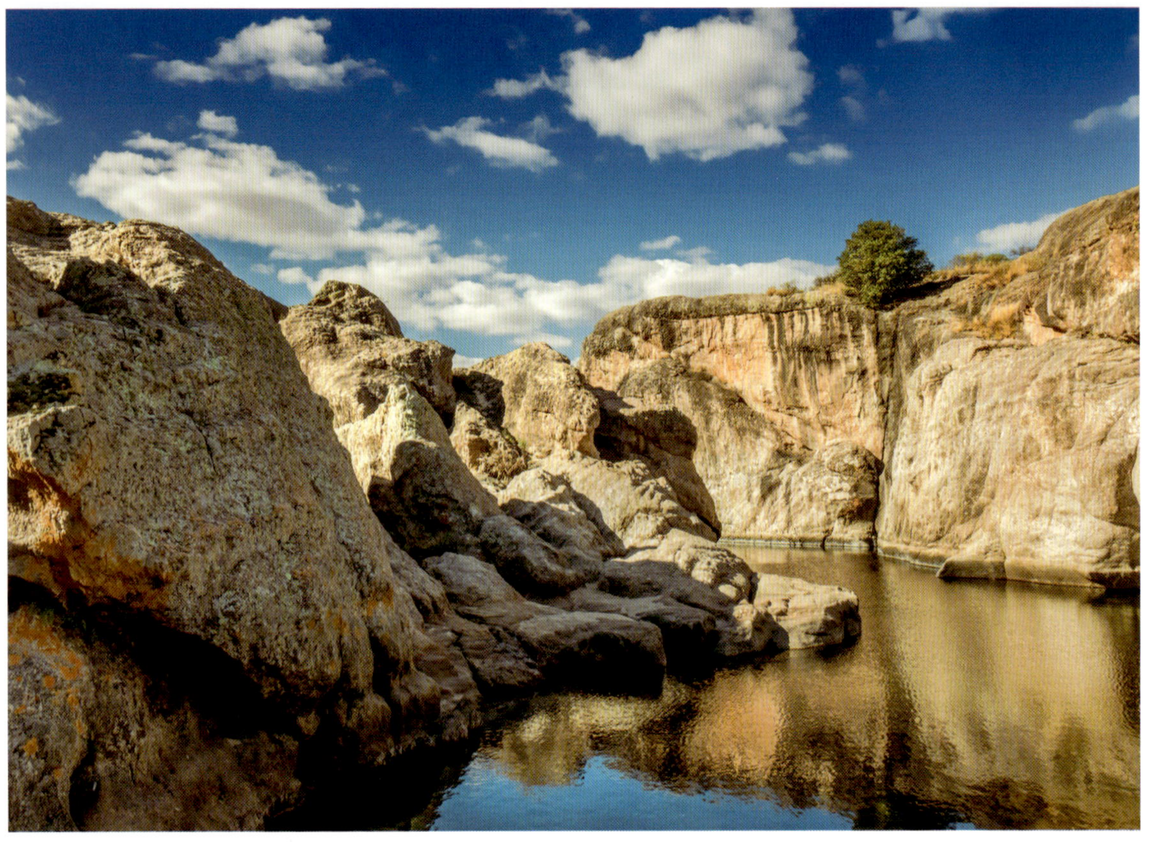

Río Mina Clavero

Cordoba

The province of Córdoba forms the centre of Argentina. It is home to 3.5 million inhabitants and engineering and military industry has developed around the capital of the same name. It is called "La Docta", or "the learned", because the first university in Latin America was founded here in 1614. The Sierra de Córdoba, a 500 km (310 mi) long mountain range, stretches from north to south. Four large, important rivers run through the fertile province in an east-west direction. At the Mina Clavero river, 162 km (100 mi) south of the capital, there are beautiful sandy beaches and the nearby Traslasierra Valley offers pure idyll. One of the "Seven Wonders of Argentina" is the bridge over the San Roque Reservoir, which is close to Córdoba.

Córdoba

La province de Córdoba occupe le centre de l'Argentine. Elle concentre 3,5 millions d'habitants et sa capitale s'est dotée d'une importante industrie. On la surnomme *La Docta* (la Savante), car c'est ici que fut fondée en 1614 la première université d'Amérique latine. La sierra de Córdoba, chaîne montagneuse de 500 km de long, s'étire du nord au sud, alors que quatre fleuves importants traversent la province fertile d'est en ouest. Sur la rive de la rivière Mina Clavero, à 162 km au sud de la capitale, une jolie plage de sable et la haute vallée de Traslasierra composent un paysage purement paradisiaque. Le pont enjambant le lac de retenue San Roque, près de Córdoba, compte parmi les « sept merveilles de l'Argentine ».

Córdoba

Die Provinz Córdoba bildet das Zentrum Argentiniens. Hier leben 3,5 Millionen Einwohner und um die gleichnamige Hauptstadt hat sich wichtige Industrie angesiedelt. Sie wird „La Docta", „die Gebildete" genannt, weil hier 1614 die erste Universität Lateinamerikas entstand. Die Sierra de Córdoba, eine 500 km lange Bergkette, zieht sich in Nord-Südrichtung. Vier große, wichtige Flüsse durchlaufen die fruchtbare Provinz in Ost-Westrichtung. Am Mina Clavero-Fluss, 162 km südlich der Hauptstadt, gibt es schöne Sandstrände und das nahe Hochtal Traslasierra bietet Idylle pur. Eines der „Sieben Wunder Argentiniens" ist die Brücke über den San Roque-Stausee, der nah bei Córdoba liegt.

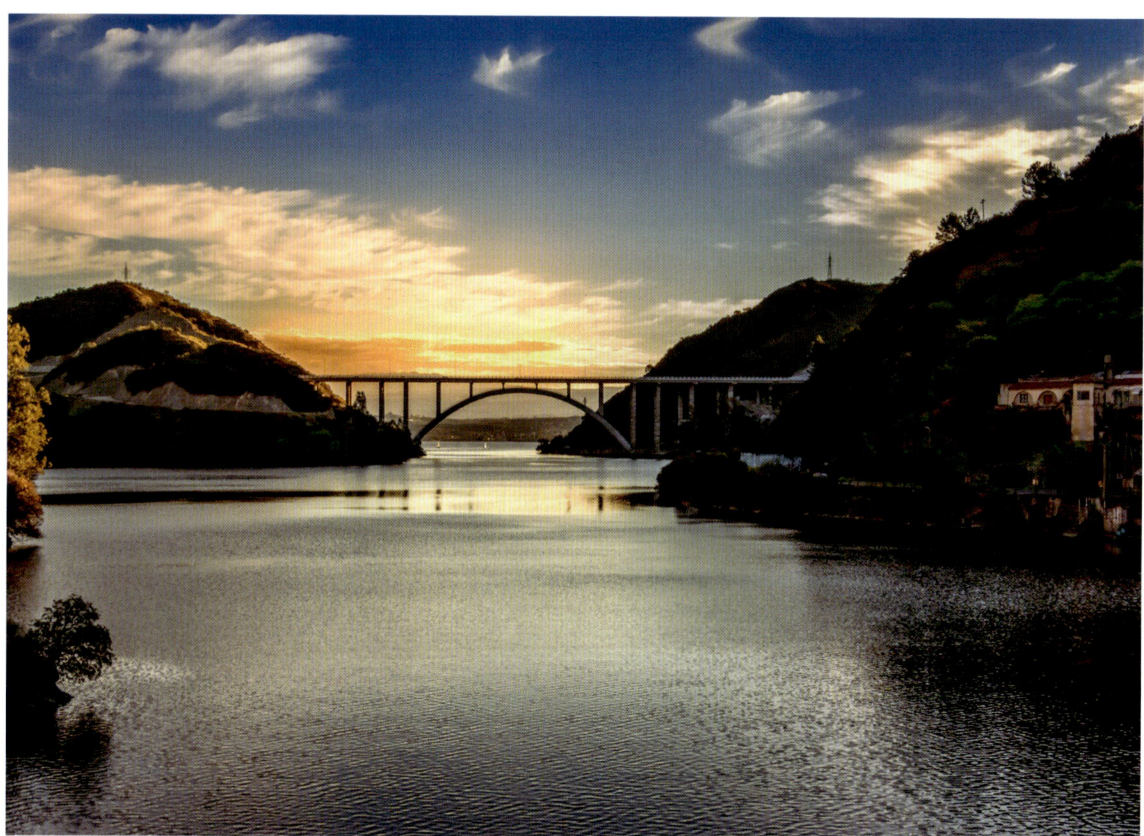

Lago San Roque

Córdoba

La provincia de Córdoba constituye el centro de Argentina. Aquí viven 3,5 millones de personas y alrededor de la capital del mismo nombre se ha establecido una importante industria. Se llama "La Docta" porque la primera universidad de América Latina se fundó aquí en 1614. La Sierra de Córdoba, una cadena montañosa de 500 km de longitud, se extiende de norte a sur. Cuatro grandes e importantes ríos atraviesan la fértil provincia en dirección este-oeste. En el río Mina Clavero, a 162 km al sur de la capital, hay hermosas playas de arena y el cercano valle alto de Traslasierra ofrece puro idilio. Una de las "Siete Maravillas de Argentina" es el puente situado sobre el embalse de San Roque, que se encuentra cerca de Córdoba.

Córdoba

A província de Córdoba forma o centro da Argentina. 3,5 milhões de habitantes vivem aqui e uma indústria importante se estabeleceu em torno da capital do mesmo nome. Chama-se "La Docta", "os educados", porque a primeira universidade da América Latina foi fundada aqui em 1614. A Serra de Córdoba, uma cordilheira de 500 km de extensão, estende-se de norte a sul. Quatro grandes e importantes rios correm através da província fértil na direção leste-oeste. No rio Mina Clavero, 162 km ao sul da capital, há belas praias de areia e o vale alto vizinho de Traslaslasierra oferece idílio absoluto. Uma das "Sete Maravilhas da Argentina" é a ponte sobre o reservatório de San Roque, que fica perto de Córdoba.

Córdoba

De provincie Córdoba vormt het centrum van Argentinië. Hier wonen 3,5 miljoen mensen en rond de gelijknamige hoofdstad heeft zich belangrijke industrie gevestigd. Het wordt "La Docta" (de intellectueel) genoemd, omdat hier in 1614 de eerste universiteit van Latijns-Amerika ontstond. De Sierra de Córdoba, een 500 km lange bergketen, strekt zich uit van noord naar zuid. Vier grote, belangrijke rivieren lopen door de vruchtbare provincie in oost-westelijke richting. Aan de Mina Clavero rivier, 162 km ten zuiden van de hoofdstad, zijn prachtige zandstranden en de nabijgelegen hoge vallei Traslasierra biedt idylle puur. Eén van de "zeven wonderen van Argentinië" is de brug over het stuwmeer San Roque dat dicht bij Córdoba ligt.

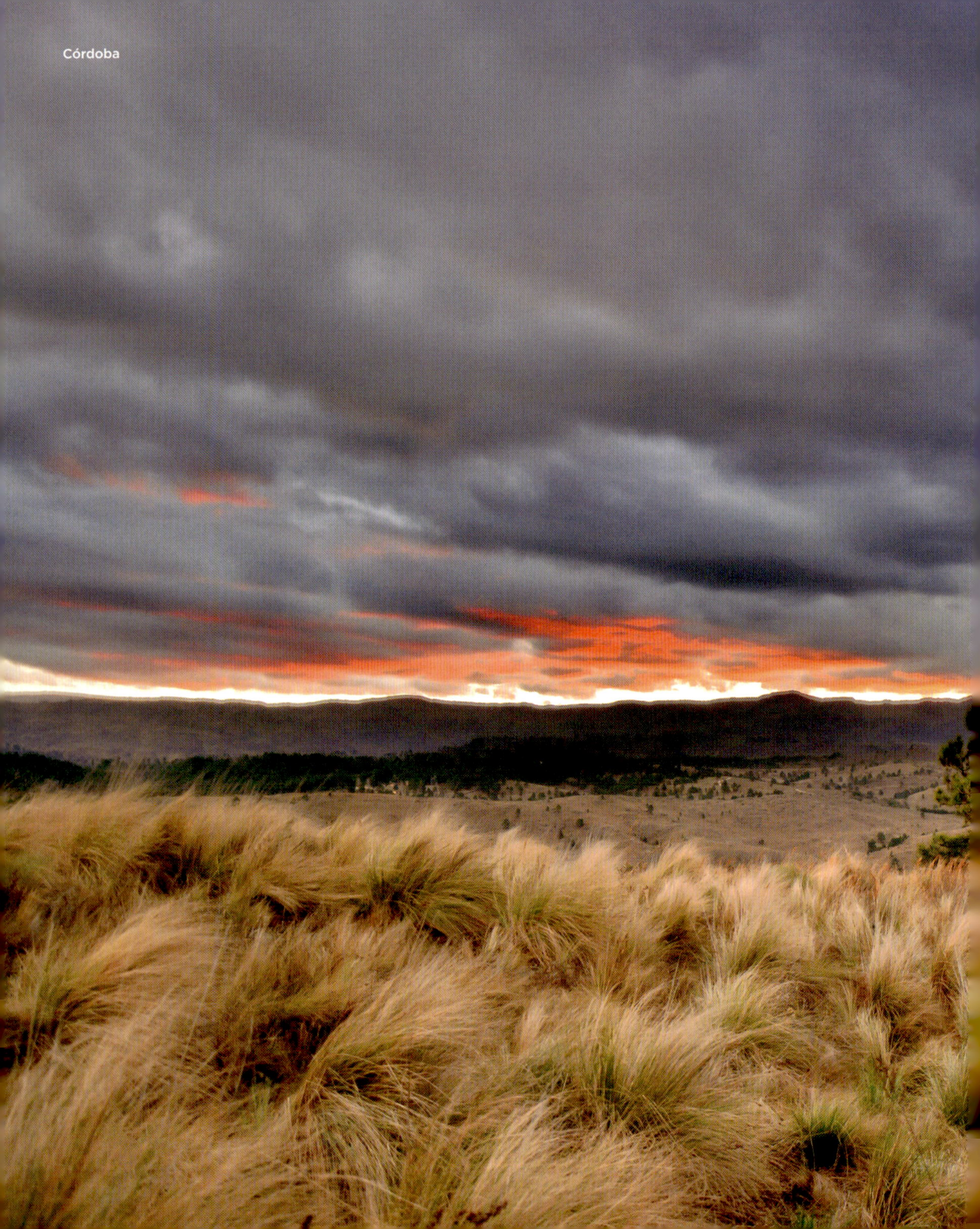
Córdoba

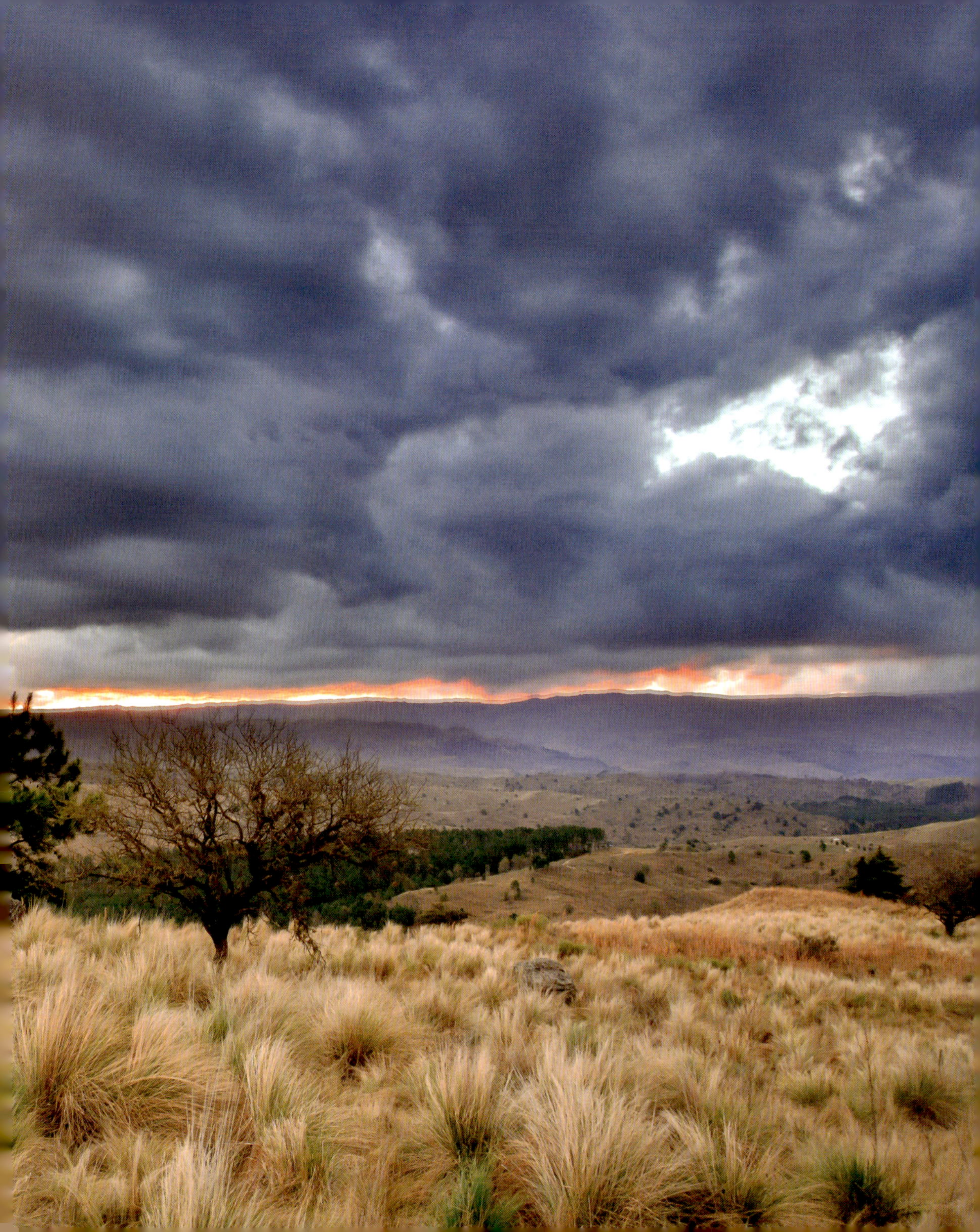

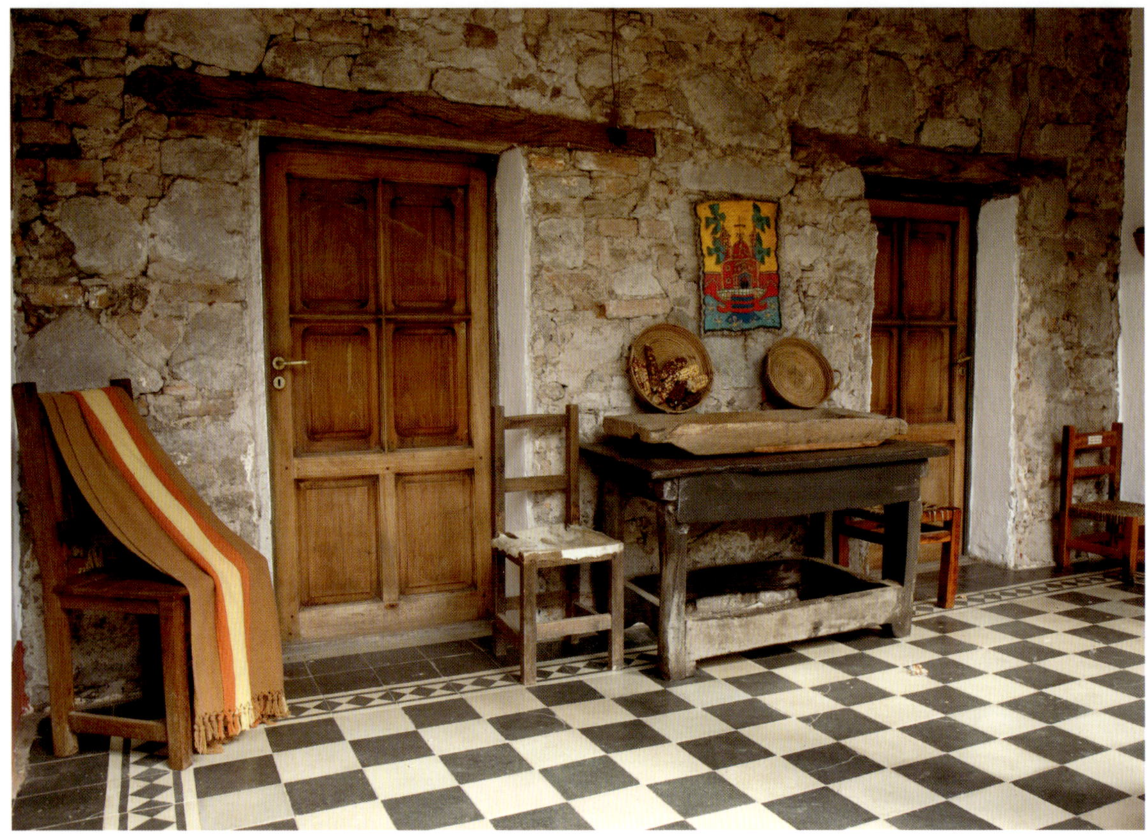

Estancia Santa Catalina

Country life around Córdoba

To the east of the Sierra de Córdoba, whose highest peak reaches 2884 m (9462 ft), lie the expanses of the pampas and large lakes. Lucrative cattle and agriculture, with rich estancias, determine the landscape, of which the Estancia Santa Catalina, 70 km (43 mi) northeast of the capital, is one of the most impressive. In 1622 the Jesuit order acquired the large estates, along with 800 Indian and African slaves, who lived in the mission. Under the guidance of five Jesuits, it mainly bred donkeys for the silver mines in Potosí. A meeting place of the political elite in the 19th century was the Estancia La Paz ("Peace"). Around the generous manor house the property offers a 100 ha (247 ac) park.

La vie rurale autour de Córdoba

La sierra de Córdoba, dont le plus haut sommet culmine à 2 884 m, est bordée à l'est par les étendues vertes de la pampa et plusieurs grands lacs. Le paysage a été modelé par les activités lucratives d'élevage et d'agriculture et par les luxueuses *estancias*. L'*estancia* Santa Catalina, située à 70 km au nord-est de la capitale régionale, est impressionnante. En 1622, l'ordre des jésuites obtint les plus grandes terres et fit travailler 800 esclaves indiens et africains sous la direction de cinq jésuites. Ils élevaient essentiellement des baudets pour les mines d'argent de Potosí. L'*estancia* La Paz («la paix») fut quant à elle le lieu de rencontre de l'élite politique du xixᵉ siècle ; la vaste demeure est sertie dans un parc d'une centaine d'hectares appartenant à la propriété.

Landleben um Córdoba

Östlich der Sierra de Córdoba, deren höchste Spitze 2884 m erreicht, liegen die Weiten der Pampa und große Seen. Lukrative Vieh- und Landwirtschaft und reiche Estanzias bestimmen die Landschaft. Beeindruckend ist die Estanzia Santa Catalina 70 km nordöstlich der Hauptstadt. 1622 erwarb der Jesuitenorden die großen Ländereien. 800 indianische und afrikanische Sklaven lebten in der Mission. Unter der Anleitung von fünf Jesuiten züchteten sie vor allem Esel für die Silberminen in Potosí. Treffpunkt der politischen Elite im 19. Jahrhundert war die Estanzia La Paz („Frieden"). Rund um das großzügige Herrenhaus wartet das Anwesen mit einer 100 ha großen Parkanlage auf.

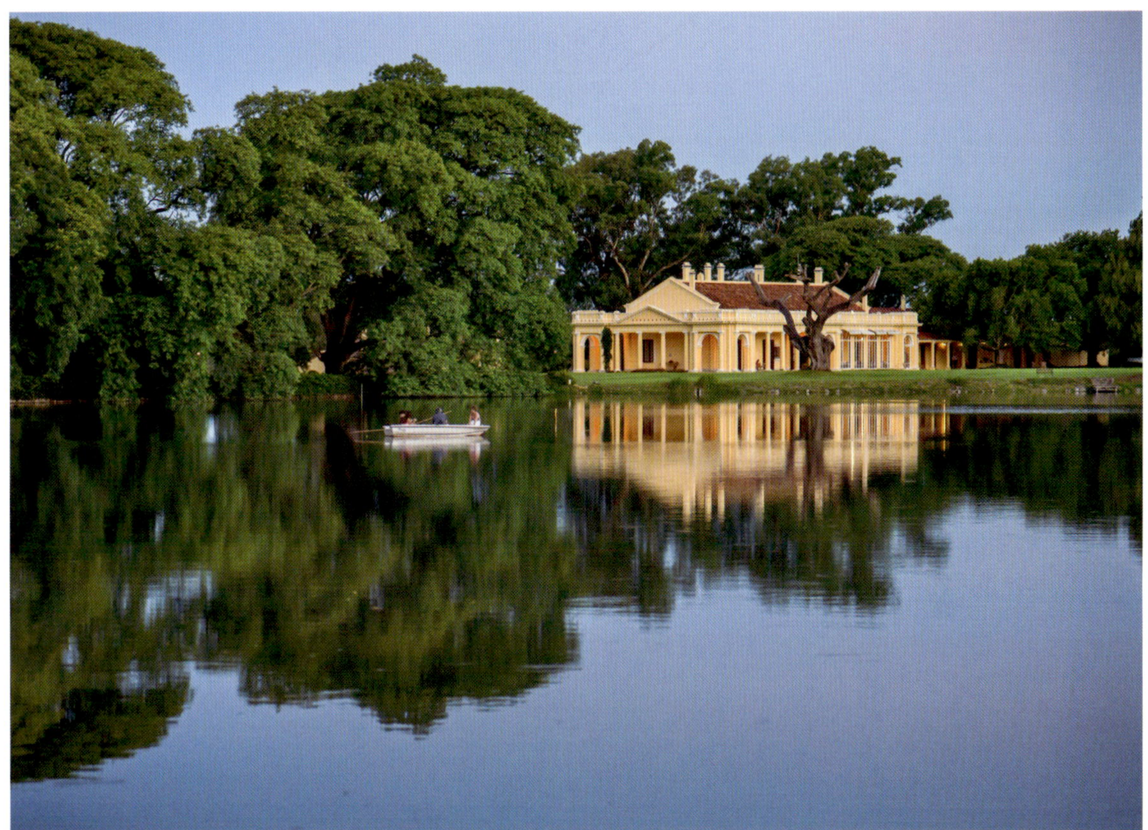

Estancia La Paz

La vida en el campo alrededor de Córdoba

Al este de la Sierra de Córdoba, cuyo pico más alto alcanza los 2884 m, se encuentran las extensiones de La Pampa y grandes lagos. La ganadería y la agricultura lucrativas y las ricas estancias determinan el paisaje. Impresionante es la Estancia Santa Catalina, que se encuentra a 70 km al noreste de la capital. En 1622 la orden jesuita adquirió las grandes propiedades. En la misión vivían 800 esclavos aborígenes y africanos. Bajo la guía de cinco jesuitas, criaban principalmente burros para las minas de plata en Potosí. El lugar de encuentro de la élite política en el siglo XIX fue la Estancia La Paz. Alrededor de la generosa casa solariega, la propiedad ofrece un parque de 100 ha.

A vida no campo ao redor de Córdoba

Ao leste da Serra de Córdoba, cujo pico mais alto atinge 2884 m, encontram-se a vastidão dos pampas e grandes lagos. O gado e a agricultura lucrativos e as ricas estâncias determinam a paisagem. Impressionante é a Estanzia Santa Catalina a 70 km ao nordeste da capital. Em 1622, a ordem jesuíta adquiriu os grandes latifúndios. 800 escravos indianos e africanos viviam na missão. Sob a orientação de cinco jesuítas, eles criavam principalmente burros para as minas de prata em Potosí. O ponto de encontro da elite política no século XIX foi a Estanzia La Paz. Ao redor da espaçosa casa senhorial a propriedade oferece um parque de 100 ha.

Het landleven rond Córdoba

Ten oosten van de Sierra de Córdoba, waarvan de hoogste top 2884 m hoog is, ligt de uitgestrekte pampa en zijn grote meren. Lucratieve veeteelt en landbouw en rijke estancias bepalen het landschap. Indrukwekkend is de Estanzia Santa Catalina, 70 km ten noordoosten van de hoofdstad. In 1622 verwierf de jezuïetenorde de grote landerijen. 800 Indiaanse en Afrikaanse slaven leefden in de missiepost. Onder leiding van vijf jezuïeten fokten ze voornamelijk ezels voor de zilvermijnen in Potosí. De Estanzia La Paz ("vrede") was in de 19e eeuw de ontmoetingsplaats van de politieke elite. Rondom het royale landhuis bevindt zich een groot park van 100 ha.

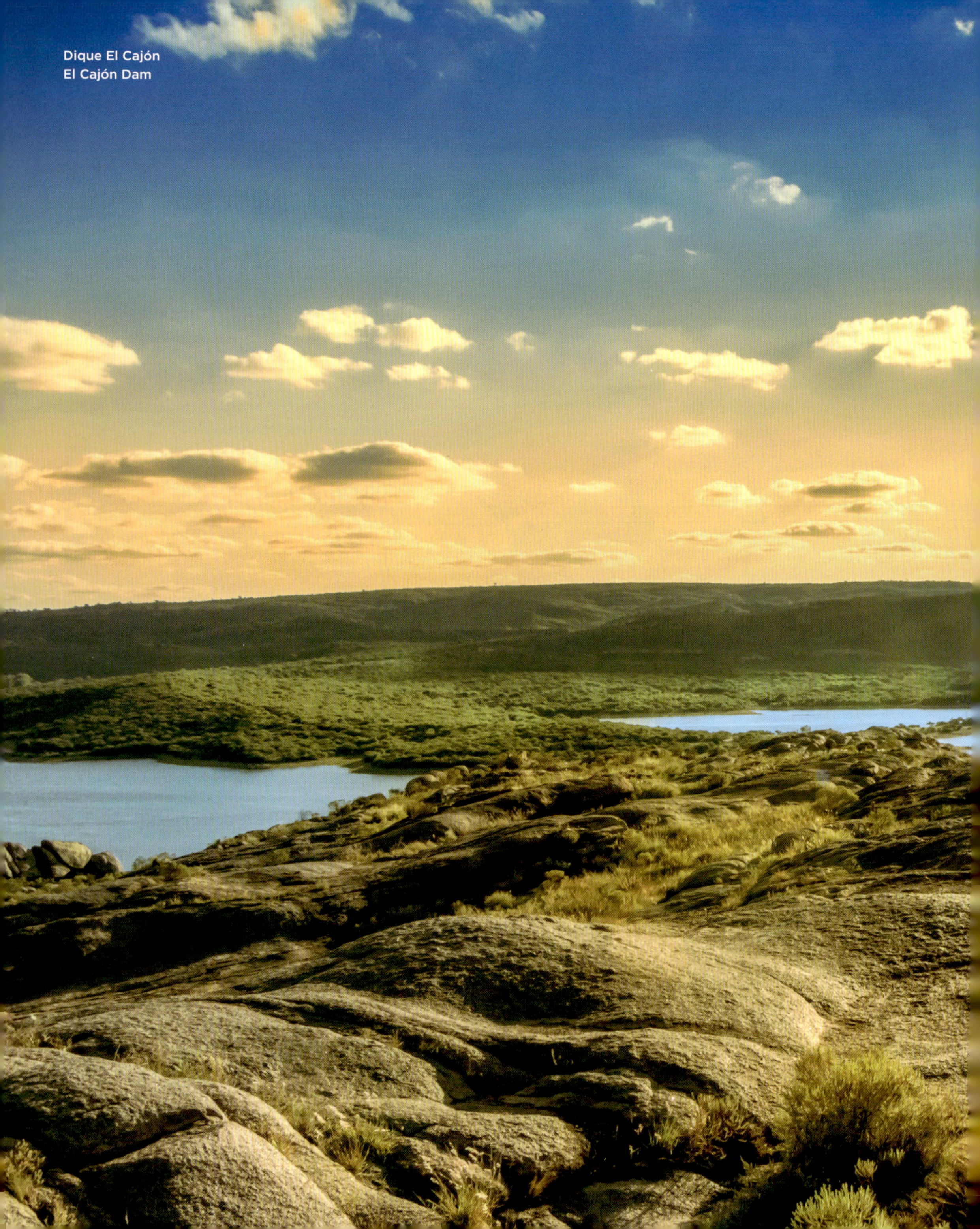
Dique El Cajón
El Cajón Dam

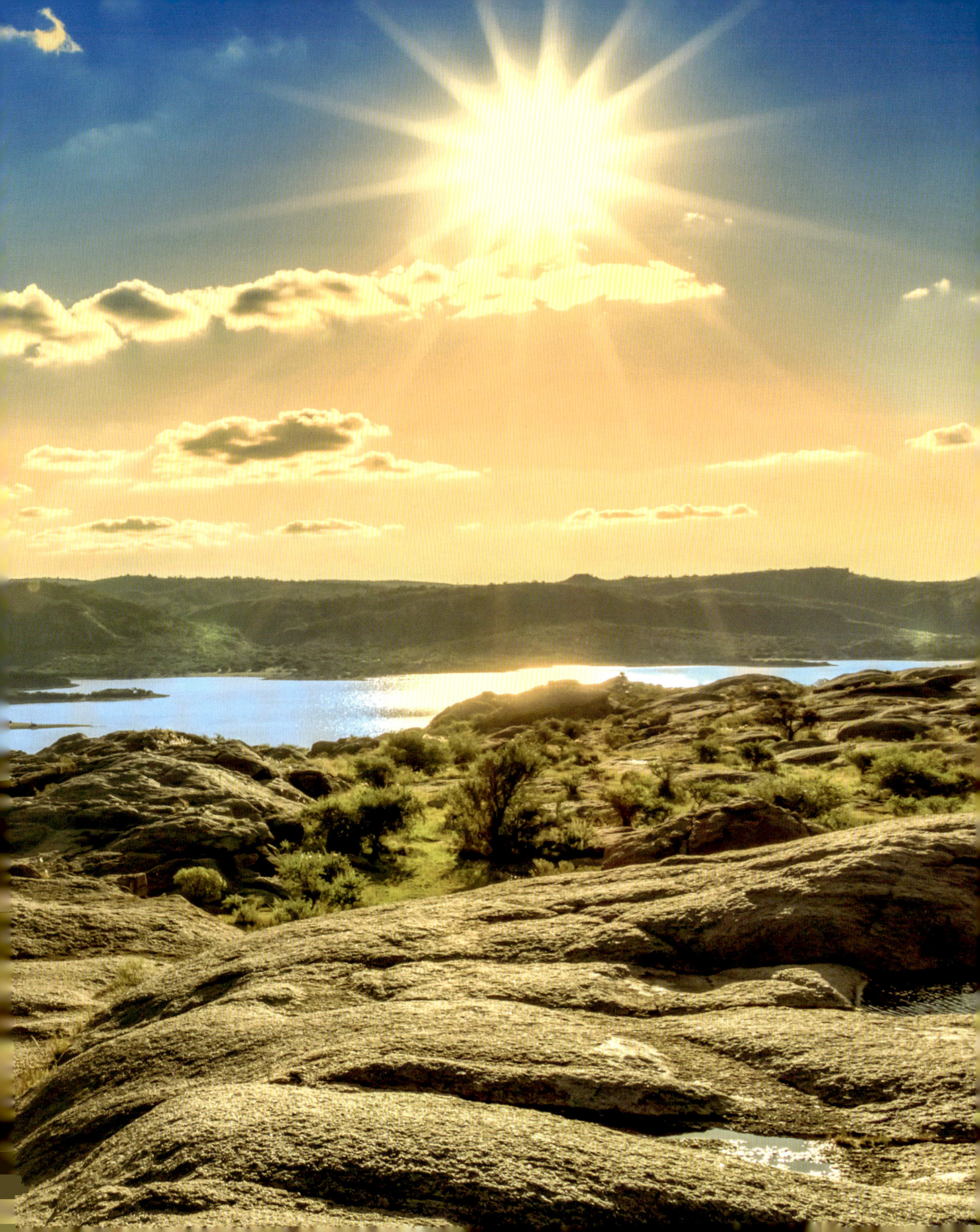

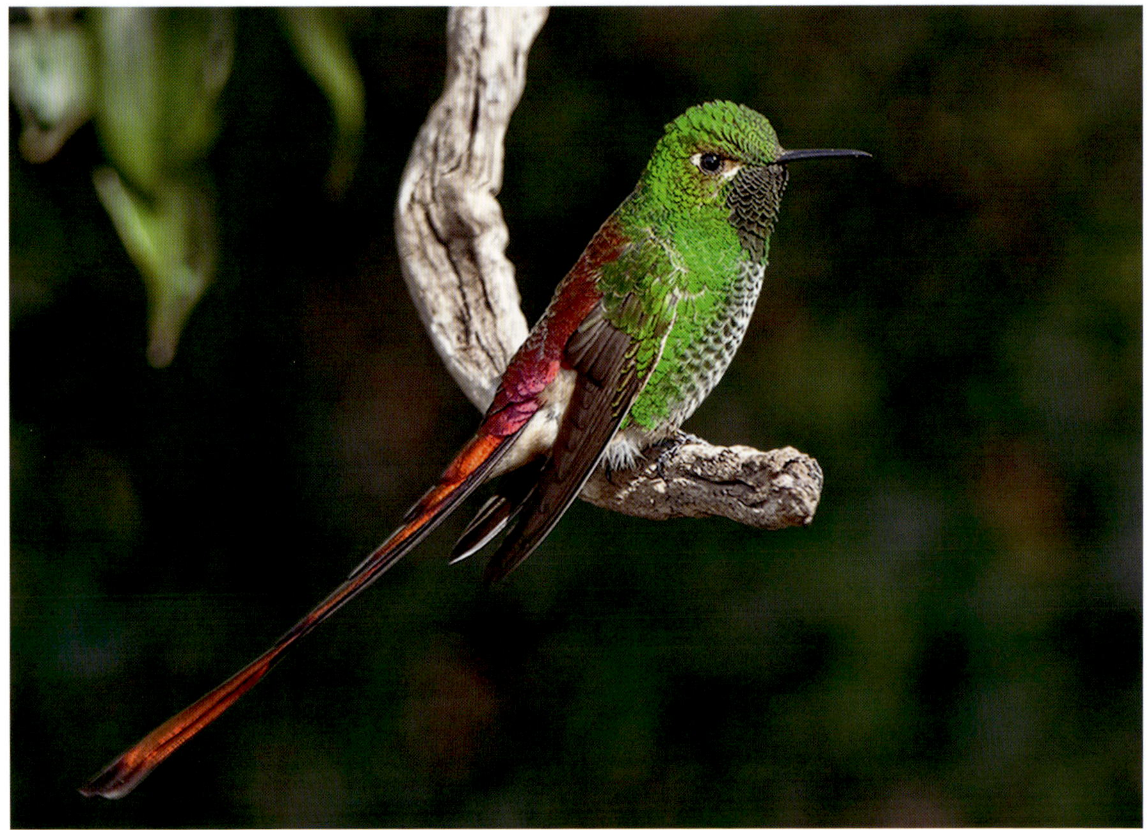

Colibrí cometa
Red-tailed comet

Pure nature

A stone's throw from Cordoba, on the Ceballos River, a large forest area invites one to relax, hike and recover. The La Quebrada reservoir is located at 900 m (2950 ft) altitude. Waterfalls and canyons can be explored here. Climatically the region is an ideal habitat for birds, and the beautiful "colibri cometa", or red-tailed comet hummingbird, is often seen. Among the vegetation the *espinillo* tree (Acacia caven) stands out. It is an ornamental tree of the Fabaceae family, growing 4-5 m (13-16 ft) tall. In spring, the bush with its sharp white thorns bears yellow flowers. They are particularly suitable for beekeeping and honey production.

Nature immaculée

À deux pas de Córdoba, sur la rive de la rivière Ceballos, une vaste forêt invite à la détente et à la balade. La région abrite également le lac de retenue La Quebrada, à 900 m d'altitude, ainsi que des chutes d'eau et ravins à explorer. Elle offre un climat idéal aux oiseaux et permet d'admirer le magnifique *colibri cometa* (colibri sapho). Parmi la végétation, l'*espinillo* (Acacia caven), surnommé «mimosa du Chili», attire le regard. Ce buisson de la famille des Fabacées atteint 4 à 5 m de haut. Au printemps, son branchage couvert d'épines blanches acérées porte des fleurs jaunes. Il est particulièrement apprécié des abeilles, et donc des apiculteurs.

Natur pur

Ein Katzensprung von Córdoba entfernt am Ceballos-Fluss lädt ein großes Waldgebiet zum relaxen, wandern und erholen ein. Der Stausee La Quebrada liegt auf 900 m Höhe. Wasserfälle und Schluchten lassen sich hier erkunden. Klimatisch ist die Region idealer Habitat für Vögel. Der wunderschöne „colibri cometa", Goldschwanz- oder Schleppensylphe genannt, ist häufig zu sehen. Unter der Vegetation sticht der Espinillo-Baum (Acacia caven) ins Auge. Es ist ein Zierbaum der Familie der Fabaceae. Er wird 4–5 m hoch. Im Frühling trägt der mit scharfen weißen Dornen bestückte Busch gelbe Blüten. Sie sind besonders geeignet zur Bienenzucht und Honiggewinnung.

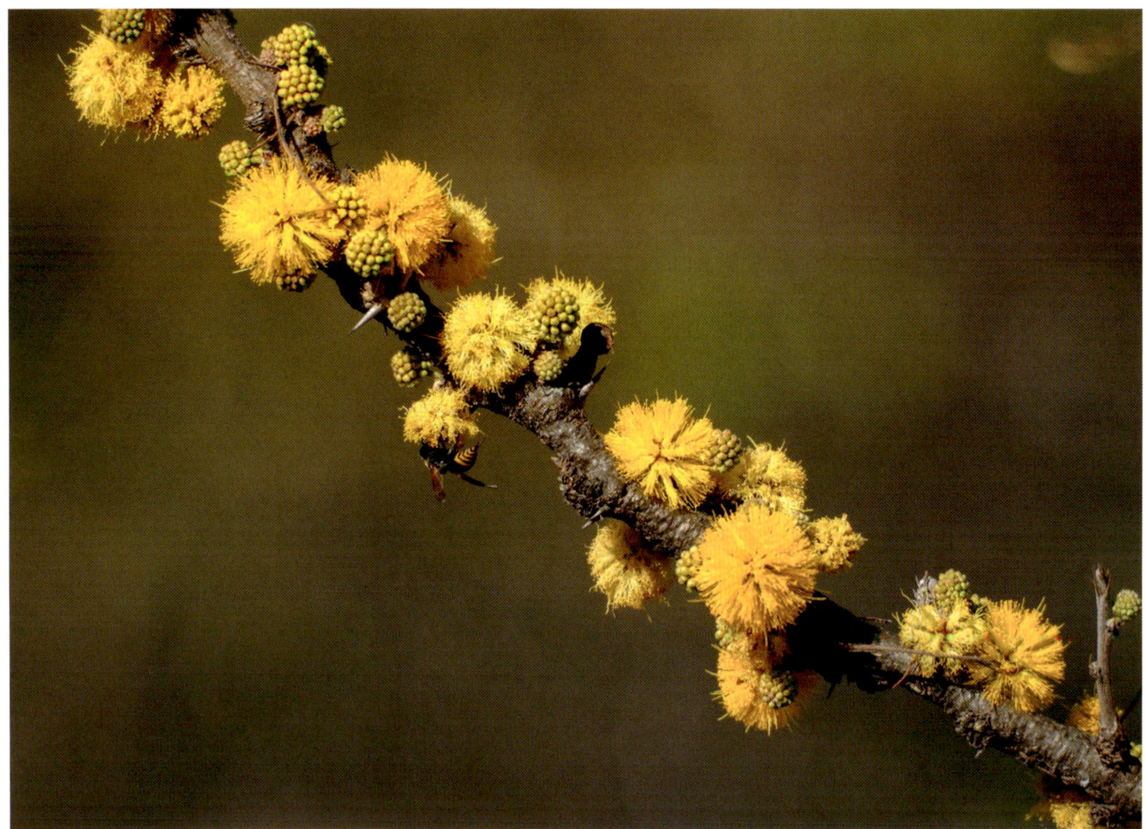

Acacia caven
Vachellia caven

Naturaleza pura

A poca distancia de Córdoba, sobre el río Ceballos, una amplia zona boscosa invita a relajarse, caminar y recuperarse. El embalse de La Quebrada está situado a 900 m de altitud. Aquí se pueden explorar las cascadas y los cañones. El clima de la región la convierte en un hábitat ideal para las aves. El hermoso "colibrí cometa" se ve a menudo. Con respecto a la vegetación, destaca el árbol espinillo (Acacia caven). Es un árbol ornamental de la familia de las fabáceas. Tendrá 4–5 metros de altura. En primavera, el arbusto con sus afiladas espinas blancas tiene flores amarillas. Son especialmente adecuados para la apicultura y la producción de miel.

Natureza pura

A um passo de Córdoba, no Rio Ceballos, uma grande área florestal convida você a relaxar, caminhar e descansar. O reservatório de La Quebrada está localizado a 900 m de altitude. Cachoeiras e desfiladeiros podem ser explorados aqui. Climaticamente a região é um habitat ideal para as aves. O belo "colibri cometa", ou chamado de Beija-flor-da-cauda-vermelha, pode ser frequentemente visto. Entre a vegetação destaca-se a árvore Espinilho (Acacia caven). É uma árvore ornamental da família Fabaceae. Ela cresce até uma altura de 4-5 metros. Na primavera, o arbusto com seus espinhos brancos afiados tem flores amarelas. Elas são particularmente adequados para a apicultura e a produção de mel.

Puur natuur

Aan de Ceballos rivier, op steenworp afstand van Córdoba, nodigt een groot bosgebied uit om te ontspannen, te wandelen en bij te komen. Het stuwmeer van La Quebrada ligt op 900 m hoogte. Hier kunnen watervallen en ravijnen worden ontdekt. Klimatologisch gezien is de regio een ideaal leefgebied voor vogels. De prachtige "colibri-cometa", ook wel sapphokomeetkolibrie genoemd, is hier vaak te zien. Onder de vegetatie springt de Espinillo boom (Acacia caven) in het oog. Het is een sierboom van de Fabaceae familie. Hij wordt 4-5 meter hoog. In het voorjaar draagt de struik met scherpe, witte doornen gele bloemen. Ze zijn bijzonder geschikt voor de bijenteelt en de honingproductie.

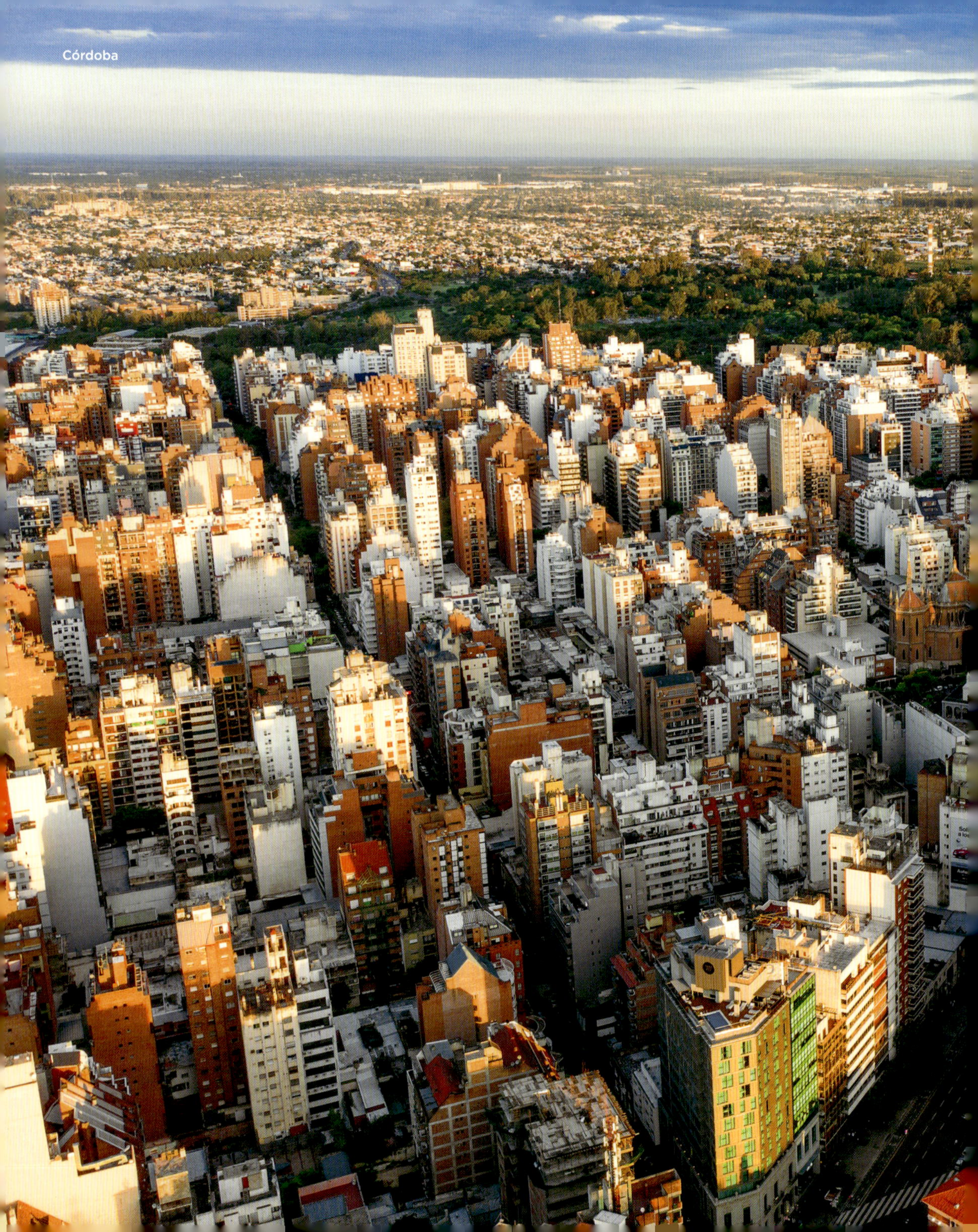

Córdoba

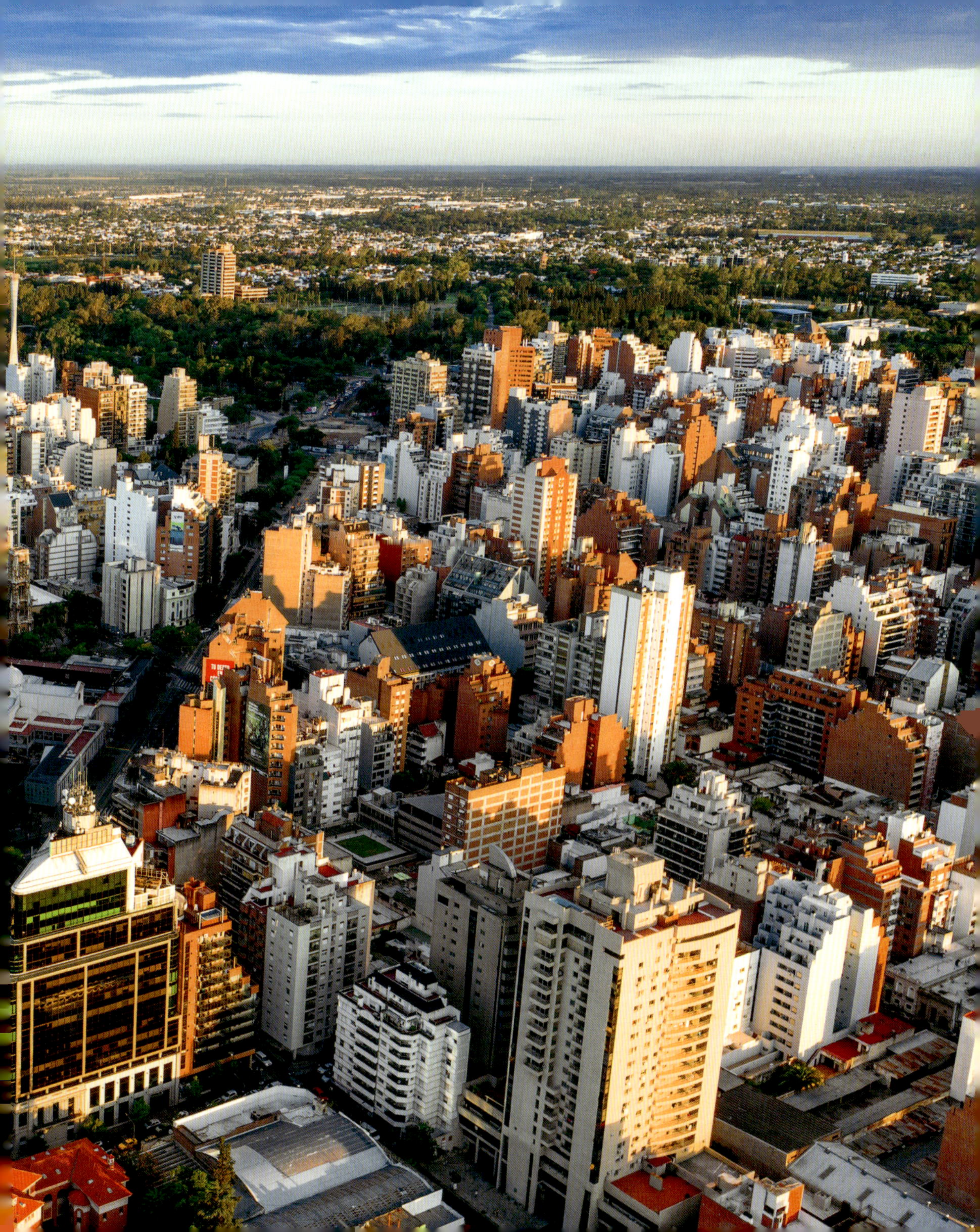

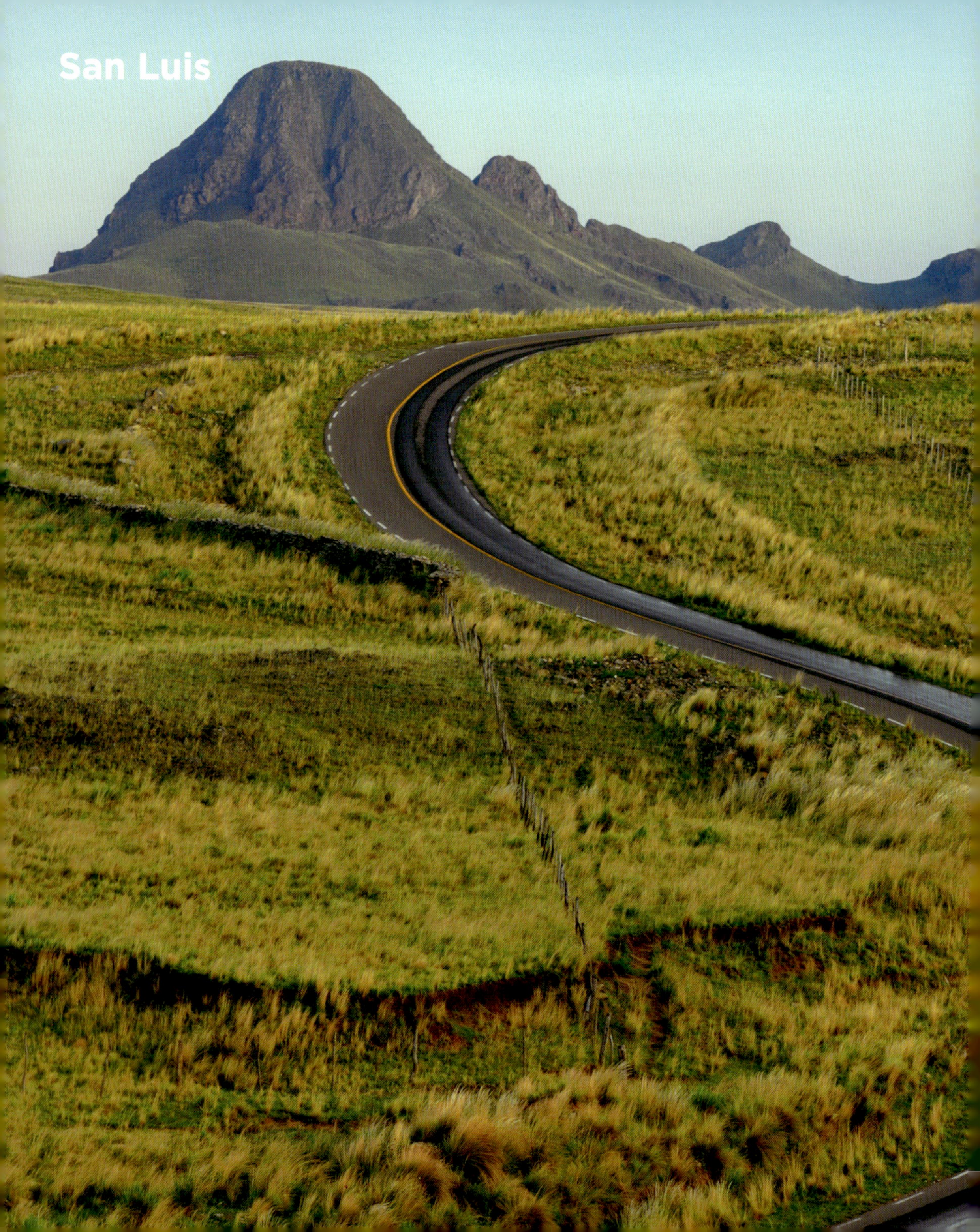
San Luis

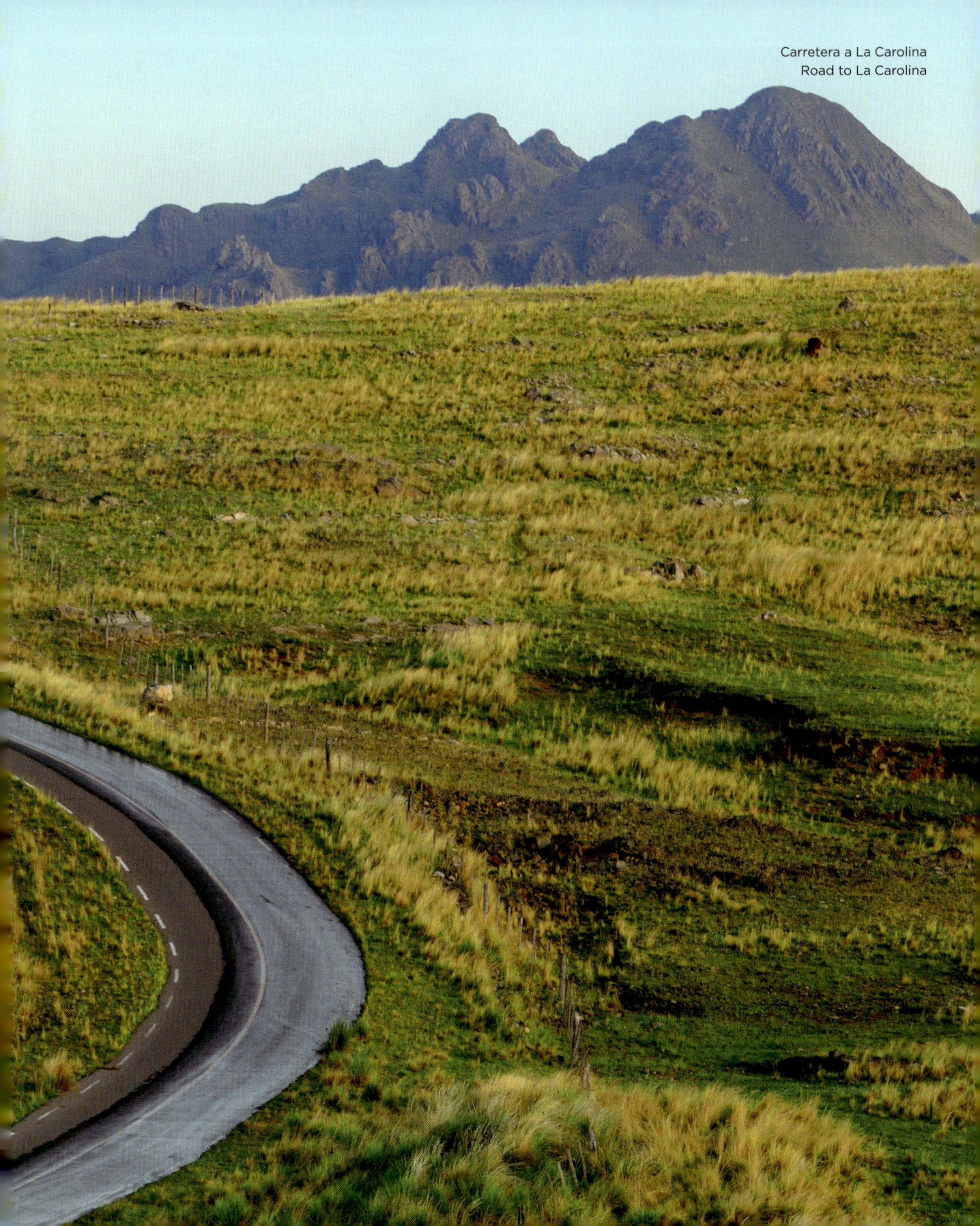

Carretera a La Carolina
Road to La Carolina

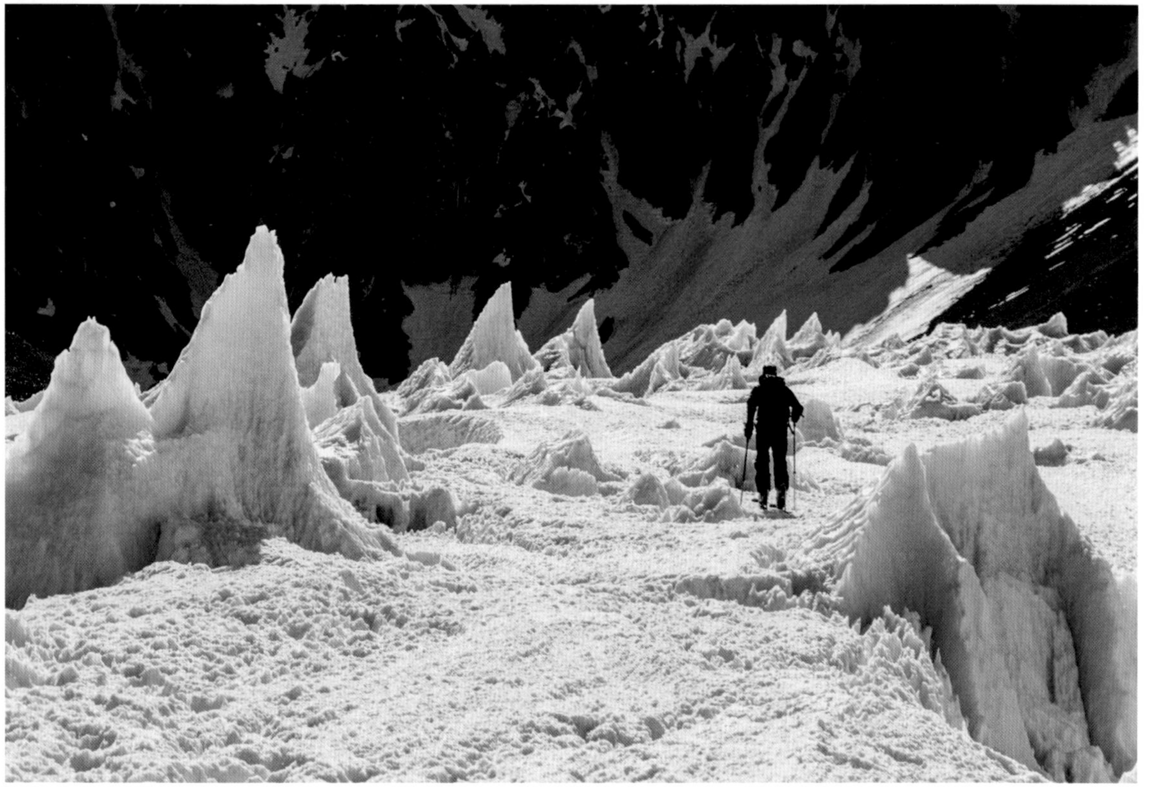

Cerro Mercedario

San Luis

The predominantly flat land of this
province borders the Andes in the extreme
southwest. In the northeast it offers
spectacular mountain and lake scenery.
With a height of 6720 m (22,047 ft),
the Cerro Mercedario is one of the most
impressive peaks of the Andes, in the area
of the high cordillera. The Potrero de Funes
reservoir beckons, 16 km (10 mi) from the
provincial capital of San Luis.

San Luis

La tierra predominantemente plana de
la provincia limita con los Andes en el
extremo suroeste. En el noreste ofrece
un interesante paisaje de montañas y
lagos. Con una altura de 6720 m, el Cerro
Mercedario es uno de los picos más
imponentes de los Andes en la zona de la
alta cordillera. A 16 km de la capital de la
provincia de San Luis, llama la atención el
embalse Potrero de los Funes.

San Luis

Le relief essentiellement plat de la province
est bordé à l'extrême sud-ouest par les
Andes, alors qu'au nord-est il fait place
à un intéressant paysage de montagnes
et de lacs. Culminant à 6 720 m, le Cerro
Mercedario est l'un des sommets les plus
imposants dans cette région de la cordillère
des Andes. Le lac de retenue Potrero de
los Funes scintille à seulement 16 km de la
capitale de la province San Luis.

San Luis

A terra predominantemente plana da
província faz fronteira com a Cordilheira
dos Andes no extremo sudoeste. O
nordeste, oferece paisagens interessantes
de montanhas e lagos. Com uma altura
de 6720 m, o Cerro Mercedario é um dos
picos mais impressionantes dos Andes na
região da Alta Cordilheira. O reservatório
de Potrero de Funes fica a 16 km da capital
provincial de San Luis.

San Luis

Das vorwiegend flache Land der Provinz
grenzt im äußersten Südwesten an die
Anden. Es wartet im Nordosten mit
interessanter Berg- und Seenlandschaft
auf. Mit 6720 m Höhe ist der Cerro
Mercedario einer der imposantesten Gipfel
der Anden im Bereich der Hochkordillere.
16 km von der Provinzhauptstadt San
Luis entfernt lockt der Stausee Potrero
de Funes.

San Luis

Het overwegend vlakke land van de
provincie grenst in het uiterste zuidwesten
aan de Andes. In het noordoosten
bevindt zich een interessant berg- en
merenlandschap. Met een hoogte van
6720 m is de Cerro Mercedario één van
de meest imposante bergtoppen van de
Andes in de hoge Cordillera. Op 16 km van
de provinciehoofdstad San Luis lonkt het
stuwmeer van Potrero de Funes.

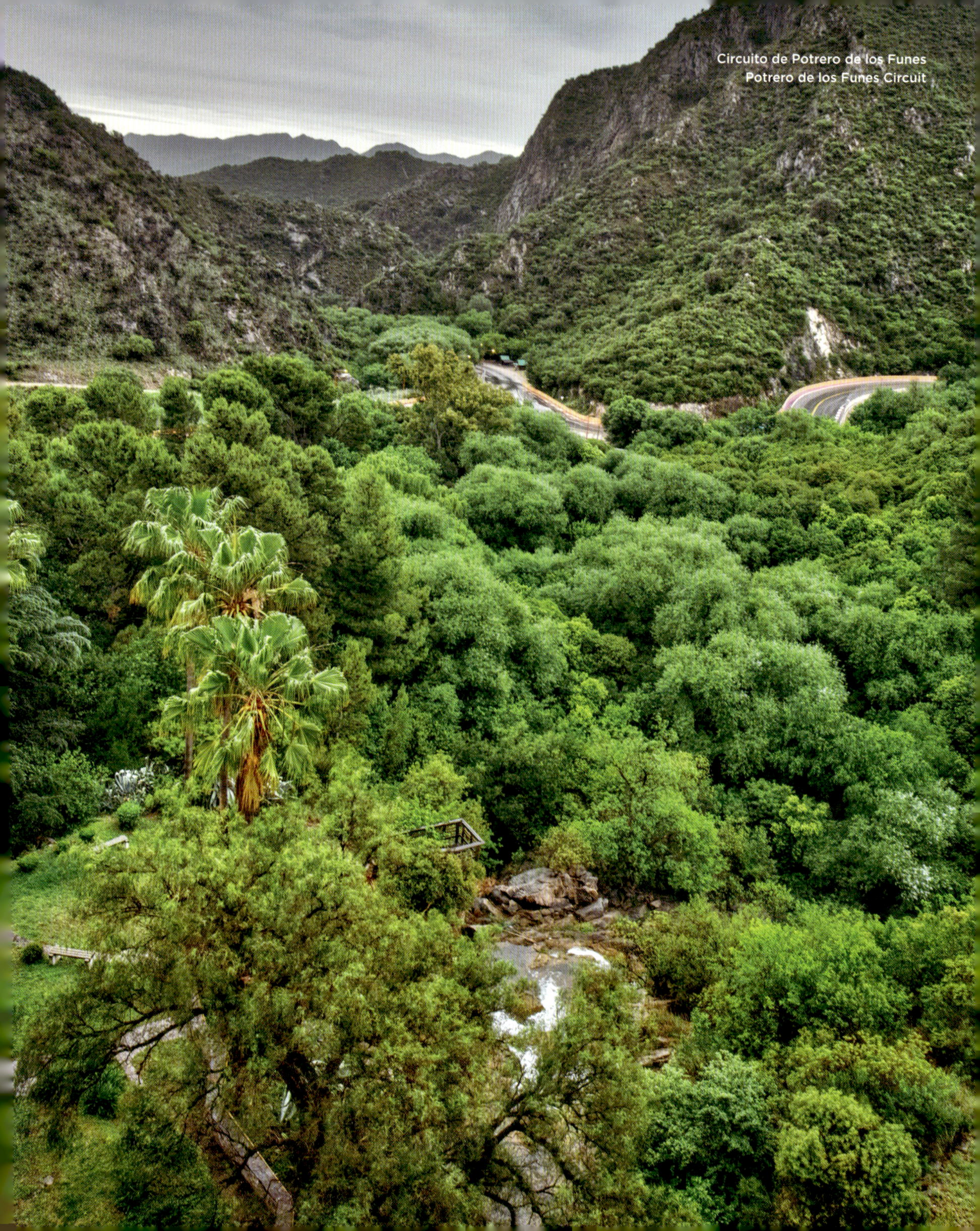

Circuito de Potrero de los Funes
Potrero de los Funes Circuit

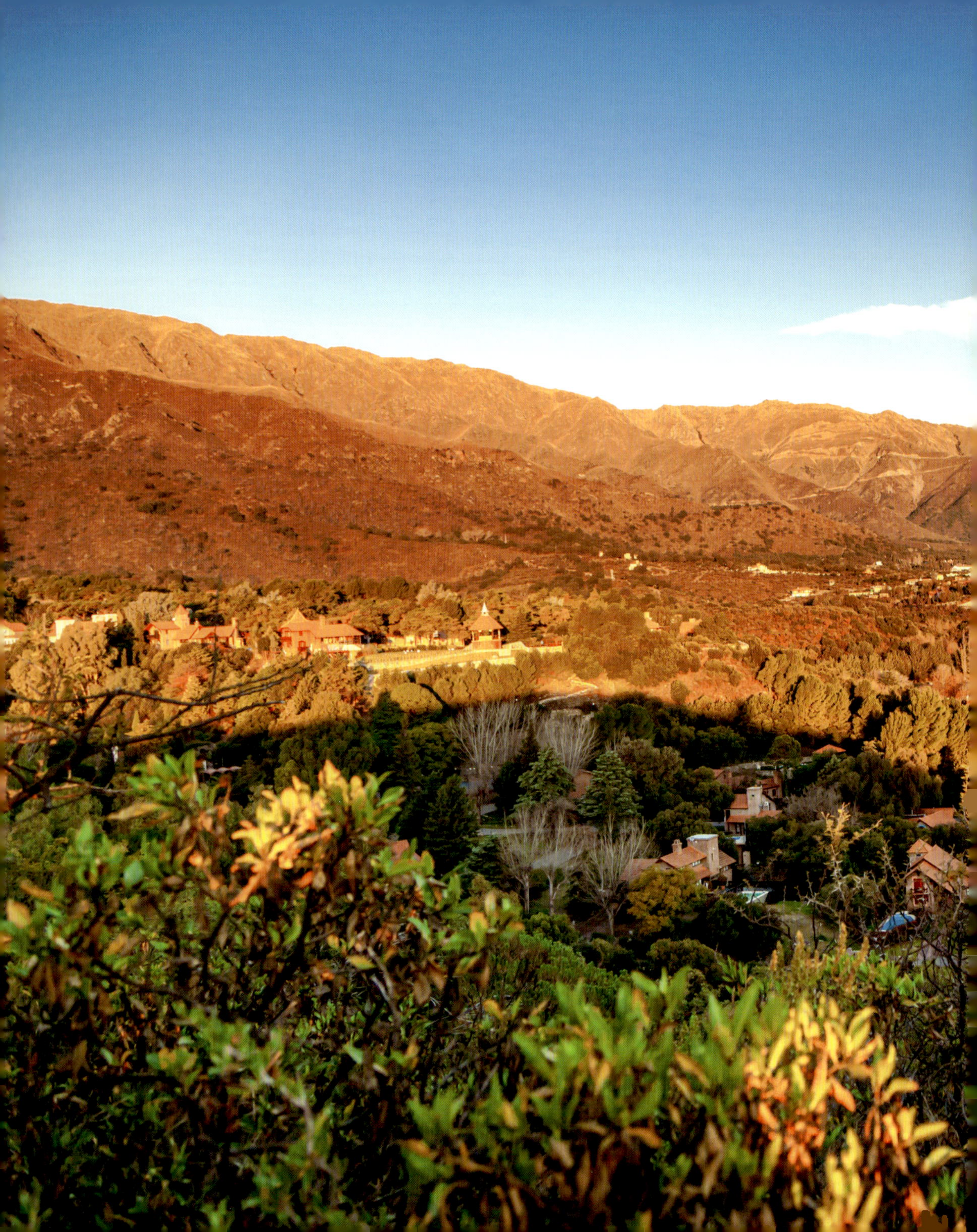

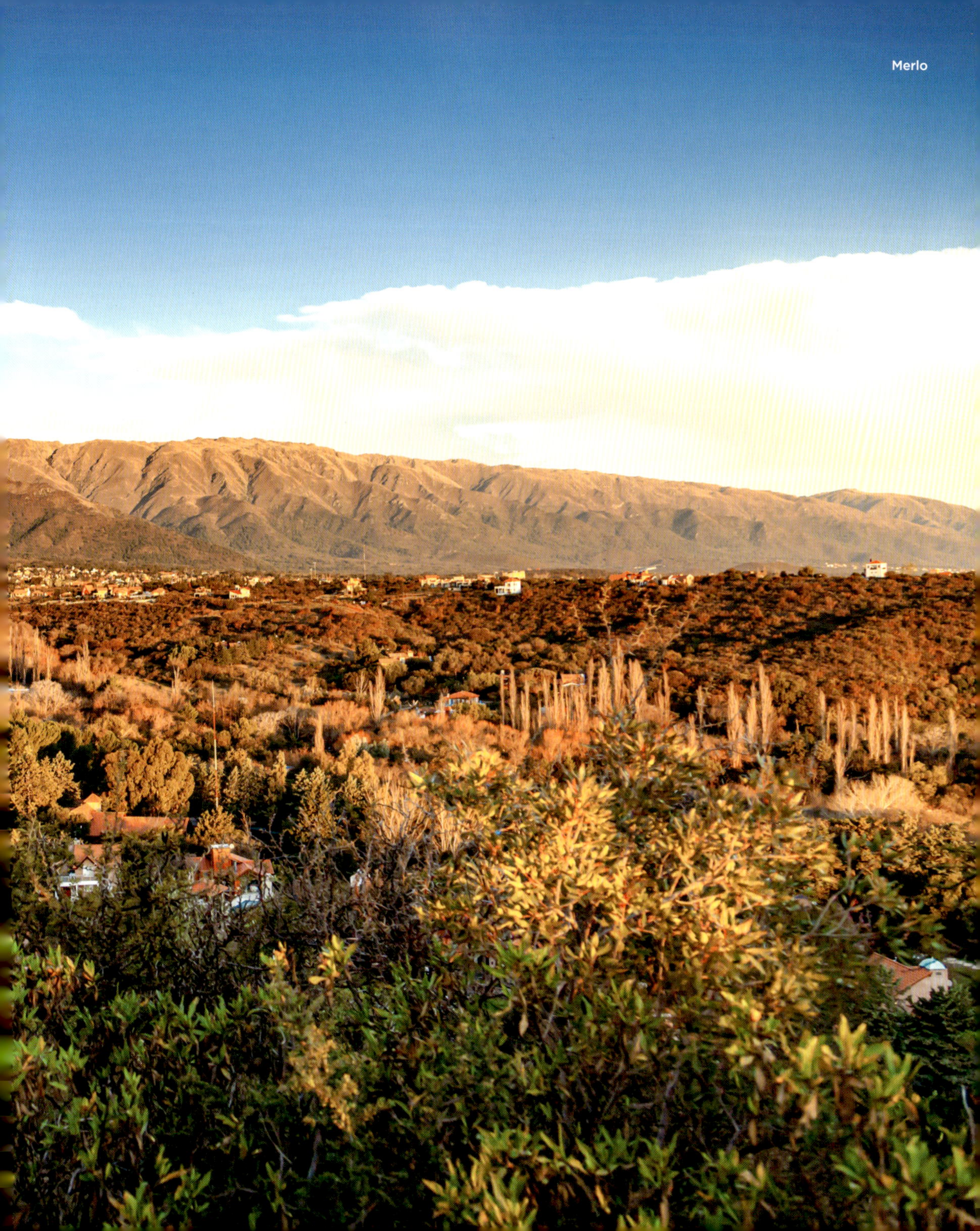

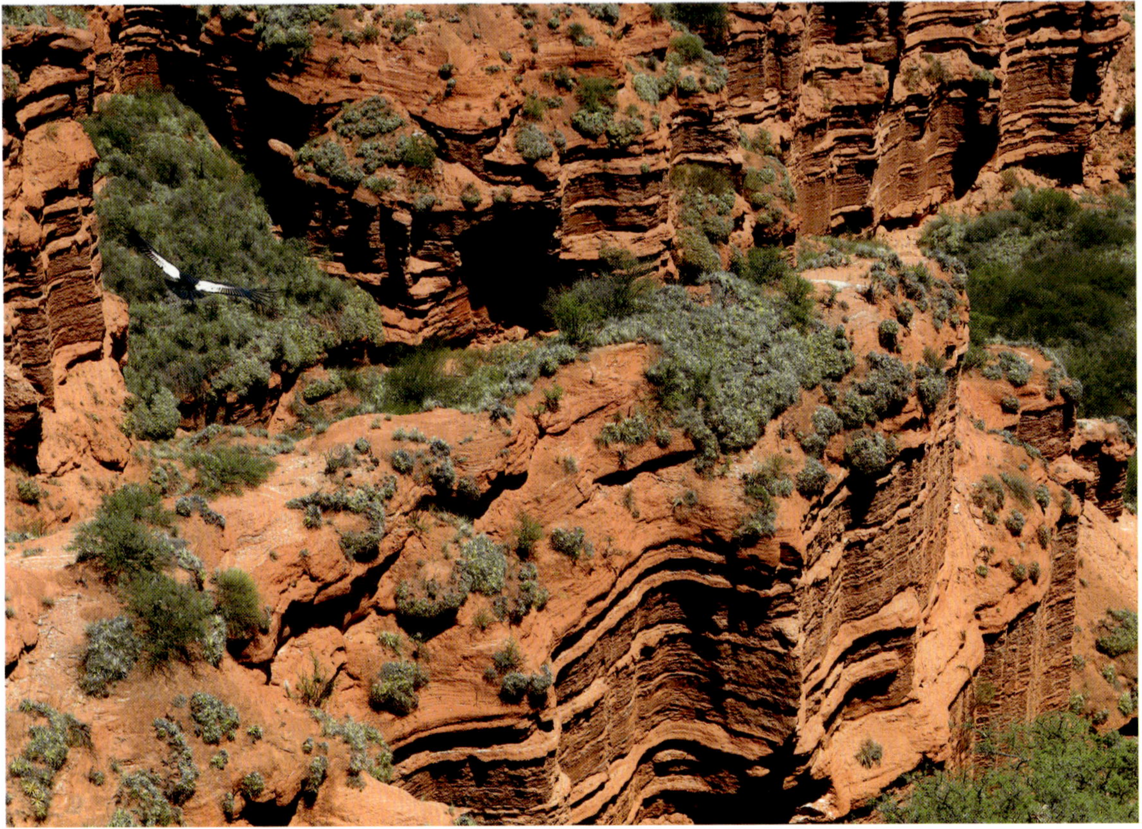

Parque Nacional Sierra de las Quijadas
Sierra de las Quijadas National Park

Sierra de las Quijadas

Wind, water and erosion have created the unique canyon mountain landscape of Sierra de las Quijadas, northeast of San Luis, over many thousands of years. The national park of the same name holds geological and paleontological treasures, where archaeologists have found the fossil of a flying reptile. The Huarpe ethnic group once lived in the region, where they used the natural rock niches as ovens to prepare food. As a reserve, the park offers favorable conditions for wild animals. Peregrine falcons and crowned eagles make their home here, alongside the rare monk parakeets.

Sierra de las Quijadas

Le vent, l'eau et l'érosion ont modelé pendant des milliers d'années le paysage de sommets et de canyons unique de la sierra de las Quijadas, qui se déploie au nord-est de San Luis. Le parc national du même nom renferme des trésors géologiques et paléontologiques. Les scientifiques y ont retrouvé le fossile d'un reptile volant. Autrefois, l'ethnie huarpe habitait la région. Ses membres utilisaient les niches creusées naturellement dans la roche comme fours pour cuire leurs aliments. En tant que réserve, le parc offre des conditions de vie idéales à la faune : faucons pèlerins, aigles couronnés et quelques rares conures veuves y trouvent refuge.

Sierra de las Quijadas

Wind, Wasser und Erosionen haben über Jahrtausende die einzigartige Canyon-Berglandschaft Sierra de las Quijadas nordöstlich von San Luis hervorgebracht. Der gleichnamige Nationalpark birgt geologische und paläontologische Schätze. Wissenschaftler fanden das Fossil eines fliegenden Reptils. Die Ethnie der Huarpe lebte einst in der Region. Sie nutzten die natürlichen Felsnischen als Öfen zur Zubereitung von Nahrung. Als Reservat bietet der Park Wildtieren günstige Bedingungen. Wanderfalken und Kronenadler haben hier ihr Revier, aber auch die seltenen Mönchssittiche.

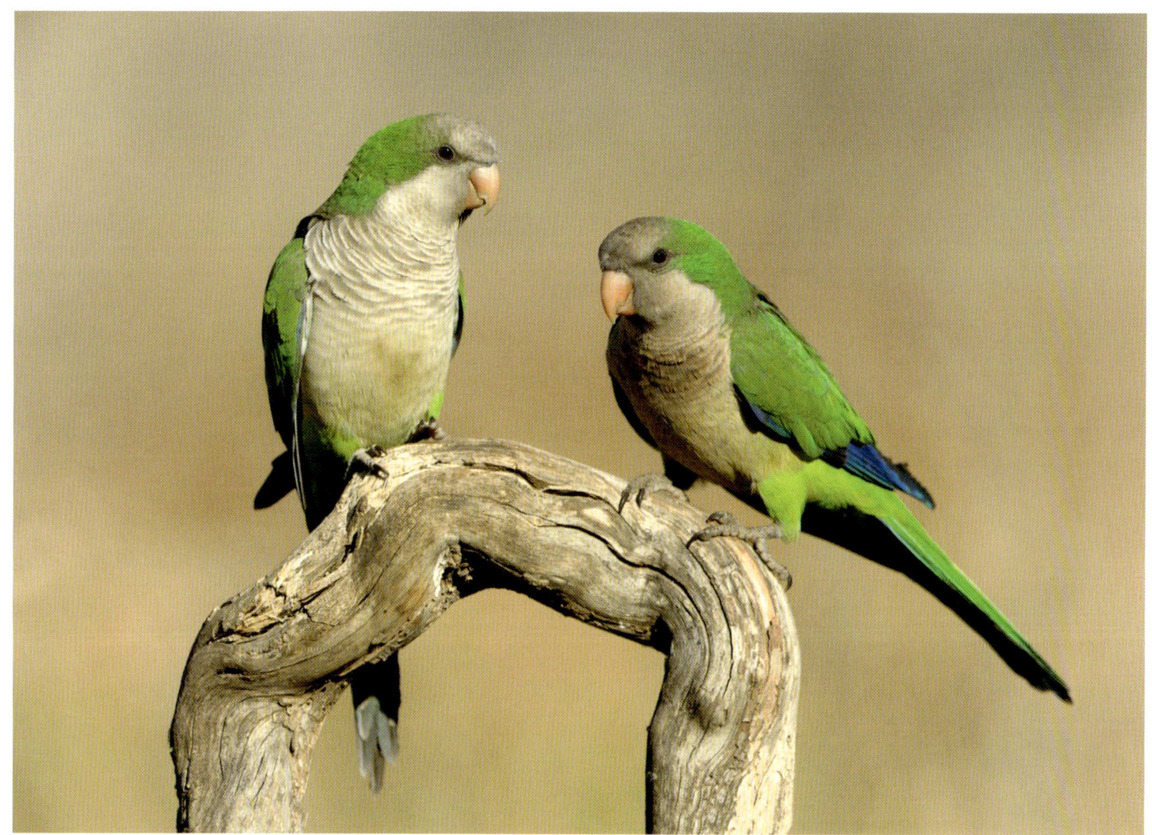

Cotorras argentinas
Monk parakeets

Sierra de las Quijadas

Durante miles de años, el viento, el agua
y la erosión han ido creando el paisaje
único de las montañas del cañón de
la Sierra de las Quijadas, al noreste de
San Luis. El parque nacional del mismo
nombre contiene tesoros geológicos
y paleontológicos. Los científicos
encontraron el fósil de un reptil volador.
La etnia Huarpe vivió en la región. Estos
pobladores utilizaban los nichos de roca
natural como hornos para preparar la
comida. Como reserva, el parque ofrece
condiciones favorables para los animales
salvajes. Los halcones peregrinos y las
águilas coronadas tienen su territorio aquí,
y también las extrañas cotorras monjes.

Sierra de las Quijadas

O vento, a água e as erosões criaram
a paisagem única montanhosa do
desfiladeiro da Serra de las Quijadas, a
nordeste de San Luis ao longo de milhares
de anos. O parque nacional do mesmo
nome guarda tesouros geológicos e
paleontológicos. Os cientistas encontraram
aqui o fóssil de um réptil voador. O grupo
étnico Huarpe já viveu na região. Eles
usavam os nichos de rochas naturais
como fornos para preparar os alimentos.
Como reserva, o parque oferece condições
favoráveis aos animais selvagens.
Falcões-peregrinos e águias-cinzenta
têm aqui o seu território, mas também os
raros caturritas.

Sierra de las Quijadas

Gedurende duizenden jaren vormden wind,
water en erosie het unieke berglandschap
van de Sierra de las Quijadas ten
noordoosten van San Luis. In het
gelijknamige nationaal park bevinden zich
geologische en paleontologische schatten.
Wetenschappers vonden het fossiel van
een vliegend reptiel. De etnische Huarpe
groep leefde ooit in de regio. Ze gebruikten
de natuurlijke nissen in de rotsen als ovens
om voedsel te bereiden. Als reservaat biedt
het park gunstige voorwaarden voor wilde
dieren. Slechtvalken en kroonarenden
hebben hier hun territorium, maar ook de
zeldzame monniksparkieten.

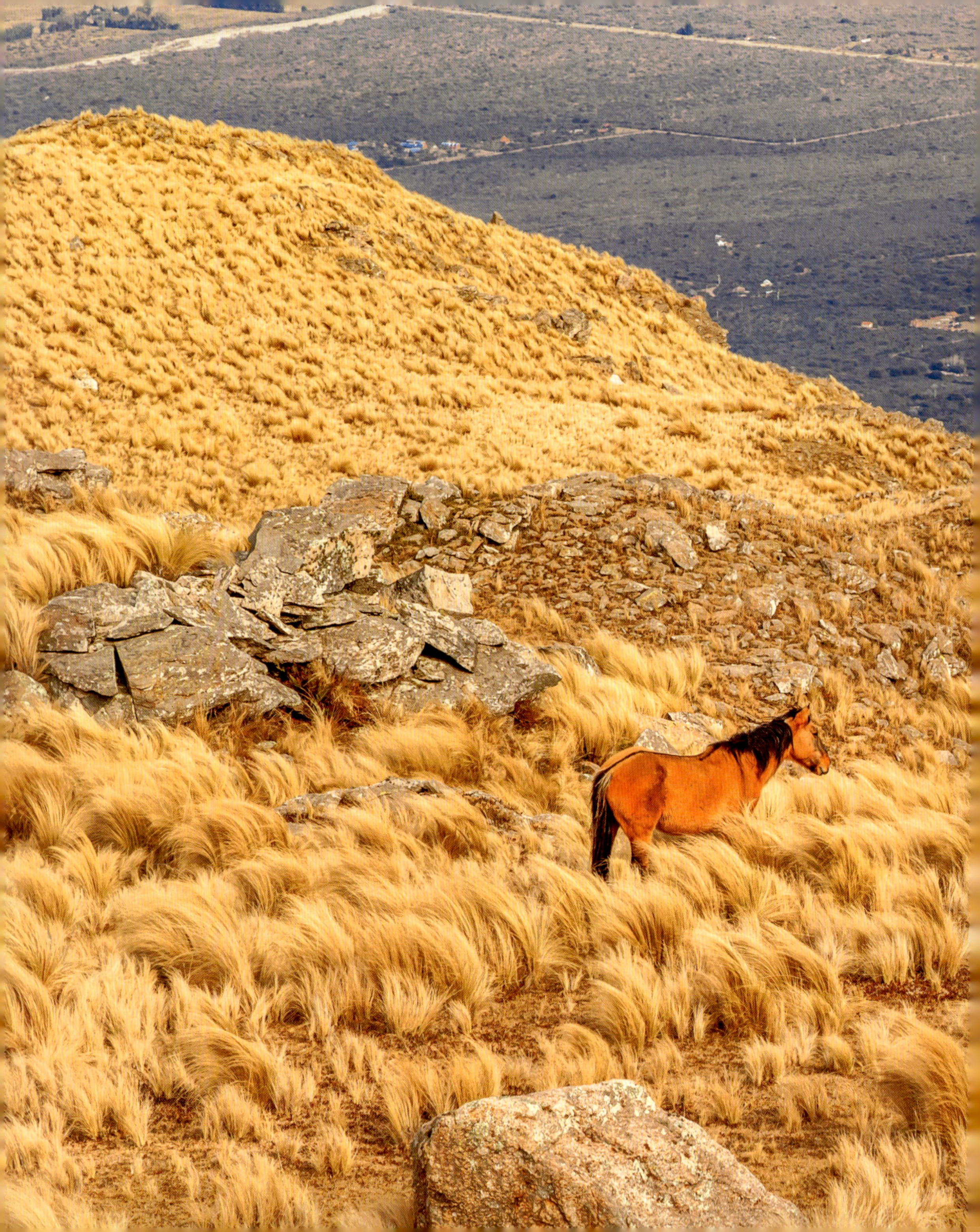

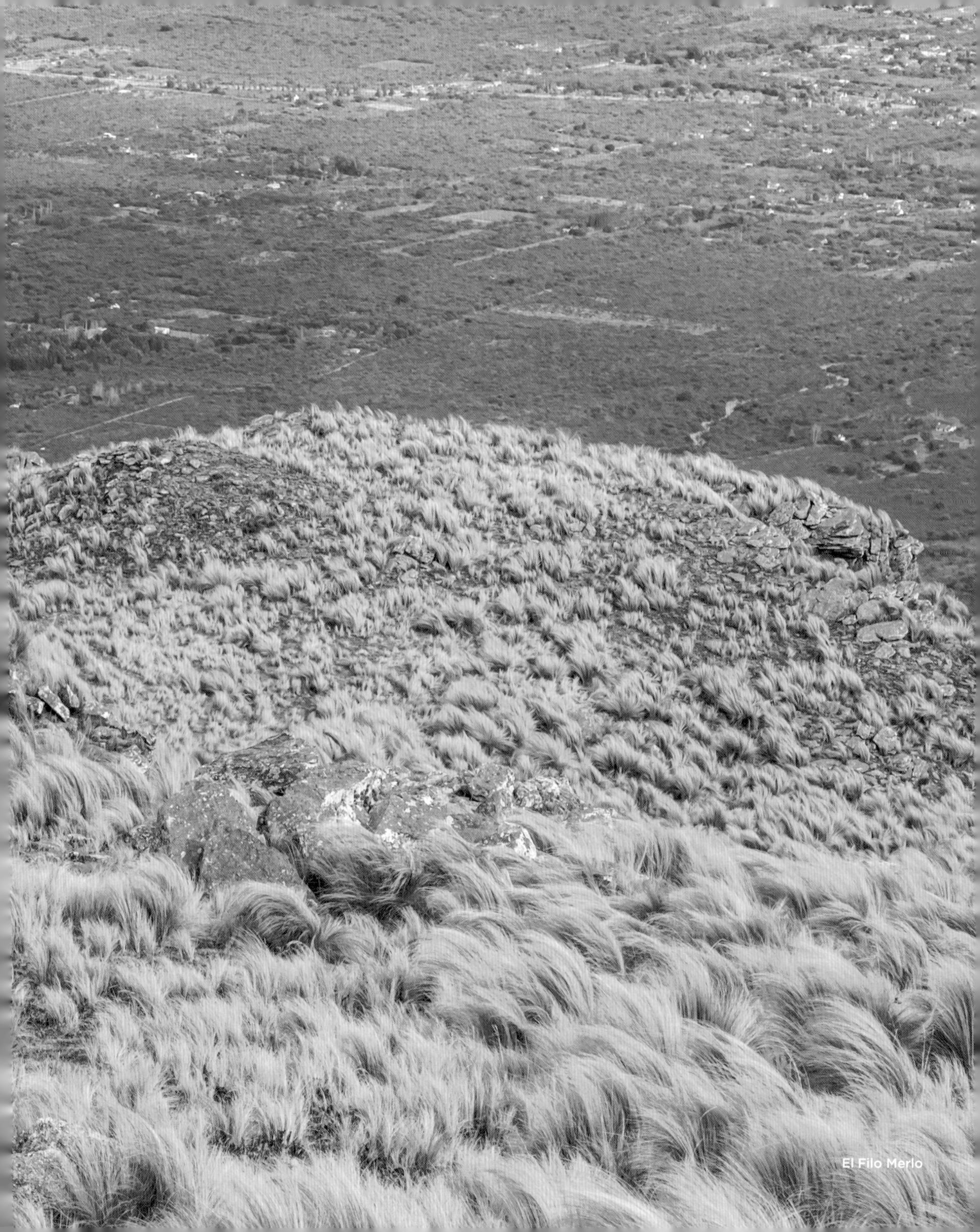
El Filo Merlo

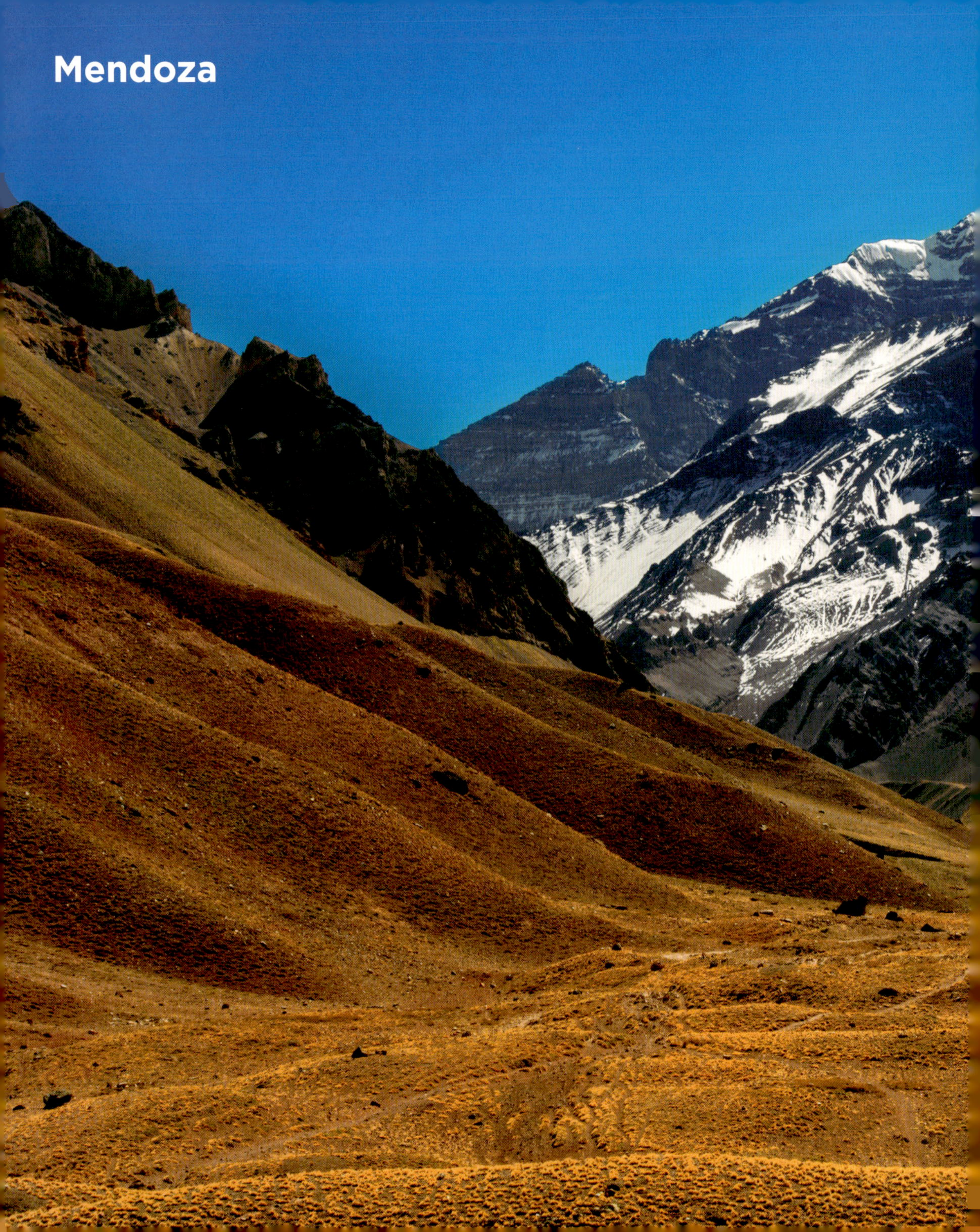
Mendoza

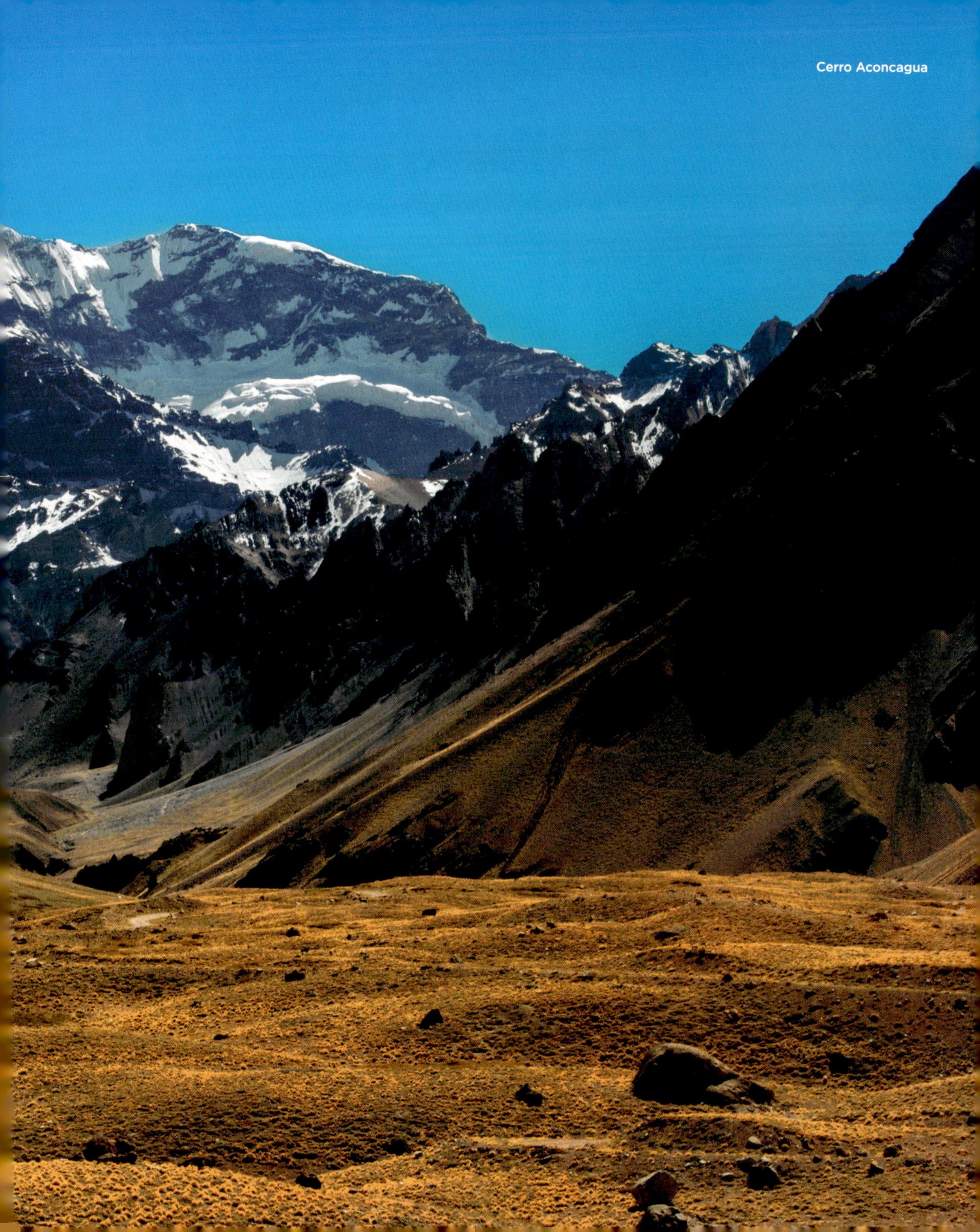
Cerro Aconcagua

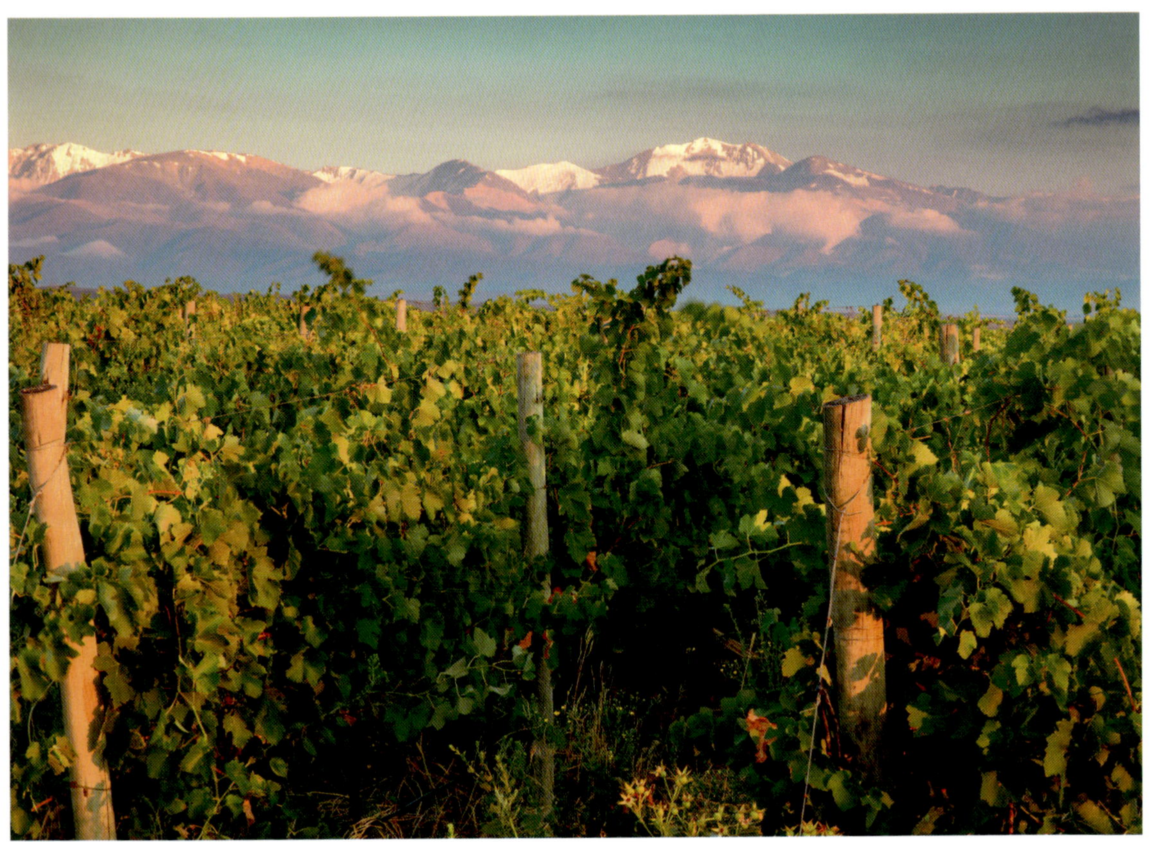

Valle de Uco
Uco Valley

Mendoza

The province of Mendoza belongs to the Cuyo region, which is what the indigenous peoples called the area because of its sandy soil. Thanks to artificial irrigation, however, magnificent vines thrive here. In the west, Mendoza borders on the high cordillera of the Andes. The permanently snow-covered Cerro Anconcagua, at 6961 m, (22,837 ft) is the highest mountain peak of the whole American continent, and also of the southern hemisphere. Southwest of the provincial capital Mendoza, which is considered the most beautiful city in the country, the Uco Valley extends along the Tunuyán River. The best vines grow here and in Luján de Cuyo, with wine production bringing great wealth to the province.

Mendoza

La province de Mendoza fait partie de la région du Cuyo. Ce nom, qui signifie « région des sables », lui fut donné par les peuples indigènes. Pourtant, l'irrigation artificielle a permis d'y cultiver de splendides vignes. À l'ouest, la province est bordée par la cordillère des Andes. Le Cerro Aconcagua, culminant à 6 961 m, est le plus haut sommet de tout le continent américain et de l'hémisphère Sud. Il est recouvert de neige éternelle. Au sud-ouest de la capitale provinciale Mendoza, considérée comme la plus belle ville du pays, la vallée d'Uco s'étire le long de la rivière Tunuyán. Les meilleurs ceps de vigne poussent ici et à Luján de Cuyo. La viticulture apporte à la province une formidable richesse.

Mendoza

Die Provinz Mendoza gehört zur Cuyo-Region. So bezeichneten die Ureinwohner das Gebiet wegen seiner „sandigen Erde". Trotzdem gedeihen hier dank künstlicher Bewässerung prächtige Weinstöcke. Im Westen grenzt Mendoza an die Hochkordillere der Anden. Der Cerro Anconcagua ist mit 6961 m die höchste Bergspitze des ganzen amerikanischen Kontinents und auch der Südhalbkugel. Er liegt im ewigen Schnee. Südwestlich der Provinzhauptstadt Mendoza, die als die schönste Stadt des Landes gilt, erstreckt sich am Tunuyan-Fluss das Uco-Tal. Hier und in Luján de Cuyo wachsen die besten Reben. Weinanbau beschert der Provinz großen Reichtum.

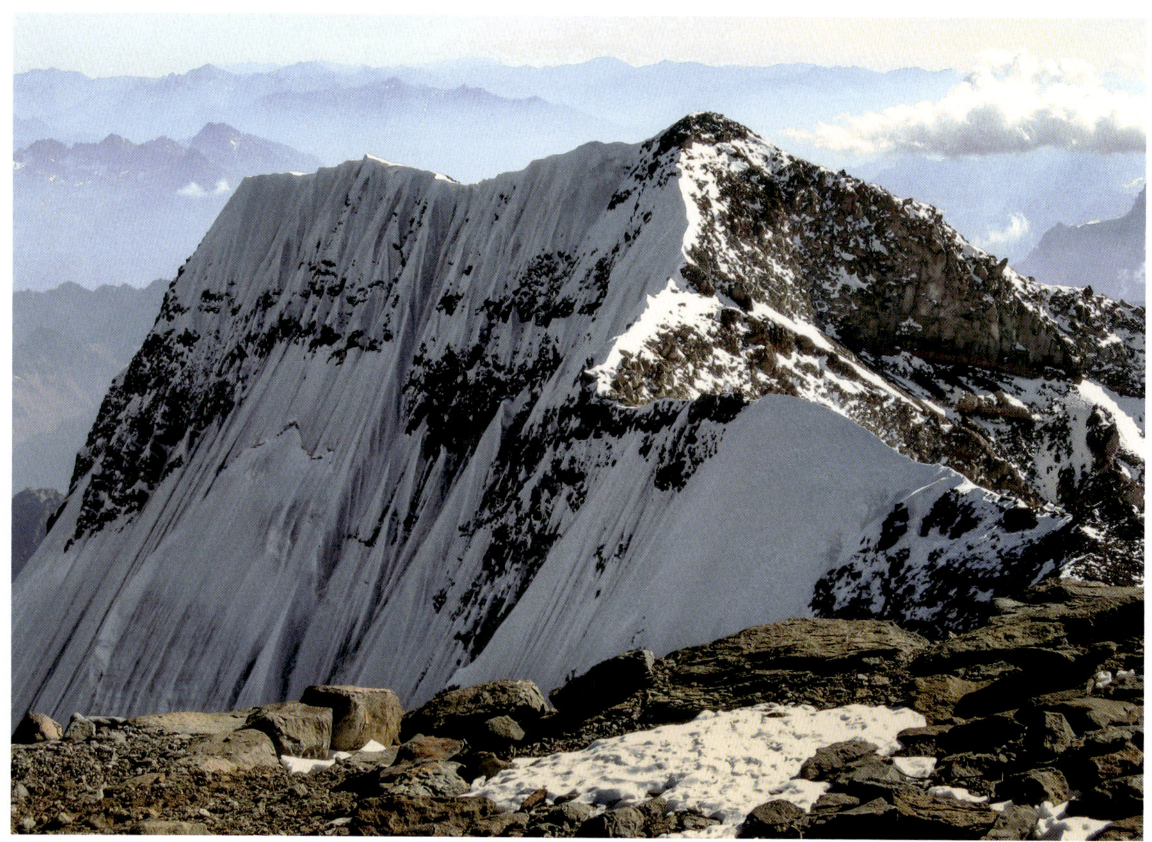

Cerro Aconcagua

Mendoza

La provincia de Mendoza pertenece a la región de Cuyo. Así es como los nativos llamaban a la zona por su "suelo arenoso". Sin embargo, gracias al riego artificial, aquí prosperan magníficas cepas. Al oeste, Mendoza limita con la alta cordillera de los Andes. El Cerro Anconcagua es, con sus 6961 m, el pico más alto de todo el continente americano y también del hemisferio sur. Siempre se encuentra nevado. Al suroeste de la capital de la provincia de Mendoza, considerada la ciudad más bella del país, el Valle de Uco se extiende a lo largo del río Tunuyán. Las mejores cepas crecen aquí y en Luján de Cuyo. La viticultura aporta una gran riqueza a la provincia.

Mendoza

A província de Mendoza pertence à região de Cuyo. Foi assim que os nativos chamavam à área por causa do seu "solo arenoso". No entanto, graças à irrigação artificial, as magníficas vinhas prosperam aqui. No oeste, Mendoza faz fronteira com a alta Cordilheira dos Andes. O Cerro Anconcagua é com 6961 m o pico mais alto da montanha de todo o continente americano e também do hemisfério sul. Ele está eternamente coberto de neve. Sudoeste da capital provincial Mendoza, considerada a cidade mais bela do país, o Vale de Uco estende-se ao longo do rio Tunuyan. As melhores videiras crescem aqui e em Luján de Cuyo. A produção de vinho traz grande riqueza para a província.

Mendoza

De provincie Mendoza behoort tot de regio Cuyo. Zo bestempelden de oerinwoners het gebied vanwege zijn "zandige aarde". Toch gedijen hier, dankzij de kunstmatige irrigatie, prachtige wijnstokken. In het westen grenst Mendoza aan de hoge cordillera van de Andes. De Cerro Anconcagua is met 6961 m de hoogste bergtop van het hele Amerikaanse continent en ook van het zuidelijk halfrond. Hij ligt in de eeuwige sneeuw. Ten zuidwesten van de provinciehoofdstad Mendoza, die als mooiste stad van het land wordt beschouwd, strekt de Uco-vallei zich langs de Tunuyan-rivier uit. Hier en in Luján de Cuyo groeien de beste wijnstokken. De wijnbouw brengt grote rijkdom in de provincie.

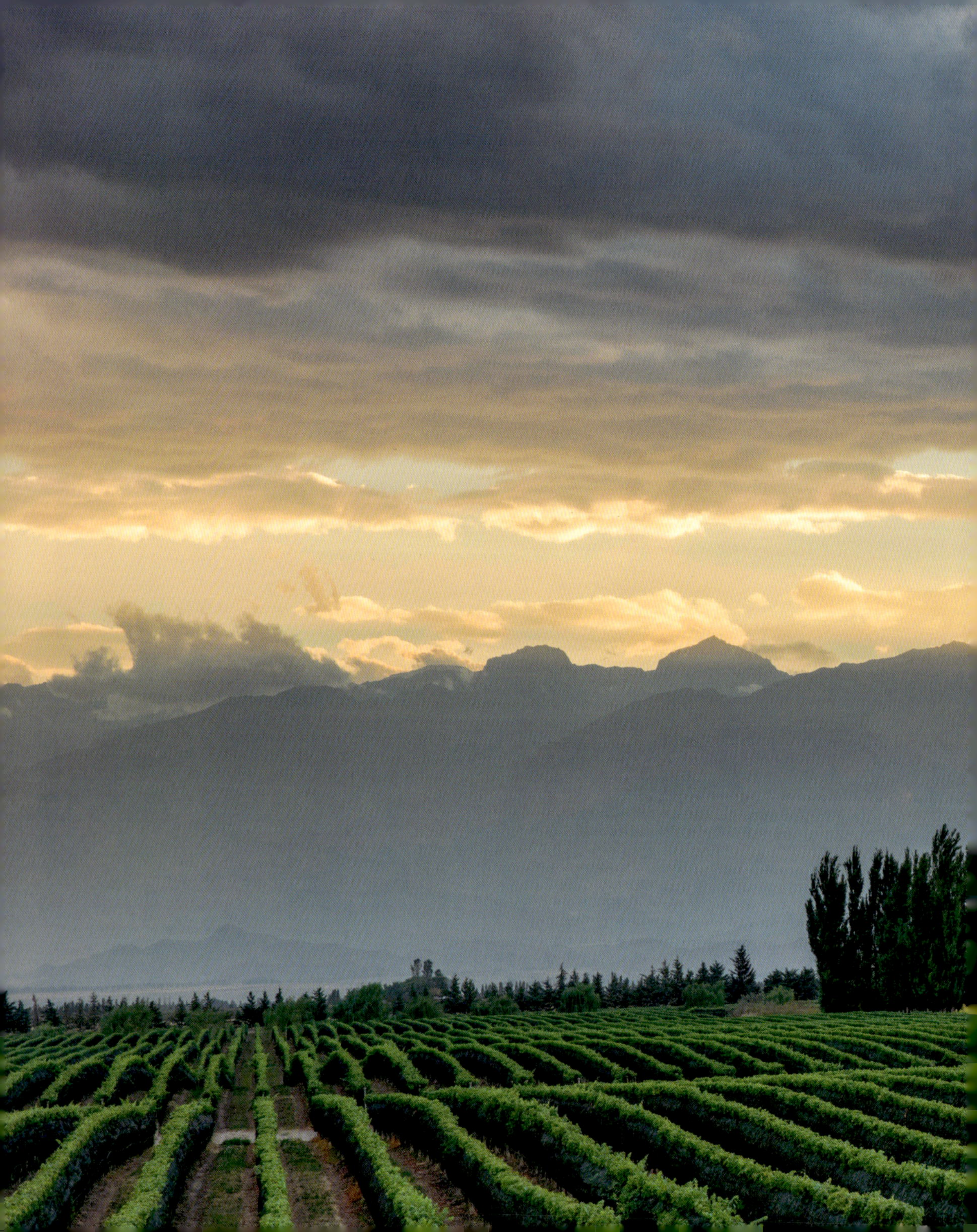

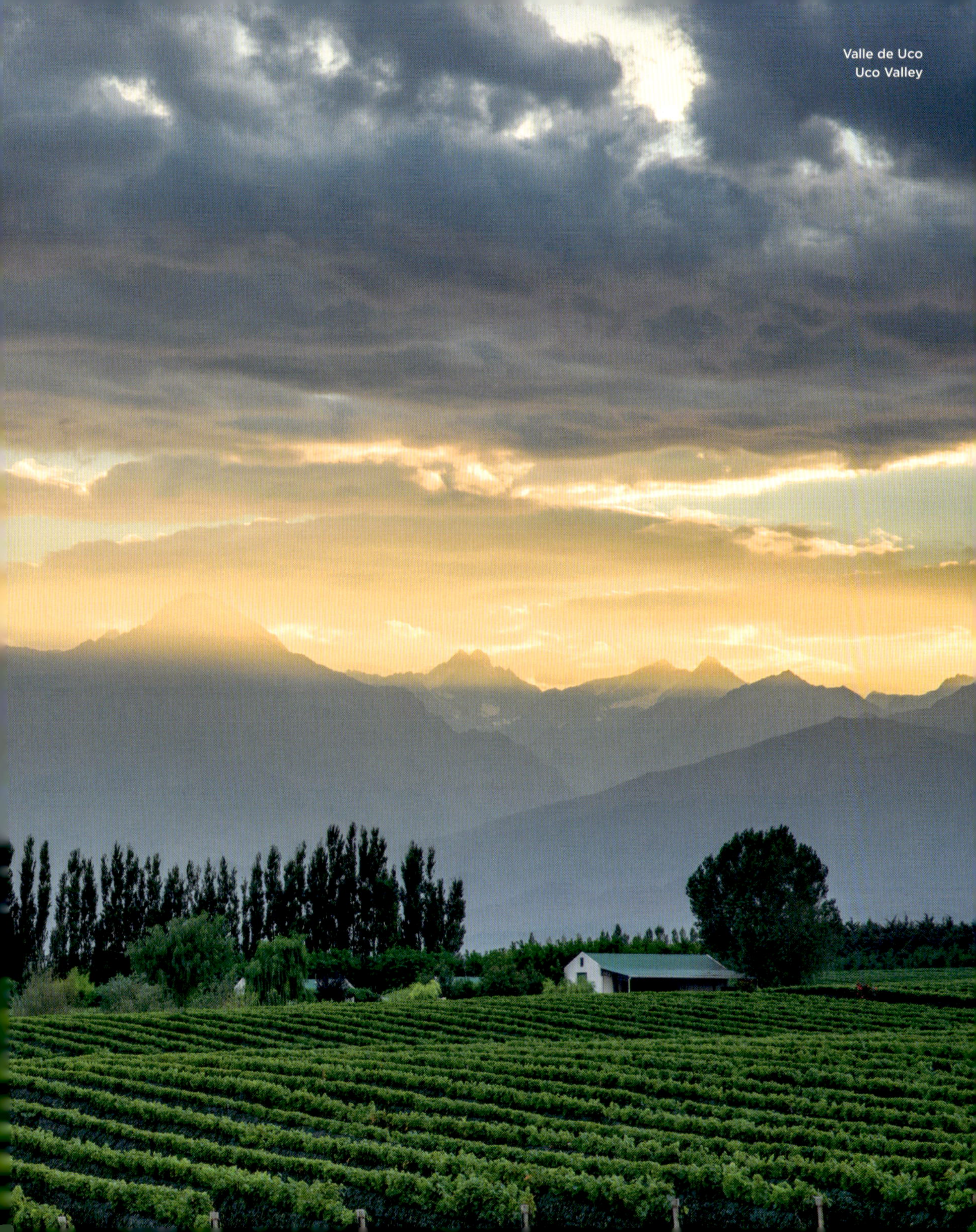
Valle de Uco
Uco Valley

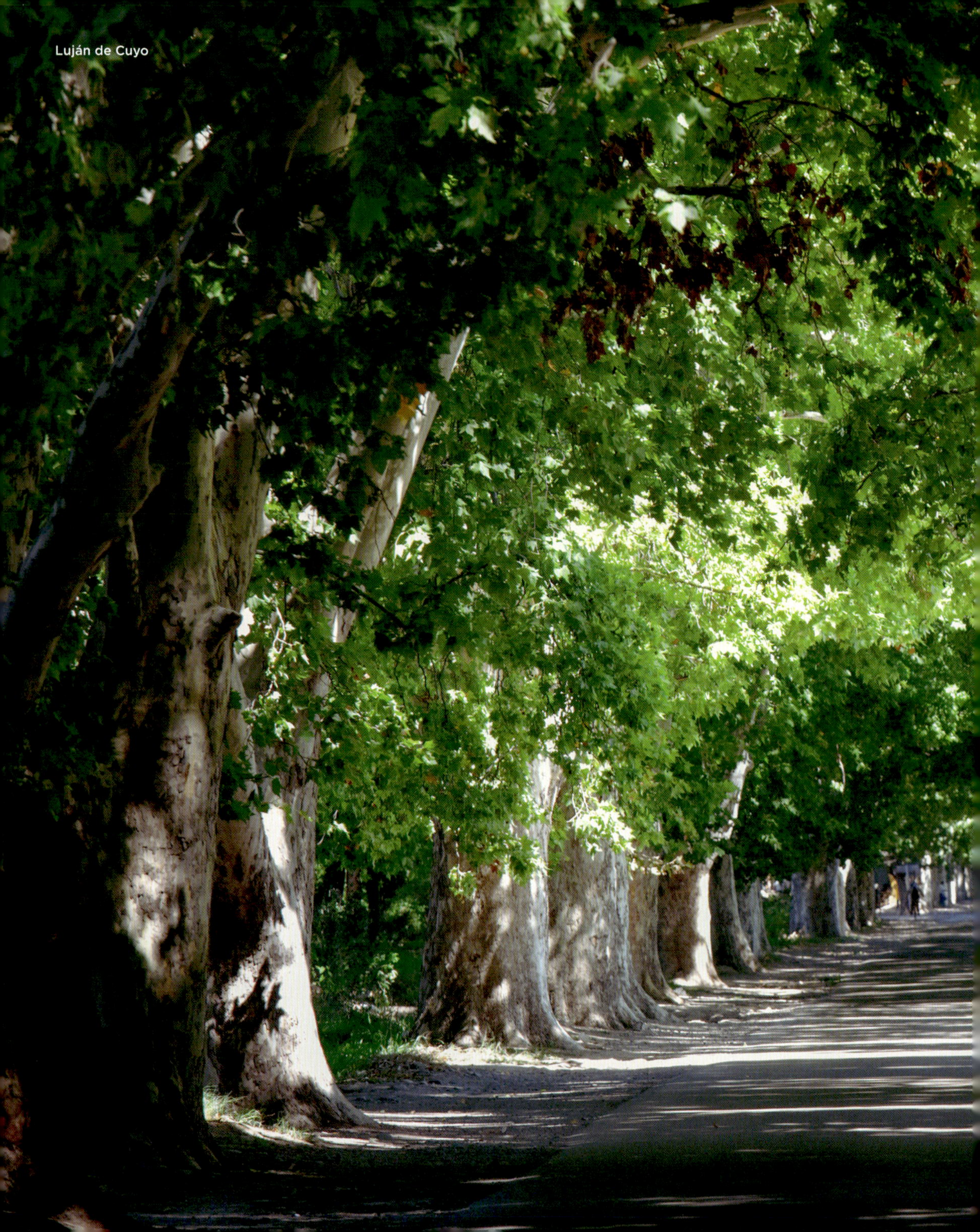
Luján de Cuyo

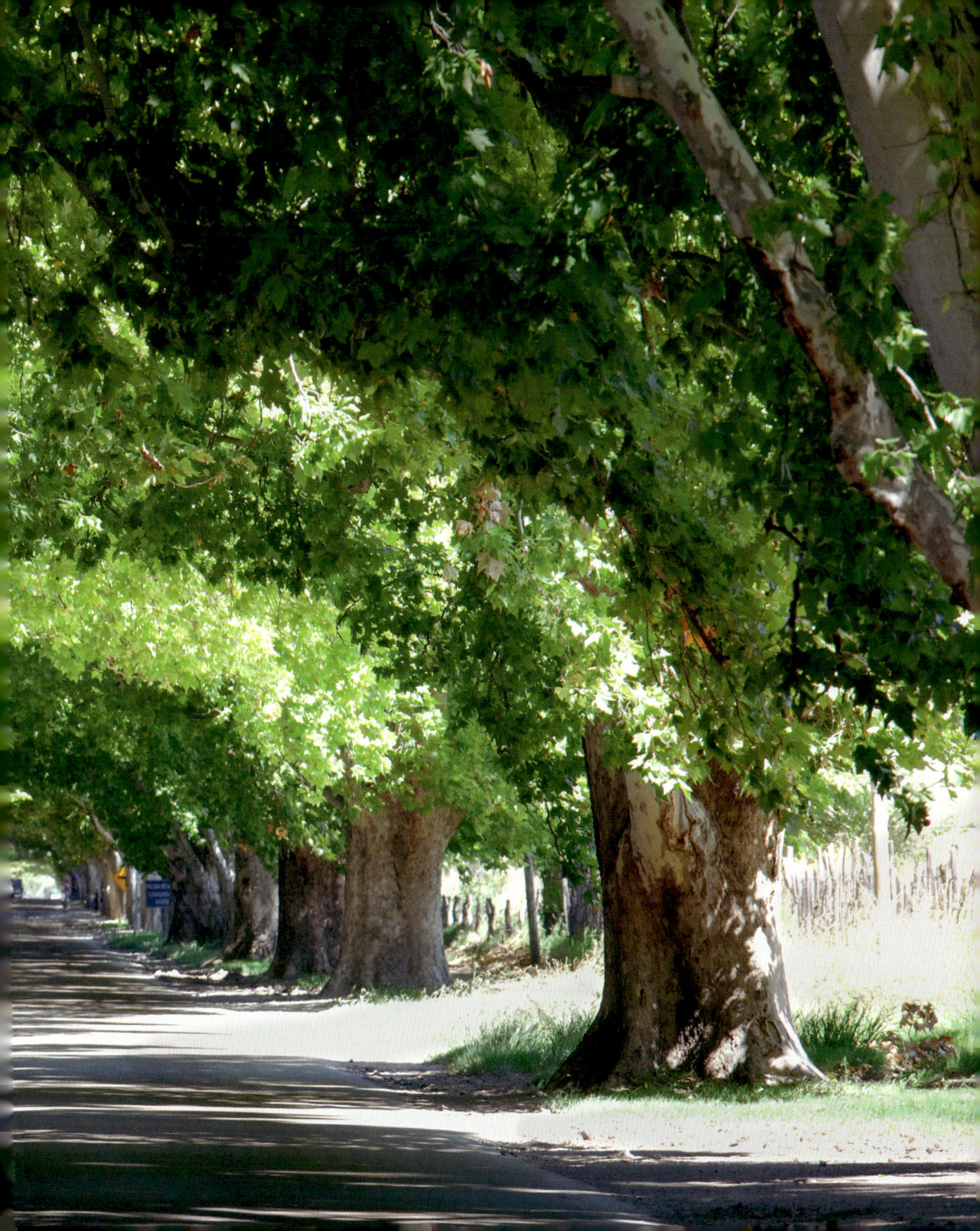

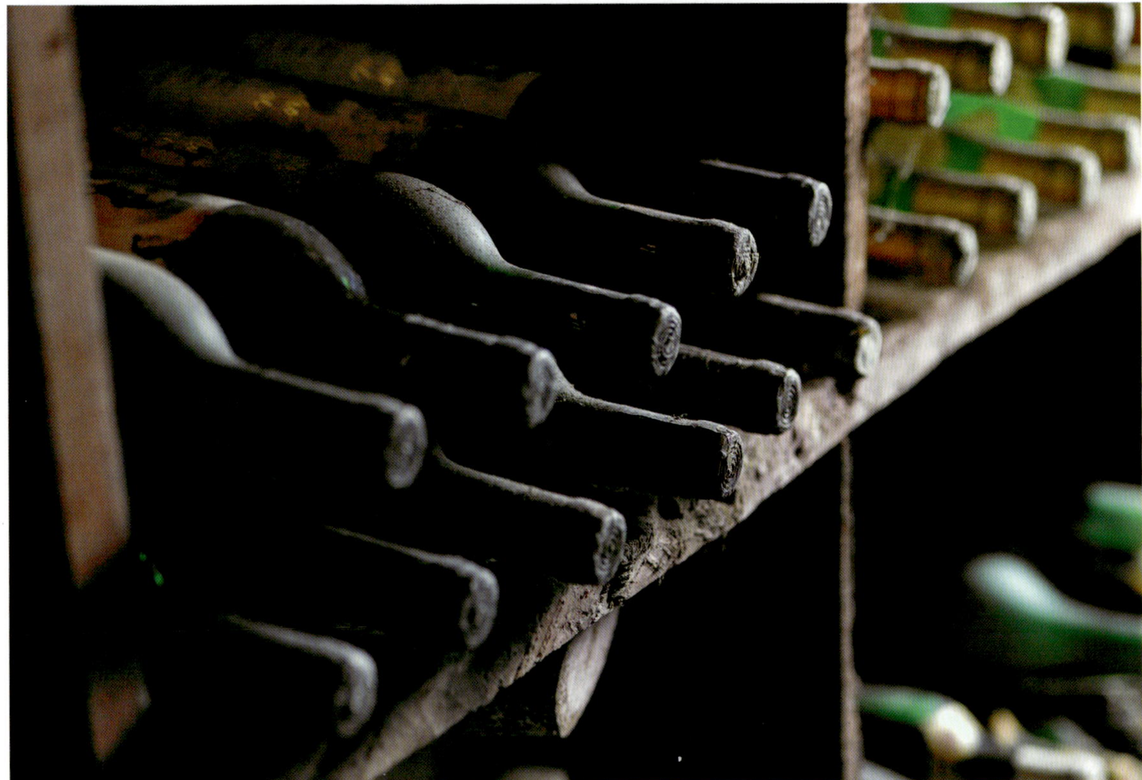

Vino
Wine

Mendoza Wines

Argentina is the fifth largest wine producer in the world. The country maintains its high position among red wine producers thanks to the Malbec grape, which thrives in the Mendoza wine region. The ideal annual average temperature of 14 °C (57 °F) is found here. Climatically, the proximity to the Andes and, of course, the constant sunshine both have a positive effect.

Vinos de Mendoza

Argentina es el quinto productor de vino del mundo. El país mantiene su primera posición entre los vinos tintos gracias a la uva malbec, que prospera en la región vitivinícola de Mendoza, ya que aquí se encuentra la temperatura media anual ideal de 14 grados. Desde el punto de vista climático, la proximidad de los Andes y, por supuesto, el sol constante tienen un efecto positivo.

Les vins de Mendoza

L'Argentine est le cinquième plus grand producteur de vins au monde. Le pays doit sa position de premier rang en matière de vin rouge à sa variété de raisin malbec, cultivée dans la région de Mendoza. Ce territoire offre en effet une température moyenne annuelle de 14 °C idéale. La proximité des Andes et, bien évidemment, l'ensoleillement constant influencent favorablement le climat.

Vinhos de Mendoza

A Argentina é o quinto maior produtor de vinho do mundo. O país mantém sua posição de liderança entre os vinhos tintos graças à uva Malbec, que prospera na região vinícola de Mendoza. A temperatura média anual ideal de 14 graus é encontrada aqui. Climaticamente, a proximidade com os Andes e, claro, o sol constante têm um efeito positivo.

Mendoza Weine

Argentinien ist der fünftgrößte Weinproduzent der Welt. Seinen Spitzenplatz unter den Rotweinen behauptet das Land durch die Malbec Traube, die in der Weinbauregion Mendoza gedeiht. Hier herrscht die ideale jährliche Durchschnittstemperatur von 14 Grad. Klimatisch schlagen die Anden-Nähe und natürlich die beständige Sonneneinstrahlung positiv zu Buche.

Mendoza wijnen

Argentinië is de op vijf na grootste wijnproducent ter wereld. Het land handhaaft zijn toppositie onder de rode wijnen dankzij de malbec druif die goed in de wijnbouwstreek van Mendoza gedijt. Hier heerst de gemiddelde jaartemperatuur van 14 graden. Klimatologisch gezien spelen de nabijheid van de Andes en natuurlijk de constante zonneschijn een positieve rol.

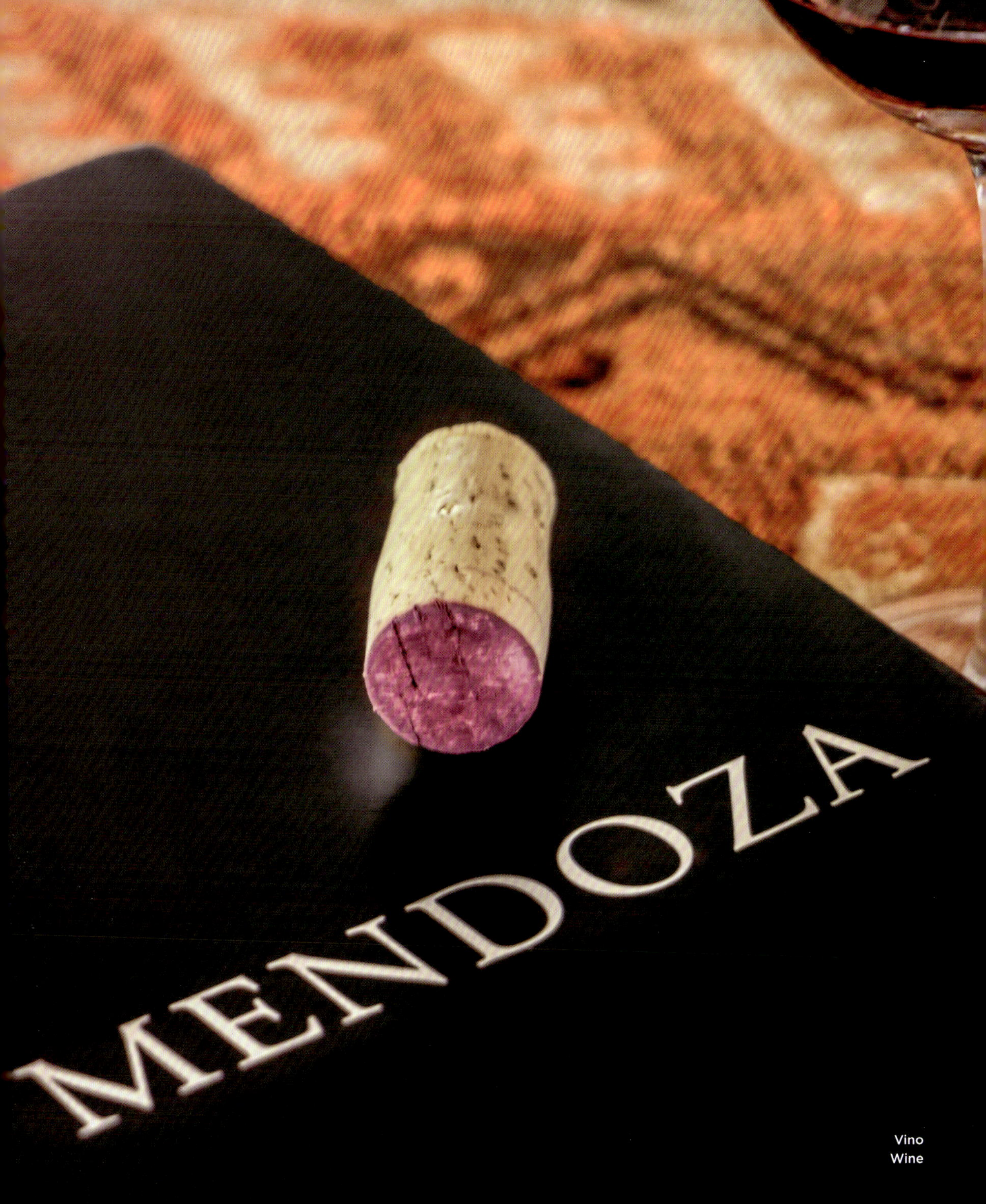

Vino
Wine

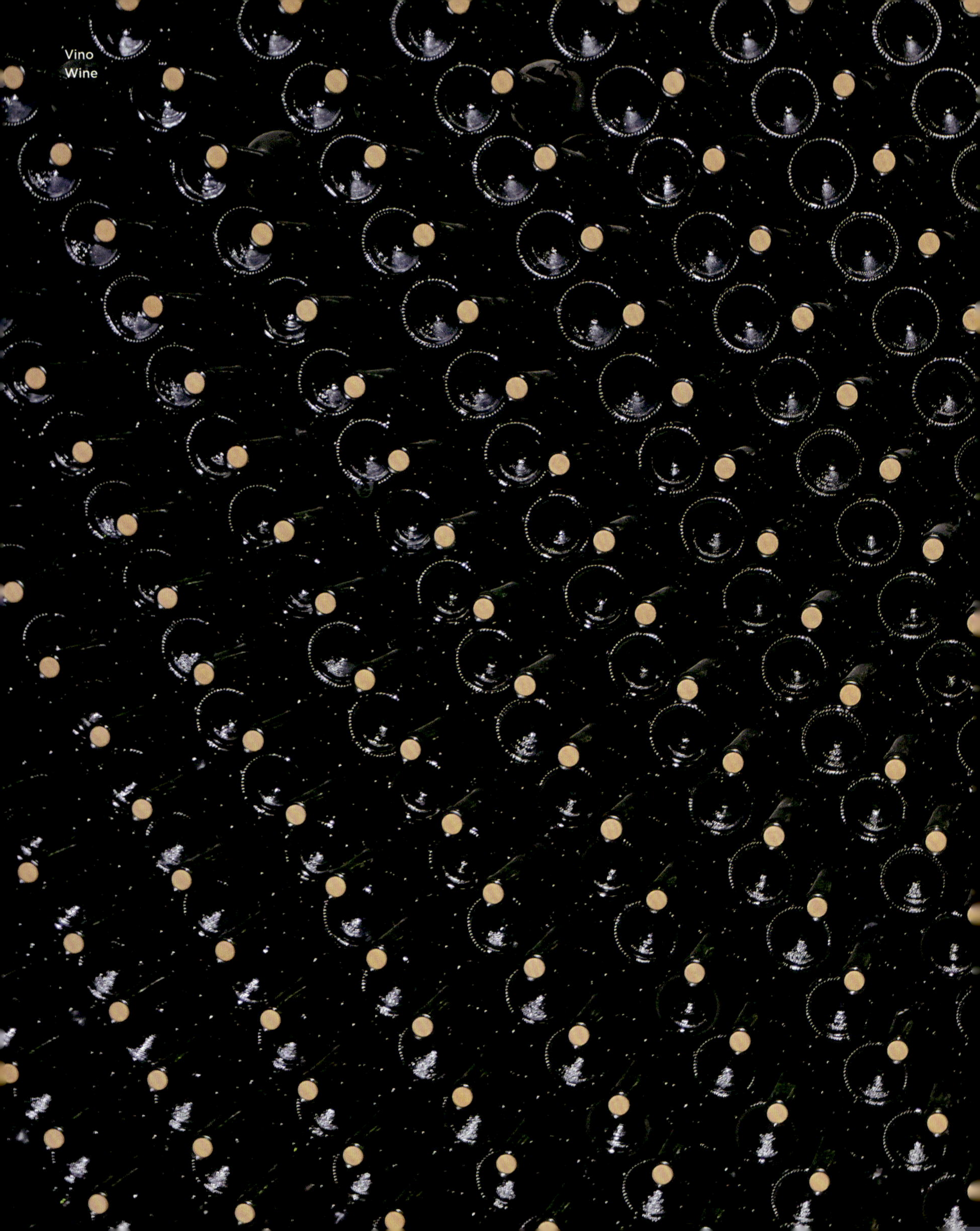

Vino
Wine

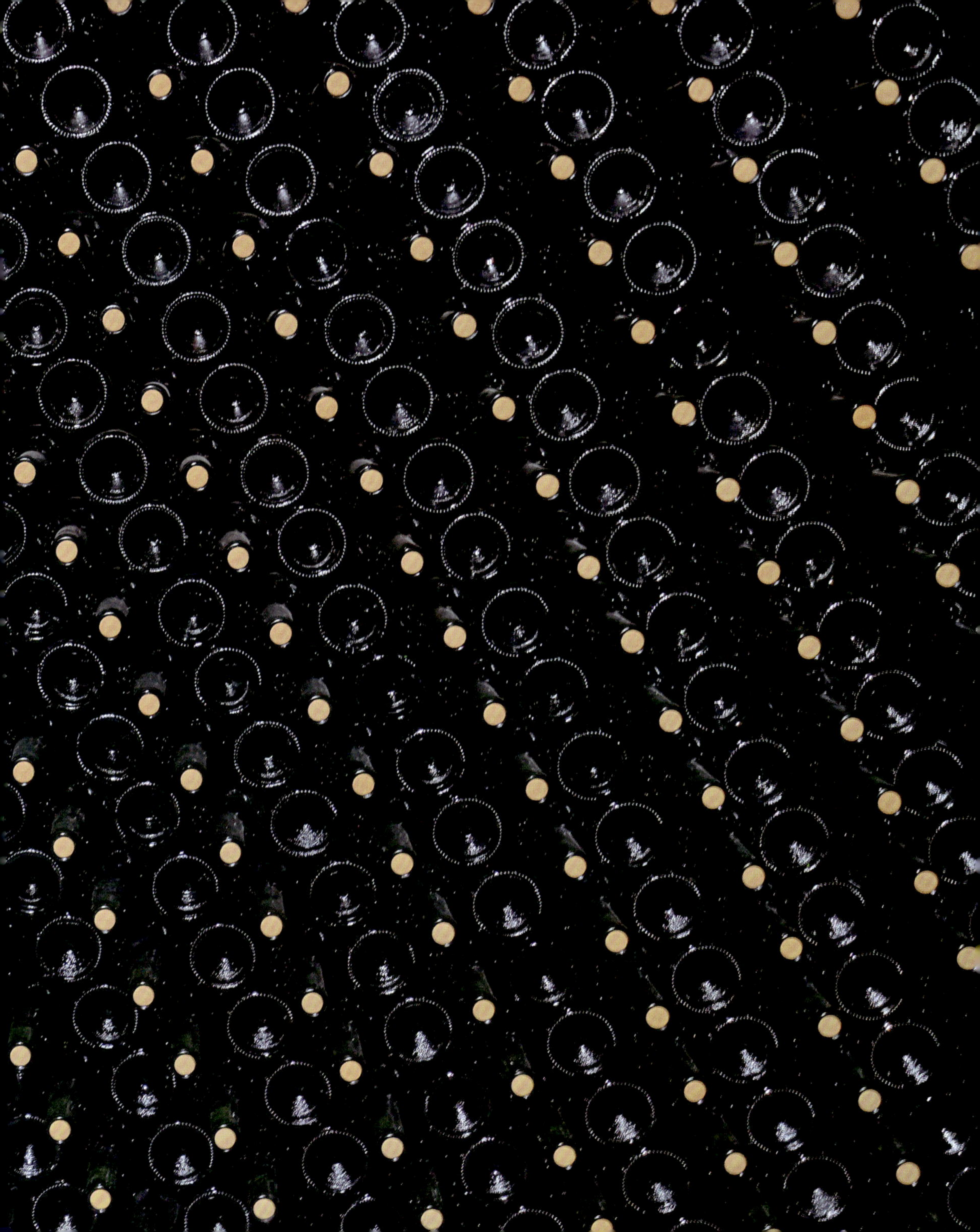

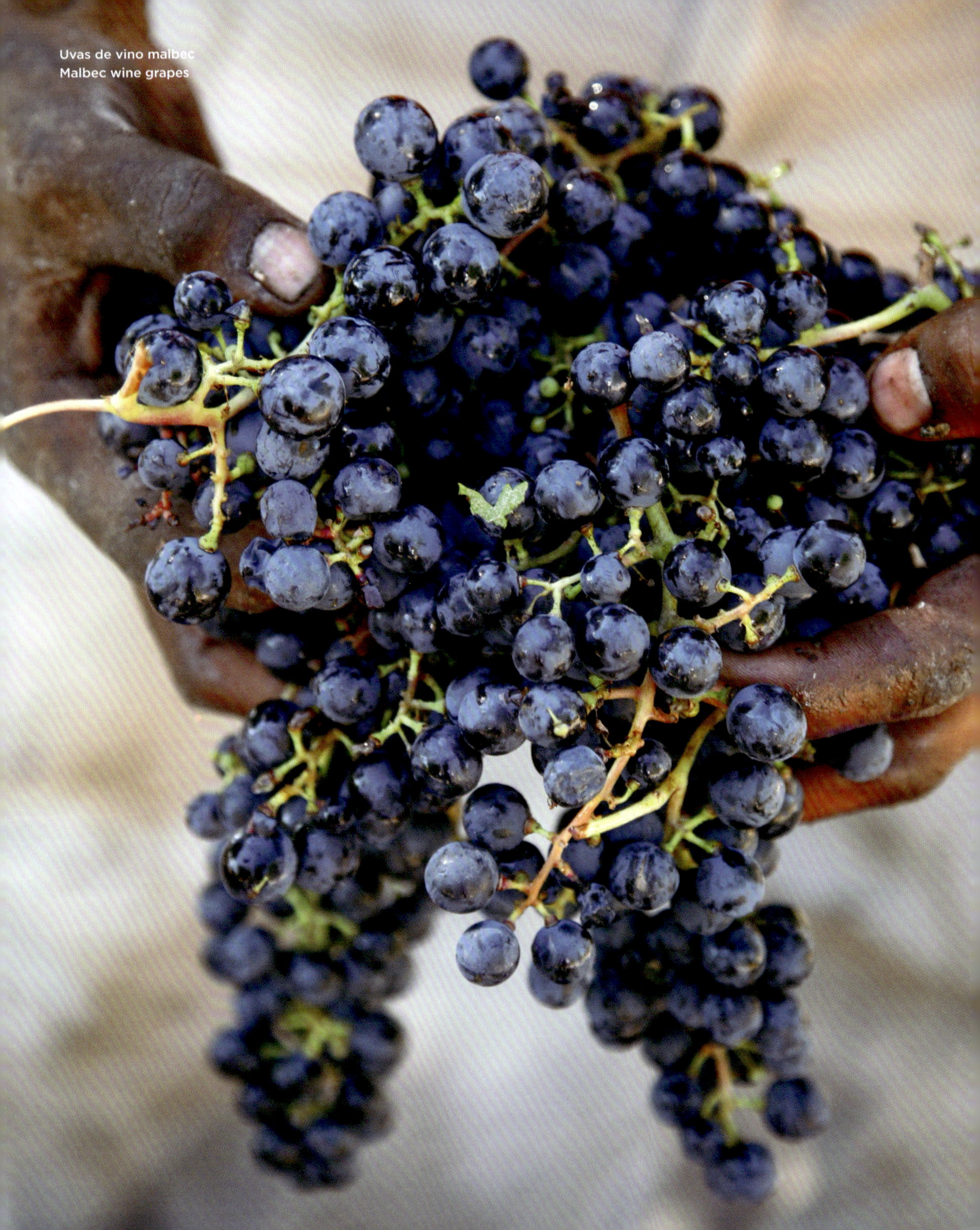

Uvas de vino malbec
Malbec wine grapes

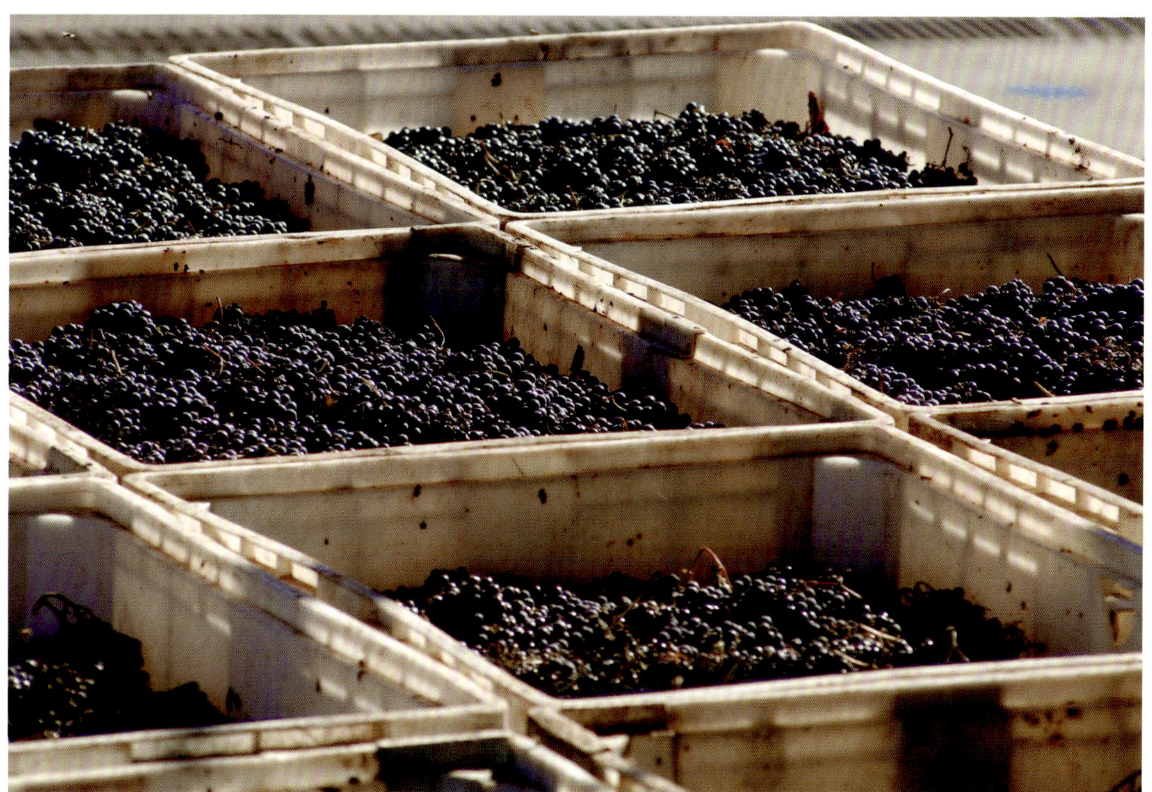

Vendimia
Grape harvest

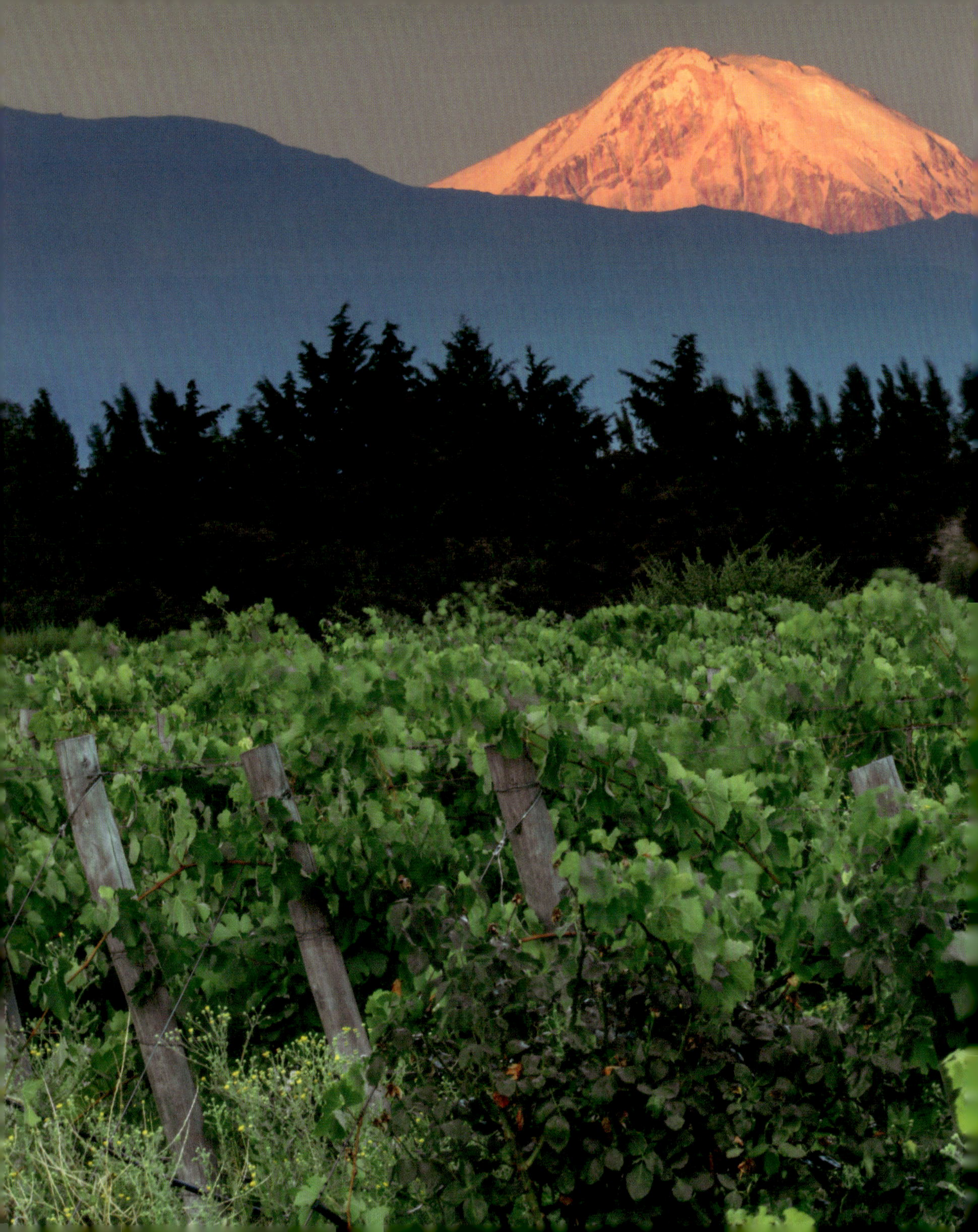

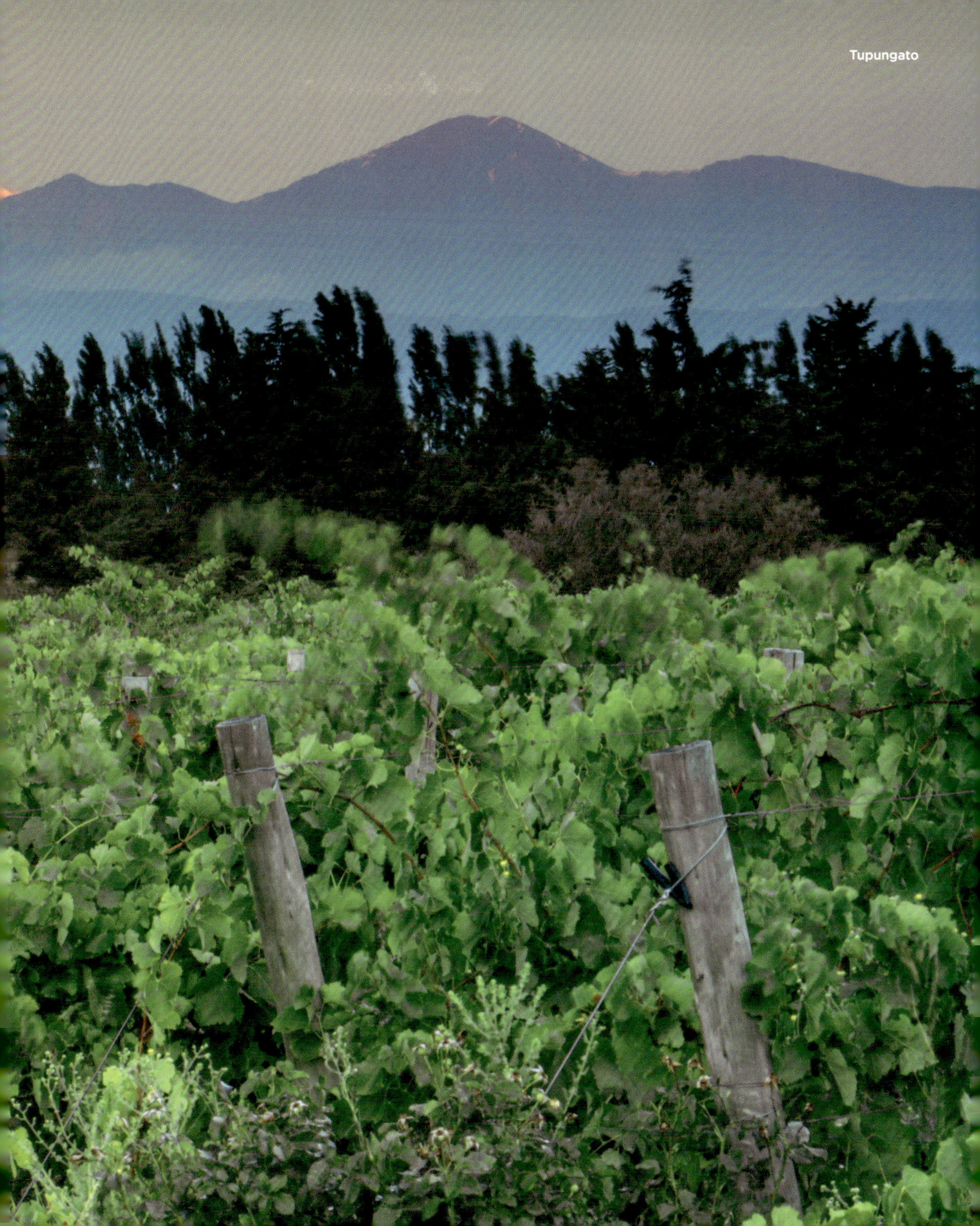
Tupungato

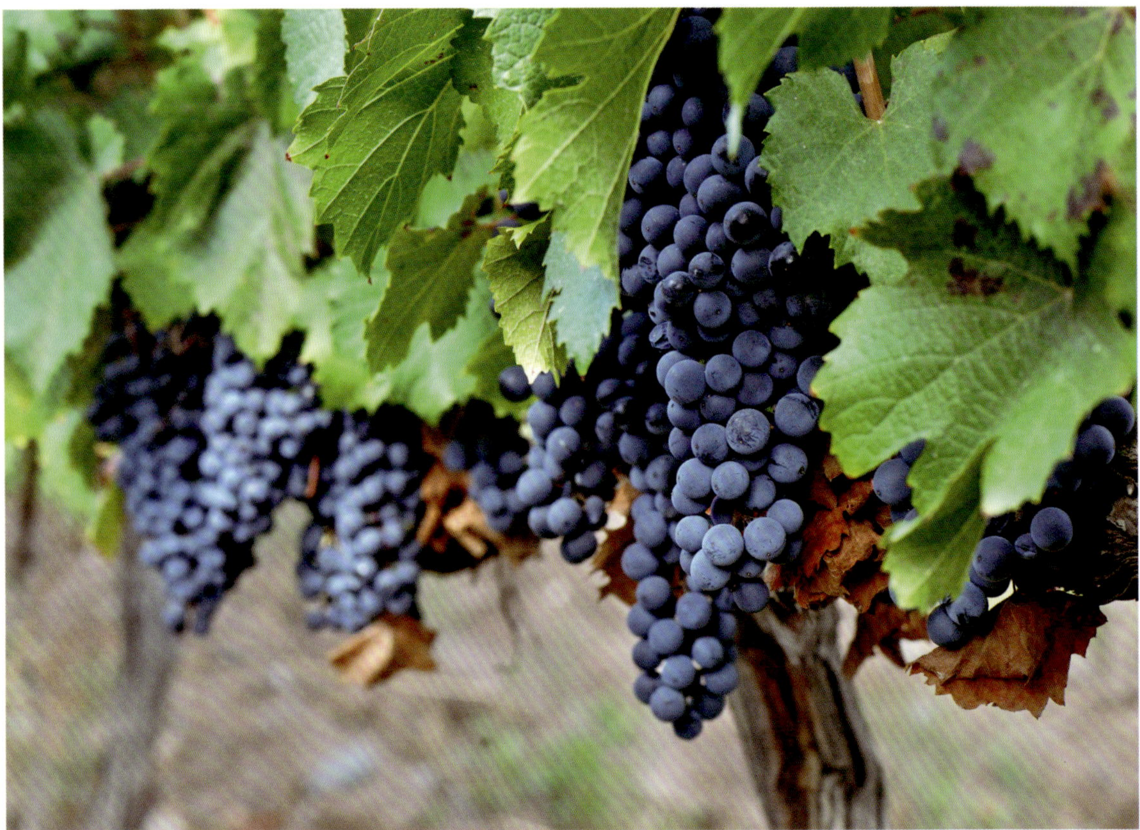

Uvas de vino malbec
Malbec wine grapes

Visit to Mendozas Bodegas

There are about 1200 wineries around
Mendoza and three-quarters of
Argentinean wines come from here. Thanks
to large investments, the number of visitors
is increasing. On the wine route, which
leads through beautiful countryside, with
views of the snow-capped mountains, you
can get to know traditional and modern
wine production in about 80 bodegas.
Most wineries are family businesses,
some of which have been producing wine
since the end of the 19th century. Besides
Malbec, Cabernet and Pinot Noir are mainly
cultivated. The deep red, intense color of
the dark grapes and the wine in the glass
is captivating.

En visite dans les bodegas de Mendoza

Environ 1200 vignobles sont cultivés
dans la région de Mendoza. Trois quarts
des vins argentins y sont produits et
d'importants investissements ont favorisé
la venue des visiteurs. En suivant la route
du vin, au cœur d'un splendide paysage
offrant une vue imprenable sur les
montagnes enneigées, l'amateur découvre
la production viticole moderne et ancienne
au cœur d'environ 80 bodegas. La majorité
des exploitations sont des entreprises
familiales qui, pour certaines, produisent du
vin depuis le xixᵉ siècle. Outre le malbec, ce
sont les cépages cabernet et pinot noir qui
y sont principalement cultivés. La couleur
intense rouge sombre des raisins et du vin
est particulièrement séduisante.

Zu Besuch in Mendozas Bodegas

Rund 1200 Weingüter gibt es rund um
Mendoza. Dreiviertel der argentinischen
Weine kommen aus Mendoza. Dank großer
Investitionen steigt die Besucherzahl. Auf
der Weinroute, die durch tolle Landschaft
mit Blick in die schneebedeckten Berge
führt, kann man in ca. 80 Bodegas die
traditionelle und moderne Weinproduktion
kennenlernen. Die meisten Winzereien
sind Familienbetriebe, die teils seit Ende
des 19. Jahrhunderts Wein keltern. Neben
Melbec werden hauptsächlich Cabernet
und Pinot Noir angebaut. Bestechend ist
die tiefrote, intensive Farbe der dunklen
Trauben und des Weins im Glas.

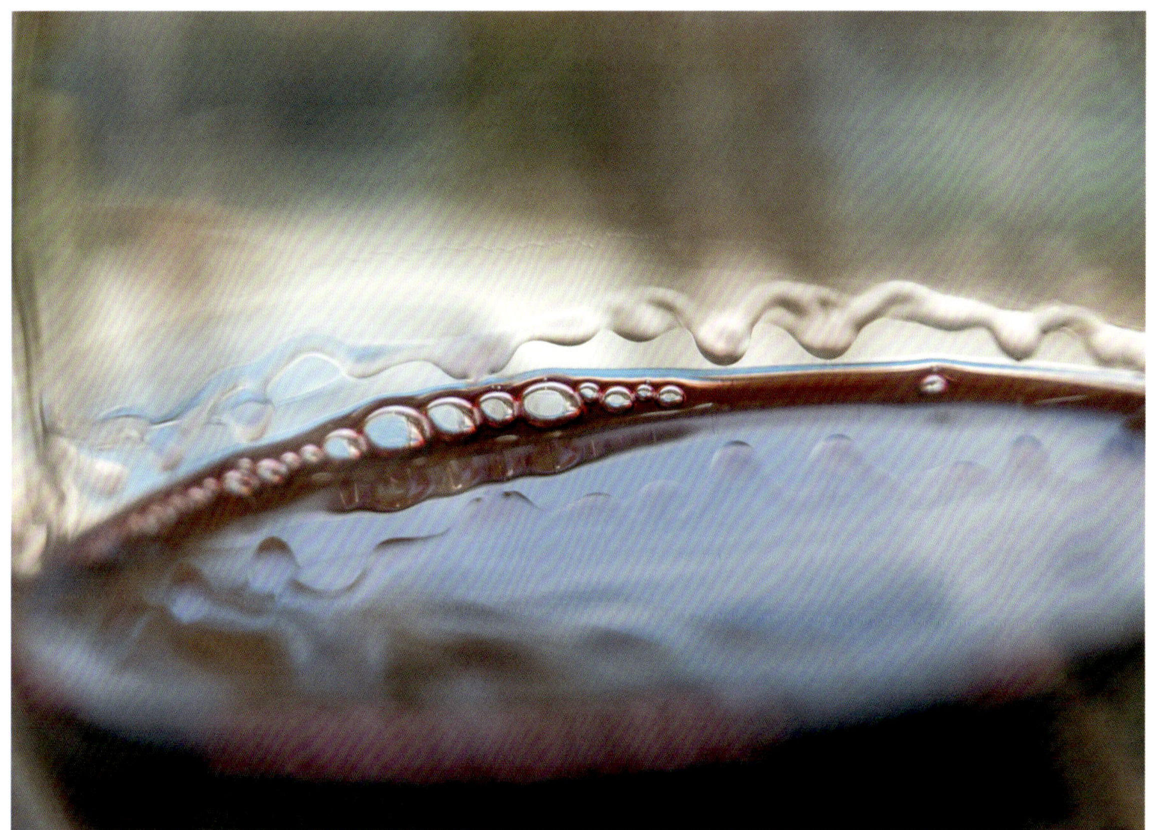

Vino
Wine

Visita a las bodegas de Mendoza

Hay aproximadamente 1200 bodegas alrededor de Mendoza. Tres cuartos de los vinos argentinos provienen de esta provincia. Gracias a las grandes inversiones, el número de visitantes está aumentando. En la ruta del vino, que atraviesa un hermoso paisaje con vistas a las montañas nevadas, se puede conocer la producción de vino tradicional y moderno en unas 80 bodegas. La mayoría de ellas son empresas familiares, algunas de las cuales han estado prensando vino desde finales del siglo XIX. Además de la uva malbec, se cultivan principalmente cabernet y pinot noir. El color rojo profundo e intenso de las uvas oscuras y el vino en la copa es cautivador.

Visita às Bodegas de Mendoza

Há cerca de 1200 vinícolas em Mendoza. Três quartos dos vinhos argentinos são provenientes de Mendoza. Graças a grandes investimentos, o número de visitantes está a aumentar. Na rota do vinho, que leva a uma excelente paisagem com vista para as montanhas cobertas de neve, você pode conhecer a produção tradicional e moderna de vinho em cerca de 80 bodegas. A maioria das adegas são empresas familiares, algumas das quais produzem vinho desde o final do século XIX. Além de Melbec, são cultivados principalmente Cabernet e Pinot Noir. A cor vermelha profunda e intensa das uvas escuras e do vinho no copo é cativante.

Bezoek aan Mendoza bodegas

Rondom Mendoza bevinden zich ongeveer 1200 landgoederen met wijngaarden. Driekwart van de Argentijnse wijnen komt uit Mendoza. Dankzij grote investeringen stijgt het aantal bezoekers. Op de wijnroute, die door een prachtig landschap met uitzicht op de besneeuwde bergen loopt, kan men in ca. 80 bodega's kennismaken met de traditionele en moderne wijnproductie. De meeste wijnmakers zijn familiebedrijven waarvan sommige al sinds het einde van de 19e eeuw wijn persen. Naast Melbec worden vooral Cabernet en Pinot Noir aangebouwd. Aantrekkelijk is de dieprode, intense kleur van de donkere druiven en van de wijn in het glas.

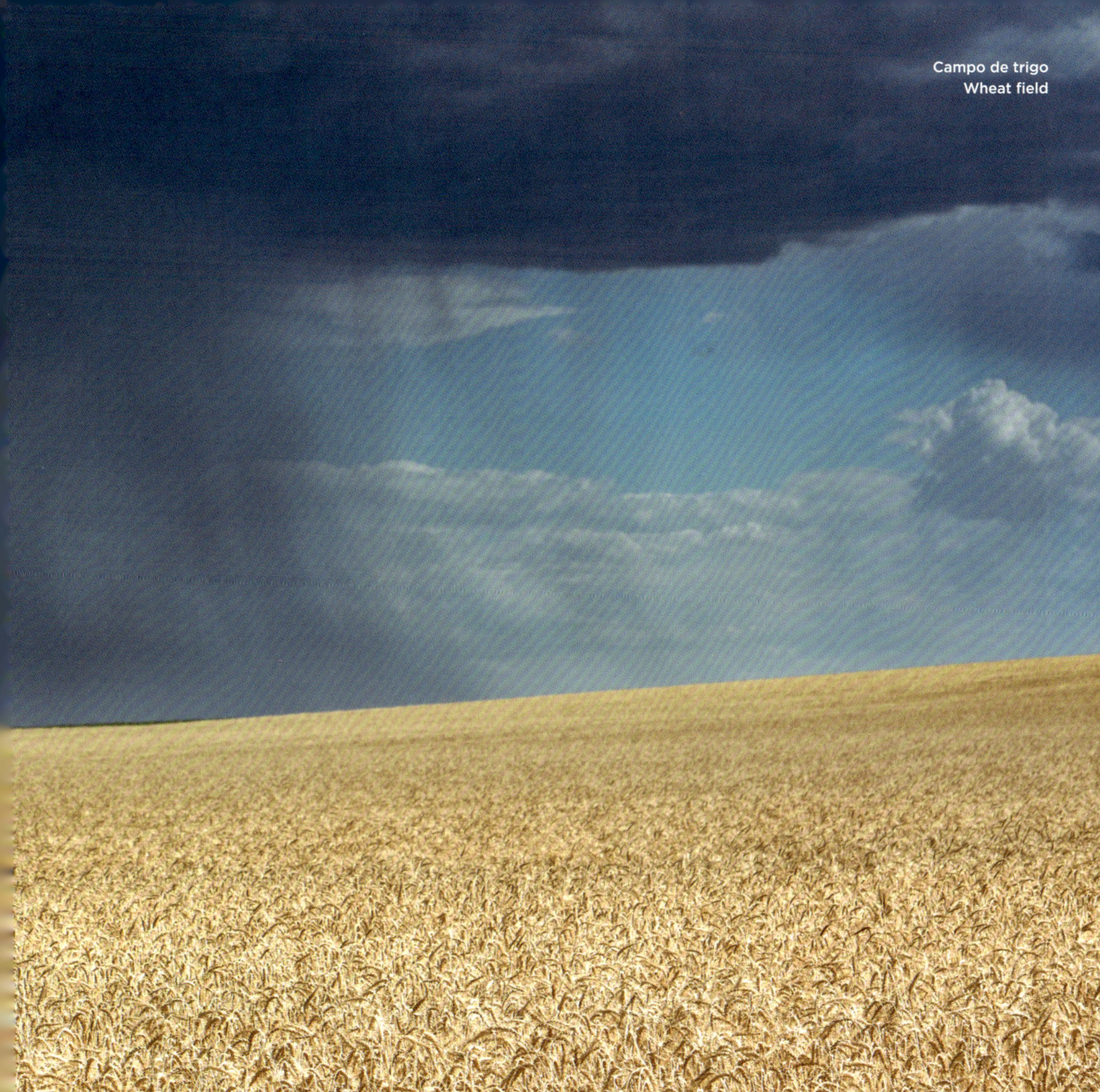

Campo de trigo
Wheat field

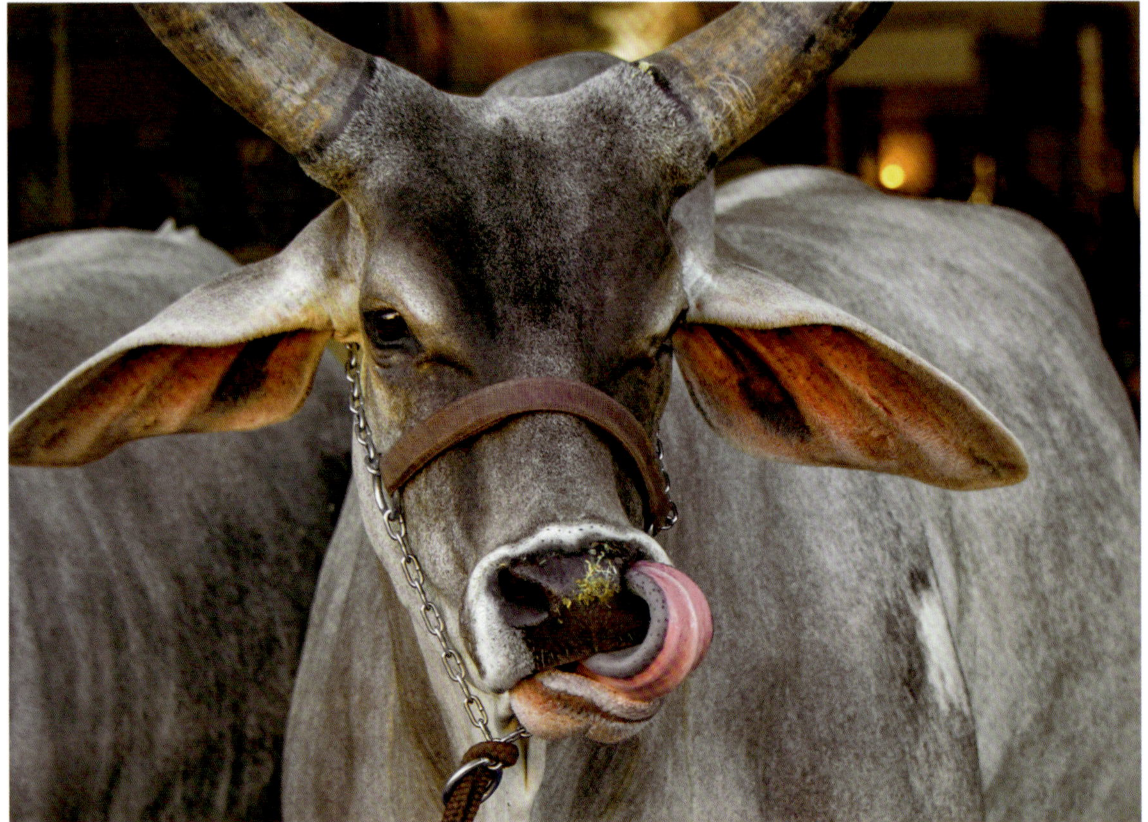

Cebú
Zebu

La Pampa

The province in the centre of the country is considered by many to epitomize Argentina because of its deserted, endless expanse. Only in the 18th century did the Spanish colonizers succeed in settling the region, against the fierce resistance of the natives. It is the granary and pantry of the country. More dense settlement is found only in the east near the city of Santa Rosa, which was chosen as the capital of the province of La Pampa in 1952, when it became independent. Zebu cattle, a particularly corpulent and hardy breed, withstand the harsh climate of the West. Gauchos complete the picture of the pampas.

La Pampa

Avec ses étendues infinies très peu peuplées, cette province au centre du pays incarne pour beaucoup l'essence de l'Argentine. Les conquistadors espagnols ne parvinrent à coloniser la région qu'au XVIII siècle, face à la forte résistance des peuples natifs. La province est aujourd'hui le grenier et le cellier du pays. La population se densifie uniquement à l'est, à proximité de Santa Rosa. La ville fut couronnée capitale régionale au moment de la fondation de la province de La Pampa en 1952. Les bovins de race zébu, particulièrement corpulents et résistants, supportent très bien le climat rude et froid des terres de l'Ouest. Les *gauchos* font partie de l'imagerie de La Pampa.

La Pampa

Die Provinz im Zentrum des Landes gilt vielen aufgrund der menschenleeren, unendlichen Weite als Inbegriff Argentiniens. Erst im 18. Jahrhundert gelang es den spanischen Kolonisatoren, die Region gegen den heftigen Widerstand der Ureinwohner zu besiedeln. Sie ist die Korn- und Speisekammer des Landes. Dichtere Besiedelung findet sich nur im Osten nahe der Stadt Santa Rosa. Sie wurde im Zuge der Eigenständigkeit der Provinz La Pampa 1952 zur Hauptstadt gekürt. Zebu-Rinder, eine besonders korpulente und widerstandsfähige Rasse, halten dem kühlen, rauen Klima im Westen stand. Gauchos gehören zum Bild der Pampa.

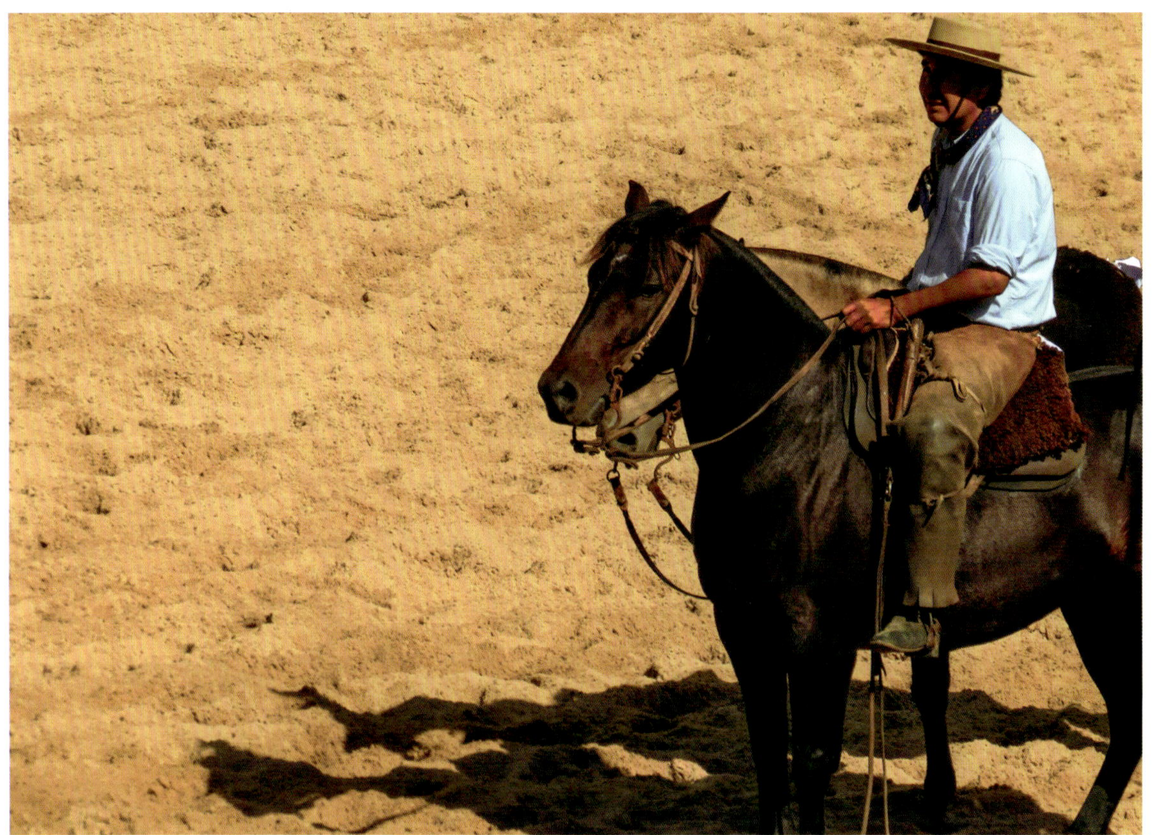

Gaucho

La Pampa

La provincia del centro del país es considerada por muchos como el epítome de Argentina por su extensión desértica e interminable. Solo en el siglo XVIII los colonizadores españoles consiguieron asentar la región contra la feroz resistencia de los nativos. Es el granero y la despensa del país. Un asentamiento más denso se encuentra solo en el este, cerca de la ciudad de Santa Rosa. Fue elegida como capital de La Pampa en 1952 cuando ésta se independizó. El ganado cebú, una raza particularmente corpulenta y resistente, soporta el clima fresco y duro del oeste. Los gauchos son una de las imágenes más típicas de La Pampa.

La Pampa

A província no centro do país é considerada por muitos como a epítome da Argentina, devido à sua vastidão desabitada. Somente no século XVIII os colonizadores espanhóis conseguiram colonizar a região contra a feroz resistência dos nativos. É o celeiro e a despensa do país. Só no leste, perto da cidade de Santa Rosa, encontra-se um povoado mais denso. Foi escolhida como a capital da província de La Pampa em 1952, quando se tornou independente. O gado zebu, uma raça particularmente corpulenta e resistente, suporta o clima frio e rigoroso do oeste. Os gaúchos pertencem à imagem dos pampas.

La Pampa

Door haar verlaten, eindeloze vergezichten wordt de provincie in het centrum van het land door velen als het toonbeeld van Argentinië beschouwd. Pas in de 18e eeuw lukten het de Spaanse kolonisatoren de regio tegen het felle verzet van de oerinwoners te koloniseren. Het is de graanschuur en de voorraadkamer van het land. Dichtere nederzettingen zijn alleen te vinden in het oosten bij de stad Santa Rosa. Deze werd als gevolg van de onafhankelijkheid van de provincie La Pampa in 1952 tot hoofdstad verkozen. Zeboe runderen, een bijzonder corpulent en sterk ras, zijn bestand tegen het koele, harde klimaat in het westen van het land. Gauchos behoren tot het beeld van de Pampa.

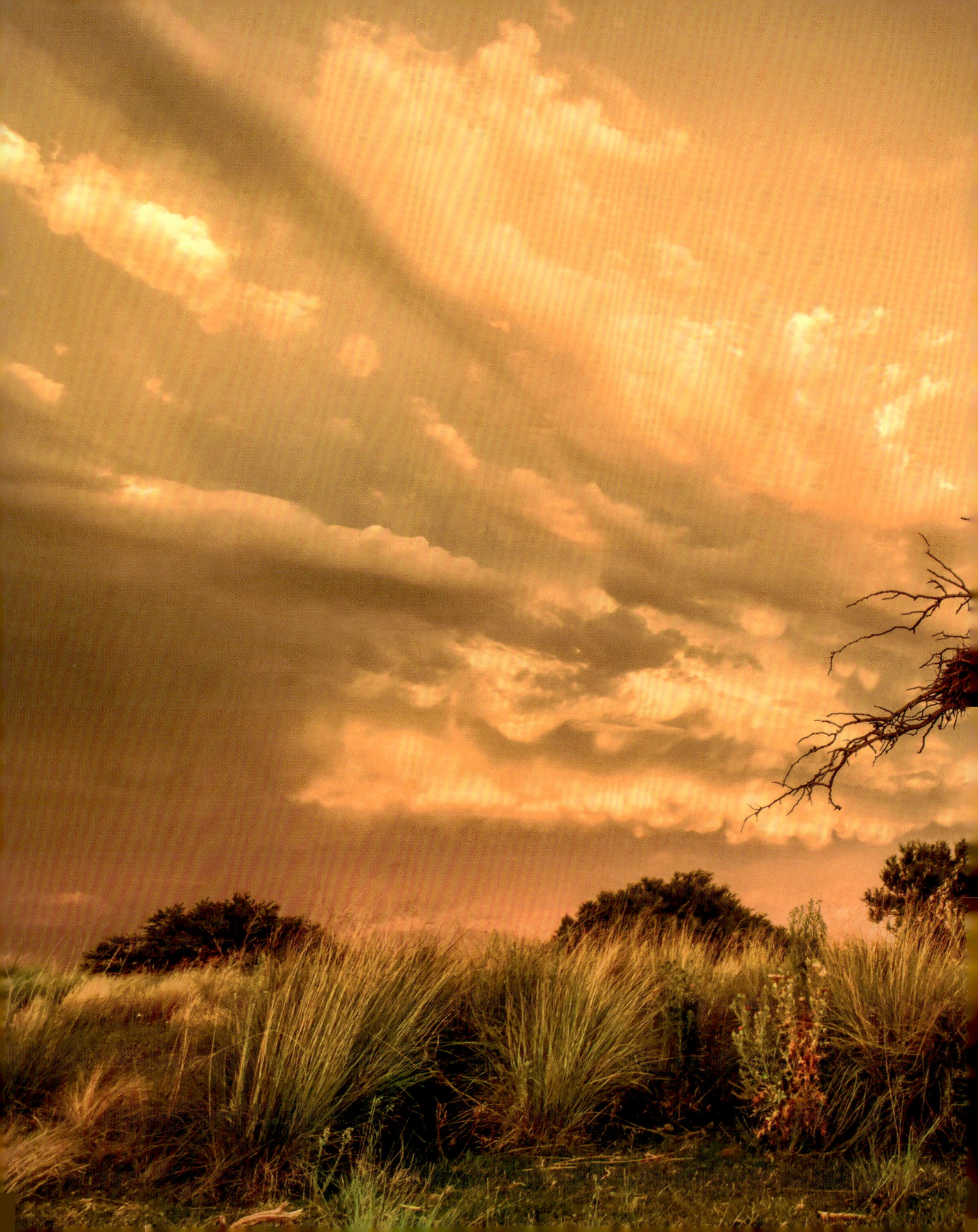

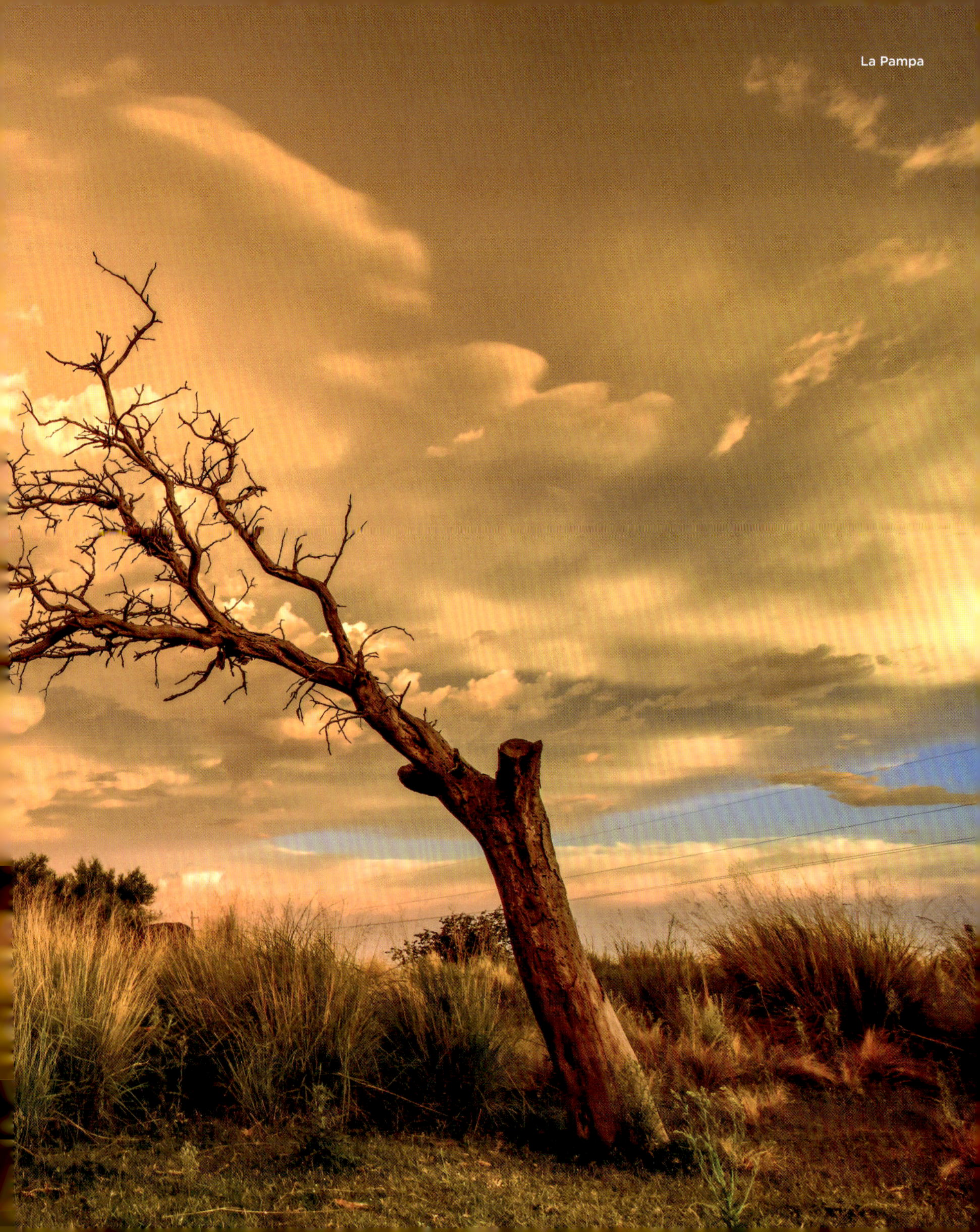
La Pampa

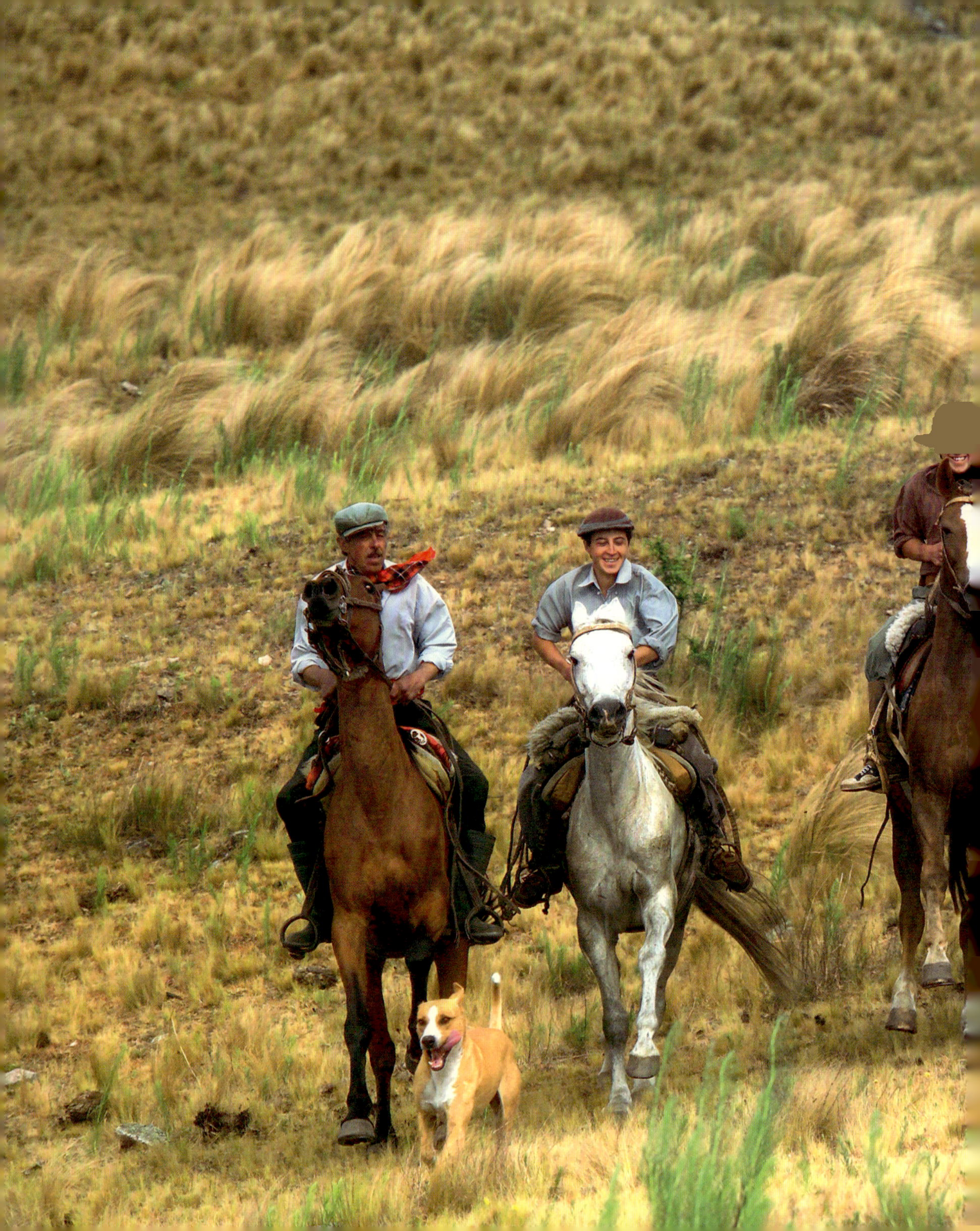

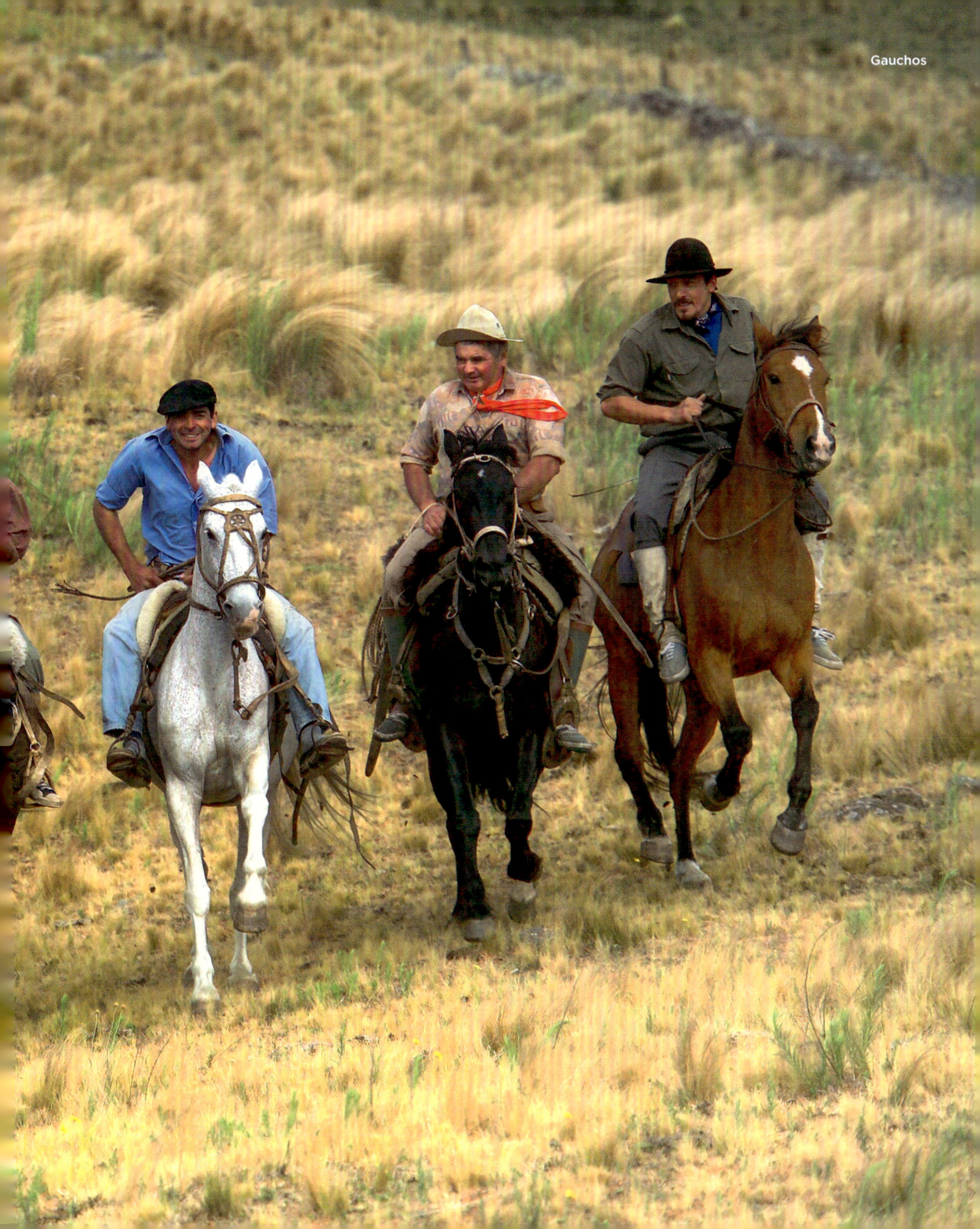
Gauchos

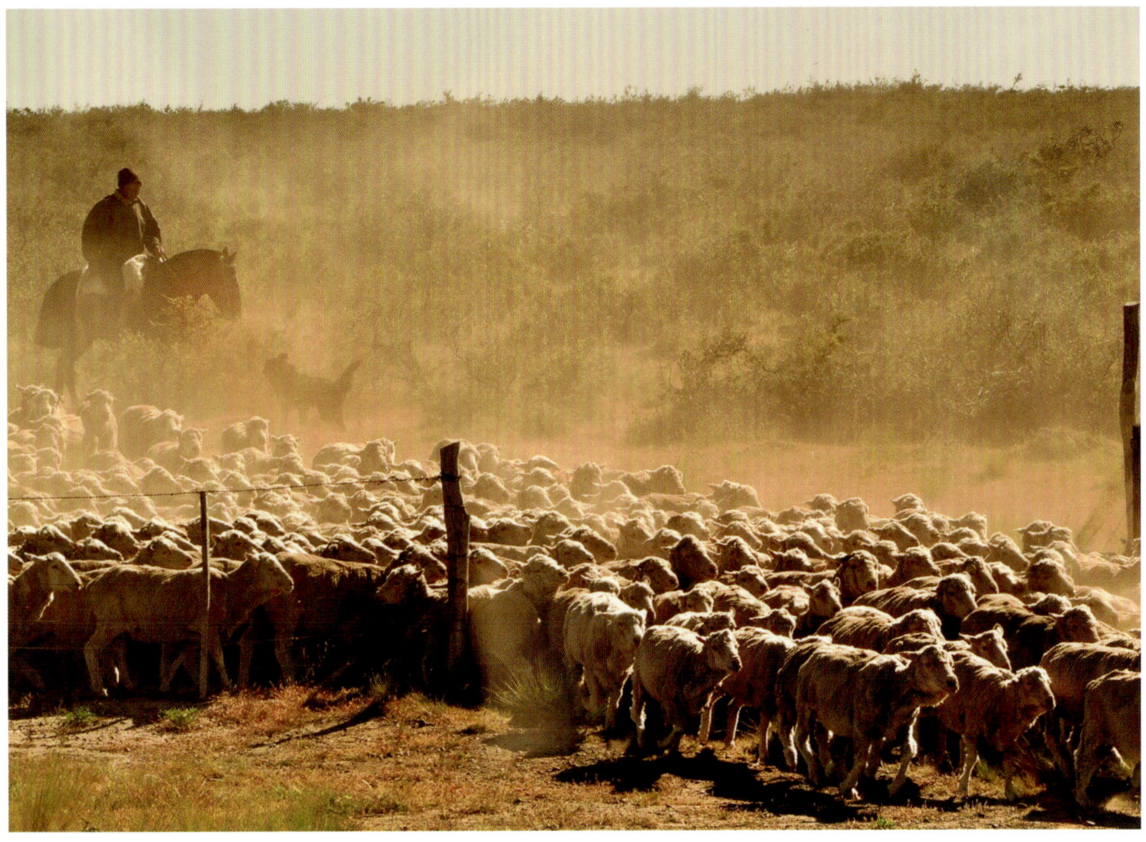

Gaucho con rebaño de ovejas
Gaucho with herd of sheep

Animal husbandry

Livestock farming in the region dates back to the 16th century, when settlers from Peru and Paraguay brought their herds and roamed the country as nomads, in search of good pastures. It was not until the middle of the 18th century that modern, lucrative livestock farming with fences and enclosures began. Dry soils and grass growth in the western part, which is a salt steppe, are more suited to the frugal sheep and goats. La Pampa has 203,000 sheep and 141,000 goats. In spite of the large herds, only a few hands are needed for work. When complex tasks, e.g. shearing the sheep, are required, seasonal workers are employed.

Élevage

L'élevage a débuté dans la région au XVIe siècle. Les colons venus du Pérou et du Paraguay y introduisirent leurs troupeaux alors qu'ils parcouraient le pays en nomades à la recherche de bons pâturages. Ce n'est qu'au XVIIIe siècle que débuta la production animale moderne lucrative, avec parcage et enclos. Les terres et la végétation sèches de la steppe salée de l'Ouest conviennent aux ovins et aux caprins. La région de La Pampa compte 203 000 moutons et 141 000 chèvres. Les immenses troupeaux ne requièrent cependant que peu de main-d'œuvre. Des saisonniers sont employés chaque année pour certaines tâches, notamment la tonte des moutons.

Viehwirtschaft

Die Viehwirtschaft der Region geht auf das 16. Jahrhundert zurück, als Siedler aus Peru und Paraguay ihre Herden mitbrachten und auf der Suche nach guten Weiden als Nomaden durch das Land zogen. Erst Mitte des 18. Jahrhundert begann die moderne, lukrative Viehwirtschaft mit Zäunen und Gehegen. Trockene Böden und Graswuchs im westlichen Teil, der eine Salzsteppe ist, eignen sich für die genügsamen Schafe und Ziegen. Mit 203 000 Schafen und 141 000 Ziegen kann La Pampa aufwarten. Trotz der großen Herden bedarf es nur weniger Hände Arbeit. Wenn aufwendige Aufgaben, z. B. die Schur der Schafe, anstehen, werden saisonale Kräfte angestellt.

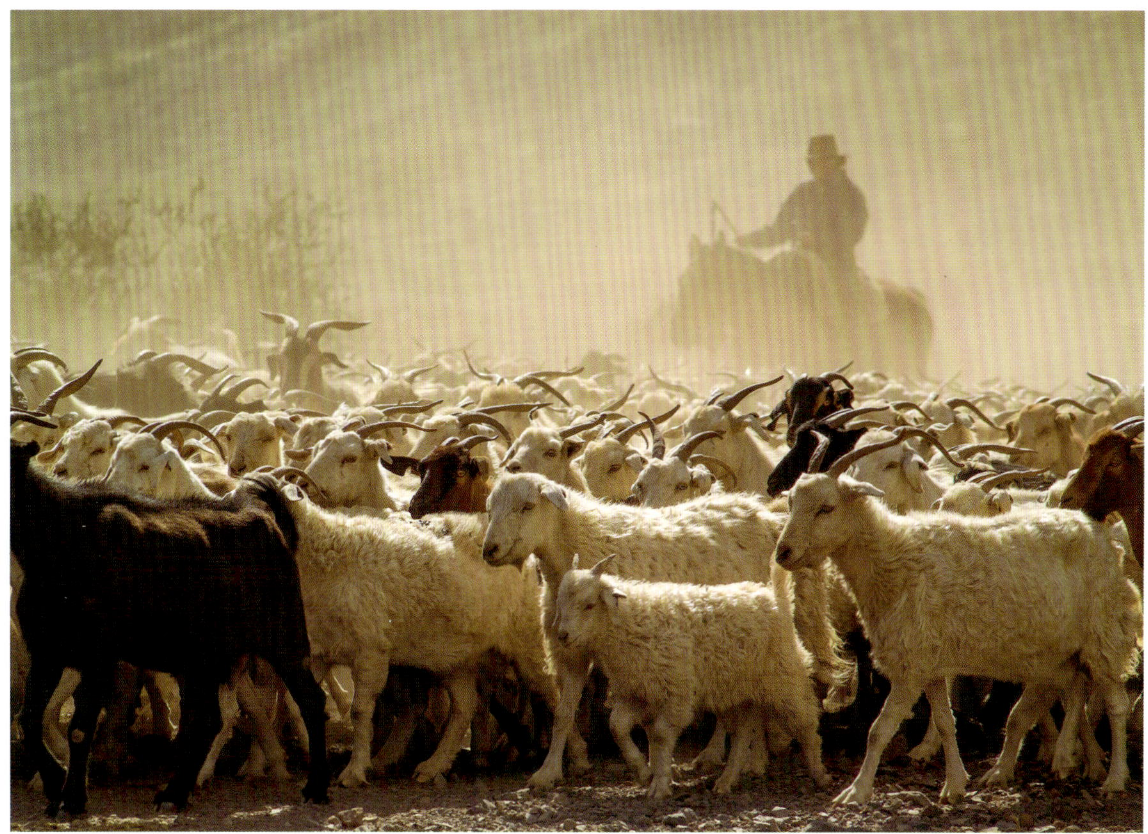

Gaucho con rebaño de cabras
Gaucho with herd of goats

Ganadería

La ganadería en la región se remonta al siglo XVI, cuando los colonos de Perú y Paraguay trajeron sus rebaños y recorrieron el país como nómadas en busca de buenos pastos. Hasta mediados del siglo XVIII no comenzó la moderna y lucrativa ganadería con vallas y cercados. Los suelos secos y el crecimiento de la hierba en la parte occidental, que es una estepa salina, son adecuados para las ovejas y las cabras. En La Pampa hay 203 000 ovejas y 141 000 cabras. A pesar de los grandes rebaños, solo se necesitan unas pocas manos para trabajar. Cuando se requieren tareas complejas, por ejemplo, esquila de ovejas, se recurre a trabajadores temporales.

Criação de gado

A pecuária na região data do século XVI, quando colonos do Peru e do Paraguai trouxeram seus rebanhos e percorreram o país como nômades em busca de bons pastos. Foi só em meados do século XVIII que começou a moderna e lucrativa pecuária com cercas e criação em cativeiros. Os solos secos e o crescimento da erva na parte ocidental, que é uma estepe salgada, são adequados para os ovinos e cabras frugais. La Pampa tem 203 000 ovelhas e 141 000 cabras. Apesar dos grandes rebanhos, apenas algumas mãos são necessárias para o trabalho. Para tarefas complexas, como por exemplo, a tosquia das ovelhas, são contratados trabalhadores sazonais.

Veehouderij

De veehouderij in de regio gaat terug tot de 16e eeuw, toen kolonisten uit Peru en Paraguay hun kuddes meenamen en als nomaden door het land zwierven op zoek naar goede weidegronden. Pas in het midden van de 18e eeuw begon de moderne, lucratieve veehouderij met hekken en omheiningen. Droge gronden en grasgroei in het westelijke deel, dat een zoutsteppe is, zijn geschikt voor de schapen en geiten die met weinig tevreden zijn. La Pampa telt 203 000 schapen en 141 000 geiten. Ondanks de grote kuddes zijn er maar weinig werkkrachten nodig. Bij grotere werkzaamheden zoals het scheren van de schapen, worden seizoenwerkers ingezet.

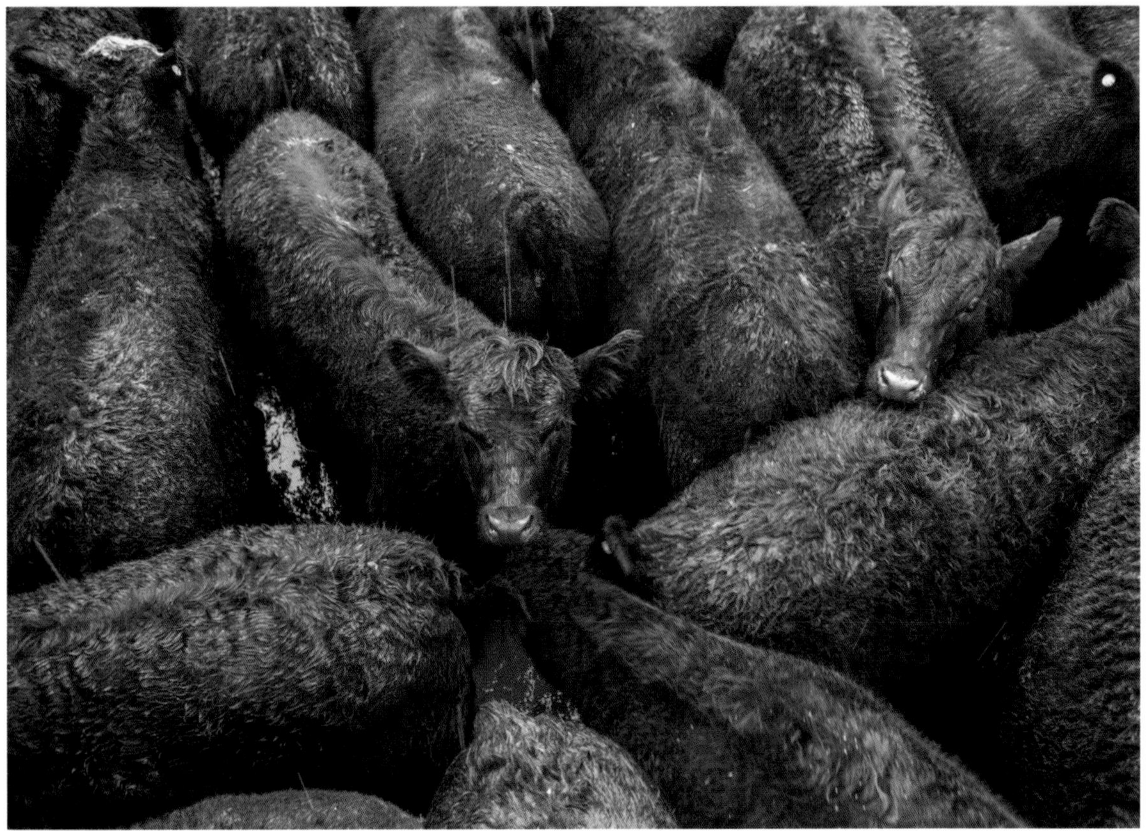

Welsh Black

The wild life

Among the cattle breeds, the Welsh Black cattle, originating from Wales, stand out in particular. Its scientific name is *Bos taurus,* which describes the stature of this strong animal excellently. Welsh Black cattle provide much high quality marbled meat, with cows of this breed weighing 800 kg (1764 lb) and bulls up to 1250 kg (2756 lb). The owner of a large herd of Welsh Black can look forward to a very lucrative business, as the demand in Argentina and abroad is enormous.

La vie au grand air

Parmi les espèces bovines, la welsh black, d'origine galloise, se remarque particulièrement. Son nom scientifique, *bos taurus,* évoque la stature de cet animal puissant. Le bœuf welsh black offre, en quantité, une viande marbrée de grande qualité. Les femelles pèsent 800 kg et les mâles jusqu'à 1250 kg. Le propriétaire d'un grand troupeau de welsh black se trouve à la tête d'une activité fort lucrative, car la demande en Argentine et à l'étranger est énorme.

Das wilde Leben

Unter den Rinderrassen ragt das Welsh-Black-Rind oder Waliser Schwarzvieh aus Wales besonders hervor. Sein wissenschaftlicher Name lautet *Bos taurus,* er beschreibt die Statur dieses kräftigen Tiers vortrefflich. Welsh-Black-Rinder bescheren nicht nur viel, sondern dazu auch hochqualitatives, marmoriertes Fleisch. Kühe dieser Rasse bringen 800 kg und Bullen bis 1250 kg auf die Waage. Dem Besitzer einer großen Herde Welsh-Black winkt ein äußerst lukratives Geschäft, denn die Nachfrage in Argentinien und im Ausland ist riesengroß.

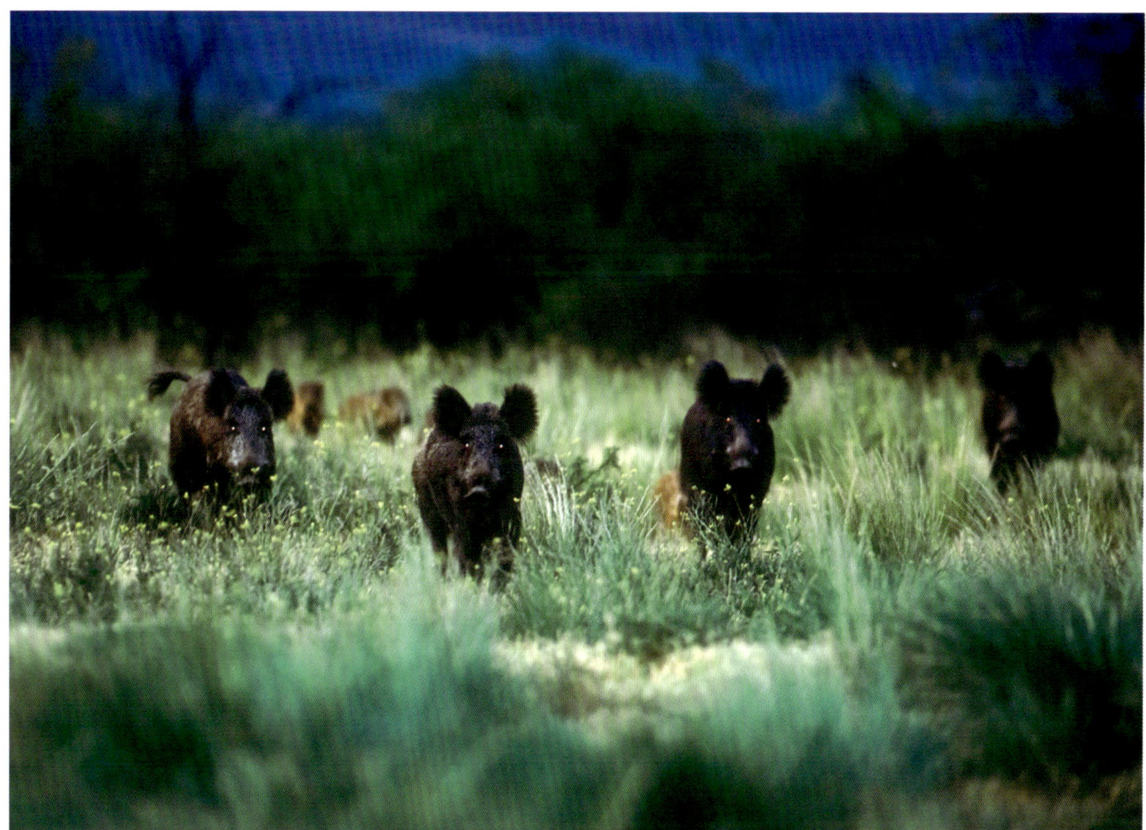

Jabalíes
Wild boars

La vida salvaje

Entre las razas de ganado, destaca el Welsh Black. Su nombre científico es *Bos taurus,* que describe de forma excelente la estatura de este fuerte animal. El ganado negro galés no solo ofrece grandes cantidades de carne marmoleada, sino también de alta calidad. Las vacas de esta raza pesan 800 kg y los toros hasta 1250 kg. El propietario de una gran manada de Welsh Black espera un negocio muy lucrativo, ya que la demanda tanto en Argentina como en el extranjero es enorme.

A vida selvagem

Entre as raças de gado, destaca-se o Gado Negro Galês ou Gado Negro Galense. O seu nome científico é *Bos taurus,* ele descreve de forma excelente a estatura deste animal forte. O gado negro galês não só fornece muita carne marmoreada, mas também de alta qualidade. As vacas desta raça pesam 800 kg e os touros até 1250 kg. O dono de uma grande manada de negros galeses atrai um negócio extremamente lucrativo, porque a demanda na Argentina e no exterior é enorme.

Het wilde leven

Onder de runderrassen steekt het Welsh Black rund of Welsh Black Cattle uit Wales boven alles uit. Zijn wetenschappelijke naam luidt *Bos taurus* en beschrijft de gestalte van dit sterke dier uitstekend. Welsh Black runderen leveren niet alleen veel, maar ook zeer kwalitatief, gemarmerd vlees op. Koeien van dit ras wegen 800 kg en stieren tot 1250 kg. De eigenaar van een grote kudde Welsh Black heeft een zeer lucratieve onderneming in het vooruitzicht, want de vraag in Argentinië en in het buitenland is enorm groot.

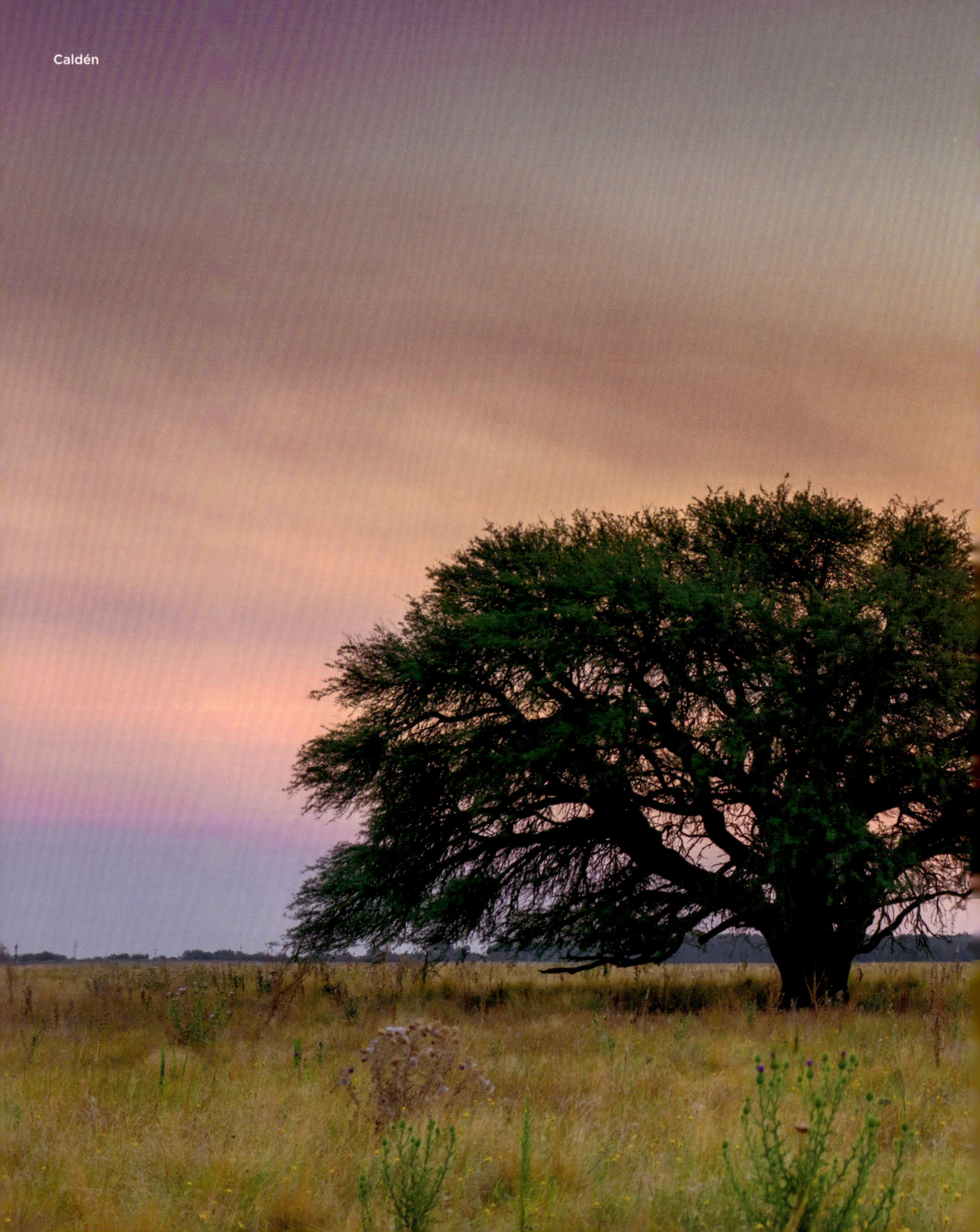
Caldén

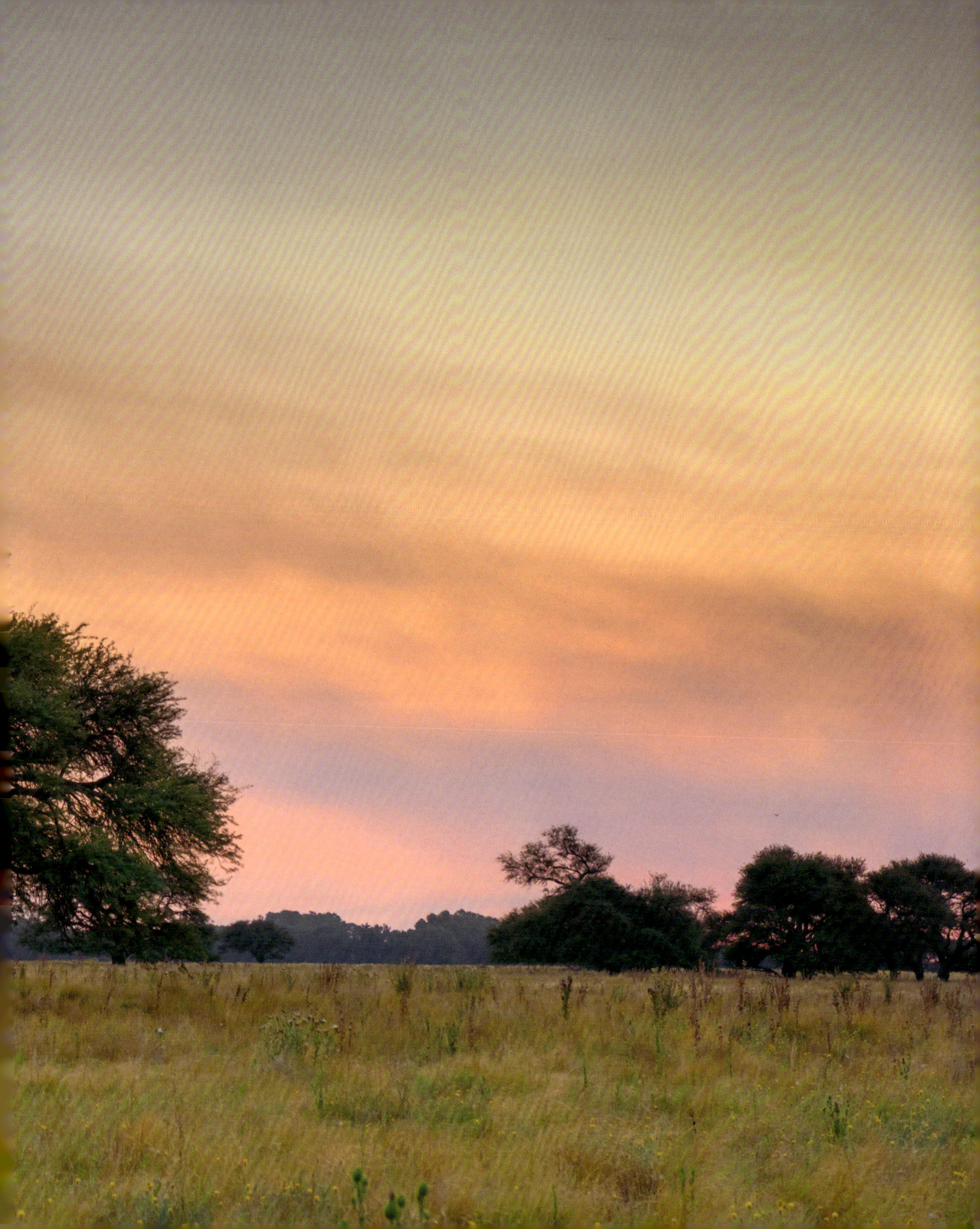

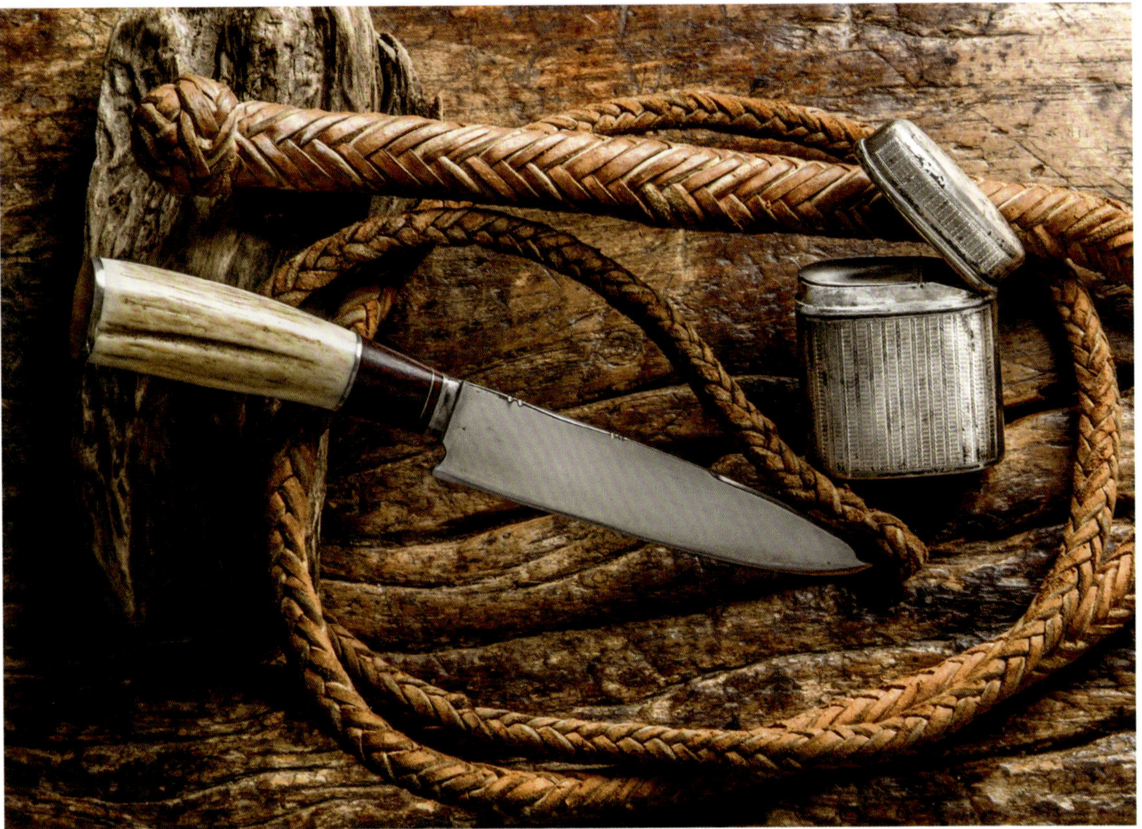

Cuchillo gaucho
Gaucho knife

Gaucho life

The typical equipment of a gaucho, who often rides in the saddle for weeks on end through the wind and weather herding cattle, includes high leather boots, a lasso, saddle and poncho as well as a large sharp knife, which fulfills many tasks. Gauchos are descendants of indigenous Indians and white settlers. They lived nomadically, like Indian ethnic groups, from hunting. From the sale of skins, some bought a silver belt, silver spurs or silver tins. In the aftermath of the fencing-off of the grazing land that had been free until 1845, they lost their livelihood and then had to work as cattle drivers and horse tamers. Despite the loss of their free life, they retained their pride.

Le mode de vie du *gaucho*

Le *gaucho* passe souvent plusieurs semaines d'affilée en selle, dans le vent et les intempéries, pour garder les troupeaux. Son équipement typique comprend des bottes de cuir hautes, un lasso, une selle et une peau animale, ainsi qu'un couteau aiguisé utile en toutes circonstances. Les *gauchos* sont des descendants des indigènes et des colons blancs. Ils menaient autrefois une vie nomade proche de celle des ethnies indiennes en pratiquant la chasse. Avec la vente des peaux, beaucoup s'achetaient des ceintures à boucle, des éperons ou des boîtes en argent. Leur moyen de subsistance disparut en 1845 avec le parcage des animaux autrefois en liberté. Contraints de travailler comme gardiens de troupeaux ou dresseurs de chevaux, ils ont perdu leur liberté, mais pas leur fierté.

Gaucholeben

Zur charakteristischen Ausstattung eines Gaucho, der oft wochenlang bei Wind und Wetter im Sattel sitzt, um Vieh zu treiben, gehören hohe Lederstiefel, Lasso, Sattel und Fell und das scharfe Messer, das viele Aufgaben erfüllt. Gauchos sind Nachfahren von indianischen Ureinwohnern und weißen Siedlern. Sie lebten nomadisch wie indianische Ethnien von der Jagd. Vom Verkauf der Felle kauften sich manche einen Silbergürtel, silberne Sporen oder Silberdosen. Im Zuge der Einzäunung der bis dahin freien Weideflächen 1845 verloren sie ihre Lebensgrundlage. Sie mussten als Viehtreiber und Pferdezähmer arbeiten. Trotz des Verlusts ihres freien Lebens behielten sie ihren Stolz.

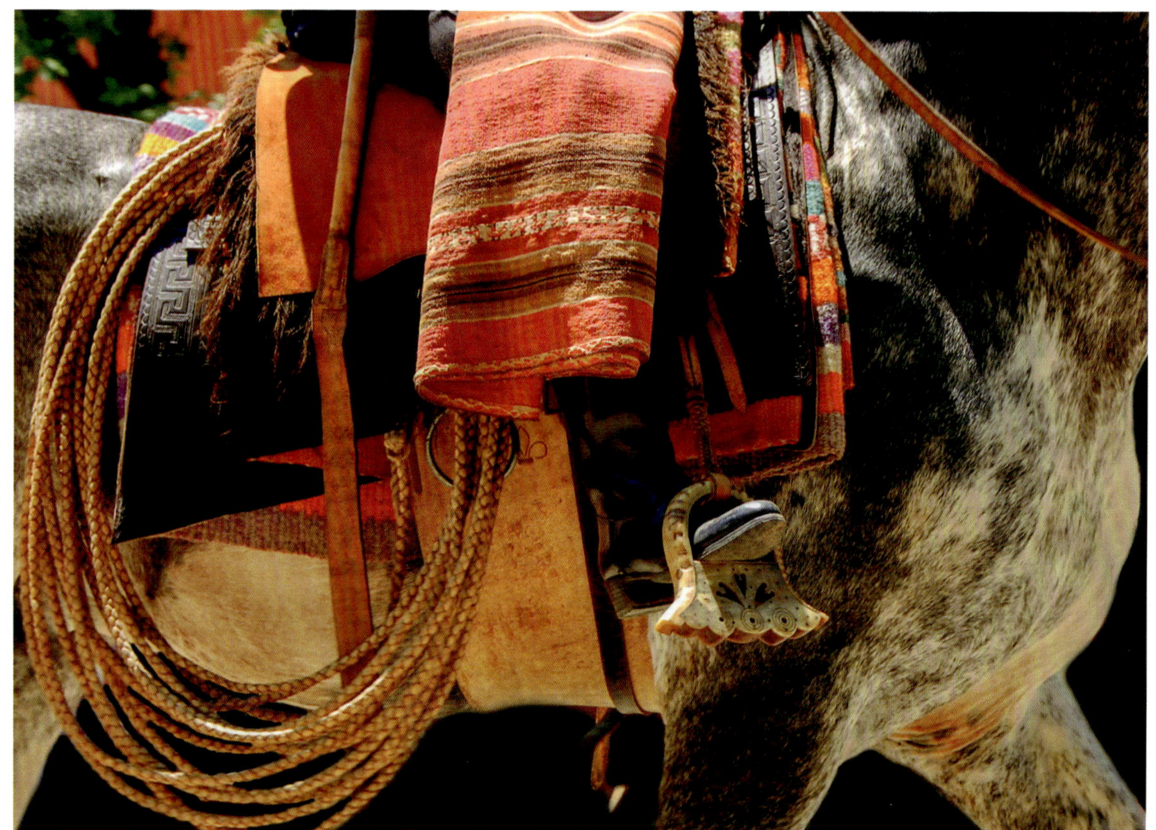

Silla con lazo
Saddle with lasso

Vida de los gauchos

El equipo característico de un gaucho, que
a menudo se sienta en la silla de montar
durante semanas para arrear ganado,
incluye botas altas de cuero, lazo, silla de
montar y pieles, y el afilado cuchillo, que
sirve para realizar numerosas tareas. Los
gauchos son descendientes de indígenas y
colonos blancos. Eran nómadas como las
etnias originarias y vivían de la caza. Con
la venta de las pieles, algunos compraban
un cinturón de plata, espuelas de plata
o latas de plata. En el transcurso de la
construcción de las vallas en los pastizales
que habían estado libres hasta entonces,
en 1845, perdieron su medio de vida.
Tenían que trabajar como arreadores de
ganado y domadores de caballos. A pesar
de la pérdida de su vida libre, conservaron
su orgullo.

Vida gaúcha

Os equipamentos característicos de um
gaúcho, que muitas vezes fica na sela por
semanas independente das condições
metereológicas para conduzir o rebanho
de gado, incluem botas altas de couro,
laço, sela e pêlo e a faca afiada, que é
usada para muitas tarefas. Os gaúchos são
descendentes de indígenas e de colonos
brancos. Eles viviam como nómades, como
os grupos étnicos indianos da caça. Com
a venda das peles, alguns compraram um
cinto de prata, esporas de prata ou latas
de prata. Devido à demarcação das áreas
de pastagem, que até então eram livres,
em 1845, perderam os seus meios de
subsistência. Eles tiveram que trabalhar
como condutores de gado e domadores de
cavalos. Apesar da perda da sua vida livre,
eles mantiveram o seu orgulho.

Gaucho leven

Tot de karakteristieke uitrusting van
een gaucho, die vaak in weer en wind
wekenlang in het zadel zit om vee
te hoeden, horen hoge leren laarzen,
lasso, zadel en vacht en het scherpe
mes dat veel taken vervult. Gaucho's
zijn afstammelingen van de Indiaanse
oerinwoners en blanke kolonisten. Ze
leefden nomadisch, zoals Indiaanse
etnische groepen van de jacht. Uit
de verkoop van de vachten kochten
sommigen een zilveren riem, zilveren
sporen of zilveren doosjes. Als gevolg
van de omheining van de tot dan toe vrije
weidegronden in 1845 verloren ze hun
broodwinning. Ze moesten als veedrijvers
en paardentemmers werken. Ondanks het
verlies van hun vrije leven, behielden ze
hun trots.

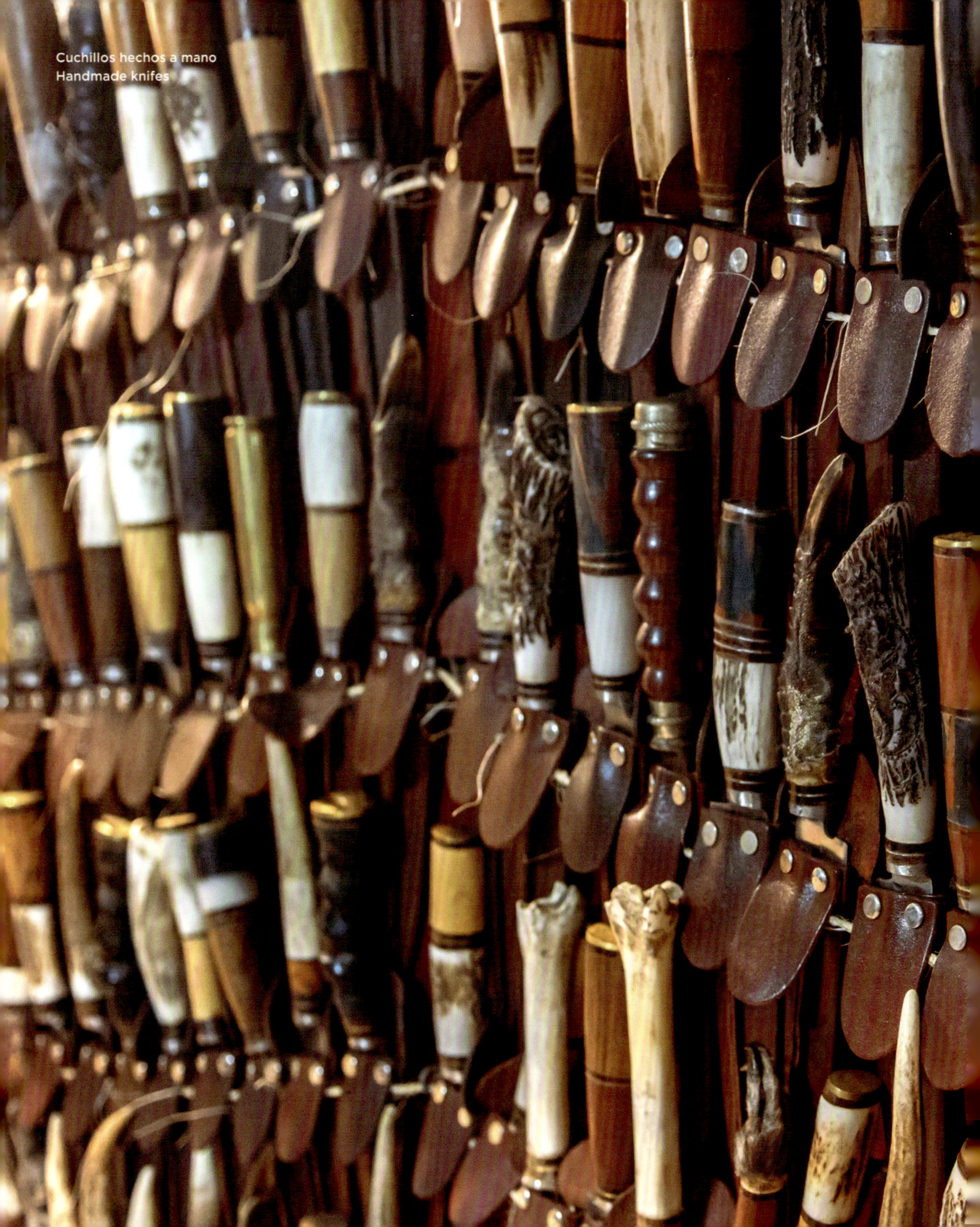
Cuchillos hechos a mano
Handmade knifes

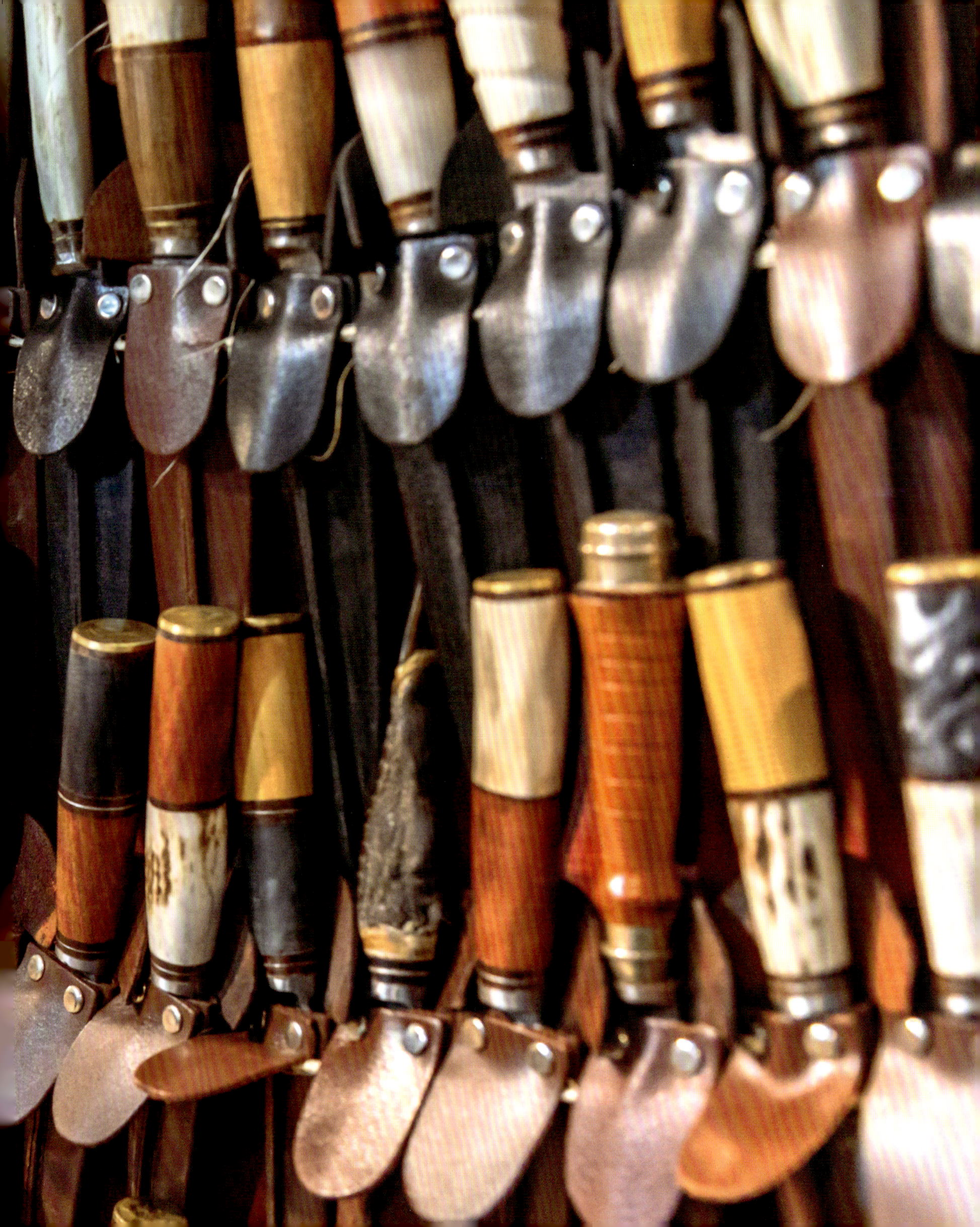

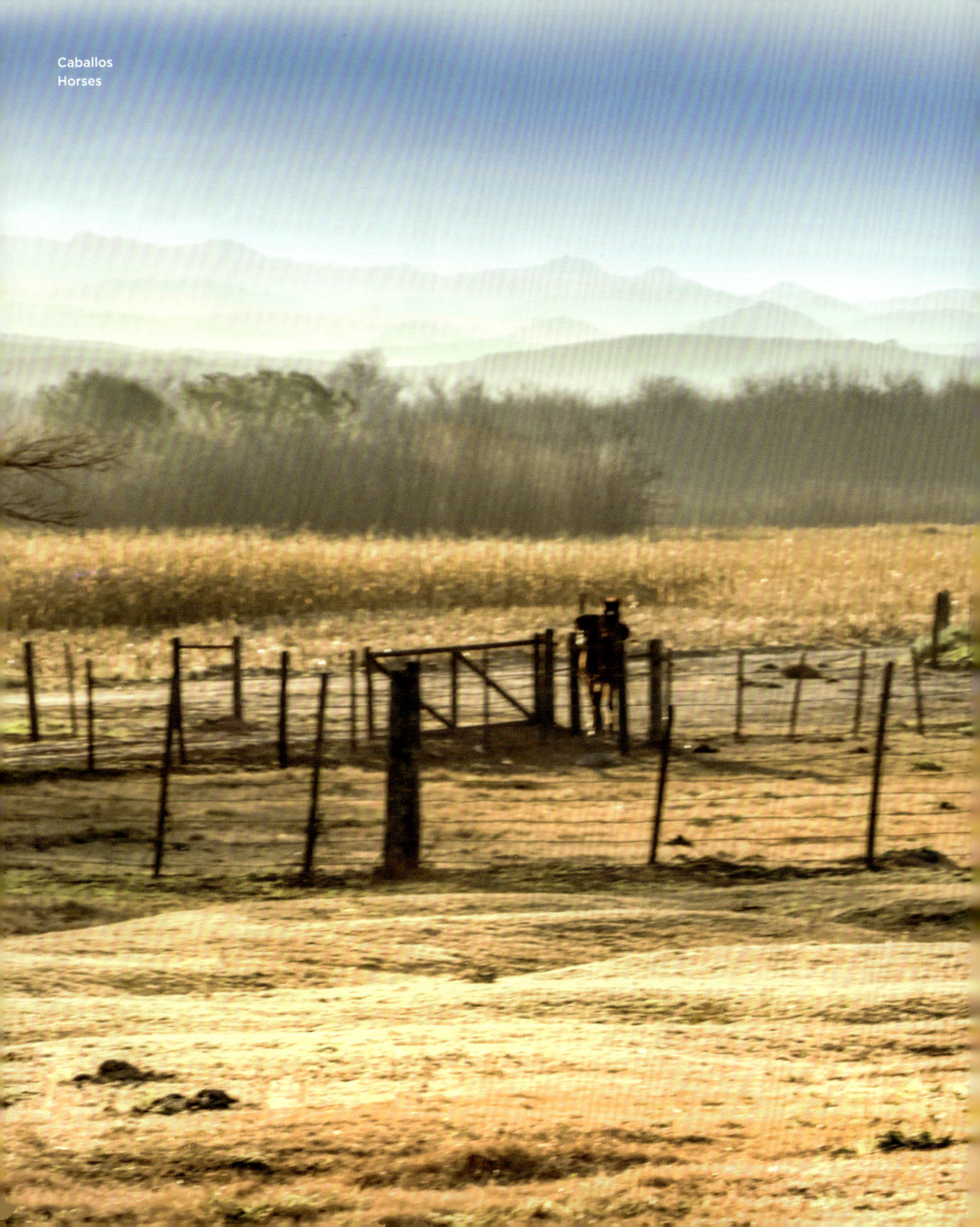

Caballos
Horses

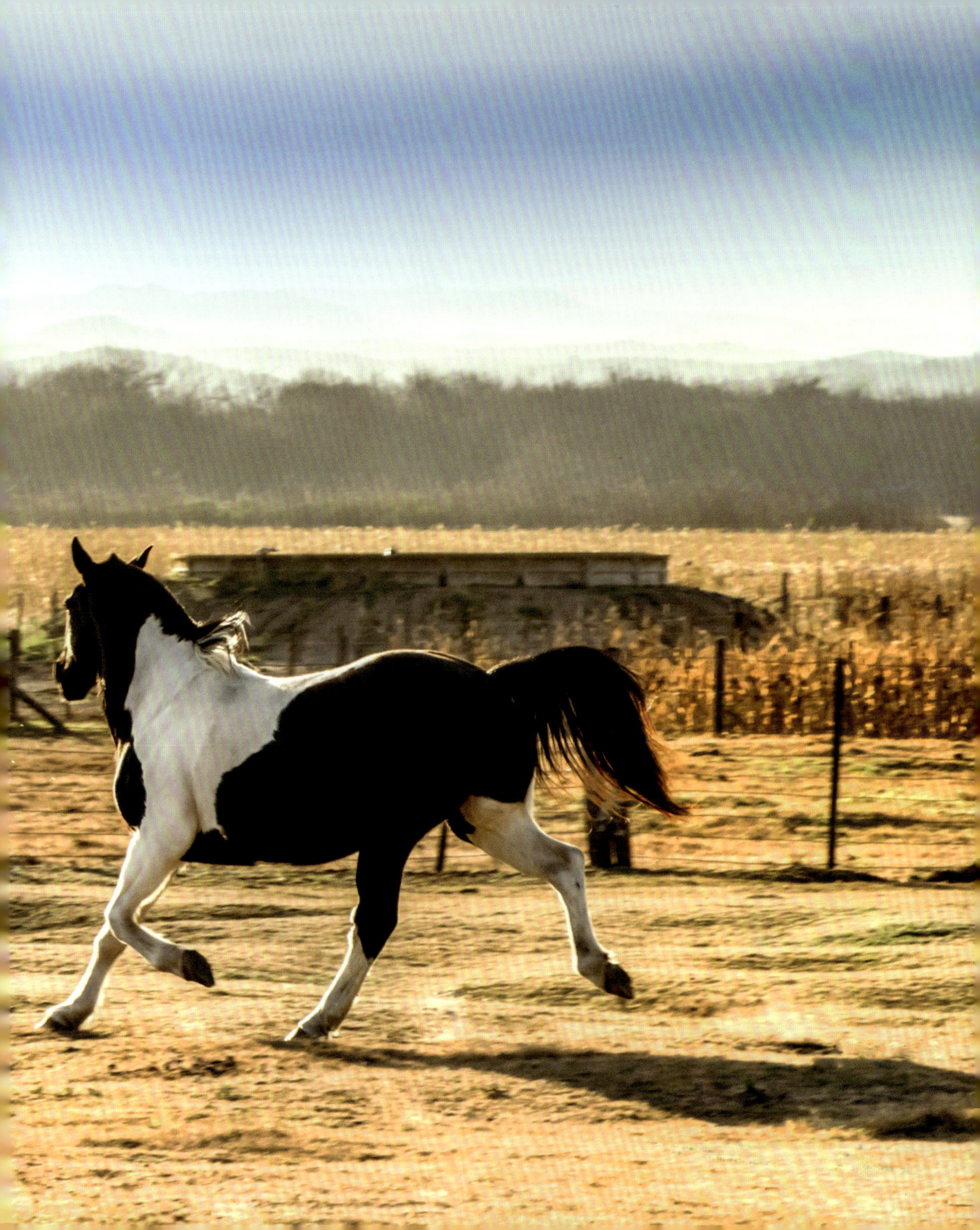

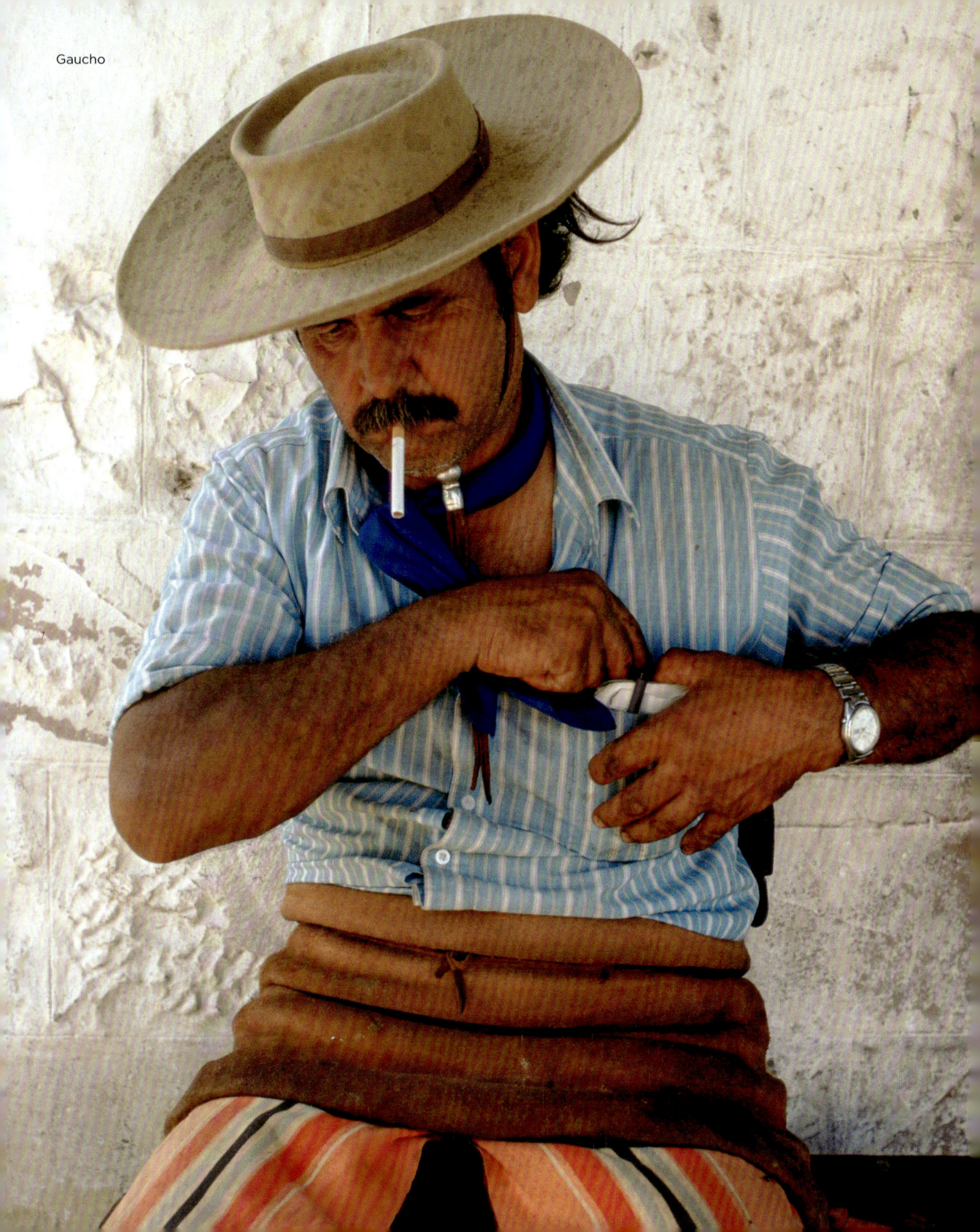

Gaucho

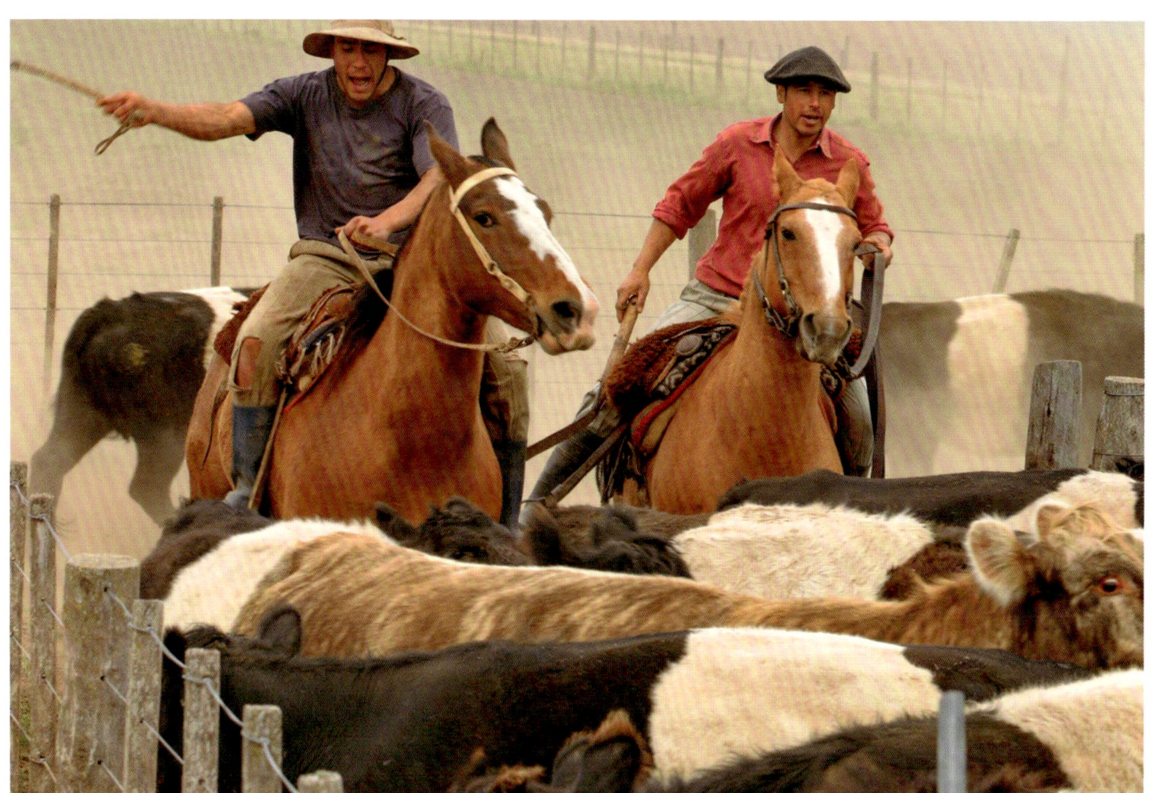

Gauchos

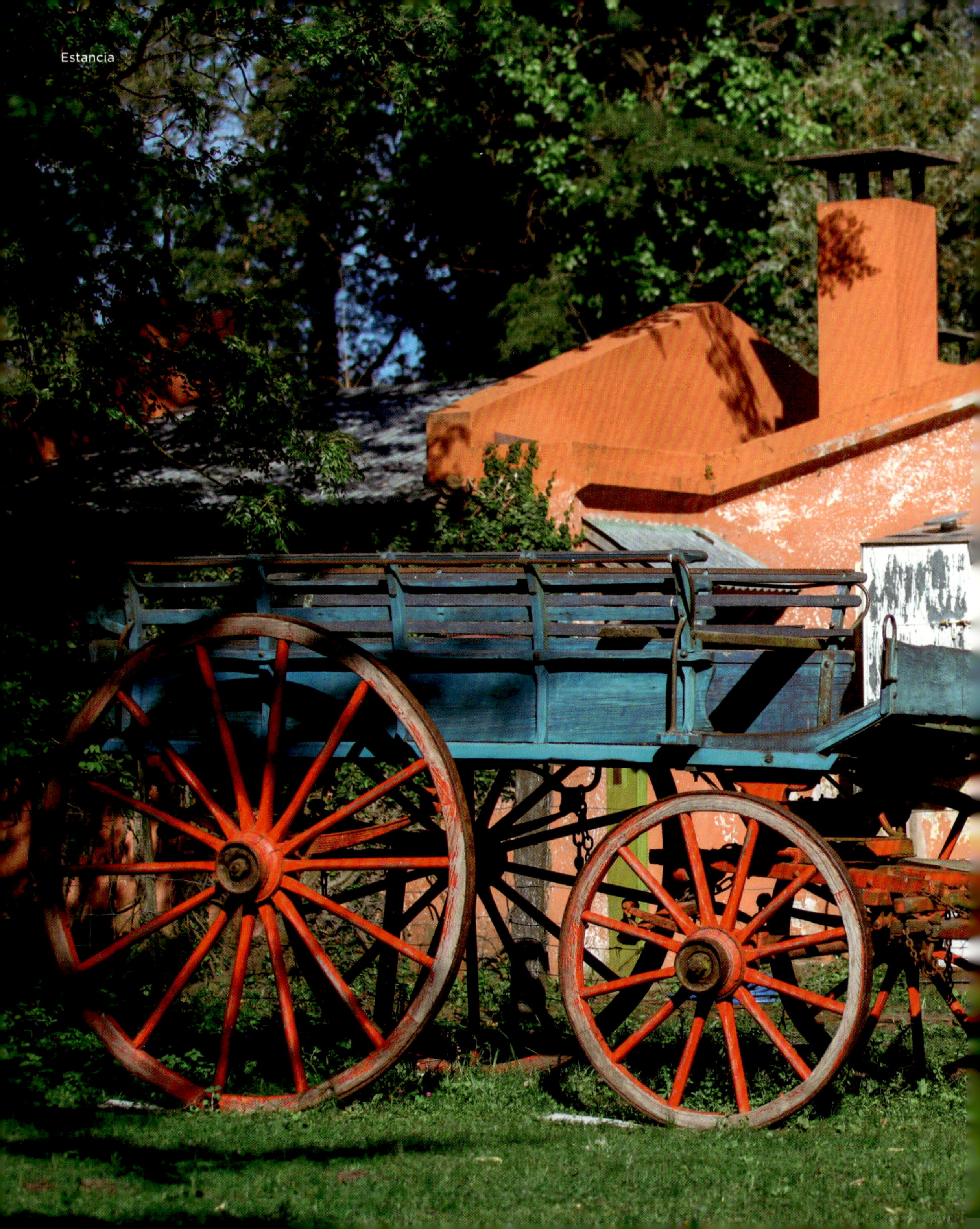

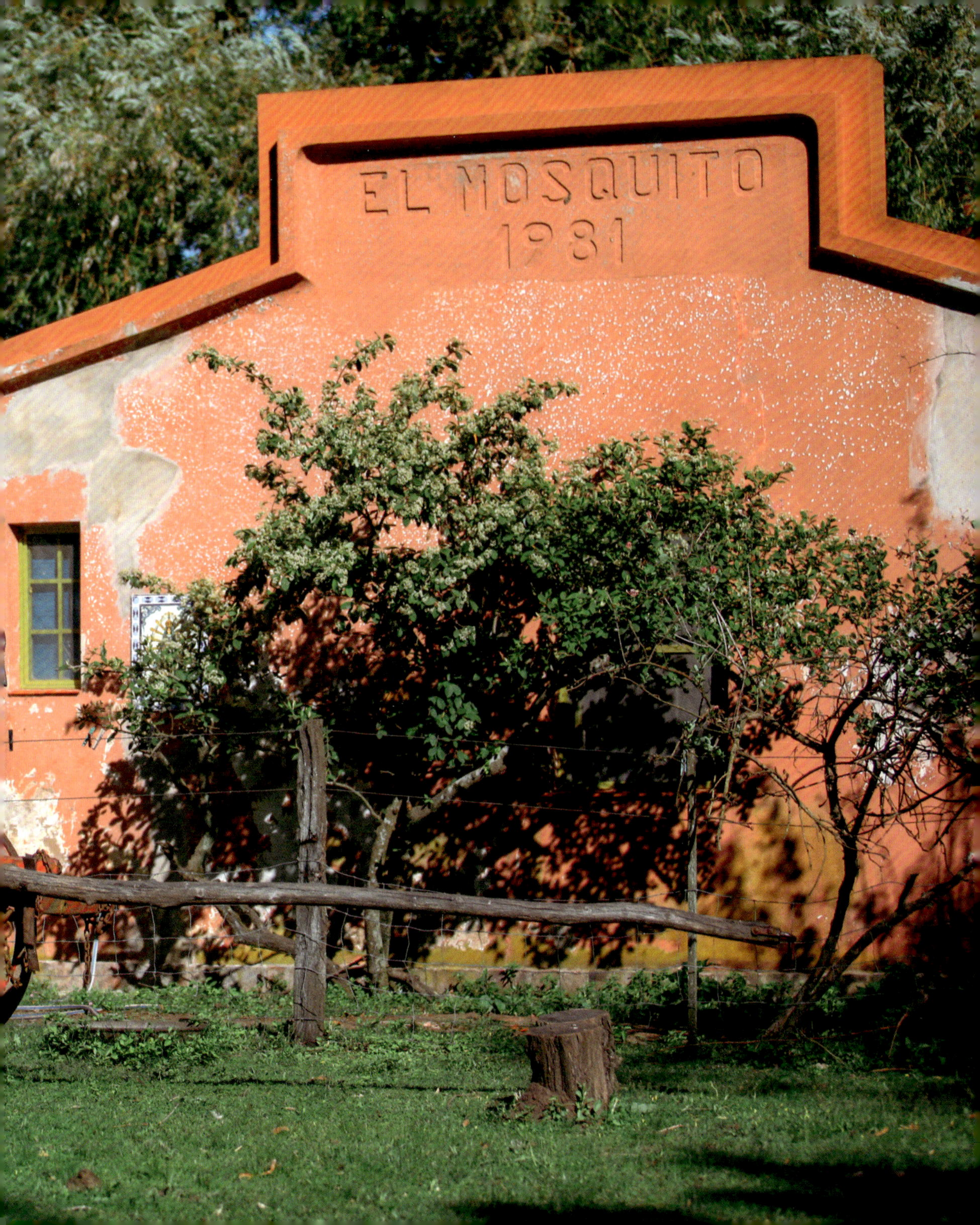

EL MOSQUITO
1981

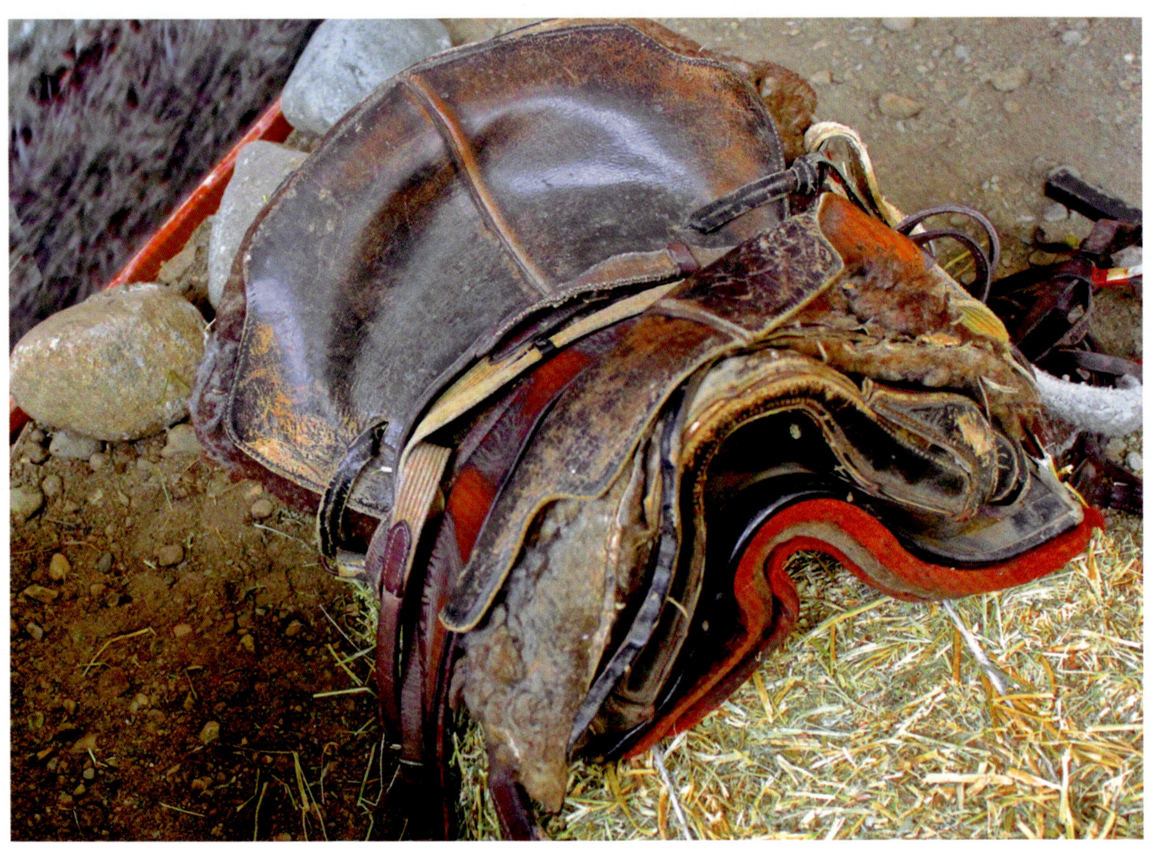

Silla
Saddle

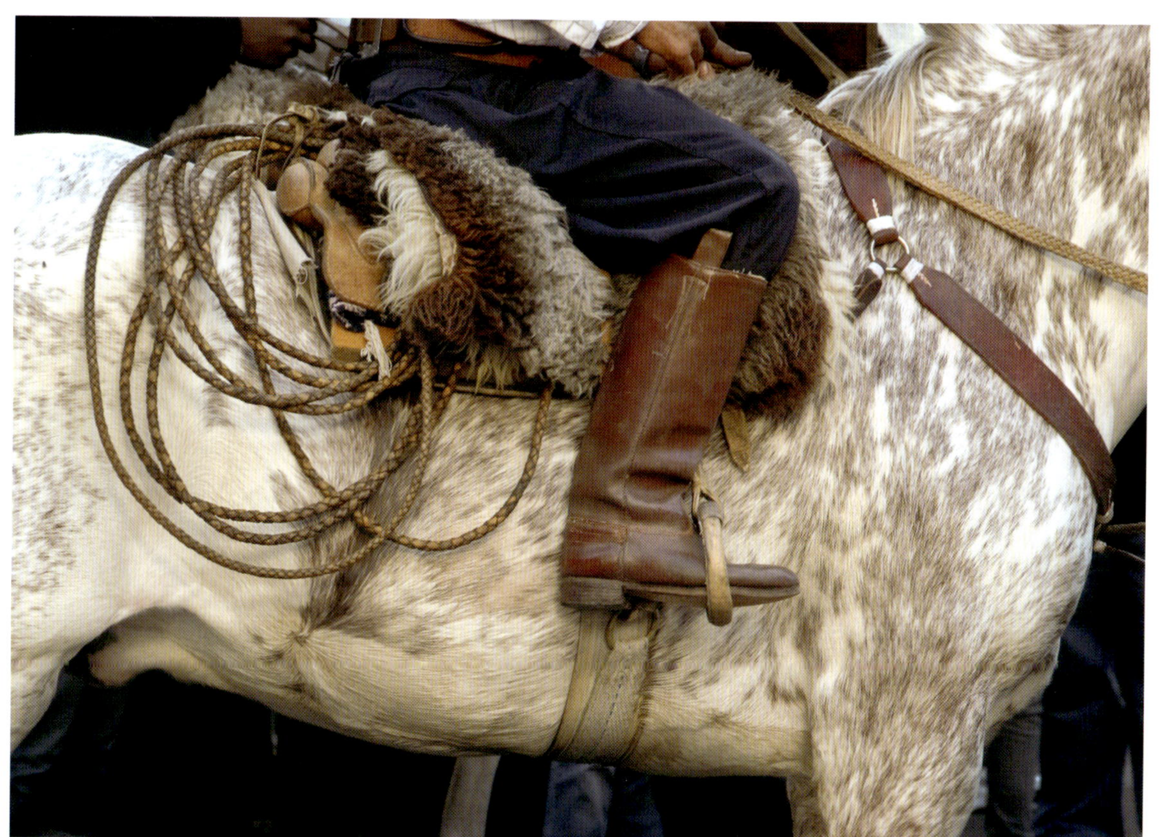

Gaucho

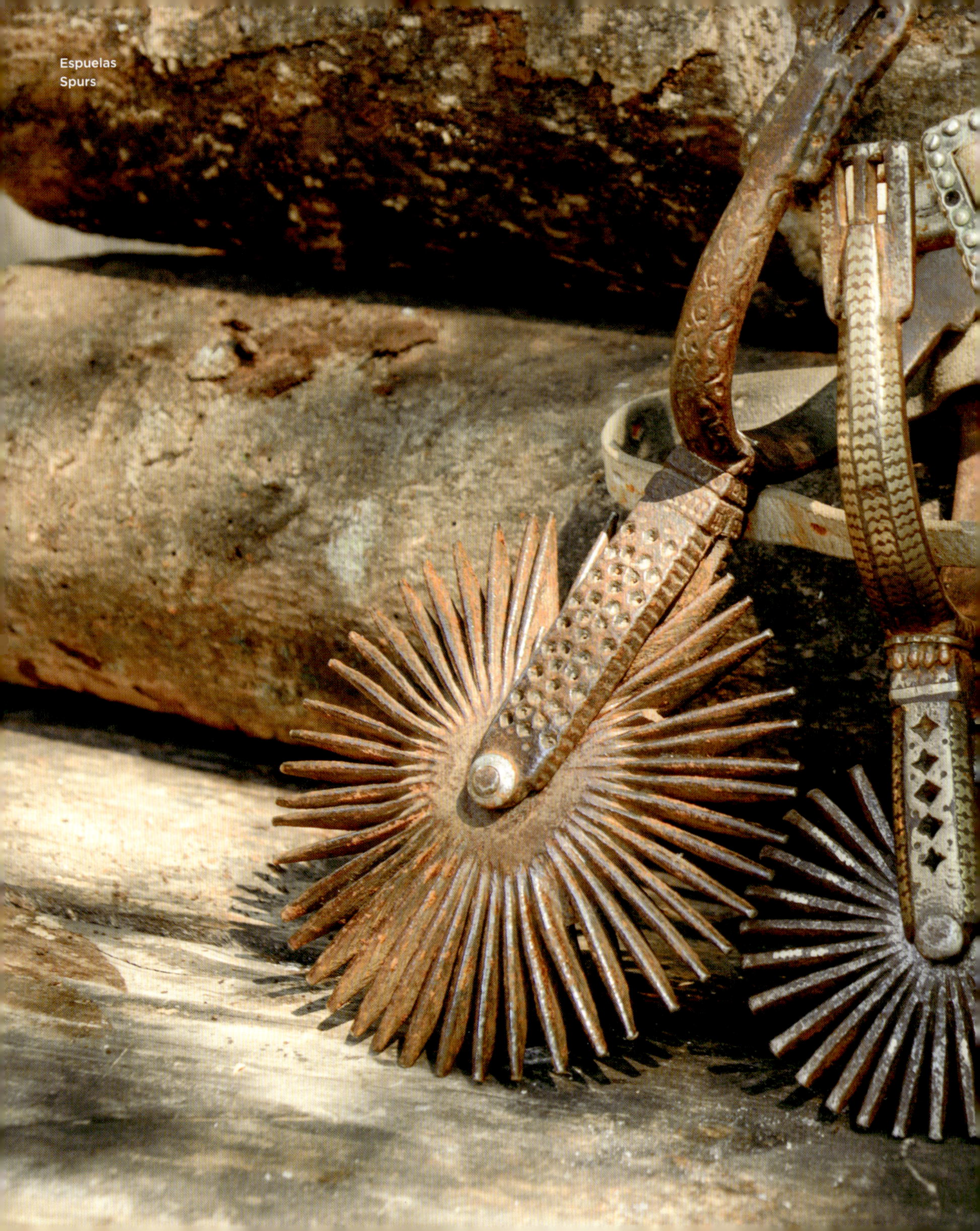
Espuelas
Spurs

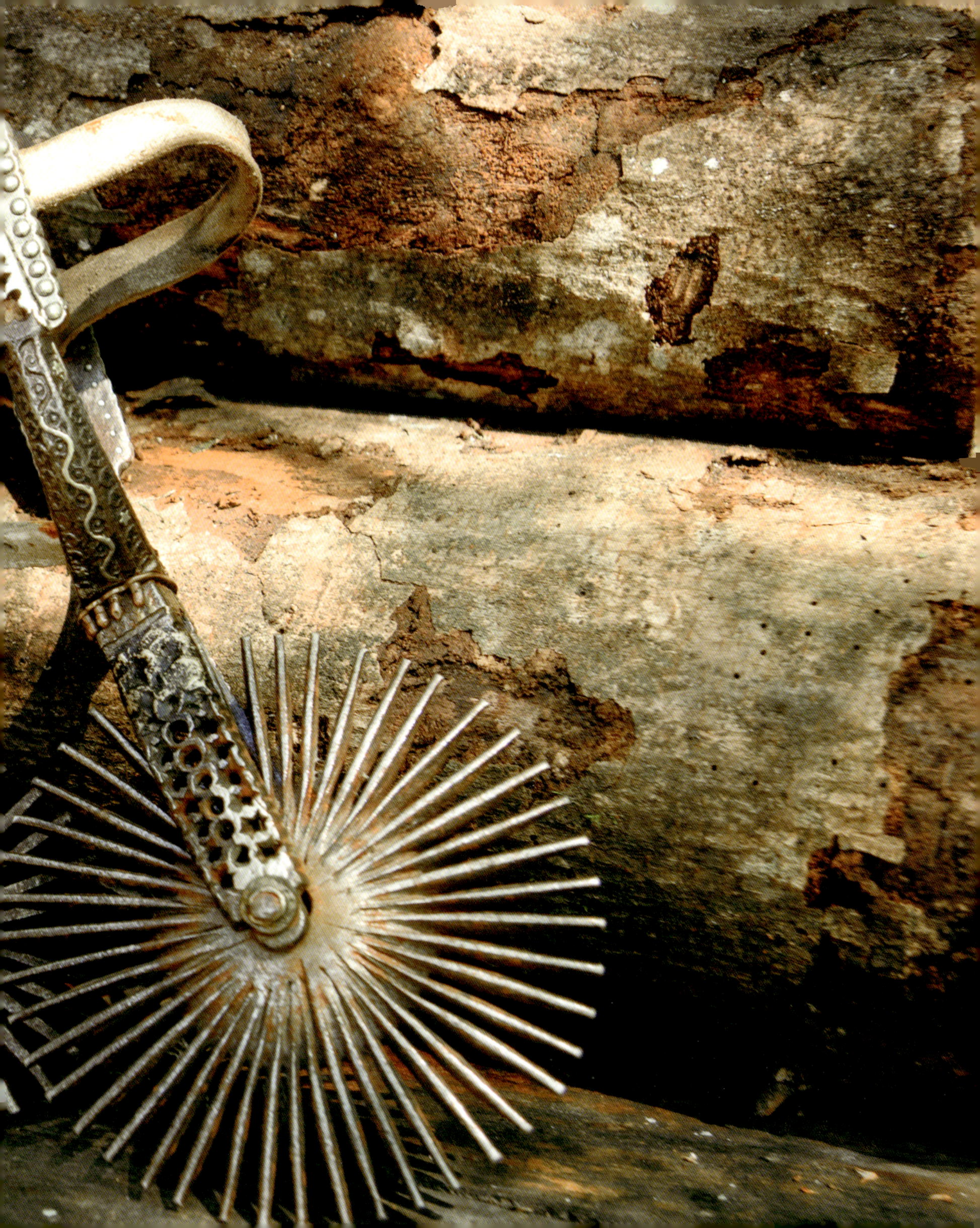

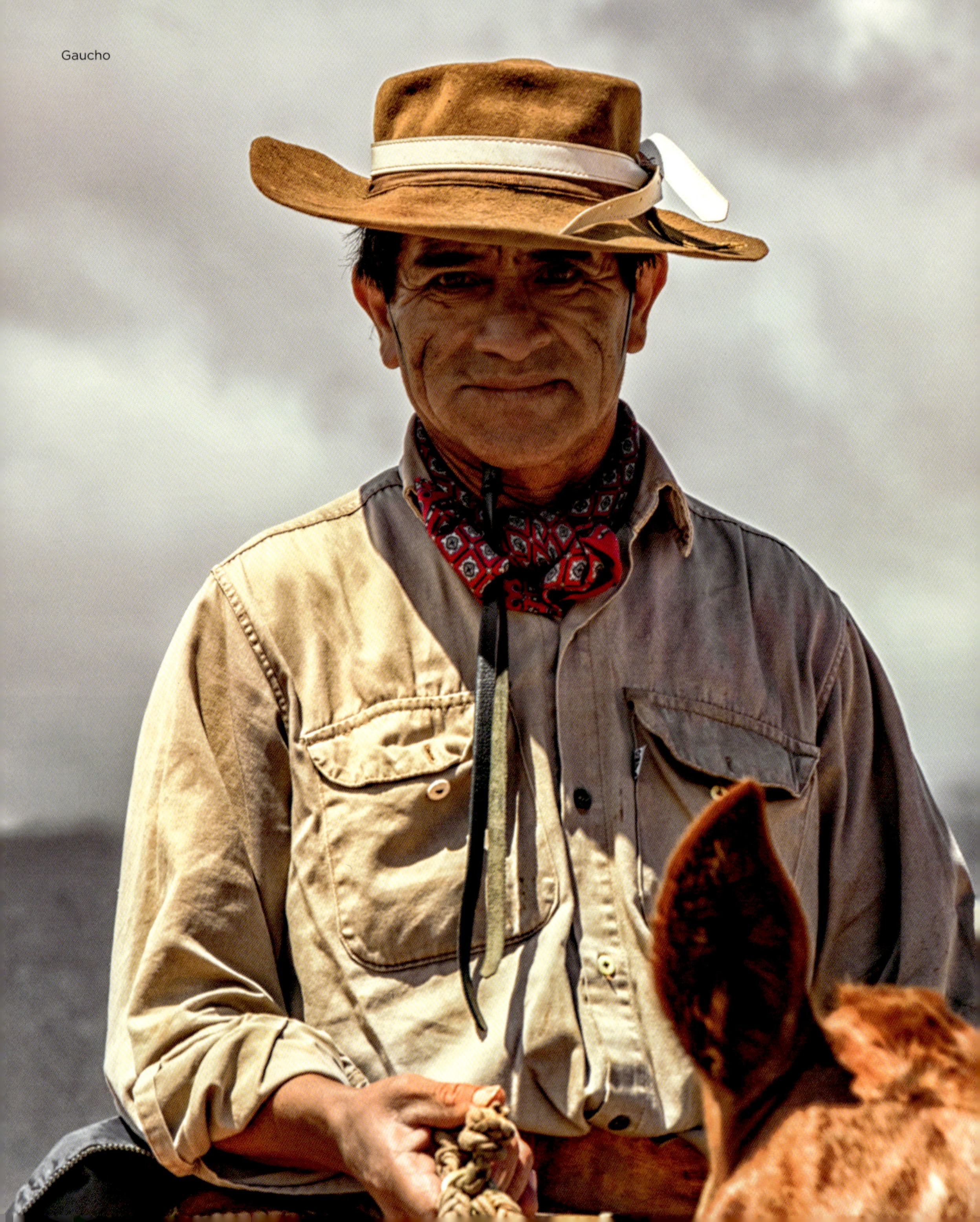

Gaucho

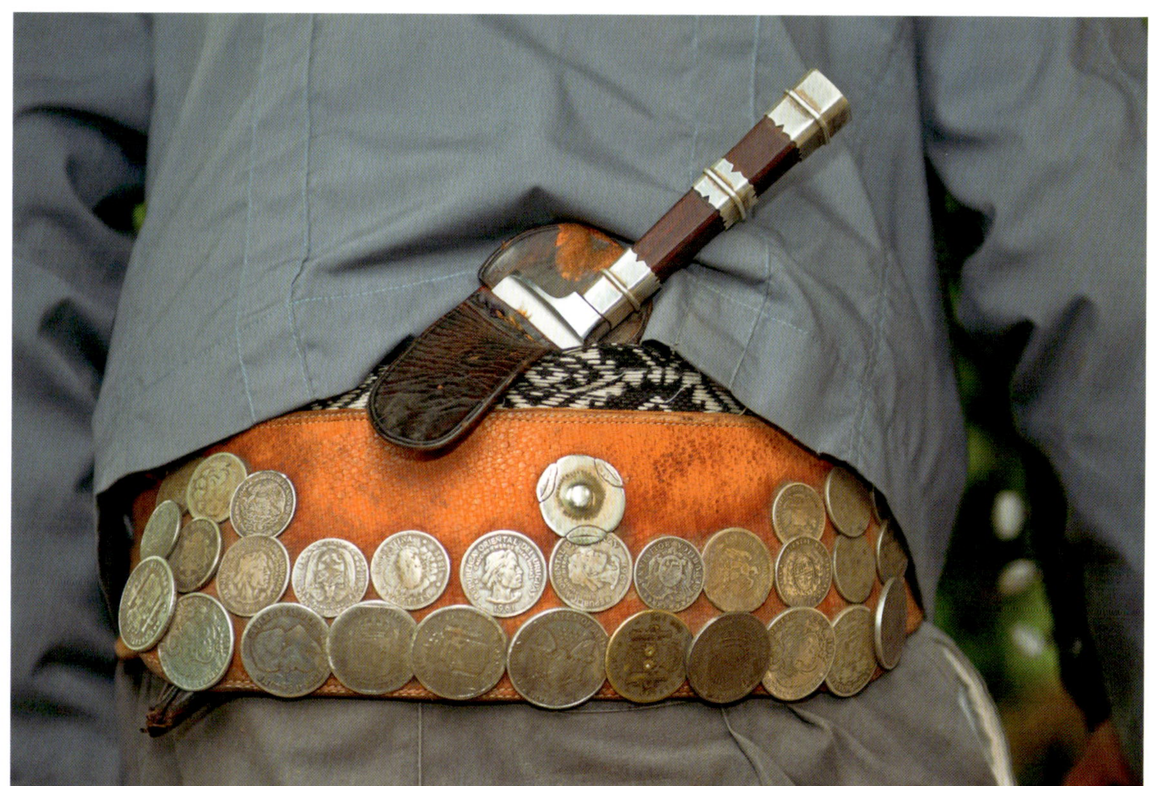

Guaica

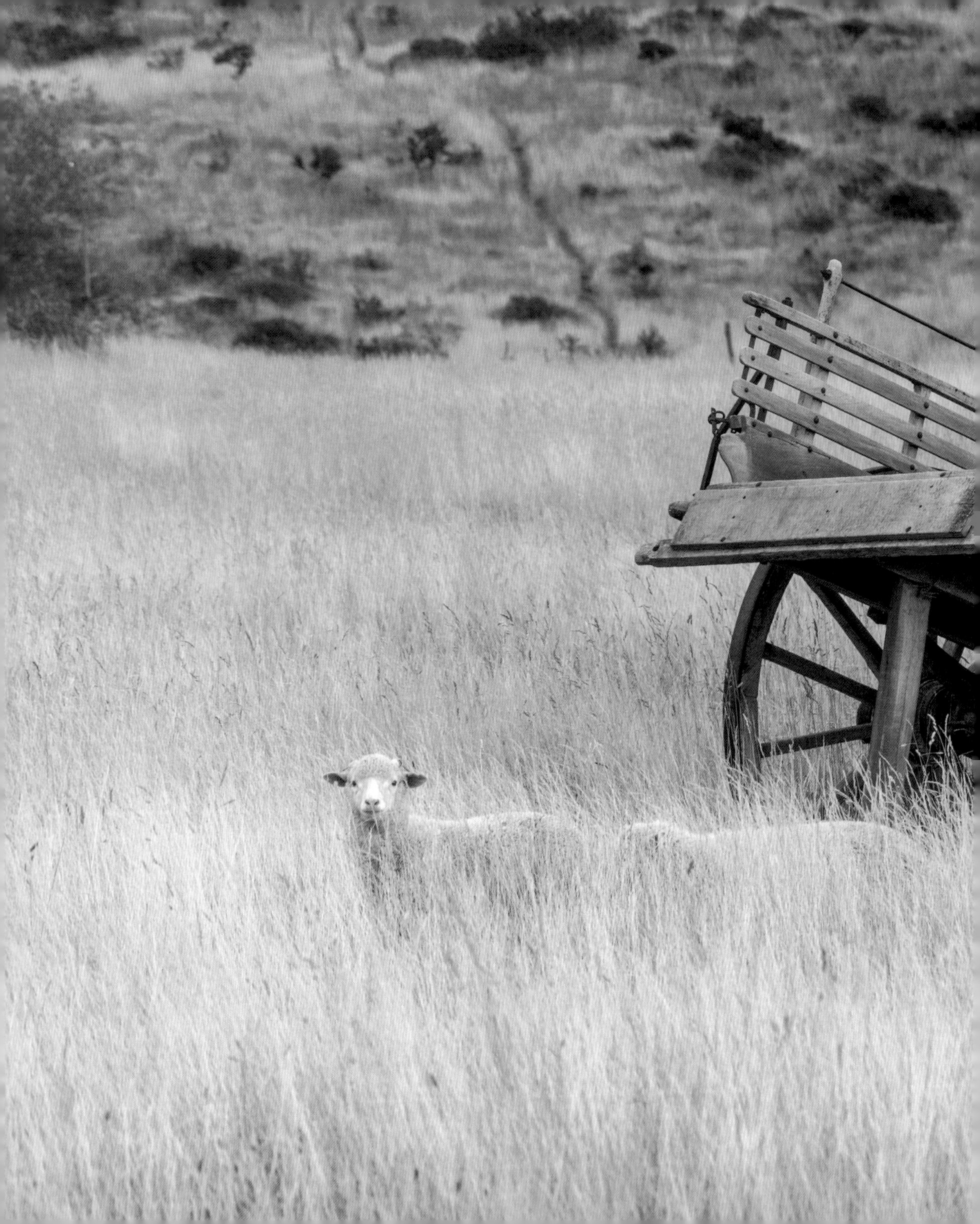

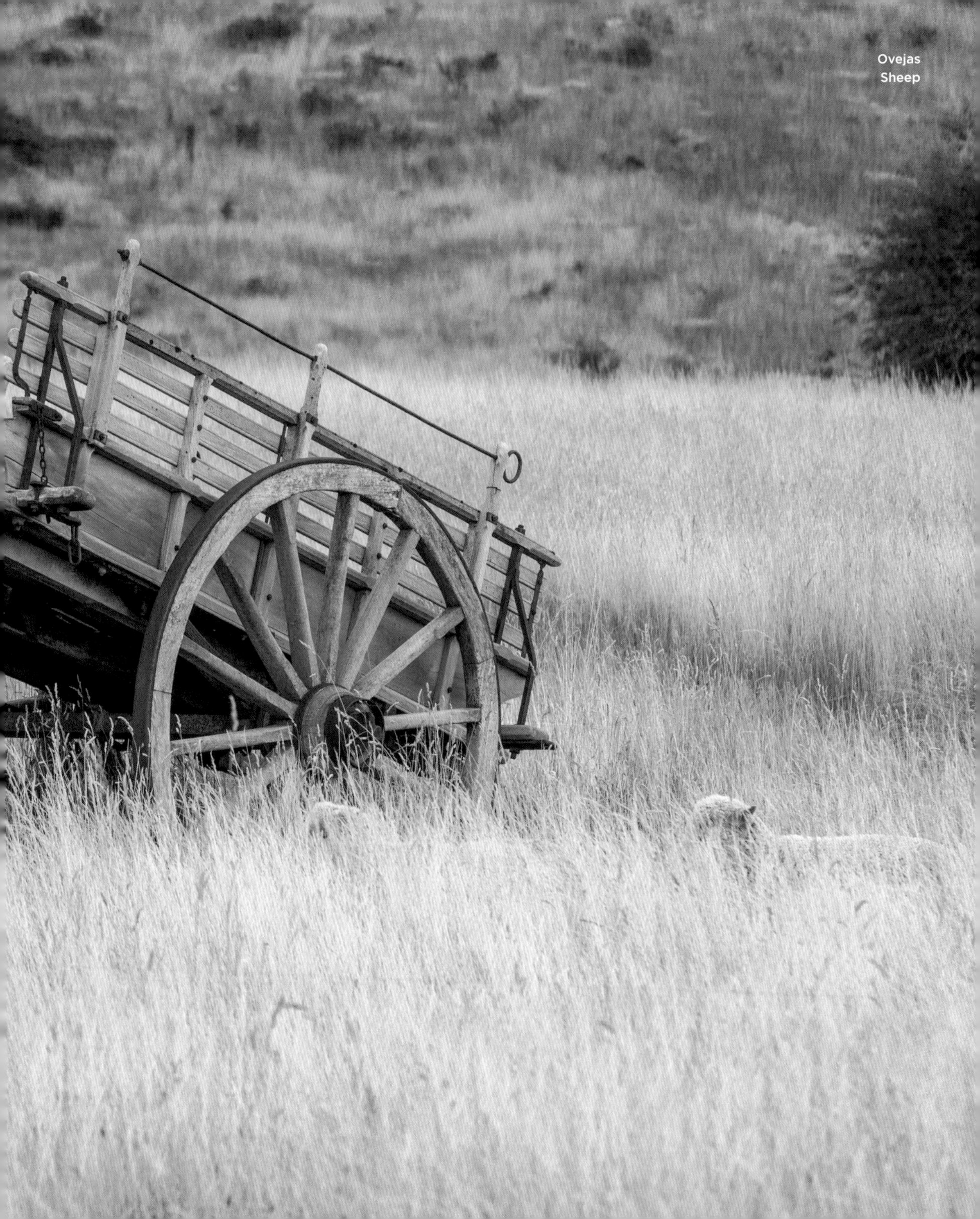
Ovejas
Sheep

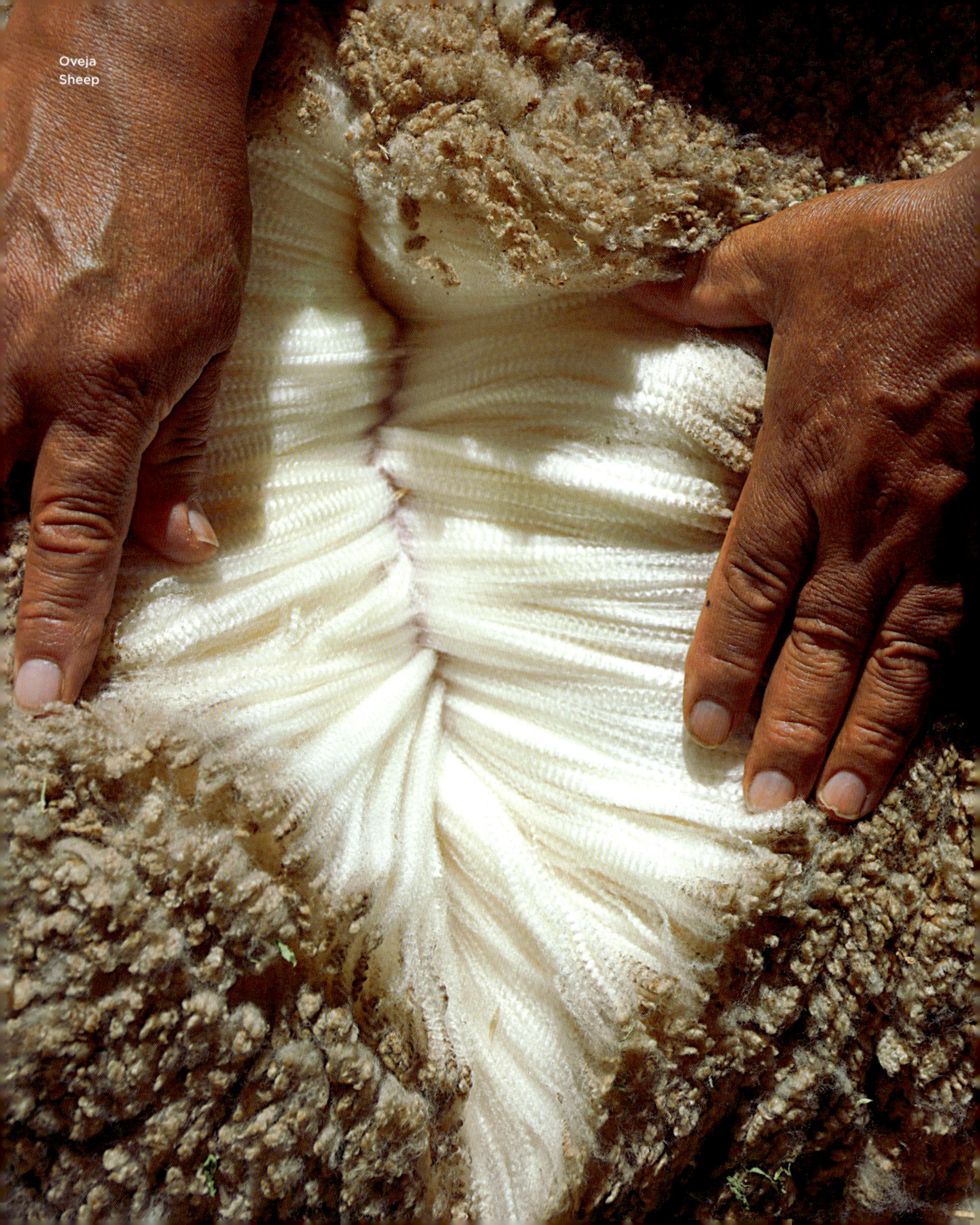
Oveja
Sheep

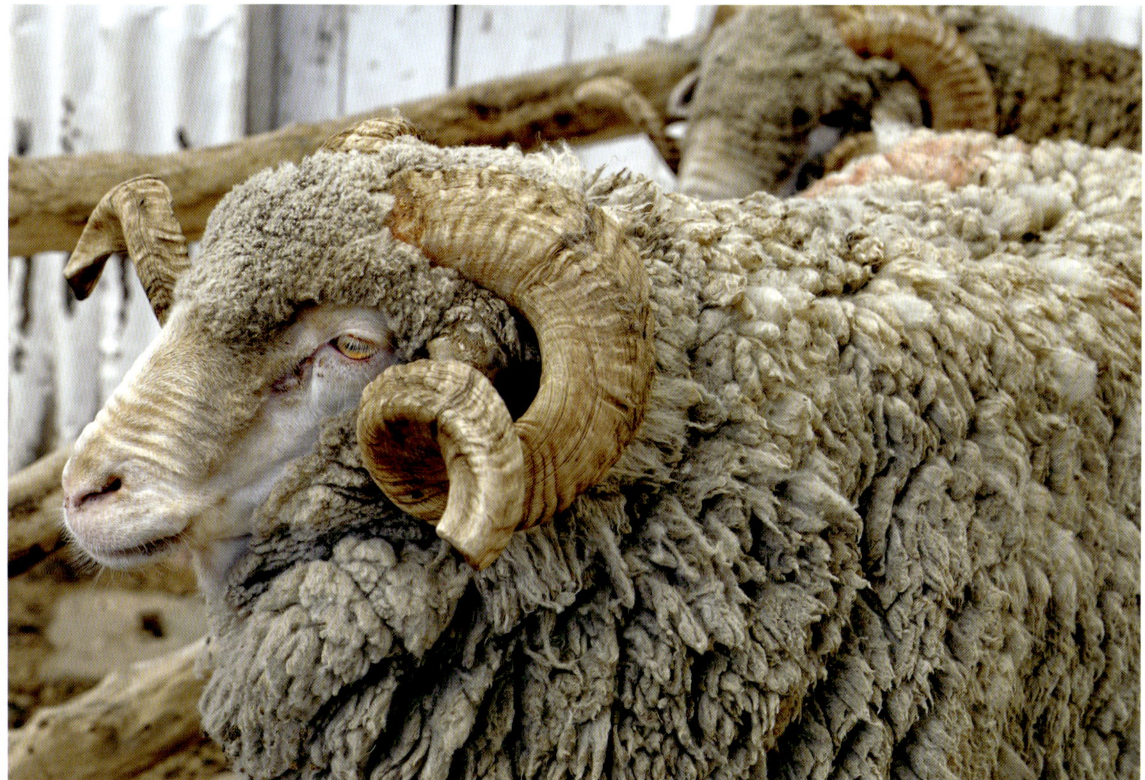

Oveja
Sheep

Sheep's wool

Argentina is the world's third largest wool exporter. Today, La Pampa is the most important sheep breeding area. Purebred sheep were introduced from Europe in the 18th century, as the wild indigenous breeds were not suitable. The Corriedale sheep, a New Zealand crossbred wool breed, is particularly lucrative.

Lana de oveja

Argentina es el tercer exportador de lana del mundo. Hoy en día, La Pampa es la zona de cría de ovejas más importante. Las ovejas de pura raza fueron introducidas desde Europa en el siglo XVIII, porque las razas autóctonas salvajes no eran adecuadas. La oveja Corriedale, una raza de lana cruzada de Nueva Zelanda, es particularmente lucrativa.

Laine de mouton

L'Argentine est le troisième exportateur de laine de mouton au monde. Actuellement, La Pampa est la première région d'élevage ovin. Au XVIIIe siècle, des moutons domestiques y furent importés d'Europe, car les espèces locales sauvages n'étaient pas adaptées à l'élevage. La plus lucrative est la corriedale, race à laine croisée d'origine néo-zélandaise.

Lã de ovelha

A Argentina é o terceiro maior exportador de lã do mundo. Hoje, La Pampa é a área mais importante para a criação de ovinos. As ovelhas de raça pura foram importadas da Europa no século XVIII porque as raças nativas selvagens não eram adequadas. A ovelha Corriedale, uma raça de lã cruzada originária da Nova Zelândia, é a mais lucrativa.

Schafwolle

Argentinien ist der drittgrößte Wollexporteur der Welt. Heute ist La Pampa das wichtigste Schafzuchtgebiet. Aus Europa wurden im 18. Jahrhundert Rasseschafe eingeführt, da die wilden einheimischen Rassen nicht geeignet waren. Lukrativ ist vor allem das Corriedale-Schaf, eine neuseeländische Crossbredwollrasse.

Schapenwol

Argentinië is de op drie na grootste wolexporteur ter wereld. Vandaag de dag is La Pampa het belangrijkste schapenhouderijgebied. Vanuit Europa werden in de 18e eeuw rasschapen ingevoerd, omdat de inheemse rassen niet geschikt waren. Lucratief is vooral het Corriedale schaap, een gekruist, Nieuw-Zeelandse wolras.

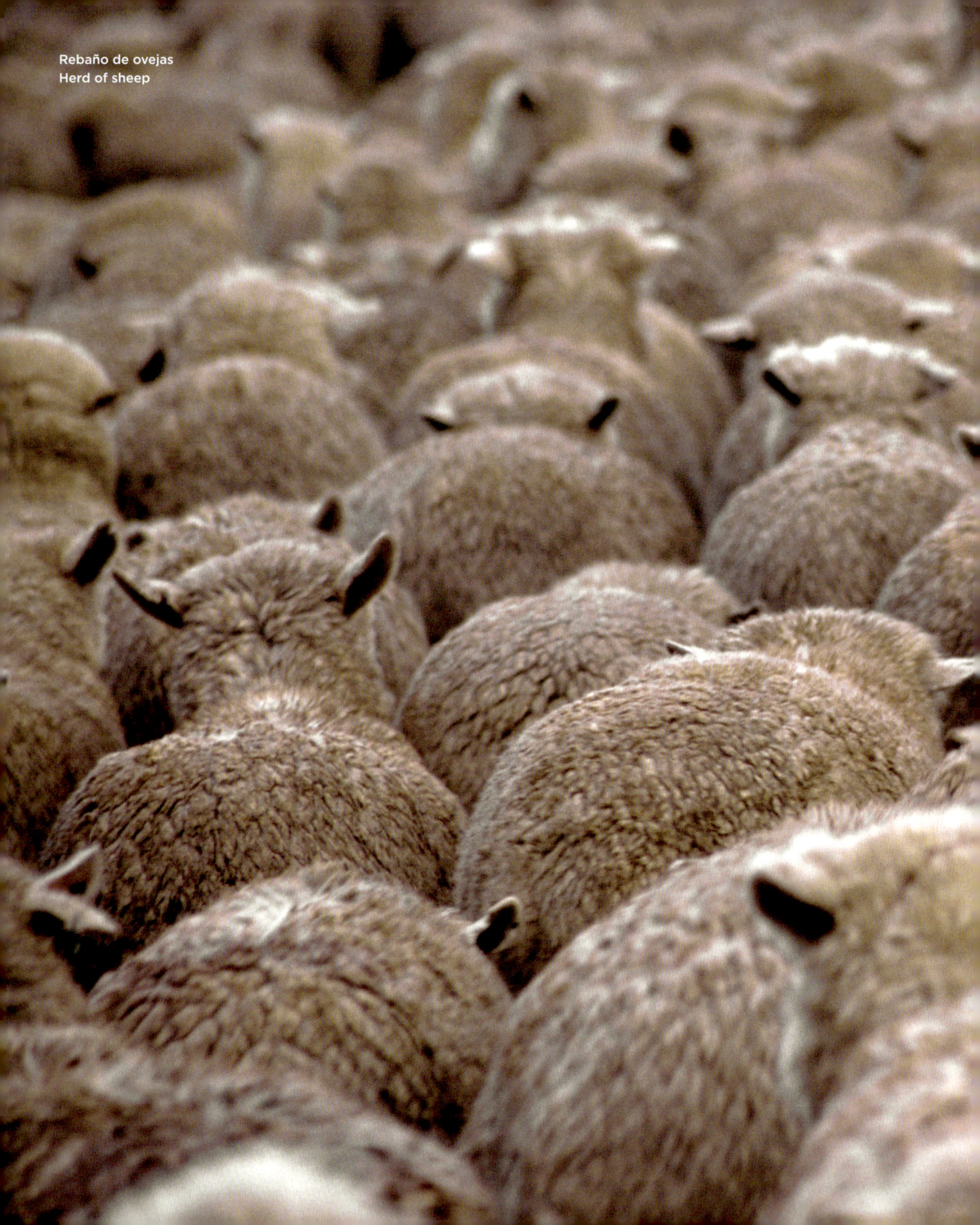
Rebaño de ovejas
Herd of sheep

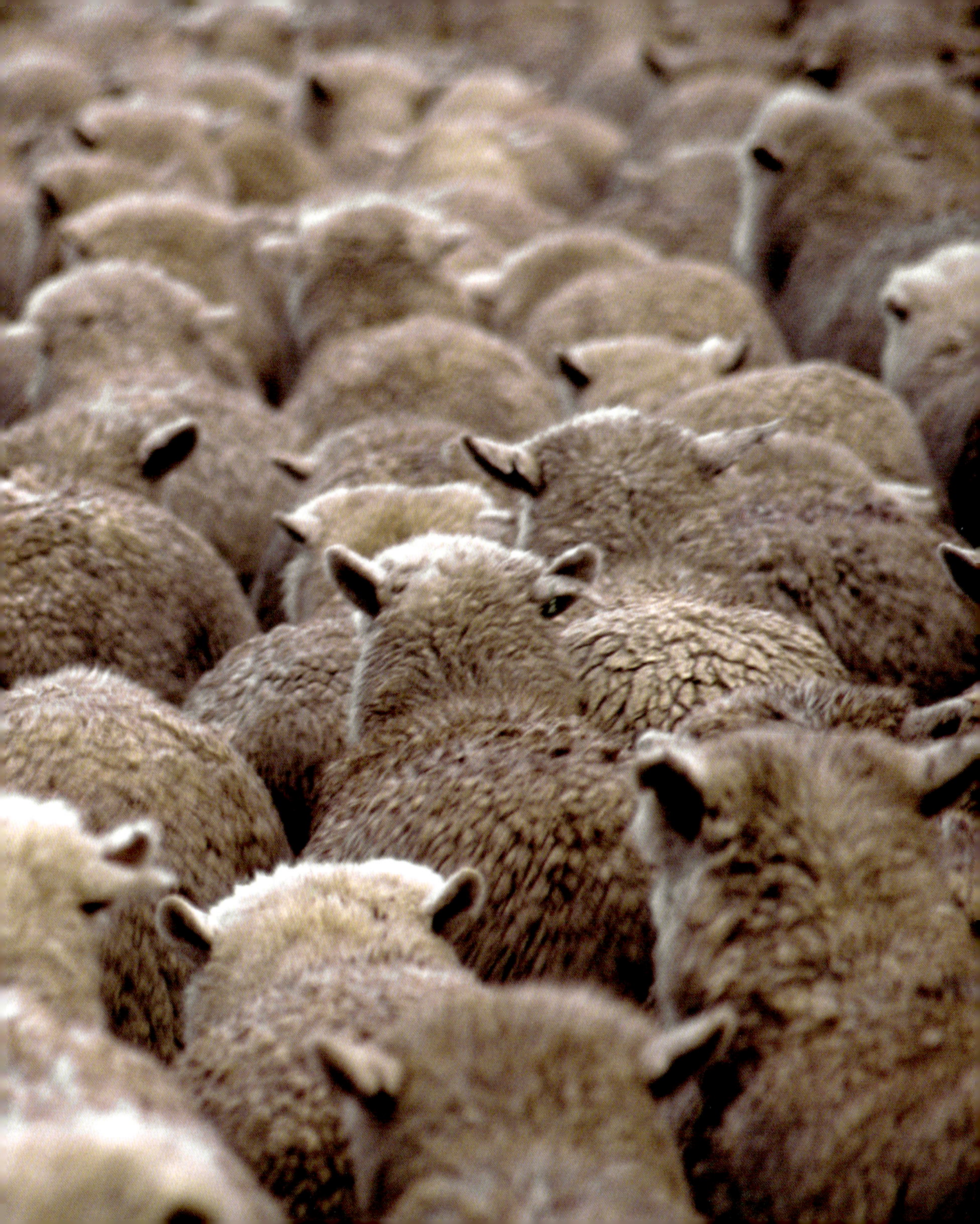

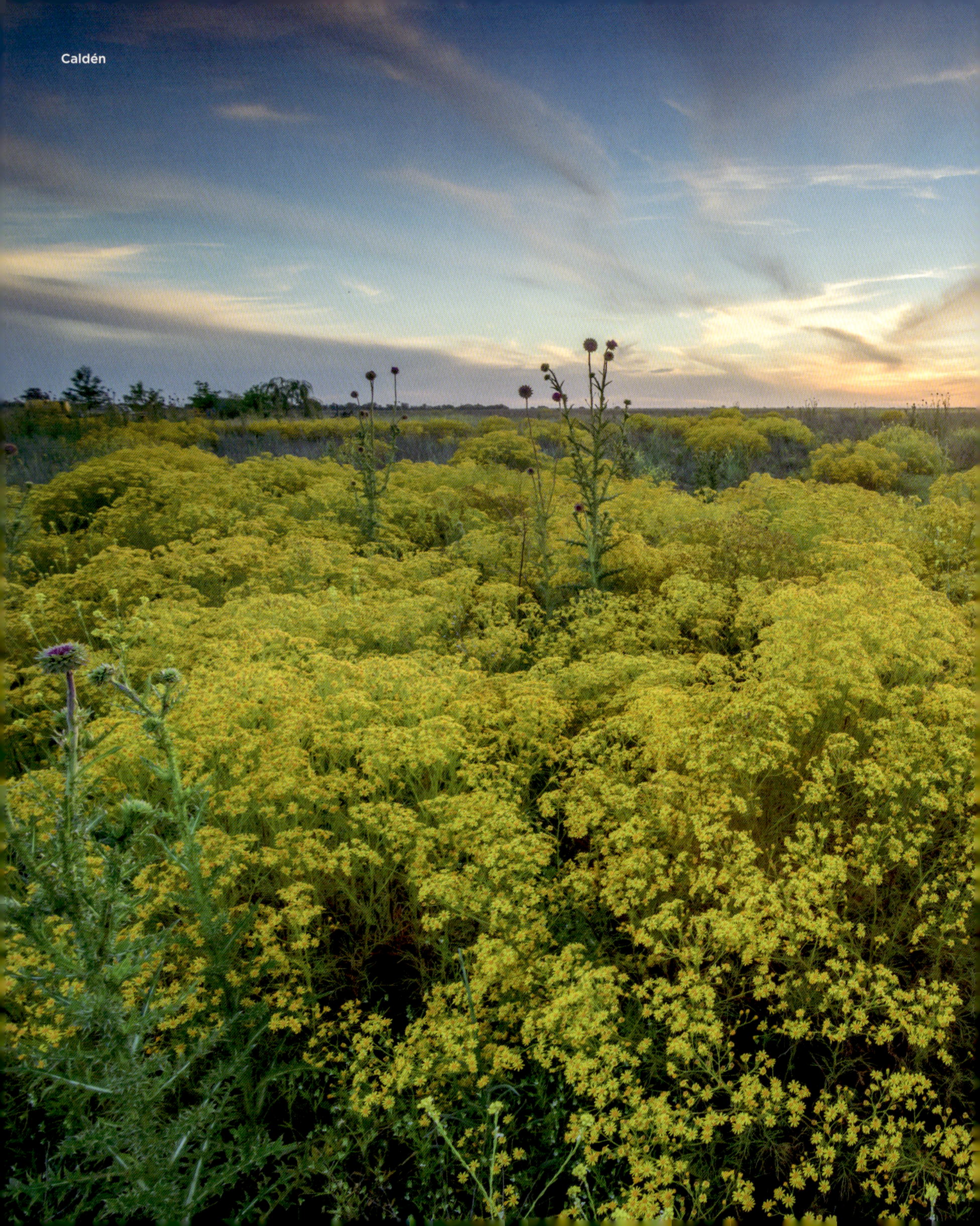
Caldén

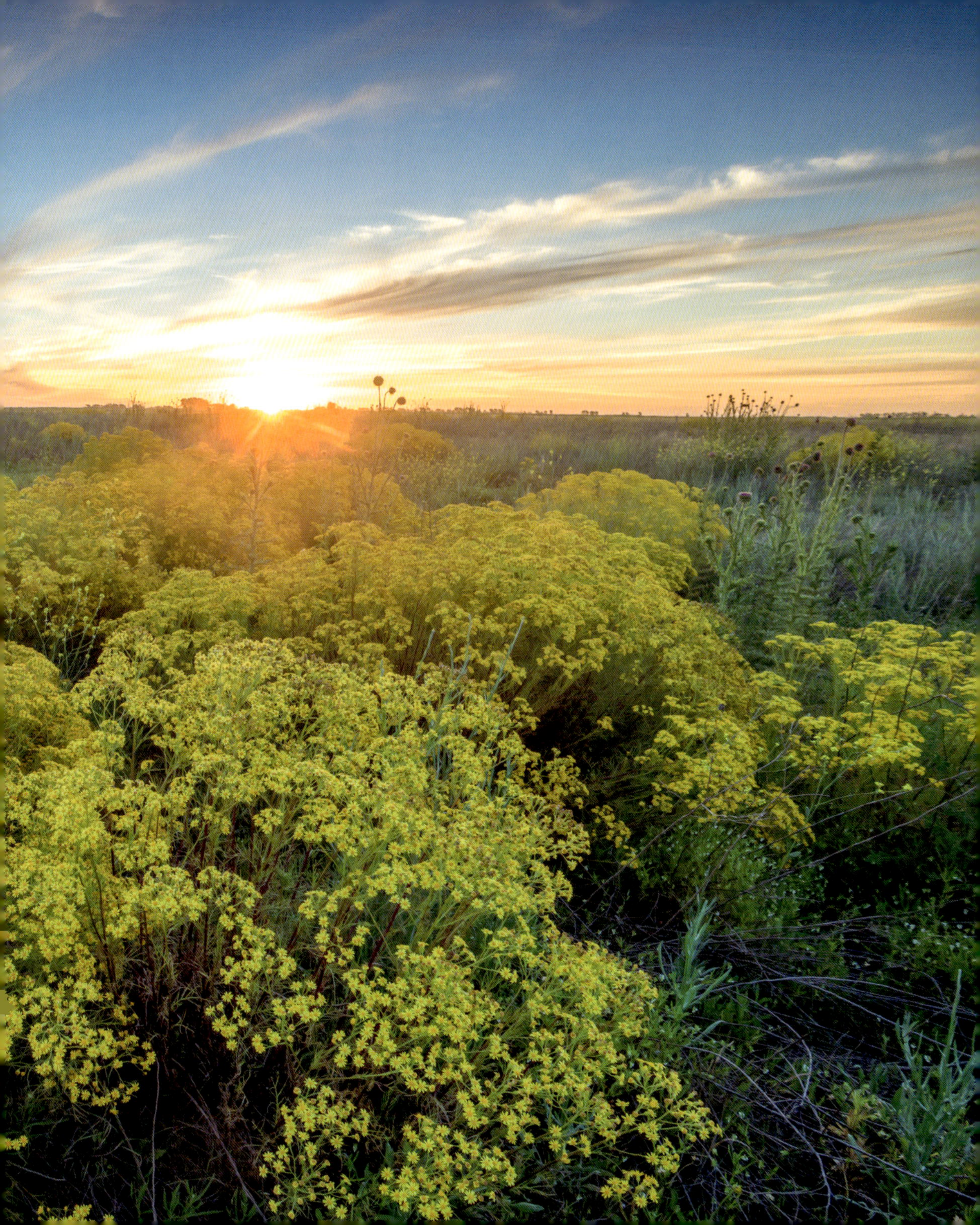

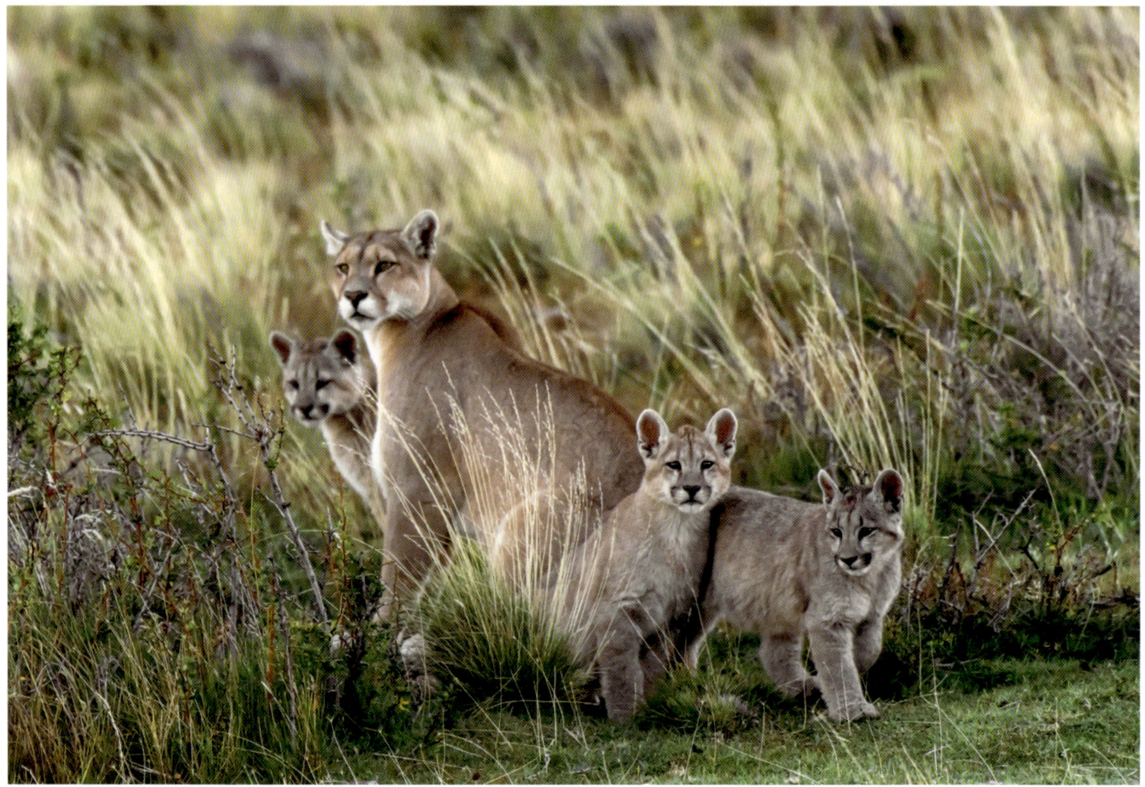

Pumas

Wildlife in La Pampa

For a long time, the concept of civilization encompassed the idea of taming wild nature and the hunting of wild animals, especially pumas, was part of the norm as they attacked cattle and sheep and disrupted the business interests of the estancias. Nevertheless, the wild cats survived. A small population lives within the Lihué Calel National Park.

Fauna y flora silvestres en La Pampa

Durante mucho tiempo predominó la idea civilizadora de domesticar la naturaleza salvaje. La caza de animales salvajes, especialmente de pumas, era de lo más normal. Se acabó con el ganado vacuno y ovino y se perturbaron los intereses comerciales de las estancias. Sin embargo, estos gatos salvajes sobrevivieron. Una pequeña población vive en el área del Parque Nacional Lihué Calel.

La faune sauvage de La Pampa

Pendant longtemps, le principe civilisateur visant à maîtriser la nature sauvage réglementait le pays. Il était tout à fait normal de chasser la faune sauvage, en particulier les pumas. Ils égorgeaient les bœufs et les moutons et contrevenaient aux intérêts économiques des *estancias*. Pourtant, ces félins sauvages ont survécu. Une petite population prospère aujourd'hui sur les terres du parc national Lihué Calel.

Vida selvagem em La Pampa

Durante muito tempo, a ideia civilizadora de domar a natureza selvagem foi o programa. A caça de animais selvagens, especialmente pumas, era normal. Estes caçavam os gados e ovelhas e perturbavam os interesses comerciais das fazendas. No entanto, os gatos selvagens sobreviveram. Uma pequena população vive na área do Parque Nacional Lihué Calel.

Wildtiere in La Pampa

Über lange Zeit war die zivilisatorische Idee, die wilde Natur zu bändigen, Programm. Die Jagd auf Wildtiere, insbesondere Pumas, gehörte zur Normalität. Sie rissen Rinder und Schafe und störten die geschäftlichen Interessen der Estanzias. Dennoch überlebten die Wildkatzen. Im Gebiet des Nationalparks Lihué Calel lebt eine kleine Population.

Wilde dieren in La Pampa

Lange tijd gold het als idee van beschaving de wilde natuur in te tomen. De jacht op wilde dieren, met name poema's, behoorde tot de normaliteit. Ze verscheurden runderen en schapen en verstoorden de zakelijke belangen van de estancias. Toch overleefden de wilde katten. In het gebied van nationaal park Lihué Calel leeft een kleine populatie.

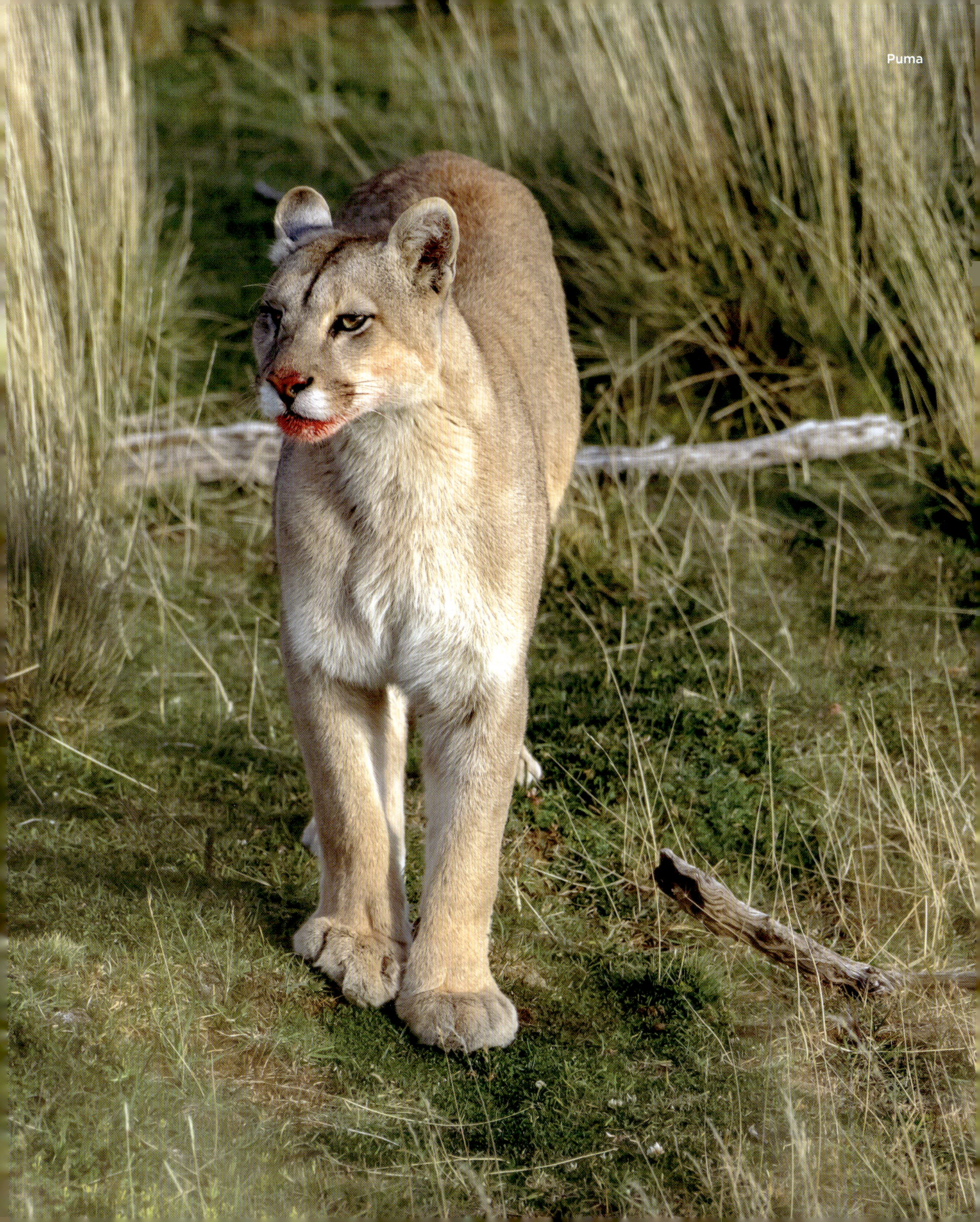

Puma

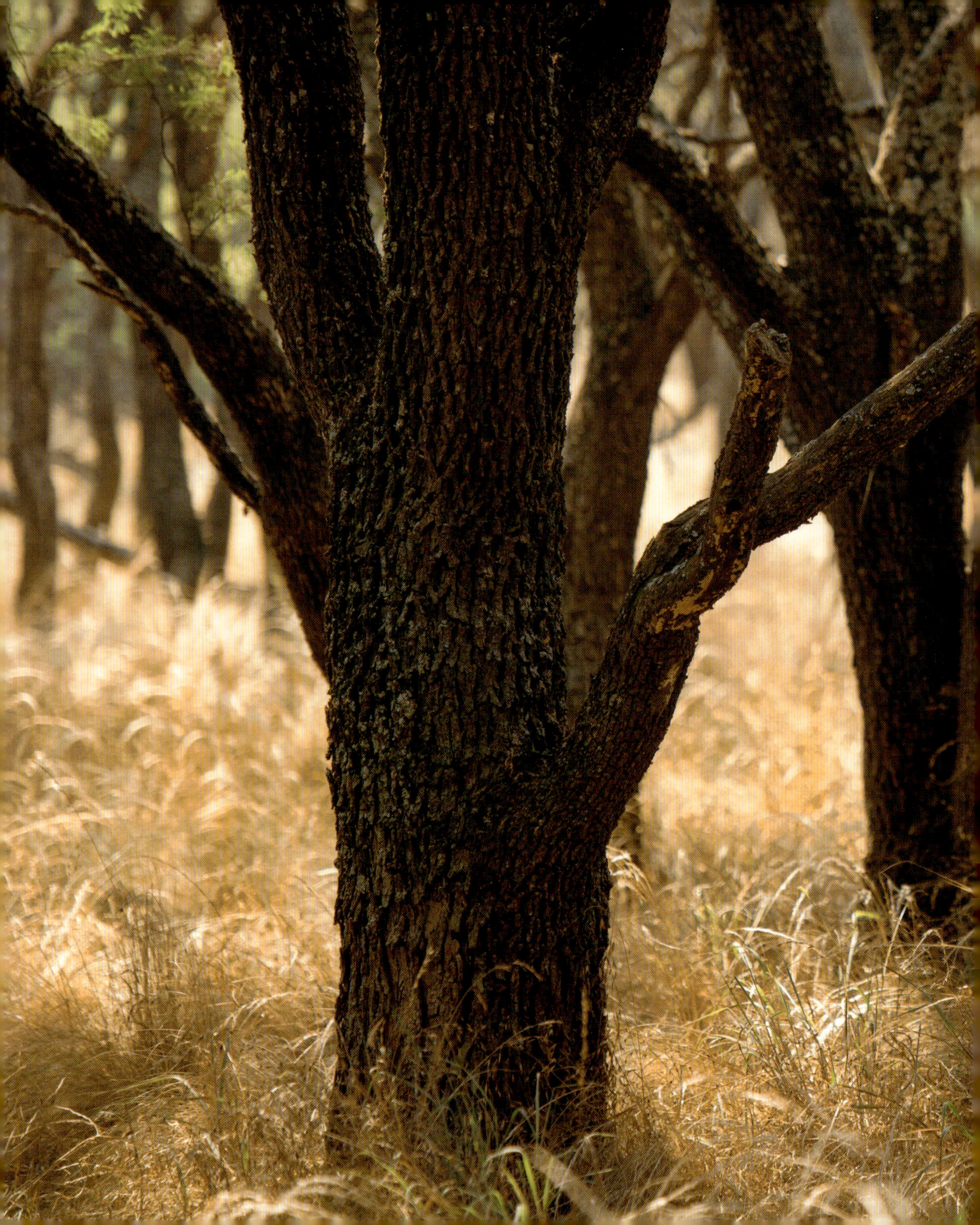

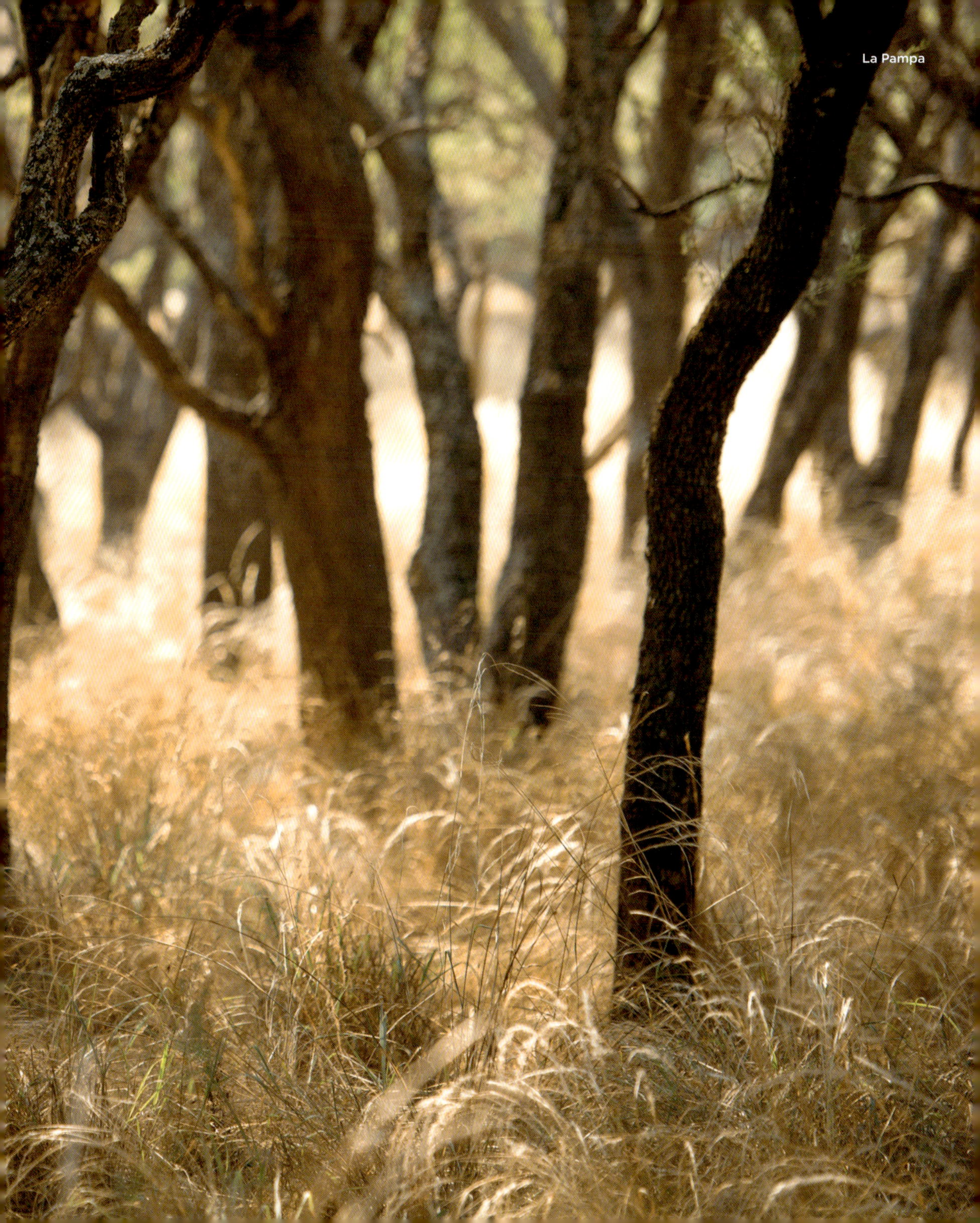
La Pampa

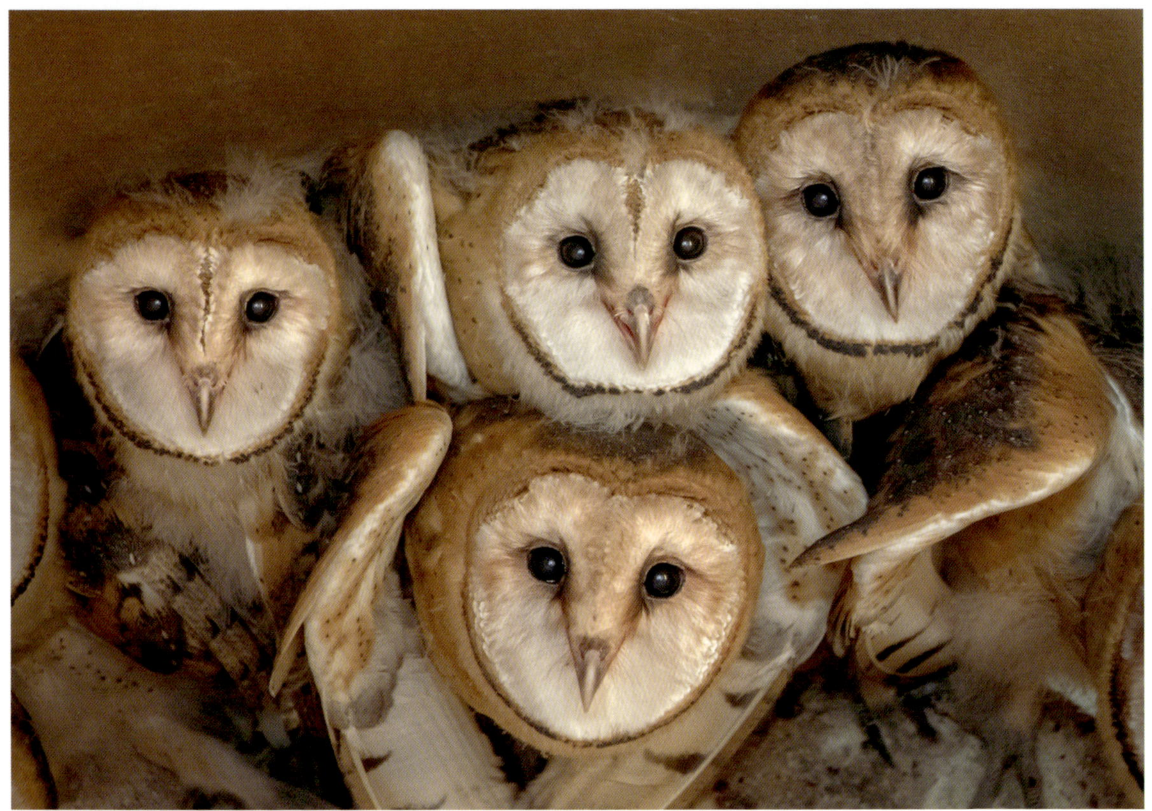

Lechuzas comunes americanas
American-barn-owls

World of Birds

In Argentina, a subtype of the American-barn-owl (*Tyto furcata tuidara*) lives. It occurs in areas with few trees, preferably semi-deserts. The adult animal grows to 33–35 cm (13–14 in) long, with a wingspan of 95 cm (37 in). Breeding grounds are tree hollows or rock crevices. Young birds are fledged at two months and train in hunting techniques after only 30 days. The blue-crowned parakeet, or sharp-tailed conure, belongs to the genus Thectocercus and is widespread in Latin America. Its plumage is green, except at the head where it displays blue feathers. It lives in the dry forest of the savannah, feeding on seeds, fruits and berries. In order to lay its eggs, it looks for an enclosure in tree hollows, so that the offspring can grow up protected.

Le monde des oiseaux

La sous-espèce de chouette effraie d'Amérique *Tyto furcata tuidara* vit en Argentine. Elle est surtout présente dans les régions peu boisées, de préférence semi-désertiques. L'adulte mesure 33 à 35 cm de long et présente une envergure de 95 cm. Elle nidifie dans les cavités des arbres ou les failles rocheuses. Les jeunes sont prêts à quitter le nid à 2 mois et s'entraînent dès 30 jours aux techniques de chasse. La conure à tête bleue, qui fait partie du genre Thectocercus, est très répandue en Amérique latine. Son plumage est entièrement vert, à l'exception de quelques plumes bleues sur la tête. Elle vit dans les arbustes secs de la savane, se nourrit de graines, de fruits et de baies. Elle nidifie dans le creux profond d'un tronc d'arbre et y cache ses oisillons.

Vogelwelt

In Argentinien lebt eine Unterart der Amerika-Schleiereule (*Tyta furcata tuidara*). Sie kommt in baumarmen Gebieten, vorzugsweise Halbwüsten vor. Das ausgewachsene Tier wird 33–35 cm lang, seine Flügelspannweite beträgt 95 cm. Brutstätten sind Baumhöhlen oder Felsspalten. Jungvögel sind mit zwei Monaten flügge, sie trainieren schon nach 30 Tagen Jagdtechniken. Der Blaukopf- oder Spitzschwanzsittich gehört zur Gattung der Thectocercus und ist in Lateinamerika weit verbreitet. Sein Federkleid ist grün, lediglich am Kopf trägt er blaue Federn. Er lebt im Trockenwald der Savanne, ernährt sich von Samen, Früchten und Beeren. Um seine Eier abzulegen, sucht er ein Gehege in Baumhöhlen, damit der Nachwuchs geschützt groß werden kann.

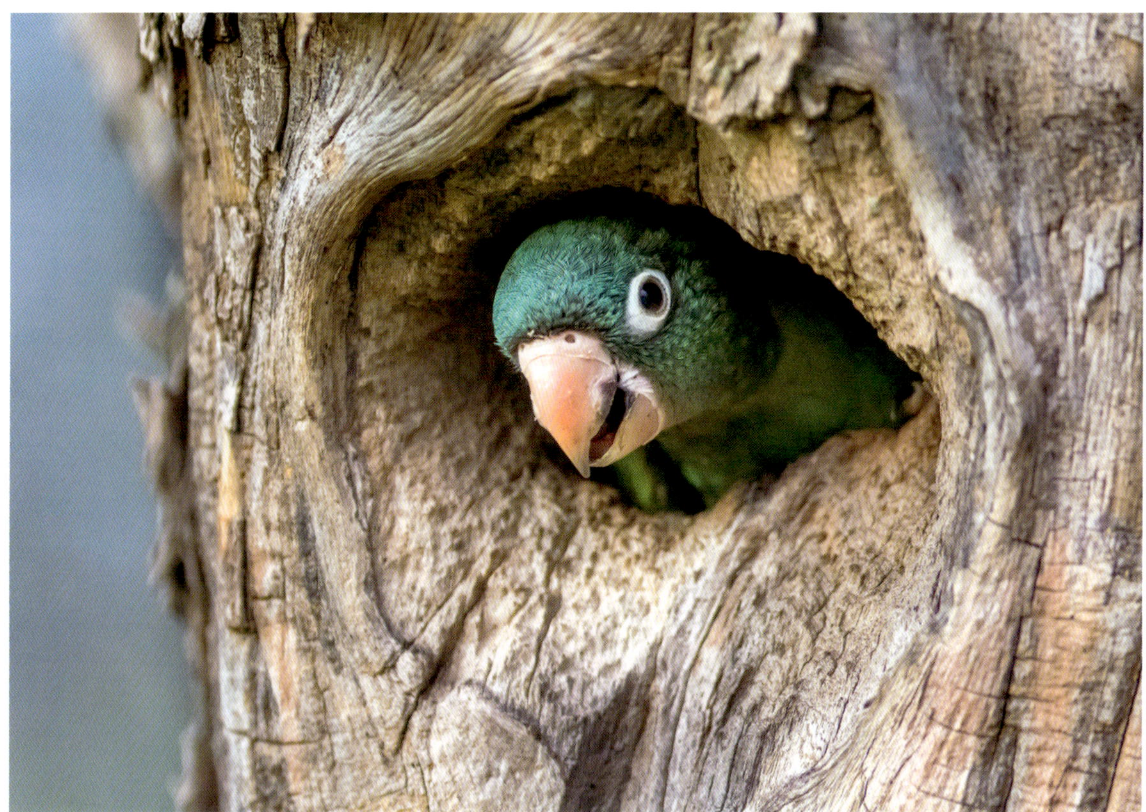

Calancate común
Blue-crowned parakeet

El mundo de las aves

En Argentina vive una subtipo de la lechuza común americana *(Tyta furcata tuidara)*. Se encuentra en zonas con pocos árboles, preferentemente en áreas semidesérticas. El animal adulto crece hasta 33–35 cm de largo, y su envergadura es de 95 cm. Las zonas de cría son huecos de árboles o grietas en la roca. Las aves jóvenes vuelan a los dos meses, y entrenan las técnicas de caza después de 30 días. El calancate común o perico de corona azul pertenece al género Thectocercus y está muy extendido en América Latina. Su plumaje es verde; tan solo en la cabeza lleva plumas azules. Vive en el bosque seco de la llanura, donde se alimenta de semillas, frutas y bayas. Para poner sus huevos, busca un lugar entre los huecos de los árboles para que las crías puedan crecer protegidas.

Mundo das Aves

Na Argentina, vive uma subespécie da coruja-de-igreja ou suindara *(Tyta furcata tuidara)*. Elas podem ser encontradas em áreas com poucas árvores, de preferência semi-desertas. O animal adulto cresce até 33-35 cm de comprimento e sua envergadura de asas é de 95 cm. Os terrenos de reprodução são cavidades de árvores ou fendas na rocha. As aves jovens são criadas em dois meses e treinam técnicas de caça após apenas 30 dias. A Aratinga-de-testa-azul ou periquito-de-bico-rosa pertence ao gênero Thectocercus e está difundido na América Latina. Sua plumagem é verde, só na cabeça carrega penas azuis. Vive na floresta seca da savana, alimentando-se de sementes, frutos e bagas. Para pôr os seus ovos, procura um recinto em cavidades de árvores, para que os filhotes possam crescer protegidos.

Vogelwereld

In Argentinië leeft een ondersoort van de Amerikaanse kerkuil *(Tyto furcata tuidara)*. Deze uil komt voor in gebieden met weinig bomen, bij voorkeur halfwoestijnen. Het volwassen dier wordt 33–35 cm lang, zijn vleugelspanwijdte is 95 cm. Broedplaatsen zijn boomholtes of spleten in rotsen. Jonge vogels kunnen na twee maanden al vliegen en trainen na 30 dagen al hun jachttechnieken. De blauwkoparatinga behoort tot het geslacht Thectocercus en is in Latijns-Amerika wijdverspreid. Zijn verenkleed is groen, alleen aan de kop heeft hij blauwe veren. Hij leeft in het droge bos van de savanne en voedt zich met zaden, vruchten en bessen. Om zijn eieren te leggen zoekt hij een behuizing in boomholtes, zodat het nageslacht beschermd kan opgroeien.

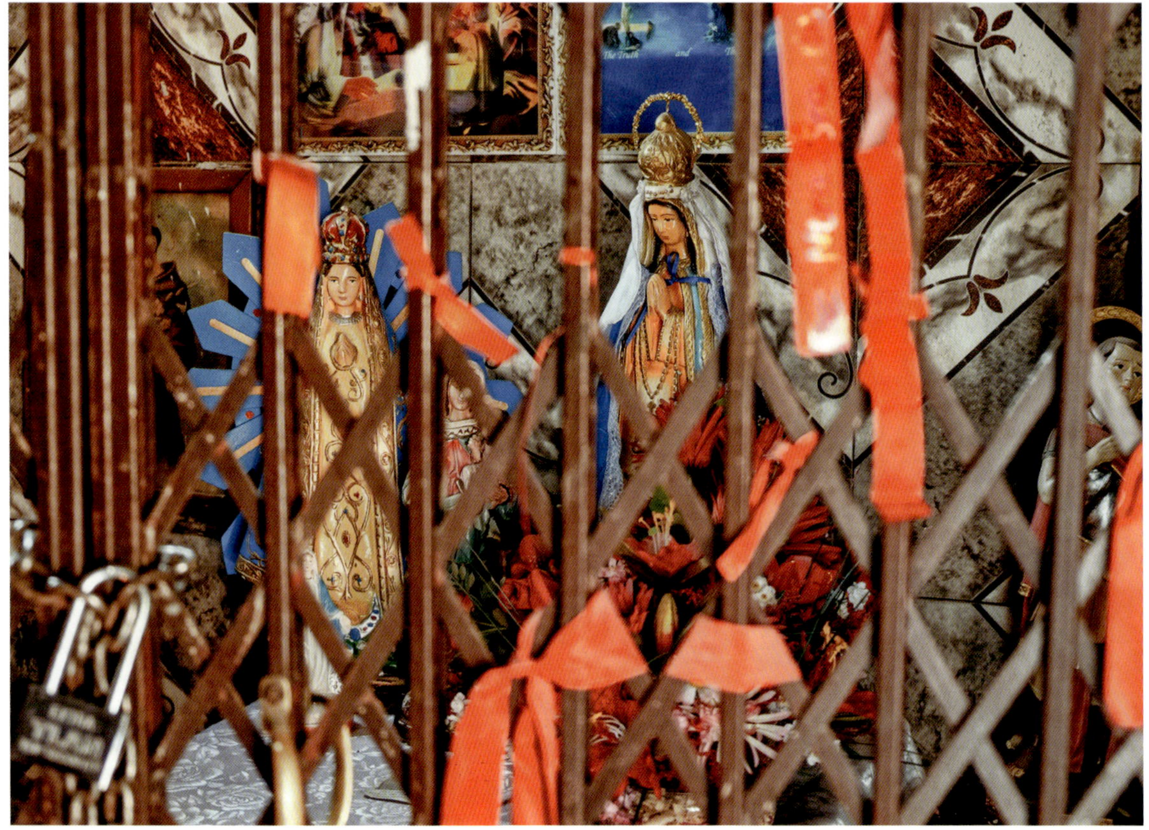

Altar para el Gauchito Gil
Altar for Gauchito Gil

The cult of the gaucho

The legend of Gauchito Gil, the fighter for the poor, spread throughout Argentina. In the 19th century, he was captured and executed in the province of Corrientes by his enemies during the Argentinian Civil Wars. Sanctuaries, Santuários Gauchito Gil, were built in many places and they are also festively decorated today. Every year, particularly on the day of his death, January 8th, crowds of pilgrims come to pay homage to the national hero. He is a symbol and support for different individuals and groups in Argentine society and the nostalgic cult of the Gaucho Gil is alive not only in rural but also in urban areas.

Le culte du *gaucho*

La légende du Gauchito Gil, défenseur des plus pauvres, s'est répandue dans toute l'Argentine. Au xixᵉ siècle, il fut arrêté dans la province de Corrientes par son ennemi du parti libéral, puis exécuté. Dans divers lieux, des sanctuaires, les *santuários Gauchito Gil,* ont été érigés et sont encore aujourd'hui ornés de décorations festives. Pour l'anniversaire de sa mort en particulier, le 8 janvier, des nuées de pèlerins se retrouvent chaque année afin d'honorer ce héros national. Il est un symbole et un soutien pour tous les individus et les groupes singuliers de la société argentine. Le culte nostalgique du Gauchito Gil est toujours vivant en campagne, mais également dans les régions urbaines.

Der Kult um den Gaucho

Die Legende um Gauchito Gil, den Kämpfer der Armen, verbreitete sich in ganz Argentinien. Im 19. Jahrhundert wurde er in der Provinz Corrientes von seinen Feinden der Liberalen Partei gefangengenommen und hingerichtet. An vielen Orten wurden Heiligenstätten, Santuários Gauchito Gil, errichtet. Sie werden auch heute festlich geschmückt. Insbesondere an seinem Todestag, dem 8. Januar, kommen jährlich Scharen von Pilgern um dem Volkshelden zu huldigen. Er ist Symbol und Halt für unterschiedliche Individuen und Gruppen der argentinischen Gesellschaft. Denn nicht nur im ländlichen, sondern auch im urbanen Raum ist der nostalgische Kult um den Gaucho Gil lebendig.

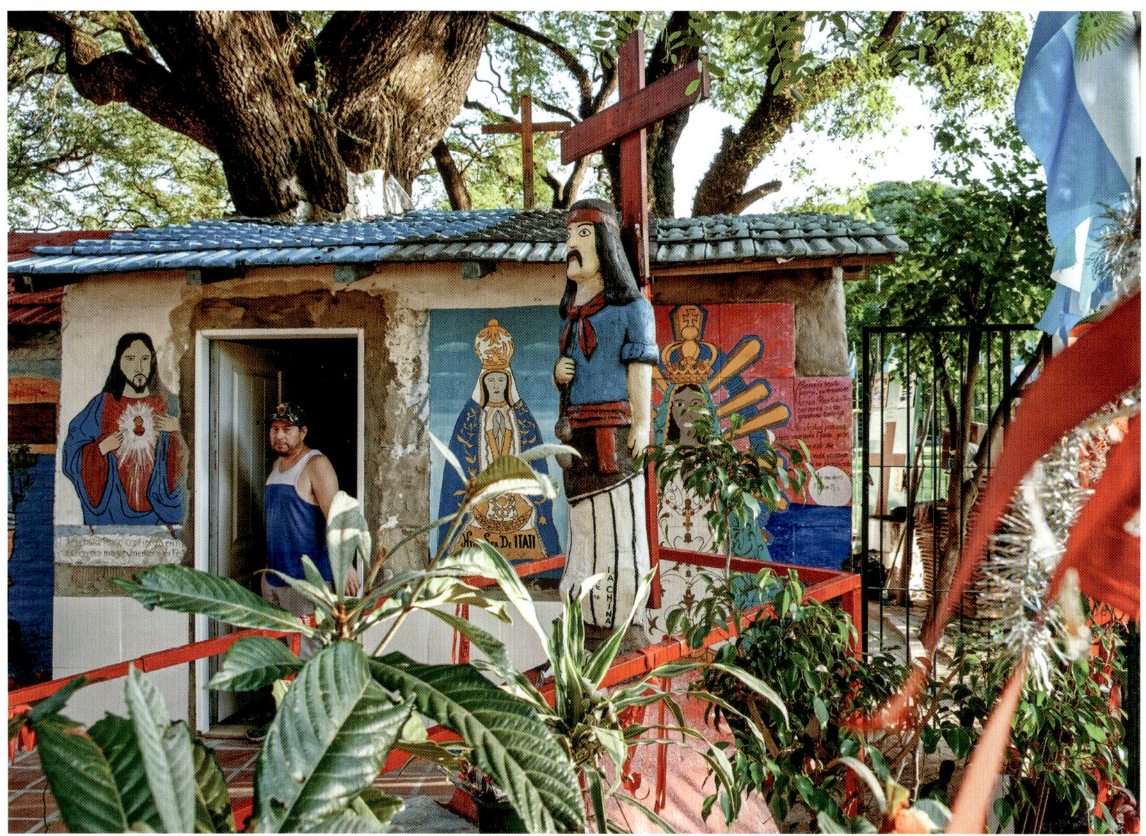

Altar para el Gauchito Gil
Altar for Gauchito Gil

El culto del gaucho

La leyenda del Gauchito Gil, el luchador de los pobres, se extendió por toda la Argentina. En el siglo XIX fue capturado y ejecutado en la provincia de Corrientes por sus enemigos del Partido Liberal. Los santuarios del Gauchito Gil fueron construidos en muchos lugares. Hoy en día también están decorados de manera festiva. Especialmente el día de su muerte, el 8 de enero, todos los años llegan multitudes de peregrinos para rendir homenaje a este héroe nacional. Es un símbolo y un apoyo para diferentes individuos y grupos de la sociedad argentina, porque el culto nostálgico del Gaucho Gil aún sigue vivo no solo en las zonas rurales, sino también en las urbanas.

O culto em torno do gaúcho

A lenda do Gauchito Gil, o justiceiro dos pobres, espalhou-se por toda a Argentina. No século XIX ele foi capturado e executado na província de Corrientes pelos seus inimigos do Partido Liberal. Em vários lugares foram construídos lugares sagrados, Santuários Gauchito Gil. Ainda hoje eles são decorados festivamente. Especialmente no dia da sua morte, 8 de janeiro, todos os anos multidões de peregrinos vêm homenagear o herói nacional. É um símbolo e um apoio para diferentes indivíduos e grupos da sociedade argentina. Pois não apenas nas áreas rurais, mas também nas áreas urbanas, o culto nostálgico do Gil Gaúcho ainda está vivo.

De cultus rondom de gaucho

De legende van Gauchito Gil, de strijder van de armen, verspreidde zich over heel Argentinië. In de 19e eeuw werd hij in de provincie Corrientes door zijn vijanden van de Liberale Partij gevangen genomen en geëxecuteerd. Op veel plaatsen werden heilige plekken, Santuários Gauchito Gil, neergezet. Ook vandaag de dag worden ze feestelijk versierd. Vooral op de dag van zijn dood, 8 januari, komen elk jaar weer massa's pelgrims om de volksheld te huldigen. Hij is een symbool en steun voor verschillende individuen en groepen in de Argentijnse samenleving. Want niet alleen in de landelijke, maar ook in de stedelijke ruimte is de nostalgische cultus van de Gaucho Gil levendig.

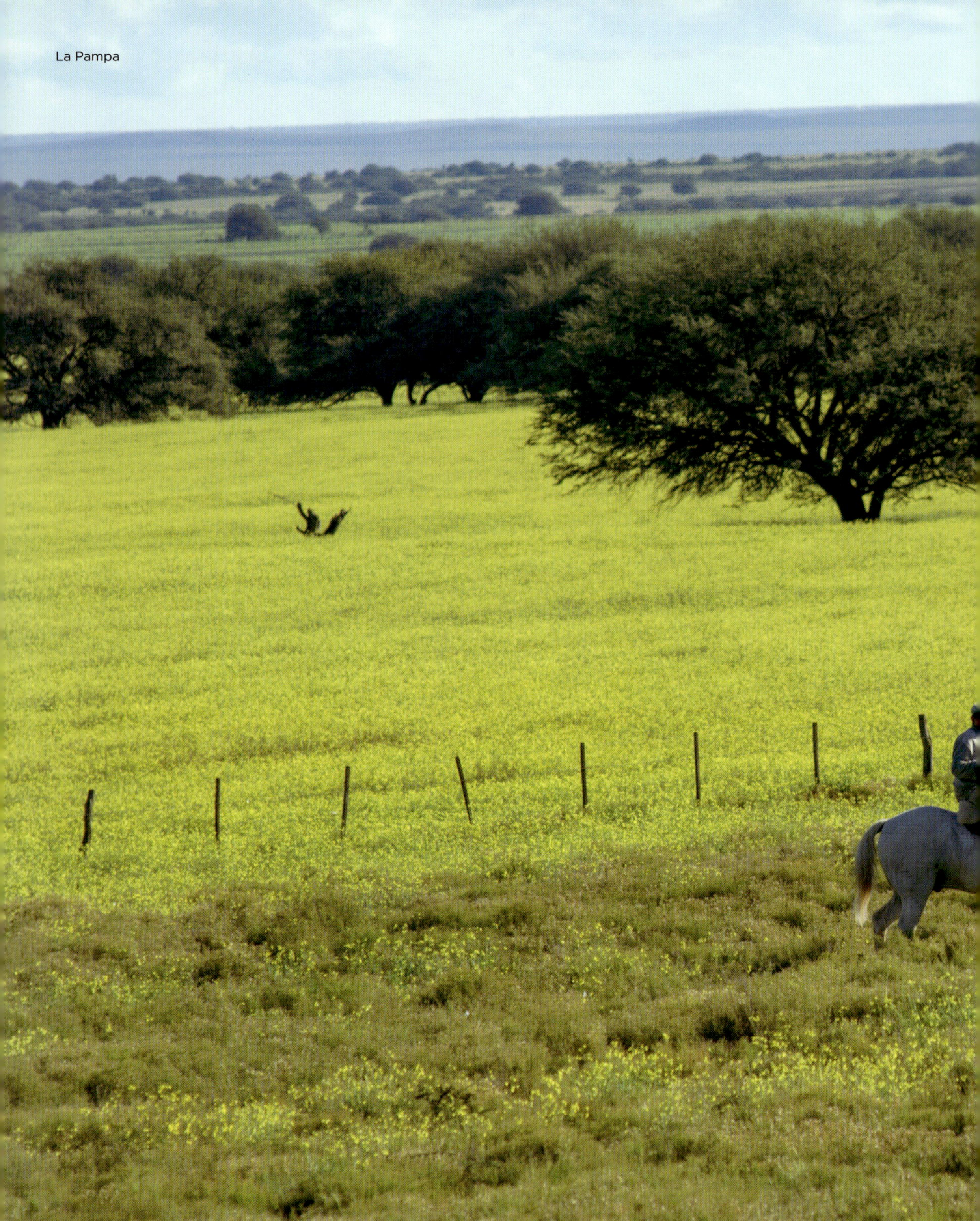
La Pampa

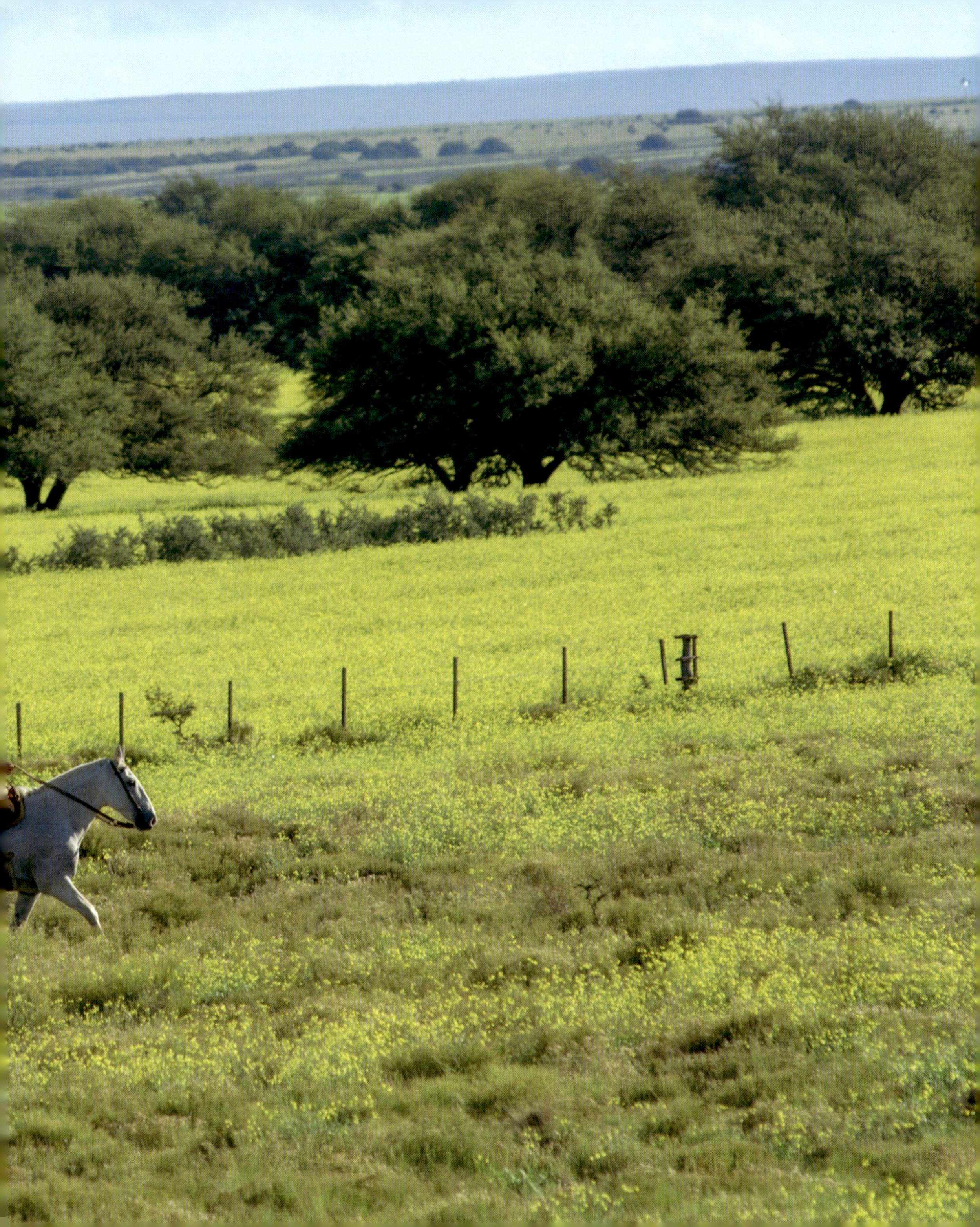

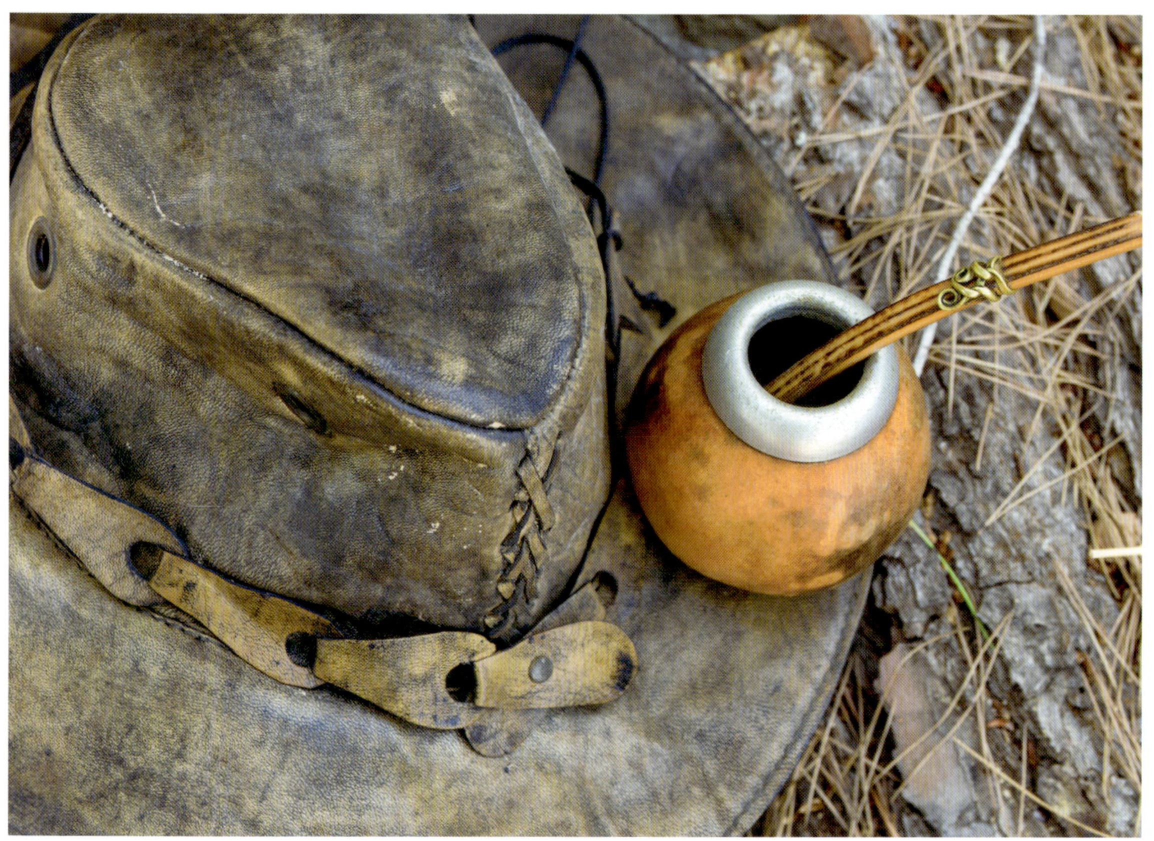

Sombrero, mate
Hat, Mate bowl

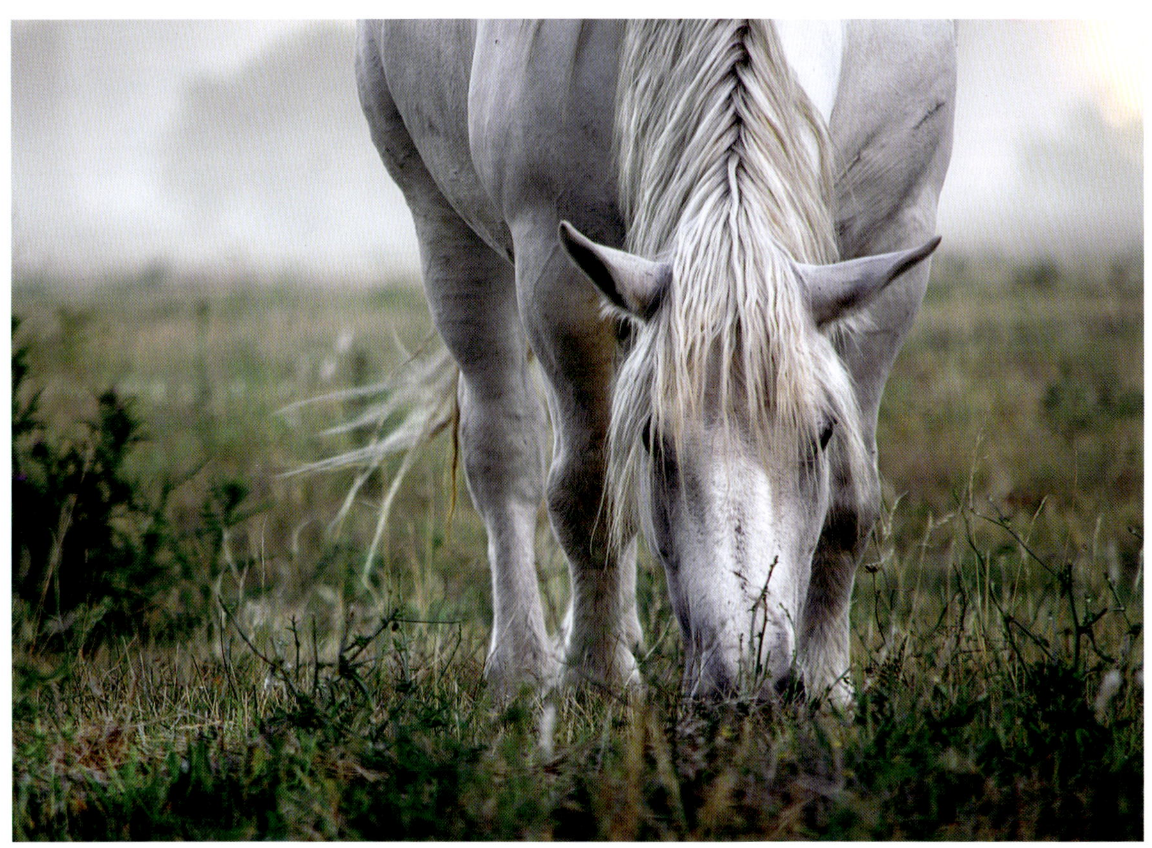

Caballo
Horse

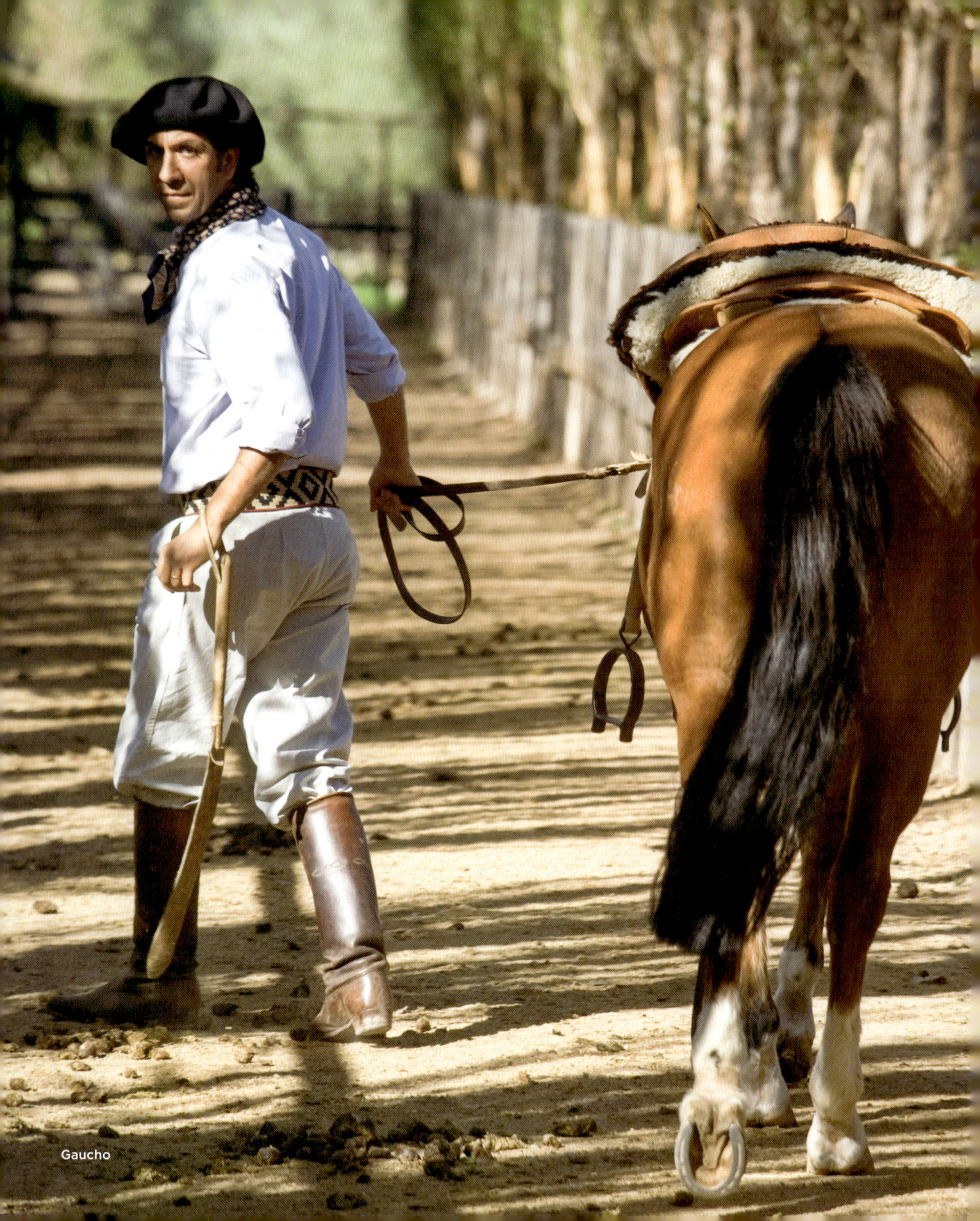

Gaucho

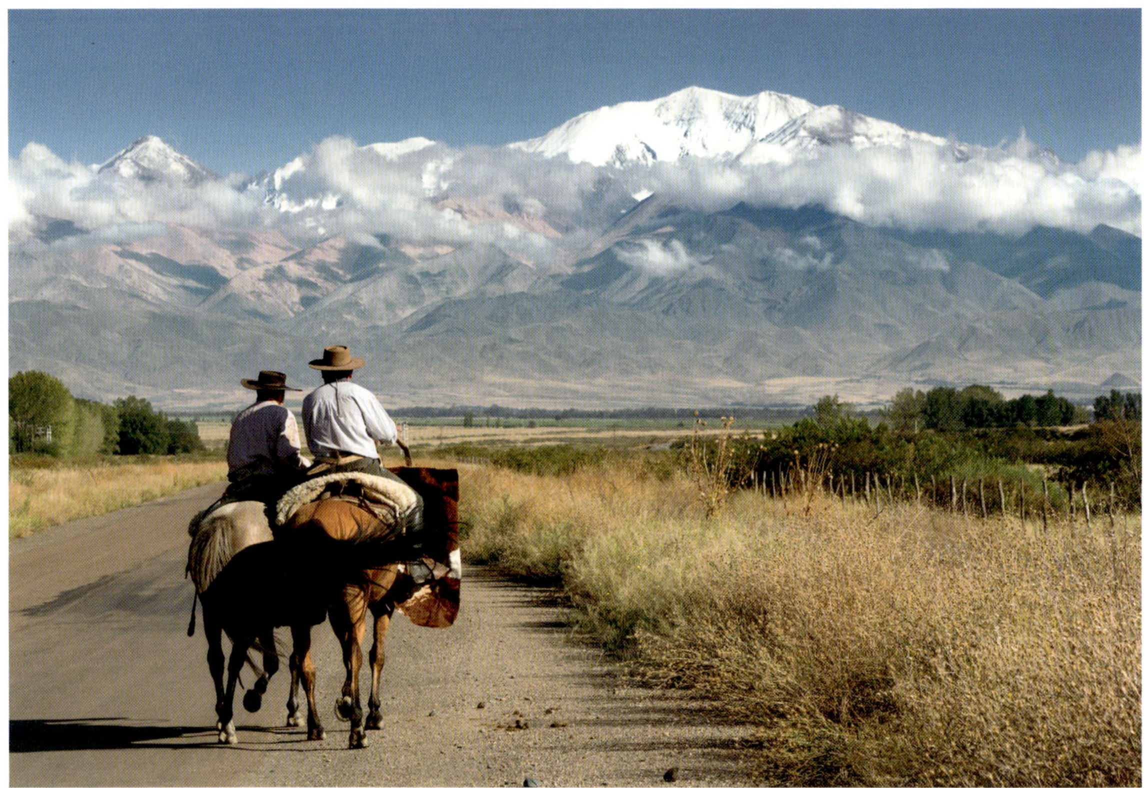

Gauchos

Heroes of the horseback

The reputation of the horse whisperers precedes them. Taming and breaking in horses is traditionally one of the tasks of the gaucho, in addition to their hard physical work, and one which requires great knowledge and skill. Although they were relegated to the status of poorly paid cattle drovers, or *peónes,* the proud attitude of the gauchos remained.

Héroes del caballo

La reputación de susurrador de caballos les precede. La doma y el jineteado de caballos es tradicionalmente una de las tareas del gaucho, así como un duro trabajo físico, que requiere gran conocimiento y habilidad. Aunque su destino los degradó a mal pagados, la actitud orgullosa de los gauchos ha pervivido.

Héros à cheval

Ils ont acquis la réputation de chuchoter à l'oreille des chevaux. Le domptage et le dressage incombent en effet traditionnellement aux *gauchos,* tout comme les travaux physiques difficiles, qui nécessitent également de nombreuses connaissances et une grande adresse. Bien que le destin les ait dégradés au rang de gardiens de troupeaux (peones) mal rémunérés, la posture fière des *gauchos* a perduré.

Heróis do cavalo

A reputação do sussurrador de cavalo precede-os. Domar e andar a cavalo tem sido tradicionalmente uma das tarefas do gaúcho, assim como o trabalho físico árduo, que requer grande conhecimento e habilidade. Embora seu destino os tenha degradado a boiadeiros mal pagos,"peones", a atitude orgulhosa dos gaúchos permaneceu.

Helden des Pferderückens

Ihnen eilt der Ruf des Pferdeflüsterers voraus. Pferde zu zähmen und zuzureiten gehört traditionell zu den Aufgaben des Gaucho, ebenso wie körperlich harte Arbeit, die großes Wissen und Geschicklichkeit erfordert. Obwohl ihr Schicksal sie zu schlecht bezahlten Viehtreibern, *peones,* degradierte, blieb die stolze Haltung der Gauchos.

Helden van de paardenrug

Met de reputatie als paardenfluisteraar waren ze hun tijd vooruit. Het temmen en africhten van paarden is traditioneel één van de taken van de gaucho, evenals hard lichamelijk werk, wat een grote kennis en vaardigheid vereist. Hoewel hun lot ze tot slecht betaalde veedrijvers, *peones,* degradeerde, hield de trotse houding van de gauchos stand.

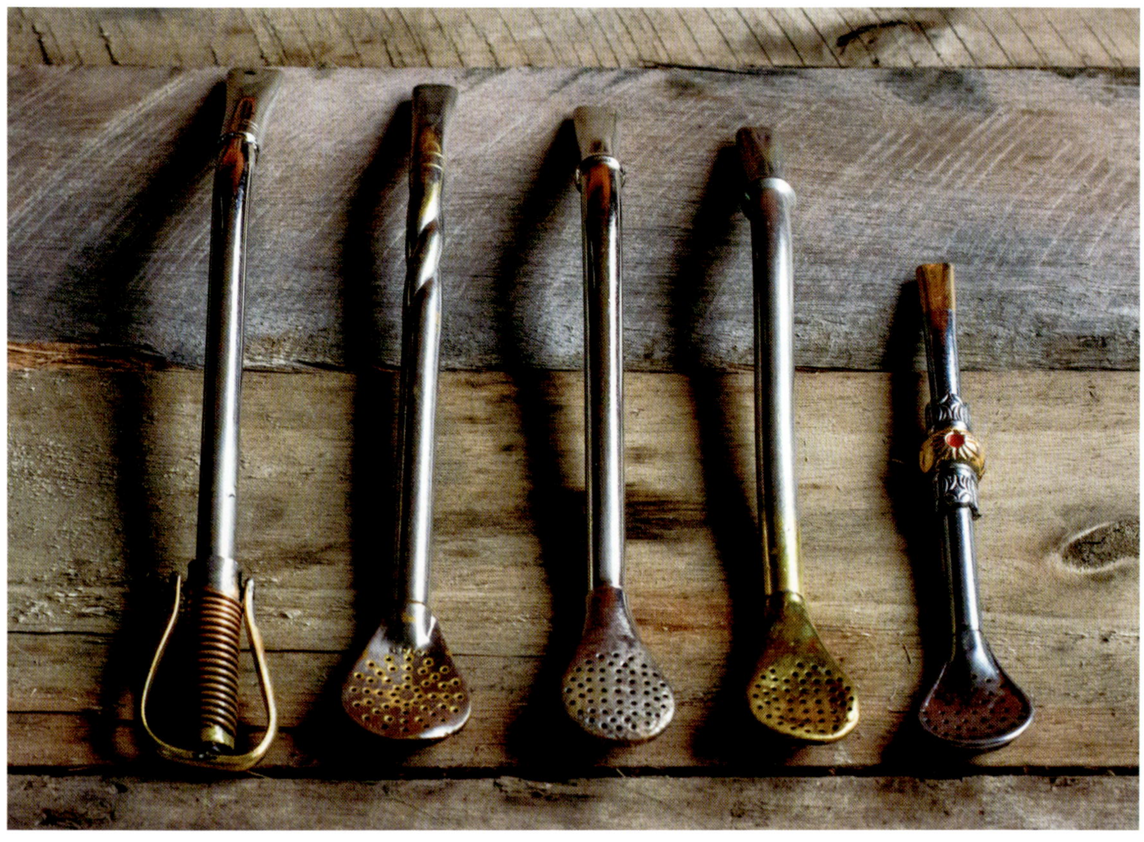

Bombillas

Mate

Drinking mate around the fire has always been an integral part of gaucho culture. Originally, it was purely a masculine thing, for men to form a silent, or sometimes a talkative group, drinking from the circulating *calabash.* Just as the indigenous groups used to do when they used drinking vessels and pipes —belonging like land and livestock—together. Mate comes from the Quechua word *mati,* which refers to the drinking vessel, a hollowed *calabash.* The filled *calabash* is always freshly infused. Mate is good for digestion and is considered a panacea, stimulating, dispelling hunger and calming the nerves.

Le maté

Déguster le maté assis autour du feu est un rituel établi de la culture *gaucho.* À l'origine, c'était une tradition purement masculine. Les hommes réunissaient une communauté, silencieuse ou parlante, d'individus parmi lesquels circulait la calebasse contenant la boisson. Ce rite était autrefois pratiqué par des groupes d'Indiens qui utilisaient en commun le récipient et la paille, comme la terre et le bétail. «Maté» vient du mot quechua *mati,* qui désigne un récipient pour boire creusé dans une calebasse. Au cours de la dégustation, on ajoute régulièrement de l'eau chaude dans la calebasse. Le maté est bon pour la circulation; considéré comme un remède universel, il stimule, atténue la sensation de faim et détend.

Mate

Rund um das Feuer Mate zu trinken war immer ein fester Bestandteil der Gaucho-Kultur. Ursprünglich war es reine Männersache, eine schweigende oder auch beredte Gemeinschaft zu bilden und aus der zirkulierenden Kalebasse zu trinken. So wie es vormals die indianischen Gruppen praktizierten, wenn sie Trinkgefäße und Pfeifen – wie Land und Vieh – gemeinschaftlich nutzten. Mate leitet sich von dem Quechua-Wort *mati* ab, das ein Trinkgefäß, die ausgehöhlte Kalebasse bezeichnete. Die gefüllte Kalebasse wird immer wieder frisch aufgegossen. Mate ist gut für die Verdauung, er gilt als Allheilmittel, putscht auf, vertreibt den Hunger und beruhigt.

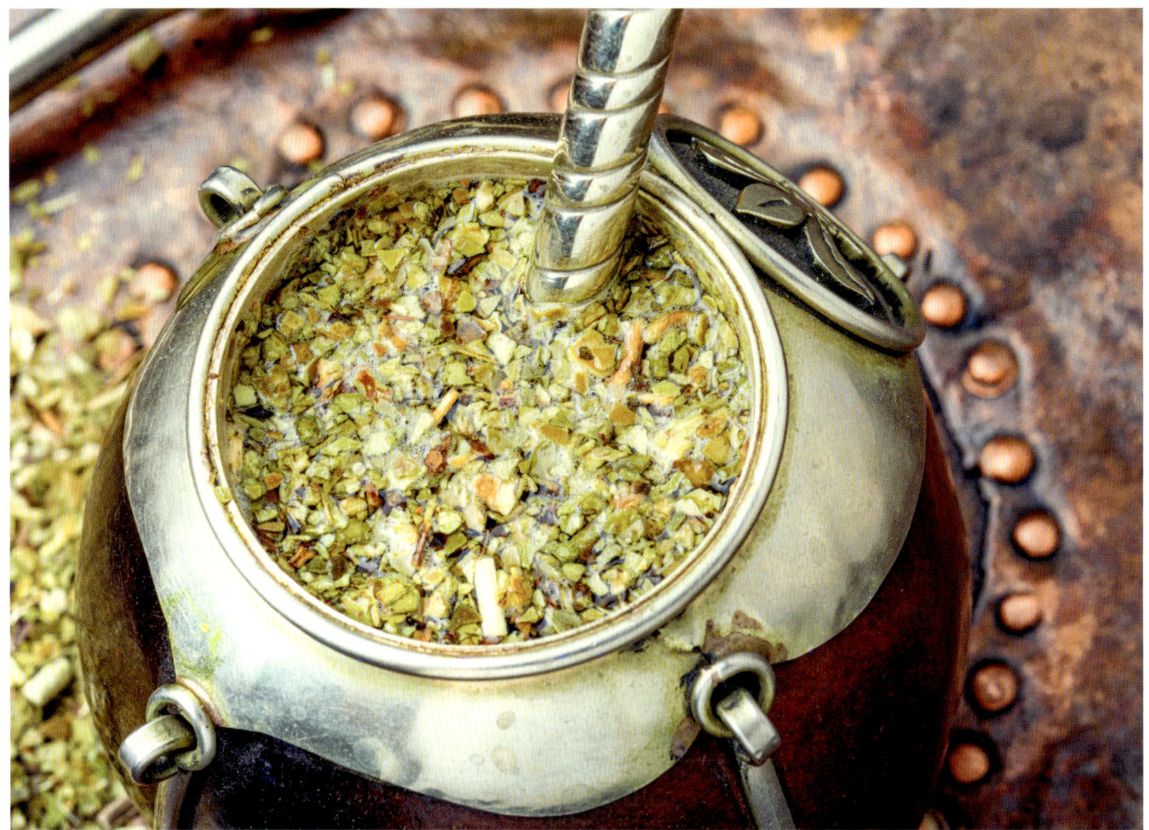

Mate

Mate

Beber mate alrededor del fuego siempre ha sido una parte integral de la cultura gaucha. Originalmente, era solo cuestión de que los hombres formaran un grupo silencioso o también hablador, para beber de la calabaza que circulaba. Tal como lo hacían los grupos indígenas cuando usaban recipientes para beber y pipas (que les eran tan propios como la tierra y el ganado) juntos. La palabra *mate* viene de la palabra quechua *mati,* que hace referencia a una vasija para beber: la calabaza hueca. La calabaza rellena siempre está recién cebada. El mate es bueno para la digestión, se considera una panacea, es un estimulante, disipa el hambre y calma los nervios.

Mate

Beber mate à volta da fogueira sempre foi parte integrante da cultura gaúcha. Originalmente, era puramente uma questão de homens formarem uma comunidade silenciosa ou mesmo eloquente, para beber da cabaça em circulação. Assim como os grupos indígenas costumavam fazer quando compartilhavam recipientes para beber e cachimbos – como terra e gado – juntos. Mate vem da palavra quíchua *mati,* que se refere a um recipiente para beber, a cabaça oca. A cabaça quando cheia é sempre servida na hora e a água é derramda várias vezes sobre o conteúdo. O mate é bom para a digestão, é considerado uma panaceia, estimula, dissipa a fome e acalma os nervos.

Mate

Het drinken van mate rond het vuur was altijd al een vast onderdeel van de gaucho-cultuur. Oorspronkelijk was het een pure mannenaangelegenheid, een zwijgende of ook welbespraakte gemeenschap te vormen, en uit de circulerende kalebas te drinken. Zoals het voorheen de Indiaanse groepen deden als ze drinkgerei en pijpen – zoals land en vee – gemeenschappelijk gebruikten. Mate stamt van het Quechua woord *mati,* dat verwijst naar een drinkkom, de uitgeholde kalebas. De gevulde kalebas wordt altijd weer vers gevuld. Mate is goed voor de spijsvertering, het geldt als wondermiddel, stimuleert, verdrijft de honger en kalmeert de zenuwen.

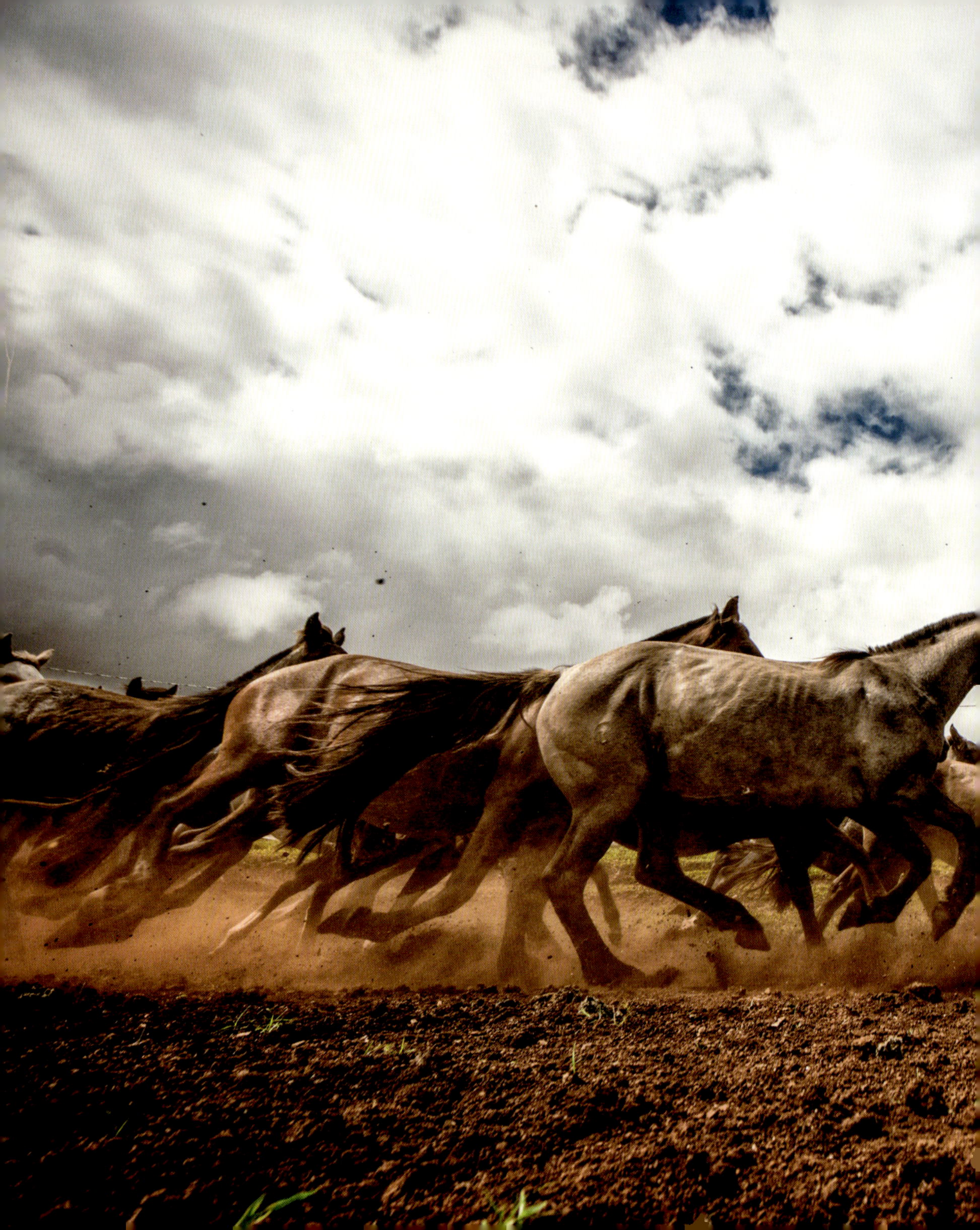

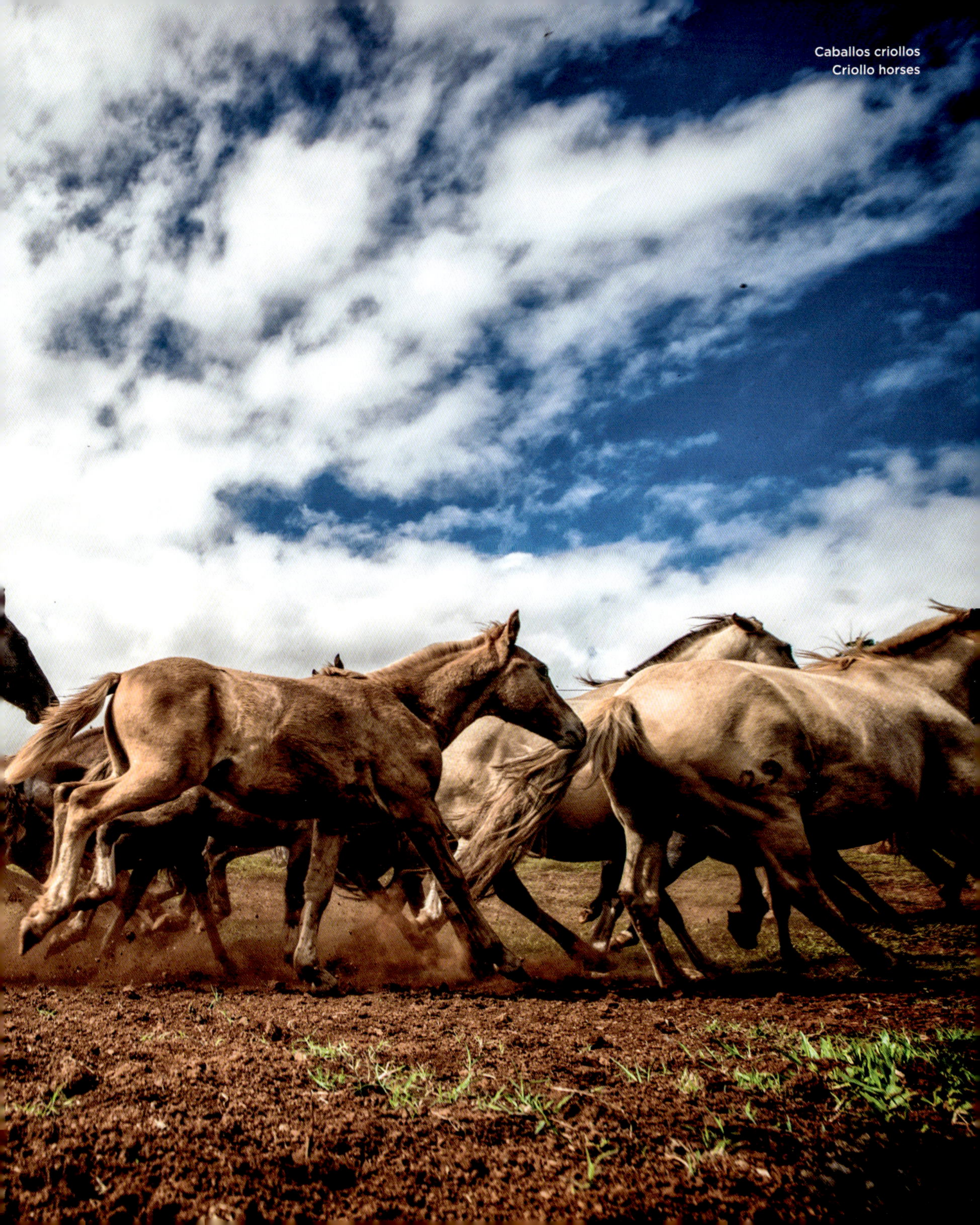

Caballos criollos
Criollo horses

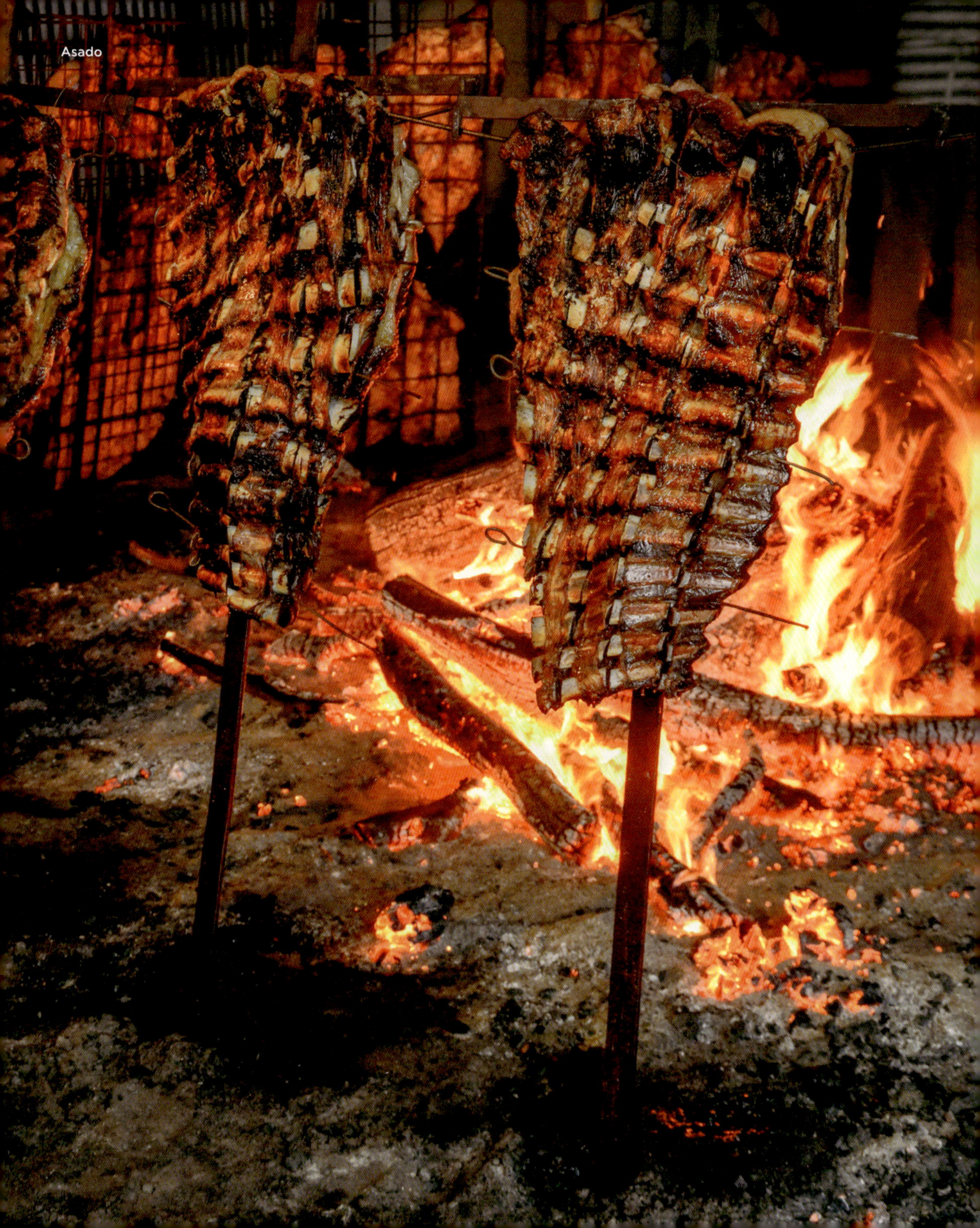
Asado

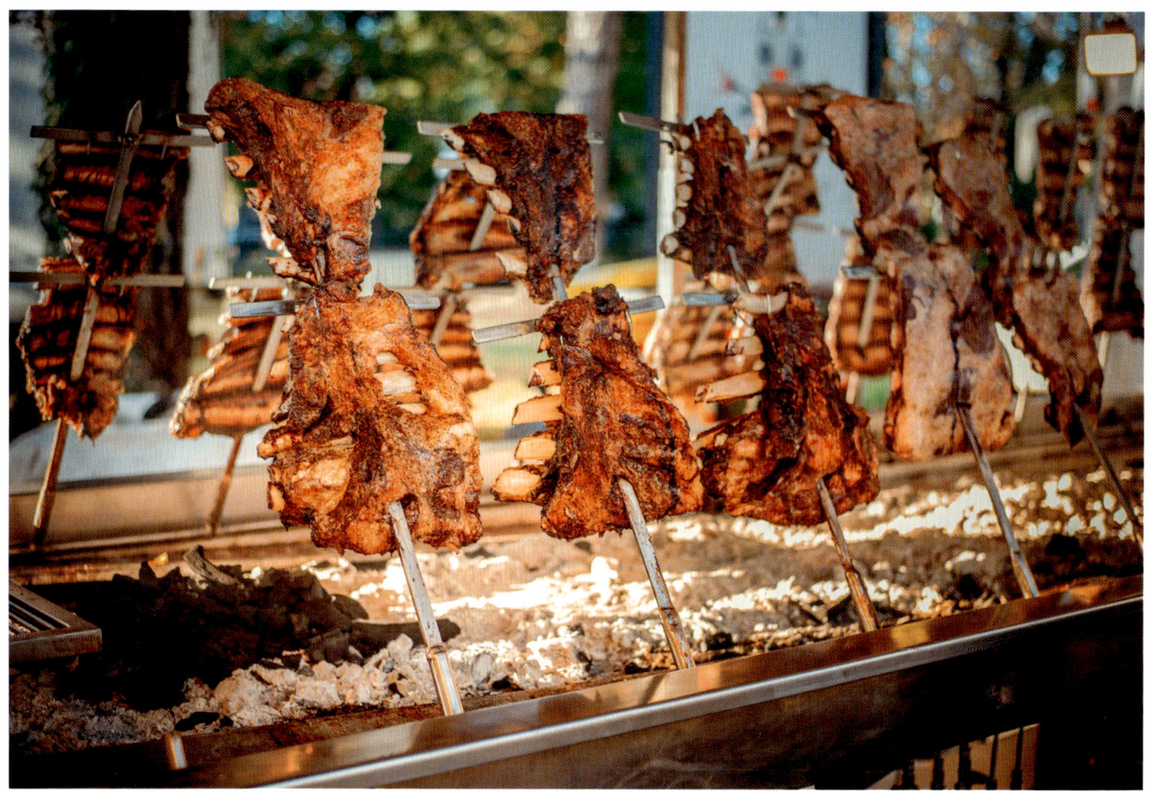

Asado

Asado a la cruz

In the countryside, the grilling method "asado a la cruz" is common, where whole sides of beef ,with skin, are placed vertically on large iron frames, which are set up over the embers. Instead of charcoal, vegetable material is used. The animal fat drips onto the embers and the resulting smoke produces special smokey notes.

Asado a la cruz

En el campo, el método de asado a la cruz es común: las mitades de carne entera con piel se colocan verticalmente en grandes parrillas de hierro, que se colocan alrededor de las brasas. En lugar de carbón, se utiliza leña. La grasa animal gotea sobre las brasas y el humo resultante produce un toque especial de ahumado.

Asado a la cruz

Dans les campagnes, la cuisson au gril est appelée *asado a la cruz* : des demi-carcasses de bœuf, avec la peau, sont installées verticalement sur de grandes grilles en fer disposées autour du brasier. Le feu est alimenté par des végétaux et non par du charbon de bois. La graisse animale tombe dans la braise, et le parfum qui s'en dégage apporte des notes aromatiques particulières.

Asado a la cruz

O método de grelhar "asado a la cruz" é comum no campo: metades inteiras de carne com pele são colocadas verticalmente em grandes grelhas de ferro, que são instaladas em torno das brasas. É usado material vegetal, em vez de carvão. A gordura animal escorre nas brasas e a fumaça resultante produz um toque defumado especial.

Asado a la cruz

Auf dem Lande ist die Grillmethode „asado a la cruz" geläufig: Ganze Rinderhälften mit Haut kommen vertikal auf große Eisengrills, die rund um die Glut aufgestellt werden. Statt Holzkohle wird pflanzliches Material verwendet. Das tierische Fett tropft auf die Glut, der entstehende Rauch produziert besondere Räuchernoten.

Asado a la cruz

Op het platteland is de grillmethode "asado a la cruz" gebruikelijk: complete stukken rund met huid worden verticaal op grote ijzeren roosters geplaatst, die rondom de vuurgloed zijn opgesteld. In plaats van houtskool wordt plantaardig materiaal gebruikt. Het dierlijk vet druipt op de gloed, de resulterende rook produceert bijzondere, gerookte geuren.

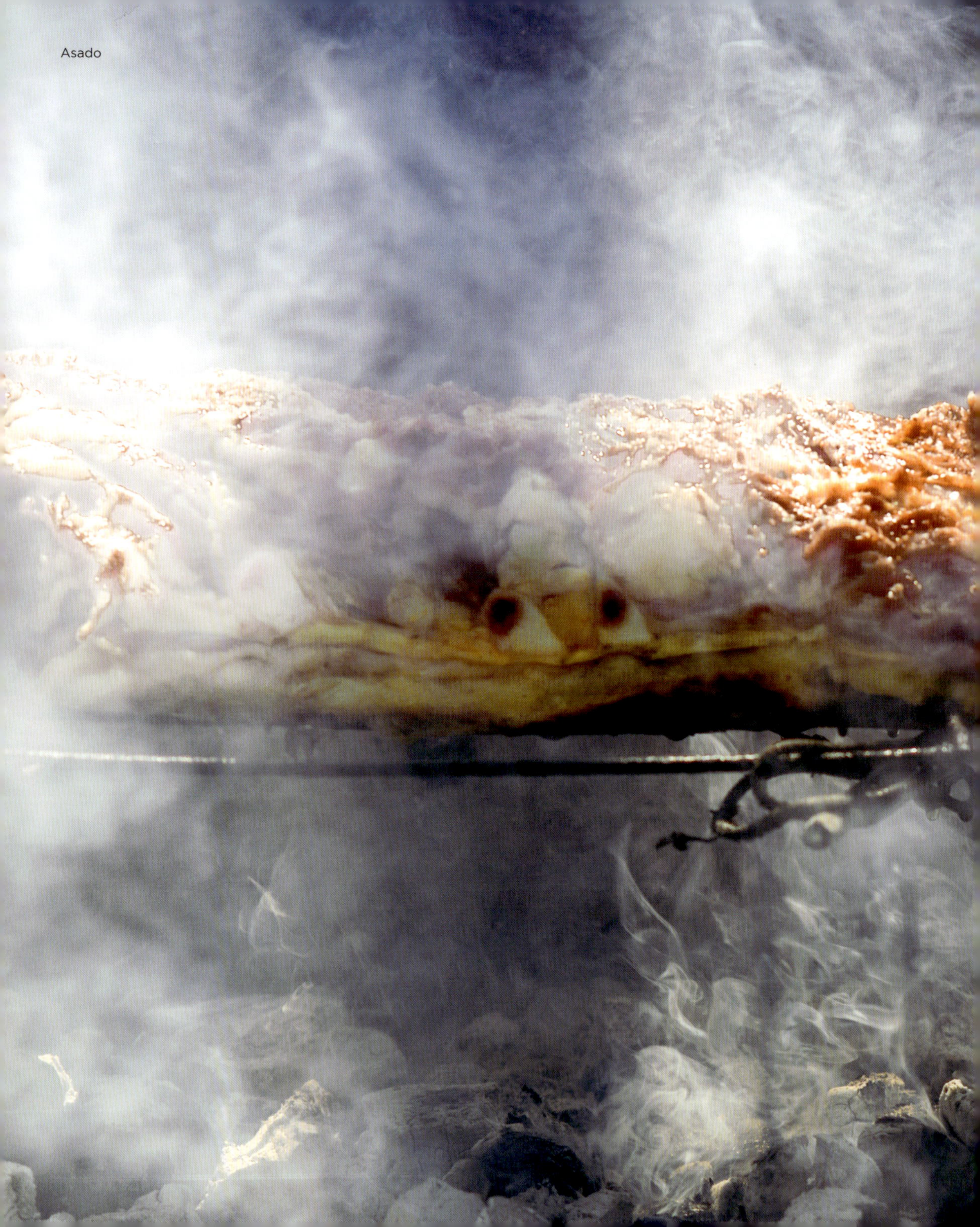

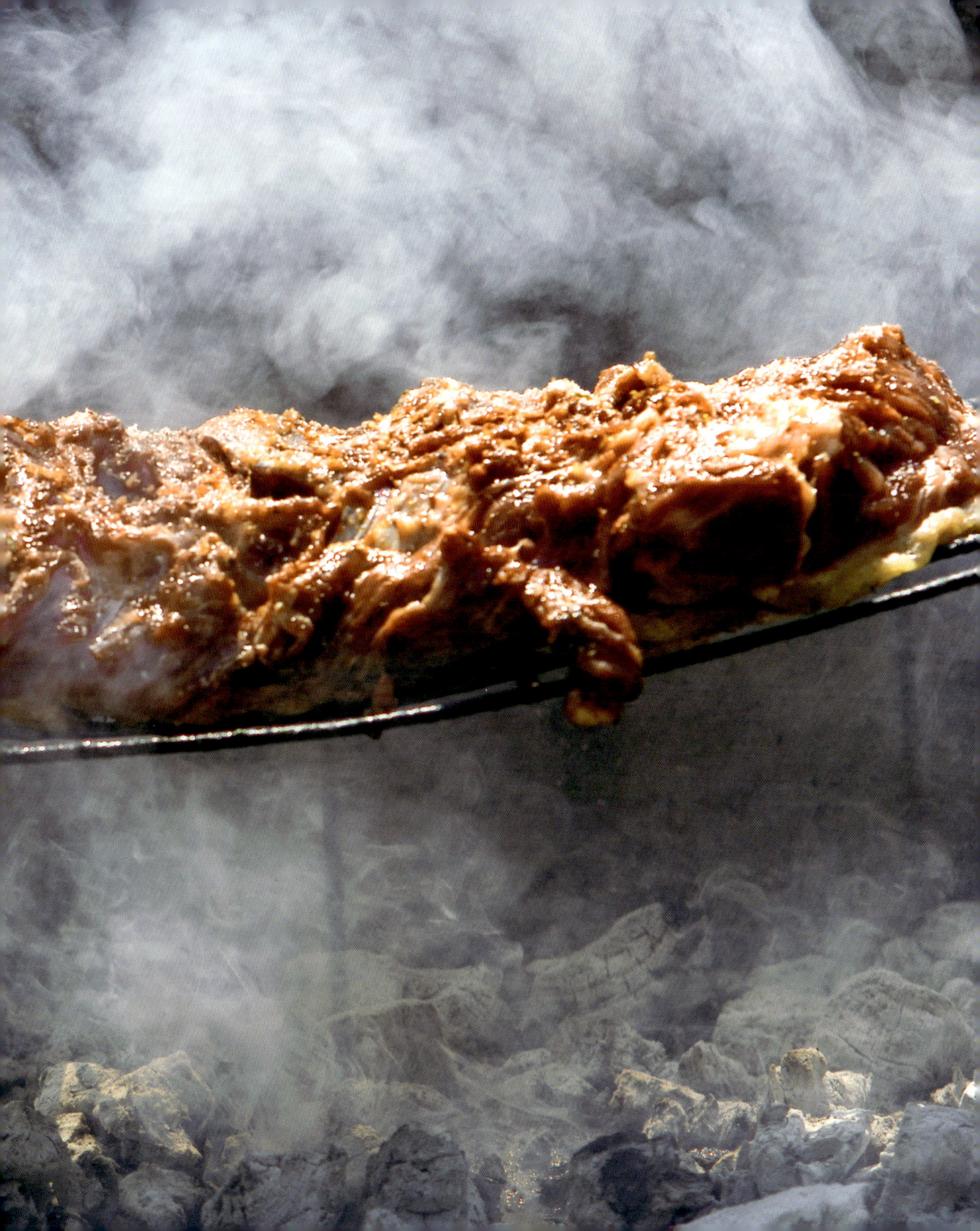

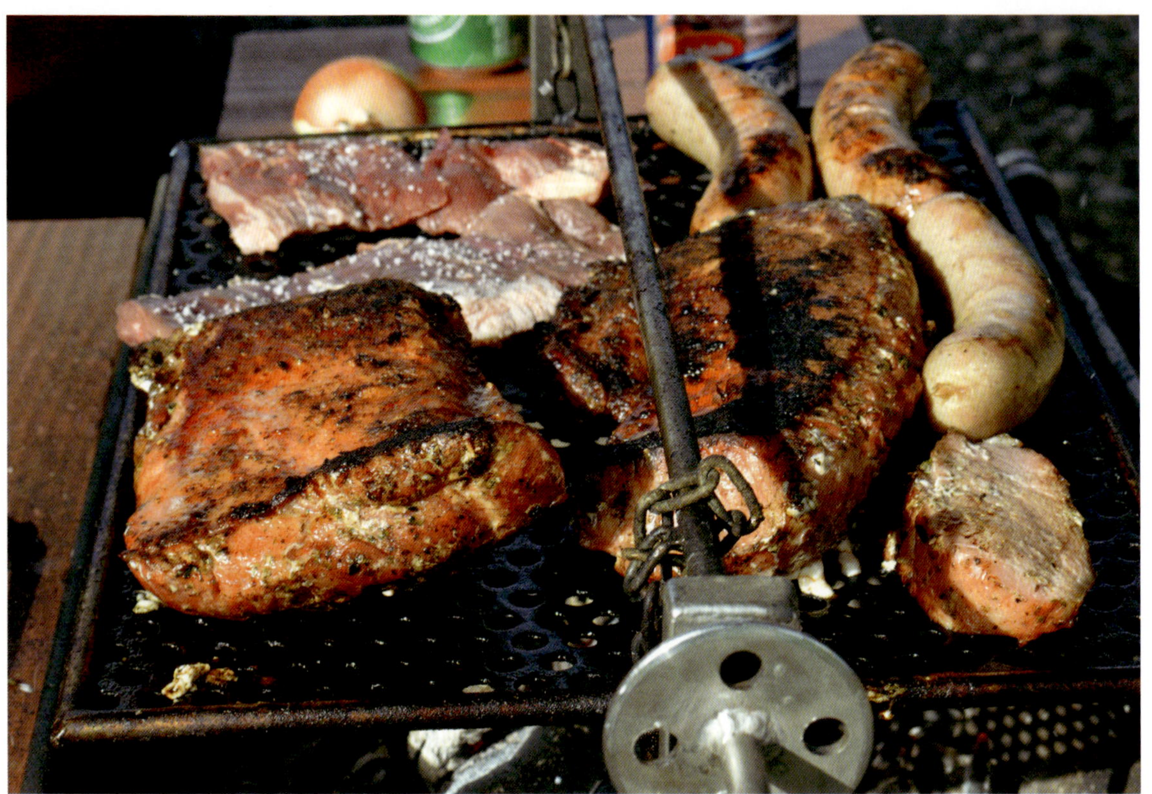

Asado

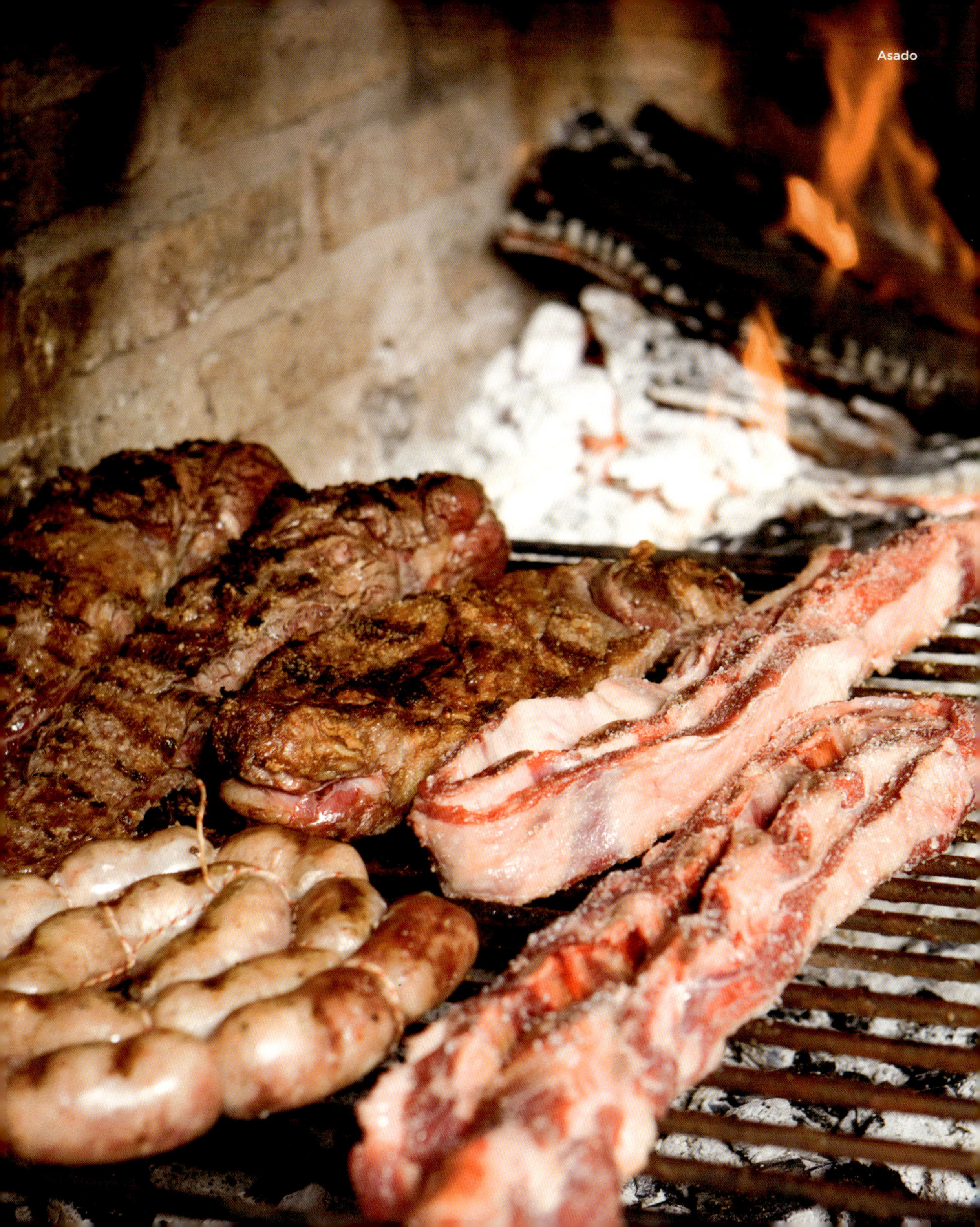
Asado

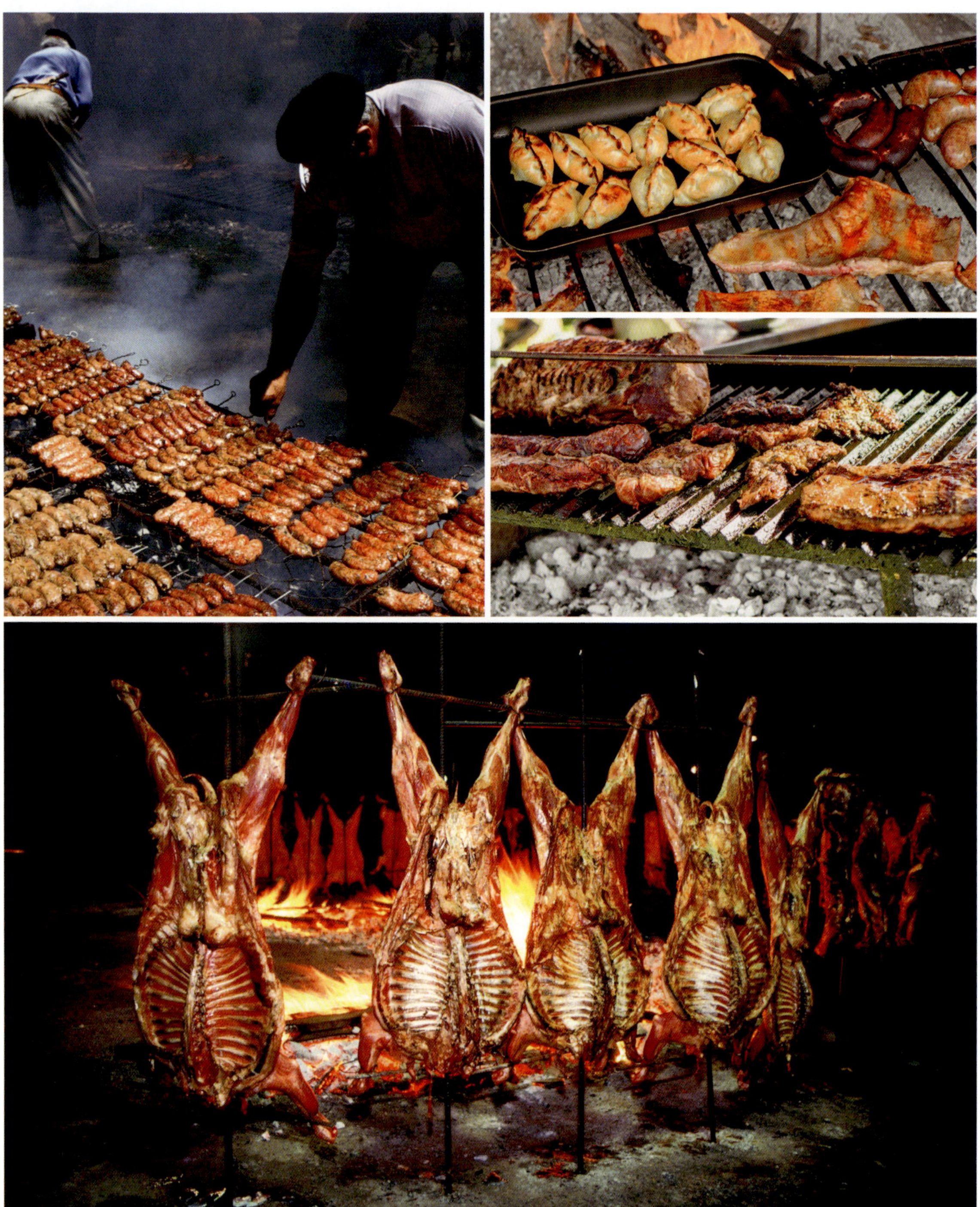

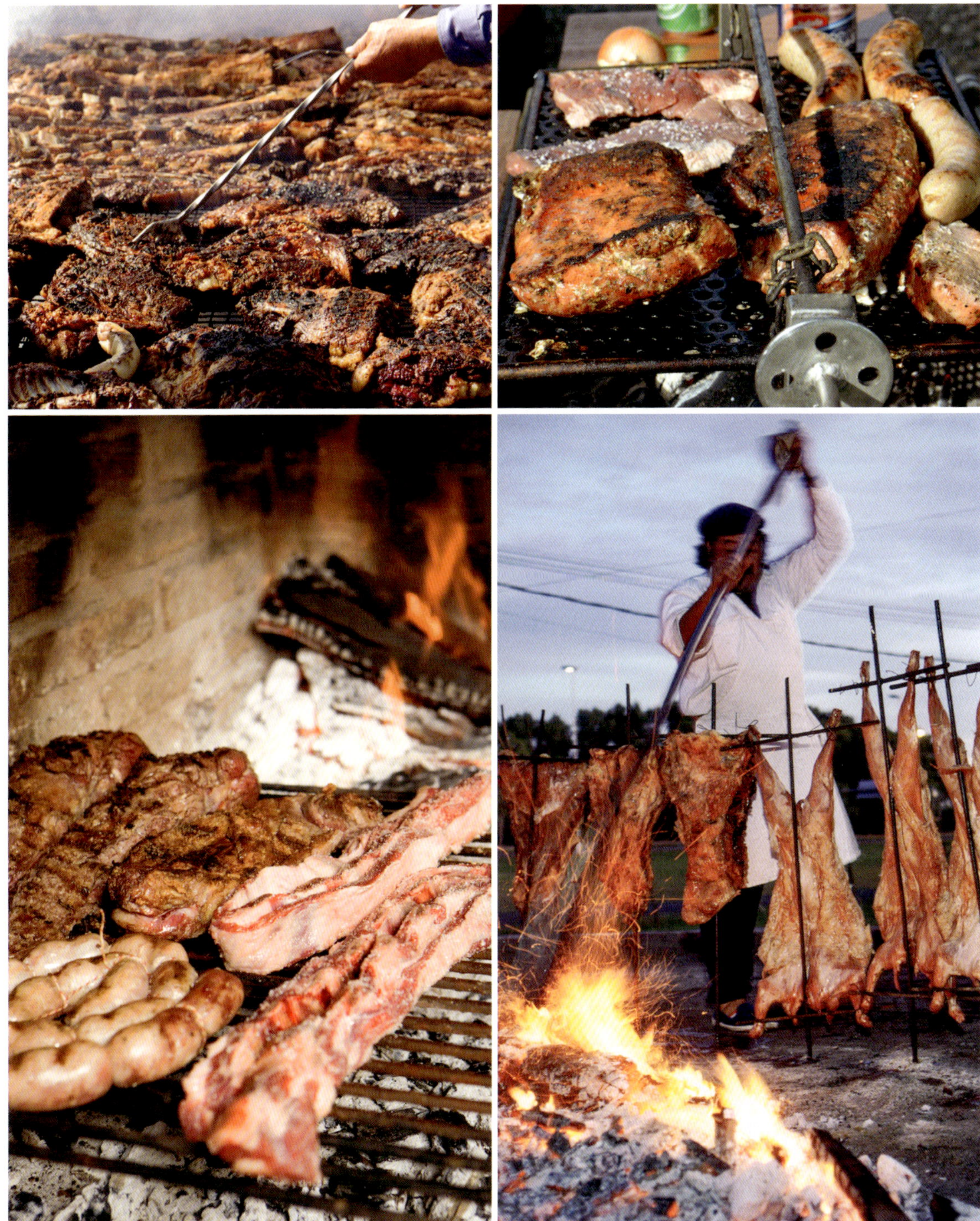

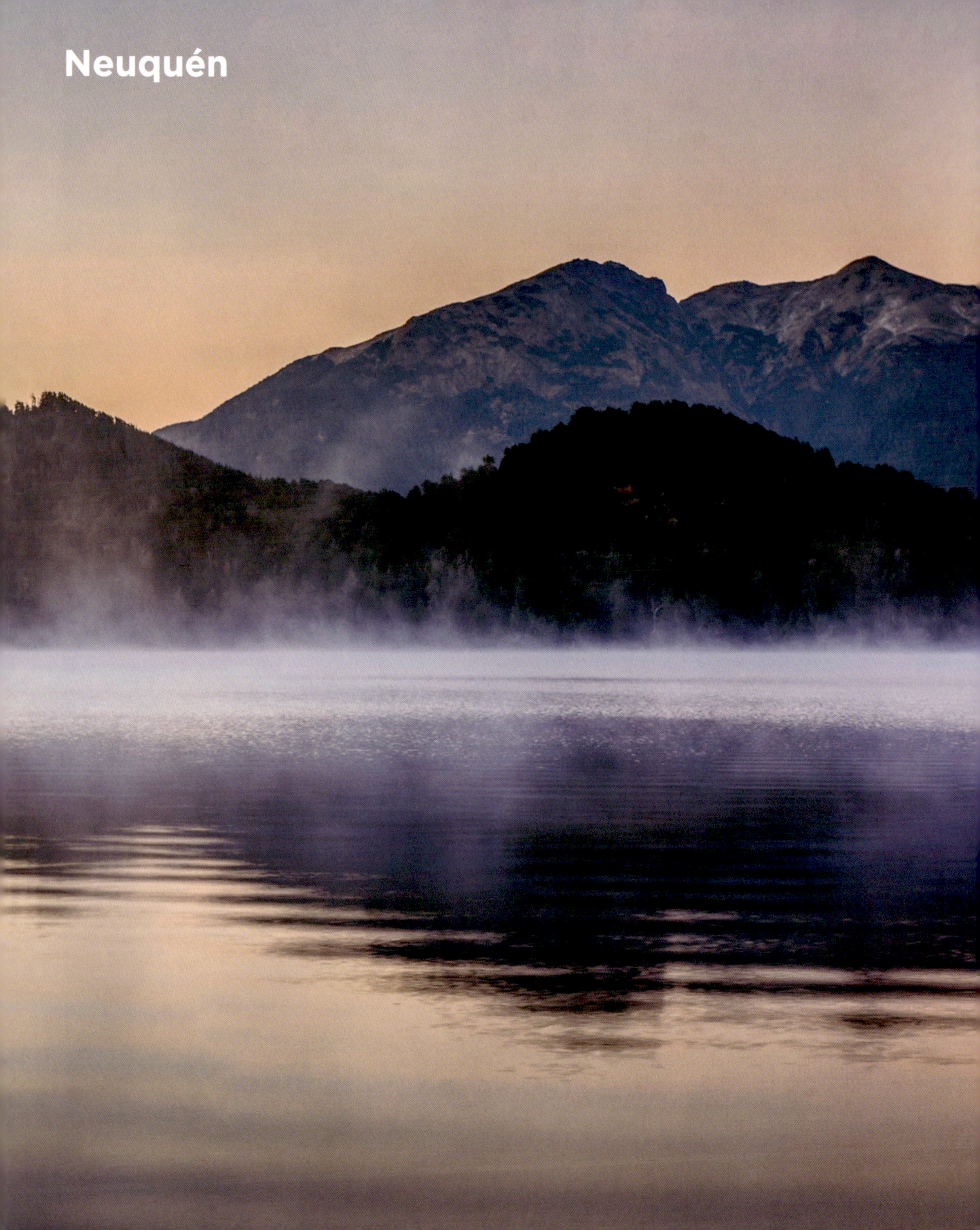
Neuquén

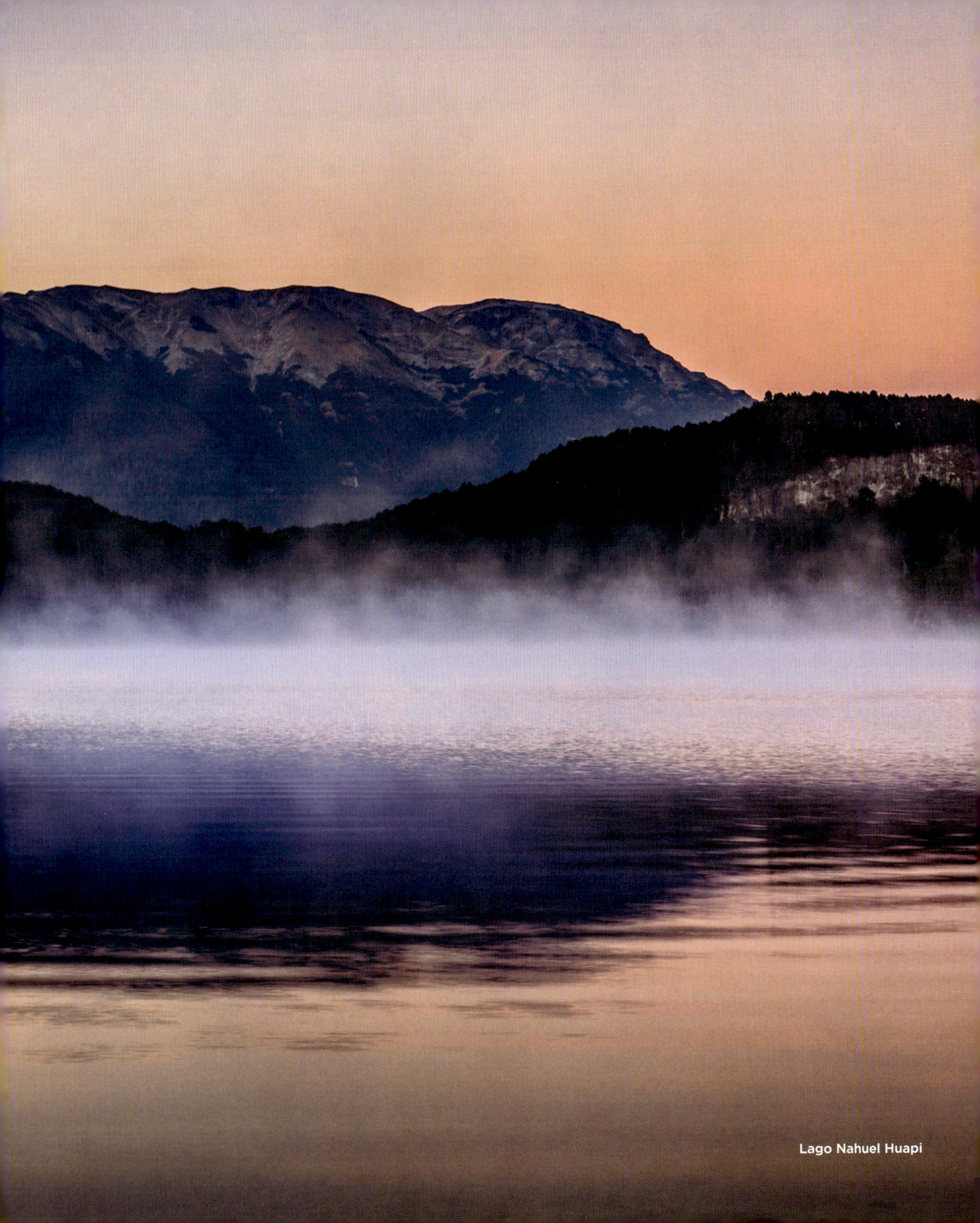
Lago Nahuel Huapi

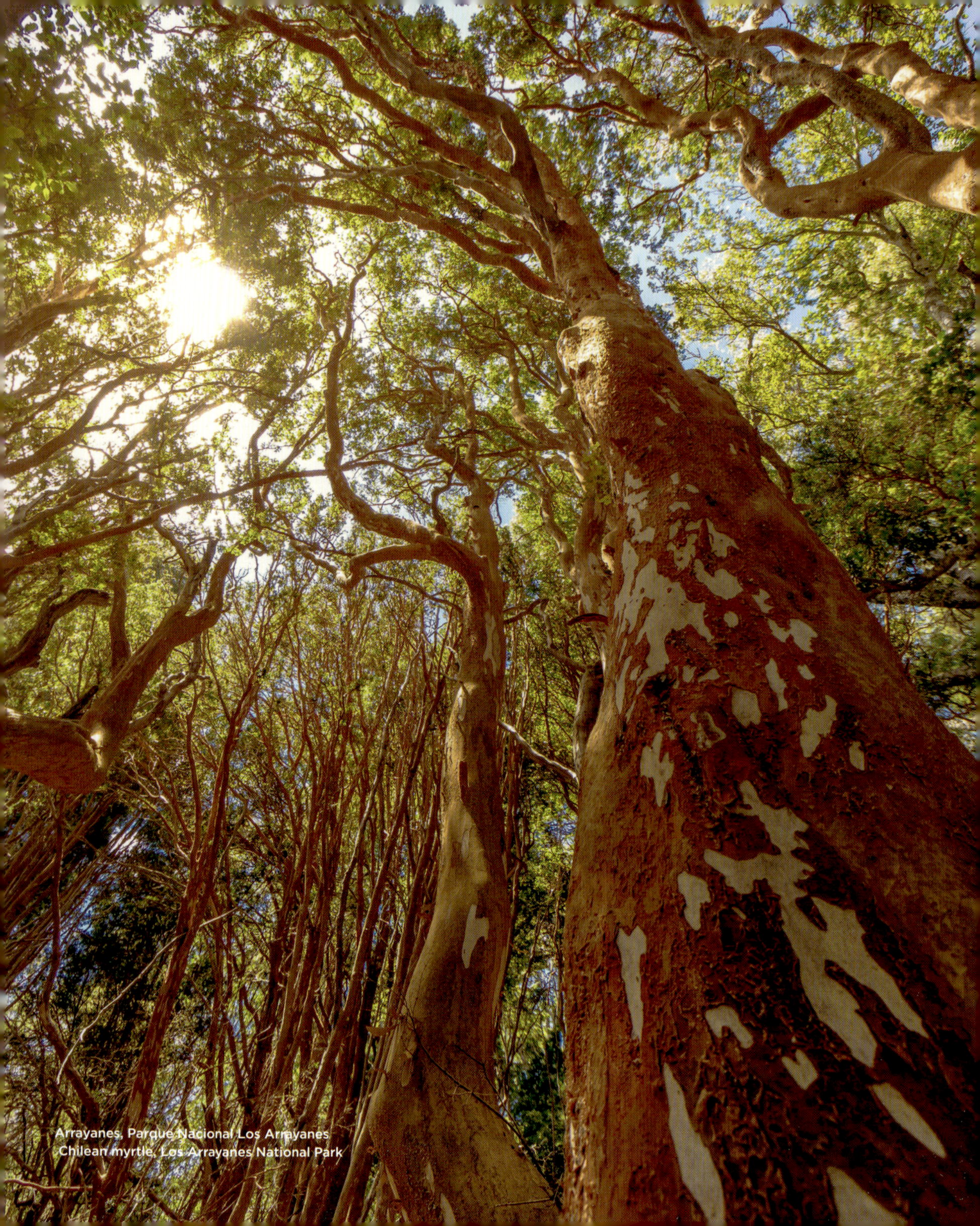

Arrayanes, Parque Nacional Los Arrayanes
Chilean myrtle, Los Arrayanes National Park

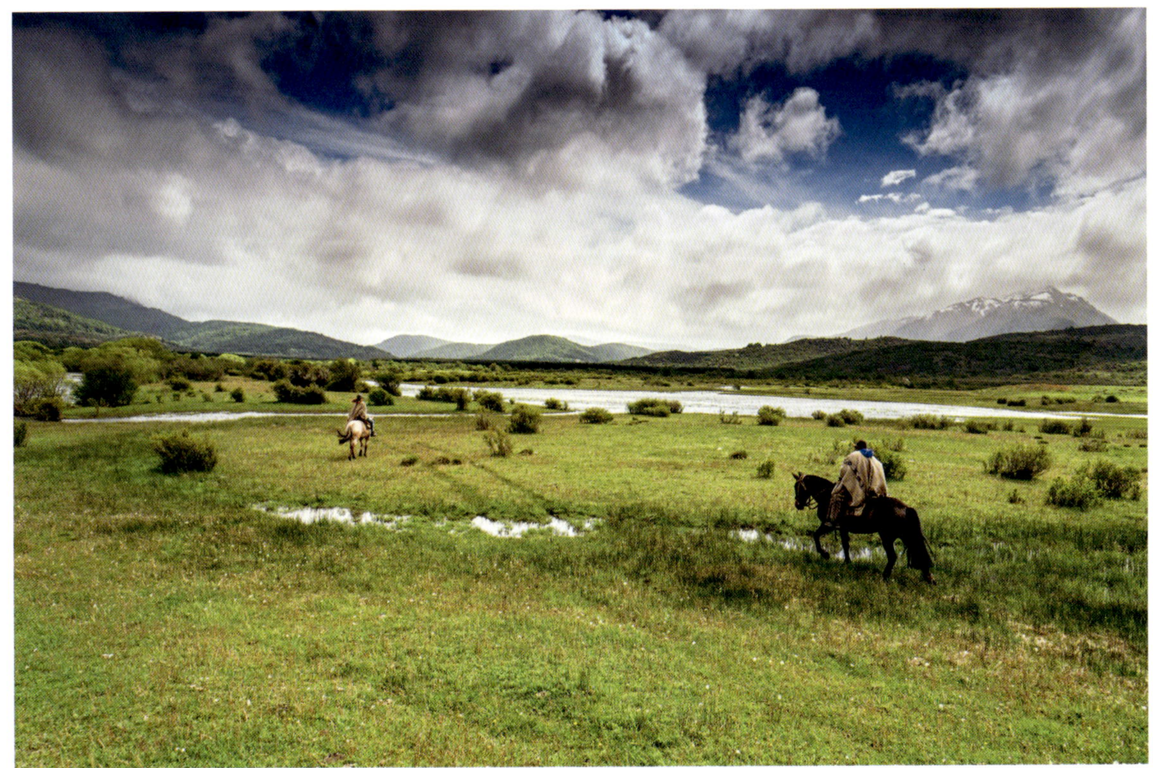

Estancia Caballadas, Río Quillén

Neuquén

The small province belongs to Patagonia and borders the Andes in the west. Mineral resources, such as oil, gold and silver, bring wealth to the region, whilst beautiful natural landscapes, large lakes and attractive national parks attract many visitors. The Los Arrayanes National Park has been established to protect rare Arrayán tree populations. These trees are also known as Chilean myrtle.

Neuquén

La pequeña provincia pertenece a la Patagonia y limita con los Andes al oeste. Los recursos minerales, como el petróleo, el oro y la plata, aportan riqueza a la región. Los hermosos paisajes naturales, los grandes lagos y los deslumbrantes parques nacionales atraen a muchos visitantes. El Parque Nacional Los Arrayanes ofrece una antigua población de árboles, también conocidos como mirtos chilenos.

Neuquén

Cette petite province de Patagonie est bordée à l'ouest par les Andes. Les richesses du sol, telles le pétrole, l'or et l'argent, ont apporté la prospérité à la région. De beaux paysages naturels, de grands lacs et des parcs nationaux splendides attirent de nombreux visiteurs. Le parc national Los Arrayanes a été créé pour préserver les arrayáns. Cette essence d'arbre ancienne est surnommée « myrte chilien ».

Neuquén

A pequena província pertence à Patagônia e faz fronteira com a Cordilheira dos Andes no oeste. Os recursos minerais, como petróleo, ouro e prata, trazem riqueza para a região. Belas paisagens naturais, grandes lagos e atraentes parques nacionais atraem muitos visitantes. O Parque Nacional Los Arrayanes oferece um conjunto de árvores antigas. As árvores também são conhecidas como murta chilena.

Neuquén

Die kleine Provinz gehört zu Patagonien und grenzt im Westen an die Anden. Bodenschätze, z. B. Erdöl, Gold und Silber, bescheren der Region Reichtum. Schöne Naturlandschaften, große Seen und attraktive Nationalparks locken viele Besucher an. Der Nationalpark Los Arrayanes bietet alten Baumbestand. Die Bäume sind auch als chilenische Myrthe bekannt.

Neuquén

De kleine provincie behoort tot Patagonië en grenst in het westen aan de Andes. Bodemrijkdommen, b.v. aardolie, goud en zilver, bezorgen de regio rijkdom. Prachtige natuurlandschappen, grote meren en aantrekkelijke nationaal parken trekken veel bezoekers. Het nationaal park Los Arrayanes biedt een oude bomenpopulatie. De bomen staan ook bekend als Chileense mirte.

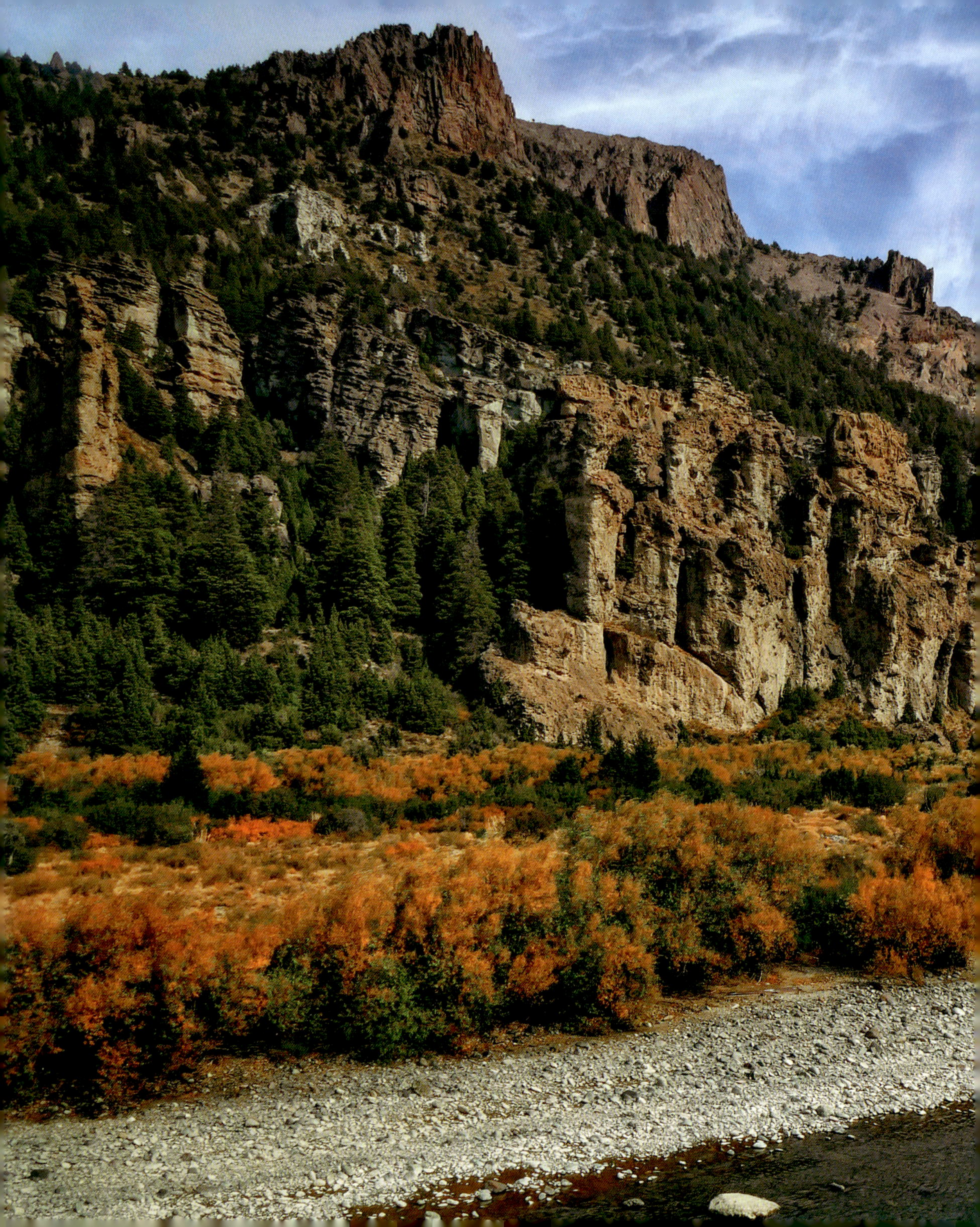

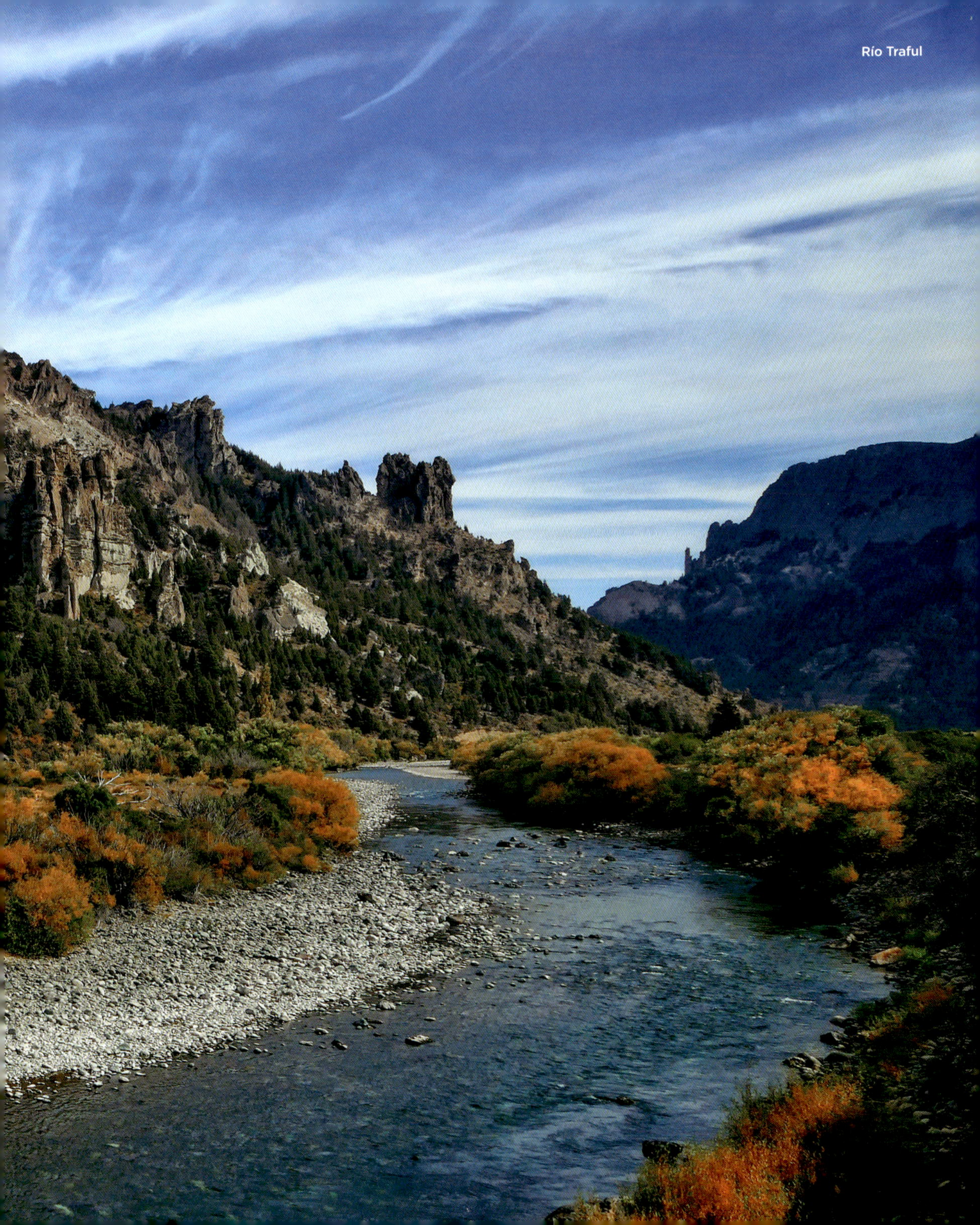
Río Traful

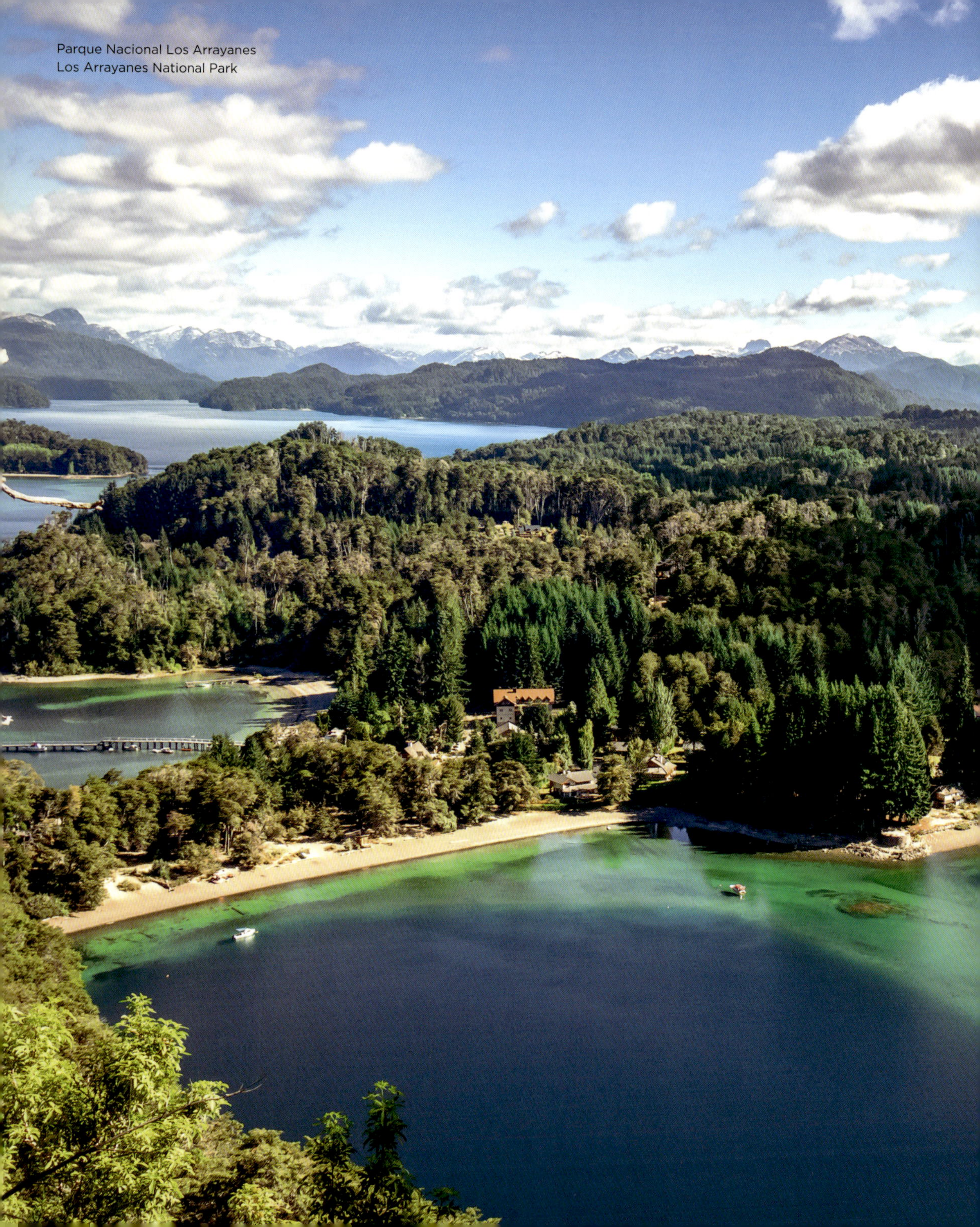

Parque Nacional Los Arrayanes
Los Arrayanes National Park

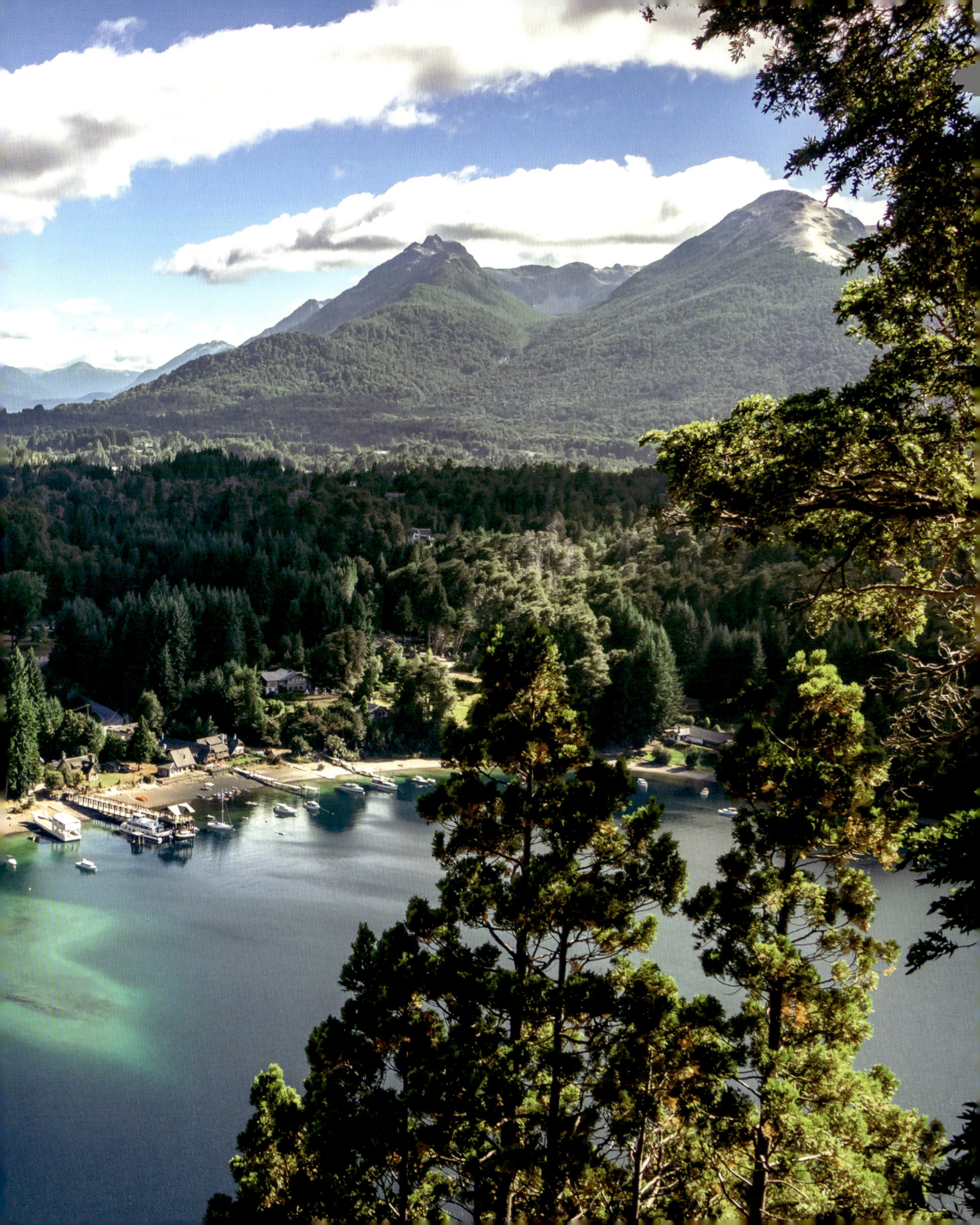

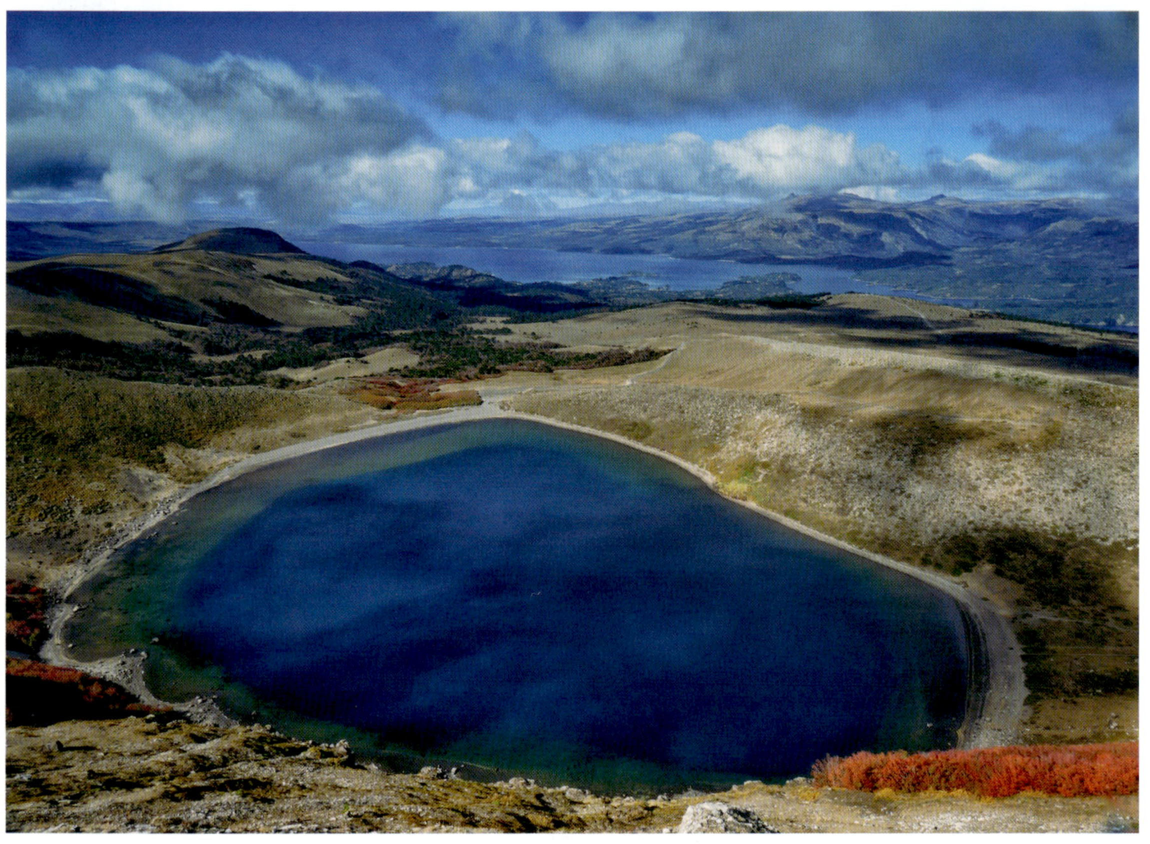

Cráter del Volcán Batea Mahuida
Crater of Batea Mahuida Volcano

Volcanic landscape

On the border with Chile and 350 km (217 mi) west of the capital, Neuquén, the volcano Batea Mahuida, with the crater lake of the same name, is located at 1948 m (6391 ft). The Mapuche Indians, who lived here until the arrival of the first white settlers in 1890, called it so because the mountain has the shape of a flat tray. The village of Villa Pehuenia is 10 km (6.2 mi) away. In winter, local Mapuche people run a small ski resort. South of the volcanic area is a large, deep lake, the Lago Aluminé. During the summer months many come here to fish for trout. It has not yet been protected, so that the rare araucaria trees, which are locally called *pehuen,* are threatened by deforestation.

Paysage de volcans

À 350 km à l'ouest de la capitale provinciale Neuquén et à la frontière du Chili, le volcan Batea Mahuida et son lac de cratère homonyme s'élèvent à 1948 m d'altitude. Les Indiens mapuches, qui vivaient là jusqu'à l'arrivée des premiers colons blancs en 1890, l'appelèrent ainsi en raison de sa forme de montagne-plateau. La localité Villa Pehuenia est située à 10 km. En hiver, les Mapuche sédentarisés gèrent une petite station de ski. Au sud de la région des volcans s'étend un immense et profond lac, le Lago Aluminé. Au cours des mois d'été, les pêcheurs de truites s'y retrouvent nombreux. Le site n'étant pour l'instant pas protégé, les rares araucarias, que les locaux appellent *pehuen,* sont menacés par le déboisement.

Vulkanlandschaft

350 km westlich der Hauptstadt Neuquén an der Grenze zu Chile liegt auf 1948 m der Vulkan Batea Mahuida mit dem gleichnamigen Kratersee. Die Mapuche-Indianer, die hier bis zur Ankunft der ersten weißen Siedler 1890 lebten, nannten ihn so, weil der Berg die Form eines flachen Tabletts hat. Die Ortschaft Villa Pehuenia befindet sich 10 km entfernt. Im Winter betreiben ansässige Mapuche ein kleines Skiresort. Südlich des Vulkangebiets schließt sich ein großer, tiefer See an, der Lago Aluminé. In den Sommermonaten kommen viele hierher, um Forellen zu fischen. Er steht bisher nicht unter Naturschutz, so dass die seltenen Araukarien, die lokal *pehuen* heißen, von der Abholzung bedroht sind.

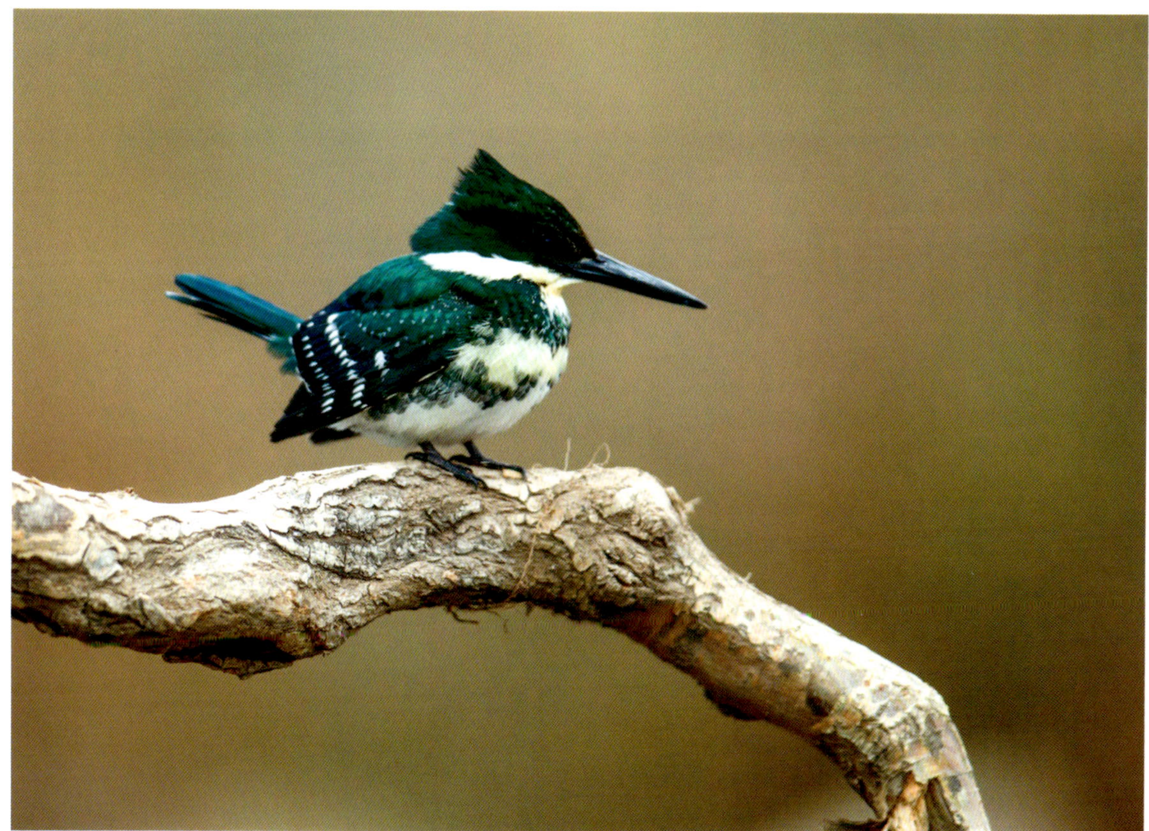

Martín pescador común
Kingfisher

Paisaje volcánico

A 350 km al oeste de la capital Neuquén, en la frontera con Chile, se encuentra el volcán Batea Mahuida con el lago del cráter del mismo nombre a 1948 m. Los mapuches, que vivieron aquí hasta la llegada de los primeros pobladores europeos en 1890, lo llamaron así porque la montaña tiene la forma de una bandeja plana. El pueblo de Villa Pehuenia se encuentra a 10 km. En invierno, los mapuches locales dirigen un pequeño centro de esquí. Al sur de la zona volcánica se encuentra un gran y profundo lago, el Aluminé. Durante los meses de verano muchos vienen aquí a pescar truchas. La zona todavía no ha sido protegida, de modo que las raras araucarias, que localmente se llaman *pehuén,* están amenazadas por la deforestación.

Paisagem vulcânica

350 km a oeste da capital Neuquén, na fronteira com o Chile, o vulcão Batea Mahuida, com o lago da cratera do mesmo nome, está localizado a 1948 m. Os índios Mapuche, que viveram aqui até a chegada dos primeiros colonos brancos em 1890, chamavam-lhe assim porque a montanha tem a forma de uma bandeja plana. A aldeia de Villa Pehuenia fica a 10 km de distância. No inverno, o povo mapuche local administra uma pequena estação de esqui. Ao sul da área vulcânica está um grande lago profundo, o Lago Aluminé. Durante os meses de verão muitos vêm aqui para pescar trutas. Como o lago ainda não está sob proteçao ambiental, as raras Araucárias, que são localmente chamadas de *pehuen,* estão ameaçadas pelo desmatamento.

Vulkaanlandschap

350 km ten westen van de hoofdstad Neuquén, op de grens met Chili, ligt op 1948 m de vulkaan Batea Mahuida met het gelijknamige kratermeer. De Mapuche-indianen, die hier tot de komst van de eerste blanke kolonisten in 1890 woonden, noemden het zo, omdat de berg de vorm van een vlak plateau heeft. Het dorp Villa Pehuenia ligt op 10 km afstand. In de winter runnen de lokale Mapuche een klein skigebied. Ten zuiden van het vulkanisch gebied ligt een groot, diep meer, het meer van Aluminé. In de zomermaanden komen velen hier naartoe om forel te vissen. Het staat nog niet onder natuurbescherming, zodat de zeldzame Araucaria, die plaatselijk *pehuen* heten, door ontbossing worden bedreigd.

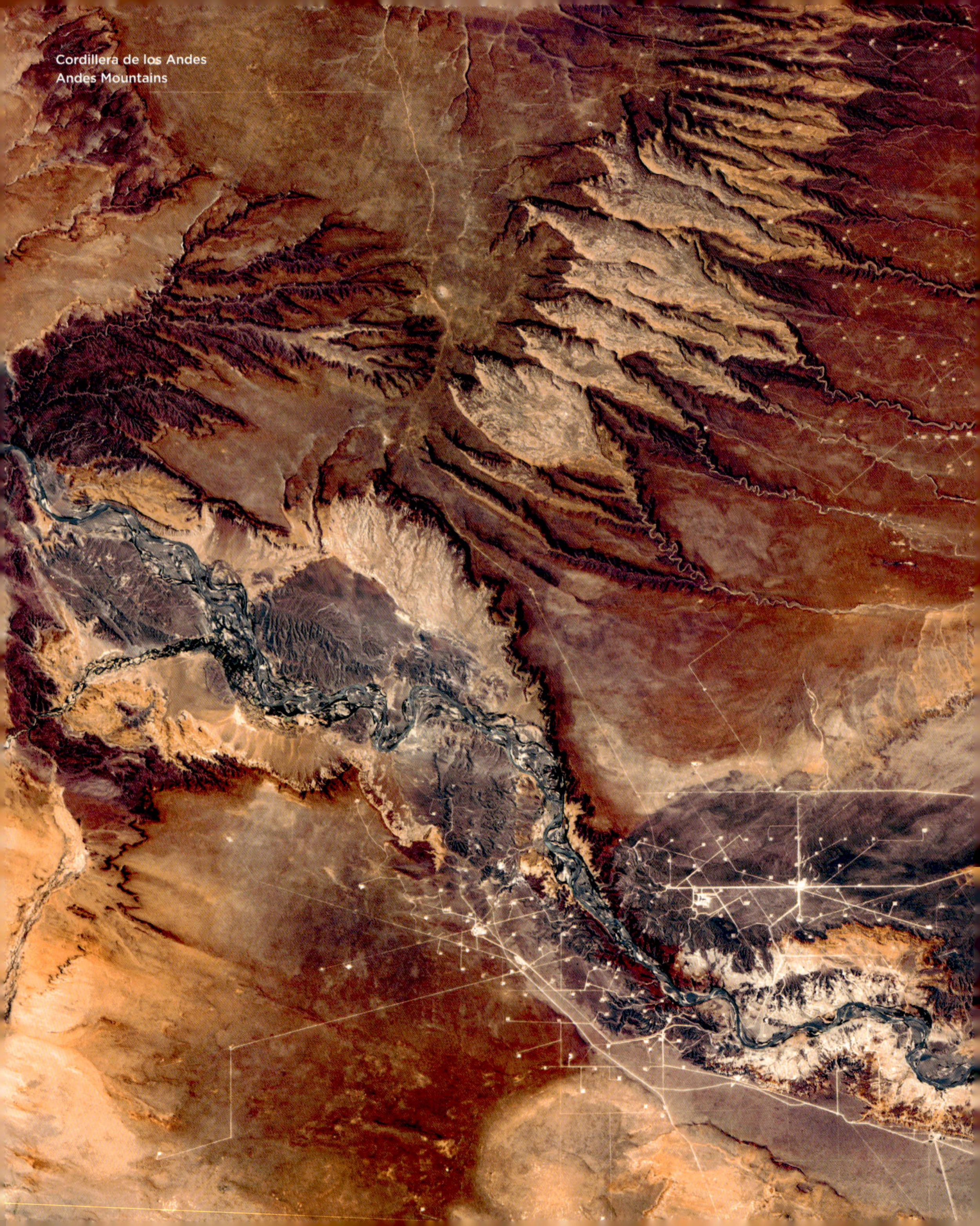

Cordillera de los Andes
Andes Mountains

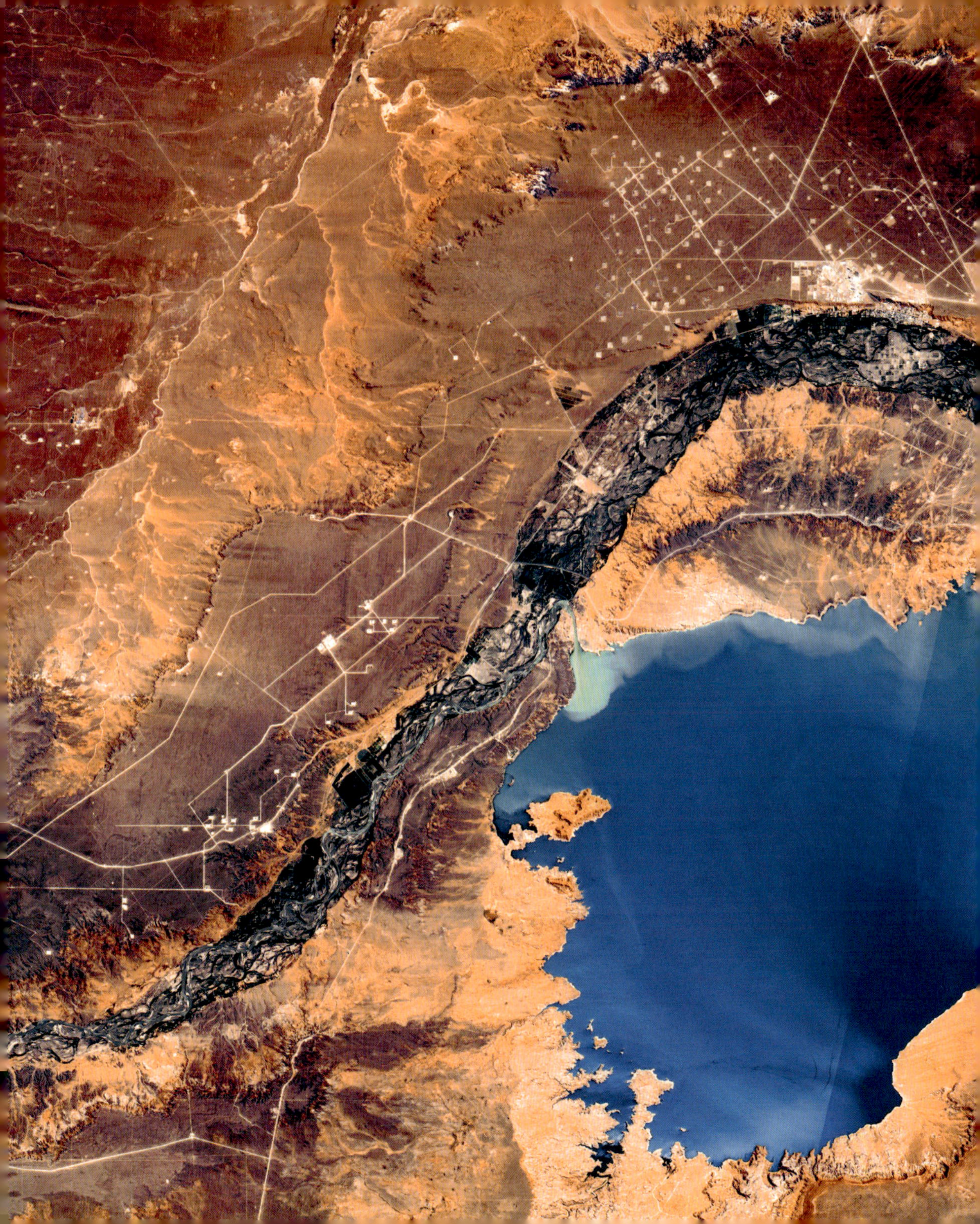

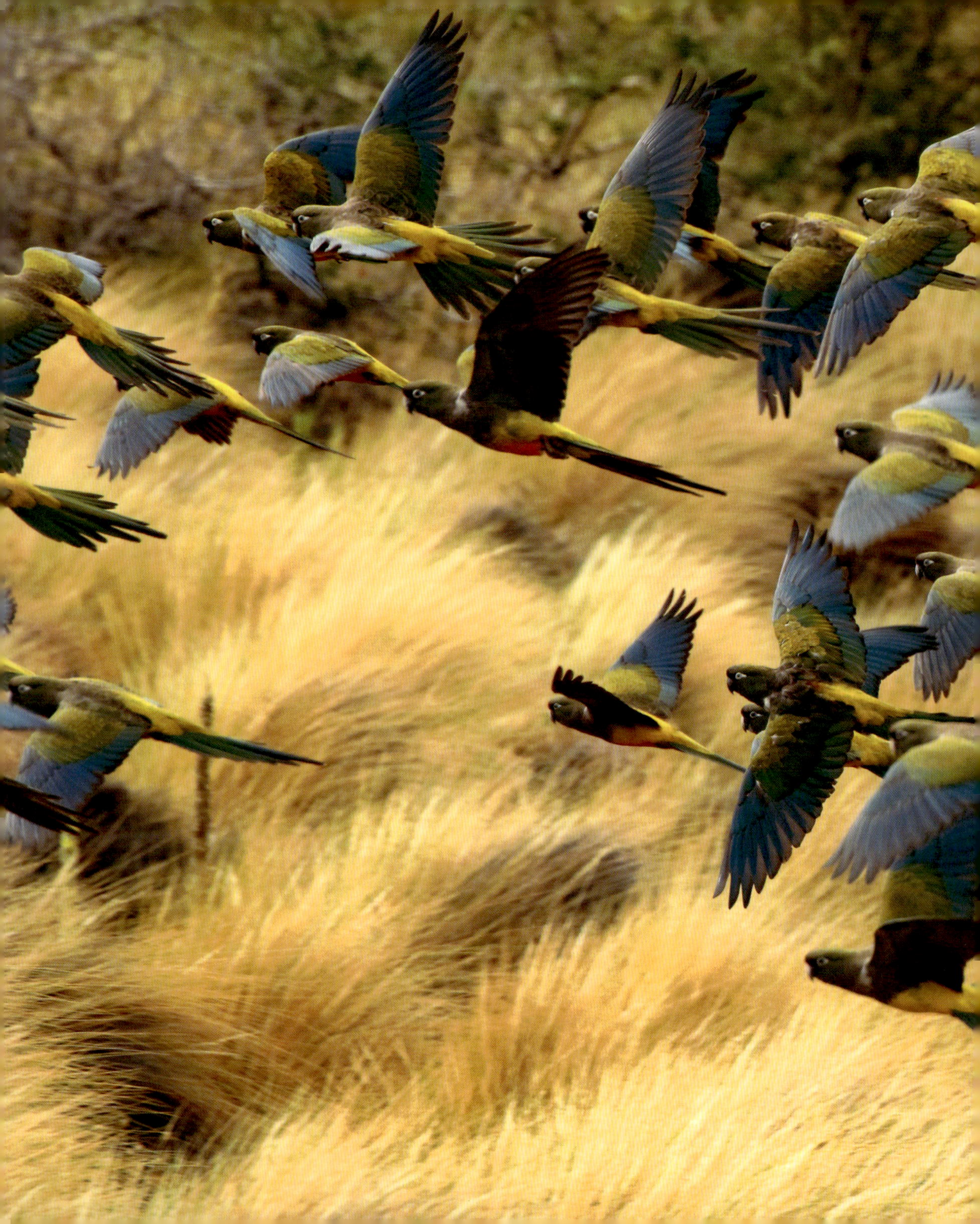

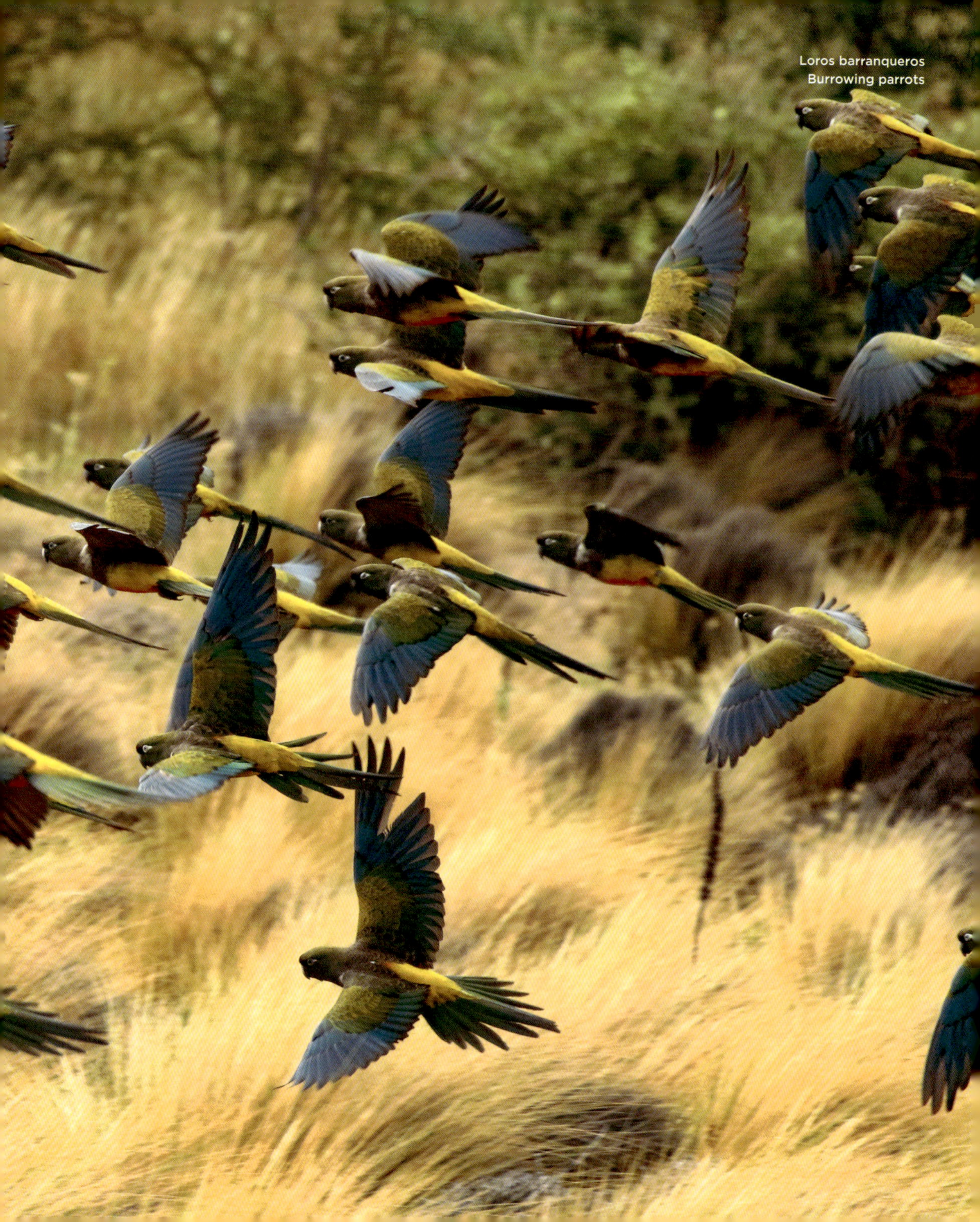
Loros barranqueros
Burrowing parrots

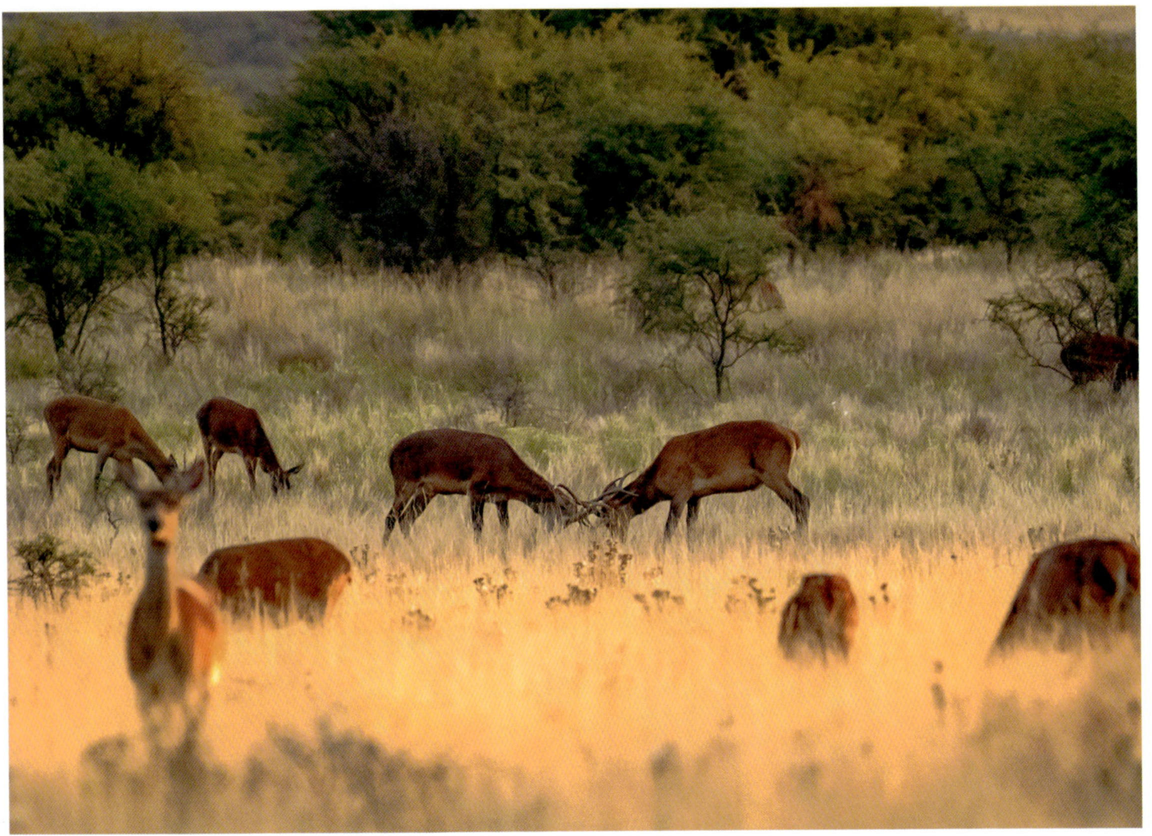

Corzos
Roe deer

Lanín National Park

A wide spectrum of wildlife can be found in Argentina's most beautiful national park, the Parque Nacional Lanín. The park, established in 1945, covers an area of 412 003 ha (1590 sq mi). In the mountainous region, which has a cold climate with temperatures of 11° to 12 °C (52 °–54 °F), there is the mainly coniferous Andean-Patagonian, or Valdivian, temperate rainforest. This is the home of one of the ten species of South American deer, the Corzuela parda, or grey deer. It resembles the European deer in physique and behaviour, but is smaller. Also, foxes are widespread, and in addition to hares, birds and lizards, young guanacos also number amongst its prey.

Parc national Lanín

Le Parque Nacional Lanín, le plus beau d'Argentine, abrite une faune exceptionnelle. Fondé en 1945, il couvre une superficie de 412 003 ha. Cette région montagneuse, dotée d'un climat froid aux températures avoisinant 11 à 12 °C, possède une forêt endémique des Andes et de Patagonie, dite valdivienne, peuplée de conifères et de résineux. L'une des dix espèces de cervidés sud-américains, le daguet gris, ou *corzuela parda,* y est chez lui. Son physique et son comportement sont proches de ceux des cervidés européens, mais il est plus petit. Les renards sont également nombreux. Outre les lapins, oiseaux et lézards, ils chassent les guanacos.

Nationalpark Lanín

Eine große Tierwelt ist im schönsten Nationalpark Argentiniens, dem Parque Nacional Lanín, anzutreffen. Der 1945 eingerichtete Park hat eine Fläche von 412 003 ha. In der Bergregion, die ein kaltes Klima bei Temperaturen von 11 bis 12 Grad aufweist, gibt es den andinisch-patagonischen bzw. Valdivianischen Wald, ein Koniferen-, Nadelholzwald. Hier ist einer der zehn Spezies des südamerikanischen Hirschs beheimatet: Corzuela parda, grauer Hirsch. Er gleicht dem europäischen Hirsch in Physis und Verhalten, ist aber kleiner als dieser. Auch Füchse sind weit verbreitet. Neben Hasen, Vögeln und Eidechsen gehören auch junge Guanakos zu seinen Beutetieren.

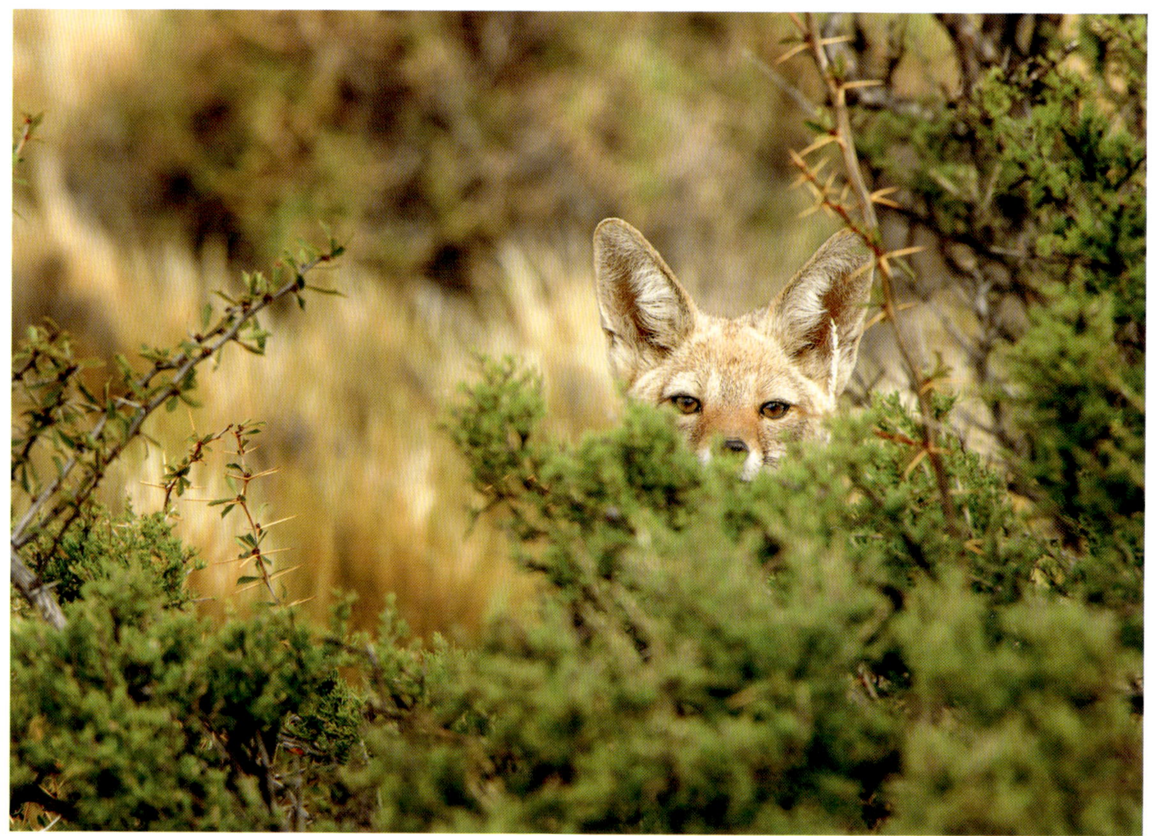

Zorro culpeo

Parque Nacional Lanín

Un gran reino animal se encuentra en el parque nacional más hermoso de Argentina, el Parque Nacional Lanín. El parque, establecido en 1945, tiene una superficie de 412 003 hectáreas. En la región montañosa, que tiene un clima frío con temperaturas de 11 a 12 grados, se encuentra el bosque andino-patagónico o valdiviano, un bosque de coníferas. Este es el hogar de una de las diez especies de ciervos sudamericanos: corzuela parda. Se asemeja al ciervo europeo en su físico y comportamiento, pero es más pequeño. También los zorros están muy extendidos. Sus presas son las liebres, las aves y los lagartos, así como los guanacos jóvenes.

Parque Nacional Lanín

Um grande reino animal pode ser encontrado no mais belo parque nacional da Argentina, o Parque Nacional Lanín. O parque, criado em 1945, cobre uma área de 412 003 hectares. Na região montanhosa, que tem um clima frio com temperaturas de 11 a 12 graus, existe a floresta andino-patagônica ou valdiviana, uma floresta de coníferas. Este é o lar de uma das dez espécies de veados sul-americanos: Corzuela parda, veado cinzento. Assemelha-se ao veado europeu no físico e no comportamento, mas é mais pequeno do que ele. Também as raposas são comuns. Para além de lebres, aves e lagartos, os jovens guanacos também pertencem às suas presas.

Lanín nationaal park

In het mooiste nationaal park van Argentinië, het Parque Nacional Lanín, is een groot dierenrijk voorhanden. Het in 1945 opgerichte park heeft een oppervlakte van 412 003 ha. In de bergachtige regio, dat met temperaturen van 11 tot 12 graden over een koud klimaat beschikt, ligt het Andes Patagonische of Valdivische bos, een coniferen-, naaldbos. Dit is de thuisbasis van één van de tien Zuid-Amerikaanse hertensoorten: Corzuela parda, grijs hert. Het lijkt qua lichaamsbouw en gedrag op het Europese hert, maar is echter kleiner. Ook vossen zijn wijdverspreid. Naast hazen, vogels en hagedissen behoren ook jonge guanaco's tot zijn prooien.

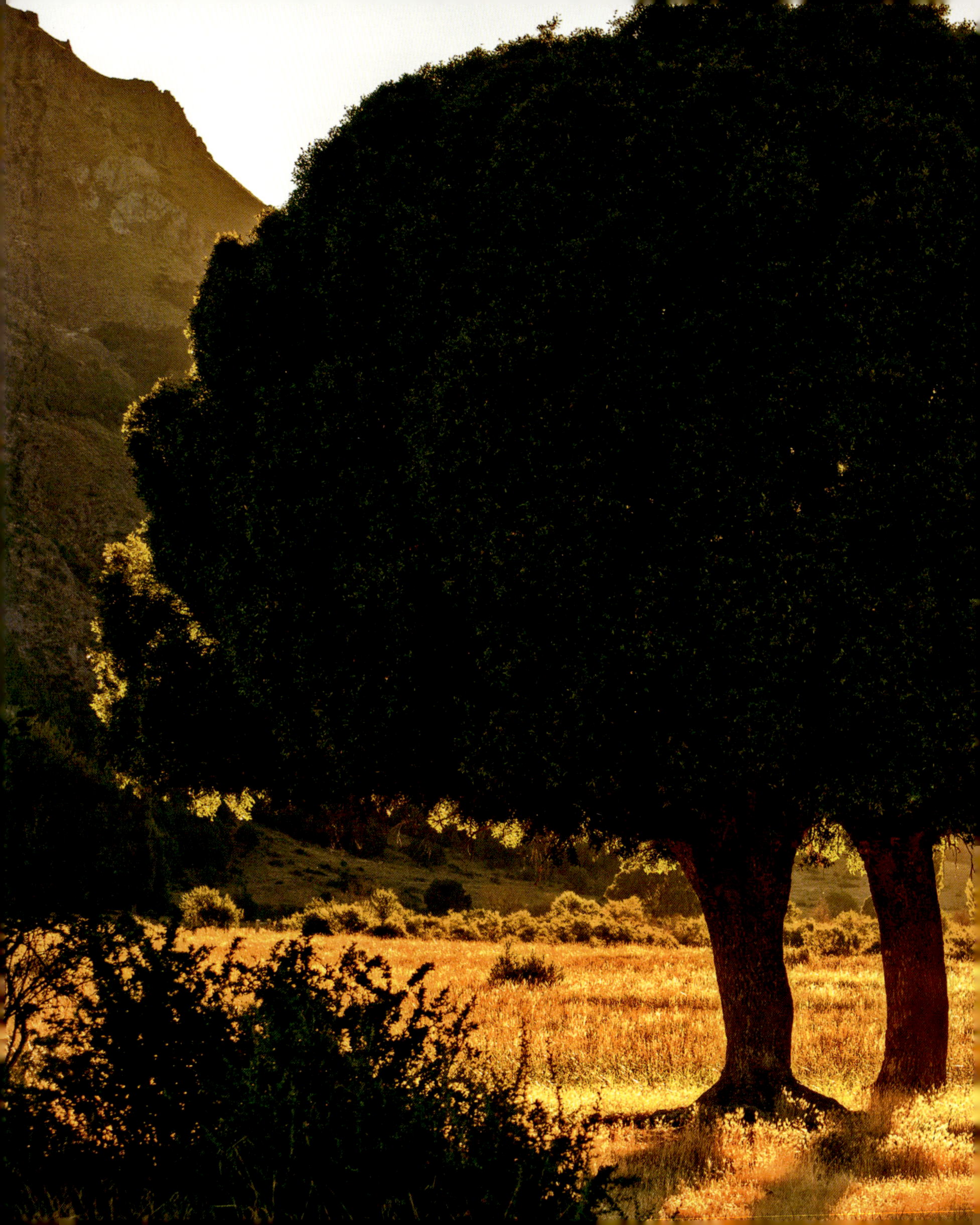

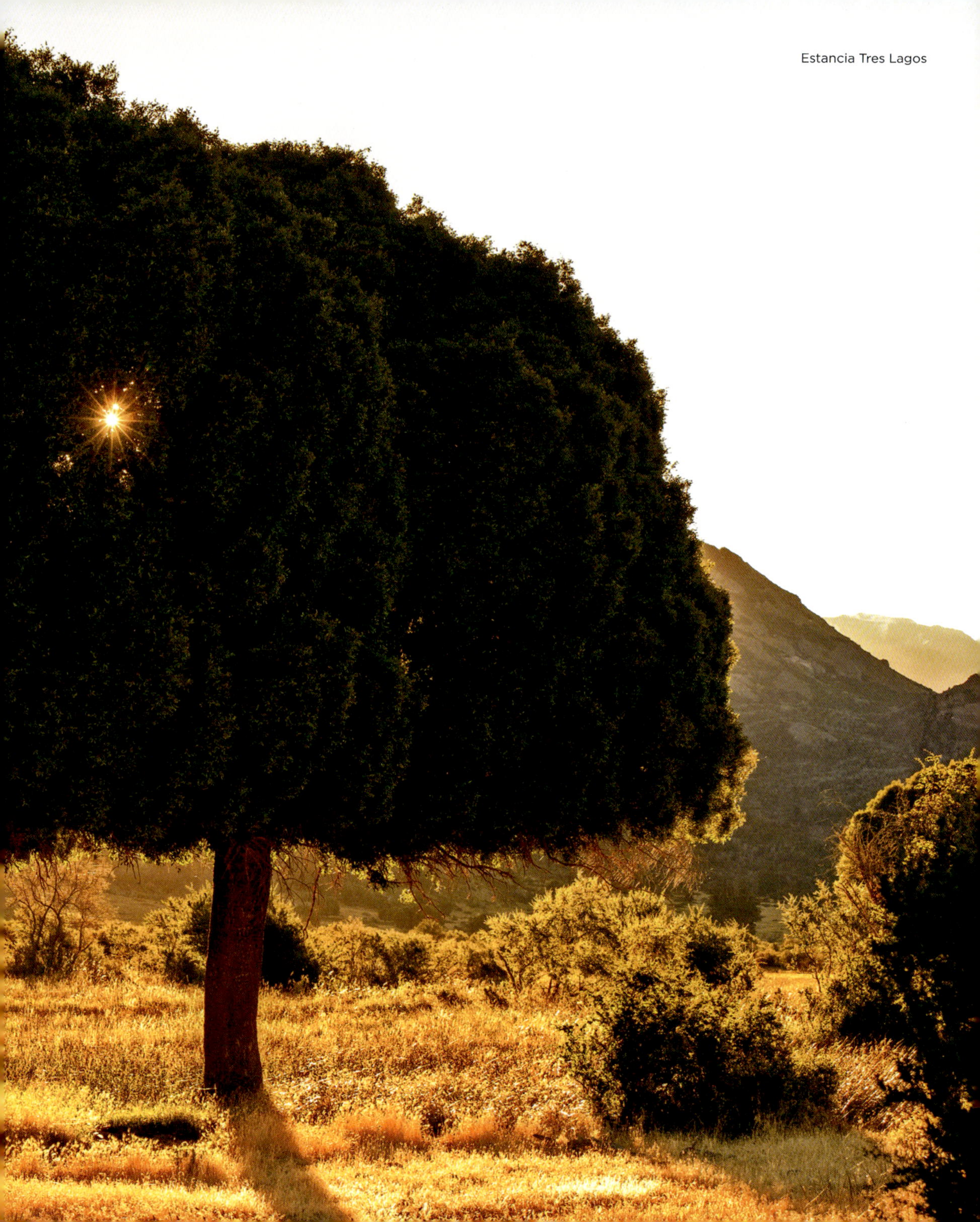
Estancia Tres Lagos

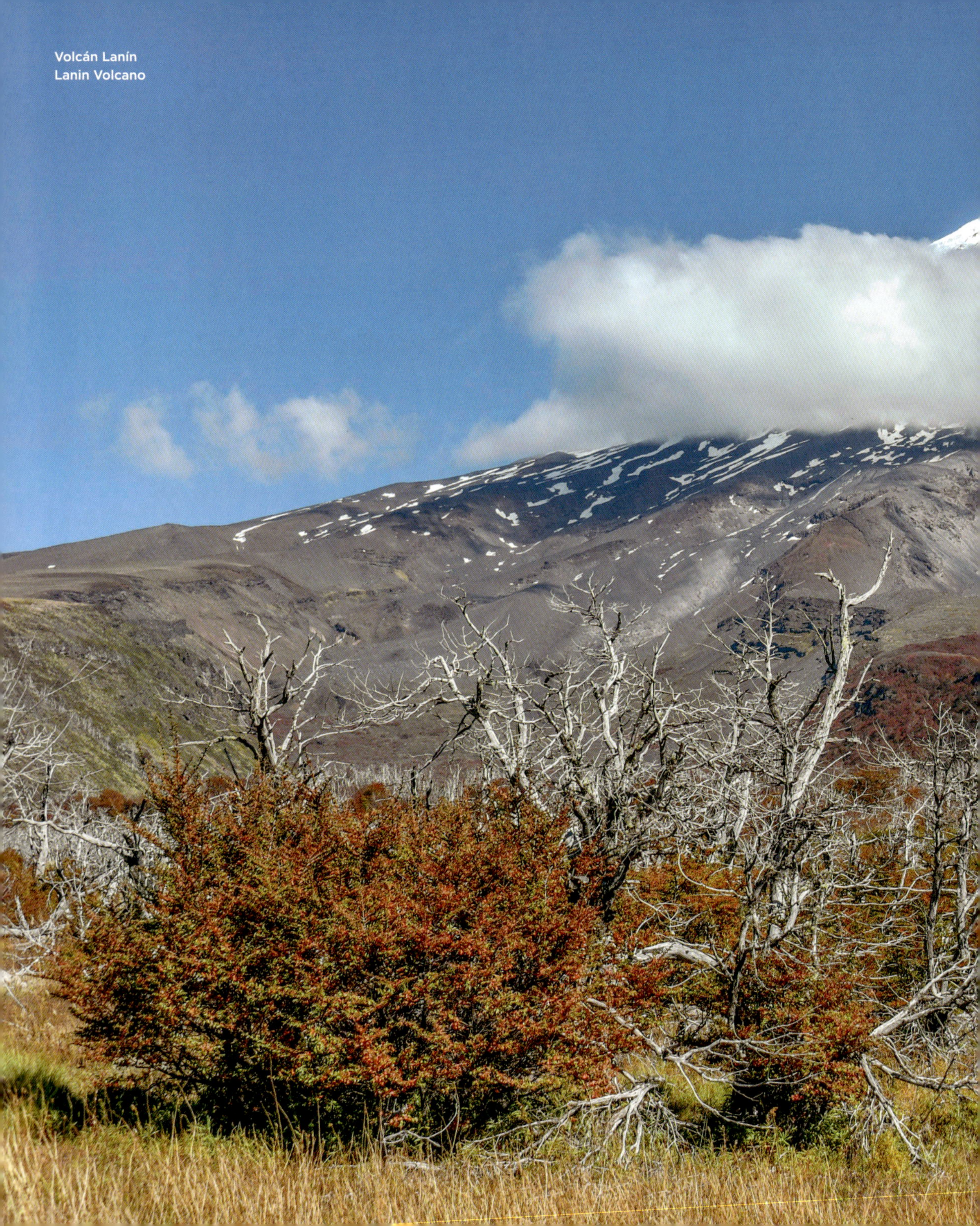
Volcán Lanín
Lanin Volcano

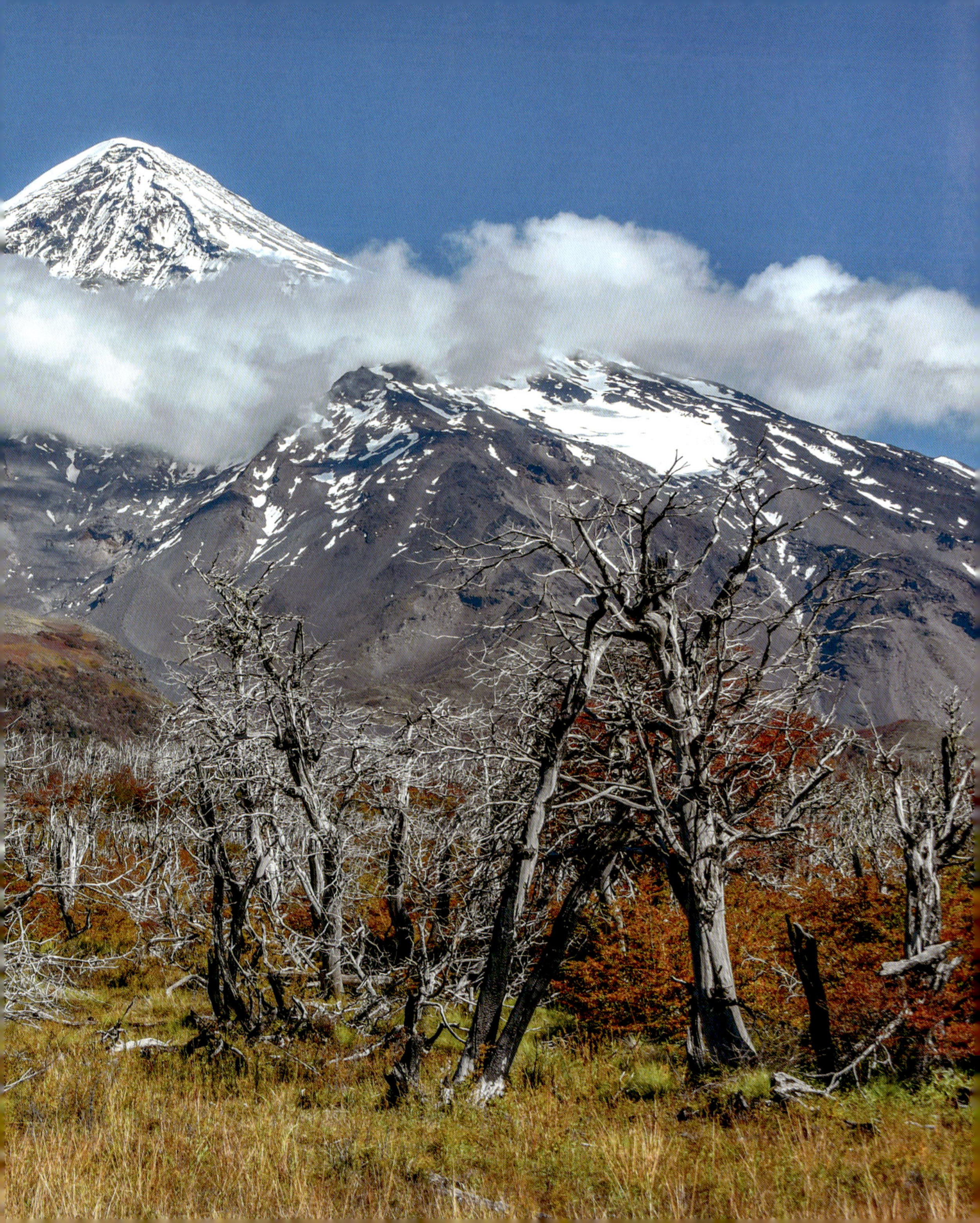

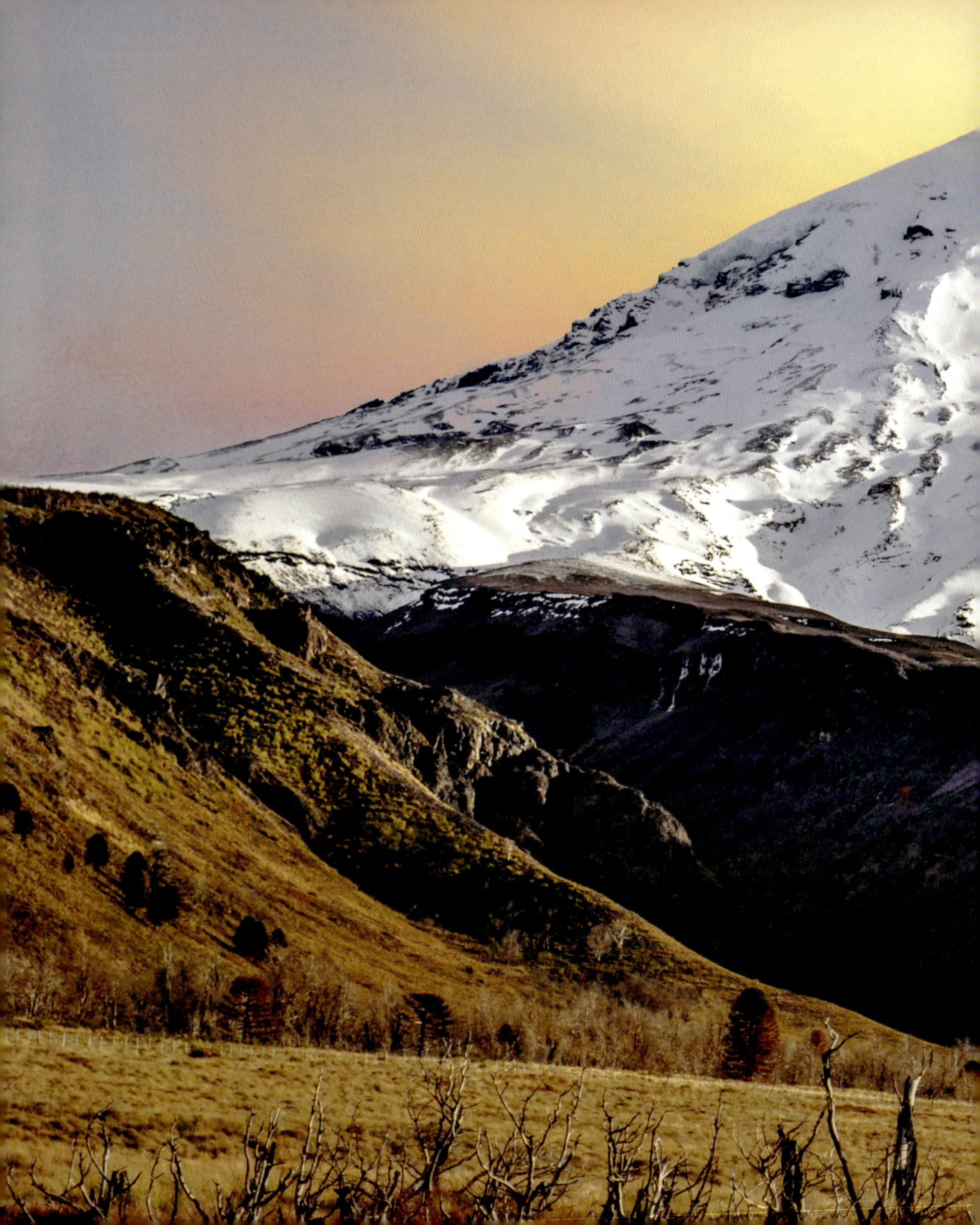

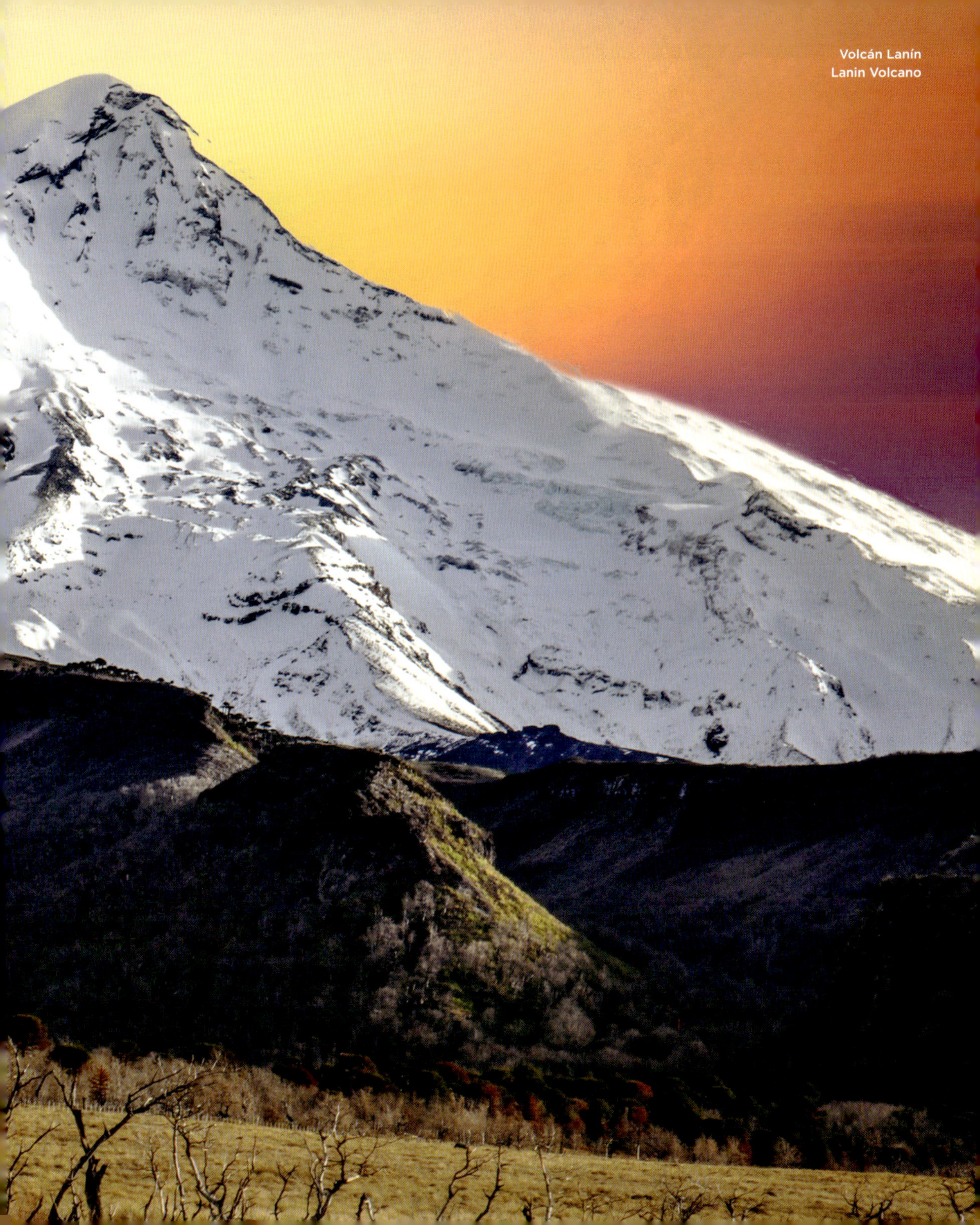
Volcán Lanín
Lanin Volcano

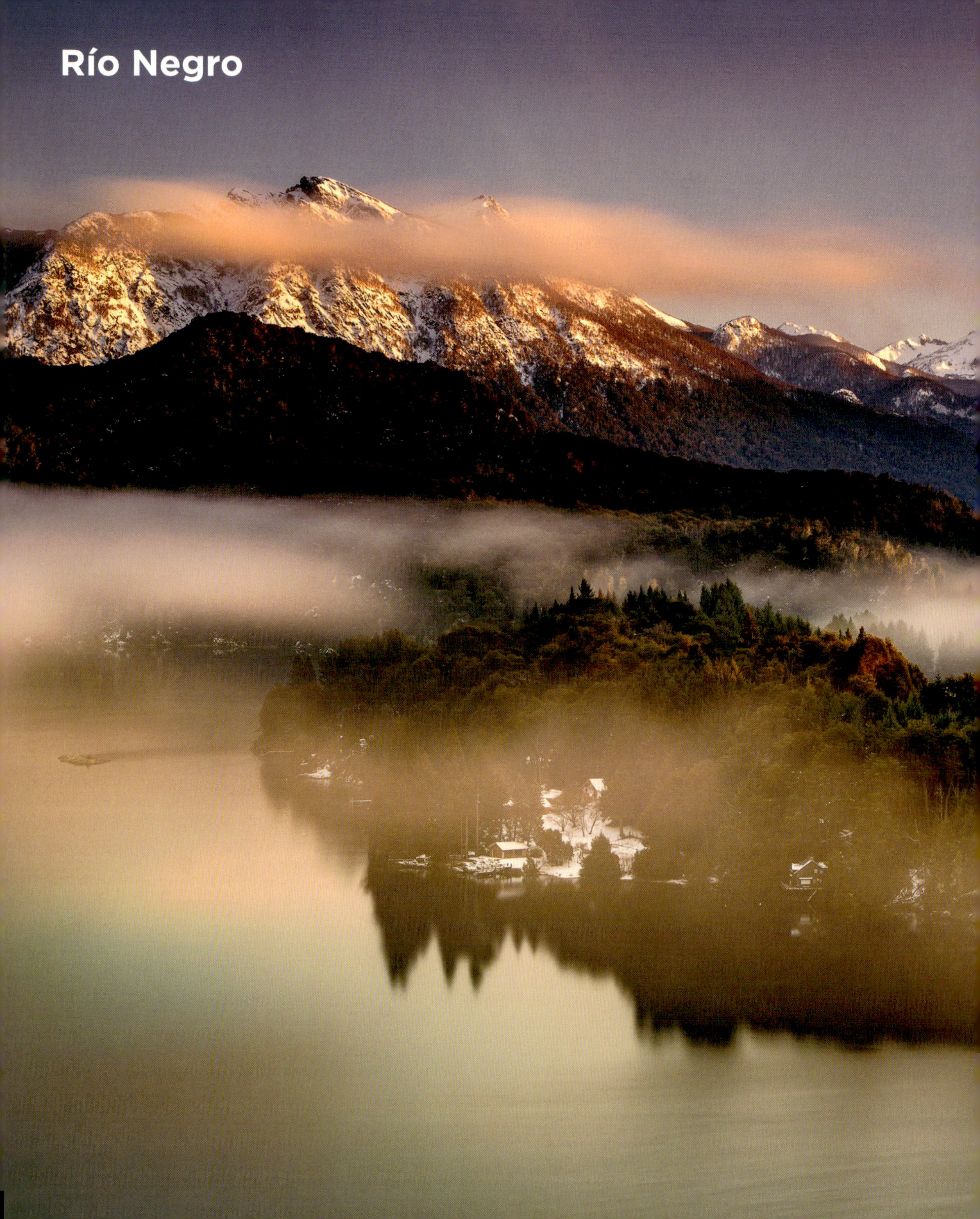
Río Negro

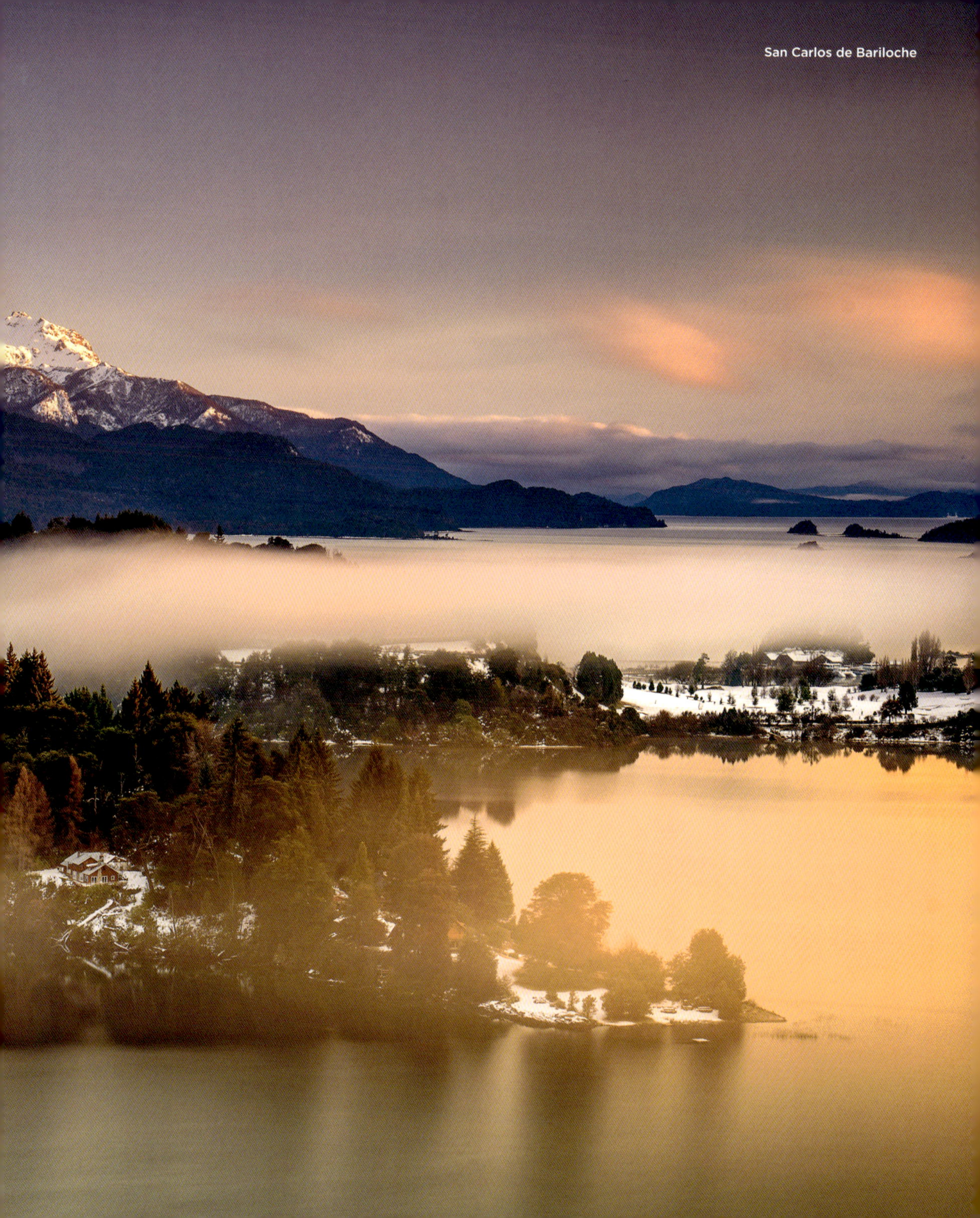
San Carlos de Bariloche

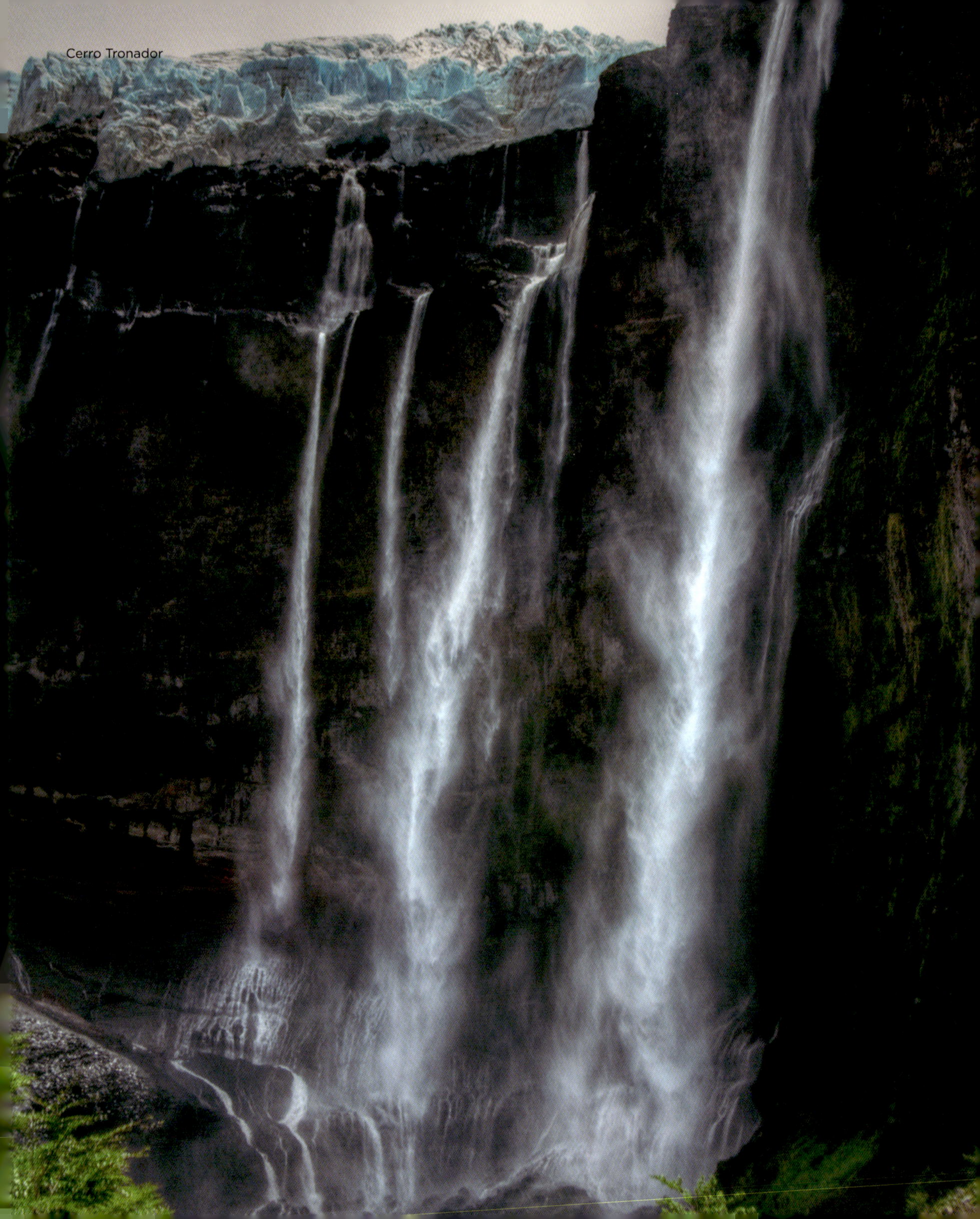

Cerro Tronador

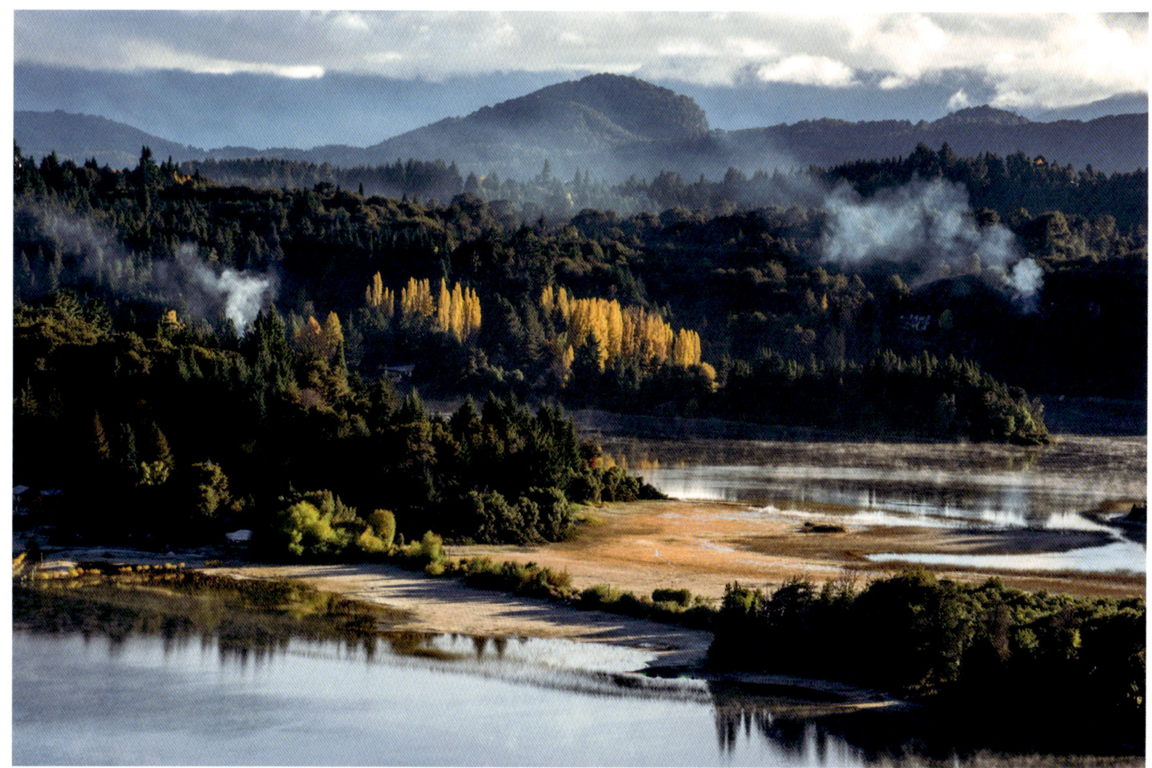

Lago Nahuel Huapi, Parque Nacional Nahuel Huapi
Nahuel Huapi Lake, Nahuel Huapi National Park

Río Negro

This province was part of the Patagonian territory until 1884. Beautiful high mountains, waterfalls, glacial lakes, including the great Nahuel Huapi Lake, attract many visitors. Due to the spectacular landscape and the people—a large part of them immigrated from Europe—the region is considered the "Switzerland of Argentina".

Río Negro

Les terres de la province de Río Negro appartenaient jusqu'en 1884 au territoire indigène de Patagonie. Les magnifiques hautes montagnes et les splendides chutes d'eau et lacs de glacier, dont le vaste lac Nahuel Huapi, attirent de nombreux visiteurs. En référence à son paysage spectaculaire et à sa population, issue en grande partie de l'immigration européenne, la région est surnommée la « Suisse argentine ».

Río Negro

Die Provinz gehörte bis 1884 zum patagonischen Territorium. Wunderschöne hohe Berge, Wasserfälle, Gletscherseen, z. B. der große Lago Nahuel Huapi, ziehen zahlreiche Besucher an. Aufgrund der spektakulären Landschaft und der Bevölkerung – ein Großteil wanderte aus Europa ein – gilt die Region als die „Schweiz Argentiniens".

Río Negro

La provincia formó parte del territorio patagónico hasta 1884. Hermosas montañas altas, cascadas, lagos glaciares, como el gran lago Nahuel Huapi, atraen a numerosos visitantes. Debido a la espectacularidad del paisaje y a la población (una gran parte de la cual son inmigrantes de Europa), la región es considerada como la "Suiza de Argentina".

Río Negro

A província fazia parte do território patagônico até 1884. Belas montanhas altas, cachoeiras, lagos glaciares, por exemplo o grande lago Nahuel Huapi, atraem numerosos visitantes. Por causa da paisagem espetacular e da população – uma grande parte deles imigrou da Europa – a região é considerada a "Suíça da Argentina".

Río Negro

De provincie maakte tot 1884 deel uit van het Patagonische grondgebied. Prachtige hoge bergen, watervallen, gletsjermeren, bijvoorbeeld het grote Nahuel Huapi-meer, trekken veel bezoekers. Vanwege het spectaculaire landschap en de bevolking – een groot deel emigreerde uit Europa – wordt de regio beschouwd als het "Zwitserland van Argentinië".

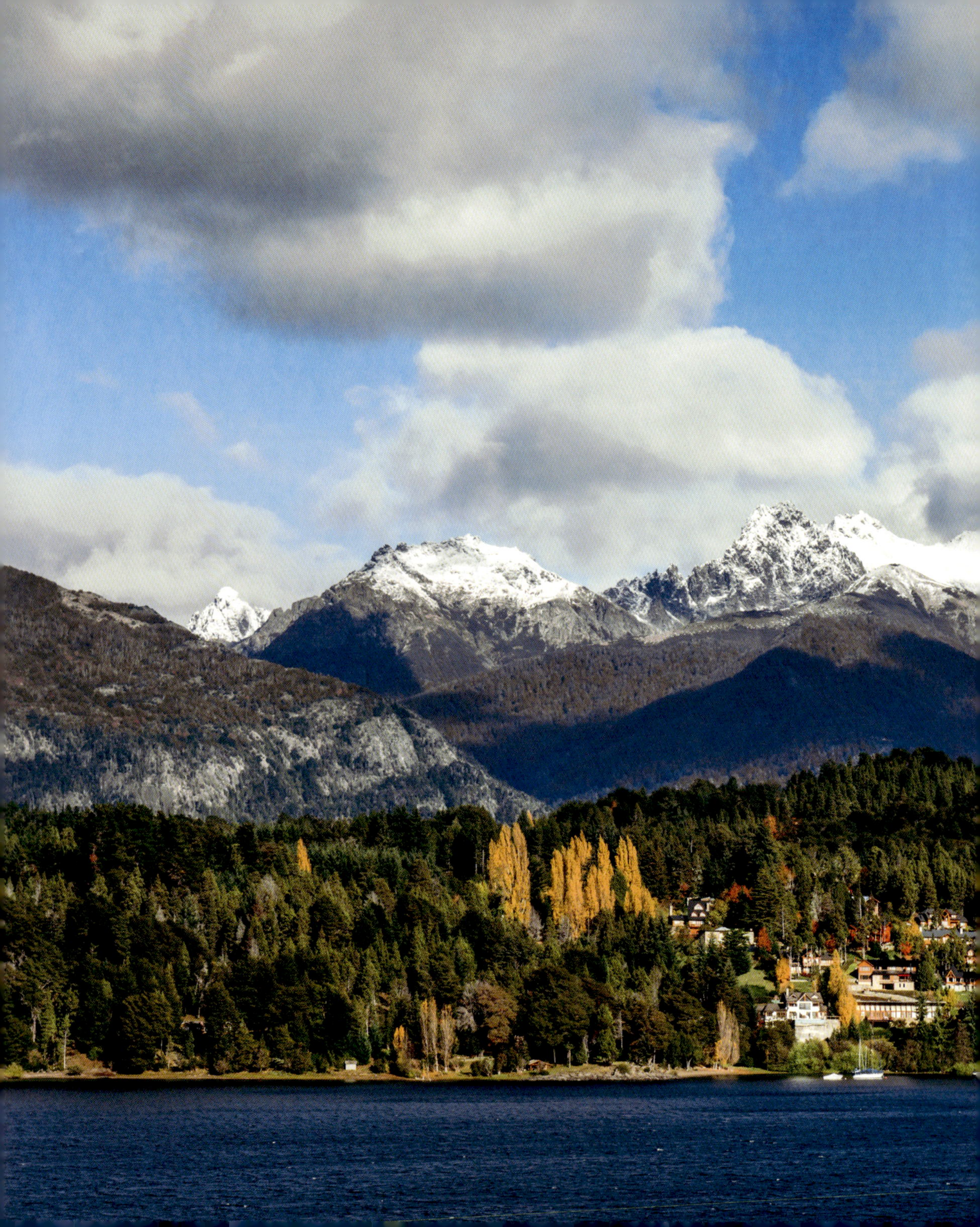

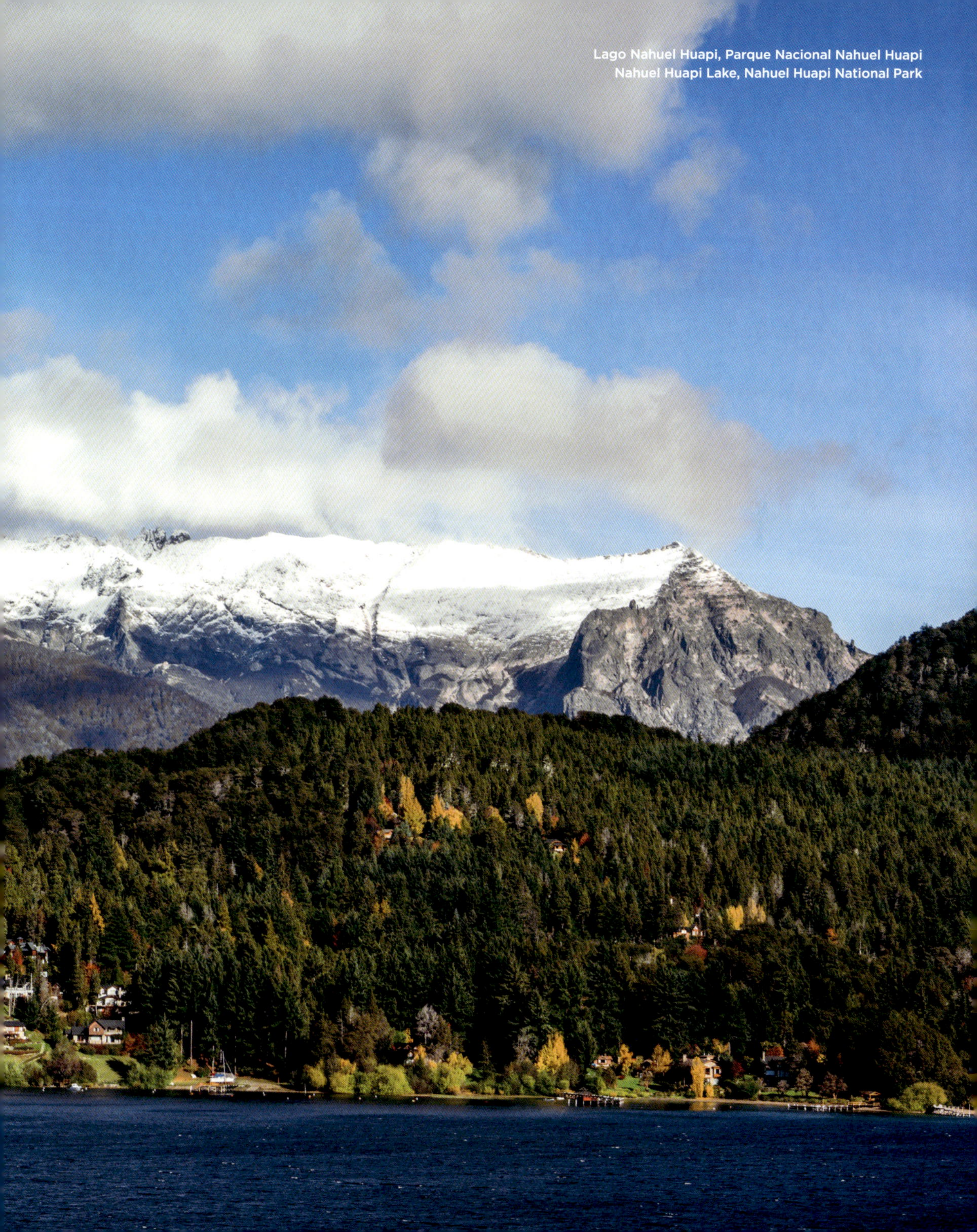

Lago Nahuel Huapi, Parque Nacional Nahuel Huapi
Nahuel Huapi Lake, Nahuel Huapi National Park

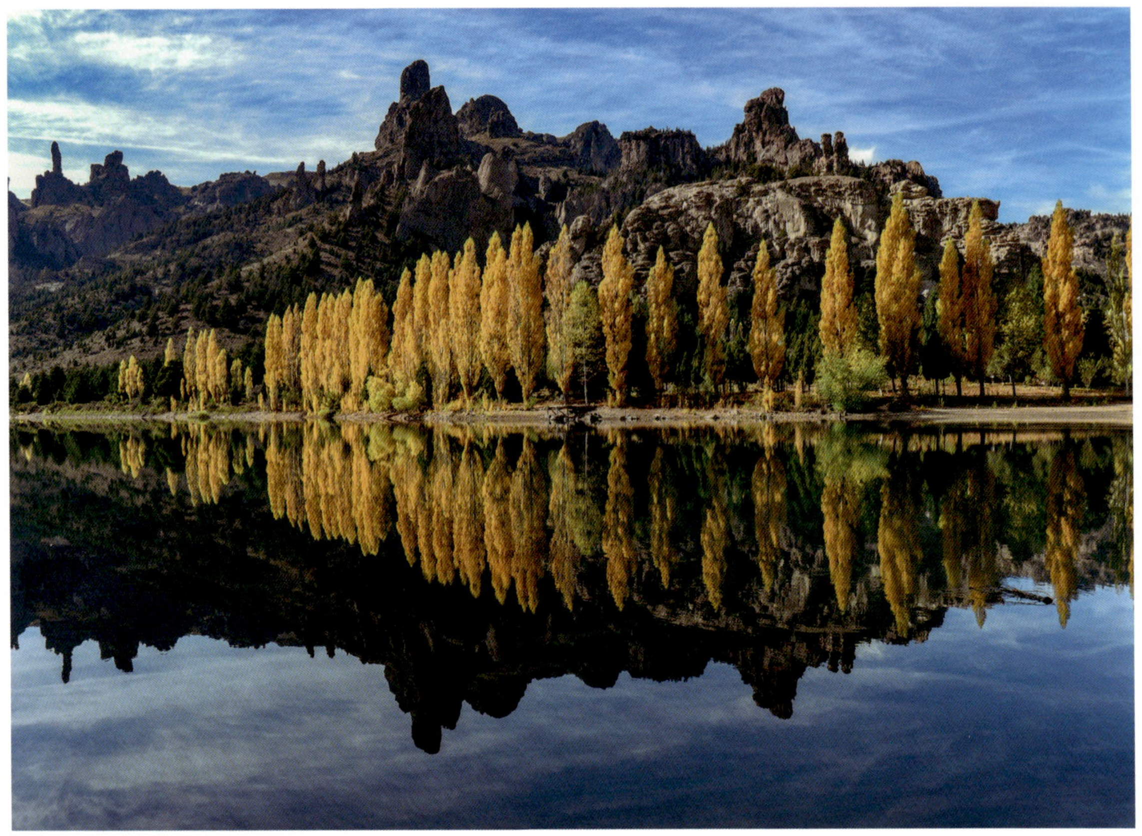

Lago Nahuel Huapi, Parque Nacional Nahuel Huapi
Nahuel Huapi Lake, Nahuel Huapi National Park

Breathtaking panoramic views

The banks of the dam of the Limay River offer a romantic scenery. The 380 km (236 mi) long river feeds from Nahuel Huapi Lake and flows into the Rio Negro at Neuquén. From the summit of the 1000 m (3280) high Cerro Campanario, the viewpoint above Bariloche, you have a breathtaking panoramic view from this unique mountain over valley landscape of the area. Even those who are not so fleet of foot can enjoy it thanks to a chair lift. The shores of the 100 km (62 mi) long Nahuel Huapi Lake, which digs deep into the mountain landscape, and the snow-covered Andean peaks on the horizon form a unique backdrop.

Panoramas époustouflants

La rive du barrage du río Limay offre un spectacle romantique. Le cours d'eau, long de 380 km, naît du lac Nahuel Huapi et coule jusqu'au confluent avec le río Negro au niveau de la ville de Neuquén. Depuis le sommet du Cerro Campanario, culminant à 1000 m, et le point de vue Bariloche, le regard embrasse un panorama époustouflant sur le paysage unique de montagnes et de vallées de la région. Un télésiège permet aux marcheurs les moins performants de profiter tout de même de la vue : les ramifications du lac Nahuel Huapi, long de 100 km, qui s'enfoncent profondément dans le paysage montagneux, et les sommets enneigés des Andes à l'horizon composent un décor unique.

Atemberaubende Panoramablicke

Eine romantische Szenerie bieten die Ufer der Talsperre des Limay-Flusses. Der 380 km lange Fluss speist sich aus dem Nahuel-Huapi-See und fließt bei Neuquén mit dem Rio Negro zusammen. Vom Gipfel des 1000 m hohen Bergs Cerro Campanario, dem Aussichtspunkt von Bariloche, hat man einen atemberaubenden Panoramablick auf die einzigartige Berg- und Tallandschaft des Gebiets. Auch wer nicht gut zu Fuß ist, kann ihn dank eines Sessellifts genießen: Die Verzweigungen des 100 km langen Nahuel-Huapi-Sees, die sich tief in die Berglandschaft graben, und die schneebedeckten Anden-Gipfel am Horizont bilden eine einmalige Kulisse.

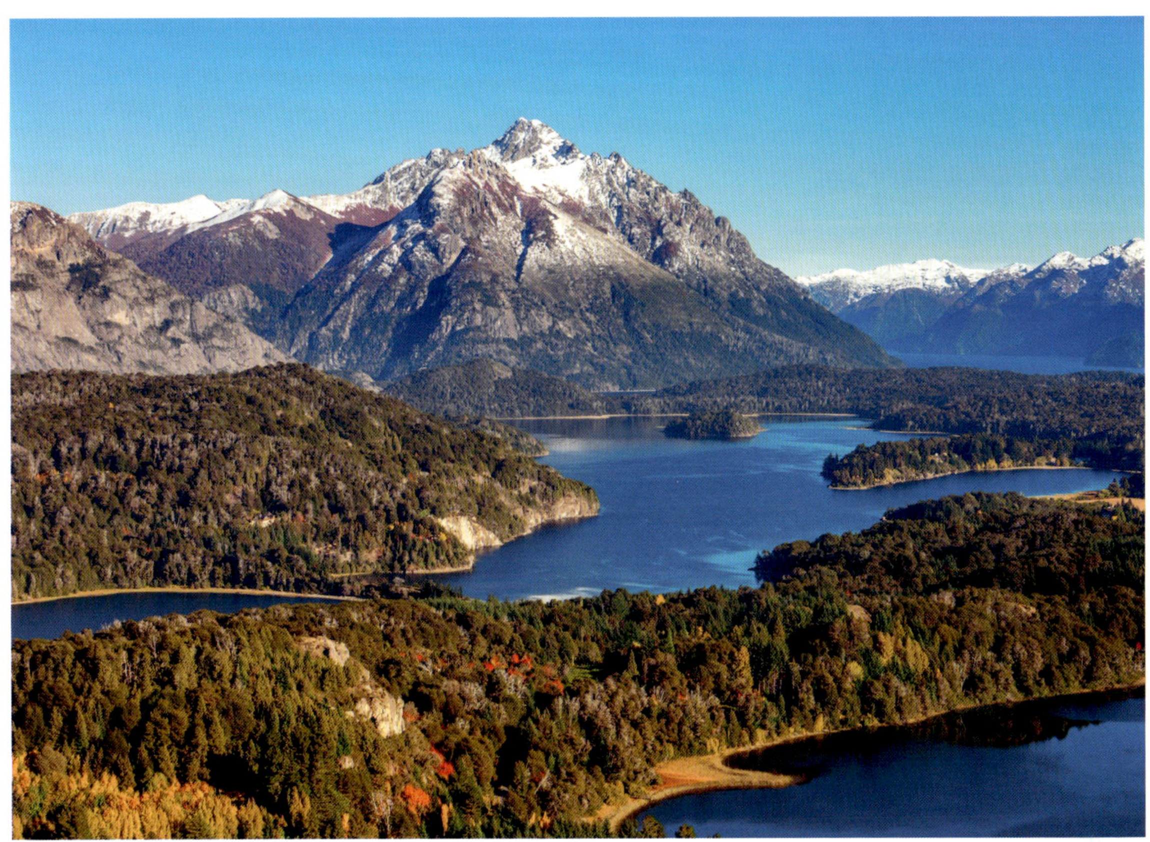

Lago Nahuel Huapi, Parque Nacional Nahuel Huapi
Nahuel Huapi Lake, Nahuel Huapi National Park

Impresionantes vistas panorámicas

Las orillas de la presa del río Limay ofrecen
un escenario romántico. El río, de 380 km
de largo, se alimenta del lago Nahuel Huapi
y desemboca en el río Negro en Neuquén.
Desde la cumbre del Cerro Campanario
de 1000 m de altura, el mirador de
Bariloche, se tiene una impresionante vista
panorámica del paisaje único de montañas
y valles de la zona. Incluso aquellos que
no quieran andar demasiado pueden
disfrutarlo gracias a una silla elevadora:
las ramificaciones del lago Nahuel Huapi,
de 100 km de largo, que se adentra en el
paisaje montañoso, y los picos andinos
nevados del horizonte forman un telón de
fondo inigualable.

Vistas panorâmicas de tirar o fôlego

As margens da barragem do rio Limay
oferecem um cenário romântico. O rio, com
380 km de extensão, alimenta-se do Lago
Nahuel Huapi e se une ao Rio Neuquén
para formar o Rio Negro. Do cume do
Cerro Campanário, com uma altura de
1000 m, o mirante de Bariloche, você tem
uma vista panorâmica de tirar o fôlego da
paisagem única da montanhas e vales da
região. Mesmo aqueles que não são bons
a pé podem desfrutar da paisagem graças
a um telefêrico: as ramificações do Lago
Nahuel Huapi, de 100 km de extensão, que
se aprofunda na paisagem montanhosa,
e os picos andinos cobertos de neve no
horizonte formam um cenário único.

Adembenemende, panoramische uitzichten

De oevers van de dam van de Limay rivier
bieden een romantisch landschap. De
380 km lange rivier krijgt water uit het
Nahuel Huapi-meer en mondt bij Neuquén
uit in de Rio Negro. Vanaf de top van de
1000 m hoge berg Cerro Campanario, het
uitzichtpunt van Bariloche, heeft men een
adembenemend, panoramisch uitzicht
op het unieke berg- en valleienlandschap
van het gebied. Ook wie niet goed ter
been is, kan er dankzij een stoeltjeslift van
genieten: de vertakkingen van het 100 km
lange Nahuel Huapi-meer, dat zich diep
in het berglandschap heeft genesteld, en
de met sneeuwde bedekte bergtoppen
van de Andes aan de horizon, vormen een
unieke coulisse.

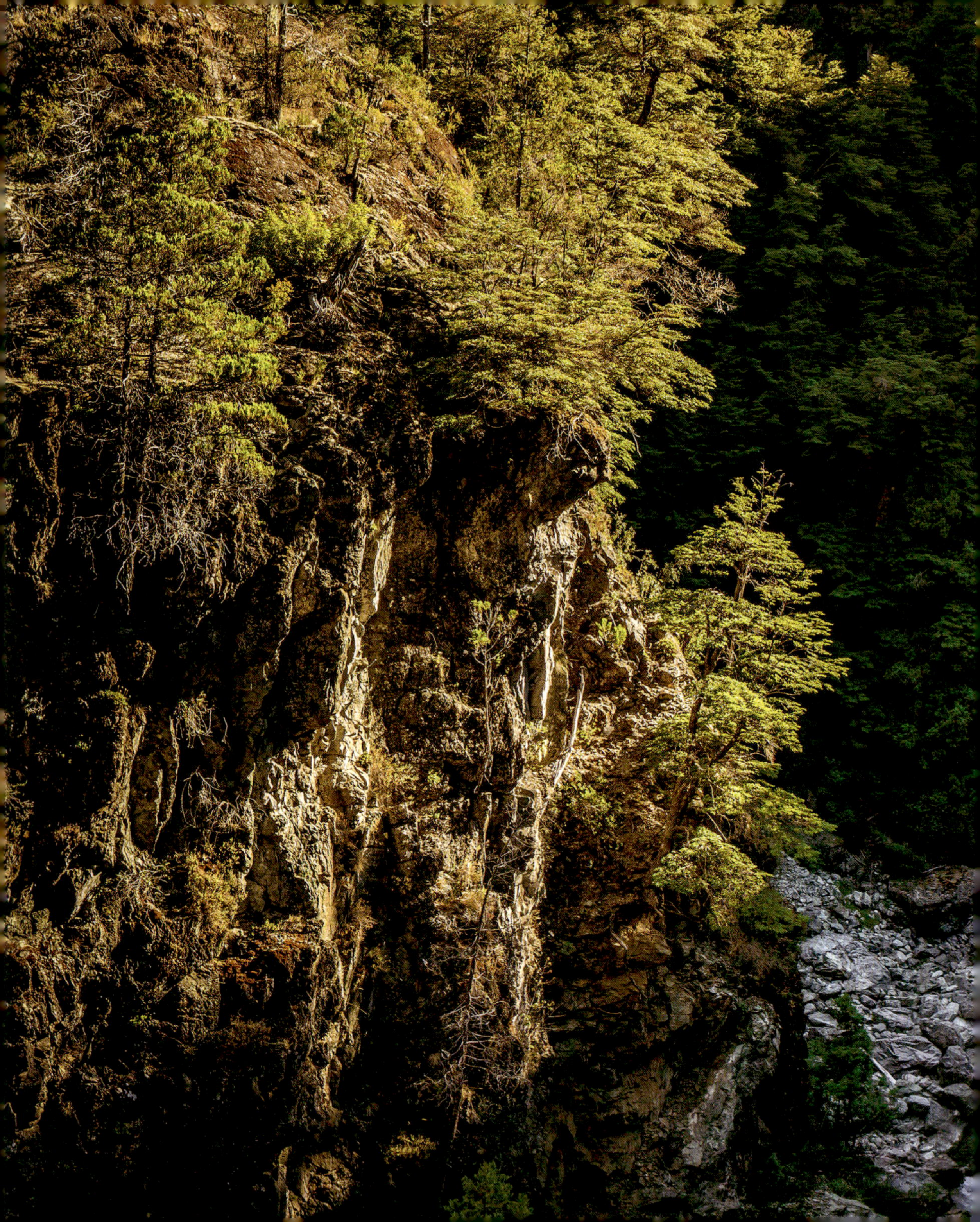

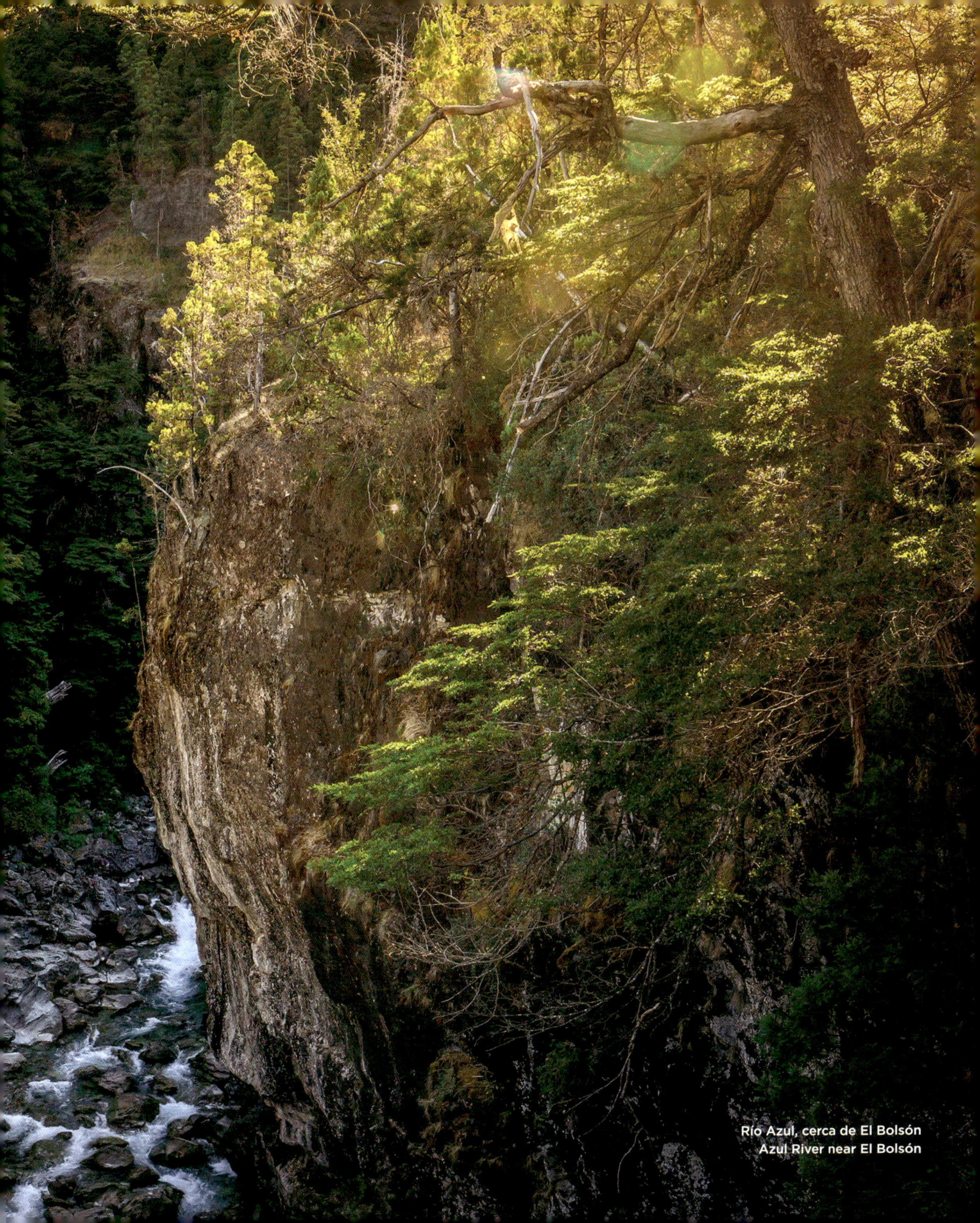

Río Azul, cerca de El Bolsón
Azul River near El Bolsón

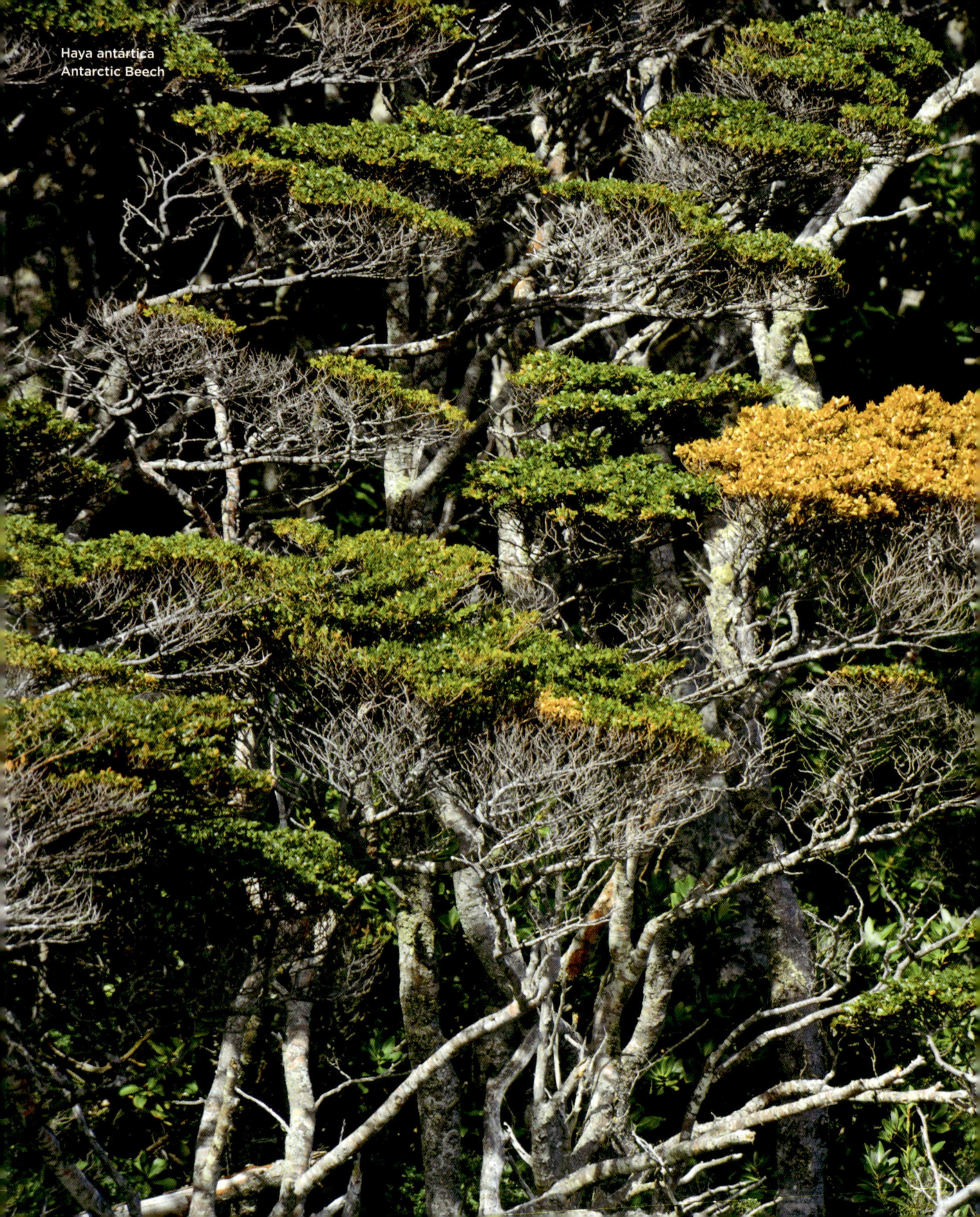

Haya antártica
Antarctic Beech

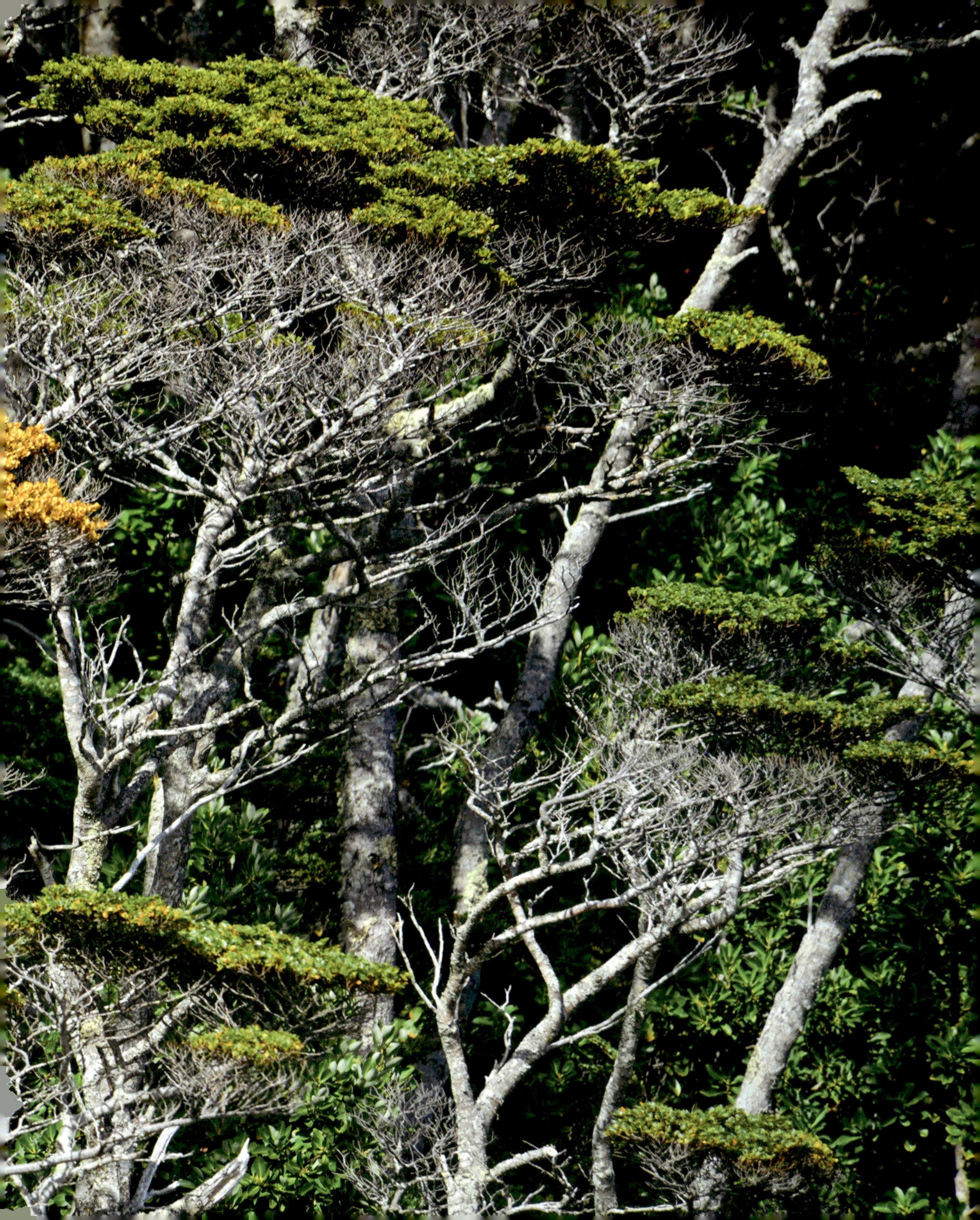

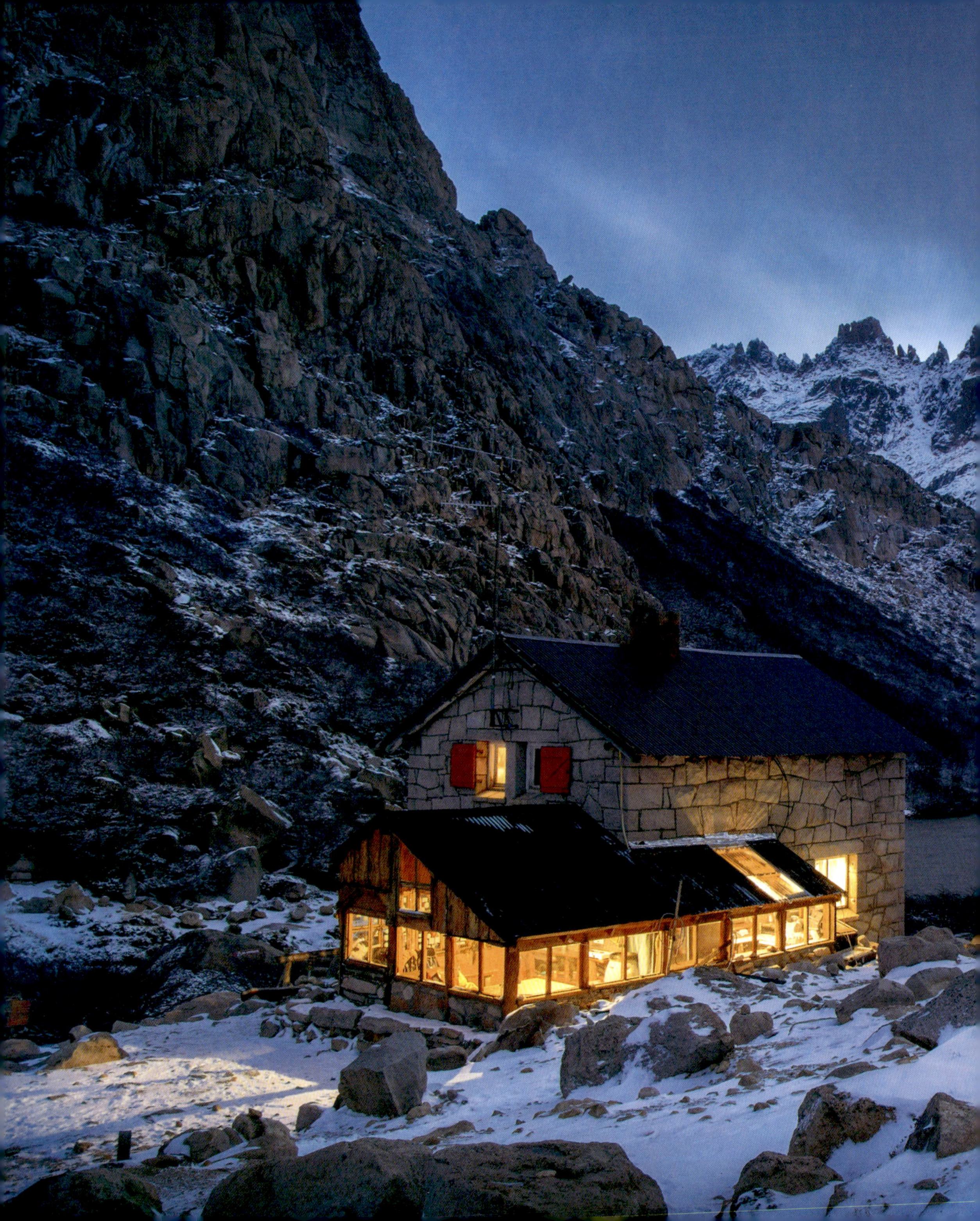

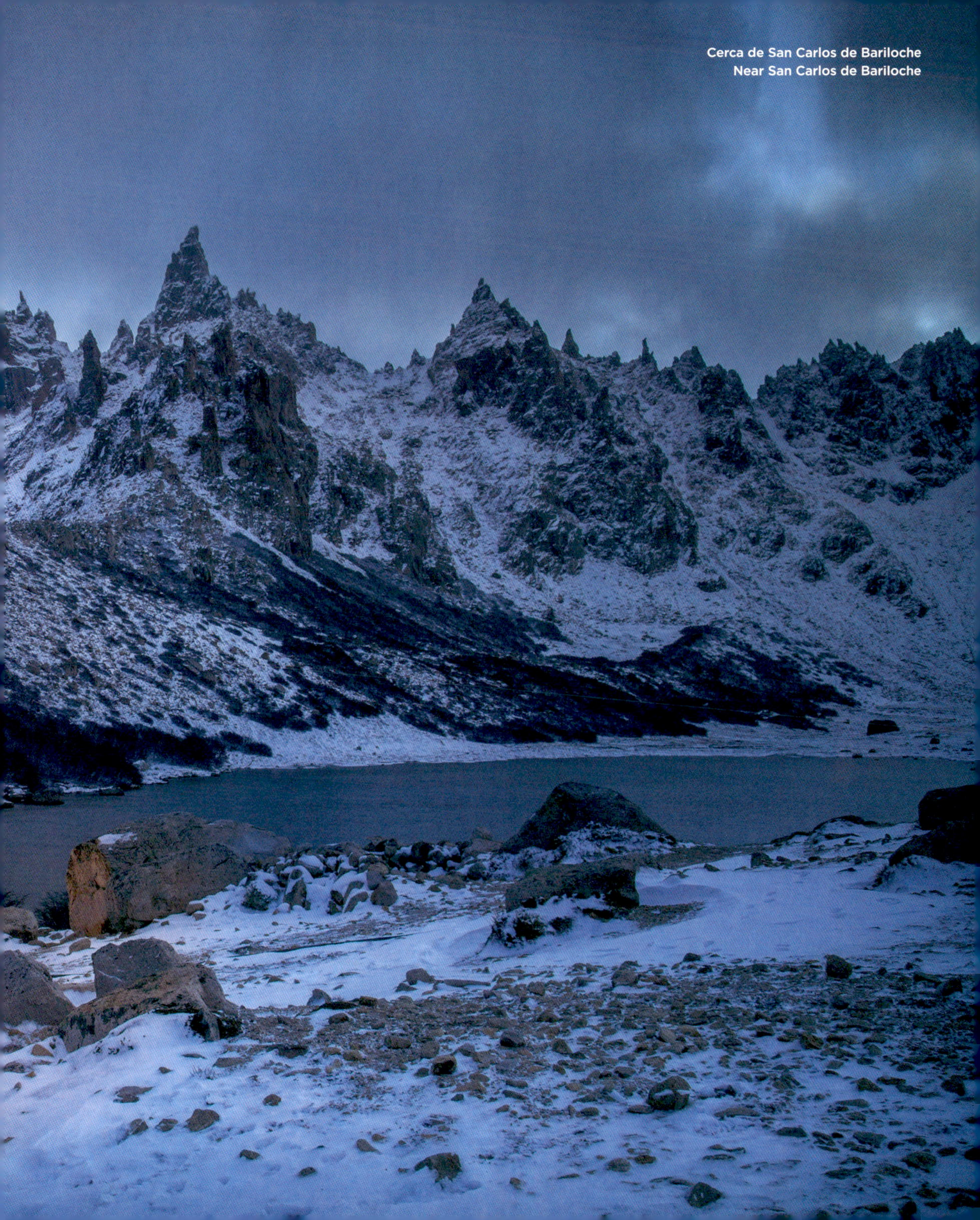

Cerca de San Carlos de Bariloche
Near San Carlos de Bariloche

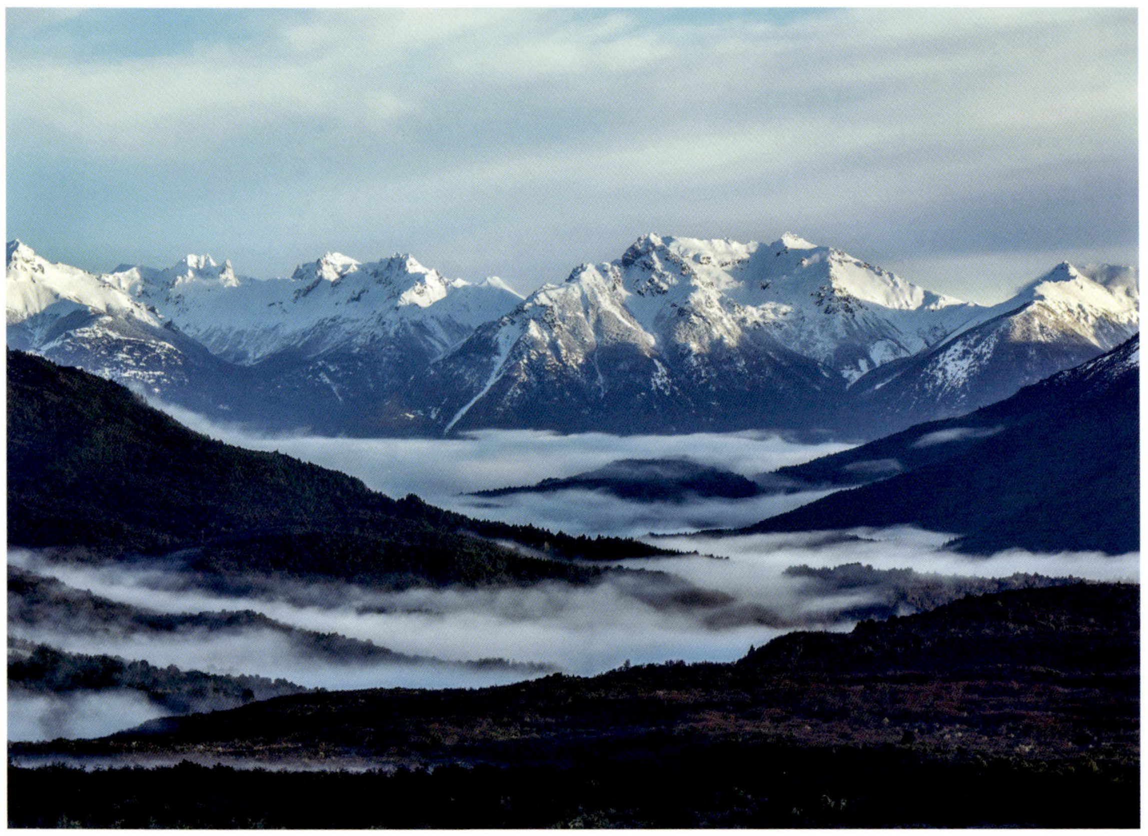

San Carlos de Bariloche

San Carlos de Bariloche

This city of 100 000 inhabitants is located
on the eastern edge of the large and
popular Nahuel Huapi National Park. It was
designated a nature reserve as early as
1903, when Francisco P. Moreno donated
land to the state. The name Nahuel Huapi
comes from the Mapuche language
and means 'puma island'. The park is
situated around the more than 500 km²
(193 sq mi), deep blue glacial lake. The
Cathedral Mountain, Cerro Catedral, is
19 km from Bariloche. The partly rocky area
of the 2405 m (7890 ft) high mountain
is considered to be the most important
skiing area of the Andes, where skiers
and snowboarders cavort during the
winter season. Mountain huts provide for
overnight stays and a refreshment stop.

San Carlos de Bariloche

Cette ville de 100 000 habitants est située
à la lisière orientale du vaste et fort prisé
parc national Nahuel Huapi. Il fut constitué
dès 1903 en réserve naturelle, lorsque
Francico P. Moreno découvrit ces terres. Le
nom *Nahuel Huapi* signifie dans la langue
des Mapuche « l'île des pumas ». Le parc
entoure le lac de glacier bleu, profond de
500 km². Bariloche est située à 19 km de
la « montagne cathédrale », Cerro Catedral.
Le territoire en partie rocheux de cette
montagne culminant à 2405 m est le plus
important domaine skiable des Andes. Les
skieurs et snowboardeurs y affluent en
hiver. Des refuges permettent d'y passer la
nuit et de se restaurer.

San Carlos de Bariloche

Die Stadt mit 100 000 Einwohnern
liegt am Ostrand des großen und
beliebten Nationalparks Nahuel Huapi.
Er wurde bereits 1903 als Naturreservat
ausgewiesen, als Francico P. Moreno
dem Staat Land schenkte. Sein Name
Nahuel Huapi kommt aus der Mapuche-
Sprache, er bedeutet Pumainsel. Der
Park liegt rund um den 500 km² großen,
tiefblauen Gletschersee. Zum Kathedralen-
Berg, Cerro Catedral, sind es 19 km von
Bariloche. Das teils felsige Gebiet des
2405 m hohen Bergs gilt als das wichtigste
Skigebiet der Anden. Hier tummeln
sich in der Wintersaison Skifahrer und
Snowborder. Für Übernachtungen und den
Einkehrschwung sorgen Berghütten.

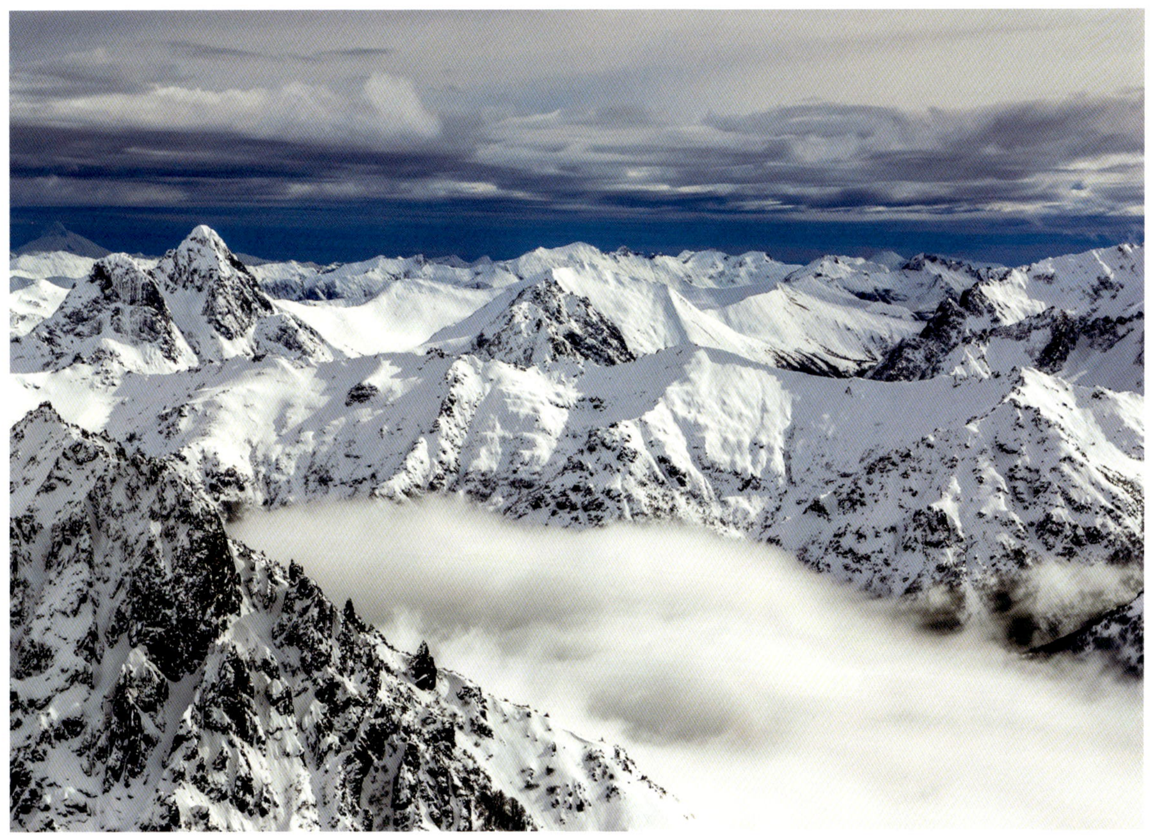

Cerro Catedral, Parque Nacional Nahuel Huapi
Cerro Catedral, Nahuel Huapi National Park

San Carlos de Bariloche

La ciudad de 100 000 habitantes está situada en el extremo oriental del gran y popular Parque Nacional Nahuel Huapi. Fue designada reserva natural ya en 1903, cuando Francisco P. Moreno donó tierras al Estado. Su nombre Nahuel Huapi proviene de la lengua mapuche, y significa "isla del puma". El parque está situado alrededor de un lago glaciar de 500 km² de superficie. El cerro Catedral se encuentra a 19 km de Bariloche. El área parcialmente rocosa de la alta montaña de 2405 m se considera la zona de esquí más importante de los Andes. Los esquiadores y los que practican snowboard vienen aquí en la temporada de invierno. Los refugios de montaña permiten pasar la noche y hacer una parada para tomar algo.

San Carlos de Bariloche

A cidade de 100 000 habitantes está localizada no extremo leste do grande e popular Parque Nacional Nahuel Huapi. Ele foi designado como reserva natural já em 1903, quando Francico P. Moreno doou terras ao Estado. O seu nome Nahuel Huapi vem da língua mapuche, significa ilha do puma. O parque está localizado em torno do lago glacial azul de 500 km² de profundidade. A montanha da catedral, o Cerro Catedral, fica a 19 km de Bariloche. A área parcialmente rochosa da montanha de 2405 m de altura é considerada a mais importante área de esqui dos Andes. Esquiadores e snowboarders podem ser encontrados aqui no inverno. As cabanas nas montanhas proporcionam noites de estadias e possibilidade de fazer uma parada para comer ou beber.

San Carlos de Bariloche

De stad met 100 000 inwoners ligt aan de oostelijke rand van het grote populaire nationaal park Nahuel Huapi. Het werd in 1903, toen Francico P. Moreno land aan de staat schonk, al tot natuurreservaat bestemd. Zijn naam Nahuel Huapi komt uit de Mapuche taal en betekent poema eiland. Het park ligt rond het 500 km² grote, diepblauwe gletsjermeer. De kathedraalberg Cerro Catedral ligt op 19 km van Bariloche. Het deels rotsachtige gebied van de 2405 m hoge berg wordt beschouwd als het belangrijkste skigebied van de Andes. Skiërs en snowboarders amuseren zich hier in het winterseizoen. Berghutten zorgen voor overnachtingen en een verfrissingsstop.

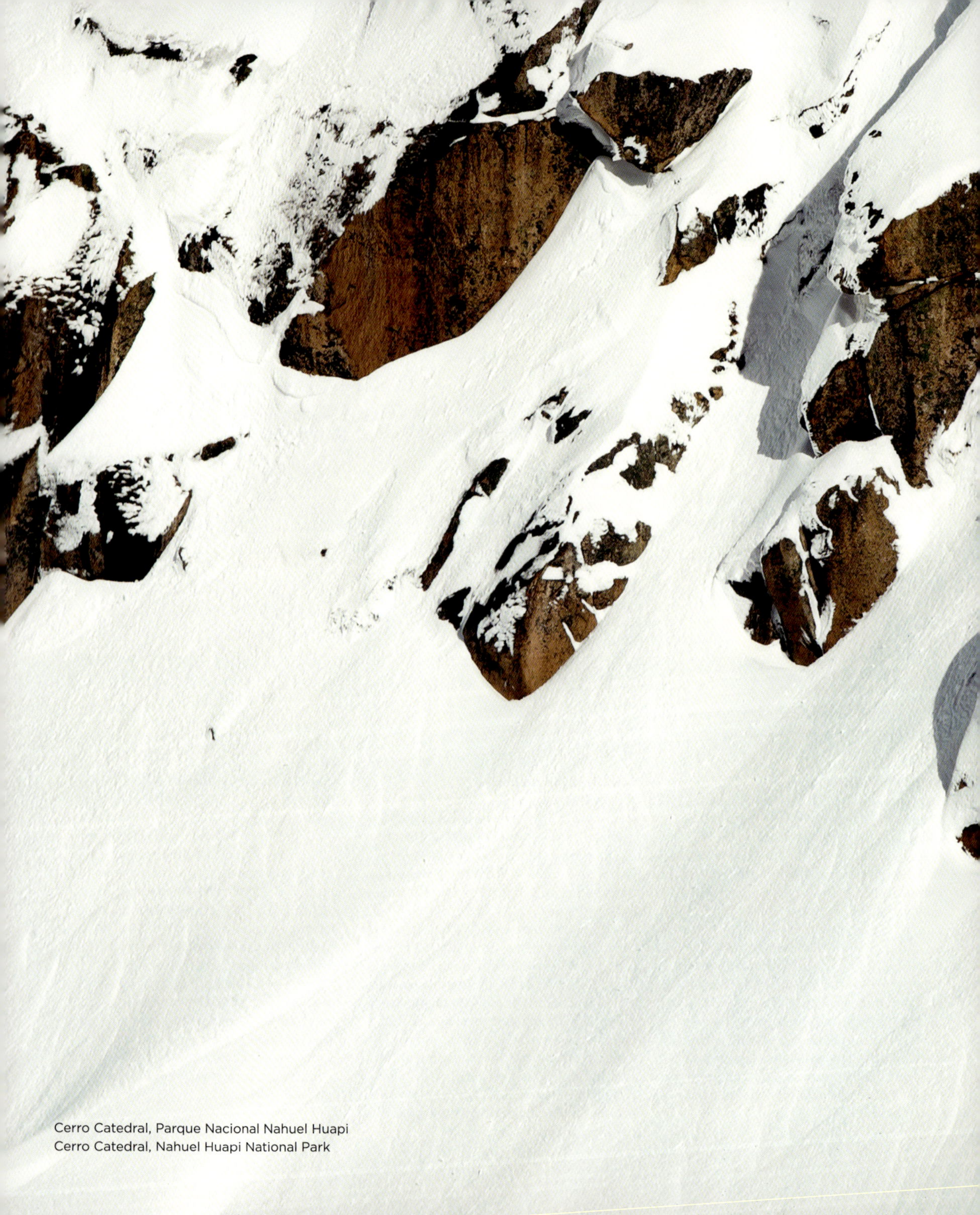

Cerro Catedral, Parque Nacional Nahuel Huapi
Cerro Catedral, Nahuel Huapi National Park

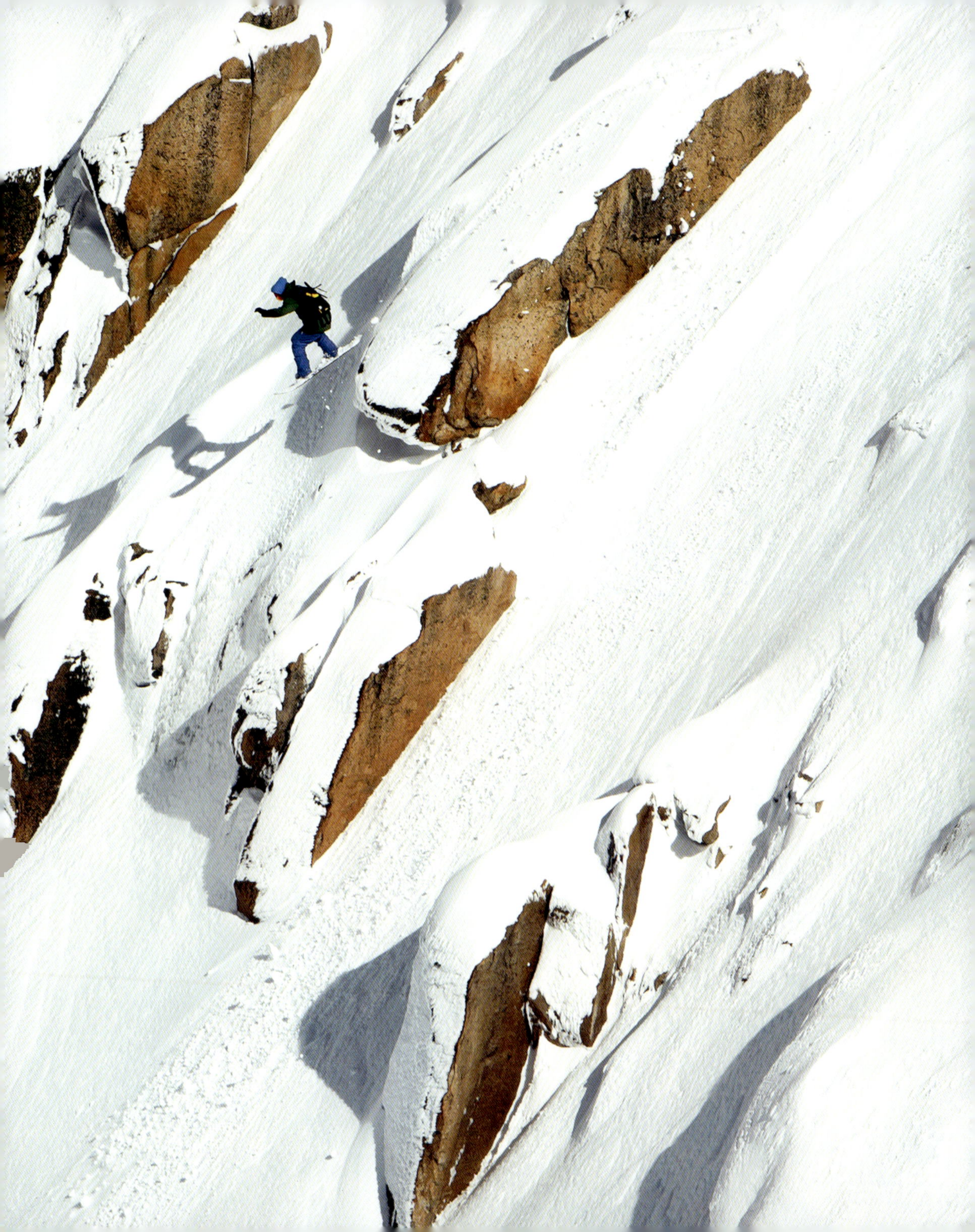

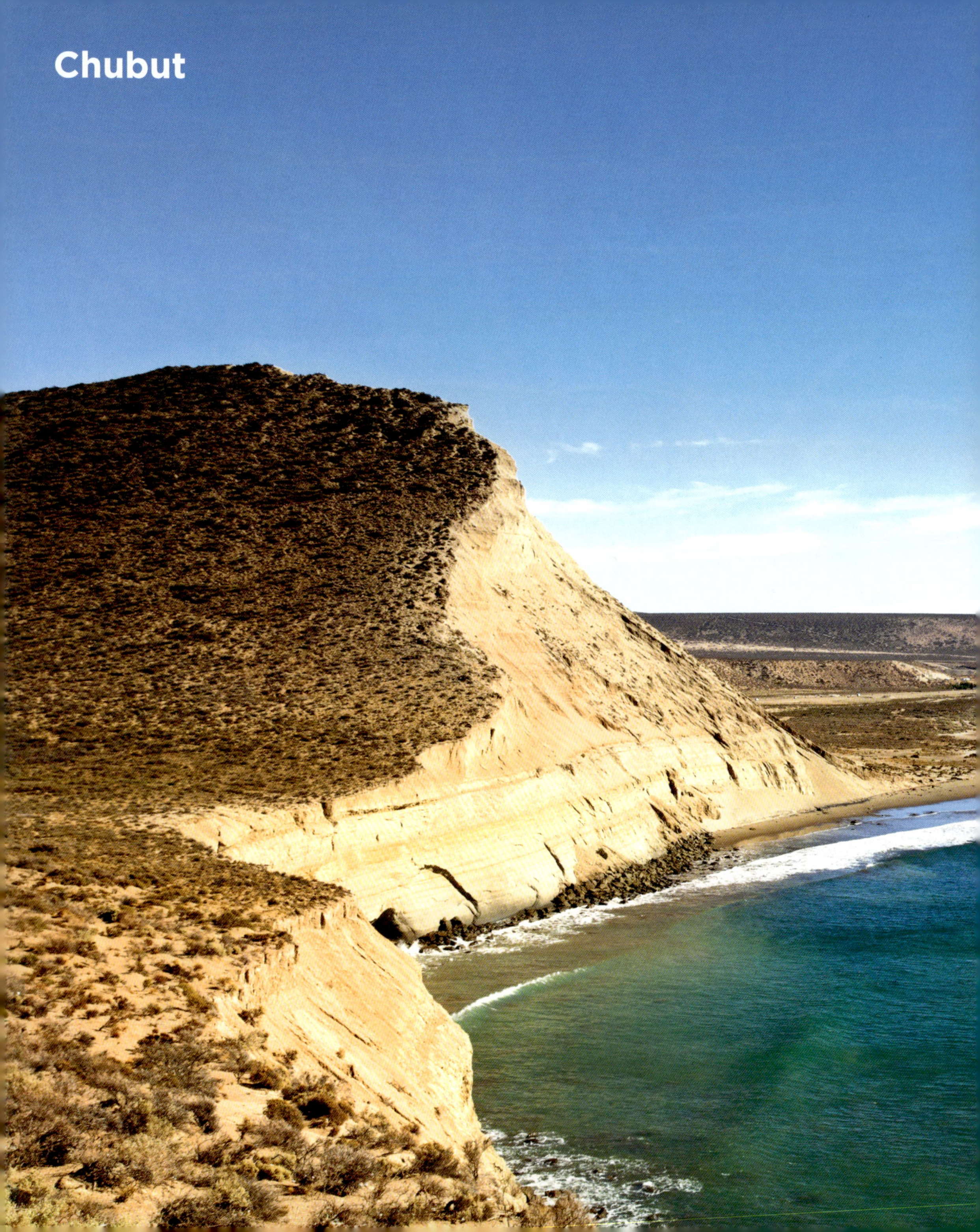
Chubut

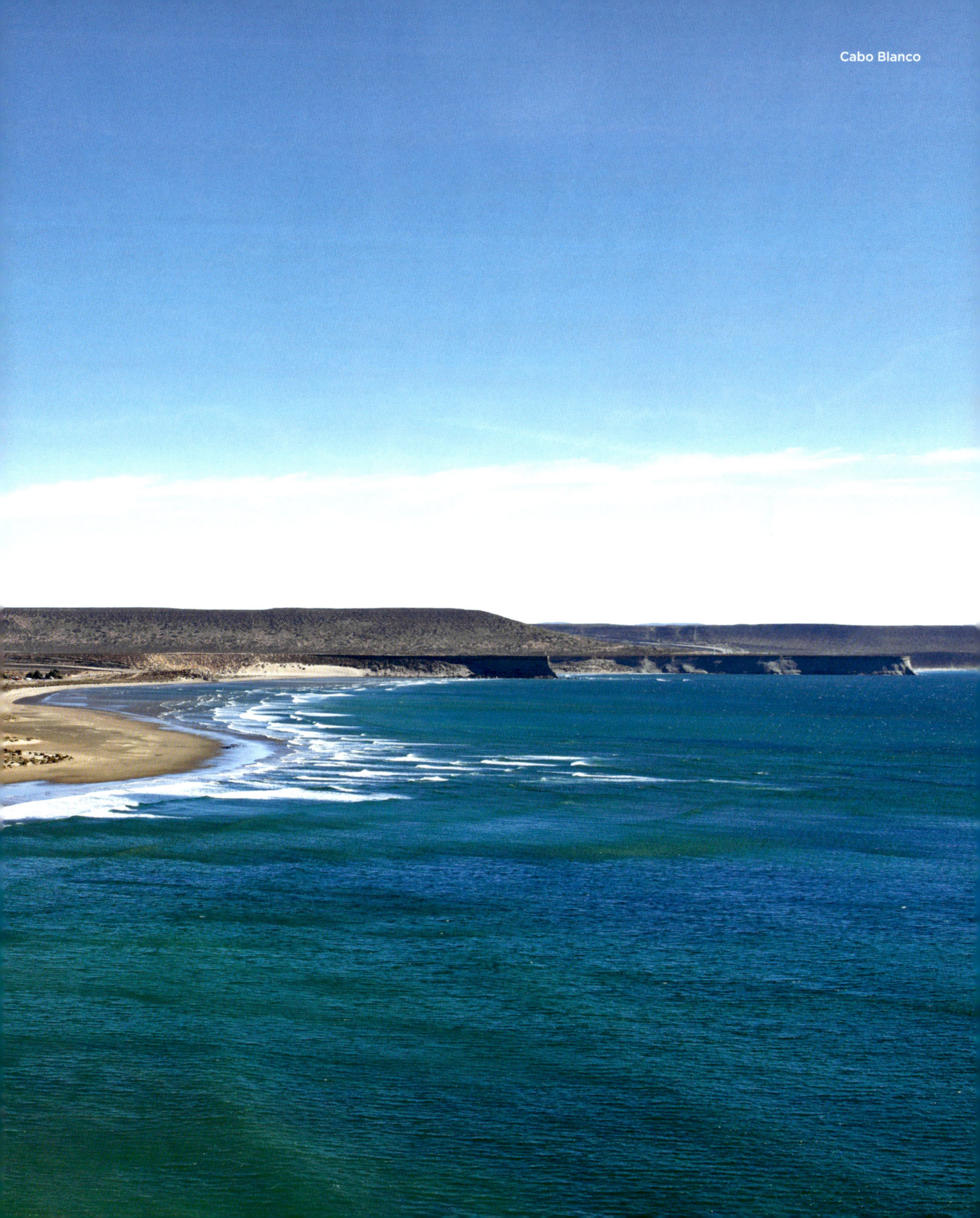

Cabo Blanco

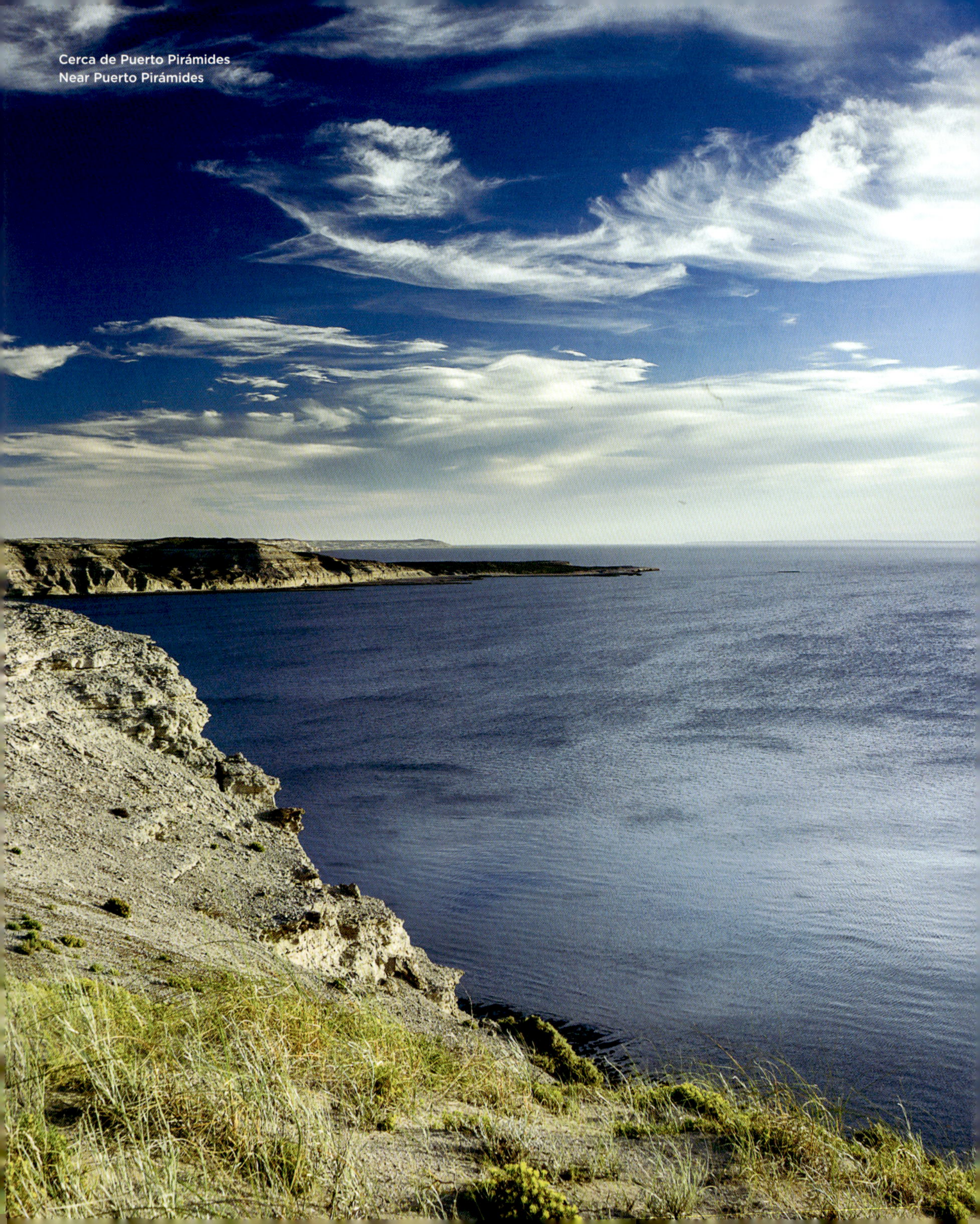

Cerca de Puerto Pirámides
Near Puerto Pirámides

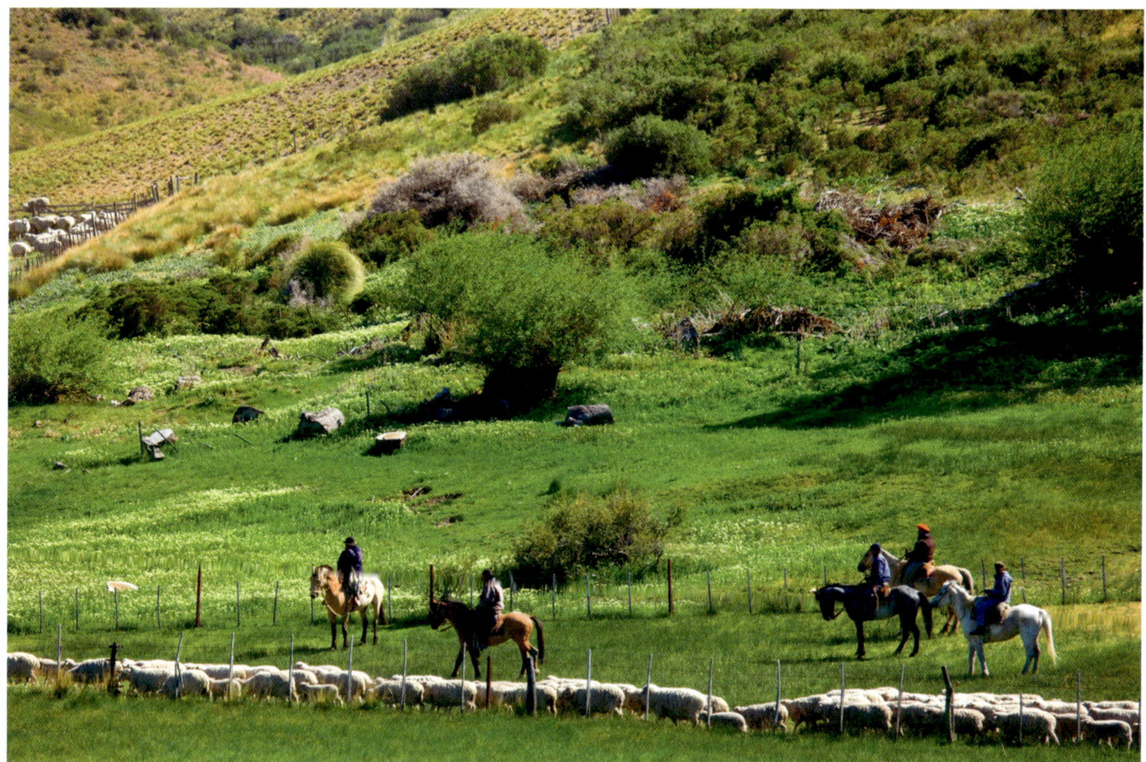

Cerca de Camarones
Near Camarones

Chubut

The province extends from the Andes in the west to the Atlantic Ocean in the east. It is the epitome of Patagonia with its large, wide steppe plain. People first settled there around 8000 BCE. In the second half of the 19th century, the south was also developed militarily and economically. The native inhabitants were made to give way for the establishment of the estancias.

Chubut

La provincia se extiende entre los Andes al oeste y el océano Atlántico al este. Es la esencia de la Patagonia, con su gran y amplia planicie esteparia. Las personas empezaron a establecerse allí a partir de 8000 a. C. En la segunda mitad del siglo XIX el sur también se desarrolló tanto militar como económicamente. Los habitantes nativos fueron obligados a ceder su territorio para que se establecieran las estancias.

Chubut

Cette province s'étend entre les Andes à l'ouest et l'Atlantique à l'est. Occupée par un vaste plateau de steppes étendues, elle est la quintessence de la Patagonie. L'homme y est installé depuis 8000 av. J.-C. Dans la seconde moitié du XIXᵉ siècle, le Sud a également été exploité militairement et économiquement. Les habitants indigènes durent céder pour que s'implantent les *estancias*.

Chubut

A província estende-se entre os Andes, a oeste, e o Oceano Atlântico, a leste. É o epítome da Patagônia, com sua grande e ampla planície de estepes. Desde 8000 a. C. as pessoas tem se estabelecido lá. Na segunda metade do século XIX, o sul também se desenvolveu militar e economicamente. Os povos indígenas tiveram que abrir mão para as estâncias.

Chubut

Die Provinz erstreckt sich zwischen den Anden im Westen und dem Atlantik im Osten. Sie ist mit ihrer großen, weiten Steppenebene der Inbegriff Patagoniens. Seit 8000 v. Chr. siedelten dort Menschen. In der zweiten Hälfte des 19. Jahrhunderts wurde auch der Süden militärisch und wirtschaftlich erschlossen. Für die Estanzias mussten die Ureinwohner weichen.

Chubut

De provincie strekt zich uit tussen de Andes in het westen en de Atlantische Oceaan in het oosten. Met zijn grote, brede steppevlakte is dit het toonbeeld van Patagonië. Sinds 8000 voor Christus vestigden zich hier mensen. In de tweede helft van de 19e eeuw werd ook het zuiden voor militaire en economische doeleinden toegankelijk gemaakt. De oerinwoners moesten plaatsmaken voor de estancias.

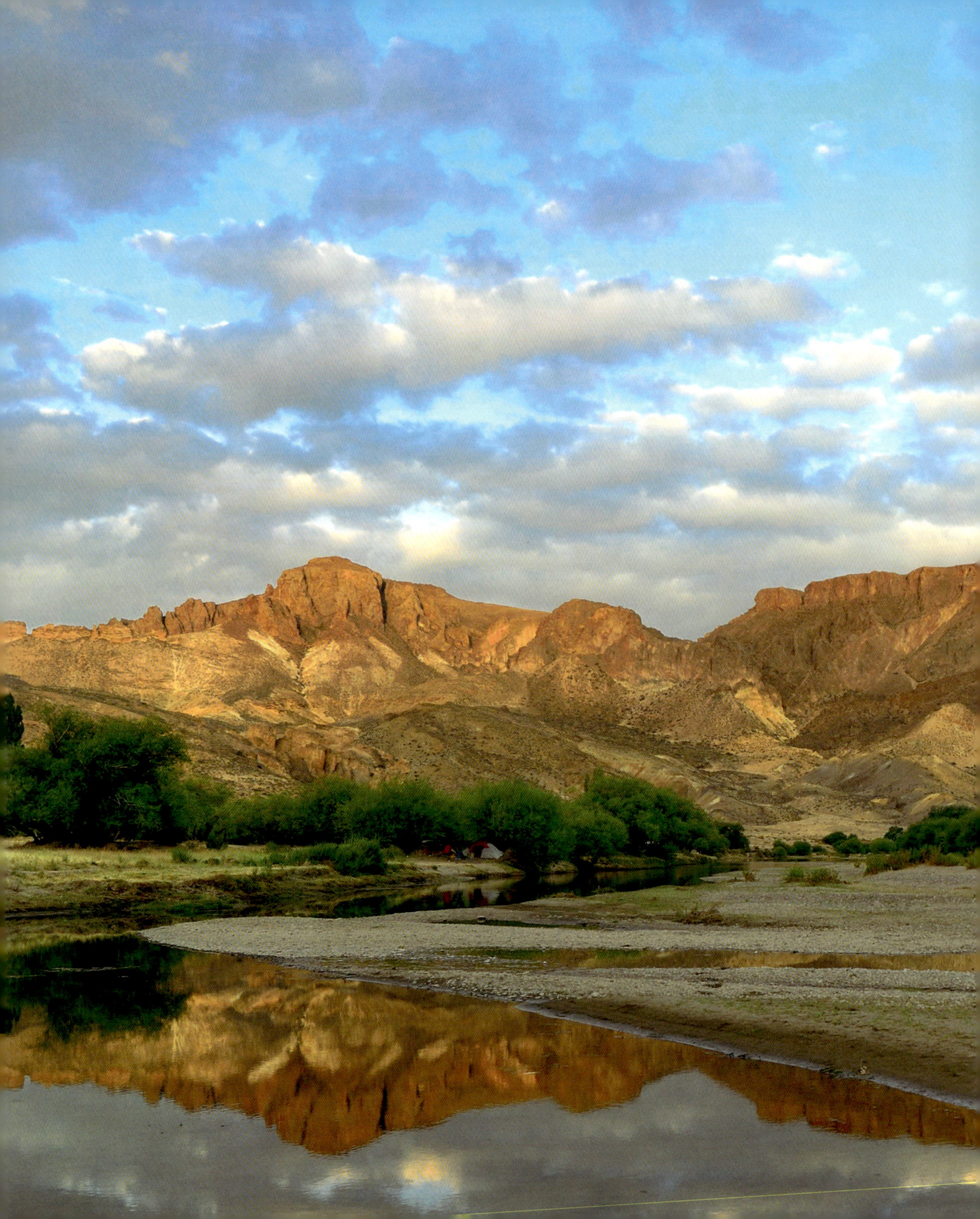

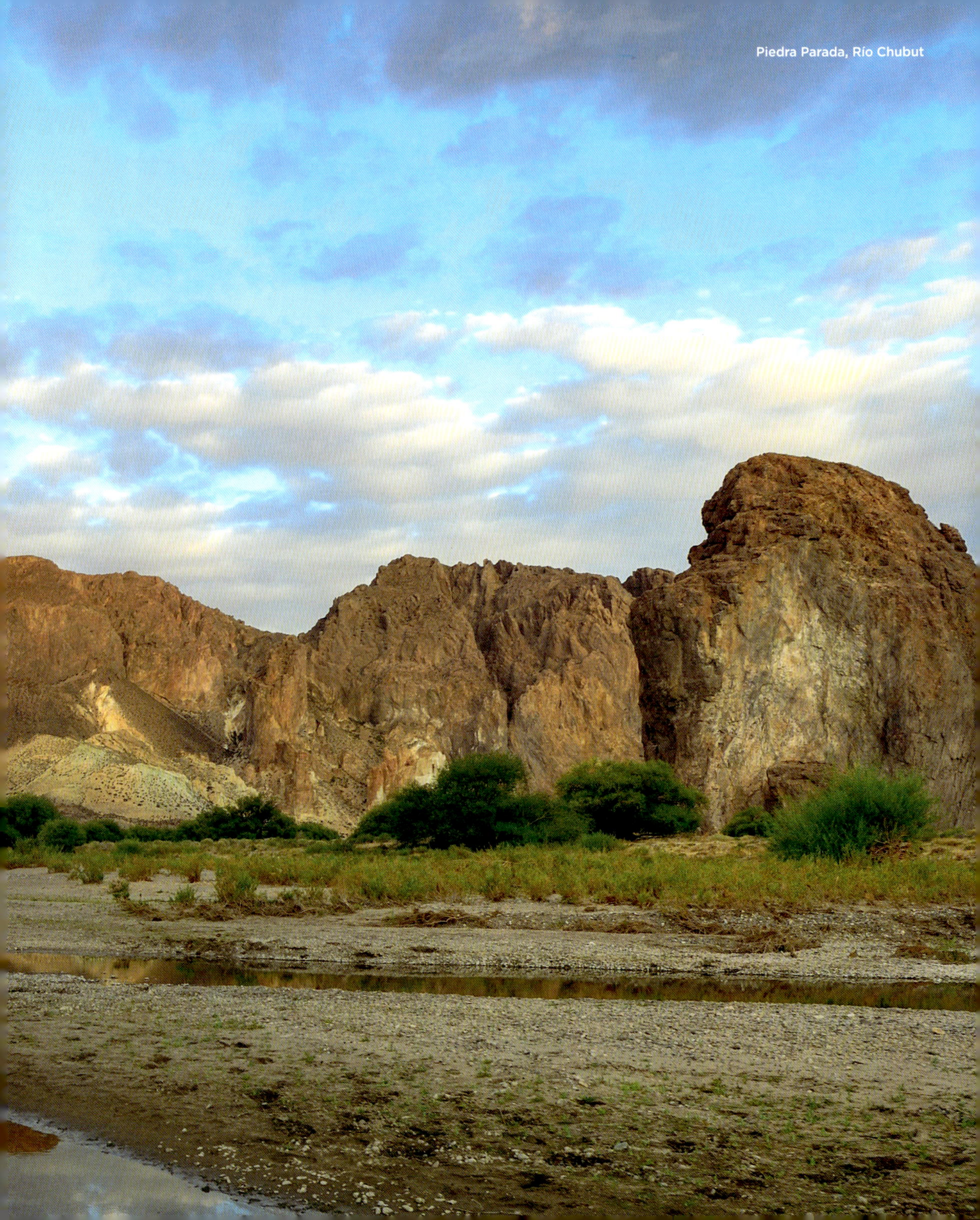

Piedra Parada, Río Chubut

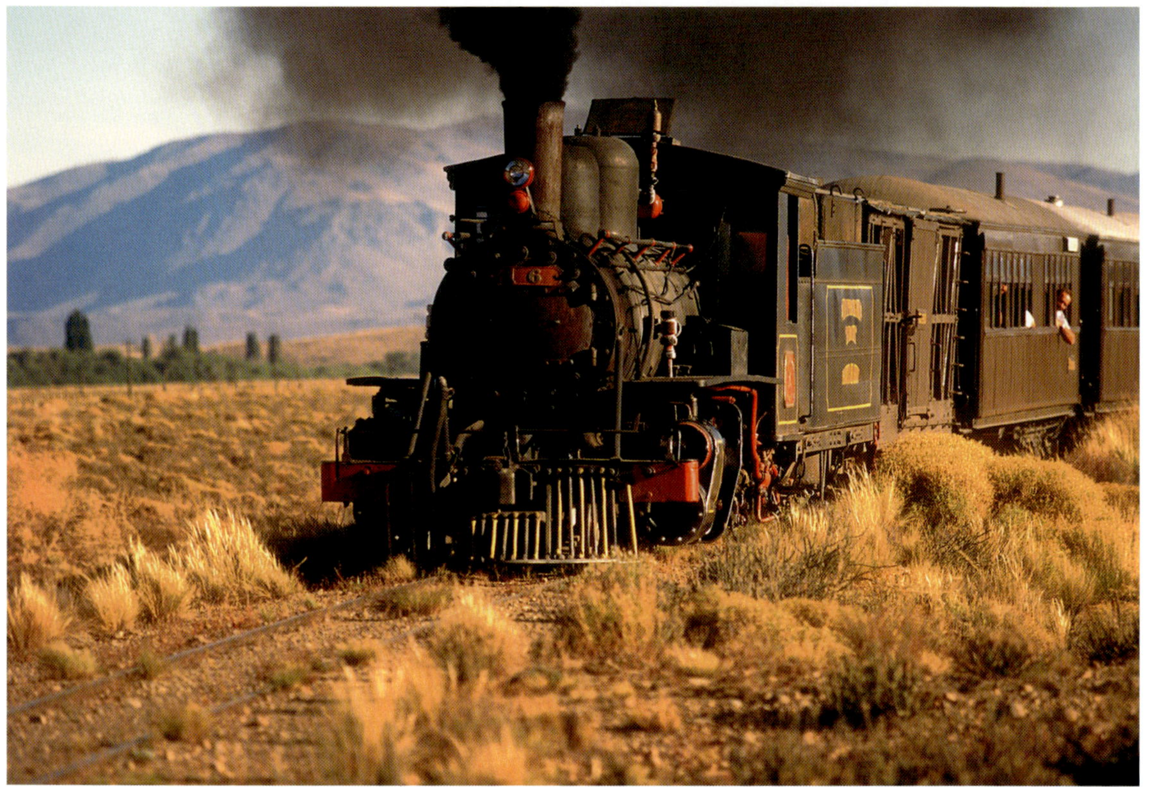

Viejo Expreso Patagónico
Old Patagonian Express

La Trochita

The Old Patagonia Express train was planned in 1908 to connect Patagonia with the capital of the country, running between Esquel at the foot of the Andes and Ingeniero Jacobacci. In between it passed all the great estancias of the region and due to its narrow gauge, it was christened "La Trochita".

La Trochita

Le réseau ferroviaire fut planifié en 1908 afin de relier la Patagonie à la capitale provinciale et de développer les transports de la région. Le tronçon du Vieil Express de Patagonie circule entre Esquel, au pied des Andes, et la station Ingeniero Jacobacci. En chemin, il dessert toutes les grandes *estancias* de la région. En référence à l'étroitesse de sa voie, il est surnommé *La Trochita.*

La Trochita

Der Patagonien-Express-Zug wurde 1908 zur Anbindung Patagoniens an die Hauptstadt des Landes und zur Vernetzung der Provinz geplant. Er verkehrte zwischen Esquel am Fuß der Anden und Ingeniero Jacobacci. Dazwischen fuhr er alle großen Estanzias der Region an. Wegen seiner schmalen Spur wurde er „La Trochita" getauft.

La Trochita

El Tren exprés de la Patagonia fue planificado en 1908 para conectar la Patagonia con la capital del país y para unir la provincia. Viajaba entre Esquel al pie de los Andes e Ingeniero Jacobacci. En su recorrido llegaba a todas las grandes estancias de la región. Por su estrecho camino recibió el nombre de "La Trochita".

La Trochita

O Trem Expresso da Patagônia foi planejado em 1908 para conectar a Patagônia com a capital do país e para ligar a província. Corria entre Esquel, aos pés dos Andes, e Ingeniero Jacobacci. Entre estas duas estações, ele passava por todas as grandes fazendas da região. Devido ao seu trilho estreito ele foi batizado de "La Trochita".

La Trochita

De Patagonië-Express werd in 1908 gepland om Patagonië met de hoofdstad van het land te verbinden en aan de provincie te koppelen. Hij reed tussen Esquel aan de voet van de Andes en Ingeniero Jacobacci. Daartussen reed hij naar alle grote estancias van de regio. Vanwege zijn smalle spoor werd hij tot "La Trochita" gedoopt.

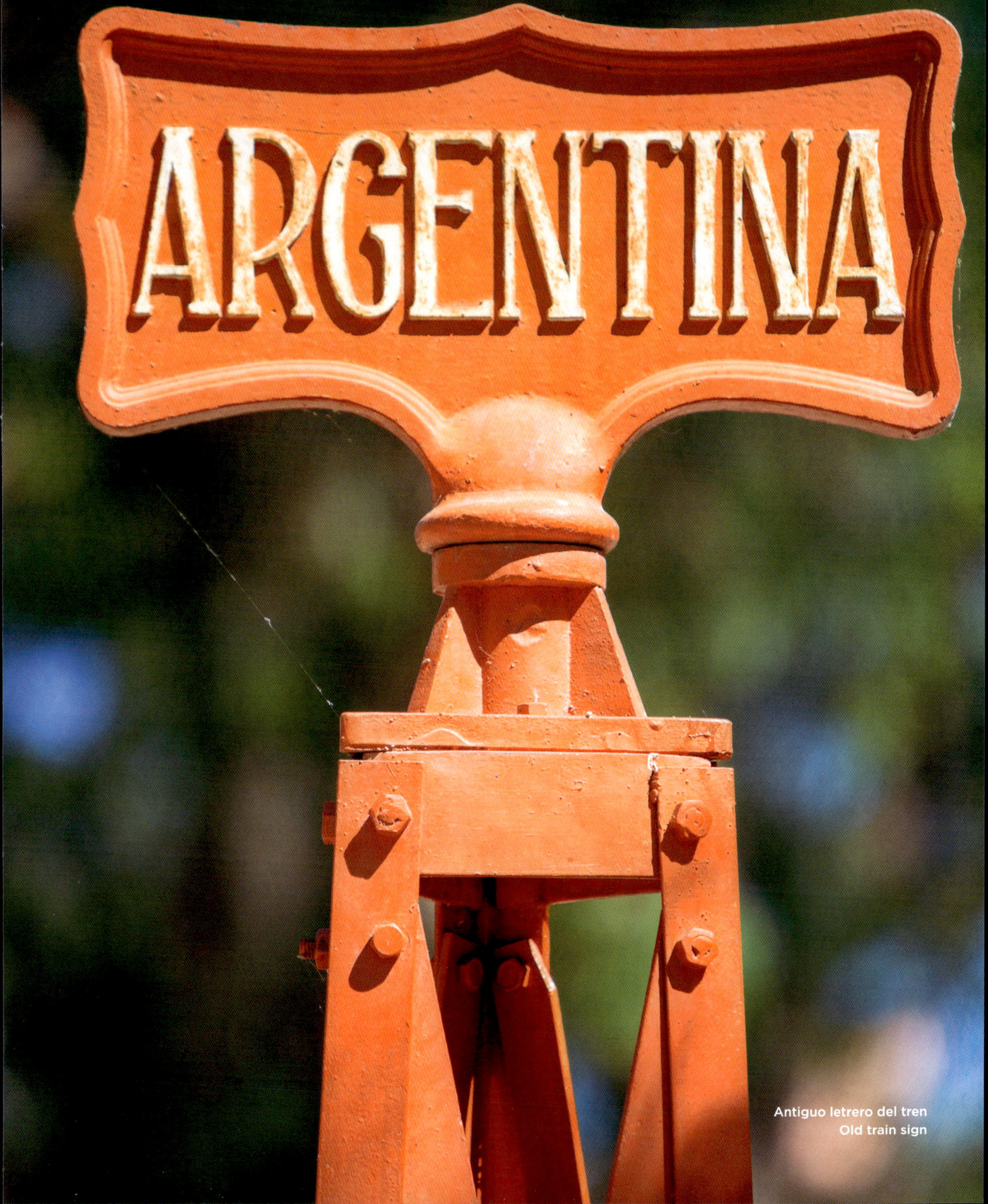

Antiguo letrero del tren
Old train sign

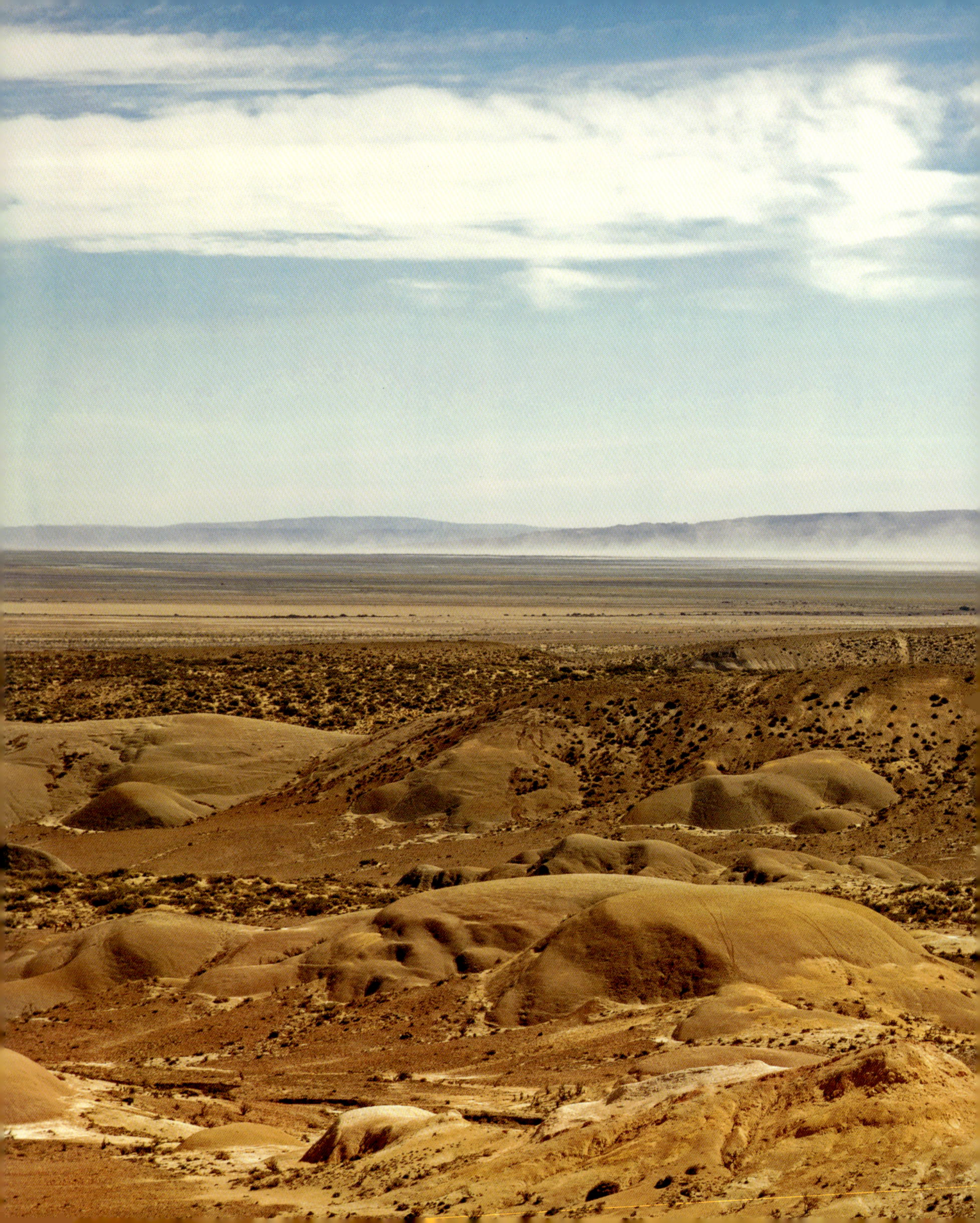

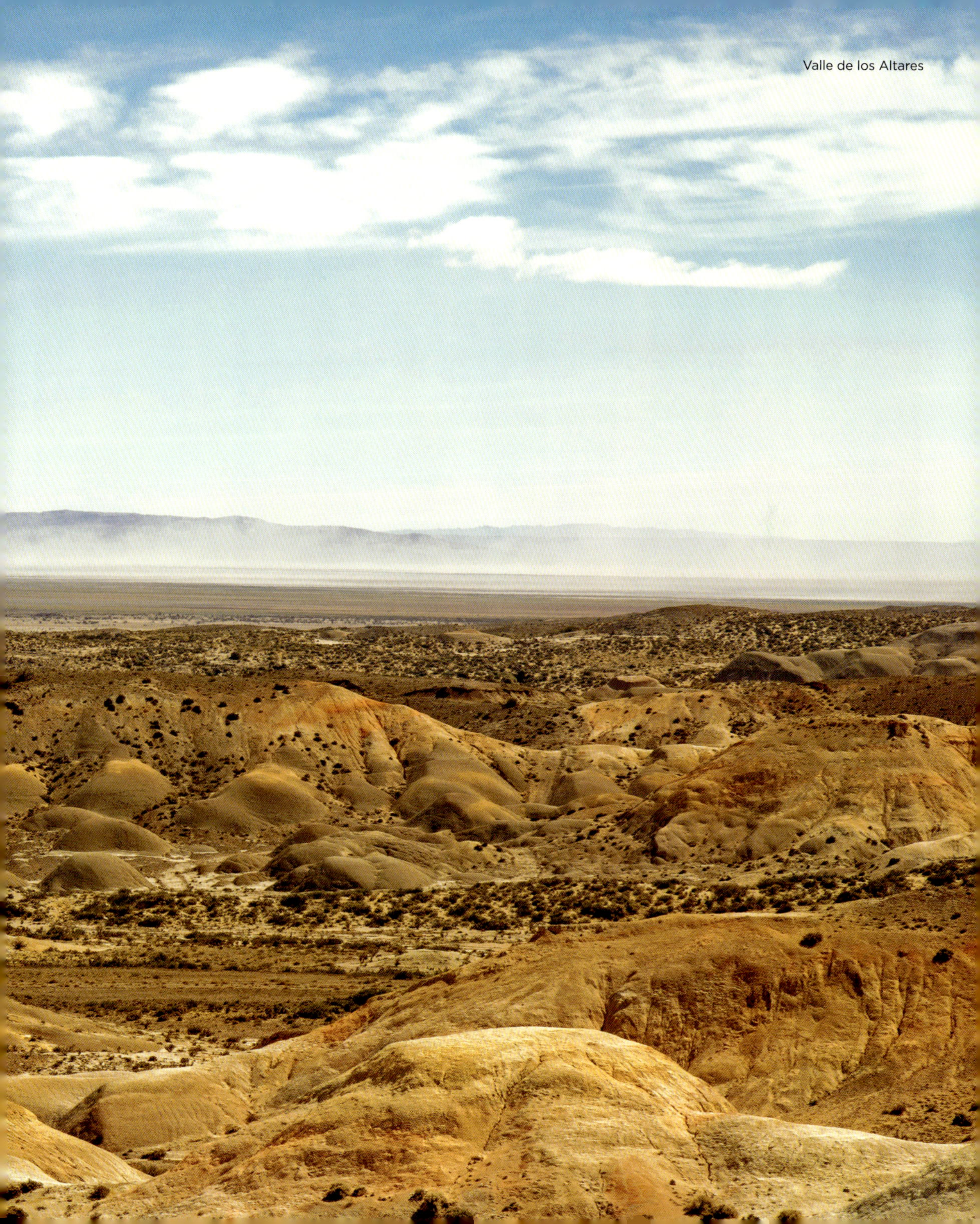
Valle de los Altares

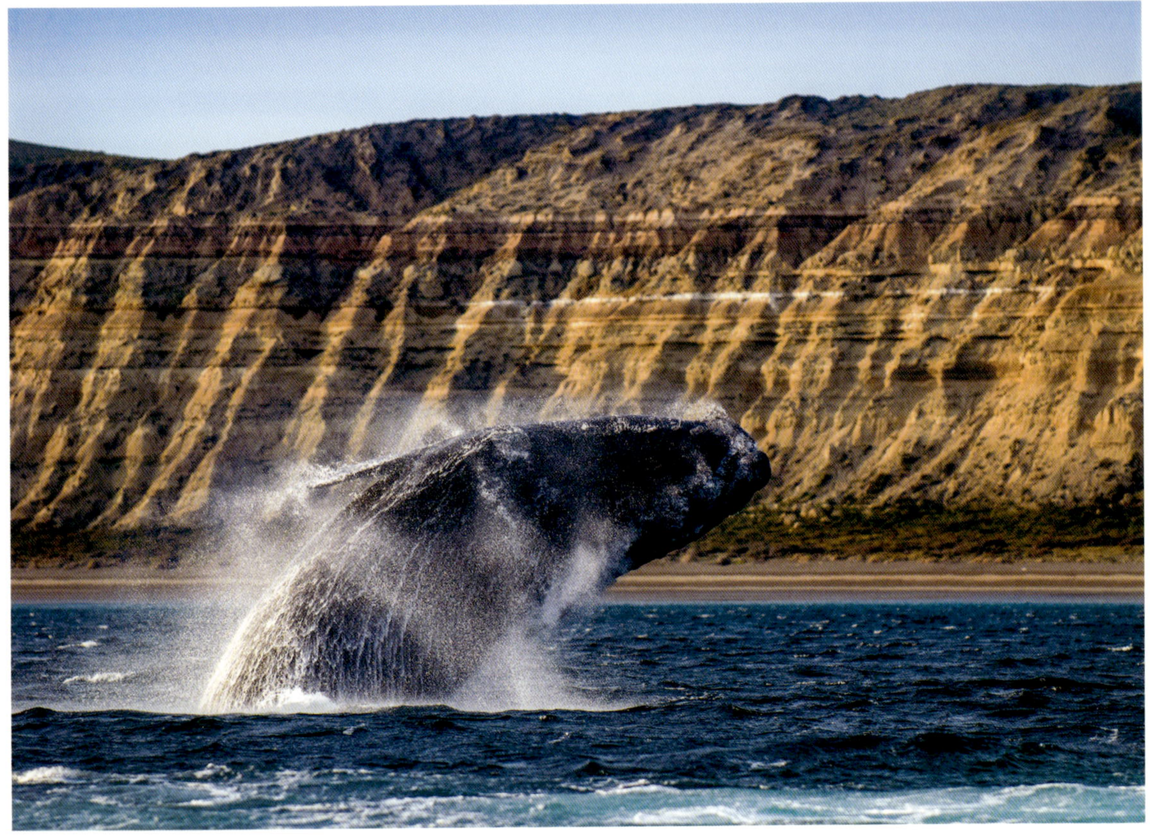

Yubarata, Península Valdés
Humpback whale, Valdés Peninsula

Valdés Peninsula

Since 1999, the Valdés peninsula has been a UNESCO World Heritage Site. It is considered one of the most oldest geological formations in southern Argentina. In the barren, rocky landscape, scientists found rocks and fossils of marine animals and oysters from the Paleogene Period. The peninsula is connected to the mainland by a narrow isthmus. In the center there are three salt lakes, 35 m (115 ft) below sea level. From May to November, southern right whales, a species of baleen whale, come to the Golfo Nuevo to give birth to their young. It is spectacular to observe how these 60 ton, 16 m (52 ft) long marine mammals rise from the water in a high arc and dive in again.

La presqu'île de Valdés

Depuis 1999, la presqu'île de Valdés est inscrite au patrimoine mondial de l'Unesco. Elle est considérée comme la formation géologique la plus authentique du sud de l'Argentine. Au cœur de son paysage rude et rocheux, les scientifiques ont découvert des roches et des fossiles d'animaux marins et d'huîtres provenant de l'époque paléocène. La presqu'île est reliée au continent par une étroite langue de terre. Elle compte en son centre trois lacs salés situés 35 m en dessous du niveau de la mer. De mai à novembre, les baleines franches australes, variété de cétacés à fanons, séjournent dans le Golfo Nuevo pour donner naissance à leurs petits. On peut observer ces mammifères marins de 60 t et 16 m de long sauter hors de l'eau puis replonger spectaculairement.

Halbinsel Valdés

Seit 1999 gehört die Halbinsel Valdés zum UNESCO-Weltkulturerbe. Sie gilt als die ursprünglichste geologische Formation Südargentiniens. In der kargen, felsigen Landschaft fanden Wissenschaftler Gestein und Fossilien von Meerestieren und Austern aus dem Paläogen-Zeitalter. Über eine schmale Landzunge ist die Halbinsel mit dem Festland verknüpft. In ihrer Mitte liegen drei Salzseen 35 m unter dem Meeresspiegel. Von Mai bis November kommen Südkaper, eine Bartenwalart, in den Golfo Nuevo, um ihre Jungen zu gebären. Es ist spektakulär zu beobachten, wie diese 60 t schweren und 16 m langen Meeressäuger im hohen Bogen aus dem Wasser aufsteigen und wieder eintauchen.

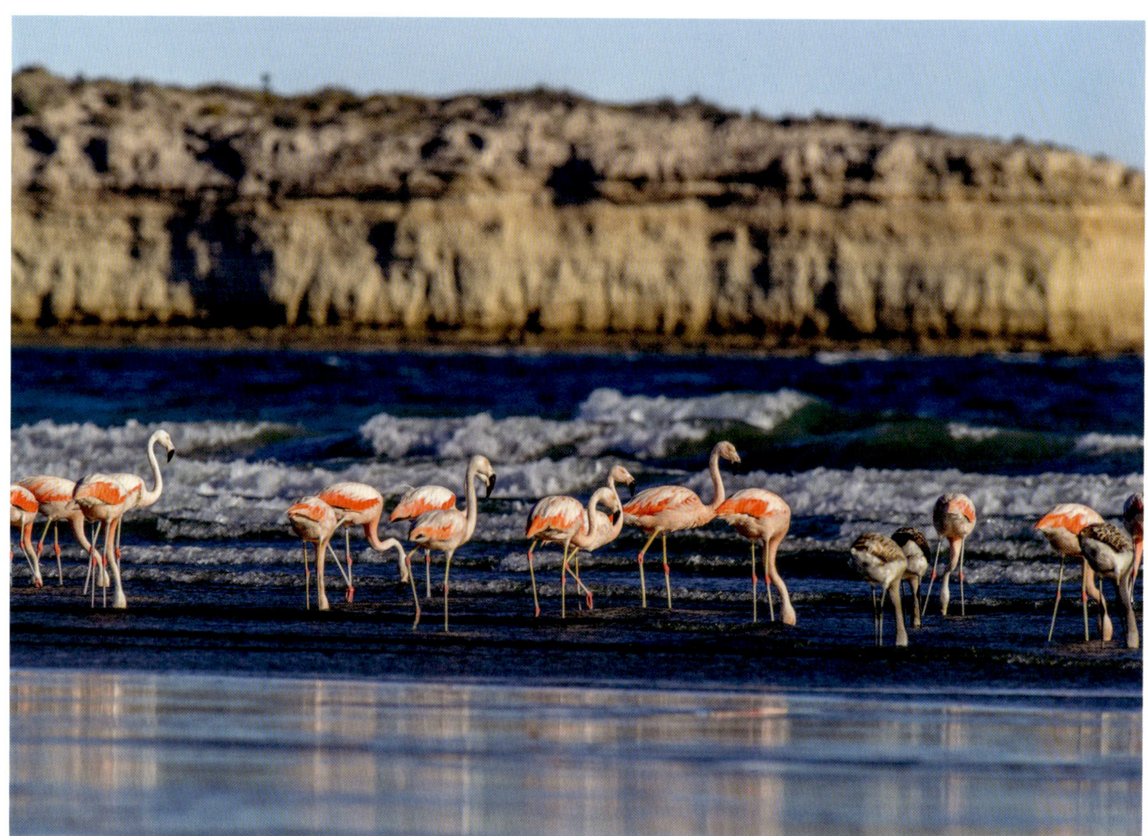

Flamencos, Península Valdés
Flamingos, Valdés Peninsula

Península Valdés

Desde 1999, la Península Valdés es
Patrimonio de la Humanidad de la
UNESCO. Es considerada la formación
geológica más original del sur de
Argentina. En su árido y rocoso paisaje, los
científicos encontraron rocas y fósiles de
animales marinos y ostras de la época del
Paleógeno. La península está conectada
al continente por un estrecho cabo. En su
centro hay tres lagos salados a 35 m bajo
el nivel del mar. De mayo a noviembre, las
ballenas francas australes, una especie de
ballena con barbas, vienen al Golfo Nuevo
para dar a luz a sus crías. Es espectacular
observar cómo estos mamíferos marinos
de 60 toneladas de peso y 16 m de largo
se elevan del agua en un arco alto y se
sumergen de nuevo.

Península Valdés

Desde 1999, a península Valdés é
Património Mundial da UNESCO. É
considerada a formação geológica
mais original do sul da Argentina. Na
paisagem árida e rochosa, os cientistas
encontraram rochas e fósseis de animais
marinhos e ostras do Período Paleógeno.
A península está ligada ao continente
por um estreito promontório. No meio
deles há três lagos de sal a 35 m abaixo
do nível do mar. De maio a novembro, as
baleias-franca-austral, uma espécie de
baleia-franca, vêm ao Golfo Nuevo para
dar à luz as suas crias. É espectacular
observar como estes mamíferos marinhos
de 60 toneladas de peso e 16 m de
comprimento sobem da água num arco
alto e mergulham novamente.

Schiereiland Valdés

Het schiereiland Valdés staat sinds 1999 op
de Werelderfgoedlijst van de UNESCO. Het
wordt beschouwd als de oorspronkelijkste
geologische formatie in het zuiden
van Argentinië. In het kale, rotsachtige
landschap vonden wetenschappers rotsen
en fossielen van zeedieren en oesters uit
het Paleogeen tijdperk. Het schiereiland
is door een smalle landtong met het
vasteland verbonden. In het midden liggen
drie zoutmeren 35 m onder de zeespiegel.
Van mei tot november komen zuidkapers,
uit de familie baleinwalvissen, naar de
Golfo Nuevo om hun kleintjes ter wereld
te brengen. Het is spectaculair om te zien
hoe deze 60 ton zware en 16 m lange
zeezoogdieren in een hoge boog uit het
water opstijgen en er weer in duiken.

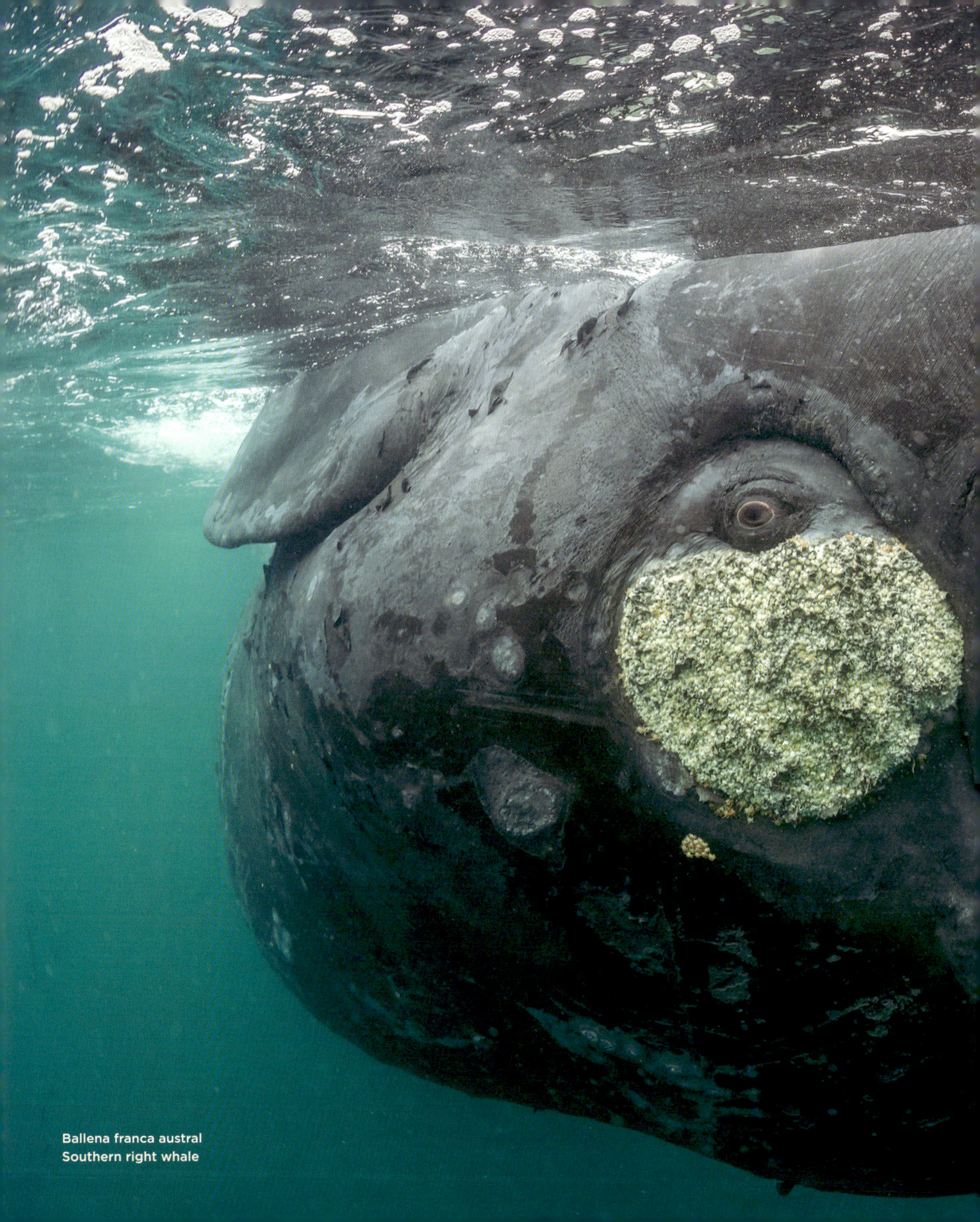

Ballena franca austral
Southern right whale

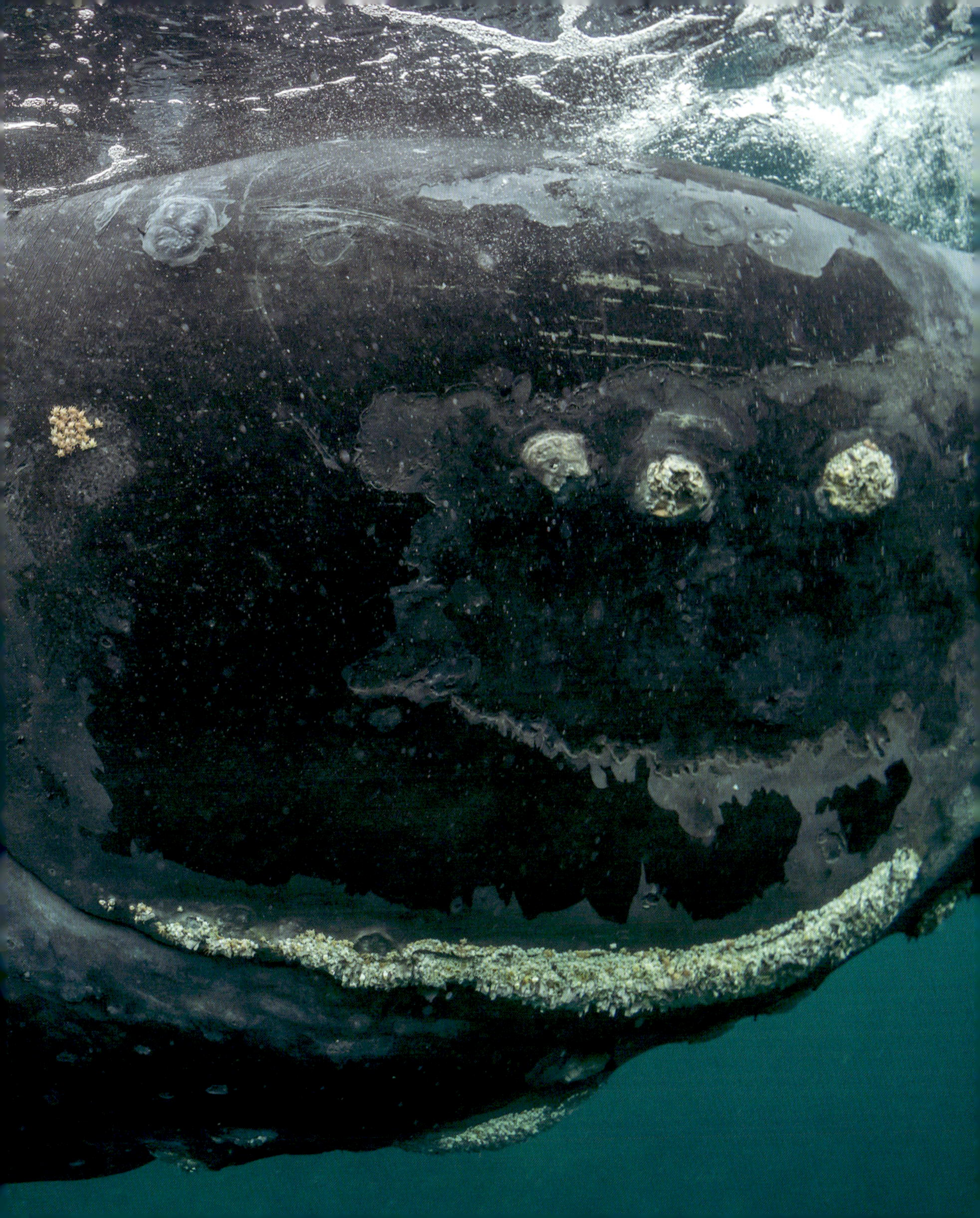

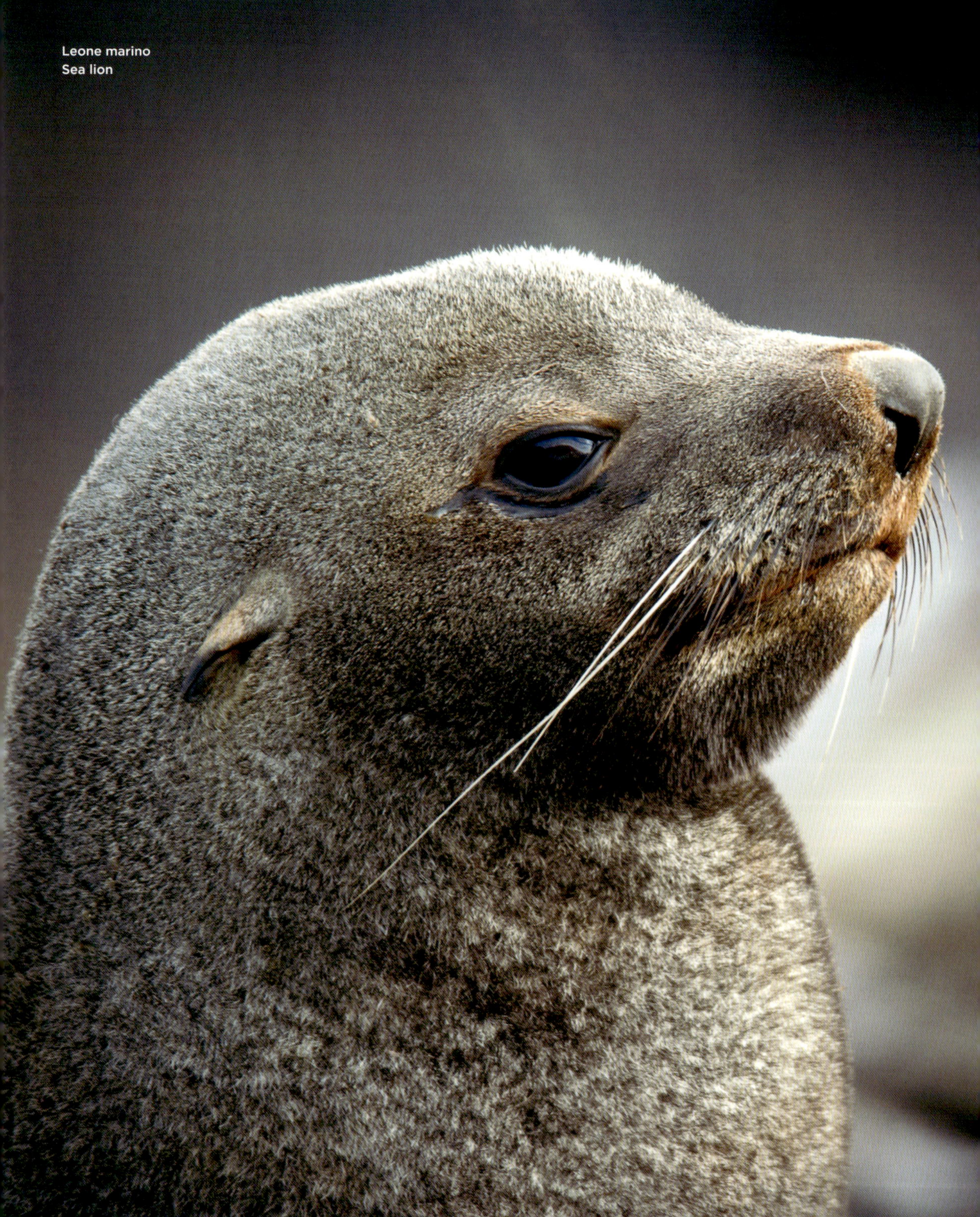

Leone marino
Sea lion

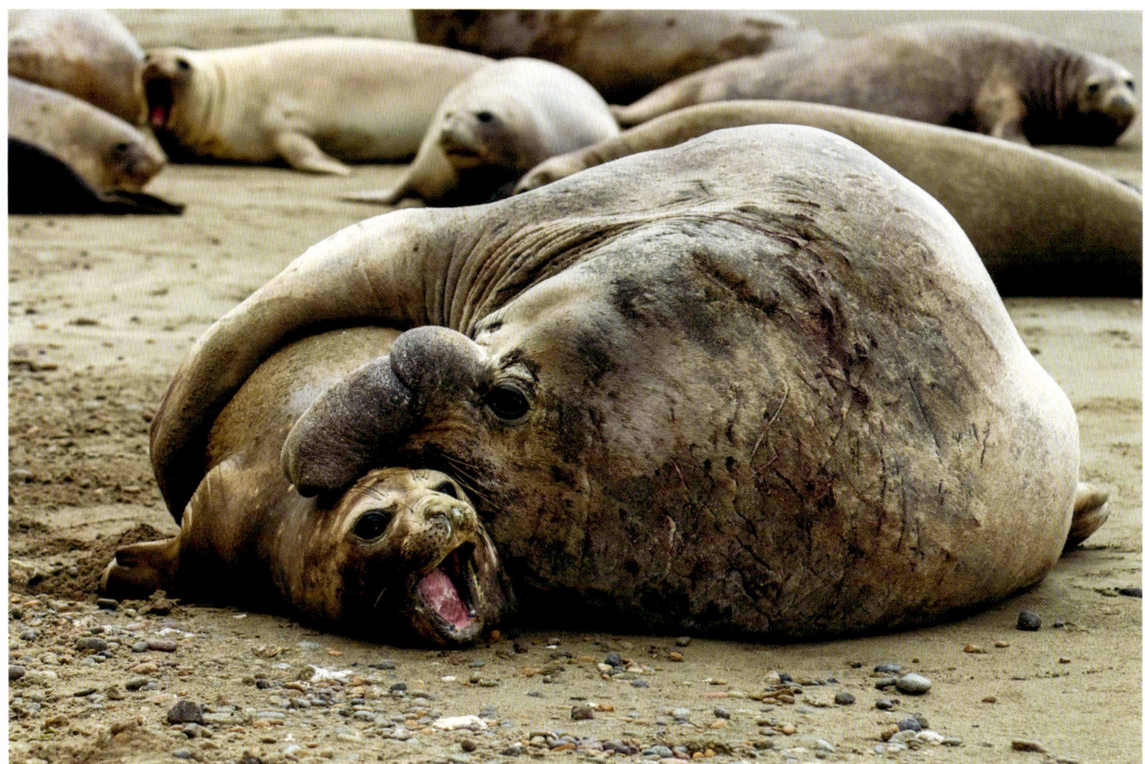

Elefante marino del sur
Southern elephant sea

Elephant seals

In August, about 800 southern elephant seals head for the coast of the Valdés peninsula to mate and give birth. These colossuses, a subspecies of seals, may be seen lazing in large herds in the sun. The males grow to 5 m (16 ft) long and weigh around 3500 kg (7700 lb), with the females being considerably smaller. The name Elephant is derived from the male's proboscis.

Elefantes marinos

En agosto, unos 800 elefantes marinos del sur se dirigen a la costa de la península Valdés para dar a luz y aparearse. Estos colosos, que son una subespecie de las focas, holgazanean juntos al sol. Los machos miden 5 m de largo y pesan 3500 kg, mientras que las hembras son bastante más pequeñas. Su nombre "elefante" se debe a la trompa que tienen los machos.

Éléphants de mer

En août, environ 800 éléphants de mer de sud mettent le cap sur la côte de la presqu'île de Valdés, pour s'y accoupler et mettre au monde leurs petits. Ces colosses, sous-espèce de la famille des phoques, paressent au soleil en groupe. Les mâles mesurent 5 m et pèsent 3500 kg, mais les femelles sont nettement plus petites. L'appellation d'éléphant de mer provient des narines des mâles qui se développent en trompe.

Elefantes-marinhos

Em agosto, cerca de 800 elefantes-marinhos-do-sul dirigem-se para a costa da península de Valdés para dar à luz e acasalar. Estes colossos, uma subespécie das focas, descansam ao sol em bandos. Os machos têm 5 m de comprimento e pesam 3500 kg, as fêmeas são consideravelmente menores. O seu nome elefante vem da tromba do macho.

Seeelefanten

Im August steuern ca. 800 Südliche Seeelefanten die Küste der Halbinsel Valdés an, um hier ihre Jungen zur Welt zu bringen und sich zu paaren. Diese Kolosse, eine Subspezie der Seehunde, faulenzen herdenweise in der Sonne. Die Männchen werden 5 m lang und wiegen 3500 kg, die Weibchen sind erheblich kleiner. Ihr Name Elefant geht auf den Rüssel der Männchen zurück.

Zeeolifanten

In augustus koersen ca. 800 zuidelijke zeeolifanten richting de kust van het schiereiland Valdés om hun kleintjes ter wereld te brengen en om te paren. Deze kolossen, een ondersoort van de zeehonden, luieren in kuddes in de zon. De mannetjes worden 5 m lang en wegen 3500 kg, de vrouwtjes zijn aanzienlijk kleiner. Hun naam olifant is afgeleid van de slurf van het mannetje.

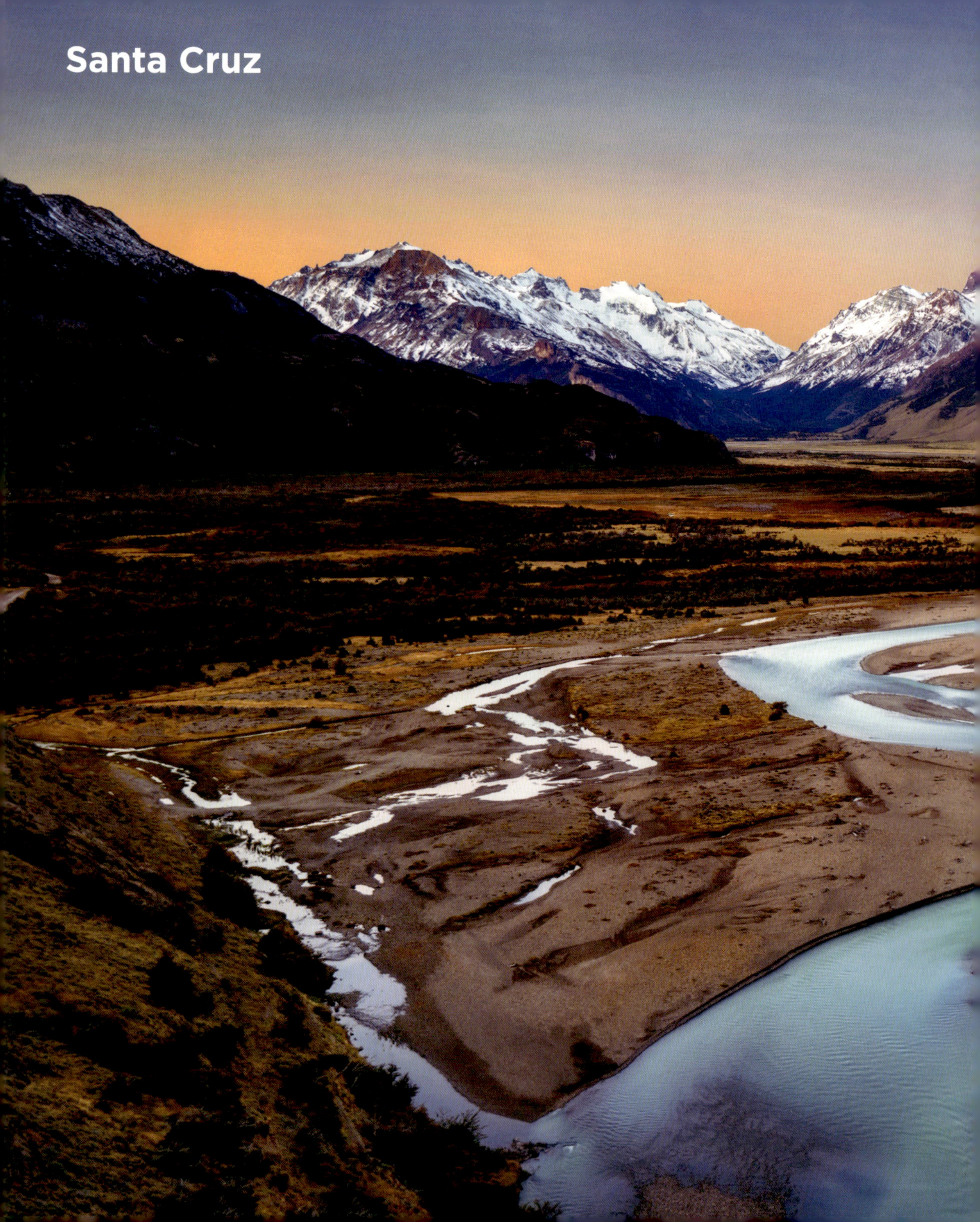
Santa Cruz

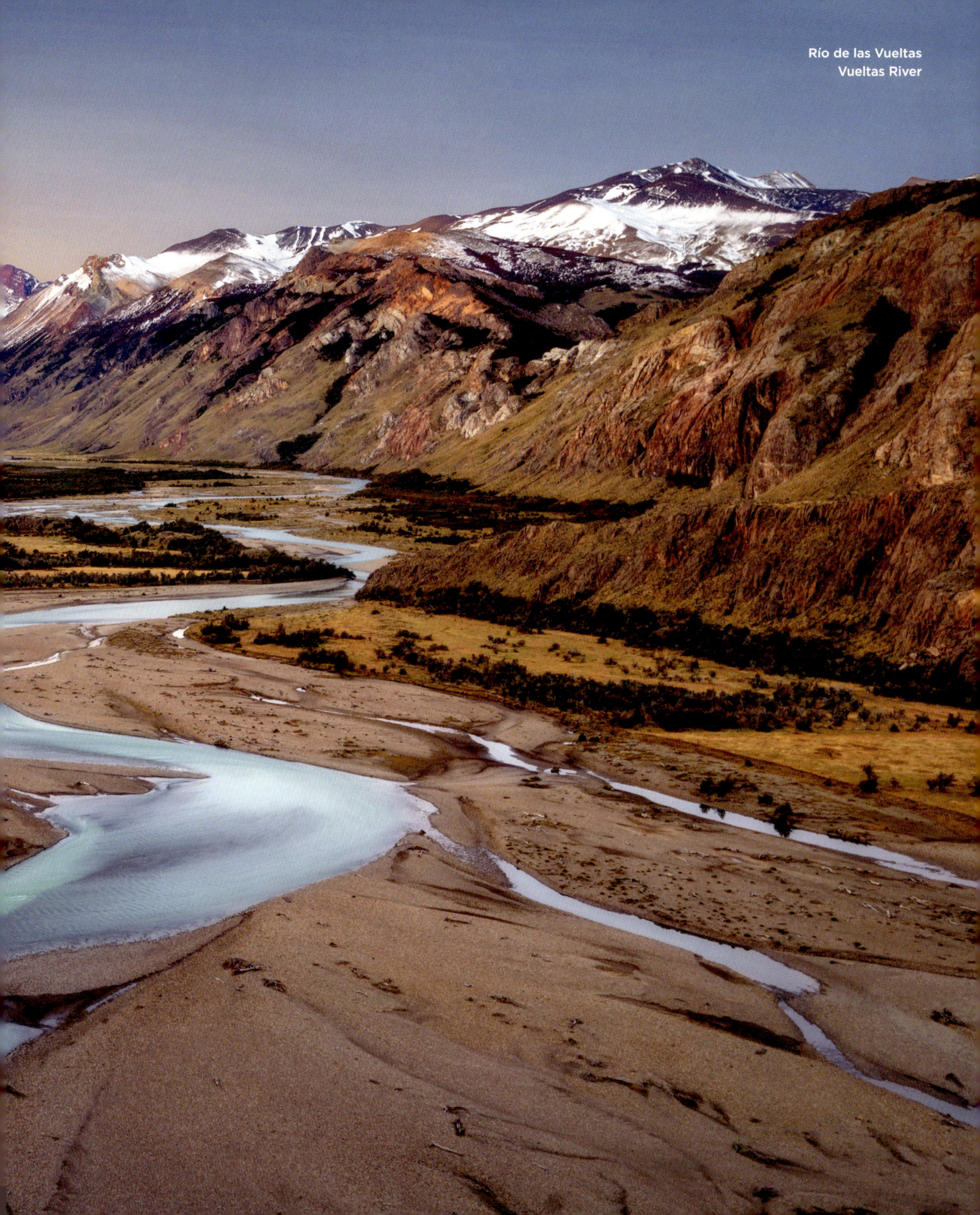
Río de las Vueltas
Vueltas River

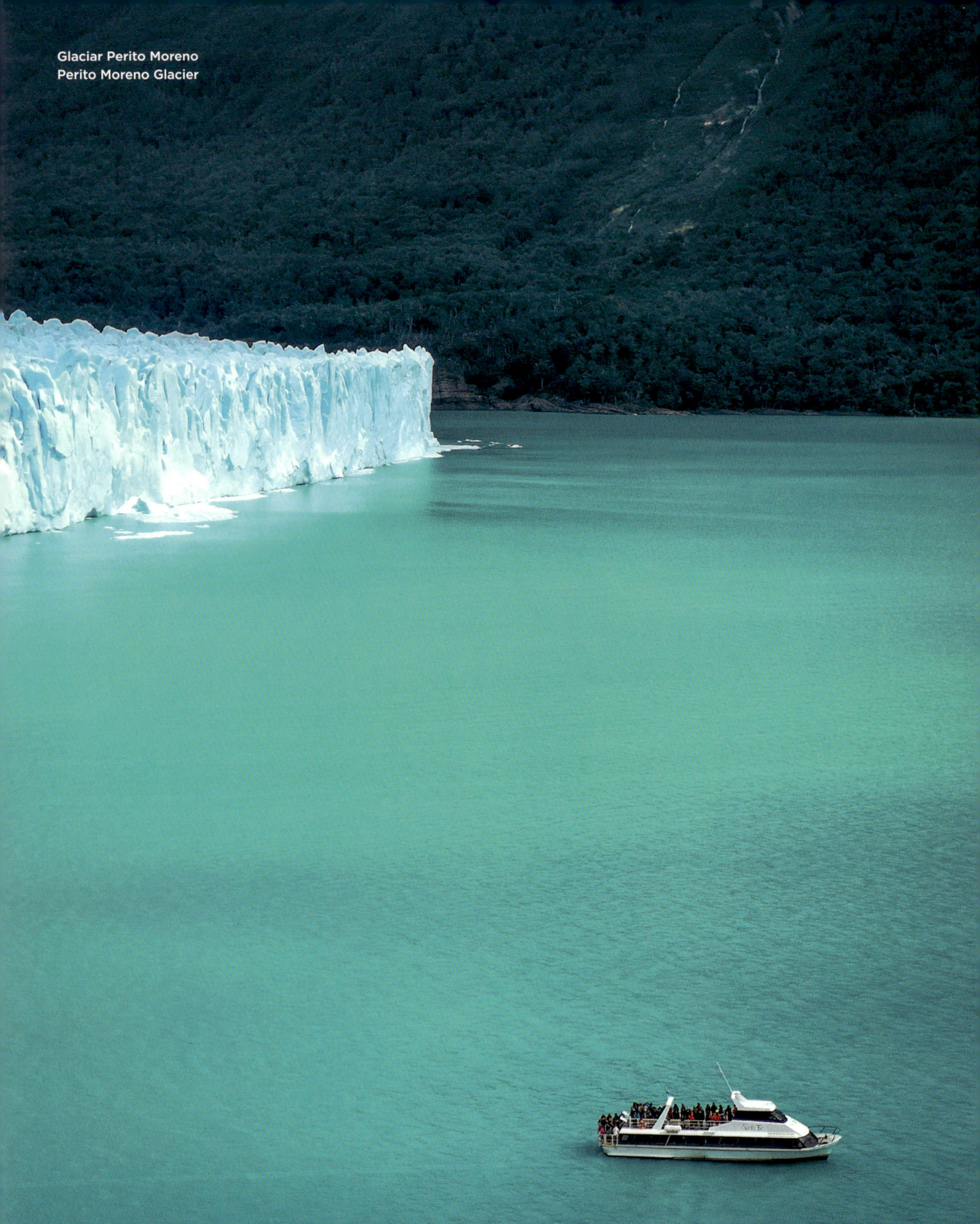
Glaciar Perito Moreno
Perito Moreno Glacier

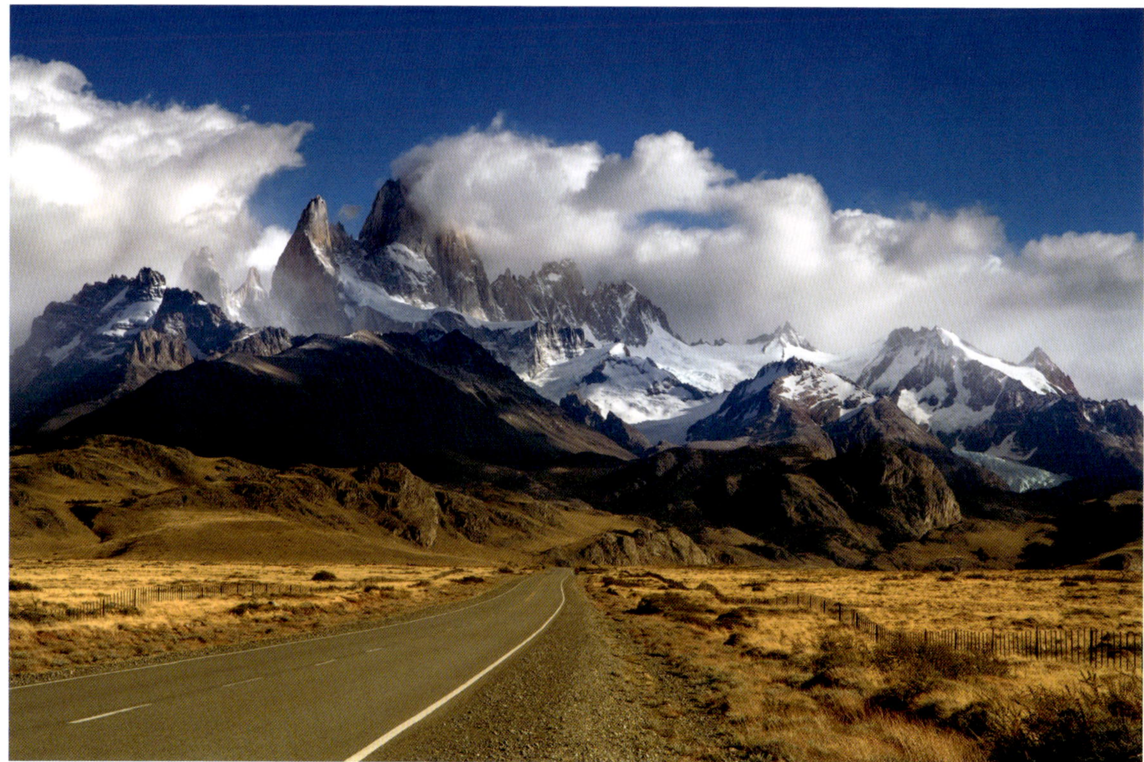

Monte Fitz Roy
Mount Fitz Roy

Santa Cruz

Although Santa Cruz is the second largest province of the country, it is very sparsely populated. In the east it borders on the Atlantic Ocean, in the west on the Andes. Livestock farming and wool are the main sources of income. With its two natural wonders, the Perito Moreno glacier and the Fitz Roy Massif, the province offers its numerous visitors particular highlights.

Santa Cruz

Santa Cruz est certes la seconde plus grande province du pays, mais elle est très peu peuplée. Elle est bordée par l'Atlantique à l'est et par les Andes à l'ouest. La production animale et la laine sont ses principales sources de revenus. Outre ses deux célèbres merveilles de la nature, le glacier Perito Moreno et le massif du Fitz Roy, la province réserve à ses visiteurs de nombreuses autres splendeurs uniques.

Santa Cruz

Santa Cruz ist zwar die zweitgrößte Provinz des Landes, aber sehr dünn besiedelt. Im Osten grenzt sie an den Atlantik, im Westen an die Anden. Viehwirtschaft und Wolle sind die Haupteinnahmequellen. Mit den beiden Naturwundern, dem Gletscher Perito Moreno und dem Fitz Roy Massiv, bietet die Provinz ihren zahlreichen Besuchern ganz besondere Highlights.

Santa Cruz

Aunque Santa Cruz es la segunda provincia más grande del país, está muy poco poblada. Al este limita con el océano Atlántico y al oeste, con los Andes. La ganadería y la lana son las principales fuentes de ingresos. Con sus dos maravillas naturales, el glaciar Perito Moreno y el macizo Fitz Roy, la provincia ofrece a sus numerosos visitantes momentos muy especiales.

Santa Cruz

Apesar de Santa Cruz ser a segunda maior província do país, é muito pouco povoada. No leste, faz fronteira com o Oceano Atlântico, a oeste, com a Cordilheira dos Andes. A pecuária e a lã são as principais fontes de rendimento. Com suas duas maravilhas naturais, o glaciar Perito Moreno e o Monte Fitz Roy, a província oferece aos seus numerosos visitantes destaques muito especiais.

Santa Cruz

Santa Cruz is weliswaar de op één na grootste provincie van het land, maar is zeer dunbevolkt. In het oosten grenst het aan de Atlantische Oceaan, in het westen aan de Andes. Veehouderij en wol zijn de belangrijkste bronnen van inkomsten. Met zijn twee natuurwonderen, de Perito Moreno gletsjer en het Fitz Roy berg, biedt de provincie zijn talrijke bezoekers zeer bijzondere highlights.

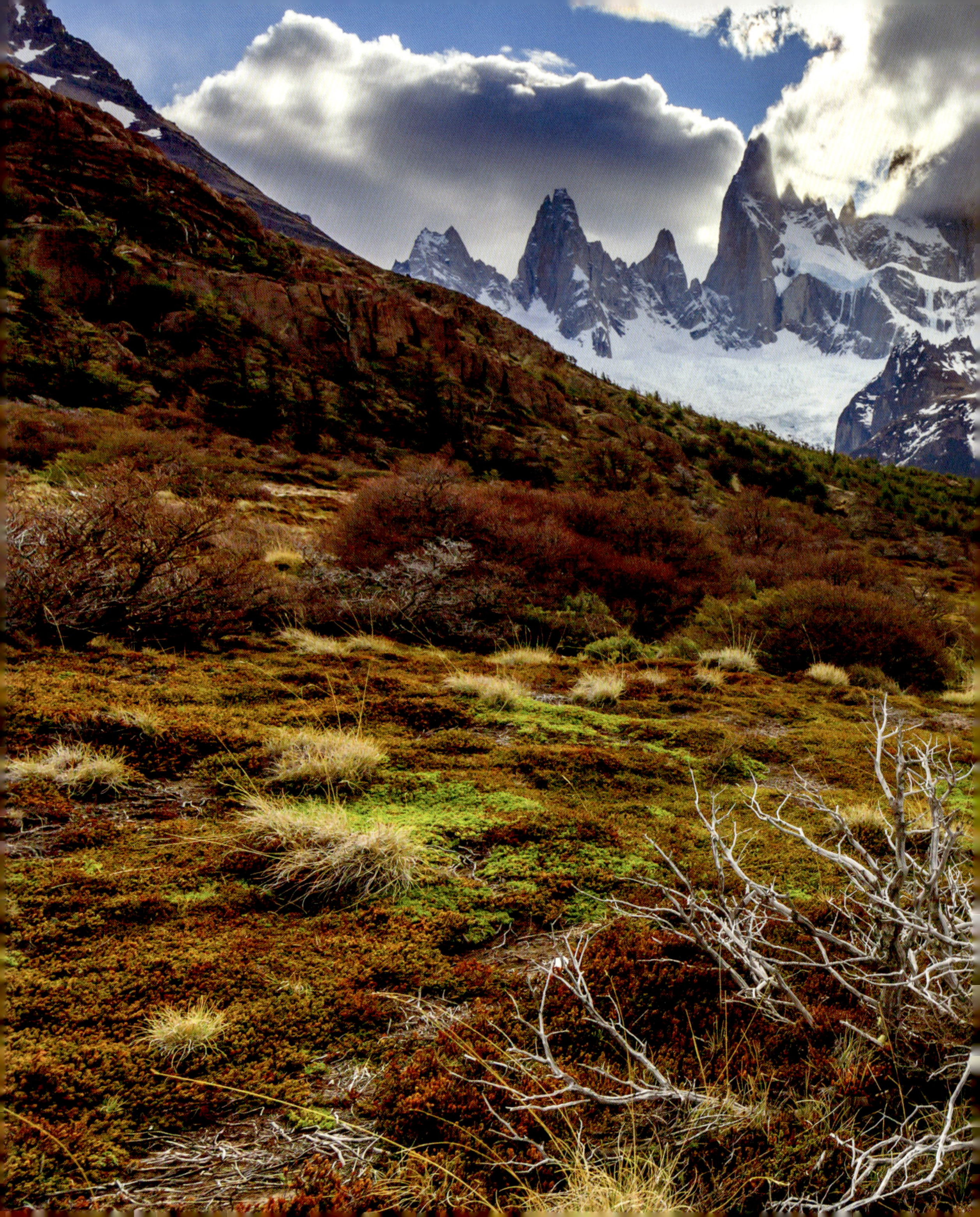

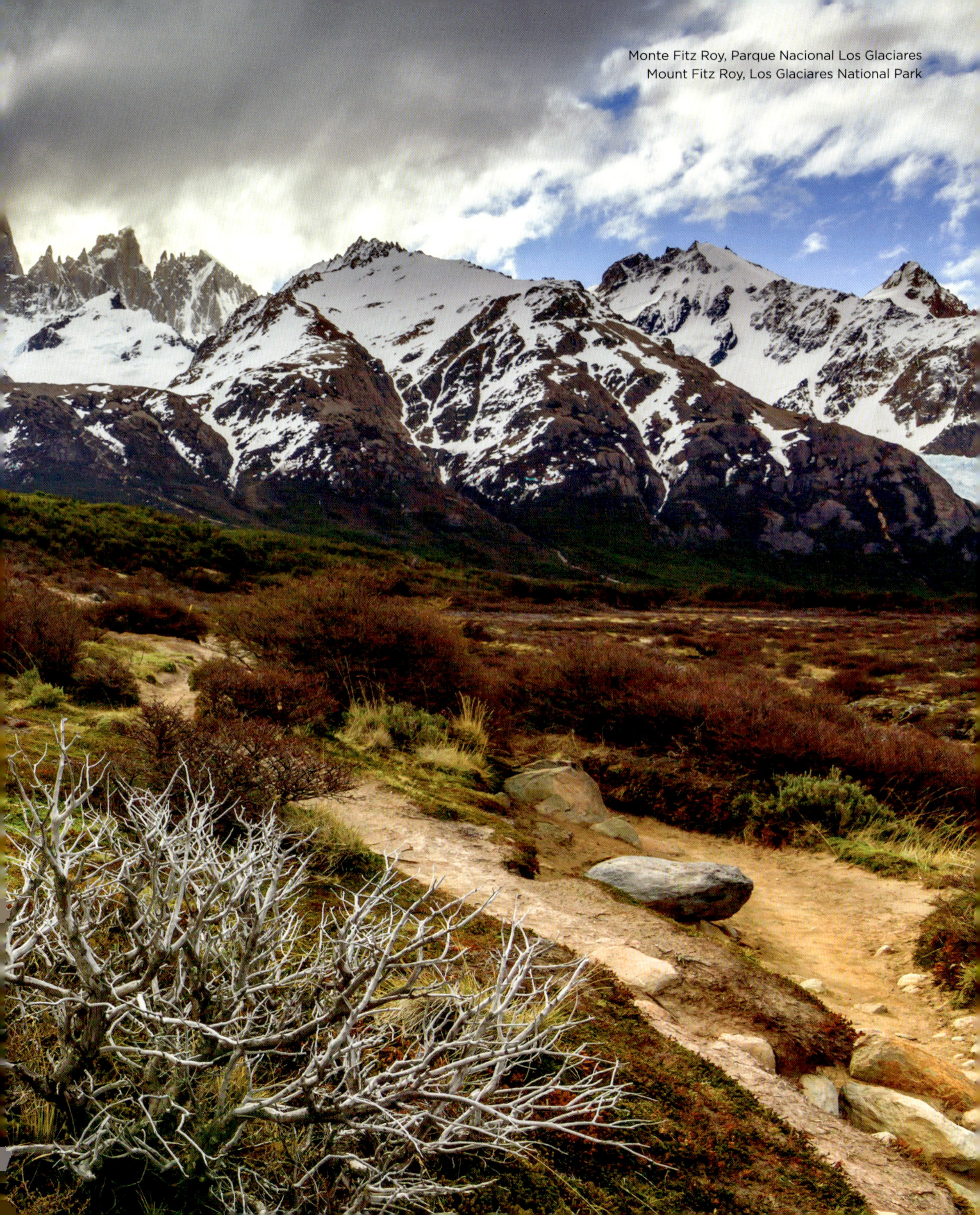

Monte Fitz Roy, Parque Nacional Los Glaciares
Mount Fitz Roy, Los Glaciares National Park

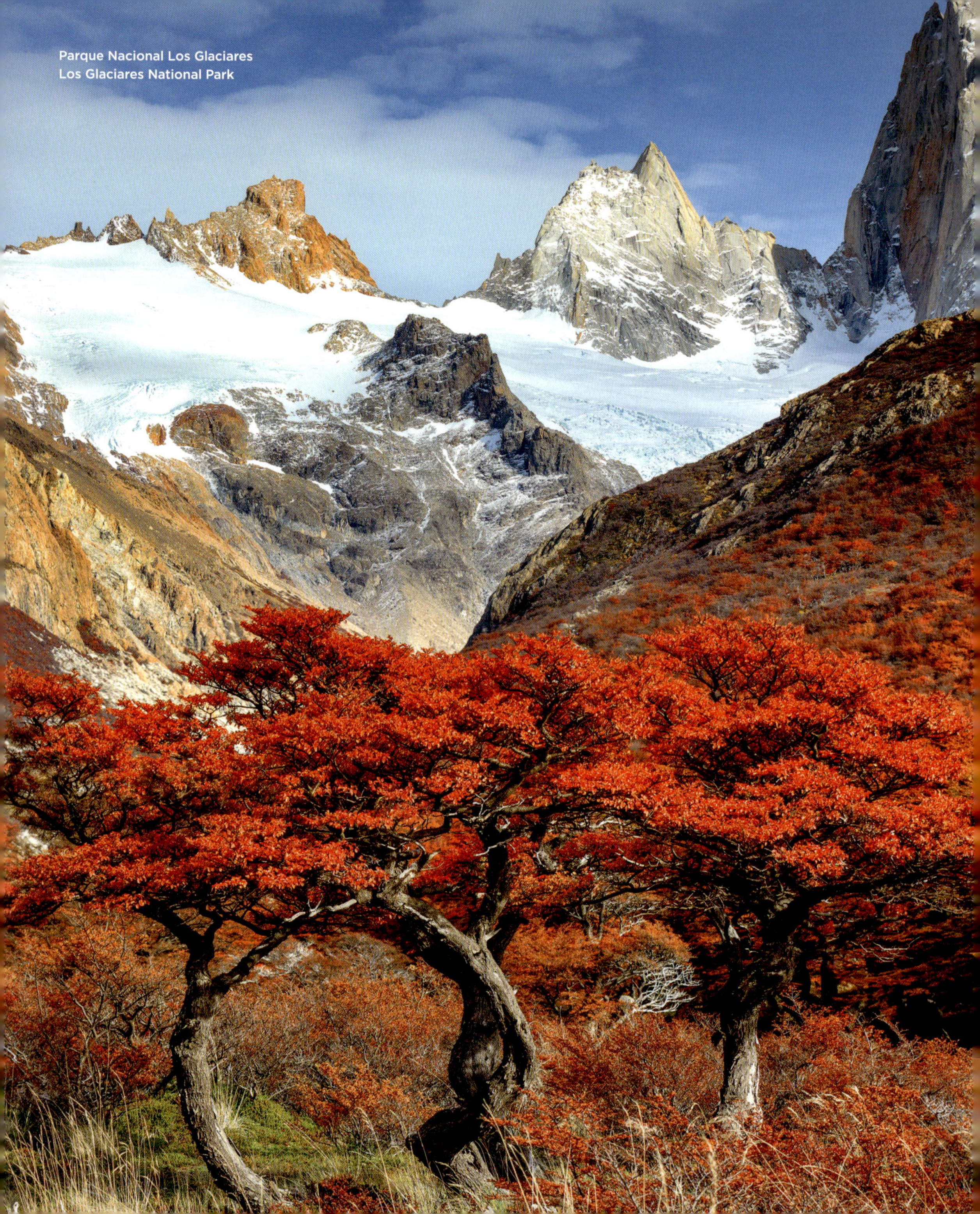

Parque Nacional Los Glaciares
Los Glaciares National Park

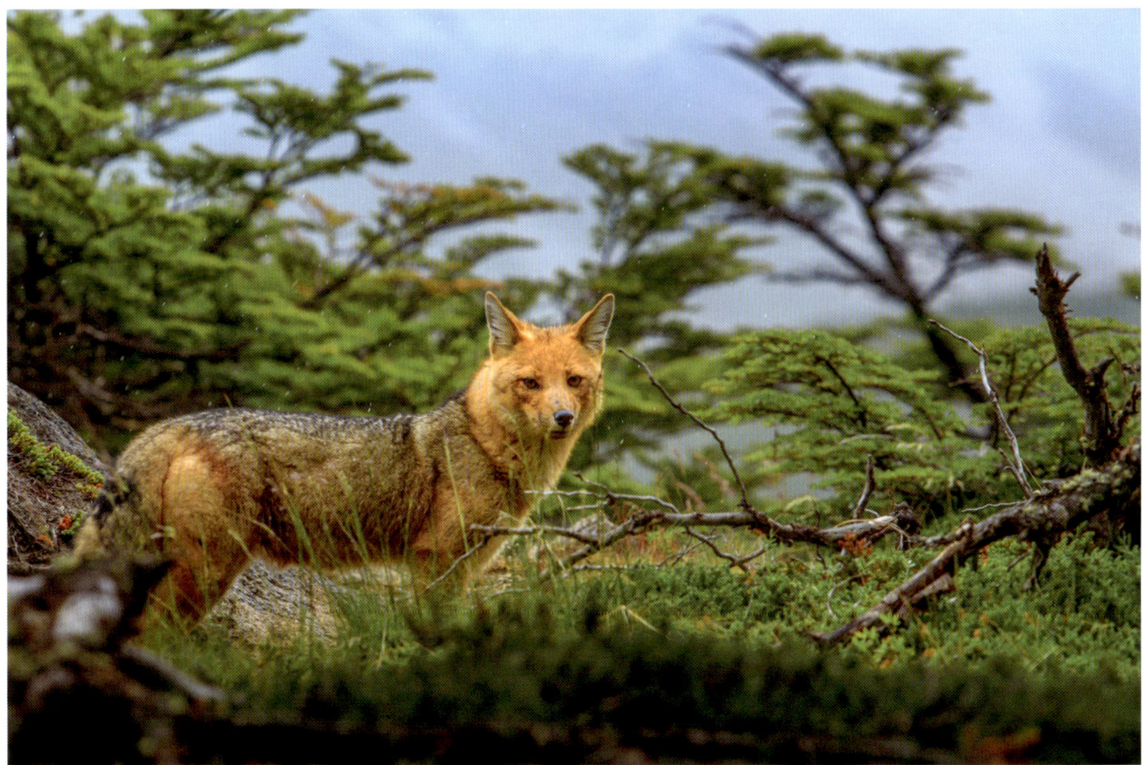

Zorro culpeo

Los Glaciares National Park

To the north of the Los Glaciares National Park lies the spectacular Fitz Roy Massif. The Tehuelche people called the mountain El Chaltén, which remains the name of the village at its foot. Although the summit is only 3405 m (11,171 ft) high, it remains a challenge even for experts among mountaineers. Lionel Terray and Guido Magnone managed the first ascent of the Fitzroy in 1952.

Parque Nacional Los Glaciares

Al norte del Parque Nacional Los Glaciares se encuentra el espectacular macizo Fitz Roy. Los tehuelches llamaban a la montaña El Chaltén. Este sigue siendo el nombre del pueblo que se encuentra a sus pies. Aunque la cumbre tiene solo 3405 m de altura, sigue siendo un desafío incluso para los alpinistas expertos. Lionel Terray y Guido Magnone realizaron el primer ascenso al Fitz Roy en 1952.

Parc national Los Glaciares

Le spectaculaire massif du Fitz Roy est situé dans le nord du parc national Los Glaciares. Les Indiens tehuelches appellent cette montagne *El Chaltén*. Tel est d'ailleurs toujours le nom du village à son pied. Bien que le mont Fitz Roy ne culmine qu'à 3 405 m, il constitue un défi pour les meilleurs alpinistes. Lionel Terray et Guido Magnone furent les premiers à réussir son ascension en 1952.

Parque Nacional Los Glaciares

Ao norte do Parque Nacional Los Glaciares está o espectacular Monte Fitz Roy. A montanha foi chamada El Chaltén pelos índios Tehuelche. Este ainda é o nome da aldeia no seu pé. Embora o cume tenha apenas 3405 m de altura, continua a ser um desafio mesmo para os mais experientes entre os alpinistas. Pela primeira vez, o Monte Fitz Roy foi escalado com sucesso em 1952 por Lionel Terray e Guido Magnone.

Nationalpark Los Glaciares

Im Norden des Nationalparks Los Glaciares liegt das spektakuläre Fitz Roy-Massiv. Von den Tehuelche-Indianern wurde der Berg El Chaltén genannt. So heißt heute noch das Dorf an seinem Fuß. Obwohl der Gipfel nur 3405 m hoch ist, bleibt er eine Herausforderung auch für Cracks unter den Bergsteigern. Lionel Terray und Guido Magnone gelang 1952 die Erstbesteigung des Fitz Roy.

Nationaal park Los Glaciares

In het noorden van het nationaal park Los Glaciares ligt de spectaculaire berg Fitz Roy. De Tehuelche-indianen noemden de berg El Chaltén. Dit is nog steeds de naam van het dorp aan zijn voet. Hoewel de top slechts 3405 m hoog is, blijft het een uitdaging, zelfs voor cracks onder de bergbeklimmers. Lionel Terray en Guido Magnone lukte het de Fitz Roy in 1952 voor het eerst te beklimmen.

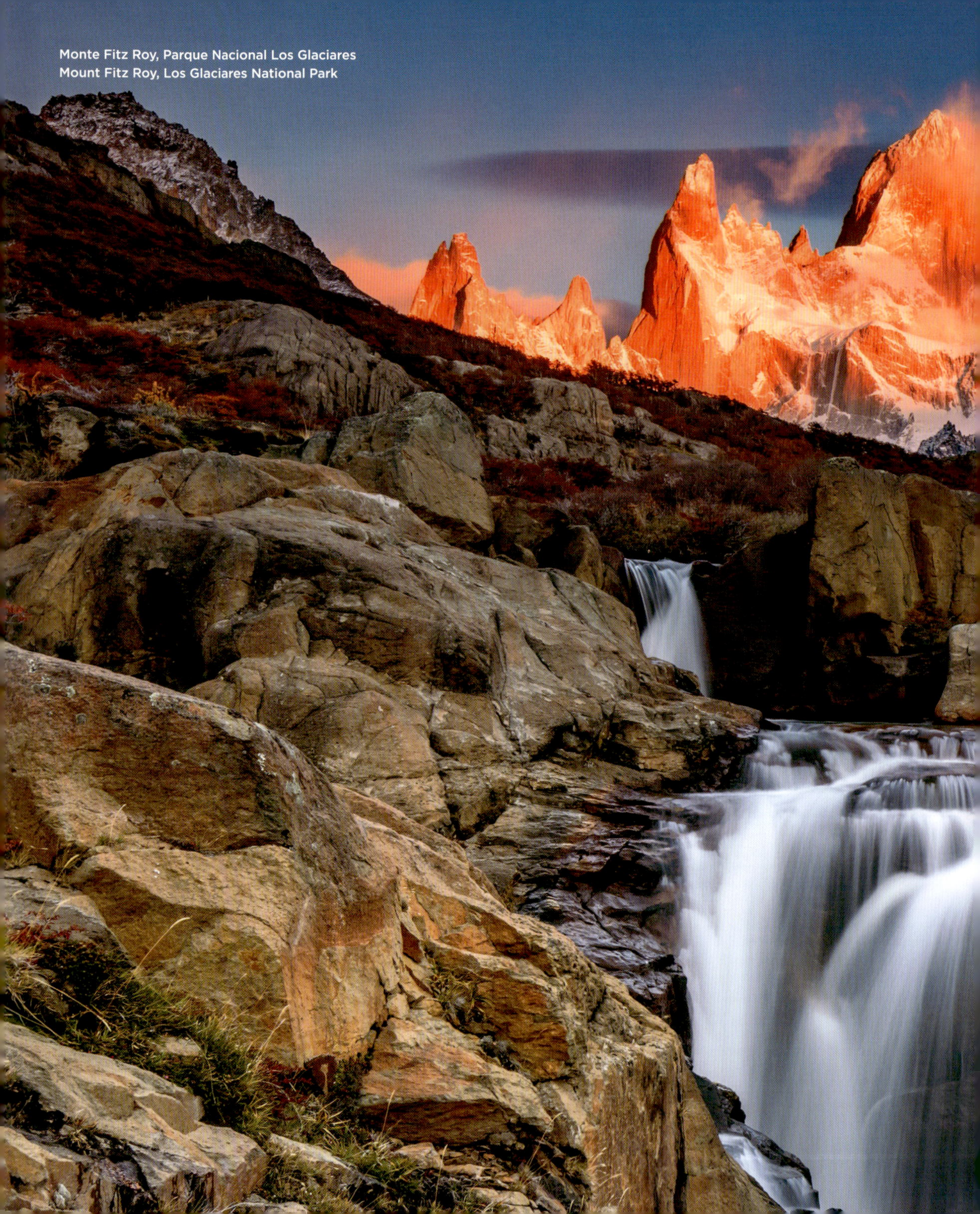
Monte Fitz Roy, Parque Nacional Los Glaciares
Mount Fitz Roy, Los Glaciares National Park

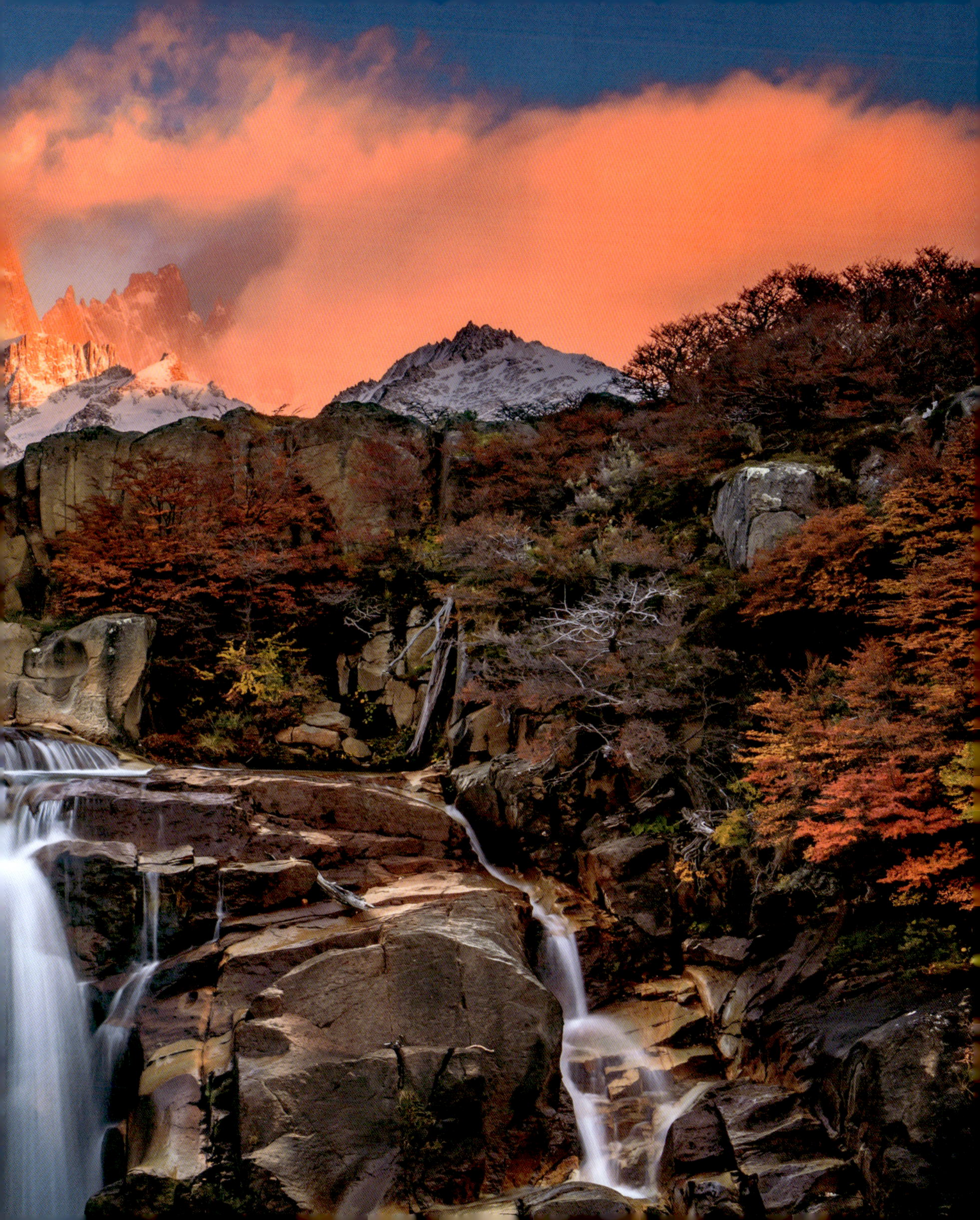

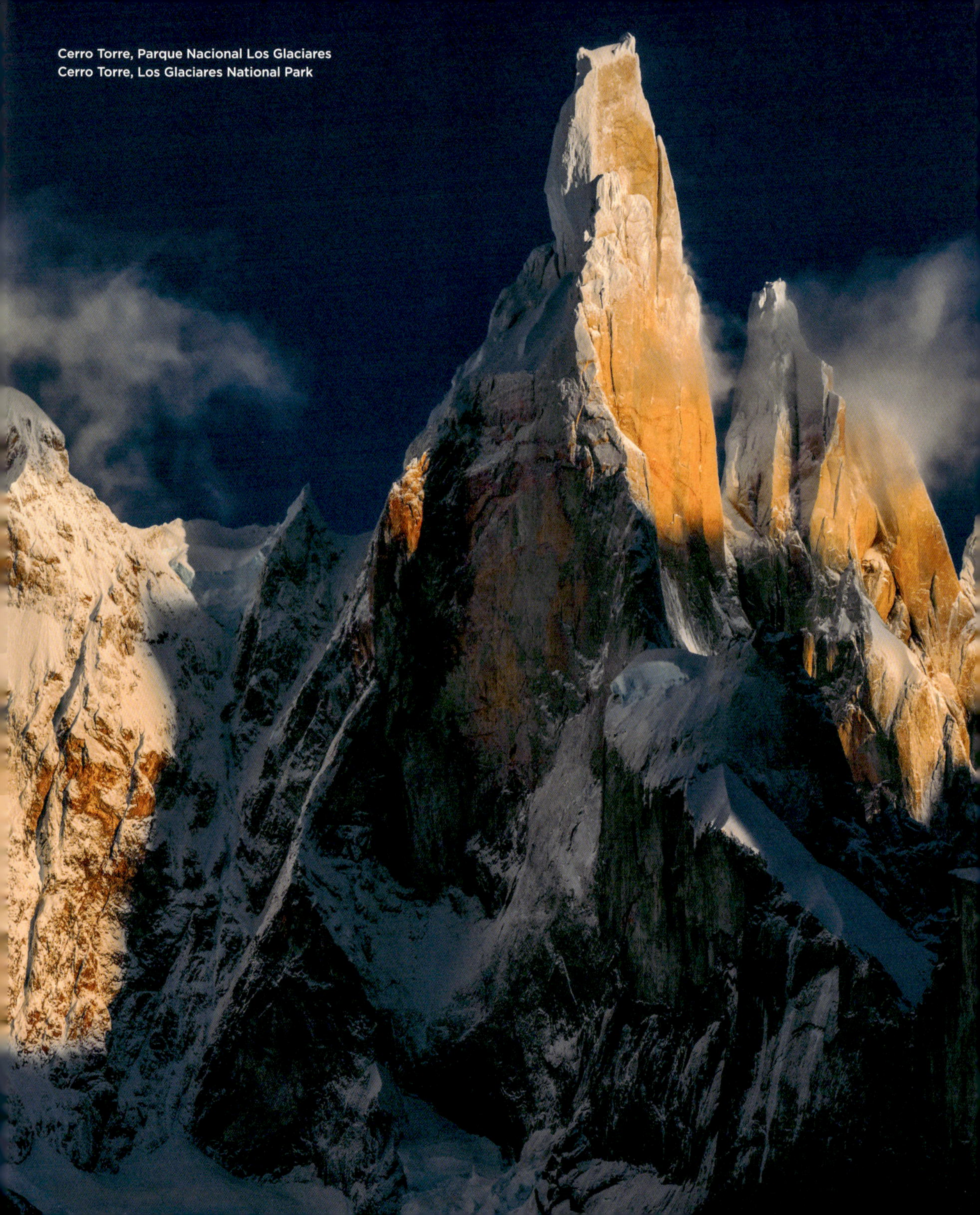
Cerro Torre, Parque Nacional Los Glaciares
Cerro Torre, Los Glaciares National Park

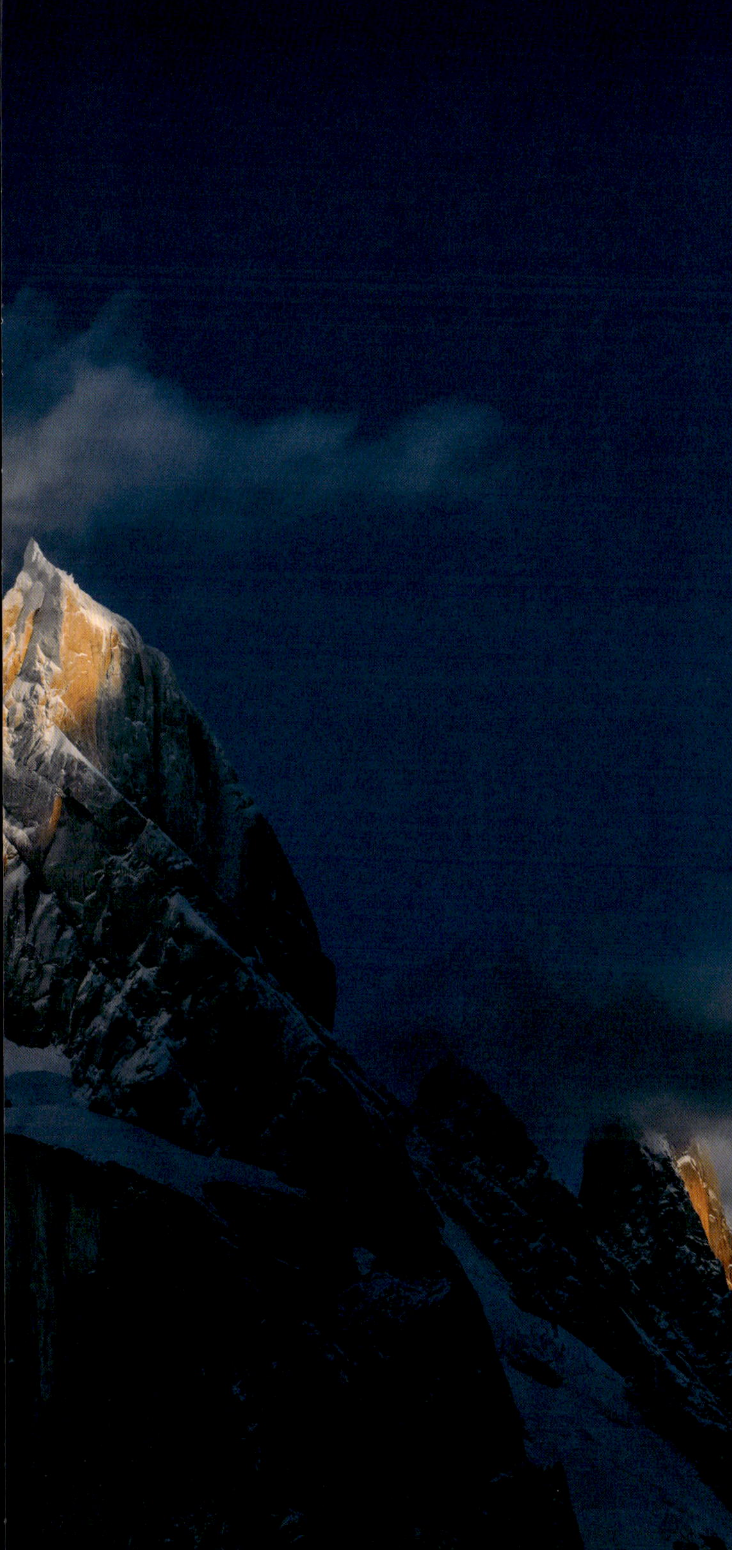

Cerro Torre

The needle top of Cerro Torre, west of the Fitz Roy peak, is only 3128 m (10,262 ft) high, but its ascent is considered more difficult than that of Fitz Roy and some expeditions have failed. There is still controversy about the first attempted ascents, and the peak of the magical Cerro Torre was probably first conquered by Casimiro Ferrari in 1974.

Cerro Torre

Les aiguilles du Cerro Torre, situé à l'ouest du mont Fitz Roy, s'élèvent à seulement 3 128 m d'altitude, mais leur ascension est encore plus difficile que celle de leur voisin et plusieurs expéditions ont échoué. Aujourd'hui encore, la première ascension porte à controverse. La gloire d'avoir vaincu en premier le Cerro Torre en 1974 reviendrait vraisemblablement à Casimiro Ferrari.

Cerro Torre

Die Nadelspitze des Cerro Torre, westlich des Fitz Roy-Gipfels, ist zwar nur 3128 m hoch, ihre Besteigung gilt aber als schwieriger als die des Fitz Roy. Einige Expeditionen scheiterten. Über die Erstbesteigung gibt es bis heute Kontroversen. Wahrscheinlich gelang es erstmals Casimiro Ferrari 1974 den magischen Cerro Torre zu bezwingen.

Cerro Torre

La cima del Cerro Torre, al oeste del pico Fitz Roy, tiene solo 3128 m de altura, pero su ascenso se considera más difícil que el del Fitz Roy. Algunas expediciones fracasaron. Todavía hay controversia sobre el primer ascenso. Probablemente Casimiro Ferrari logró por primera vez en 1974 conquistar el mágico Cerro Torre.

Cerro Torre

O extremidade do topo do Cerro Torre, a oeste do pico do Fitz Roy, tem apenas 3128 m de altura, mas a sua subida é considerada mais difícil do que a do Fitz Roy. Algumas expedições falharam. Ainda há controvérsia sobre a primeira subida. Provavelmente Casimiro Ferrari tenha conseguido, pela primeira vez em 1974, conquistar o mágico Cerro Torre.

Cerro Torre

De 'naald' van de Cerro Torre, ten westen van de top van Fitz Roy, is slechts 3128 m hoog, maar de beklimming geldt als moeilijker dan die van Fitz Roy. Sommige expedities mislukten. Nu bestaat er nog steeds controverse over de eerste beklimming. Waarschijnlijk lukte het Casimiro Ferrari in 1974 om voor het eerst de magische Cerro Torre te bedwingen.

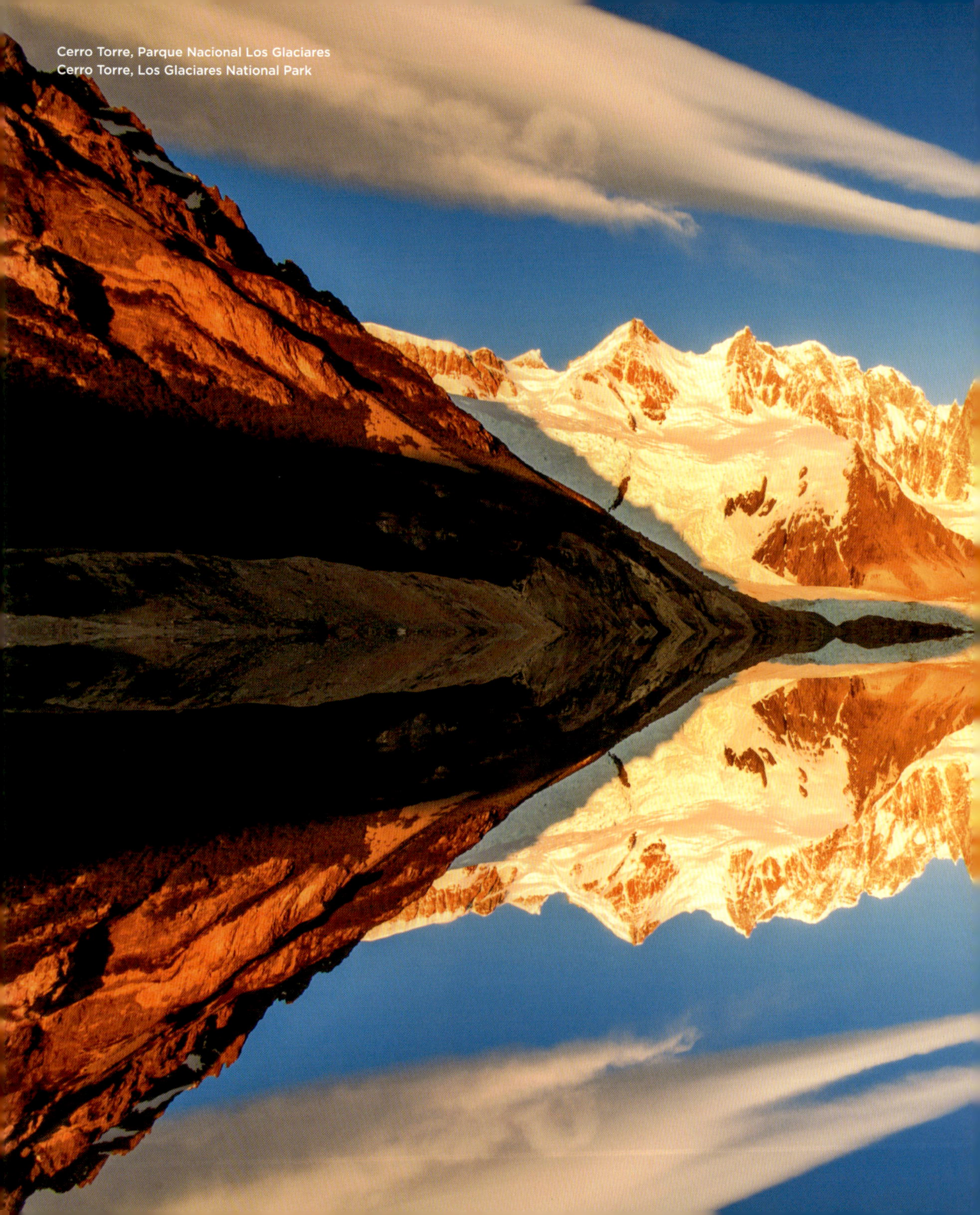
Cerro Torre, Parque Nacional Los Glaciares
Cerro Torre, Los Glaciares National Park

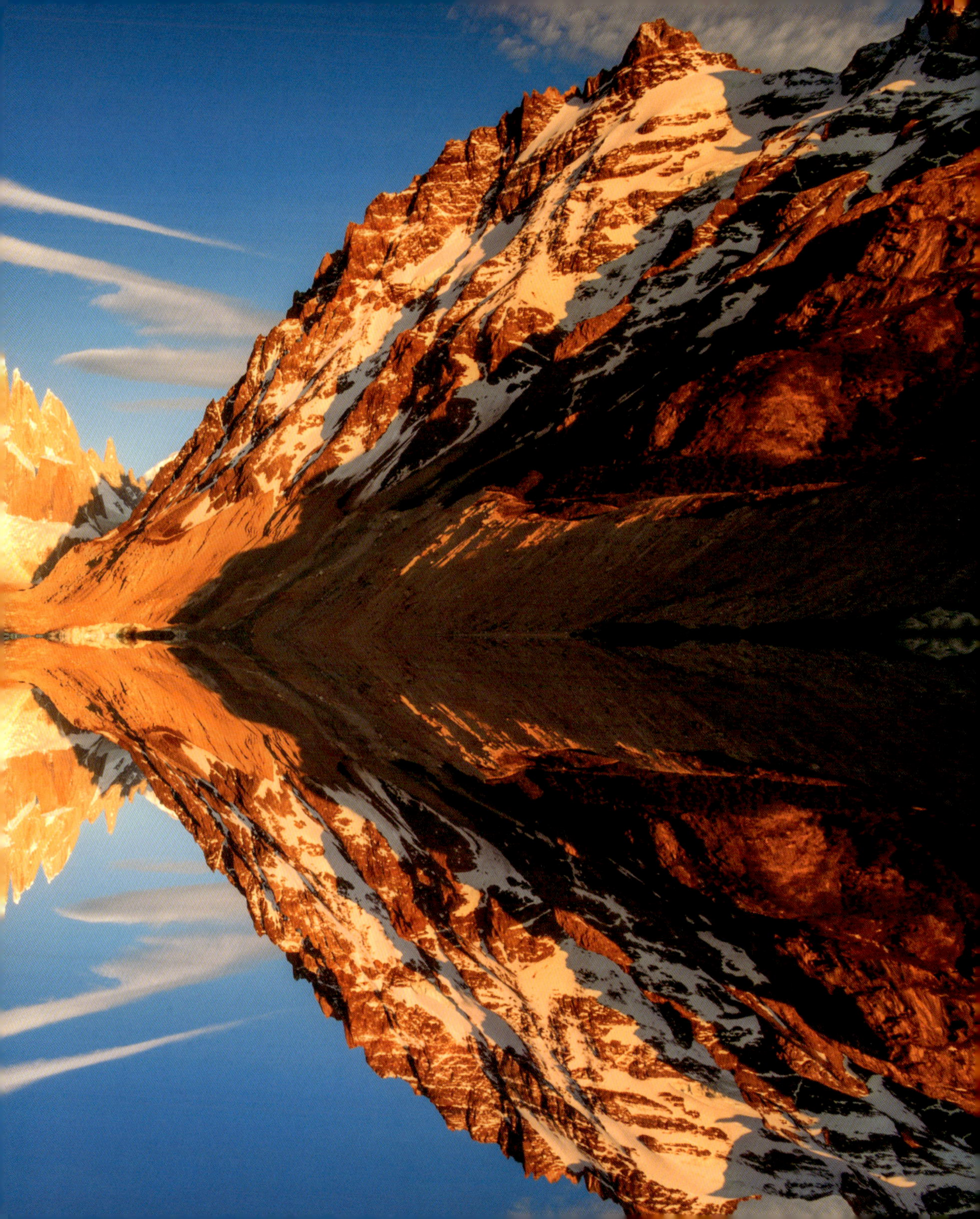

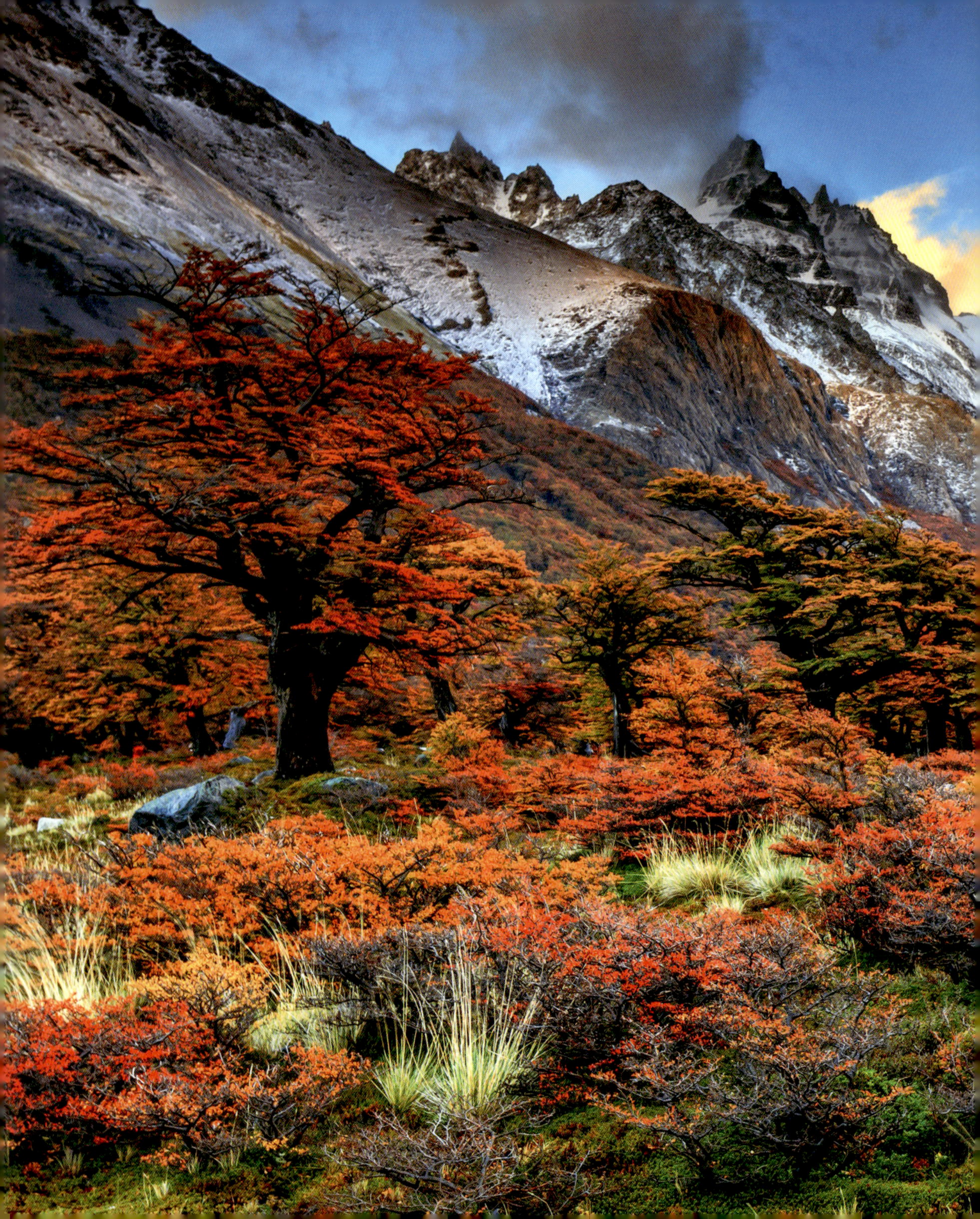

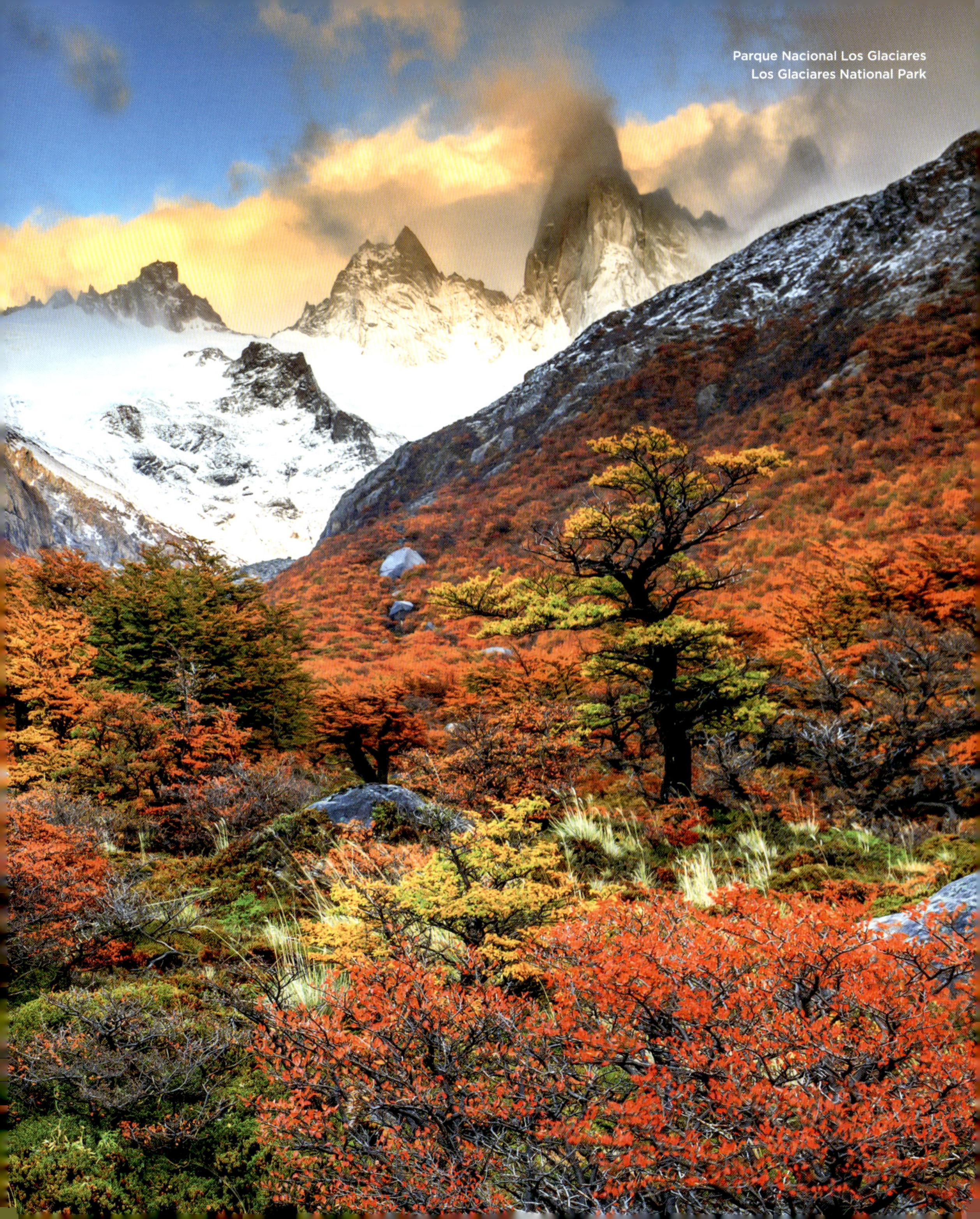

Parque Nacional Los Glaciares
Los Glaciares National Park

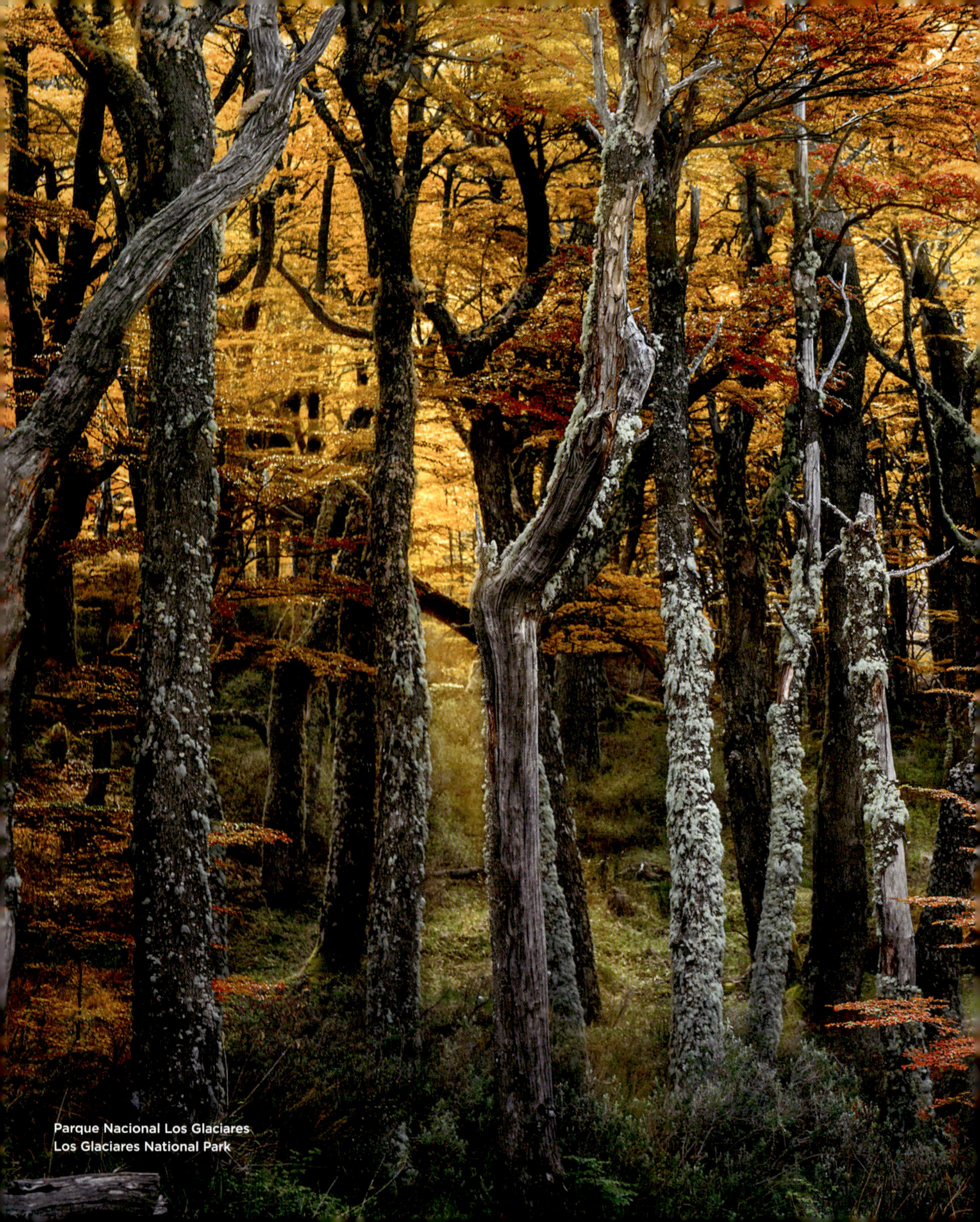
Parque Nacional Los Glaciares
Los Glaciares National Park

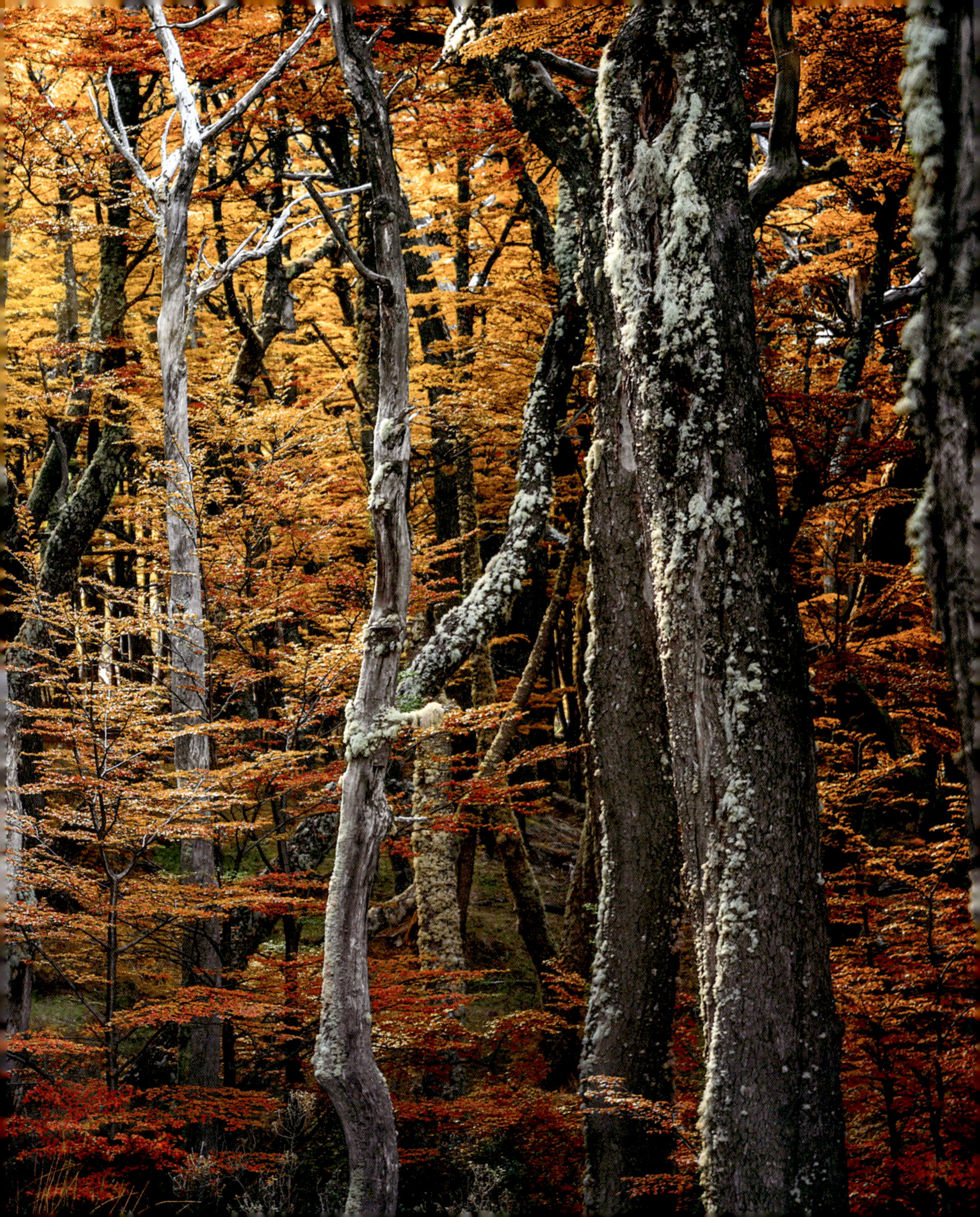

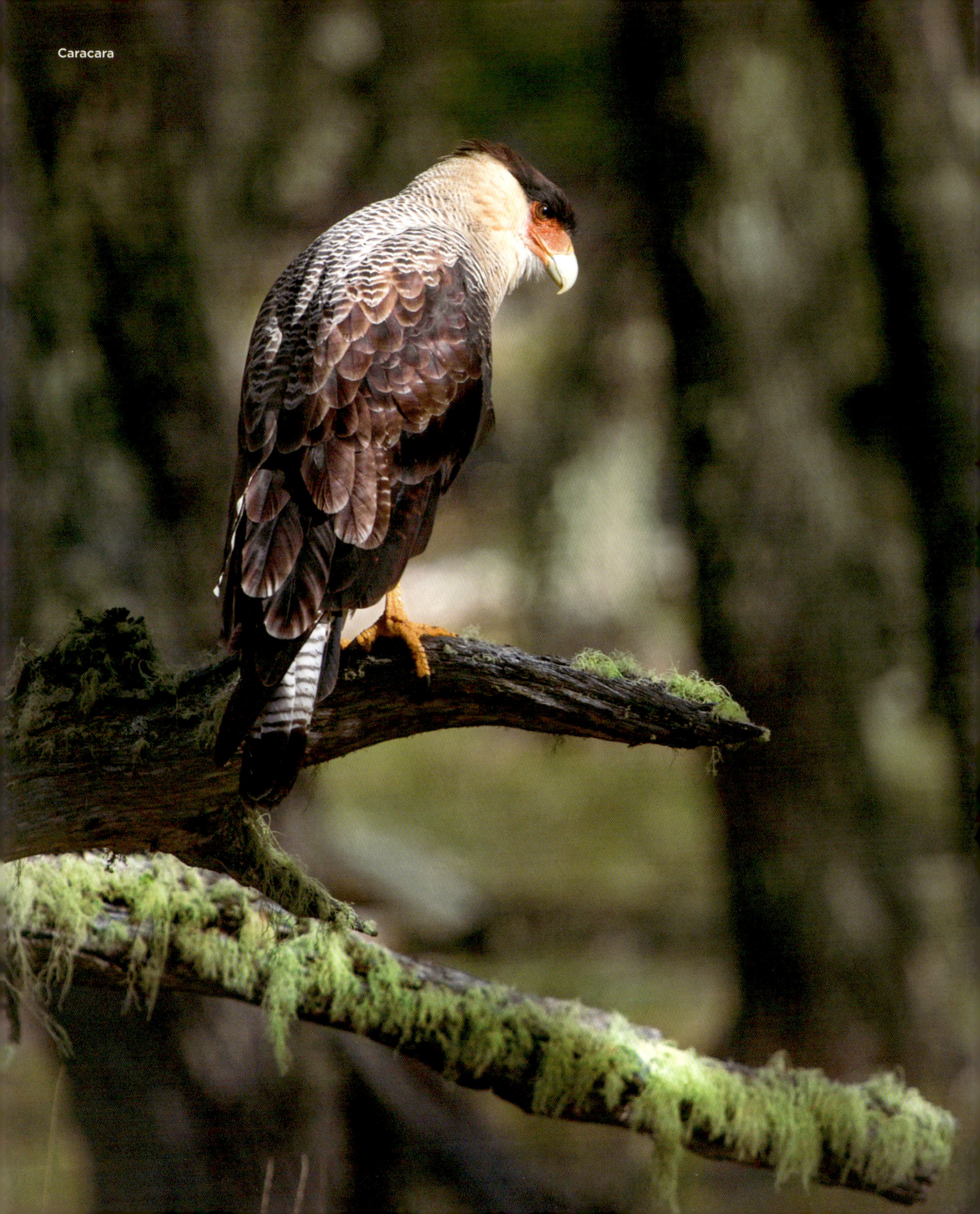
Caracara

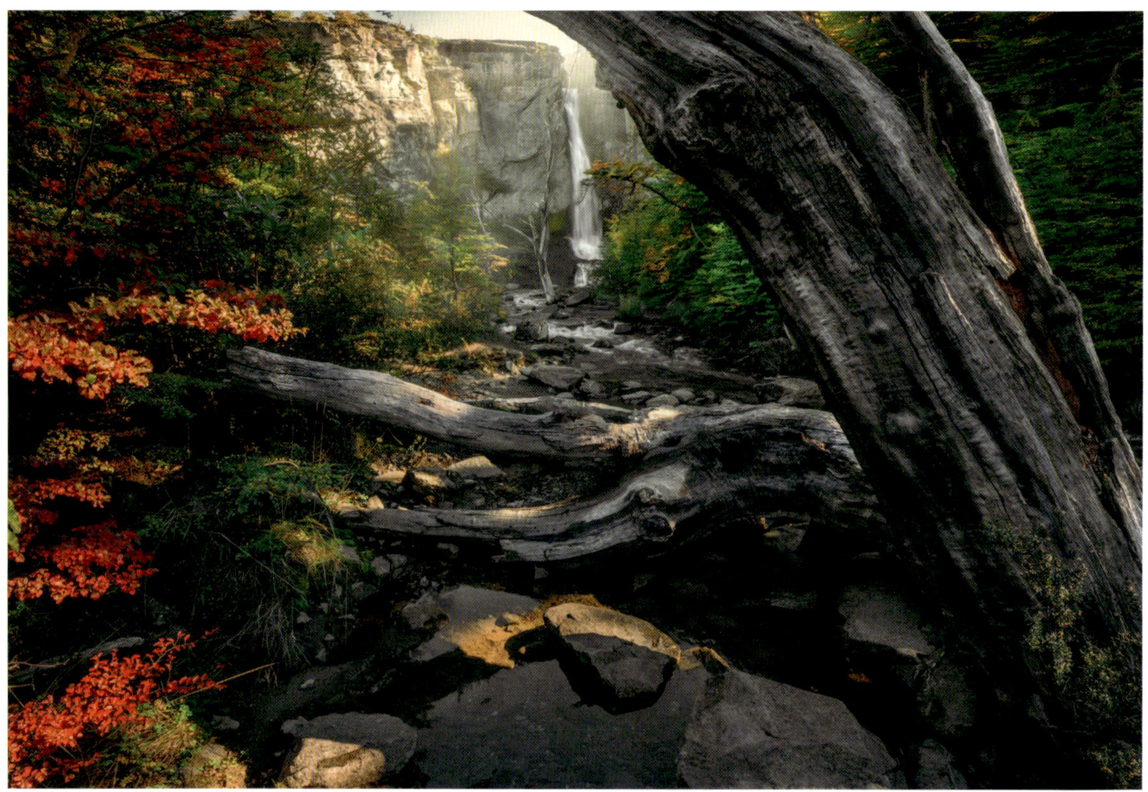

Chorrillo del Salto

Hiking in the Fitz Roy area

A beautiful excursion from the village of El Chaltén leads to the waterfall of Chorrillo del Salto. The path runs through a former glacier bed and after 4 km (2.5 mi) you reach the 20 m (66 ft) high waterfall. Bird fans may see the Southern crested caracara bird of prey, with a little luck.

Senderismo en la zona del Fitz Roy

Una hermosa excursión desde el pueblo de El Chaltén conduce a la cascada Chorrillo del Salto. El sendero pasa por un antiguo lecho glaciar. Después de 4 km se llega a la cascada de 20 m de altura. Con un poco de suerte, los amantes de las aves pueden ver el ave de rapiña caracara.

Randonner dans le massif du Fitz Roy

Une belle excursion à partir de la localité El Chaltén mène aux chutes d'eau Chorrillo del Salto. Le chemin traverse le lit d'un ancien glacier. Après 4 km, il atteint la chute d'eau de 20 m. Les amateurs d'ornithologie viennent y admirer, avec un peu de chance, le rapace *caracará*.

Caminhadas na área do Fitz Roy

Uma bela excursão desde o povoado de El Chaltén conduz à cascata Chorrillo del Salto. O caminho passa por uma antiga geleira. Após 4 km, você alcança a cachoeira de 20 m de Altura. Com um pouco de sorte, os fãs das aves podem ver a ave de rapina Caracará.

Wandern im Gebiet des Fitzroy

Ein schöner Ausflug von der Ortschaft El Chaltén führt zum Wasserfall Chorrillo del Salto. Der Weg verläuft durch ein ehemaliges Gletscherbett. Nach 4 km erreicht man den 20 m hohen Wasserfall. Vogelfans können mit etwas Glück den Raubvogel Caracará sehen.

Wandelen in het gebied bij Fitzroy

Een mooie excursie vanuit het dorp El Chaltén leidt naar de waterval Chorrillo del Salto. Het pad loopt door een voormalige gletsjerbedding. Na 4 km bereikt men de 20 m hoge waterval. Vogelfans kunnen met een beetje geluk de Caracará roofvogel zien.

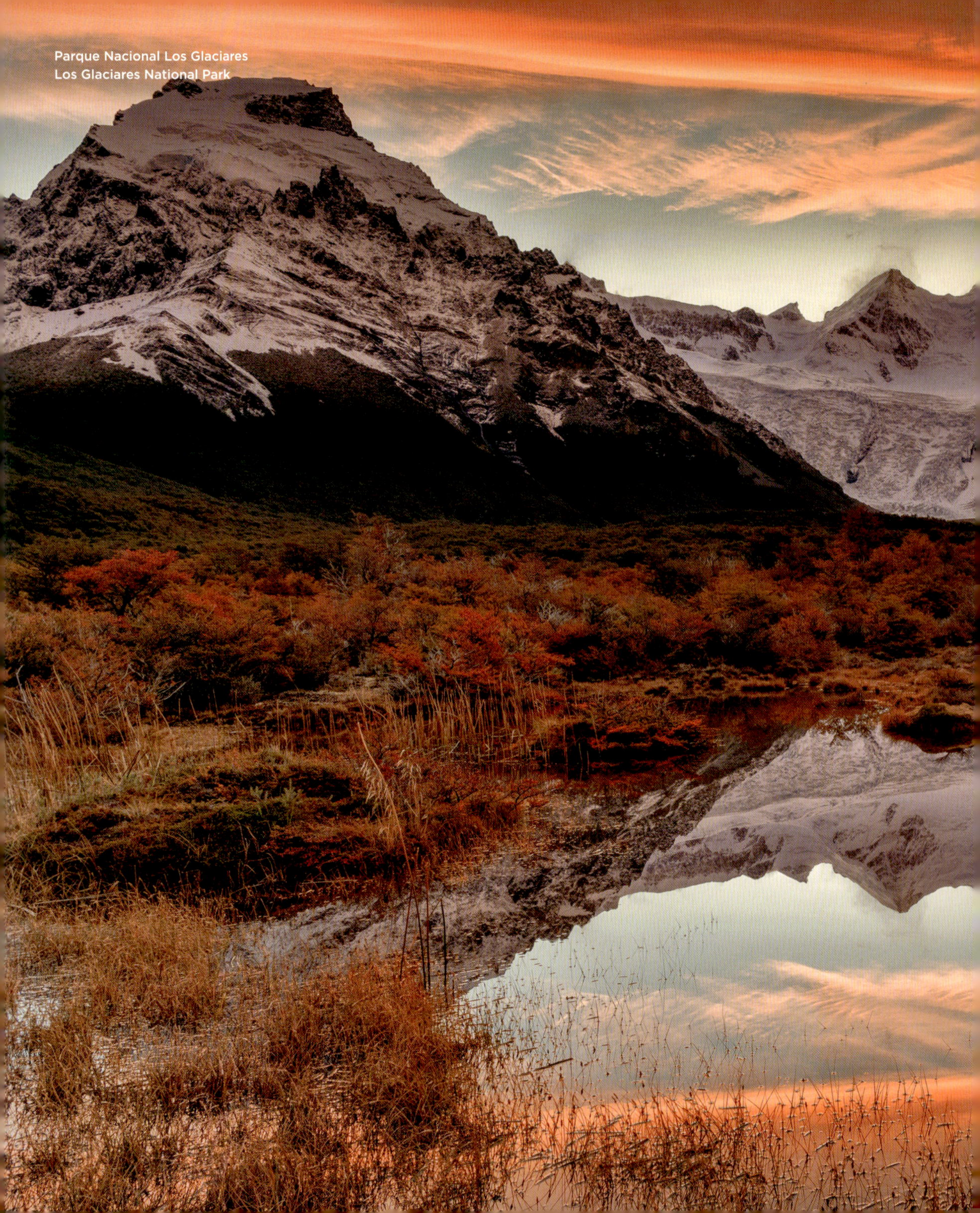
Parque Nacional Los Glaciares
Los Glaciares National Park

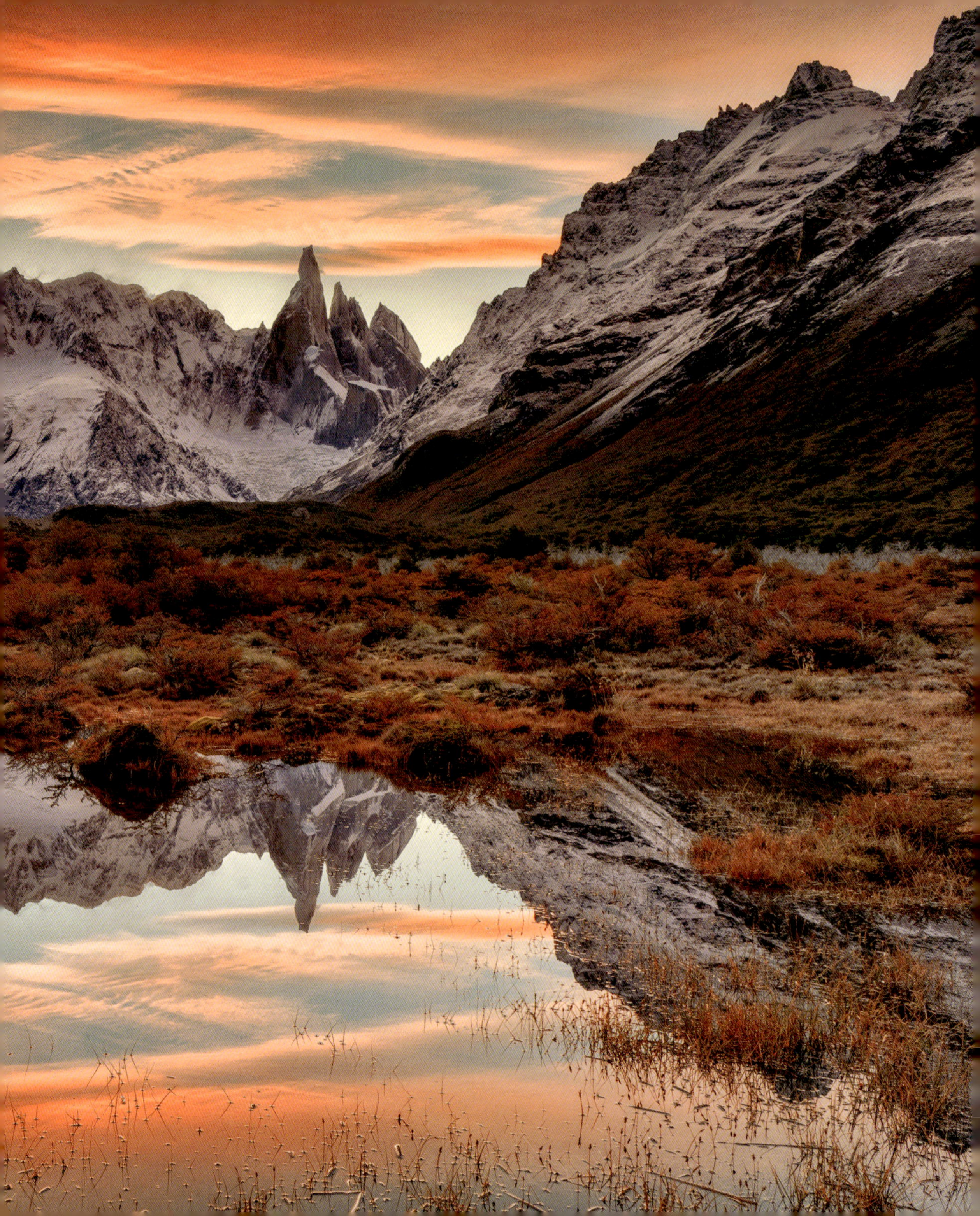

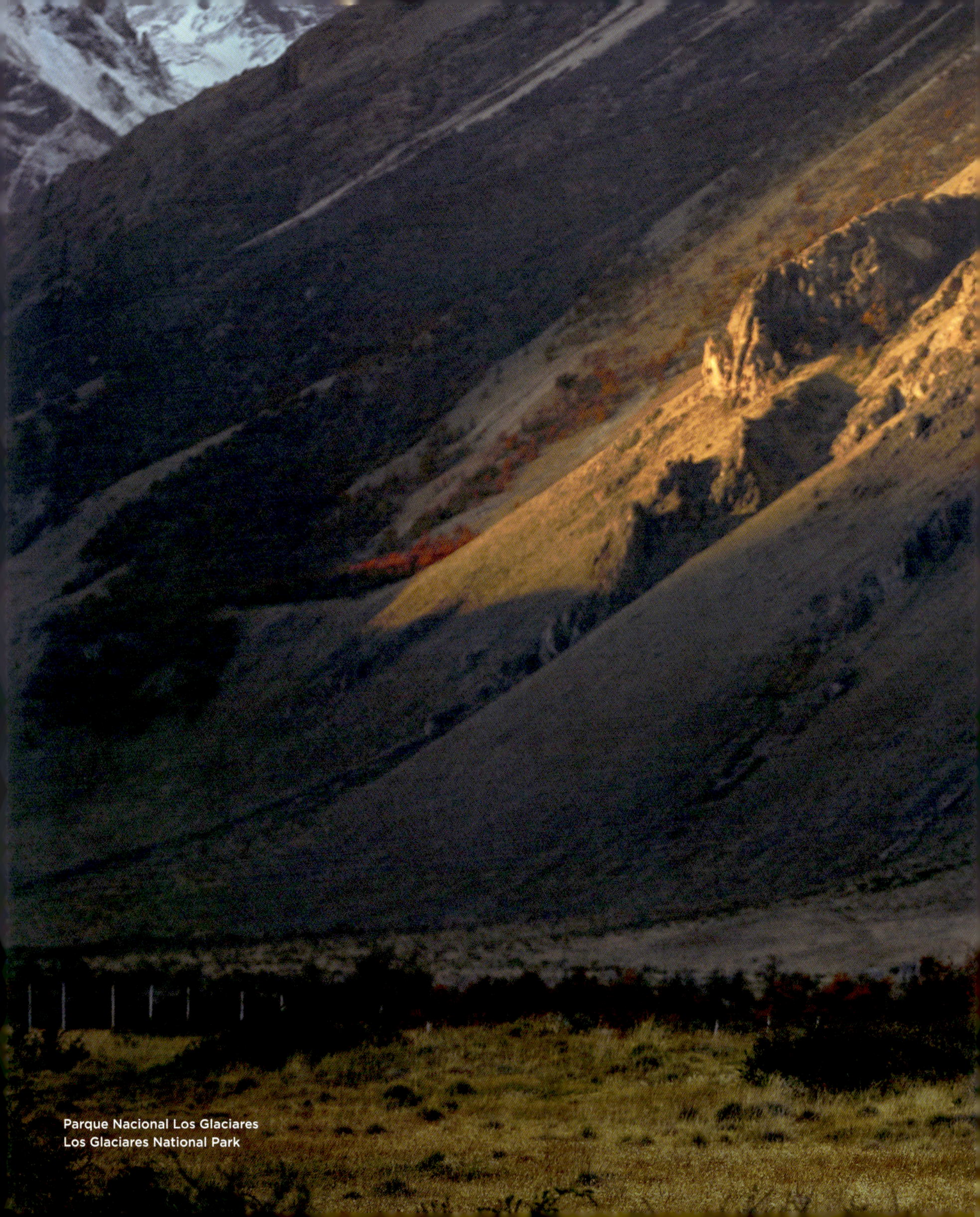

Parque Nacional Los Glaciares
Los Glaciares National Park

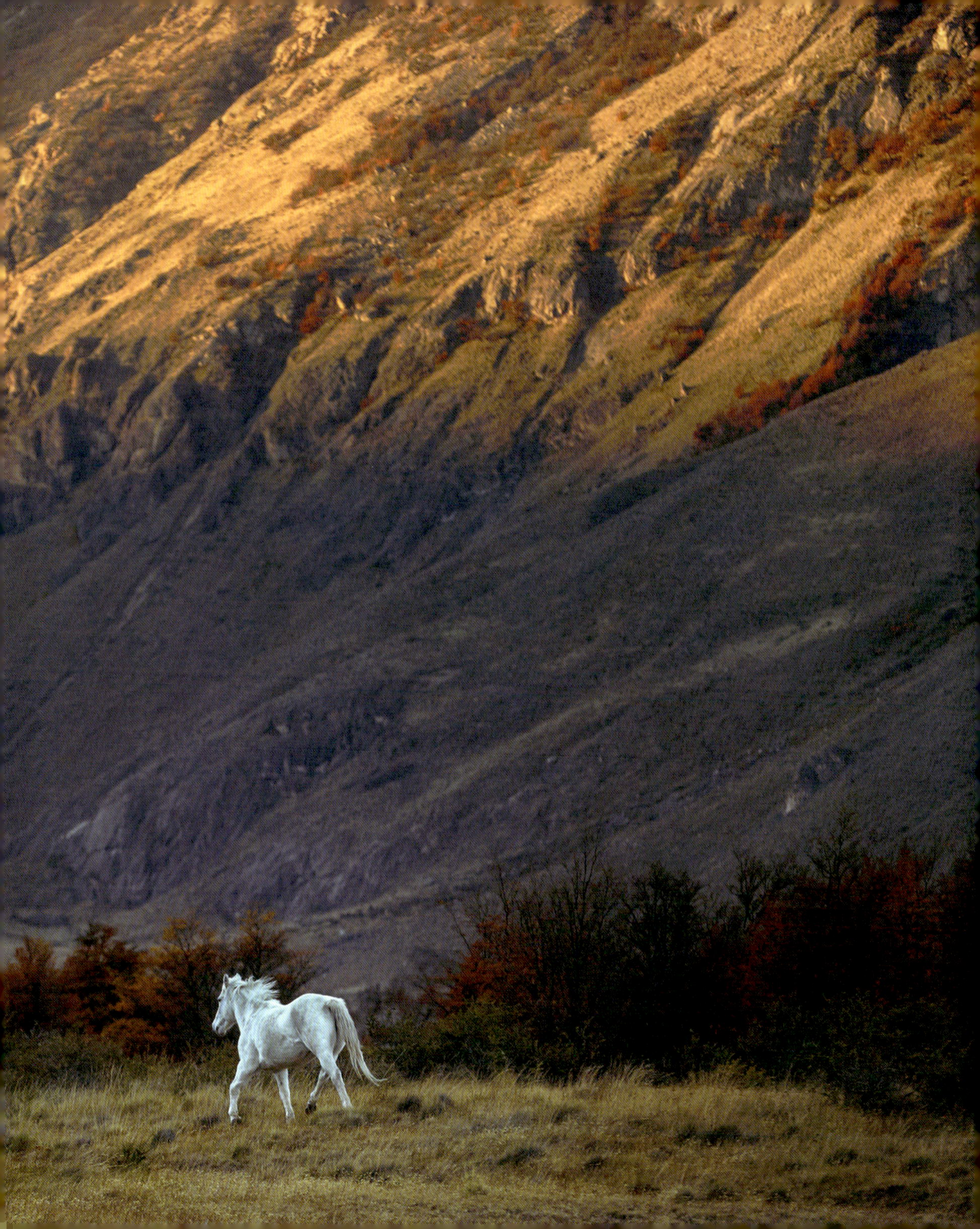

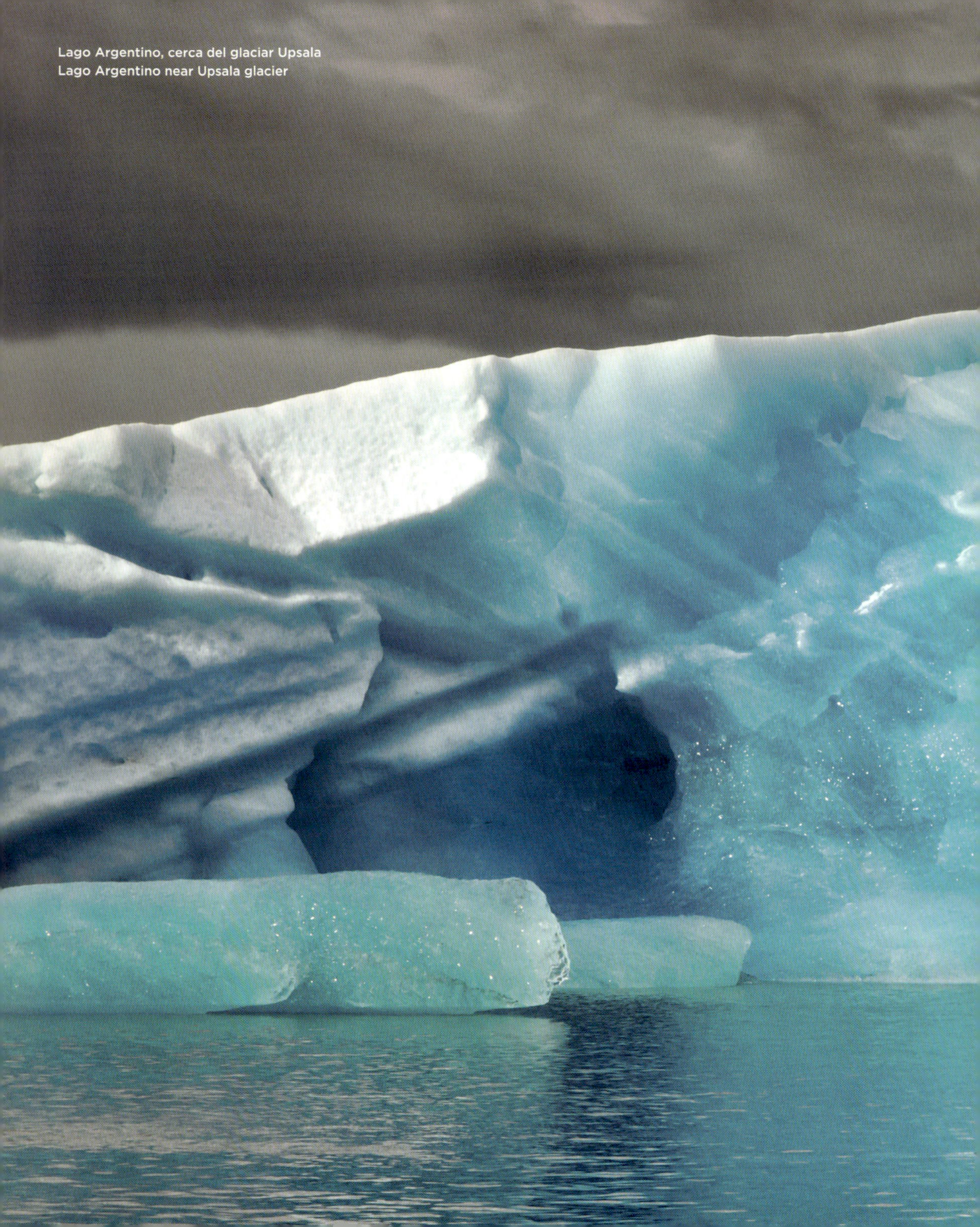
Lago Argentino, cerca del glaciar Upsala
Lago Argentino near Upsala glacier

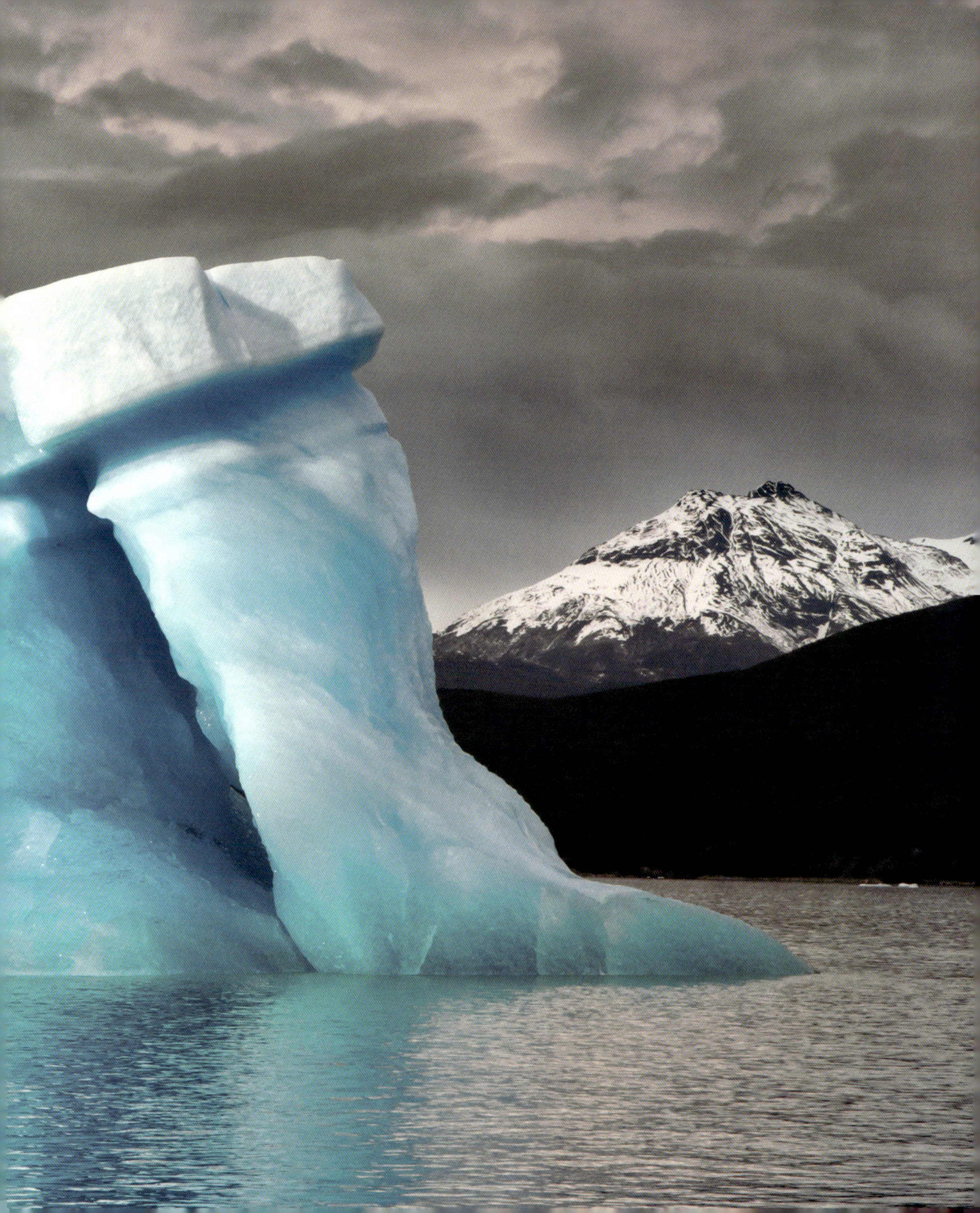

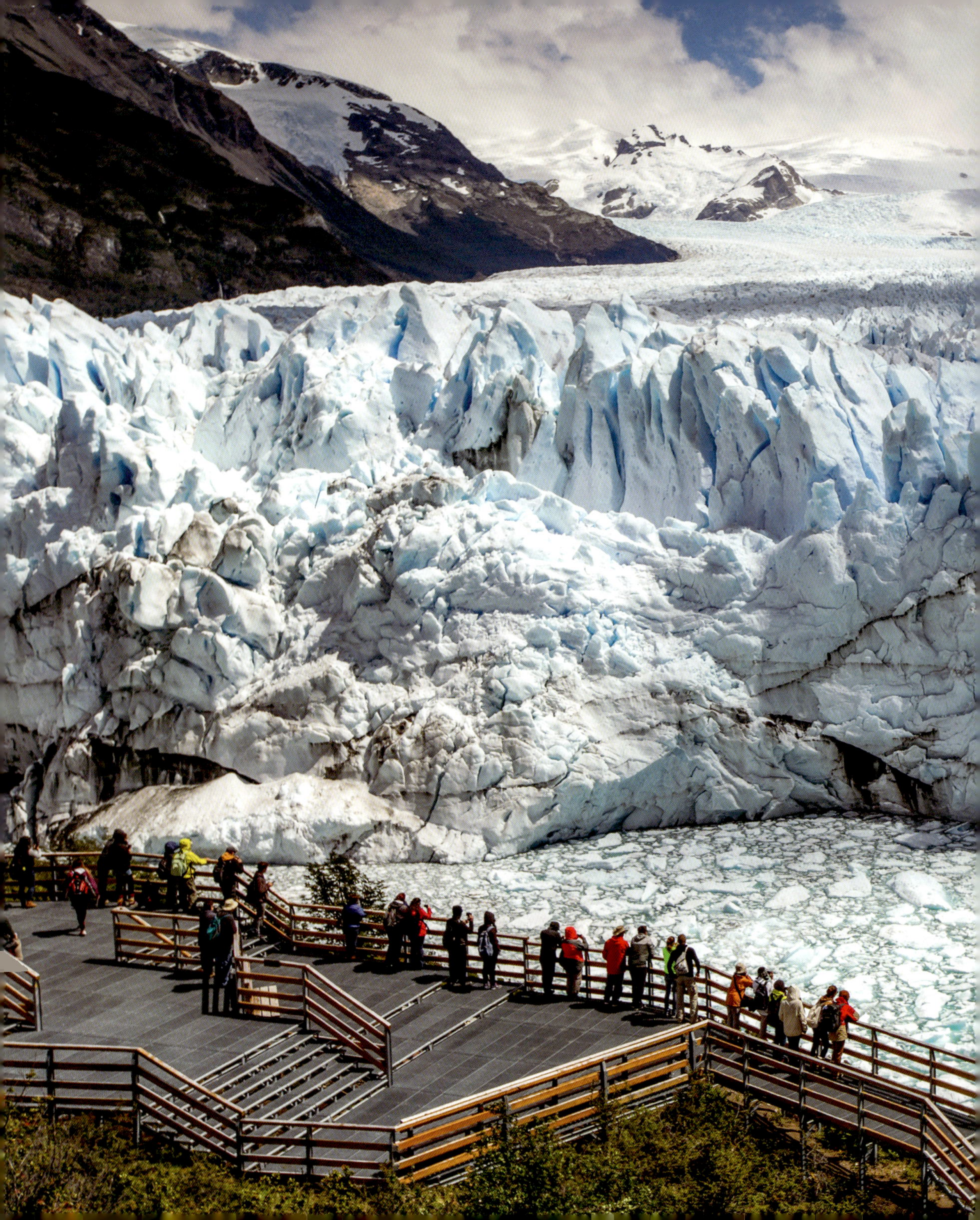

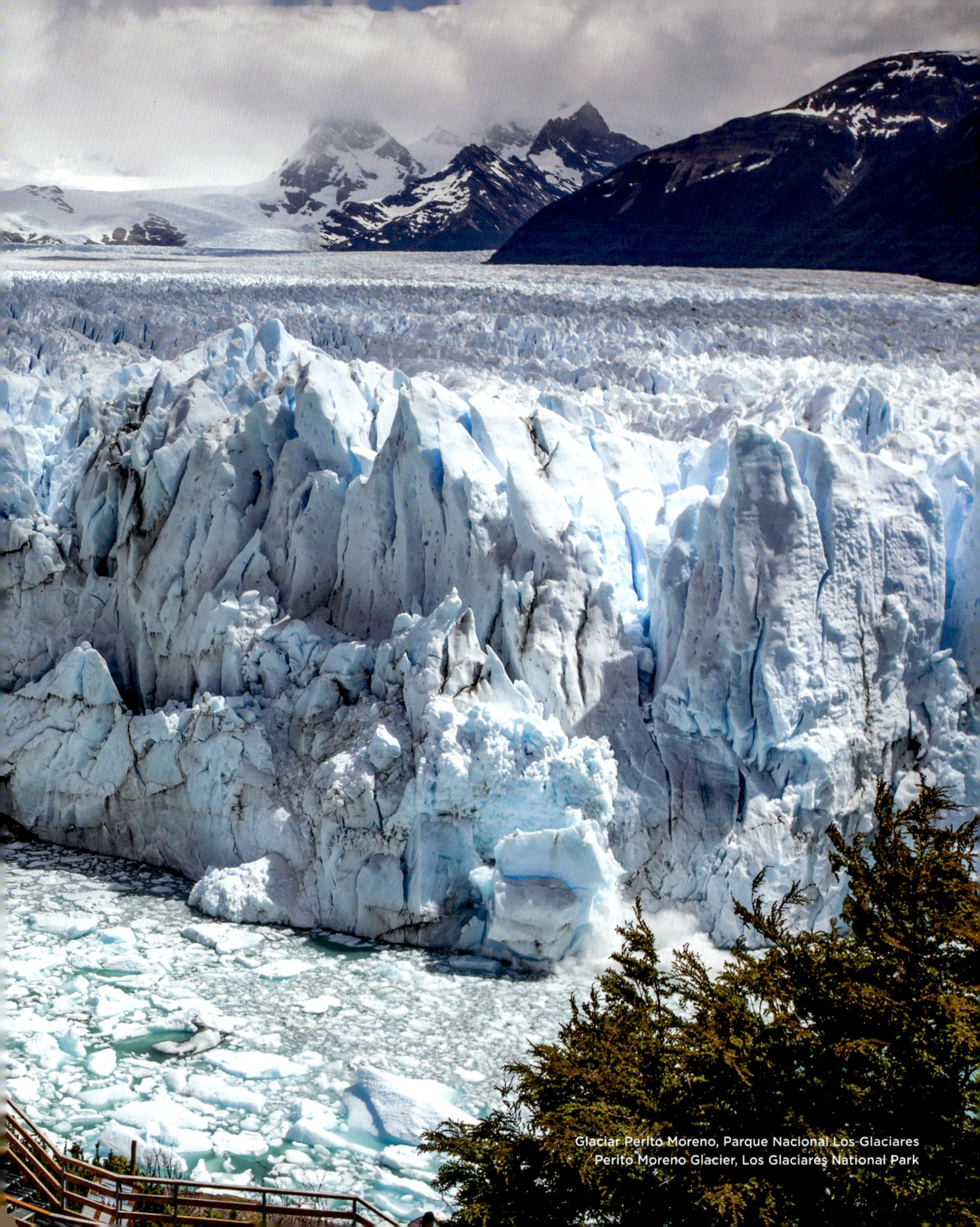

Glaciar Perito Moreno, Parque Nacional Los Glaciares
Perito Moreno Glacier, Los Glaciares National Park

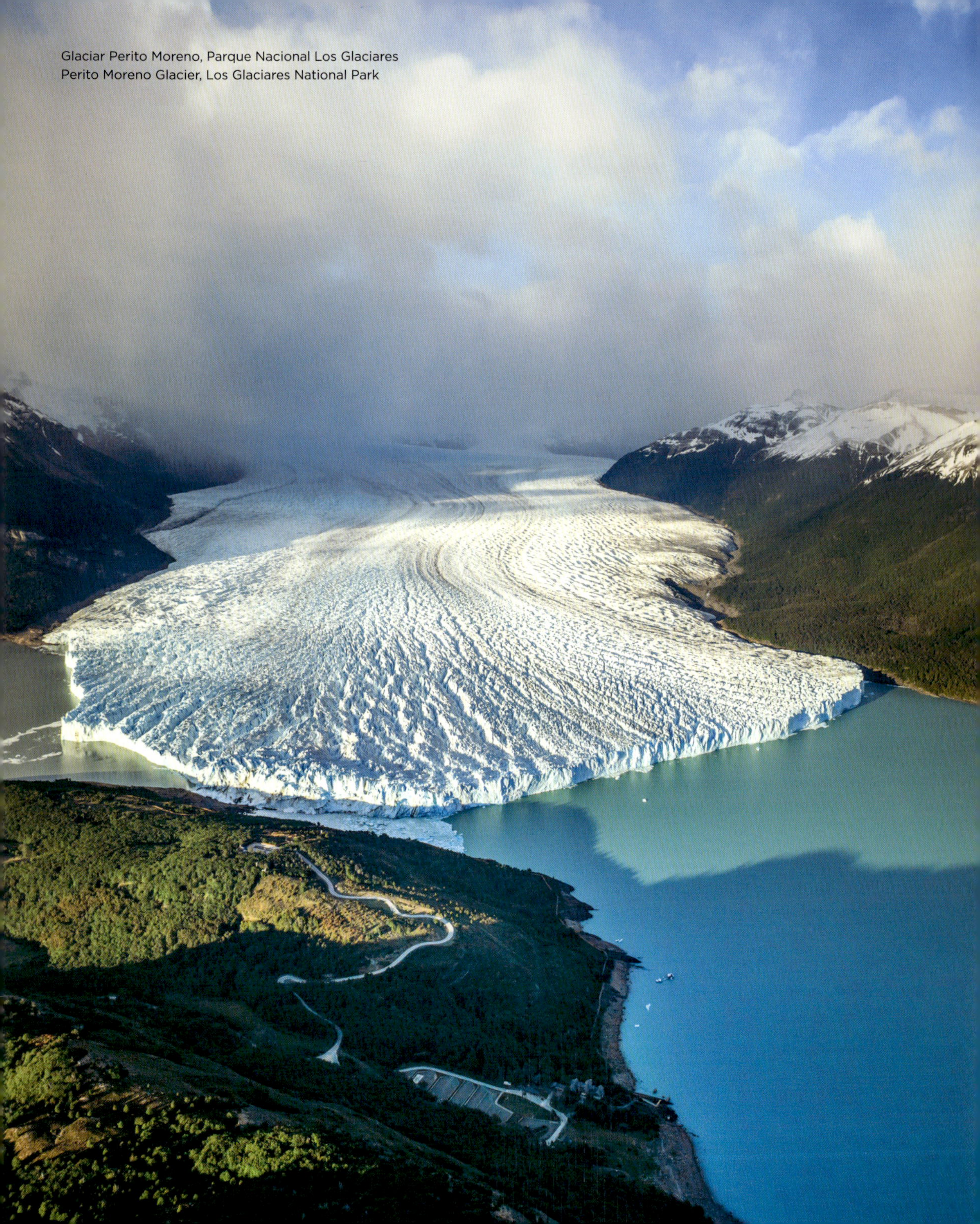

Glaciar Perito Moreno, Parque Nacional Los Glaciares
Perito Moreno Glacier, Los Glaciares National Park

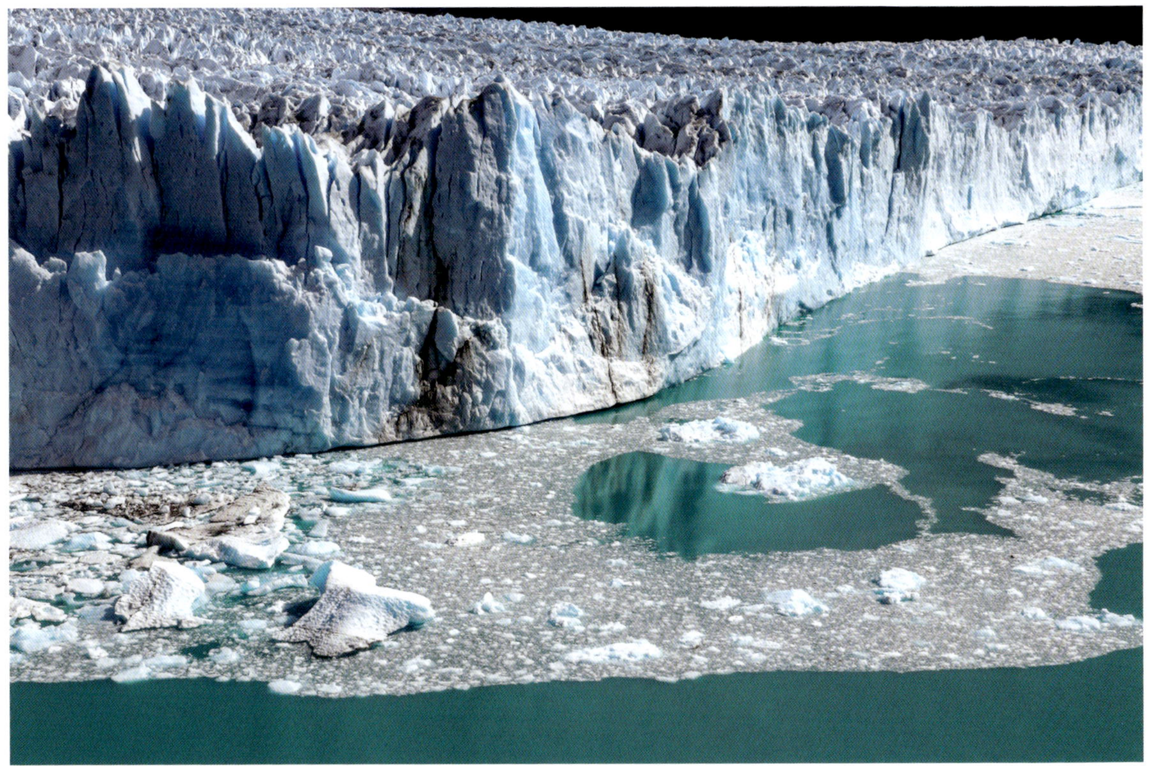

Glaciar Perito Moreno, Parque Nacional Los Glaciares
Perito Moreno Glacier, Los Glaciares National Park

Perito Moreno Glacier

In the south of the Los Glaciares National Park, which covers glacial areas of 22,000 km² (8494 sq mi), lies the most famous of the glaciers, the Perito Moreno. Its glacier tongue rises 60 m (197 ft) above Lake Argentino. It is 4 km (2.5 mi) wide, with fissures and crevices. Since the glacier is constantly moving, every now and then a large ice block breaks away from the wall and crashes into the lake.

Glaciar Perito Moreno

En el sur del Parque Nacional Los Glaciares, que cubre una superficie de 22 000 km², se encuentra el más famoso de los glaciares: el Perito Moreno. Su lengua glaciar se eleva a 60 m del Lago Argentino. Tiene 4 km de ancho y presenta grietas. Dado que el glaciar se encuentra en constante movimiento, de vez en cuando se desprende un gran bloque de hielo de la pared y se estrella contra el lago.

Le glacier Perito Moreno

Au sud du parc national Los Glaciares, qui comprend 22 000 km² de glaciers, s'élève le plus célèbre d'entre eux, le Perito Moreno. Son front glaciaire s'élève à 60 m au-dessus de la surface du Lago Argentino. Il couvre une largeur de 4 km et présente des fissures. Le glacier étant toujours en mouvement, de gros blocs de glace se détachent régulièrement de sa paroi et s'effondrent avec fracas dans le lac.

Glaciar Perito Moreno

No sul do Parque Nacional Los Glaciares, que abrange áreas glaciais de 22 000 km², encontra-se o mais famoso dos glaciares: o Perito Moreno. A sua língua glaciar sobe 60 m do Lago Argentino. Tem 4 km de largura e possui fendas. Como a geleira está em constante movimento, de vez em quando, um grande bloco de gelo se rompe e cai no lago.

Perito Moreno Gletscher

Im Süden des Nationalparks Los Glaciares, der Gletscherflächen von 22 000 km² umfasst, liegt der berühmteste der Gletscher: der Perito Moreno. Seine Gletscherzunge ragt 60 m aus dem Lago Argentino. Sie ist 4 km breit und hat Risse. Da der Gletscher ständig in Bewegung ist, bricht ab und zu ein großer Eisquader aus der Wand und stürzt krachend in den See.

Perito Morenogletsjer

In het zuiden van het nationaal park Los Glaciares, dat een gletsjergebied van 22 000 km² beslaat, ligt de beroemdste van de gletsjers: de Perito Moreno. Zijn gletsjertong stijgt 60 m uit het Argentinomeer. Hij is 4 km breed en heeft scheuren. Aangezien de gletsjer voortdurend in beweging is, breekt af en toe een groot ijsblok uit de wand en stort in het meer.

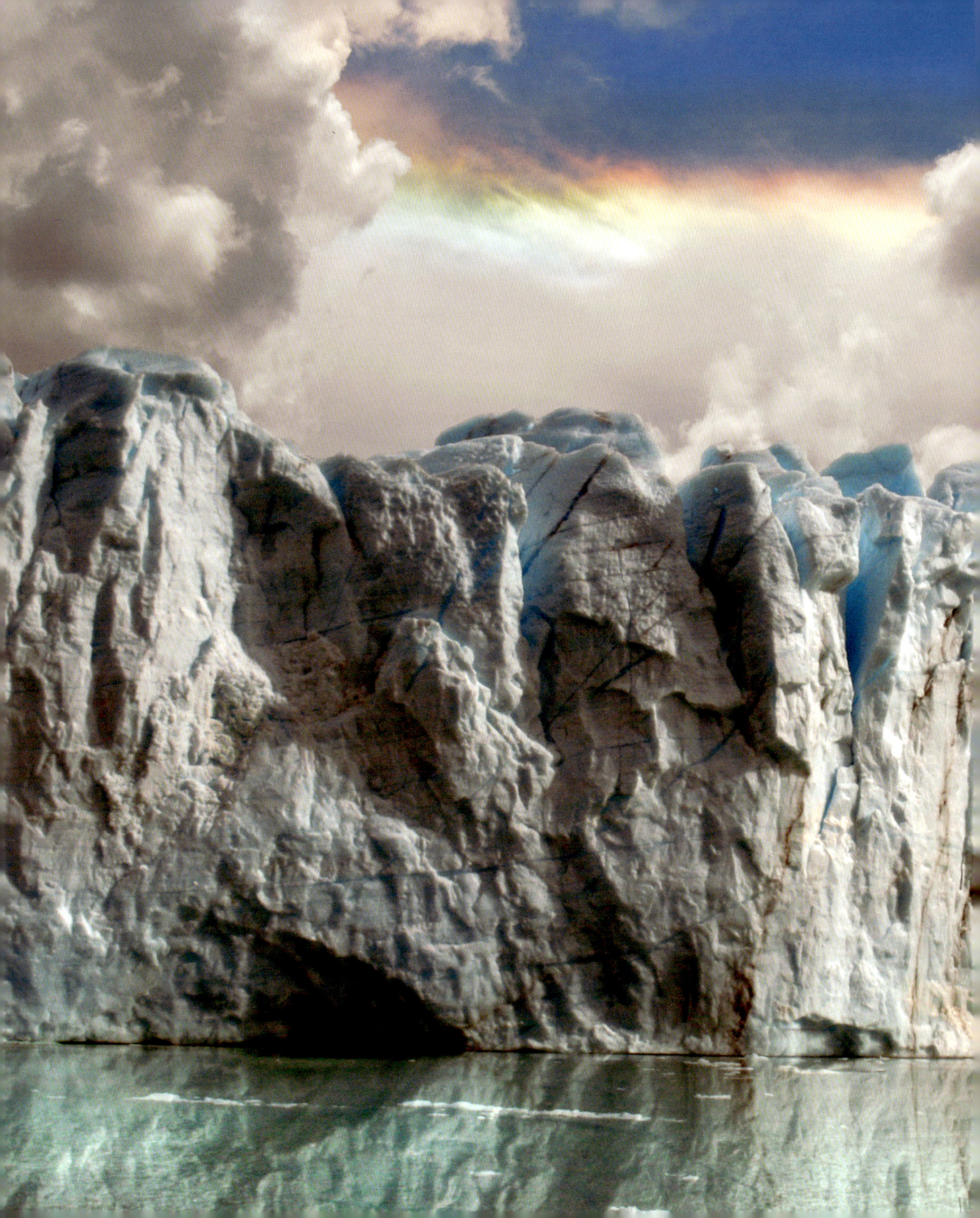

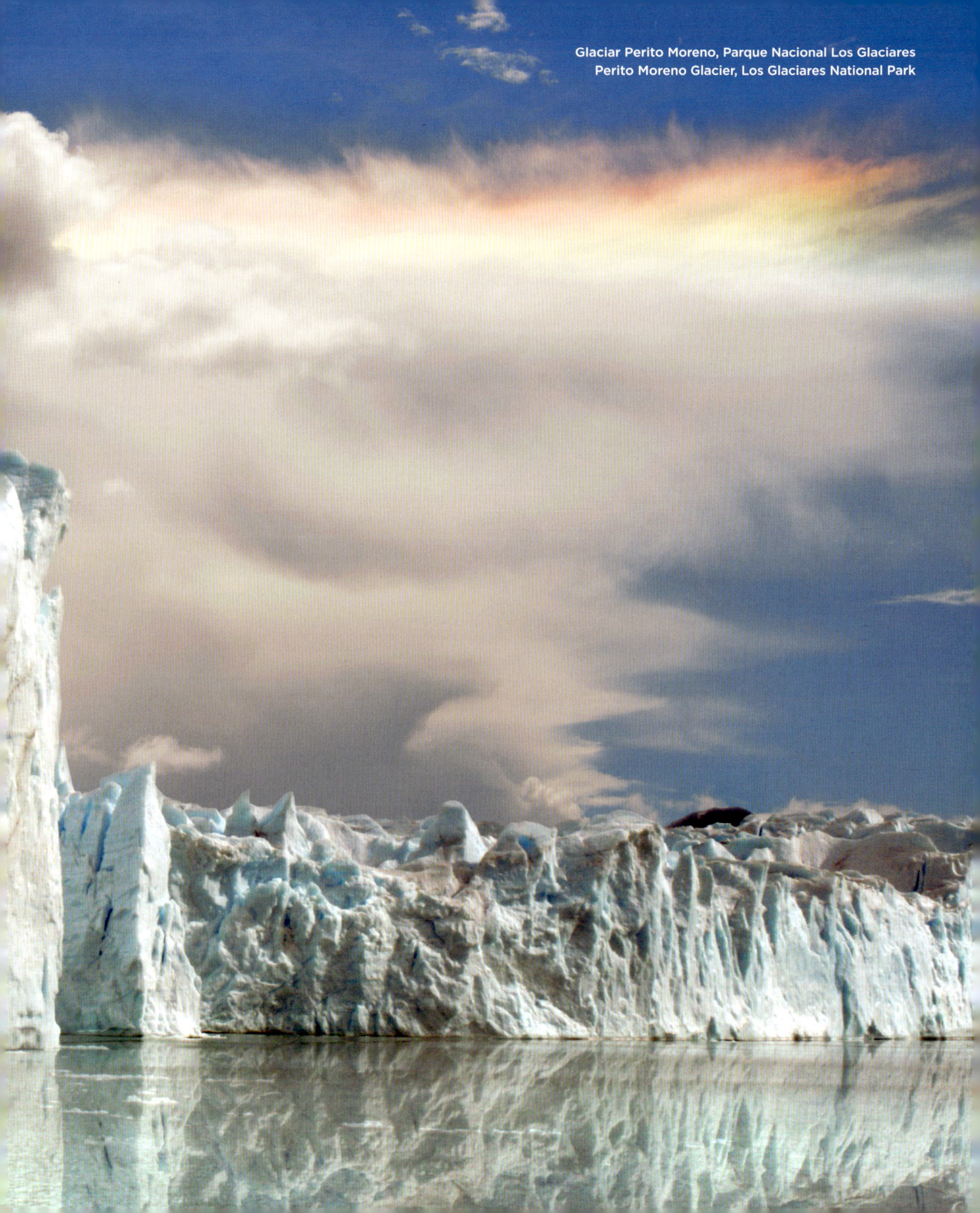

Glaciar Perito Moreno, Parque Nacional Los Glaciares
Perito Moreno Glacier, Los Glaciares National Park

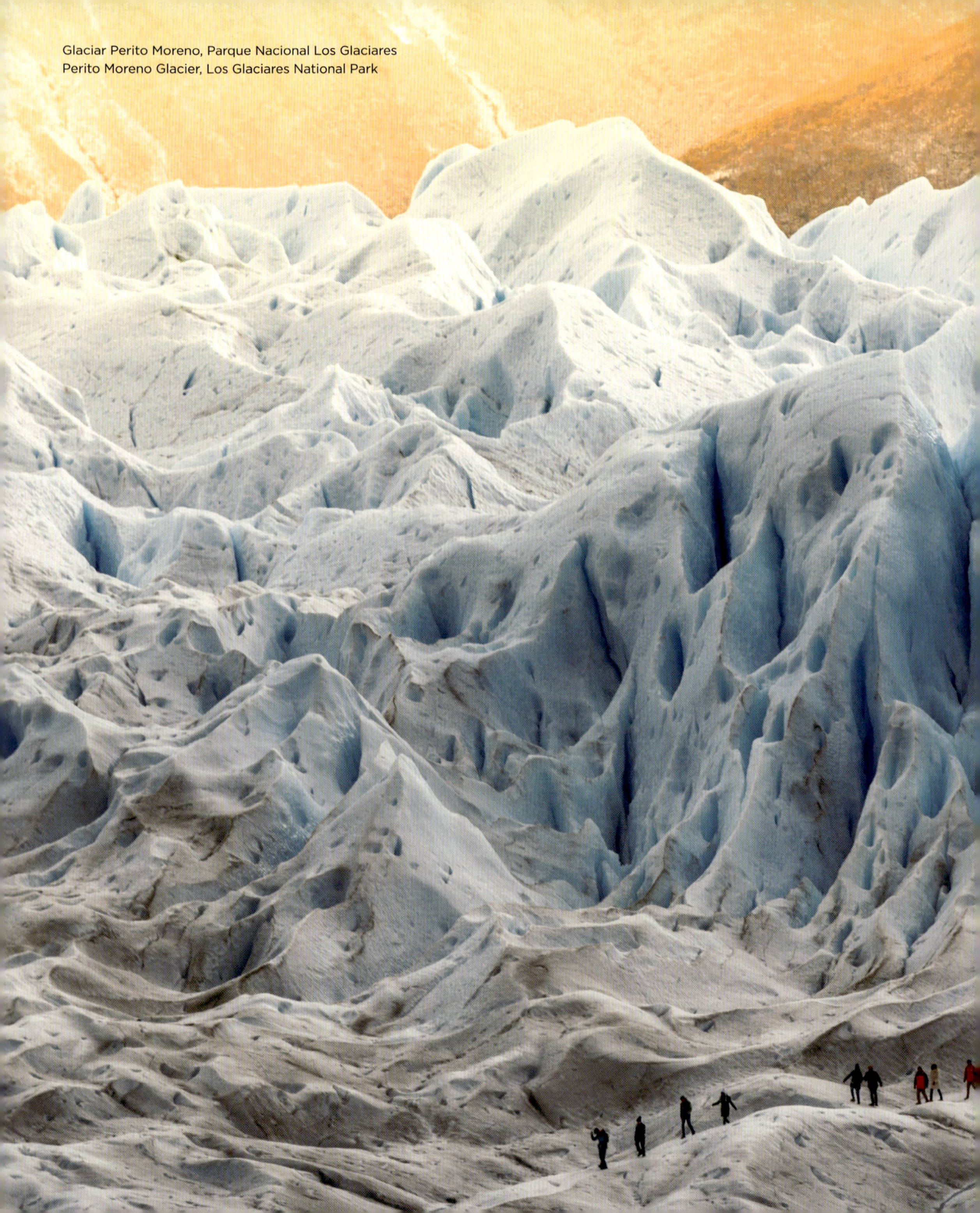
Glaciar Perito Moreno, Parque Nacional Los Glaciares
Perito Moreno Glacier, Los Glaciares National Park

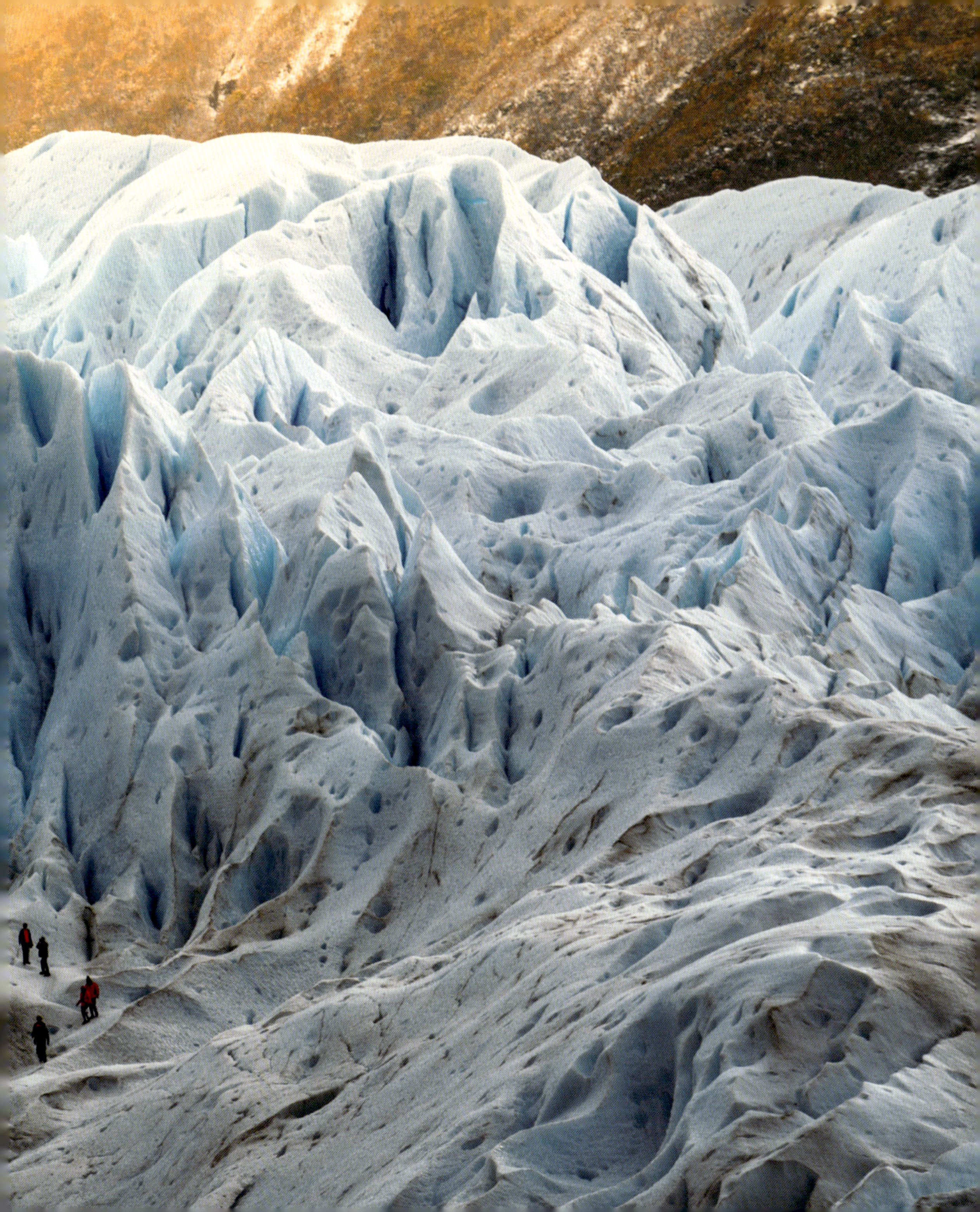

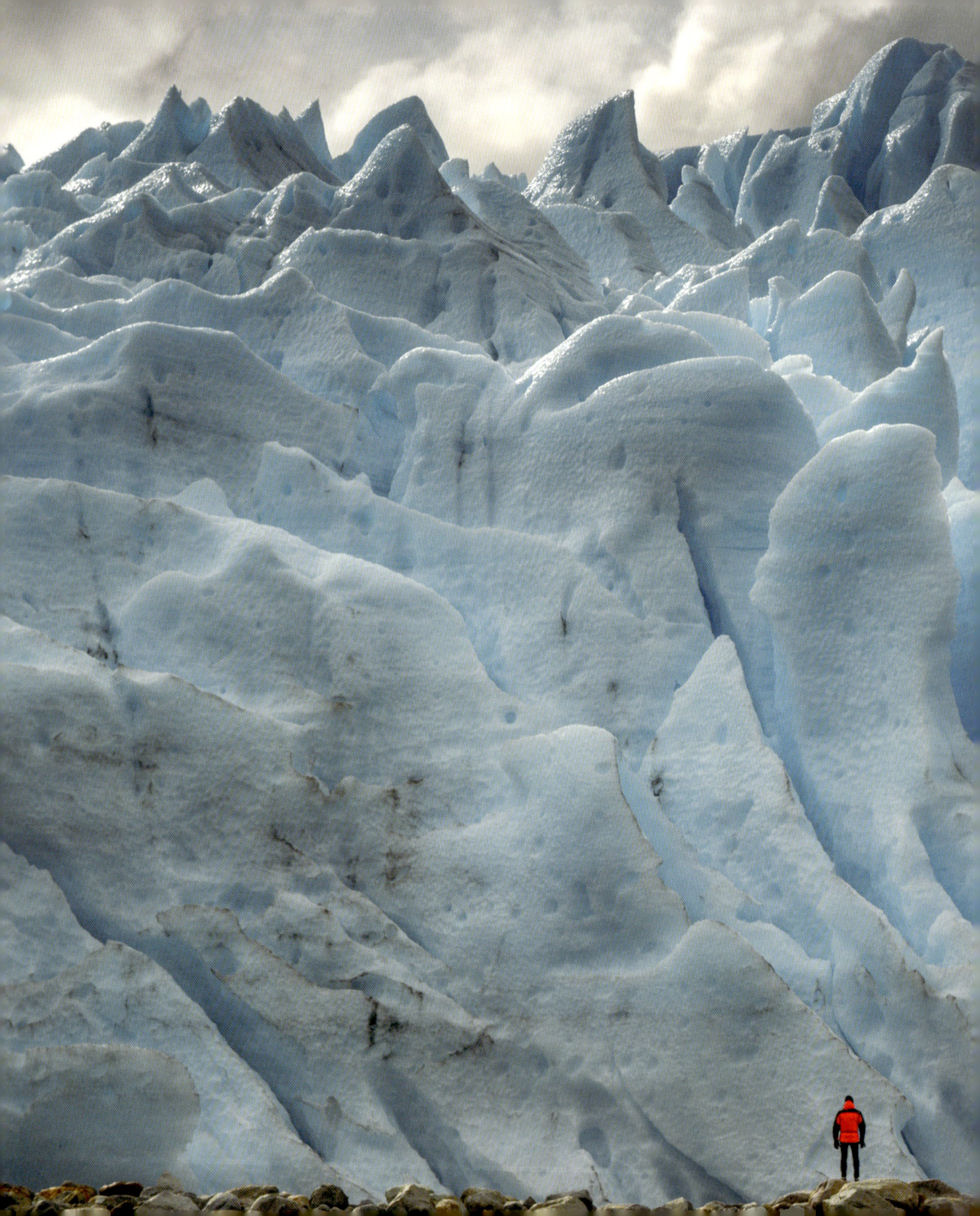

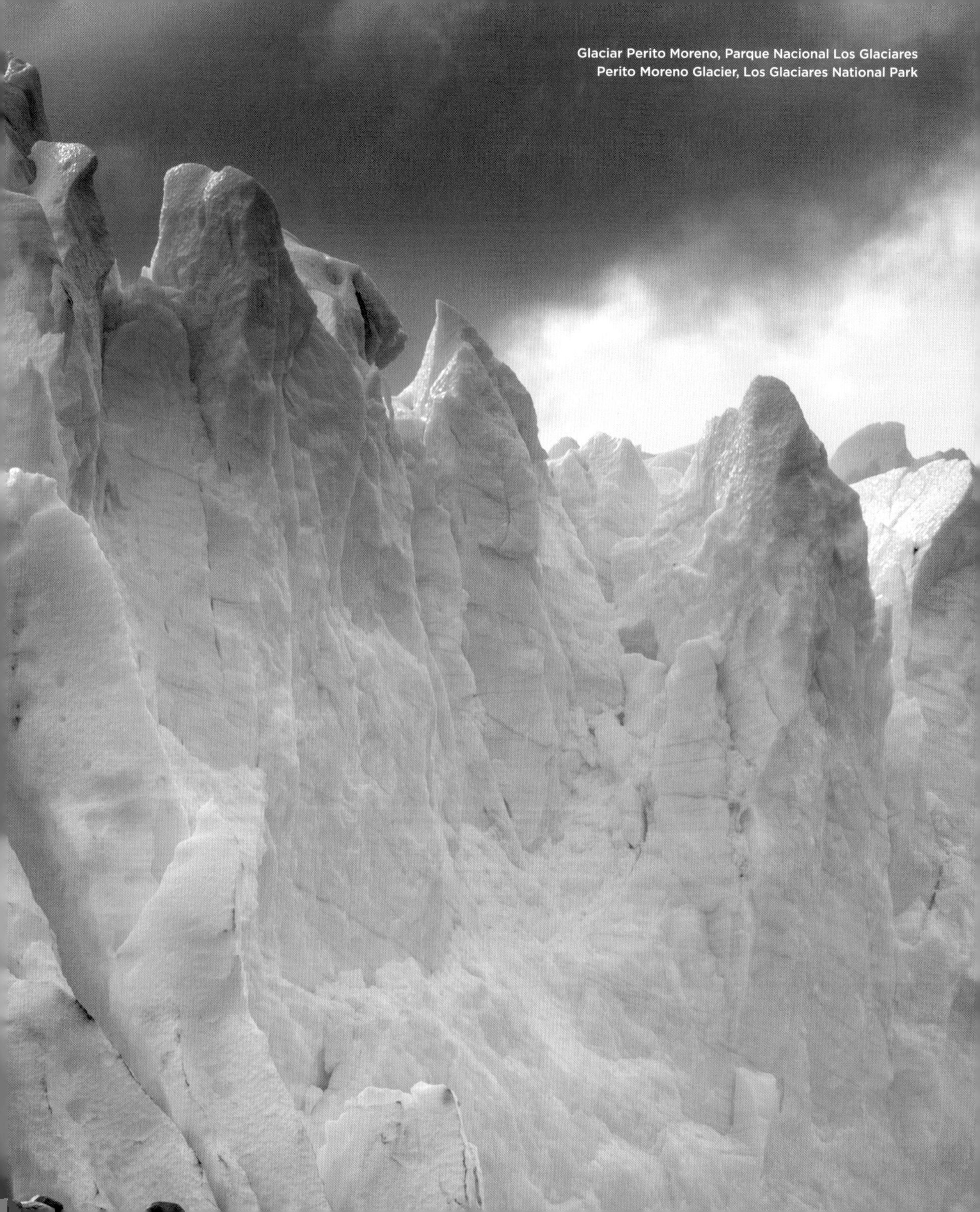
Glaciar Perito Moreno, Parque Nacional Los Glaciares
Perito Moreno Glacier, Los Glaciares National Park

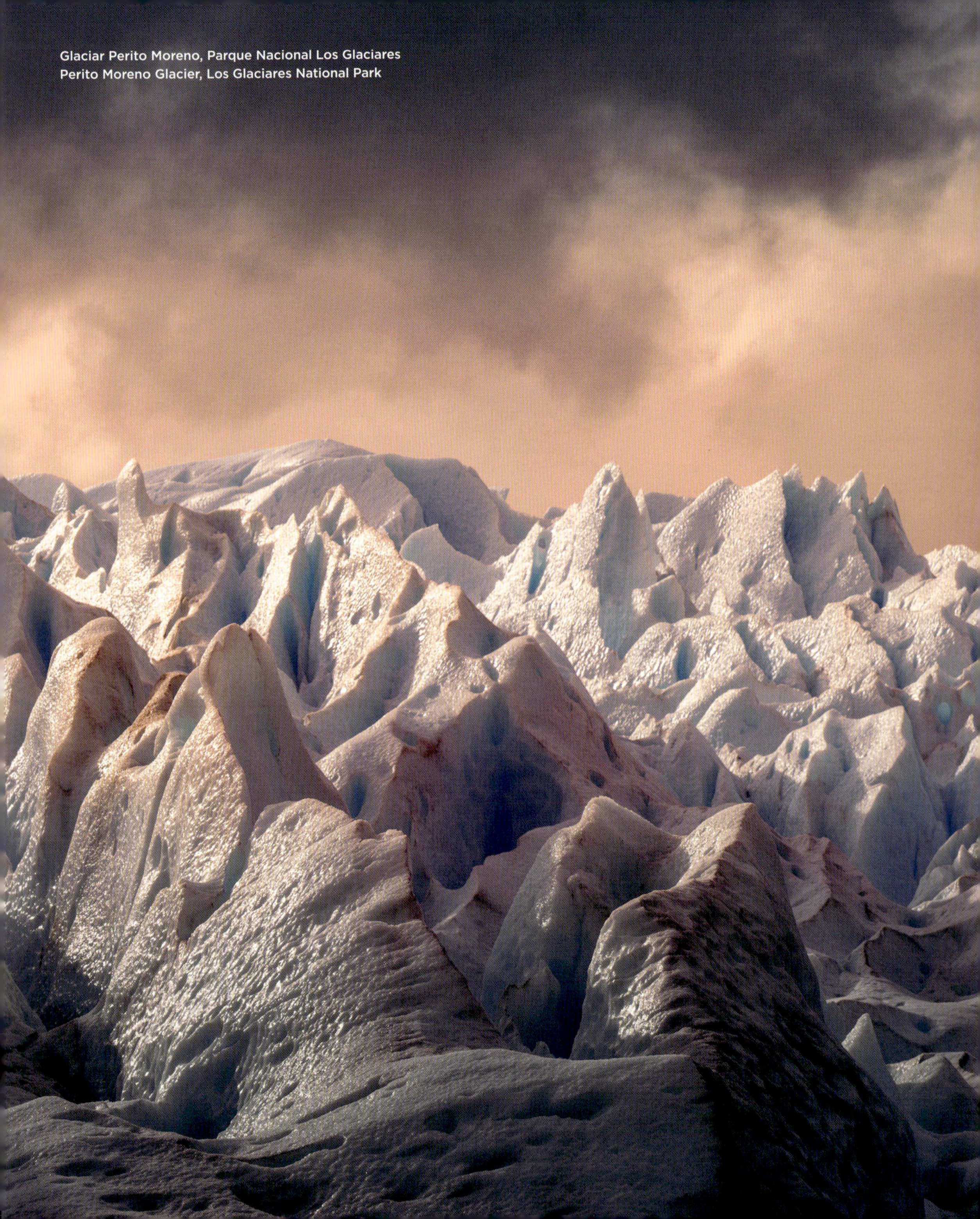

Glaciar Perito Moreno, Parque Nacional Los Glaciares
Perito Moreno Glacier, Los Glaciares National Park

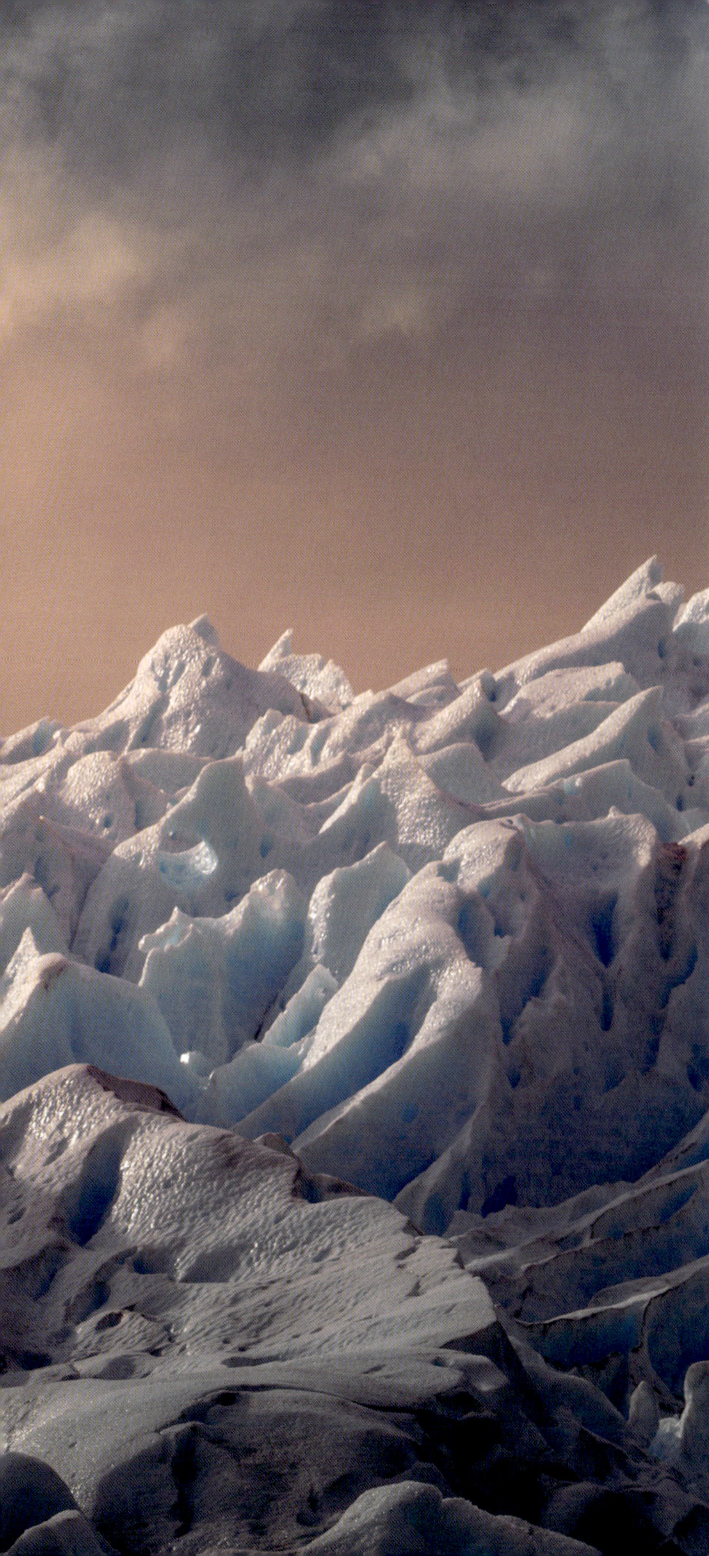

Glacier Adventure

The compressed glacier ice of Perito Moreno forms a cratered landscape on its surface. With special permits and good equipment, including spikes under your shoes, you can go on a guided hike on the ice mass, a unique experience. The gigantic dimensions of Perito Moreno can only be properly grasped when a human being serves as a comparison.

Aventure dans les glaciers

La glace compressée du Perito Moreno façonne un paysage de cratères. Sous couvert d'une autorisation spéciale, et avec un bon équipement et des crampons montés sur les chaussures, il est possible d'effectuer une randonnée sur les masses glacées. Une expérience inoubliable! La présence d'êtres humains sur les photos permet de réellement appréhender les dimensions gigantesques du Perito Moreno.

Gletscherabenteuer

Das gepresste Gletschereis des Perito Moreno bildet an der Oberfläche eine Kraterlandschaft. Mit Sondergenehmigungen kann man mit guter Ausstattung, Spikes unter dem Schuhwerk, eine geführte Wanderung auf den Eismassen unternehmen: ein einmaliges Erlebnis. Die gigantische Dimension des Perito Moreno lässt sich erst richtig erfassen, wenn ein Mensch als Maßstab dient.

Aventura en el glaciar

El hielo compacto del glaciar Perito Moreno forma un paisaje de cráteres en la superficie. Con permisos especiales, buen equipo y púas bajo los zapatos, se puede hacer una caminata guiada sobre las masas de hielo: una experiencia única. La gigantesca dimensión del Perito Moreno solo puede entenderse bien cuando un ser humano sirve de referencia.

Aventura Glaciar

O glaciar prensado de Perito Moreno forma uma paisagem de crateras na superfície. Com licenças especiais e bom equipamento, spikes debaixo dos sapatos, você pode fazer uma caminhada guiada sobre as massas de gelo: uma experiência única. A dimensão gigantesca de Perito Moreno só pode ser devidamente entendida quando o tamanho de um ser humano serve como referência.

Gletsjeravontuur

Het geperste gletsjerijs van Perito Moreno vormt aan de oppervlakte een kraterlandschap. Met speciale vergunningen en een goede uitrusting, spikes onder de schoenen, kan men een begeleide wandeling over de ijsmassa's maken: een unieke ervaring. De gigantische dimensie van Perito Moreno kan alleen goed worden begrepen als de mens als maatstaf dient.

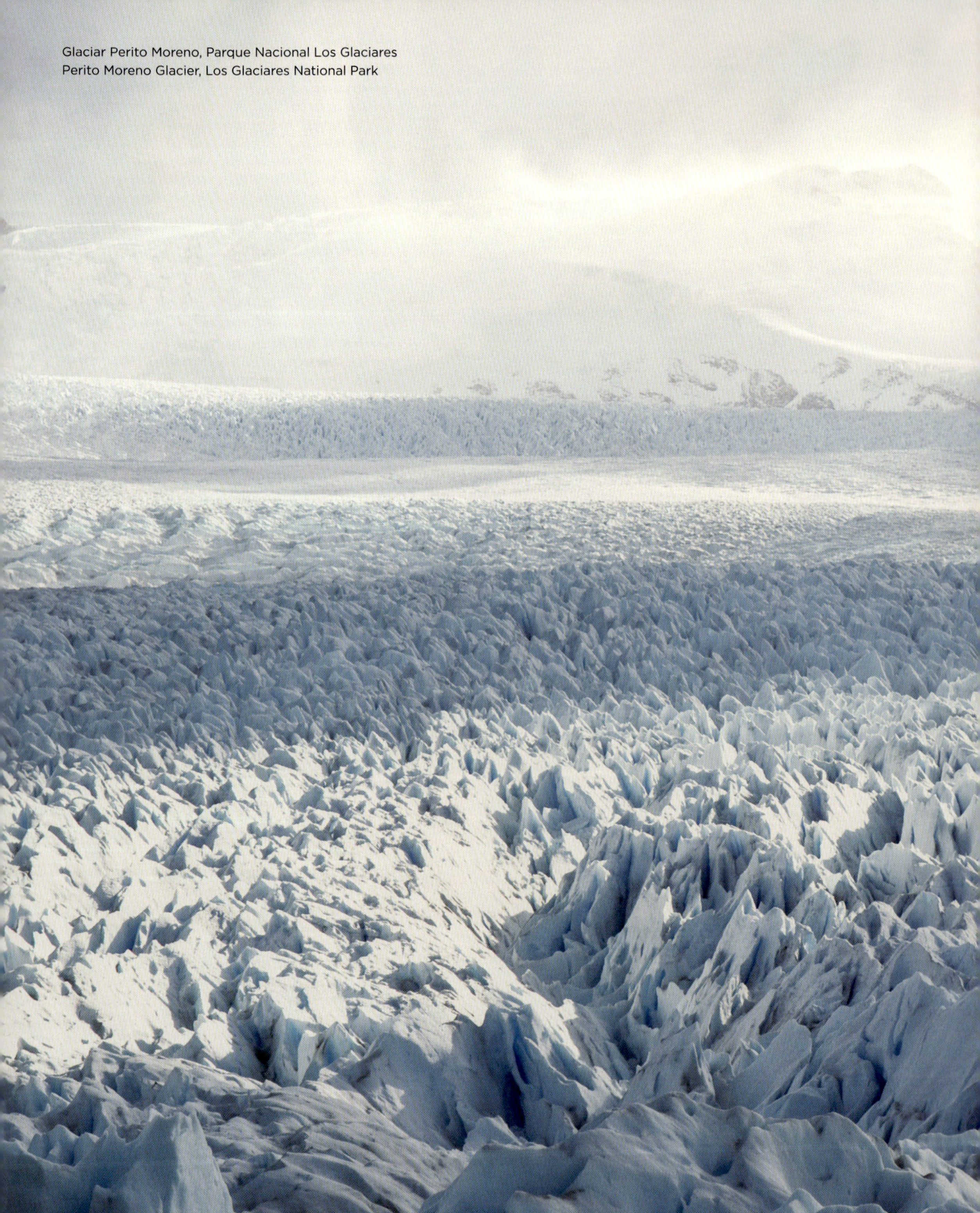

Glaciar Perito Moreno, Parque Nacional Los Glaciares
Perito Moreno Glacier, Los Glaciares National Park

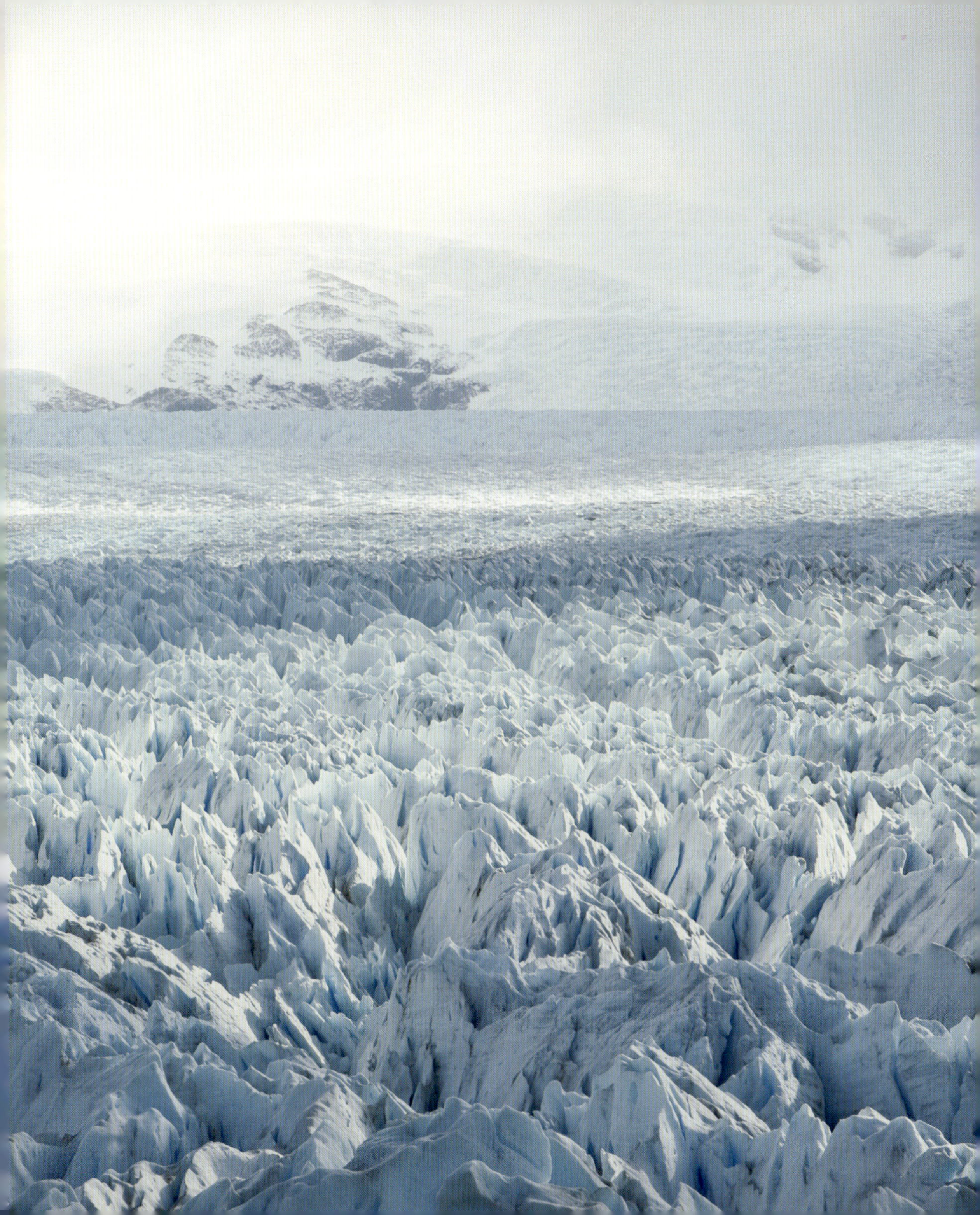

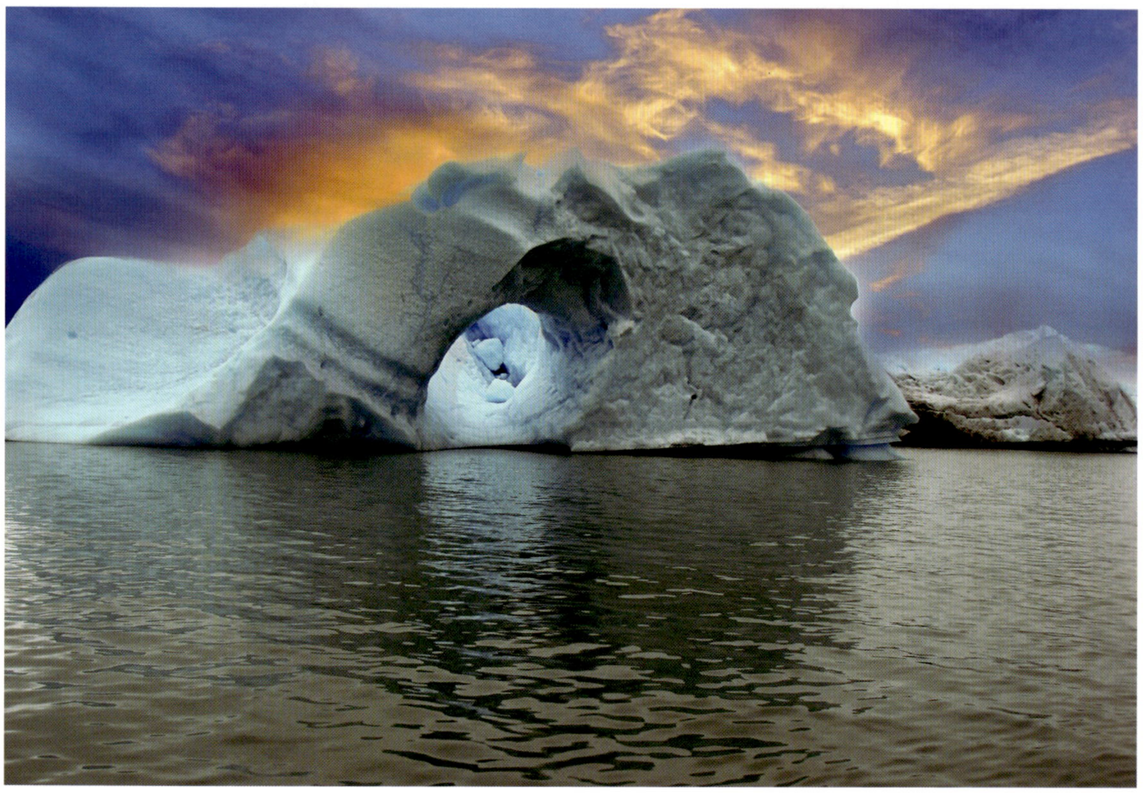

Glaciar Spegazzini, Parque Nacional Los Glaciares
Spegazzini Glacier, Los Glaciares National Park

Spegazzini Glacier

The Perito Moreno offers blue ice channels and gullies as well as crevasses, but the highest and most important glacier of the National Park is the Spegazzini Glacier. It was named after the botanist Carlos Luis Spegazzini and has its origin in the Chilean part of Patagonia.

Glaciar Spegazzini

El Perito Moreno ofrece tanto canales de hielo azul y barrancos, como grietas. Pero el glaciar más alto e importante del Parque Nacional es el Glaciar Spegazzini. Fue nombrado en honor al botánico Carlos Luis Spegazzini. Tiene su origen en la parte chilena de la Patagonia.

Le glacier Spegazzini

Si le Perito Moreno offre pistes glacées bleues, rigoles et crevasses, le plus haut et le plus vaste glacier du parc national est le glacier Spegazzini, qui porte le nom du botaniste Carlos Luis Spegazzini. Il naît dans la partie chilienne de la Patagonie.

Glaciar Spegazzini

O Perito Moreno oferece canais de gelo azul além de valetas. Mas o glaciar mais alto e mais importante do Parque Nacional é o Glaciar Spegazzini. Foi nomeado em homenagem ao botânico Carlos Luis Spegazzini. Tem a sua origem na parte chilena da Patagônia.

Spegazzini-Gletscher

Blaue Eiskanäle und Rinnen sowie Gletscherspalten bietet der Perito Moreno. Doch der höchste und wichtigste Gletscher des Nationalparks ist der Spegazzini-Gletscher. Er wurde nach dem Botaniker Carlos Luis Spegazzini benannt. Seinen Ursprung hat er im chilenischen Teil Patagoniens.

Spegazzini gletsjer

De Perito Moreno biedt blauwe ijskanalen, geulen en ook gletsjerspleten. Maar de hoogste en belangrijkste gletsjer van het nationaal park is de Spegazzini gletsjer. Deze is vernoemd naar de botanicus Carlos Luis Spegazzini. Hij komt oorspronkelijk uit het Chileense deel van Patagonië.

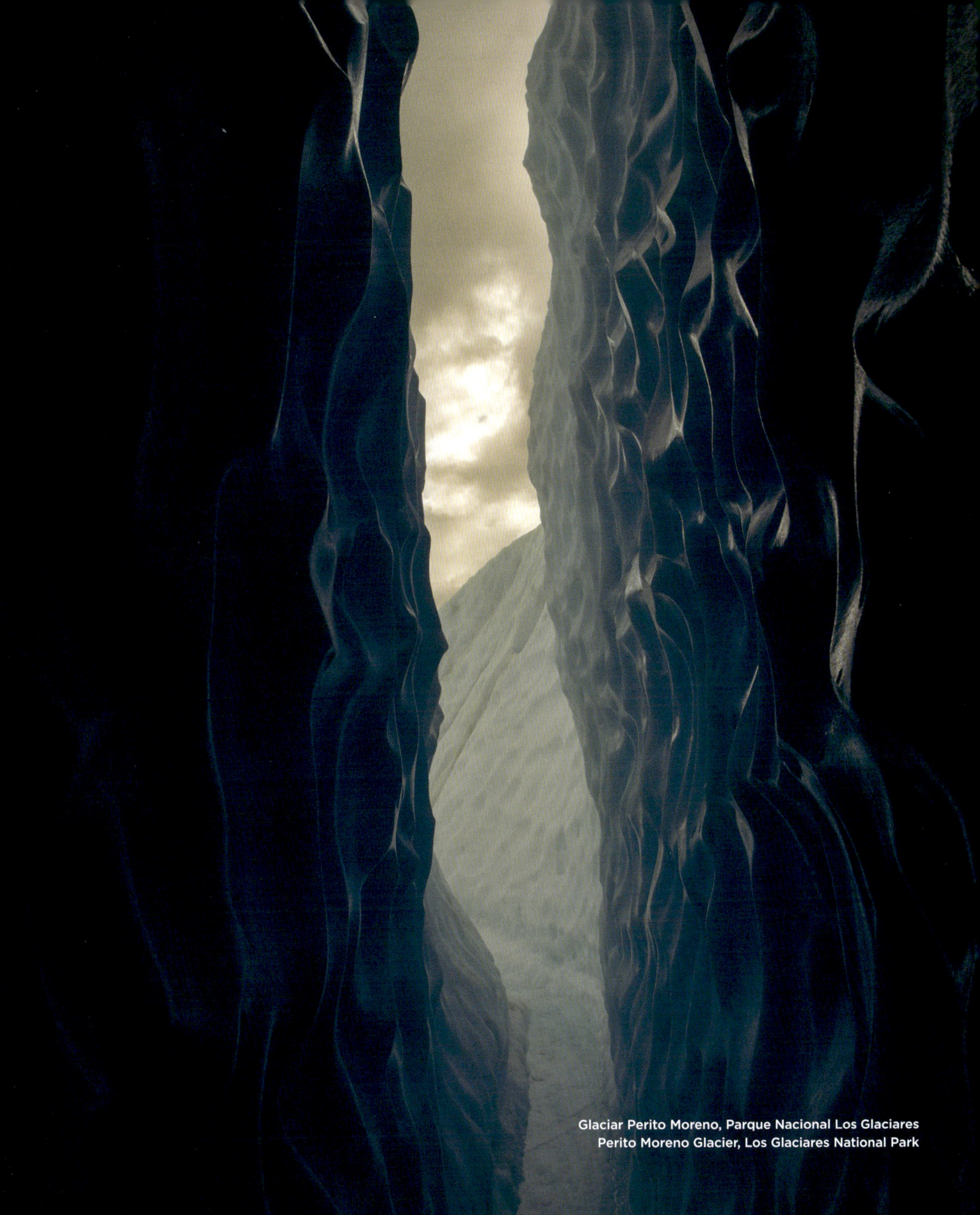

Glaciar Perito Moreno, Parque Nacional Los Glaciares
Perito Moreno Glacier, Los Glaciares National Park

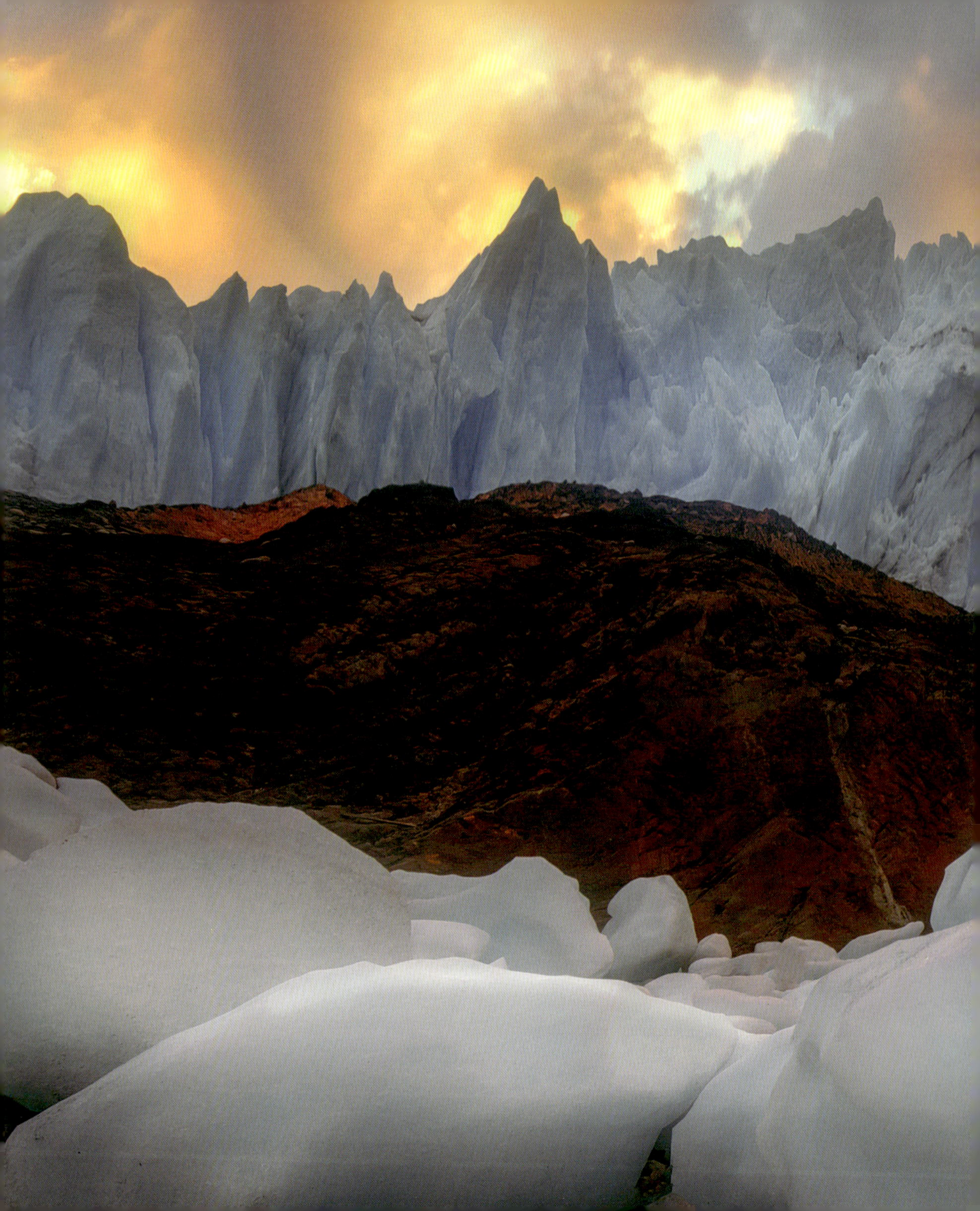

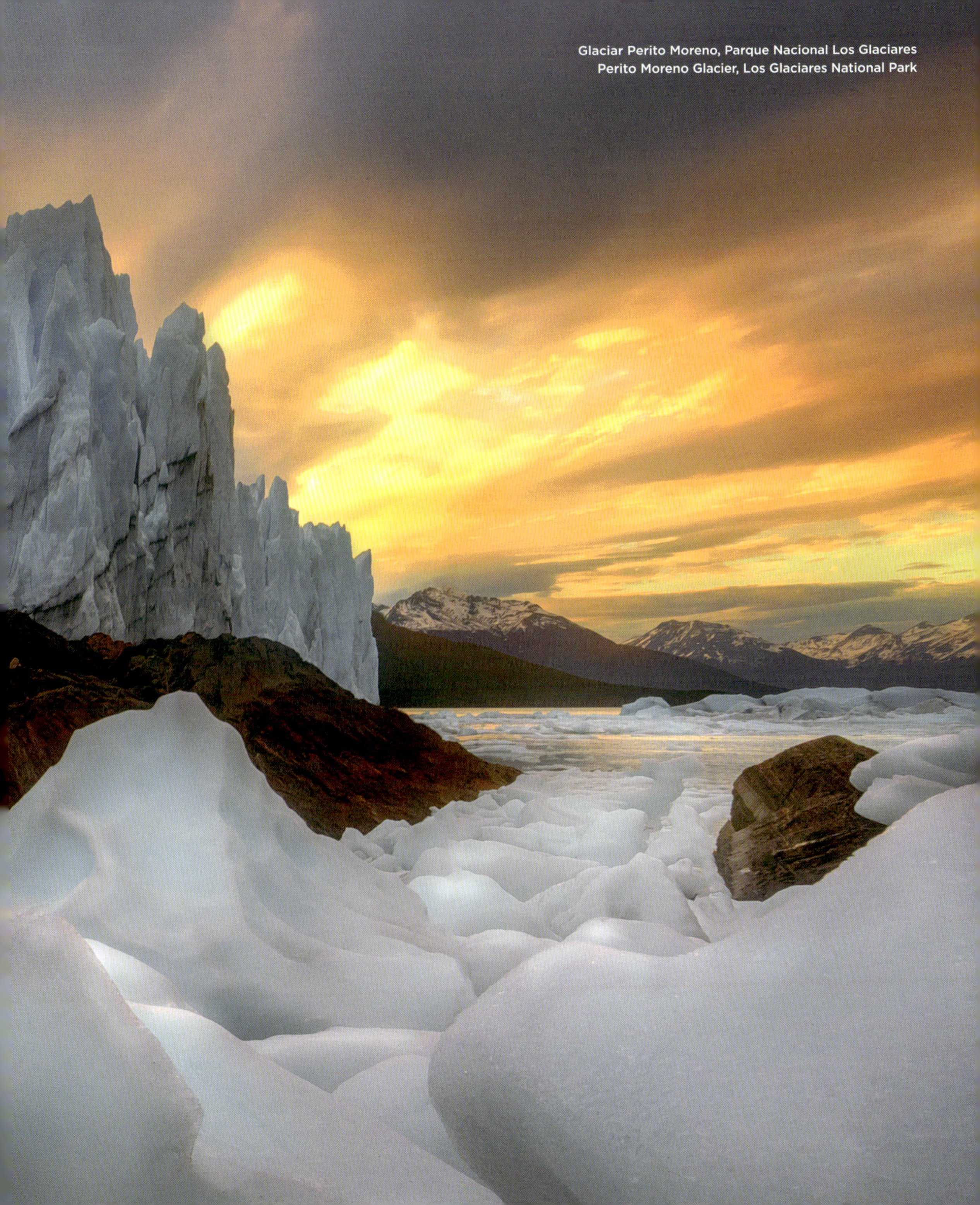

Glaciar Perito Moreno, Parque Nacional Los Glaciares
Perito Moreno Glacier, Los Glaciares National Park

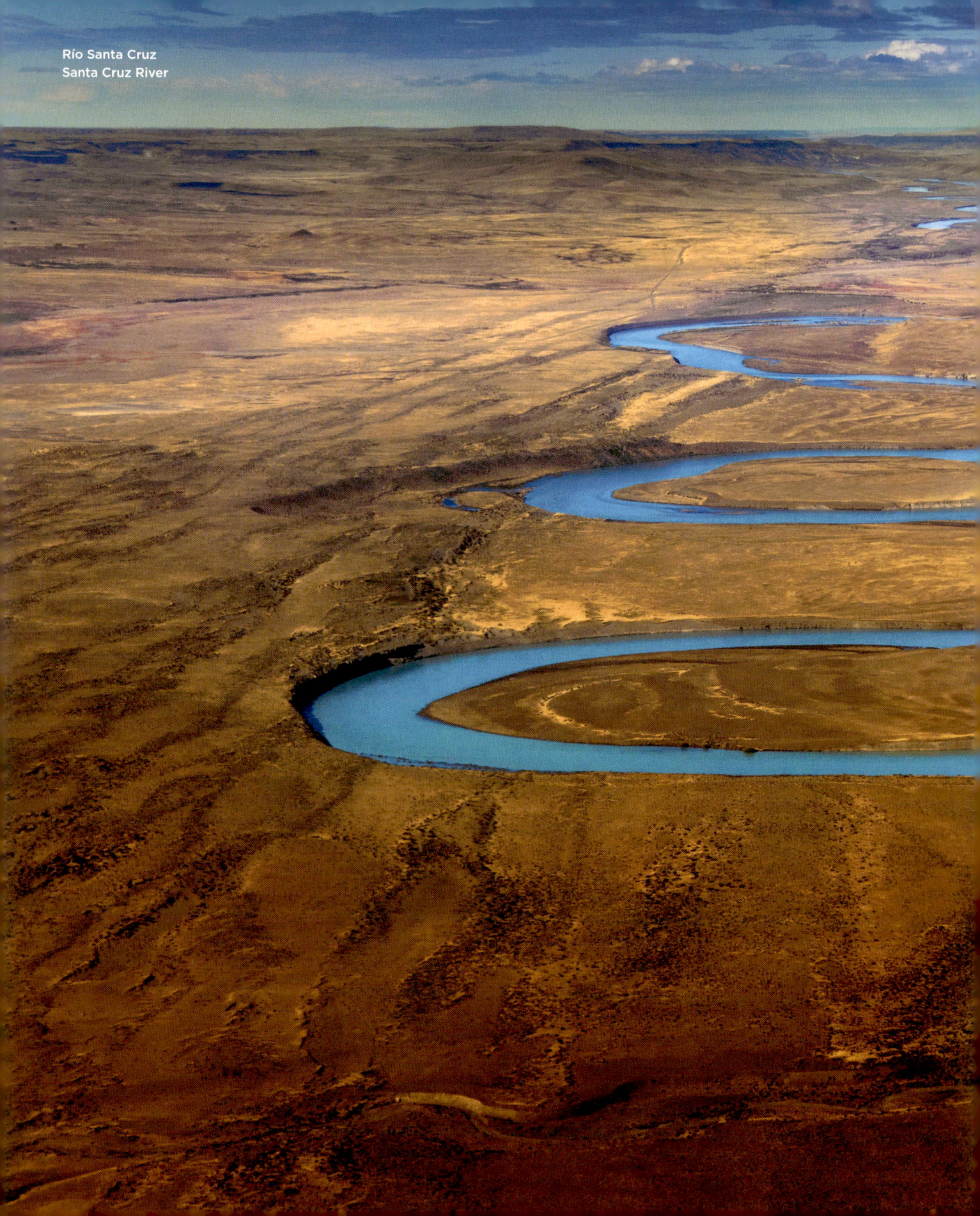
Río Santa Cruz
Santa Cruz River

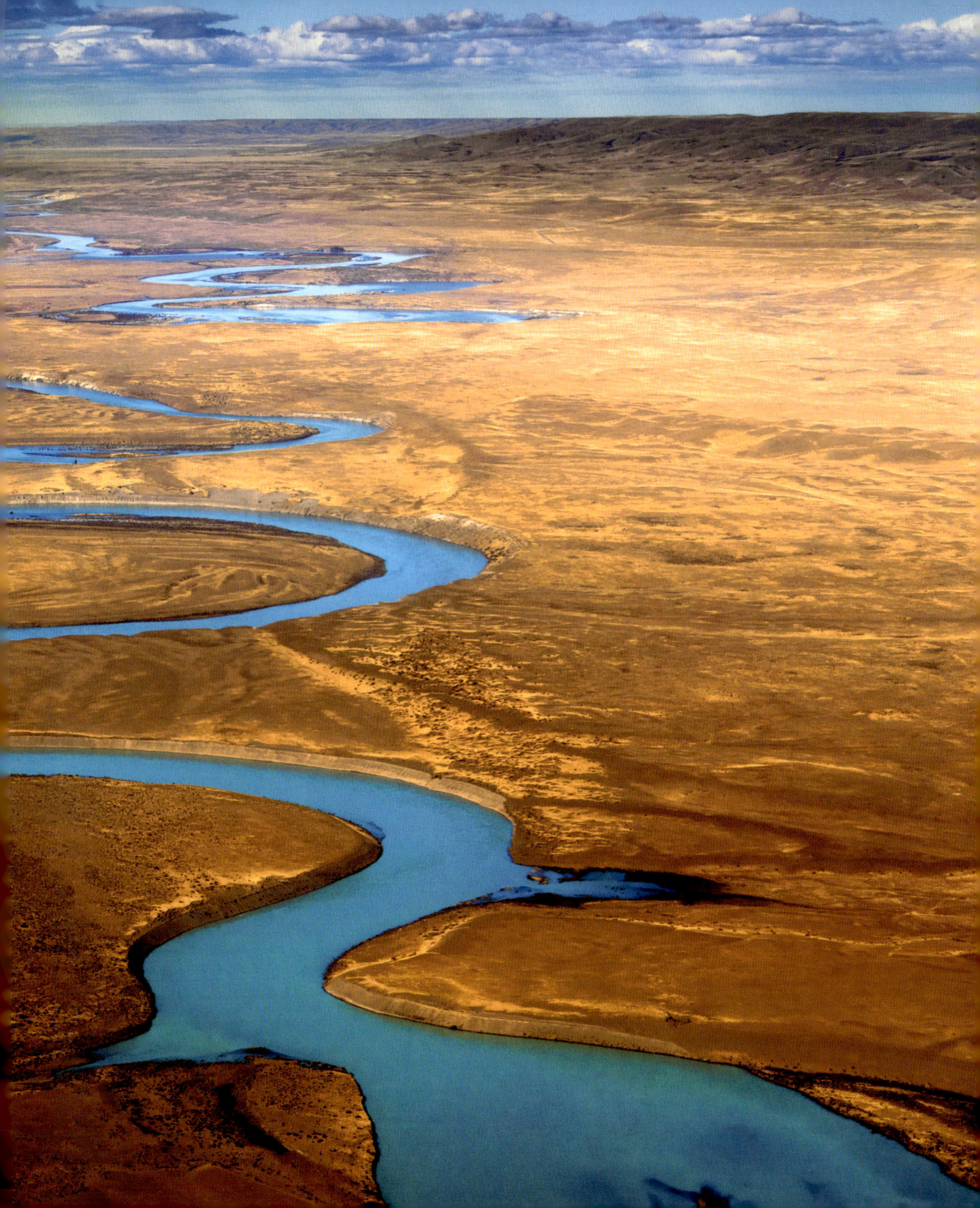

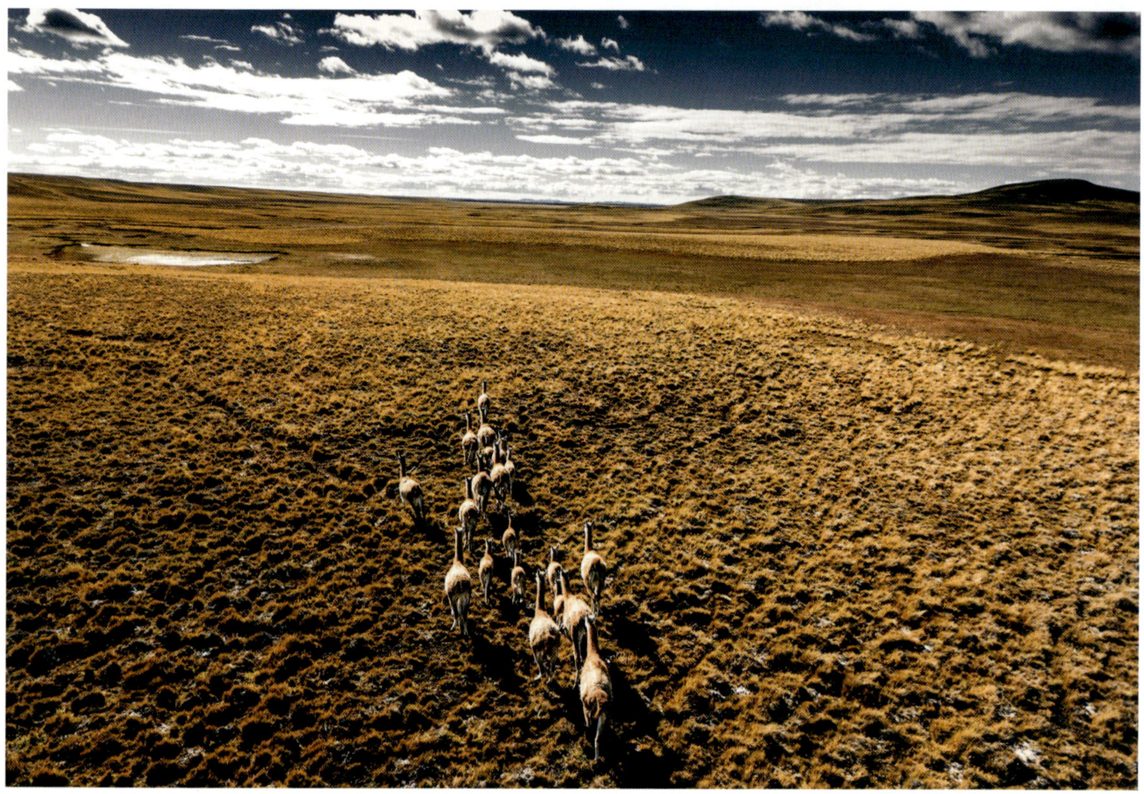

Guanacos

Guanacos

In the Andean region and in the vast grassland of southern Patagonia one will encounter small, wild herds of guanacos. Before the arrival of the Spanish, there were 50 million guanacos in South America. Guanacos were hunted for their fur and later to gain grazing land for sheep. By crossing- breeding the guanaco, the domesticated lama was created.

Guanacos

Dans la région des Andes et dans les plaines herbeuses du sud de la Patagonie prospèrent de nombreux petits guanacos sauvages. Avant l'arrivée des Espagnols, 50 millions de guanacos vivaient en Amérique du Sud. Ils furent chassés pour leur fourrure, puis pour exploiter les terres destinées à l'élevage ovin. Le lama domestique est le descendant par croisement du guanaco.

Guanakos

Im Andengebiet und im weiten Grasland Süd-Patagoniens trifft man auf kleine, wilde Guanakoherden. Vor der Ankunft der Spanier gab es 50 Millionen Guanakos in Südamerika. Wegen ihres Fells und später, um Weidefläche für Schafe zu gewinnen, wurden Guanakos gejagt. Durch Kreuzung entstand aus dem Guanako das Haustier Lama.

Guanacos

En la región andina y en las vastas praderas del sur de la Patagonia, se encuentran pequeñas y salvajes manadas de guanacos. Antes de la llegada de los españoles, había 50 millones de guanacos en Sudamérica. Los guanacos eran cazados por su piel y más tarde para ganar pastos para las ovejas. Al cruzar el guanaco se creó la llama como animal domesticado.

Guanacos

Na região andina e na vasta pastagem do sul da Patagônia você encontrará pequenos rebanhos selvagens de guanacos. Antes da chegada dos espanhóis, existiam 50 milhões de guanacos na América do Sul. Os guanacos eram caçados por causa das suas peles e mais tarde para ganhar terras de pasto para ovelhas. Devido ao cruzamento do guanaco, surgiu o lama, como animal de estimação.

Guanaco's

In het Andesgebied en in het uitgestrekte grasland van Zuid-Patagonië komt men kleine, wilde kuddes guanaco's tegen. Vóór de komst van de Spanjaarden waren er in Zuid-Amerika 50 miljoen guanaco's. Er wordt op ze gejaagd vanwege hun vacht en later om weidegrond voor schapen te winnen. Door kruising ontstond uit de guanaco het huisdier lama.

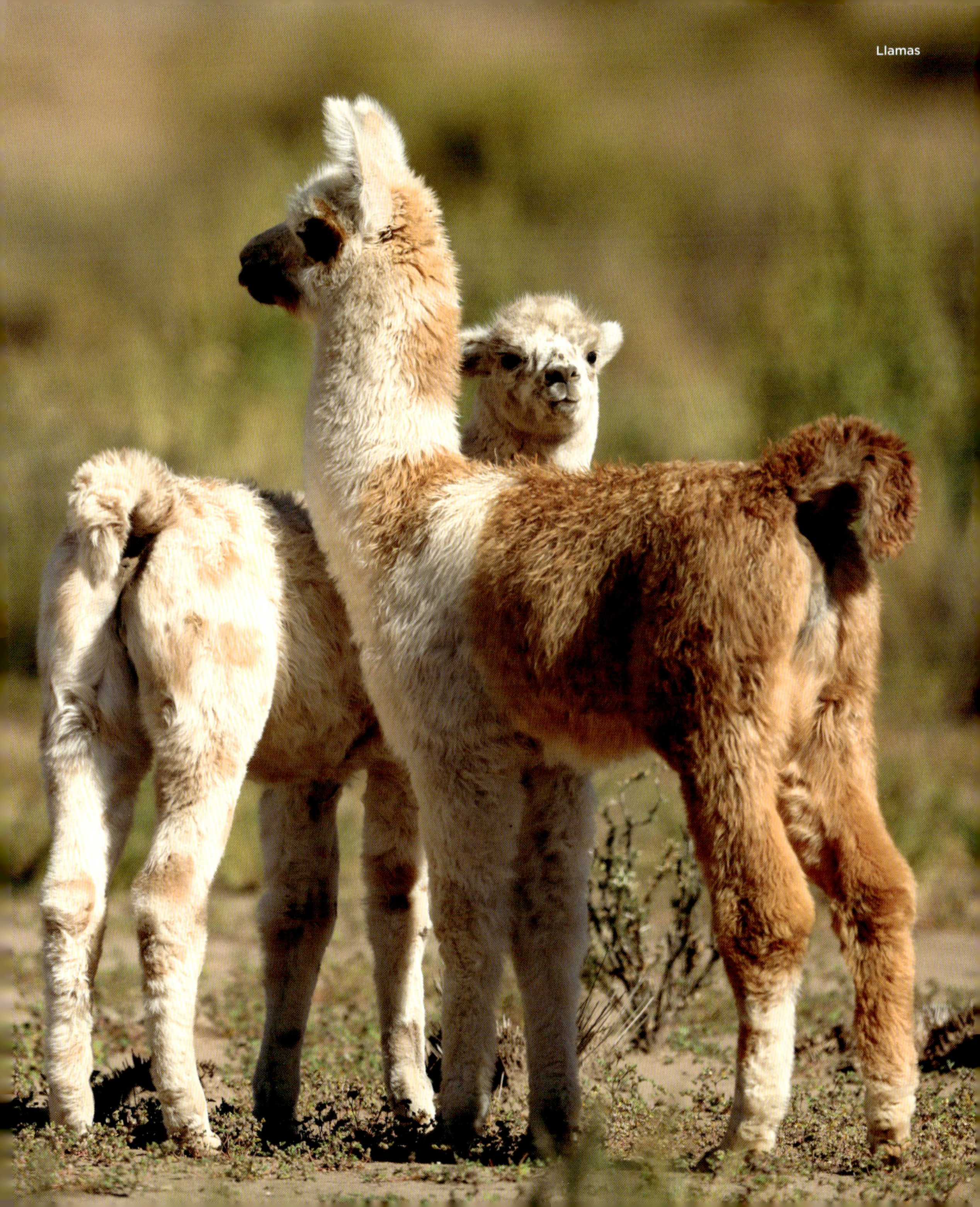
Llamas

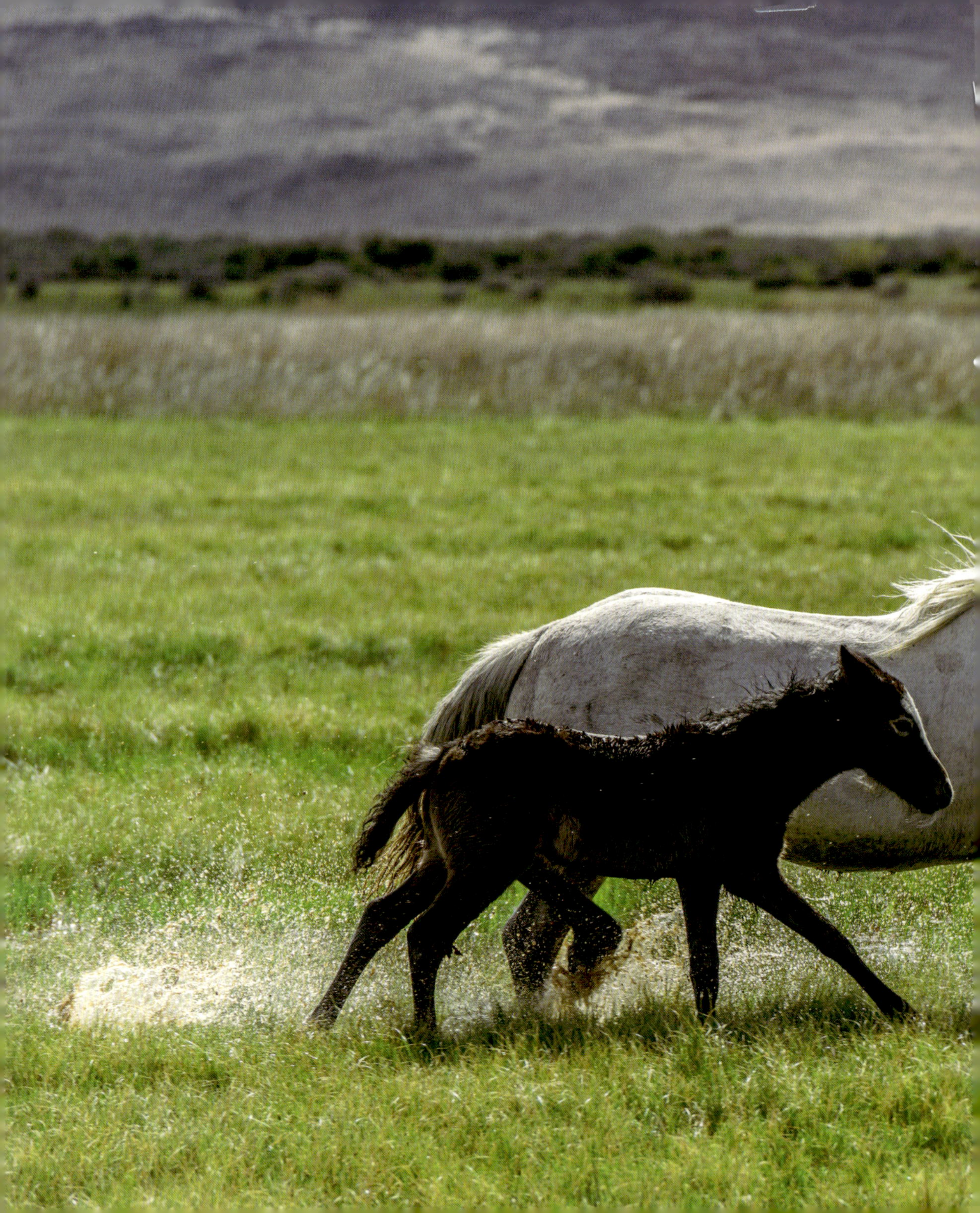

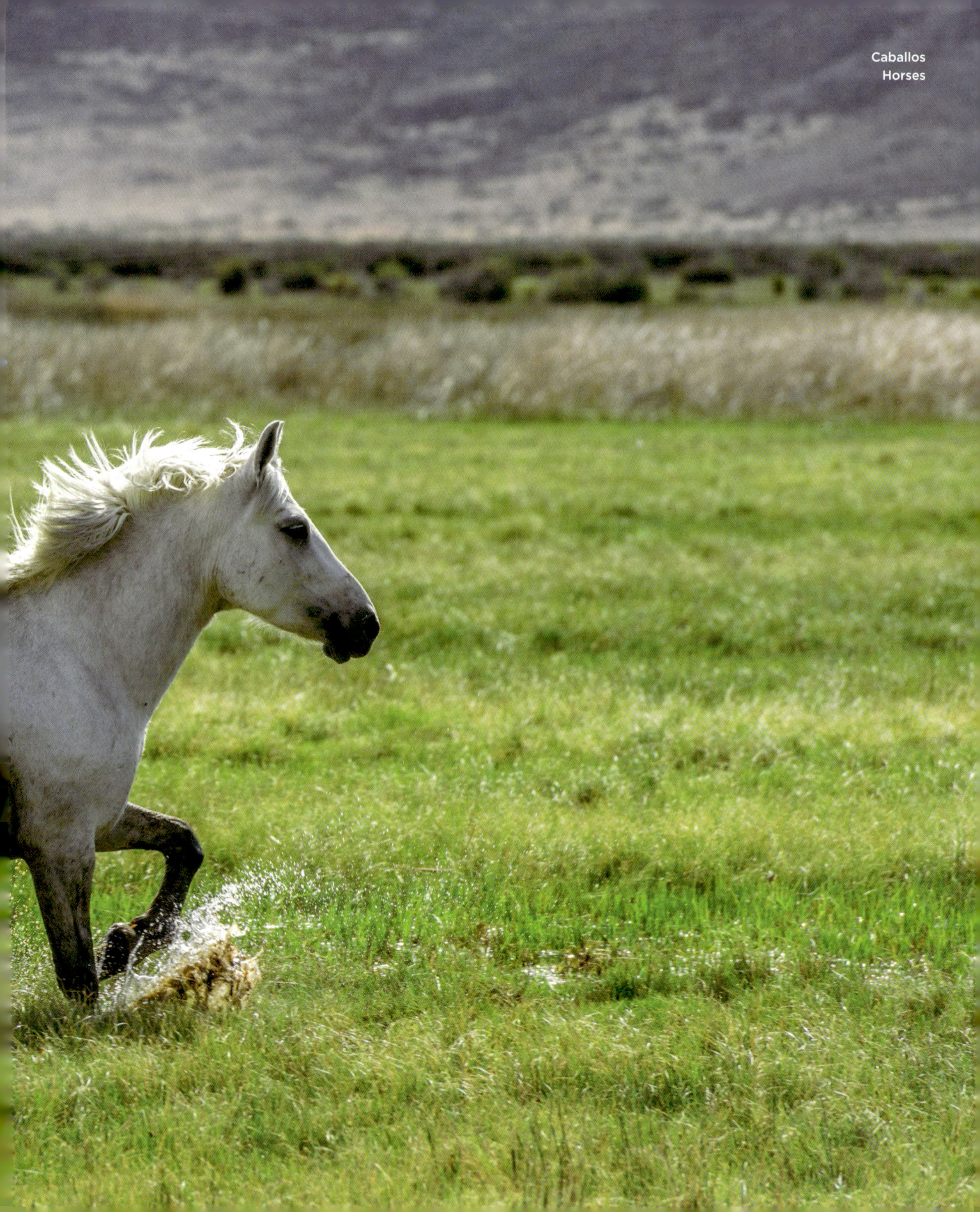
Caballos
Horses

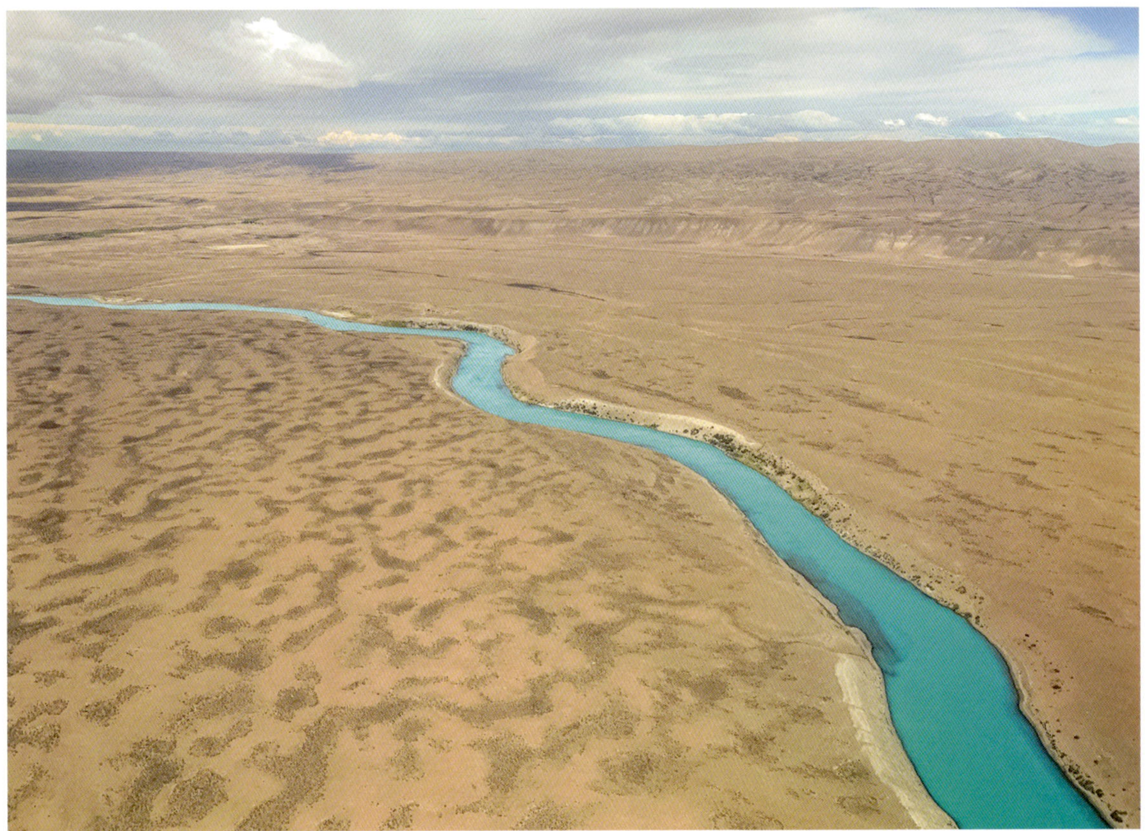

Río Santa Cruz
Santa Cruz River

El Calafate

Near the source of the Santa Cruz River, which feeds from the glacial Lake Argentino, the prevalent image is that of the flat Patagonian landscape, featuring grasslands, sheep estancias and horses. The most important settlement today is El Calafate, located on the southern shore of Lake Argentino. It is the starting point for excursions to the Los Glaciares National Park. El Calafate owes its name to the local berry bush, which bears blue fruit. In 1834, Captain Robert FitzRoy, who gave his name to the Fitz Roy Massif, and Charles Darwin of *HMS Beagle* undertook an expedition up the Rio Santa Cruz, but they turned back after 161 km (100 mi) and did not reach El Calafate.

El Calafate

Dans la région du fleuve Santa Cruz, émissaire du lac glaciaire Argentino, le plat paysage naturel typique de Patagonie se définit ainsi : plaines herbeuses, *estancias* vivant de l'élevage ovin et chevaux. La plus grande communauté actuelle, El Calafate, est située sur la rive sud du Lago Argentino. Cette petite ville, qui a emprunté son nom à un buisson à baies bleues local, est un parfait point de départ pour les randonnées dans le parc naturel de Los Glaciares. En 1834, le capitaine Robert FitzRoy, éponyme du massif, et Charles Darwin, arrivés à bord du navire *HMS Beagle,* menèrent une expédition destinée à remonter le río Santa Cruz. Ils durent cependant faire demi-tour après 161 km et n'atteignirent jamais El Calafate.

El Calafate

Im Gebiet des Santa Cruz-Flusses, der sich aus dem Gletschersee Lago Argentino speist, ist ein Bild bestimmend für die ebene patagonische Naturlandschaft: Grasland, Schaf-Estanzias und Pferde. Die wichtigste Siedlung heute ist El Calafate, die am Südufer des Lago Argentino liegt. Sie ist Ausgangspunkt für Ausflüge in den Naturpark Los Glaciares. Seinen Namen hat El Calafate dem hier heimischen Blaubeerbusch zu verdanken. 1834 unternahmen Kapitän Robert FitzRoy, Namensgeber des Fitz-Roy-Massivs, und Charles Darwin von der *HMS Beagle* eine Expeditionsreise den Rio Santa Cruz aufwärts. Sie kehrten aber nach 161 km um und kamen nicht bis El Calafate.

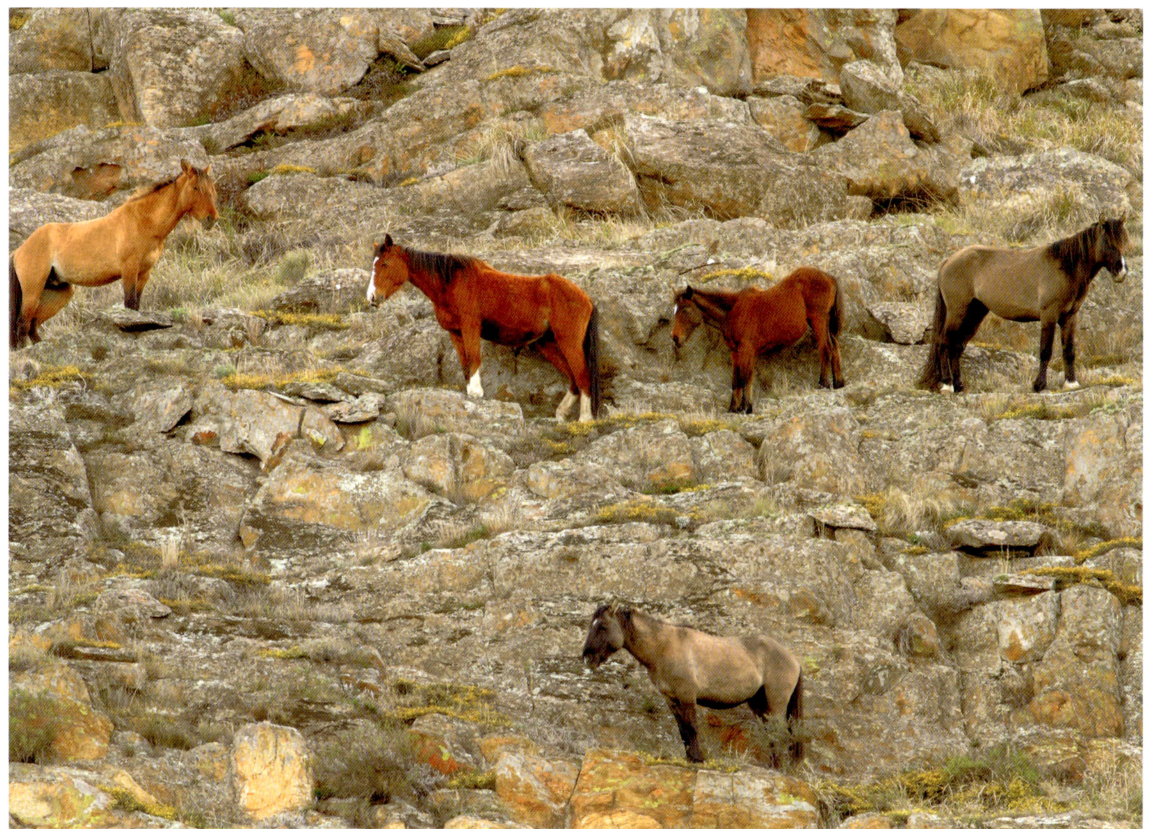

Caballos
Horses

El Calafate

En la zona del río Santa Cruz, que se
alimenta del lago glaciar Argentino, una
imagen domina el paisaje natural de la
llanura patagónica: pastizales, estancias
de ovejas y caballos. El asentamiento
más importante hoy en día es El Calafate,
ubicado en la ribera sur del Lago
Argentino. Es el punto de partida de
las excursiones al Parque Nacional Los
Glaciares. El Calafate debe su nombre
al arbusto de arándanos local. En 1834,
el capitán Robert FitzRoy, que dio su
nombre al macizo Fitz Roy, y Charles
Darwin del *HMS Beagle* emprendieron
una expedición por el río Santa Cruz, pero
regresaron después de 161 km y no llegaron
a El Calafate.

El Calafate

Na área do Rio Santa Cruz, que se alimenta
do lago glacial Lago Argentino, uma
imagem é dominante na paisagem natural
plana da Patagônia: prados, fazendas
de ovelhas e cavalos. O povoado mais
importante hoje é El Calafate, localizado
na margem sul do Lago Argentino. É o
ponto de partida para excursões ao Parque
Natural Los Glaciares. El Calafate deve o
seu nome ao arbusto de mirtilo local. Em
1834, o Capitão Robert FitzRoy, que deu
seu nome ao Maciço Fitz Roy, e Charles
Darwin, do *HMS Beagle,* empreenderam
uma expedição pelo Rio Santa Cruz. Mas
eles voltaram depois de 161 km e não
chegaram a El Calafate.

El Calafate

In het gebied van de rivier Santa Cruz,
die water krijgt uit het gletsjermeer
Argentinomeer, is één beeld bepalend voor
het vlakke Patagonische natuurlandschap:
de graslanden, schaap-estancias en
paarden. De belangrijkste nederzetting
vandaag de dag is El Calafate, gelegen aan
de zuidelijke oever van het Argentinomeer.
Het is het startpunt voor excursies naar het
natuurpark Los Glaciares. El Calafate dankt
zijn naam aan de lokale bosbessenstruik.
In 1834 ondernamen kapitein Robert
FitzRoy, naamgever van de Fitz Roy-berg,
en Charles Darwin met de *HMS Beagle*
een expeditie naar de Rio Santa Cruz.
Ze keerden echter na 161 km terug en
bereikten El Calafate niet.

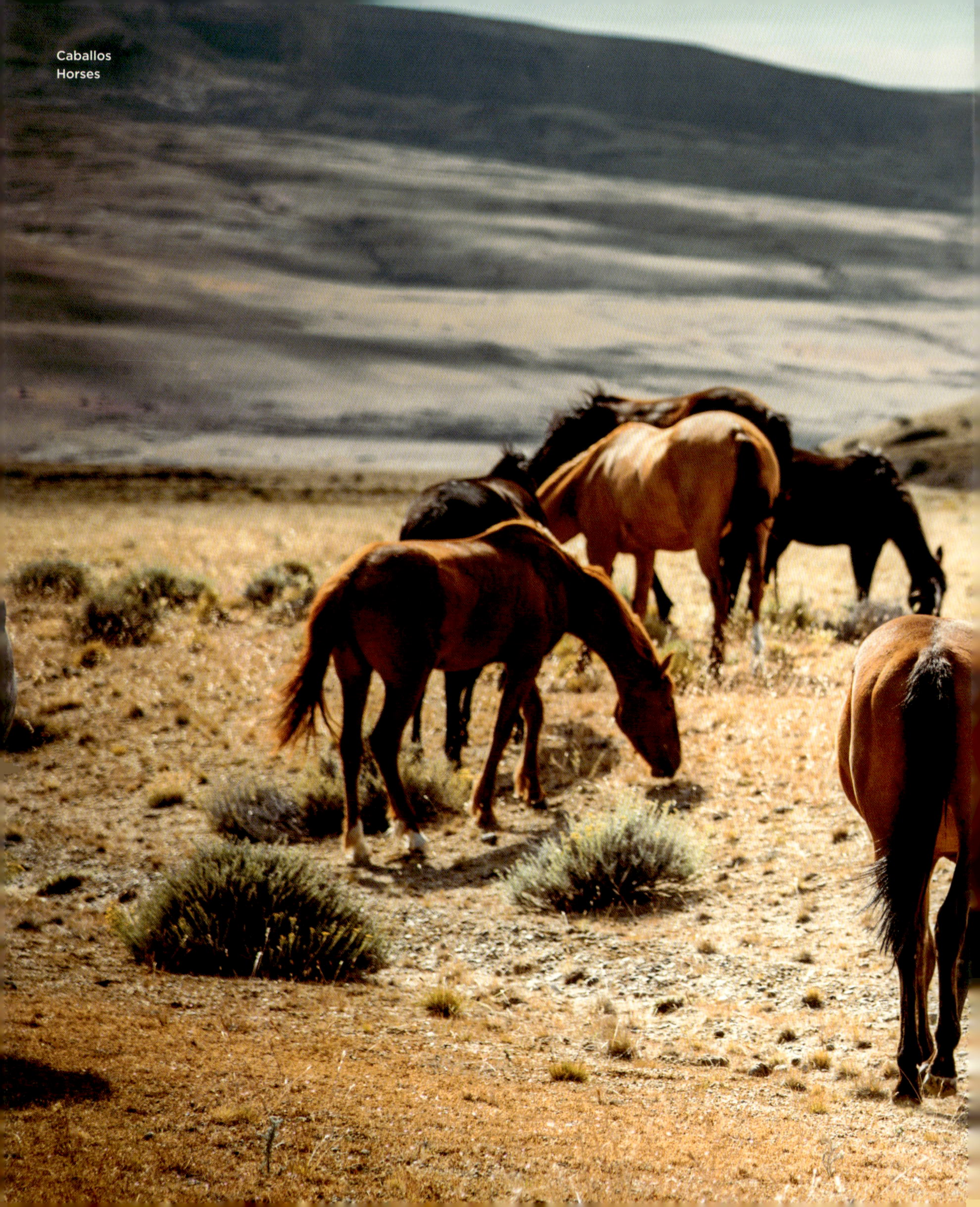
Caballos
Horses

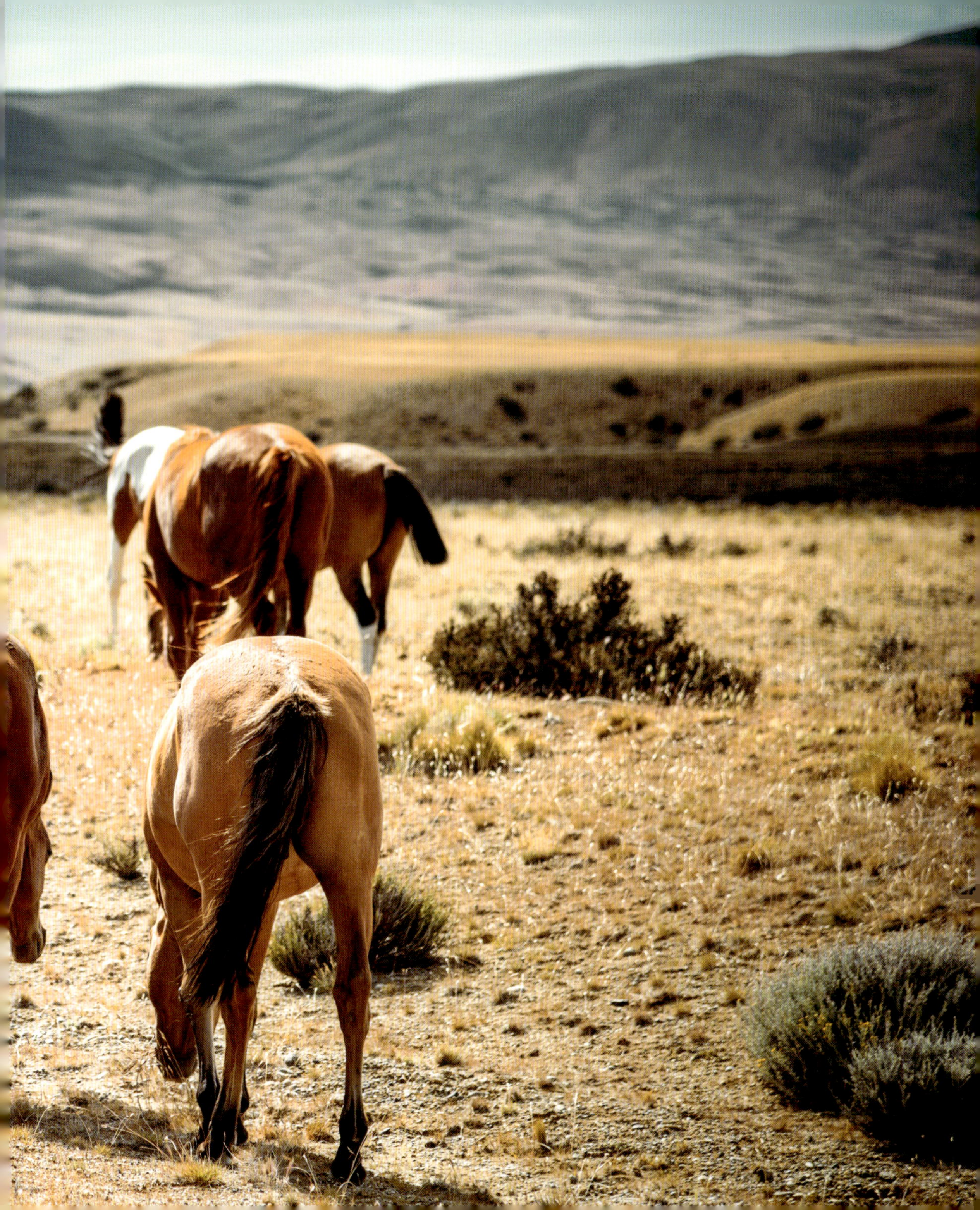

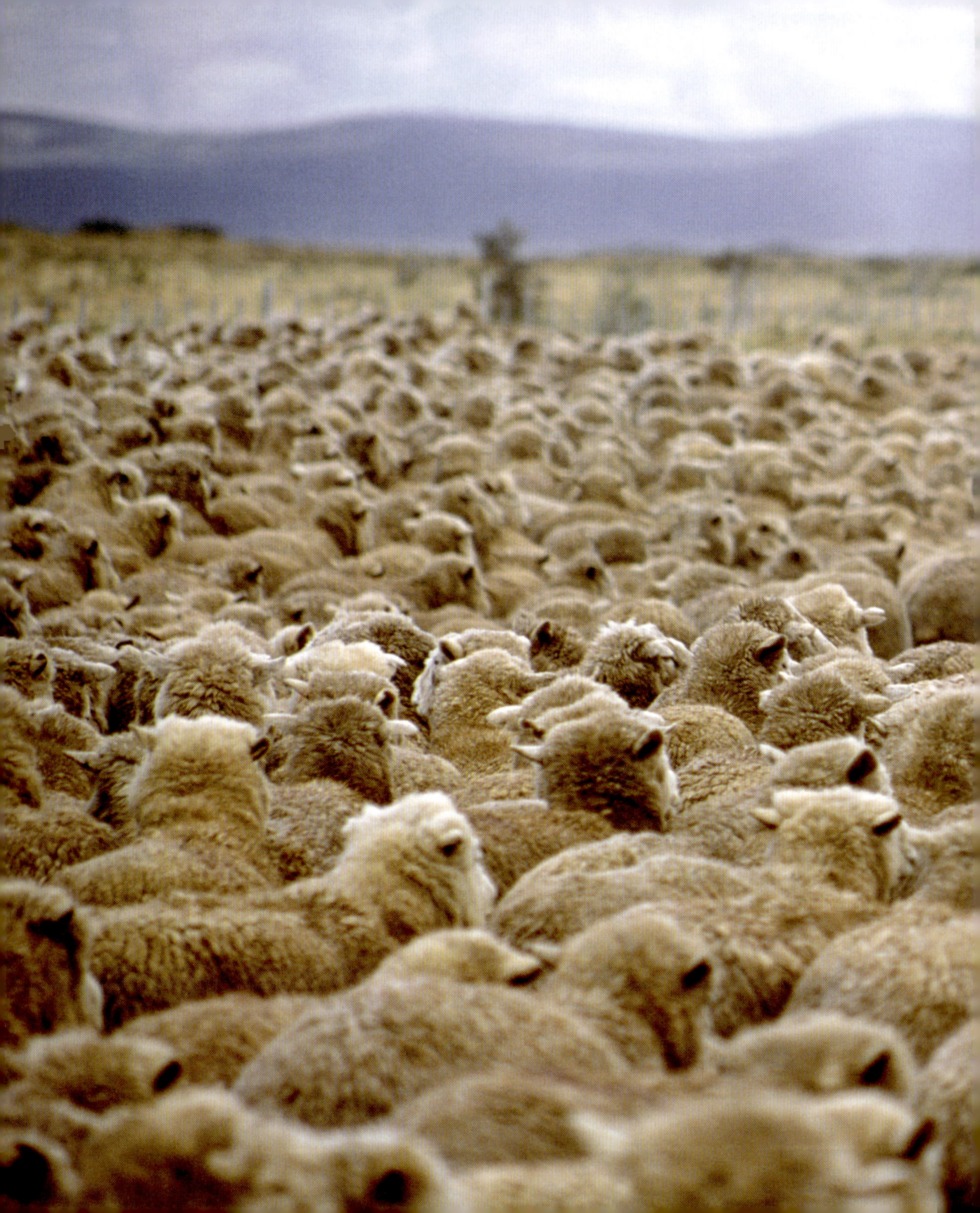

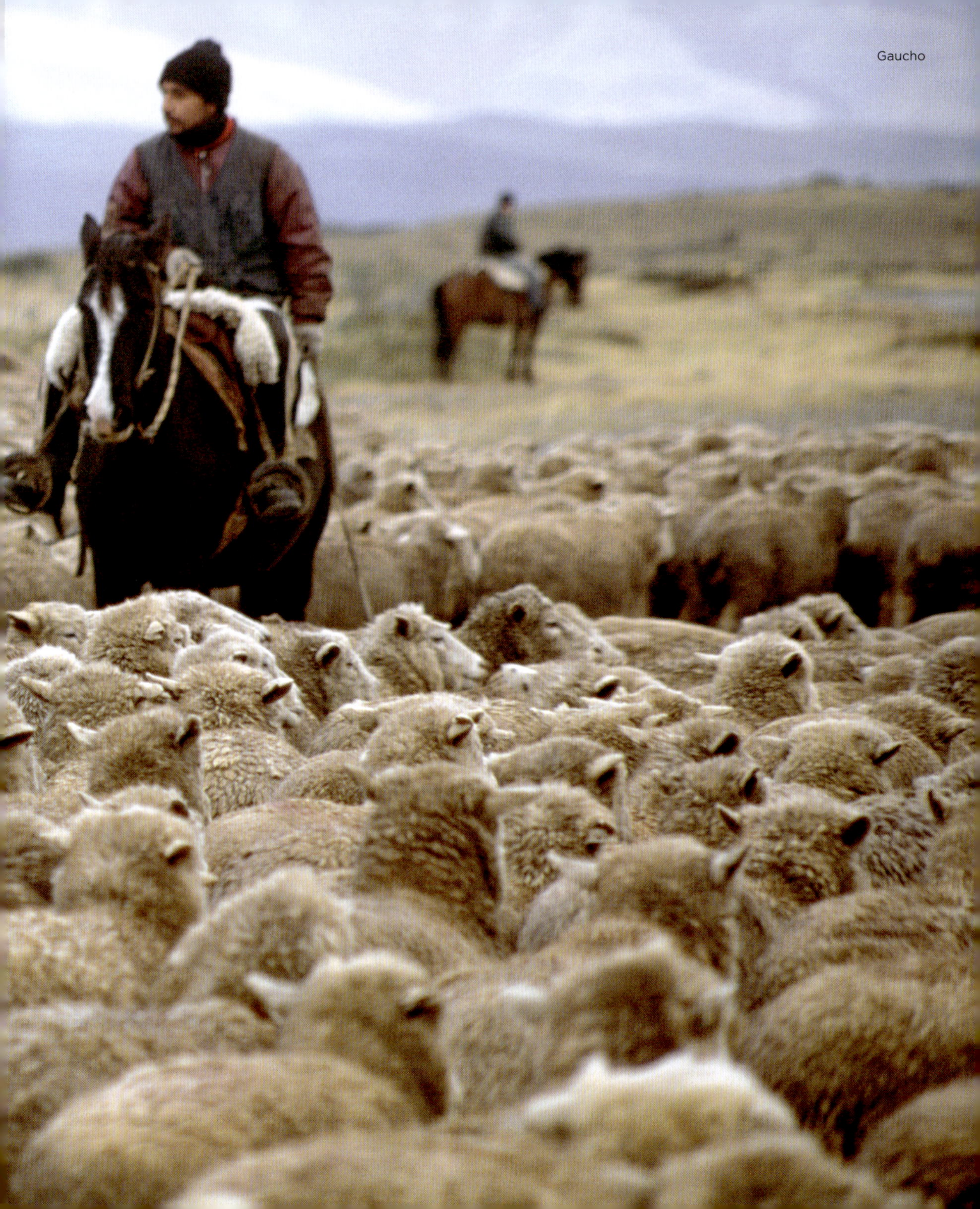
Gaucho

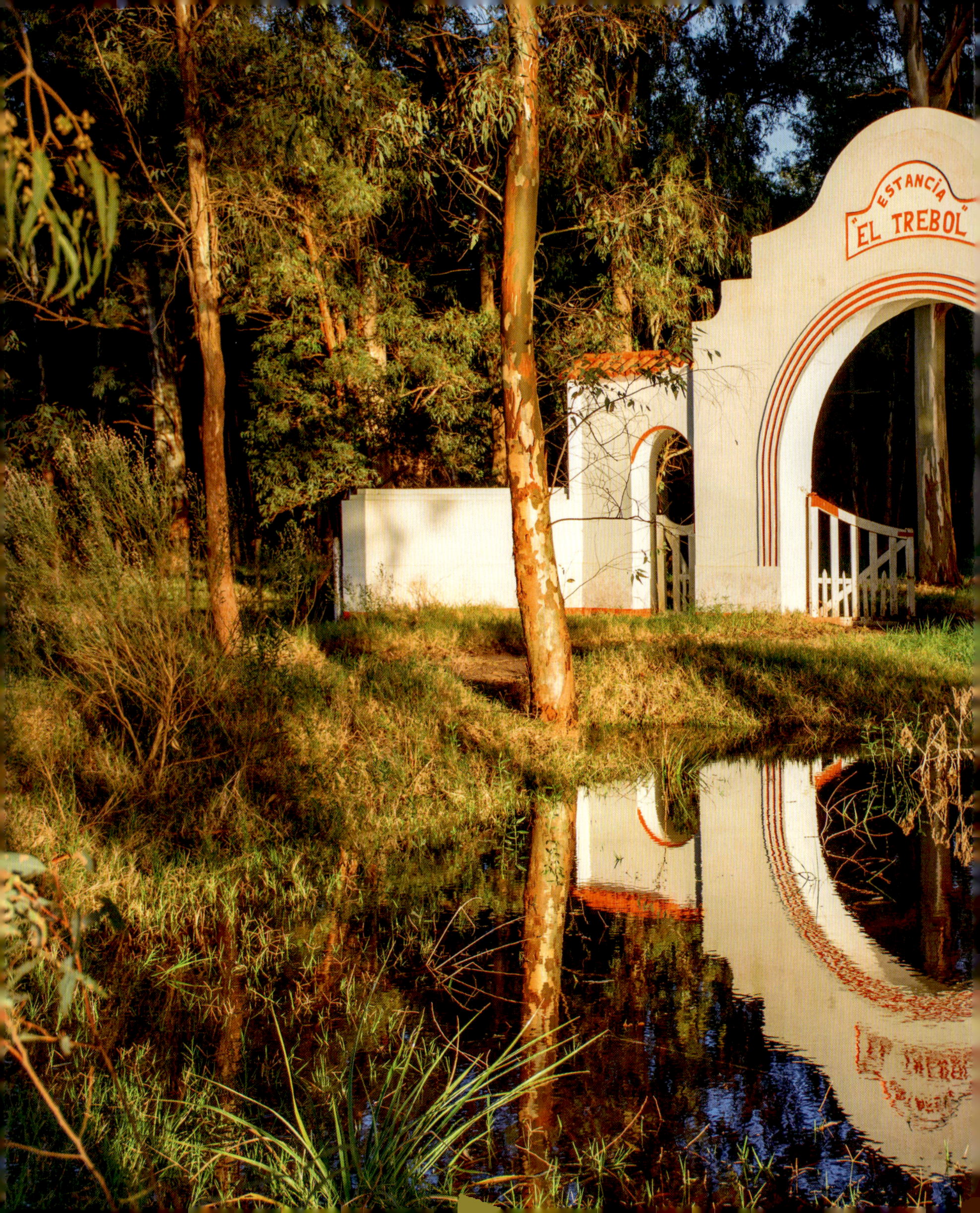

ESTANCIA
"EL TREBOL"

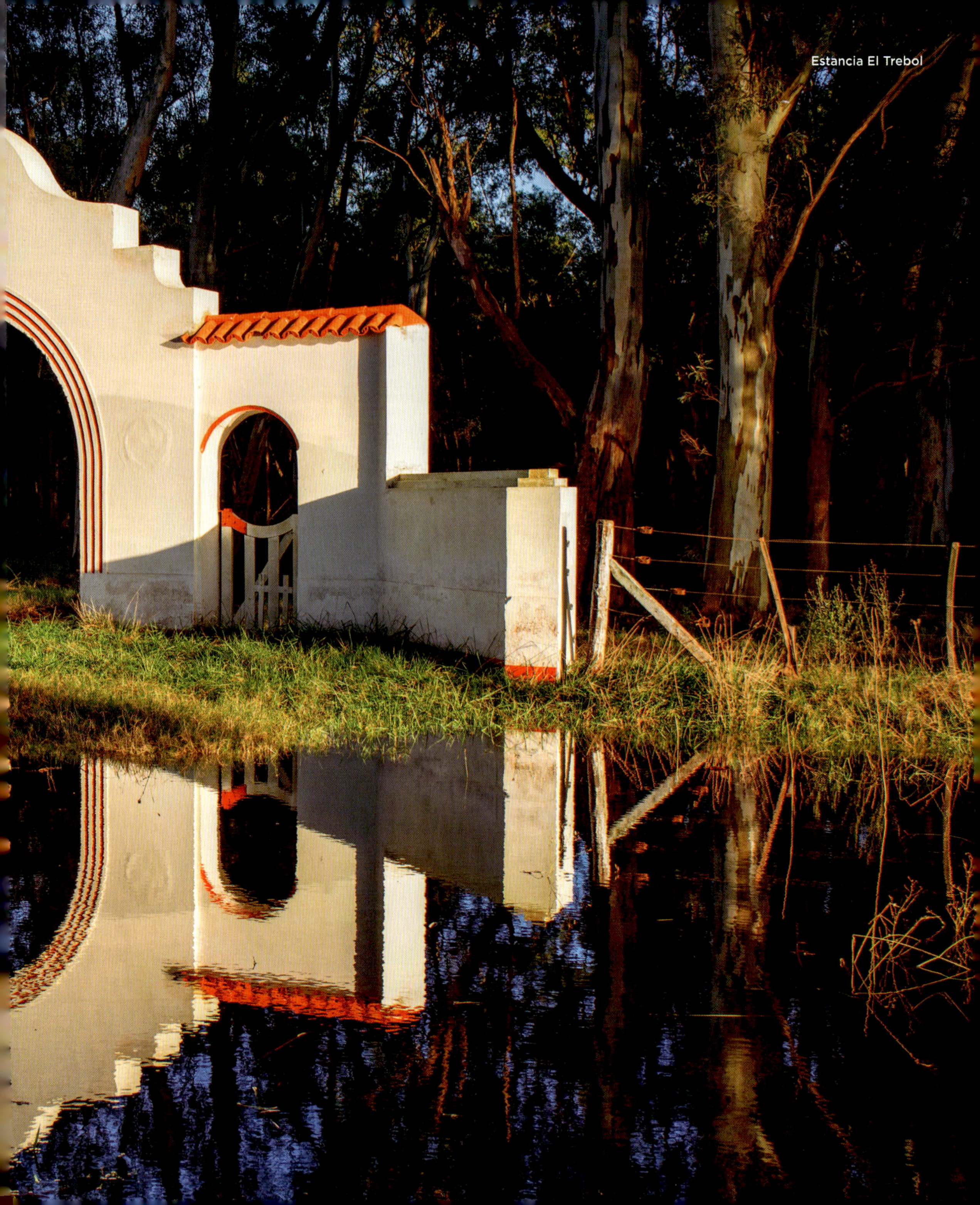
Estancia El Trebol

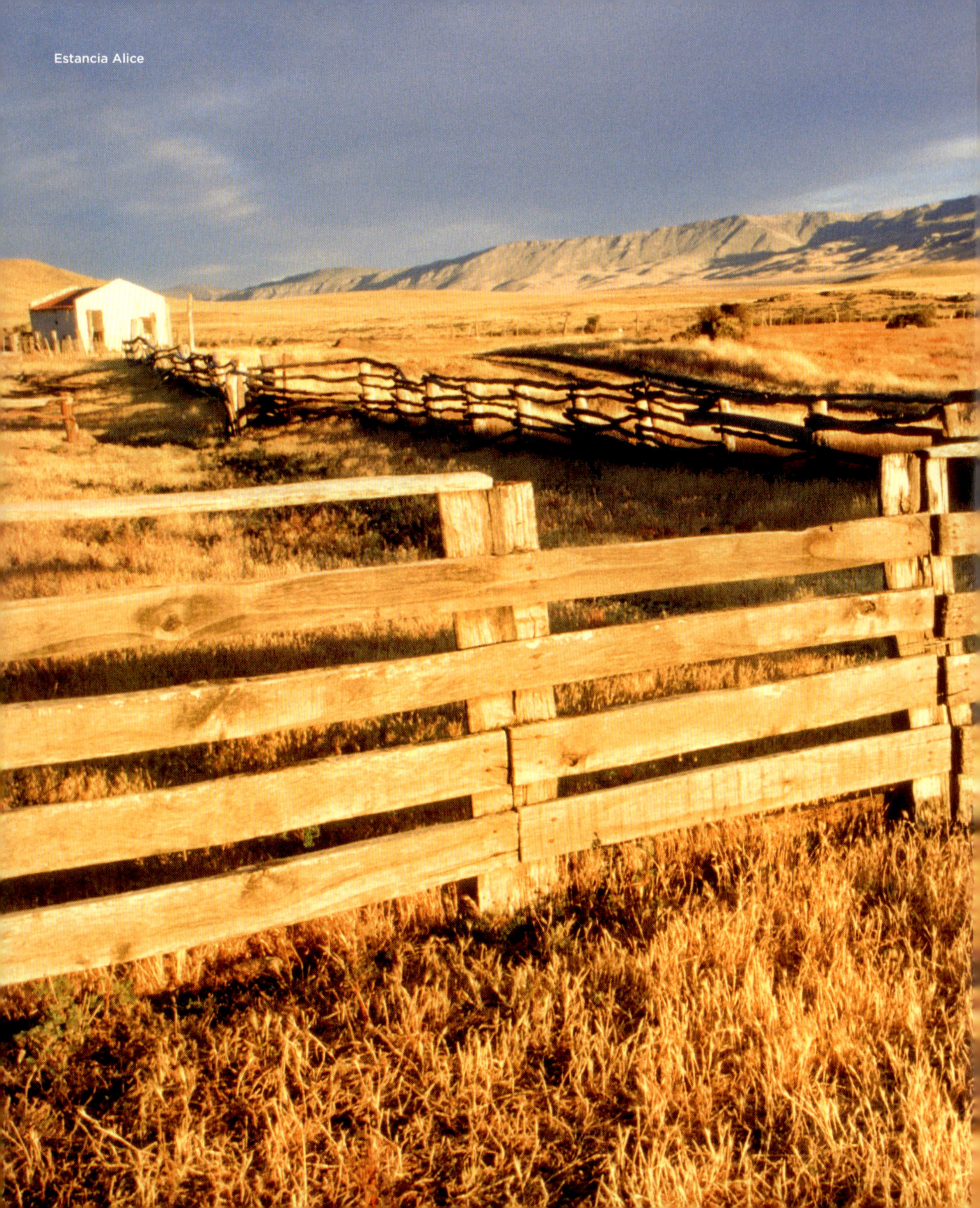
Estancia Alice

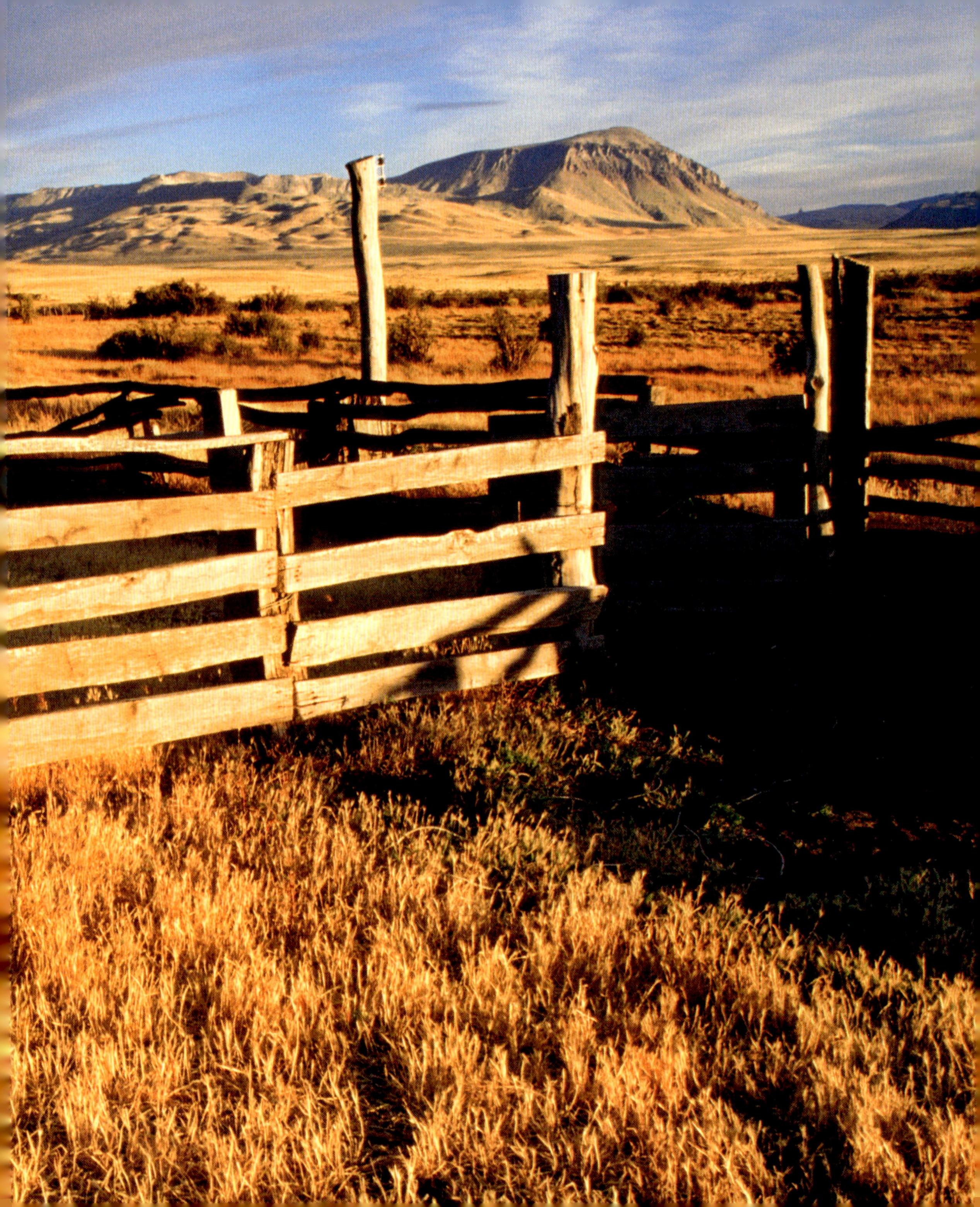

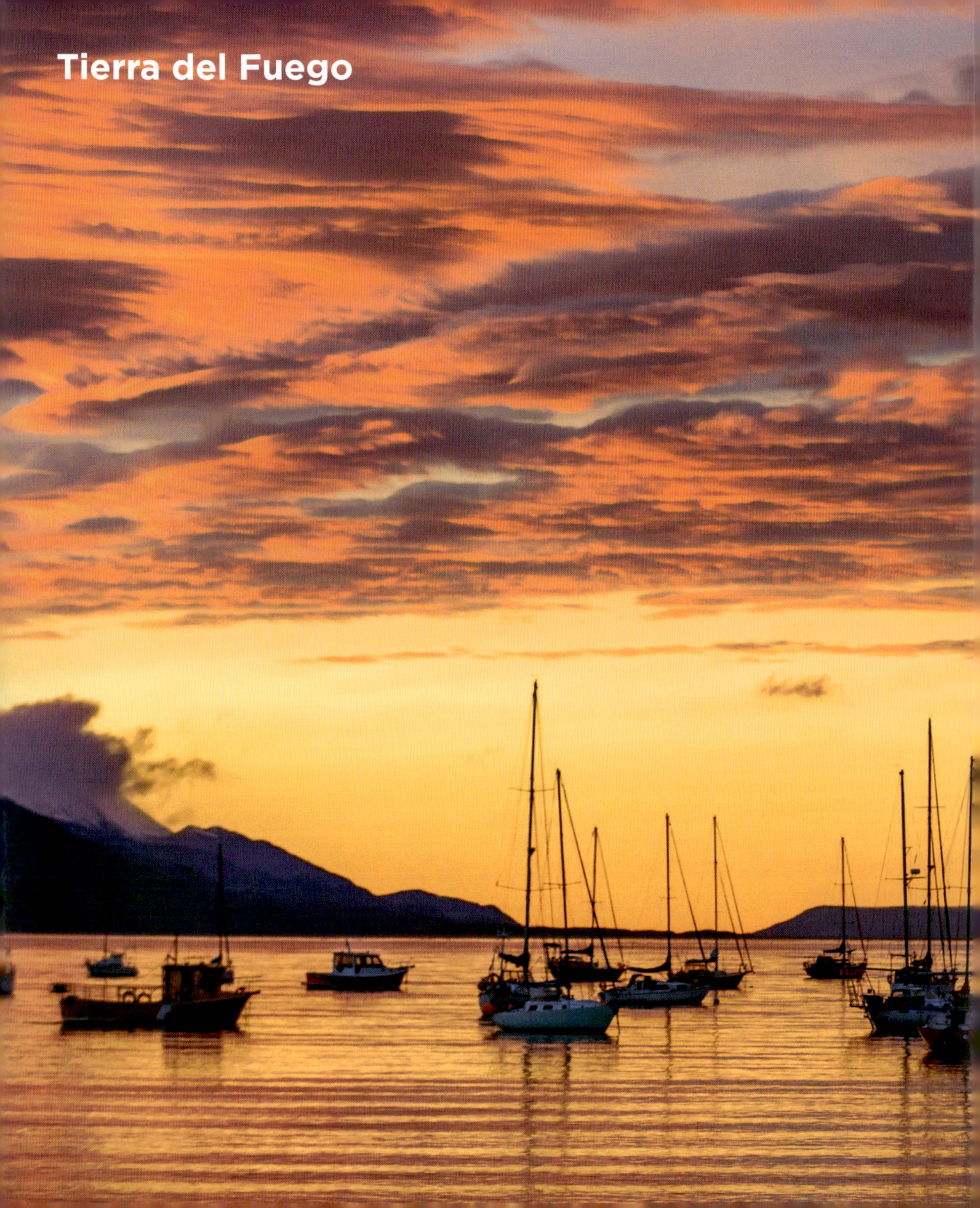
Tierra del Fuego

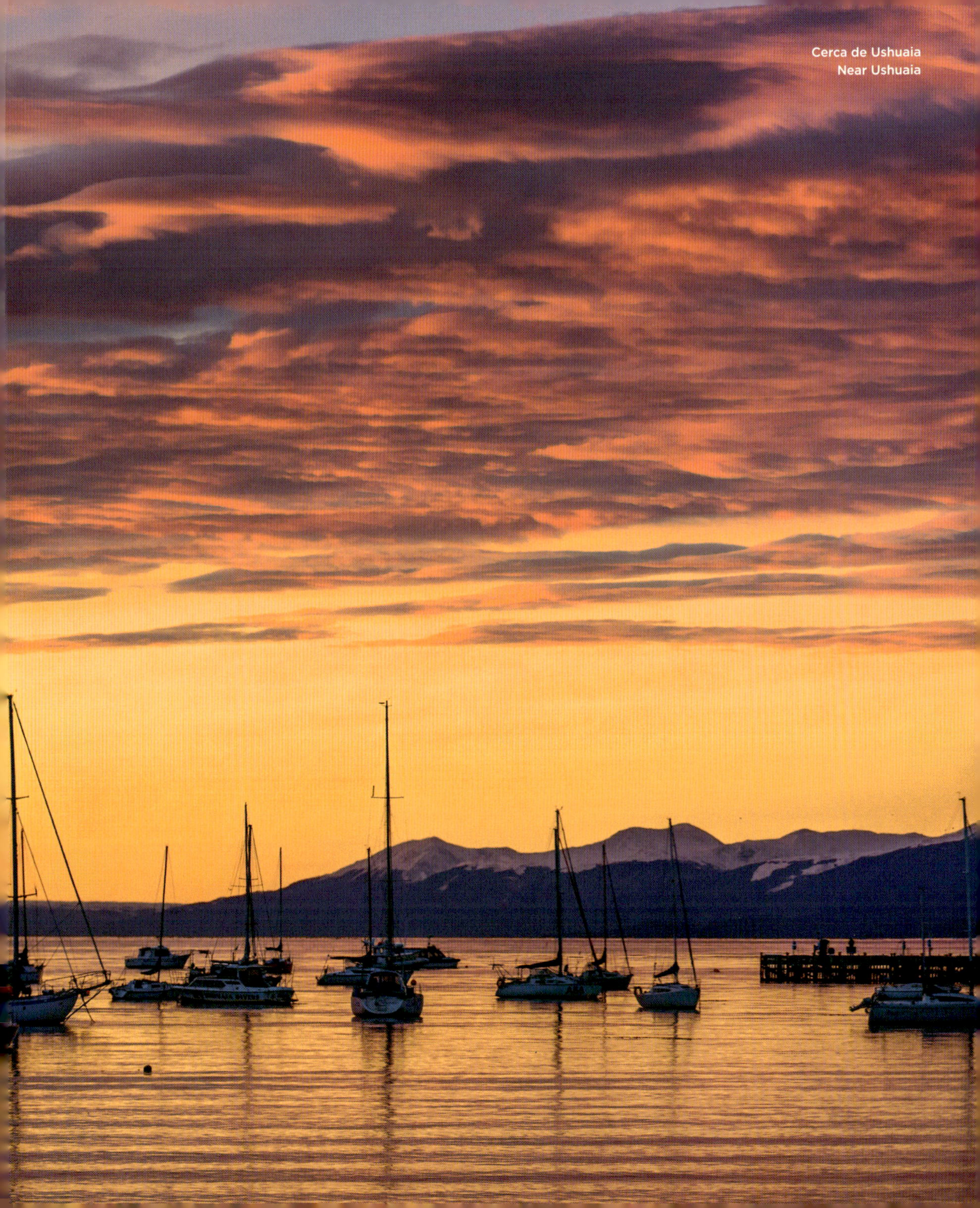

Cerca de Ushuaia
Near Ushuaia

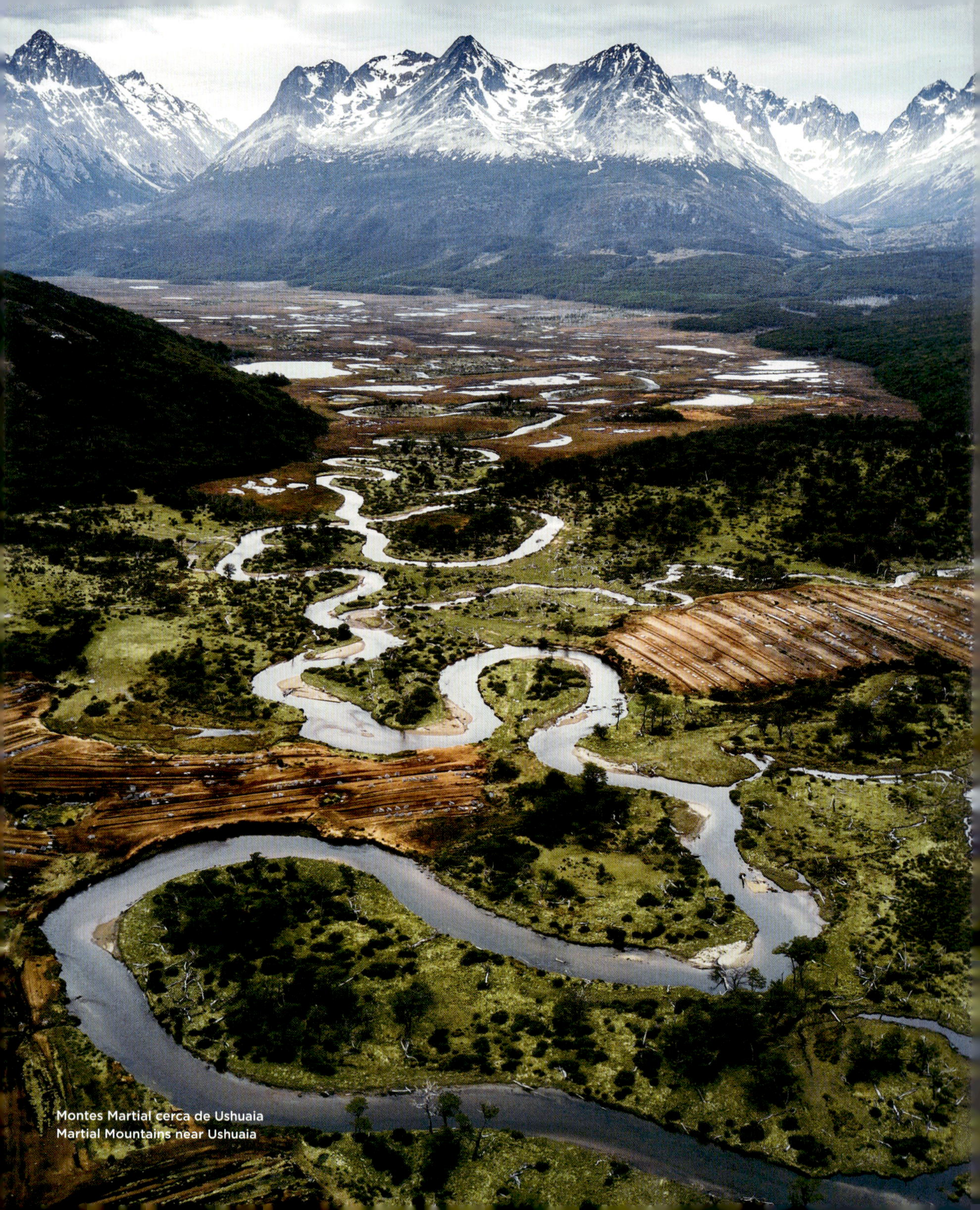

Montes Martial cerca de Ushuaia
Martial Mountains near Ushuaia

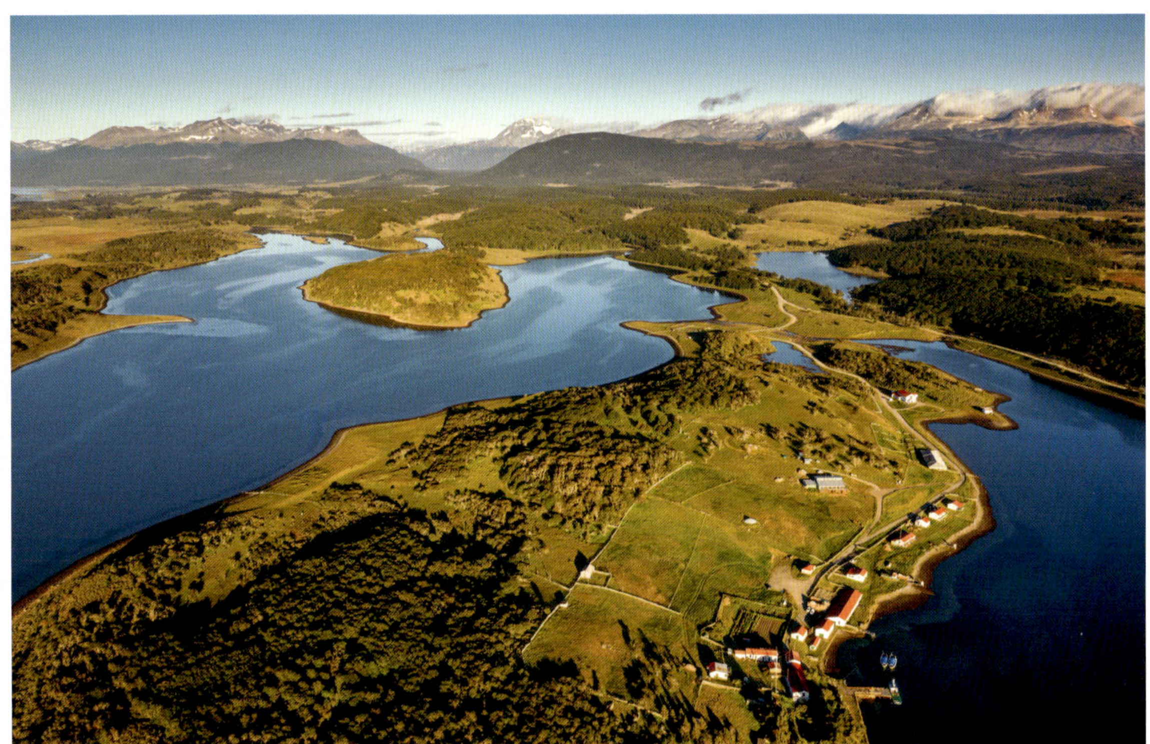

Estancia Harberton, Canal Beagle
Estancia Harberton, Beagle Channel

Tierra del Fuego

Tierra del Fuego is the southernmost point of the Americas. The archipelago consists of a main island, which together with the offshore islands, forms an area of 73,500 km² (28,378 sq mi). When Magellan sailed south of the mainland in 1520, he could see from the ship fires burning everywhere on land, which is how the name came about. Behind the capital Ushuaia the Martial Mountain with glacier rises picturesquely.

Tierra del Fuego

Tierra del Fuego es el punto más meridional de América. El archipiélago está formado por una isla principal que, junto con las islas de ultramar forman un área de 73 500 km². Cuando Magallanes navegó al sur de tierra firme en 1520, se podían ver fuegos ardiendo por todas partes desde el barco; de ahí el nombre. Detrás de la capital Ushuaia se eleva de manera pintoresca el los montes Martial con su glaciar.

Terre de Feu

« Terre de Feu » est le nom donné à l'archipel situé à l'extrême sud du continent américain. Il est composé d'une île principale et de nombreuses petites îles, qui totalisent une superficie de 73 500 km². Lorsque Magellan doubla le cap en 1520, on ne voyait depuis le voilier qu'un immense incendie, d'où le nom donné à cette terre. Derrière la capitale provinciale Ushuaia se dressent le pittoresque Cerro Martial et son glacier.

Terra do Fogo

Tierra del Fuego é o ponto mais ao sul da América. O arquipélago é constituído por uma ilha principal que, juntamente com as ilhas da costa, forma uma área de 73 500 km². Quando Magalhães navegou para sul do continente em 1520, podia-se ver fogos ardendo por todos os lados desde o navio. Foi assim que o nome surgiu. Atrás da capital Ushuaia, a Montanha Marcial com geleira ergue-se pitorescamente.

Feuerland

Feuerland ist der südlichste Punkt Amerikas. Der Archipel besteht aus einer Hauptinsel, die mit den vorgelagerten Inseln eine Fläche von 73 500 km² bildet. Als Magellan 1520 südlich des Festlands segelte, sah man vom Schiff aus überall Feuer brennen. So kam der Name zustande. Hinter der Hauptstadt Ushuaia erhebt sich malerisch der Martial-Berg mit Gletscher.

Vuurland

Vuurland is het meest zuidelijke punt van Amerika. De archipel bestaat uit een hoofdeiland, dat samen met de kleinere eilanden een oppervlakte van 73 500 km² vormt. Toen Magellaan in 1520 ten zuiden van het vasteland voer, zag men vanaf het schip overal branden. Zo is de naam ontstaan. Achter de hoofdstad Ushuaia verheft zich pittoresk de Martial berg met gletsjer.

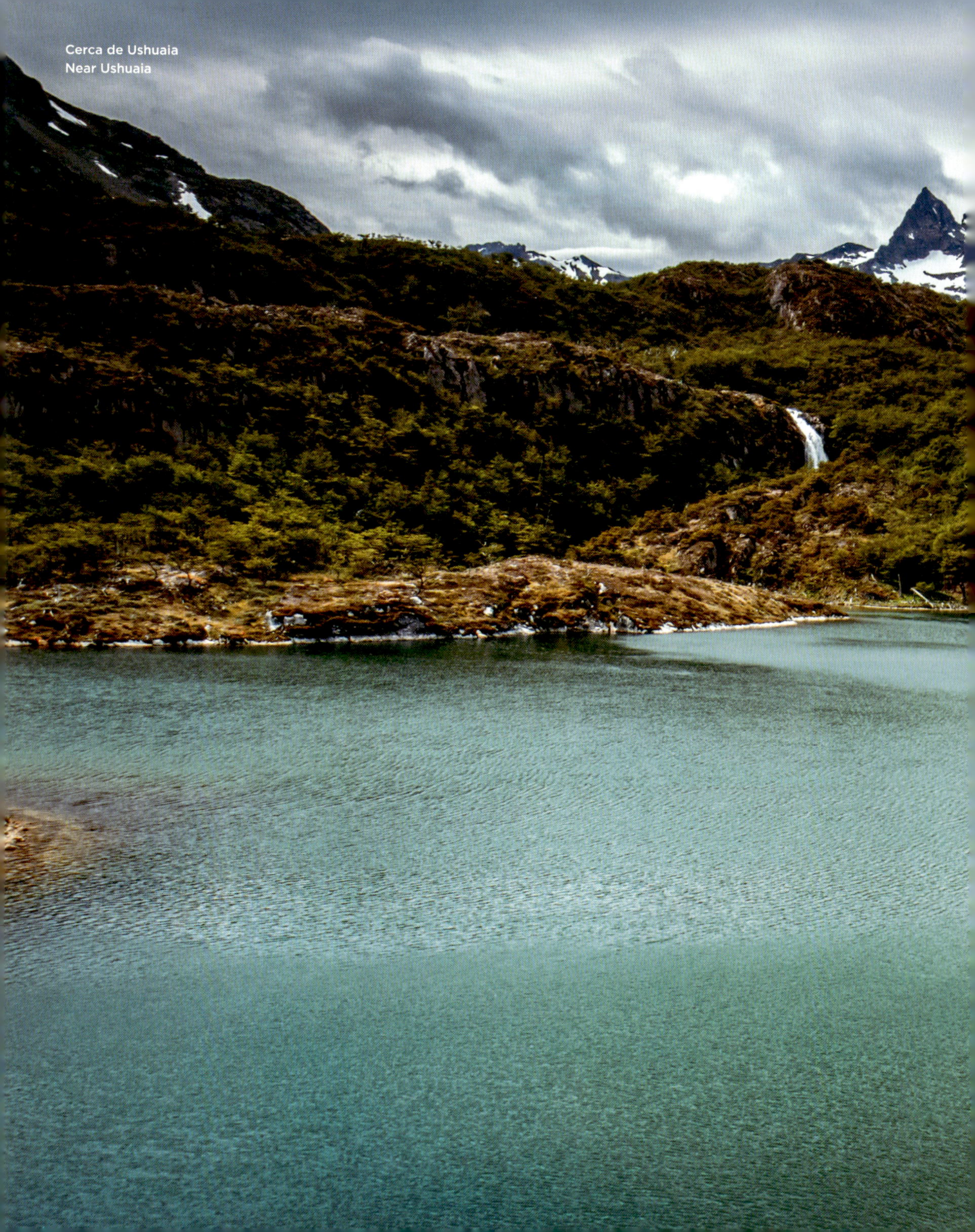
Cerca de Ushuaia
Near Ushuaia

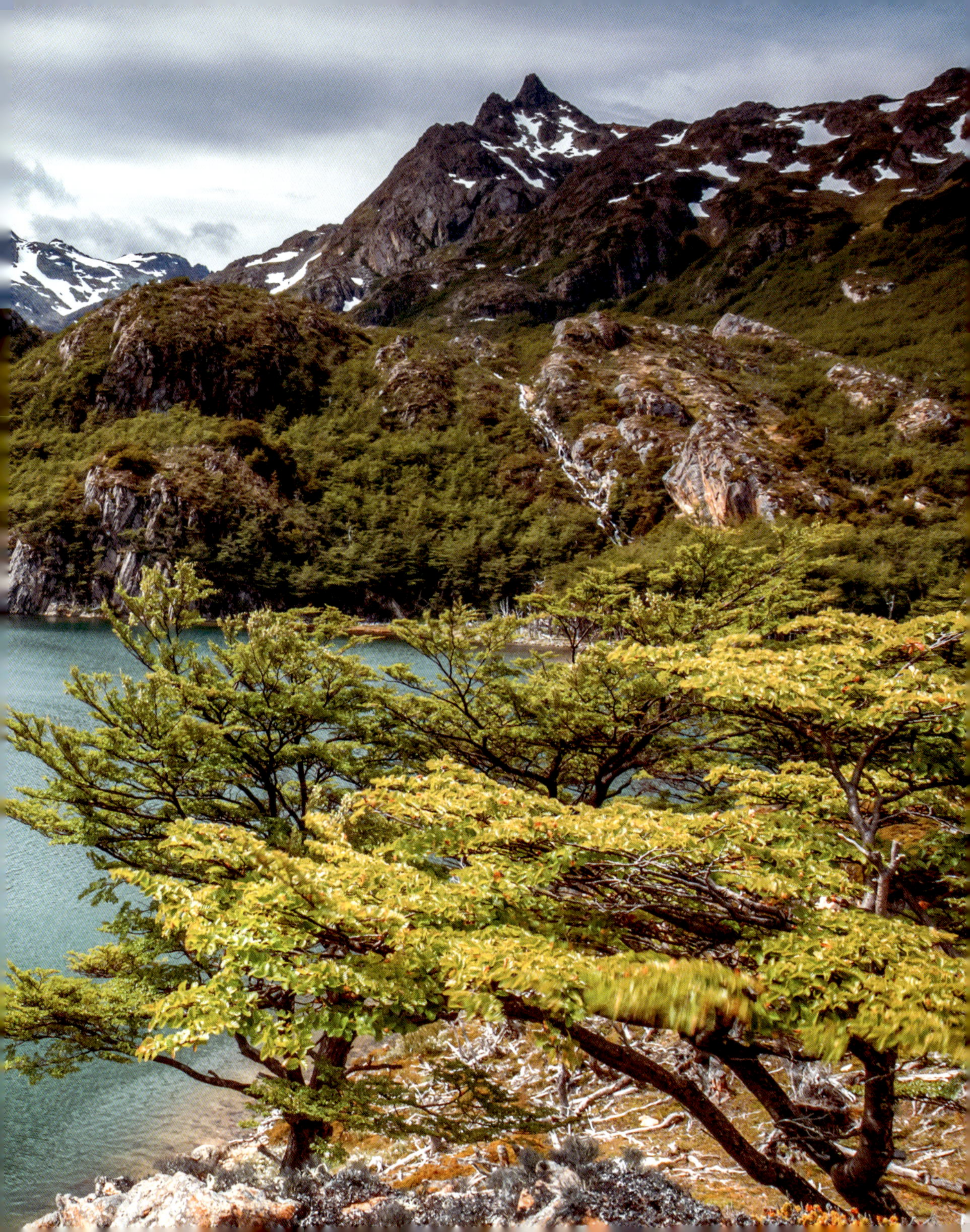

Old canoe trails

The coast off the Tierra del Fuego archipelago is criss-crossed by countless waterways and channels. Before the settlement by the Europeans, indigenous groups lived here as hunters and fishermen. They were canoe-born nomads, who lived from fishing and also hunted seals, sea lions and elephant seals.

Les anciennes voies des canots

Les côtes de l'archipel de la Terre de Feu sont parcourues par une myriade de voies d'eau et de chenaux. Avant la colonisation des Européens, les peuples indigènes vivaient ici de la chasse et de la pêche. Ils étaient nomades, se déplaçaient en canot, pêchaient et chassaient le phoque, le lion de mer et les éléphants de mer.

Alte Kanuwege

Die Küste vor dem Feuerlandarchipel ist von unzähligen Wasserwegen und Kanälen durchzogen. Vor der Besiedlung durch die Weißen lebten hier indigene Gruppen als Jäger und Fischer. Sie waren Kanunomaden, zogen umher, fischten und jagten Robben, Seelöwen und Seeelefanten.

Antiguos caminos de canoa

La costa del archipiélago de Tierra del Fuego está atravesada por innumerables vías de agua y canales. Antes del asentamiento de los europeos, los pueblos originarios vivían aquí como cazadores y pescadores. Eran nómadas en canoa, deambulaban, pescaban y cazaban focas, leones marinos y elefantes marinos.

Trilhas antigas de canoagem

A costa ao largo do arquipélago da Terra do Fogo é atravessada por inúmeras vias navegáveis e canais. Antes da colonização pelos brancos, grupos indígenas viviam aqui como caçadores e pescadores. Eram nômades de canoa, vagueavam, pescavam e caçavam focas, leões-marinhos e elefantes-marinhos.

Oude kanogebieden

De kust voor de archipel Vuurland wordt door talloze waterwegen en kanalen doorkruist. Vóór de vestiging door de blanken leefden hier inheemse groepen als jagers en vissers. Ze waren kano-nomaden, dwaalden rond, visten en joegen op zeehonden, zeeleeuwen en zeeolifanten.

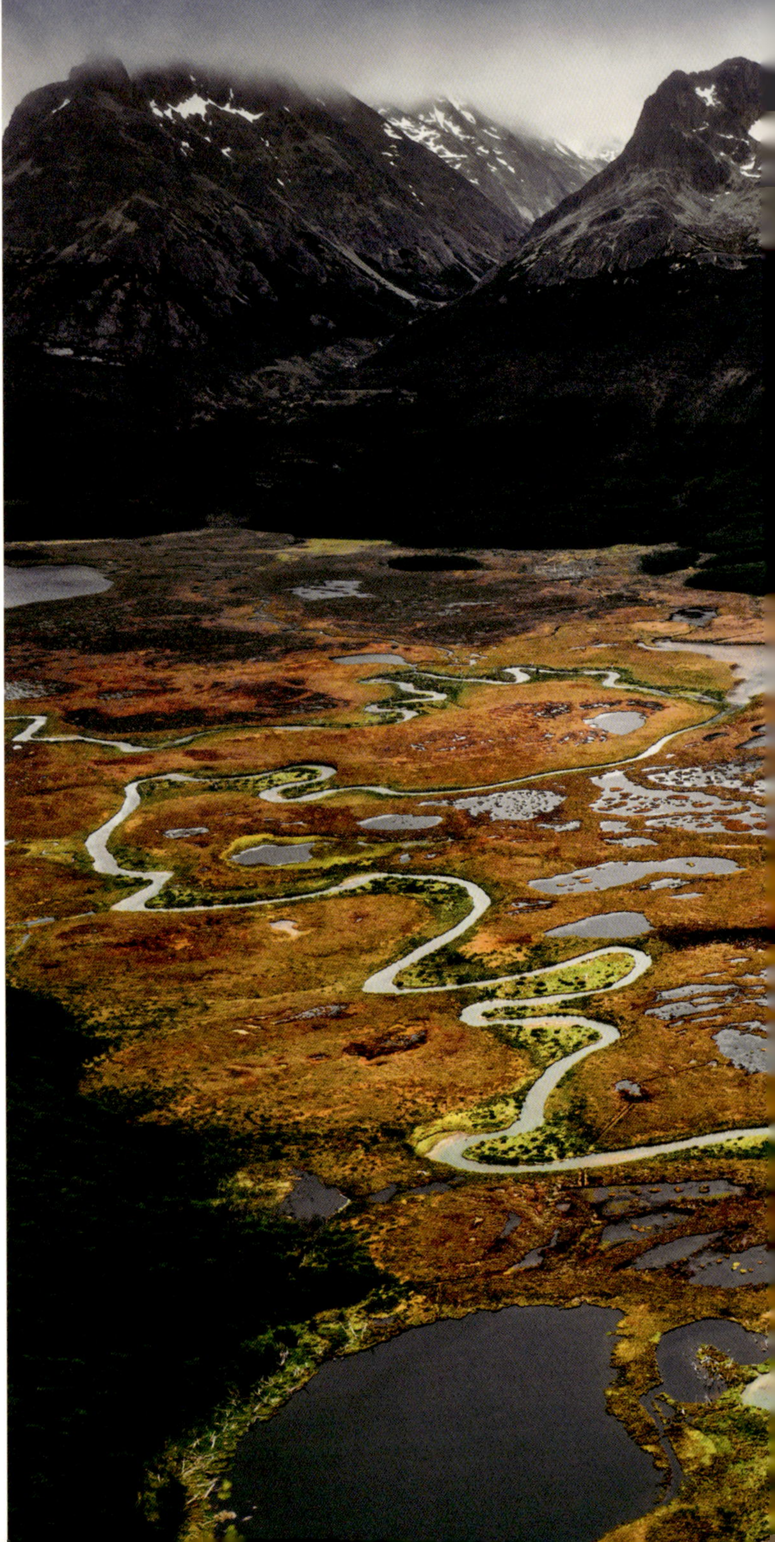

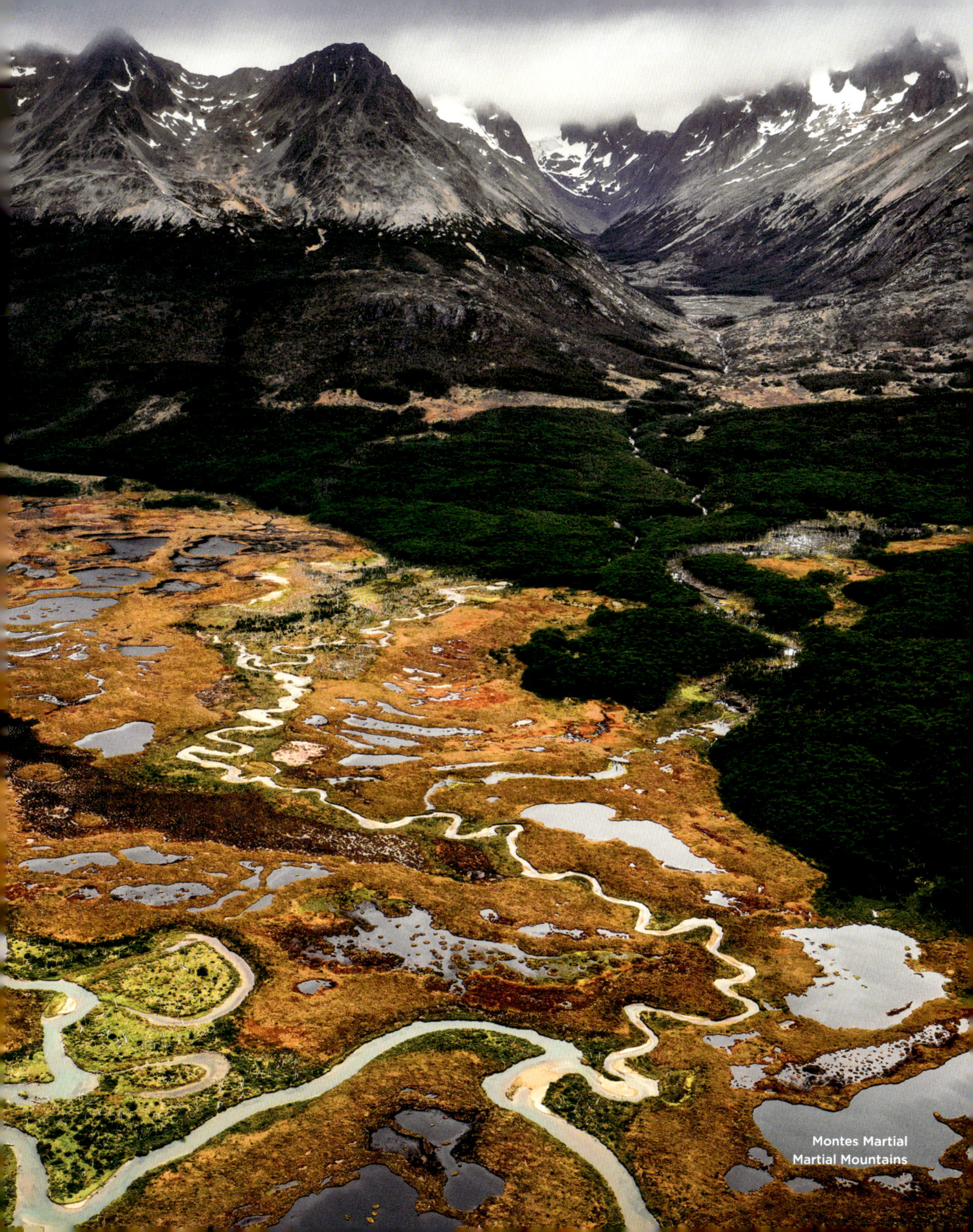

Montes Martial
Martial Mountains

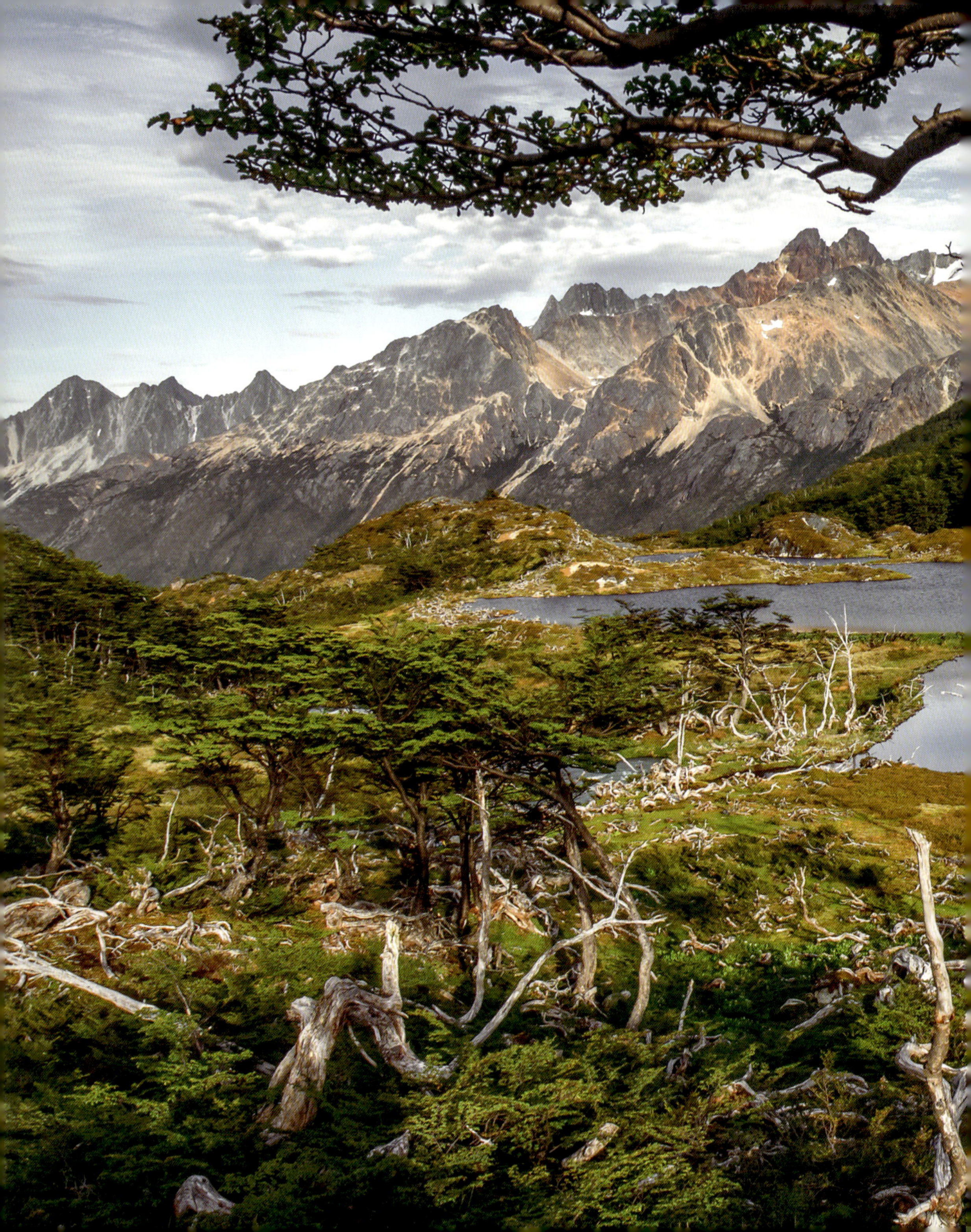

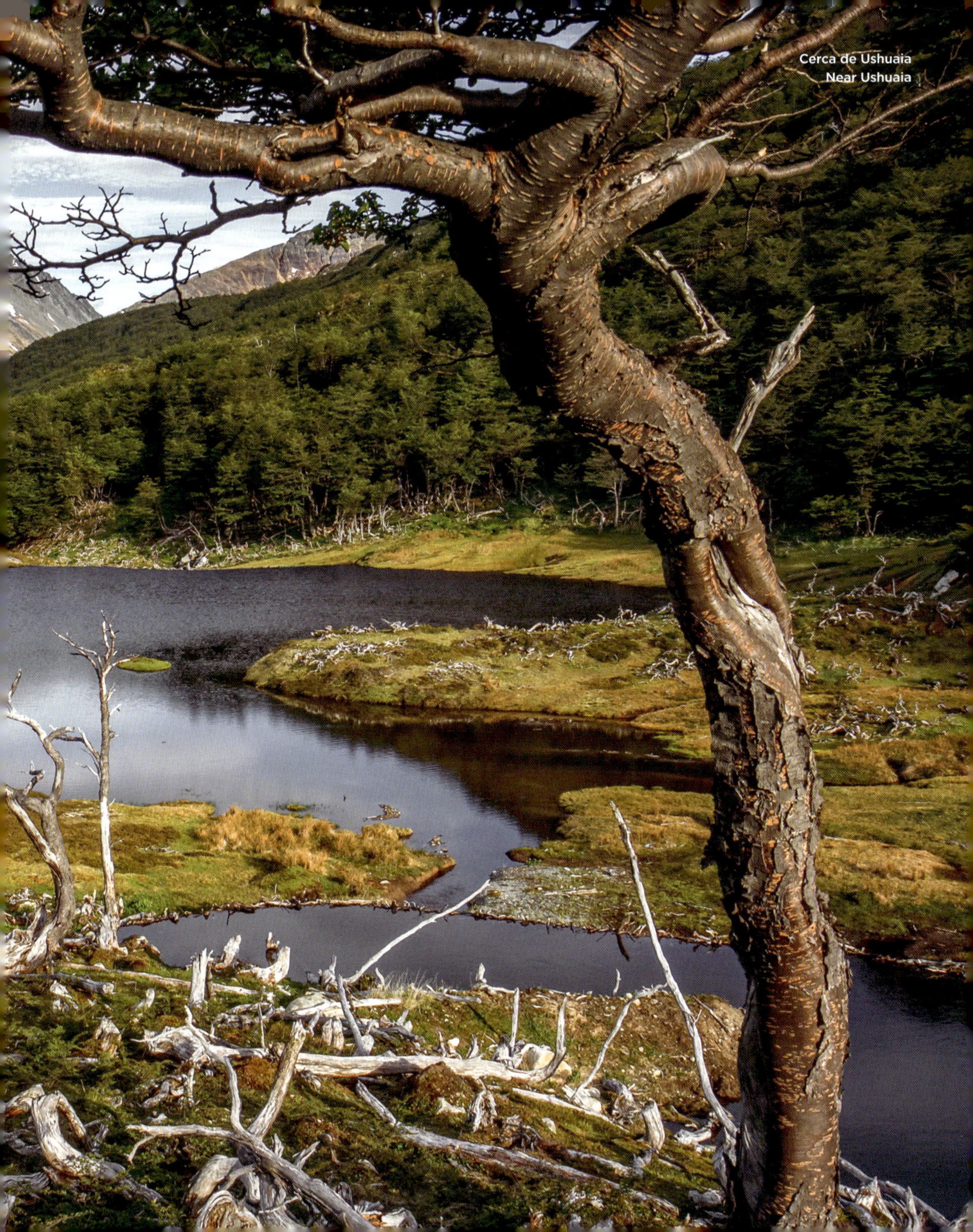

Cerca de Ushuaia
Near Ushuaia

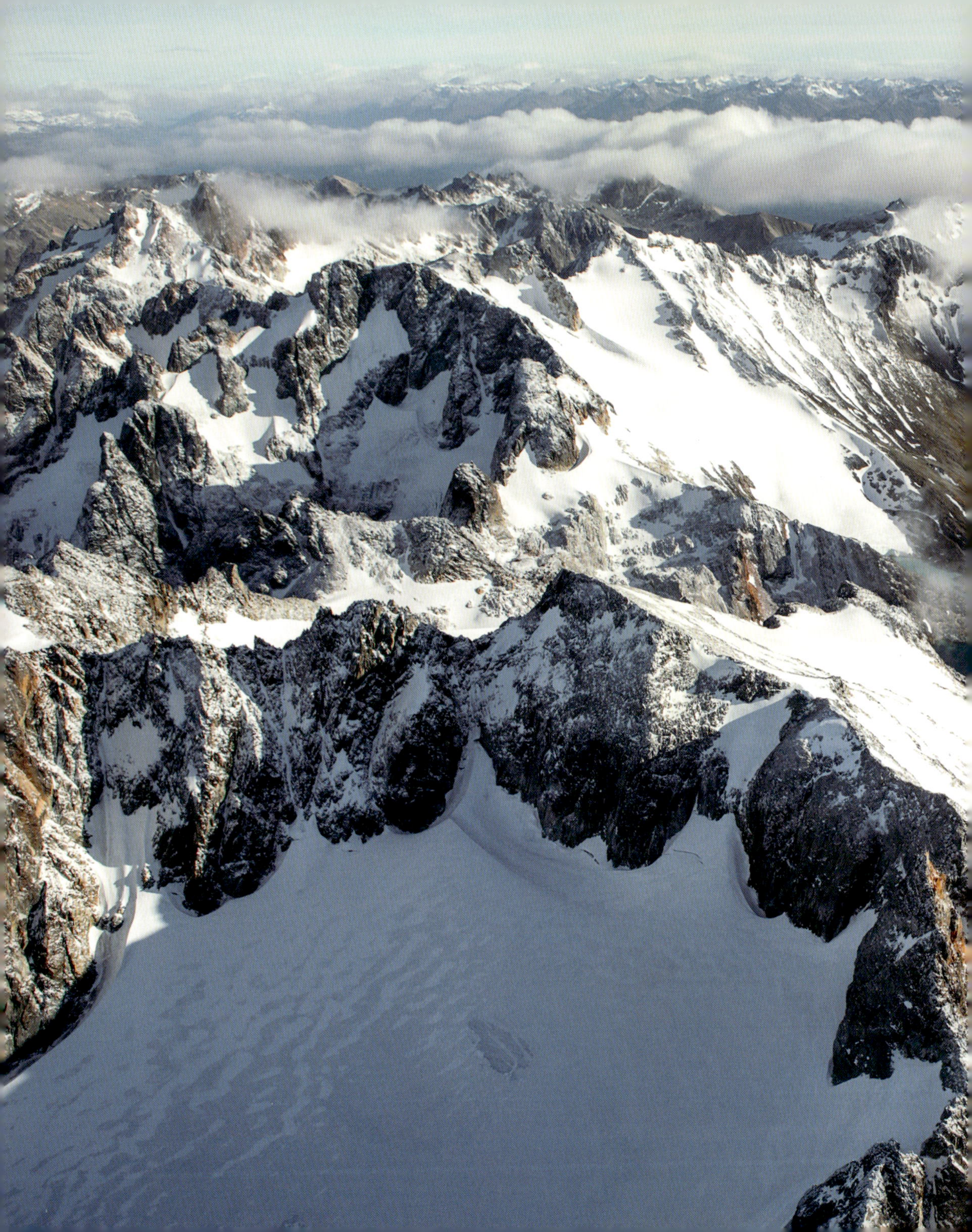

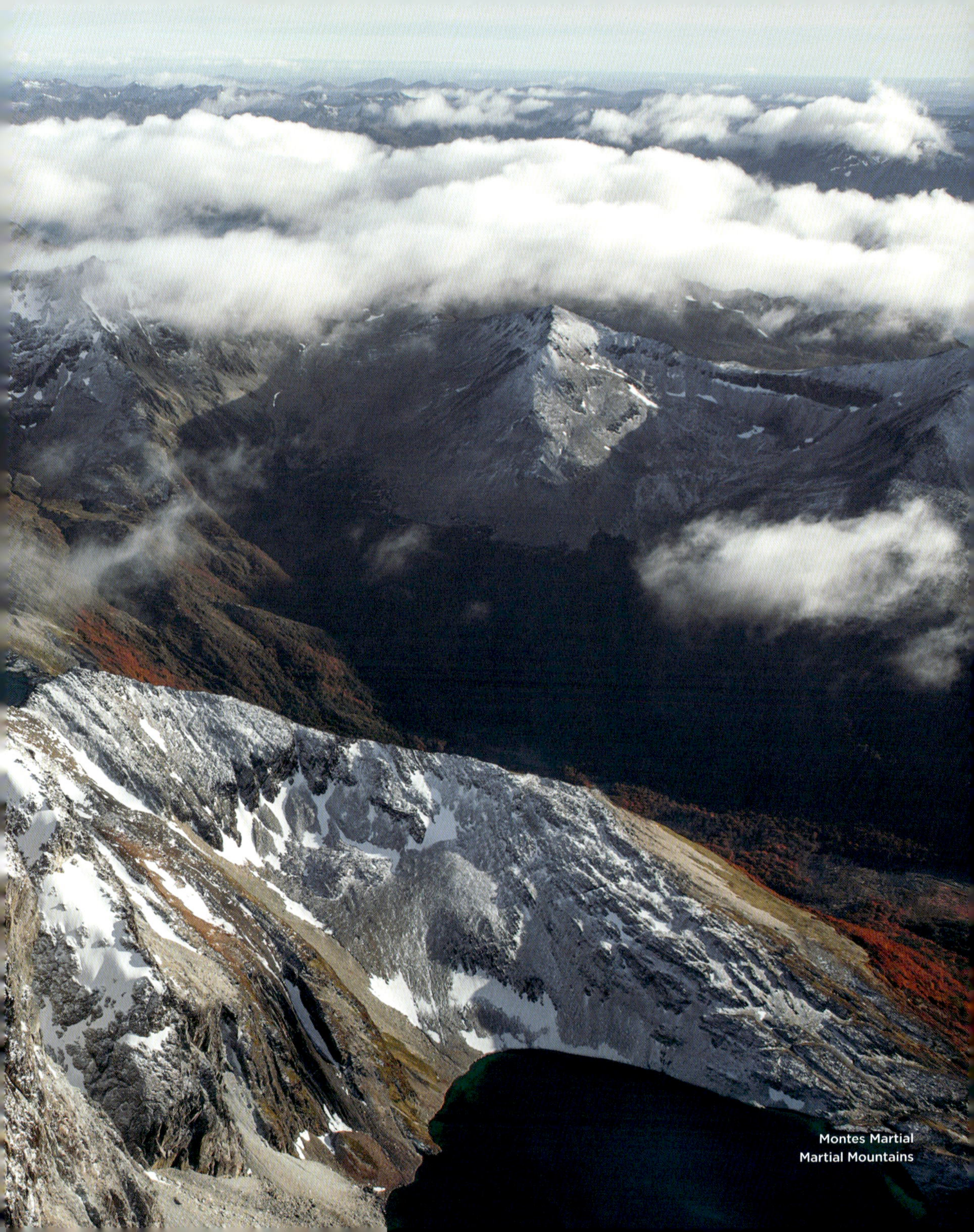
Montes Martial
Martial Mountains

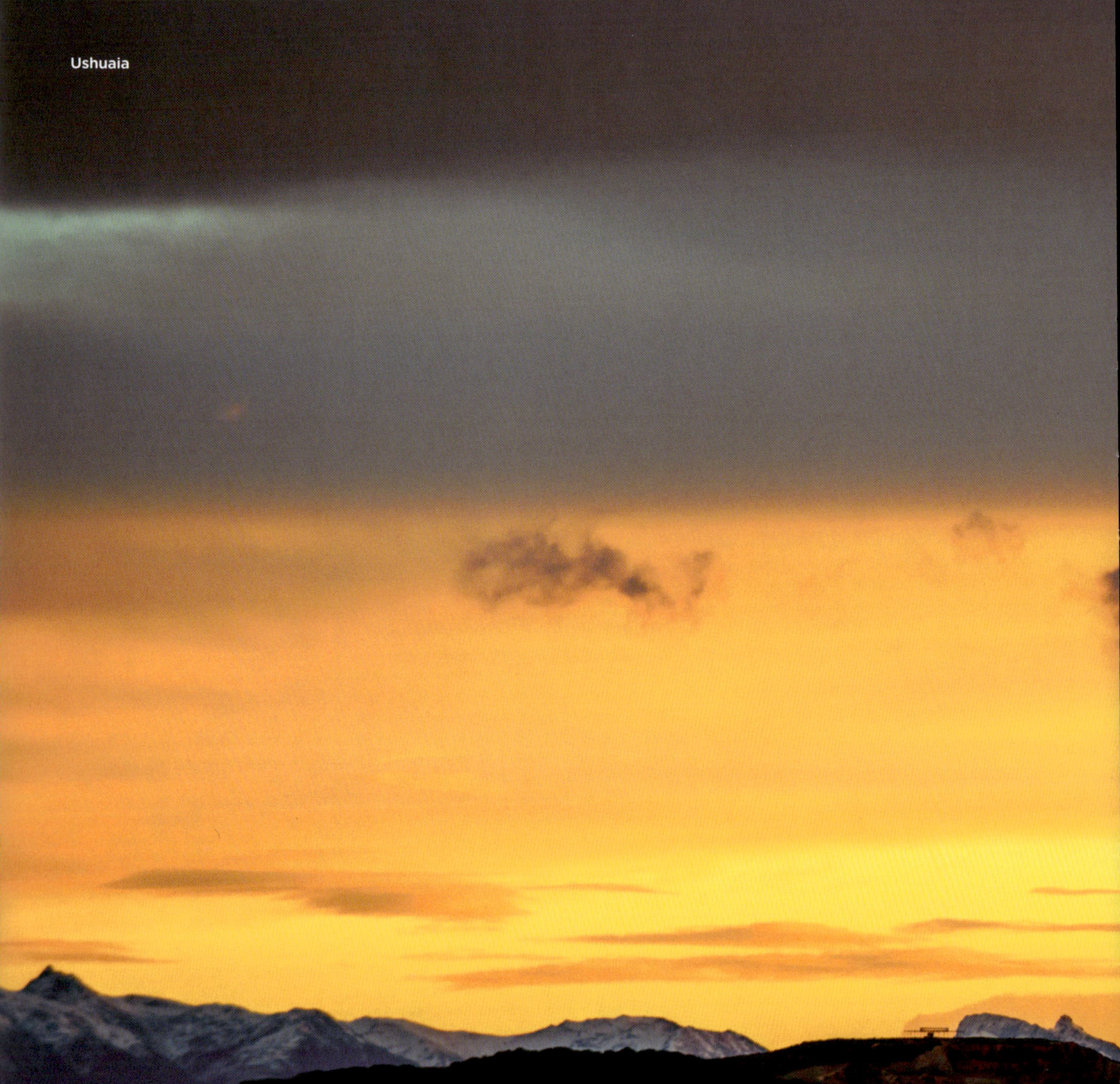
Ushuaia

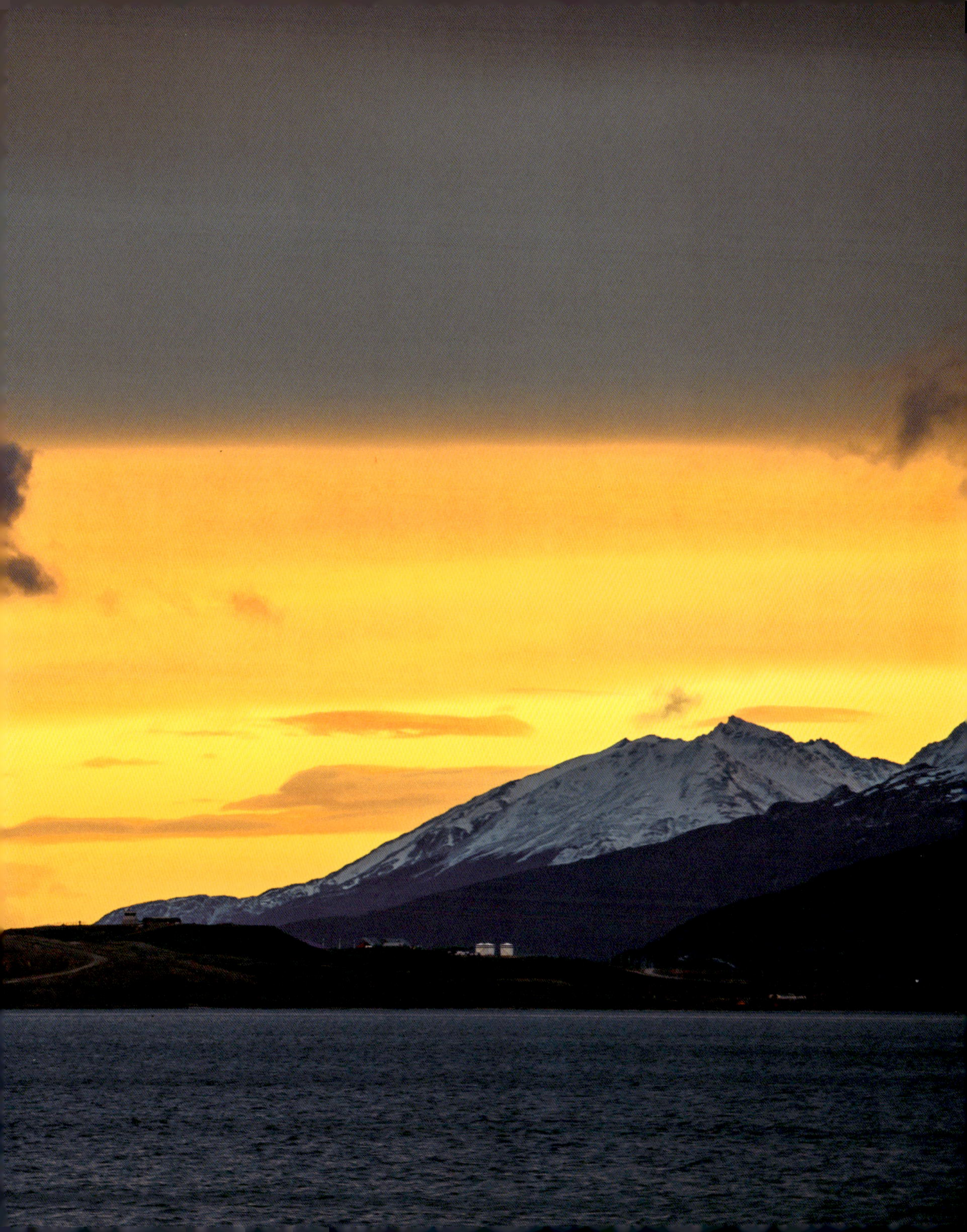

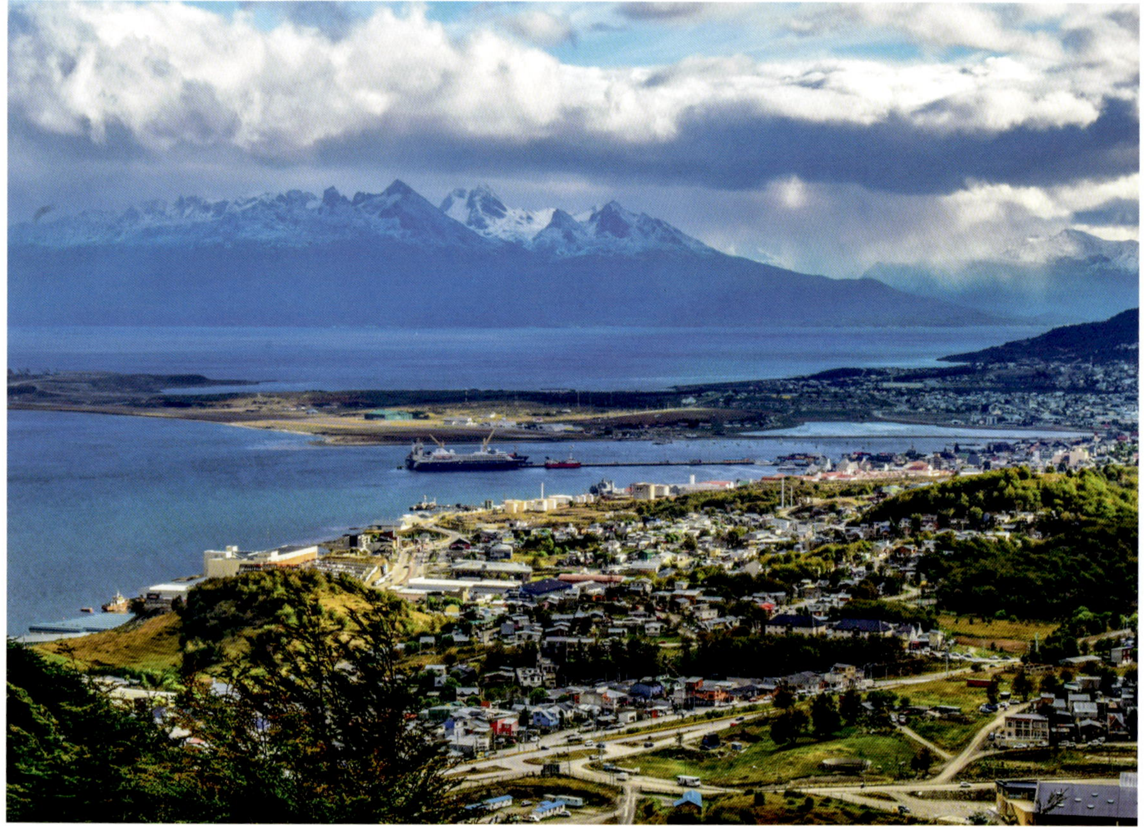

Ushuaia

Ushuaia

The indigenous name *Ushuaia* means "the bay that looks to the east". The city is located on the northern bank of the Beagle Channel, which was discovered by Captain FitzRoy in 1834 during Charles Darwin's second circumnavigation of the world. In 1902 the settlement consisted of a prison and the wooden houses of rich estancia owners. In 1947 the southernmost city in the world became a military base. Today, 50,000 inhabitants live in the port city, which is prospering through tourism. Colorful rows of wooden houses line the deep blue sea bay. With the background of the mountains, which are also snow-covered in summer, Ushuaia provides a romantic backdrop.

Ushuaia

Le nom indien *Ushuaia* signifie « la baie orientée vers l'est ». La ville est installée sur la rive nord du canal Beagle, découvert en 1834 par le capitaine FitzRoy au cours du deuxième voyage d'exploration de Charles Darwin. En 1902, la colonie était constituée d'une prison et de maisons en bois des riches propriétaires d'*estancias.* En 1947, la ville la plus méridionale du monde devint une base militaire. Aujourd'hui, cette ville portuaire prospère grâce au tourisme et compte 50 000 habitants. Des rangées de maisons en bois colorées bordent la baie maritime d'un bleu profond. À l'arrière-plan, les sommets couverts de neige éternelle offrent à Ushuaia un décor des plus romantiques.

Ushuaia

Der indianische Name *Ushuaia* bedeutet „die Bucht, die nach Osten sieht". Die Stadt liegt am nördlichen Ufer des Beagle-Kanals, der 1834 von Kapitän FitzRoy während der zweiten Weltumseglung Charles Darwins entdeckt wurde. 1902 bestand die Siedlung aus einem Gefängnis und Holzhäusern reicher Estanziabesitzer. 1947 wurde die südlichste Stadt der Welt Militärstützpunkt. Heute leben 50 000 Einwohner in der durch Tourismus prosperierenden Hafenstadt. Bunte Holzhäuserreihen säumen die tiefblaue Meeresbucht. Mit dem Hintergrund der auch im Sommer schneebedeckten Berge liefert Ushuaia eine romantische Kulisse.

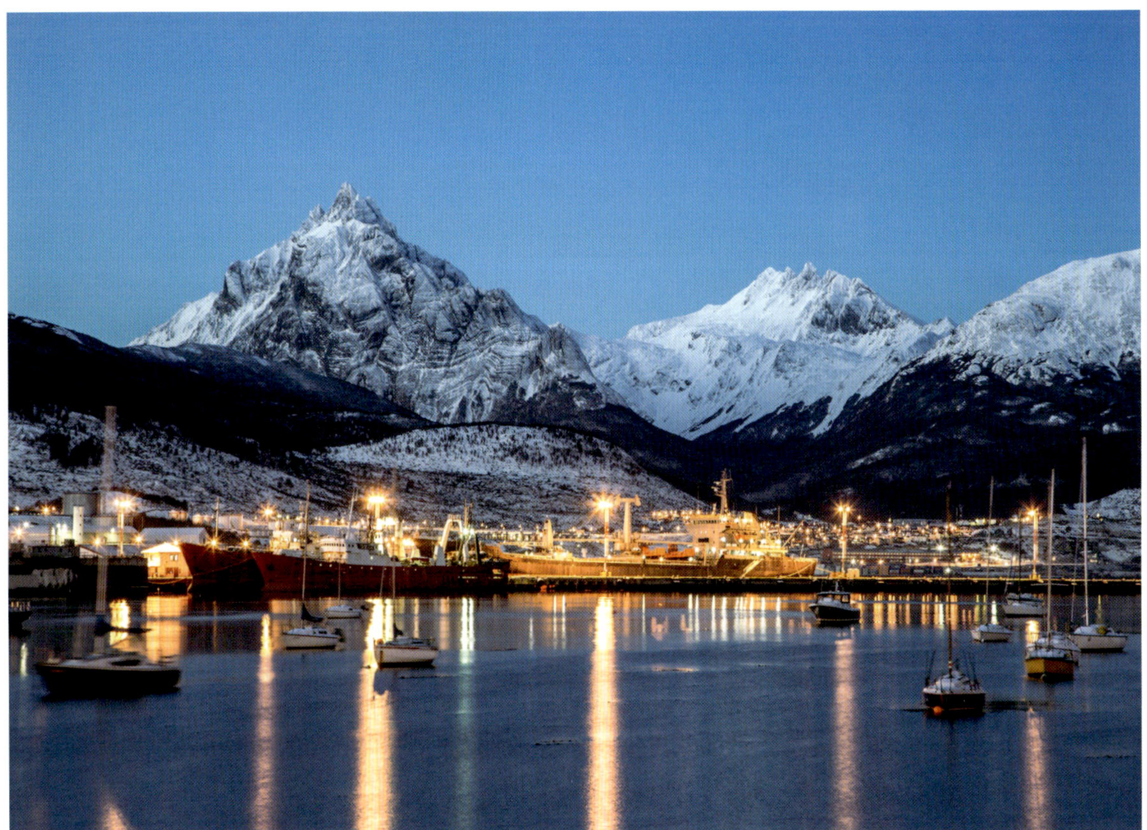

Ushuaia

Ushuaia

El nombre en lengua originaria *Ushuaia* significa "la bahía que mira hacia el este". La ciudad está situada en la orilla norte del Canal Beagle, que fue descubierto por el capitán FitzRoy en 1834 durante la segunda circunnavegación del mundo de Charles Darwin. En 1902, el asentamiento consistía en una prisión y casas de madera de ricos propietarios de estancias. En 1947, la ciudad más meridional del mundo se convirtió en una base militar. Hoy en día, 50 000 habitantes viven en la ciudad portuaria, que está prosperando gracias al turismo. Coloridas hileras de casas de madera se alinean en la bahía del mar azul profundo. Con el fondo de las montañas, que también están cubiertas de nieve en verano, Ushuaia ofrece un escenario romántico.

Ushuaia

O nome indiano *Ushuaia* significa "a baía que se extende amplamente em direção ao oeste". A cidade está localizada na margem norte do Canal Beagle, que foi descoberta pelo Capitão FitzRoy em 1834, durante a segunda circum-navegação do mundo de Charles Darwin. Em 1902 o assentamento consistia em uma prisão e casas de madeira de ricos proprietários de fazendas. Em 1947, a cidade mais meridional do mundo tornou-se uma base militar. Hoje, 50 000 habitantes vivem na cidade portuária, que está a prosperar através do turismo. Linhas coloridas de casas de madeira alinhadas na baía do mar azul profundo. Com o fundo das montanhas, que também estão cobertas de neve no verão, Ushuaia oferece um cenário romântico.

Ushuaia

De Indiase naam *Ushuaia* betekent "de baai die naar het oosten kijkt". De stad ligt op de noordelijke oever van het Beaglekanaal dat in 1834 tijdens Charles Darwins tweede zeiltocht om de wereld door kapitein Fitz Roy werd ontdekt. In 1902 bestond de nederzetting uit een gevangenis en houten huizen van rijke estancia eigenaren. In 1947 werd de zuidelijkste stad ter wereld een militaire basis. Vandaag de dag wonen er 50 000 inwoners in de door het toerisme florerende havenstad. Langs de diepblauwe baai staan rijen bontgekleurde, houten huizen. Met op de achtergrond de ook in de zomer met sneeuw bedekte bergen, vormt Ushuaia een romantische coulisse

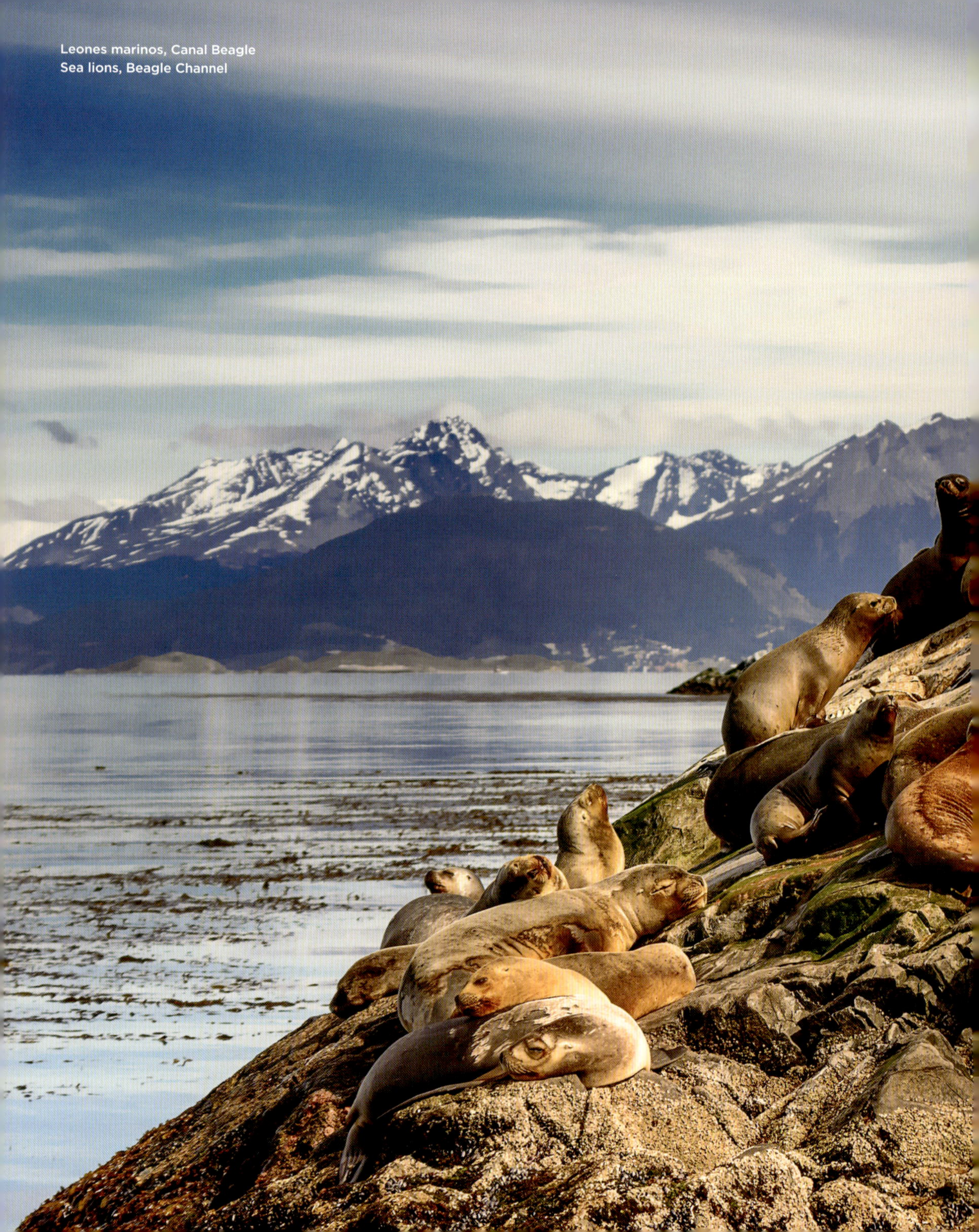

Leones marinos, Canal Beagle
Sea lions, Beagle Channel

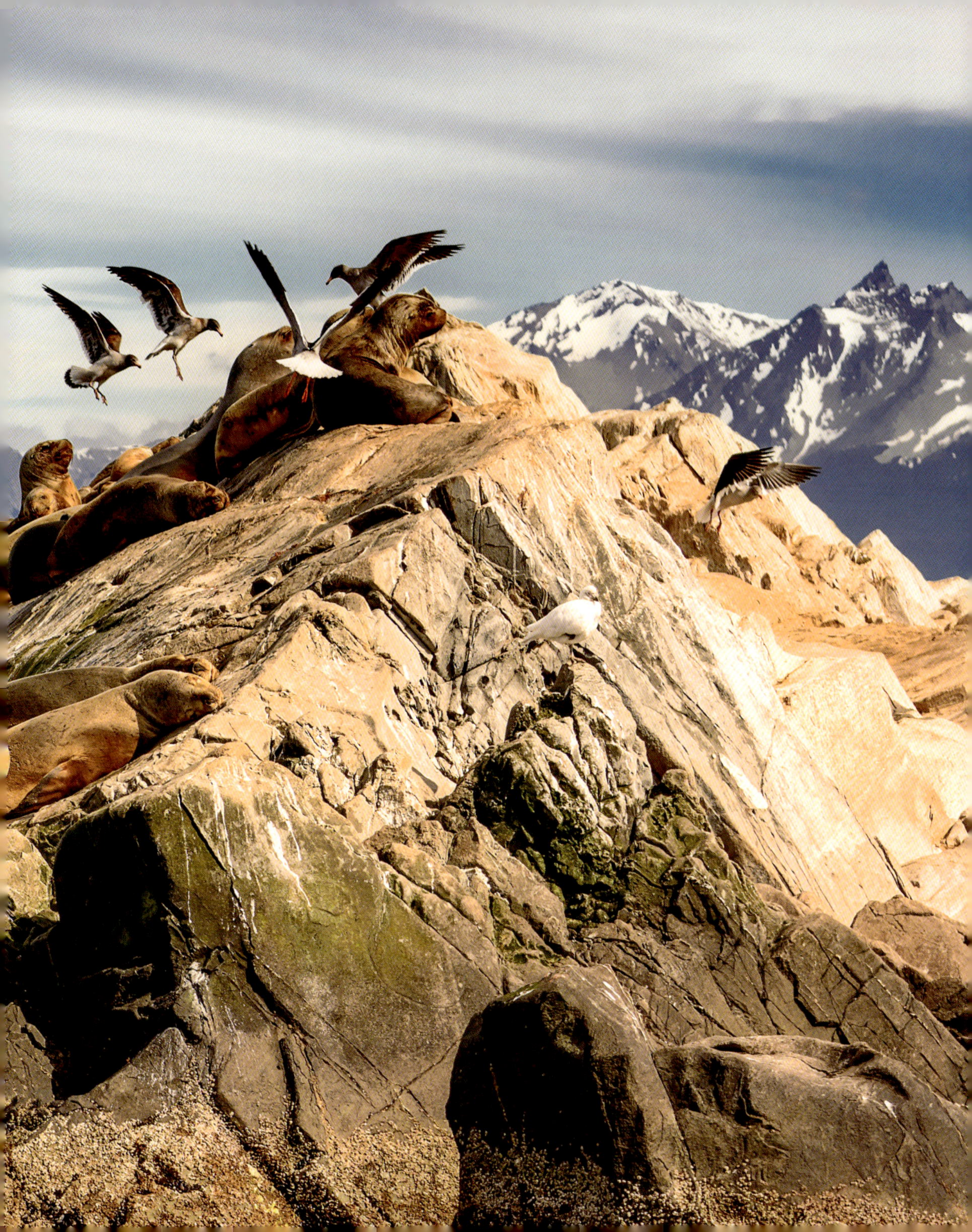

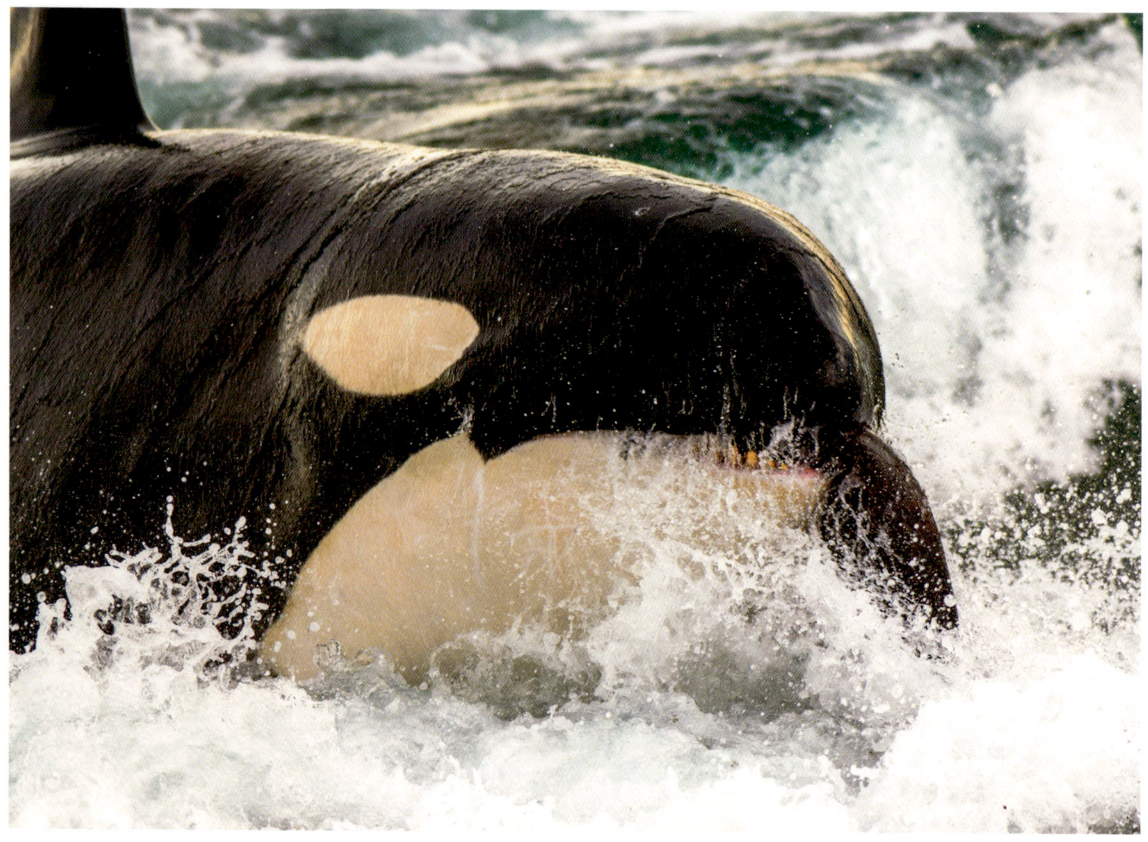

Orca

Spectacular hunt

Orcas, or killer whales, are the largest genus of the dolphin species. Male specimens grow between 5 and 9.8 m (16-30 ft) long and weigh up to 7 tons, with a maximum speed of 56 km per hour (35 mph). They are characterized by complex social structures. Up to four generations form part of a matriarchal managed group. They often hunt their prey in groups. Recently, killer whales have been observed to successfully hunt, in groups of four or five, sea lions resting on the shore. The animals run a great risk of injury, because they have to go ashore with a large part of their body for a short time.

Chasse spectaculaire

Les orques, ou épaulards, représentent l'espèce la plus nombreuse de la famille des Delphinidés. Les mâles mesurent entre 5 et 9,8 m de long et pèsent 7 t. Ces animaux peuvent atteindre une vitesse maximale de 56 km/h et présentent la particularité de vivre selon des structures sociales complexes, notamment au sein de groupes dirigés par des femelles réunissant jusqu'à quatre générations. Les orques chassent souvent en groupe. On a récemment observé la technique de chasse mise en œuvre par quatre ou cinq individus pour attraper les lions de mer sur le rivage. Lors de ces manœuvres, les orques s'exposent à un très grand risque de blessures, car elles sont obligées de sortir de l'eau une grande partie de leur corps pendant un court instant.

Spektakuläre Jagd

Orcas oder Killerwale sind die größte Gattung aus der Spezies der Delfine. Männliche Exemplare werden zwischen 5 und 9,8 m lang und wiegen 7 t. Ihre Geschwindigkeit liegt maximal bei 56 km pro Stunde. Sie zeichnen sich durch komplexe Sozialstrukturen aus. Bis zu vier Generationen bilden Teil einer matriarchalisch geführten Gruppe. Oft jagen sie gemeinsam ihre Beute. Inzwischen beobachtete man, wie Killerwale in der Gruppe zu viert oder fünft erfolgreich Jagd auf am Ufer ruhende Seelöwen machten. Dabei gehen die Tiere ein großes Verletzungsrisiko ein, denn sie müssen kurzfristig mit einem großen Teil ihres Körpers an Land.

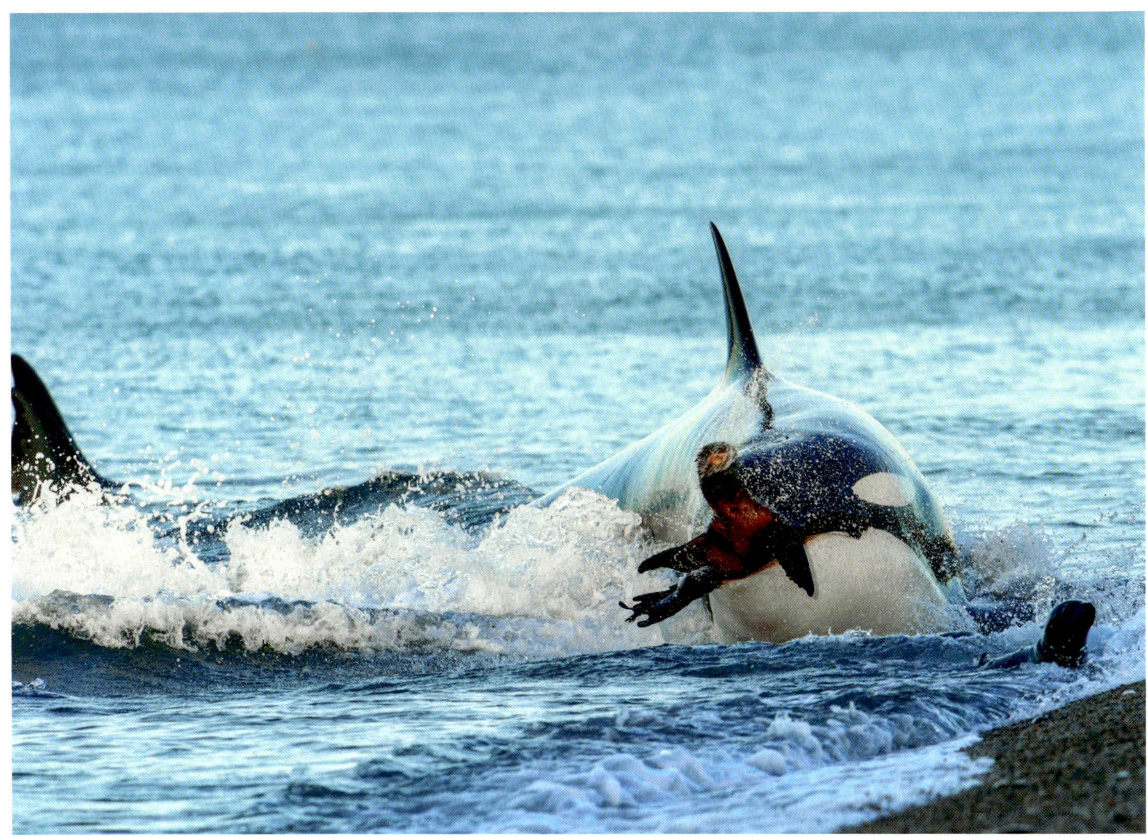

Orcas cazando lobos marinos
Orcas hunting Sea lions

Caza espectacular

Las orcas son el género más grande de
la especie de los delfines. Los ejemplares
machos crecen entre 5 y 9,8 m de largo y
pesan 7 toneladas. Su velocidad máxima
es de 56 km por hora. Se caracterizan por
sus complejas estructuras sociales. Hasta
cuatro generaciones forman parte de un
grupo administrado matriarcalmente. A
menudo cazan su presa juntos. Mientras
tanto, se ha observado que las orcas
cazan con éxito a los leones marinos que
descansan en la orilla en grupos de cuatro
o cinco. Los animales corren un gran riesgo
de sufrir lesiones, ya que tienen que salir a
tierra con una gran parte de su cuerpo por
un corto tiempo.

Caça espectacular

As orcas ou baleias assassinas são o
maior gênero da espécie de golfinhos. Os
exemplares machos crescem até 5 e 9,8 m
de comprimento e pesam 7 toneladas. A
sua velocidade máxima é de 56 km por
hora. São caracterizados por estruturas
sociais complexas. Até quatro gerações
fazem parte de um grupo matriarcal. Eles
costumam caçar as suas presas juntos.
Pôde-se já observar, um grupo de quatro
ou cinco baleias assassinas caçando com
sucesso leões-marinhos, que estavam
descansando na costa. Os animais correm
um grande risco de lesões, porque têm de
ir a terra com uma grande parte do corpo
por um curto período de tempo.

Spectaculaire jacht

Orka's of zwaardwalvissen zijn het
grootste geslacht van de familie dolfijnen.
Mannelijke exemplaren worden tussen
5 en 9,8 m lang en wegen 7 ton. Hun
maximale snelheid ligt bij 56 km per uur. Ze
onderscheiden zich door complexe sociale
structuren. Tot vier generaties maken
deel uit van een matriarchaal geleide
groep. Vaak jagen ze samen op hun prooi.
In de tussentijd observeerde men hoe
zwaardwalvissen in groepjes van vier of
vijf succesvol jaagden op aan de oever
uitrustende zeeleeuwen. Daarbij lopen de
dieren een groot risico op verwonding op,
omdat ze kort met een groot deel van hun
lichaam aan land moeten gaan.

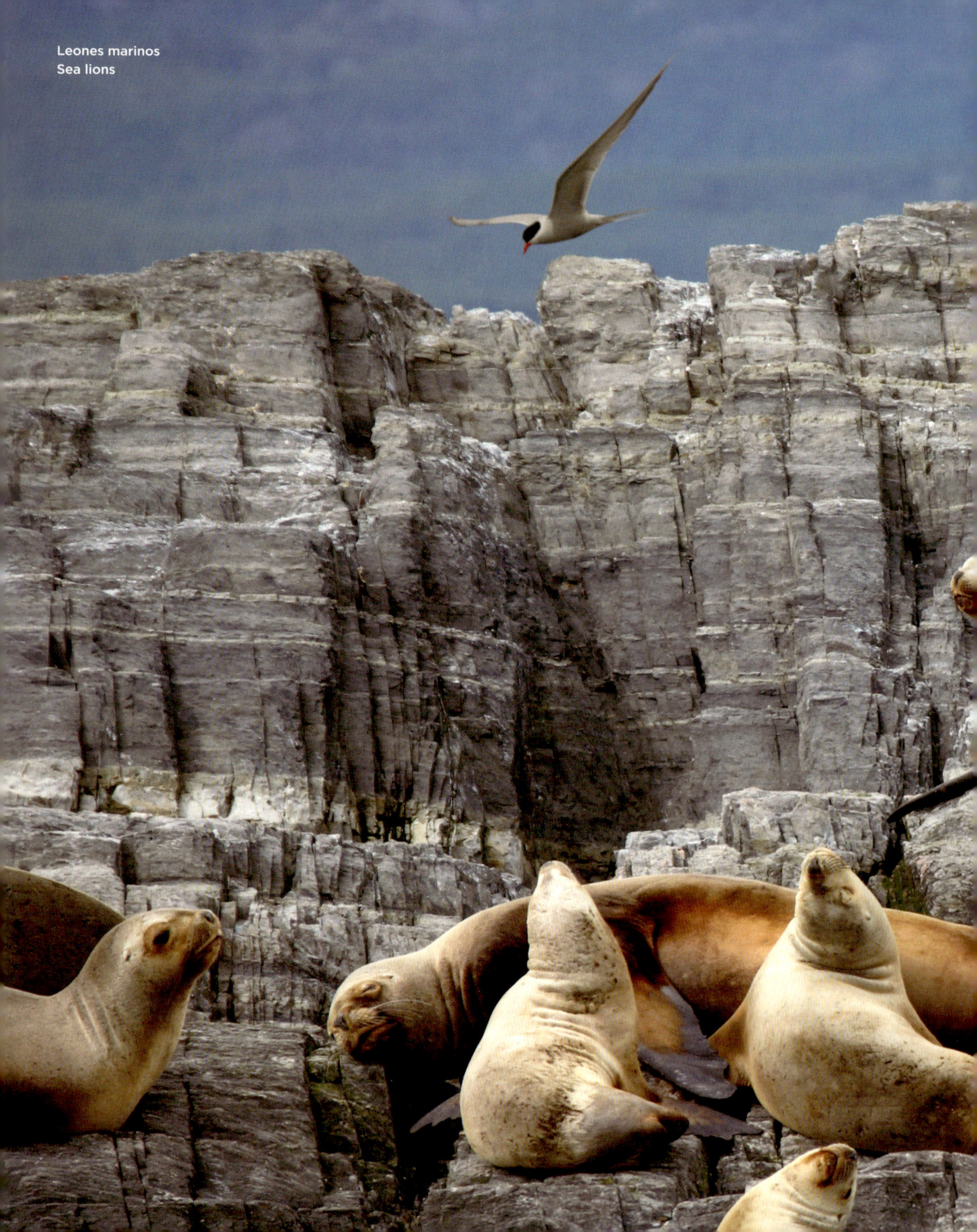

Leones marinos
Sea lions

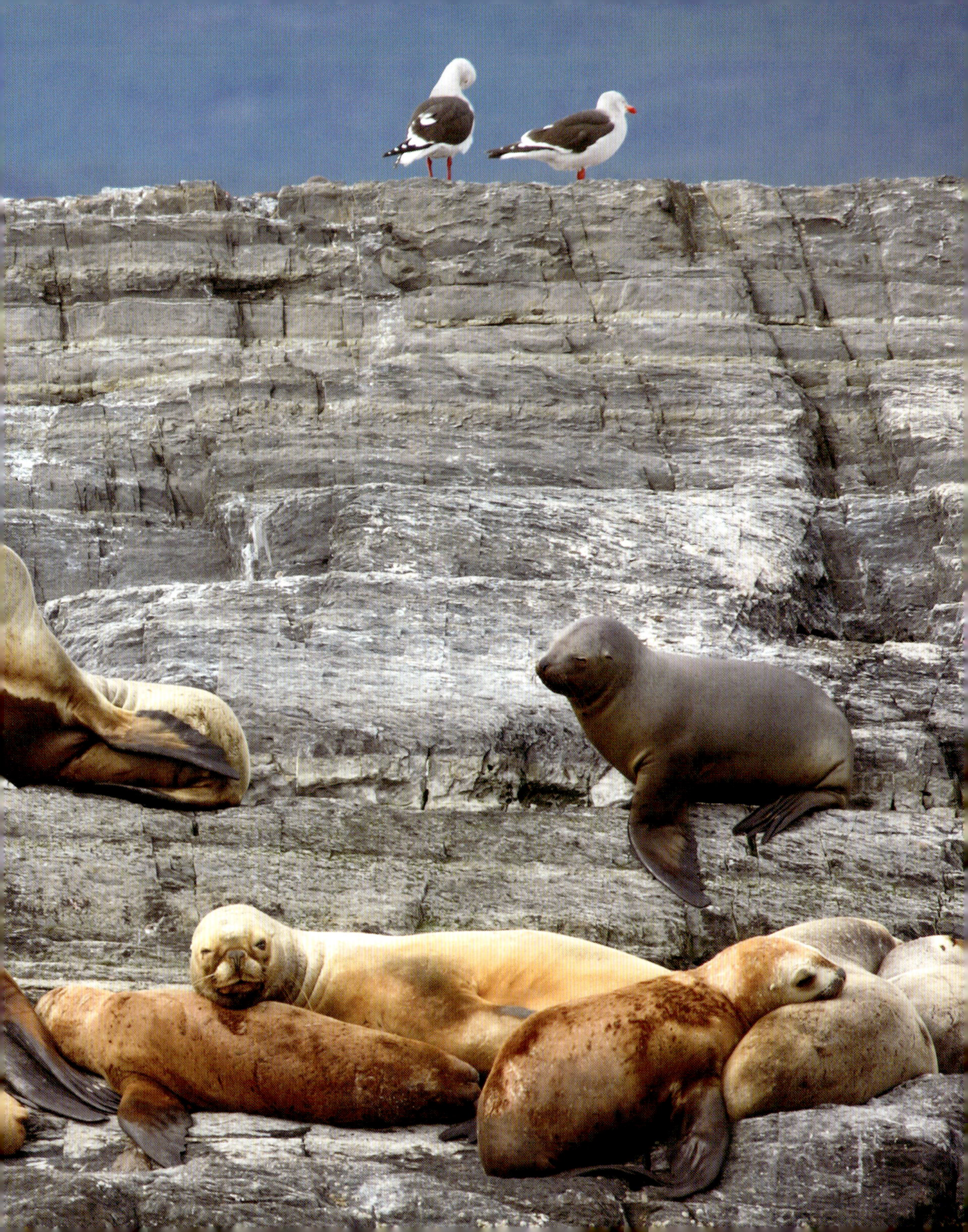

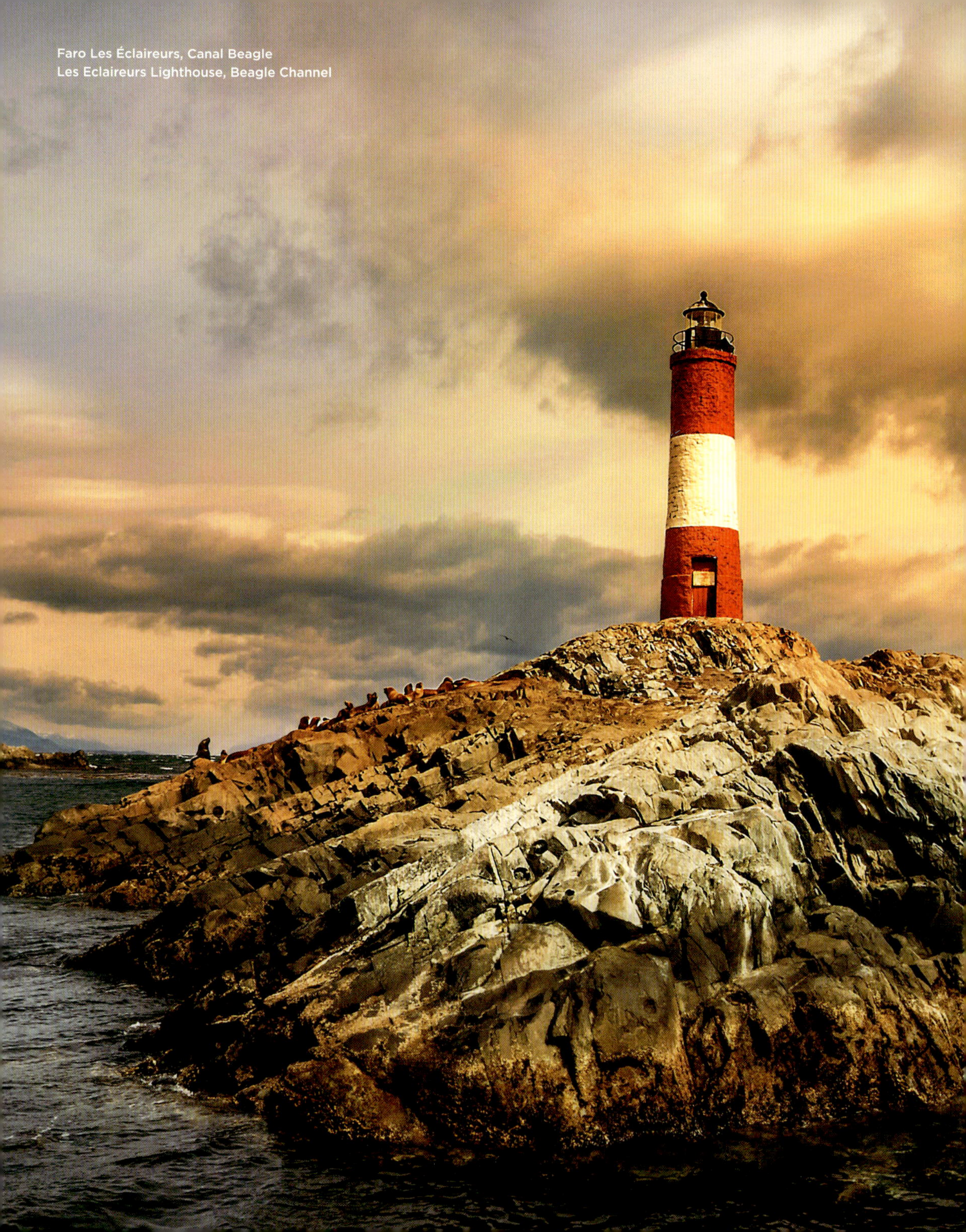
Faro Les Éclaireurs, Canal Beagle
Les Eclaireurs Lighthouse, Beagle Channel

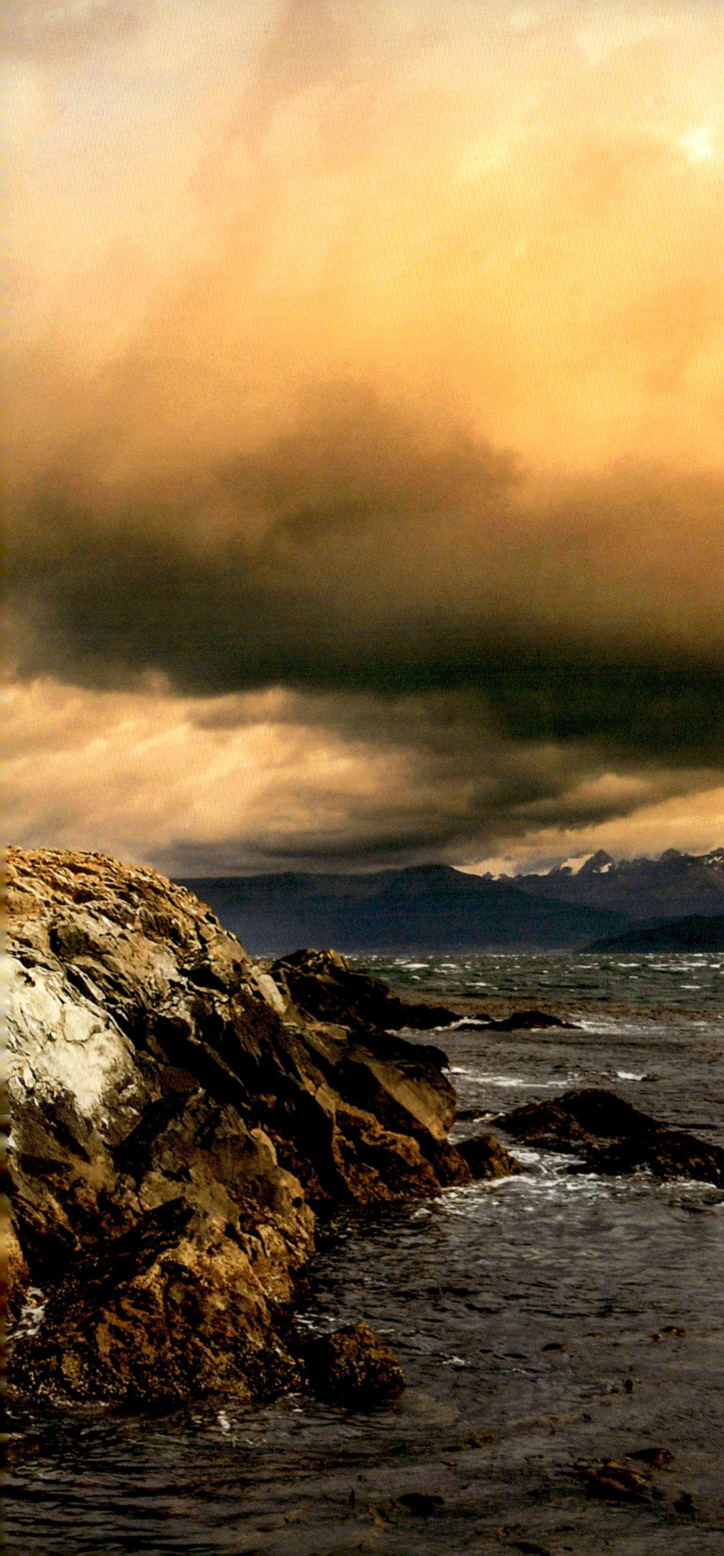

The Enlightened One

In the middle of the Beagle Channel, 9 km (5.6 mi) east of Ushuaia, lies the picturesque lighthouse Les Éclaireurs, or 'the scouts'. The 11 m (36 ft) high, windowless brick tower has only one door facing west. It lies 22 m (72 ft) above sea level and guards the entrance to the channel. Every 10 seconds it emits a light signal that can be seen 14 km (8.7 mi) away.

Les Éclaireurs

Au milieu du canal Beagle, à 9 km à l'est d'Ushuaia, se dresse un phare pittoresque, baptisé « Les Éclaireurs ». Cette tour de 11 m de haut, dépourvue de fenêtre et construite en brique, ne possède qu'une porte orientée à l'ouest. Le phare est à bâti à 22 m au-dessus du niveau de la mer et protège l'entrée du canal. Il envoie un éclat toutes les 10 secondes, visible jusqu'à 13,9 km.

Der Erleuchtete

In der Mitte des Beagle-Kanals, 9 km östlich von Ushuaia liegt der pittoreske Leuchtturm Les Éclaireurs: der Erleuchtete. Der 11 m hohe, fensterlose Turm aus Ziegelsteinen hat nur eine nach Westen ausgerichtete Tür. Er liegt 22 m über dem Meeresspiegel und bewacht die Kanal-Einfahrt. Alle 10 Sekunden gibt er ein Lichtsignal ab, das 13,9 km weit zu sehen ist.

Los iluminadores

En medio del canal Beagle, a 9 km al este de Ushuaia, se encuentra el pintoresco faro Les Éclaireurs: los iluminadores. La torre de ladrillo de 11 m de altura, sin ventanas, solo tiene una puerta que da al oeste. Se encuentra a 22 m sobre el nivel del mar y vigila la entrada al canal. Cada 10 segundos emite una señal luminosa que se puede ver a 13,9 km de distancia.

O Iluminado

No meio do Canal Beagle, 9 km a leste de Ushuaia, encontra-se o pitoresco farol Les Éclaireurs: o iluminado. A torre de tijolos de 11 m de altura, sem janelas, tem apenas uma porta voltada para o oeste. Fica a 22 m acima do nível do mar e protege a entrada do canal. A cada 10 segundos ele emite um sinal luminoso que pode ser visto a 13,9 km de distância.

De verlichte

In het midden van het Beaglekanaal, 9 km ten oosten van Ushuaia, ligt de pittoreske vuurtoren Les Éclaireurs: de verlichte. De 11 m hoge, raamloze bakstenen toren heeft slechts één naar het westen gerichte deur. Hij ligt 22 m boven de zeespiegel en bewaakt de ingang van het kanaal. Om de 10 seconden zendt hij een lichtsignaal uit dat op 13,9 km afstand te zien is.

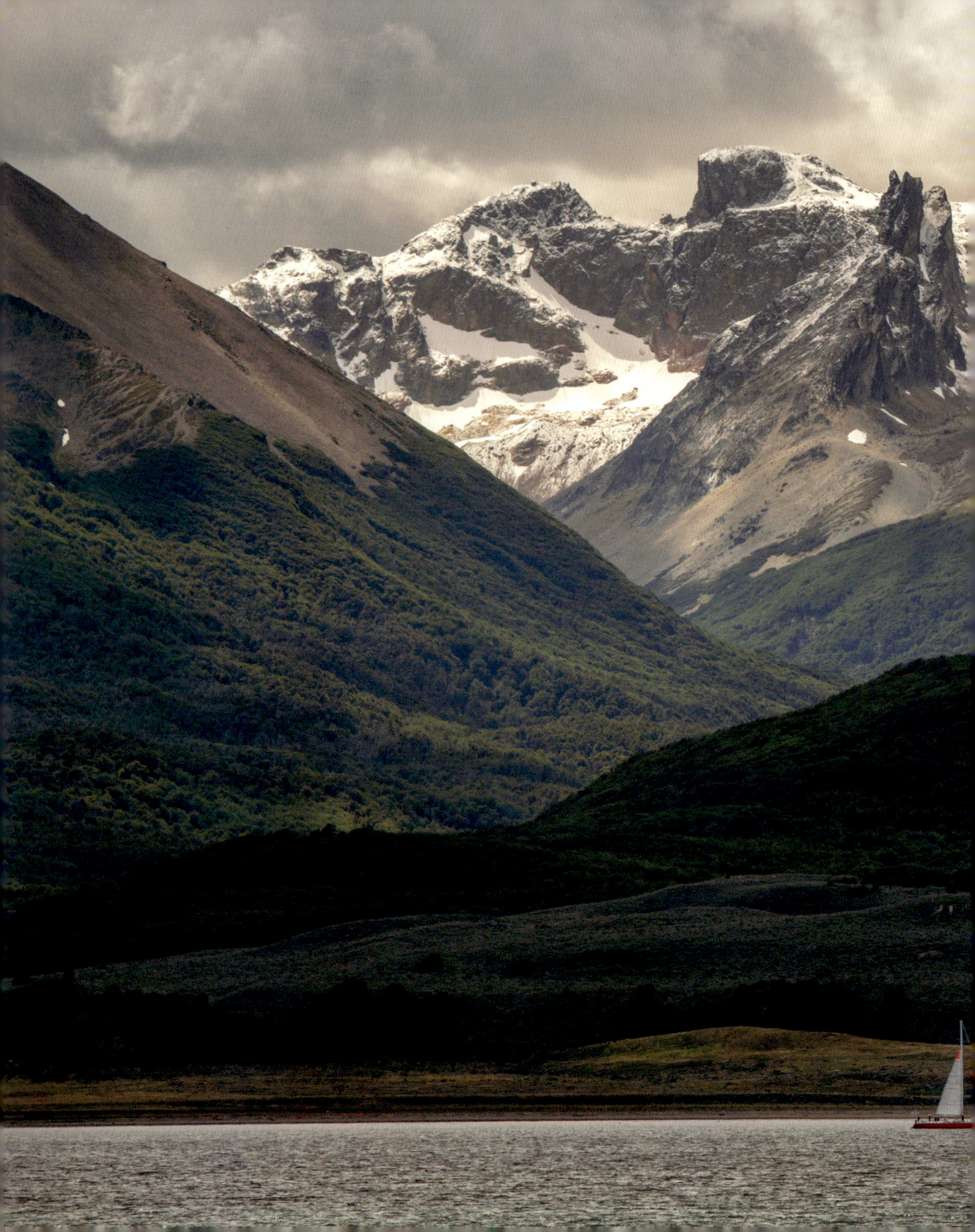

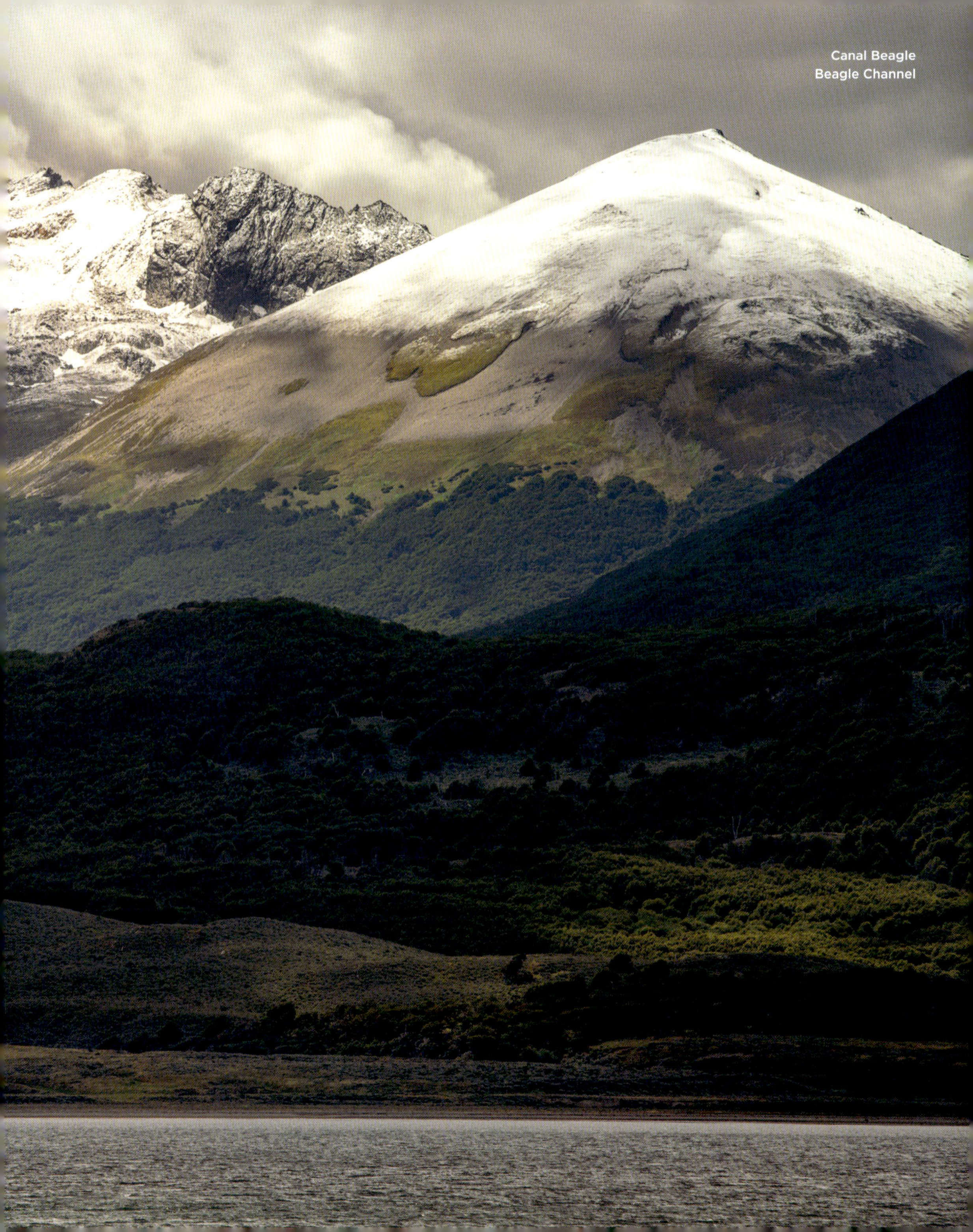
Canal Beagle
Beagle Channel

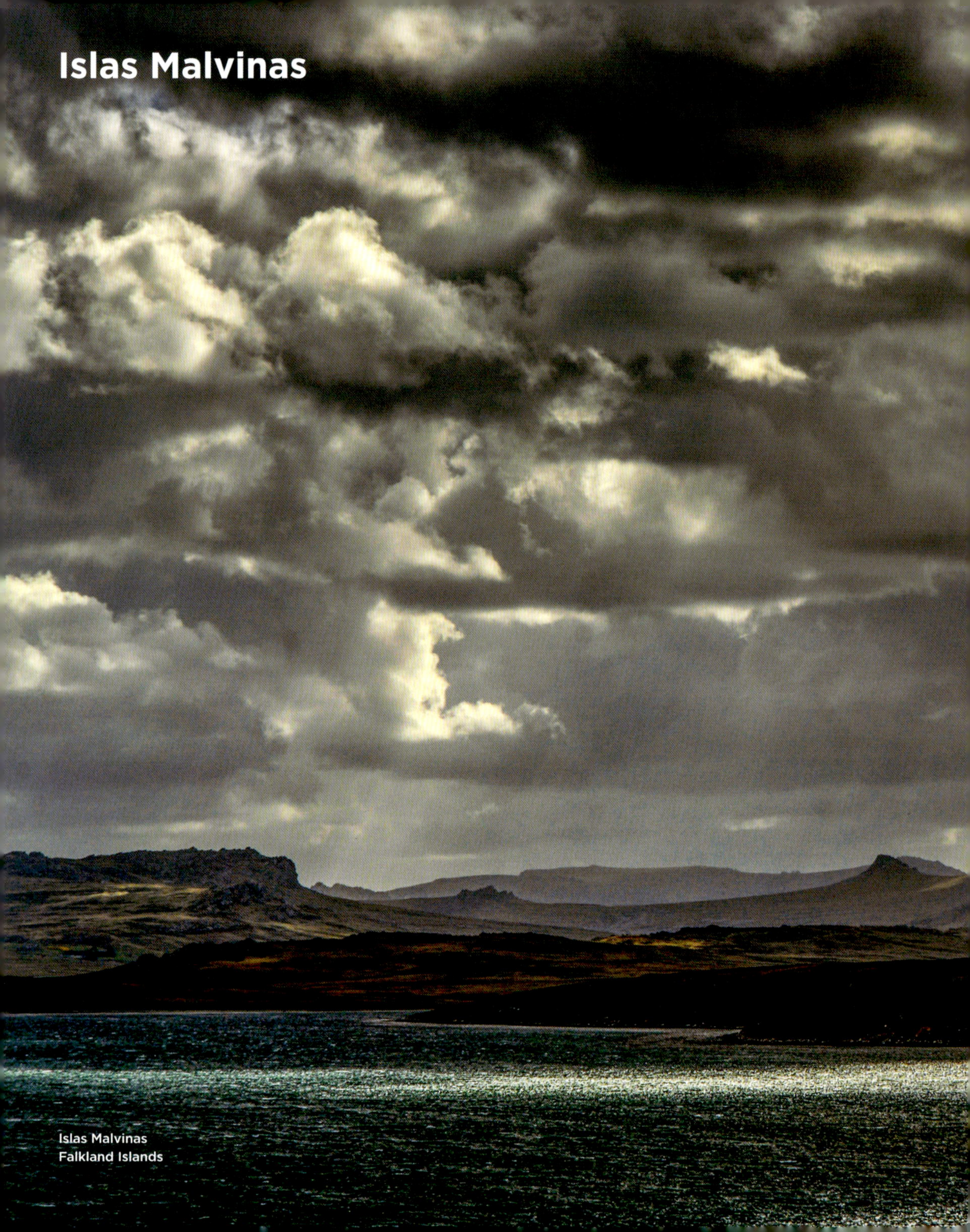

Islas Malvinas
Falkland Islands

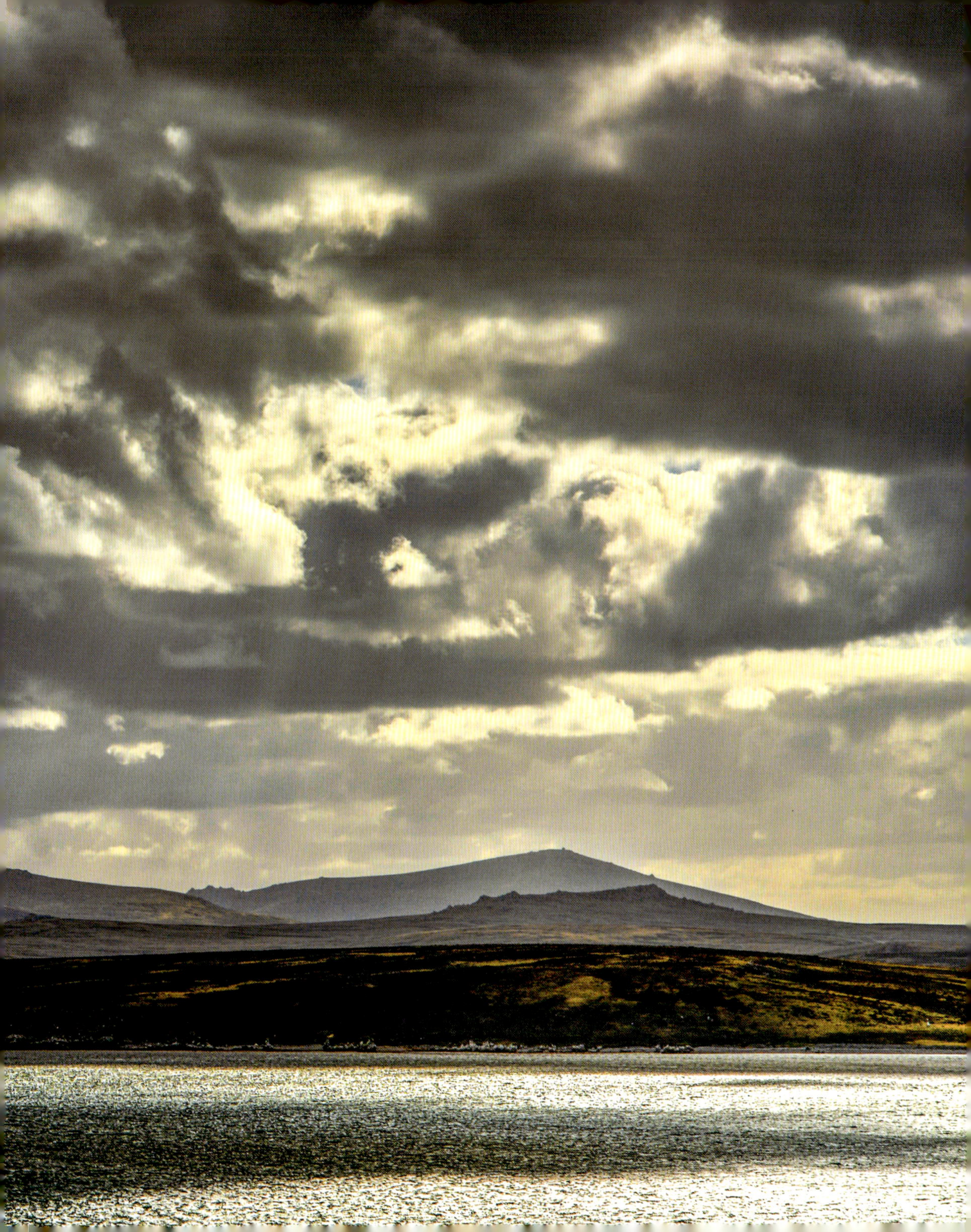

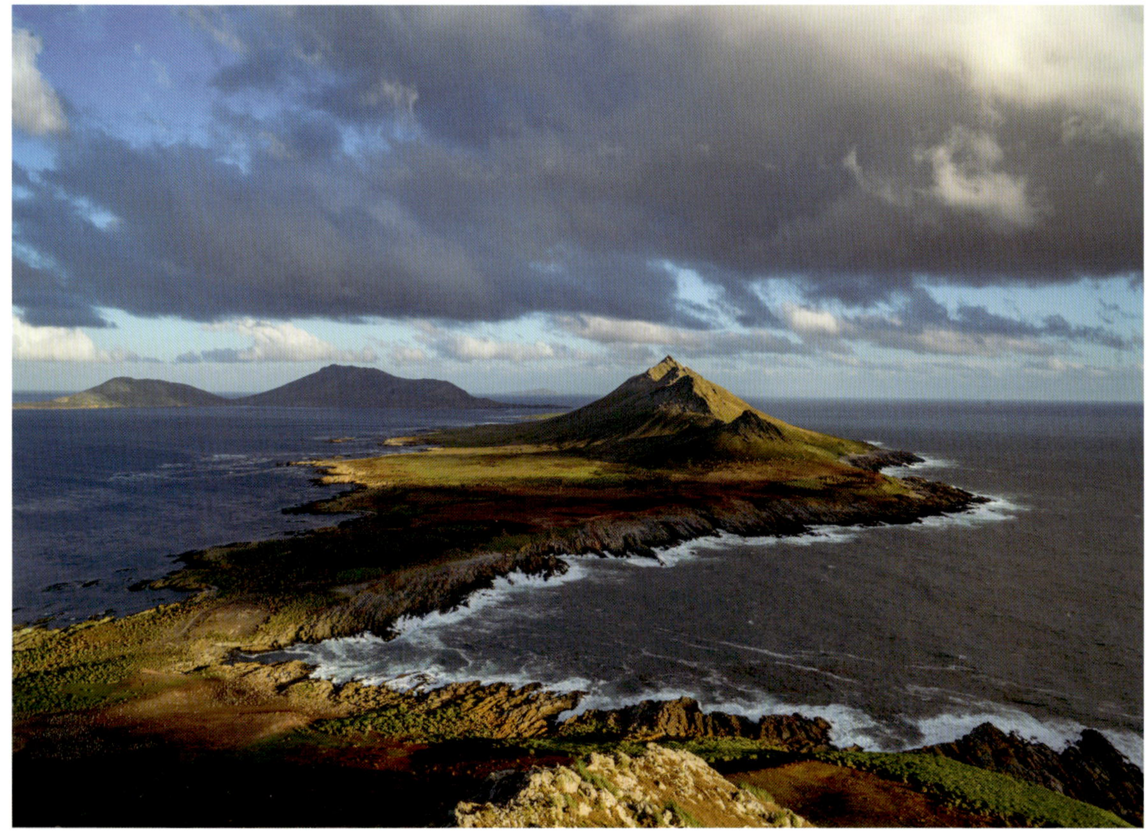

Isla Trinidad
Saunders Island

Malvinas

The Malvinas archipelago is located in
the South Atlantic, 395 km (245 mi) east
of Tierra del Fuego and consists of 200
islands. The largest islands in the west
and east each have an area of 6000 km²
(2316 sq mi). Argentina has claimed the
Malvinas for itself since 1833. The climate
here is cold, windy and rainy, and only
in summer will the thermometer rise
to 20 degrees (68 °F). On the 120 km²
(46 sq mi) large Isla Trinidad, northwest
of the western main island of Isla Gran
Malvina, sheep farming is carried out . The
eastern islands offer white sandy beaches,
turquoise water and rocky coastline. In
spring the yellow gorse flowers bloom.

Les îles Malouines

Les îles Malouines, ou îles Falkland,
sont un archipel de 200 îles situé dans
l'Atlantique sud, à 395 km à l'est de la Terre
de Feu. Les deux îles principales, Grande
Malouine (Isla Gran Malvina ou Falkland
occidentale) et Malouine orientale (Isla
Soledad ou Falkland orientale), mesurent
chacune environ 6 000 km². L'Argentine
revendique les Malouines depuis 1833. Il y
règne un climat froid, venteux et pluvieux,
et le thermomètre n'atteint 20 °C qu'en
été. L'île Saunders (Isla Trinidad) est située
au nord-ouest de la Isla Gran Malvina et
couvre 120 km². L'élevage de moutons y
est pratiqué. Les îles les plus orientales
de l'archipel arborent des plages de
sable blanc, des eaux turquoise et des
côtes rocheuses. Au début du printemps
fleurissent les ajoncs jaunes.

Malwinen

Die Malwinen liegen im Südatlantik,
395 km östlich von Feuerland und
bestehen aus 200 Inseln. Die größten
Inseln im Westen und Osten haben jeweils
eine Fläche von 6000 km². Argentinien
beansprucht die Malwinen seit 1833 für
sich. Hier herrscht ein kaltes, windiges
und regnerisches Klima, nur im Sommer
steigt das Thermometer auf 20 Grad.
Auf der 120 km² großen Isla Trinidad
nordwestlich der Ost-Hauptinsel Isla
Gran Malvina wird Schafzucht betrieben.
Die östlichen Inseln warten mit weißen
Sandstränden, türkisfarbenem Wasser und
felsiger Küste auf. Im Frühjahr blüht der
gelbe Stechginster.

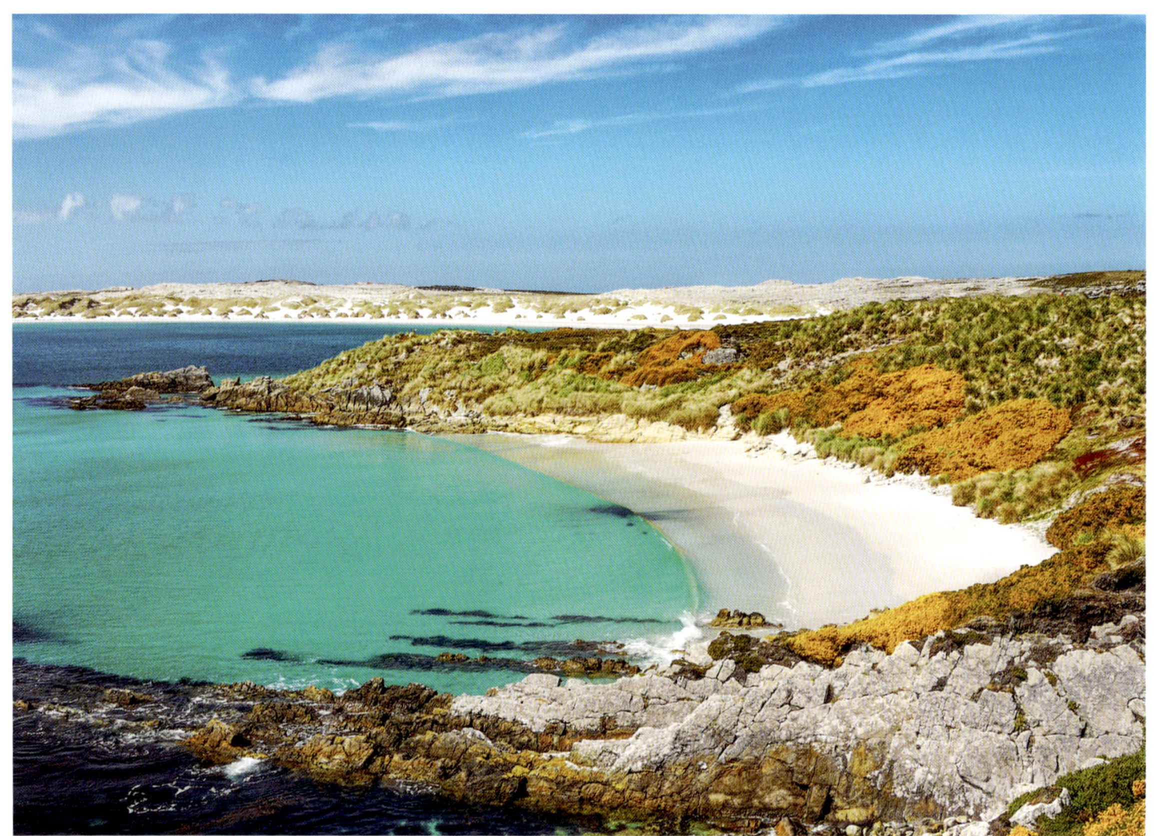

Isla Soledad
East Falkland Island

Islas Malvinas

Las Islas Malvinas están situadas en el
Atlántico Sur, a 395 km al este de Tierra
del Fuego, y están formadas por 200
islas. Las islas más grandes del oeste y
del este tienen cada una una superficie
de 6000 km². Argentina ha reclamado las
Malvinas para sí desde 1833. El clima aquí
es frío, ventoso y lluvioso; solo en verano
el termómetro sube a 20 grados. En los
120 km² de la Isla Trinidad, al noroeste
de la isla principal del este, se practica la
cría de ovejas en la Isla Gran Malvina. Las
islas orientales ofrecen playas de arena
blanca, agua turquesa y costa rocosa. En
primavera, florece el espinillo amarillo.

Malvinas

As Malvinas estão localizadas no Atlântico
Sul, 395 km a leste da Terra do Fogo
e consistem em 200 ilhas. As maiores
ilhas do oeste e do leste têm uma área
de 6000 km² cada uma. A Argentina
reivindica as Malvinas desde 1833. O clima
aqui é frio, ventoso e chuvoso, só no
verão o termômetro sobe para 20 graus.
Nos 120 km² da grande Isla Trinidad é
praticada a criação de ovinos, a noroeste
da ilha principal do leste, a Isla Gran
Malvina. As ilhas orientais oferecem praias
de areia branca, águas azul-turquesa e
costa rochosa. As moitas de tojo amarelo
florescem na primavera.

Malvinas

De Malvinas liggen in het zuiden van de
Atlantische Oceaan, 395 km ten oosten van
Vuurland en bestaan uit 200 eilanden. De
grootste eilanden in het westen en oosten
hebben elk een oppervlakte van 6000 km².
Argentinië heeft sinds 1833 de Malvinas
voor zichzelf opgeëist. Hier heerst een
koud, winderig en regenachtig klimaat,
alleen in de zomer stijgt de thermometer
tot 20 graden. Op het 120 km² grote eiland
Isla Trinidad, ten noordwesten van het
oostelijke hoofdeiland Isla Gran Malvina,
houdt met zich met schapenfokkerij
bezig. De oostelijke eilanden bieden witte
zandstranden, turquoise water en een
rotsachtige kustlijn. In het voorjaar bloeit
de gele gaspeldoorn.

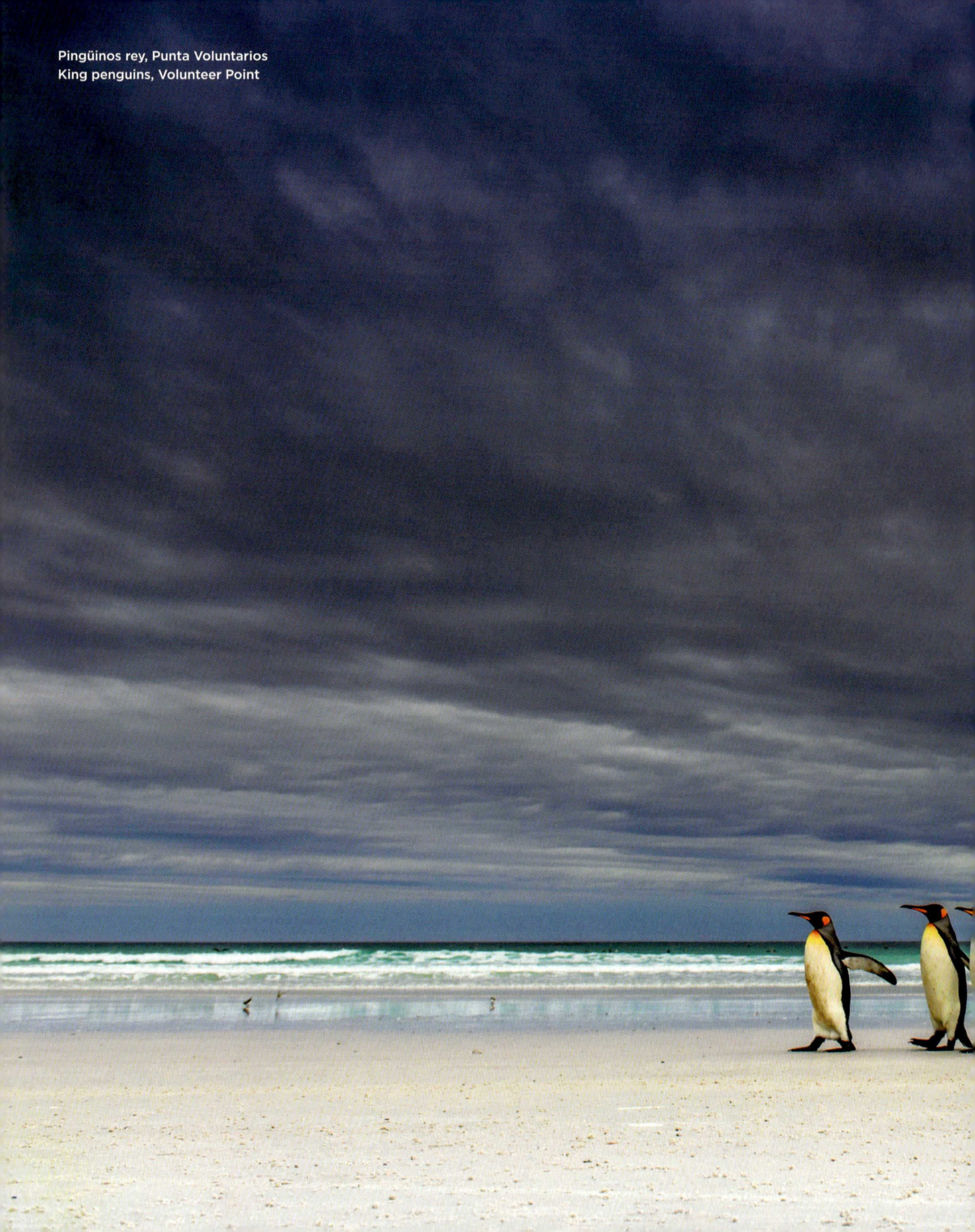
Pingüinos rey, Punta Voluntarios
King penguins, Volunteer Point

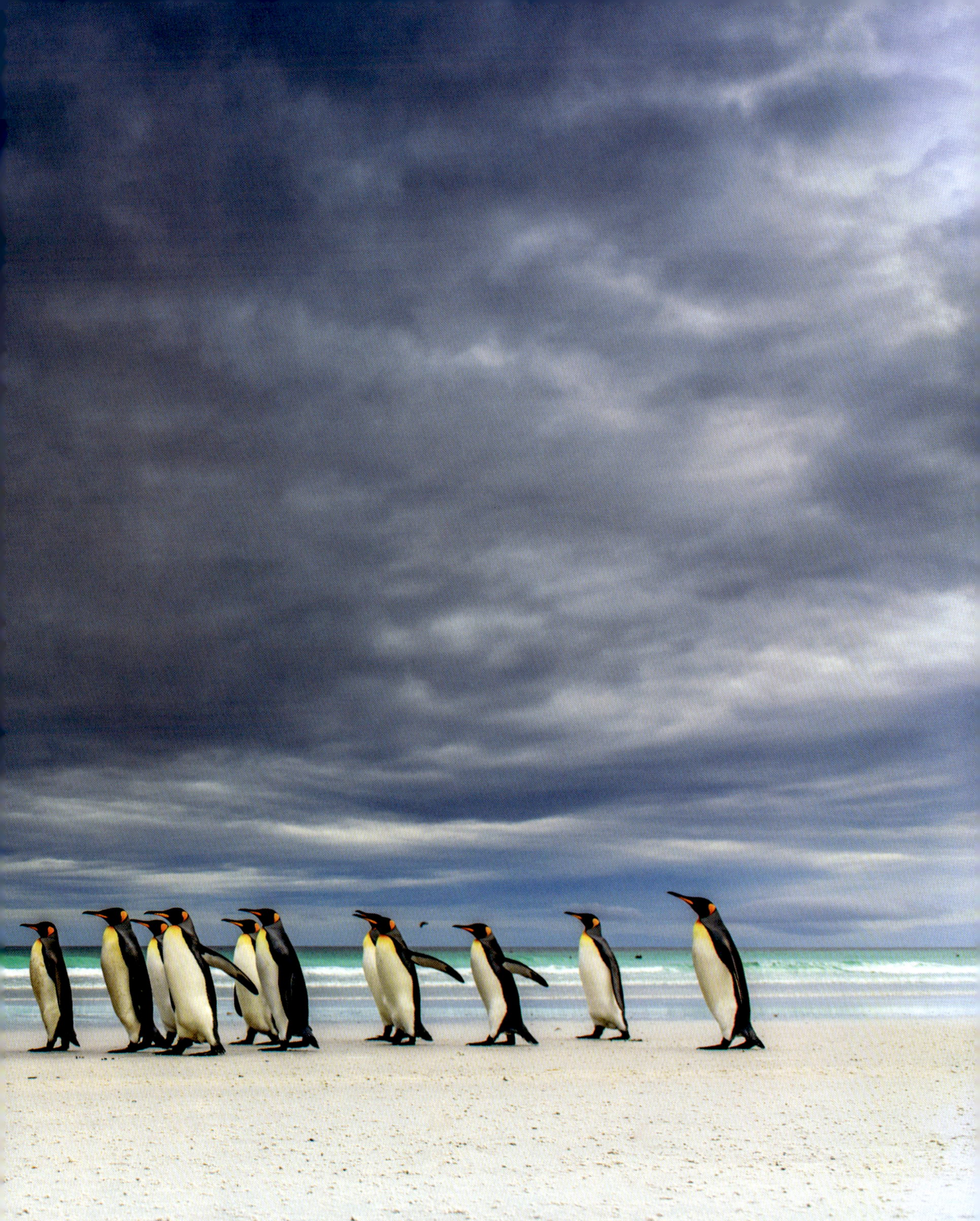

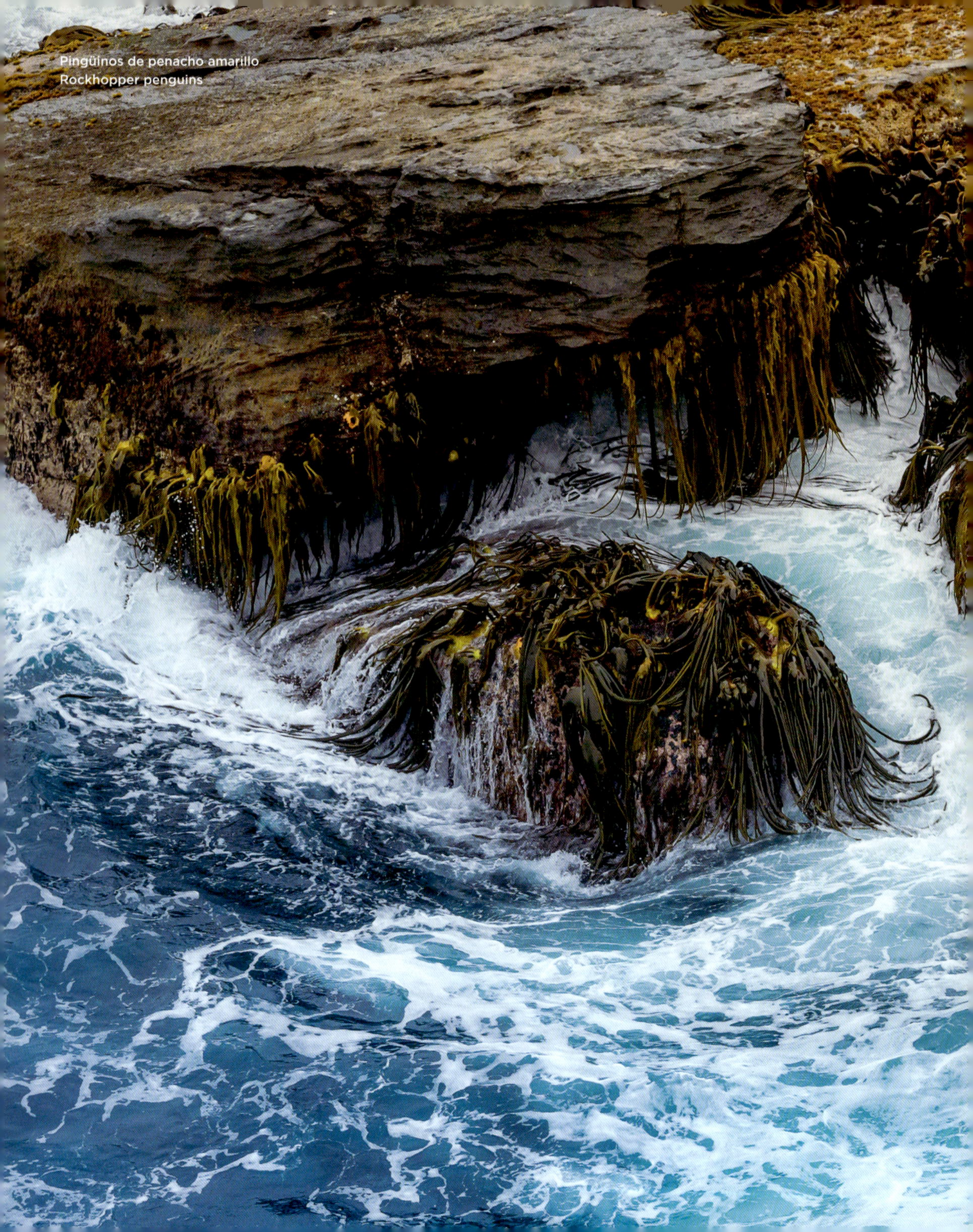

Pingüinos de penacho amarillo
Rockhopper penguins

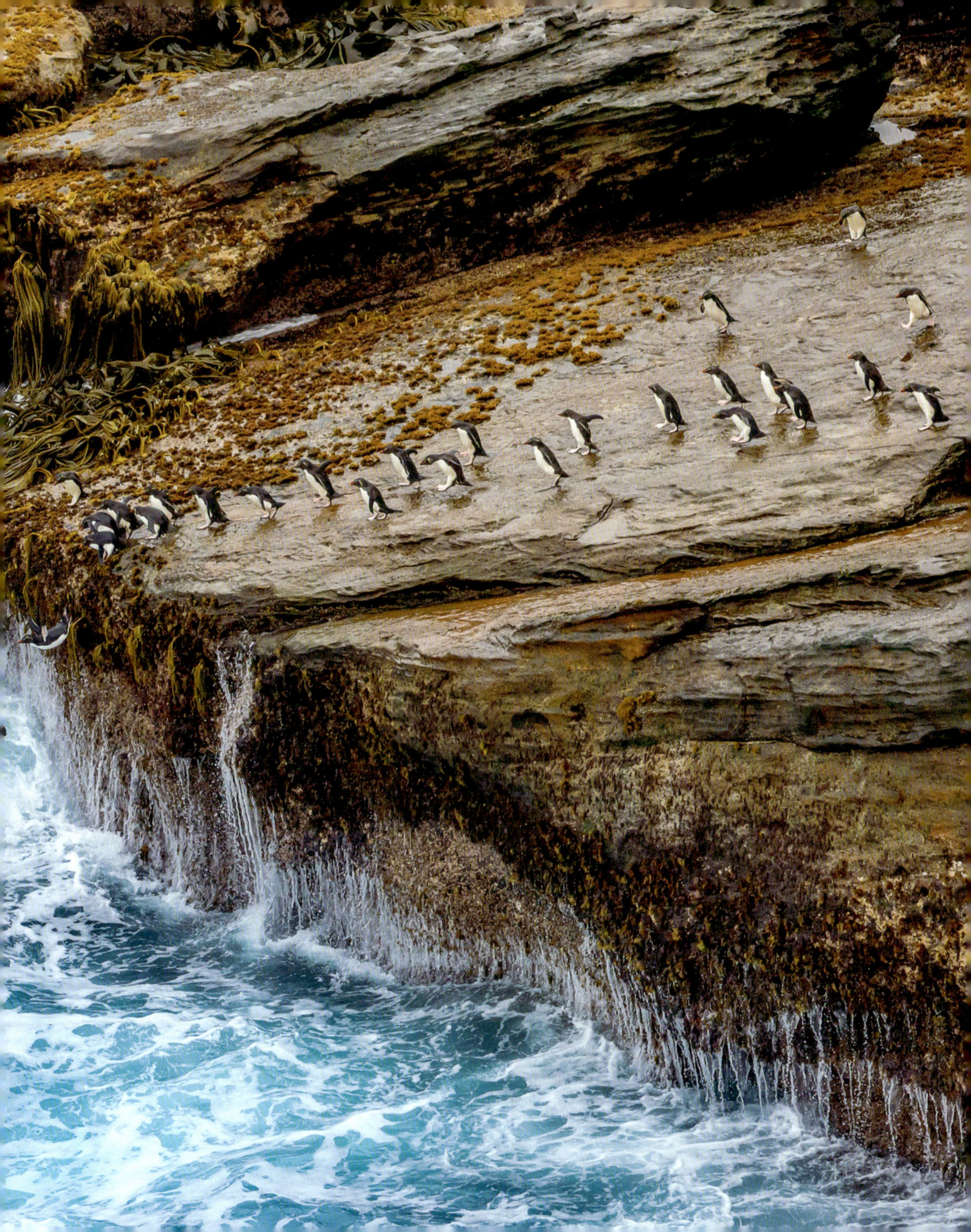

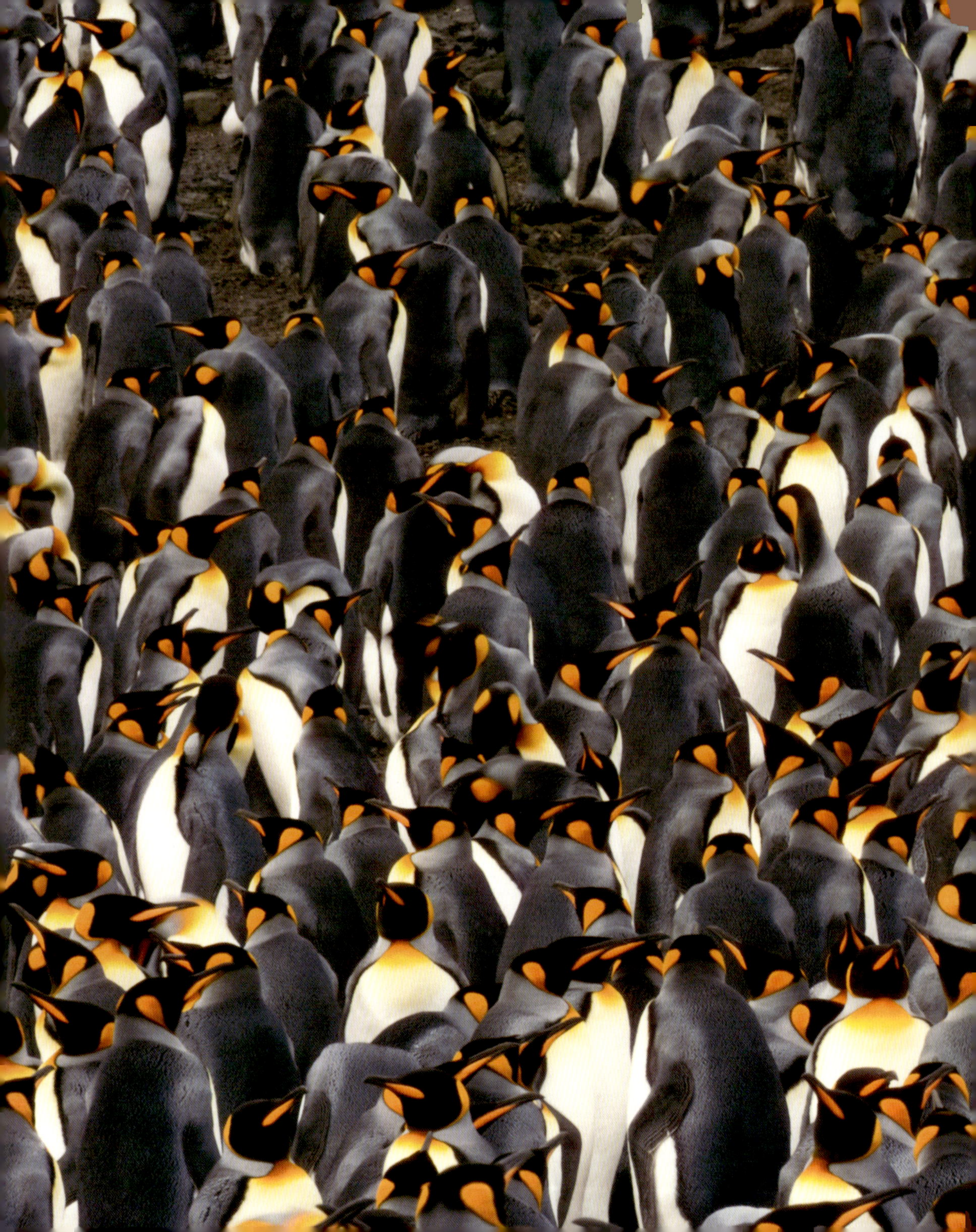

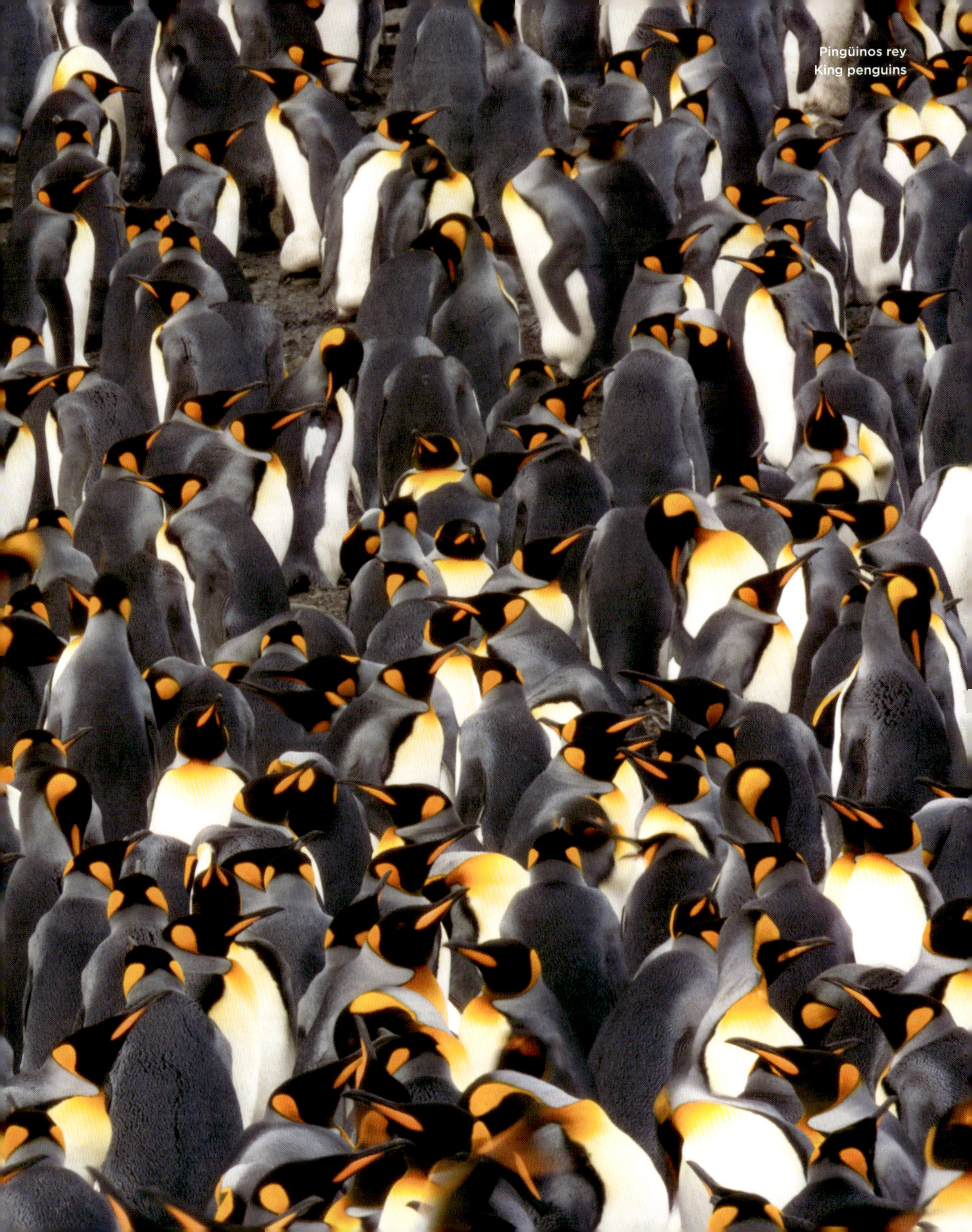
Pingüinos rey
King penguins

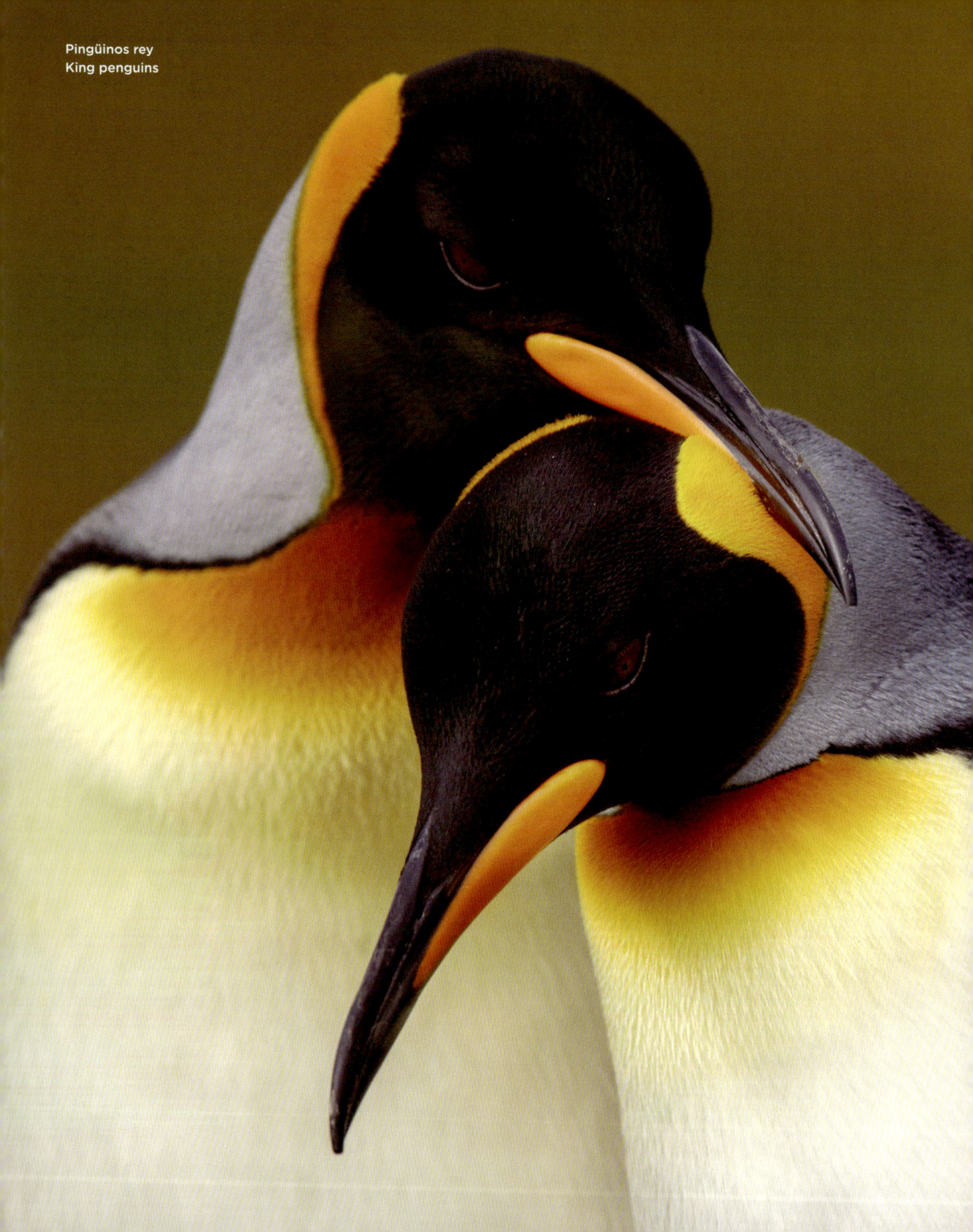

Pingüinos rey
King penguins

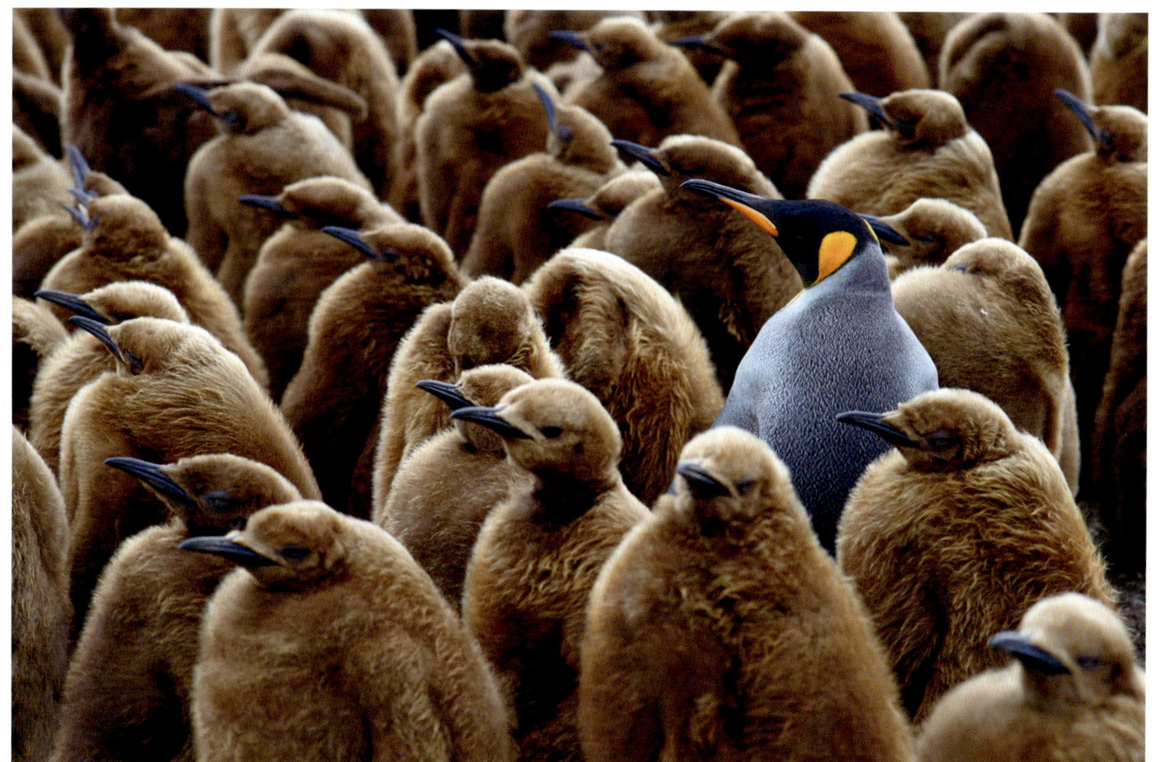

Pingüinos rey
King penguins

King Penguins

King penguins have small colonies on the Malvinas, next to the breeding grounds of the gentoo penguins. Standing 85–95 cm (33–37 in) tall and weighing 10–16 kg (22–35 lb), the king penguin is almost as big as the stately emperor penguin. The female lays a 310 g (11 oz) egg, with the pair sharing the duties of incubating and raising the offspring over a 9 month period.

Pingüinos rey

Los pingüinos Aptenodytes tienen pequeñas colonias en las Malvinas junto a las zonas de reproducción de los pingüinos papúa. Con 85–95 cm de tamaño y 10–16 kg de peso, el pingüino rey es casi tan grande como el majestuoso pingüino emperador. La hembra pone un huevo pesado de 310 g, la pareja lo incuba alternativamente y comparte la crianza de las crías durante 9 meses.

Manchots royaux

Ces grands manchots vivent en petites colonies sur les Malouines, à proximité des sites de reproduction des manchots papous. Mesurant 85 à 95 cm et pesant 10 à 16 kg, le manchot royal est pratiquement aussi grand que l'imposant manchot empereur. La femelle pond un œuf de 310 g que le couple couve tour à tour, puis les deux parents s'occupent conjointement d'élever l'oisillon pendant plus de 9 mois.

Pinguim-rei

Os pinguims-rei vivem em pequenas colónias nas Malvinas, junto aos locais de reprodução dos pinguins-gentoo. Com 85–95 cm de tamanho e 10–16 kg de peso, o penguim-rei é quase tão grande quanto o imponente penguim-imperador. A fêmea põe um ovo pesado de 310 g, o par alimenta alternadamente e compartilha a criação dos filhotes ao longo de 9 meses.

Königspinguine

Die Großpinguine haben auf den Malwinen kleine Kolonien neben den Brutstätten der Eselspinguine. Mit 85–95 cm Größe und 10–16 kg Gewicht ist der Königspinguin fast so groß wie der stattliche Kaiserpinguin. Das Weibchen legt ein 310 g schweres Ei, das Paar brütet abwechselnd und teilt sich über 9 Monate die Aufzucht des Nachwuchses.

Koningspinguïns

Op de Falklandeilanden hebben de Aptenodytes pinguïns kleine kolonies naast de broedplaatsen van de ezelspinguïns. Met een grootte van 85–95 cm en een gewicht van 10–16 kg is de koningspinguïn bijna net zo groot als de statige keizerspinguïn. Het vrouwtje legt een 310 g zwaar ei, het paar broedt afwisselend en deelt de opvoeding van het nageslacht gedurende 9 maanden.

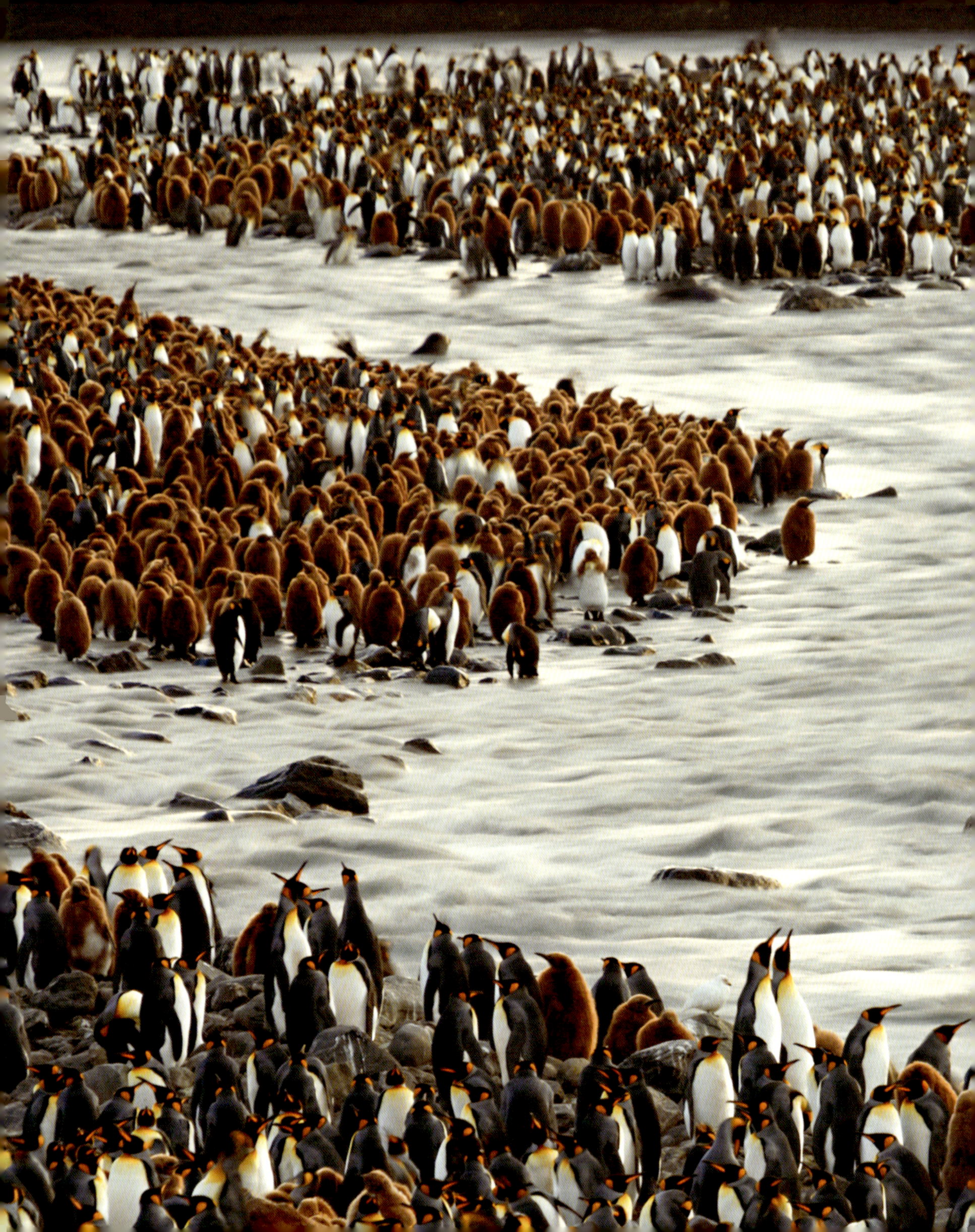

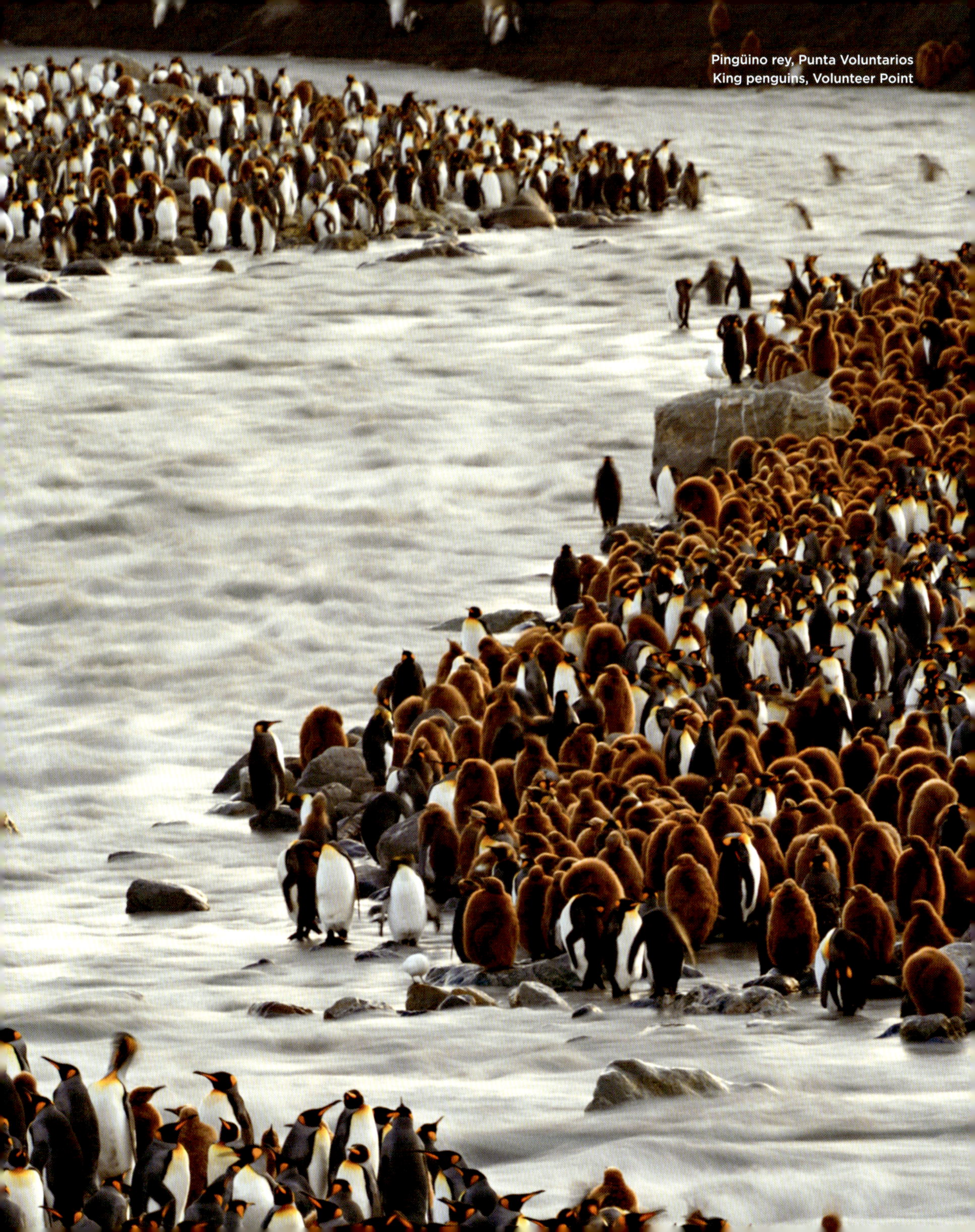
Pingüino rey, Punta Voluntarios
King penguins, Volunteer Point

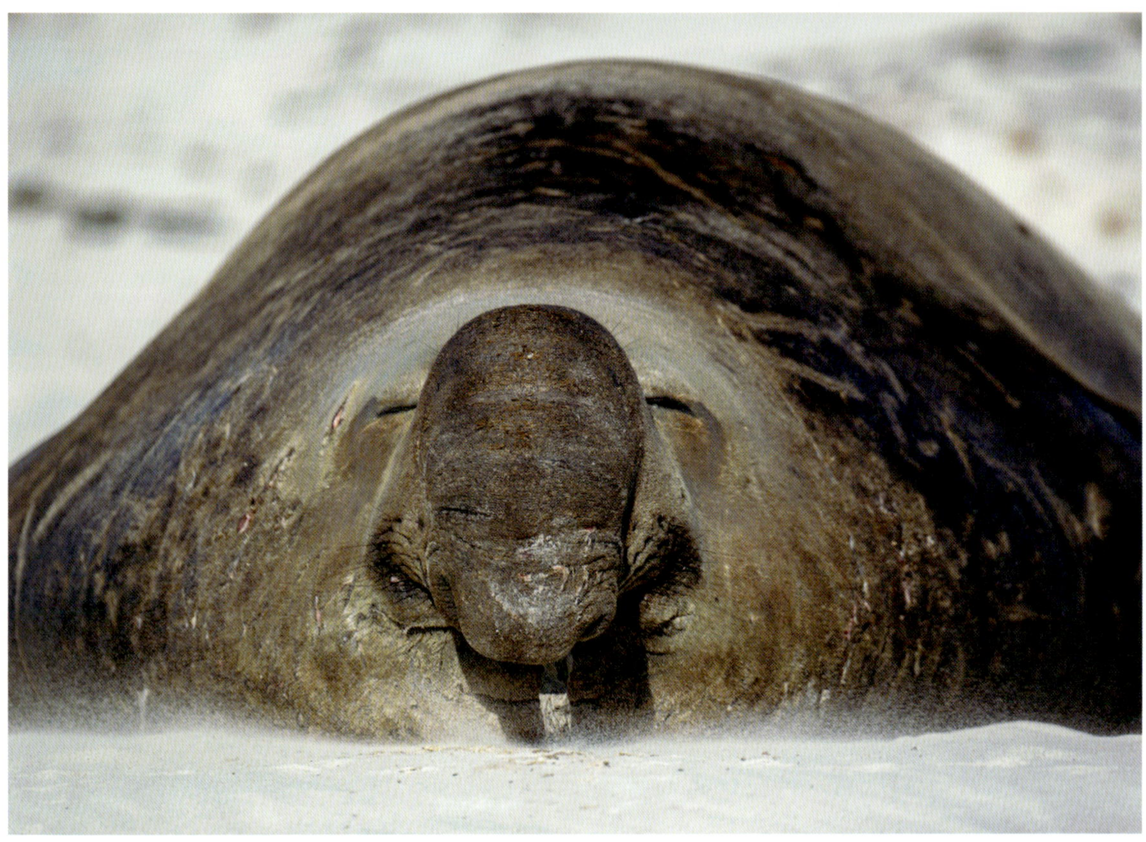

Elefante marino del sur
Southern elephant seal

Southern elephant seal

With a length of 6.5 m (21 ft) and a weight
of 3.5 tons, the southern elephant seals
are the largest in the seal family. They have
a short, stiff coat. The 10 cm (4 in) long
trunk of the bulls can be expanded. Over
the course of the year they may cover
4800 km (2982 mi), meaning that they
spend most of their time at sea. During the
mating season and for giving birth, they
form colonies on land. The males arrive
before the females and determine their
territory, after which the dominant males
establish harems of up to 60 females,
which they will protect from rivals by
posturing and fighting. Females carry their
young for 8 months, after which the young
animals are suckled for 23 days and must
then fend for themselves.

Éléphant de mer du Sud

L'éléphant de mer du Sud mesure 6,5 m,
pèse environ 3,5 t et représente ainsi la
plus grosse espèce de phoques (Phocidés).
Il est doté d'une fourrure courte et rêche.
Le mâle possède une trompe de 10 cm
qu'il peut gonfler. Au cours d'une année,
les éléphants de mer du Sud parcourent
4 800 km, ce qui signifie qu'ils passent la
majeure partie de leur temps en mer. Ils
forment des colonies sur terre à l'époque
des amours et pour la mise bas. Les mâles
arrivent avant les femelles et défendent
âprement leur territoire. Leur harem peut
compter jusqu'à 60 femelles. La gestation
dure 8 mois et les jeunes sont allaités
23 jours avant d'être livrés à eux-mêmes.

Südlicher Seeelefant

Mit 6,5 m Länge und einem Gewicht von
3,5 t sind die Südlichen Seeelefanten die
größten in der Familie der Robben. Sie
tragen ein kurzes, hartes Fell. Der 10 cm
lange Rüssel der Bullen ist aufblasbar. Im
Lauf des Jahres legen sie 4800 km zurück,
d. h. sie verbringen die meiste Zeit auf dem
Meer. Zur Paarungszeit und zum Gebären
bilden sie Kolonien an Land. Die Männchen
kommen vor den Weibchen an und legen
ihr Revier fest. Ihr Harem umfasst bis
zu 60 Weibchen, um die Rivalenkämpfe
ausgetragen werden. Weibchen tragen
ihre Jungen 8 Monate aus. Die Jungtiere
werden 23 Tage gesäugt, dann sind sie auf
sich gestellt.

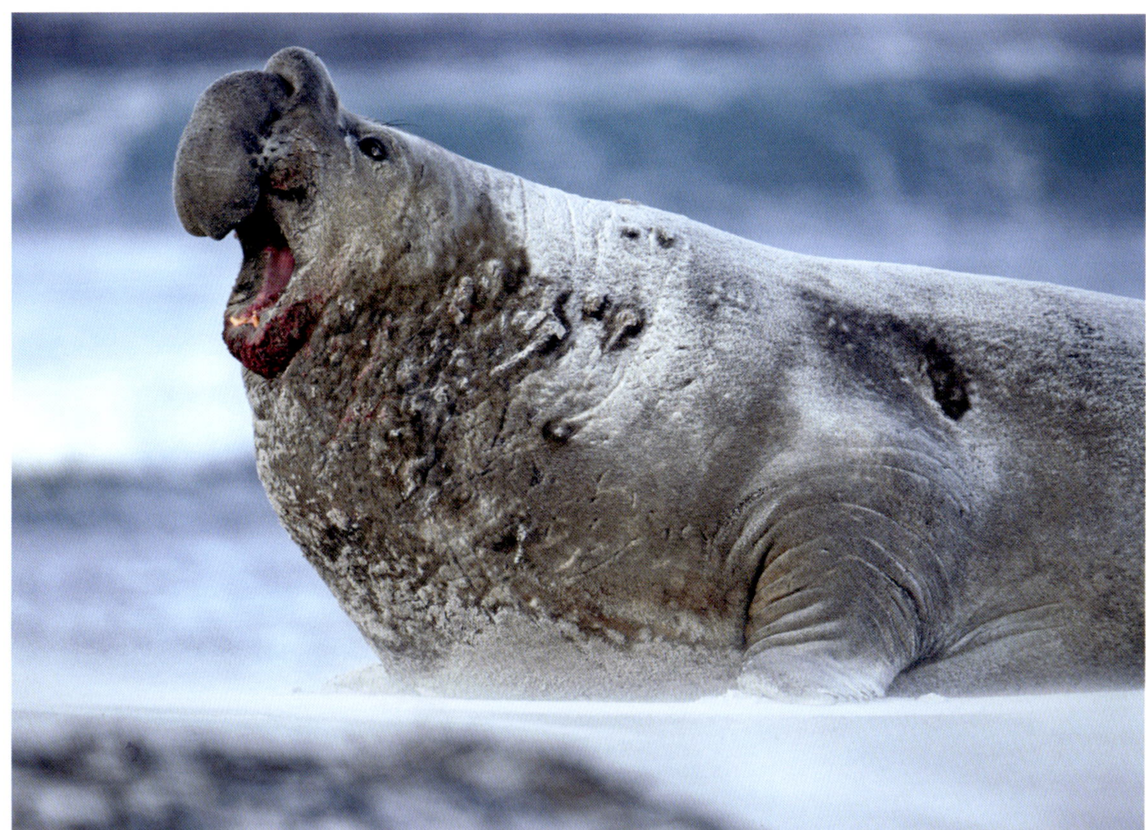

Elefante marino del sur
Southern elephant seal

Elefante marino del sur

Con una longitud de 6,5 m y un peso
de 3,5 t, los elefantes marinos del sur
son los más grandes de la familia de los
Pinnípedos. Tienen un pelaje corto y duro.
El hocico de los machos, de 10 cm de
largo, se hincha. En el transcurso del año
recorren 4800 km, lo que significa que
pasan la mayor parte del tiempo en el mar.
Durante la temporada de apareamiento
y para el parto forman colonias en tierra.
Los machos llegan antes que las hembras
y determinan su territorio. Su harén
incluye hasta 60 hembras para competir
en las peleas rivales. Las hembras llevan
a sus crías durante 8 meses. Las crías son
amamantadas durante 23 días y luego se
quedan solas.

Elefante-marinho-do-sul

Com um comprimento de 6,5 m e um peso
de 3,5 t, os elefantes-marinhos-do-sul são
os maiores da família das focas. Eles têm
uma pelagem curta e rígida. Os machos
possuem um focinho inflável de 10 cm de
comprimento. No decorrer do ano, eles
cobrem 4800 km, o que significa que
passam a maior parte do seu tempo no
mar. Durante a época do acasalamento e
para dar à luz formam colónias em terra.
Os machos chegam antes das fêmeas e
determinam o seu território. O seu harém
inclui até 60 fêmeas para as lutas rivais a
serem combatidas. As fêmeas carregam os
seus filhotes durante 8 meses. Os animais
jovens são amamentados durante 23 dias,
depois ficam por conta própria.

Zuidelijke zeeolifant

Met een lengte van 6,5 m en een gewicht
van 3,5 ton zijn de zuidelijke zeeolifanten
de grootste in de zeehondenfamilie.
Ze hebben een korte, harde vacht. De
10 cm lange slurf van het mannetje is
opblaasbaar. In de loop van het jaar
leggen ze 4800 km af, wat betekent dat
ze het grootste deel van hun tijd op zee
doorbrengen. Tijdens de paartijd en bij
de bevalling vormen ze kolonies op het
land. De mannetjes komen eerder aan dan
de vrouwtjes en bepalen hun territorium.
Hun harem omvat tot 60 vrouwtjes waar
de mannetjes rivaliserend om vechten.
Vrouwtjes dragen hun jongen 8 maanden
lang. De jonge dieren worden 23 dagen
gezoogd, daarna staan ze er alleen voor.

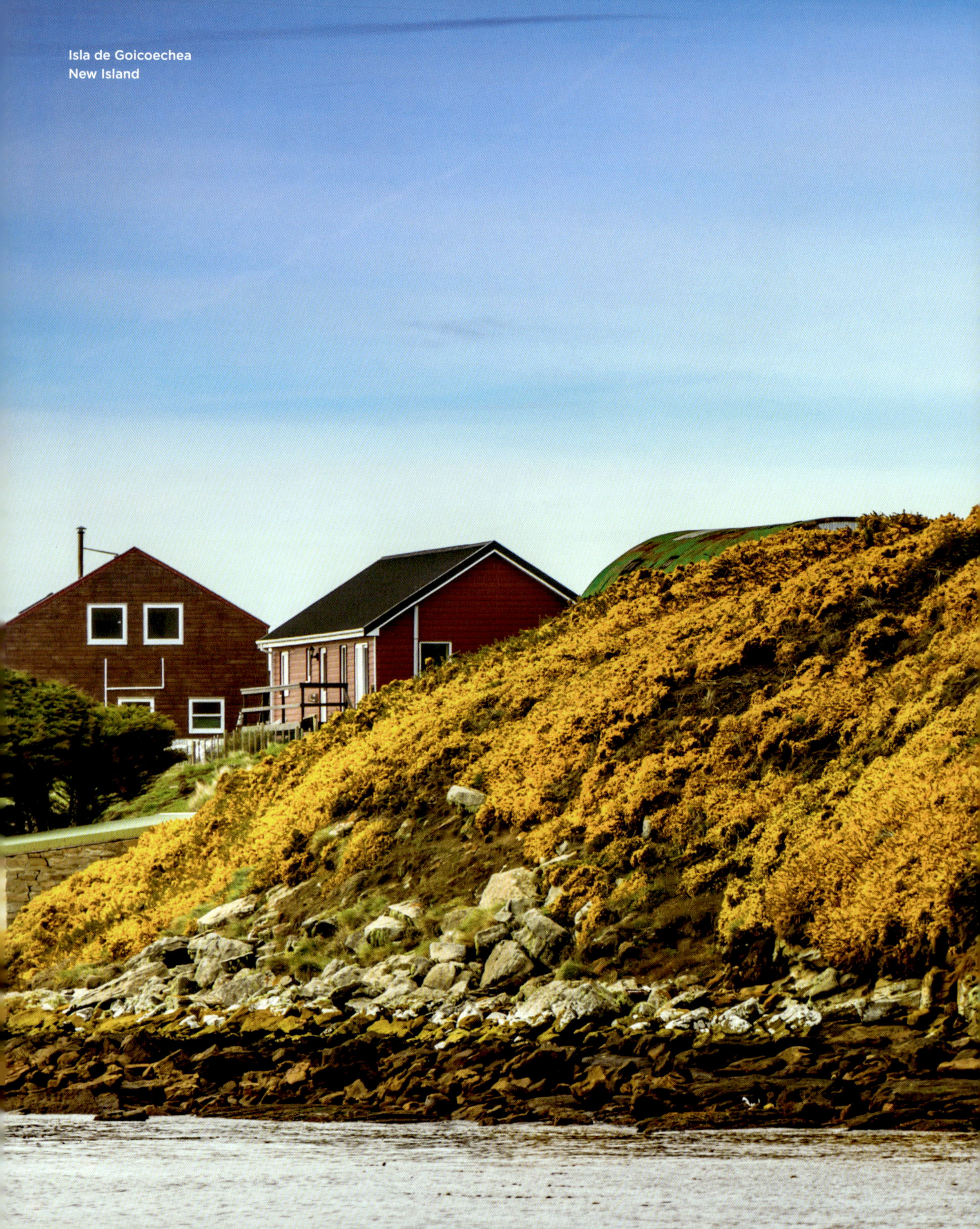
Isla de Goicoechea
New Island

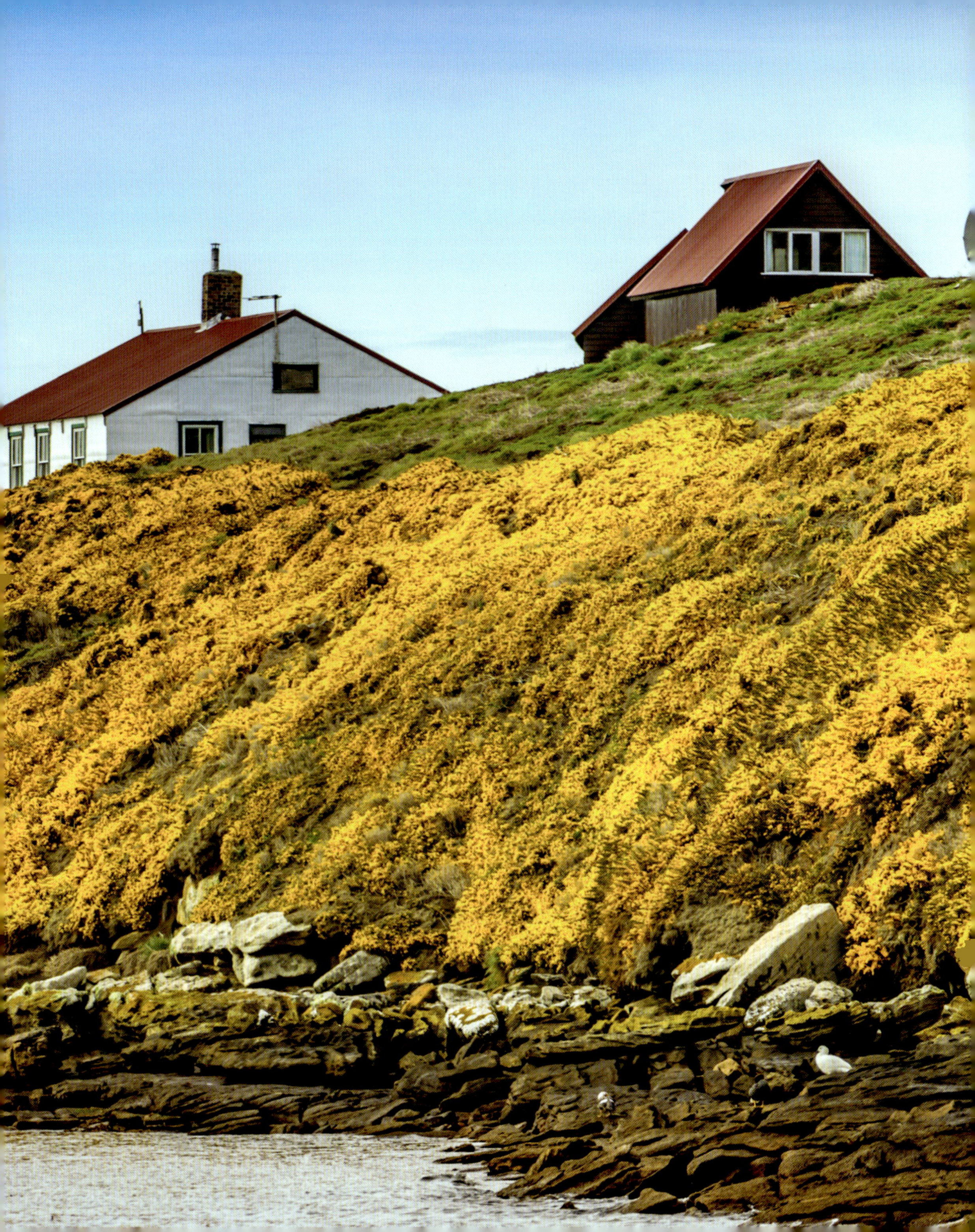

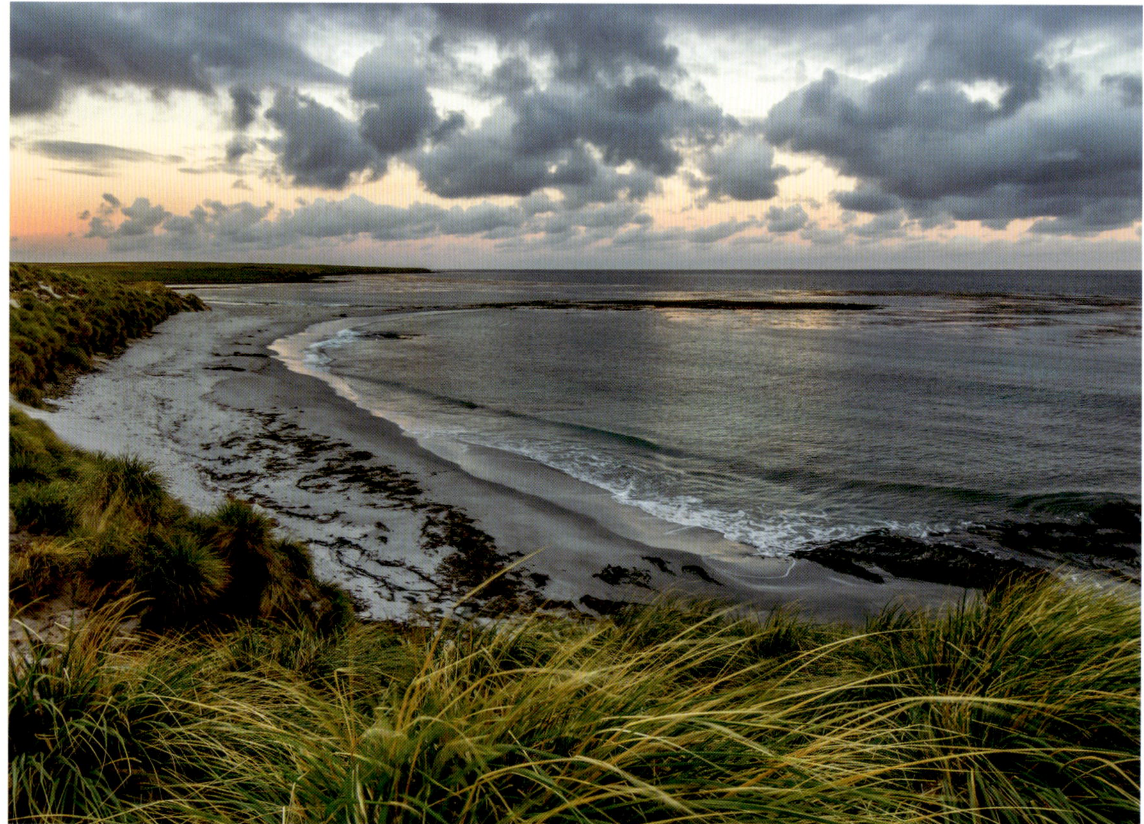

Islas Malvinas
Falkland Islands

Signpost forest

Near the capital of the Malvinas, Puerto
Argentino, or Stanley, on the eastern
main island there is a signpost, which was
made by British soldiers, who between
April and June 1982, during their wartime
deployment on the islands, put up signs
with the names of their home towns and
the distance to them. In the short war
655 Argentines and 253 British died,
and 12,000 Argentines were taken into
captivity. Island visitors, especially cruise
tourists, have added several city names to
the signpost at the port city.

Poteau indicateur

Près de Puerto Argentino (ou Stanley),
la capitale des îles Malouines, sur l'île
principale orientale, se dresse un pieu
portant des panneaux indicateurs. Il a été
installé par les soldats britanniques venus
combattre entre avril et juin 1982. Ils y ont
inscrit le nom de leur localité de résidence
ainsi que sa distance. Lors de ce court
conflit, 655 Argentins et 253 Britanniques
perdirent la vie et 12 000 Argentins furent
faits prisonniers de guerre. Les touristes
venus en visite sur l'île, et en particulier les
croisiéristes, ont complété le poteau situé
non loin du port en y ajoutant leur propre
ville d'origine.

Schilderwald

Nahe der Hauptstadt der Malwinen
Puerto Argentino bzw. Stanley auf der
östlichen Hauptinsel steht ein Pfahl mit
Wegweisern. Er stammt von britischen
Soldaten, die zwischen April und Juni
1982 während ihres Kriegseinsatzes auf
den Inseln Schilder anbrachten, auf die
die Namen ihrer Heimatorte samt der
Entfernung eingetragen wurden. In dem
Kurzkrieg starben 655 Argentinier und
253 Briten, 12 000 Argentinier gingen
in Kriegsgefangenschaft. Inselbesucher,
vor allem Kreuzfahrttouristen, haben den
Wegweiser bei der Hafenstadt um etliche
Städtenamen ergänzt.

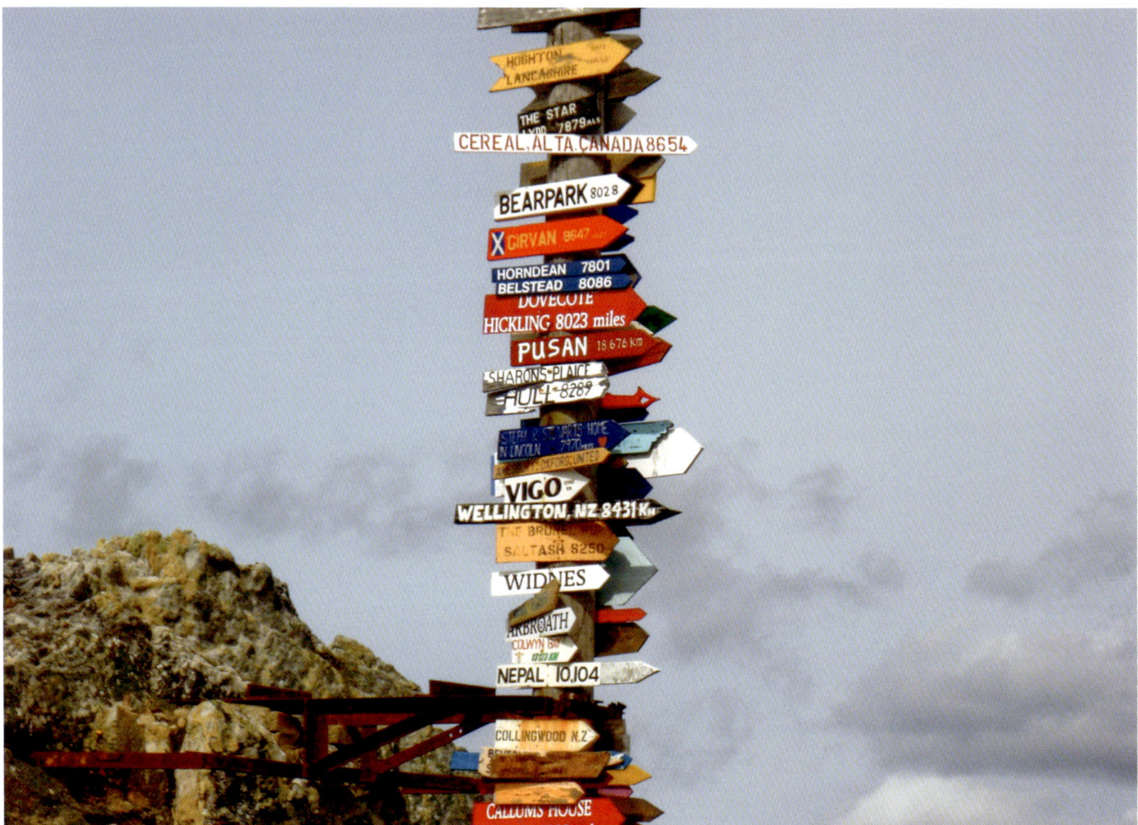

Puerto Argentino, Isla Soledad
Stanley, East Falkland Island

Bosque de señales

Cerca de la capital de las Malvinas, Puerto Argentino, en la isla principal del este, hay un poste con señales. Fue realizado por soldados británicos que entre abril y junio de 1982, durante su despliegue de guerra en las islas, colocaron carteles con los nombres de sus ciudades de origen y la distancia a ellas. En la corta guerra murieron 655 argentinos y 253 británicos, y se tomaron como prisioneros de guerra 12 000 argentinos. Los visitantes de la isla, especialmente los turistas de cruceros, han añadido varios nombres de ciudades al conjunto de señales de la ciudad portuaria.

Floresta de Placas

Perto da capital das Malvinas Puerto Argentino ou Stanley, na ilha principal oriental, há um poste com placas de sinalização. Foi feita por soldados britânicos que, entre abril e junho de 1982, durante o seu esforço nas ilhas em tempo de guerra, colocaram placas com os nomes das suas cidades de origem e a distância até elas. Na guerra curta, 655 argentinos e 253 ingleses morreram, 12 000 argentinos foram para o cativeiro. Os visitantes das ilhas, especialmente os turistas de cruzeiro, adicionaram vários nomes de cidades à sinalização da cidade portuária.

Wegwijzer

Op het oostelijke hoofdeiland, in de buurt van Puerto Argentino of Stanley, de hoofdstad van de Falklandeilanden, staat een paal met wegwijzers. Deze stamt van de Britse soldaten die tussen april en juni 1982, tijdens hun inzet in de Falkland-oorlog, borden hebben opgehangen met de namen van hun woonplaats en de afstand tot de eilanden. In de korte oorlog stierven 655 Argentijnen en 253 Britten, 12 000 Argentijnen werden krijgsgevangene gemaakt. Eilandbezoekers, vooral cruisetoeristen, hebben verschillende plaatsnamen aan de wegwijzer in de havenstad toegevoegd.

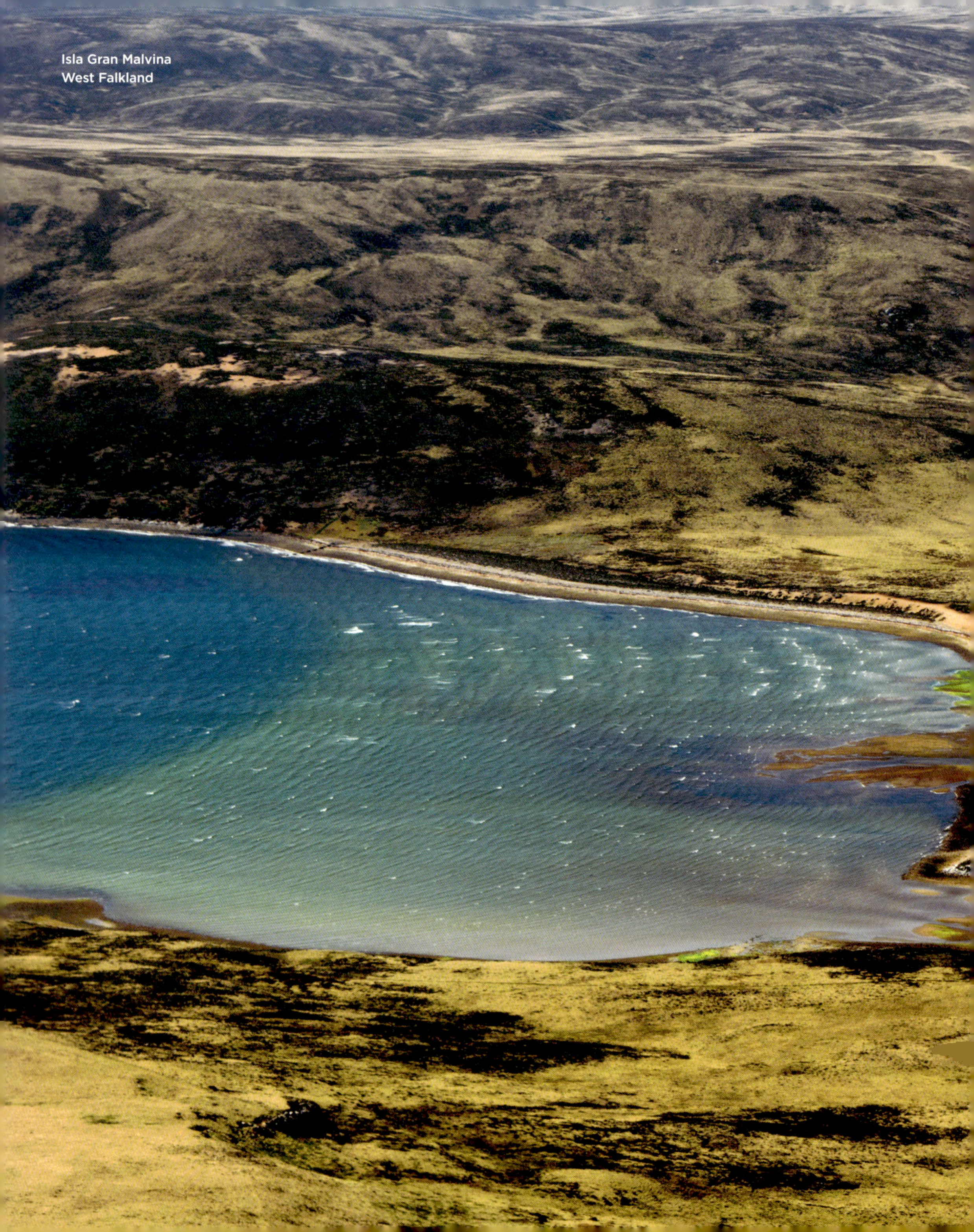

Isla Gran Malvina
West Falkland

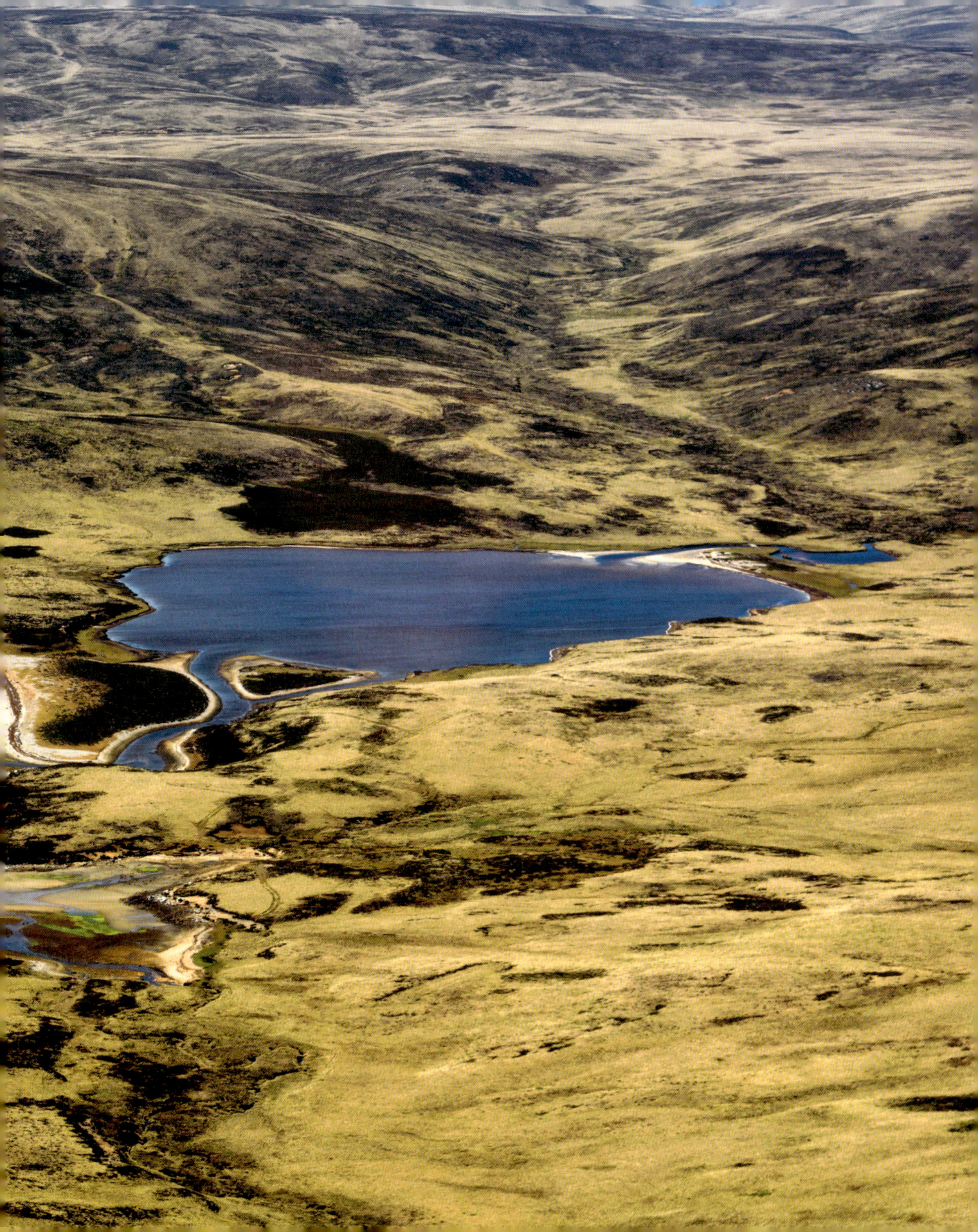

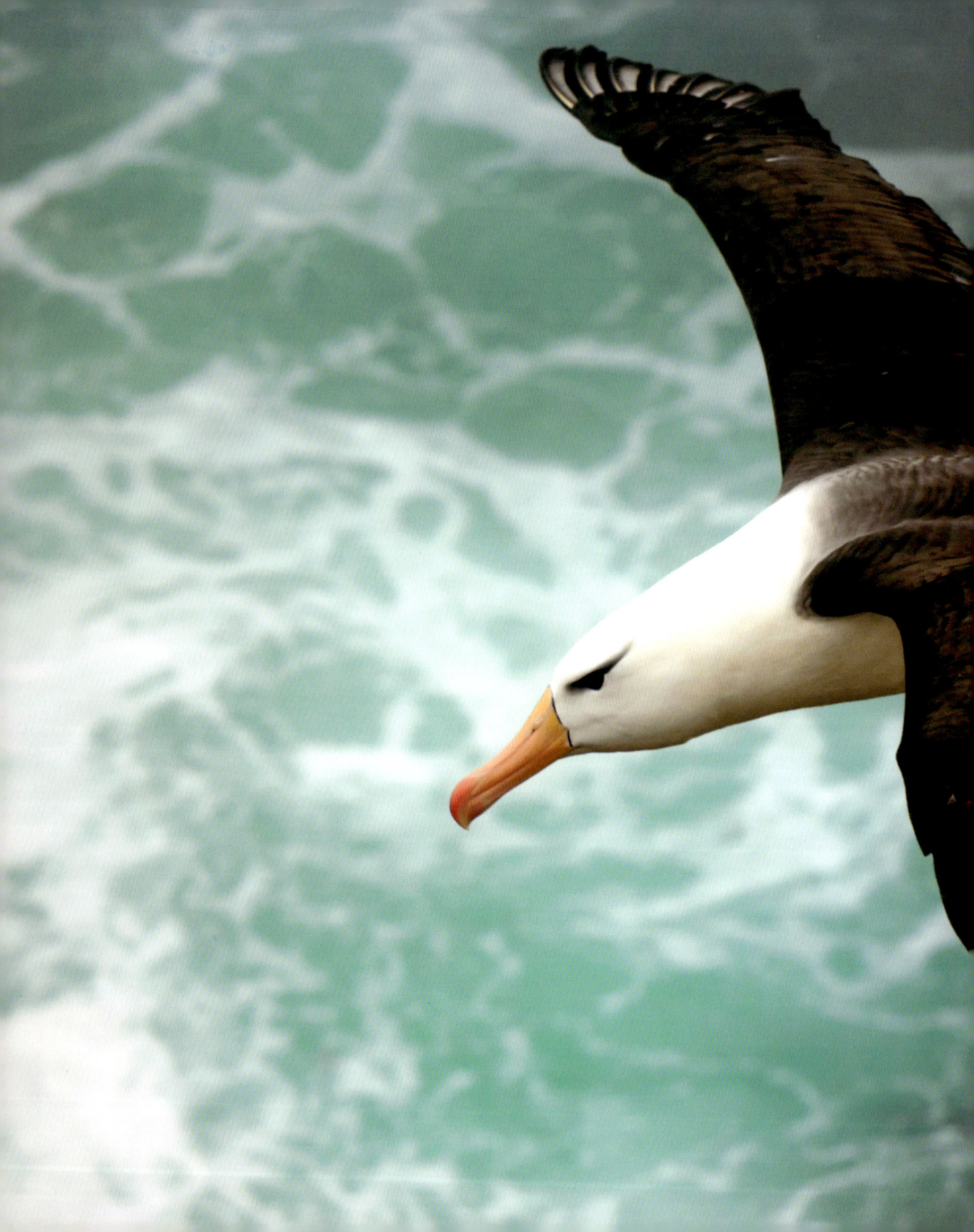

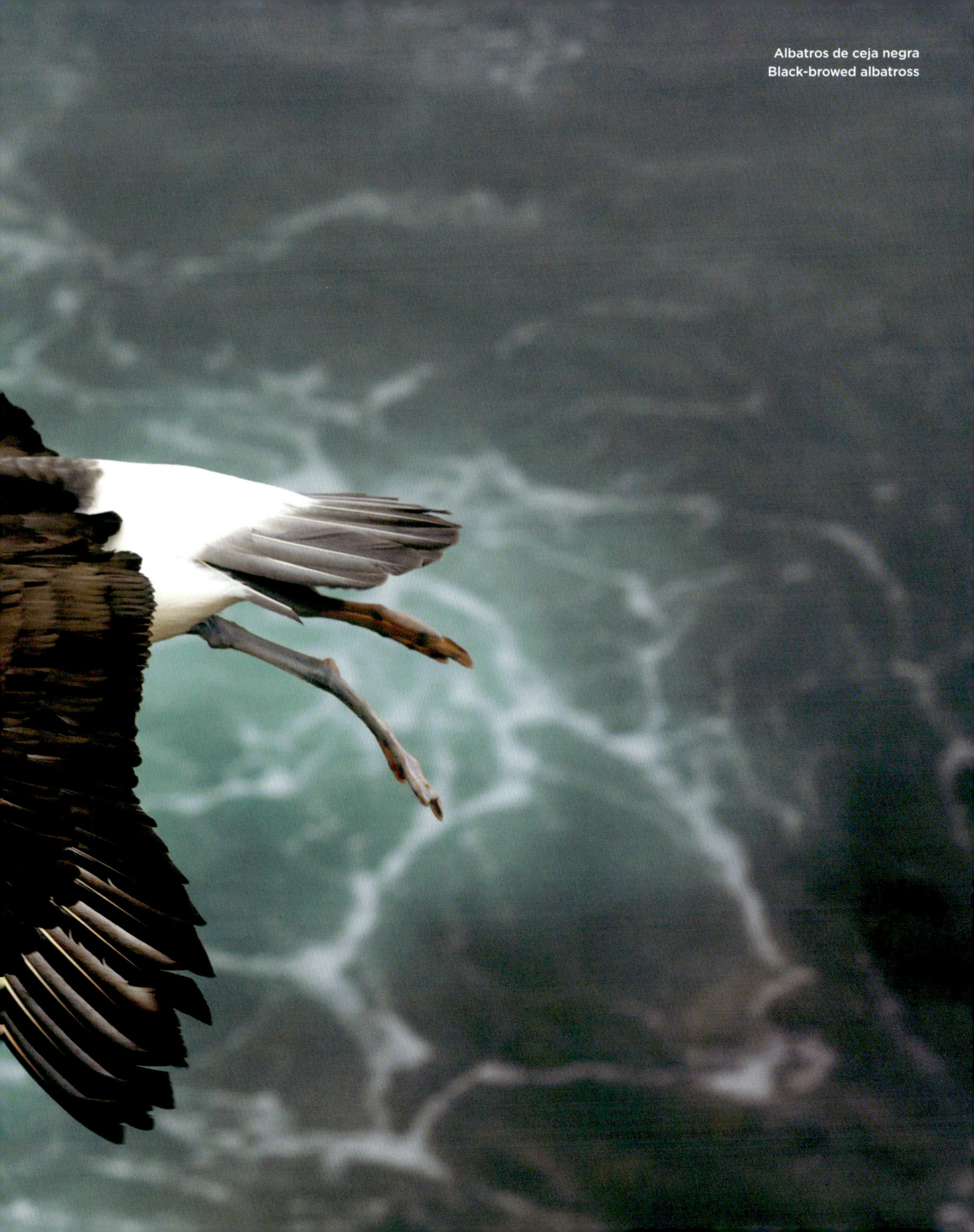
Albatros de ceja negra
Black-browed albatross

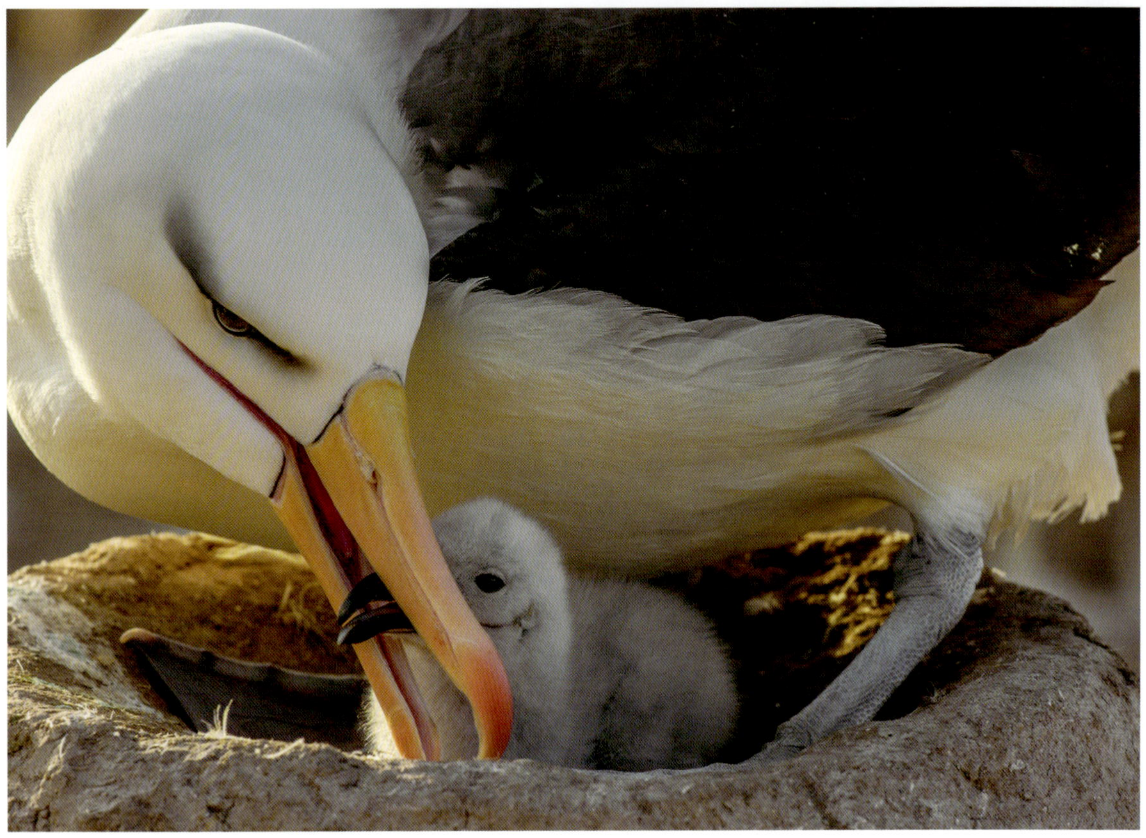

Albatros de ceja negra
Black-browed albatross

Albatrosses

These seabirds belong to the order of procellariiformes (the tubenoses). There are 21 species, 17 of which live in the southern oceans. The black-browed albatross is the smallest of the albatrosses and can live to be 30 years old. Its wingspan may reach 245 cm (96 in). It is able to glide over the waves for hours without flapping its wings. The birds nest on 12 islands around the polar circle. Up to 400,000 black-browed albatrosses breed on the Malvinas, with the largest nesting colony on Steeple Jason Island, northwest of the main islands. They lay only one egg, which is then incubated for 70 days. The young spend 120 days in the nest before becoming fledged.

Albatros

Cette famille d'oiseaux de mer appartient à l'ordre des Procellariiformes et comprend 21 espèces, dont 17 vivent dans l'océan austral. L'albatros à sourcils noirs est le plus petit. Il peut vivre jusqu'à 30 ans et présente une envergure de 245 cm. Il peut planer au-dessus des vagues pendant des heures sans un battement d'ailes. Ces oiseaux nidifient sur 12 îles autour du cercle polaire et 400 000 choisissent les Malouines. La plus grande colonie est installée sur l'île Steeple Jason, au nord-ouest de l'île principale occidentale. La femelle ne pond qu'un œuf qui est couvé pendant 70 jours. Le jeune passe ensuite 120 jours au nid avant de prendre son envol.

Albatrosse

Die Seevögel gehören zur Ordnung der Röhrennasen. Es gibt 21 Arten, davon leben 17 in den südlichen Ozeanen. Der Schwarzbrauenalbatross ist der kleinste der Albatrosse. Er kann 30 Jahre alt werden. Seine Flügel haben eine Spannweite von 245 cm. Ohne einen Flügelschlag kann er stundenlang über den Wellen gleiten. Die Vögel nisten auf 12 Inseln rund um den Polarkreis. 400 000 Schwarzbrauenalbatrosse brüten auf den Malwinen. Die größte Nistkolonie liegt auf Steeple Jason Island nordwestlich der Hauptinseln. Sie legen nur ein Ei, das 70 Tage lang ausgebrütet wird. Das Junge verbringt 120 Tage im Nest, bis es flügge wird.

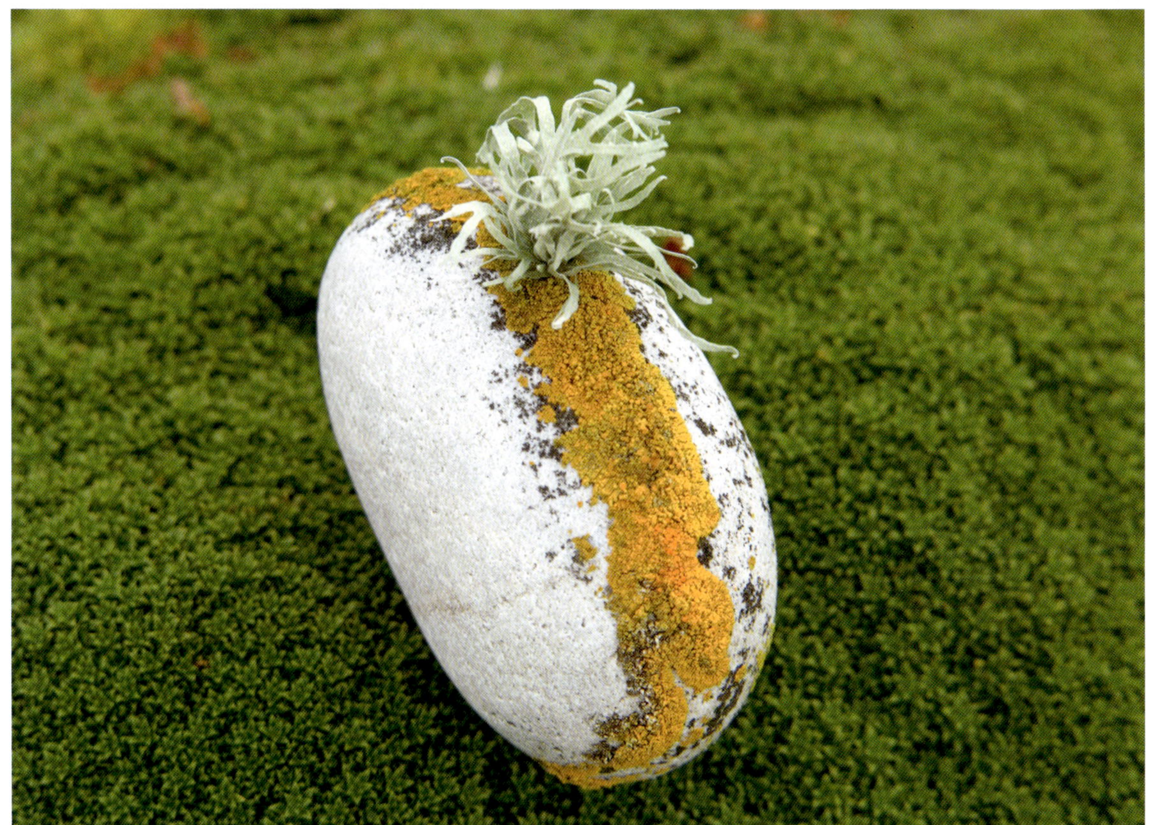

Liquen
Lichen

Albatros

Las aves marinas pertenecen al orden de los Procellariiformes. Hay 21 especies, 17 de las cuales viven en los océanos del sur. El albatros de ceja negra es el más pequeño de los albatros. Puede vivir hasta los 30 años. Sus alas tienen una envergadura de 245 cm. Puede deslizarse sobre las olas durante horas sin batir las alas. Los pájaros anidan en 12 islas alrededor del círculo polar. Unos 400 000 albatros de ceja negra se reproducen en las Malvinas. La mayor colonia de anidación se encuentra en la isla Salvaje del Oeste, al noroeste de las islas principales. Solo ponen un huevo, que se incuba durante 70 días. La cría pasa 120 días en el nido antes de convertirse en un polluelo.

Albatrozes

As aves marinhas pertencem à ordem dos Procellariiformes, também conhecidos como bobos, painhos ou almas-de-mestre. Existem 21 espécies, 17 das quais vivem nos oceanos do sul. O albatroz-de-sobrancelha é o menor dos albatrozes. Ele pode viver até os 30 anos de idade. As suas asas têm uma envergadura de 245 cm. Pode deslizar sobre as ondas durante horas sem bater as asas. As aves nidificam em 12 ilhas ao redor do Círculo Polar. 400 000 albatrozes-de-sobrancelha se reproduzem nas Malvinas. A maior colónia de nidificação está localizada na Steeple Jason Island, a noroeste das ilhas principais. Só põem um ovo, que é incubado durante 70 dias. As crias passam 120 dias no ninho antes de se tornarem independentes.

Albatrossen

Zeevogels behoren tot de orde van de buissnaveligen. Er zijn 21 soorten, waarvan er 17 in de zuidelijke oceanen leven. De wenkbrauwalbatros is de kleinste van de albatrossen. Hij kan 30 jaar oud worden. Zijn vleugels hebben een spanwijdte van 245 cm. Hij kan urenlang over de golven glijden zonder met zijn vleugels te slaan. De vogels nestelen op 12 eilanden rond de poolcirkel. Op de Falklandeilanden broeden 400 000 wenkbrauwalbatrossen. De grootste broedkolonie bevindt zich op Steeple Jason Island ten noordwesten van de hoofdeilanden. Ze leggen maar één ei dat 70 dagen lang wordt uitgebroed. De jongen blijven 120 dagen in het nest voordat ze kunnen vliegen.

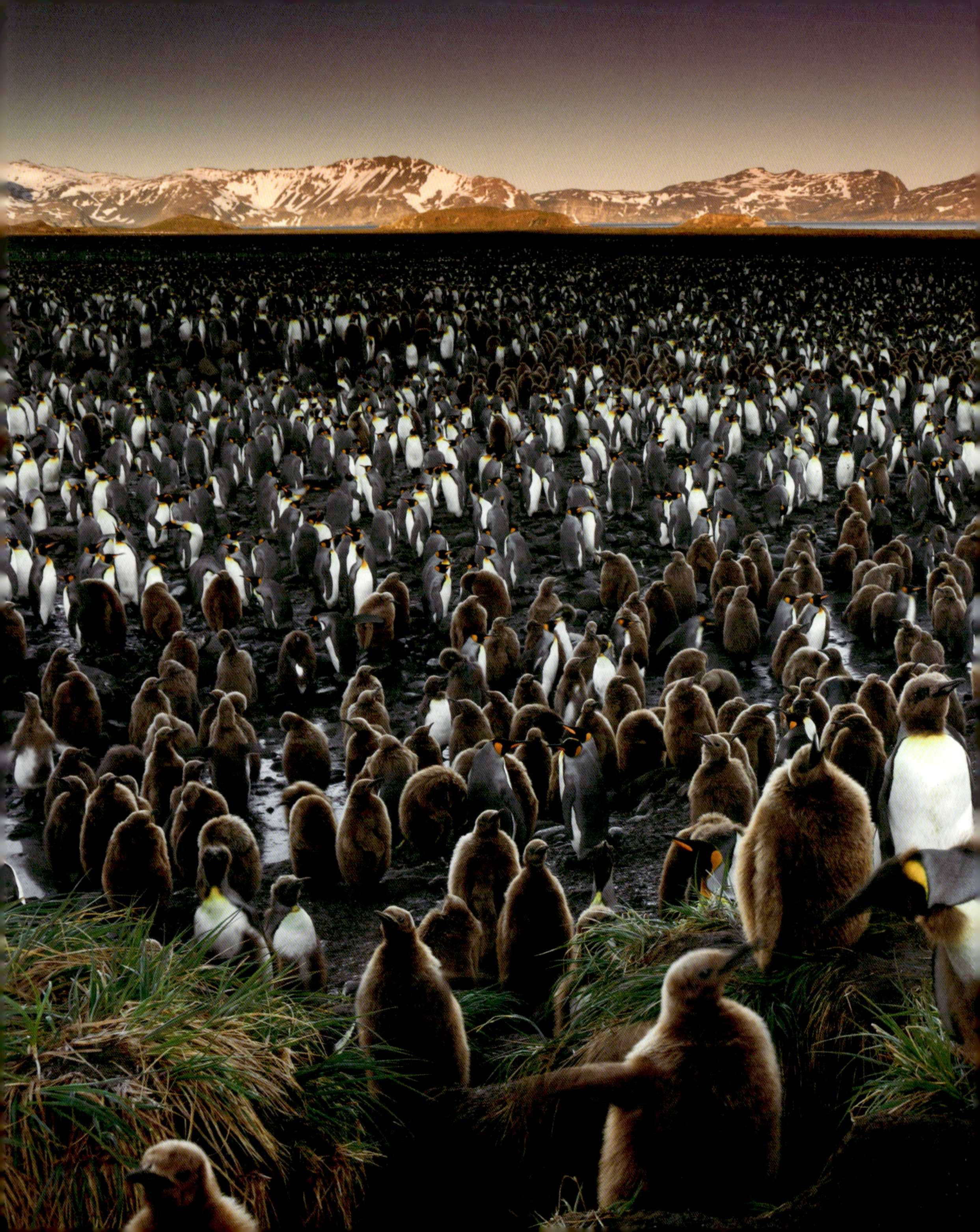

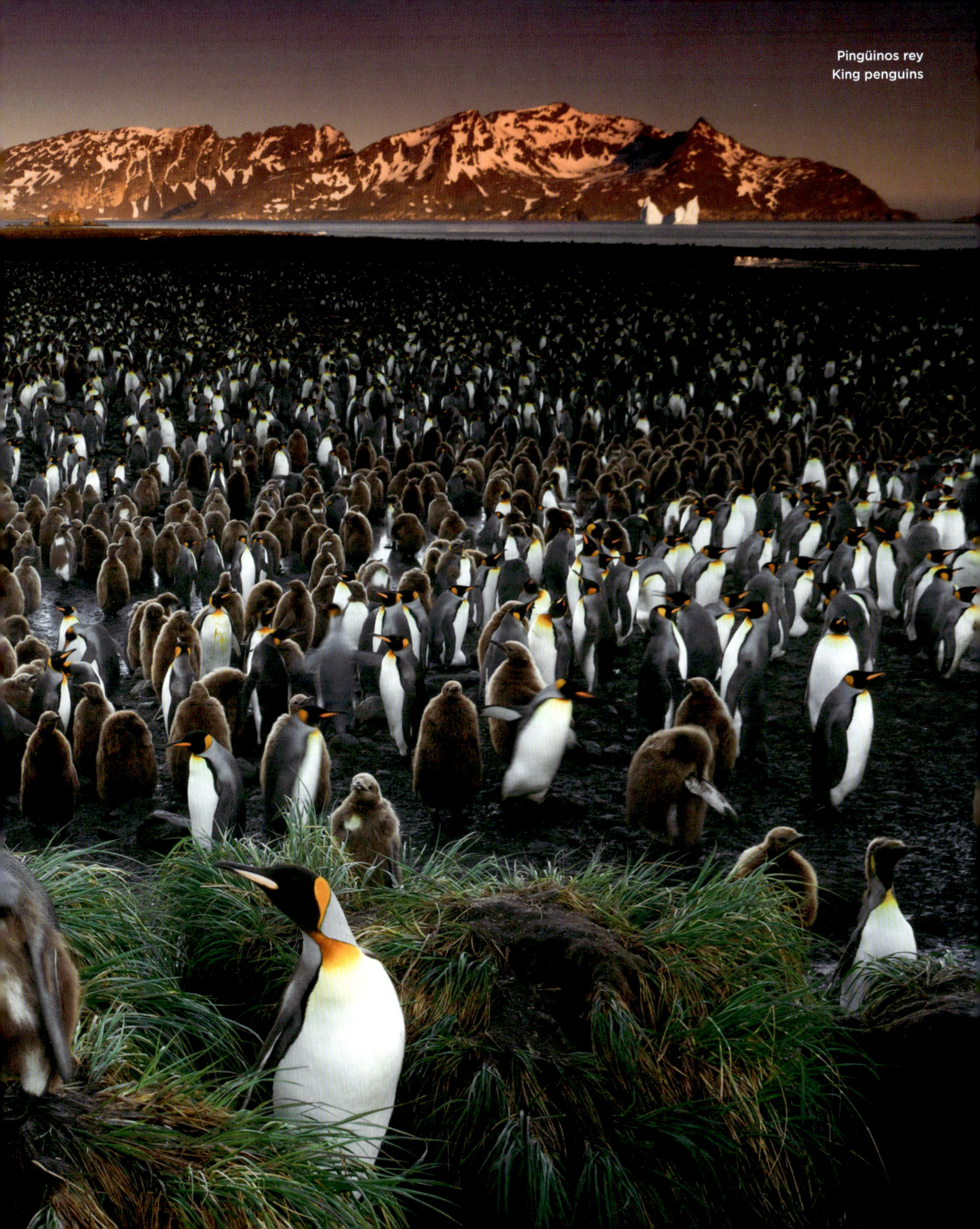
Pingüinos rey
King penguins

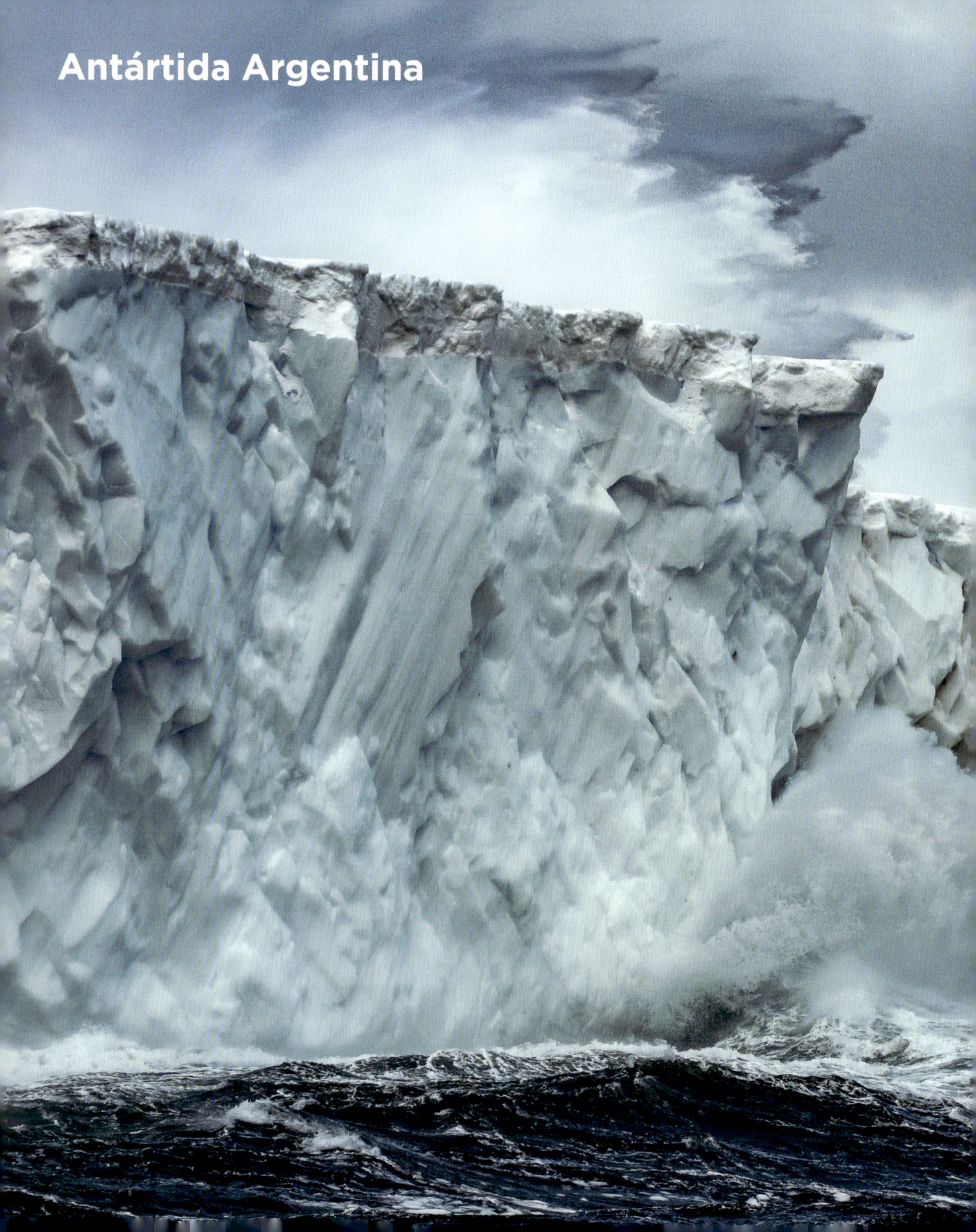
Antártida Argentina

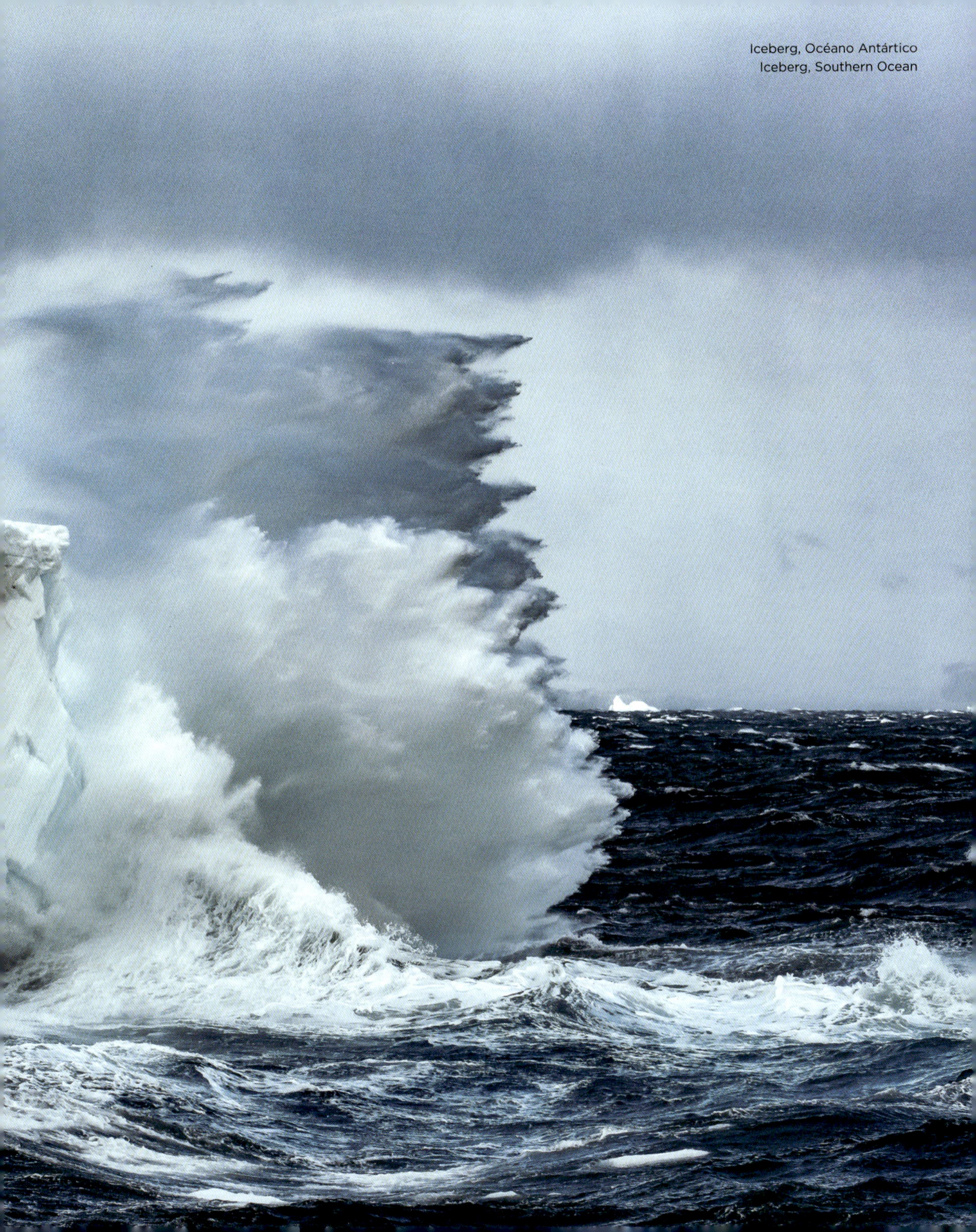

Iceberg, Océano Antártico
Iceberg, Southern Ocean

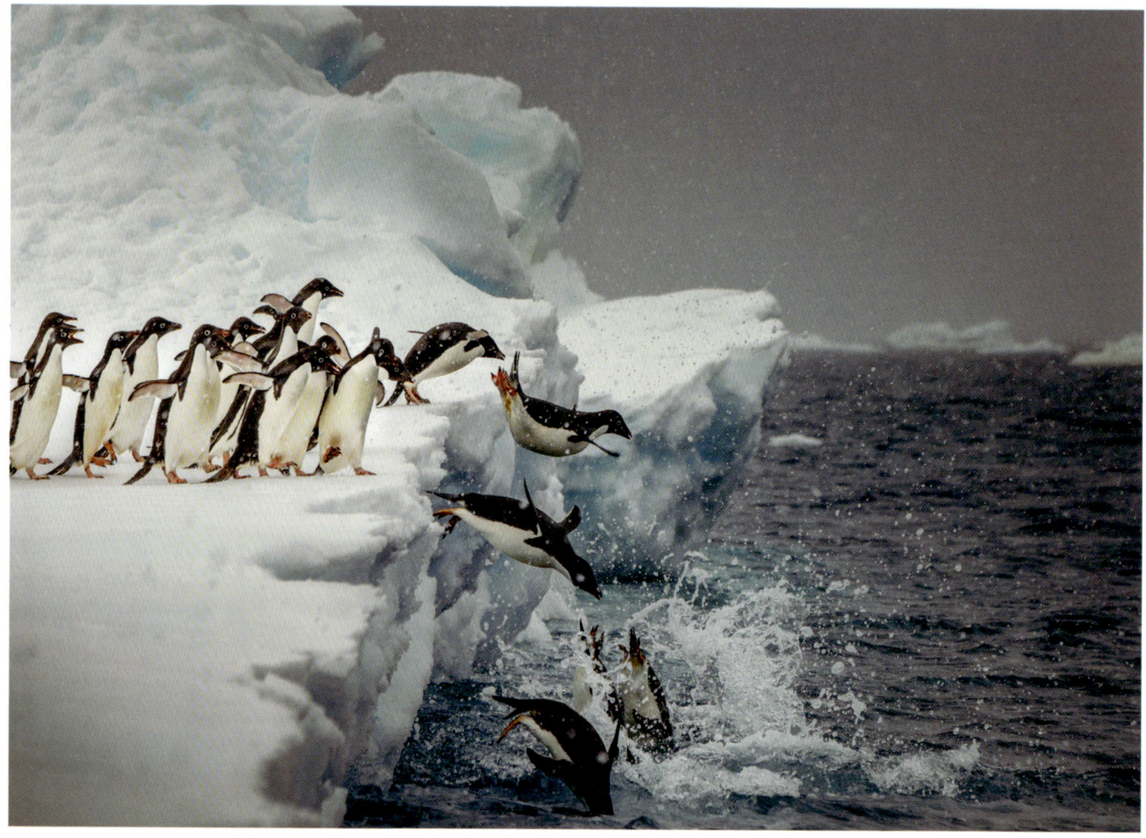

Pingüinos de Adelia
Adélie penguins

Argentine Antarctica

Argentina has claimed Antarctic territory since 1942. In 1946, it defined the boundaries as from the 25th longitude west to the 74th longitude west, and the 60th parallel South. The districts are: "Argentine Antarctic Territory of Tierra del Fuego", "Argentine Antarctica" and the "South Atlantic Islands", largely encompassing an area between the South Pole and the Antarctic peninsula Tierra de San Martín. Argentina operates a total of six stations in Antarctica, partly for military and partly for scientific purposes, where around 230 people live. On excursions, e.g. a trip through the La Maire Strait, which is the sea route between the Isla de los Estados and the eastern foothills of Tierra del Fuego, one may see impressive icebergs and penguins.

L'Antarctique argentine

L'Argentine revendique depuis 1942 une portion du continent antarctique. En 1946, elle l'a délimitée par une section triangulaire entre les méridiens 25° ouest et 74° ouest. Le nom exact de ce territoire est « Département de la province argentine de Terre de Feu, Antarctique et îles de l'Atlantique sud » et il s'étend entre le pôle Sud et la péninsule Antarctique (appelée en Argentine « Tierra de San Martín »). L'Argentine compte au total six stations en Antarctique, à des fins scientifiques ou militaires, habitées par 230 personnes. Une excursion maritime, par exemple dans le détroit de Le Maire, qui sépare l'île des États (Isla de los Estados) et les contreforts orientaux de la Grande Île de la Terre de Feu, permet d'admirer d'imposants icebergs et des manchots.

Argentinische Antarktis

Argentinien beansprucht seit 1942 Gebiete der Antarktis. 1946 legte es die Grenzen vom 25. Längengrad bis zum 74. Längengrad West fest. Die Distrikte sind: „argentinisch Antarktisches Territorium Feuerland", „argentinische Antarktis" und „Inseln im Südatlantik". Es handelt sich um das Gebiet zwischen dem Südpol und der antarktischen Halbinsel Tierra de San Martín. Insgesamt betreibt Argentinien sechs Stationen in der Antarktis, zum Teil zu militärischen, zum Teil zu wissenschaftlichen Zwecken. 230 Menschen wohnen hier. Bei Ausflügen, z. B. einer Fahrt auf der La Maire-Straße, dem Seeweg zwischen der Isla de los Estados und den östlichen Ausläufern Feuerlands, sieht man imposante Eisberge und Pinguine.

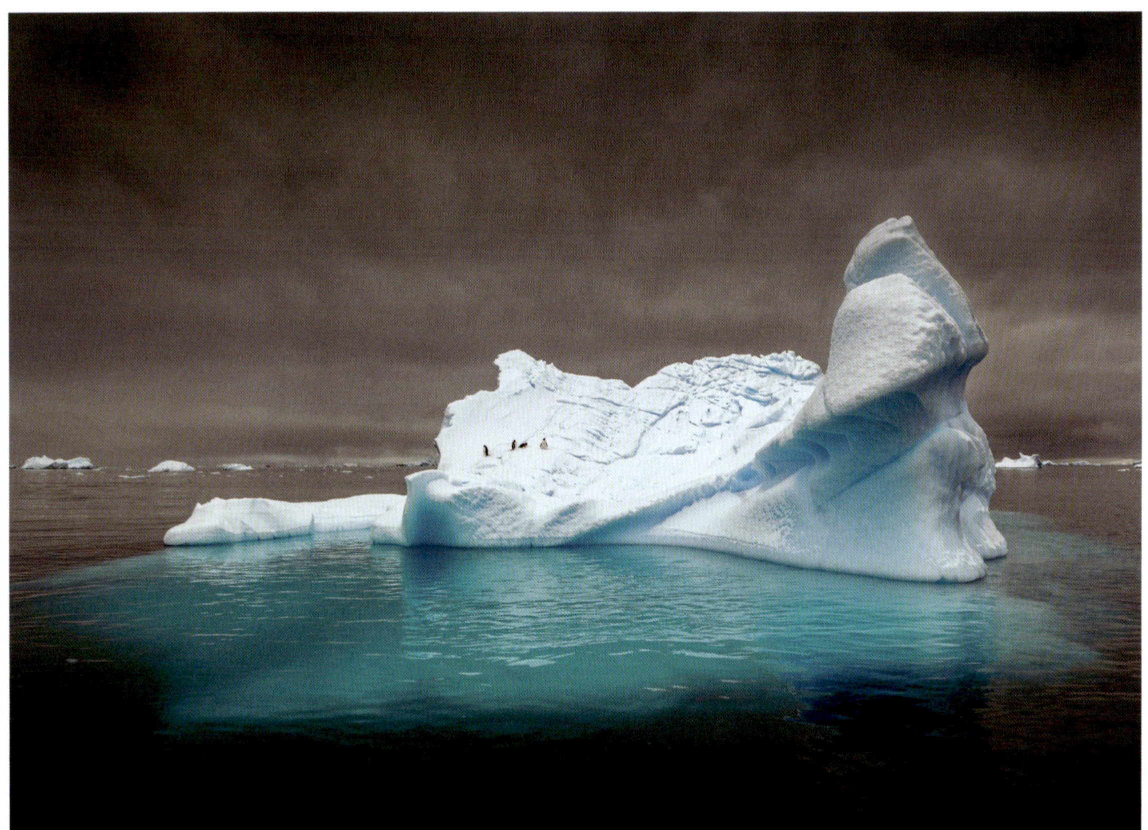

Iceberg

Antártida Argentina

Argentina ha reclamado el territorio antártico desde 1942. En 1946 definió los límites desde la 25.ª longitud oeste hasta la 74.ª longitud oeste. Los distritos son: Territorio Antártico Argentino de Tierra del Fuego, Antártida Argentina e Islas del Atlántico Sur. Es la zona comprendida entre el Polo Sur y la península Antártica Tierra de San Martín. Argentina opera un total de seis estaciones en la Antártida, en parte para fines militares y en parte para fines científicos. Aquí viven 230 personas. En las excursiones, por ejemplo, un viaje por el Estrecho de Le Maire, la ruta marítima entre la Isla de los Estados y las estribaciones orientales de Tierra del Fuego, se pueden ver impresionantes icebergs y pingüinos.

Antárctida argentina

A Argentina reivindica território antártico desde 1942. Em 1946 definiu os limites da 25ª longitude até a 74ª longitude oeste. Os distritos são: "Território Antártico Argentino da Terra do Fogo", "Antártica Argentina" e "Ilhas do Atlântico Sul". Esta é a área entre o Pólo Sul e a Península Antártica "Tierra de San Martín". A Argentina opera um total de seis estações na Antártica, em parte para fins militares e em parte para fins científicos. Aqui vivem 230 pessoas. Em excursões, por exemplo, um passeio no Estreito de La Maire, a rota marítima entre a Ilha dos Estados Unidos e o sopé oriental da Terra do Fogo, você pode ver impressionantes icebergs e pinguins.

Argentijns Antarctica

Sinds 1942 eist Argentinië gebieden van Antartica op. In 1946 bepaalde het de grenzen van de 25e lengtegraad tot de 74e lengtegraad in het westen. De districten zijn: "Argentijns Antarctisch Gebied van Vuurland", "Argentijns Antarctica" en "Eilanden in de Zuid-Atlantische Oceaan". Dit is het gebied tussen de Zuidpool en het Antarctisch schiereiland Tierra de San Martín. Argentinië exploiteert in totaal zes stations op Antarctica, deels voor militaire en deels voor wetenschappelijke doeleinden. Hier wonen 230 mensen. Tijdens excursies, bijvoorbeeld een tocht over de Straat Le Maire, de zeeweg tussen de Isla de los Estados en de oostelijke uitlopers van Vuurland, ziet men indrukwekkende ijsbergen en pinguïns.

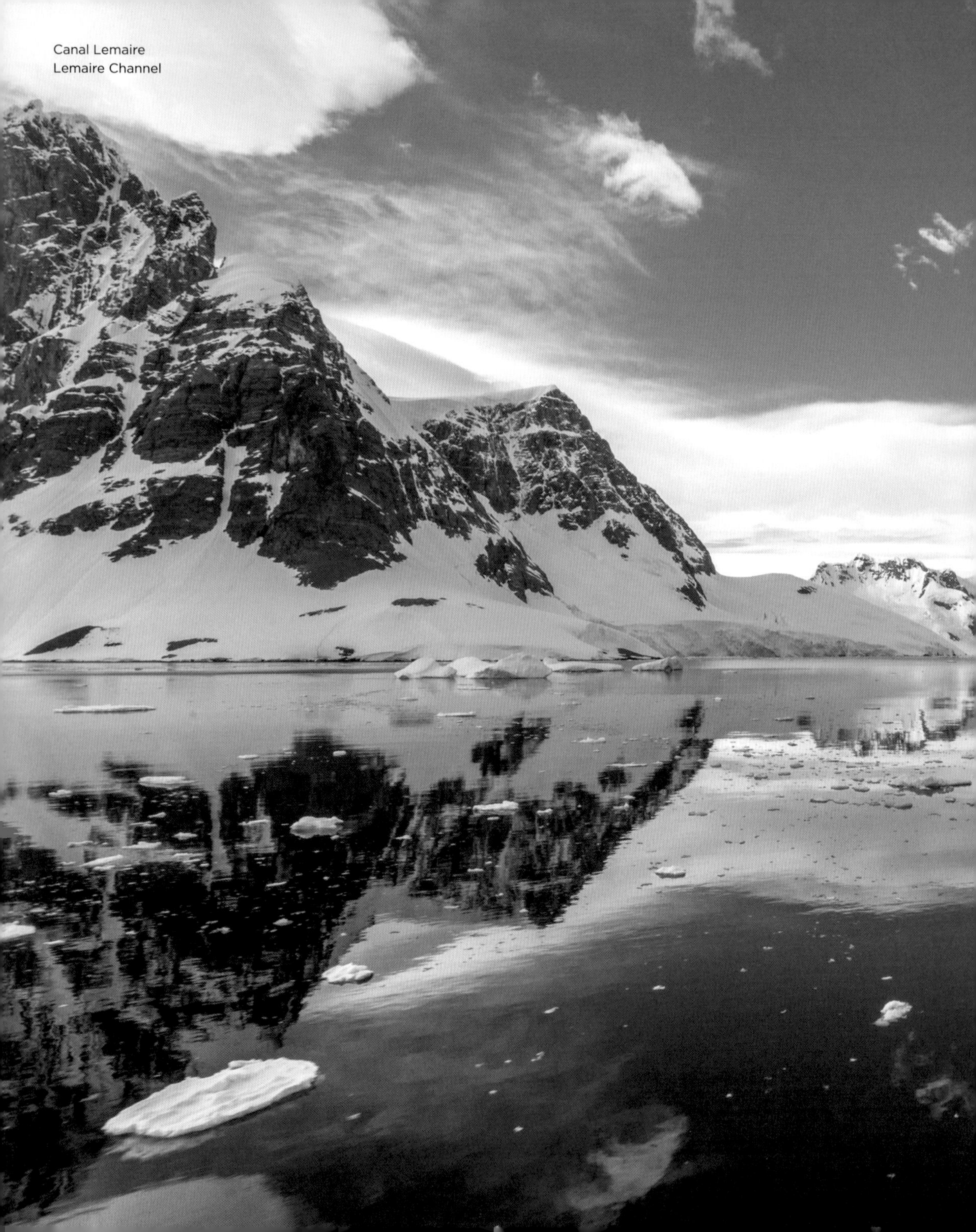

Canal Lemaire
Lemaire Channel

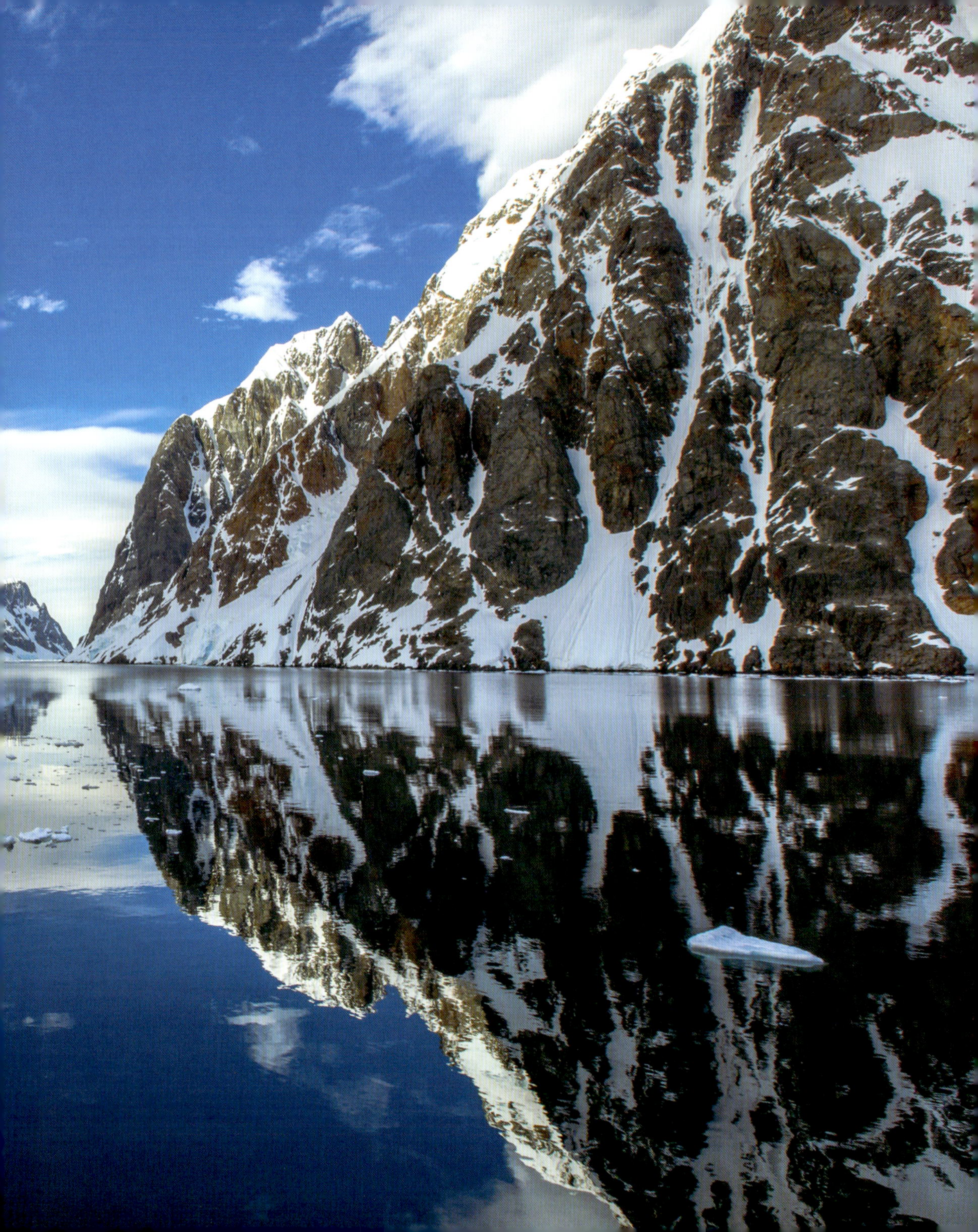

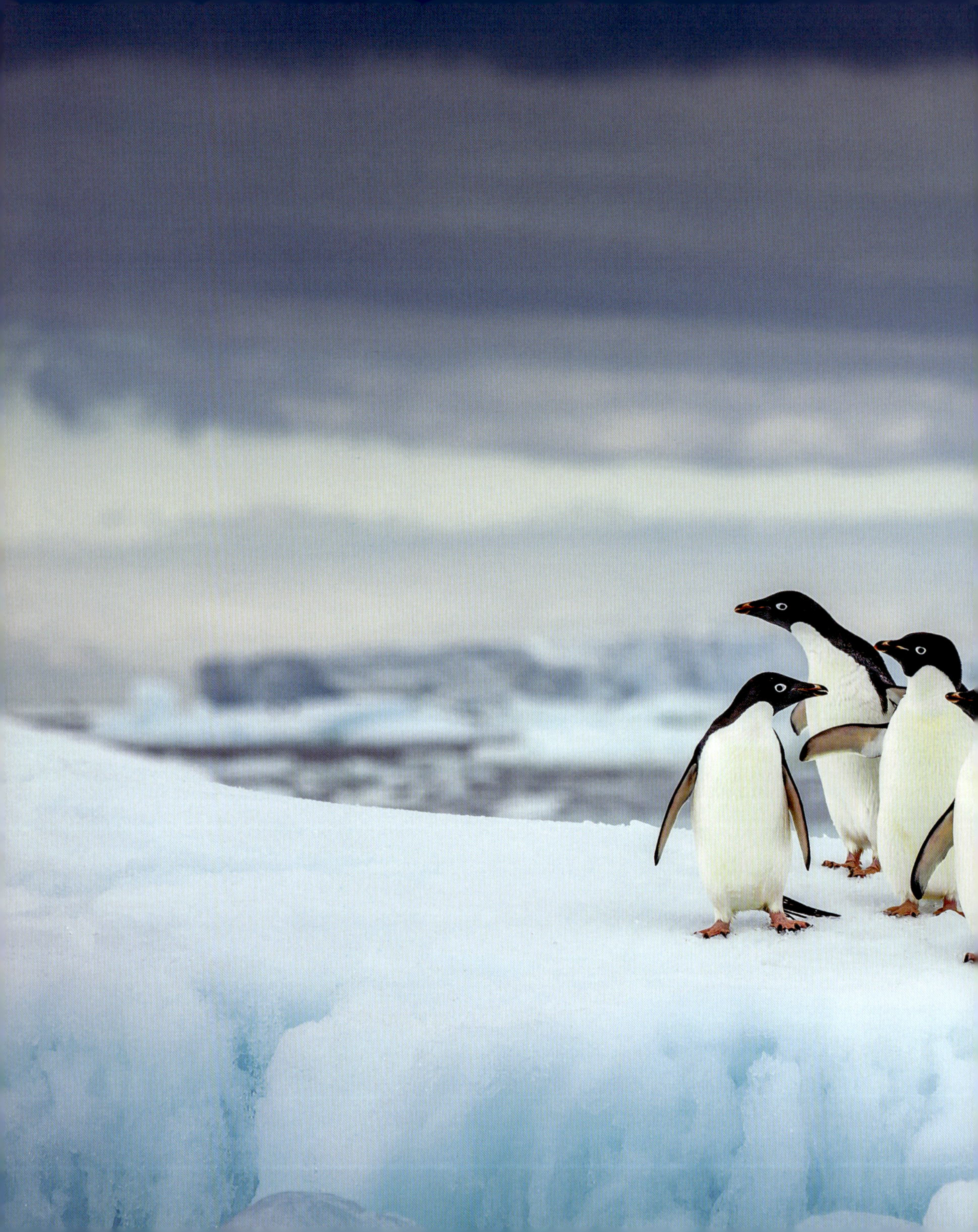

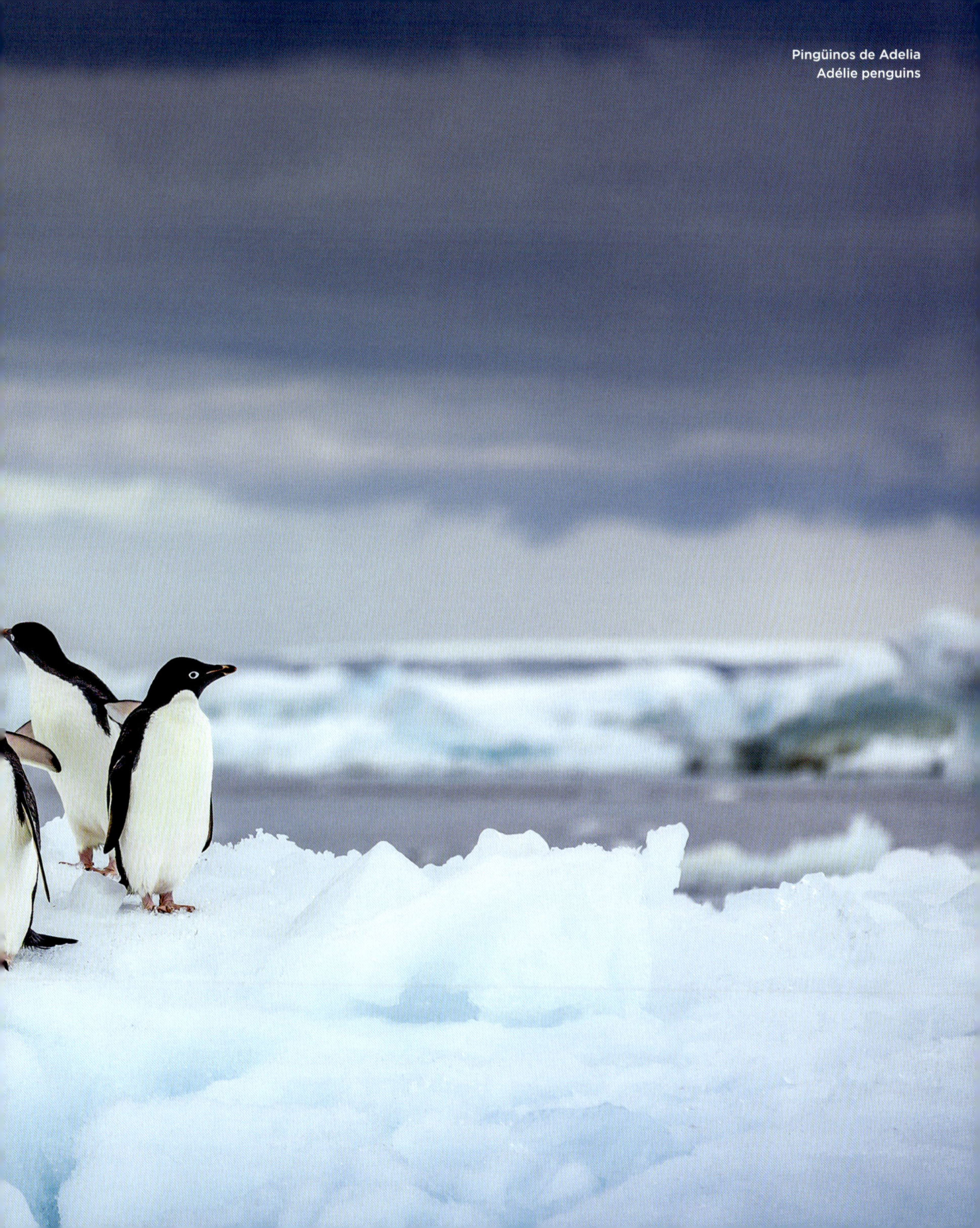
Pingüinos de Adelia
Adélie penguins

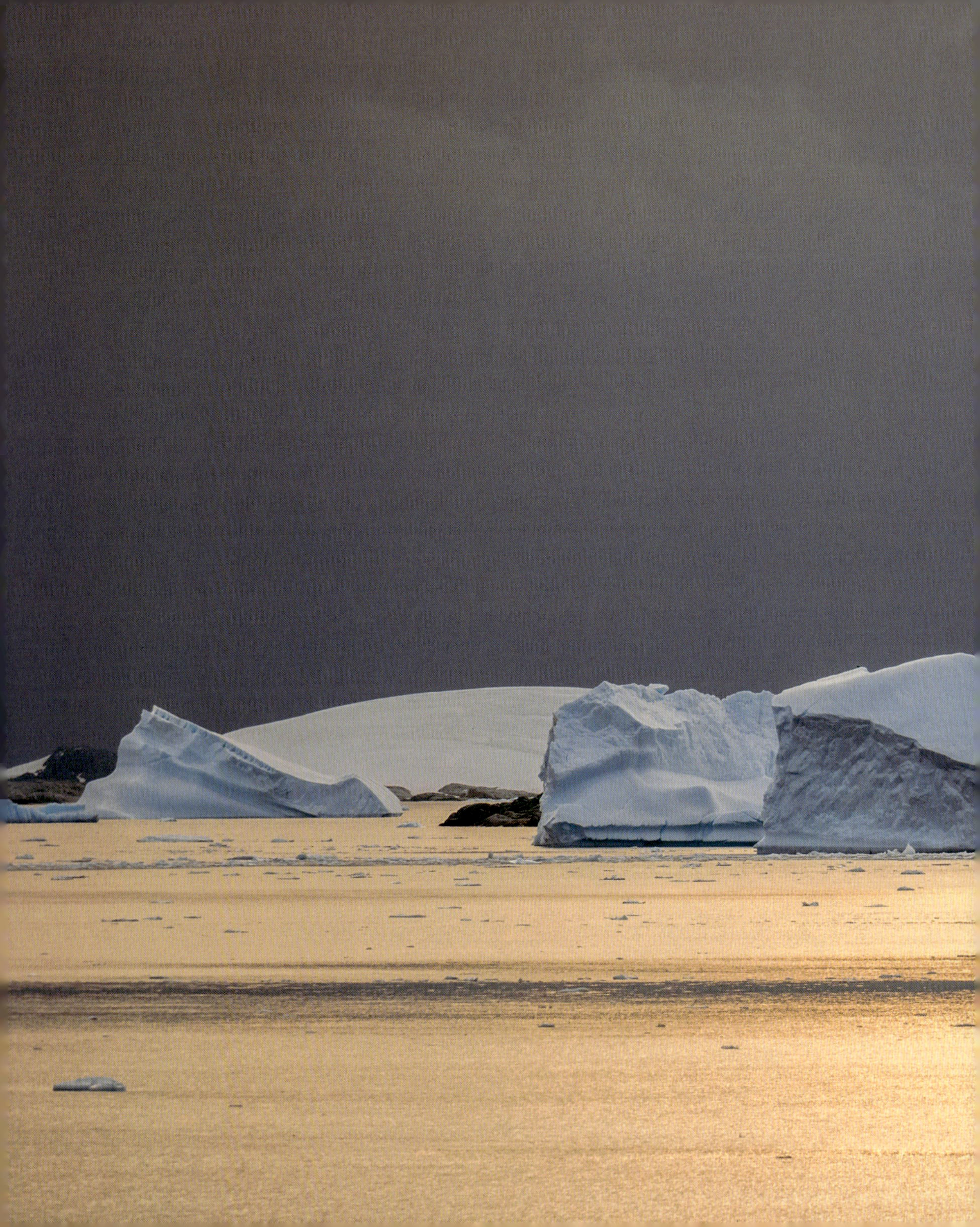

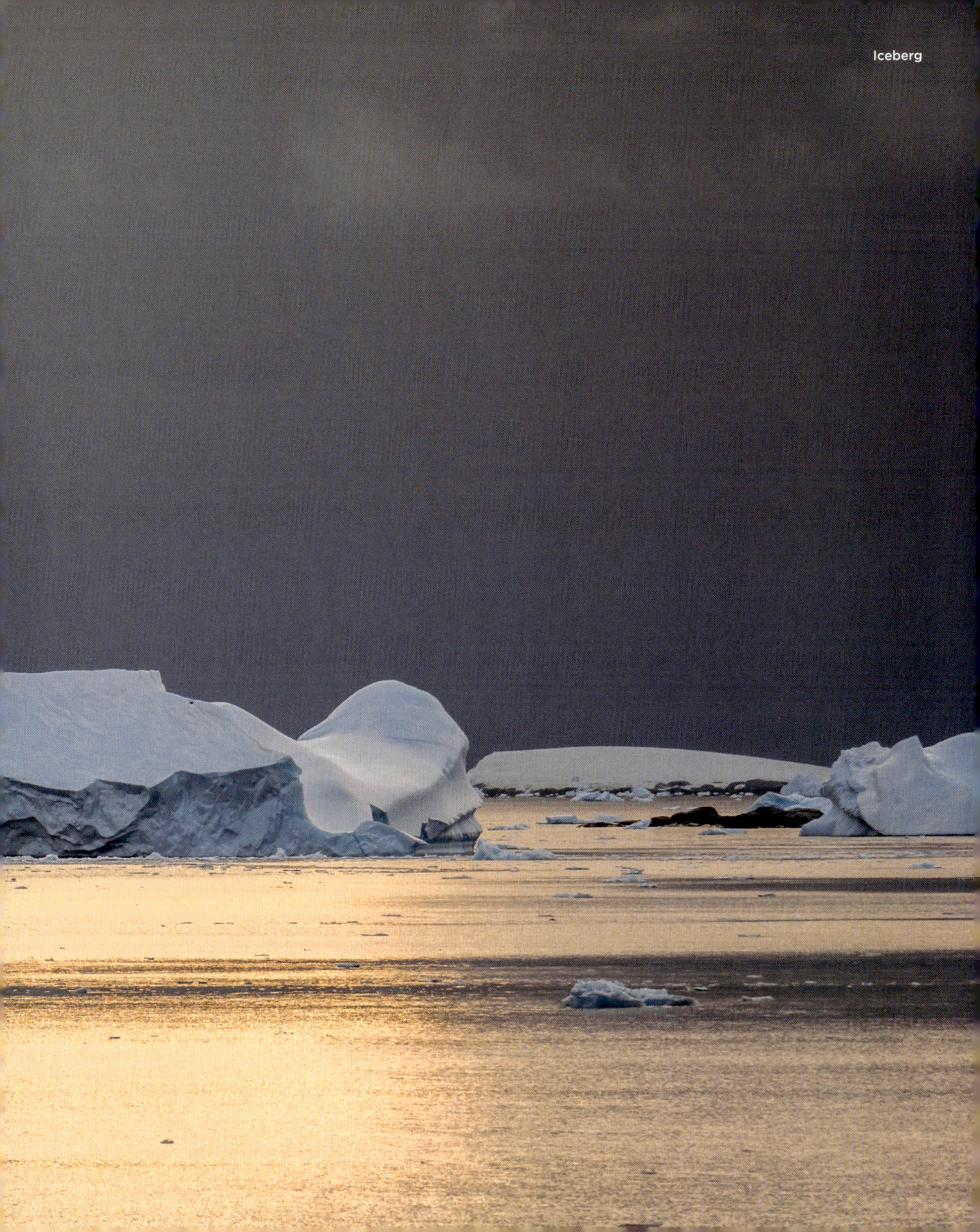

Iceberg

Acacia caven 237
Adélie penguins 504, 508/509
Aguada, La 218
Albatros de ceja negra 496–498
Albatross, black-browed 496–498
Alfajores 132
Altar for Gauchito Gil 118, 119, 312, 313
Altar para el Gauchito Gil 118, 119, 312, 313
American-barn-owl 310
Andes Mountains 14/15, 32/33, 342/343
Ardeida 101
Arrayanes 334
Asado (argentino) 172, 174/175, 324–331
Atacama Plateau 26
Avenida 9 de Julio 122
Azul River 362/363

Bailarines de tango 160, 161
Ballena franca austral 384/385
Band, Hans 156
Bandoneón 156
Batea Mahuida Volcán 340
Beagle Channel 451, 464, 470–473
Beech, Antarctic 364/365
Boars, wild 279
Boca, La 164, 165
Bombillas 320
Buenos Aires 22, 120/121, 123, 124, 206
Buschiazzo, Juan Antonio 131

Caballos 18, 286/287, 317, 436/437, 439–441
Caballos criollos 322/323
Cabo Blanco 372/373
Cabras 86, 87, 277
Calancate común 311
Calchaquí Indians 62
Calchaquí Valley 56–59
Caldén 280/281, 304/305
Camarones 375
Campo da Piedra Pómez 8/9, 82/83
Campo de trigo 268/269
Canal Beagle 451, 464, 470–473
Canal Lemaire 506/507
Capybaras 100
Caracara 406, 407
Carolina, La 241
Carpinchos 100
Castro y Bazán, Domingo 224
Catamarca 9, 83, 85, 89
Cataratas del Iguazú 4/5, 90–95
Cattle, herd of 70/71
Cattle, Welsh Black 278

Cebú 270
Cementerio de la Recoleta 150–155
Cerro Aconcagua 250/251, 253
Cerro Catedral 369–371
Cerro de los Siete Colores 40, 41
Cerro Mercedario 242
Cerro Torre 398–401
Cerro Tronador 356
Chilecito 224, 225
Chimehuin River 10/11
Chivos 216/217
Chorillo del Salto 407
Chinchulines rellenos 173
Churrasco 134/135
Ciénaga 218
Circuito de Potrero de los Funes 243
Club de Regatas La Marina 186
Coatí 96
Cocina argentina 80/81
Colibri cometa 236
Comet, red-tailed 236
Cóndor andino 54, 55
Condor, Andean 54, 55
Cordillera de los Andes 14/15, 32/33, 342/343
Córdoba 230/231, 238/239
Corrientes 101, 103, 105, 113, 114
Corzo 346
Cotorras argentinas 247
Criollo horses 322/323
Cuchillo gaucho 282
Cuchillos 284/285
Cuesta de Miranda 215
Cuisine, Argentinean 80/81

Darwin, Charles 438, 462, 463
Dique El Cajón 234, 235
Docta, La 228, 229
Dunas de Tatón 88/89

East Falkland Island 477, 493
El Ateneo Grand Splendid 148/149
El Bolsón 363
El Cajón Dam 234, 235
El Filo Merlo 248/249
Elefante marino del sur 387, 488, 489
Southern elephant seal 387, 488, 489
Empanadas salteñas 78, 79
Encomienda 86
Espuelas 294/295
Estancia 290/291
Estancia Alice 446/447

Estancia Caballadas 335
Estancia El Trebol 444/445
Estancia Harberton 451
Estancia Iberá 112, 113
Estancia La Bamba de Areco 195–197
Estancia La Candelaria del Monte 194
Estancia La Paz 232, 233
Estancia La Porteña 199
Estancia Santa Catalina 232
Estancia Santa Cecilia 106, 111, 115
Estancia Santa Susana 198
Estancia Tres Lagos 348/349
Estancia Yapeyú 114
Esteros del Iberá 101–105
Evita 155

Falkland Islands 474/475, 492
Faro Les Éclaireurs 470/471
Ferrari, Casimiro 399
FitzRoy, Robert 438, 462, 463
Flamenco 223, 383
Flamingo 223, 383

Gardel, Carlos 156
Gauchito Gil 118, 119, 312, 313
Gaucho knife 282
Gauchos 107–113, 200/201, 271, 274–277, 288, 289, 293, 296, 318, 319, 442/443
Glaciar Perito Moreno 16/17, 390, 414–427, 429–431
Glaciar Spegazzini 428
Glaciar Upsala 412
Goats 86, 87, 216/217, 277
Graffiti 142, 143
Grape harvest 263
Guaica 297
Guanacos 2, 36, 434
Guaraní 106
Güiraldes, Ricardo 198

Hat 316
Haya antáctica 364/365
Herbs and plants, medical 69
Heron 101
Hierbas y plantas medicinales 69
Hombre Argentino 37
Horses 18, 286/287, 317, 436/437, 439–441
Horses, criollo 322/323
Huarpe 246, 247
Humpback whale 382

Iberá Wetlands 101–105
Iceberg 502/503, 505, 510/511
Iguazu Falls 4/5, 90–95
Incas 54, 62, 63, 214, 215
Incense 68
Incienso 68
Indigenous people of the Pilagás 116, 117
Indios calchaquíes 63
Iruya 64/65
Isla de Goicoechea 490/491
Isla Gran Malvina 494/495
Isla Soledad 477, 493
Isla Trinidad 476
Islas Malvinas 474/475, 492

Jabalíes 279
Jaguar 74

King penguins 478/479, 482–487, 500/501
Kingfisher 341
Knifes 284/285

La Boca 22
La Pampa 6/7, 21, 272/273, 308/309,
    314/315
Lago Argentino 412/413
Lago Nahuel Huapi 332/333, 357–361
Lago San Roque 226/227, 229
Laguna brava 214, 220–222
Laguna Verde 84/85
Lanín Volcán 350–353
Lechuza común americana 310, 311
Lemaire Channel 506/507
Leones marinos 386, 464/465, 467–469
Les Éclaireurs Lighthouse 470/471
Letrero del tren, antiguo 379
Lichen 499
Linda, La 78
Liquen 499
Llamas 26, 36, 67, 435
Loros barranqueros 344/345
Los Arrayanes National Park 334, 338/339
Los Cardones National Park 72/73, 76/77
Los Glaciares National Park 2, 17, 393, 394,
    396, 398, 400, 402–405, 408–411, 415–
    417, 419, 420, 423, 424, 426, 428, 429,
    431
Luján de Cuyo 256/257

Magallanes 451
Magellan 451

Magnone, Guido 395
Maimara 40
Malbec vineyards 12/13
Malbec wine grape 258, 262, 266
Man, Argentinean 37
Mapuches 340, 341
Mar del Plata 204–211
Martial Mountains 450, 454/455, 458/459
Martin pescador común 341
Mate 141, 221, 316
Mate bowls 141, 316
Mendoza 13
Mercado de San Telmo 128–131, 137–140
Merlo 244/245
Misiones 91, 92, 93, 95, 106, 115
Monk parakeets 247
Monte Fitz Roy 2, 18, 391–393, 396/397
Monte Pissis 214, 221
Montes Martial 450, 454/455, 458/459
Merello, Tita 156
Moreno, Francisco P. 368, 369
Mount Fitz Roy 2, 18, 391–393, 396/397
Museo de Arte Tigre Intendente Ricardo
    Ubieto 187
Myrtle, Chilean 334

Nahuel Huapi Lake 357–361
Nahuel Huapi National Park 357, 359–361,
    369, 370
New Island 490/491

Océano Antártico 503
Old Patagonian Express 378
Orcas 466, 467
Ovejas 276, 298–303

Palacio de Gobierno de la República
    Argentina 125
Palermo 123, 169
Pampa, La 6/7, 21, 272/273, 308/309,
    314/315
Parakeets 247, 311
Parque Nacional Los Arrayanes 334,
    338/339
Parque Nacional Los Cardones 72/73,
    76/77
Parque Nacional Los Glaciares 2, 17, 393,
    394, 396, 398, 400, 402–405, 408–411,
    415–417, 419, 420, 423, 424, 426, 428,
    429, 431
Parque Nacional Nahuel Huapi 357, 359–

361, 369, 370
Parque Nacional Sierra de las Quijadas 246
Parque Nacional Talampaya 212/213, 218,
    219
Parrilla al Carbon 166/167
Parrilla Don Julio 169
Parrots, burrowing 344/345
Paso de Jama 27
Patagonia 375
Pavo real común 98/99
Peafowl, Indian 98/99
Pehuen 340
Peónes 319
Perezoso de dos dedos de Linnaeus 97
Perito Moreno Glacier 16/17, 390, 414–427,
    429–431
Perón, Eva 154, 155
Piedra Parada 376/377
Pilagás 116/117
Pingüinos de Adelia 504, 508/509
Pingüinos de penacho amarillo 480/481
Pingüinos rey 478/479, 482–487, 500/501
Plaza Dorrego 126/127
Polo 202/203
Potrero de los Funes Circuit 243
Puente de la Mujer 146/147
Puerto Argentino 493
Puerto de Frutos 179
Puerto Madero 144/145
Puerto Pirámides 374
Pumas 48, 49, 306, 307
Puna de Atacama 26
Punta Voluntarios 478, 487
Purmamarca 25, 29–31, 35, 41

Quebrada de Humahuaca 40
Quebrada de las Conchas 52/53
Quebrada de Las Flechas 60/61

Recoleta 148
Recoleta Cemetery 150–155
Reserva Provincial Serranías del Famatina
    217
Reses, manada de 70/71
Restaurante 168
Río Azul 362/363
Río Chimehuin 10/11
Río Chubut 377
Río de la Plata 184/185
Río de las Vueltas 388/389
Río Luján 189, 192/193
Río Mina Clavero 228

Río Paraná 176/177, 181
Río Quillén 335
Río Santa Cruz 432/433, 438
Río Sarmiento 178
Río Traful 336/337
Rockhopper penguins 480/481
Roe deer 346

Saddle 292
Saddle with lasso 283
Salinas Grandes del noroeste 42–45
Salta 47, 50–52, 57, 59, 60, 64, 66, 70, 73, 76, 78
San Carlos de Bariloche 354/355, 366–368
San Telmo 127, 133, 136, 142, 143, 160, 168
Santa Cruz 18
Santa Cruz River 432/433, 438
Saunders Island 476
Sea lions 386, 464/465, 467–469
Seal, elephant 488, 489
Serranía de Hornocal 38/39, 46/47
Serranías del Famatina Provincial Wildlife Reserve 217
Sheep 276, 298–303, 442/443
Sierra de las Quijadas National Park 246
Silla 292
Silla con lazo 283
Sloth, Linnaeus's two-toed 97
Solomillo en tiras 170/171
Sombrero 316

Southern Ocean 503
Spegazzini Glacier 428
Spegazzini, Carlos Luis 428
Spurs 294/295
Stanley 493
Striploin Steak 170/171

Talampaya National Park 212/213, 218, 219
Tango 156–159, 162/163
Tango dancers 160, 161
Tatón Dunes 88/89
Tehuelche 395
Tejidos 31
Terray, Lionel 395
Textiles 31
Tigre 177–183, 185, 186, 188–191, 193
Tomb of Eva Perón 154, 155
Train sign, old 379
Tren a las Nubes 66
Tumba de Eva Perón 154, 155
Tomb of Eva Perón 154, 155
Tupungato 264/265

Uco Valley 13, 252, 254/255
Upsala glacier 412
Ushuaia 449, 450, 452, 457, 460–463, 471
Uvas de vino malbec 262, 266

Vachellia caven 237
Valdés Península 382, 383

Valle de los Altares 380/381
Valle de Uco 13, 252, 254/255
Valles Calchaquíes 56–59
Velazco, Juan Ramirez de 214
Vendimia 263
Vicuñas 62
Viejo Expreso Patagónico 378
Viñedo de malbec 12/13
Vino 258–261, 267
Volcanes 340, 350–353
Volunteer Point 478, 487
Vueltas River 388/389

Welsh Black cattle 278
West Falkland 494/495
Whale, southern right 384/385
Wheat field 268/269
Wine 258–261, 267

Xuxuyoc 26

Yubarata, 382
Yungas 75

Zebu 270
Zorro culpeo 63, 347, 395

Photo credits

Lisovskaya; 172 Fernando de Noguera Arnal; 174 Lisovskaya, THEPALMER, Foto4440; 175 Aleksandr_Vorobev, Mariana Lebed; 176 Gabrielle Therin-Weise; 178, 179 Rebeca Mello; 186 diegograndi; 188 Jose Fernando Ogura/Curitiba/Brazil; 203 Marcelo Endelli; 206 Ricardo Guledjian/EyeEm; 207 Agustín Faggiano - Fotografía; 212 Antonio Spiller/500px; 214 Dmitry_Saparov; 218, 219 Javier Ghersi; 220, 222 Dmitry_Saparov; 223 Nick Dale/EyeEm; 224, 225 Juan Forner/EyeEm; 226, 228, 229 Edsel Querini; 230 Nahuel Ludueña/EyeEm; 234 Edsel Querini; 236 Cesar Hugo Storero; 237 Roberto Michel; 238 Guillermo Mansilla/EyeEm; 243 Eric Kitayama; 244 Flavia Morlachetti; 246 Eric Kitayama; 247 Javier Parigini/500px; 248 Flavia Morlachetti; 258 Gary John Norman; 259 EAQ; 260 reisegraf; 266 Westend61; 267 funebre; 270 Paulo Hoeper; 276 By Ronaldo Melo; 278 Augusto Famulari/EyeEm; 280 Foto4440; 282 Marilia Ferraz; 283 Eduardo Amorim; 284 Lautaro Federico; 286 Edsel Querini; 293 T-Immagini; 294 Buenaventuramariano; 297 Gabrielle Therin-Weise; 298 Juergen Schonnop/EyeEm; 300 Misael Maria Garro Alemany Casal/EyeEm; 301 zixian; 304 Foto4440; 306, 307 Terry Allen/500px; 308 nickalbi; 316 olindana; 317 juliatedesco-imágenes; 318 cristianl; 321 Nikolay_Donetsk; 324 Foto4440; 325 scalatore1959; 326 jopstock; 328 diegoboettiger; 329 Javier Pierini; 330 Christopher Pillitz; Aleksandr_Vorobev; 331 Christopher Pillitz, gabrielabertolini; 336 Jeff Miller; 338 diegograndi; 340 Jeff Miller; 341 Mario Tizón/EyeEm; 342 Tom Jaksztat/500px; 344 Cagan Hakki Sekercioglu; 346 Maximiliano Cagel/500px; 347 Belen Martinez/EyeEm; 352 pabloborca; 354 Nicolas Falduti/EyeEm; 356 McKay Savage; 357, 358 xeni4ka; 360 Harald von Radebrecht; 361 saiko3p; 362 Manuel Sulzer; 364 Kike Calvo; 366 Luxy Images; 368 Juan Manuel Iglesias/EyeEm; 369, 370 Ben Girardi; 374 Sergio Herrera Soria; 376 Peter Giovannini; 378 Stryker3; 379 piccaya; 382, 383 Foto4440; 384 wildestanimal; 386 Foto4440; 387 wildestanimal; 388 Lukas Bischoff; 390 Sergio Toro/EyeEm; 391 Adria Photography; 392 Anton Petrus; 394 Olga Tarasyuk; 395 Edson Vandeira; 396 Anton Petrus; 398 Siraphob Tatiyarat; 400 Anton Petrus; 402 Helminadia; 404 Gustavo Rodríguez/500px; 406 Joseph Shelly; 407 Mo Sharaf/500px; 408 mmphoto; 410 Patrick Fraser; 412 Anna

Tuzel; 414 Manuel ROMARIS; 416 Mint Images; 417 Thomas Janisch; 418 Gina Pricope; 420, 422, 424 Marco Bottigelli; 426 Grafissimo; 428 Elijah-Lovkoff; 429 Paul Arnfield; 430 SinghaphanAllB; 432 coolbiere photograph; 434 franckreporter; 435 Cagan Hakki Sekercioglu; 436 Christian Handl; 438 David Madison; 439 Pablo Dolsan; 440 franckreporter; 448 YONGRONG YU; 450 Johannes Hulsch/EyeEm; 451 Posnov; 452 Gustavo Borsone/EyeEm; 455 Posnov; 456 Gustavo Borsone/EyeEm; 458 Westend61; 460 YONGRONG YU; 462 Sandra Marisa Antonelli/EyeEm; 463 leonardospencer; 464 Angelo D'amico/EyeEm; 466 Foto4440; 468 Steve Allen; 470 Marco_Piunti; 472 Posnov; 474 Neil Bussey; 476 Cristina Mittermeier; 477 Cheryl Ramalho; 478 Mark Roberts; 480 Ralph Lee Hopkins; 482 Mint Images - Art Wolfe; 484 Ben Cranke; 485 JeremyRichards; 486 Mint Images - Art Wolfe; 488, 489 Marco Simoni; 490 Laura Grier/robertharding; 492 Daniel Nicholson/500px; 493 Jason Auch; 494 Sergio Pitamitz; 496 drferry; 498 Cristina Mittermeier; 499 Tom Murphy; 500 Mint Images - Art Wolfe; 502 Ray Hems; 504 David Merron/500px; 505 David Merron; 506 Nan Yang/500px; 508 David Merron; 510 Ruben Earth

Huber Images
102, 104 Matt Williams-Ellis

Laif
106 Heeb; 108, 112, 113 Beth Wald/Aurora; 114, 115 Heeb; 196 Thomas Linkel; 199 Gonzalez; 263 Heeb; 289 Diego Giudice/Archivolatino; 335 Thomas Linkel

mauritius images
26 Novarc Images/Jutta Riegel; 37 Reiner Harscher; 40 Emiliano Rodriguez/Alamy; 52 Minden Pictures/Chris Stenger/; 55 robertharding/Pablo Cersosimo; 56 Walter Bibikow; 60 Reiner Harscher; 62 imageBROKER/Peter Giovannini; 63 Minden Pictures/Chris Stenger/; 76 Alamy/Zena Elea; 80 Sabena Jane Blackbird/Alamy; 81 JerÛnimo Alba/Alamy; 82 imageBROKER/Peter Giovannini; 87 Alamy/Watchtheworld; 96 Jason Friend/Alamy; 107 robertharding/Matthew Williams; 110 Alamy/Heebphoto; 116 imageBROKER/Florian Kopp; 117 imageBROKER; 122 John Warburton-Lee/Michele Fal; 148 Alamy/Wim Wiskerke; 155 Rene Meyer; 160 Alamy/travelstock44.de/Juerg; 163 Hemis.fr/RIEGER Bertrand; 166 Alamy/Wiskerke; 168 John Warburton-Lee/Demetrio Ca; 180 Alamy/Bernardo

Galmarini; 181 Alamy/David R. Frazier Photoli; 182 Alamy/Bernardo Galmarini; 183 Alamy/Sara Armas; 187 robertharding/Karol Kozlowski; 189 Alamy/Karol Kozlowski Premium; 191 Alamy/Bernardo Galmarini; 192 Alamy/Henri Martin; 194 Alamy/Tim Moore; 195 Hemis.fr/RIEGER Bertrand; 200 Etcheverry Images/Alamy; 202 imageBROKER/Christian Prandl, buteo/Alamy; 203 buteo/Alamy, frederic cholin/Alamy; 232 Rupert Sagar-Musgrave/Alamy; 233 robertharding/Yadid Levy; 240 robertharding/Pablo Cersosimo; 242 Whit Richardson/Alamy; 250 Alamy/Kari; 252 Alamy/David Noton Photography; 254 David Noton Photography/Alamy; 256 Walter Bibikow; 262 robertharding/Yadid Levy; 264 David Noton Photography/Alamy; 274 Alamy/Paul Springett 08; 279 nature picture library/Gabriel; 288 christopher Pillitz/Alamy; 290 Alamy/Nicholas Tinelli; 302 Alamy/Jon Crwys-Williams; 310, 311 nature picture library/Gabriel; 314 Javier Etcheverry/Alamy; 322 Alamy/Chris Schmid Photography; 330 Michele Molinari/Alamy; 332 robertharding/Matthew Williams; 334 Alamy/Diego Grandi; 348 Novarc Images/Jutta Riegel; 350 imageBROKER/Harald von Radebre; 372 Novarc Images/Jutta Riegel; 375 Alamy/JUAN CARLOS MUÑOZ; 380 Novarc Images/Jutta Riegel; 442 Alamy/Jon Crwys-Williams; 444 Alamy/Nicholas Tinelli; 446 Alamy/JORDI CAMÍ; 467 robertharding/Pablo Cersosimo

Shutterstock
6 Andrzej Rostek; 42 andrmoel; 64 Guillermo Caffarini; 80 MARCELA ALONSO GIORDANA; 81 AS Food studio, J. Filirovska, Mariana L, Nora Claudia Mazzini; 92 Zhosan Olexandr; 128 shu2260; 130 Stefano Ember; 133 caroldejorge.fotografia; 142, 143 Aleksandra H. Kossowska; 154 Aleksandar Todorovic; 162 Goran Bogicevic; 162 Joni Hanebutt; 163 elbud, Gabriela Rosell, Gerardo C.Lerner, LongJon, Luis War, salvatore ferri; 164 gg-foto; 173 Larisa Blinova; 175 de Dios Editores, Foto 4440; 184 Alexandr Vorobev; 190 Christian Saez; 203 Mana Photo; 203 sunsinger; 204 altzaga; 208 Diegomezr; 210 Nick Photoworld; 211 Tom Payne; 215 Guillermo Caffarini; 216 Emiliano Barbieri; 253 Santiago_78; 268 Nick Photoworld; 271 NRuArg; 272 Foto 4440; 277 panoglobe; 292 Reimund Boderke; 296 MindStorm; 312, 313 buteo; 319 Nick Photoworld; 320 Pablo Bauza

KÖNEMANN

© 2020 koenemann.com GmbH
www.koenemann.com

© Éditions Place des Victoires
6, rue du Mail – 75002 Paris
www.victoires.com
Dépôt légal : 1er trimestre 2020
ISBN : 978-2-8099-1792-5

Series Concept: koenemann.com GmbH

Responsible Editor: Jennifer Wintgens
Picture Editing: Katja Sassmannshausen
Layout: Regine Ermert
Colour Separation: Prepress GmbH, Cologne
Text: Ellen Spielmann
Translation into French: Véronique Valentin
Translation into English, Spanish, Portuguese and Dutch: koenemann.com GmbH

Printed in China by Shyft Publishing / Hunan Tianwen Xinhua Printing Co., Ltd.

ISBN 978-3-7419-2532-0